ScottForesman

EXPLORING MATHEMATICS

AUTHORS

L. Carey Bolster
Coordinator of Mathematics
Baltimore County Public Schools
Towson, Maryland

Clem Boyer
Coordinator of Mathematics, K-12
District School Board of Seminole County
Sanford, Florida

Thomas Butts
Associate Professor,
Mathematics Education
University of Texas at Dallas
Richardson, Texas

Mary Cavanagh
Math/Science Coordinator
Solana Beach School District
Solana Beach, California

Marea W. Channel
Mathematics Resource Teacher
Los Angeles Unified School District
Los Angeles, California

Warren D. Crown
Associate Professor of
Mathematics Education, Rutgers,
The State University of New Jersey
New Brunswick, New Jersey

Jan Fair
Mathematics Department
Allan Hancock College
Santa Maria, California

Robert Y. Hamada
District Mathematics Specialist, K-12
Los Angeles Unified School District
Los Angeles, California

Margaret G. (Peggy) Kelly
Associate Professor
California State University, San Marcos
San Marcos, California

Miriam Leiva
Professor of Mathematics
University of North Carolina at Charlotte
Charlotte, North Carolina

Mary Montgomery Lindquist
Callaway Professor of Mathematics Education
Columbus College
Columbus, Georgia

William B. Nibbelink
Professor, Division of Early Childhood and
Elementary Education, University of Iowa
Iowa City, Iowa

Linda Proudfit
University Professor of Mathematics
and Computer Education, Governors State
University, University Park, Illinois

Cathy Rahlfs
Mathematics Coordinator
Humble Independent School District
Humble, Texas

Rosie Ramirez
Assistant Principal
Highland Elementary School
Silver Spring, Maryland

Jeanne F. Ramos
Assistant Principal
Nobel Middle School
Northridge, California

Gail Robinette
Vice-Principal
Fresno Unified School District
Fresno, California

David Robitaille
Head, Department of Mathematics
and Science Education
University of British Columbia
Vancouver, British Columbia,
Canada

James E. Schultz
Project LITMUS
University of Georgia
Athens, Georgia

Richard Shepardson
Professor, Division of Early Childhood
and Elementary Education
University of Iowa
Iowa City, Iowa

Jane Swafford
Professor of Mathematics
Illinois State University, Normal, Illinois

Benny Tucker
Dean, School of Education and Human Studies
Union University
Jackson, Tennessee

John Van de Walle
Professor of Education
Virginia Commonwealth University
Richmond, Virginia

David E. Williams
Former Director of Mathematics Education
School District of Philadelphia
Philadelphia, Pennsylvania

Robert J. Wisner
Professor of Mathematics
New Mexico State University
Las Cruces, New Mexico

Multicultural Reviewers

Cherry McGee Banks
University of Washington
Seattle, Washington

Armando Ayala
Director of Bilingual Education
Placer County, California

Diane Deckert Jost
Field Museum of Natural History, Chicago, Illinois

Patricia Locke
(Ta Wacin Waste Win)
Lakota, Chippewa Educator
Wakpala, South Dakota

Vicky Owyang Chan
Multicultural Educator
Fremont, California

Seree Weroha
Kansas State University, Manhattan, Kansas

Efrain Melendez
Dakota School, Los Angeles, California

Linda Skinner
Choctaw Educator, Edmond, Oklahoma

ScottForesman
A Division of HarperCollins*Publishers*

Editorial Offices: Glenview, Illinois   Regional Offices: Sunnyvale, California • Tucker, Georgia • Glenview, Illinois • Oakland, New Jersey • Dallas, Texas

CONTRIBUTING AUTHOR

Janet K. Scheer
Director of Field Services for Mathematics
ScottForesman, Glenview, Illinois

CONSULTANTS

Reading
Robert A. Pavlik
Professor and Chairperson,
Reading/Language Arts Department,
Cardinal Strich College
Milwaukee, Wisconsin

At-Risk Sudents
Edgar G. Epps
Marshall Field Professor of Urban Education
Department of Education,
University of Chicago
Chicago, Illinois

Limited-English-Proficient Students
Walter Secada
Department of Curriculum and Instruction
University of Wisconsin
Madison, Wisconsin

Mainstreaming
Roxie Smith
Associate Provost
Northwestern University
Evanston, Illinois

Gifted Students
Christine Kuehn Elbert
Assistant Professor of Education
University of South Carolina
Columbia, South Carolina

Junior High School
Edward A. Silver
Professor of Cognitive Studies
and Mathematics Education
University of Pittsburgh
Pittsburgh, Pennsylvania

CRITICAL READERS

Jennifer Allen
Muscogee County School District
Columbus, Georgia

Shirley Brady
Community School District 19
Brooklyn, New York

Sister Carole Cierniak
Our Lady of Perpetual Help School
Glenview, Illinois

Tom Daly
Pitt County Schools
Greenville, North Carolina

Susan Davis
Pinellas County School System
Largo, Florida

Margaret Foster
Calleyville Middle School
Calleyville, Texas

Linda Hayden
Timberland Junior High School
Pennington, New Jersey

Diana D. Heafey
St. Brendan School
San Francisco, California

Dicky Jackson
Terrebonne Parish School Board
Houma, Louisiana

Jean Reherman
Taft Middle School
Oklahoma City, Oklahoma

Betty VandenBosch Shaw
Flint Community Schools
Flint, Michigan

Linda A. Tangretti
Greensburg Salem School District
Greensburg, Pennnsylvania

Mary Soniat Thompson
Orleans Parish School Board
New Orleans, Louisiana

Harold M. Weymouth
Portsmouth Middle School
Portsmouth, Rhode Island

Acknowledgments appear after the index

ISBN: 0-673-45528-9

23456789-VU-99989796959493

Contents

Chapter 3 Integers and Rational Numbers

Chapter 4 Expressions and Equations

Chapter 5 Graphing

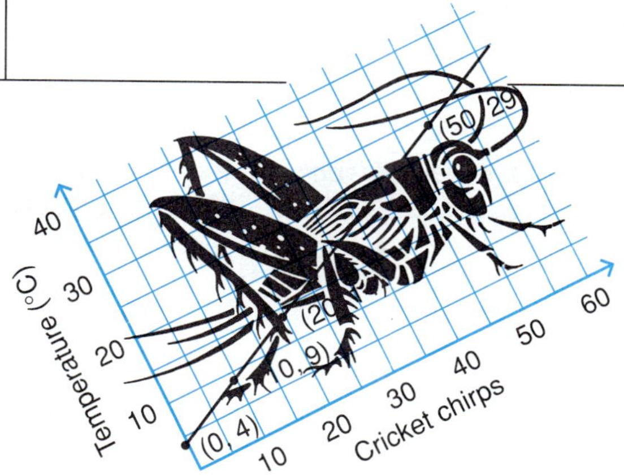

Chapter 6 Ratio, Proportion, and Percent

Chapter 7 Consumer Topics

Chapter 8 Systems of Measurement

Chapter 9 Geometry

Chapter 10 Measurement in Geometry

Chapter 11 Rational and Irrational Numbers

Chapter 12 Indirect Measurement

Chapter 13 Statistics

Chapter 14 Probability

Chapter 15 Mathematical Reasoning

WELCOME TO

EXPLORING MATHEMATICS

Mathematics is valuable and interesting. The next ten pages describe some of the ways your book will help you explore and discover more of the wonders of mathematics.

Your book will help you build your

Math Power

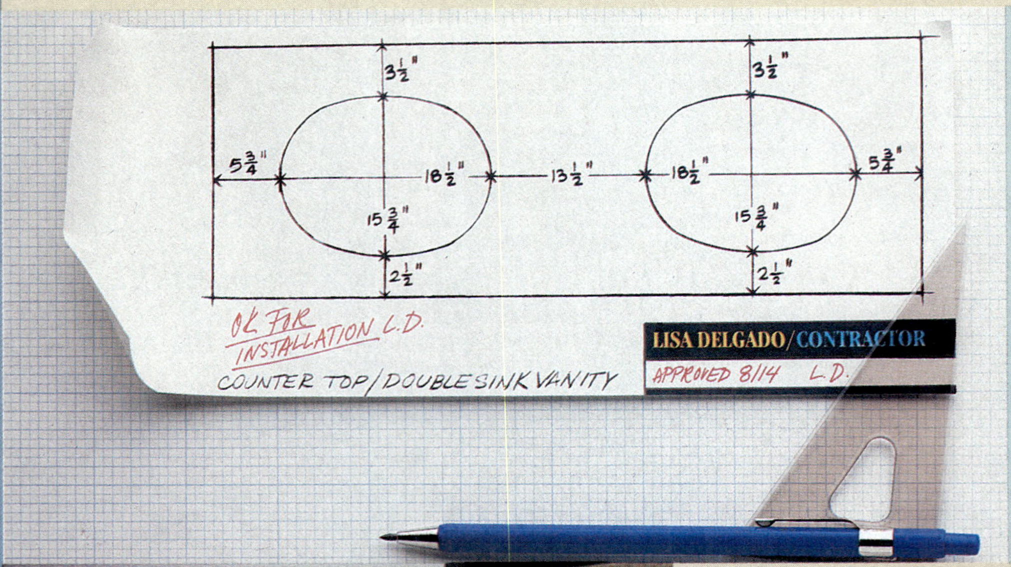

Build your math power by doing

Problem Solving and Critical Thinking

You'll need to use math to solve problems all your life. So, as you solve problems in your book, you will do more than find answers, you will also learn how to think mathematically.

In Chapter 1, tell the page numbers where these first occur.

1 "Problem-Solving Guide"
- Understand
- Plan and Solve
- Look Back

2 "Tips for Problem Solvers"

3 An exercise called "Critical Thinking"

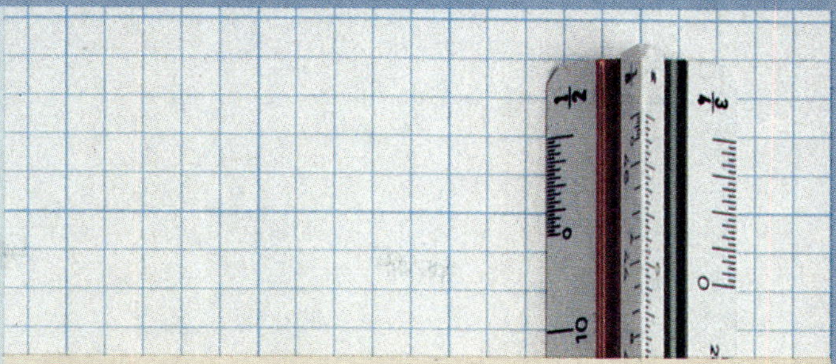

Build your math power by looking for
Connections

Your book will help you explore connections between mathematics, the real world, and other school subjects. Multicultural connections show the part mathematics plays in many cultures and societies.

4 On what page does "Multicultural Connection" first appear at the top?

5 On page 61, find a problem which involves a science activity.

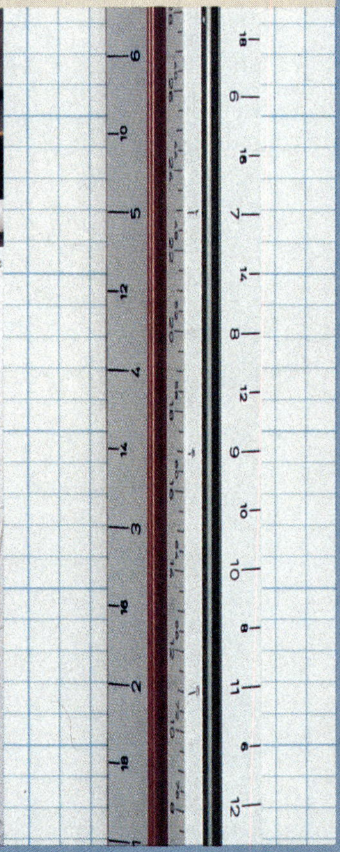

Build your math power by working on

Number Sense and Using Data

To work with numbers sensibly, you need to understand numbers, estimate, and do mental math. To read and use data, you need to be able to gather, organize, display, and analyze data.

1 Find a chapter that begins with a Number Sense Project about the New York Stock Exchange. Then find where this project is continued. (Hint: Find the Problem-Solving Workshop within the chapter.) On what page is the project continued?

2 On page 64, Problems 31–40, you are asked to estimate each sum by what method?

3 On what pages is the Data File that you'll use with exercise 34 on page 74?

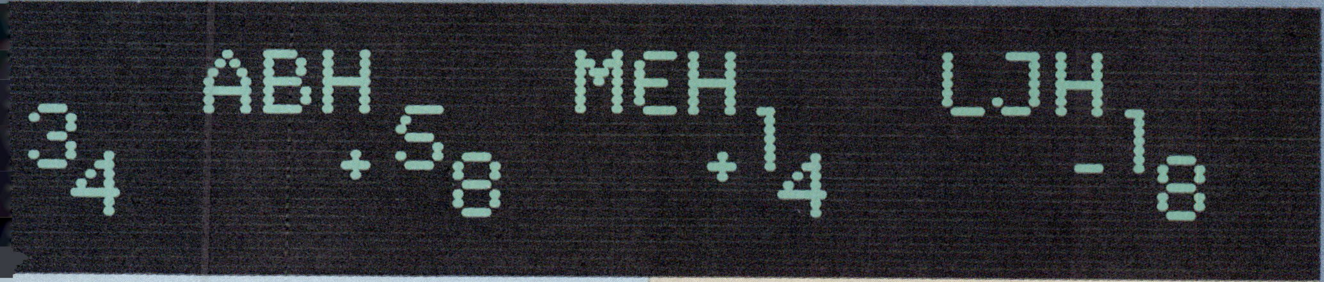

Build your math power by using Calculators and Computers

Calculators and computers can help you solve problems and learn mathematics. It's important to know when calculators can help you and when they are not needed.

4 On page 21, which problem suggests you use a calculator?

5 Which exercises on page 57 ask you to tell whether or not you would use a calculator?

6 What pages in the Independent Study Handbook explain how to use a calculator?

7 On page 59, what math topic does a computer help you learn?

0 12587 00180 6

Use your book to help you

Do Your Best

To do your best

Expect to Succeed

When you want to learn something, it helps to believe in yourself. Whether you are learning a sport, a musical instrument, or mathematics, a positive attitude can make a big difference.

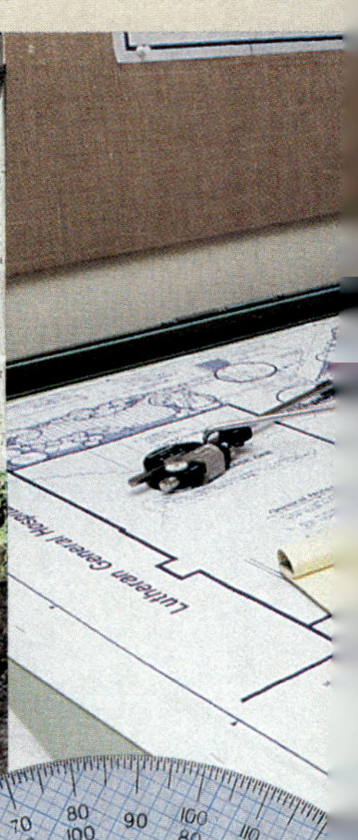

To do your best

Build Your Understanding

When you understand what you're doing, you do it better and remember it longer. So it pays to study the "Build Understanding" part of the lessons.

1 On page 28, why is it easy to see what new math words are being taught?

To do your best, learn ways to do
Independent Study

One of the most important things you can learn from a math book is how to learn math even when a teacher is not there to help.

2 On page 7, look to the right of the words "Check Understanding." On what pages can you find another example for that lesson?

3 On page 8, look to the right of the word "Practice". On what pages can you find more practice for that lesson?

4 There is an Independent Study Handbook in the back of your book. On what page does the "Math Study Skills" section begin?

5 Name the first and last words defined in the glossary on page 605.

Your book will help you experience

Active Learning

You'll learn math by doing

Math Activities

Activities help you understand math. Some activities use materials that help you show numbers, measure objects, do experiments, explore shapes, and solve problems.

1 What materials are used in the activity on page 130?

2 Draw one-third of a circle using the "Math Sketcher" (or a compass and a straightedge). Then draw one-third of other figures such as a regular hexagon and an equilateral triangle.

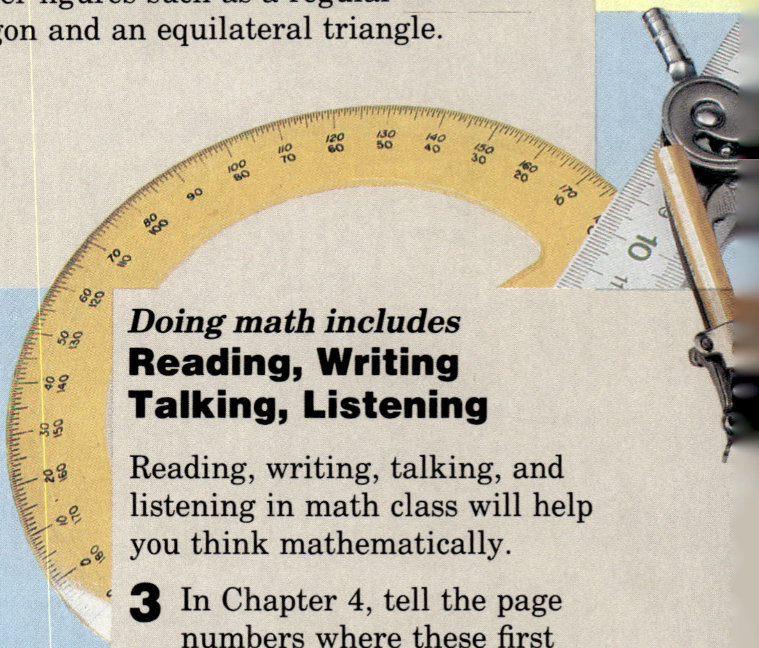

Doing math includes

Reading, Writing Talking, Listening

Reading, writing, talking, and listening in math class will help you think mathematically.

3 In Chapter 4, tell the page numbers where these first occur.

"Talk About Math"

"Write About Math"

"Reading Math"

A good way to learn is by

Working in Groups

In real life, and in math class, people can often solve problems better by working together.

4 How many students should work together in a group to do the activity in the "Estimating Sums and Differences of Fractions" lesson on page 62?

5 In the "Explore As a Team" on page 16, what is the "Tip for Working Together"?

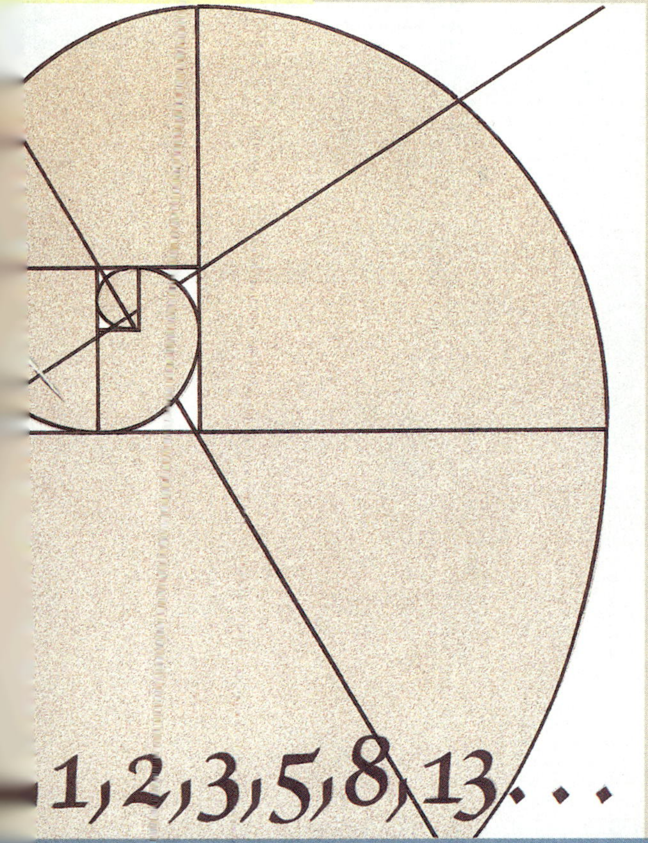

To have a math adventure, catch the spirit of

Exploration

Be a Math Explorer and discover new things. Look for patterns, check out your hunches, and try different approaches to problems.

6 What lesson in Chapter 1 begins by exploring the sequence of a number of branches growing on a plant?

7 In the "Explore Math" on page 69 you are asked to explore an alternative method for what type of computation?

A key ingredient to learning math is

Enjoying Math

Your book will help you

Enjoy Math at School

The explorations in your book will help you enjoy and discover the wonders of math.

1 In Chapter 1, what lesson involves exploring the patterns in an array of numbers shaped in a triangle?

2 In the game of bowling, the ten pins are placed in a triangular array. Draw diagrams to show all the different ways you could still have a triangular array if you knocked down one or more pins.

To make math a part of your life

Enjoy Math at Home

Outside of school, share math ideas with others and continue to explore math your whole life.

3 What item or equipment do you need in order to do the Math-at-Home activity on page 520?

4 What are you asked to draw in the family activity suggested in the Problem-Solving Workshop in Chapter 3?

5 Play a game with a family member. To help build thinking skills, choose a strategy game like checkers, chess, or backgammon; to sharpen number, computation, money, and other math skills, play darts, dominoes, cards, or a boardgame that involves numbers or money.

Getting Started 1

Did You Know: Decibels give a scale of the intensity of sound. Hearing for humans begins at 0 decibels and becomes painful at 140 decibels. On the decibel scale, leaves rustling would be about 10 decibels and a jet taking off would be about 140 decibels.

Number-Sense Project

Estimate
List three sounds that you hear each day and guess where they would be on the decibel scale.

Gather Data
Find examples of the decibel levels of at least 5 sounds.

Analyze and Report
Combine the examples found by the class and make a bar graph to show the decibel levels of various sounds.

Using a Problem-Solving Guide

Build Understanding

Use this guide to solve the problem below and other problems you will find in this book.

The number 13 is an example of a 2-digit number with 2 different digits in increasing order. How many such numbers are there?

PROBLEM SOLVING **GUIDE**

Understand
QUESTION
FACTS
KEY IDEA

Plan and Solve
STRATEGY
ANSWER

Look Back
SENSIBLE ANSWER
ALTERNATE APPROACH

PROBLEM SOLVING **GUIDE**

Understand

QUESTION
What are you asked to find?

FACTS
What facts are given?

KEY IDEA
How are the facts and question related?

Plan and Solve

STRATEGY
What can you do to solve the problem?

ANSWER
Give the answer in a sentence.

Look Back

SENSIBLE ANSWER
Did you check your work?

ALTERNATE APPROACH
Is there another way to get the same answer?

Understand

QUESTION How many 2-digit numbers fit the conditions?

FACTS The number has 2 different digits in increasing order.

KEY IDEA The ones digit is greater than the tens digit.

Plan and Solve

STRATEGY You might *make a table* and *find a pattern*.

Tens Digit	Numbers	Number of Numbers
9		0
8	89	1
7	79, 78	2
6	69, 68, 67	3
5	59, 58, 57, 56	4
4		5
3		6
2		7
1		8
	Total	36

ANSWER There are 36 numbers.

Look Back

SENSIBLE ANSWER For 9 tens, there is no greater digit for the ones place. For 8 tens there is only one greater digit, and so on. The pattern above makes sense.

ALTERNATE APPROACH List the numbers 10–99 and circle those that fit the conditions.

Talk About Math Suppose the two different digits were in decreasing order. Would there be 36 of these numbers?

Check Understanding

Use the problem-solving guide to answer the questions.

1. What is the first step in solving a problem?

2. How does the "Facts" step help you solve a problem?

3. In which steps do you describe or explain how to solve a problem?

4. How do you decide whether you obtained a sensible answer?

Practice

How many 3-digit numbers are there in which the sum of the digits is 18? Exercises 5–8 should help you solve this problem.

5. Give three examples of numbers that fit the conditions.

6. Can such a number include both the digit 2 and the digit 5? Explain.

7. Give all such numbers with 9 hundreds and 9 tens; with 9 hundreds and 8 tens.

8. Give all such numbers greater than 900.

9. Explain how you will solve the problem. What is the answer?

10. Did you use a pattern to solve the problem? If so, describe the pattern.

Solve each problem. **Remember** to refer to the problem-solving guide for help and tips.

11. How many digits are written to list the numbers 0–99?

12. How many digits are written to list the numbers 0–999?

13. How many of the digits in Problem 11 are 2s?

14. How many of the digits in Problem 12 are 2s?

The 31-digit number shown is formed by writing all the digits of the numbers 1 to 20 in order.

1234567891011121314151617181920

Remove 16 of these digits and, without rearranging the digits that remain, form a 15-digit number with the given property.

15. Largest

16. Smallest

17. Closest to 500,000,000,000,000

ALGEBRA

Sequences

Build Understanding

A. Susie is planning to fence a 1-meter-wide piece of land for a garden. To order materials, she needs to know how the amount of fencing will increase as the length of the garden increases.

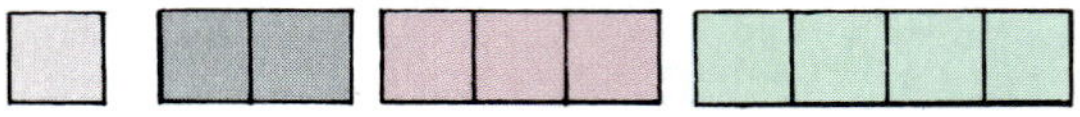

$P =$ 4 m $P = 6$ m $P = 8$ m $P = 10$ m

Make a table to show how the length of the garden and its perimeter are related.

Number of squares	1	2	3	4	5	6	7	8
Perimeter	4	6	8	10	12	14	16	18

As the length of the garden increases by 1 m, the perimeter of the garden increases by 2 m. The perimeter of the garden, 4, 6, 8, 10, . . . , forms a ***sequence,*** or an ordered list of numbers that can be generated from a pattern or rule.

The sequence, 4, 6, 8, 10, . . . , is an ***arithmetic sequence.*** The difference between consecutive terms in an arithmetic sequence is the same.

B. What is the eighth term in the sequence 2, 4, 8, 16, . . . ?

Notice that each term is twice the preceding term. Continue this pattern: 2, 4, 8, 16, 32, 64, 128, 256. The eighth term is 256.

This is a ***geometric*** sequence because each term is obtained from the preceding term by multiplying or dividing by the same number.

C. Write the 20th term of the sequence 2, 4, 8, 16, . . . as a power of 2.

2 is the first power of 2. $2 = 2^1$
4 is the second power of 2. $4 = 2 \times 2 = 2^2$
8 is the third power of 2. $8 = 2 \times 2 \times 2 = 2^3$

An ***exponent*** tells how many times the ***base*** is used as a factor. The base in this example is 2.

The 20th term, written as a power of 2, is 2^{20}.

D. Is the sequence 1, 8, 27, 64, . . . arithmetic, geometric, or neither? Give the next 3 terms.

Since $8 - 1 = 7$, but $27 - 8 \neq 7$, it is not arithmetic.

Since $1 \times 8 = 8$, but $8 \times 8 \neq 27$, it is not geometric.

The sequence is neither arithmetic nor geometric. But notice the following pattern.

Second term $8 = 2 \times 2 \times 2 = 2^3$
Third term $27 = 3 \times 3 \times 3 = 3^3$
Fourth term $64 = 4 \times 4 \times 4 = 4^3$

The next 3 terms are 5^3 or 125, 6^3 or 216, and 7^3 or 343.

■ **Write About Math** Write 5 terms of an arithmetic sequence and 5 terms of a geometric sequence that each start with the number 7.

Check Understanding

For another example, see Set A, pages 40–41.

For Exercises 1–3, use the figures at the right.

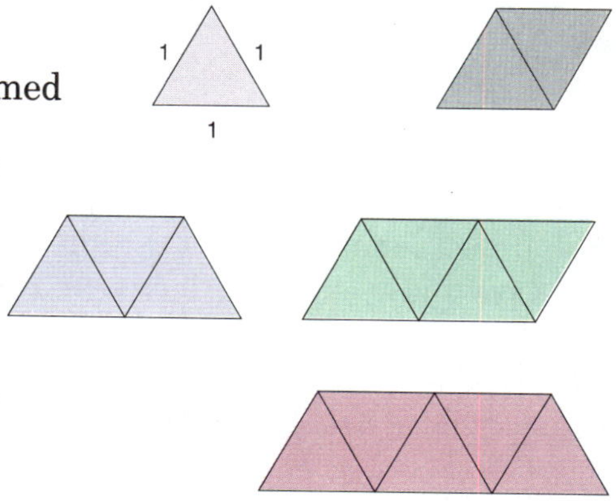

1. Write the first 8 numbers in the sequence formed by the perimeters of these figures. Is this an arithmetic sequence or a geometric sequence?

2. What is the 34th number in the sequence in Exercise 1?

3. If the perimeter of the figure is 70, how many triangles make up the figure?

Tell whether the sequence is arithmetic, geometric, or neither. Give the next 3 numbers in the sequence.

4. 4, 12, 36, 108, . . .

5. 0, 3, 8, 15, . . .

6. 4, 12, 20, 28, . . .

Find the answer.

7. Give the missing terms in this arithmetic sequence.
30, ▦, ▦, ▦, 90

8. Give the missing terms in this geometric sequence.
1, ▦, ▦, 1,000,000

Practice

For More Practice, see Set A, pages 42–43.

Tell whether the sequence is arithmetic, geometric, or neither. Then write the next 3 terms. **Remember** to show how each term in a sequence is found from the preceding term.

9. 5, 7, 9, 11, . . .

10. 95, 91, 87, 83, . . .

11. 2, 8, 32, 128, . . .

12. 1, 5, 25, 125, . . .

13. 1, 4, 9, 16, . . .

14. 1, 2, 5, 10, . . .

15. 0, 5, 10, 15, . . .

16. $11^1, 11^2, 11^3, 11^4$, . . .

17. 1, 2, 3, 5, 8, 13, . . .

18. $\frac{1}{2}, 1\frac{1}{2}, 2\frac{1}{2}, 3\frac{1}{2}$, . . .

19. $\frac{1}{2}, \frac{1}{3}, \frac{1}{4}, \frac{1}{5}$, . . .

20. 0.8, 2.4, 7.2, 21.6, . . .

Find the missing terms in each arithmetic sequence. Tell whether you used mental math or paper and pencil.

21. ▒, ▒, 13, 17, 21

22. 6, ▒, 20, ▒, 34

23. ▒, 35, ▒, 67, ▒

24. 40, ▒, 30, ▒, 20, ▒

25. 4, 10, ▒, ▒, ▒, 34

26. ▒, ▒, 18, 27, ▒, 45

27. ▒, 15, ▒, 35, ▒

28. 98, 91, ▒, ▒, 70, ▒

29. ▒, 13, ▒, 37, ▒

Find the missing terms in each geometric sequence. Tell whether you used mental math or paper and pencil.

30. 6, 24, ▒, 384, ▒

31. ▒, ▒, 72, 144, 288

32. 3, 12, ▒, ▒, 768

33. ▒, 30, ▒, ▒, 30,000

34. 1, 0.1, 0.01, ▒, ▒, ▒

35. 1,024, 256, 64, ▒, ▒, ▒

36. 3, 21, ▒, ▒, ▒

37. ▒, ▒, 36, 6, ▒

38. 243, 162, 108, ▒, ▒, 32

39. If the perimeter in Example A is 72, how many squares form the rectangle?

40. Find the 34th number in the sequence in Example A.

41. The first 5 numbers in the *triangular number sequence* are 1, 3, 6, 10, and 15. Notice that 3 = 1 + 2, 6 = 1 + 2 + 3, and so on. Write the next five triangular numbers.

42. Susie puts tomatoes in piles containing different numbers of tomatoes. The first four piles contain 1, 4, 10, and 20 tomatoes. The numbers in the sequence are the sum of the first triangular number, the first and second triangular numbers, and so on. How many tomatoes will be in each of the next four piles?

Problem Solving

Use the method shown in Example A to form a sequence of perimeters of figures made up of regular octagons connected as shown in the figure.

43. Write the first 6 numbers in this sequence.

44. What will be the 34th number?

45. In what position in the sequence is 602?

Number Sense Write 6 numbers of any arithmetic sequence. Do you still have an arithmetic sequence if you do the following?

46. Add 3 to each number.

47. Multiply each number by 3.

Number Sense Write 6 numbers of any geometric sequence. Do you still have a geometric sequence if you do the following?

48. Add 3 to each number.

49. Multiply each number by 3.

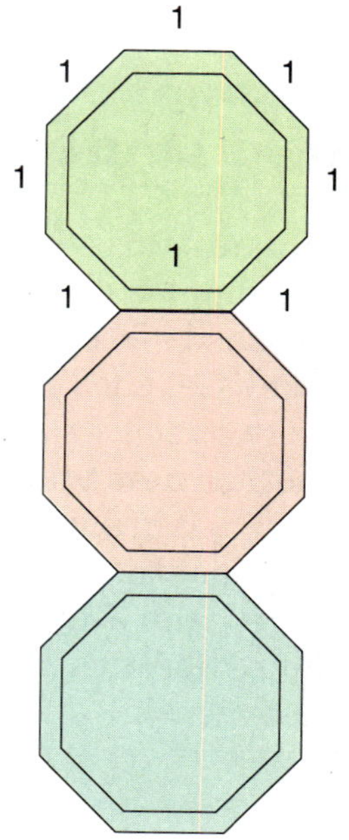

This represents the third number in the sequence.

Skills Review

Review, pages 577–578

Find each answer. **Remember** to check your answers.

1. 672 + 19 **2.** 427 − 208 **3.** 18 × 53 **4.** 648 ÷ 8

5. 243 − 107 + 19 **6.** 111 + 28 + 63 **7.** 720 ÷ 5 **8.** 21 × 16 × 10

9. 117 ÷ 9 **10.** 515 − 4 − 219 **11.** 1,021 + 7 + 213 + 89

12. 151 × 20 **13.** 15 + 32 + 208 + 45 **14.** 534 ÷ 6

15. 317 × 4 **16.** 892 − 42 − 350 **17.** 18,216 − 9,108

18. 9,677 + 630 **19.** 29,475 ÷ 5 **20.** 23,863 + 32,594 + 8,506

21. 1,366 × 45 **22.** 1,309 ÷ 7 **23.** 10,000 − 899

24. 6,214 + 5,027 **25.** 19 × 1,078 **26.** 1,585 ÷ 5

27. 1,000 − 452 **28.** 12 × 503 **29.** 354 − 90 − 214

Fibonacci Sequence

Build Understanding

A plant started growing in January. The plant will need to grow for two months before it can add a new branch. Likewise, each new branch must grow for two months before it can add another new branch. After the second month, a branch adds a new branch each month. How many branches will there be in July? In the diagram below, the red branch shows the new growth that month.

You can look at the diagram to find the answer. By July there will be 13 branches.

The number of branches from January through July form the first seven numbers of the ***Fibonacci sequence,*** which bears the nickname of the thirteenth-century mathematician, Leonardo of Pisa. These numbers are 1, 1, 2, 3, 5, 8, 13, ...

Write About Math Write a rule that tells how each number in the Fibonacci sequence is related to the two numbers before it.

Check Understanding

For another example, see Set B, pages 40–41.

Find each answer.

1. Write the first 15 numbers in the Fibonacci sequence.

2. Which of the first 15 Fibonacci numbers are even numbers?

3. In which positions in the sequence do you think the next 3 even numbers will occur?

4. Write more numbers in the Fibonacci sequence to check your answer to Exercise 3.

5. In what positions in the sequence do you think the multiples of 3 will occur?

6. Use the drawing. Write the sequence for the number of new branches each month from August through December.

Practice

For More Practice, see Set B, pages 42–43.

Where in the Fibonacci sequence do multiples of each number occur?

7. Multiples of 13

8. Multiples of 55

9. Multiples of 144

The sequence 3, 4, 7, 11, . . . is formed as follows: 4 + 3 = 7, 7 + 4 = 11, and so on.

10. Give the next 4 terms of this sequence.

11. What is the 12th term of the sequence?

The rule for the Fibonacci sequence is used to construct each sequence below. Tell whether you used mental math or paper and pencil to fill in the missing numbers.

12. 3, 7, 10, ■, ■, ■

13. 1, 5, ■, ■, ■, ■

14. 2, 2, ■, ■, ■, 16, ■

15. 2, 5, 7, ■, ■, ■

16. 2, ■, 8, ■, ■, ■

17. 5, ■, 10, ■, 25, ■

18. ■, ■, ■, ■ 57, 88

19. 9, ■, 28, ■, ■, ■

20. ■, ■, 16, 24, ■, ■

21. 3, ■, ■, 7, ■, ■

22. 7, ■, ■, 9, ■, ■, ■

23. 8, ■, ■, ■, 49, ■, 128

24. 1, 3, 4, 7, 11, 18, . . . is called the Lucas sequence. How are the Lucas numbers related to the Fibonacci numbers? Find a pattern.

25. **Number Sense** If you multiply each term in the Fibonacci sequence by 5, will the relationship between the terms in the new sequence follow the Fibonacci rule? Explain.

Problem Solving

Solve each problem.

26. A male bee has 1 parent. A female bee has 2 parents. Extend the diagram to show the number of ancestors in the 7th generation (G7) for a male bee.

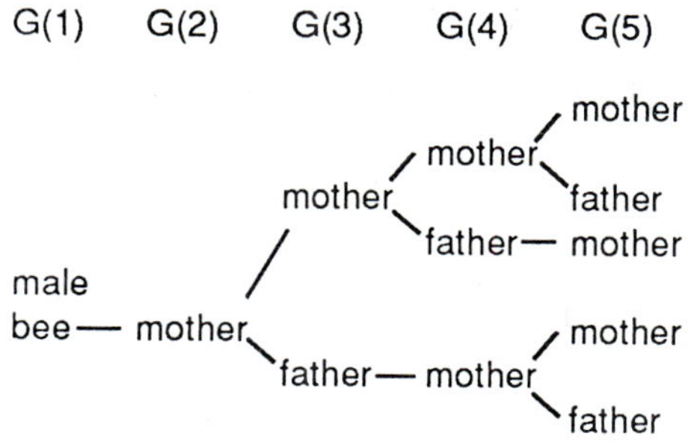

27. How many bees should there be in the fifteenth generation?

Critical Thinking Repeat Problems 28 and 29 until you find a pattern. Describe the pattern in words.

28. Select any 3 consecutive Fibonacci numbers. Multiply the first and last numbers. Square the middle number. What is true about the two products?

29. Select any 4 consecutive Fibonacci numbers. Multiply the first and last numbers and the two middle numbers. What is true about the two products?

ALGEBRA

Pascal's Triangle

Build Understanding

This interesting number array is called Pascal's triangle. The triangle begins with 1 and continues as shown. It has many uses in arithmetic and unexpected links to other areas of mathematics.

ACTIVITY

That Magic Triangle
Groups: 4 students

a. What is the number on each end of each row of the triangle?

b. Look at row 2. How is the number 2 related to the numbers in row 1?

c. Look at row 3. How are the second and third number related to the numbers in row 2? Do you see a pattern?

d. Test your pattern on rows 4 and 5. If it works, use the pattern to complete rows 6 and 7. If it does not work, try to find a pattern that does work.

e. Complete rows 8 through 10 of Pascal's triangle.

Talk About Math Explain how Pascal's triangle is developed.

Check Understanding

For another example, see Set C, pages 40–41.

Find each answer.

1. Write the sequence formed by adding the first 2 numbers in each of rows 0 through 10 in Pascal's triangle. The sum of row 0 is 1.

2. What is the sum of the first two numbers in the 22nd row? Hint: what pattern do you see in the sequence in Exercise 1?

Calculator Find each product. Then explain how each product is related to Pascal's triangle.

3. 11 × 11

4. 11 × 11 × 11

5. 11 × 11 × 11 × 11

6. Does 11 × 11 × 11 × 11 × 11 fit the pattern? Explain.

Practice

For More Practice, see Set C, pages 42–43.

Use Pascal's triangle to find each answer. **Remember** that row 0 is the first row of the triangle.

7. Write the sequence formed by the sum of all the numbers in each of rows 0 through 10.

8. What pattern do you see in Exercise 7? What is the sum of the numbers in row 15?

9. Except for the 1s, which rows contain all even numbers? Which of the rows 11 through 30 do you think will follow this pattern?

10. Which rows contain all odd numbers? Which of rows 11 through 30 do you think will follow this pattern?

11. The sum of all numbers above row 1 is 1, above row 2 is 1 + 2, or 3, and above row 3 is 7. Write a sequence for the first 10 such numbers.

12. Compare the sequence in Exercise 11 with that in Exercise 7. What is the sum of all the numbers above row 23?

13. Write each of the numbers in the sequence in Exercise 7 as a power of 2.

14. If n is the row number, write an expression for the sum of the numbers in the row n.

15. Write the first three numbers in the tenth row.

16. What are the terms of the row whose sum is 2,048?

Problem Solving

Solve each problem.

For each of Problems 17–20, write a sequence of 8 numbers with terms that are the first number on the diagonal, the sum of the first 2 numbers on the diagonal, the sum of the first 3 numbers, and so on. You will need to extend the terms on the diagonal to get a sequence with 8 terms.

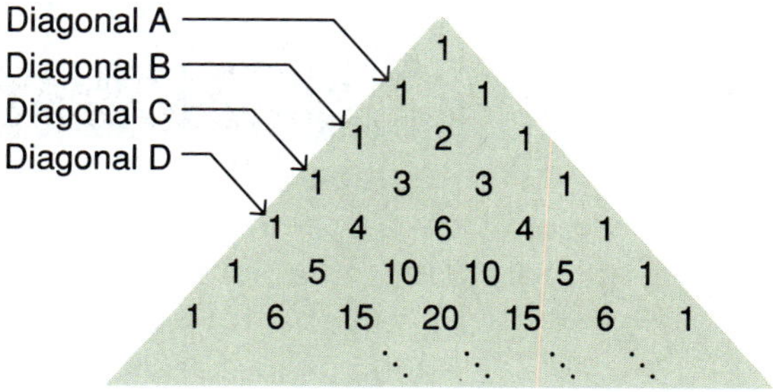

17. Diagonal *A*

18. Diagonal *B*

19. Diagonal *C*

20. Diagonal *D*

Critical Thinking Solve these problems about Pascal's triangle.

21. Find each of the sequences in Problems 17–20 elsewhere in Pascal's triangle. Write a generalization to tell where the sequence is located.

22. You have worked with the sequence in Diagonal *B* before. What are these numbers called?

C A R E E R   C O N N E C T I O N

Solve a Simpler Problem

PROBLEM SOLVING GUIDE

Understand
QUESTION
FACTS
KEY IDEA

Plan and Solve
STRATEGY
ANSWER

Look Back
SENSIBLE ANSWER
ALTERNATE APPROACH

Build Understanding

A landscaper is making a 12-foot path with patio tiles that are 1 foot wide by 2 feet long. He can lay the tiles vertically or horizontally. If the path is 2 feet wide, how many different arrangements of the tiles are possible?

Understand Find how many ways 1-foot by 2-foot patio tiles can be laid to make a path 2 feet wide and 12 feet long.

Plan and Solve STRATEGY *Solve a simpler problem* and *find a pattern*. The drawing shows all possible arrangements for 1-foot, 2-foot, and 3-foot long paths.

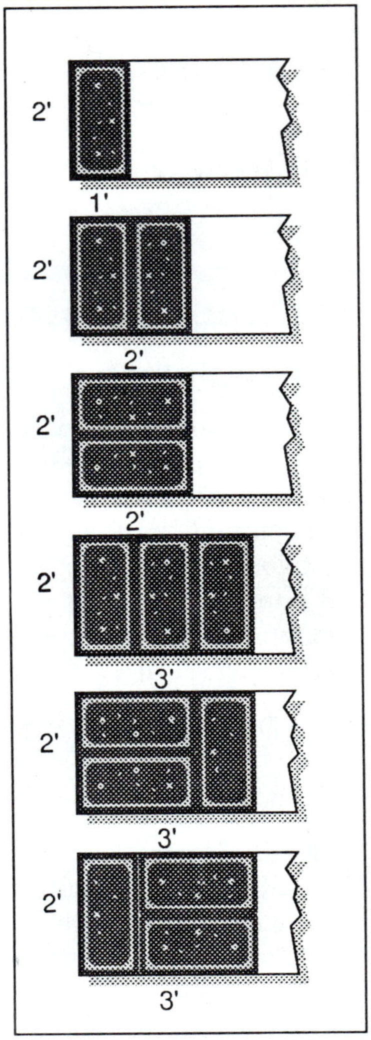

Draw pictures to complete the table for 4-foot and 5-foot long paths. Look for a pattern in the table to determine the number of tiles in a twelve-foot path.

Length of path	1 ft	2 ft	3 ft	4 ft	5 ft
Number of arrangements	1	2	3	5	8

The numbers 1, 2, 3, 5, and 8 are the second through sixth Fibonacci numbers. The sixth Fibonacci number tells the number of possible arrangements for a path 5 feet long. Find the 13th Fibonacci number to determine the number of arrangements for a path 12 feet long.
1, 1, 2, 3, 5, 8, 13, 21, 34, 55, 89, 144, **233**

ANSWER There are 233 ways to tile the pathway.

Look Back Check the pattern by drawing the arrangements for a 6-foot-long path.

■ **Talk About Math** How can you be sure that the pattern in the Fibonacci sequence is the correct one for this problem?

Check Understanding

Use the information in Build Understanding to find each answer.

1. How many arrangements are possible for a 10-foot-long path? a 14-foot-long path?

2. If the pattern did not hold for a 6-foot-long path, what would you conclude?

Practice

Sandra Day O'Connor is the first woman on the Supreme Court.

Solve each problem.

3. What is the sum of the first 1,000 odd numbers?

4. What is the sum of the first 1,000 even numbers?

5. What is the sum of the numbers 1 through 1,000?

6. There are 9 Supreme Court Justices. Each October every Justice shakes hands with every other Justice just before the first session. How many handshakes take place? *Hint:* Use Pascal's triangle.

The following rules apply to a certain team tournament:

a. All teams are paired off in the first round.
b. If there is a team that cannot be paired at a round, it passes that round and must play in the next round.
c. Only winning teams and passed teams can go on to another round.

How many games will be played to establish the winner in a(n)

7. 8-team tournament? **8.** 12-team tournament? **9.** 32-team tournament?

ALGEBRA

10. Critical Thinking Refer to Problems 7–9. Write an expression for the number of games played if there are x teams in the tournament.

Midchapter Checkup

Tell whether the sequence is arithmetic, geometric, or neither. Give the next three terms.

1. 1, 3, 5, 7, . . . **2.** 1, 3, 9, 27, . . . **3.** 1, 2, 4, 7, 11, . . .

4. Use the rule for constructing the Fibonacci sequence to find the missing terms.
3, ▒, 6, ▒, 15, ▒, ▒, ▒, . . .

If row 4 of Pascal's triangle is 1, 4, 6, 4, 1, what is

5. row 3? **6.** row 5?

Problem-Solving Workshop

Number-Sense Project

Look back at pages 2-3. The hertz is a unit of measure for the frequency of sound waves. When sound frequencies are too high or too low, we cannot hear the sounds. The table shows how the human hearing range compares to that of several animals.

1. Which animals can hear frequencies above those of humans?

2. Which animals can hear frequencies below those of humans?

Animal	Hearing range in hertz
Human	20 - 20,000
Dolphin	150 - 150,000
Robin	250 - 21,000
Dog	15 - 50,000
Cat	65 - 65,000
Grasshopper	100 - 15,000

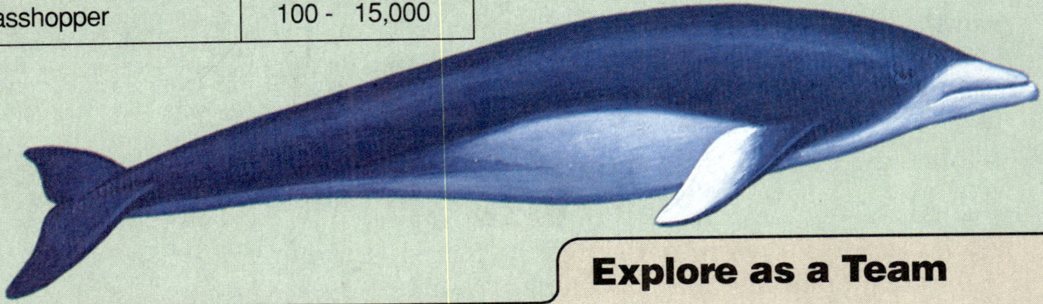

Explore as a Team

1. Have one member of your team fill in a 3×3 square grid using three different letters of the alphabet. Each letter is put in three squares and squares marked with the same letter must share a common side.

2. Have the other members of the team try to copy the first player's pattern by asking how many of each letter are in a specific row or column.

3. The first member answers but does not give the order in which the letters appear. Continue until one member of your team thinks he or she has copied the pattern correctly. The first person to copy the pattern correctly is the winner.

4. Repeat the game taking turns drawing a pattern and asking questions.

TIPS FOR WORKING TOGETHER

Involve your whole group.
Help everyone to participate.

Explore with a Computer

Use the *Spreadsheet Workshop Project* for this activity.

1. At the computer, change the number in row 0 of Pascal's Triangle to any other number. What happens to the rest of the numbers?

2. Change all of the 1's in the outside diagonals to 2's. What happens?

3. Experiment with changing the outside diagonals to other numbers.

4. What number would have to be placed in each spot in the outside diagonals in order to have the sum of the bottom row be four times what it is now?

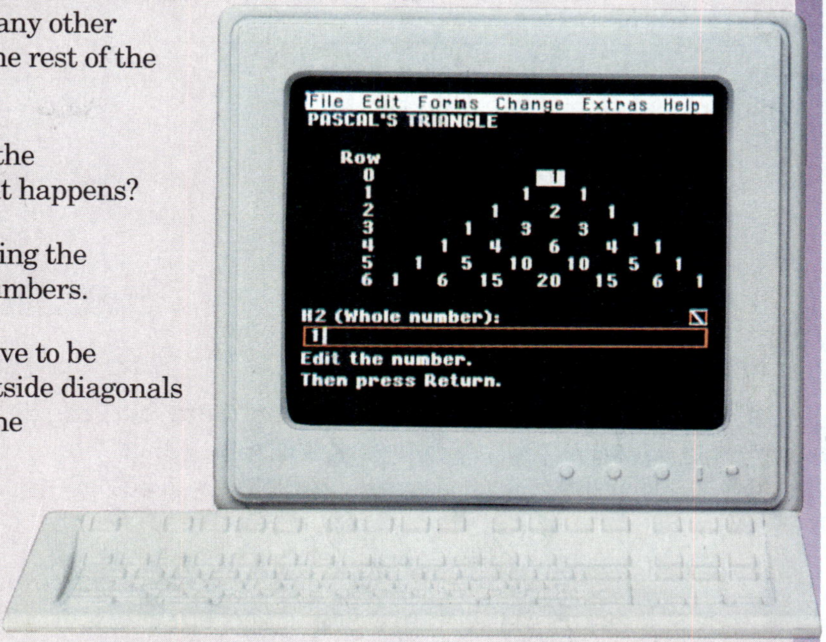

Critical-Thinking Activity

Four friends started a music group. Their names are Dan, Pam, Sam, and Betty. They play the drums, piano, saxophone, and guitar. Each person also serves in another capacity for the group, as a dancer, singer, press agent, or general manager. When they perform, each wears a costume which is green, purple, sequined, or has diamonds. Dan plays the piano and sings and Pam is the dancer.

Each person's name, instrument they play, capacity they serve in, and costume begins with a different letter.

Describe each person.

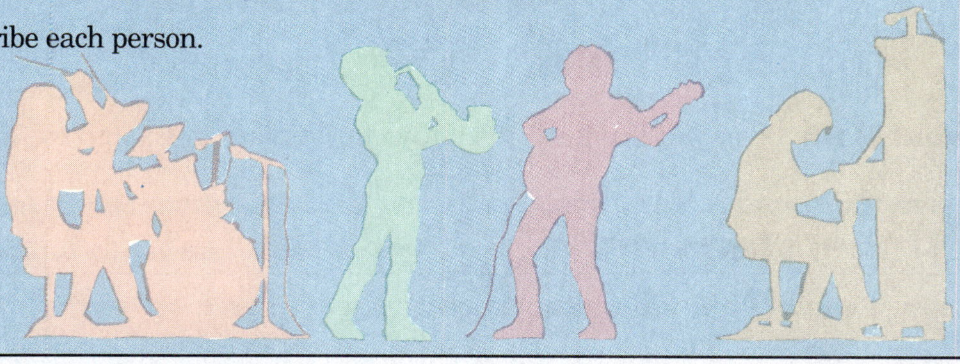

Estimation Strategies

Build Understanding

City	Mileage to Chicago	Highway
Champaign	135	I-57
E. St. Louis	288	I-55
Joliet	42	I-55
Kankakee	56	I-57
Moline	183	I-80
Mt. Vernon	274	I-57
Peru	83	I-80
Springfield	197	I-55

A. One week Ms. Jordan, a salesperson, made round trips from Chicago to Kankakee, Champaign, and East St. Louis. Estimate the total distance she drove on the three trips.

The one-way distances are 56 miles, 135 miles, and 288 miles. You can estimate the one-way distances, add them, and double the result.

One way you can estimate is to add the ***front-end digits*** and then adjust.

56	Add the front-end digits:	**100 + 200 → 300**	
135	Then adjust: 56 + 35 ≈ 100.	**Add 100 → 400**	The symbol ≈ means
+288	88 ≈ 90.	**Add 90 → 490**	"is approximately equal to."

You can also estimate by rounding to the nearest hundred.

56 + 135 + 288 ⇒ 100 + 100 + 300 = 500

Ms. Jordan drove about 500 miles one way, or about 1,000 miles round trip.

B. Estimate the product by ***rounding*** each factor to one nonzero digit.

42 × 288

40 × 300 = 12,000

42 × 288 ≈ 12,000

C. Estimate the sum by ***clustering.***

$6.55	Three of the numbers
6.90	cluster around 7.
2.04	3 × 7 = 21
+ 7.18	21 + 2 = 23

The estimated sum is $23.

D. Estimate 738 ÷ 19 by using ***compatible numbers.*** Compatible numbers are numbers close to the numbers given that are easy to work with. Here are some ways to estimate the quotient.

$19\overline{)738}$ $\quad \overset{40}{20\overline{)800}}$ $\quad \overset{37}{20\overline{)740}}$ $\quad \overset{40}{19\overline{)760}}$ $\quad \overset{40}{18\overline{)720}}$ $\quad$ **738 ÷ 19 ≈ 40**

■ **Talk About Math** Can you think of other ways to estimate in Examples A–D?

Check Understanding

For another example, see Set D, pages 40–41.

Estimate each answer. Tell which estimation strategy you used.

1. 218 × 4.95 **2.** 38.7 + 2.14 + 91 **3.** 2,467 ÷ 49 **4.** 13.6 + 15.2 + 14.7 + 16.7

Practice

For More Practice, see Set D, pages 42–43.

Estimate each answer. Tell which estimation strategy you used.

5. 20.3 + 3.12 + 58.2 **6.** 4,316 + 1,529 + 997 **7.** 524 − 379

8. 61.30 − 199.8 **9.** $7\overline{)3{,}386}$ **10.** $68\overline{)2{,}017}$

11. 37.9 × 413 **12.** 2.13 + 19.8 + 207 **13.** 34 × 97 × 61

14. 6,849 − 4,963 **15.** 492 × 41 **16.** 38,641 ÷ 89

17. 4.7 × 36.8 **18.** 322 + 43 + 137 **19.** 2,124 − 688

20. 12 × 9 × 11 × 3 **21.** $489\overline{)12{,}225}$ **22.** 184 × 319 × 5

23. 325,214 − 197,196 **24.** 208 + 582 + 614 + 949 **25.** 16 × 168 × 208

26. 138 + 147 + 141 + 290 + 45 + 292 **27.** 52.465 + 49.117 + 51.092 + 47.983

Estimate and then compute the exact answers.

28. 479 × 27 **29.** 357 + 285 **30.** 231 × 83 **31.** 128 + 347

32. **Number Sense** Compare your estimated answers with your exact answers in Exercises 28–31. When will the estimated answer be greater than the exact answer? less than the exact answer?

Problem Solving

Estimate each answer. Use the table on page 18.

33. The total number of miles traveled on a round trip between Chicago and Springfield and a round trip between Chicago and Kankakee

34. The number of gallons of gasoline used on a trip from Chicago to East St. Louis in a car that averages 28 miles per gallon.

35. The total gasoline charges: $15.36, $14.47, $16.08, $14.98

36. The distance between Springfield and East St. Louis traveling on I-55

37. The number of miles in 19 round trips between Joliet and Chicago

38. The number of miles in 9 round trips from Chicago to Mt. Vernon

Critical Thinking Look at each exercise. Without checking the answers, determine why the computation is incorrect.

39. 234 × 63 = 297 **40.** 43 + 32 + 26 + 19 = 1,120 **41.** $\begin{array}{r} 3{,}943 \\ 12\overline{)472{,}836} \end{array}$

ALGEBRA

Evaluating Expressions

Build Understanding

A. A fast-food restaurant has 18 full-time employees who are paid weekly. Eleven each earn $180, 5 each earn $237, and 2 each earn $330. Find their average weekly salary.

Write an expression for the average amount earned per week. Then evaluate.

The average salary equals the total amount of all the salaries divided by the number of employees, or

$$\frac{11 \times 180 + 5 \times 237 + 2 \times 330}{11 + 5 + 2}.$$

> **The Standard Order of Operations**
>
> - Multiply and divide from left to right.
> - Add and subtract from left to right.
>
> If the expression contains parentheses or a division bar:
>
> - First compute inside the parentheses, using the standard order.
> - Compute above and below the division bar, using the standard order.
> - Do the remaining computations using the standard order.

How should this computation be performed?

Use the standard order of operations:

$$\frac{11 \times 180 + 5 \times 237 + 2 \times 330}{11 + 5 + 2} = \frac{1{,}980 + 1{,}185 + 660}{11 + 5 + 2} = \frac{3{,}825}{18} = 212.5$$

Multiply from left to right above the division bar. — Add above and below the division bar. — Divide.

The average weekly salary is $212.50.

B. Evaluate the expression $\frac{42 + 4d}{2e}$ when $d = 9$ and $e = 13$.

$$\frac{42 + 4 \times 9}{2 \times 13} = \frac{42 + 36}{26} = \frac{78}{26} = 3$$

Substitute for d and e in the expression. Multiply. — Add above the division bar. — Divide.

■ **Write About Math** Describe how you could use your calculator to perform the computation in Example A.

Check Understanding

For another example, see Set E, pages 40–41.

Compute by using the standard order of operations.

1. 24 − 6 + 2 **2.** 24 − 6 × 2 **3.** 24 × 6 − 2 **4.** 24 ÷ 6 × 2 **5.** 24 ÷ 6 ÷ 2

6. 5 + 2 × 4 + 3 **7.** (5 + 2) × (4 + 3) **8.** 5 + 2 × (4 + 3) **9.** (5 + 2) × 4 + 3

Practice

For More Practice, see Set E, pages 42–43.

Compute. **Remember** to use the standard order of operations.

10. $10 - 4 + 1$ **11.** $9 + 4 - 2$ **12.** $10 \div 2 - 2$ **13.** $10 \times 9 + 2$

14. $8 \times 6 + 2$ **15.** $8(6 + 2)$ **16.** $(5 - 2)(5 - 2)$ **17.** $5 \times 5 - 2 \times 2$

18. $13 + 3 - 40 \div 4$ **19.** $100 \times 3 \div 6 + 4 - 4$ **20.** $5 + 5 - 5 \times 5 \div 25$

21. $17(10 - 7)$ **22.** $17 - (10 - 7)$ **23.** $(17 - 10) - 7$

24. $\frac{2(2 - 2)}{6(5 + 4)} + 9$ **25.** $\frac{6(14 - 7)}{7(1 + 5)} - 1$ **26.** $\frac{33 - 7(3 + 1)}{27 \div 9 + 2}$

27. $\frac{8 \times 9 + 8 \times 6}{4 \times 9 + 4 \times 6}$ **28.** $\frac{15 \times 3 + 56 \div 8}{56 \div 8 - 1 \times 3}$ **29.** $\frac{(586 - 186)(29 + 61)}{45(438 - 38)}$

30. $\frac{7 - 2}{7 + 2} \times \frac{3 \times 9}{5 \times 3}$ **31.** $24 \div \frac{10 + 2 \times 3 + 8}{10 - 2 \times 3}$ **32.** $\frac{48 - 15 + 2}{48 - (15 + 2)} \div 7$

Evaluate each expression if $x = 8$ and $y = 6$.

33. $2x + y$ **34.** $2(x + y)$ **35.** $5x - 3y$ **36.** $\frac{x + y}{x - y}$ **37.** $2(x - y)$

38. Evaluate each expression in Exercises 33–37 when $x = -1$ and $y = 1$.

Insert parentheses to make the statement true.

39. $4 + 3 \times 2 = 14$ **40.** $5 \times 4 + 8 \div 2 - 6 = 8$ **41.** $6 \times 8 \div 4 + 4 = 6$

42. $13 - 4 \times 3 - 1 = 0$ **43.** $8 \times 10 \div 2 + 3 = 64$ **44.** $9 + 3 \times 9 - 3 = 72$

Problem Solving

Write an expression for the problem. Then evaluate it.

45. Compute the average monthly salary if 7 employees each earn $1,250 per month and 5 employees each earn $1,035 per month.

46. **Calculator** Find the average yearly salary if 18 employees each earn $24,550, 15 each earn $49,900, and 2 each earn $75,812. Round your answer to the nearest cent.

Number Sense For 1 ▦ 2 ▦ 3 ▦ 4, insert +, −, ×, or ÷ for each ▦, and insert parentheses to make

47. a whole number as large as possible.

48. a whole number as small as possible.

49. a fraction.

50. a mixed number.

Interpret the Remainder

PROBLEM SOLVING GUIDE

Understand
QUESTION
FACTS
KEY IDEA

Plan and Solve
STRATEGY
ANSWER

Look Back
SENSIBLE ANSWER
ALTERNATE APPROACH

Build Understanding

Teela Martinez is a motion picture animator. For a movie segment showing a dog chasing a cat, 24 pictures represent one second of viewing time. Teela drew 204 pictures. How long will the chase segment last?

Understand QUESTION How long will the segment last?

FACTS There are 204 pictures; and 24 pictures take 1 second of viewing time.

KEY IDEA How many groups of 24 are in 204?

Plan and Solve STRATEGY To find the number of groups of 24 in 204, you can divide.
First, estimate:

$$204 \div 24 \rightarrow 200 \div 20 = 10$$

Next, divide.

$$\begin{array}{r} 8 \\ 24\overline{)204} \\ \underline{192} \\ 12 \end{array} \text{ R12 or } 8\tfrac{12}{24} = 8\tfrac{1}{2} \text{ or } 8.5$$

ANSWER Before you can give the answer, you must decide how to use the remainder. Since a fraction of a second makes sense, you can use $8\frac{1}{2}$ or 8.5.

The chase segment will last $8\frac{1}{2}$ seconds.

Look Back The answer is reasonable since it is close to the estimate.

In division, you often have to interpret the remainder to answer the question. If the answer must be a whole number, decide whether you should round the quotient up or down. If an exact answer makes sense, you can express it as a decimal or a mixed number. Sometimes, just the remainder is the answer.

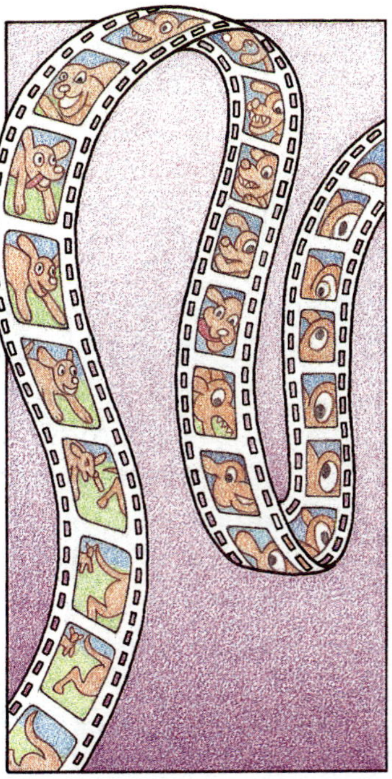

A cartoon sequence that takes 3 months to draw by hand can be done on a computer in just 2 weeks.

■ **Talk About Math** What kinds of problems require a whole-number answer? When might the remainder be the answer?

Check Understanding

Solve each problem. Explain how the remainder is used in giving the answer.

1. Teela drew an 889-picture scene. How many seconds does it run?

2. If art paper comes in packs of 48 sheets, how many packs will Teela need to get 889 sheets?

Practice

Solve each problem. **Remember** to decide how the remainder should be used.

3. Teela's pictures are photographed at a rate of 8 feet per second. How long will it take to photograph 150 feet of film?

4. **Mental Math** Teela has 625 pictures for a 30-second commercial. If 20 pictures represent 1 second of viewing time, how many extra pictures does she have?

5. A full-length animated movie could require as many as 100,000 separate pictures. At 24 pictures per second, how long would such a movie last?

6. **Number Sense** Can the remainder in division be greater than the divisor? Explain why or why not.

Choose a ______ Strategy

Granola Grab More than 16 boys are seated around a table. They pass around a box containing 49 granola bars. Each boy takes one bar each time the box comes to him. Manolo took the first and last bar in the box. How many boys are seated at the table?

7. How many granola bars are in the box?

8. How many bars do you know for certain that Manolo gets?

9. How many boys would be seated at the table if Manolo got 2 bars?

10. What is the greatest number of bars that Manolo could get?

11. How many boys would be seated at the table if Manolo gets the greatest number of bars?

12. How many boys could be seated at the table? List all possibilities.

ALGEBRA

Mental Math Strategies

Build Understanding

A. Dee likes to solve problems "in her head." One way that Dee finds sums and differences mentally is by using ***compensation.***

a. Find \$1.49 + \$2.45.

1.50 + 2.44 = 3.94

\$1.49 + \$2.45 = \$3.94

Add 1¢ to \$1.49 and compensate by subtracting 1¢ from \$2.45. In effect, 0 has been added.

b. Find \$3.64 − \$0.98.

3.64 − 1.00 = 2.64

2.64 + 0.02 = 2.66

\$3.64 − \$0.98 = \$2.66

Add 2¢ to 98¢. Subtract. To compensate, add 2¢ to the answer.

B. Dee also uses the properties of operations to break numbers into convenient parts.

Commutative Properties of Addition and Multiplication The order of numbers can be changed without changing the sum or product.	$6 + 8 = 8 + 6$ $5 \times 9 = 9 \times 5$
Associative Properties of Addition and Multiplication The grouping of numbers can be changed without changing the sum or product.	$(5 + 7) + 3 = 5 + (7 + 3)$ $(2 \times 3) \times 5 = 2 \times (3 \times 5)$
Distributive Properties Multiplication distributes over addition and subtraction.	$3 \times (2 + 4) = (3 \times 2) + (3 \times 4)$ $4 \times (7 - 3) = (4 \times 7) - (4 \times 3)$
Properties of 0 and 1 The sum of zero and a number is that number. The product of one and a number is that number.	$8 + 0 = 8$ $7 \times 1 = 7$

Which property did Dee use to find each answer?

45 + 37	**25 × 28**	**15 × 19**
45 + (30 + 7)	**25 × (4 × 7)**	**15 × (20 − 1)**
(45 + 30) + 7	**(25 × 4) × 7**	**(15 × 20) − (15 × 1)**
75 + 7	**100 × 7**	**300 − 15**
82	**700**	**285**
Associative Property of Addition	**Associative Property of Multiplication**	**Distributive Property**

■ **Talk About Math** Why did Dee add 2¢ to the answer in the subtraction problem in Example A?

Check Understanding

For another example, see Set F, pages 40–41.

1. Complete the table.

n	2	4	5	10	12	24	124
$10 \times n$							
$5 \times n$							

Use the table to help you describe a mental math strategy for multiplying by

2. 5. **3.** 15.

Use mental math to find the product.

4. $5 \times 85 \times 20$. **5.** $349 + 68 + 51$

Practice

For More Practice, see Set F, pages 42–43.

Identify the property. Then compute mentally on one side of the equal sign. Explain why you chose that side.

6. $6 \times (40 + 5) = (6 \times 40) + (6 \times 5)$

7. $18 + (2 + 37) = (18 + 2) + 37$

8. $(30 - 1) \times 8 = (30 \times 8) - (1 \times 8)$

9. $5 \times (8 \times 3) = (5 \times 8) \times 3$

10. $5 \times 49 \times 2 = 5 \times 2 \times 49$

11. $15 + 79 + 5 = 15 + 5 + 79$

Use mental math to do each computation. **Remember** to use the properties of operations correctly.

12. $79 - 43$ **13.** $239 + 247$ **14.** $25 \times 3 \times 7 \times 4$ **15.** 8×53

16. $58 + 77$ **17.** $28 + 154$ **18.** $119 + 198$ **19.** $81 - 57$

20. $(89 + 3) + 67$ **21.** $122 + 0$ **22.** $1{,}129 \times 1$ **23.** $5 \times 4 \times 0 \times 8$

24. $5{,}002 - 2{,}887$ **25.** $38{,}491 - 16{,}378$ **26.** 7×62

27. 75×99 **28.** $8 \times 4 \times 25 \times 15$ **29.** $150 \times 8{,}640$

30. $87 \times 321 + 13 \times 321$ **31.** $137 \times 78 + 137 \times 22$ **32.** $49 \times 119 - 49 \times 19$

Problem Solving

33. Critical Thinking Develop a mental math strategy for multiplying a number by 25. Explain your strategy in writing.

Write and solve a problem using

34. one of the associative properties.

35. one of the distributive properties.

36. one of the commutative properties.

37. either the property of 0 or 1.

Choose a Computation Method

Build Understanding

When you compute, sometimes you can do the work mentally. Otherwise, you use paper and pencil or, if the computation is tedious, a calculator.

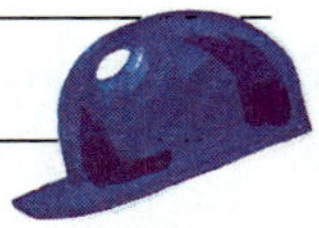

Seating Capacity

Stadium	Football	Baseball
Candlestick	61,413	58,000
Fulton County	59,673	52,003
Kingdome	64,984	59,850
Metrodome	62,212	55,244
Riverfront	59,574	52,392
Three Rivers	59,000	58,727

A. Candlestick Park had 15 consecutive sellouts for baseball games. What was the total attendance for those games?

Find the product: 15 × 58,000.

Recall the mental math strategy for multiplying a number by 15.

(10 + 5) × 58,000	Think of 15 as 10 + 5. Multiply 58,000 by 10 and then by 5.
10 × 58,000 = 580,000	Think: 10 × 58,000
5 × 58,000 = 290,000	Think: 5 × 58,000 = (10 × 58,000) ÷ 2
580,000 + 290,000 = 870,000	Add.

The attendance for the 15 games was 870,000.

B. Find the difference in the seating capacities for football and baseball games at Riverfront Stadium.

Find 59,574 − 52,392.

$$\begin{array}{r} \mathbf{59{,}574} \\ \mathbf{-52{,}392} \\ \hline \mathbf{7{,}182} \end{array}$$

Subtract by using paper and pencil.

A football game has 7,182 more seats than a baseball game.

C. **Calculator** Both the Kingdome and the Metrodome are sellouts for all 81 home baseball games. Find the total attendance for the two stadiums:

(59,850 + 55,244) × 81

The computation would be tedious with paper and pencil. Use a calculator.

Press: 59,850 [+] 55,244 [×] 81 [=]

Display: 9,322,614

The total attendance is 9,322,614.

Talk About Math Give an example of a subtraction problem involving two different 5-digit numbers which could be solved more quickly mentally than with a calculator.

Check Understanding

Refer to the table on page 26. For each stadium, find the difference in the football and baseball seating capacities. Use mental math, paper and pencil, or a calculator. Tell which method you used.

1. Candlestick **2.** Metrodome **3.** Three Rivers **4.** Fulton County

5. The average ticket price at Candlestick Park is $5.00. What is the approximate revenue for a sellout baseball game?

Practice

Use mental math, paper and pencil, or a calculator to find the answer. Tell which method you used.

6. 52,396 + 41,647 − 20,099 **7.** (12 × 61,413) + (12 × 64,984) **8.** 3,800 × 22

9. 81,196 − 79,804 **10.** 1,250,000 + 50,000 + 2,700,000 **11.** 550 × 100

12. 25 × 59,000 **13.** 20,100 × 13,507 **14.** 7,512 − 10

Estimation Estimate each answer. Then compute.

15. 59,856 + 61,274 **16.** 48,620 − 22,307 **17.** 25 × 58,727

18. 50 × 137 × 20 **19.** 5,231 × 78 **20.** 348.7 + 652.3

21. 56,131 − 19,392 **22.** 65 + 387 + 35 **23.** 100,000 − 68,952 − 1,048

Problem Solving

Solve each problem. Tell whether you used mental math, paper and pencil, or a calculator.

24. If there is a sellout for each of the 81 baseball games at the Metrodome this season, what will the total attendance be for the year?

25. Suppose baseballs cost $5.95 each and an average of six dozen are used per game. What is the cost of the baseballs for all 81 home games?

26. The Rousseaus bought 5 tickets at $4.50 each, 2 score cards at $1.25 each, a pennant for $6.25, 5 orange drinks for $1.50 each, and 6 hot dogs for $2.25 each. How much did they spend?

27. Parking costs $3 per car. If everyone drove to the game with an average of 3 people per car, how much money would be collected for parking at a sellout football game at Fulton County Stadium?

Factors and Divisibility

Build Understanding

A. The Chinese calendar groups years under 12 animal designations—one for each year. Mr. Lyn's students are painting the animals on separate square pieces of canvas to make a mural. How many different ways can they make a rectangular mural using all 12 squares?

To find the possible rectangles, list the factors of 12.

1 × 12
2 × 6
3 × 4

Each product represents the dimensions of a rectangle.

There are 3 possible ways.

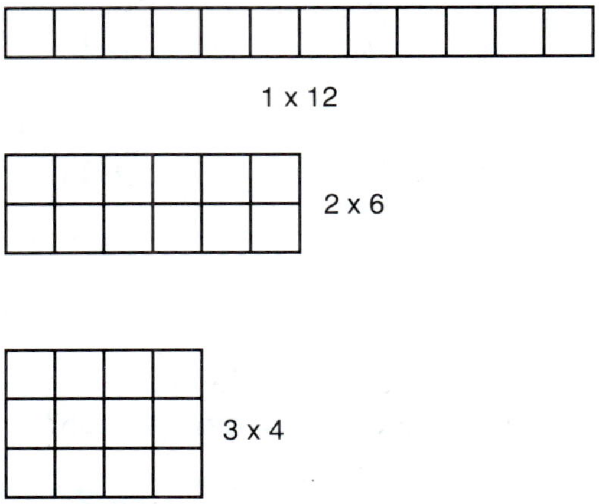

1, 2, 3, 4, 6, and 12 are all the ***factors,*** or ***divisors,*** of 12.

B. Find a number that has exactly 2 factors.

The only product for 19 is 1 × 19. So 19 has exactly 2 factors.

A whole number with exactly 2 factors is a ***prime number.*** A whole number with more than 2 factors is a ***composite number.*** Zero and one are neither prime nor composite.

C. Mental Math Find the first 5 whole numbers divisible by 7.

Think: 1 × 7, 2 × 7, 3 × 7, and so on.

A whole number that is divisible by another whole number is a ***multiple*** of that number.

The first 5 multiples of 7 are 7, 14, 21, 28, and 35.

D. The Mayan civilization used three systems simultaneously for counting days. One calendar was based on a 260-day cycle. Which of the whole numbers 1 through 6 are divisors of 260? You can use divisibility rules to find the answers.

1? Yes. Every number is divisible by 1.
2? Yes. Even numbers are divisible by 2.
3? No. Since the sum of the digits $(2 + 6 + 0)$ is not divisible by 3, you know that 260 is not divisible by 3.
4? Yes. The number formed by the last two digits (60) is divisible by 4, so 260 is also divisible by 4.
5? Yes. Any number with 0 or 5 as the ones digit is divisible by 5.
6? No. Since 260 is not divisible by both 2 and 3, it is not divisible by 6.

The first band from the center of the Aztec Calendar Stone shows the 20 different signs representing the days of the month.

■ **Write About Math** The number 9 was considered magical in ancient China because any multiple of 9 "returned" to 9. What do you think this means?

Check Understanding

For another example, see Set G, pages 40–41.

Complete each statement. A number is divisible by

1. 2 if ___?___ **2.** 3 if ___?___ **3.** 4 if ___?___ **4.** 5 if ___?___ **5.** 6 if ___?___ **6.** 9 if ___?___

7. Which of the whole numbers 1 through 9 are divisors of 735?

8. Explain a systematic way to determine whether 83 is prime or composite.

Practice

For More Practice, see Set G, pages 42–43.

Find all the factors of the given number. Tell whether it is prime or composite. **Remember** to use the divisibility rules.

9. 90	**10.** 91	**11.** 92	**12.** 93	**13.** 95	**14.** 97
15. 49	**16.** 88	**17.** 105	**18.** 127	**19.** 361	**20.** 570
21. 40	**22.** 16	**23.** 51	**24.** 11	**25.** 112	**26.** 529

27. Mental Math Give the first ten multiples of 6. Can you give all of the multiples of 6?

28. Number Sense For any whole number greater than 1, can you find a factor of the number that is also a multiple of the number?

Problem Solving

Critical Thinking Tell if each statement is *true* or *false*. Explain your answer.

29. A multiple of 3 is always divisible by 9.

30. A multiple of 9 is always divisible by 3.

31. Every prime number is an odd number.

32. A multiple of 10 is always even.

TIPS FOR PROBLEM SOLVERS

Be confident so you can do your best.

Solve each problem.

33. Use Data Refer to Pascal's triangle on page 12. In which of the rows 3–6 is the third number a multiple of the row number? Which of rows 7–20 should follow this pattern?

34. The year 1990 is Chinese Lunar Year 4688, the Year of the Horse. Is 4688 a prime number? Why?

35. List the next three years after 1990 that will also be the Year of the Horse.

36. Reggie is thinking of 3 numbers. Use these clues to find them.
a. Their product is 72.
b. Their sum is a multiple of 7.
c. Two of the numbers are prime.

37. Use these clues to find Marcia's three numbers.
a. Their product is 72.
b. Their sum is prime.
c. Each number has only one digit.

38. Think of a set of three numbers, and write three clues that can be used to find them.

39. Repeat Problem 38 but write clues for a set of four numbers.

Each column in this Babylonian calendar shows a different month. The Babylonians also had a seven-day week.

40. The use of 60 minutes in an hour and 60 seconds in a minute dates back to the Babylonians. What are the factors of 60?

41. The ancient Egyptians based their calendar on the return of the Dog Star, Sirius, to its sunrise location on the horizon every 365 days. Their calendar had 12 months, each of which had 30 days. The extra days at the end of the 12 months were festival days. How many festival days were there?

Explore ________ Math

A school has 100 lockers and 100 students. All of the lockers are closed. As the students enter, the first student, S1, opens every locker. Next, the second student, S2, begins with locker L2, and closes every other locker. S3 begins with L3 and changes every third locker—from open to closed or from closed to open. S4 changes every fourth locker, S5 every fifth locker, and so on.

	L1	L2	L3	L4	L5	L6	L7	L8
Start	C	C	C	C	C	C	C	C
S1	O	O	O	O	O	O	O	O
S2		C		C		C		C
S3			C			O		
S4				O				O
S5					C			
S6						C		
S7							C	
S8								C

42. Make a table like the one shown but include the first 12 lockers and students. Write O if the student opened a door and C if the student closed the door.

43. For each of students 1–12, list which of lockers 1–12 that student touches. What do you notice about these numbers? Which lockers will student 20 touch?

44. For each of lockers 1–12, list which of students 1–12 touch that locker. What do you notice about these numbers? Which students will touch locker 36?

45. After student 5 passes, which lockers are no longer changed?

46. After student 12 passes, which lockers are no longer changed?

47. After all students pass, which of lockers 1–12 are open? of lockers 1–25? of lockers 1–100?

48. After all students pass, which of lockers 1–12 were touched by exactly 3 students? of lockers 1–25? of lockers 1–100?

Exponents and Prime Factorization

Build Understanding

Prime numbers are sometimes called the building blocks for whole numbers. Do you know why?

A. An ***exponent*** tells how many times a number is used as a factor.

$3 \times 3 = 3^2$ Read 3^2 as "three squared" or "three to the second power."

3^2, or 9, is the 2nd power of 3.

The square root of 9 is 3. $\sqrt{9} = 3$. Nine is a perfect square because its square root is a whole number.

$2 \times 2 \times 2 = 2^3$ Read 2^3 as "two cubed" or "two to the third power."

$5 \times 5 \times 5 \times 5 = 5^4$ Read 5^4 as "five to the fourth power."

Any number raised to the first power is that number: $3^1 = 3$. Any nonzero number raised to the zero power is 1: $3^0 = 1$.

B. Study what happens when powers of a number are multiplied.

$$3^2 \times 3^3 = (3 \times 3) \times (3 \times 3 \times 3)$$
$$= 3^5$$
$$5^2 \times 5^2 = (5 \times 5) \times (5 \times 5)$$
$$= 5^4$$
$$7 \times 7^4 = 7 \times 7 \times 7 \times 7 \times 7$$
$$= 7^5$$
$$2^3 \times 3^2 = 2 \times 2 \times 2 \times 3 \times 3$$
$$= 2^3 \times 3^2$$

C. Any composite number can be written as a product of primes.

Write 180 as a product of primes.

You can use a ***factor tree*** to write a product of primes. Start with any 2 factors whose product is 180. Keep writing factors until all factors are prime.

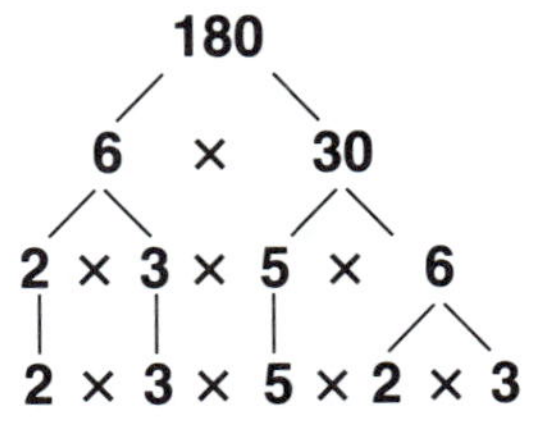

$180 = 2 \times 3 \times 5 \times 2 \times 3$

Or you can use ***successive division.***

Divide by prime factors until the quotient is 1.

2	180	$180 \div 2 = 90$
2	90	$90 \div 2 = 45$
3	45	$45 \div 3 = 15$
3	15	$15 \div 3 = 5$
5	5	$5 \div 5 = 1$
	1	

The ***prime factorization*** of 180 is $2 \times 2 \times 3 \times 3 \times 5$. This can be written in exponential form as $2^2 \times 3^2 \times 5$.

■ **Talk About Math** Give a rule for writing $6^5 \times 6^8$ as a power of 6.

Check Understanding

For another example, see Set H, pages 40–41.

1. Make two different factor trees for 60. Is the prime factorization always the same?

Write the prime factorization in exponential form for Exercises 2 and 3.

2. 315 (Use a factor tree.)
3. 220 (Use successive division.)
4. Write $5^2 \times 5^3$ as a power of 5.
5. **Calculator** Is 1,225 a perfect square?

Practice

For More Practice, see Set H, pages 42–43.

Write the prime factorization of each number in exponential form. **Remember** to include all the factors in your answer.

6. 24
7. 225
8. 325
9. 363
10. 593
11. 972
12. 2,058
13. 4,000
14. 6,422
15. 12,155
16. 32,400
17. 165,375
18. **Calculator** Which of the numbers 100 through 1,000 are perfect squares?

Express each product as a power of 7. Tell whether you use mental math or paper and pencil.

19. $7^2 \times 7^3$
20. $7^3 \times 7^5$
21. $7^4 \times 7^4$
22. 7×7^9
23. $7^2 \times 7^{12} \times 7^{100}$

Problem Solving

Solve each problem.

24. Find the least perfect square that has 60 as a factor. Why is this the least such number?
25. Show how you can use the prime factorization of 45 to list all the factors of 45.

You can write 3^2 as $3^0 \times 3^2$ and $3^1 \times 3^1$. Tell how many ways you can write the following as a product of 2 factors.

26. 3^3
27. 3^4
28. 3^5
29. 3^6
30. 3^7
31. 3^8
32. 3^9
33. How many ways can you write 3^n as a product of two factors if n is odd? if n is even?

Critical Thinking Show why these number sentences are false. Then change one exponent or one base in each number sentence so that it becomes true.

34. $2^3 \times 2^5 = 2^{15}$
35. $(3^1)(3^0) = 3^0$
36. $2^4 \times 4^2 = 8^8$
37. $4^4 + 4^4 = 2^8$

Common Factors and Equal Fractions

Build Understanding

A. Some people say that *smiles* is the longest word in the English language because there is a *mile* between the first and last letters. *Webster's Third International Dictionary* lists the longest word as *pneumonoultramicroscopicsilicovolcanoconiosis*. Nine of the 45 letters in this word are *o*s. What fraction of the letters is this? Write this fraction three ways.

$\frac{9}{45} = \frac{3}{15} = \frac{1}{5}$ So, $\frac{1}{5}$ of the letters are *o*'s.

You can divide both the numerator and the denominator of a fraction by a ***common factor*** to find an equal fraction.

Factors of 9: 1, 3, 9

Factors of 45: 1, 3, 5, 9, 15, 45

Common factors: 1, 3, 9

Greatest Common Factor: 9

Divide by the ***greatest common factor (GCF)*** to find the fraction in lowest terms.

$$\frac{9}{45} = \frac{9 \div 9}{45 \div 9} = \frac{1}{5}$$

$\frac{1}{5}$ is in lowest terms because the GCF of its numerator and denominator is 1.

The dictionary Noah Webster published in 1828 contained 12,000 more words and 40,000 more definitions than any previous English dictionary.

B. Use prime factorization to find the GCF of 252 and 360. Then, write $\frac{252}{360}$ in lowest terms.

Write the prime factorization of each number. For common prime factors, choose the term with the smaller exponent.

$252 = 2^2 \times 3^2 \times 7$

$360 = 2^3 \times 3^2 \times 5$

GCF: $2^2 \times 3^2 = 36$

$$\frac{252}{360} = \frac{252 \div 36}{360 \div 36} = \frac{7}{10}$$

To write $\frac{252}{360}$ in lowest terms, divide the numerator and denominator by the GCF.

■ **Talk About Math** If the GCF of two numbers is 1, the numbers are ***relatively prime.*** What is true of a fraction that has a numerator and a denominator that are relatively prime?

Check Understanding

For another example, see Set I, pages 40–41.

Use prime factorization to find the GCF of each pair of numbers.

1. 9 and 12 **2.** 28 and 56 **3.** 13 and 89 **4.** 65 and 195

Write each fraction in lowest terms.

5. $\frac{9}{12}$ **6.** $\frac{13}{89}$ **7.** $\frac{24}{30}$ **8.** $\frac{105}{150}$

Practice

For More Practice, see Set I, pages 42–43.

Find the GCF for the given numbers. **Remember** to find all the common factors.

9. 6 and 48 **10.** 18 and 54 **11.** 17 and 67 **12.** 55 and 115

13. 30 and 105 **14.** 24 and 168 **15.** 25 and 175 **16.** 20 and 75

17. 8, 15, and 60 **18.** 12, 18, and 36 **19.** 100, 215, and 450

20. Number Sense Can two even numbers be relatively prime? Explain.

Write each fraction in lowest terms.

21. $\frac{18}{54}$ **22.** $\frac{8}{15}$ **23.** $\frac{100}{450}$ **24.** $\frac{14}{90}$ **25.** $\frac{39}{65}$

26. $\frac{24}{72}$ **27.** $\frac{57}{190}$ **28.** $\frac{47}{140}$ **29.** $\frac{39}{77}$ **30.** $\frac{60}{75}$

31. $\frac{32}{224}$ **32.** $\frac{72}{108}$ **33.** $\frac{135}{216}$ **34.** $\frac{429}{572}$ **35.** $\frac{252}{882}$

Problem Solving

Write a word in which one third of the letters are vowels and that has the given number of letters.

36. 3 letters **37.** 6 letters **38.** 9 letters **39.** 12 letters

40. What fraction of the letters in your full name are vowels? Write the fraction in lowest terms.

41. Can two odd numbers have a GCF greater than one? Give an example to explain your answer.

42. Number Sense The GCF of 2 and another number is 1. Describe the other number.

43. Critical Thinking What is the GCF of two prime numbers?

Common Multiples and Common Denominators

Build Understanding

A. The Cougars and the Lions played the same number of soccer games. The Cougars won $\frac{7}{12}$ of the games they played and the Lions won $\frac{5}{8}$ of the games they played. Which team won more games?

Since both fractions refer to the same number of games played, you can find the answer by comparing the fractions.

It is easier to compare fractions when they have a common denominator. A ***common denominator*** of two fractions is a common multiple of their denominators. The ***least common multiple,*** LCM, is the least common denominator.

Multiples of 8: 8, 16, 24, 32, 40, 48, . . .
Multiples of 12: 12, 24, 36, 48, 60, . . .
The LCM of 8 and 12 is 24.

The least common denominator (LCM) of $\frac{5}{8}$ and $\frac{7}{12}$ is 24.

$\frac{5}{8} = \frac{5 \times 3}{8 \times 3} = \frac{15}{24}$ and $\frac{7}{12} = \frac{7 \times 2}{12 \times 2} = \frac{14}{24}$

Since $15 > 14$, $\frac{15}{24} > \frac{14}{24}$.

So $\frac{5}{8} > \frac{7}{12}$.

The Lions won more games.

B. Use prime factorization to find the LCM of 84 and 180.

Write the prime factorization of each number. For any common prime factors, choose the term with the largest exponent.

$84 = 2^2 \times 3 \times 7$

$180 = 2^2 \times 3^2 \times 5$

$\text{LCM} = 2^2 \times 3^2 \times 5 \times 7$

The LCM of 84 and 180 is 1,260.

Talk About Math Can the GCF and LCM of two numbers be the same?

Check Understanding

For another example, see Set J, pages 40–41.

1. Find the LCM of 28 and 56.

2. Which is greater, $\frac{23}{28}$ or $\frac{53}{56}$? Explain.

Practice

For More Practice, see Set J, pages 42–43.

Find the LCM for the given numbers.

3. 9, 12 **4.** 18, 60 **5.** 9, 15 **6.** 13, 89

7. 40, 100 **8.** 32, 64, 80 **9.** 14, 35, 49 **10.** 34, 102

Tell which fraction is larger. **Remember** to find the least common multiple.

11. $\frac{5}{9}, \frac{11}{15}$ **12.** $\frac{4}{9}, \frac{7}{12}$ **13.** $\frac{11}{18}, \frac{31}{60}$ **14.** $\frac{7}{10}, \frac{13}{15}$

15. $\frac{5}{9}, \frac{7}{12}$ **16.** $\frac{13}{20}, \frac{7}{10}$ **17.** $\frac{7}{32}, \frac{5}{24}$ **18.** $\frac{9}{16}, \frac{8}{15}$

Write the fractions in order from smallest to largest.

19. $\frac{1}{2}, \frac{5}{8}, \frac{5}{11}$ **20.** $\frac{5}{6}, \frac{2}{3}, \frac{7}{12}$ **21.** $\frac{1}{3}, \frac{1}{9}, \frac{1}{5}$ **22.** $\frac{7}{12}, \frac{11}{20}, \frac{13}{24}$

23. $\frac{9}{14}, \frac{3}{4}, \frac{5}{7}$ **24.** $\frac{2}{3}, \frac{5}{6}, \frac{2}{9}$ **25.** $\frac{8}{15}, \frac{3}{5}, \frac{7}{12}$ **26.** $\frac{1}{2}, \frac{4}{13}, \frac{1}{3}, \frac{7}{39}$

Mixed Practice For each pair of numbers, find the LCM and the GCF.

27. 4 and 6 **28.** 8 and 12 **29.** 7 and 15 **30.** 11 and 13

31. 2 and 11 **32.** 14 and 70 **33.** 16 and 25 **34.** 121 and 143

Problem Solving

Solve each problem.

35. In June, Laura has a soccer game every 4th day starting June 4 and a baseball game every 6th day beginning June 6. On which June days will she play both soccer and baseball?

36. The Hawks and the Eagles played the same number of games. The Hawks won $\frac{2}{3}$ of their games, and the Eagles won $\frac{3}{4}$. Which team won fewer games?

37. If the Hawks and Eagles from Problem 36 played 24 games, how many games did each team win?

38. **Number Sense** Write a rule for finding the LCM of two numbers that are relatively prime.

ALGEBRA **Critical Thinking** Solve each problem.

39. If the prime factors of x are a and b, and the prime factors of y are b and c, what is the LCM of x and y?

40. If the GCF of x and y is 1, what is the LCM of x and y?

Skills Review

Tell whether the sequence is arithmetic, geometric, or neither. Then write the next three terms

1. 75, 72, 69, 66, . . . **2.** 3, 9, 27, 81, . . .

3. 50, 62, 74, 86, . . . **4.** 0, 3, 7, 12, . . .

Estimate each answer.

5. $4{,}361 \div 72$ **6.** $45.87 - 12.44$

7. $212 + 195 + 188$ **8.** $58 \times 92 \times 103$

Compute. **Remember** to use the standard order of operations.

9. $5 \times 6 - 2$ **10.** $72 \div 8 + 5 \times 3$

11. $\frac{3(7-4)}{3(9-8)}$ **12.** $\frac{42 - 6(4+2)}{81 \div 9 \div 3}$

Use mental math to do each computation.

13. $2.98 + $3.15 **14.** 25×28

15. $16{,}998 - 5{,}312$ **16.** $20 \times 7 \times 6 \times 5$

Use mental math, paper and pencil, or a calculator to find each answer.

17. $25 \times 40{,}000$ **18.** $7 \times 5{,}624 \times 9$

19. $2{,}692 - 1{,}371$ **20.** $1{,}450 + 90 + 400$

Write the prime factorization of each number in exponential form.

21. 90 **22.** 144 **23.** 252

Find the grestest common factor and the least common multiple for each pair of numbers.

24. 6 and 8 **25.** 4 and 12

26. 16 and 25 **27.** 7 and 11

Problem-Solving Review

Solve each problem.

28. How many 3-digit numbers are there in which the sum of the digits is 16?

29. Five teams are in a volleyball tournament. Each team plays every other team once. How many games are played in all?

30. The Pine Hill Walnuts make 6 round trips each season to play the Cairo Pecans. If Pine Hill is about 88 miles from Cairo, approximately how many miles do the Walnuts travel for these games in a season?

31. On a trip, Ms. Alvarez drove 472 miles and used 13 gallons of gasoline. About how many miles did her car travel per gallon of gas?

32. The Anacondas played twice as many games as the Rattlers. The Rattlers won $\frac{2}{3}$ of their games and the Anacondas won $\frac{1}{2}$ of their games. Which team won more games?

33. **Data File** Use the data on pages 110–111. What part of its state's total rail-trails is each of the five longest rail-trails?

34. **Make a Data File** Use a dictionary to find 30 words having at least 12 letters. List the words alphabetically in a column. In a second column, list the number of vowels in each word. In a third column, list the fraction of each word composed of vowels.

Cumulative Skills Review • Chapter 1

Use the Fibonacci Sequence (1, 1, 2, 3, 5, 8, 13, . . .) for each exercise.

1. What two terms of the sequence are added to get the ninth term?

2. What are the ninth, tenth and eleventh terms of the sequence?

Use Pascal's triangle on page 12 to find each answer.

3. What numbers will be in row 12?

4. Which numbers in row 9 are divisible by 3?

Estimate each answer.

5. 43.2×292 **6.** $6.13 + 18.2 + 909.12$ **7.** $97 \times 504 \times 22$ **8.** $6{,}586 \div 11$

Evaluate each expression if $x = 4$ and $y = 8$.

9. $5x - 2y$ **10.** $7(x + y)$ **11.** $7x + y$ **12.** $(x + y) \div (y - x)$

13. $x + 13y$ **14.** $(y)(x)4$ **15.** $\frac{x + 7}{y}$ **16.** $(x + 3)y$

Insert parentheses to make the statement true.

17. $8 - 3 \times 2 = 10$ **18.** $6 \times 6 - 1 \div 5 = 6$ **19.** $10 + 10 \times 10 \div 5 = 40$

Use mental math to compute.

20. 6×52 **21.** $12 \times 77 + 88 \times 77$ **22.** $2{,}476 + 1{,}324$ **23.** $6{,}003 - 1{,}557$

Use mental math, paper and pencil, or a calculator to find the answer.

24. 50×680 **25.** $78{,}291 - 67{,}009$ **26.** $97 + 249 + 503$ **27.** 760×240

28. $72{,}012 + 16{,}092$ **29.** \$7.98 + \$3.42 **30.** $17{,}420 \div 16$ **31.** \$15.67 − \$2.99

Write the prime factorization of each number in exponential form.
Tell whether it is prime or composite.

32. 43 **33.** 100 **34.** 39 **35.** 72 **36.** 97 **37.** 77

Write each fraction in lowest terms.

38. $\frac{20}{36}$ **39.** $\frac{16}{72}$ **40.** $\frac{51}{170}$ **41.** $\frac{13}{78}$ **42.** $\frac{120}{270}$ **43.** $\frac{36}{78}$

Write the fractions in order from smallest to largest.

44. $\frac{7}{8}, \frac{7}{11}, \frac{7}{9}$ **45.** $\frac{6}{7}, \frac{5}{8}, \frac{1}{2}$ **46.** $\frac{1}{5}, \frac{1}{9}, \frac{1}{4}$ **47.** $\frac{4}{9}, \frac{5}{6}, \frac{2}{3}$

48. $\frac{4}{5}, \frac{3}{8}, \frac{-1}{7}, \frac{1}{2}$ **49.** $\frac{3}{5}, 0, \frac{1}{4}, \frac{7}{8}$ **50.** $\frac{1}{8}, \frac{1}{16}, \frac{3}{32}, \frac{7}{64}$ **51.** $\frac{9}{10}, \frac{4}{5}, \frac{1}{2}, \frac{2}{3}$

Reteaching

Set A pages 6–9

The sequence 9, 17, 25, 33, 41, . . . is an arithmetic sequence. Here, the difference between consecutive terms is 8.

The sequence 1, 3, 9, 27, 81, . . . is a geometric sequence. Here, each consecutive term is 3 times the preceding term.

Remember to look for a pattern between consecutive terms in a sequence.

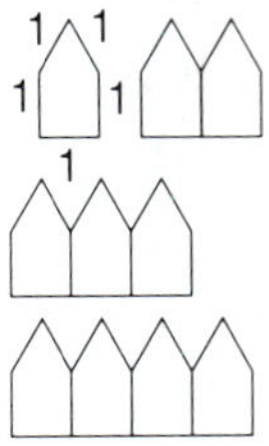

1. Write the first 7 terms in the sequence formed by the perimeters of these figures.

2. What is the 25th term?

3. If the perimeter is 125, how many pentagons make up the figure?

Set B pages 10–11

Study this pattern for the Fibonacci sequence 1, 1, 2, 3, 5, 8, . . .

3rd term: 1 + 1 = 2
4th term: 1 + 2 = 3

Remember that the Fibonacci sequence is neither arithmetic nor geometric.

1. What are the first and second terms of the Fibonacci sequence?

2. What two terms are added to get the 3rd term? To get the 4th term?

3. Write the 7th through 12th terms.

Set C pages 12–13

Part of Pascal's triangle is shown here. Row 2 has three terms. The first and last terms are both 1. The middle term is the sum of the two terms above it.

Row
0: 1
1: 1 1
2: 1 2 1
3: 1 3 3 1
4: 1 ■ ■ ■ 1

Remember that the first and last term in any row of Pascal's triangle is 1.

1. Write the terms in rows 4 and 5 of Pascal's triangle.

2. Write a rule for finding each term between the first and last terms in any row.

Set D pages 18–19

Estimate 59 + 37 by using front-end digits and adjusting.
Front-end digits: 50 + 30 = 80
Adjust: 9 + 7 = 16, which rounds to 20
Add: 80 + 20 = 100

Remember that front-end digits and clustering work best for addition and subtraction.

1. Estimate 59 + 37 by rounding and then using compatible numbers. Compare your answers.

2. Clustering doesn't work for the sum 59 + 37. Explain why.

Set E pages 20–21

To compute 48 − 24 ÷ 3, use the standard order of operations.
First, multiply and divide.
Then add and subtract.

Divide: 24 ÷ 3 = 8. Subtract: 48 − 8 = 40.

Remember to first multiply and divide, and then add and subtract.

1. Compute 112 − 9 × 3.
2. Compute 72 + 8 ÷ 8.

Set F pages 24–25

Use mental math to add 87 + 66.

Think: 87 + 3 = 90; 66 − 3 = 63

90 + 63 = 153

Remember to use compensation and the properties of operations to break numbers into easier parts for mental math.

1. What strategy is used in the example?
2. What mental math strategy can you use to compute 15 × 24?
3. Use mental math to compute 15 × 24.

Set G pages 28–31

List the factors of 22.
Since 22 is even, it is divisible by 2.

Factors: 1 × 22 and 2 × 11

The number 22 is composite since it has more than two factors. It is a multiple of 1, 2, 11, and 22.

Remember to use divisibility rules for 2, 3, 5, 9, and 10, and your knowledge of prime numbers to find factors of a number.

Is the number divisible by 2, 3, 5, 9, or 10? List all the possibilities.

1. 50
2. 42
3. 185
4. 200

Set H pages 32–33

Use successive division to find the prime factorization of 210.

2 | 210
3 | 105
5 | 35
7 | 7
1

Divide by prime factors. Start with 2, then 3, then 5, and so on. Continue until the quotient is 1.

210 = 2 × 3 × 5 × 7

Remember that you can use exponents to show how many times a number is used as a factor.

1. Use a factor tree to write 210 as a product of primes.
2. Write $3^3 \times 3^5$ as a power of 3.
3. Write the prime factorization of 882 in exponential form.

Set I pages 34–35

Find the greatest common factor (GCF) of 12 and 30. Use prime factorization.

$12 = 2^2 \times 3$ $30 = 2 \times 3 \times 5$

The GCF is 2 × 3, or 6.

Remember that the GCF of two numbers is the largest of the common factors.

Use prime factorization to find the GCF.

1. 30 and 45
2. 20 and 75

Set J pages 36–37

To compare fractions, find the least common multiple (LCM) of their denominators, and rewrite each fraction. Compare $\frac{17}{30}$ and $\frac{23}{45}$.

$30 = 2 \times 3 \times 5$ $45 = 3^2 \times 5$ LCM = $2 \times 3^2 \times 5$, or 90

$\frac{17}{30} = \frac{51}{90}$ and $\frac{23}{45} = \frac{46}{90}$

Since 51 > 46, then $\frac{17}{30} > \frac{23}{45}$.

Remember that the LCM is the smallest of the common multiples of two numbers.

1. Find the LCM of 16 and 40.
2. Which fraction is greater, $\frac{3}{16}$ or $\frac{7}{40}$?

More Practice

Set A pages 6–9

Tell whether the sequence is arithmetic, geometric, or neither. Then write the next 3 terms.

1. 1, 4, 5, 9, 14, . . .

2. 2, 11, 20, 29, . . .

3. 1, 4, 16, 64, . . .

Find the missing term in each arithmetic sequence.

4. 1, ▒, 23, 34, ▒, . . .

5. 5, ▒, ▒, 26, 33, . . .

6. ▒, 13, ▒, 19, ▒, . . .

Find the missing term in each geometric sequence.

7. 2, ▒, 50, 250, ▒, . . .

8. 1, 7, ▒, ▒, 2401, . . .

9. ▒, 9, ▒, 81, ▒, . . .

Set B pages 10–11

Use the Fibonacci Sequence, 1, 1, 2, 3, 5, 8, 13, . . . , to answer Exercises 1 and 2.

1. Write a sequence that gives the positions of the odd numbers in the Fibonacci sequence.

2. Write a rule that describes the sequence you found in Exercise 1.

Construct each of these sequences by using the same rule that is used to construct the Fibonacci sequence.

3. 1, 4, ▒, 9, ▒, 23, . . .

4. 3, 2, ▒, ▒, 12, ▒, . . .

Set C pages 12–13

Use Pascal's triangle on page 12 to find each answer.

1. Write the sequence found by adding the first 3 numbers in each of rows 0 through 10. The sum of row 0 is 1, and the sum of row 1 is 2.

2. Describe the pattern of the sequence in Exercise 1.

3. What is the 12th term in the sequence? What is the 22nd term?

Set D pages 18–19

Estimate each answer.

1. 88 + 42 + 91 + 39

2. 276 + 814 + 431

3. 89,719 − 28, 284

4. 626 − 243

5. 9,687 − 8,833

6. 21,975 + 37,647

7. 70 × 5,001

8. 628 ÷ 91

9. 236 × 92

Set E pages 20–21

Compute.

1. 11 − 5 + 2

2. 18 ÷ 3 + 3

3. 12 × 4 + 12

4. 11 + 4 − 6 ÷ 3

5. 50 × 4 ÷ 8 + 6 − 10

6. 16 + 3 − 8 × 3 ÷ 6

7. $\frac{8 + 9 \times 4}{8 + 7 - 4}$

8. $\frac{66 - 6(2 + 3)}{2 + 60 \div 6}$

Set F pages 24–25

Use mental math to do each computation.

1. 67 + 38 **2.** 101 − 87 **3.** 9 × 43 **4.** 236 + 64

5. 231 − 89 **6.** 13 × 19 **7.** 57 + 82 + 23 + 18 **8.** 25 × 82

9. 355 − 27 **10.** 41 × 39 **11.** 139 + 93 **12.** 1042 − 142

Set G pages 28–31

Find all factors of the given number.

1. 53 **2.** 84 **3.** 191 **4.** 308

5. 108 **6.** 35 **7.** 48 **8.** 71

9. 105 **10.** 121 **11.** 100 **12.** 101

Set H pages 32–33

Write the prime factorization of each number in exponential form.

1. 63 **2.** 80 **3.** 300 **4.** 96 **5.** 105

6. 162 **7.** 1,125 **8.** 1,470 **9.** 6,048 **10.** 18,865

11. 19 **12.** 72 **13.** 240 **14.** 560 **15.** 20,000

Set I pages 34–35

Find the GCF for the given numbers.

1. 18 and 45 **2.** 36 and 42 **3.** 63 and 56 **4.** 90, 108, and 630

Write each fraction in lowest terms.

5. $\frac{42}{90}$ **6.** $\frac{36}{56}$ **7.** $\frac{108}{630}$ **8.** $\frac{45}{63}$ **9.** $\frac{51}{306}$ **10.** $\frac{34}{323}$

11. $\frac{32}{8}$ **12.** $\frac{27}{45}$ **13.** $\frac{24}{108}$ **14.** $\frac{105}{225}$ **15.** $\frac{120}{320}$ **16.** $\frac{297}{432}$

Set J pages 36–37

Find the LCM for the given numbers.

1. 24 and 42 **2.** 12 and 63 **3.** 49 and 735 **4.** 24, 30, and 48

Tell which fraction is larger.

5. $\frac{2}{3}, \frac{19}{21}$ **6.** $\frac{24}{25}, \frac{13}{15}$ **7.** $\frac{11}{24}, \frac{19}{42}$ **8.** $\frac{41}{56}, \frac{51}{63}$

Find the GCF and the LCM for each pair.

9. 6 and 8 **10.** 3 and 12 **11.** 5 and 6 **12.** 18 and 60

13. 12 and 20 **14.** 9 and 11 **15.** 22 and 33 **16.** 10 and 20

Enrichment

Number Sense

Fill in each blank in the story below.

Sam, Letha, Kelly, and David Barnett drove from their home in New York to California last summer. The morning they started their trip the temperature was ___1.___ (7°, 27°, 77°) Fahrenheit. They packed all of their luggage into their new car that weighed ___2.___ (2, 20, 200) tons and they were on their way. The Barnetts drove about ten hours each day, taking time to stop for meals and rest. Sam and Letha drove just under the speed limit, and the family traveled approximately ___3.___ (100, 500, 2,000) miles per day. As they were traveling across Iowa, they drove through a thunderstorm with wind gusts of ___4.___ (5, 50, 200) miles per hour. In one hour, ___5.___ (2, 20, 50) inches of rain fell.

The Barnetts reached California in ___6.___ (1, 3, 6) days. Along the way they passed through ___7.___ (2, 10, 45) states and ___8.___ (4, 12, 60) time zones. Kelly read in her guidebook that California has a population of ___9.___ (1 million, 25 million , 1 billion) people and an area of ___10.___ (100, 1,000, 150,000) square miles.

While in California they saw many attractions. They visited Mount Whitney, the highest mountain in the continental United States, with a height of ___11.___ (140, 1,400, 14,000) feet and camped in Yosemite National Park. In Yosemite they hiked for three hours, covering ___12.___ ($\frac{1}{2}$, 6, 30) miles. David saw a kingsnake that was ___13.___ (1 mm, 1 cm, 1 m) long and a deer that weighed about ___14.___ (15, 125, 800) pounds. On the way back to their campsite they waded across a cold stream. The temperature of the water was about ___15.___ (−40°, −4°, 40°) Fahrenheit.

The Barnetts were away from home about $\frac{1}{3}$ of the summer. They were happy to return home after their ___16.___ (1-, 4-, 9-) week vacation.

Chapter 1 Review/Test

1. How many times is the digit 3 used in the numbers between 0 and 100?

2. Tell whether the sequence 4, 8, 12, 16 is geometric, arithmetic, or neither.

In Exercises 3 and 4, write the next three terms in the sequences, and tell how each term is found.

3. 64, 32, 16, 8, . . .

4. 4, 4, 8, 12, 20, . . .

5. The numbers in row four of Pascal's triangle are: 1, 4, 6, 4, 1. What are the numbers in rows five and six?

6. Complete the table below to find the answer for this problem.
Starting from 2, what is the sum of the first 10 even numbers?

Step	Addends	Total
1	2	2
2	2 +4	6
3	2 + 4 + 6	?
4	2 + 4 + 6 + 8	?
5	2 + 4 + 6 + 8 + 10	?

7. Tell which compatible numbers you would multiply to estimate the answer to the problem.
Last summer, Carlos's family drove to the lake 11 times. The round trip is 58 miles. How many miles did they drive?

Compute.

8. $16 - 8 \times 2$

9. $14 + 2 \times 3 - 10$

Evaluate each expression if $c = 7$ and $y = 4$.

10. $3(c + y)$

11. $\frac{2c+y}{c-4}$

12. The World Series Baseball Company packs 24 baseballs in a carton. One team needs 818 baseballs for July. How many cartons should the manager order so she will have enough?

13. Which property is used in this number sentence? Tell whether you would use pencil and paper, mental math, or a calculator to compute.

$23 \times 29 = (23 \times 30) - (23 \times 1)$

14. Find all of the factors of 24.

15. Write the prime factorization of 96.

Find the greatest common factor.

16. 18 and 24

17. 11 and 12

Find the least common multiple.

18. 9 and 15

19. 7 and 28

Write each fraction in lowest terms.

20. $\frac{13}{39}$

21. $\frac{36}{100}$

22. $\frac{11}{121}$

Which is greater?

23. $\frac{4}{9}$ or $\frac{1}{2}$

24. $\frac{7}{12}$ or $\frac{11}{18}$

25. **Write About Math** Rephrase the information given in this problem.
Kate bought 3 new horse statues, which she added to her collection of 6 horse statues and 12 dog statues. How many statues are in her collection now?

Decimals and Fractions 2

Did You Know: Mark Wellman, a paraplegic, was the first climber to scale El Capitan in Yosemite National Park using only his arms. Wellman figured that scaling the 3,569 feet of sheer rock was equivalent to doing 7,000 pull-ups.

Number-Sense Project

Estimate

To do a pull-up, hang by two arms from a horizontal bar and pull your body up until your chin is over the bar. How many pull-ups do you think you can do at one time?

Gather Data

Each day for a week do as many pull-ups as you can at one time. Keep track of the number of pull-ups and the amount of time they take. Determine how far off the floor you raise your body with each pull-up.

Analyze and Report

Use your data to find how many pull-ups you would have to do to raise yourself 3,569 feet. How long would this many pull-ups take?

Dividing a Decimal by a Whole Number

Build Understanding

Together, Jordi and Lisa bought 12 audio tapes for the listening library at the Teen Center. The tapes they selected, shown at the right, cost $103.74. What was the average cost per tape?

Since you want to find an average cost, you can divide the total cost by the number of audio tapes.

Use compatible numbers to estimate.
$103.74 ÷ 12 → 100 ÷ 10 = 10

Pencil and Paper

```
      8.645
12)103.740
    96
     7 7
     7 2
       54
       48
        60
        60
         0
```

Calculator

Press: 103.74 [÷] 12 [=]

Display: 8.645

8.645 ≈ 8.65   Since you are finding an average cost, round to the nearest hundredth.

The average cost per tape was $8.65.

Check: Is the answer reasonable? Is it close to the estimate?

■ **Talk About Math** Why can an ending zero be written in 103.74 when you divide to find the average cost of the tapes?

Check Understanding

For another example, see Set A, pages 76–77.

Number Sense Place the decimal point correctly in the quotient. Write zeros if needed.

1. 0.75 ÷ 6 → 125   **2.** 737.2 ÷ 388 → 19   **3.** 150.9 ÷ 3 → 503

Find the quotient.

4. 109.06 ÷ 38   **5.** 9.682 ÷ 206   **6.** 3,139.56 ÷ 81

Practice

For More Practice, see Set A, pages 78–79.

Estimation Show how to use compatible numbers to decide if the quotient is reasonable. Write *yes* or *no*.

7. 385 ÷ 45 = 0.73 **8.** 29.16 ÷ 27 = 1.08 **9.** 8.4 ÷ 15 = 0.56

10. 493.68 ÷ 68 = 726 **11.** 23.1768 ÷ 58 = 0.3996 **12.** 103.439 ÷ 49 = 2.111

13. 342.07 ÷ 79 = 4.33 **14.** 192.4 ÷ 26 = 0.74 **15.** 346.15 ÷ 35 = 98.9

Use the information on page 48 to find the average cost. **Remember** to place the decimal point in the quotient and to round to the nearest cent.

16. Jordi's tape selections **17.** Lisa's tape selections

18. 3 compact disks, which total $53.97 **19.** 23 posters, which total $65.78

Mixed Practice First estimate. Then divide to find the exact answer. Tell whether you used paper and pencil or calculator.

20. 78 ÷ 12 **21.** $51\overline{)3{,}223.2}$ **22.** $3\overline{)15.009}$ **23.** 422 ÷ 59 **24.** 23.56 ÷ 38

25. $\frac{0.068}{16}$ **26.** $\frac{87.36}{24}$ **27.** $\frac{57.0024}{8}$ **28.** $\frac{68.579}{97}$ **29.** $\frac{0.4455}{11}$

30. 0.4 ÷ 3 **31.** $\frac{7.2}{120}$ **32.** 8,100 ÷ 8 **33.** 29.25 ÷ 15 **34.** $\frac{10.1}{101}$

Problem Solving

Use the information on page 48 to solve each problem.

35. Each tape in the library was given a code. The tapes coded with the letter R and a number are rock music tapes. What is the average cost of the rock music tapes?

36. The tapes coded with the letter T and a number are country music tapes. What is the average cost of the country music tapes?

37. Number Sense The tapes coded with the letter V and a number feature a male or a female vocalist. Without computing, determine whether the average cost of the vocalist tapes is higher or lower than the average cost of the country music tapes.

38. The tapes coded R44, T89, C73, and V74 were checked out most often during the first month the library was open. What is the average cost of the most popular tapes? Was this price higher or lower than the average price for all the tapes?

Multiplying and Dividing by Multiples of 10

Build Understanding

Changing from one metric measure to another is easier than changing from one customary measure to another. Do you know why?

A. A college rowing course is about 6.4 kilometers long. How many meters long is the course?

Since 1 km = 1,000 m, multiply 6.4 by 1,000.

6.4 × 1,000 = 6.4 0 0 = 6,400

3 zeros — Move the decimal point 3 places to the right.

The course is about 6,400 m long.

B. An Olympic-size swimming pool is 50 meters long. Express this length in kilometers.

Since 1,000 m = 1 km, divide 50 by 1,000.

50 ÷ 1,000 = 0 5 0. = 0.05

3 zeros — Move the decimal point 3 places to the left.

The pool is 0.05 km long.

C. Find 1.093 × 200. Compute mentally as much as you can.

1.093 × 100 = 1.0 9 3 = 1 0 9.3

109.3 × 2 = 218.6

Talk About Math Explain how you can divide 6.2 by 50 mentally.

Check Understanding

For another example, see Set B, pages 76–77.

Compute. Do as much of the work as you can mentally.

1. 1,000 × 37 **2.** 682 ÷ 10 **3.** 2.5 × 400 **4.** 10.4 ÷ 200

5. When you multiply or divide by a power of 10, how do you know how many places to move the decimal point?

6. Write a mental math strategy for multiplying by a power of 10 and for dividing by a power of 10.

Practice

For More Practice, see Set B, pages 78–79.

Tell whether you would use mental math or paper and pencil. Then compute.

7. 10×4.5 **8.** $4{,}284 \div 20$ **9.** $525 \div 500$ **10.** $0.075 \times 2{,}000$

11. $0.37 \div 1{,}000$ **12.** 1.28×500 **13.** 32.8×50 **14.** $5{,}678 \div 10{,}000$

Calculator Use a calculator to divide.

15. $0.02 \div 100$ **16.** $4.6 \div 600$ **17.** $0.34 \div 100$ **18.** $0.012 \div 2{,}000$

ALGEBRA

Evaluate the expression $6.8n$ for each value of n.

19. $n = 100$ **20.** $n = 1{,}000$ **21.** $n = 10{,}000$ **22.** $n = 4{,}000$ **23.** $n = 300$

Evaluate the expression $6.8 \div n$ for each value of n.

24. $n = 10$ **25.** $n = 100$ **26.** $n = 1{,}000$ **27.** $n = 200$ **28.** $n = 40$

Evaluate each expression for $p = 100$.

29. $5.64p$ **30.** $\frac{74.256}{p}$ **31.** $0.07p$ **32.** $4 \div p$ **33.** $23.5p$

Number Sense Multiply a number by 50. Multiply the same number by 100. Then write a mental math strategy for multiplying by

34. 50. **35.** 500. **36.** 5,000. **37.** 0.5.

Problem Solving

Find each length in meters.

38. A 91.4 centimeter-long baseball bat

39. A rowing course that is 0.2 kilometer long

40. An ant that is 6.83 millimeter long

41. **Use Data** Sounds, Inc. ordered 1,000 copies of tape #R31. What will be the income from the sale of these tapes? Use the information on page 48.

TIPS FOR PROBLEM SOLVERS

Share your thinking with others. Explaining your ideas helps you think better.

Skills Review pages 20–21, 32–33

Evaluate each expression for $a = 3$, $b = 9$, and $c = 0$.

1. $a + 3b$ **2.** $b - 6c + 9a$

Write the prime factorization of each number using exponents.

3. 100 **4.** 144 **5.** 250

Dividing a Decimal by a Decimal

Build Understanding

Some service jobs and typical weekly earnings are shown in the table. What is the hairstylist's hourly rate?

Service Occupations		
Occupation	Earnings	Hours Worked
Hairstylist	\$435.63	42.5
Nurse	\$566.35	48.2
Computer programmer	\$873.38	41.1
Social worker	\$416.25	37.5
Custodian	\$299.93	38.7

Since you want to find the amount earned per hour, you can divide the total amount earned (\$435.63) by the number of hours worked (42.5 hours).

Use compatible numbers to estimate.
$435.63 \div 42.5 \rightarrow 400 \div 40 = 10$

Pencil and Paper

```
          10.250
42.5)435.6300
     425
      106
        0
      1063
       850
       2130
       2125
          50
           0
          50
```

Calculator

Press: 435.63 [÷] 42.5 [=]

Display: *10.250117*

10.250117 ≈ 10.25 — Since the hourly rate of pay is expressed in dollars and cents, round to the nearest hundredth.

The hairstylist earns about \$10.25 per hour.

Check: The answer is reasonable since it is close to the estimate.

■ **Talk About Math** In the pencil-and-paper method, can the division process be continued? How? What would be the next digit in the quotient?

Check Understanding

For another example, see Set C, pages 76–77.

Name the power of 10 by which you would multiply both divisor and dividend before dividing.

1. $37.995 \div 1.5$ **2.** $37.995 \div 0.15$ **3.** $\frac{1.5}{25.12}$ **4.** $\frac{1.25}{0.125}$

Practice

For More Practice, see Set C, pages 78–79.

Estimation Using compatible numbers, estimate each worker's hourly pay rate. Use the table on page 52.

5. Nurse **6.** Computer programmer **7.** Social worker **8.** Custodian

Divide. Round your answers to the nearest hundredth if necessary.

9. $\frac{14.75}{3.15}$ **10.** $\frac{1.06}{0.2}$ **11.** $\frac{52.66}{1.333}$ **12.** $\frac{1{,}566.1}{1.55}$ **13.** $\frac{147.375}{4.5}$

14. $\frac{0.365}{3.65}$ **15.** $\frac{1{,}047.48}{8.7}$ **16.** $\frac{57.512}{3.64}$ **17.** $\frac{0.02975}{0.035}$ **18.** $\frac{590.27}{7.2}$

Mixed Practice Find the quotient. Tell whether you used paper and pencil, mental math, or a calculator.

19. $\frac{1.001}{0.26}$ **20.** $\frac{138.38}{17}$ **21.** $\frac{208.74}{4.9}$ **22.** $\frac{385}{500}$ **23.** $\frac{410.2}{70}$

24. $3.6\overline{)2{,}880}$ **25.** $\frac{29.61}{0.07}$ **26.** $\frac{81.27}{0.03}$ **27.** $5.4\overline{)4{,}352.4}$ **28.** $7.6 \div 0.02$

29. $\frac{48.626}{8.2}$ **30.** $573.5 \div 37$ **31.** $\frac{600}{25.5}$ **32.** $\frac{3.8175}{0.75}$ **33.** $0.32\overline{)0.512}$

Calculator Use a calculator to find the hourly rate of each worker. Round your answers to the nearest cent.

Occupation	Earnings	Hours Worked
34. Police officer	$532.13	47.3
35. Librarian	$307.32	37.25

Occupation	Earnings	Hours Worked
36. Auto mechanic	$592.86	48.2
37. Tile setter	$424.46	36.75

Problem Solving

Solve each problem.

38. A car repair bill for $96.71 included $35.96 for parts. The rest was for 2.3 hours of labor. Another repair bill for $91.55 included $32.75 for parts and 2.4 hours of labor. What was the hourly labor charge for each?

39. Which hourly labor charge was greater? How much more is that charge for 40 hours of labor? for 50 weeks at 40 hours per week?

TIPS FOR PROBLEM SOLVERS

Organize your work to help you think clearly.

Choose an Operation

Understand
QUESTION
FACTS
KEY IDEA

Plan and Solve
STRATEGY
ANSWER

Look Back
SENSIBLE ANSWER
ALTERNATE APPROACH

Build Understanding

In 1894 French educator Baron Pierre de Coubertin proposed that the ancient Olympic games be revived on an international scale. The first Modern Olympics were held in 1896 in Athens, Greece, where 311 athletes from 13 nations competed.

In the 1936 Olympics in Berlin, Jesse Owens won the 200-meter dash in 20.7 seconds for an Olympic record. What was his average speed in meters per second? Round the answer to the nearest tenth.

Understand FACTS Jesse Owens ran 200 m in 20.7 sec.
KEY IDEA 20.7 times the average equals 200.

Plan and Solve STRATEGY To find a missing factor, choose the operation of *division*. Divide 200 by 20.7.

Estimate: $200 \div 20 = 10$

$\mathbf{200 \div 20.7 \approx 9.66}$

ANSWER Jesse Owens' average speed was 9.7 m/sec.

Look Back SENSIBLE ANSWER 9.7 is close to 10, so 9.7 is reasonable.

■ **Talk About Math** If you know Jesse Owens' average speed, how would you find his total running time?

Jesse Owens was an Olympic champion from the United States who won 4 gold medals.

Check Understanding

Tell what operation you would use to solve each problem.

1. Jean ran 100 m in 10.8 sec. What was her average speed?

2. How much faster is a speed of 9.3 m/sec than one of 8.7 m/sec?

Practice

Solve each problem and tell which operation you used.

3. In 1948 Sammy Lee from the United States won the gold medal for platform diving with 130.05 points. He won again in 1952 with 156.28 points. How many more points did he get in 1952 than in 1948?

4. In 1936 the 400-meter four-man relay was won by the United States team, which included Jesse Owens, in 39.8 sec. What was the average running time of each team member?

5. In three winter Olympics, skier Uhlrich Wehling won the Nordic Combined for East Germany. His scores were 413.34, 423.39, and 432.20 points. Find the total number of points he scored.

6. How many more points did Uhlrich Wehling score the third time he won the Nordic Combined than the first time he won? (See Problem 5.)

7. In the 1948 Olympics in London, the women's 400-meter relay was won by the team from Holland. The four women on the team had an average running time of 11.875 sec. What was the total time for the team?

8. In the 1988 Olympics Christa Rothenburger from East Germany set a record time of 1:17.65 in the women's 1,000 meters. In 1992 Bonnie Blair won the gold medal for the United States with a time of 1:21.90. How much faster was Christa than Bonnie?

9. Use data from Problems 1–8 to write a problem that requires the use of addition and division.

Countries all over the world have recognized sports and Olympic champions on their stamps.

Choose a ________ Strategy

Who's Ahead? The list shows the current positions of runners A–E. If runner B has gone 200 meters, how far has each of the others run?

A is 20 meters ahead of C.
B is 10 meters behind A.
C is 5 meters behind E.
D is 15 meters ahead of B.
E is 20 meters behind D.

10. List runners A–E in order, starting with the lead runner.

11. Find the distance each runner has gone

Fractions and Decimals

Build Understanding

A. Write the lens magnification as a fraction in lowest terms. Since 0.52 means 52 hundredths, you can write 0.52 as 52 ÷ 100.

$$0.52 = \frac{52}{100} = \frac{13}{25}$$

B. Write the flash recycle time as a fraction of a minute and then as a decimal.

Since there are 60 seconds in 1 minute, you can write 8 seconds as $\frac{8}{60}$ of a minute.

$\frac{8}{60} = \frac{2}{15}$ $\quad \frac{2}{15}$ means 2 ÷ 15.

Find 2 ÷ 15.

$$\begin{array}{r} 0.133 \\ 15\overline{)2.000} \\ 1\,5 \\ \hline 50 \\ 45 \\ \hline 50 \\ 45 \\ \hline 5 \end{array}$$

Write zeros in the dividend and divide. If you continue dividing, the remainder will always be 5 and the digit 3 will repeat in the quotient. There will never be a remainder of 0.

0.133... is a ***repeating decimal.*** The repeating digit or group of digits is the ***repetend***. One way to write a repeating decimal is to put a bar over the digit or digits that repeat.

$$\frac{2}{15} = 0.133... = 0.1\overline{3}$$

C. Write the shutter speed, $\frac{1}{500}$ sec, as a decimal.

$$\begin{array}{r} 0.002 \\ 500\overline{)1.000} \\ 1\,000 \\ \hline 0 \end{array}$$

Write zeros in the dividend and divide. For this division, the remainder is 0.

$$\frac{1}{500} = 0.002$$

0.002 is a ***terminating decimal***.

D. Write $0.\overline{27}$ as a fraction.

You can let n represent the decimal. $\quad n = 0.2727...$

Since there are two repeating digits, multiply both sides of the equation by 100. Subtract the first equation from the second equation.

$$\begin{array}{rl} 100n = & 27.2727... \\ -\ n = & 0.2727... \\ \hline 99n = & 27 \end{array}$$

Solve the resulting equation. $\quad n = \frac{27}{99} = \frac{3}{11}$

$$0.\overline{27} = \frac{3}{11}$$

Talk About Math How can you mentally find the decimal for $\frac{1}{2}$?

Check Understanding

For another example, see Set D, pages 76–77.

Write as a decimal.

1. $\frac{9}{50}$ **2.** $\frac{1}{6}$ **3.** $\frac{7}{22}$

Write as a fraction in lowest terms.

4. 0.425 **5.** 0.66 **6.** $0.\overline{6}$

Practice

For More Practice, see Set D, pages 78–79.

Tell whether you would use paper and pencil or a calculator. Then write each fraction as a repeating or terminating decimal.

7. $\frac{1}{4}$ **8.** $\frac{3}{10}$ **9.** $\frac{9}{25}$ **10.** $\frac{2}{3}$ **11.** $\frac{7}{15}$ **12.** $\frac{5}{9}$ **13.** $\frac{4}{11}$ **14.** $\frac{7}{8}$

Write each decimal as a fraction in lowest terms.

15. 0.7 **16.** 0.99 **17.** 0.25 **18.** 0.375 **19.** $0.\overline{8}$ **20.** $0.9\overline{54}$

Mental Math Write each fraction with either 10, 100, or 1,000 in the denominator. Then write each new fraction as a decimal.

21. $\frac{3}{4}$ **22.** $\frac{2}{5}$ **23.** $\frac{7}{20}$ **24.** $\frac{4}{25}$ **25.** $\frac{27}{250}$ **26.** $\frac{1}{200}$ **27.** $\frac{6}{125}$ **28.** $\frac{499}{500}$

Compare the repeating decimals, using >, <, or =.

29. $0.4\overline{37}$ ▒ $0.\overline{437}$ **30.** $0.\overline{24}$ ▒ $0.\overline{242}$ **31.** $0.8\overline{65}$ ▒ $0.8\overline{6}$ **32.** $0.2\overline{121}$ ▒ $0.21\overline{212}$

Problem Solving

Critical Thinking Solve each problem.

33. Study Exercises 21–28. Explain how and when you can change some fractions to decimals using mental math.

34. How can you tell from the denominator of a fraction whether the decimal will terminate or repeat? Hint: Find the prime factors of the denominators.

Midchapter Checkup

Estimate. Then compute. Tell if you used mental math or paper and pencil.

1. 12.6 ÷ 18 **2.** 4.98 ÷ 1.2 **3.** 5.8 × 100 **4.** 2.5 × 500

Write as a fraction in lowest terms.

5. 0.28 **6.** $0.\overline{7}$ **7.** 0.07

Write as a decimal.

8. $\frac{3}{5}$ **9.** $\frac{3}{20}$ **10.** $\frac{96}{120}$

Problem-Solving Workshop

Real-Life Decision Making

Suppose you want to buy a new jacket that costs $85.95. You have saved $12. Your grandmother told you that she will pay you if you do one of the following chores for her:

a. Feed and walk her dog daily for $1.00 per day.

b. Yardwork Saturday mornings for $10.00 each Saturday.

c. Cook dinner three nights a week for $3.00 per meal.

1. In which plan would you earn money the fastest?

2. Which choice would you make? Explain your answer.

Number-Sense Project

Look back at pages 46-47.

1. The table shows how the time is spent in a 45-minute exercise class. What fraction of the time is spent doing each exercise?

2. Suppose the class is 60 minutes long and the time per exercise is the same as in the 45-minute class. What fraction of the 60 minutes is spent doing each exercise? What fraction of the period is left over for more exercises?

MATH laugh

Father to son: I thought I told you to be home by a quarter of 12.

Son to father: Yes, but I learned in math class that $\frac{1}{4}$ of 12 is 3!

Exercise Class (45 minutes)	
Warm-up/cool down	10 min
Leg/hip exercises	9 min
Arm exercises	5 min
Aerobic exercises	15 min
Stomach exercises	6 min

Explore with a Computer

Use the *Fractions Workshop Project* for this activity.

1. At the computer, make a rectangular unit that is divided like the one shown at the right. Shade parts of the unit to show $\frac{7}{8} \times \frac{5}{8}$. What is the overlap area of shading?

2. If you change $\frac{7}{8}$ to $\frac{3}{8}$, predict what will happen to the overlap area of shading. Make a new figure to verify your answer.

3. If you change $\frac{5}{8}$ to $\frac{6}{8}$, predict what will happen to the overlap area of shading. Make a new figure to verify your answer.

4. How can you end up with a "square overlap" area of shading?

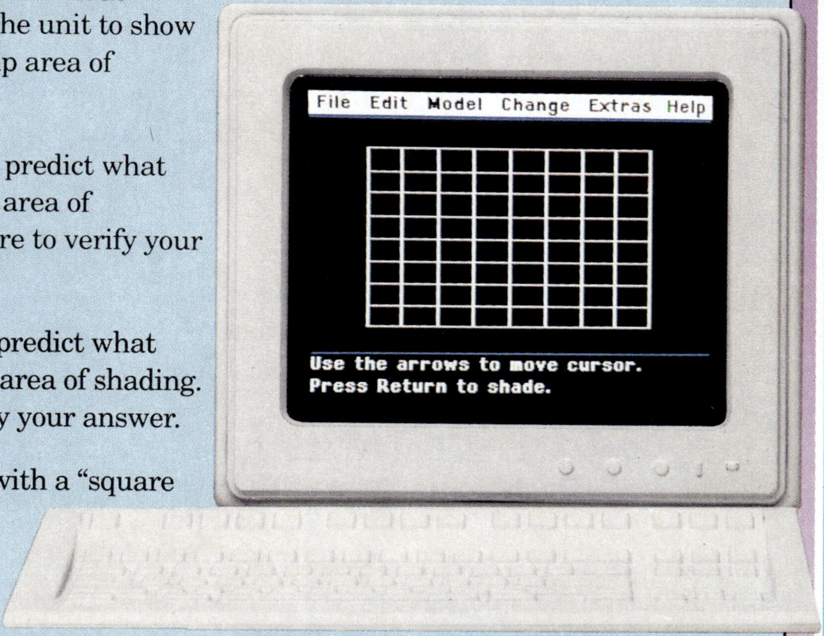

Math-at-Home Activity

Take a survey of the people in your family. Ask them what time, to the nearest half hour, they fall asleep at night and wake up in the morning.

1. What was the most common time to go to sleep?

2. What was the most common time to wake up?

3. What fraction of the people in your family got at least eight hours of sleep?

4. What fraction of the people in your family go to sleep after 10:30 P.M.?

Fractions and Mixed Numbers

Build Understanding

A. The wingspan of the mourning cloak butterfly is $2\frac{3}{4}$ in. A number like $2\frac{3}{4}$ is a ***mixed number***. A mixed number has a whole number part and a fraction part.

B. Every mixed number or whole number greater than zero can be written as an ***improper fraction***. Write $2\frac{3}{4}$ as an improper fraction. You can write the whole number 2 as an improper fraction, $\frac{8}{4}$. Then add $\frac{8}{4}$ and $\frac{3}{4}$.

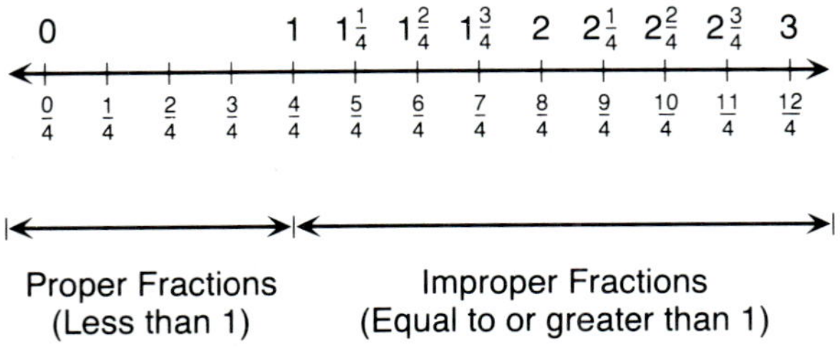

$$\mathbf{2\frac{3}{4} = 2 + \frac{3}{4} = \frac{8}{4} + \frac{3}{4} = \frac{11}{4}}$$

C. Mental Math Express $\frac{24}{9}$ as a mixed number.

$\mathbf{\frac{24}{9} = \frac{8}{3} = 8 \div 3 = 2\frac{2}{3}}$ Rename if possible. Divide the numerator by the denominator.

$\mathbf{\frac{24}{9} = 2\frac{2}{3}}$

D. List $1\frac{1}{2}$, $2\frac{1}{3}$, and $1\frac{2}{5}$ from least to greatest.

$\mathbf{1\frac{1}{2}, 1\frac{2}{5}, 2\frac{1}{3}}$ First compare the whole numbers. $2\frac{1}{3}$ is the greatest number.

$\mathbf{1\frac{5}{10}, 1\frac{4}{10}, 2\frac{1}{3}}$ Compare the fraction parts of $1\frac{1}{2}$ and $1\frac{2}{5}$.

$\mathbf{1\frac{4}{10}, 1\frac{5}{10}, 2\frac{1}{3}}$ Since $\frac{5}{10} > \frac{4}{10}$, $1\frac{1}{2} > 1\frac{2}{5}$.

$\mathbf{1\frac{2}{5}, 1\frac{1}{2}, 2\frac{1}{3}}$ Write the numbers in increasing order.

The io moth does not feed and therefore lives only a few days.

■ **Talk About Math** How can you tell if a fraction is a proper fraction or an improper fraction?

Check Understanding

For another example, see Set E, pages 76–77.

1. Write $10\frac{3}{4}$ as an improper fraction.

2. Write 8 with a denominator of 3.

3. Write $\frac{30}{8}$ as a mixed number.

4. Compare $5\frac{1}{2}$ and $5\frac{1}{3}$. Use $<$ and $>$.

Practice

For More Practice, see Set E, pages 78–79.

Write each mixed number as an improper fraction. Write each improper fraction as a mixed number or a whole number. Tell whether you used mental math or paper and pencil.

5. $6\frac{2}{3}$ **6.** $1\frac{3}{5}$ **7.** $7\frac{5}{8}$ **8.** $\frac{18}{10}$ **9.** $\frac{57}{13}$ **10.** $\frac{63}{12}$

11. $\frac{189}{12}$ **12.** $4\frac{1}{2}$ **13.** $\frac{35}{35}$ **14.** $5\frac{3}{10}$ **15.** $\frac{294}{7}$ **16.** $13\frac{5}{6}$

Compare. Use $<$, $>$, or $=$.

17. $4\frac{1}{2}$ ▒ $4\frac{2}{5}$ **18.** $6\frac{6}{10}$ ▒ $6\frac{3}{5}$ **19.** $3\frac{1}{4}$ ▒ $3\frac{1}{3}$ **20.** $1\frac{8}{9}$ ▒ $2\frac{5}{6}$

21. $\frac{8}{5}$ ▒ $1\frac{3}{5}$ **22.** $7\frac{3}{5}$ ▒ $7\frac{3}{10}$ **23.** $1\frac{5}{12}$ ▒ $1\frac{2}{12}$ **24.** $2\frac{2}{5}$ ▒ $2\frac{3}{8}$

List the mixed numbers in order from least to greatest.

25. $3\frac{5}{6}$, $2\frac{3}{5}$, $2\frac{3}{10}$ **26.** $4\frac{1}{3}$, $4\frac{5}{6}$, $4\frac{7}{12}$, $3\frac{5}{8}$ **27.** $1\frac{2}{3}$, $1\frac{5}{6}$, $1\frac{1}{6}$, $1\frac{7}{12}$

Mixed Practice Write each decimal as a mixed number, and each mixed number as a decimal.

28. 4.28 **29.** $8\frac{9}{16}$ **30.** 1.008 **31.** $7\frac{8}{15}$ **32.** 3.396 **33.** $6\frac{5}{7}$

List the numbers in order from least to greatest.

34. $1\frac{3}{10}$, [illegible].23, $1\frac{1}{5}$, 1.5 **35.** 7.7, 7.07, $7\frac{7}{7}$, $7\frac{7}{20}$ **36.** 3.28, $3\frac{9}{32}$, 3.283, $3\frac{1}{4}$

Problem Solving

Solve each problem.

37. List the insects shown on page 60 in order from the least wingspan to the greatest wingspan.

38. A cloudless sulphur butterfly has a wingspan between those of the dogface and io. Give three mixed numbers that fit this description.

Estimating Sums and Differences of Fractions and Mixed Numbers

Build Understanding

A. What's the Half of It?
Materials: Math Sketcher
Groups: 4 students

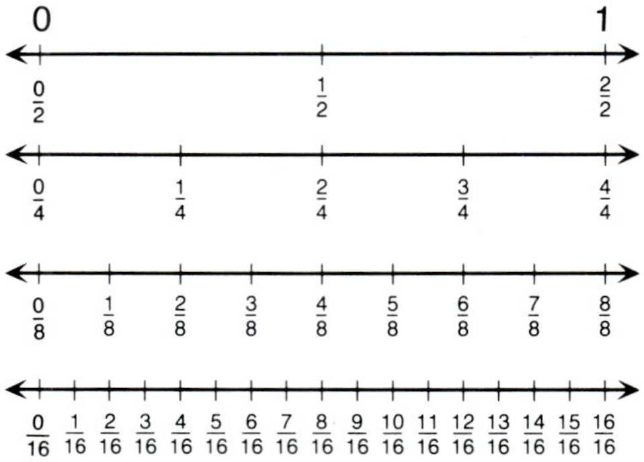

a. Draw four number lines, and mark 0 and 1 above the first line. Below the first number line, mark $\frac{0}{2}$, $\frac{1}{2}$, and $\frac{2}{2}$. Below the second number line, mark $\frac{0}{4}$, $\frac{1}{4}$, $\frac{2}{4}$, $\frac{3}{4}$, and $\frac{4}{4}$. On the third number line, mark $\frac{0}{8}$, $\frac{1}{8}$, $\frac{2}{8}$, and so on. On the fourth number line, mark all the sixteenths.

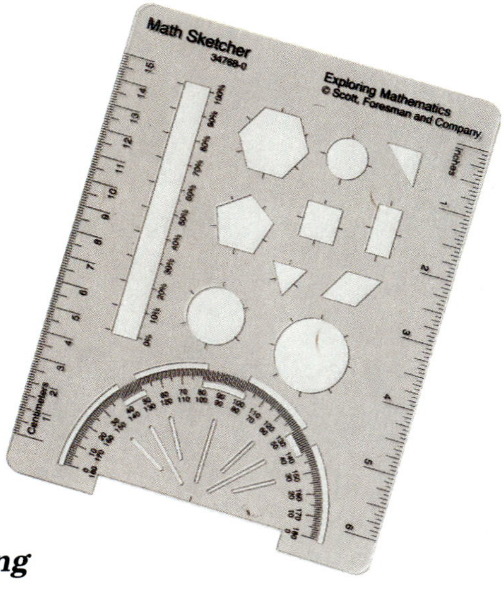

b. Compare the marked fractions with $\frac{1}{2}$. How can you tell by looking at the numerator and the denominator whether a fraction is equal to $\frac{1}{2}$? less than $\frac{1}{2}$? greater than $\frac{1}{2}$?

c. Which fractions are closer to 0 than to $\frac{1}{2}$? How can you tell? Which fractions are closer to $\frac{1}{2}$ than to 0 or 1? How can you tell? Which fractions are closer to 1 than to $\frac{1}{2}$? How can you tell?

B. You can estimate sums of fractions by ***comparing*** each fraction with the reference point $\frac{1}{2}$.

Estimate $\frac{5}{8} + \frac{2}{3}$.

$$\begin{array}{l} \quad \frac{5}{8} > \frac{1}{2} \\ + \frac{2}{3} > \frac{1}{2} \\ \hline \end{array}$$

The sum is greater than 1 since each addend is greater than $\frac{1}{2}$.

Estimate $\frac{1}{3} + \frac{2}{5}$.

$$\begin{array}{l} \quad \frac{1}{3} < \frac{1}{2} \\ + \frac{2}{5} < \frac{1}{2} \\ \hline \end{array}$$

The sum is less than 1 since each addend is less than $\frac{1}{2}$. The sum is between $\frac{2}{5}$ and 1.

Estimate $\frac{5}{8} + \frac{1}{4}$.

$$\begin{array}{l} \quad \frac{5}{8} > \frac{1}{2} \\ + \frac{1}{4} < \frac{1}{2} \\ \hline \end{array}$$

You cannot tell if the sum is greater than 1 or less than 1. The sum is greater than the larger addend, $\frac{5}{8}$.

C. You can estimate sums of fractions or mixed numbers by finding a range.

Estimate $24\frac{7}{8} + 12\frac{1}{2} + 6\frac{3}{11}$.

$25 + 13 + 7 = 45$ Round up.
$24 + 12 + 6 = 42$ Round down.

The sum is between 42 and 45.

D. You can estimate sums or differences with fractions or mixed numbers by rounding to the nearest whole number.

Estimate $12\frac{5}{8} - 4\frac{1}{3}$.

$13 - 4 = 9$ Round $12\frac{5}{8}$ up.
Round $4\frac{1}{3}$ down.

The estimated difference is 9.

Talk About Math If you round both addends to the nearest whole number, when will the actual sum be greater than the estimated sum? When will it be less?

Check Understanding

For another example, see Set F, pages 76–77.

Answer the questions.

$\frac{3}{8}$	$\frac{5}{10}$	$\frac{1}{3}$	$\frac{5}{6}$	$\frac{5}{12}$	$\frac{8}{16}$	$\frac{9}{10}$	$\frac{3}{4}$

1. Which fractions above equal $\frac{1}{2}$?

2. Which are less than $\frac{1}{2}$?

3. Which are greater than $\frac{1}{2}$?

Estimate by comparing each fraction to the nearest half. Tell if the sum is greater than 1, less than 1, or if you can only determine if the sum is greater than the larger fraction.

4. $\frac{5}{6} + \frac{1}{3}$

5. $\frac{1}{4} + \frac{1}{6}$

6. $\frac{2}{3} + \frac{1}{8}$

7. $\frac{7}{10} + \frac{7}{8}$

8. $\frac{4}{9} + \frac{1}{10}$

9. $\frac{3}{4} + \frac{3}{6}$

Find the range of each sum.

10. $1\frac{5}{6} + 3\frac{3}{4}$

11. $6\frac{1}{3} + 2\frac{1}{4}$

12. $2\frac{7}{8} + 7\frac{5}{6}$

13. $9\frac{1}{6} + 4\frac{9}{10}$

Estimate by rounding to the nearest whole number.

14. $\frac{5}{9} + \frac{1}{3} + \frac{3}{8}$

15. $21\frac{1}{4} - 7\frac{1}{8}$

16. $9\frac{3}{8} - 5\frac{5}{6}$

17. $1\frac{2}{5} + 3\frac{1}{2} - \frac{9}{10}$

18. $4\frac{1}{2} + 9\frac{1}{8} + \frac{3}{4}$

19. $\frac{15}{16} + 5\frac{1}{3} + 7\frac{7}{10}$

20. $2\frac{2}{3} + 5\frac{2}{9} - 3\frac{1}{4}$

21. $14\frac{4}{5} - 1\frac{7}{8} + 2\frac{1}{4}$

22. $5\frac{7}{10} + 3\frac{5}{6} - \frac{1}{2}$

Practice

For More Practice, see Set F, pages 78–79.

Round each number to the nearest half.

23. $\frac{1}{9}$ **24.** $2\frac{3}{5}$ **25.** $\frac{2}{3}$ **26.** $3\frac{9}{10}$

27. $\frac{3}{4}$ **28.** $1\frac{2}{11}$ **29.** $\frac{5}{6}$ **30.** $1\frac{5}{12}$

Estimate each sum by comparing each fraction to $\frac{1}{2}$.

31. $\frac{2}{3} + \frac{4}{5}$ **32.** $\frac{1}{6} + \frac{1}{4}$ **33.** $\frac{6}{7} + \frac{7}{10}$ **34.** $\frac{3}{8} + \frac{2}{9}$ **35.** $\frac{4}{9} + \frac{1}{10}$

36. $\frac{2}{7} + \frac{5}{6}$ **37.** $\frac{9}{10} + \frac{1}{10}$ **38.** $\frac{3}{4} + \frac{7}{8}$ **39.** $\frac{1}{7} + \frac{3}{5}$ **40.** $\frac{2}{3} + \frac{4}{5}$

Name all the proper fractions with a denominator of 8 that are

41. less than $\frac{1}{2}$. **42.** greater than $\frac{1}{2}$. **43.** equal to $\frac{1}{2}$.

Estimate each sum or difference. Tell which method of estimation you used.

44. $36\frac{1}{3} + 17\frac{8}{9}$ **45.** $41\frac{3}{10} - 26\frac{1}{2}$ **46.** $28\frac{1}{3} + 10\frac{1}{4}$

47. $35 - 6\frac{1}{3}$ **48.** $11\frac{2}{3} + 22\frac{3}{4}$ **49.** $15\frac{1}{5} - 5\frac{4}{5}$

50. $17\frac{5}{6} + 4\frac{1}{2}$ **51.** $33\frac{3}{10} - 16\frac{5}{12}$ **52.** $23\frac{2}{3} + 14\frac{5}{6}$

53. $75\frac{2}{5} - 46\frac{7}{9}$ **54.** $56\frac{2}{5} + 23\frac{1}{8}$ **55.** $61\frac{11}{12} - 23\frac{1}{2}$

56. $89\frac{4}{9} - 44\frac{7}{8} + 10\frac{3}{7}$ **57.** $29\frac{1}{2} + 32\frac{2}{3} + 21\frac{4}{5} + 8\frac{1}{4}$

Number Sense If you know that the actual sum or difference will be greater than or less than your estimate, write *greater than* or *less than*. If you cannot tell without computing, write *cannot tell.*

58. In Exercise 44 **59.** In Exercise 46 **60.** In Exercise 47

61. In Exercise 48 **62.** In Exercise 51 **63.** In Exercise 52

64. In Exercise 54 **65.** In Exercise 56 **66.** In Exercise 53

Problem Solving

Solve each problem.

67. The sum of two fractions greater than $\frac{1}{2}$ is always greater than what number?

68. The sum of two proper fractions is always less than what whole number?

69. The sum of three proper fractions is always less than what whole number?

ALGEBRA **Number Sense** For the fraction $\frac{a}{b}$, what is true about a and b if the fraction is

70. equal to 0?

71. equal to 1?

72. greater than $\frac{1}{2}$?

73. equal to $\frac{1}{2}$?

74. less than $\frac{1}{2}$?

75. greater than 1?

A helicopter service transports patrons between Cedar City Airport *(C)* and the Business District *(D)*. It also provides emergency transportation from Ashton Island *(A)* to Birch Hill Hospital *(B)*. The map is drawn to scale, with $\frac{1}{2}$ inch representing $2\frac{1}{2}$ miles. Give a reasonable estimate of each distance.

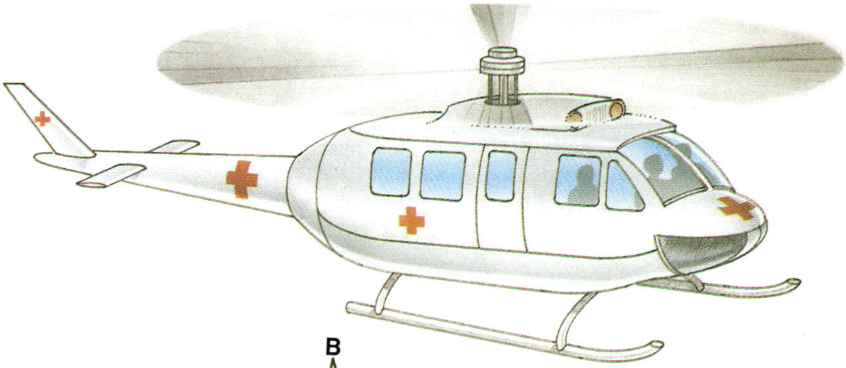

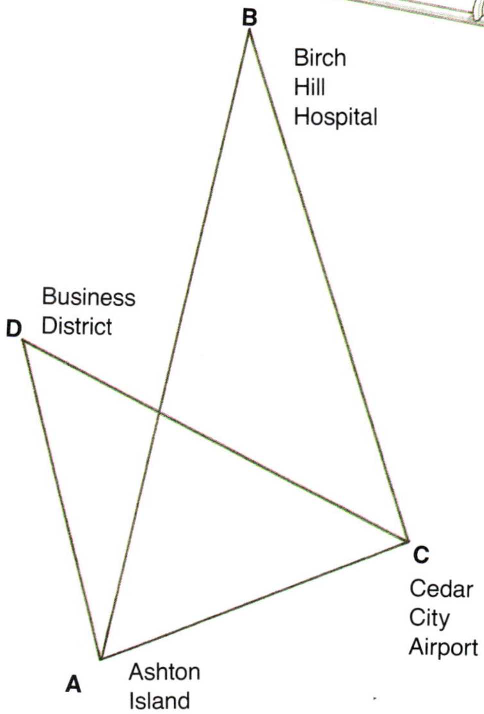

76. From *A* to *D*

77. From *A* to *B*

78. From *C* to *D*

79. From *B* to *C*

80. A pilot must make 10 round-trip flights from the Cedar City Airport to the Business District in one day. How many miles does she travel in one day?

Adding and Subtracting Fractions and Mixed Numbers

Build Understanding

LOOKOUT MOUNTAIN TRAIL

FROM	TO	MILES
Deer Lodge	Hanging Rock	$\frac{4}{5}$
Hanging Rock	Bear Creek	$\frac{9}{10}$
Bear Creek	Crater Lake	$\frac{1}{2}$
Crater Lake	Logging Road	$1\frac{1}{3}$
Logging Road	Lone Tree	1

FROM	TO	MILES
Lone Tree	Star Mine	$1\frac{2}{5}$
Star Mine	High Cliff	$\frac{7}{8}$
High Cliff	Rock Falls	$2\frac{5}{6}$
Rock Falls	Lookout Pass	$1\frac{3}{4}$

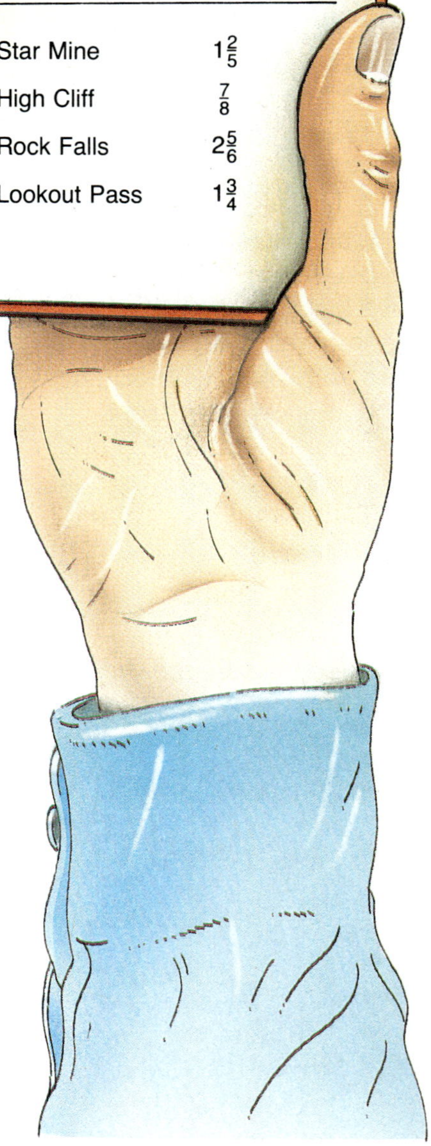

A. Salvadore and Maria Santos are hiking on Mount Lookout to enjoy the scenery while they improve their fitness. How many miles will they hike if they go from Deer Lodge to Crater Lake?

Since you want to find a total, you can add.

Find $\frac{4}{5} + \frac{9}{10} + \frac{1}{2}$.

First estimate by rounding to the nearest whole number.

$1 + 1 + 1 = 3$

Then add.

$$\frac{4}{5} = \frac{8}{10}$$
$$\frac{9}{10} = \frac{9}{10}$$

Write the fractions with a common denominator. Notice that one of the denominators is the least common denominator.

$$+\frac{1}{2} = \frac{5}{10}$$

Add the numerators.

$$\frac{22}{10} = 2\frac{2}{10} = 2\frac{1}{5}$$

Rename the sum as a mixed number. Write the fraction in lowest terms.

They will hike $2\frac{1}{5}$ miles from Deer Lodge to Crater Lake.

B. Salvadore hiked to High Cliff. How much farther is it to Lookout Pass?

Find $2\frac{5}{6} + 1\frac{3}{4}$.

Estimate: 3 + 2 = 5.

$$\begin{array}{r} 2\frac{5}{6} = 2\frac{10}{12} \\ +1\frac{3}{4} = 1\frac{9}{12} \\ \hline 3\frac{19}{12} = 3 + 1\frac{7}{12} \\ = 4\frac{7}{12} \end{array}$$

Remember: The least common multiple of 6 and 4 is the least common denominator.

Rename the sum.

It is $4\frac{7}{12}$ miles from High Cliff to Lookout Pass.

C. On another day, Maria hiked from Star Mine to High Cliff. Salvadore hiked from Bear Creek to Crater Lake. How much farther did Maria hike than Salvadore?

Find the difference $\frac{7}{8} - \frac{1}{2}$.

$$\begin{array}{r} \frac{7}{8} = \frac{7}{8} \\ -\frac{1}{2} = \frac{4}{8} \\ \hline \frac{3}{8} \end{array}$$

Write the fractions with a common denominator. Then subtract the numerators.

Maria hiked $\frac{3}{8}$ mile farther than Salvadore.

D. Find $9\frac{3}{4} - 3\frac{1}{6}$.

Estimate: 10 − 3 = 7.

$$\begin{array}{r} 9\frac{3}{4} = 9\frac{9}{12} \\ -3\frac{1}{6} = 3\frac{2}{12} \\ \hline 6\frac{7}{12} \end{array}$$

Write the fractions with a common denominator. Subtract the fractions. Then subtract the whole numbers.

E. Find $7\frac{1}{3} - 4\frac{1}{2}$.

Estimate: 7 − 5 = 2.

$$\begin{array}{r} 7\frac{1}{3} = 7\frac{2}{6} = 6\frac{8}{6} \\ -4\frac{1}{2} = 4\frac{3}{6} = 4\frac{3}{6} \\ \hline 2\frac{5}{6} \end{array}$$

Rename $7\frac{2}{6}$ to show more sixths.

$7\frac{2}{6} = 6 + 1 + \frac{2}{6}$

$= 6 + \frac{6}{6} + \frac{2}{6}$

$= 6\frac{8}{6}$

Write About Math When is the product of two denominators the least common denominator?

Check Understanding

For another example, see Set G, pages 76–77.

Find the least common denominator.

1. $\frac{5}{6}, \frac{7}{8}$

2. $\frac{1}{2}, \frac{9}{10}, \frac{5}{8}$

Find the missing numbers.

3. $10\frac{1}{3} = ▒\frac{4}{3}$

4. $15\frac{3}{8} = 14\frac{▒}{8}$

Add. Write your answer in lowest terms.

5. $4\frac{5}{6} + 10\frac{4}{9}$

6. $\frac{4}{5} + \frac{1}{2} + \frac{7}{10}$

7. $9\frac{2}{3} + 5\frac{4}{15} + 2\frac{1}{5}$

Subtract. Write your answer in lowest terms.

8. $\frac{4}{9} - \frac{1}{6}$

9. $15\frac{2}{3} - 7\frac{1}{4}$

10. $30 - 6\frac{7}{10}$

11. $25\frac{3}{4} - 13\frac{5}{6}$

Practice

For More Practice, see Set G, pages 78–79.

Add or subtract. **Remember** to rename your answers when necessary.

12. $\frac{2}{3} + \frac{1}{2}$

13. $\frac{2}{3} + \frac{3}{4}$

14. $12\frac{1}{2} + 17\frac{2}{9}$

15. $8\frac{1}{3} + \frac{7}{8}$

16. $\frac{2}{5} - \frac{1}{3}$

17. $\frac{5}{8} - \frac{1}{10}$

18. $6 - \frac{4}{9}$

19. $27\frac{1}{2} - 9\frac{2}{7}$

20. $\frac{4}{5} + \frac{8}{15}$

21. $5\frac{1}{2} + 9\frac{1}{6}$

22. $9\frac{3}{8} - 5$

23. $8\frac{13}{20} - \frac{4}{5}$

24. $13\frac{3}{10} + 9\frac{2}{5}$

25. $10\frac{1}{3} - 6\frac{6}{7}$

26. $34\frac{3}{10} - 4\frac{3}{4}$

27. $41 + 27\frac{7}{10}$

28. $32\frac{3}{4} - 18\frac{4}{9}$

29. $23\frac{11}{12} + 14\frac{3}{8}$

30. $9\frac{1}{6} - 5\frac{3}{8}$

31. $53\frac{1}{2} + 16\frac{1}{2}$

32. $4\frac{2}{3} + 2\frac{3}{5} + 7\frac{4}{5}$

33. $9\frac{5}{8} + 15\frac{1}{2} + 10\frac{3}{4}$

34. $10\frac{1}{3} + 47\frac{1}{4} + 16$

Mental Math Find each missing number mentally.

35. $\frac{3}{4} + \frac{\square}{4} = 1$

36. $5\frac{7}{9} - 3\frac{\square}{9} = 2\frac{1}{3}$

37. $\frac{\square}{16} + \frac{9}{16} = 1$

38. $1\frac{5}{6} - \frac{\square}{\square} = 1\frac{1}{3}$

39. $4\frac{3}{10} + \frac{\square}{\square} = 5$

40. $\frac{5}{8} + \frac{3}{8} + \frac{2}{5} = \frac{2}{5} + \square = \square$

41. $\frac{5}{16} + \frac{11}{12} + \frac{11}{16} = \frac{11}{12} + \square = \square$

Problem Solving

Solve each problem. Use the table on page 66. **Remember** to estimate before you add or subtract.

42. Find a segment of the trail that is about 5 miles long.

43. Find a segment of the Lookout Mountain Trail that is about 10 miles long.

44. How much farther is it from Deer Lodge to Bear Creek than from Deer Lodge to Hanging Rock?

45. Salvador hiked from Crater Lake to the Logging Road. Maria hiked from Hanging Rock to Bear Creek. How much farther did Salvador hike than Maria?

Fill in the mileage chart for the trails on Lookout Mountain.

To / From	Deer Lodge	Hanging Rock	Bear Creek	Crater Lake	Logging Road	Lone Tree	Star Mine
Deer Lodge	—	$\frac{4}{5}$	**46.**	**47.**	**48.**	**49.**	**50.**
Hanging Rock	$\frac{4}{5}$	—	$\frac{9}{10}$	**51.**	**52.**	**53.**	**54.**
Bear Creek		$\frac{9}{10}$	—	$\frac{1}{2}$	**55.**	**56.**	**57.**
Crater Lake			$\frac{1}{2}$	—	$1\frac{1}{3}$	**58.**	**59.**
Logging Road				$1\frac{1}{3}$	—	1	**60.**

61. How much farther is the distance from Logging Road to Star Mine than from Deer Lodge to Bear Creek?

62. One day Salvador and Maria hiked from Deer Lodge to Star Mine and back. How far did they hike?

Explore Math

Explore an alternate method for adding $\frac{2}{7} + \frac{5}{9}$.

63. First, find the sum in the usual manner.

64. Use the following steps to explore another method.

a. Find the product of the first numerator times the second denominator.

b. Find the product of the second numerator times the first denominator.

c. Add the products you found in steps a and b to find the numerator of the sum.

d. Multiply the two denominators to find the denominator of the sum.

65. Are the answers to Exercises 63 and 64 the same?

66. Describe a method for subtracting fractions similar to the rule for adding fractions that was used in Exercise 64. Try a few cases.

67. Do the methods of Exercises 64 and 66 work for mixed numbers? Try a few cases.

68. Explain how you can use this method to add fractions by using a calculator.

Multiplying and Dividing Fractions and Mixed Numbers

Build Understanding

A. Gramercy Park in New York City is about $\frac{2}{3}$ of a city block long and $\frac{1}{4}$ of a block wide. What is the area of Gramercy Park in square blocks?

The diagram represents one city block, and the green part represents the park. You can see that the area of the park is $\frac{2}{12}$, or $\frac{1}{6}$, square block.

You can also find the area of the rectangle by multiplying the length times the width.

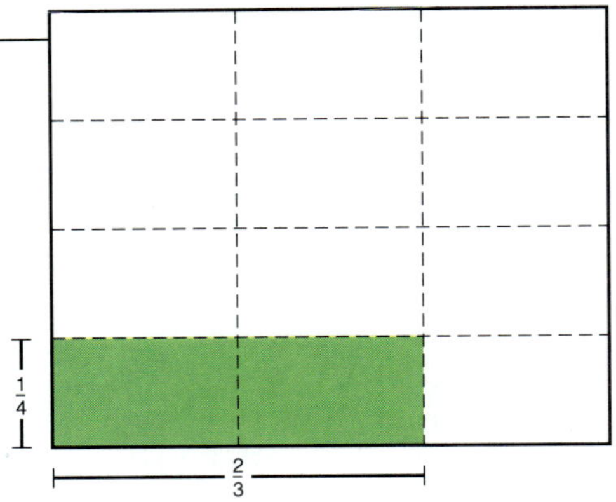

$$\frac{2}{3} \times \frac{1}{4} = \frac{2 \times 1}{3 \times 4} = \frac{2}{12} = \frac{1}{6}$$

Multiply the numerators. Then multiply the denominators.

$$\frac{\overset{1}{\cancel{2}}}{3} \times \frac{1}{\underset{2}{\cancel{4}}} = \frac{1 \times 1}{3 \times 2} = \frac{1}{6}$$

Whenever possible, divide a numerator and a denominator by a common factor before you multiply. This will simplify your work.

B. Find $6 \div \frac{3}{4}$.

$$6 \div \frac{3}{4} = \frac{6}{1} \times \frac{4}{3} = 8$$

To divide by a number, multiply by the ***reciprocal*** of the divisor. Two numbers are reciprocals if their product is 1.

C. Find $2\frac{1}{4} \times 3\frac{1}{3}$.

Estimate: $2 \times 3 = 6$

$$2\frac{1}{4} \times 3\frac{1}{3} = \frac{9}{4} \times \frac{10}{3}$$

Write each number as a fraction. Then multiply.

$$= \frac{\overset{3}{\cancel{9}} \times \overset{5}{\cancel{10}}}{\underset{2}{\cancel{4}} \times \underset{1}{\cancel{3}}}$$

$$= \frac{15}{2} = 7\frac{1}{2}$$

D. Find $6\frac{3}{4} \div 1\frac{1}{2}$.

$$6\frac{3}{4} \div 1\frac{1}{2} = \frac{27}{4} \div \frac{3}{2}$$

Write the mixed numbers as improper fractions. Then multiply by the reciprocal of the divisor.

$$= \frac{27}{4} \times \frac{2}{3}$$

$$= \frac{\overset{9}{\cancel{27}} \times \overset{1}{\cancel{2}}}{\underset{2}{\cancel{4}} \times \underset{1}{\cancel{3}}}$$

$$= \frac{9}{2} = 4\frac{1}{2}$$

Write About Math Write a rule for finding the reciprocal of any number.

Check Understanding

For another example, see Set H, pages 76–77.

Find each product or quotient.

1. $\frac{3}{4} \times \frac{4}{5} \times \frac{1}{6}$ **2.** $\left(\frac{3}{8}\right)\left(2\frac{2}{3}\right)$ **3.** $\frac{1}{6} \div \frac{2}{3}$ **4.** $3\frac{1}{2} \div \frac{3}{4}$ **5.** $\frac{5}{8} \div 5$

Practice

For More Practice, see Set H, pages 78–79.

Name the reciprocal of each number.

6. $\frac{7}{8}$ **7.** $5\frac{2}{3}$ **8.** 6 **9.** $\frac{1}{3}$ **10.** $\frac{12}{5}$ **11.** 1

Multiply or divide. **Remember** to multiply the dividend by the reciprocal of the divisor whenever you divide.

12. $\frac{1}{3} \times \frac{3}{5}$ **13.** $\frac{1}{3} \div \frac{3}{5}$ **14.** $\frac{1}{2} \times 2$ **15.** $\frac{1}{2} \div 2$ **16.** $2 \div \frac{1}{2}$

17. $\frac{3}{8} \times \frac{1}{2}$ **18.** $\frac{5}{8} \times \frac{8}{5}$ **19.** $\frac{2}{3} \div \frac{5}{6}$ **20.** $\frac{3}{16} \div \frac{7}{8}$ **21.** $12 \times \frac{3}{8}$

22. $4\frac{2}{3} \div \frac{2}{7}$ **23.** $\frac{3}{5} \div 2$ **24.** $\frac{3}{5} \times \frac{11}{12}$ **25.** $1\frac{4}{9} \div 1\frac{4}{9}$ **26.** $\frac{4}{5} \div 6\frac{2}{3}$

27. $\left(\frac{3}{4}\right)^2$ **28.** $\left(2\frac{1}{5}\right)\left(6\frac{1}{2}\right)$ **29.** $\left(\frac{3}{4}\right)\left(\frac{4}{3}\right)\left(\frac{1}{2}\right)$ **30.** $\dfrac{\frac{3}{4}}{\frac{2}{3}}$ **31.** $\dfrac{2\frac{4}{5}}{\frac{3}{3}}$

Mixed Practice Compute each answer.

32. $3\frac{3}{4} \times 5\frac{1}{3}$ **33.** $\frac{11}{12} - \frac{3}{8}$ **34.** $25\frac{3}{4} + 37\frac{5}{8}$ **35.** $\frac{4}{9} \div 1\frac{2}{3}$

36. $11\frac{2}{3} - 5\frac{5}{6}$ **37.** $4\frac{4}{5} \div 8$ **38.** $2\frac{1}{2} \times 1\frac{3}{5}$ **39.** $\frac{13}{15} + \frac{4}{25}$

Problem Solving

Solve each problem.

40. The city is going to subdivide 12 acres into lots for townhouses. How many $\frac{3}{4}$-acre lots can be made?

41. If the 12 acres in Problem 40 were divided into $1\frac{1}{2}$-acre lots for apartment buildings, how many lots would be formed?

42. **Critical Thinking** Multiply $8 \times 4\frac{1}{2}$. Then show how you can compute without changing the numbers to improper fractions. Give a rule for multiplying a whole number and a mixed number.

43. Use the work at the right to explain the rule for dividing fractions. Then state the rule in your own words.

$$\frac{3}{4} \div \frac{3}{8} = \frac{\frac{3}{4}}{\frac{3}{8}} = \frac{\frac{3}{4} \times \frac{8}{3}}{\frac{3}{8} \times \frac{8}{3}} = \frac{\frac{3}{4} \times \frac{8}{3}}{1} = \frac{3}{4} \times \frac{8}{3}$$

Too Much or Too Little Information

PROBLEM SOLVING GUIDE

Understand
QUESTION
FACTS
KEY IDEA

Plan and Solve
STRATEGY
ANSWER

Look Back
SENSIBLE ANSWER
ALTERNATE APPROACH

Build Understanding

Underground cities have been proposed in Japan to ease the land shortage. Alice City would feature two concrete cylinders, each 262 ft in diameter and 197 ft high. Each lower base would be 500 ft below ground. Alice City could house 100,000 people and would cost $4.2 billion to build.

A. How much "ground" space would the bottom of each of Alice City's cylinders provide?

Understand QUESTION What is the area of one base of each cylinder?

FACTS Each cylinder is 262 ft in diameter and 197 ft tall.

KEY IDEA Each base is circular. You need only the diameter.

Plan and Solve STRATEGY Use the formula for the area of a circle.

$A = \pi r^2$ π is about 3.14.

$A \approx (3.14)(131)^2$ The radius is half the diameter: $262 \div 2 = 131$. $(131)^2 = 131 \times 131$

$A \approx 53{,}885.54$

ANSWER The bottom of each cylinder would provide about 53,886 sq ft of space.

Look Back SENSIBLE ANSWER Estimate by using compatible numbers.
$3 \times 100^2 = 3 \times 10{,}000 = 30{,}000$
The answer is reasonable.

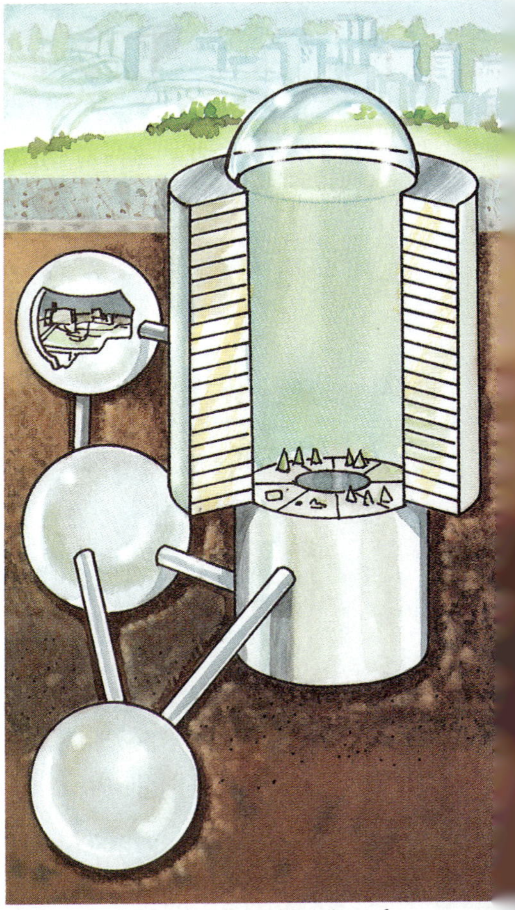

Although Japan is about the size of California, its population is almost half that of the U.S.

B. How much area will be provided by the center floor of each sphere connected to the cylinders?

The diameter of the spheres is not given. There is too little information to solve this problem.

■ **Write About Math** Write a problem that uses \$4.2 billion and 100,000 people.

Check Understanding

The Urban Geo Grid is another proposed underground city.

Urban Geo Grid

Area: 435 sq mi
Depth of base: 164 ft below ground
Population: 500,000
Cost: \$80.2 billion

Find the per-person cost of this city.

1. What information do you need to solve this problem?

2. What given data are not needed to solve the problem?

3. What units will you need in your answer?

4. What is the per-person cost of the Geo Grid?

Practice

Tell whether you would use mental math, paper and pencil, or calculator. Then solve each problem. If not enough information is provided, write *too little information.*

5. About how many Alice Cities equal the cost of one Geo Grid?

6. How much deeper will Alice City extend than Geo Grid?

7. How many years will it take to complete Alice City?

8. How much more is the per-person cost of Geo Grid than of Alice City?

9. Compare the total area of Alice City with that of Geo Grid.

10. Compare the total numbers of people the two cities can support.

11. To the nearest tenth of a mile, how far will Alice City extend below ground?

12. Japan's Asahi TV Studio is 66 ft underground. Geo Grid extends to about how many times this depth?

13. Use $V = \pi r^2 h$ to find the volume of one of the cylinders for Alice City.

14. How does the volume of a cylinder compare with the area of a base?

Skills Review

First estimate. Then divide.

1. $3\overline{)27.03}$ **2.** $50.6 \div 23$ **3.** $\frac{115.2}{12}$

Evaluate the expression $3.7k$ for each value of k.

4. $k = 10$ **5.** $k = 1{,}000$ **6.** $k = 400$

Evaluate the expression $8.4 \div x$ for each value of x.

7. $x = 100$ **8.** $x = 10{,}000$ **9.** $x = 400$

Divide. Round your answer to the nearest hundredth.

10. $\frac{1.82}{0.7}$ **11.** $\frac{3.69}{2.05}$

12. $\frac{16.75}{1.75}$ **13.** $\frac{200.2}{1.9}$

Write each fraction as a repeating or terminating decimal.

14. $\frac{5}{6}$ **15.** $\frac{13}{20}$ **16.** $\frac{1}{8}$

Write each decimal as a fraction in lowest terms.

17. 0.15 **18.** $0.\overline{7}$ **19.** 0.4

Compare the mixed numbers. Use >, <, or =.

20. $4\frac{5}{6}$ ▒ $4\frac{4}{5}$ **21.** $9\frac{4}{9}$ ▒ $9\frac{1}{3}$

Estimate each sum or difference.

22. $2\frac{2}{3} + 7\frac{1}{8}$ **23.** $56\frac{5}{9} - 2\frac{1}{2}$

Compute each answer.

24. $\frac{5}{9} - \frac{1}{6}$ **25.** $\frac{1}{2} + \frac{1}{5} + \frac{3}{10}$

26. $4\frac{3}{8} + 2\frac{1}{2}$ **27.** $\frac{7}{12} \times \frac{4}{7}$

28. $\frac{3}{4} \div \frac{1}{8}$ **29.** $\left(\frac{5}{6}\right)^2$

Problem-Solving Review

Solve each problem.

30. The bill for Fran's car repairs was $100.00. Parts cost $28.75 and the rest of the bill was for 2.5 hours of labor. What was the hourly charge for labor?

31. Ari, Ben, and Rita had the same homework assignment. It took Ari $2\frac{3}{4}$ hours to finish. Ben did the work in $2\frac{5}{6}$ hours. Rita spent $2\frac{7}{10}$ hours. Who spent the least amount of time on homework?

32. On three successive days, Juanita hiked $7\frac{1}{5}$ km, $11\frac{1}{4}$ km, and $10\frac{9}{10}$ km. She estimated that she hiked 29 km in all. Is the actual distance greater or less than Juanita's estimate?

33. The area of Pang's new house is $2\frac{1}{2}$ times the area of his uncle's apartment. The apartment is $1\frac{1}{2}$ times the size of Pang's cousin's dormitory room. If his uncle's apartment has an area of 840 square feet, what is the area of Pang's house?

34. Data File Use the data on pages 110–111. Suppose you wanted to exchange 500 U.S. dollars into local currency in each of these countries: Ireland, Great Britain, France, and Spain. How much of each currency would you receive?

35. Make a Data File Prepare 5 yes and no questions about current school or local issues. Survey 30 students from your school. Record your results in a double bar graph.

Cumulative Skills Review • Chapters 1 and 2

Tell whether the sequence is arithmetic, geometric, or neither. Then write the next three terms.

1. 96, 90, 85, 81, . . . **2.** 3, 6, 12, 24, . . . **3.** 17, 23, 29, 35, . . .

Estimate each answer.

4. $78.2 - 33.4$ **5.** $96 \times 12 \times 302$ **6.** $785 + 797 + 822$ **7.** $93 - 56.71$

8. 40.5×24.5 **9.** $8{,}150 \div 92$ **10.** $29.8 + 52.1$ **11.** $3{,}683 \div 65$

Compute. **Remember** to use the standard order of operations.

12. $\frac{9(3 + 2) + 3}{2(48 \div 6) - 4}$ **13.** $\frac{6 + 3 \times 2 + 8}{40 \div 8 + 5}$ **14.** $9 \times 6 \div 2 - 17$ **15.** $90 \div 10 + 5 \times 3$

Write the prime factorization of each number in exponential form.

16. 200 **17.** 99 **18.** 441 **19.** 81

Find the greatest common factor and the least common multiple for each pair of numbers.

20. 8 and 10 **21.** 12 and 15 **22.** 2 and 13 **23.** 24 and 16

Multiply or divide. Round your answers to the nearest tenth if necessary.

24. $9.23 \times 1{,}000$ **25.** $2.3 \times 10{,}000$ **26.** 8.6×200 **27.** 0.7×500

28. $6.8 \div 0.4$ **29.** $\frac{12.12}{0.4}$ **30.** $7.2 \div 3.1$ **31.** $\frac{225.5}{7.5}$

Write each mixed number as an improper fraction. Write each improper fraction as a mixed number or a whole number.

32. $2\frac{4}{5}$ **33.** $\frac{17}{12}$ **34.** $4\frac{9}{10}$ **35.** $\frac{65}{6}$

36. $\frac{45}{9}$ **37.** $3\frac{12}{13}$ **38.** $\frac{24}{4}$ **39.** $10\frac{5}{12}$

Add or subtract. Write your answer in simplest form.

40. $\frac{7}{8} - \frac{3}{4}$ **41.** $\frac{5}{9} + \frac{2}{3}$ **42.** $2\frac{1}{2} - 1\frac{7}{10}$ **43.** $6 - 4\frac{8}{11}$

44. $3\frac{3}{4} + 1\frac{5}{8} + 12\frac{1}{2}$ **45.** $\frac{13}{16} + \frac{7}{8} + \frac{3}{4} + \frac{5}{8}$

Multiply or divide. Write your answer in simplest form.

46. $\frac{15}{16} \times \frac{4}{5}$ **47.** $\frac{20}{21} \div \frac{5}{7}$ **48.** $3\frac{1}{3} \times 1\frac{1}{2}$ **49.** $6\frac{1}{4} \div \frac{5}{8}$

50. $2\frac{1}{6} \times 7$ **51.** $3\frac{1}{8} \div 4$ **52.** $12 \div \frac{4}{5}$ **53.** $\frac{1}{6} \times 47$

Reteaching

Set A pages 48–49

To divide a decimal by a whole number, place the decimal point in the quotient. Follow the steps for whole number division.

Divide \$73.15 by 22.

```
     3.325      Place the decimal point directly over
22)73.150       the decimal point in the dividend.
   66
    7 1         Write a zero to get 3 decimal places
    6 6         in the answer in order to round to the
      55        nearest cent.
      44
      110
      110
        0       Round 3.325 to $3.33.
```

Remember that you can write zeros in the dividend so that you can continue dividing.

1. 12)24.072 **2.** 16)38.4

3. 60)11.25 **4.** 29)4.524

5. 16.1 ÷ 46 **6.** 17.5 ÷ 5

7. 0.6 ÷ 48 **8.** 1.26 ÷ 21

9. $\frac{0.912}{25}$ **10.** $\frac{35.97}{33}$

11. $\frac{10.4}{4}$ **12.** $\frac{4.26}{3}$

Set B pages 50–51

When multiplying or dividing by a multiple of 10, count the zeros and move the decimal point.

Multiply—move right.
0.87 × 1,000 = 0.870 = 870 (3 zeros, 3 places)

Divide—move left.
4.2 ÷ 100 = 04.2 = 0.042 (2 zeros, 2 places)

Remember to write zeros when more places are needed in the answer.

1. 341.8 ÷ 1,000 **2.** 42.81 × 100

3. 41.234 ÷ 10,000 **4.** 9.02 × 1,000

5. 0.725 × 100,000 **6.** 3.62 ÷ 100

Set C pages 52–53

1. When dividing by a decimal, move the decimal point to make the divisor a whole number.
2. Move the decimal point in the dividend the same number of places.

0.02)0.70 = 2)70 Write a zero to have enough places to move the decimal point.

Remember to place the decimal point in the answer.

1. 33.58 ÷ 7.3 **2.** 4.8 ÷ 0.06

3. 3.2 ÷ 0.004 **4.** 7.14 ÷ 2.04

Set D pages 56–57

To write a fraction as a decimal, divide the numerator by the denominator. Make sure that the fraction is in lowest terms first.

$\frac{9}{75} = \frac{3}{25} = 25\overline{)3.00}$ (quotient 0.12) $\frac{9}{75} = 0.12$

Remember that the line between the numerator and denominator means "divided by."

Write each decimal as a fraction in lowest terms.

1. 0.6 **2.** 0.07 **3.** 0.625 **4.** $0.\overline{3}$

Write each fraction as a decimal.

5. $\frac{3}{8}$ **6.** $\frac{11}{20}$ **7.** $\frac{4}{25}$ **8.** $\frac{10}{36}$

Set E pages 60–61

To write an improper fraction as a mixed number, divide.

$$\frac{74}{13} = 13\overline{)74} \quad 5\frac{9}{13}$$
$$\begin{array}{r} 74 \\ \underline{65} \\ 9 \end{array}$$

Write the remainder over the divisor as the fraction part of the mixed number.

To write a mixed number as an improper fraction, rename the whole number.

$5\frac{9}{13}$ $\quad 5 = \frac{65}{13} \quad \frac{65}{13} + \frac{9}{13} = \frac{74}{13}$

Remember that the denominator of a fraction is the divisor.

Write each mixed number as an improper fraction and each improper fraction as a mixed number.

1. $\frac{55}{16}$ **2.** $\frac{65}{12}$

3. $36\frac{1}{8}$ **4.** $14\frac{5}{6}$

5. $7\frac{4}{5}$ **6.** $\frac{49}{6}$

Set F pages 62–65

Rounding is one method of estimation that can be used with fractions or mixed numbers—for both sums and differences.

$7\frac{5}{8} - 3\frac{2}{9}$ **Round:** $7\frac{5}{8} \rightarrow 8$

$3\frac{2}{9} \rightarrow 3$

$8 - 3 = 5$

Remember that you can find a range for a sum after rounding.

1. $8\frac{3}{5} + 3\frac{1}{7}$ Sum is between ▒ and ▒.

2. $31\frac{7}{8} - 14\frac{2}{3}$ Estimate is ▒.

3. $3\frac{7}{10} + 4\frac{3}{5}$ Sum is between ▒ and ▒.

4. $16\frac{2}{3} - 14\frac{1}{3}$ Estimate is ▒.

Set G pages 66–69

Follow these steps to subtract mixed numbers:

a) Rewrite with a common denominator.
b) Rename if necessary to subtract the fractions.
c) Subtract the fractions.
d) Subtract the whole numbers.

Remember that the whole number can be renamed as a fraction.

1. $5\frac{1}{8} - 1\frac{1}{4}$ **2.** $14\frac{2}{10} - 9\frac{3}{4}$ **3.** $47\frac{5}{8} - 20\frac{5}{6}$

Set H pages 70–71

Dividing by a number is the same as multiplying by its reciprocal.

$$2\frac{3}{16} \div 1\frac{1}{4} = \frac{35}{16} \div \frac{5}{4}$$

$$\frac{\overset{7}{\cancel{35}}}{\underset{4}{\cancel{16}}} \times \frac{\overset{1}{\cancel{4}}}{\underset{1}{\cancel{5}}} = \frac{7}{4} = 1\frac{3}{4}$$

The reciprocal of $\frac{5}{4}$ is $\frac{4}{5}$.

Remember to write mixed numbers as improper fractions.

1. $4\frac{1}{4} \div 7\frac{7}{8}$ **2.** $2\frac{1}{12} \div 3\frac{3}{4}$

3. $6\frac{1}{4} \div 2\frac{1}{2}$ **4.** $13\frac{1}{3} \div 8$

5. $3\frac{2}{3} \times 4\frac{1}{5}$ **6.** $1\frac{1}{4} \times 6$

7. $8 \times 4\frac{2}{3}$ **8.** $1\frac{1}{5} \times 9\frac{3}{8}$

More Practice

Set A pages 48–49

First estimate. Then divide.

1. 75 ÷ 15 **2.** 45.92 ÷ 82 **3.** 105.28 ÷ 47 **4.** 72.8 ÷ 112

5. $6\overline{)0.0078}$ **6.** $39\overline{)4{,}898.4}$ **7.** $172\overline{)29{,}721.6}$ **8.** $99\overline{)197.01}$

9. 73.224 ÷ 24 **10.** 3209.2 ÷ 71 **11.** 0.0272 ÷ 8 **12.** 999.4 ÷ 19

13. $33\overline{)9.24}$ **14.** $210\overline{)191.1}$ **15.** $88\overline{)2.4112}$ **16.** $96\overline{)0.912}$

Set B pages 50–51

Multiply each number by 10, 100, 1,000, and 10,000. Then divide each number by these multiples of 10.

1. 6.25 **2.** 0.00365 **3.** 20.02 **4.** 85.1

5. 9.438 **6.** 12,987 **7.** 0.399 **8.** 378.02

9. 2.05 **10.** 0.9 **11.** 194.1 **12.** 10,461

13. 819 **14.** 172,000 **15.** 0.039 **16.** 78.7

17. 5.4 **18.** 38.9 **19.** 210 **20.** 0.904

Set C pages 52–53

Divide. Round your answer to the nearest tenth.

1. 29.16 ÷ 4.7 **2.** 5.05 ÷ 1.01 **3.** 68.42 ÷ 3.21 **4.** 11.11 ÷ 1.21

5. 394.8 ÷ 23.5 **6.** 4.97 ÷ 0.03 **7.** 3,495.2 ÷ 9.7 **8.** 15.09 ÷ 4.5

Divide. Round your answer to the nearest hundredth.

9. 516.29 ÷ 49.7 **10.** 3.787 ÷ 21.9 **11.** 111.1 ÷ 121 **12.** 9,376.3 ÷ 63.9

13. 11.002 ÷ 8.4 **14.** 185.22 ÷ 0.54 **15.** 35.68 ÷ 2.9 **16.** 247.6 ÷ 9.3

Set D pages 56–57

Write each fraction as a repeating or a terminating decimal.

1. $\frac{3}{4}$ **2.** $\frac{7}{100}$ **3.** $\frac{9}{32}$ **4.** $\frac{5}{11}$ **5.** $\frac{11}{12}$ **6.** $\frac{9}{13}$

7. $\frac{14}{21}$ **8.** $\frac{8}{15}$ **9.** $\frac{5}{8}$ **10.** $\frac{16}{5}$ **11.** $\frac{4}{27}$ **12.** $\frac{37}{45}$

Write each decimal as a fraction in lowest terms.

13. 0.95 **14.** 0.1875 **15.** $0.\overline{2}$ **16.** $0.\overline{834}$

17. 0.32 **18.** $0.\overline{8}$ **19.** $0.\overline{729}$ **20.** 0.095

Set E pages 60–61

Write each number as an improper fraction.

1. $3 = \frac{\blacksquare}{7}$ **2.** $5 = \frac{\blacksquare}{11}$ **3.** $10 = \frac{\blacksquare}{3}$ **4.** $4\frac{2}{9}$ **5.** $2\frac{5}{6}$ **6.** $5\frac{7}{10}$

7. $3\frac{5}{8}$ **8.** $9\frac{1}{7}$ **9.** $4\frac{2}{3}$ **10.** $11\frac{3}{5}$ **11.** $2\frac{3}{4}$ **12.** $21\frac{1}{2}$

Write each fraction as a mixed number or a whole number.

13. $\frac{37}{4}$ **14.** $\frac{39}{13}$ **15.** $\frac{49}{9}$ **16.** $\frac{55}{14}$ **17.** $\frac{108}{25}$ **18.** $\frac{57}{7}$

19. $\frac{23}{4}$ **20.** $\frac{18}{11}$ **21.** $\frac{52}{3}$ **22.** $\frac{212}{4}$ **23.** $\frac{93}{8}$ **24.** $\frac{78}{6}$

List the numbers in order from greatest to least.

25. $\frac{20}{7}, \frac{10}{4}, \frac{21}{8}$ **26.** $1\frac{5}{6}, 1\frac{2}{3}, 2\frac{2}{9}$ **27.** $3\frac{13}{14}, 4\frac{3}{25}, 3\frac{6}{7}, 4\frac{1}{4}$ **28.** $2\frac{5}{8}, \frac{7}{3}, 2\frac{2}{3}, \frac{5}{2}$

Set F pages 62–65

Estimate each sum or difference.

1. $57\frac{1}{2} + 22\frac{5}{6}$ **2.** $16\frac{4}{9} - 5\frac{1}{3}$ **3.** $98\frac{1}{5} + 32\frac{1}{6}$ **4.** $5 - 2\frac{8}{9}$

5. $21\frac{13}{15} + 18\frac{1}{11}$ **6.** $100\frac{17}{25} - 50\frac{15}{32}$ **7.** $39\frac{1}{4} - 24\frac{5}{6}$ **8.** $20 - 9\frac{3}{5}$

9. $12\frac{3}{4} + 2\frac{5}{8}$ **10.** $31\frac{7}{8} + 12\frac{1}{3}$ **11.** $7\frac{1}{9} - 4\frac{7}{8}$ **12.** $8\frac{9}{11} + 41\frac{3}{4}$

Set G pages 66–69

Add or subtract.

1. $1\frac{3}{4} + 7\frac{11}{16}$ **2.** $6\frac{2}{3} + 9\frac{5}{6}$ **3.** $3\frac{6}{7} - 1\frac{4}{21}$ **4.** $14\frac{5}{8} - 7\frac{3}{10}$

5. $42\frac{1}{4} + 6\frac{4}{9}$ **6.** $10 - 4\frac{6}{11}$ **7.** $9\frac{1}{3} + 4\frac{4}{5}$ **8.** $22\frac{5}{6} - 11\frac{8}{9}$

9. $35 + 9\frac{4}{5}$ **10.** $62\frac{1}{3} - 33\frac{3}{5}$ **11.** $91\frac{3}{8} + 17\frac{5}{6}$ **12.** $14\frac{4}{7} + 18\frac{9}{14}$

Set H pages 70–71

Multiply or divide.

1. $\frac{1}{4} \times \frac{7}{8}$ **2.** $\frac{4}{9} \times \frac{2}{3}$ **3.** $\frac{1}{15} \div \frac{4}{5}$ **4.** $\frac{9}{14} \div \frac{3}{7}$

5. $1\frac{5}{6} \times 3\frac{4}{5}$ **6.** $\frac{4}{7} \div 4$ **7.** $\frac{2}{11} \div 3\frac{1}{33}$ **8.** $1\frac{5}{16} \times 6\frac{2}{3}$

9. $\frac{4}{5} \times 20$ **10.** $\frac{4}{5} \div 20$ **11.** $12\frac{2}{9} \times 5\frac{1}{4}$ **12.** $1\frac{5}{6} \times \frac{4}{11}$

Enrichment

Division Patterns with Nines

Use paper and pencil or a calculator to find each quotient.

1. 2 ÷ 9
2 ÷ 99
2 ÷ 999
2 ÷ 9,999

2. 3 ÷ 9
3 ÷ 99
3 ÷ 999
3 ÷ 9,999

3. 4 ÷ 9
4 ÷ 99
4 ÷ 999
4 ÷ 9,999

4. 5 ÷ 9
5 ÷ 99
5 ÷ 999
5 ÷ 9,999

5. What pattern do you notice?

For Problems 6–8, try to discover a pattern as soon as possible. Then use mental math to write the remaining answers. Then check your answers. Do the same for Problems 9–11.

6. 12 ÷ 9
12 ÷ 99
12 ÷ 999
12 ÷ 9,999
12 ÷ 99,999
12 ÷ 999,999

7. 26 ÷ 9
26 ÷ 99
26 ÷ 999
26 ÷ 9,999
26 ÷ 99,999
26 ÷ 999,999

8. 47 ÷ 9
47 ÷ 99
47 ÷ 999
47 ÷ 9,999
47 ÷ 99,999
47 ÷ 999,999

9. 9 ÷ 9
9 ÷ 99
9 ÷ 999
9 ÷ 9,999
9 ÷ 99,999
9 ÷ 999,999

10. 1 ÷ 0.9
2 ÷ 0.9
3 ÷ 0.9
4 ÷ 0.9
6 ÷ 0.9
8 ÷ 0.9

11. 1 ÷ 0.09
2 ÷ 0.09
3 ÷ 0.09
5 ÷ 0.09
7 ÷ 0.09
9 ÷ 0.09

12. 10 ÷ 99
20 ÷ 99
30 ÷ 99
40 ÷ 99
60 ÷ 99
90 ÷ 99

13. 1 ÷ 99
10 ÷ 99
100 ÷ 99
1,000 ÷ 99
10,000 ÷ 99
100,000 ÷ 99

14. Study the pattern in Problems 6–8. Do you think the pattern will hold for all 2-digit numbers? Try others to find out.

15. Division by other numbers may also result in recognizable quotient patterns. For example, use the numbers 1–10 as dividends and use 11 and 111 as divisors. Describe any patterns you notice.

Chapter 2 Review/Test

For Exercises 1 and 2, use compatible numbers to decide which quotient is reasonable.

1. $38.82 \div 12$

a. 323.5 **b.** 32.35 **c.** 3.235

2. $0.37 \div 0.8$

a. 0.04625 **b.** 0.4625 **c.** 4.625

3. How many kilometers long is a 440 m racetrack?

Multiply or divide.

4. 0.038×400 **5.** $3.24 \div 0.08$

6. Sarah had a job baby-sitting for her neighbor. She worked 4.5 hours and made $11.25. How much did Sarah earn per hour?

7. Which operation should be used to solve this problem?

Brian's family went on a summer vacation. They drove an average of 180 miles per day for 13 days. How far did they travel?

a. addition
b. multiplication
c. division

8. What part of a minute is 15 seconds? Write your answer as a fraction and as a decimal.

Write each fraction as a repeating or terminating decimal.

9. $\frac{5}{8}$ **10.** $\frac{3}{11}$ **11.** $\frac{5}{16}$

Write each decimal as a fraction in lowest terms.

12. 0.125 **13.** 0.45 **14.** 0.34

15. List these mixed numbers in order from least to greatest.

$4\frac{5}{6}, 5\frac{11}{12}, 4\frac{2}{3}$

Change each improper fraction to a mixed number and each mixed number to an improper fraction.

16. $\frac{27}{6}$ **17.** $7\frac{3}{8}$ **18.** $\frac{17}{2}$

Tell whether each sum is less than 1 or greater than 1.

19. $\frac{2}{3} + \frac{3}{5}$ **20.** $\frac{7}{16} + \frac{2}{5}$

Solve.

21. $7\frac{3}{5} - 2\frac{2}{10}$ **22.** $\frac{5}{6} + \frac{1}{4}$

23. $\frac{4}{5} \times \frac{5}{4}$ **24.** $4\frac{3}{4} \div \frac{1}{4}$

25. Ronald ate $\frac{1}{3}$ of a pizza for lunch Saturday and his sister Freda ate $\frac{1}{4}$ of it. How much of the pizza did they eat?

26. Mr. Smith ordered wallpaper for his son's room. The room was 8 feet wide, 9 feet long, and 8 feet high. What information would you use to find out how much wallpaper Mr. Smith should buy for the *biggest* wall?

27. **Write About Math** Discuss what compatible numbers you used to answer Problem 2 and why you chose them.

Integers and Rational Numbers

3

Did You Know: In 1987, about 50 billion shares of stock were traded on the New York Stock Exchange. Newspaper reports give the daily changes in the value of stocks using rational numbers like $+1\frac{1}{4}$ (a gain of $1.25) and $-\frac{5}{8}$ (a loss of $0.625).

Number-Sense Project

Estimate

Use a newspaper and select a stock on the New York Stock Exchange. Follow its gains and/or losses for 3 days. Then predict if it will gain or lose in the next week.

Gather Data

Make an imaginary purchase of $5,000 of the stock you selected. Chart its performance for a week.

Analyze and Report

Make a graph to show the performance of your stock. After one week did you make money or lose money?

ALGEBRA

Meaning of Integers

Build Understanding

A. Every place on earth is either above, below, or at sea level. ***Integers*** can be used to describe elevations.

Mount Everest is 29,028 feet above sea level, or +29,028 (positive 29,028) feet.

The Dead Sea is 1,312 feet below sea level, or −1,312 (negative 1,312) feet.

Highest and Lowest Altitudes of Continents

Continent	Highest Elevation	Feet Above Sea Level	Lowest Elevation	Feet Below Sea Level
Asia	Mount Everest	29,028	Dead Sea	1,312
South America	Mount Aconcagua	22,834	Valdes Peninsula	131
North America	Mount McKinley	20,320	Death Valley	282
Africa	Kilimanjaro	19,340	Lake Assal	512
Europe	Mount Elbrus	18,510	Caspian Sea	92
Antarctica	Vinson Massif	16,864	Unknown	—
Australia	Mount Kosciusko	7,310	Lake Eyre	52

B. All integers can be shown on a number line.

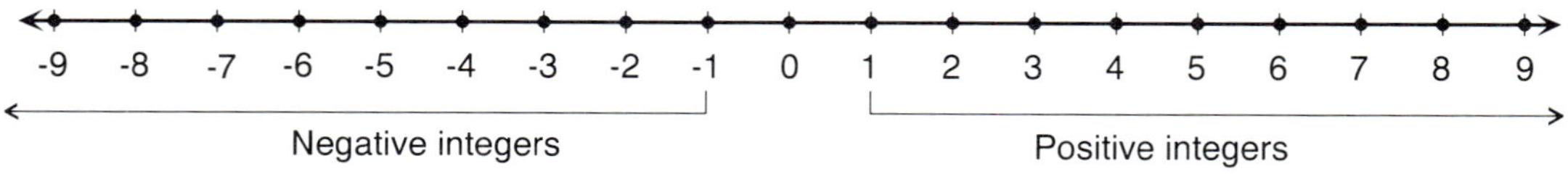

Positive integers are usually written without the plus sign. Negative integers are always written with the negative sign. Zero is neither positive nor negative.

C. For every positive integer, there is a corresponding negative integer. On a number line, an integer and its ***opposite*** are located the same distance from zero, but on opposite sides of zero.

The opposite of 6 is −6. $\mathbf{-(6) = -6}$

The opposite of −4 is 4. $\mathbf{-(-4) = 4}$

D. The ***absolute value*** of an integer tells the number of units the integer is from zero on the number line.

The absolute value of 7 is 7. $\mathbf{|7| = 7}$

The absolute value of −5 is 5. $\mathbf{|-5| = 5}$

The absolute value of 0 is 0. $\mathbf{|0| = 0}$

E. You can use a horizontal number line to compare two integers. The integer farther to the right on a number line is the greater integer.

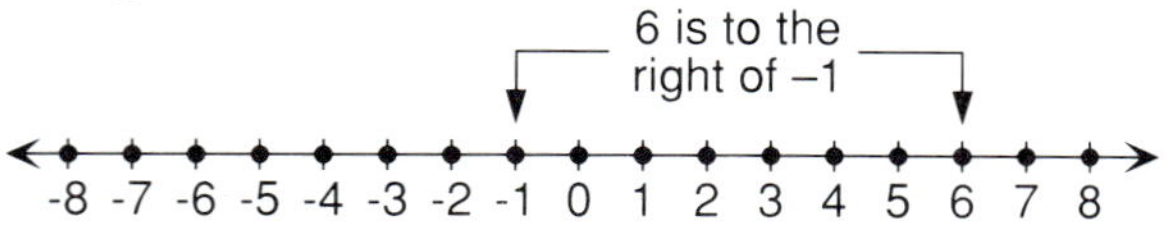

6 > −1

■ **Talk About Math** Is the absolute value of 1 greater than the absolute value of −75? Explain.

Check Understanding

For another example, see Set A, pages 104–105.

Solve.

1. If 12 represents a gain of 12 yards on a football field, what does -12 represent?

Write an integer for each exercise.

2. $-(-8)$ **3.** $-(50)$ **4.** $-|93|$

Practice

For More Practice, see Set A, pages 106–107.

Write an integer for each exercise. **Remember** to write a negative sign for a negative integer.

5. A loss of \$2 **6.** 55 feet above sea level **7.** 9° below zero

8. 23 feet below sea level **9.** A gain of \$6 **10.** 32° above zero

11. A deposit of \$3 **12.** A loss of 2 yards **13.** A withdrawal of \$5

Give the value for each exercise.

14. $|-1|$ **15.** $|63|$ **16.** $|-715|$ **17.** $|23{,}501|$ **18.** $|456|$

19. $|-7|$ **20.** $|42|$ **21.** $|-66|$ **22.** $|-1{,}263|$ **23.** $-|13|$

24. $|0|$ **25.** $-|-8|$ **26.** $|-(-8)|$ **27.** $|x|$ if $x \geq 0$ **28.** $|y|$ if $y < 0$

Number Sense Compare each pair of integers. Use $<$ or $>$.

29. -4 ▒ 4 **30.** -9 ▒ -12 **31.** 6 ▒ 3 **32.** -14 ▒ 14 **33.** -8 ▒ 2

34. 0 ▒ 17 **35.** -19 ▒ 0 **36.** -5 ▒ -1 **37.** 0 ▒ -101 **38.** -19 ▒ 17

39. -5 ▒ -8 **40.** 75 ▒ 57 **41.** -1 ▒ -2 **42.** $|-1|$ ▒ $|-2|$ **43.** $|5|$ ▒ $|-7|$

Problem Solving

Solve each problem.

44. Use the table on page 84. Write the elevations as integers in order from greatest to least.

45. **Visual Thinking** Is there a least positive integer? a greatest positive integer? a least negative integer? a greatest negative integer?

46. What integer would you write to show a detour of 3 miles? Explain.

47. What integer would you use to show that you waited 15 minutes? Explain.

Adding and Subtracting Integers

Build Understanding

A. Thermometers measure air temperature. The scale of a thermometer is similar to a number line. It has integers showing temperatures above and below zero degrees. Positive integers are shown above zero and negative integers are shown below zero.

B. Between 3:00 P.M. and 4:00 P.M. the temperature dropped 2 degrees. Between 4:00 P.M. and 5:00 P.M. the temperature dropped 3 degrees. What was the total change in temperature?

To find the total, add -2 and -3.

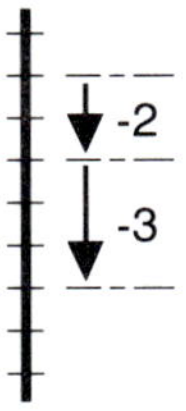

To add integers with the same sign, add without regard to the signs. Then use the sign of the numbers in your answer.

$$-2 + (-3) = -5$$

The change in temperature was $-5°$.

C. The temperature rose 3 degrees between noon and 1:00 P.M. and dropped 7 degrees between 1:00 P.M. and 2:00 P.M. Find the total change in temperature between noon and 2:00 P.M.

Add 3 and (-7).

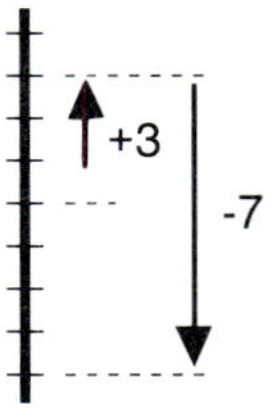

To add two integers with different signs, consider the distance each integer is from zero. Subtract the shorter distance from the longer distance. Then use the sign of the number farther from zero in your answer.

$$3 + (-7) = -4$$

The change in temperature was $-4°$.

D. When adding more than two integers, rearrange the numbers to make the addition easier. Find this sum.

$$-7 + 6 + 5 + (-8) + (-12) + 9 + 15$$
$$-7 + (-8) + (-12) + 6 + 5 + 9 + 15$$
$$-27 \quad + \quad 35$$
$$8$$

E. How would you find $3 - (-7)$? $-6 - 9$?

To subtract an integer, add its opposite.

$3 - (-7)$	$-6 - 9$
$3 + (+7) = 10$	$-6 + (-9) = -15$

Talk About Math Explain how the commutative property of addition makes the addition in Example D easier.

Check Understanding

For another example, see Set B, pages 104–105.

Write an addition expression for each exercise.

1. The temperature was −8 degrees. It rose 7 degrees.

2. The temperature was −8 degrees. It dropped 7 degrees.

Practice

For More Practice, see Set B, pages 106–107.

Number Sense Will the answer be positive or negative?

3. $-5 + (-1)$ **4.** $-3 - (-5)$

Calculator Solve by using the key sequence shown.

5. $7 + (-10)$ **Press:** 7 [+] 10 [+/-] [=]

Compute. Tell whether you used mental math, paper and pencil, or a calculator to find each answer. **Remember** to look at the signs.

6. $-4 + (-6)$ **7.** $9 + 5$ **8.** $-35 - (-28)$ **9.** $-7 + 7$

10. $9 + (-4)$ **11.** $-11 + 27$ **12.** $-42 + 38$ **13.** $25 + (-16)$

14. $33 - (-12)$ **15.** $-6 + 18$ **16.** $-4 + (-26)$ **17.** $-23 - 23$

18. $-4 + 2 + (-32) + 4$ **19.** $-17 + 9 + 9 + (-1)$ **20.** $7 - (-14) - (9) + (-3)$

Complete each table.

a	$6 + a$
1	**21.**
−1	**22.**
−3	**23.**

b	$9 + b$
24.	5
−3	**25.**
26.	−6

c	$c - 8$
0	**27.**
28.	−14
29.	−4

d	$7 - d$
30.	9
7	**31.**
32.	−7

Problem Solving

Solve the following.

33. The temperature on the surface of the moon can vary from 127°C to −153°C. What is the difference in these temperatures?

34. On Mars the low temperature is −84°C and the high temperature is −33°C. What is the difference in these temperatures?

Critical Thinking Solve each problem.

35. The sum of two integers is −8. When the lesser integer is subtracted from the greater integer, the difference is 4. What are the integers?

36. The sum of two integers is 2. When the lesser integer is subtracted from the greater integer, the difference is 8. What are the integers?

ALGEBRA

Multiplying and Dividing Integers

Build Understanding

ACTIVITY

A. Describe That Pattern
Groups: 4 students

Column A	Column B
(3) (3) = 9	(-3)(3) = -9
(3) (2) = 6	(-3)(2) = -6
(3) (1) = 3	(-3)(1) = -3
(3) (0) = ?	(-3) (0) = ?
(3) (-1) = ?	(-3) (-1) = ?
(3) (-2) = ?	(-3) (-2) = ?
(3) (-3) = ?	(-3) (-3) = ?

a. Discuss the pattern you see in Column A. By how much does the product decrease each time?

b. By how much does each product in Column B increase?

c. Copy and complete Columns A and B.

d. In Columns A and B, if two integers have the same sign, what is their product? If two integers have different signs, what is their product? Is this true for all integers?

B. **Calculator** Find each product.

(4)(5) **Press:** 4 [×] 5 [=]
Display: 20

(4)(−5) **Press:** 4 [×] 5 [+/−] [=]
Display: −20

(−4)(−5) **Press:** 4 [+/−] [×] 5 [+/−] [=]
Display: 20

(−4)(5) **Press:** 4 [+/−] [×] 5 [=]
Display: −20

C. To find the quotient of two integers, think of the related multiplication.

Find 54 ÷ (−6).

$(-6)(-9) = 54$, so $54 \div (-6) = (-9)$

Find −48 ÷ (−8).

$(-8)(6) = -48$, so $-48 \div (-8) = 6$

The quotient of two integers that have the same sign is positive. The quotient of two integers that have different signs is negative.

■ **Talk About Math** What is the sign of the product of three positive integers? of three negative integers?

Check Understanding

For another example, see Set C, pages 104–105.

Tell whether each product or quotient is positive or negative.

1. 9×15 **2.** $5\,(-7)$ **3.** $(-4)(-8)$ **4.** $-14 \div (-7)$ **5.** $-6 \div 3$

Practice

For More Practice, see Set C, pages 106–107.

Compute. Tell whether you used mental math or paper or pencil to find each answer. **Remember** to write a negative sign for negative products and quotients.

6. $(-9)(3)$	**7.** $(18)(7)$	**8.** $9\,(-45)$	**9.** $(-8)(-4)$
10. $-49 \div (-7)$	**11.** $-64 \div (8)$	**12.** $0 \div (-7)$	**13.** $36 \div (-6)$
14. -5×12	**15.** $52 \div (-4)$	**16.** $(-24) \div (-6)$	**17.** $(-14)(-3)$
18. $0 \times (-77)$	**19.** $72 \div (-12)$	**20.** $(11)(-5)$	**21.** -9×7
22. $-14\,(400)$	**23.** $(13) \times (-6)$	**24.** $(-4)(-21)(2)$	**25.** $(-6)(-4)(-7)$

Mixed Practice Compute.

26. $-19 - 8$	**27.** $53 + (-3)$	**28.** $72 \div (-9)$	**29.** $(-6)(-8)$
30. $-81 \div (-3)$	**31.** $6(-15)(0)$	**32.** $87 - (-7)$	**33.** $-45 + 15$
34. $-39 - 13$	**35.** $-7 - (-12)$	**36.** $8 + (-2) - 2$	**37.** $5(-17)$

Problem Solving

Solve each problem.

38. **Critical Thinking** *Closure Under Addition of Integers* means the sum of two integers is always another integer. Is division of integers closed? Explain your answer.

39. Isa's average golf score has dropped 7 strokes every year for six years. If her average was 138 six years ago, what is her average score now?

Explore Math

Find each product.

40. $(-3)^2$ **41.** $(-3)^3$ **42.** $(-3)^4$ **43.** $(-3)^5$ **44.** $(-3)^6$

45. Study Problems 40–44. When -3 is raised to an even power, what is the sign of the answer? When -3 is raised to an odd power, what is the sign of the answer?

46. State a rule for predicting the sign of a negative number raised to an even or to an odd power. Check your rule using -2.

Use Data from a Table

PROBLEM SOLVING **GUIDE**

Understand
QUESTION
FACTS
KEY IDEA

Plan and Solve
STRATEGY
ANSWER

Look Back
SENSIBLE ANSWER
ALTERNATE APPROACH

Build Understanding

Have you ever been outside on a windy day when the temperature seemed much colder than the temperature indicated on the thermometer? The wind makes you feel colder and this effect is called the ***wind-chill factor.*** What temperature does it seem to be when the wind speed is 20 miles per hour and the air temperature is 20°F?

Understand QUESTION What is the wind-chill factor when the temperature is 20°F and the wind speed is 20 miles per hour?

FACTS The air temperature is 20°F. The wind is blowing at 20 miles per hour.

KEY IDEA The wind makes you feel colder, so the wind-chill factor is lower than the air temperature.

Plan and Solve STRATEGY Use the table at the right to find the wind-chill factor at various air temperatures and wind speeds. In the first column of the table, find the air temperature of 20°F. Read across the row to the wind-speed column marked 20. The number where the row and the column meet is the wind-chill factor.

ANSWER The wind-chill factor for an air temperature of 20°F and a wind speed of 20 miles per hour is −10°F.

Look Back SENSIBLE ANSWER The wind-chill factor is less than 20°F, so the answer is reasonable.

Wind-Chill Temperature Table

Air temp.	Wind speed in miles per hour			
	10	20	30	40
40°F	28	18	13	10
30°F	16	4	−2	−6
20°F	4	−10	−18	−21
10°F	−9	−25	−33	−37
0°F	−21	−39	−48	−53
−10°F	−32	−53	−63	−69
−20°F	−46	−67	−79	−85
−30°F	−58	−82	−94	−100

■ **Talk About Math** Does the wind-chill factor decrease at the same rate as the air temperature? Explain.

Check Understanding

Use the table on page 90 for Exercises 1 and 2.

1. What is the wind-chill factor when the air temperature is −10°F and the wind speed is 30 miles per hour?

2. If the wind-chill factor is −37°F, what is the air temperature and the wind speed?

Practice

Solve each problem.

3. From 2:00 P.M. to 3:00 P.M. the air temperature fell from 10°F to 0°F and the wind speed rose from 10 miles per hour to 20 miles per hour. What was the change in wind-chill factor?

4. From 8:00 A.M. to 2:00 P.M. the air temperature rose from −10°F to 30°F and the wind speed fell from 30 miles per hour to 10 miles per hour. What was the change in wind-chill factor?

The wind-chill factor on Mt. Washington Observatory in New Hampshire often drops below −100°F.

5. Yesterday the wind-chill factor was 16°F. Today it is −25°F. How much greater was the wind-chill factor yesterday than today?

Estimation Use the table on page 90 to estimate the answers to Exercises 6–9.

6. About how fast must the wind be blowing for a temperature of 40°F to feel like 24°F?

7. About how fast must the wind be blowing for a temperature of 30°F to feel like −5°F?

8. Estimate the wind-chill factor when the air temperature is 30°F and the wind speed is 50 miles per hour.

9. Estimate the wind-chill factor when the wind speed is 30 miles per hour and the air temperature is 50°F.

Midchapter Checkup

Mental Math Find each answer.

1. −14 + (−6) **2.** 12 × (−6) **3.** −72 ÷ 9 **4.** −2 − (−8) **5.** 9 − 12

Complete each table.

m	0	10	−15
$m + (-6)$	**6.**	**7.**	**8.**

b	**9.**	**10.**	12
$\frac{b}{-3}$	0	−3	**11.**

Problem-Solving Workshop

Critical Thinking Activity

1. Solve each number riddle.

a. I am the only two-digit number that is a square and a cube. Who am I?

b. I am a two-digit palindrome. Who am I?

c. We are both even integers. Our sum is negative. Our product is −96. Neither of us is a factor of the other. Who are we?

d. We are both two-digit even integers. Our product is a cube and our sum is −30. Who are we?

Number-Sense Project

1. *Look back at pages 82-83.* Listed below is a portfolio of six stocks and the closing price on September 6.

a. Find the total value of the portfolio at closing on September 6.

b. How much did the stocks gain or lose on September 6?

Stock	Shares	Closing Price	Change
A	300	30	$-2\frac{1}{8}$
B	100	$37\frac{7}{8}$	$-2\frac{1}{4}$
C	100	$46\frac{1}{8}$	$-2\frac{3}{4}$
D	200	61	$+\frac{5}{8}$
E	200	$117\frac{3}{4}$	$+\frac{5}{8}$
F	100	139	$+1\frac{3}{4}$

MATH laugh

When is seven even?

When you take away the "s"!

Explore with a Computer

Use the *Graphing and Probability Workshop Project* for this activity.

In February, Joey had $100.00 in his savings account. The next month he decided to start a lawn mowing business. To buy a lawn mower, Joey had to use all his money in savings, and borrow $75.00 from his father. He earns $5.00 for each lawn he mows. He also pays for lawnmower repairs.

1. At the computer, the table shows how much money Joey had at the end of each month. View the data in the table as a line graph.

2. In which month did he earn the most money? In which two months did he earn the same amount of money?

3. After one month's work did he still owe money to his father?

4. How many months did it take him to have more money than when he started?

Math-at-Home Activity

Talk to members of your family about important family events that occurred before and after you were born. Record these events on a number line like the one shown below. Use zero to represent the year you were born.

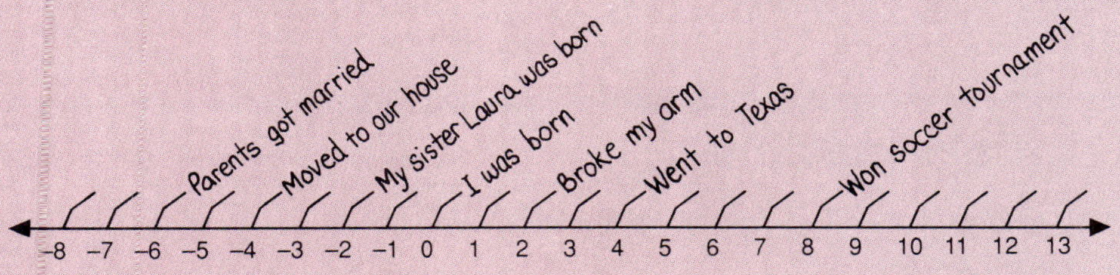

Meaning of Rational Numbers

Build Understanding

A. Consider the numbers -5, $2\frac{1}{3}$, and 0.25. Each of these numbers can be written in many other ways.

Each of these numbers is a ***rational number.*** Any number that can be written as the quotient of two integers is a rational number. However, the divisor, or denominator, cannot be 0.

$$-5 = \frac{-5}{1} = \frac{5}{-1} = \frac{-10}{2} = \frac{-15}{3}$$

$$2\frac{1}{3} = \frac{7}{3} = \frac{-7}{-3} = -\frac{-7}{3} = \frac{14}{6} = -\frac{7}{-3}$$

$$0.25 = \frac{1}{4} = \frac{-1}{-4} = \frac{2}{8} = \frac{-4}{-16}$$

B. Rational numbers can be shown on a number line.

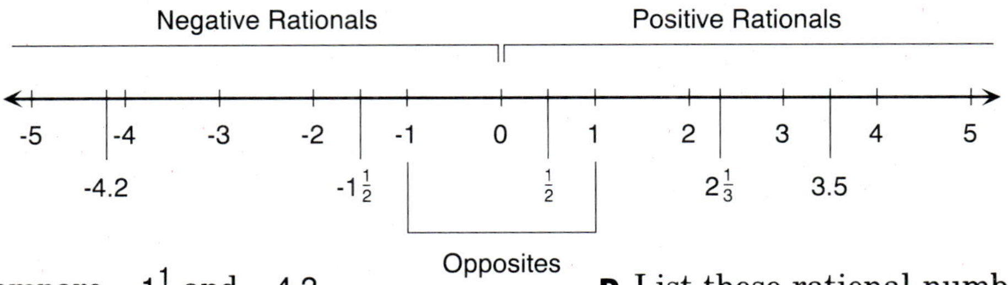

C. Compare $-1\frac{1}{2}$ and -4.2. Use <, >, or =.

The greater of two rational numbers is the number farther to the right on a number line.

$-1\frac{1}{2} > -4.2$

D. List these rational numbers in order from least to greatest: -1.5, $2\frac{1}{3}$, 0, -3, $1\frac{4}{5}$.

Write the numbers in the order in which they appear, from left to right, on a number line.

$-3 \quad -1.5 \quad 0 \quad 1\frac{4}{5} \quad 2\frac{1}{3}$

■ **Talk About Math** Is there a rational number that is neither positive nor negative?

Check Understanding

For another example, see Set D, pages 104–105.

Express the rational number in two different ways.

1. The length of a sofa that is $60\frac{1}{4}$ inches long

2. The thickness of a table that is 0.75 inches thick

Use the number line for Exercises 3–4.

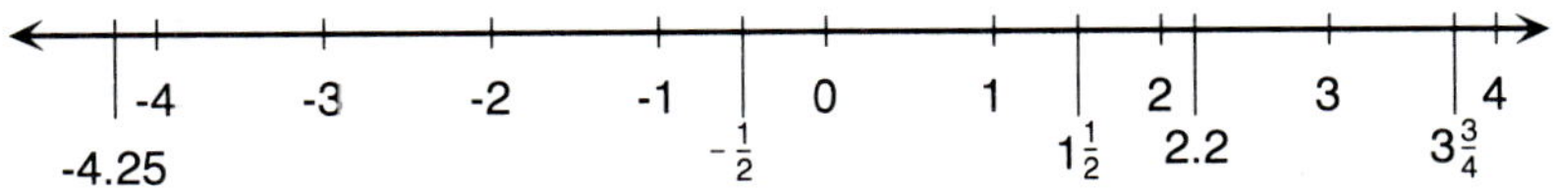

3. Name the greatest and the least rational numbers shown on this number line.

4. List these rational numbers in order from greatest to least: 3, −4.25, −4, $-\frac{1}{2}$, $3\frac{3}{4}$.

Practice

For More Practice, see Set D, pages 106–107.

Write each number as the quotient of two integers. **Remember** to write each answer in lowest terms.

5. -7 **6.** $1\frac{3}{4}$ **7.** $-2\frac{3}{5}$ **8.** -1.6 **9.** 2.3

Write the opposite of each rational number.

10. $-\frac{3}{4}$ **11.** 5.1 **12.** $2\frac{1}{3}$ **13.** $-1\frac{4}{5}$ **14.** -0.4

Number Sense Compare. Use <, >, or =.

15. $-\frac{1}{6}$ ▒ $\frac{1}{4}$ **16.** $-\frac{1}{9}$ ▒ $\frac{1}{9}$ **17.** $-\frac{2}{3}$ ▒ $-\frac{4}{6}$ **18.** 0.8 ▒ -0.7

List the numbers in order from least to greatest.

19. 0 $-\frac{1}{2}$ $\frac{3}{4}$ **20.** $-\frac{1}{3}$ $-\frac{1}{10}$ $-\frac{1}{5}$ **21.** $2\frac{4}{5}$ -1 $\frac{3}{2}$ **22.** 0.6 -0.6 -1.6

Problem Solving

Solve each problem.

23. Geraldo is a meteorologist and records a low temperature of fourteen-and-a-half degrees below zero Fahrenheit. Write this as a rational number.

24. Kathy signed a 2.5-year lease for her furniture store. Write 2.5 as the quotient of two integers.

25. Georgio charted his weight gains and losses as follows: Week 1: gain $2\frac{1}{2}$ lb; Week 2: lose $1\frac{3}{4}$ lb; Week 3: gain 3 lb. Write these changes as rational numbers.

26. Critical Thinking Tell whether the following statement is true. Fractions are always rational numbers and rational numbers are always fractions. Explain your answer.

Adding and Subtracting Rational Numbers

Build Understanding

A. Joel is a nurse. The temperature of one of his patient's rose $\frac{1}{10}$ of a degree during the first hour and dropped $\frac{1}{2}$ of a degree during the second hour. What was the change in temperature for the two-hour period?

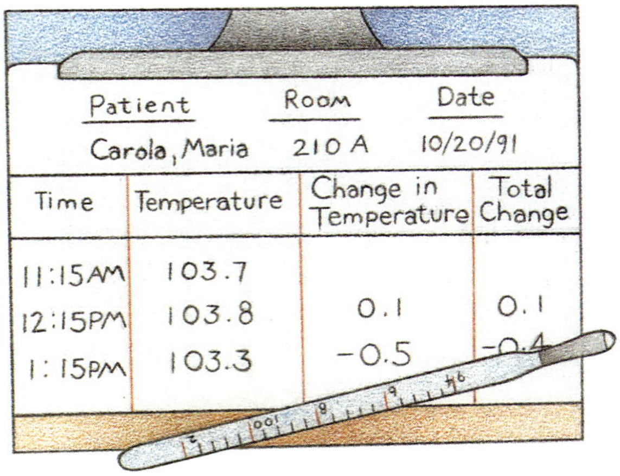

Find $\frac{1}{10} + \left(-\frac{1}{2}\right)$.

$$\frac{1}{10} + \left(-\frac{1}{2}\right) = \frac{1}{10} + \left(\frac{-5}{10}\right)$$
$$= \frac{1+(-5)}{10}$$
$$= \frac{-4}{10} \text{ or } -\frac{4}{10}$$

Write the numbers as fractions with a common positive denominator. Add the numerator the same way you add integers.

The change in temperature for the two-hour period was a decrease of $\frac{4}{10}$ degrees, or $-\frac{4}{10}°$.

B. Find $-\frac{2}{5} - \frac{7}{4}$.

$$-\frac{2}{5} - \frac{7}{4} = -\frac{2}{5} + \left(-\frac{7}{4}\right)$$
$$= -\frac{2}{5} + \frac{-7}{4}$$
$$= \frac{-8}{20} + \frac{-35}{20}$$
$$= \frac{(-8) + (-35)}{20}$$
$$= \frac{-43}{20}$$
$$= -2\frac{3}{20}$$

To subtract a rational number, add its opposite.

C. Find $-2.4 + 0.58$.

$$-2.4 + 0.58 = -2.40 + 0.58$$
$$= -1.82$$

Calculator

Press: 2.4 [+/-] [+] .58 [=]

Display: *−1.82*

■ **Write About Math** Explain how to use a calculator to find $1.52 - (-3.47)$.

Check Understanding

For another example, see Set E, pages 104–105.

Solve.

1. Subtract $3.64 - (-2.33)$. **2.** Add $-9.56 + 1.37$. **3.** $-\frac{5}{8} + \frac{3}{4}$

Practice

For More Practice, see Set E, pages 106–107.

Add or subtract. **Remember** to add the opposite when you need to subtract a rational number.

4. $\frac{2}{5} + \left(-\frac{7}{5}\right)$ **5.** $\frac{3}{5} + \left(-\frac{3}{5}\right)$ **6.** $\frac{-12}{5} + \left(-\frac{1}{2}\right)$ **7.** $-5 + \frac{1}{4}$

8. $\frac{-2}{3} + 6$ **9.** $\frac{7}{8} - \left(-\frac{3}{8}\right)$ **10.** $\frac{-1}{13} - \frac{1}{2}$ **11.** $\frac{-3}{4} - \left(-\frac{7}{8}\right)$

12. $\frac{3}{5} + \left(-\frac{1}{4}\right)$ **13.** $\frac{-3}{7} - \left(\frac{1}{3}\right)$ **14.** $\frac{2}{3} + \frac{-4}{11}$ **15.** $\left(-\frac{11}{3}\right) - \left(-\frac{7}{2}\right)$

16. $-9.7 + 9.7$ **17.** $4 + (-7.82)$ **18.** $-0.7 - 0.5$ **19.** $0 - 37.1$

20. $-3.87 + 1.37$ **21.** $11.54 - 12.66$ **22.** $1.15 - (-2.3)$ **23.** $-7.6 - (-9.6)$

24. $-7.65 + 11.32 - (4.1)$ **25.** $-9.3 + 2.45 - 6.7$ **26.** $6.59 - (-4.31) + (-4.9)$

Problem Solving

Solve each problem.

27. Tony's temperature increased 0.6°F during the first hour, 0.2°F during the second hour, and 0.1°F during the third hour; it decreased 0.8°F during the fourth hour. What was his overall change in temperature?

28. Vera's temperature was 103.9°F when she was admitted to the hospital. In the first hour it rose 0.7°F and in the second hour 0.2°F. In the third hour it dropped 1.1°F. What was her temperature then?

TIPS FOR PROBLEM SOLVERS

Compare problems to help you relate new problems to ones you've solved before.

Critical Thinking Will the answer be positive or negative when you

29. add a negative rational number to a negative rational number?

30. subtract a negative rational number from a positive rational number?

Skills Review pages 52–53, 56–57

For Exercises 1–3, divide. Round each answer to the nearest hundredth. For Exercises 4–6, write each fraction as a decimal.

1. $\frac{3.14}{2.7}$ **2.** $\frac{9.8}{3.1}$ **3.** $\frac{31.62}{16.9}$ **4.** $\frac{2}{5}$ **5.** $\frac{7}{20}$ **6.** $\frac{5}{8}$

Multiplying and Dividing Rational Numbers

Build Understanding

Patient Name B.Chandler

WEIGHT LOSS

Week 1 1.5 lb

Week 2 1.5 lb

Week 3 1.5 lb

Week 4 ______

Week 5 ______

A. Mr. Chandler's doctor wants him to lose weight. He has lost 1.5 pounds per week for the past 3 weeks. What is his total weight loss?

Since each week's loss was the same, multiply.

Use the same rules for multiplying rationals that you use to multiply integers.

$3 \times (-1.5) = -4.5$ When one number is positive and the other is negative, their product is negative.

Mr. Chandler's weight loss was 4.5 pounds.

B. If Mr. Chandler continues to lose 1.5 pounds per week, how many weeks will it take for him to lose 30 pounds?

Use the same rules for dividing rational numbers that you use for integers.

Total change		Weekly change		
-30	$\div$	(-1.5)	$=$	20

Two numbers with the same sign have a positive quotient.

He will lose 30 pounds in 20 weeks.

C. Find $\frac{2}{3} \div \left(-4\frac{1}{2}\right)$.

$$\frac{2}{3} \div \left(-4\frac{1}{2}\right) = \frac{2}{3} \div \left(-\frac{9}{2}\right)$$ Write $-4\frac{1}{2}$ as an improper fraction.

$$= \frac{2}{3} \times \left(-\frac{2}{9}\right)$$ Multiply by the reciprocal of $-\frac{9}{2}$.

$$= \frac{2}{3} \times \left(\frac{-2}{9}\right)$$

$$= -\frac{4}{27}$$ When one number is positive and the other is negative, their product is negative.

■ **Talk About Math** Is division of rational numbers closed? In other words, is the quotient of two rational numbers always a rational number when the divisor is not 0?

Check Understanding

For another example, see Set F, pages 104–105.

Refer to Example A. What is Mr. Chandler's weight loss for each time period?

1. 5 weeks **2.** 9 weeks **3.** 17 weeks

For Exercises 4–7, tell whether each product or quotient is positive or negative.

4. $-6 \div 2.8$ **5.** $\frac{1}{2} \times \left(-\frac{3}{8}\right)$ **6.** $\frac{5}{6} \div \left(-\frac{2}{3}\right)$ **7.** $\left(-\frac{3}{5}\right)\left(-\frac{1}{8}\right)$

8. **Calculator** Write a key sequence for finding -0.4×8.2. Then find the product.

Practice

For More Practice, see Set F, pages 106–107.

Multiply or divide.

9. $\frac{-5}{6}\left(\frac{-2}{5}\right)$

10. $\frac{-3}{4}\left(\frac{4}{7}\right)$

11. $\frac{-1}{2}\left(\frac{3}{8}\right)$

12. $\frac{-1}{8}(-12)$

13. $\left(3\frac{1}{2}\right)\left(\frac{-7}{9}\right)$

14. $\frac{-1}{2}(-2)$

15. $\frac{3}{5} \div \frac{7}{10}$

16. $\frac{5}{8} \div \left(\frac{-1}{2}\right)$

17. $\frac{-1}{2} \div \left(\frac{-1}{4}\right)$

18. $\frac{3}{4} \div (-2)$

19. $4\frac{1}{2} \div \left(\frac{-1}{2}\right)$

20. $\frac{-3}{7} \div 5\frac{1}{3}$

21. $\left(-\frac{2}{3}\right)\left(-\frac{5}{6}\right)$

22. $\frac{7}{8}(-32)$

23. $\left(-1\frac{1}{3}\right) \div \frac{3}{4}$

24. $\left(-3\frac{1}{8}\right) \div \left(-\frac{5}{8}\right)$

25. $-4(1.5)$

26. $-0.7(-0.3)$

27. $-16 \div (-0.5)$

28. $(-1.2)(0.8)$

29. $40 \div (-0.5)$

30. $-21 \div 0.07$

31. $(-1.05)(-8)$

32. $(-3.2)(1.5)$

33. $(3.4)(-100)$

34. $-18.6 \div (-0.6)$

35. $(0.8)(-0.8)$

36. $(-6)(-0.25)$

Mixed Practice Complete each table.

a	$3a - 4$
0	**37.**
$\frac{1}{2}$	**38.**
$\frac{3}{2}$	**39.**
40.	−1

y	$\frac{y}{2} + 5$
3.8	**41.**
−2.2	**42.**
43.	5
−0.8	**44.**

m	$-6m + 2$
−2	**45.**
−4	**46.**
47.	−4
$-\frac{1}{2}$	**48.**

Problem Solving

Solve each problem.

49. Mrs. Chandler has lost 2.5 pounds per week for the past 3 weeks. If her weight loss continues at the same rate, in how many weeks will Mrs. Chandler lose 40 pounds?

50. The doctor told Mr. Chandler's son that he needs to lose a total of 25 pounds. If he loses 1.5 pounds per week, how many weeks does he need to diet?

51. Will Mrs. Chandler or her son reach the weight-loss goal first? How much sooner?

52. Mrs. Chandler exercised $1\frac{1}{2}$ hours every day. How many hours per week is this?

ALGEBRA

Use a Formula

Build Understanding

Lebanese cooking is famous for its many *mezze* dishes. A mezze dish is an appetizer. Before dinner Lebanese diners are presented with a wide variety of mezze such as fruits, vegetables, cheese, yogurt, and olives.

Akram was teaching Emily how to make *baba ganouche,* or eggplant dip, a favorite mezze. The recipe said to preheat the oven to 200°C. They wondered what 200°C is equal to in degrees Fahrenheit.

Understand QUESTION What is 200°C in degrees Fahrenheit?

FACT You can compare temperatures on the two scales by using thermometers or by using a formula.

KEY IDEA Use a formula to convert between the two scales.

Plan and Solve STRATEGY You know the Celsius temperature, so *use the formula* for finding a Fahrenheit temperature.

$F = \frac{9}{5}C + 32$

$$F = \frac{9}{5}C + 32$$
$$F = \frac{9}{5}(200) + 32$$
$$F = 360 + 32$$
$$F = 392$$

ANSWER 200°C is the same as 392°F.

Look Back ALTERNATE APPROACH Use the Celsius formula to work backward and check your answer.

$$C = \frac{5}{9}(F - 32)$$
$$C = \frac{5}{9}(392 - 32)$$
$$C = \frac{5}{9}(360)$$
$$C = 200$$

200°C is the same as 392°F.

PROBLEM SOLVING GUIDE

Understand
QUESTION
FACTS
KEY IDEA

Plan and Solve
STRATEGY
ANSWER

Look Back
SENSIBLE ANSWER
ALTERNATE APPROACH

Many Middle-Easterners buy their fruits, vegetables, and other goods in the *souk,* or open-air market.

Talk About Math Is water at 100°C hotter than water at 212°F? Explain.

Check Understanding

What temperature on the Fahrenheit scale corresponds to 150°C?

1. **Estimation** Will your answer be more or less than 400°F?

2. Write the formula you will use. Find the answer.

Practice

Tell which formula you would use to find the corresponding temperature on the other scale. Then find the temperature. Label your answer.

3. 20°C
4. 10°F
5. −5°F
6. −10°C
7. 77°F
8. 15°C

Solve each problem.

9. Dfina is a hearty stew eaten by many Israelis. Dfina is placed in the oven at 190°C and cooked overnight. What is the Fahrenheit temperature at which dfina is cooked?

10. Lahm bil Ajeen is also a Lebanese mezze. Sometimes this dish is called Arab pizza because the name means "meat in dough." If Lahm bil Ajeen is cooked at 450°F, at what Celsius temperature is it cooked?

Falafel, fried vegetables in pita bread, can be purchased from street vendors throughout the Middle East.

Choose a Strategy

The Great Race Wanda and Freddie raced around the $\frac{1}{4}$-mile track three times. Wanda ran each lap at the rate of 8 miles per hour. Freddie ran the first lap at the rate of 10 miles per hour, the second lap at 8 miles per hour, and the third lap at 6 miles per hour. Use the formulas to solve each problem. Write answers to the nearest tenth of a minute.

Distance = *Rate* × *Time* or $d = rt$

PROBLEM SOLVING STRATEGIES

Choose an Operation
Solve a Simpler Problem
Use a Formula

11. How much time did it take Wanda to run one lap?

12. How much time did it take Freddie to run each lap?

13. Who won the race? by how many minutes?

Skills Review

Give the value for each exercise.

1. $|-9|$ **2.** $|14|$ **3.** $-|5|$

Compare. Use <, >, or =.

4. -18 ■ 9 **5.** -11 ■ -17

6. 14 ■ -14 **7.** $-\frac{2}{3}$ ■ $-\frac{8}{12}$

8. -3.6 ■ 1.4 **9.** $\frac{4}{5}$ ■ $-\frac{4}{5}$

Write each number as the quotient of two integers.

10. 3.8 **11.** -9 **12.** $5\frac{2}{3}$

13. $-2\frac{1}{2}$ **14.** -1.4 **15.** 18

Add or subtract.

16. $14 - (-5)$ **17.** $-11 + -11$

18. $-3 + (-6)$ **19.** $-12 - (-4)$

20. $\frac{2}{3} + \left(-\frac{2}{3}\right)$ **21.** $-\frac{1}{2} + \frac{4}{5}$

22. $7 - \left(-\frac{6}{7}\right)$ **23.** $-3\frac{3}{4} - 5$

24. $-2.6 + 1.7$ **25.** $-6.8 - (-6.8)$

26. $-5.5 + (-3.2)$ **27.** $7.8 - 1.2$

Multiply or divide.

28. $-42 \div (-7)$ **29.** $-7(12)$

30. $(-2)(-3)(5)$ **31.** $-72 \div 3$

32. $200 \div (-4)$ **33.** $(5)(-2)(5)(-2)$

34. $-\frac{1}{2}\left(-\frac{1}{2}\right)$ **35.** $\left(-\frac{1}{5}\right)(5)$

36. $-8 \div \frac{8}{9}$ **37.** $-2.6 \div (2.6)$

38. $0.9(-0.5)$ **39.** $-\frac{3}{2} \div (-1.5)$

Problem-Solving Review

Solve each problem.

40. One day the temperature ranged from a low of −12°F to a high of 38°F. What was the difference between the high and low temperatures for that day?

41. In a football game, Carlos lost 4 yards on each of three consecutive running plays. On the next two plays he gained 3 yards and 5 yards. Express his total running yardage for the five plays as an integer.

42. Mary jogged 2.5 miles during the first week of the year. She plans to increase her total distance by 0.25 mile each week. In which week will Mary run a total of 5 miles?

43. Starting at 2:00 P.M., the temperature in the solarium rose 0.8 degree during the first hour, rose 1.1 degrees during the second hour, and dropped 0.75 degree during the third hour. What was the overall change in temperature?

44. Elaine recorded a low temperature of thirteen and three fourths degrees below zero Fahrenheit. Write this as a rational number.

45. **Data File** Use the data on pages 110–111. Which of the baseball players listed has the highest slugging average? Who has the best isolated power rating?

46. **Make a Data File** Use an almanac. Make a table listing the ten cities in the United States with the greatest difference between their lowest and highest temperatures.

Cumulative Skills Review • Chapters 1–3

Use mental math to do each computation.

1. 11×22 **2.** $\$15.03 + \$7.98$ **3.** $17 + 55 + 83 + 42$ **4.** $25{,}695 - 14{,}551$

5. $6{,}789 - 889$ **6.** 76×25 **7.** 92×40 **8.** $65 \times 76 + 35 \times 76$

Write the prime factorization of each number in exponential form. Tell whether it is prime or composite.

9. 175 **10.** 69 **11.** 83 **12.** 120

13. 225 **14.** 29 **15.** 128 **16.** 97

Write each fraction as a repeating or terminating decimal.

17. $\frac{7}{10}$ **18.** $\frac{8}{9}$ **19.** $\frac{3}{5}$ **20.** $\frac{15}{16}$

21. $\frac{7}{11}$ **22.** $\frac{3}{40}$ **23.** $\frac{1}{9}$ **24.** $\frac{11}{12}$

Write each decimal as a fraction in lowest terms.

25. 0.25 **26.** $0.\overline{3}$ **27.** 0.23 **28.** 0.2

Evaluate the expression $0.88m$ for each value of m.

29. $m = 100$ **30.** $m = 10{,}000$ **31.** $m = 10$ **32.** $m = 7{,}000$

Evaluate the expression $864 \div p$ for each value of p.

33. $p = 10$ **34.** $p = 200$ **35.** $p = 1{,}000$ **36.** $p = 10{,}000$

Evaluate each expression when $a = 6$ and $b = -2$.

37. $a - b$ **38.** $b + a$ **39.** $-a + b - a$ **40.** $8 + b - a$

41. $b + \left(-\frac{a}{2}\right)$ **42.** $2b - a$ **43.** $-5a - b$ **44.** $b + \left(\frac{12}{a}\right)$

Add or subtract.

45. $\frac{3}{4} + \frac{1}{12}$ **46.** $2\frac{1}{2} - 1\frac{3}{8}$ **47.** $5\frac{1}{9} + 4\frac{5}{6}$ **48.** $9 - 5\frac{15}{16}$

49. $-\frac{11}{13} + \frac{11}{13}$ **50.** $-\frac{7}{4} - \left(-\frac{5}{8}\right)$ **51.** $1.4 + \left(-\frac{3}{2}\right)$ **52.** $0 - \left(-\frac{7}{9}\right)$

Multiply or divide.

53. $6.5(-0.1)$ **54.** $-8 \div (0.4)$ **55.** $-\frac{1}{4}(-4)$ **56.** $-\frac{2}{7} \div 3\frac{1}{2}$

57. $7\frac{1}{2} \div -\frac{3}{4}$ **58.** $-\frac{5}{7}\left(-\frac{7}{5}\right)$ **59.** $\frac{6}{11} \div -3$ **60.** $\frac{9}{10}\left(-\frac{6}{5}\right)$

Reteaching

Set A pages 84–85

Positive integers are to the right of zero on this number line.

Negative integers are to the left of zero.

Each integer has an opposite, located the same distance from zero on the number line.

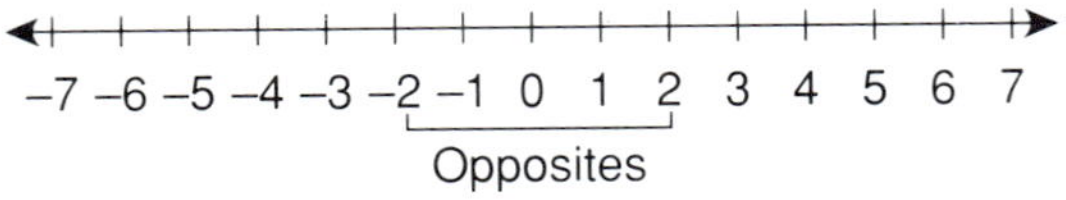

Remember to use zero as a reference point.

Write an integer to represent each amount.

1. 3°C below zero
2. A gain of 6 yards
3. A loss of \$45
4. 645 feet above sea level
5. The opposite of 19
6. An increase of 12 points
7. A profit of \$300
8. 36° below normal

Set B pages 86–87

Find −1 + (−4).

On a number line, start at 0 and move 1 unit to the left. Then move another 4 units to the left.

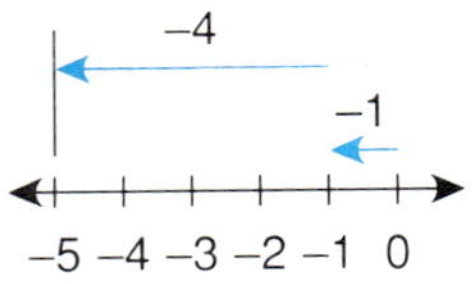

−1 + (−4) = −5

Find −2 + 5.

Start at 0 and move 2 units to the left. Then move 5 units to the right.

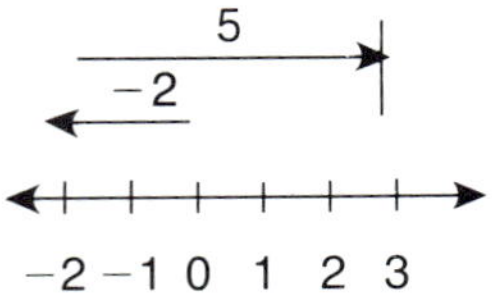

−2 + 5 = 3

To subtract an integer, add its opposite.

Remember that the sum of two integers that have the same sign also has that sign.

1. −7 + (−3)
2. 4 − 5
3. −29 + 17
4. −12 + (−7)
5. −10 + (−21) + (−13)
6. 16 + (−11) + (−4)
7. −15 + 12 + 19
8. −6 + 20 + (−14)
9. 18 − (−7) + 6
10. −1 − (−7) −45
11. 24 − (−2) − 30

Set C pages 88–89

If two integers have the same sign, their product is positive.

If two integers have different signs, their product is negative.

If two integers have the same sign, their quotient is positive.

If two integers have different signs, their quotient is negative.

(5)(−7) = −35

Since the signs are different, the product is negative.

Remember that you can tell the sign of your answer by looking at the signs of the integers being multiplied or divided.

1. (−4)(9)
2. 8(−21)
3. −44 ÷ 11
4. (−6)(−8)
5. −63 ÷ (−9)
6. 85 ÷ (−5)
7. (−8)(16)(−4)
8. (−2)(−7)(−14)
9. (−4)(−9)(−2)
10. (−2)(−6)(8)(2)
11. −72 ÷ 36
12. −49 ÷ (−7)
13. $\frac{-51}{-17}$
14. $\frac{800}{-20}$

Set D pages 94–95

This number line shows how integers and rational numbers are related.

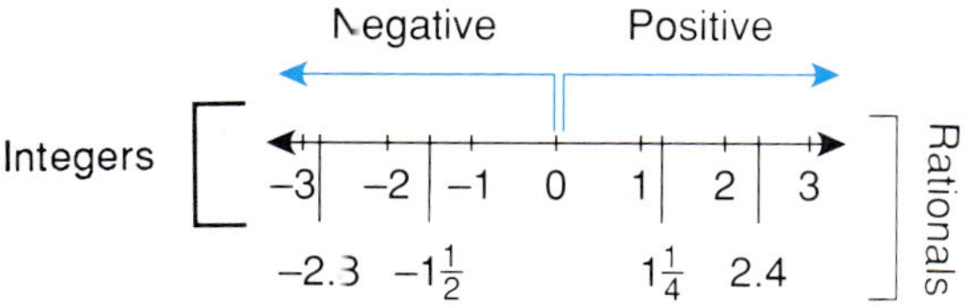

Remember that any number that can be written as the quotient of two integers is a rational number.

Write each number as a quotient of two integers.

1. $-7\frac{2}{3}$ **2.** 0.2 **3.** $4\frac{4}{5}$

4. −5.2 **5.** −8 **6.** 1.4

7. 2.3 **8.** $-2\frac{1}{2}$ **9.** −4

Set E pages 96–97

Find $\frac{-1}{3} - \frac{3}{4}$.

$$\frac{-1}{3} - \frac{3}{4}$$

$$\frac{-1}{3} - \frac{3}{4} = \frac{-1}{3} + \left(-\frac{3}{4}\right)$$

To subtract a rational number, add its opposite.

$$= \frac{-1}{3} + \frac{-3}{4}$$

Write $-\frac{3}{4}$ as $\frac{-3}{4}$.

$$= \frac{-4}{12} + \frac{-9}{12}$$

$$= \frac{-4 + (-9)}{12}$$

$$= \frac{-13}{12} = -1\frac{1}{12}$$

Remember that you add rational numbers the same way you add integers.

1. $\frac{2}{5} + \left(-\frac{1}{2}\right)$ **2.** $-3.3 + (-0.5)$

3. $-\frac{1}{3} + \frac{2}{7}$ **4.** $\frac{5}{8} - \left(-\frac{3}{4}\right)$

5. $6 + (-8.17)$ **6.** $-\frac{1}{12} - \frac{4}{9}$

7. $4.2 - 4.75$ **8.** $-0.4 - 0.8$

9. $-1.2 + 4.5$ **10.** $0 - 37.1$

11. $-\frac{1}{8} + \left(-\frac{3}{4}\right)$ **12.** $\frac{1}{5} - \left(-\frac{2}{3}\right)$

Set F pages 98–99

Find $\left(-\frac{2}{5}\right)\left(-\frac{1}{8}\right)$.

$$\left(-\frac{2}{5}\right)\left(-\frac{1}{8}\right) = \frac{2}{40} = \frac{1}{20}$$

Find $\frac{5}{6} \div \left(-1\frac{1}{2}\right)$.

$$\frac{5}{6} \div \left(-1\frac{1}{2}\right) = \frac{5}{6} \div \left(-\frac{3}{2}\right)$$

$$= \frac{5}{6} \times \left(-\frac{2}{3}\right)$$

$$= -\frac{10}{18} = -\frac{5}{9}$$

Remember that the rules for multiplying and dividing rational numbers are the same as for multiplying and dividing integers.

1. $-\frac{1}{6}\left(-\frac{3}{5}\right)$ **2.** $\frac{8}{3}\left(-\frac{1}{4}\right)$

3. $-12 \div (-0.4)$ **4.** $\frac{4}{5} \div (-10)$

5. $2\frac{3}{4} \div \left(-\frac{3}{4}\right)$ **6.** $-18 \div (-0.2)$

7. $7.5(-0.1)$ **8.** $\frac{5}{6} \div \frac{11}{12}$

9. $-\frac{1}{8}(-12)$ **10.** $\frac{3}{4} \div (-2)$

More Practice

Set A pages 84–85

Write an integer for each exercise.

1. A loss of \$50 **2.** 6° below zero **3.** A deposit of \$345

4. 115 feet below sea level **5.** A gain of 4 pounds **6.** A rise of 12°

7. $-(-25)$ **8.** $-(9)$ **9.** $-(-150)$ **10.** $-(13)$

Give the value for each exercise.

11. $|-7|$ **12.** $|28|$ **13.** $-|10|$ **14.** $|-1{,}476|$ **15.** $-|16|$

Compare each pair of integers. Write $<$ or $>$.

16. -16 ▒ 4 **17.** 8 ▒ 2 **18.** -11 ▒ -13 **19.** -7 ▒ 7 **20.** 5 ▒ -5

21. -12 ▒ -15 **22.** 7 ▒ 8 **23.** -14 ▒ 2 **24.** 50 ▒ 9 **25.** -31 ▒ -3

Set B pages 86–87

Add or subtract.

1. $32 - (-8)$ **2.** $6 + 3$ **3.** $-5 + (7)$ **4.** $4 - 9$

5. $-15 + 15$ **6.** $-41 - (-26)$ **7.** $9 - (-11) - (6) + (-4)$

Evaluate each expression when $x = 3$ and $y = -5$.

8. $x - y$ **9.** $x + y$ **10.** $y - x$ **11.** $x - y + x$

12. $x + y + x$ **13.** $x + y - x$ **14.** $y - x + y$ **15.** $5 + x + y$

Complete each table.

16.

c	$c - 5$
1	▒
−1	▒
−7	▒
11	▒

17.

d	$7 + d$
▒	6
−2	▒
▒	−5
▒	−3

18.

e	$8 + e$
▒	0
−14	▒
▒	3
−9	▒

Set C pages 88–89

Multiply or divide.

1. $-36 \div (-6)$ **2.** $(12)(3)$ **3.** $0 \div 15$ **4.** $(-6)(-3)$

5. $-8(200)$ **6.** $64 \div (-8)$ **7.** $24(-5)(-2)$ **8.** $-320 \div (-40)$

9. $(-3)(-9)(-2)$ **10.** $8(-48)$ **11.** $-78 \div (-6)$ **12.** $-128 \div (8)$

13. $(-8)(2)(-5)$ **14.** $-120 \div (-24)$ **15.** $84 \div 12$ **16.** $6(-4)(-2)(-1)$

Set D pages 94–95

Write each number as the quotient of two integers.

1. 4.7 **2.** −5 **3.** $2\frac{2}{5}$ **4.** −6.4 **5.** $-3\frac{1}{4}$

Write the opposite of each rational number.

6. −0.8 **7.** $3\frac{4}{5}$ **8.** 6.9 **9.** $-\frac{3}{4}$ **10.** $-2\frac{5}{8}$

Compare. Use <, >, or =.

11. $-\frac{3}{4}$ ▒ $-\frac{4}{5}$ **12.** $-\frac{2}{5}$ ▒ $-\frac{8}{20}$ **13.** −2.5 ▒ −2.4 **14.** $\frac{5}{6}$ ▒ $-\frac{5}{6}$

List the numbers in order from least to greatest.

15. $-\frac{2}{3}, \frac{3}{5}, 0$ **16.** $-\frac{1}{4}, -\frac{3}{10}, -\frac{1}{5}$ **17.** $\frac{2}{3}, -2, \frac{7}{2}$ **18.** 0.2, −0.2, −1.2

Set E pages 96–97

Add or subtract.

1. $\frac{5}{8} + \left(-\frac{5}{8}\right)$ **2.** $\left(-\frac{1}{6}\right) + \frac{1}{2}$ **3.** $-7 + \frac{3}{4}$ **4.** $\frac{3}{5} + \left(-\frac{8}{5}\right)$

5. $2.6 + \left(-\frac{1}{4}\right)$ **6.** $-\frac{19}{4} + \left(-\frac{5}{6}\right)$ **7.** $-1.2 + 4.5$ **8.** $0 - \frac{3}{8}$

9. $-1 - \frac{5}{16}$ **10.** $\frac{1}{3} - \left(-\frac{2}{3}\right)$ **11.** $-\frac{2}{5} + \left(-\frac{4}{5}\right)$ **12.** $\left(-\frac{1}{6}\right) + \left(-7\frac{5}{6}\right)$

13. $-3.8 - 3.4$ **14.** $-1.5 + (-0.05)$ **15.** $6 + (-9.37)$ **16.** $0 - 21.6$

Set F pages 98–99

Multiply or divide.

1. $-\frac{1}{6}(-6)$ **2.** $4\frac{2}{3}\left(-\frac{5}{6}\right)$ **3.** $-\frac{4}{5}\left(-\frac{5}{7}\right)$ **4.** $-\frac{1}{2}\left(\frac{3}{5}\right)$

5. $\frac{8}{5}\left(-\frac{2}{14}\right)$ **6.** $\frac{9}{14}\left(-\frac{14}{9}\right)$ **7.** $\frac{1}{4} \div (-3)$ **8.** $-6 \div \left(-\frac{1}{5}\right)$

9. $\frac{4}{5} \div -4.5$ **10.** $-14 \div (-1.4)$ **11.** $0.8(-0.5)$ **12.** $-\frac{4}{7} \div 2\frac{3}{4}$

Complete each table.

13.

b	$\frac{b}{3} + 4$
1.2	▒
−2.1	▒
▒	−6
−0.9	▒

14.

x	$-5x + 2$
−2	▒
−4	▒
▒	$\frac{3}{4}$
$-\frac{1}{5}$	▒

15.

m	$4m - 3$
0	▒
$\frac{1}{5}$	▒
$-\frac{5}{2}$	▒
▒	−7

Enrichment

Rational Numbers

What kinds of plants grow best in the math lab?

To find out, copy and complete each magic square. In magic squares 1 and 2, the numbers in each row, column, and diagonal have the same ***sum***. In magic square 3 they have the same ***product***. If the number that you write in a square appears in the answer grid at the bottom of the page, find the letter in the square and write it above the number in the grid.

S **1.**	-10	B **2.**
O **3.**	T **4.**	E **5.**
$-7\frac{1}{4}$	12	$-1\frac{3}{4}$

-9.4	R **6.**	20.3	U **7.**
4.1	-1.3	W **8.**	M **9.**
Q **10.**	9.5	6.8	T **11.**
23	-14.8	R **12.**	14.9

1	S **13.**	H **14.**
I **15.**	2	O **16.**
16	A **17.**	4

Answer: Plants ___ ___ ___ ___

-4 $\quad \frac{1}{2}$ $\quad 1$ $\quad \frac{1}{4}$

___ ___ ___ ___ ___ ___   ___ ___ ___ ___ ___

$3\frac{3}{4}$ $\quad -6.7$ $\quad -17.5$ $\quad \frac{1}{8}$ $\quad 17.6$ $\quad -4\frac{1}{2}$ $\qquad -12.1$ $\quad 8$ $\quad 6\frac{1}{2}$ $\quad 1.4$ $\quad 32$

Chapter 3 Review/Test

Write an integer for each of the following.

1. An increase of 47 ft

2. $-(-14)$

3. A loss of 3 yards

4. $7°$ above zero

5. The opposite of -11

6. $-(3)$

Compare. Use <, >, or =.

7. -12 ▒ -7

8. $\frac{1}{4}$ ▒ $\frac{3}{12}$

9. -0.6 ▒ -0.8

10. 2 ▒ 4

Solve.

11. The price of one share of a company's stock rose $\frac{5}{8}$ one day and then fell $\frac{1}{2}$ the next day. Find the total change in price.

12. Below is a table for making hot cereal. How many cups of dry cereal and how many cups of water do you need to make seven servings?

Dry cereal	$\frac{1}{3}$ cup	$\frac{2}{3}$ cup	2 cups
Water	$\frac{3}{4}$ cup	$1\frac{1}{2}$ cups	$4\frac{1}{2}$ cups
Servings	1	2	6

Add or subtract.

13. $-13 + (-4)$

14. $-2.4 + (-0.5)$

15. $36 - (-15)$

16. $-\frac{1}{11} - \frac{3}{4}$

17. $-22 - (-7)$

18. $-\frac{4}{5} - \left(-\frac{9}{10}\right)$

19. $-2.6 + (-0.04)$

20. $17 + (-9)$

Multiply or divide.

21. $-\frac{1}{6}(-15)$

22. $-64 \div (-8)$

23. $17(-4)$

24. $\frac{2}{5} \div \left(-\frac{3}{10}\right)$

25. $4.5(-0.01)$

26. $-12 \div (-0.2)$

27. $-52 \div 4$

28. $(-7)(-9)(-2)$

Give each value.

29. $|-2|$

30. $|85|$

Write each number as the quotient of two integers.

31. $2\frac{5}{8}$

32. -3.4

Use the given solution method to find the answer to this problem.

33. The computer in Mr. Jackson's car tells him that he has been traveling at a rate of 54.8 miles per hour. If he continues at the same rate, how far will Mr. Jackson have driven in $2\frac{1}{2}$ hours?

Solution method: Use this formula.
rate × time = distance

a. 137 miles per hour
b. 137 hr
c. 137 mi
d. 137 hours per mile

34. **Write About Math** Explain why your answer to Problem 33 is sensible.

1. Sports Statistics

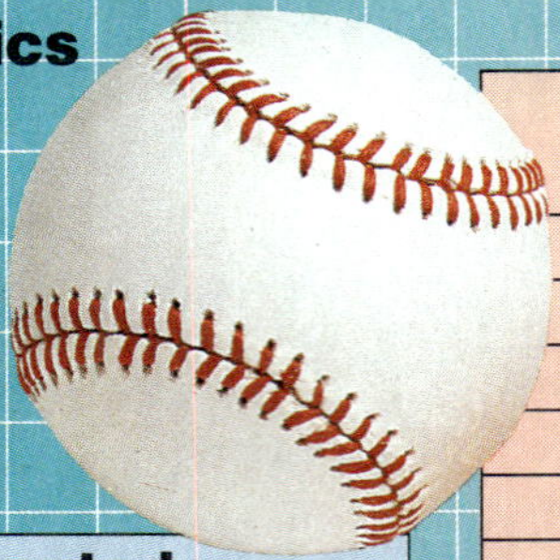

Top Ten			
Player	AB	H	TB
Kevin Mitchell, S.F.	377	109	245
Howard Johnson, Mets	380	112	228
Fred McGriff, Tor.	385	107	215
Darryl Strawberry, Mets	326	76	164
Mickey Tettleton, Bal.	364	95	185
Bo Jackson, K.C.	334	90	174
Eric Davis, Cin.	299	82	156
Lonnie Smith, Atl.	327	106	188
Rob Deer, Mil.	391	88	184
Ruben Sierra, Tex.	431	139	242

How they're computed

Slugging Average $= \frac{\text{Total bases (TB)}}{\text{At-bats(AB)}}$

Isolated Power $= \frac{\text{Total bases–hits (H)}}{\text{At-bats(AB)}}$

1. Sports Statistics: A baseball player's slugging average is a combination of both batting average and power. The isolated power rating determines how often a batter hits for extra bases.

2. Table: The currencies in twenty-two countries are each expressed as a number of U.S. dollars.

3. Map: Rail-trains are abandoned railroad lines that have been made over into hiking trails.

4. Double Bar Graph: This style of graph makes it easy to compare information about two different groups.

2. Table

Currency Exchange Rates
As of May 23, 1989

Country	Unit	Value in U.S. dollars
Argentina	peso	0.0239
Australia	dollar	0.7878
Austria	schilling	0.0739
Bahamas	dollar	1.017
Canada	dollar	0.8664
Egypt	pound	0.4505
France	franc	0.1534
Great Britain	pound	1.643
India	rupee	0.0737
Ireland	pound	1.3937
Israel	shekel	0.6156
Italy	lira	0.000734
Jamaica	dollar	0.1771
Japan	yen	0.00735
Kenya	schilling	0.0605
Korea	won	0.00175
Mexico	peso	0.000439
Norway	krone	0.1453
Russia	ruble	1.1716
Spain	peseta	0.00849
Thailand	baht	0.0435
W. Germany	mark	0.5186

3. Map

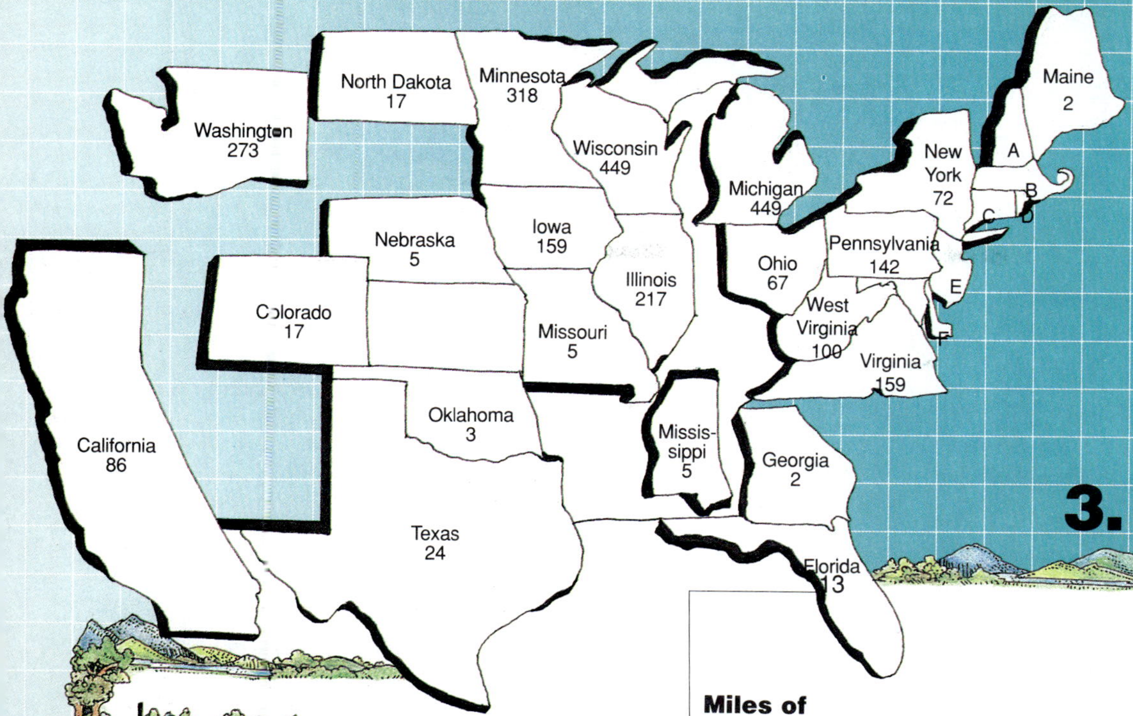

Miles of Rail Trails By State*

A. New Hampshire 20
B. Massachusetts 57
C. Connecticut 15
D. Rhode Island 14
E. New Jersey 51
F. Maryland 22

*Includes trails under construction

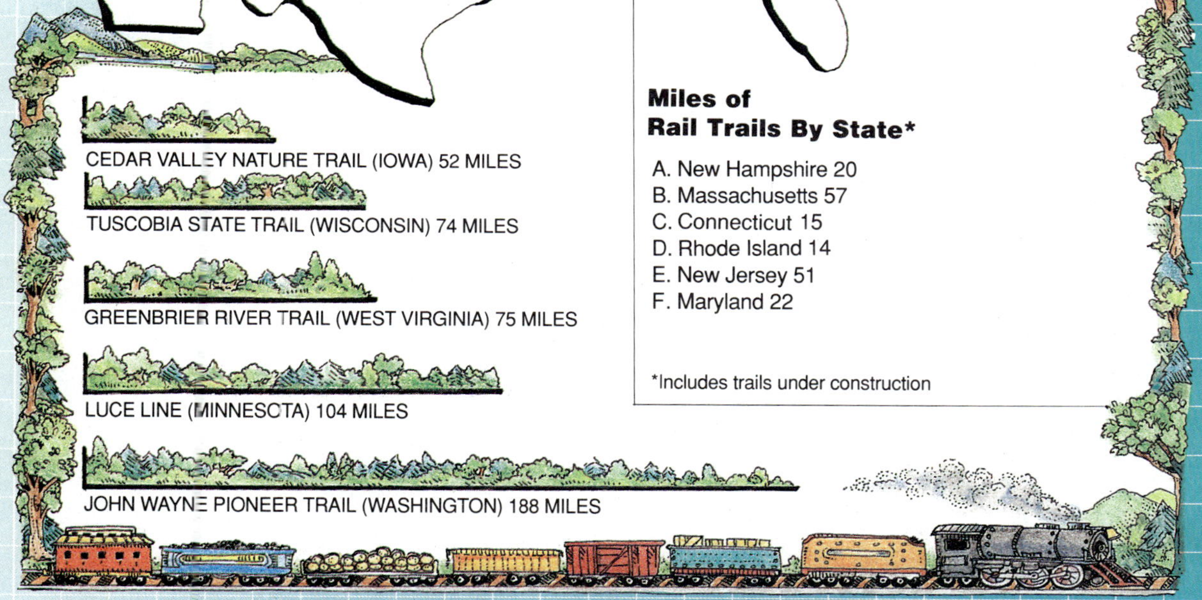

4. Double Bar Graph

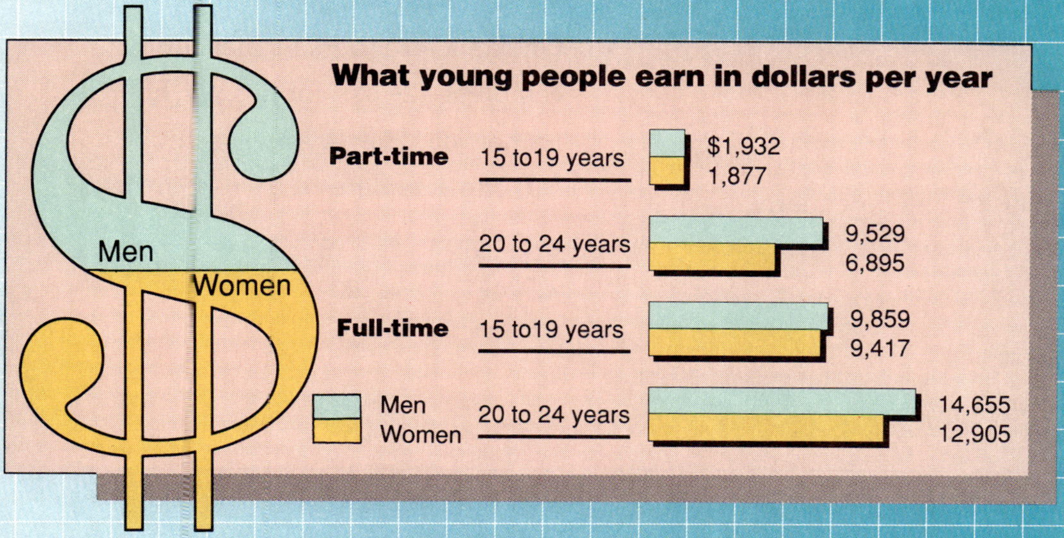

CUMULATIVE REVIEW/TEST

Cumulative Review/Test Chapters 1–3

Choose the letter for the correct answer.

1. What are the next three terms in the sequence 1, 3, 7, 15, . . . ?

a. 17, 19, 21 **b.** 31, 63, 127
c. 23, 31, 39 **d.** 29, 67, 129

2. The numbers in row three of Pascal's triangle are 1, 3, 3, 1. What are the numbers in row five?

a. 1 4 6 7 1
b. 1 4 6 4 1
c. 1 1 5 10 10 5 1
d. 1 5 10 10 5 1

3. Which expression would be best to use to *estimate* the answer? Gloria bought 4.79 pounds of stew meat that cost $1.44 per pound. What was the cost of the meat?

a. $5 \times 1\frac{1}{2}$ **b.** 5×1 **c.** 4×1

4. Evaluate the expression when $c = 5$ and $f = 2$. (Hint: Remember the standard order of operations.)

$$\frac{8 + 3c \times 2f}{f}$$

a. 68
b. 46
c. 34
d. not given

5. Choose the operation that should be performed first to evaluate this expression.

$4 + 5 \times 13 + 6 \times 18$

a. $13 + 6$ **b.** 5×13 **c.** $4 + 5$

6. The number 36 has how many factors?

a. 8 **b.** 9 **c.** 10

7. Which is equal to $2^2 \times 2^3$?

a. $2 \times 2 \times 2 \times 2 \times 2$
b. $2 \times 2 \times 2 \times 2 \times 2 \times 2$
c. $2 \times 2 \times 2 \times 2$
d. not given

8. How can the number 100 be written using only prime factors?

a. $(5 \times 2)^{10}$ **b.** $5 \times 5 \times 4$
c. 25×4 **d.** $2^2 \times 5^2$

9. All 123 children went on a trip to the museum. Each bus can only hold 35 people. How many buses should the principal order?

a. 6 **b.** 5 **c.** 4 **d.** 3

10. Use compatible numbers to decide which answer is reasonable.

$0.65 \div 0.4$

a. 0.1625 **b.** 1.625 **c.** 16.25

11. Multiply.

7.2×300

a. 2,160
b. 21,600
c. 21.6
d. not given

12. Divide.

$4.56 \div 1.2$

a. 38
b. 0.38
c. 3.8
d. not given

13. On the average, Sid's mother can complete $12\frac{2}{5}$ assemblies per hour on her job. How many assemblies can she complete in a $7\frac{1}{2}$-hour day?

a. $19\frac{3}{10}$ **b.** $19\frac{9}{10}$
c. $84\frac{1}{5}$ **d.** 93

14. After finishing their salad, Ann ate $\frac{1}{4}$ of a pizza, Sue ate $\frac{3}{8}$, and Bill ate $\frac{1}{3}$. Who ate the *least* pizza?

a. Ann **b.** Sue **c.** Bill

15. Which fractions are written in order from least to greatest?

a. $\frac{1}{3}$ $\frac{1}{4}$ $\frac{1}{5}$
b. $\frac{5}{7}$ $\frac{5}{10}$ $\frac{5}{11}$
c. $\frac{3}{7}$ $\frac{6}{11}$ $\frac{2}{9}$
d. $\frac{4}{11}$ $\frac{4}{7}$ $\frac{7}{9}$

16. Which fraction, when written as a decimal, gives a repeating decimal?

a. $\frac{3}{25}$ **b.** $4\frac{1}{10}$
c. $\frac{5}{6}$ **d.** $\frac{8}{250}$

17. Subtract.

$$6\frac{1}{7} - 2\frac{2}{3}$$

a. $4\frac{1}{4}$
b. $4\frac{11}{21}$
c. $4\frac{10}{21}$
d. not given

18. Divide.

$4\frac{3}{4} \div \frac{1}{8}$

a. $1\frac{13}{19}$
b. $\frac{1}{38}$
c. 38
d. not given

19. Which integers are in order from least to greatest?

a. −6, 0, 4
b. 0, 4, −6
c. 4, 0, −6
d. 0, −6, 4

20. Add.

12 + (−18)

a. −30
b. 30
c. 6
d. not given

21. Multiply.

15(−9)

a. 135
b. 6
c. −135
d. not given

22. Subtract.

3.7 − (−2.1)

a. 5.8
b. 1.6
c. −1.6
d. not given

23. Divide.

$-\frac{3}{5} \div \frac{9}{20}$

a. $-1\frac{1}{3}$
b. $1\frac{1}{3}$
c. $\frac{27}{100}$
d. not given

24. From the surface, the Deep Water submarine submerged 60 feet. Then it rose 25 feet and finally submerged 100 feet. How far was it below the surface then?

a. 185 feet **b.** 135 feet
c. 160 feet **d.** 125 feet

25. Use the given solution method to find the answer to this problem.

Corey drives 8 miles to school at an average of 25 miles per hour. How long does the trip take?
Solution method: Use this formula:
$\text{Time} = \frac{\text{Distance}}{\text{Rate}}$

a. 0.32 hours **b.** 3.13 hours
c. 2.0 hours **d.** 3.125 hours

Expressions and Equations

4

Did You Know: For a 12-month period, the record rainfall in the United States occurred in 1981–1982 when 739 inches fell in Kukui, Hawaii. The record snowfall, 1,122 inches, occurred on Mt. Rainier, Washington, in 1971–1972. Some weather forecasters consider 10 inches of snow equivalent to 1 inch of rain.

Number-Sense Project

Estimate
Guess the annual amount of precipitation in your area.

Gather Data
Find the normal precipitation for each month of the year in your area or the closest area for which data are available.

Analyze and Report
Graph your data for each month. What is the annual amount of precipitation in your area?

ALGEBRA

Order of Operations

Build Understanding

A. Amy and Beth computed $4 + 2 \times 5$. Which answer is correct?

If there are no grouping symbols, the ***standard order*** of operations is:

First, compute all powers.

Second, multiply and divide from left to right.

Third, add and subtract from left to right.

Beth is correct because she used the standard order of operations.

If an expression contains grouping symbols or division bars:

First, compute inside the grouping symbols using standard order.

Second, compute above and below the division bars before you divide.

Third, do the remaining computations using standard order.

B. Compute $3 \div \frac{4^2 + 2 \times 7}{(2 + 3) \times (-2)}$.

$$3 \div \frac{4^2 + 2 \times 7}{(2 + 3) \times (-2)} = 3 \div \frac{16 + 14}{5 \times (-2)} = 3 \div \frac{30}{-10} = 3 \div -3 = -1$$

Talk About Math Explain why it is important for everyone to use the same standard order of operations.

Check Understanding

For another example, see Set A, pages 136–137.

Mental Math Compute.

1. $8 + 4 \div 2$ **2.** $(8 + 4) \div 2$ **3.** $3 + 2^3$ **4.** $4 \times \frac{5}{5 + 3}$

Practice

For More Practice, see Set A, pages 138–139.

Compute. Use mental math or pencil and paper.

5. $\frac{1}{4} + 8 \div 6$

6. $\left(\frac{1}{4} + 8\right) \div 6$

7. $8 \times 4 \div \frac{2}{3}$

8. $(10 - 2)^2$

9. $10 - 2^2$

10. $-15 - (18 - 3)$

11. $(7 + 4)^2$

12. $9 \div 9 \times 9 + 9$

13. $0.6(2.2 - 0.2)$

14. $-5.8 \times 1.2 + 6$

15. $6^2 - 6$

16. $4^2 - 3^2$

17. $-33.6 \div 2 + 6.8$

18. $\frac{8}{3} \div 3 \times 3$

19. $4\left(\frac{1}{8} + \frac{5}{8}\right)$

20. $\left(\frac{1}{7} - \frac{1}{14}\right)7$

21. $\frac{5}{8} \div \frac{3}{16} \times 1\frac{2}{5}$

22. $\frac{(5 + 5)^2}{5^2 + 5^2}$

23. $\left(\frac{3}{5} + \frac{1}{2}\right)^2\left(\frac{1}{11}\right)^2$

24. $8 \div \frac{2^2 + 3 \times 4}{(5 + 6) \times (-2)}$

Insert parentheses so that the equations are true.

25. $3 \times 2 + 4 = 18$

26. $7 - 4 - 2 - 1 = 4$

27. $7 - 4 - 2 - 1 = 2$

28. $6 \times 5 \div 15 - 5 = 3$

29. $-7 + 8 \times 5 - 3 = 2$

30. $24 \div 2 - 8 - 4 = -8$

31. $3 + 4^2 = 49$

32. $2 + 3 \times 5 - 1 = 24$

33. $2 + 3 \times 5 - 1 = 14$

Problem Solving

Solve each problem.

34. Fran bought 3 tacos for \$0.59 each and 4 burritos for \$0.89 each. Which expression tells how much she paid?

a. $(3 + 4) \times (0.59 + 0.89)$
b. $(3 \times 0.59) + (4 \times 0.89)$
c. $(4 \times 0.59) + (3 \times 0.89)$

35. Marisa bought 6 pears for 25¢ each and 5 plums for 20¢ each. Which expression tells how much she paid?

a. $(6 \times 25) + (5 \times 20)$
b. $(6 + 5)(25 + 20)$
c. $(5 \times 20) \times (6 \times 25)$

36. From Problem 34, write an expression that tells how much change Fran would receive from a \$10 bill.

37. Write a problem similar to Problems 34 and 35. Exchange papers with a classmate and solve.

38. **Critical Thinking** The area of the trapezoid is the sum of the areas of a rectangle and a right triangle. Insert parentheses in the equation so that it expresses the area of the trapezoid.

$A = 6 \times 9 + \frac{1}{2} \times 13 - 9 \times 6 = 66$

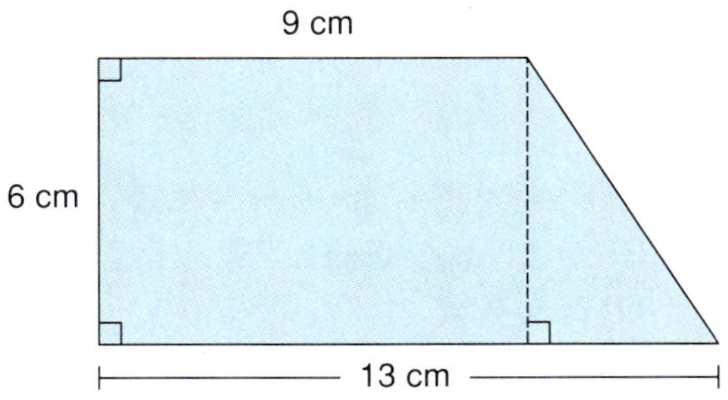

ALGEBRA

Evaluating Expressions

Build Understanding

Ikebana is the Japanese name for the art of flower arranging. In the moribana arrangement, the longest stem represents heaven, the second longest, humans, and the shortest, earth.

The ancient Egyptians, Greeks, and Romans practiced the art of flower arranging. Today you can decorate with floral arrangements using flowers that grow all over the world.

Moribana is a type of Japanese floral arrangement in which the lengths of the three main stems depend on the distance across the bowl, d, and the height of the bowl, h. The lengths of the three stems from longest to shortest are represented by the ***variables,*** a, b, and c, respectively. A variable is a letter or symbol used to represent a number.

A. The shortest stem is half as long as the length of the second longest stem, b, so the expression $\frac{1}{2}b$ could be used for its length. This table gives the values for $\frac{1}{2}b$ when $b = 1, 2, 3, 4, 5, 6$.

b	1	2	3	4	5	6
$\frac{1}{2}b$	$\frac{1}{2}$	1	$1\frac{1}{2}$	2	$2\frac{1}{2}$	3

B. The second longest stem is two thirds the length of the longest stem, a. Evaluate $\frac{2}{3}a$ for $a = 1, 2, 3, 4, 5, 6$.

a	1	2	3	4	5	6
$\frac{2}{3}a$						

C. The expression $1\frac{1}{2}d + h$ represents the length of the longest stem. To evaluate the expression when $d = 9$ and $h = 2$, substitute the numbers for the variables.

$$1\frac{1}{2}d + h = 1\frac{1}{2}(9) + 2$$
$$= 13\frac{1}{2} + 2$$
$$= 15\frac{1}{2}$$

Write About Math Write an expression for the length of the shortest stem in terms of the longest stem.

Check Understanding

For another example, see Set B, pages 136–137.

The values of the following expressions for $t = 2$ are incorrect. Explain the errors.

1. $4 + 7t = 4 + 72 = 76$ **2.** $5t + 6 = 5 \times 2 + 6 = 40$ **3.** $(t + 3)^2 = 2^2 + 3^2 = 13$

Practice

For More Practice, see Set B, pages 138–139.

Evaluate each expression when $a = 7$, $b = \frac{1}{2}$, and $c = -5$. **Remember** to do the operations within the parentheses first.

4. $2a + 2a$ **5.** $4a$ **6.** $3a - a$ **7.** $5b - a$ **8.** $(a + b)a$

9. $\frac{2a}{c}$ **10.** $\frac{c(c - a)}{a}$ **11.** $\frac{(2 - a)0.7}{ab}$ **12.** $\frac{3}{4}(a + 2b)$ **13.** $a^2 + ab$

Evaluate $f + 3g$ when

14. $f = 3\frac{1}{4}, g = \frac{3}{8}$ **15.** $f = 1.4, g = -2$ **16.** $f = -9, g = 3$ **17.** $f = \frac{1}{8}, g = -\frac{3}{4}$

Evaluate $4p - q$ when

18. $p = 3.6, q = 3.6$ **19.** $p = -1.5, q = 6$ **20.** $p = -3.8, q = -19.2$

Evaluate $xy - z$ when

21. $x = -3, y = 5, z = 7$ **22.** $x = 0, y = 4, z = -9$ **23.** $x = -5, y = 9, z = 0$

Problem Solving

Solve. Use the information on page 118.

24. Find b in a moribana arrangement if the longest stem is to be a 10-inch dahlia, a flower that originally came from Mexico.

25. Find a in a moribana arrangement that has African bird-of-paradise flowers if the bowl is 6 inches across and $2\frac{1}{2}$ inches high.

N

Explore ________ Math

Which of Exercises 26–29 are true for $x = 4$? Which are true for $x = 10$?

26. $7x + 1 + 2x = 10x$ **27.** $7x + 1 + 2x = 9x + 1$

28. $x + x = x^2$ **29.** $x + x = 2x$

30. What is a shortcut for finding $3m + 9m - m$ for $m = 6.7$?

ALGEBRA

Writing Expressions and Equations

Build Understanding

NUMBER OF HOURS	1	2	3	4	5	6
COST ($)	7	9	11	13	15	17

A. Susan wants to write a mathematical expression for the cost of renting a canoe, so that she doesn't have to refer to the table in back of her every time she has a customer.

She notices that the cost is always $2 more for an extra hour. She tries the expression $2h$ (where h represents the number of hours), but her answers are always $5 too low. She writes the expression $2h + 5$ to fit this new fact. The new expression works.

B. A ***mathematical sentence*** contains a relation sign, such as $=$, $<$, $>$, or $\neq$. Sentences may be open, true, or false. A sentence containing a variable is an ***open sentence.*** An open sentence is neither true nor false. A sentence that contains an equal sign is an ***equation.***

The two sentences below are open.

$2n + 3 = 17$ $\qquad$ $x + 1 < 7$

Only the first sentence below is true.

$4 + 3 = 7$ $\qquad$ $3 + 2 = 4$

C. Word phrases can be translated into mathematical expressions.

Word Phrases	Expressions
7 added to a number 7 more than n the sum of n and 7	$n + 7$
3 less than a number n minus 3 3 subtracted from n	$n - 3$

D. Write an equation for y in terms of x.

x	0	1	2	3	5	10
y	0	4	8	12	20	40

The equation is $y = 4x$.

■ **Talk About Math** Can you find a value for n that makes the open sentence $4 + n = n + 4$ false? Can you find a value for n that makes the open sentence $6n - 3n = 2n$ true? Explain your answers.

Check Understanding

For another example, see Set C, pages 136–137.

Number Sense Choose the letter of the correct expression.

1. 5 less than n
a. $n - 5$ **b.** $5 - n$ **c.** $5n$

2. The total of n and 5
a. $5n$ **b.** $n + 5$ **c.** $n - 5$

Practice

For More Practice, see Set C, pages 138–139.

Write a mathematical expression for each of the following.

3. The product of 7 and x

4. 7 less than x

5. 7 more than x

6. $\frac{1}{3}$ the sum of x and 7

7. The sum of $\frac{2}{3}p$ and q

8. 5 divided by n

9. $\frac{22}{7}$ times the square of r

10. The square of the sum of a and b

11. The square of the product of m and n

For each table, choose the correct equation.

12.

x	1	2	3	4
y	4	8	12	16

a. $x = y + 3$
b. $y = 4x$
c. $y = x + 3$

13.

x	1	2	3	4
y	3	5	7	9

a. $y = 3x$
b. $y = x - 3$
c. $y = 2x + 1$

Tell whether the sentence is true, false, or open.

14. $9 = x + 3$

15. $14 = t + 3(2)$

16. $8 + 1 < 6$

17. $-3 < -1$

18. $10 > -2r + 10$

19. $-6 - 2 = -4$

20. $0 > -2$

21. $3p + 1 = 7$

Problem Solving

Solve the problems. Use the information given on page 120.

22. Write an expression for finding the average cost per hour when a canoe is rented for n hours.

23. A camper rented a canoe at 8:00 A.M. and returned it at 1:00 P.M. Find the average cost per hour.

24. In winter Susan rents ski equipment. She uses the expression $4h + 2$ (where h is the number of hours) to find the cost per person. A family of three went cross-country skiing for 4 hours. How much did it cost the family to go skiing?

25. Use Data When a ski team left at 8:00 A.M. the temperature was 25°F and calm. When they returned at noon the temperature had climbed to 40°F with wind speeds of 20 mi/h. Did it feel colder at 8:00 A.M. or noon? Explain your answer. (See page 90.)

ALGEBRA

Writing and Solving Addition and Subtraction One-Step Equations

Build Understanding

A. A total of 762 people attended a health fair. If 386 were adults, how many were students?

Let n represent the number of students. The total attendance equals the number of adults plus the number of students.

$$762 = n + 386$$

To solve an equation, you must find a number that will make the sentence true when the variable is replaced by the number.

$$762 = n + 386$$

$$762 + (-386) = n + 386 + (-386)$$ Add the opposite of 386 to both sides.

$$376 = n$$

Check: $762 = n + 386$

$762 \stackrel{?}{=} 376 + 386$ Substitute 376 for n in the original equation.

$762 = 762$

There were 376 students at the fair.

B. Solve $x - 8 = 12$.

$$x - 8 = 12$$

$$x - 8 + (8) = 12 + (8)$$ Add 8 to both sides.

$$x = 20$$

Check: $20 - 8 \stackrel{?}{=} 12$

$12 = 12$

C. Solve $12.9 = a + 2.5$.

$$12.9 = a + 2.5$$

$$12.9 + (-2.5) = a + 2.5 + (-2.5)$$

$$10.4 = a$$

Check: $12.9 \stackrel{?}{=} 10.4 + 2.5$

$12.9 = 12.9$

Talk About Math Yori, a first grader, is to solve the number sentence, $\square + 3 = 5$. Explain why she is solving an equation.

Check Understanding

For another example, see Set D, pages 136–137.

Tell what you would do to solve each equation. Then solve the equation.

1. $k + 5 = 12$ **2.** $y - 7 = 3$ **3.** $3.5 + c = 20$ **4.** $97 = 14 + m$

Practice

For More Practice, see Set D, pages 138–139.

Solve each equation and check your solution.

5. $n + 15 = 20$ **6.** $3 = c - 5$ **7.** $w - 1.2 = 3$ **8.** $4 + y = -2$

9. $w + 1.2 = 3$ **10.** $-6 + m = -8$ **11.** $30 + z = -30$ **12.** $26 = q + 26$

13. $9.5 = p - 3.5$ **14.** $r - 0.5 = 0.75$ **15.** $52 = t - 52$ **16.** $x - (-2) = 0$

17. $d + 10.5 = 0.5$ **18.** $-32 = b - 32$ **19.** $17 = a - 17$ **20.** $-19 = 9 + f$

21. $3.6 + k = -7.4$ **22.** $h - 1\frac{1}{3} = \frac{2}{3}$ **23.** $g - (8 - 12) = 7$ **24.** $-x + 8 = 0$

Write and solve an equation to find each number.

25. Seven more than n is eighteen.

26. Seven less than n is four.

27. Twenty-five is nine more than b.

28. The sum of a and one is negative two.

29. The opposite of m minus one is one.

30. Two subtracted from x is twelve.

31. Five is three tenths more than c.

32. Three tenths is five more than c.

Problem Solving

Write an equation for each problem and then solve it.

33. If 150 adults attend a fair that has a total attendance of 762, how many students are there?

34. If 212 students attend the same fair, with a total attendance of 762, how many adults are there?

35. Critical Thinking Study the six equations below. Group together all those equations that have the same solution. Explain how each equation can be derived from one of the others in the same group.

$n + 8 = 12$ $n - 8 = 12$ $8 + n = 12$ $12 = n + 8$ $12 = -8 + n$ $12 = n + (-8)$

Midchapter Checkup

1. Evaluate $2a - b$ when a is -5 and b is -2.

2. Write an expression for one third the sum of eight and y.

Compute.

3. $3 \times 4 \div 6$ **4.** $\frac{3^2 - 5}{2 \times 5 + 5}$

Solve and check.

5. $n - (-5) = 14$ **6.** $5 + x = -5$

Explore As A Team

A square is a "magic square" if the sum of the numbers in each row, column, and diagonal are the same. This special sum is called the magic constant.

Your team can make 3 × 3 magic squares by using the square at the right and assigning values to x, y, and z and determining the value of each expression.

For example, if $x = 5$, $y = 4$, and $z = 1$, then the magic square is:

$x + y$	$(x + z) - y$	$x - z$
$(x - y) - z$	x	$x + y + z$
$x + z$	$(x + y) - z$	$x - y$

5 + 4	(5 + 1) − 4	5 − 1
(5 − 4) − 1	5	5 + 4 + 1
5 + 1	(5 + 4) − 1	5 − 4

=

9	2	4
0	5	10
6	8	1

1. Have each person make a 3 × 3 magic square using fractions, decimals, and whole numbers.

2. Exchange magic squares and work as a team to find the magic constant for each square.

3. Work as a team to determine the values for x, y, and z for each magic square.

TIPS FOR WORKING TOGETHER

To make sure your group understands the task or solution have each group member say it in his/her own words, summarize the steps, or give an example.

Number-Sense Project

Look back at pages 114-115.

1. The record snowfall on Mt. Rainier is equivalent to how many inches of rain?

2. The record rainfall in Kukui, Hawaii, is equivalent to about how many feet of snow?

Explore with a Computer

Use the *Spreadsheet Workshop Project* for this activity.

1. The eighth-grade class decided to earn money to cover the cost of a science field trip. Each student gave up one gym class a week to help clean the school grounds. They earned $1.25 per hour. Each student had to earn $6.25 to go on the trip. How many hours did each student have to work?

2. Admission would cost $4.00 per student and they would pay $78.75 for the bus. The students collected $218.75 in all. How many students went on the trip? At the computer, study the equation set up in the spreadsheet. Apply this equation to find the answer.

Real-Life Decision Making

Suppose you manage a movie theater which has four auditoriums. Since there is only a small lobby you want to schedule the movies so that no two audiences are in the lobby at the same time. After a movie has ended, it takes 15 minutes to clear out an audience and seat a new one.

The running time for the four films you are showing are 2 hours, $1\frac{1}{2}$ hours, $1\frac{3}{4}$ hours and $1\frac{1}{2}$ hours. Suppose you want to run each movie three times, starting no earlier than 5:30 P.M. and ending at midnight. More than one movie may end by midnight.

Devise a schedule.

ALGEBRA

Solving One-Step Multiplication and Division Equations

Build Understanding

A. An object on Jupiter weighs about $2\frac{3}{5}$ times its weight on Earth. If a spacecraft weighs 4,914 pounds on Jupiter, what is its weight on Earth?

Let w represent the weight of the spacecraft on Earth. Then $2\frac{3}{5}w = 4{,}914$. To solve the equation, multiply both sides by the reciprocal of $2\frac{3}{5}$.

$$2\frac{3}{5}w = 4{,}914$$

$$\frac{13}{5}w = 4{,}914 \qquad \text{Write } 2\frac{3}{5} \text{ as } \frac{13}{5}.$$

$$\left(\frac{5}{13}\right)\frac{13}{5}w = \left(\frac{5}{13}\right)4{,}914 \qquad \text{Multiply both sides by the reciprocal of } \frac{13}{5}.$$

$$w = 1{,}890$$

The spacecraft weighs 1,890 pounds on Earth.

Check: $2\frac{3}{5} \times 1{,}890 \stackrel{?}{=} 4{,}914$

$4{,}914 = 4{,}914$

Even though Jupiter is 318 times the size of Earth, one day lasts less than 10 hours. One Jupiter year is 43,433 10-hour days.

B. Solve $50t = 1{,}020$.

$$50t = 1{,}020$$

$$\left(\frac{1}{50}\right)50t = \left(\frac{1}{50}\right)1{,}020$$

$$t = 20.4$$

C. Solve $\frac{1}{3}x = -12$.

$$\frac{1}{3}x = -12$$

$$\left(\frac{3}{1}\right)\frac{1}{3}x = \left(\frac{3}{1}\right)(-12) \qquad \text{Multiply both sides by the reciprocal of } \frac{1}{3}.$$

$$x = -36$$

■ **Write About Math** Write a rule in words and in symbols for finding the reciprocal of a fraction. Write a rule for finding the reciprocal of an integer.

Check Understanding

For another example, see Set E, pages 136–137.

Tell what must be done to solve each equation.

1. $5n = 15$ **2.** $-5n = 15$ **3.** $y + 3 = 6$

4. $3.2y = 4.16$ **5.** $2\frac{1}{4}y = 2\frac{1}{4}$ **6.** $\frac{d}{12} = 4\frac{1}{2}$

Practice

For More Practice, see Set E, pages 138–139.

Solve each equation.

7. $4n = 8$ **8.** $\frac{1}{2}d = 8$ **9.** $\frac{5}{8}x = \frac{3}{4}$ **10.** $0.5a = 8.2$

11. $\frac{3}{4}t = 2\frac{1}{2}$ **12.** $2\frac{1}{2}k = \frac{5}{6}$ **13.** $36.8 = \frac{m}{2}$ **14.** $1.2d = 18$

15. $25.6 = 3.2y$ **16.** $7m = -39.2$ **17.** $-6q = 510$ **18.** $-24 = -5w$

19. $5s = 7.5$ **20.** $\frac{3}{8}g = 0$ **21.** $1.6f = -16$ **22.** $6z = 0.6$

Mixed Practice Solve each equation.

23. $x - 4 = 7$ **24.** $2\frac{1}{3} + y = 5$ **25.** $3\frac{1}{4}y = 13$ **26.** $3 = 1\frac{1}{2} + d$

27. $17 = t + 17$ **28.** $-\frac{1}{3}r = 1\frac{2}{3}$ **29.** $-4.9 = c + 4.9$ **30.** $1 = 2\frac{4}{5}p$

31. $\frac{7}{8}x = 5\frac{1}{4}$ **32.** $55 = 11 + m$ **33.** $\frac{7x}{8} = 42$ **34.** $3\frac{1}{2} = \frac{1}{6}t$

Problem Solving

Solve. Use the information on page 126.

35. Greg would weigh 325 pounds on Jupiter. Find his weight, *w*, on Earth.

36. Find the weight, *w*, on Earth of a rock that weighs 260 pounds on Jupiter.

37. **Estimation** An object on Earth weighs about 6 times as much as on the moon. A moon rock sample weighs about 22.75 lb on the moon. Estimate its weight on Earth.

Critical Thinking Explain why each sentence is true.

38. $1n = n$ **39.** $-1x = -x$ **40.** $3 - y = 3 + (-y)$ **41.** $\frac{1}{3}m = \frac{m}{3}$

Reading ______ Math

Vocabulary Complete each sentence.

1. A(n) ___?___ is a statement containing an equal sign.

2. An equation containing a variable is called a(n) ___?___ statement.

3. To compute $4 + (3 - 1) \times 9$, the first operation is ___?___.

4. To compute $2 + 15 \div 3 \times 8$, the first operation is ___?___ .

ALGEBRA

Write an Equation

Build Understanding

In two weeks, Darci will have enough money to buy her favorite video tape. The tape costs $39 and she earns $12 per week. How much money does Darci have now? Write and solve an equation to solve the problem.

PROBLEM SOLVING GUIDE

Understand
QUESTION
FACTS
KEY IDEA

Plan and Solve
STRATEGY
ANSWER

Look Back
SENSIBLE ANSWER
ALTERNATE APPROACH

Understand QUESTION How much money does Darci have now?

FACTS The tape costs $39. In two weeks she will earn $24.

KEY IDEA The amount of money already saved plus the amount earned is $39.

Plan and Solve STRATEGY Let a variable represent the amount of money she has now. Write a sentence that translates the key idea into an equation and solve the equation.

Let n represent the amount she has.

$$n + 24 = 39$$

$$n + 24 + (-24) = 39 + (-24)$$

$$n = 15$$

ANSWER Darci has $15.

Look Back SENSIBLE ANSWER The amount of money saved, $15, plus the amount earned, $24, is equal to the cost of the tape, $39.

Talk About Math In solving $n + 24 = 39$, why do you add (-24) to both sides of the equation?

Check Understanding

Mr. Chavez gave $\frac{2}{3}$ of his baseball cards to his daughter. His daughter received 192 cards. How many cards did Mr. Chavez own?

1. How might you represent all of Mr. Chavez's cards?

2. How many cards did Mr. Chavez give to his daughter?

3. Write an equation to determine the number of cards Mr. Chavez owned.

4. Solve the equation.

Practice

Write and solve an equation. **Remember** to perform the same operation on both sides of each equation.

5. At \$4.50 an hour, how many hours must Winema work to earn \$90?

6. Stan worked 7 hours and received \$39.20. How much does he earn per hour?

7. After Darci bought the tape, she began to save for a video game that cost \$84. How many weeks must she work to save enough money to buy the game if she saves \$12 per week?

Choose a ______ Strategy

Sound Thinking A scientist fired an explosive flare in the desert. A second scientist, located 924 meters from the first, observed that 2.8 seconds elapsed between the flash and the explosion. Estimate the speed of sound.

8. How many seconds after the flare was fired was the explosion heard? How far had the sound traveled?

9. Based on this information, what is the speed of sound?

PROBLEM SOLVING
STRATEGIES

Choose an Operation
Solve a Simpler Problem
Use a Formula
Write an Equation

ALGEBRA

Writing and Solving Two-Step Equations

Build Understanding

ACTIVITY

A. Don't Lose Your Balance
Materials: Two-pan balance, small paper clips, and envelopes
Groups: 4 students

a. Put 2 envelopes and 3 paper clips on the left pan. Add paper clips to the right pan until the pans balance.

b. Write an equation that expresses the equal weights. Let w represent the weight of each envelope and $2w + 3$ the weight on the left pan. Suppose 19 paper clips are added to the right pan. Then $2w + 3 = 19$.

c. Find w, the weight of one envelope, by first removing 3 paper clips from each pan. This action is the same as subtracting 3 from both sides of the equation.

$$2w + 3 = 19$$
$$2w + 3 - 3 = 19 - 3$$
$$2w = 16$$

d. Divide the contents in each pan into two equal piles. Remove 1 envelope and 8 paper clips. This action is the same as multiplying both sides of the equation by $\frac{1}{2}$.

$$2w = 16$$
$$\left(\frac{1}{2}\right) 2w = \left(\frac{1}{2}\right) 16$$
$$w = 8$$

One envelope weighs 8 paper clips.

B. Miss Berg started math class with this riddle: "I'm thinking of a number. If you multiply the number by $\frac{2}{3}$ and then subtract 7, the result is 9. What's the number?"

One student wrote an equation to solve the problem.

$$\frac{2}{3}x - 7 = 9$$
$$\frac{2}{3}x - 7 + 7 = 9 + 7 \quad \text{Add the opposite of } -7.$$
$$\frac{2}{3}x = 16$$
$$\left(\frac{3}{2}\right)\frac{2}{3}x = 16\left(\frac{3}{2}\right) \quad \text{Multiply both sides by the reciprocal of } \frac{2}{3}.$$
$$x = 24$$

Talk About Math When two steps are needed to solve an equation, why do you add the opposite of a number before you multiply by the reciprocal of the other number?

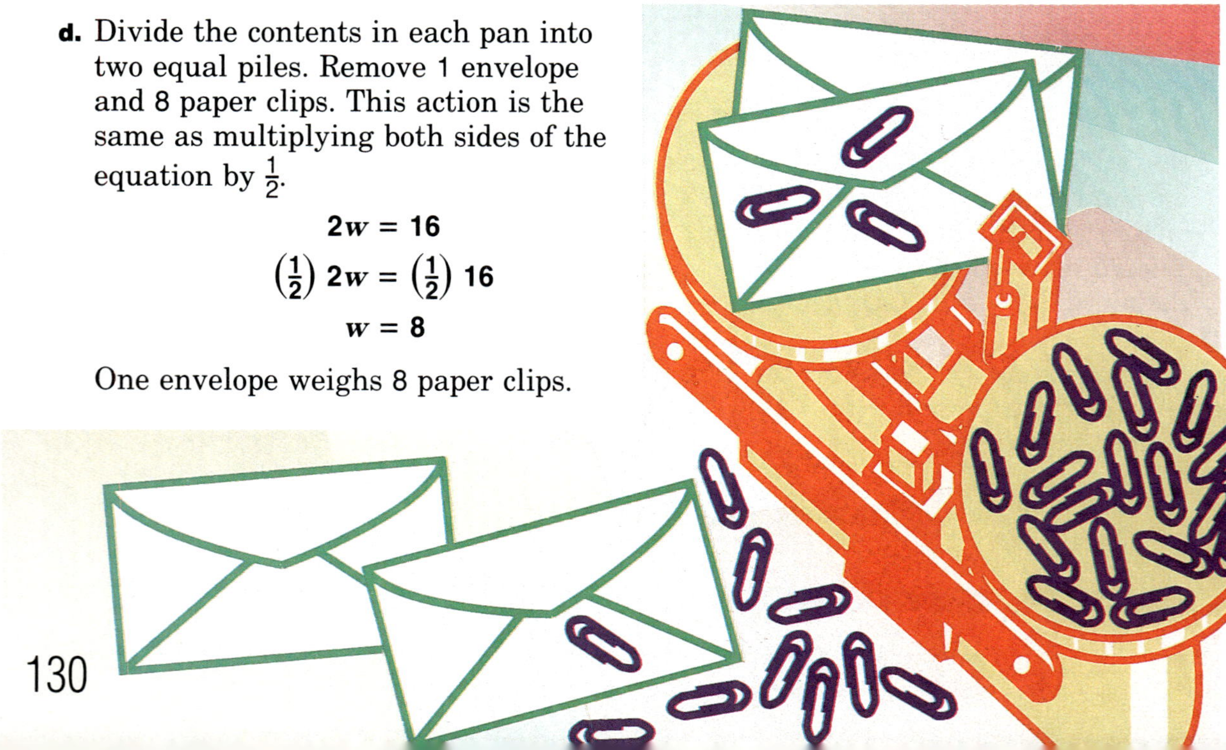

Check Understanding

For another example, see Set F, pages 136–137.

Indicate the two steps, in order, that you would use to solve each equation.

1. $6n - 3 = 39$ **2.** $4 + 3g = 19$ **3.** $\frac{2}{3}k - \frac{2}{3} = \frac{7}{12}$ **4.** $-\frac{3}{4}y + \frac{1}{3} = \frac{4}{3}$

Practice

For More Practice, see Set F, pages 138–139.

Solve each equation.

5. $3n + 5 = 26$ **6.** $4t - 5 = 23$ **7.** $-3 + 6x = 39$ **8.** $5w + 4 = -16$

9. $4c + 3 = 83$ **10.** $0.5m - 3.5 = 40$ **11.** $8h - 17 = 55$ **12.** $6.8 = 7.5r - 8.2$

13. $38 = 6 + \frac{1}{2}k$ **14.** $\frac{x}{4} - 3 = 7$ **15.** $8 = \frac{d}{7} + 2$ **16.** $5 + \frac{5}{8}t = 25$

17. $-4z + 3 = 7$ **18.** $11 = 27 + (-8x)$ **19.** $0 = 12d - 3$ **20.** $-8 = -4 - 6n$

Mixed Practice For each equation, make and complete a table for $x = -3, -2, -1, 0, 1, 2, 3$.

21. $\frac{2}{3}x = y$ **22.** $x + 3.2 = y$ **23.** $y = x \div 2$ **24.** $y = x^2$

Problem Solving

Write and solve an equation to find the answer to each problem.

25. If $\frac{2}{3}$ of a number is increased by 15, the result is 73. What is the number?

26. When the quotient of a number divided by 8 is decreased by 5, the result is 2. What is the number?

27. Seven more than five times a number is 62. Find the number.

28. If $\frac{1}{4}$ is $\frac{3}{8}$ of a number, what is the number?

29. **Critical Thinking** To solve $\frac{3}{4}x - 6 = 3$, Max multiplied by $\frac{4}{3}$ before adding. How did he get the correct answer?

Skills Review pages 28–31, 32–33

For Exercises 1–3, tell whether the numbers are divisible by 2, 3, or 5.

1. 450 **2.** 651 **3.** 1,224

For Exercises 4–6, give the prime factors of each number.

4. 56 **5.** 100 **6.** 24

ALGEBRA

Write an Equation

PROBLEM SOLVING GUIDE

Understand
QUESTION
FACTS
KEY IDEA

Plan and Solve
STRATEGY
ANSWER

Look Back
SENSIBLE ANSWER
ALTERNATE APPROACH

Build Understanding

The cost for students to use the Elmtown Recreation Center is \$355 for the first year. The cost includes an initial \$25 membership fee and 12 equal monthly payments. Write and solve an equation to find the amount of each monthly payment.

Understand

QUESTION What is the amount of each monthly payment?

FACTS The total cost is \$355. There is a \$25 membership fee and 12 equal payments.

KEY IDEA The membership fee plus 12 times the amount of each monthly payment is \$355.

Plan and Solve

STRATEGY Translate the key idea into an equation and solve the equation.

Let n represent the amount of each monthly payment.

$$25 + 12n = 355$$
$$(-25) + 25 + 12n = 355 + (-25)$$
$$12n = 330$$
$$n = 27.5$$

ANSWER Each monthly payment is \$27.50.

Look Back

SENSIBLE ANSWER Substitute \$27.50 into the original equation.

$$25 + 12(27.50) = 25 + 330$$
$$= 355$$

In one day, Americans jog about 28 million miles. That's 7 times the total length of all roads in the United States.

Talk About Math Is it possible to solve the problem above by adding (−355) to both sides of the equation? Why or why not?

Check Understanding

Solve each problem.

1. If x represents the amount of money earned per hour, what does $32x$ represent?

2. If n represents Miguel's age in 6 years, what does $n + 6$ represent?

Practice

Write and solve an equation for each problem.

3. The Recreation Center's rate for adults is \$35 a month plus a \$50 membership fee. What is the cost for the first year?

4. A special rate is offered for senior citizens. They pay \$325 a year, which includes a membership fee of \$40. What is the monthly cost?

5. Glenda joined the Center at the senior citizen rate and used the Center 57 times. Excluding the membership fee, what was her cost per visit?

6. During the month of June a six-month membership is offered for \$126 instead of \$35 per month. What is the monthly savings over the regular membership?

7. Tara's father will let her join the Elmtown recreation center when she has saved \$355, which is the total fee for the year. Tara has \$83 and she has a job paying \$4 an hour. How many hours must she work before she can join the recreation center?

8. A special limited membership for students is offered. It costs \$75 to join, and there is a charge of \$7 each time you use the center. How many times a year can you use the center before the limited membership equals a regular student membership?

Choose a ______ Strategy

It's All Relative Solve this problem.

9. When Mrs. Spry was asked her age, she gave the following reply:
"My only grandson is $\frac{1}{4}$ as old as I am and my only granddaughter is $\frac{3}{8}$ as old as I am. If the sum of the ages of my grandchildren is decreased by 6, the result is 39." How old is Mrs. Spry?

PROBLEM SOLVING
STRATEGIES

- Choose an Operation
- Solve a Simpler Problem
- Use a Formula
- Write an Equation

Skills Review

Compute.

1. $\frac{5}{8} + 6 \div 3$

2. $20 - 3^2$

3. $9 \times 3 \div \frac{1}{3}$

4. $(5 + 4)^2$

Insert parentheses in each of the following so that the given equations are true.

5. $8 + 3 \times 5 = 23$

6. $5 - 2^2 = 9$

7. $8 + 2 \times 5 \div 10 - 8 = 25$

Find the value of each expression when $m = 8$, $n = \frac{3}{4}$, and $p = -4$.

8. $5m$

9. $4n - p$

10. $(10 - m)p$

11. $p^2 + 8n$

12. $\frac{4p}{(mn)}$

13. $(m + p)n$

Write a mathematical expression for each of the following.

14. 12 more than k

15. 2 times h

16. the product of 9 and v

17. $\frac{1}{8}$ the difference between r and t

Solve.

18. $y + 12 = 25$

19. $1.5 - n = 0.7$

20. $-2 = c + 3$

21. $r + (-1) = -4$

22. $s - \frac{4}{5} = 2$

23. $6t = 18$

24. $\frac{2}{5}n = 4$

25. $9 = 0.3v$

26. $3\frac{1}{2}p = 14$

27. $\frac{5}{6}m = \frac{5}{18}$

28. $3x - 2 = 13$

29. $8t + 3 = 23$

30. $\frac{h}{4} - 3 = 0$

31. $10 = \frac{h}{9} + 1$

Problem-Solving Review

Solve each problem.

32. Jenny bought 4 lemons for 25¢ each and 6 limes for 30¢ each. Write an expression that tells how much she paid.

33. The expression $4n$ is used to compute the boat rental charge at Falcon Lake. The variable n stands for the number of hours, and the 4 stands for the price per hour. Use the expression to determine the cost of renting a boat from 10 A.M. to 4 P.M.

34. An object on the moon weighs about $\frac{1}{6}$ of what it would weigh on the earth. If the trash Wally takes out every night would weigh about 2.5 pounds on the moon, estimate its weight in Wally's yard.

35. Lulu gave $\frac{2}{5}$ of her comic book collection to her friend. If she gave her friend 30 comic books, how many were in her collection?

36. If $\frac{3}{5}$ of a number is decreased by 14, the result is 10. What is the number?

37. **Data File** Use the data on pages 252–253. Write an equation for finding the length of a pin if you know its size. Write an equation for finding the size of a pin if you know its length.

38. **Make a Data File** Use a newspaper or magazine to find the cost of buying a compact car and a mid-sized car. Find the prices of four different makes of cars. Record the results in a double bar graph.

Cumulative Skills Review • Chapters 1–4

Use mental math, paper and pencil, or a calculator to find the answer.

1. $5 \times 16 \times 20$ **2.** $4{,}505 - 2{,}309$ **3.** $1{,}250 + 3{,}717$ **4.** $56{,}312 \times 255$

5. $5{,}682 - 100$ **6.** $25 \times 48{,}000$ **7.** $9 \times 16 + 9 \times 84$ **8.** $45{,}000 + 7 + 230$

Write the prime factorization of each number in exponential form.

9. 625 **10.** 360 **11.** 70 **12.** 131

Divide. Round to the nearest hundredth if necessary.

13. $8.65 \div 5$ **14.** $43.7 \div 19$ **15.** $304.2 \div 26$ **16.** $39.2 \div 7$

17. $3.32 \div 0.4$ **18.** $3.71 \div 1.06$ **19.** $12.8 \div 2.35$ **20.** $525.5 \div 5.5$

Estimate by rounding to the nearest whole number.

21. $\frac{5}{6} - \frac{2}{5}$ **22.** $2\frac{1}{5} + \frac{1}{4}$ **23.** $6\frac{1}{9} - 5\frac{15}{16}$ **24.** $7\frac{3}{4} \div 9\frac{1}{8}$

Give the value for each exercise.

25. $|18|$ **26.** $-|3|$ **27.** $|-8|$ **28.** $|1|$

Compare. Use >, <, or =.

29. $13 \ \square \ -13$ **30.** $-19 \ \square \ -9$ **31.** $-\frac{4}{5} \ \square \ -0.8$ **32.** $4.5 \ \square \ -7.7$

Add or subtract.

33. $15 + (-3)$ **34.** $-18 - (-12)$ **35.** $-10 + (-20)$ **36.** $19 - (-9)$

37. $-\frac{2}{3} + \frac{1}{3}$ **38.** $-\frac{7}{8} - \frac{1}{8}$ **39.** $-\frac{4}{5} + \left(-\frac{4}{5}\right)$ **40.** $3.9 - (-0.9)$

Find the value of each expression when $r = -9$, $s = \frac{1}{3}$, and $t = 3$.

41. $r - t$ **42.** $5r$ **43.** st **44.** $(r + t)s$

45. $r^2 - t$ **46.** $15s + 2t$ **47.** $r + s - t$ **48.** rs

Solve.

49. $m - 9 = 8$ **50.** $2.4 + v = 3.9$ **51.** $z + -1 = 5$ **52.** $5g = 55$

53. $\frac{w}{8} = 5$ **54.** $2.5s = -10$ **55.** $7h - 4 = 24$ **56.** $\frac{f}{6} + 3 = 6$

57. $213 = r - 60$ **58.** $7.3t = 65.7$ **59.** $200 = 4y + 68$ **60.** $543 = \frac{p}{2} + 432$

Reteaching

Set A pages 116–117

When a problem involves several operations, always compute in the order listed below. This is the standard order of operations.

- Compute all powers.
- Multiply and divide from left to right.
- Add and subtract from left to right.

Remember to compute inside the parentheses first, following the standard order of operations.

1. $20 + 4 \times 5$

2. $13 - 3^2$

3. $3^2 - 8 \div 1$

4. $(7 + 8)\,5$

5. $6 \times (7 - 3) + 6$

6. $12 \div 2 \times 5$

7. $(9 - 4 \div 2) + 10$

8. $17\,(10 - 7)$

9. $5^2 \times 2 + 4^2$

10. $17 \times 10 - 7$

11. $5 + 5 - 5 \times 5 \div 5$

12. $6 + 8 \times 5 - 2$

Set B pages 118–119

In the expression $5a - 2$, the letter a is called a variable because the value of a may vary.

To evaluate (or give the value of) the expression $5a - 2$, substitute the given value of a.

If $a = 4$:

$5a - 2 =$

$5(4) - 2 =$

$20 - 2 = 18$

If $a = 5$:

$5a - 2 =$

$5(5) - 2 =$

$25 - 2 = 23$

Remember that there may be more than one variable in an expression.

Give the value of each expression when $y = 8$ and $z = 12$.

1. $10z$

2. $10z + y$

3. $6y - y$

4. $7z + 7y$

5. $3(y + z)$

6. $(15 - z)^2$

Evaluate $a + 2b$ when

7. $a = 4, b = 3.$

8. $a = 9, b = 8.$

Set C pages 120–121

Write an equation to show the relationship between x and y.

x	1	2	3	4
y	4	7	10	13

Look for a pattern. Guess and check.
Try $y = 3x$.
For $x = 1$, $3x = 3(1) = 3$. But $3 \neq 4$.
Notice that 3 is 1 less than 4.
Try $y = 3x + 1$.
For $x = 1$, $3x + 1 = 3(1) + 1 = 4$.
For $x = 2$, $3x + 1 = 3(2) + 1 = 7$.
For $x = 3$, $3x + 1 = 3(3) + 1 = 10$.
For $x = 4$, $3x + 1 = 3(4) + 1 = 13$.

The equation is $y = 3x + 1$.

Remember that an equation may be in terms of either variable.

1. Write an equation for a in terms of b.

a	2	4	6	8	10
b	1	2	3	4	5

2. Write an equation for b in terms of a.

a	1	3	5	7	9
b	5	17	29	41	53

Set D pages 122–123

To solve an addition or subtraction equation, isolate the variable on one side. To do this, add the same number to both sides.

Solve $s + 46 = 89$.

Since 46 is added to s, add -46 to both sides.

$$s + 46 + (-46) = 89 + (-46)$$

$$s = 43$$

Solve $k - (-92) = 50$.

Since -92 is subtracted from k, add -92 to both sides.

$$k - (-92) + (-92) = 50 + (-92)$$

$$k = -42$$

Remember to add the same amount to both sides of the equation.

1. $8 + d = 26 \quad d = ▒$
2. $3.7 = e - 0.9 \quad e = ▒$
3. $f - (-16) = 43 \quad f = ▒$
4. $55 + g = -17 \quad g = ▒$
5. $m + 6.5 = -7 \quad m = ▒$
6. $n - 4.4 = 1.7 \quad n = ▒$
7. $15.2 + x = -4.8 \quad x = ▒$
8. $w - 212 = -8 \quad w = ▒$

Set E pages 126–127

To solve a multiplication or division equation, isolate the variable on one side. To do this, multiply both sides by the same number.

Solve $22t = 4{,}466$.

Since t is multiplied by 22, multiply each side by $\frac{1}{22}$.

$$\left(\frac{1}{22}\right) \times 22t = \left(\frac{1}{22}\right) \times 4{,}466$$

$$t = 203$$

Remember that if the variable is multiplied by a fraction, you multiply by its reciprocal.

1. $129 = 3p \quad p = ▒$
2. $\frac{4}{5}q = 36 \quad q = ▒$
3. $7\frac{1}{2}r = \frac{3}{4} \quad r = ▒$
4. $7\frac{2}{5} = 6\frac{1}{6}s \quad s = ▒$
5. $-6n = 84 \quad n = ▒$
6. $-\frac{3}{4}a = -9 \quad a = ▒$

Set F pages 130–131

Some equations require two steps to solve.

a) Add the opposite of a number first.

b) Then multiply by the reciprocal.

Remember that a variable in a fraction such as $\frac{y}{2}$ means $\frac{1y}{2}$ or $\frac{1}{2}y$.

1. $100 = 8j - 4 \quad j = ▒$
2. $\frac{2}{9}m + 5 = 36 \quad m = ▒$
3. $\frac{n}{3} - 3 = 3 \quad n = ▒$
4. $-0.24y + 0.1 = -3.2 \quad y = ▒$
5. $-10x - 8 = -13 \quad x = ▒$

Independent Study MORE PRACTICE

More Practice

Set A pages 116–117

Compute.

1. $\frac{6}{5} + 3$
2. $4 \times 7 \div 20$
3. $14 - 5 \times 6$
4. $(14 - 7)^2$
5. $\frac{10}{3} + 14$
6. $7 - 3 \times 6$
7. $6 - (8 - 5)$
8. $\frac{10}{15} - 5$
9. $\frac{20}{2 + 4 \times 3}$
10. $3 + \frac{6 \times 4}{3}$
11. $3 + \frac{4 \times 7}{14}$
12. $\frac{6^2 - 3}{6 + 5} + 4$

Insert parentheses in each of the following so that the given equations are true.

13. $4 \times 2 + 6 = 32$
14. $2 + 4 \times 6 - 3 = 23$
15. $3 + 7 - 5 \times 2 = 0$

Set B pages 118–119

Find the value of each expression when $a = 2$, $b = \frac{6}{5}$, and $c = 4$.

1. $a - 5$
2. ac
3. $\frac{a}{5} - b$
4. $3b - 3b$
5. $c - c$
6. $5ab$
7. $3ac - 5b$
8. $a(a - 1)$
9. $(6 - c)21$
10. c^3
11. $(a + 4)^3$
12. $2ac + 5$
13. $(2 - c)40$
14. $\frac{c}{4}$
15. $6b$
16. $(2a + 1)b$
17. Copy and complete the table.

x	0		1	
$2x + 3$		4		7

Set C pages 120–121

Write a mathematical expression for

1. the product of 16 and a.
2. 16 less than a.
3. the product of 10 and the sum of a and b.
4. one-fourth the sum of a and c.

Choose the correct equation.

5.

x	1	2	3	4
y	0	1	2	3

a. $y = x - 1$
b. $y = x + 1$
c. $y = 2x$

Tell whether the sentence is true, false, or open.

6. $10 = x + 2$
7. $15 = 7 + 6(2)$
8. $6 = 3t - 2$
9. $-5 < -3$
10. $x + 2 = x$
11. $t + 0 = t$

Set D pages 122–123

Solve.

1. $a + 13 = 28$
2. $b + 2.5 = 10$
3. $c - 2\frac{1}{2} = 5$
4. $21 = d + 7$
5. $f + 6 = 13$
6. $g - 14 = 30$
7. $15 + h = -9$
8. $-12 = k - 4$
9. $n - 6.2 = 40$
10. $2.9 + p = -12.9$
11. $q + 17 = 10$
12. $51\frac{2}{3} = 3\frac{1}{3} + v$
13. $64 + x = -9$
14. $u - 17.1 = -12$
15. $r + 6\frac{7}{8} = 4\frac{1}{3}$
16. Find w, if 2 more than a number w is $5\frac{3}{7}$.
17. Find y, if 10 less than a number y is 0.8.
18. Find m, if 6 more than a number m is 21.
19. Find x, if 8 less than a number x is 7.

Set E pages 126–127

Solve.

1. $\frac{2}{3}k = 8$
2. $4n = 13$
3. $1.6a = 8$
4. $\frac{a}{4} = 3$
5. $10t = 23.9$
6. $3\frac{1}{2}b = 9$
7. $\frac{4}{3}m = -24$
8. $-5k = -2.5$
9. $2.9v = 9.86$
10. $10c = \frac{4}{5}$
11. $\frac{w}{7} = -8$
12. $\frac{3}{4}f = 4\frac{1}{2}$
13. $\frac{u}{-11} = -\frac{3}{22}$
14. $\frac{5}{9}h = 15$
15. $-2b = -17$
16. $\frac{n}{12} = 8$
17. $4.2k = 46.2$
18. $-3m = 5.7$

Set F pages 130–131

Solve.

1. $2x + 3 = 9$
2. $6a - 14 = 3$
3. $\frac{1}{2}t + 3 = 4$
4. $1\frac{1}{3}b + 2\frac{1}{6} = 5$
5. $\frac{n}{4} + 3 = 5$
6. $1.5m - 4 = 2.6$
7. $\frac{v}{9} - 6 = -1$
8. $\frac{2}{3}a + 6\frac{1}{2} = 7\frac{1}{2}$
9. $5q - 12 = -11$
10. $\frac{5}{6}c + \frac{1}{3} = \frac{1}{6}$
11. $\frac{1}{8}m - 9 = \frac{1}{2}$
12. $\frac{3}{7}b - 14 = -4$
13. $-12d + 1 = \frac{1}{2}$
14. $\frac{x}{5} + 2 = -7$
15. $20y - 6 = 44$
16. $4n - 0.5 = -22$
17. $2g + 30 = 8$
18. $\frac{w}{-3} + 4 = 6$

Enrichment

Function Notation

A ***function*** is a rule that explains how to get a resulting number by operating on a given number, x. If the rule is "Add 11 to x," then using 60 for x results in 71.

The notation $f(x)$, read "f of x," indicates a function. The function $f(x) = 3x - 4$ means multiply 3 and x and subtract 4 from the product.

To evaluate a function for a particular value of x, replace x by that number and perform the operations indicated.

If $f(x) = 3x - 4$, find $f(9)$.
$f(9) = 3(9) - 4 = 27 - 4 = 23$

Explain the meaning of each function.

1. $f(x) = 8x + 25$ **2.** $f(x) = \frac{2}{3}x - 7$ **3.** $f(x) = x^2 + x$ **4.** $f(x) = \frac{x - 8}{5}$

Evaluate these functions for the given values of x.

$f(x) = 8x - 5$	**5.** $f(-3)$	**6.** $f(0)$	**7.** $f(1)$	**8.** $f(8.5)$
$f(x) = \frac{6 - x}{7}$	**9.** $f(-15)$	**10.** $f(-1)$	**11.** $f(13)$	**12.** $f(62)$
$f(x) = 25 - x^2$	**13.** $f(-3)$	**14.** $f(0)$	**15.** $f(3)$	**16.** $f(5)$
$f(x) = x^3 + x$	**17.** $f(-2)$	**18.** $f(0)$	**19.** $f(2)$	**20.** $f(4)$

21. For which functions did your answers increase as x increased?

22. For which functions did your answers decrease as x increased?

23. What values do you have to use for x to get a negative answer for $f(x) = 25 - x^2$?

24. What values do you have to use for x to get a negative answer for $f(x) = x^3 + x$?

25. Write a function for which the results are always 0 or less than 0, no matter what x is.

26. The number of feet that an object will fall in x seconds is given by $f(x) = 16x^2$. What is your reaction to a trial witness who says a beam falling from a construction site 1,000 feet above the street reached the ground in 5 seconds?

Chapter 4 Review/Test

Which operation should be performed first?

1. $4 \times (3^2 + 2) - 6$ **2.** $(6 - 2)^2 + 18$

Insert parentheses in each of the following so that the equation is true.

3. $16 \div 8 \div 2 = 4$ **4.** $10 - 3^2 + 6 = 7$

Evaluate each expression when $x = -8$ and $z = \frac{1}{4}$.

5. $12z + x$ **6.** $x(6 + z)$ **7.** $\frac{96z}{x}$

8. Choose the correct equation for this rental table.

Hours (x)	1	2	3	4	5
Cost in Dollars (z)	6	10	14	18	22

a. $z = 4x - 2$ **b.** $z = 4x + 2$
c. $z = 3x + 3$ **d.** $z = 5x + 1$

Solve each equation.

9. $8 = d + 3$ **10.** $9 + h = -2$

11. $r - 3 = 11.5$ **12.** $6 = w - 6$

13. Write an equation and then solve the problem.

Only 380 students saw the school play. A total of 1,155 students and adults were present. How many adults saw the play?

Find the reciprocal of each number.

14. $\frac{41}{52}$ **15.** 7.3 **16.** 1 **17.** 63

Solve each equation.

18. $7r = 21$ **19.** $\frac{3}{4}n = 4\frac{1}{2}$

20. $5z + 6 = 26$ **21.** $4z - 3 = 5$

22. $12 = 4 + \frac{1}{2}k$ **23.** $\frac{n}{2} + 6 = 11$

Write an equation for each problem and then solve the problem.

24. Cynthia wants to buy a ten-speed bicycle that costs $132. She has saved $85. How much money does she need before she can buy the bicycle?

25. Judy's family spent $432 on a short trip to New York. They spent an average of $108 per person. How many people are in Judy's family?

26. Maria paid a total of $425 for a stereo system. She made a down payment and then paid $50 a month for 6 months. How much was the down payment?

27. **Write About Math** Would you prefer to use a table similar to the one in Item 8, or an equation to find out how much something costs? Why?

Graphing

5

Did You Know:
A tomato is a fruit and not a vegetable. Botanists classify tomatoes as fruits because they come from the part of the plant that contains the seeds. There are over 4,000 varieties of tomatoes. Tomato seeds require about 80 days to develop into plants with ripe fruits.

Number-Sense Project

Estimate
Plant some seeds, such as popcorn seeds. Keep them watered and in a sunny place. How long do you think it will take before they start to grow?

Gather Data
Observe your seeds each day. Once the seeds sprout select one plant and record its growth each day for 2 weeks.

Analyze and Report
How long did it take before the seeds began to grow? During which period of time was the growth of the plant the greatest?

Graphing Equations and Inequalities

Build Understanding

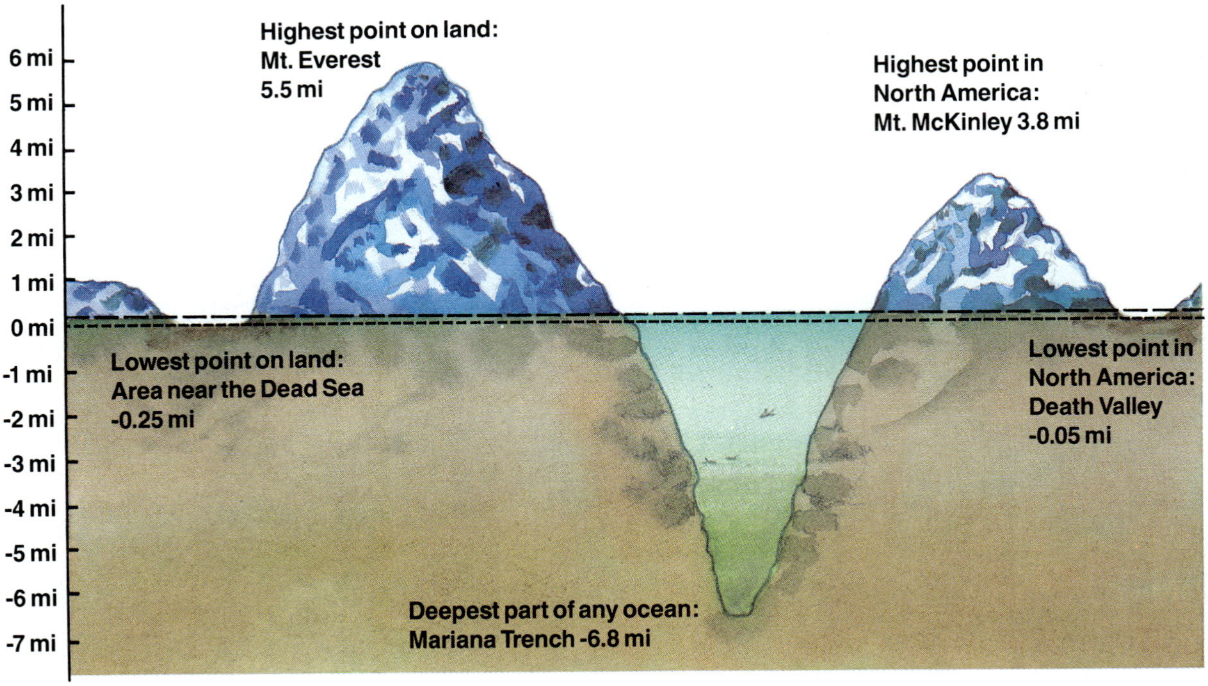

A. Elevations on or below the earth's surface are equal to or less than 5.5 mi. This can be expressed by the ***inequality*** $x \leq 5.5$. The symbol $\leq$ means "is less than or equal to."

All numbers that make $x \leq 5.5$ true are solutions. Is 0 a solution? Is 3.2? Is 4? Is 5.5? Is 5.8?

Since 5.5 and all numbers less than 5.5 are solutions, first graph the equation $x = 5.5$ with a filled-in circle.

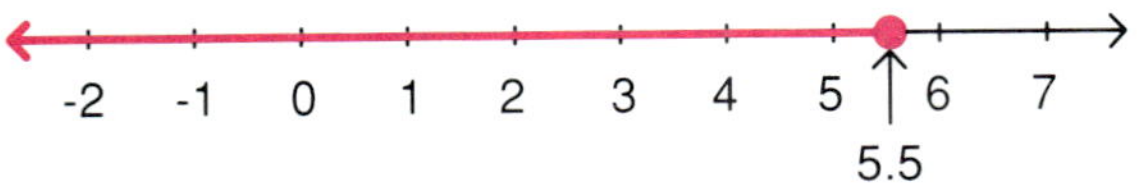

Then draw a solid line to the left of 5.5 to show that all numbers less than 5.5 are solutions.

B. Many aircraft can fly at altitudes higher than 5.5 miles.

All numbers greater than 5.5 are solutions of $x > 5.5$.

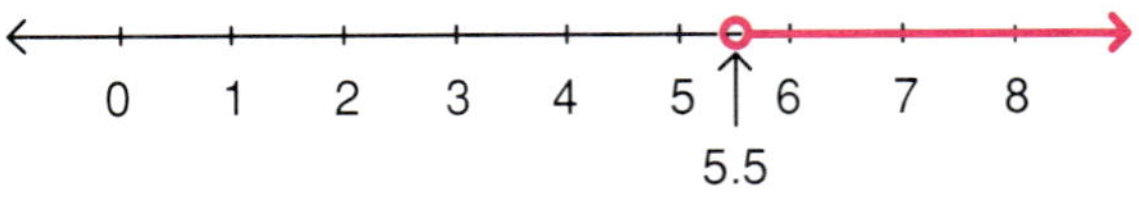

Use an open circle at 5.5 since 5.5 is not a solution. Use a solid line to the right of 5.5 to show that all numbers greater than 5.5 are solutions.

C. A tour bus left Colorado Springs for the top of Pikes Peak. Colorado Springs has an elevation of 1 mile above sea level and Pikes Peak is 2.7 miles above sea level. Write an inequality to express all the elevations of the bus, h, during the trip. Then graph the inequality. What is the solution set?

This inequality shows the elevation of the bus will be greater than or equal to 1 mile above sea level. $\boldsymbol{h \geq 1}$

This inequality shows the elevation of the bus will be less than or equal to 2.7 miles above sea level. $\boldsymbol{h \leq 2.7}$

The two inequalities can be written as a ***compound inequality.*** $\boldsymbol{h \geq 1}$ ***and*** $\boldsymbol{h \leq 2.7}$

Lightly sketch the graphs for $h \geq 1$ and $h \leq 2.7$ above the same number line. Select values for h from each graph. Is 1 a solution of the compound inequality? Is 2? Is 2.7? Is 3?

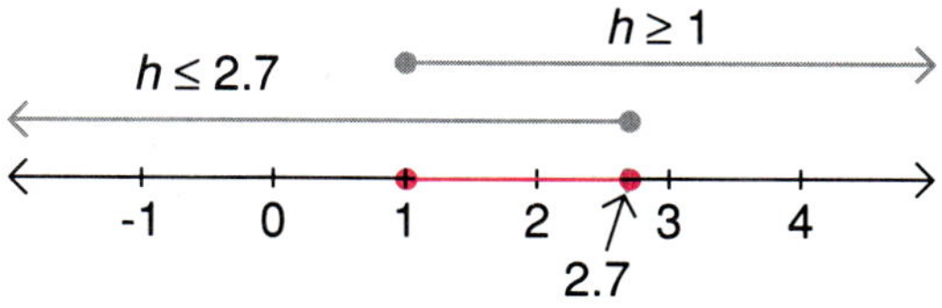

The numbers 1 and 2.7 and all numbers between them are solutions. Draw a solid line between 1 and 2.7 and fill in the circles for 1 and 2.7. The solution set is 1 mile, 2.7 miles, and all elevations between 1 mile and 2.7 miles.

D. Graph the solution set of $m < -1$ *or* $m \geq 3$.

Each solution is either less than -1, or greater than 3, or equal to 3.

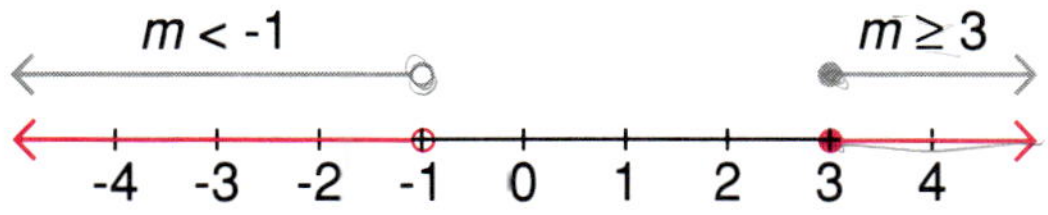

E. Graph the solution set of $m < -1$ *and* $m \geq 3$.

Since no number can be both less than -1 and greater than 3, the solution set is the empty set, $\emptyset$.

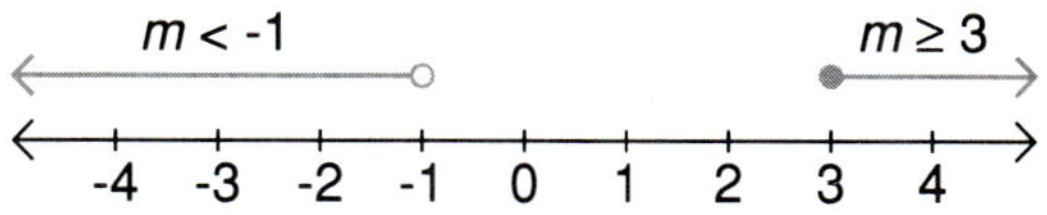

Talk About Math Explain how to graph the compound inequality $h > 1$ or $h < 2.7$. What is the solution set?

Check Understanding

For another example, see Set A, pages 176–177.

Graph the inequality. Then describe the solution set.

1. $x \geq -6$ **2.** $x < 5$ **3.** $x \geq -6$ and $x < 5$ **4.** $x \geq -6$ or $x < 5$

Practice

For More Practice, see Set A, pages 178–179.

Which of these numbers, -6, $-3\frac{1}{2}$, -2, 0, 2, $3\frac{1}{2}$, 6, 7.5, and 15, is in the solution set for

5. $x > 6$ and $x \geq 2$?
6. $x > 6$ or $x \geq 2$?
7. $x \geq -2$ and $x < 6$?

Graph each equation or inequality on a number line.

8. $x > -2$
9. $y + 3 \leq 4$
10. $y - 2 = 5$
11. $p \geq 3\frac{3}{4}$
12. $q < -1\frac{1}{2}$
13. $r \leq 5.8$
14. $m < 4$
15. $n < 1$ or $n < 2$
16. $g \geq 2$ and $g \leq 0$
17. $t \geq -5$ and $t \leq -2$
18. $a < -2\frac{1}{2}$ or $a \geq 1\frac{1}{2}$
19. $b > 0.5$ and $b < -2$
20. $t > -4$ or $t < 4$
21. $m > 2$ or $m = 1$
22. $c \leq 2$ and $c > 0$

Give an equation or an inequality for each graph.

23. 

24. 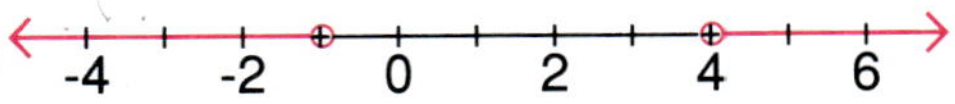

25. 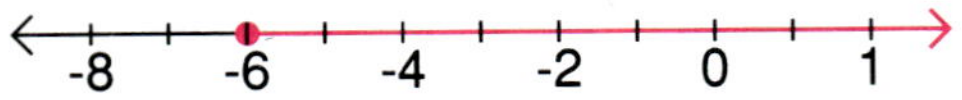

26. 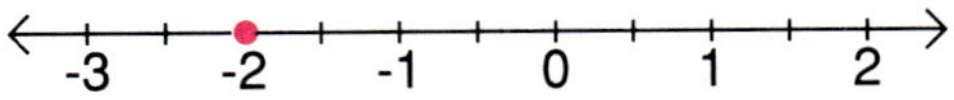

27. 

28. 

Calculator Find the elevation to the nearest hundred feet.

29. Mt. Everest
30. Mariana Trench
31. Death Valley

Problem Solving

For each situation, write an equation or inequality. Use the data on page 144.

32. An airplane directly over Mt. McKinley

33. A tourist on the shore of the Dead Sea

34. A bathyscaphe descending into the Mariana Trench

35. A mountain climber more than halfway up Mt. McKinley

TIPS FOR PROBLEM SOLVERS

Visualize the problem in your mind to help you understand it better.

Give each answer. Use the data on page 144.

36. The deepest part of the Dead Sea is 0.45 miles below sea level. What is the difference between this and the elevation around the Dead Sea?

37. The average depth of the Pacific Ocean is 2.4 miles. How much deeper is the Mariana Trench?

38. What is the difference between the lowest point and the highest point in North America?

39. What is the difference between the lowest and highest points shown in the diagram?

Choose a ________ Strategy

Locate Big Bear Big Bear Lodge is more than 5 miles from Wolf River Bridge but less than 3 miles from Beaver Falls. It is within 2 miles of Fox Lake. Trace the map and show where the lodge is located.

PROBLEM SOLVING STRATEGIES

Choose an Operation
Solve a Simpler Problem
Use a Formula
Write an Equation

40. Which figure shows locations 5 miles from the bridge? Draw the figure and shade the area representing more than 5 miles. Hint: Think about a circle.

41. Draw the figure that shows all points 3 miles from the falls. Shade the appropriate area.

42. Which figure represents locations 2 miles from the lake? Draw the figure and shade the appropriate area.

43. Show where the Big Bear Lodge is located.

ALGEBRA

Solving Inequalities by Graphing

Build Understanding

A. More or Less?
Groups: 4 students

Draw a number line. In order to graph $r + 3 \geq -2$, each of you substitute a number for r to test if it is a solution. If a number is a solution, graph it with a filled-in circle. Continue testing numbers until you can predict all the solutions of the inequality. How many numbers did you test? Graph the solution set and write an inequality that describes it.

B. Graph the solution set of $t - 3 \leq 2$.

The solution to $t - 3 = 2$ is 5. Since $5 - 3 \leq 2$, you know that 5 is a solution of the inequality. Put a filled-in circle at 5.

Decide if the graph goes to the right or left by testing a number greater than 5 and a number less than 5. Test 0 and 6.

Is $0 - 3 \leq 2$? Yes; 0 is a solution.

Is $6 - 3 \leq 2$? No; 6 is not a solution. Since 0 is a solution and 6 is not, the graph goes to the left of 5.

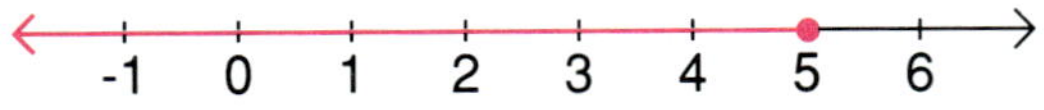

The solution set is $t \leq 5$.

C. Graph $-4t > 12$.

The solution of $-4t = 12$ is -3. Test to see if -3 is a solution of the inequality.

Since $-4(-3)$ is not greater than 12, -3 is not a solution. Put an open circle at -3.

Now test a number greater than -3 and a number less than -3.

Is $-4(0) > 12$? No; 0 is not a solution.

Is $-4(-10) > 12$? Yes; -10 is a solution, so the graph goes to the left of -3.

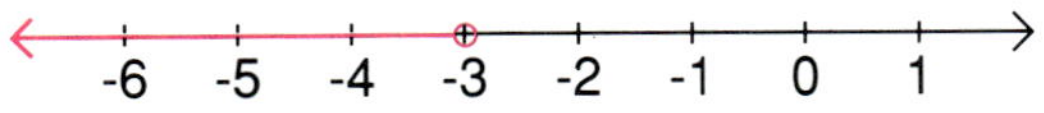

The solution set is $t < -3$.

■ **Talk About Math** Which numbers are the easiest to substitute in an inequality to check if the graph goes left or right?

Check Understanding

For another example, see Set B, pages 176–177.

Answer these questions about the graph of $\frac{1}{3}m \leq -2$.

1. Which number is circled? Is the circle filled in?

2. Does the graph go to the right or left of the circled number?

Practice

For More Practice, see Set B, pages 178–179.

Find the solution set. Draw a graph to help you.

3. $x + 6 > 8$ **4.** $c - 6 \geq -2$ **5.** $8x \leq 16$ **6.** $\frac{1}{2}w < -1$

7. $y + 7 \leq 3$ **8.** $m + 5 > -7$ **9.** $-8 > 2 + p$ **10.** $4 + x \leq 3.3$

11. $k - 9.6 \geq 0$ **12.** $m - 9 \geq -12$ **13.** $\frac{1}{2}m \geq -2$ **14.** $5x < -25$

15. $-5x < 25$ **16.** $-5x > -25$ **17.** $3x > -9$ **18.** $-3x < -9$

Mixed Practice Match each equation or inequality with the graph of its solution set.

19. $2x > -6$ **20.** $20 + 7x = -1$

21. $-4x > -12$ **22.** $x \geq 3$ and $x \leq -3$

23. $3 + x < 6$ **24.** $x \geq -3$ or $x \leq 3$

25. $10 < 13 + x$ **26.** $x \leq -3$ or $x \geq 3$

27. $3x + 7 = -2$ **28.** $x \leq 3$ and $x \geq -3$

29. $x^2 \geq 0$ **30.** $x + 6 \leq 3$ or $-x \leq -3$

31. $|x| \geq 3$ **32.** $|x| \leq 3$

a.
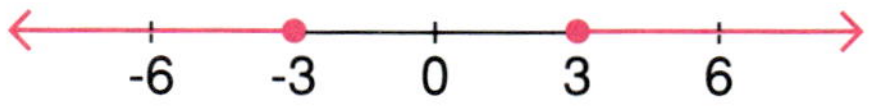

b.
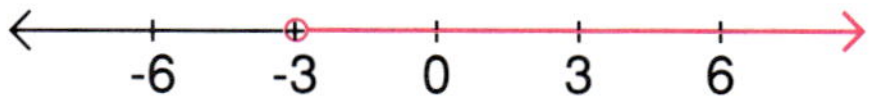

c.
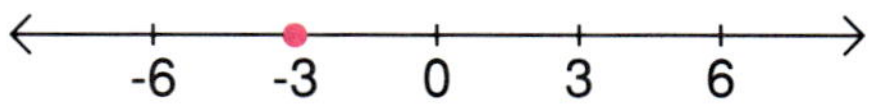

d.
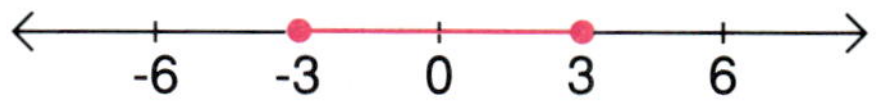

e.
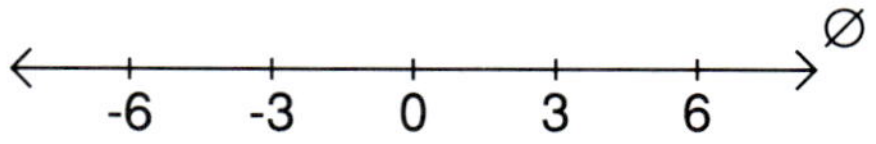

f.
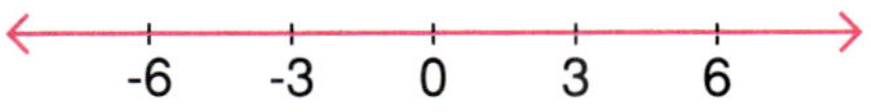

g.
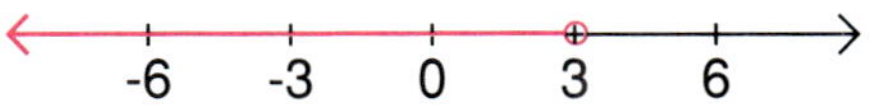

Problem Solving

Solve each problem.

33. Critical Thinking Look at Exercises 14–18. What do you notice about the inequality signs in the solutions when both sides of the inequality are multiplied by a negative number? a positive number?

Write an inequality to describe each solution.

34. The temperature has risen 6° since 7:00, but it is still less than 30°. What was the temperature at 7:00?

35. Joe has covered 5 miles of the trail and has more than 3.5 miles to go. What is the length of the trail?

36. After Betsy wrote a $100 check, she had less than $250 left in her account. How much did she have in her account before she wrote the check?

37. Use Data Use the graph on page 144. If an airplane ascends 1.2 miles, it will be higher than Mt. McKinley. How high is the airplane now?

Use Data from a Diagram

PROBLEM SOLVING GUIDE

Understand
QUESTION
FACTS
KEY IDEA

Plan and Solve
STRATEGY
ANSWER

Look Back
SENSIBLE ANSWER
ALTERNATE APPROACH

Build Understanding

Locations in Chicago are given east or west of State Street and north or south of Madison Street. It is one mile between each group of 800 street numbers.

Estimate how far Wrigley Field is from the intersection of State and Madison Streets.

Understand QUESTION About how far is Wrigley Field from State and Madison Streets?

FACT Each group of 800 street numbers is about 1 mile. Use the data from the map. Wrigley Field is located at about 1000 W and 3600 N of State and Madison.

Plan and Solve Divide to find miles.

$1{,}000 \div 800 = 1\frac{1}{4}$

$3{,}600 \div 800 = 4\frac{1}{2}$

ANSWER Wrigley Field is about $1\frac{1}{4}$ miles west and $4\frac{1}{2}$ miles north of State and Madison.

Look Back SENSIBLE ANSWER Each square block is 1 mile by 1 mile. Wrigley Field is a little more than 1 mile west and 4 miles north of State and Madison.

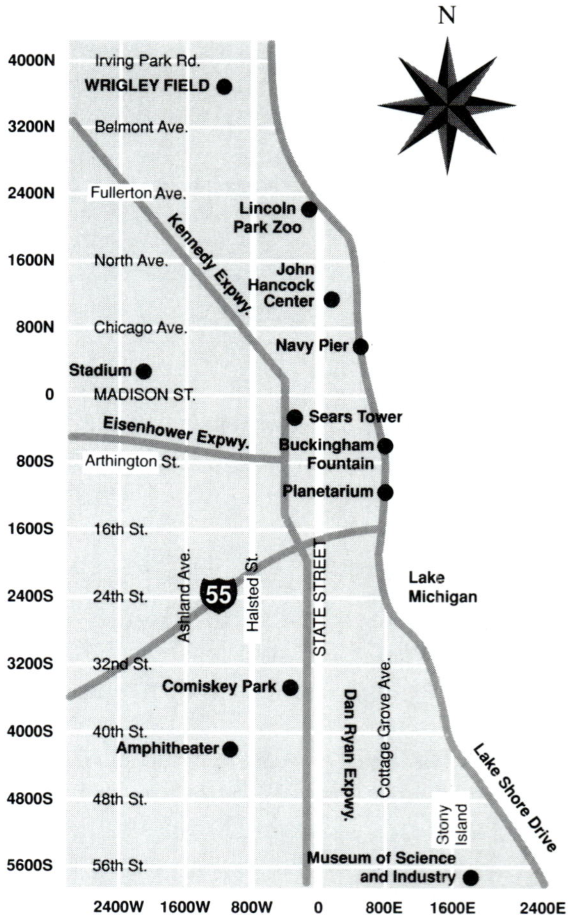

■ **Talk About Math** Very few streets are east of State Street. Why do you think this was chosen as the zero point?

Check Understanding

Use the map on page 150 to answer each question.

1. What streets intersect at about 1600W and 2500S?

2. How many miles is the Museum of Science and Industry from State and Madison?

3. What street is about $2\frac{1}{2}$ mi south and 2 mi east of Comiskey Park?

4. About how far east from the lake is the Stadium?

Practice

For each location, give the street number east or west of State Street and north or south of Madison Street.

5. Intersection of 16th and Halsted

6. John Hancock Center

7. Planetarium

Estimation For each location estimate the number of miles east or west of State Street and north or south of Madison Street.

8. 2400W and 2400N

9. 800E and 4800S

10. 800W and 3000N

11. Comiskey Park

12. Sears Tower

13. Buckingham Fountain

Tell what is shown on the map at the given distances from State and Madison.

14. $\frac{3}{4}$ mi east and $\frac{3}{4}$ mi north

15. $2\frac{1}{4}$ mi west near Madison

16. 1 mi west and $\frac{3}{4}$ mi south

17. $\frac{1}{4}$ mi west and $2\frac{3}{4}$ mi north

Reading ______ Math

Number Lines Estimate the location of each point to the nearest tenth. For example, point *A* is about 3.2.

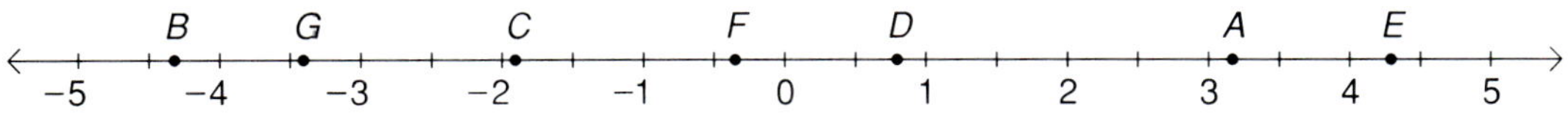

1. *B* **2.** *C* **3.** *D* **4.** *E* **5.** *F* **6.** *G*

ALGEBRA

Graphing in the Coordinate Plane

Build Understanding

Equations such as $x + 3 = 7$ and $3x = -15$ have one variable and the solution can be graphed on a number line. Equations like $x + 3 = y$ and $3x = y$ have two variables and many solutions. These solutions can be graphed in the ***coordinate plane,*** or coordinate grid.

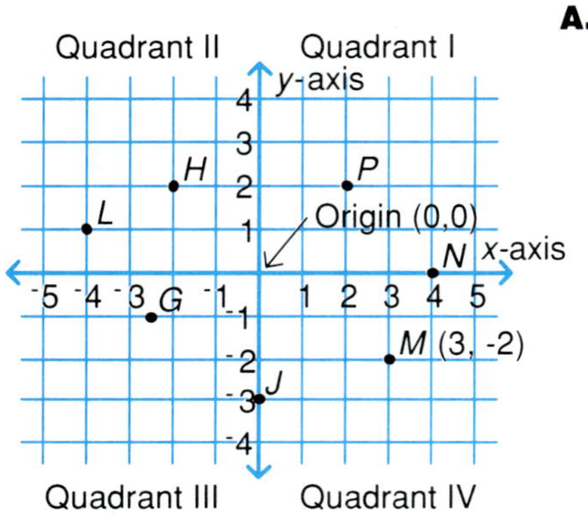

A. The coordinate plane is formed by two perpendicular number lines, called the ***x-axis*** and the ***y-axis***, which intersect at a point called the ***origin.*** This forms Quadrants I, II, III, and IV, which are numbered counterclockwise.

Every point in the coordinate plane can be located by an ordered pair of numbers (x, y) called the ***coordinates*** of the point. The coordinates of the origin are (0, 0).

The coordinates of point M are $(3, -2)$ because M is 3 units to the right of the origin and 2 units down.

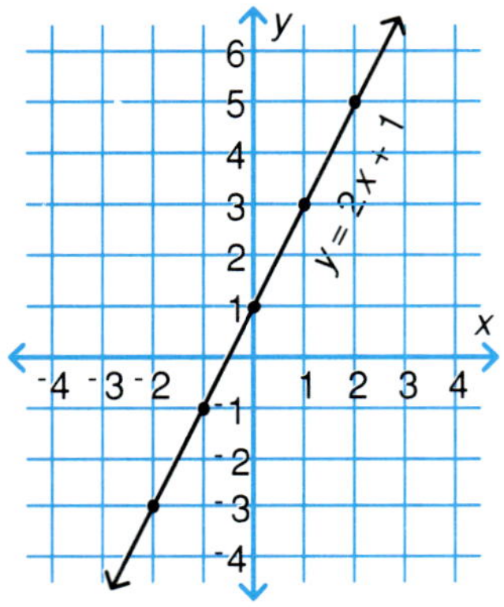

(1.5, 4) is on the line.
$4 = 2(1.5) + 1$, so it is a solution.
$(-3, -5)$ is on the line.
$-5 = 2(-3) + 1$,
so it is a solution.

B. Graph the equation $y = 2x + 1$.

Make a table. Select values for x and solve for y.

x	y	(x, y)
0	1	(0, 1)
−1	−1	(−1, −1)
−2	−3	(−2, −3)
1	3	(1, 3)

Graph these points on a coordinate grid. Notice that they appear to fall on a line. Draw the line. Are other points on the line solutions of the equation? Can you find a point on the line that is not a solution?

Every point on the line is a solution of $y = 2x + 1$. The graph of $y = 2x + 1$ is a line, so $y = 2x + 1$ is a ***linear equation.***

C. Graph $y = x^2$.

x	y	(x, y)
−2	4	(−2, 4)
−1	1	(−1, 1)
0	0	(0, 0)
1	1	(1, 1)
2	4	(2, 4)

Make a table. Then graph the points.

Choose zero and some negative and positive integers for x. This helps you to determine all the quadrants in which the graph is located.

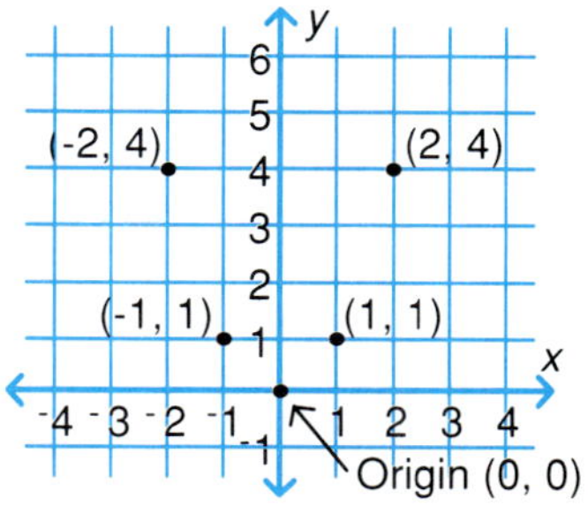

You can see that the graph is not a line. Find the coordinates of more points and connect them with a smooth curve. You might want to use a calculator.

x	y	(x, y)
3	9	(3, 9)
2.5	6.25	(2.5, 6.25)
−2.5	6.25	(−2.5, 6.25)
−3	9	(−3, 9)

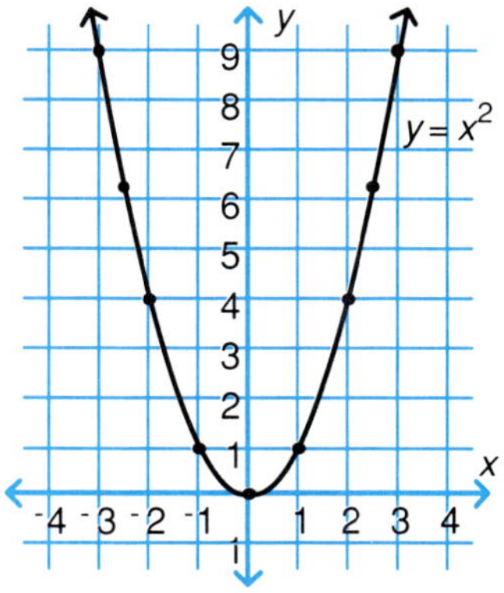

Notice that the same y value is obtained for $x = 2$ and $x = -2$, for $x = 2.5$ and $x = -2.5$, and so on. Since the point (1.5, 2.25) is on the graph of $y = x^2$, the point (−1.5, 2.25) is also on the graph because $(1.5)^2 = (-1.5)^2$.

Graph the points. (You will have to estimate the positions of points with coordinates that are not whole numbers.) Connect the points with a smooth curve.

Since the graph is not a line, $y = x^2$ is called a ***nonlinear equation.*** A graph with this shape is called a ***parabola.***

Talk About Math What do the coordinates of points on the x-axis have in common? the y-axis?

Check Understanding

For another example, see Set C, pages 176–177.

Where is $P(x, y)$ located on the coordinate plane if

1. $x > 0$ and $y < 0$? **2.** $x < 0$ and $y < 0$? **3.** $x > 0$ and $y > 0$?

Give two more points on the graph of

4. $y = 2x + 1$ in Example B. **5.** $y = x^2$ in Example C.

Graph each equation.

6. $y = -5x$ **7.** $y = -5x + 2$ **8.** $y = \frac{1}{3}x$ **9.** $y = \frac{1}{3}x - 1$

Practice

For More Practice, see Set C, pages 178–179.

Plot the points on the same coordinate grid and connect them in order. Connect point J with point A.

10. $A(0, 7)$ **11.** $B(1.5, 2)$ **12.** $C(7, 1)$ **13.** $D(3, -1)$ **14.** $E(4, -6)$

15. $F(0, -3)$ **16.** $G(-4, -6)$ **17.** $H(-3, -1)$ **18.** $I(-7, 0)$ **19.** $J(-2, 2)$

For each point, name the quadrant or axis in which the point is located. Do not graph the point.

20. $K(25, -12)$ **21.** $L(-31, 0)$ **22.** $M(-20, -47)$ **23.** $N(0, -76)$

24. $P(-102, 54)$ **25.** $Q(88, -23)$ **26.** $R(93, 67)$ **27.** $S(71, 0)$

Graph each equation on a different coordinate plane. **Remember** to make a table with enough ordered pairs so that you can establish the graph.

28. $y = x - 5$ **29.** $y = 5x$ **30.** $y = \frac{1}{5}x$ **31.** $y = 3 - x$

32. $y = x^2 - 1$ **33.** $y = -x^2$ **34.** $y = -2$ **35.** $x = 5$

Graph each set of equations on the same coordinate plane.

36. $y = 2x$
$y = 2x + 1$
$y = 2x + 3$
$y = 2x - 3$
$y = 2x - 4$

37. $y = 8x$
$y = 2x$
$y = x$
$y = \frac{1}{2}x$
$y = \frac{1}{8}x$

38. $y = -4x$
$y = -2x$
$y = -\frac{1}{2}x$
$y = -\frac{1}{4}x$

39. $y = 4x - 3$
$y = -\frac{1}{4}x - 3$
$y = x$
$y = -x$

What do you notice about the sets of equations and their graphs in

40. Exercise 36? **41.** Exercise 37? **42.** Exercise 38? **43.** Exercise 39?

Study the graph below. If the equation of the line is $y = mx + b$,

44. what does b equal?

45. is the sign of m positive or negative?

46. what is the equation of ℓ?

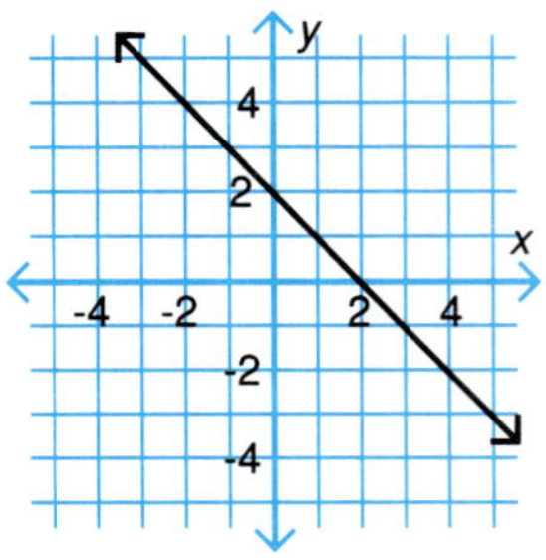

What is the equation of

47. the x-axis? **48.** the y-axis?

Calculator Graph each equation on a coordinate grid.

49. $y = x^2 + 1$ **50.** $y = -x^2 + 2$ **51.** $y = x^3$ **52.** $xy = 12$

Problem Solving

Visual Thinking Picture in your mind the graph of each equation. Then match each statement with one or more of the equations.

53. The equation is linear.

54. The equation is nonlinear.

55. The graph goes through the origin.

56. The graph rises from left to right.

57. The graph falls from left to right.

58. The graph is parallel to the x-axis.

59. The graph is parallel to the y-axis.

a. $y = x + 45$

b. $y = 23x$

c. $y = -61x^2$

d. $x = -2$

e. $y = x^2 - 55$

f. $y = -44x$

g. $y = -2$

h. $y = -x + 36$

Solve each problem.

Use the same coordinate grid for Exercises 60 and 61. Let the x-axis represent the length and let the y-axis represent the width. For example, consider length 6, width 4 as different from length 4, width 6.

60. A rectangle has a perimeter of 24 inches. Make a graph of possible widths and lengths.

61. A rectangle has an area of 24 inches. Make a graph of possible widths and lengths.

62. Estimate the approximate length and width of a rectangle with a perimeter of 24 inches and an area of 24 square inches.

63. **Number Sense** Since the coordinates represent lengths and widths, in which quadrant do all of the points lie?

Skills Review pages 122–123

Solve each equation.

1. $m + 6 = 14$

2. $k - 4 = 9$

3. $6 + n = 35$

4. $8 + a = 6$

5. $12 + y = 3$

6. $14 + g = -3$

7. $4x = 19$

8. $12b = -36$

9. $9t = 117$

10. $\frac{1}{2}n = 12$

11. $\frac{3}{4}n = 16$

12. $\frac{8x}{3} = 15$

13. $4b - 2 = 18$

14. $6n + 3 = 51$

15. $9 + 5a = 49$

16. $\frac{1}{2}x + 3 = 8$

17. $5b - 6 = -11$

18. $\frac{5}{8}m + 3 = 1$

ALGEBRA

Graphing Pairs of Linear Equations

Build Understanding

Have you ever heard the saying, "A picture is worth a thousand words"? Sometimes making a graph, or a picture, of an equation is the easiest way to solve a problem.

A. What two numbers have a sum of 4 and a difference of 1?

If x and y represent the numbers, then we can write the equations $x + y = 4$ and $x - y = 1$.

Make tables and graph both equations on the same coordinate grid.

$x + y = 4$

x	y	(x, y)
0	4	(0, 4)
1	3	(1, 3)
2	2	(2, 2)
4	0	(4, 0)

$x - y = 1$

x	y	(x, y)
1	0	(1, 0)
2	1	(2, 1)
0	−1	(0, −1)
−2	−3	(−2, −3)

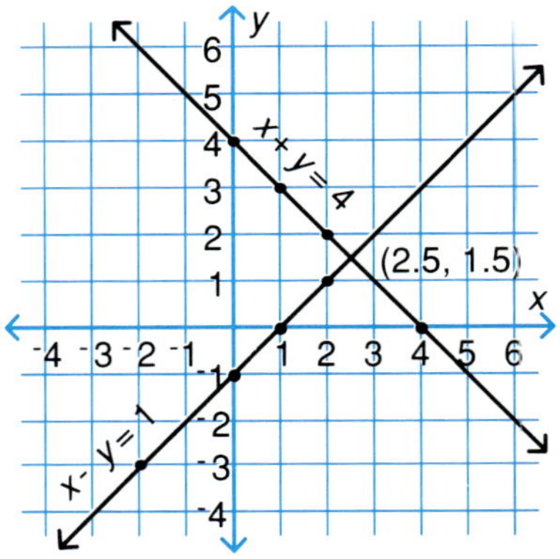

The lines intersect at (2.5, 1.5). Notice that $2.5 + 1.5 = 4$ and $2.5 - 1.5 = 1$. The two numbers are 2.5 and 1.5.

B. Graph $y = -2$ and $x = -2$.

For $y = -2$, y is -2 for every value of x. The graph is parallel to and 2 units below the x-axis.

The graph of $x = -2$ is parallel to and 2 units to the left of the y-axis.

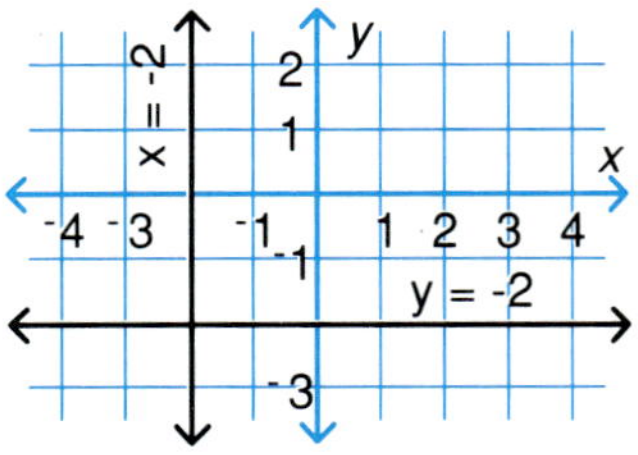

Talk About Math Describe a line that is parallel to $y = -2$.

Check Understanding

For another example, see Set D, pages 176–177.

Graph each pair of equations on the same coordinate grid. If the lines intersect, describe the point or points of intersection.

1. $y = 2x + 2$ and $y = x + 2$

2. $y = x - 1$ and $y = \frac{2x - 2}{2}$

Practice

For More Practice, see Set D, pages 178–179.

Graph each pair of equations on the same coordinate grid.

3. $y = x$
$y = -x$

4. $y = x + 4$
$y = 2x - 3$

5. $y = x + 4$
$y = x - 4$

6. $y = 3 - x$
$y = x - 2$

7. $y = 2x - 1$
$y = 2x + 1$

8. $y = 4x - 2$
$y = 4x + 1$

9. $x = 4$
$y = 3$

10. $y = 0$
$y = -1$

11. $y = \frac{1}{2}x + 3$
$y = 2x - 3$

12. $2x + y = 3$
$x - y = 9$

13. $y = 3x + 1$
$y = 2x - 3$

14. $y = -2x + 2$
$y = 3x - 3$

In $y = 2x + 3$, the number 2 is called the ***coefficient*** of x. The number 3 is called the ***constant term.*** In $y = -x$, the coefficient of y is 1, the coefficient of x is -1, and the constant term is 0.

What do you notice about the coefficients of x when the graphs of two equations

15. intersect?

16. are parallel?

17. What do you notice about the constant term and the point at which the graph crosses the y-axis?

Mental Math Without graphing, tell whether the graphs of these pairs of equations intersect or are parallel.

18. $y = 7x + 1.5$
$y = 7x - 19$

19. $y = 9x + 4$
$y = 5x - 6$

20. $y = -32x$
$y = 17x$

21. $y = 43$
$y = -28$

Problem Solving

Find each pair of numbers.

22. Two numbers with a sum of 5 and a difference of 5

23. Two numbers with a sum of -6 and a difference of 2

24. Two numbers, one twice the other, with a sum of 8

25. Approximate two numbers with a sum of 6 and a product of 6.

Critical Thinking Solve each problem.

26. If two different lines intersect, how many possible points of intersection are there?

27. Look at the graphs of $x + y = 4$ and $x - y = 1$ in Example A on page 156. Describe how the graphs of $x + y = -4$ and $x - y = -1$ are related to the graphs of $x + y = 4$ and $x - y = 1$.

Make a Graph

Build Understanding

Lin Chen wants to join one of two video clubs. Based only on cost, which club should he join?

Vista Video: Membership: \$3.00 per month
Rental: \$2.00 per tape

Star Video: Membership: \$5.00 per month
Rental: \$1.50 per tape

Understand QUESTION When is one club cheaper than the other?

KEY IDEA Find when the costs are equal. Make the decision based on the number of tapes to be rented per month.

Plan and Solve STRATEGY *Make a graph* for each club showing costs and number of rentals.

The graph shows that Vista Video is cheaper for fewer than 4 rentals, but more expensive for more than 4 rentals. The cost is the same at both stores for 4 rentals.

ANSWER If Lin plans to rent more than 4 tapes per month, he should join Star Video Club. If he plans to rent fewer, Vista Video is cheaper.

Look Back SENSIBLE ANSWER For 4 tapes, the cost at Vista Video is 3 + 2.00(4), or \$11. At Star Video the cost is 5 + 1.50(4), or \$11.

Talk About Math What are some of the other factors Lin should consider?

PROBLEM SOLVING GUIDE

Understand
QUESTION
FACTS
KEY IDEA

Plan and Solve
STRATEGY
ANSWER

Look Back
SENSIBLE ANSWER
ALTERNATE APPROACH

Vista: $c = 2t + 3$

t	c
0	3
1	5
2	7
5	13

Star: $c = 1.50t + 5$

t	c
0	5
1	6.50
2	8
5	12.50

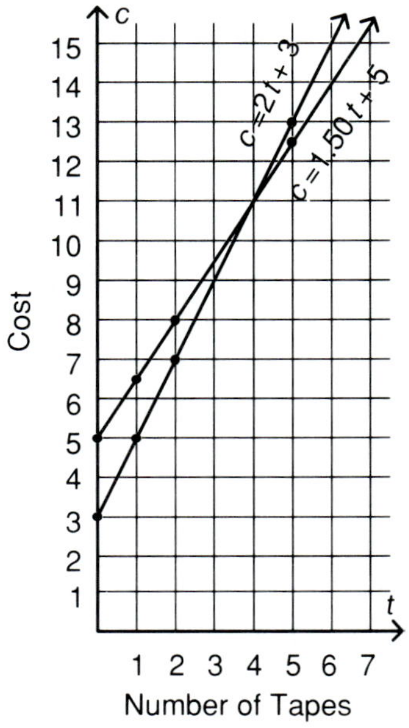

Check Understanding

Tell what the answer to Lin's problem would be if each of the following changes were made.

1. There is no membership fee at either store.

2. Vista Video charges $3.00 per tape.

Practice

Lin can rent a VCR from Vista Video for $5 per day. Star Video rents the same VCR for $20 for the first 3 days and then $4 for each additional day.

3. How much will the VCR from Vista cost for 1 day? 2 days? 10 days?

4. How much will the VCR from Star cost for 1 day? 2 days? 10 days?

5. Make a graph to show the costs at each store.

6. You expect to rent about 6 tapes per month. Which store would you choose?

Solve the problem.

7. Kim started with $30 and saved $2 a week. Tim started on the same day with $20 and saved $3 a week. For how long did Kim have more money saved than Tim? When did Tim have more?

Midchapter Checkup

Graph each inequality on a number line.

1. $a \leq -4$ **2.** $t < 7$ **3.** $x > -4$ **4.** $m \geq -5$

Write each solution set as an inequality. Draw a graph to help you.

5. $a - 5 > 4$ **6.** $m + 3 \geq 2$ **7.** $4a < -8$ **8.** $\frac{1}{3}x \geq -1$

Name the quadrant or axis in which each point is located.

9. $A(-4, 6)$ **10.** $B(3, \frac{1}{2})$ **11.** $C(0, -23)$ **12.** $D(-0.5, 0)$

13. Graph $y = 2x + 1$ and $y = x - 3$ on the same coordinate grid. Name the point of intersection.

Real-Life Decision Making

1. Suppose this is a map of your town. As you walk from one place to another, walk along the streets and do not cut across any spaces. How many direct routes are there from

a. Santa Maria High School at the corner of Morrison and Broadway to the public library at the corner of Broadway and Oak?

b. Fesler Junior High School at the corner of Cypress and Concord to Town Center West Mall at the corner of Broadway and Cook?

c. Santa Maria High School at the corner of Morrison and Broadway to Allan Hancock College at the corner of College and Park?

d. Rose's Market at the corner of Cypress and College Drive to Simas Park at Orange and Miller?

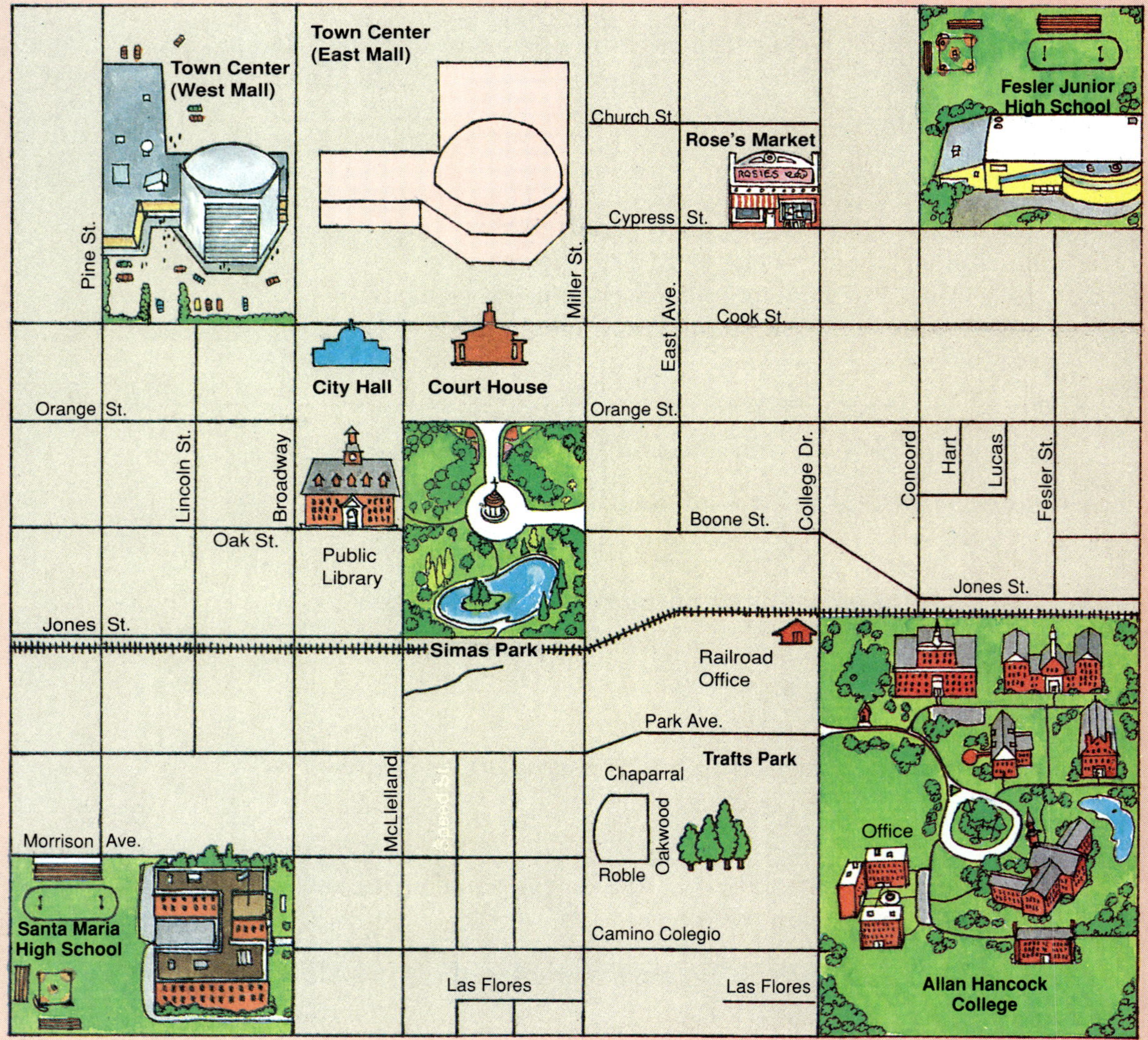

Explore with a Computer

Use the *Graphing and Probability Workshop Project* for this activity.

The Fesler Junior High School marching band is raising money for new uniforms by selling painters' caps. Each cap costs $2. There is a one-time setup fee of $3 for producing all of the caps. The students plan to sell the caps for $2 each.

Cost: $y = 2x + 3$
Price: $y = 2x$

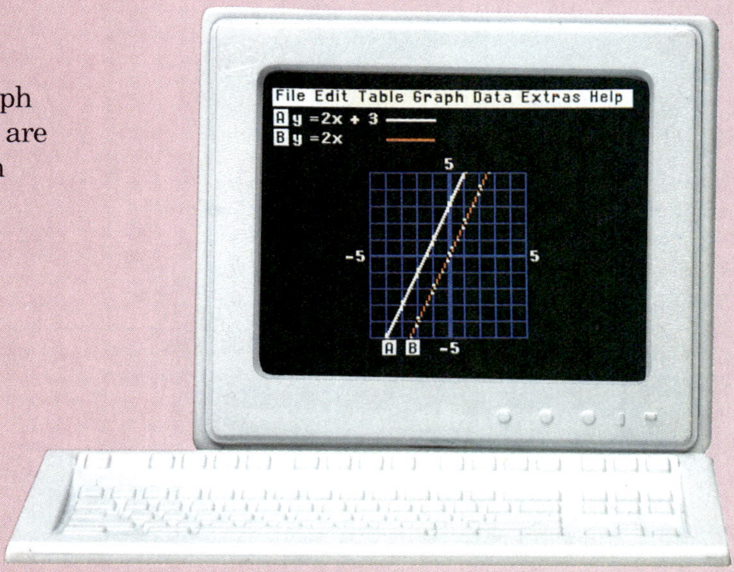

1. At the computer, graph the two equations. How are the graphs similar? Can the marching band earn more money than they spend?

2. Suppose the setup fee increased to $4. In the first equation, change the 3 to a 4 to show this increase. How did the graph change?

3. Suppose they decide to sell the caps for $3 apiece. Change the second equation to show this increase. How did the graph change?

4. How many caps do they have to sell to earn more money than they spend?

Number-Sense Project

Look back at pages 142–143.

1. The following measurements show the growth of an avocado plant.

a. Graph the data.

b. Estimate the height on Day 19. How did you determine this?

c. Estimate the height on Day 23.

DAY	1	13	14	15	16	17	18	20	21	22	26
HEIGHT (mm)	0	0	8	14	20	26	34	49	63	78	160

ALGEBRA

Writing Equations from Graphs

Build Understanding

Cricket chirps are affected by air temperature. In fact, you can estimate the temperature by counting cricket chirps. This relationship is shown on the graph. Write an equation for this line.

c	*t*
0	4
10	9
20	14
50	29

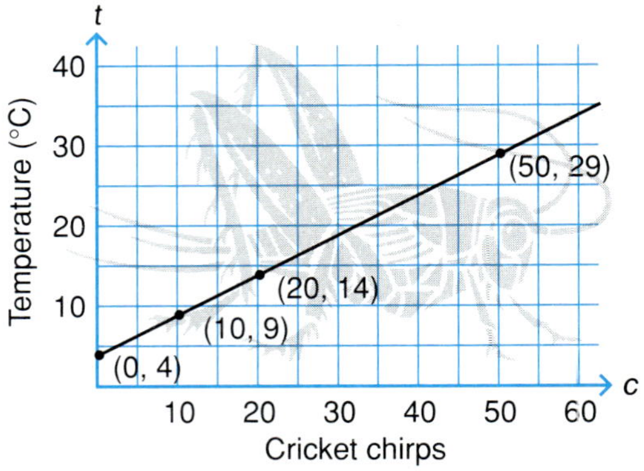

Some species of crickets can chirp up to 200 times per second.

Make a table of chirps (c) and temperature (t) using points on the line.

Now look for a relationship between c and t. The ordered pair (0, 4) shows that when the temperature is 4, there are no chirps. This tells you that 4 will probably appear in the equation.

Notice that when you divide the number of chirps by 2 and add 4, you get the temperature. This suggests $t = \frac{1}{2}c + 4$. Can you find a point on the line whose coordinates do not fit the equation?

Since all points on the graph fit the equation, the equation for the graph is $t = \frac{1}{2}c + 4$.

■ **Talk About Math** If one of the points on a line has coordinates (0, 0), what does this tell you about the equation for the graph?

Check Understanding

For another example, see Set E, pages 176–177.

Write the equations. **Remember** to notice negative signs.

1. Write an equation for the graph.

2. Write an equation that fits the data in the table.

x	0	1	−1	2	3
y	−1	0	−2	1	2

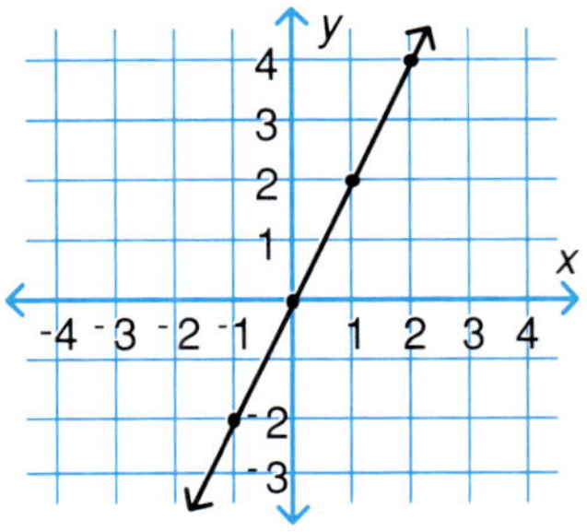

Practice

For More Practice, see Set E, pages 178–179.

For each exercise, write an equation that fits the data in the table or graph.

3.

x	y
−2	2
−1	1
0	0
1	−1
3	−3

4.

x	y
−4	−2
−2	−1
0	0
2	1
4	2

5.

x	y
−2	0
−1	1
0	2
1	3
2	4

6.

x	y
−2	−5
−1	−3
0	−1
2	3
3	5

7.

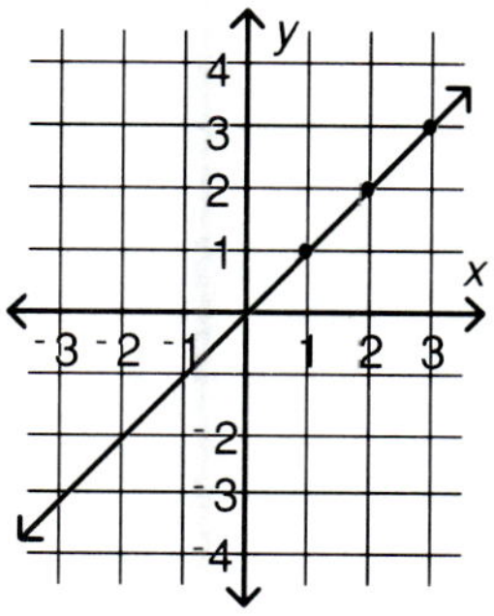

8.

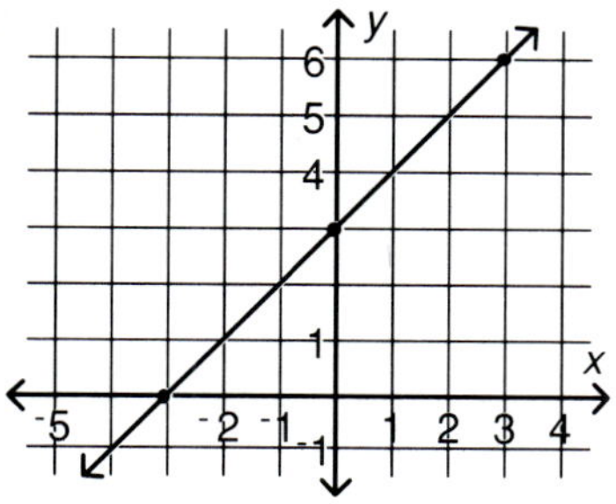

9.

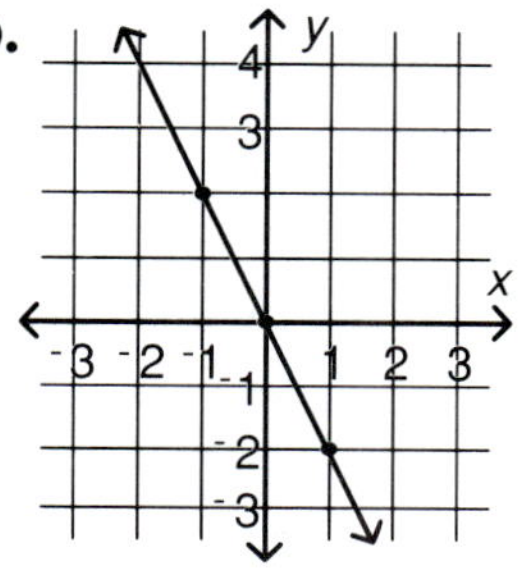

10. Write an equation for a line that goes through the origin and falls from left to right.

11. Write an equation for a line that goes through the origin and rises from left to right.

12. Write an equation for a line parallel to $y = \frac{1}{2}x + 3$. Then graph both equations.

Problem Solving

Air temperature changes with elevation. Suppose it is 0°C at a mountain camp. The graph shows how the temperature (in Celsius) changes as a hiker moves above or below (−) the camp (in meters).

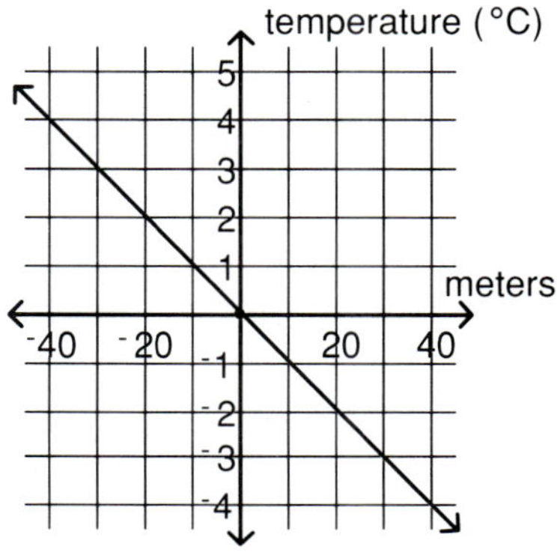

13. Write an equation for the graph.

14. Find the temperature 500 meters above camp.

15. Find the temperature 350 meters below camp.

16. At how many meters from camp does the temperature read −2.5°C?

ALGEBRA

Graphing Inequalities in Four Quadrants

Build Understanding

A. During his first week on the job, Frederico could work no more than 10 hours per week on the computerized grinder. For each additional week of experience, he could work 2 additional hours per week on the grinder. The number of hours Frederico could work on the grinder is given by $h \leq 10 + 2w$. Since neither variable can be negative, graph this inequality in the first quadrant.

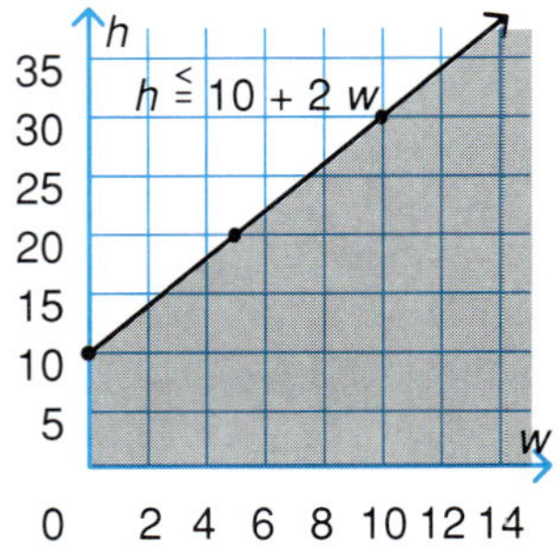

The inequality is a combination of $h = 10 + 2w$ and $h < 10 + 2w$. First graph the equation. Since the equation is part of the inequality, draw a solid line.

Now select points on each side of the line and check to see if they make the inequality true. Try (2, 20). Is $20 \leq 10 + 2(2)$? No. Try (3, 10). Is $10 \leq 10 + 2(3)$? Yes.

Can you find a point in the region below the line that is not a solution? No. Can you find a point above the line that is a solution? No. Shade the area below the line. The line and the shaded region are the graph of $h \leq 10 + 2w$.

B. Graph $y > 2 - x$.

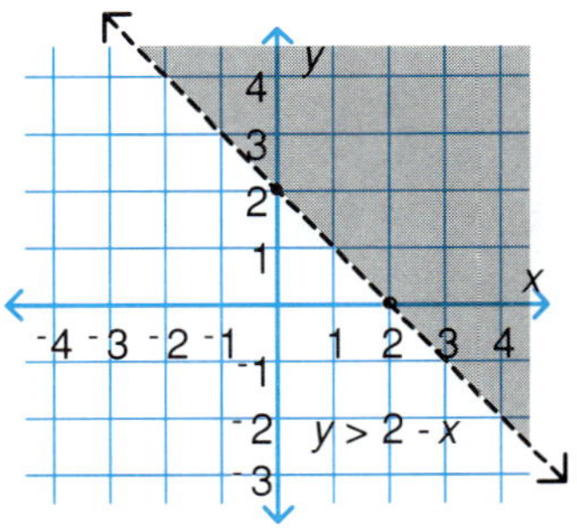

First graph $y = 2 - x$. Since this equation is not part of the inequality, use a dashed line.

(0, 0) is below the line. Is it a solution?
(3, 2) is above the line. Is it a solution?

All points above the line are solutions. Shade the area above the dashed line. The shaded region is the graph of $y > 2 - x$.

■ **Talk About Math** How many points do you need to check in order to determine whether the shaded region is above or below the line?

Check Understanding

For another example, see Set F, pages 176–177.

1. Graph $y < -2x$. Is the line included in the graph?

2. Graph $y \geq x + 1$. Is the line included in the graph?

Practice

For More Practice, see Set F, pages 178–179.

Graph each inequality on a coordinate plane.

3. $y \leq -x$ **4.** $y > x + 3$ **5.** $y \geq x - 1$ **6.** $y < 3x$

7. $y \geq 1 - x$ **8.** $y > 2x + 4$ **9.** $y \leq \frac{1}{2}x$ **10.** $y < -x + 1$

11. $y \leq 4x - 1$ **12.** $y > \frac{1}{4} + x$ **13.** $y \geq 1 - 2x$ **14.** $y < -1 - 2x$

15. $y > \frac{2}{3}x + 1$ **16.** $y < x - 5$ **17.** $y \leq 3x - 2$ **18.** $y \geq 3 - x$

Mixed Practice Graph

19. $y > -2$ on a number line.

20. $y \leq x - 2$ on a coordinate plane.

21. $y \geq 7$ on a number line.

22. $y \geq 7 + x$ on a coordinate plane.

23. $x \leq 7$ and $x > -3$ on a number line.

24. $x \leq 7$ and $x > -3$ on a coordinate plane.

Problem Solving

Solve each problem.

25. During her first week Pam was limited to less than 5 hours on a milling machine. For each additional two weeks of experience, she could use the machine an additional hour per week. Graph $h < 0.5w + 5$.

26. After how many weeks can Pam work on the machine more than 15 hours a week?

27. **Critical Thinking** Graph the inequality $x < -2$ on a number line and on a coordinate plane. In what ways are the graphs similar? In what ways are they different?

TIPS FOR PROBLEM SOLVERS

Compare problems to help you relate new problems to ones you've solved before.

Explore Math

Solve.

28. Graph $y > x$ and $y < 3 - x$ on the same coordinate plane.

29. What does the double-shaded region represent?

30. Give three solutions of $y > x$ and $y < 3 - x$.

31. Describe the graph of $y > x$ or $y < 3 - x$.

ALGEBRA

Translating Figures

Build Understanding

ACTIVITY

A. Sliding on the Grid

Materials: Graph paper, rulers, tracing paper, scissors

a. Draw a coordinate grid. Label each axis from −10 to 10.

b. Draw a figure with vertices $R(-5, 5)$, $S(-3, 2)$, $T(-5, 2)$, and $U(-1, 2)$. Trace the figure on another piece of paper and cut it out. Replace the tracing on $RSTU$. Then slide it 5 units to the right. Copy the figure at the new location. Give the coordinates of the vertices. What happens to the coordinates of the vertices when you move a figure 5 units to the right?

c. Use figure $RSTU$ and its tracing again. What happens to the coordinates of the vertices when you move left? when you move up? when you move down?

B. Lucia is playing a video game that involves moving the "video ghost" left, right, up, or down. How can she move from the green ghost to the red ghost?

First ***translate*** (slide) $\triangle LMN$ 5 units down by subtracting 5 from each y-coordinate. Use the rule $(x, y) \rightarrow (x, y - 5)$.

$L(-3, 2) \rightarrow L'(-3, -3)$
$M(-2, 1) \rightarrow M'(-2, -4)$
$N(-4, 1) \rightarrow N'(-4, -4)$

Read L' as "L prime."

Now translate $\triangle L'M'N'$ 4 units right by adding 4 to each x-coordinate. Use the rule $(x, y) \rightarrow (x + 4, y)$.

$L'(-3, -3) \rightarrow L''(1, -3)$
$M'(-2, -4) \rightarrow M''(2, -4)$
$N'(-4, -4) \rightarrow N''(0, -4)$

Read L'' as "L double prime."

$\triangle L''M''N''$ is a ***translation*** of $\triangle LMN$ using the rule $(x, y) \rightarrow (x + 4, y - 5)$.

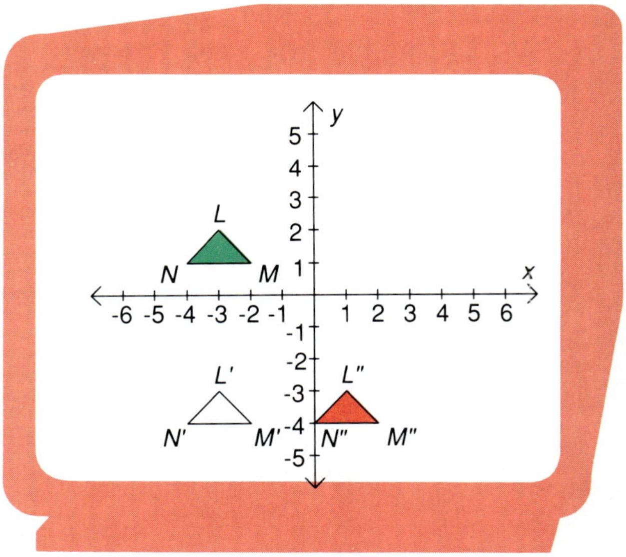

BASIC programmers use a grid system to move video game figures across the screen.

■ **Talk About Math** Describe a way Lucia can move the green ghost so that it touches the other two ghosts. Give the rule for this translation.

Check Understanding

For another example, see Set G, pages 176–177.

Draw a coordinate grid and label each axis from −6 to 6. Graph point G with coordinates (3, −2). For each exercise, translate point G as indicated. Label the new point and give its coordinates.

1. P: right 3 units **2.** Q: left 4 units **3.** R: up 4 units

4. S: down 1 unit **5.** T: left 5 units and up 5 units

Practice

For More Practice, see Set G, pages 178–179.

Give the rule for the translation.

6. Pentagon $ABCDE$ to $A'B'C'D'E'$

7. Rectangle $JKLM$ to $J'K'L'M'$

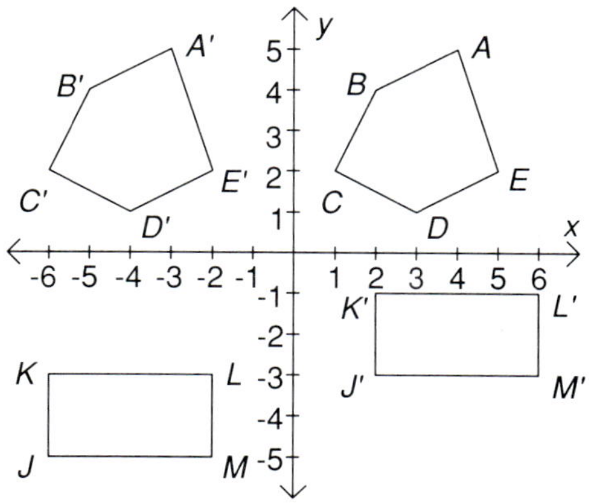

Copy the figure on a coordinate grid and translate it using the given rule.

8. $ABCDE$ using $(x, y) \rightarrow (x, y - 7)$

9. $JKLM$ using $(x, y) \rightarrow (x + 4, y + 8)$

Draw a triangle with vertices $P(3, -5)$, $Q(4, -3)$, and $R(6, -4)$ on a coordinate grid. Translate it using the given rule. Label the resulting figure $P'Q'R'$.

10. $(x, y) \rightarrow (x - 4, y + 2)$ **11.** $(x, y) \rightarrow (x + 1, y - 1)$ **12.** $(x, y) \rightarrow (x - 7, y + 5)$

Draw a square with vertices $W(-3, 4)$, $X(0, 4)$, $Y(0, 1)$ and $Z(-3, 1)$ on a coordinate grid. Translate it using the given rule. Label the resulting figure $W'X'Y'Z'$.

13. $(x, y) \rightarrow (x + 2, y - 3)$ **14.** $(x, y) \rightarrow (x - 5, y + 1)$ **15.** $(x, y) \rightarrow (x + 4, y + 4)$

Problem Solving

Give a rule that will move the video ghost from the first color to the second.

16. Red to blue **17.** Blue to black

18. Purple to blue **19.** Yellow to red

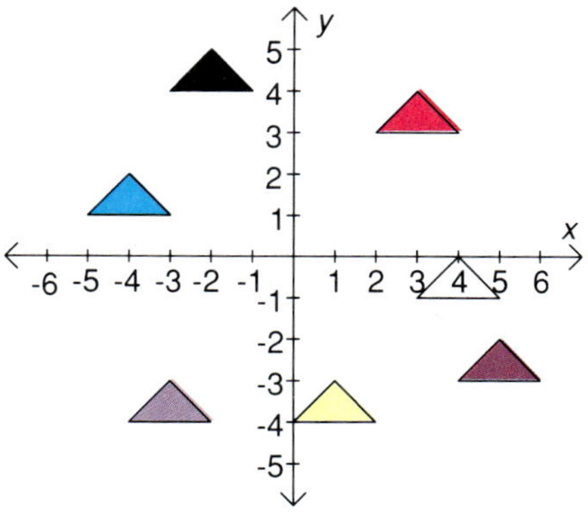

Where will the red video ghost be after these moves?

20. Right 1, down 4; then right 1, down 2

21. Left 7, up 1; then right 1, down 8

ALGEBRA

Reflections and Rotations

Build Understanding

Geometric figures like the one at the right appear in some art of the Kuba people in west central Africa. Designs made from such figures are used to decorate clothing, carved masks, and shields. Many of the patterns that are used can be made by applying translations, reflections, or rotations to geometric figures.

ACTIVITY

A. Pattern Folding

Materials: Tracing paper

a. Make a coordinate grid. Trace the triangular figure at the right in the first quadrant. Fold the paper on the y-axis as shown and trace the image in the second quadrant. The two figures are ***reflections*** of one another over the y-axis.

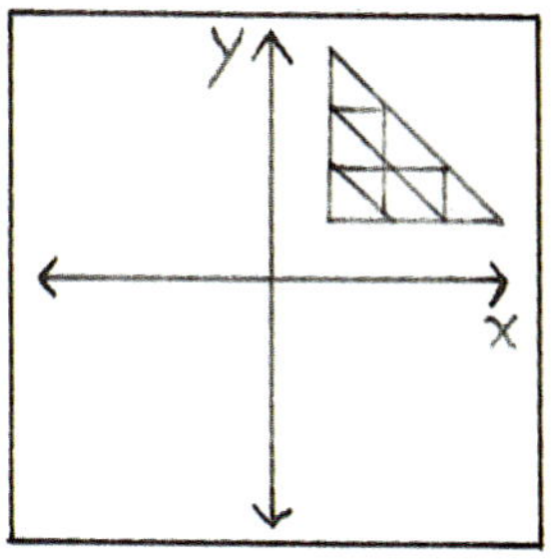

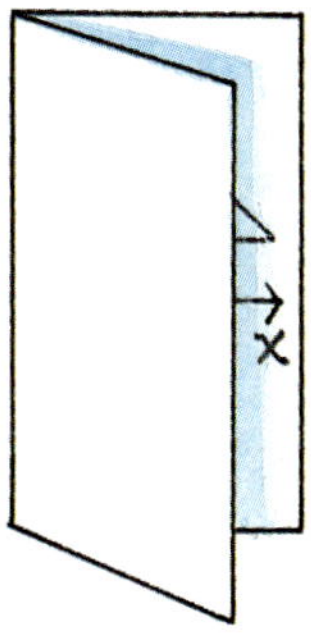

b. Label $\triangle ABC$ as shown. Reflect A, B, and C over the y-axis by folding and marking the images in the second quadrant. Label the reflections A', B', and C'. Compare the coordinates of a point and its reflection over the y-axis.

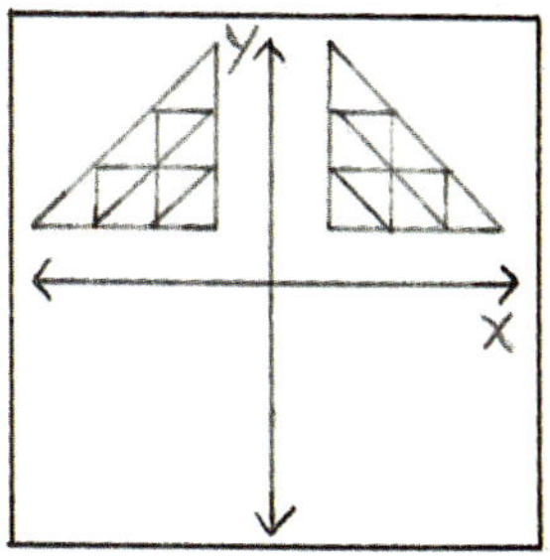

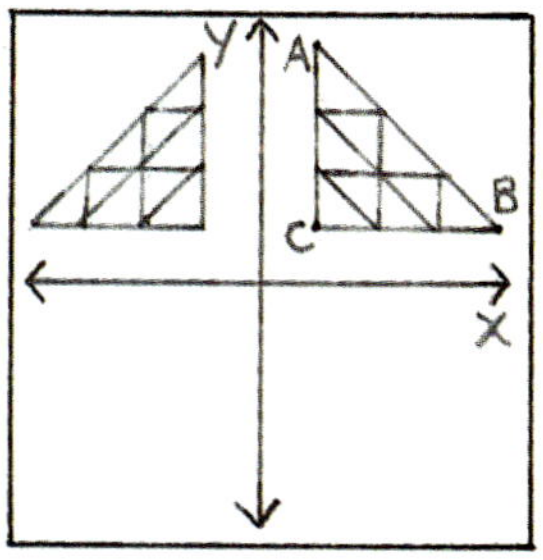

c. Repeat step b, this time reflecting A', B', and C' over the x-axis to find A'', B'', and C''. Then reflect A'', B'', and C'' over the y-axis to find A''', B''', and C'''. Finally, reflect A''', B''', and C''' over the x-axis.

d. What do you notice about the coordinates of points reflected over the y-axis? over the x-axis? What happened when A''', B''', and C''' were reflected over the x-axis?

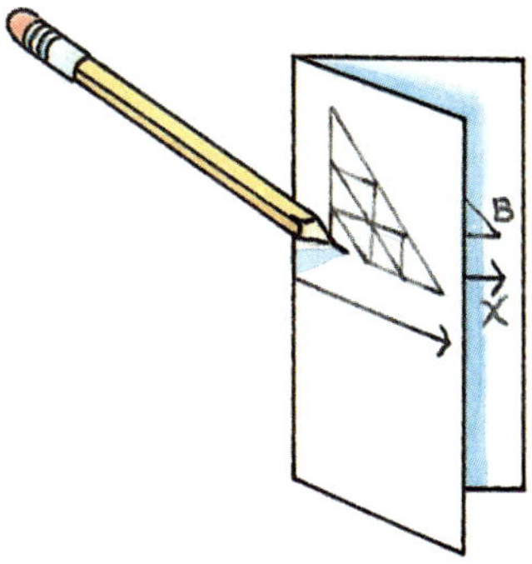

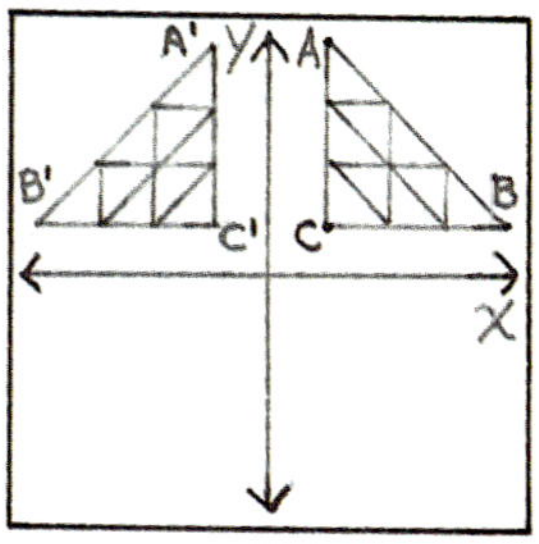

B. Spinning Around Zero
Materials: Paper, scissors, brass fastener or pin

a. Draw a coordinate grid and any triangle, KLM, with vertex K at the origin and side KL on the x-axis. Make a pattern of $\triangle KLM$ and cut it out. Attach vertex K at the origin with a fastener. Then rotate the triangle around the origin. Trace various positions on the grid.

b. $\triangle K'L'M'$ is a 90° counterclockwise ***rotation*** of $\triangle KLM$. Rotate your triangle 90° and give the coordinates of the vertices. Compare them to the coordinates of K, L, and M. What do you notice?

c. $\triangle K''L''M''$ is a 180° rotation of $\triangle KLM$. Rotate your triangle 180° and give the coordinates.

d. Predict the coordinates of each of these rotations of $\triangle KLM$: 270° counterclockwise, 90° clockwise, and 360° rotation. Rotate your triangle to check your predictions.

e. As $\triangle KLM$ is rotated around the origin, what figure is formed by point L? by point M? Draw these figures on your grid.

f. $\triangle K''L''M''$ is a 180° rotation of $\triangle KLM$. Show how you can reflect $\triangle KLM$ to get $\triangle K''L''M''$. Hint: You might have to reflect $\triangle KLM$ more than once.

Translations, reflections, and rotations transform one figure into another. They are called ***transformations.***

Talk About Math Why do you think translations, reflections, and rotations are often called *slides, flips,* and *turns?*

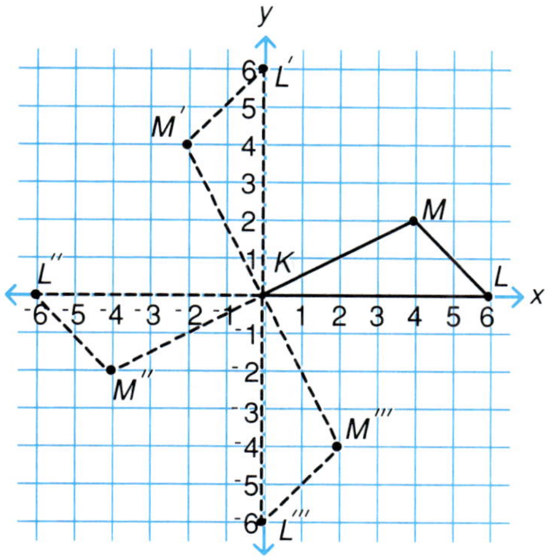

Since point K does not move, K', K'', and K''' also have coordinates (0, 0).

This carved wooden mask is from the Congo. Called a *shene malula* mask, it was worn by the *babende,* those who performed police functions in each village.

Check Understanding

For another example, see Set H, pages 176–177.

Use the Math Sketcher for Exercises 1–3.

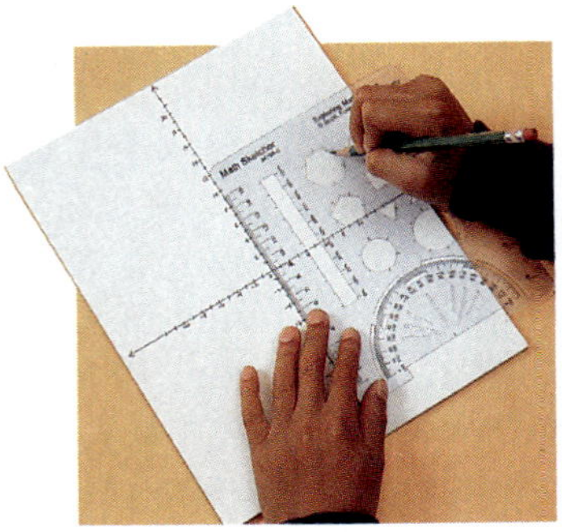

1. On a coordinate grid copy one of the figures given on the Math Sketcher. Give the coordinates of the vertices or the center.

2. Reflect the figure over the x-axis and give the new coordinates. Repeat, using the y-axis. Then give a rule for reflecting over each axis.

3. Copy another figure from the Math Sketcher. Rotate it 90° clockwise around the origin. Give the new coordinates. Repeat, rotating it 180° counterclockwise.

Practice

For More Practice, see Set H, pages 178–179.

Copy the figure on a coordinate grid and draw the new figure on the same grid. Give the original and the new coordinates.

4. Reflect over the x-axis.

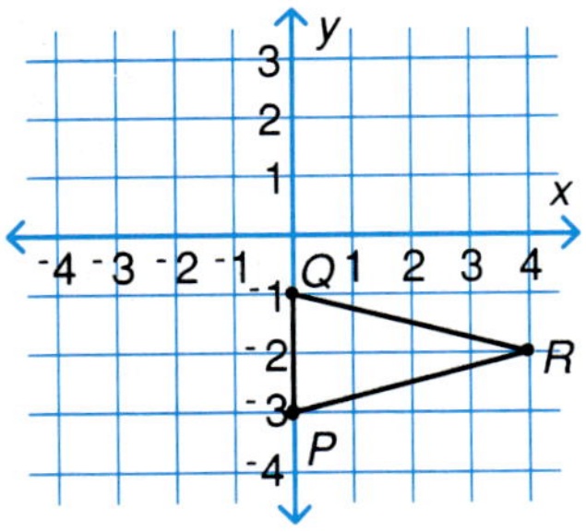

5. Reflect over the y-axis.

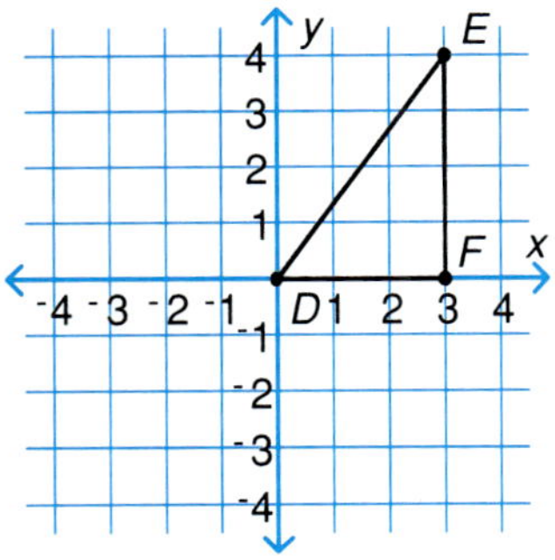

6. Reflect over the dotted line.

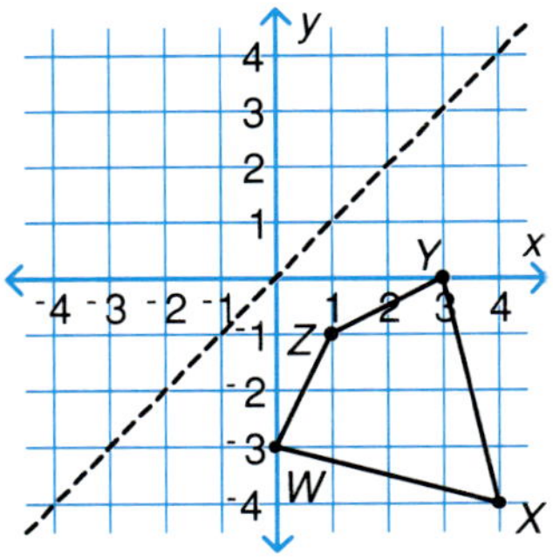

Copy $\triangle DEF$ from Exercise 5.

7. Rotate $\triangle DEF$ 90° clockwise about D to get $\triangle D'E'F'$.

8. Now rotate $\triangle D'E'F'$ 90° clockwise about D' to get $\triangle D''E''F''$.

9. How could you rotate $\triangle DEF$ to get $\triangle D''E''F''$?

10. How could you rotate $\triangle DEF$ so it fits back on itself?

11. Two reflections over two perpendicular lines give the same result as a 180° rotation. Show that this is true with $\triangle DEF$.

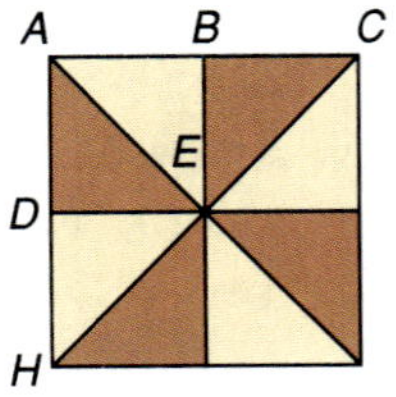

Use the figure at the right. Give a transformation that moves triangle DEH onto triangle

12. BEA.

13. BCE.

14. DEA.

Draw $\triangle PQR$ with vertices $P(4, -2)$, $Q(0, 2)$, and $R(-4, -2)$. Perform each transformation. Draw the new triangle and give its coordinates.

15. Rotate $\triangle PQR$ 90°clockwise about the origin.

16. Rotate $\triangle PQR$ 180° about the origin.

17. **Number Sense** How many degrees do you have to rotate $\triangle PQR$ before it fits back on itself?

Problem Solving

Solve.

This Navajo rug is in the Two Gray Hills style. These rugs are noted for their high quality and geometric designs.

18. **Critical Thinking** If you rotate a figure around its center and it fits back on itself in less than a 360° rotation, the figure has ***point symmetry.*** Find a polygon that has point symmetry.

19. **Visual Thinking** If you reflect a figure over a line through its center and it fits back on itself, the figure has ***reflection symmetry.*** The line over which you reflect the figure to fit back on itself is called a ***line of symmetry.*** Look at the *shene malula* mask on page 169. Does the mask appear to have reflection symmetry? If so, identify the line of symmetry.

20. The figures at the right are used by some Navajo rug weavers. Draw one of these figures on a coordinate grid and use translations, reflections, and rotations to create a design of your own. Describe each transformation you use.

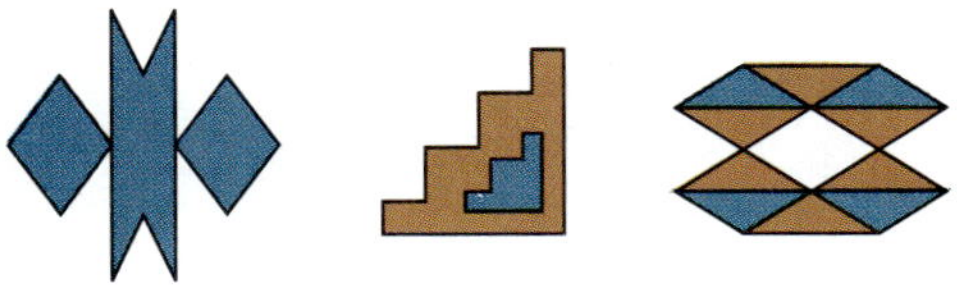

Explore Math

Solve.

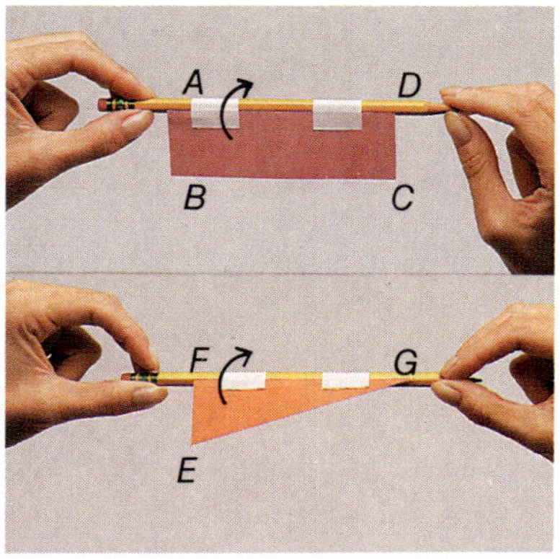

21. Cut rectangle $ABCD$ out of heavy paper and tape side AD to a straw or pencil. Rotate the pencil. What figure is suggested by the rotation of point C? point D? the entire rectangle?

22. Repeat Exercise 21 using a right triangle EFG with side FG taped to the pencil. What figure is suggested by the point E? point G? the entire triangle?

Dilations

Build Understanding

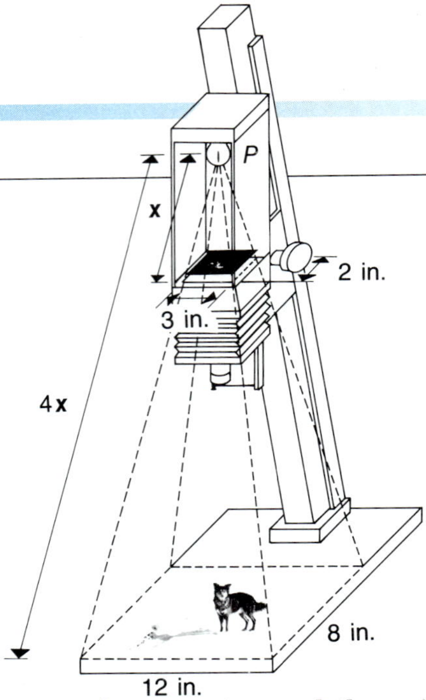

A. Joe Lukins, a professional photographer, uses an enlarger like the one shown to make prints from negatives.

The diagram shows how Joe makes an 8-in. by 12-in. picture from a 2-in. by 3-in. negative. Notice that on each ray from the light source (point P), the distance of the negative is one-fourth the distance of the print from the light.

The negative and the picture are similar but not congruent. A transformation that changes the size but not the shape of a figure is a ***dilation.***

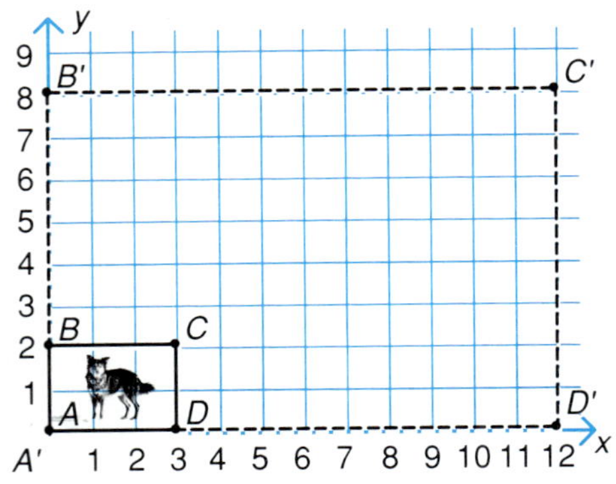

B. Represent the negative and the print on a coordinate grid. Compare the lengths of the corresponding sides. Give a rule for the dilation.

Both the length and the width of rectangle $A'B'C'D'$ are 4 times that of rectangle $ABCD$. The rule is: (x, y) becomes $(4x, 4y)$.

Notice that the area of rectangle $A'B'C'D'$ is 4×4, or 16 times the area of rectangle $ABCD$.

Talk About Math Give a rule for reducing the size of a figure.

Check Understanding

1. Give a rule for the dilation of $\triangle LMN$ to $\triangle L'M'N'$.

2. Draw any rectangle on a coordinate grid. Then draw a dilation using the rule: (x, y) becomes $(2x, 2y)$. Compare their coordinates.

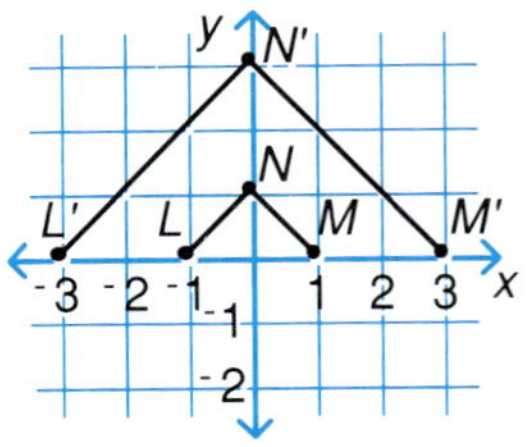

Practice

On a coordinate grid draw a rectangle with vertices $A(-4, 2)$, $B(-4, 4)$, $C(2, 4)$, $D(2, 2)$. Use this figure for Exercises 3–8.

3. Dilate rectangle $ABCD$ using the rule (x, y) becomes $(3x, 3y)$. Label the new figure $A'B'C'D'$.

4. Compare the lengths of the sides of rectangle $ABCD$ and $A'B'C'D'$. Then compare the areas.

5. Now dilate rectangle $ABCD$ using the rule (x, y) becomes $(\frac{1}{2}x, \frac{1}{2}y)$. Label the new figure $A''B''C''D''$.

6. Compare the lengths of the sides of rectangles $ABCD$ and $A''B''C''D''$. Then compare the areas.

7. Give the new coordinates when rectangle $ABCD$ is dilated using the rule (x, y) becomes $(12x, 12y)$.

8. Give the new coordinates when rectangle $ABCD$ is dilated using (x, y) becomes $(0.25x, 0.25y)$.

Mixed Practice Name the triangle that is a result of the transformation.

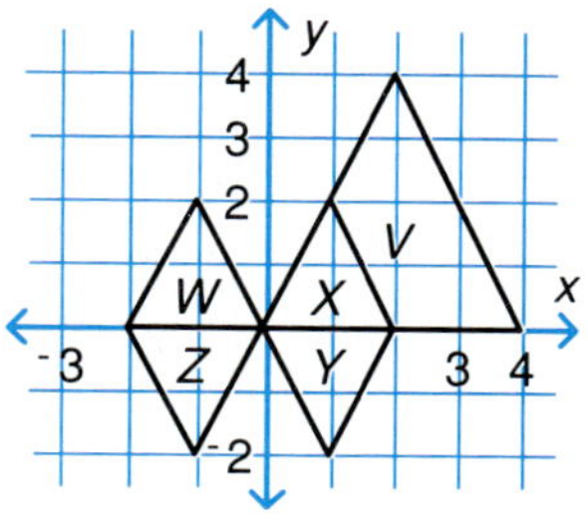

9. A translation of $\triangle X$

10. A dilation of $\triangle X$

11. A 180° rotation of $\triangle X$ about (0, 0)

12. Two reflections of $\triangle X$

Problem Solving

For a print 5 times the size of a negative, the distance between the light source and the negative is one fifth of the distance between the light source and the print. A 2.5-in. by 3.5-in. negative is 4 in. from the light. Find the distance between the negative and the print for the given print sizes.

13. 10 in. by 14 in.

14. 5 in. by 7 in.

15. 15 in. by 21 in.

16. Draw a triangle on a coordinate grid with vertices $P(0, 0)$, $Q(0, 8)$, $R(4, 0)$. Rotate it clockwise 90° about the origin. Reflect that rotation over the y-axis. Dilate the reflection using the rule (x, y) becomes $(0.5x, 0.5y)$. Slide the dilation up 4 units. Then slide the dilation up 4 more units. What object does your figure look like?

Skills Review

Graph each equation or inequality on a number line.

1. $x > -3$

2. $n + 4 = 2$

3. $f \leq 4$ and $f \geq -1$

4. $m > 1$ or $m = 0$

Write each solution set as an inequality. You may want to draw a graph.

5. $p + 4 > -1$

6. $7x \leq 14$

7. $k - 6 < 0$

8. $\frac{1}{2}r \geq -2$

Graph each equation.

9. $y = -2x$

10. $y = -x + 2$

Graph each pair of equations on the same coordinate grid. If the lines intersect, describe the point of intersection.

11. $y = x + 4$
$y = x - 2$

12. $y = -2x$
$y = x - 3$

Write an equation for the table.

13.

x	−1	0	1	2	3
y	4	0	−4	−8	−12

Graph each inequality on a coordinate grid.

14. $y < 2x + 2$

15. $y \geq x + 2$

Use parallelogram *ABCD* for each exercise.

16. Draw *ABCD* on a coordinate grid. $A(1, 1)$, $B(2, 3)$, $C(5, 3)$, $D(4, 1)$

17. Translate *ABCD* so that (x, y) becomes $(x + 2, y + 1)$.

18. Reflect *ABCD* over the y-axis.

19. Dilate *ABCD* using the rule (x, y) becomes $(2x, 2y)$.

Problem-Solving Review

Solve each problem.

20. A climber is at least halfway up a mountain that is 2.5 miles high. Write an inequality to express the height the climber has reached.

21. Two joggers ran 6 miles and have at least 2.5 miles more to go. What is the length of their route?

22. A gondola takes skiers to the top of Powder Peak. Graph the equation, $y = x + 1$, to show the gondola's path. A tow rope takes skiers up Peter Rabbit Path. Graph the equation, $y = \frac{1}{2}x - 2$, to show the path of the tow rope. Which path is steeper?

23. Two numbers, one 2 times greater than the other, have a sum of −12. What are the numbers?

24. Val and Sal started doing sit-ups the same day. Val did 30 and Sal did 20. Every day Val did 3 more sit-ups than the day before, and Sal did 5 more than the day before. On which day did Sal begin doing more sit-ups than Val?

25. Write an equation for a line parallel to the line expressed by the equation $y = 2x + 2$.

26. **Data File** Use the data on pages 252–253. Write an equation to find the number of furlongs in $3\frac{3}{4}$ miles. Solve the equation.

27. **Make a Data File** Find out the membership costs and rental fees for at least two video stores. Make a multiple line graph to display your findings.

Cumulative Skills Review • Chapters 1–5

Use the standard order of operations to compute.

1. $15 \div 3 + 2$ **2.** $6 \times 4 + 25 \div 5$ **3.** $9 + 7 - 8 \div 4$ **4.** $(5 + 4) \times 6 - 10$

5. $(13 - 6)^2 - 5$ **6.** $1 + \frac{2 \times 9}{6}$ **7.** $\frac{2^2 + 8}{3 + 1} - 3$ **8.** $\frac{64}{4} - 9$

Find the greatest common factor (GCF) and the least common multiple (LCM) for each pair of numbers.

9. 12 and 15 **10.** 20 and 8 **11.** 29 and 18 **12.** 36 and 24

Write each mixed number as an improper fraction. Write each improper fraction as a mixed number or a whole number.

13. $20\frac{3}{7}$ **14.** $9\frac{5}{8}$ **15.** $14\frac{9}{10}$ **16.** $10\frac{7}{12}$

17. $\frac{115}{5}$ **18.** $\frac{100}{9}$ **19.** $\frac{222}{11}$ **20.** $\frac{49}{4}$

Compare each pair of integers. Write < or >.

21. $-4 \;\square\; 0$ **22.** $6 \;\square\; -6$ **23.** $-19 \;\square\; 8$ **24.** $-17 \;\square\; -12$

Multiply or divide.

25. $-40 \div (-8)$ **26.** $(8)(-5)$ **27.** $880 \div (-20)$ **28.** $20(-40)$

29. $0.9(-0.7)$ **30.** $\frac{11}{15}\left(-\frac{15}{11}\right)$ **31.** $-\frac{5}{7} \div \left(-\frac{5}{8}\right)$ **32.** $-3.6 \div 3$

Evaluate each expression when $x = -4$, $y = \frac{4}{5}$, and $z = 5$.

33. $x - z$ **34.** yz **35.** $\frac{x}{z}$ **36.** $x(x + z)$

37. $2y$ **38.** $(z - x)^2$ **39.** $5y + 5z$ **40.** $(z \div x)y$

Graph each inequality on a number line.

41. $m < 1$ **42.** $n \geq 0$ **43.** $b > -1$ and $b < 1$ **44.** $r = 3$ or $r < 2$

Write each solution set as an inequality.

45. $p + 1 > 4$ **46.** $4w < 12$ **47.** $\frac{t}{2} < 8$ **48.** $c - 7 < 3$

49. $12 > 1.5z$ **50.** $\frac{f}{4} + 9 < 10$ **51.** $16 > s + 7$ **52.** $\frac{1}{3}g > 18$

Tell whether each pair of equations is parallel or intersects.

53. $y = 2x + 1$, $y = x + 1$ **54.** $y = 3x - 5$, $y = 3x + 5$ **55.** $y = 2x + 2$, $y = \frac{x}{2}$ **56.** $y = x - 1$, $y = x - 6$

Reteaching

Set A pages 144–147

To graph the solution set of an inequality, begin with a number line.

Graph $x \geq 3$.

Draw a closed circle at 3. 3 is included.

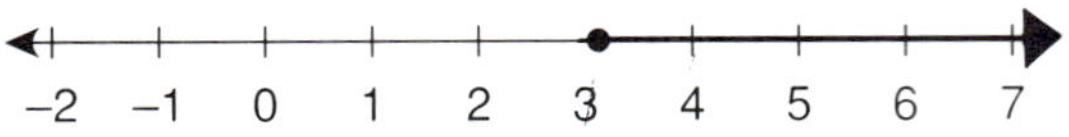

Shade in all numbers to the right of, or greater than, 3.

Remember use an open circle when the number is not a solution and a closed circle when it is.

Graph.

1. $y < -2$ **2.** $x \geq 0$ **3.** $x \leq 2$

4. $b \geq -3$ **5.** $y + 3 = 7$ **6.** $x \geq 2$ and $x \leq -1$

7. $y > 3.5$ or $y \leq -1.5$

8. $x < 3$ and $x < -2$

Set B pages 148–149

To solve an inequality by graphing, first solve the related equation. Then test which numbers solve the inequality.

Solve $t + 7 \geq 3$ by graphing.

The numbers to the right are solutions.

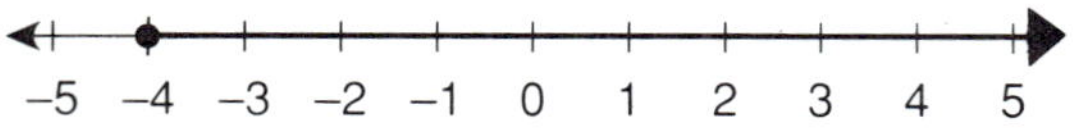

−4 is a solution.

Remember to use an open circle when the solution to the related equation is not a solution to the inequality.

Solve. Draw a graph to help you.

1. $x + 6 < 5$ **2.** $y - 2 \geq 1$

3. $-2x > 4$ **4.** $5x \leq 10$

5. $-3x \geq 9$ **6.** $4 + y \leq 1.1$

7. $x - 4 > -3$ **8.** $-1y \geq 5$

Set C pages 152–155

To graph an equation on the coordinate plane, make a table. Then graph the points.

Remember the first coordinate of each ordered pair is the *x*-coordinate, or distance along the horizontal axis. The second coordinate is the *y*-coordinate, or the distance along the vertical axis.

Plot the points on the same coordinate grid and connect them in order. Then connect point *F* to point *A*.

1. $A(0, 3)$ **2.** $B(3, 1)$ **3.** $C(3, -1)$

4. $D(0, -3)$ **5.** $E(-3, -1)$ **6.** $F(-3, 1)$

Graph each equation.

7. $y = 2x$ **8.** $y = -2x$ **9.** $y = 4x$

Set D pages 156–157

To graph a pair of equations on the same coordinate plane, make a table of values for each equation and then graph the equations.

Remember to choose *x*-values that are easy to evaluate. Then find the corresponding *y*-values.

Graph each pair of equations on the same coordinate grid.

1. $y = 3x$, $y = -3x$ **2.** $y = x + 4$, $y = 2x - 1$

3. $x = 2$, $y = 3$ **4.** $y = 0$, $y = -3$

Set E pages 162–163

To write an equation for a table, look for a relationship between x and y.

x	-2	-1	0	2	4
y	-7	-5	-3	1	5

Since $y = -3$ when $x = 0$, -3 will appear in the equation. Try doubling each value and subtracting 3. The rule is $y = 2x - 3$.

Remember to use the y-value for $x = 0$ to help decide if something is added to or subtracted from x.

Write an equation that fits the data.

1.

x	-4	-2	0	1	3
y	-8	-4	0	2	6

2.

x	-3	-1	0	2	4
y	6	4	3	1	-1

Set F pages 164–165

To graph an inequality in the plane, graph the related equation and check points to see which ones are on the graph. Shade above or below the line.

Remember to use a dashed line if the equation is not part of the inequality.

Graph each inequality

1. $y \leq 3x$

2. $y > 2x + 1$

3. $y < -x + 1$

4. $y \geq -x + 1$

5. $y \leq -\frac{1}{2}x$

6. $y > 3 - x$

Set G pages 166–167

To write a rule for a translation, see how the coordinates change. Then write a rule.

To move the triangle, 8 is subtracted from each x and 2 is added to each y. Use the rule $(x, y) \rightarrow (x - 8, y + 2)$.

Remember that each coordinate changes by the same amount.

1. Give the rule for the translation of $ABCD$ to $A'B'C'D'$.

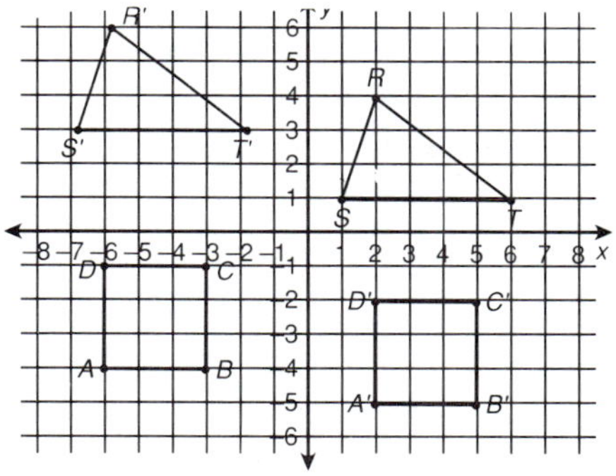

Set H pages 168–171

The rule for reflecting coordinates over the x-axis is $(x, y) \rightarrow (x, -y)$. The rule for reflecting coordinates over the y-axis is $(x, y) \rightarrow (-x, y)$.

Remember that reflecting a figure over the x-axis means the same as flipping it over the x-axis.

1. Copy triangle RST in Set G. Reflect it over the x-axis. Draw the figure and give the new coordinates.

2. Copy square $ABCD$ in Set G. Reflect it over the y-axis. Draw the figure and give the new coordinates.

3. Draw triangle MNO with coordinates $O(0, 0)$, $M(4, 0)$, and $N(4, 3)$. Rotate it counterclockwise 90° about point O and give the new coordinates.

More Practice

Set A pages 144–147

Graph each inequality on a number line.

1. $y \geq -4$ **2.** $x \leq -7$ **3.** $x > -2$ **4.** $b < 4$

5. $a \geq 2$ or $a \leq 1$ **6.** $b < 4$ and $b < 3$ **7.** $c > -3$ and $c \leq 4$

8. $w \leq -3$ or $w \geq 1$ **9.** $m > 3$ or $m = 0$ **10.** $z > 3$ and $z < -2$

11. $n > -4$ or $n \leq 2$ **12.** $u \leq 9$ and $u \geq 0$ **13.** $x > -1$ and $x = 3$

Set B pages 148–149

Write each solution set as an inequality. Draw a graph to help you.

1. $x + 3 > 4$ **2.** $w - 4 \leq -2$ **3.** $-6 > p + 1$ **4.** $8y \leq 24$

5. $5 + a < 2.4$ **6.** $-4a \leq -12$ **7.** $\frac{1}{2}m > -1$ **8.** $n - 4 > -11$

9. $3x \geq -3$ **10.** $k - 5 < 7$ **11.** $\frac{3}{5}n \leq 4$ **12.** $c + 8 \geq 3$

Set C pages 152–155

Plot the points on the same coordinate grid and connect them in order. Connect point F with point A.

1. $A(2, 0)$ **2.** $B(2, 4)$ **3.** $C(3, 4)$ **4.** $D(3, 1)$ **5.** $E(5, 1)$ **6.** $F(5, 0)$

Name the quadrant or axis in which each point is located. Do not graph the point.

7. $(23, 17)$ **8.** $(0, 32)$ **9.** $(-12, -3)$ **10.** $(0, 25)$ **11.** $(-12, 18)$ **12.** $(-4, 0)$

Graph each equation.

13. $y = -2x$ **14.** $y = \frac{1}{2}x$ **15.** $y = 2x + 1$ **16.** $y = -3x - 4$

Set D pages 156–157

Graph each pair of equations on the same coordinate grid.

1. $y = 3x$, $y = x + 1$ **2.** $y = x + 3$, $y = 2x - 4$ **3.** $y = 4$, $y = -3$ **4.** $y = 3 + x$, $y = 2 - x$

Do not graph these equations. Tell whether they are parallel or they intersect.

5. $y = 2x + 1$, $y = 2x - 3$ **6.** $y = 3x + 5$, $y = 2x + 5$ **7.** $y = 12x - 13$, $y = 12x + 14$ **8.** $y = 24$, $y = 2x + 1$

9. $y = \frac{x}{2} + 8$, $y = \frac{x}{2} - 8$ **10.** $y = -2x$, $y = -2x + 9$ **11.** $y = 4x - 6$, $y = -4x$ **12.** $y = 3x + 42$, $y = \frac{x}{3} + 42$

Set E pages 162–163

Write an equation for the table or graph.

1.

x	−2	−1	0	1	2
y	−5	−4	−3	−2	−1

2.

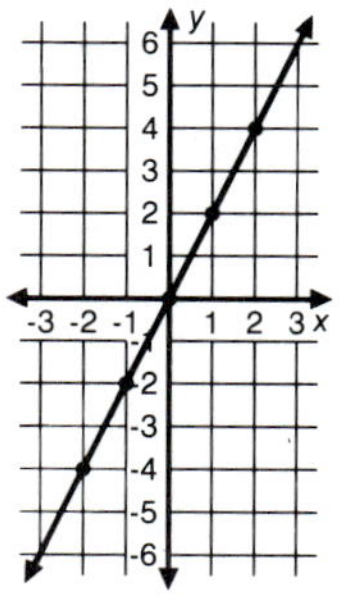

3.

x	−4	−2	0	2	4
y	−1	0	1	2	3

4.

x	−2	−1	0	1	2
y	−4	−2	0	2	4

5.

x	−2	−1	0	1	2
y	−7	−4	−1	2	5

6.

x	−6	−3	0	3	6
y	−1	0	1	2	3

7.

x	−2	−1	0	1	2
y	0	1	2	3	4

Set F pages 164–165

Graph each inequality on a coordinate grid.

1. $y \leq x$

2. $y > x + 1$

3. $y \geq 2x$

4. $y < 2x + 1$

5. $y \geq -2x$

6. $y \leq 3x - 2$

7. $y > -x + 3$

8. $y < 2 - x$

Set G pages 166–167

1. Give the rule for translation of rectangle $ABCD$ to $A'B'C'D'$.

2. Give the rule for the translation of triangle RST to $R'S'T'$.

3. Copy $ABCD$ on a coordinate grid and translate it so that (x, y) becomes $(x + 6, y - 3)$.

4. Copy triangle RST on a coordinate grid and translate it so that (x, y) becomes $(x, y + 2)$.

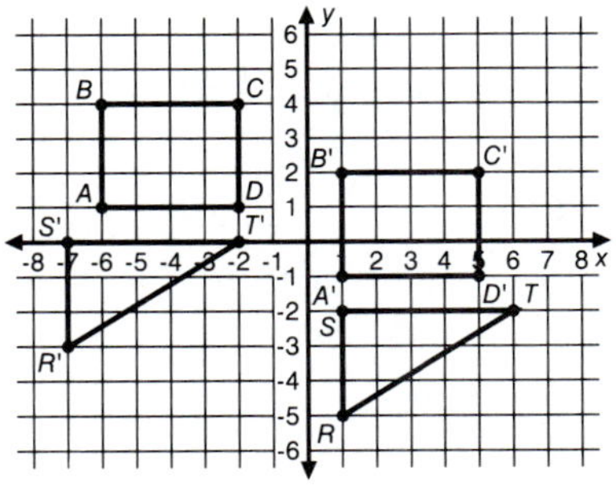

Set H pages 168–171

1. Copy rectangle $ABCD$ above. Reflect it over the x-axis. Draw the figure and give its new coordinates.

2. Copy rectangle $ABCD$ above. Reflect it over the y-axis. Draw the figure and give its new coordinates.

3. Copy triangle RST above. Rotate it 90° clockwise to get $R'S'T'$.

4. Now rotate $R'S'T'$ 90° clockwise to get $R''S''T''$.

5. How could you rotate RST to get $R''S''T''$?

Enrichment

Solving Inequalities

Inequalities can be solved by the same methods you use to solve equations. Use inverse operations to isolate the variable on one side of the inequality.

Solve.
$3x + 7 > 13$

Subtract 7.
$3x + 7 - 7 > 13 - 7$
$3x > 6$

Divide by 3.
$\frac{3x}{3} > \frac{6}{3}$

Solution
$x > 2$

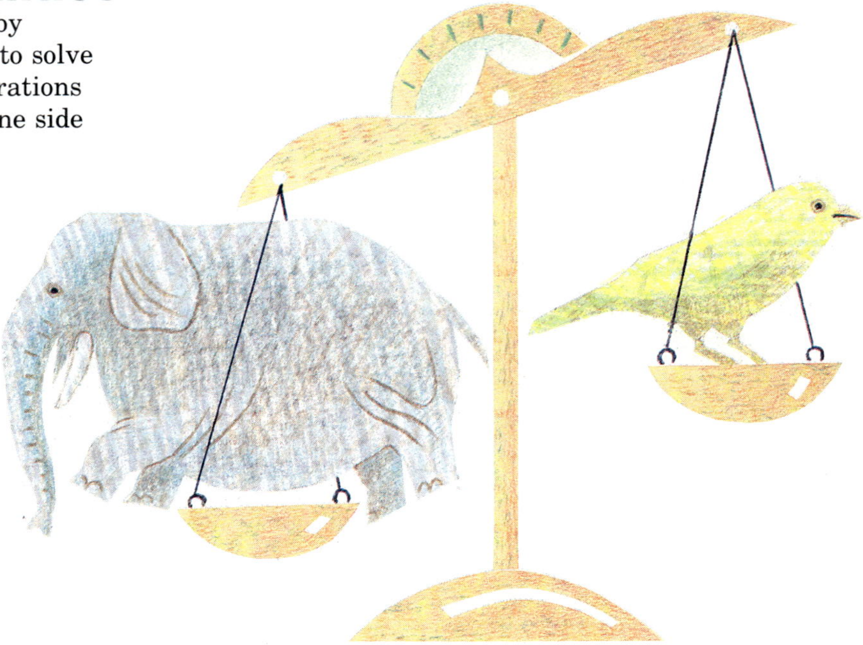

Solve each inequality.

1. $6x > 30$ **2.** $x - 9 \leq 21$ **3.** $\frac{n}{7} \geq 4$ **4.** $k + 11 < 15$

5. $3p - 5 > 25$ **6.** $13 \leq \frac{h}{4} + 6$ **7.** $8 + 5y > 21$ **8.** $17 < 12c + 5$

Notice what happens if you multiply or divide both sides of an inequality by a negative number:

	$6 < 7$			**$10 > 8$**
Multiply by −3:	**$-3(6)$? $-3(7)$**	**Direction of inequality changes**	**Divide by −2:**	**$\frac{10}{-2}$? $\frac{8}{-2}$**
	$-18 > -21$			**$-5 < -4$**

Reverse the direction of an inequality if you multiply or divide both sides of the inequality by a negative number.

Solve: **$-8x \leq 24$**
Divide by −8: **$\frac{-8x}{-8} \geq \frac{24}{-8}$**
Solution: **$x \geq -3$**

Solve each inequality.

9. $-6x > 54$ **10.** $\frac{r}{-5} \leq -4$ **11.** $27 < -9c$ **12.** $16 \geq \frac{-1n}{2}$

13. $-7x + 11 > 39$ **14.** $\frac{e}{-4} - 5 \leq 2$ **15.** $-2 > \frac{m}{-3} + 9$ **16.** $35 < -12k - 13$

17. $8 - 5k \leq -10$ **18.** $\frac{4}{3}y > -12$ **19.** $v - 19 \leq -1$ **20.** $3.8 - 0.5x \geq 21.2$

Chapter 5 Review/Test

Graph each on a number line.

1. $x > -1$

2. $y + 4 \leq 2$

3. Which statement describes best why the answer given for this problem is *not* reasonable?

A diver descended 100 feet to search for sunken gold. He rose 25 feet to cross a ridge, then descended 50 feet to the ocean floor. How far below the surface was the diver?
Answer: 175 feet

a. He descended *only* 100 feet when he began.
b. The ocean floor was *only* 50 feet below the ridge.
c. The answer does not account for the fact that he *rose* to cross a ridge.

Write each solution set as an inequality.

4. $4x < 20$

5. $2x + 3 \geq 11$

Read the story to answer the questions below.

Sue made a coordinate grid of her home town. She put her home at the origin and her school in quadrant I. Her best friend lives at coordinates (17, −29).

6. Write the coordinates where Sue lives.

7. Tell whether each coordinate of Sue's school is positive or negative.

8. In what quadrant does her best friend live?

9. Graph $y = x + 2$ and $y = x + 3$ on the same coordinate grid. Do the lines intersect or are they parallel?

10. Draw two graphs on the same coordinate grid, and answer the following question.

Alex and Clara are saving for new bicycles. Alex has $23 and can save $15 each month. Clara has $51 and can save $8 each month. At the end of which month will Alex have as much money saved as Clara?

Write an equation that fits the data.

11.

x	y
0	0
1	−3
2	−6
3	−9

12.

x	y
0	−1
2	0
4	1
6	2

13.

x	y
−1	−2
0	1
1	4
2	7

14. Graph $y > 2x + 1$ on a coordinate grid.

The vertices of rectangle *ABCD* are (0, 3), (0, 0), (−1, 0), (−1, 3). Use this information for Problems 15 and 16.

15. What are the new coordinates when the rectangle is translated 5 units to the right?

16. What are the new coordinates when the rectangle is reflected over the *y*-axis?

17. A different rectangle has coordinates (0, 0), (4, 0), (4, 2), and (0, 2). What are the new coordinates when the rectangle is dilated using this rule: (x, y) becomes $(3x, 3y)$?

18. **Write About Math** Suppose there are two equations $y = \blacktriangle x + \blacksquare$ and $y = \bullet x + \rule{0.5em}{1em}$. How can you tell whether the two equations are parallel or intersect?

Ratio, Proportion, and Percent

6

Did You Know: The average person burns up calories at the following rates per minute:

Sleeping	1	Walking fast	5
Watching TV	1	Volleyball	6
Walking	3	Bicycling	8
Jogging	11	Running	19
Swimming	80		

Number-Sense Project

Estimate
Estimate how many calories you burn each day in the activities listed.

Gather Data
Keep track of the number of minutes you participate in each activity for one day.

Analyze and Report
Determine the number of calories you burn up participating in each activity.

ALGEBRA

Ratio and Proportion

Build Understanding

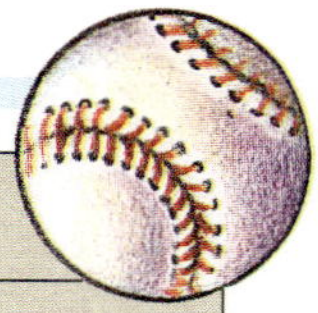

Junior High League		
Team	Won	Lost
Lions	19	1
Tigers	17	3
Braves	15	5
Hawks	11	9
Bulldogs	8	12
Griffins	4	16

A. The Lions baseball team finished the season with 19 wins and 1 loss. The ratio that compares the number of games won by the Lions to the number of games lost is 19 to 1. A ***ratio*** is a pair of numbers that makes a comparison or describes a rate. A ratio can be written in the following ways.

19 to 1 **19:1** $\frac{19}{1}$

The two numbers of a ratio are called its ***terms.***

B. A ratio is in ***simplest form*** when the GCF of the two numbers is 1. Write the ratio of games won to games lost by the Bulldogs in simplest form.

$$\frac{8}{12} = \frac{2}{3} \quad \begin{matrix}\leftarrow \text{Games won} \\ \leftarrow \text{Games lost}\end{matrix}$$

(8 ÷ 4 for the first terms; 12 ÷ 4 for the second terms)

When you multiply or divide both terms of a ratio by the same nonzero number, you get an ***equal ratio.***

C. Roberto is the fastest backstroke swimmer on the swim team. His record for swimming 100 meters is 80 seconds. What was his rate per second?

A ratio that compares two different units is called a ***rate.*** To find a rate, write a ratio and then find an equal ratio with a second term of 1.

$$\frac{100}{80} = \frac{1.25}{1} \quad \begin{matrix}\leftarrow \text{Meters} \\ \leftarrow \text{Seconds}\end{matrix}$$

(100 ÷ 80 for the first terms; 80 ÷ 80 for the second terms)

Roberto swims 1.25 meters every second. His rate is 1.25 meters per second.

D. An equation stating that two ratios are equal is called a ***proportion.*** The ***cross-products*** of a proportion are equal.

$$\frac{38}{4} \stackrel{?}{=} \frac{19}{2}$$

4 × 19 and 38 × 2 are *cross-products.* The cross-products are equal, so the ratios form a proportion.

$$4 \times 19 \stackrel{?}{=} 38 \times 2$$

$$76 = 76$$

$$\frac{38}{4} = \frac{19}{2}$$

$$\frac{17}{2} \stackrel{?}{=} \frac{34}{3}$$

$$2 \times 34 \stackrel{?}{=} 17 \times 3$$

$$68 \neq 51$$

$$\frac{17}{2} \neq \frac{34}{3}$$

The cross-products are not equal, so the ratios do not form a proportion.

E. Mr. Burke races cars. In his first race, he drove a 12-mile course in 10 minutes. In his next race, he drove a 30-mile course in 25 minutes. Do the two ratios of miles to minutes form a proportion?

Method 1: Check the cross-products.

$$\frac{12}{10} = \frac{30}{25} \quad \begin{array}{l}\leftarrow \text{Miles} \\ \leftarrow \text{Seconds}\end{array}$$

$$10 \times 30 = 12 \times 25$$

$$300 = 300$$

The cross-products are equal, so the ratios do form a proportion.

Method 2: Write the ratios in simplest form and compare.

$$\frac{12}{10} = \frac{6}{5} \quad \begin{array}{l} 12 \div 2 \\ 10 \div 2 \end{array} \qquad \frac{30}{25} = \frac{6}{5} \quad \begin{array}{l} 30 \div 5 \\ 25 \div 5 \end{array}$$

$$\frac{6}{5} = \frac{6}{5}$$

The ratios are equal, so the ratios do form a proportion.

F. **Calculator** Use a calculator to solve this proportion.

$$\frac{4.6}{n} = \frac{1.84}{6.32}$$

$$(4.6)(6.32) = 1.84n$$ Express the cross-products.

$$n = \frac{(4.6)(6.32)}{1.84}$$ Divide both sides of the equation by 1.84.

Press: 4.6 [×] 6.32 [÷] 1.84 [=]

Display: 15.8

$n = 15.8$

Talk About Math For Example C, could you find Roberto's rate as seconds per meter? Explain.

Check Understanding

For another example, see Set A, pages 210–211.

Use the table in Example A. Write the ratio of wins to losses in simplest form for each team.

1. Tigers **2.** Hawks **3.** Griffins **4.** Bulldogs **5.** Braves

Tell whether each statement is true or false.

6. If the cross-products are not equal, then the ratios form a proportion.

7. A proportion is formed by two equal ratios.

8. A rate is a ratio that uses a different form of measurement for both terms.

Practice

For More Practice, see Set A, pages 212–213.

For Exercises 9–16, write a ratio in simplest form.

9. 10 to 4 **10.** 1,200:1,500 **11.** 45:55 **12.** 15 to 90

13. 3 out of 4 **14.** \$6 out of \$48 **15.** 1,000,000 to 1 **16.** 360 to 240

Solve each proportion. Tell whether you would use mental math, paper and pencil, or a calculator.

17. $\frac{3}{5} = \frac{m}{25}$ **18.** $\frac{d}{8} = \frac{70}{80}$ **19.** $\frac{18}{63} = \frac{4}{x}$ **20.** $\frac{8}{n} = \frac{6}{15}$ **21.** $\frac{5}{6} = \frac{t}{72}$

22. $\frac{s}{13} = \frac{99}{117}$ **23.** $\frac{20}{65} = \frac{96}{m}$ **24.** $\frac{4}{5} = \frac{r}{50}$ **25.** $\frac{1}{21} = \frac{8}{x}$ **26.** $\frac{24}{k} = \frac{8}{37}$

Write a rate for each problem. Then write the rate in simplest form.

27. \$120 for 20 tickets **28.** 240 km in 3 h **29.** 385 mi in 7 h

30. \$12 for 4 lb **31.** 75 mi for 3 gal **32.** 1,200 mi in 6 days

Calculator Use a calculator to decide whether each pair of ratios is equal. Write *yes* or *no*.

33. $\frac{5{,}280}{440} \stackrel{?}{=} \frac{204}{17}$ **34.** $\frac{0.053}{0.0424} \stackrel{?}{=} \frac{1.75}{1.4}$ **35.** $\frac{1.728}{12} \stackrel{?}{=} \frac{2.520}{18}$ **36.** $\frac{142}{65} \stackrel{?}{=} \frac{563}{268.1}$

In each of Exercises 37–44, rewrite one measurement so that the two units are the same. Then write a ratio in simplest form.

37. 9 in. to 3 ft **38.** 8 oz to 1 lb **39.** 20 mg to 10 g **40.** 48 min to 4 h

41. 2 ft to 5 yd **42.** 9 c to 1 qt **43.** 5 m to 25 cm **44.** 10¢ to \$4

Problem Solving

Use the proportions given to solve each problem.

45. Maria gets 1 hit out of every 3 times at bat. If she got 12 hits, how many times was she at bat?
$\frac{1}{3} = \frac{12}{x}$

46. A race car driver drives around a 5-mile track in 4 minutes. How long does it take to drive 35 miles?
$\frac{4}{5} = \frac{r}{35}$

47. If a bicyclist covers 10 miles in 25 minutes, what is her speed in miles per hour?
$\frac{10}{25} = \frac{m}{60}$

48. In 2 minutes, Joel can skate 1,500 meters. At that rate, how far could Joel skate in 5 minutes?
$\frac{1{,}500}{2} = \frac{n}{5}$

49. Carlos bowled a 240-point game. How many points did he average per frame in a 10-frame game?
$\frac{240}{10} = \frac{c}{1}$

50. It takes Mitch 175 seconds to swim 200 meters. How far would you expect Mitch to swim in 35 seconds?
$\frac{175}{200} = \frac{35}{s}$

Write and solve a proportion for each problem.

51. If Ruth runs 15 miles in 1 hour 45 minutes, how long will it take her, on average, to run 1 mile?

52. A baseball pitcher has given up 80 runs in 210 innings. How many runs would you expect him to give up in 9 innings?

Critical Thinking Write a problem that would describe each proportion.

53. $\frac{12}{n} = \frac{30}{36}$ **54.** $\frac{c}{80} = \frac{7}{20}$ **55.** $\frac{1.2}{2.4} = \frac{x}{1.2}$ **56.** $\frac{17}{28} = \frac{102}{m}$

Number Sense Tell whether each proportion is equal to $\frac{x}{y} = \frac{a}{b}$. Write *yes* or *no*.

57. $\frac{b}{a} = \frac{y}{x}$ **58.** $\frac{2a}{2b} = \frac{x}{y}$ **59.** $\frac{x}{b} = \frac{a}{y}$ **60.** $\frac{x}{a} = \frac{y}{b}$

Skills Review

pages 122–123, 126–127 130–131

Solve each equation.

1. $k - 63 = 27$ **2.** $h + 449 = 573$ **3.** $46 + 56 + f = 215$

4. $4m = 288$ **5.** $92 = 23t$ **6.** $\frac{c}{9} = 38$

7. $3x - 7 = 11$ **8.** $12 = \frac{1}{4}g + 6$ **9.** $\frac{y}{8} - 7 = 0$

Using Proportions to Solve Percent Problems

Build Understanding

A. Out of 130,000 voters, 104,000 favored the purchase of a large amount of land for a wildlife refuge. What percent of the 130,000 voters is this? Write a proportion.

$\frac{104,000}{130,000} = \frac{r}{100}$ Since percent means "hundredths," use 100 as the second term.

$\frac{4}{5} = \frac{r}{100}$ Write the ratio in its simplest form to simplify the calculation.

$4(100) = 5r$ Write the cross-products.

$\frac{400}{5} = r$

$80 = r$

Of the 130,000 voters, 80% voted for the wildlife refuge.

This circle graph shows that the majority of the voters favored a wildlife refuge.

B. A radio was originally priced at \$20. If it is on sale at a 12.5% discount, how much is the discount?

$\frac{12.5}{100} = \frac{n}{20}$ ←Discount ←Original Price Write a proportion.

$(12.5)(20) = 100n$ Write the cross-products.

$\frac{250}{100} = \frac{100n}{100}$ Divide both sides of the equation by 100.

$2.5 = n$

The discount was \$2.50.

C. 15.5% of what number is 12.4?

$\frac{15.5}{100} = \frac{12.4}{s}$ Write a proportion.

$15.5s = 100(12.4)$ Write the cross-products.

$\frac{15.5s}{15.5} = \frac{1,240}{15.5}$ Divide both sides of the equation by 15.5.

$s = 80$

■ **Talk About Math** In Example A, what percent of the voters were not in favor of the land purchase?

Check Understanding

For another example, see Set B, pages 210–211.

Tell which proportion you would use to solve Exercises 1–2.

1. 35% of what number is 77?

a. $\frac{35}{100} = \frac{n}{77}$ **b.** $\frac{35}{100} = \frac{77}{n}$

2. 12 is 2% of what number?

a. $\frac{n}{12} = \frac{2}{100}$ **b.** $\frac{12}{n} = \frac{2}{100}$

Practice

For More Practice, see Set B, pages 212–213.

Solve each proportion.

3. $\frac{n}{100} = \frac{4}{25}$ **4.** $\frac{12.5}{100} = \frac{1}{n}$ **5.** $\frac{n}{100} = \frac{5}{6}$ **6.** $\frac{n}{100} = \frac{360}{450}$

7. $\frac{15}{n} = \frac{30}{100}$ **8.** $\frac{1.5}{7.5} = \frac{n}{100}$ **9.** $\frac{3.8}{5.7} = \frac{n}{100}$ **10.** $\frac{2.4}{n} = \frac{62.5}{100}$

11. $\frac{8.2}{n} = \frac{28.5}{1,000}$ **12.** $\frac{0.25}{100} = \frac{0.1}{n}$ **13.** $\frac{n}{96} = \frac{9.375}{100}$ **14.** $\frac{15.2}{10.4} = \frac{n}{1,000}$

15. $\frac{n}{20} = \frac{95}{100}$ **16.** $\frac{n}{48} = \frac{37.5}{100}$ **17.** $\frac{60}{n} = \frac{15}{100}$ **18.** $\frac{4.5}{90} = \frac{n}{100}$

Write and solve a proportion.

19. 50% of n is 12. **20.** 35% of 40 is n. **21.** 87.5% of n is 8.4.

22. 5% of n is 80. **23.** $24\frac{1}{2}$% of 30 is n. **24.** 18% of n is 17.1.

25. n% of 150 is 12. **26.** n% of 52 is 78. **27.** 13.4% of 950 is n.

28. n% of 1 is 10. **29.** 2.5% of 125 is n. **30.** 0.5% of n is 2.

31. 11% of 111 is n. **32.** n% of 56 is 7. **33.** 7.5% of 6,000 is n.

34. $\frac{1}{2}$% of n is 8. **35.** 134% of 55 is n. **36.** n% of 53.6 is 0.536.

Problem Solving

Write and solve a proportion for each problem.

37. Kim received a discount of $3.99 on a sweater originally priced at $19.95. What percent of the original price was the discount?

38. A software disk was originally priced at $55. If the original price is discounted 35%, find the amount of the discount.

39. Of a group of people polled, 55% favored chocolate frozen yogurt over vanilla. If 330 people favored chocolate, how many people were polled?

40. A serving of a cereal contains 11.25 mg of vitamin C. If the recommended daily requirement of vitamin C is 45 mg, what percent does a serving contain?

41. **Critical Thinking** Morgan said, “Fifty percent of one number plus ten percent of another number is the same as sixty percent of the sum of the two numbers.” Do you agree? Explain.

ALGEBRA

Write an Equation

PROBLEM SOLVING GUIDE

Understand
QUESTION
FACTS
KEY IDEA

Plan and Solve
STRATEGY
ANSWER

Look Back
SENSIBLE ANSWER
ALTERNATE APPROACH

Build Understanding

Breads are enjoyed by most cultures around the world. Some breads are flat like Middle Eastern *pita* or Indian *chapatis*. Others are light and airy like Ukrainian *chernyl klib* or Swedish *limpa*.

Eight cups of corn meal are used to make 3 dozen *tortillas*, flat Mexican bread. How much corn meal is needed to make 60 tortillas?

Understand QUESTION How much corn meal is needed for 60 tortillas?

FACTS Eight cups of corn meal are needed for 3 dozen tortillas.
60 tortillas equals 5 dozen tortillas.

KEY IDEA The amounts of the ingredients are proportional.

Plan and Solve STRATEGY Write a proportion. You know that 8 cups of corn meal are needed for 3 dozen tortillas. Let n represent the amount of corn meal needed for 5 dozen tortillas.

Cups of corn meal → / Number of dozen → $\frac{8}{3} = \frac{n}{5}$ ← Cups of corn meal / ← Number of dozen

$$8 \times 5 = 3n$$

$$\frac{40}{3} = \frac{3n}{3}$$

$$13\frac{1}{3} = n$$

ANSWER To make 60 tortillas, $13\frac{1}{3}$ cups of corn meal are needed.

Look Back SENSIBLE ANSWER The amount of tortillas increased from 3 dozen to 5 dozen. Since $1\frac{2}{3}$ times 3 is 5, multiply 8 by $1\frac{2}{3}$. Since $1\frac{2}{3} \times 8 = 13\frac{1}{3}$, the answer makes sense.

Tortillas are often served with a filling of meat, vegetables, cheese, and spices.

Write About Math Could you solve the problem by finding the number of cups of corn meal needed to make one dozen tortillas? Rewrite the strategy to see if you get the same answer.

Check Understanding

Tell whether each proportion can be used to solve the problem on page 190. Write *yes* or *no*. Explain.

1. $\frac{3 \text{ dozen}}{8 \text{ cups}} = \frac{5 \text{ dozen}}{n \text{ cups}}$ **2.** $\frac{3 \text{ dozen}}{5 \text{ dozen}} = \frac{n \text{ cups}}{8 \text{ cups}}$ **3.** $\frac{8 \text{ cups}}{3 \text{ dozen}} = \frac{5 \text{ dozen}}{n \text{ cups}}$

Practice

Write and solve an equation for each problem.

4. To make 3 dozen tortillas, 4 cups of water are used. How much water is needed to make 60 tortillas?

5. *Grissini* are long Italian bread sticks. Three teaspoons of yeast are needed to make 16 sticks. How much yeast is needed for 4 dozen sticks?

6. *Challah* is a braided Jewish egg bread. Seven cups of flour make 2 loaves. Would 16 cups of flour be enough for 5 loaves? Explain your answer.

7. In Tunisia, Africa, a round bread called *khobaz* is enjoyed. Two loaves contain 1 cup of whole wheat flour, $\frac{1}{2}$ cup of rye flour, and $4\frac{1}{2}$ cups of semolina flour. What is the total amount of flour in 15 loaves?

In India, this woman makes *chapatis* from a dough of water and flour.

Choose a ______ Strategy

Ayes and Nays A small group voted to determine if they should go to a movie or go swimming. The results were 3 to 2 for going swimming.

8. Can you use the ratio 3 to 2 to determine the number of people who voted? Explain.

9. Write a ratio that shows the number who voted to go swimming to the number who voted.

10. What percent did not want to go swimming?

PROBLEM SOLVING STRATEGIES

Choose an Operation
Solve a Simpler Problem
Use a Formula
Write an Equation
Make a Graph

Ratios in Geometry

Build Understanding

Many consider the Parthenon to be the best example of ancient Greek architecture. The front of the building is a ***golden rectangle.*** The ratio of the length of a golden rectangle to its width is about 1.6 to 1.

A. Finding Golden Rectangles
Materials: Ruler, index cards of different sizes
Groups: With a partner

a. Measure a small index card. Write a ratio comparing the card's length to its width.

b. Is the ratio equal or close to the ratio of a golden rectangle? Write a proportion. If the ratios are equal, the index card is a golden rectangle.

c. Repeat steps a and b for a larger index card to determine whether other objects are golden rectangles.

B. For each circle, calculate the ratio of the circumference, C to the diameter d. What pattern do you see in the ratios?

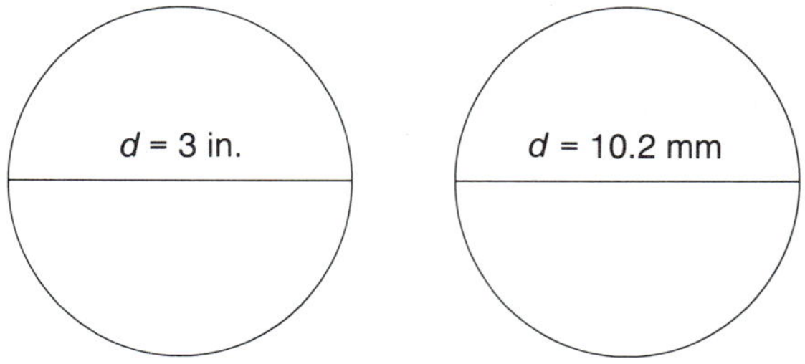

C = 9.4 in. $\quad$ **C = 32.0 mm**

$\frac{9.4}{3} \approx 3.13$ $\quad$ $\frac{32.0}{10.2} \approx 3.14$

The ratio of the circumference to the diameter is about 3 to 1.

Write About Math Measure the diameter of a quarter. Show how you could use ratios to estimate the circumference of the coin.

Check Understanding

For another example, see Set C, pages 210–211.

Tell which ratios $\frac{a}{b}$ are golden rectangle ratios.

1. $a = 10.4$, $b = 3.5$ **2.** $a = 18.6$, $b = 11.8$ **3.** $a = 233$, $b = 144$

Tell if each circumference and diameter represents a circle.

4. $C = 45$ mm, $d = 11$ mm **5.** $C = 10.8$ in., $d = 3.44$ in. **6.** $C = 30.8$ cm, $d = 9.8$ cm

Practice

For More Practice, see Set C, pages 212–213.

Find the length of a golden rectangle with each of these widths.

7. 6 in. **8.** 12 mm **9.** 7.5 in. **10.** 33 m

11. 8 ft **12.** 16 yd **13.** 43 cm **14.** 100 m

Find the width of a golden rectangle with each of these lengths.

15. 14.4 cm **16.** 32 ft **17.** 25.6 m **18.** 11 in.

19. 6 ft **20.** 100 cm **21.** 76 m **22.** 10 cm

Estimation Estimate the diameter of each circle.

23. $C = 381$ cm **24.** $C = 31.2$ in. **25.** $C = 128.4$ mm **26.** $C = 4.5$ ft

Problem Solving

Solve each problem.

27. What is the ratio of the circumference of a circle to its radius?

28. A rectangular picture frame is 23.2 inches long. Find the width if the frame is a golden rectangle.

29. How much longer or shorter must a football field (100 yd × 160 ft) be to make a golden rectangle?

30. How much wider or narrower must a basketball court (94 ft × 50 ft) be to make a golden rectangle?

Explore ______ Math

Recall that these numbers form a ***Fibonacci sequence.***
1, 1, 2, 3, 5, 8, 13, 21, 34, 55, 89, 144, 233, . . .

31. **Calculator** Calculate the ratio of each number in the Fibonacci sequence to the preceding term starting at 5. What pattern do you notice?

Percents, Fractions, and Decimals

Build Understanding

Fahad kept track of the time he spent on various activities and put the results in a table.

ACTIVITY	HOURS
Sleeping 	8
Going to classes 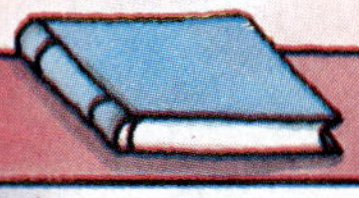	6
Doing homework	3
Playing with friends	2.5
Eating	2
Traveling	1
Other Activities	1.5

A. What part of the day did Fahad spend eating?

2 hours out of 24, or $\frac{2}{24} = \frac{1}{12}$

What percent of the day did Fahad spend eating?

To write a *fraction as a percent,* first express the fraction as a decimal.

$$\begin{array}{r} 0.08\frac{1}{3} \\ 12\overline{)1.00} \\ \underline{96} \\ 4 \end{array}$$

$\frac{1}{12} = 0.08\frac{1}{3}$

To write a *decimal as a percent,* move the decimal point 2 places right.

$0.08\frac{1}{3} = 8\frac{1}{3}\%$**, or** 8.33%

Fahad spent $8\frac{1}{3}\%$ of his day eating.

B. Write 2.5% as a decimal. To write a *percent as a decimal,* move the decimal point 2 places to the left and omit the percent sign. Write zeros as needed.

$2.5\% = 0.025$

C. Write $\frac{1}{4}\%$ as a decimal.

$\frac{1}{4}\% = 0.25\% = 0.0025$

D. Write $14\frac{2}{7}\%$ as a fraction.

$$\begin{aligned} 14\tfrac{2}{7}\% &= 0.14\tfrac{2}{7} \\ &= \frac{14\frac{2}{7}}{100} \\ &= 14\tfrac{2}{7} \div 100 \\ &= \frac{100}{7} \times \frac{1}{100} \\ &= \frac{1}{7} \end{aligned}$$

■ **Write About Math** How would you represent 0% as a decimal? as a fraction?

Check Understanding

For another example, see Set D, pages 210–211.

Refer to the table on page 194 for Exercises 1–3. Write each answer as a fraction and as a percent. What part of each day did Fahad spend

1. sleeping? **2.** going to class? **3.** doing homework?

Practice

For More Practice, see Set D, pages 212–213.

Write each fraction as a percent and each percent as a fraction.

4. $\frac{31}{40}$ **5.** 8% **6.** $\frac{0}{8}$ **7.** $\frac{5}{9}$ **8.** $16\frac{2}{3}\%$ **9.** $\frac{3}{4}$ **10.** $\frac{1}{2}\%$

11. $1\frac{1}{2}$ **12.** 87.5% **13.** $\frac{7}{25}$ **14.** $4\frac{2}{3}$ **15.** $\frac{9}{9}$ **16.** $\frac{11}{5}$ **17.** $\frac{37}{30}$

Mental Math Write each decimal as a percent, and each percent as a decimal.

18. 0.005 **19.** 300% **20.** 5.0 **21.** $8\frac{1}{2}\%$ **22.** $0.37\frac{1}{2}$ **23.** 0.065 **24.** 1.46

25. 37% **26.** 8% **27.** $\frac{3}{4}\%$ **28.** 4.355 **29.** 550% **30.** 2.3% **31.** 0.9

32. 0.7% **33.** 2.5 **34.** 2.5% **35.** 120% **36.** 22.0 **37.** 0.13% **38.** 4,000%

Problem Solving

Use the table on page 194 for Problems 39–40.

39. What percent of the day did Fahad spend in classes and doing homework?

40. What combination of activities take up 50% of Fahad's day? List every possible combination.

41. **Critical Thinking** How can you tell if a fraction is equivalent to a percent that is less than 100%, equal to 100%, or greater than 100%? Give an example of each case.

Midchapter Checkup

Write each ratio in simplest form.

1. 10 cm to 45 cm **2.** 3.5 to 5

Write as percents.

6. $\frac{14}{50}$ **7.** $\frac{7}{12}$ **8.** 0.145

Solve.

3. $\frac{8}{n} = \frac{1.5}{3.0}$ **4.** $\frac{15}{100} = \frac{4.2}{n}$ **5.** $\frac{85}{100} = \frac{n}{20}$

Write as fractions.

9. 65% **10.** $12\frac{1}{2}\%$ **11.** 150%

Problem-Solving Workshop

Critical Thinking Activity

1. Two years ago, PQR Cable Television and XYZ Cable Television each charged $10.00 a month for their services. Last year, PQR Cable increased its rates by 15% and XYZ decreased its rates by 15%. This year, PQR Cable decreased its rates by 15% and XYZ increased its rates by 15%.

a. How much does each cable company charge for its monthly services this year?

b. Which cable company charges more?

c. Do they charge more or less than they did two years ago?

Number-Sense Project

Look back at pages 182–183.

1. Tina kept track of the number of calories she ate at one meal.

Tina's meal	Calories
one 6-ounce hamburger patty	185 per 3 ounces
2 cups milk	150 per cup
1 cup green beans	35 per cup
1 banana	100 each

To burn off the calories in the hamburger and banana, about how long would Tina have to do each activity?

a. Walk fast

b. Run

c. Bicycle

d. Swim

e. How many calories are in Tina's meal?

Explore with a Computer

Use the *Spreadsheet Workshop Project* for this activity.

The 8th-grade students are making pumpkin costumes for the 1st-grade play. The list shows how much material of each color they need to make 2 costumes.

Orange	45 sq ft
Brown	12 sq ft
Green	7 sq ft

1. At the computer, change the equation to find how much material is needed to make 10 costumes. Record on a sheet of paper the total amount of material needed.

2. Predict how much material would be needed for 15 costumes. Change the equations to check your prediction.

Visual-Thinking Activity

1. 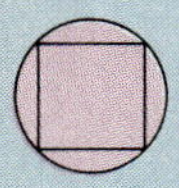 compares to 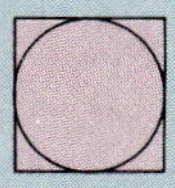 as 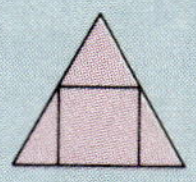 compares to __?__.

2. 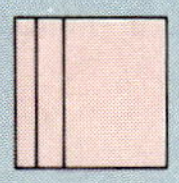 compares to 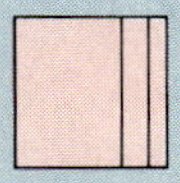 as 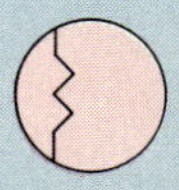 compares to __?__.

3. 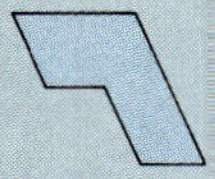 compares to 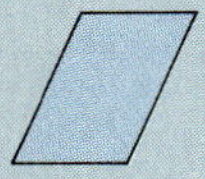 as  compares to __?__.

ALGEBRA

Equations for Percent Problems

Build Understanding

A. To learn about the political process, Angela Bufford ran for Student Council president. In the election, she received 45% of the votes. If 600 students voted, how many votes did Angela receive?

Write an equation to find what number is 45% of 600.

What number is 45% of 600?

$v = 45\% \times 600$

$v = 0.45 \times 600$ Write 45% as a decimal.

$v = 270$

Angela received 270 votes.

B. Julio received 25% of 600 votes. How many votes did he receive?

What number is 25% of 600?

$v = 25\% \times 600$ Write an equation.

$v = \frac{1}{4} \times 600$ Substitute $\frac{1}{4}$ for 25%.

$v = 150$

Julio received 150 votes.

C. Mary Lee received 120 of 600 votes. What percent did she receive?

120 is what percent of 600?

$120 = p \times 600$ Write an equation.

$\frac{120}{600} = p$

$0.2 = p$

Mary Lee received 20% of the votes.

D. 12 is 30% of what number?

$12 = 30\% \times n$

$12 = 0.3n$

$\frac{12}{0.3} = n$

$40 = n$

E. 75% of what number is 30?

$75\% \times n = 30$

$\frac{3}{4}n = 30$

$n = \frac{30}{1} \times \frac{4}{3}$

$n = 40$

Talk About Math Explain why either a proportion or another form of an equation can be used to solve a percent problem. Give an example.

Check Understanding

For another example, see Set E, pages 210–211.

Write an equation for each exercise. Then solve.

1. Find 7.5% of 180.

2. What percent of 80 is 100?

Practice

For More Practice, see Set E, pages 212–213.

Tell whether you would use mental math, paper and pencil, or a calculator for Exercises 3–6. Then solve.

3. $25\% \times 40 = m$

4. $m \times 1.5 = 3$

5. $m \times 30 = 15$

6. $0.8\% \times 100 = m$

Write an equation for each problem. Then solve.

7. Find 4% of 20.

8. What number is 30% of 40?

9. 30 is what percent of 90?

10. What percent of 100 is 6.5?

11. What is 66% of 333?

12. What percent of 500 is 62.5?

13. 48 is 96% of what number?

14. What is 186% of 7,000?

15. 8 is what percent of 3,200?

16. 12 is $\frac{3}{4}$% of what number?

Mixed Practice Write a proportion and another equation for each question. Solve them.

17. 80 is what percent of 40?

18. What percent of 10 is 0.5?

19. 25% of what number is 6.4?

20. What is 5% of 50?

21. 25 is what percent of 125?

22. 125% of what number is 400?

Problem Solving

The Student Council has a budget of $2,150. For Problems 23–26 tell how much money is available.

Student Council Budget	
Publicity	25%
Refreshments	40%
Supplies	20%
Other expenses	15%

23. Publicity

24. Supplies

25. Refreshments

26. Other expenses

Write and solve an equation.

27. The Student Council spent 35% of its refreshment budget. How much money is left for refreshments?

28. Flyers cost $217. What percent of the publicity budget is this?

CONSUMER CONNECTION

Mental Math with Percents

Build Understanding

Percent	Fraction
100%	$\frac{1}{1}$
75%	$\frac{3}{4}$
$66\frac{2}{3}\%$	$\frac{2}{3}$
50%	$\frac{1}{2}$
40%	$\frac{2}{5}$
$33\frac{1}{3}\%$	$\frac{1}{3}$
30%	$\frac{3}{10}$
25%	$\frac{1}{4}$
20%	$\frac{1}{5}$

A smart consumer knows the fractional equivalent of commonly used percents.

A. Linda received a 20% discount on a book that originally cost $30. How much was her discount?

Find 20% of 30 mentally.

Think: $20\% = \frac{1}{5}$

$\frac{1}{5}$ **of 30 is 30 ÷ 5, or 6.**

Linda received a $6 discount.

B. A 10% discount on a sweater amounted to $4. What was the original price of the sweater?

10% of what number is 4? Find the answer mentally.

Think: $10\% = \frac{1}{10}$. **If** $\frac{1}{10}$ **of a number is 4, then the number must be 10 × 4, or 40.**

The original price was $40.

C. Johnette paid for a coat in installments. After two months, she has paid $50 of the total purchase price, which was $150. What percent of the purchase price has she paid?

Find what percent 50 is of 150 mentally.

Think: $\frac{50}{150} = \frac{1}{3} = 33\frac{1}{3}\%$

She has paid $33\frac{1}{3}\%$ of the purchase price.

Talk About Math How could you use the information in the table to find 80% of a number?

Check Understanding

For another example, see Set F, pages 210–211.

Match each percent and fraction.

1. 30% **2.** 75% **3.** $33\frac{1}{3}\%$ **4.** 50% **5.** 20% **6.** 25%

a. $\frac{1}{3}$ **b.** $\frac{3}{10}$ **c.** $\frac{1}{2}$ **d.** $\frac{1}{4}$ **e.** $\frac{1}{5}$ **f.** $\frac{3}{4}$

Use mental math to find each correct answer.

7. 25% of 32
a. 80 **b.** 8 **c.** 4

8. 6 is what percent of 3?
a. 50% **b.** 200% **c.** 18%

Practice

For More Practice, see Set F, pages 212–213.

Mental Math Use mental math to find each answer.

9. 75% of 20 is what number?

10. 6 is what percent of 30?

11. $33\frac{1}{3}$% of what number is 10?

12. 300% of 20 is what number?

13. 40 is what percent of 60?

14. 150% of 10 is what number?

15. 22 is what percent of 44?

16. 25% of what number is 5?

Mixed Practice Tell whether you would use mental math or paper and pencil. Then find each answer.

17. 15 is what percent of 30?

18. 30 is what percent of 15?

19. 15 is 30% of what number?

20. 25% of what number is 12?

21. 12 is what percent of 25?

22. 12 is what percent of 3?

23. What percent of 27 is 9?

24. 96 is 40% of what number?

Problem Solving

Solve each problem.

25. Roy made a 20% down payment on a $12,000 car. How much was the down payment?

26. Marvin earned $320 one summer and decided to put 75% of it in the bank. How much did Marvin save?

27. Tina received a discount of $15 on computer software that had a list price of $60. Find the percent of the discount.

28. A local amusement park gives 15% discounts to students. If the admission fee is normally $8, how much do students pay?

Reading ______ **Math**

ALGEBRA

Numbers and Symbols Convert each problem to numbers and symbols.

1. Five plus four times the sum of two and five.

2. *Y* is greater than one half times *x*.

3. *Y* equals the quantity negative *x* minus five divided by two.

Estimating Percents

Build Understanding

Oxygen, carbon, hydrogen, and nitrogen make up 91% of our body weight. About 4% is made up of minerals like calcium, iron, zinc, and copper.

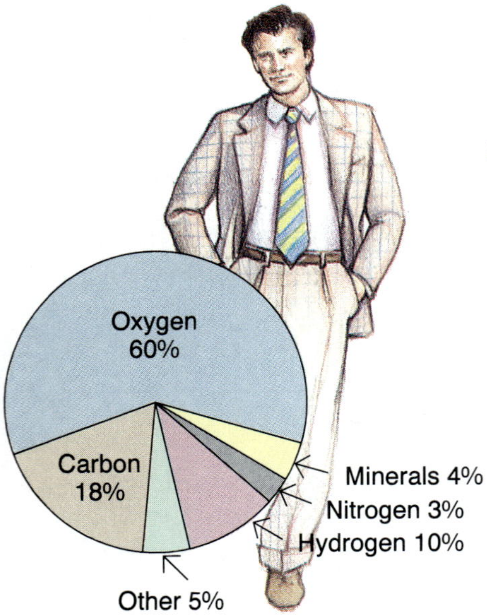

A. Marcus weighs 150 pounds. If 18% of the average person's body weight is carbon, approximately how much of Marcus's body weight is carbon?

To estimate 18% of 150, round 18% up to 20%. 20% is the same as $\frac{1}{5}$.

$$\frac{1}{5} \times 150 = 30$$

About 30 pounds of Marcus's body weight is carbon.

B. Judith calculated that minerals make up about 6 pounds of her body weight. If 4% of the average person's body weight is made up of minerals, about how much does Judith weigh?

To estimate the solution of the equation $0.04w = 6$, round 4% up to 5%. 5% is the same as $\frac{1}{20}$.

$$\frac{1}{20} \times w = 6$$

$$\frac{w}{20} = 6$$

$$20\left(\frac{w}{20}\right) = 6(20)$$

$$w = 120$$

Judith weighs about 120 pounds.

C. Joe weighs 105 pounds. About how much of his body weight is hydrogen if the average person's body is about 10% hydrogen?

Think: 10% is 0.1 and 105 is about 100.

$$0.1 \times 100 = 10$$

About 10 pounds is hydrogen.

D. 12 is about what percent of 49?

Think: $\frac{12}{49}$ is close to $\frac{12}{48}$; $\frac{12}{48} = \frac{1}{4}$ and $\frac{1}{4} = 25\%$.

So 12 is about 25% of 49.

Check: 49 is about 50.

$50 \div 2 = 25$, and $25 \div 2 = 12.5$.

Therefore, 12 is about $\frac{1}{4}$, or 25%, of 50.

Talk About Math Find the word clues in the questions and answers of the examples that let you know you are estimating.

Check Understanding

For another example, see Set G, pages 210–211.

Mental Math Which is the best estimate?

1. 24.5% of 80 is what number?
a. 30 **b.** 20 **c.** 15

2. Find 30% of 19.7.
a. 60 **b.** 6 **c.** 10

3. 1.95 is what percent of 9.95?
a. 20% **b.** 15% **c.** 10%

4. 40% of what number is 19.95?
a. 80 **b.** 8 **c.** 50

Practice

For More Practice, see Set G, pages 212–213.

Estimate. **Remember** to use common percents and equivalent fractions or decimals.

5. What is 24% of 45?

6. Find 66% of 36.

7. What number is 25% of 31.8?

8. 8 is 24% of what number?

9. 48% of what number is 60?

10. Find 11% of 960.

11. What is 32% of 600?

12. Find 76.5% of 20.

13. Find 48% of 110.

14. What is 50% of 201.3?

15. 3.9 is 21% of what number?

16. Find 15% of $24.95.

17. 3.94 is what percent of 15.5?

18. What number is 68% of 31?

19. 13 is what percent of 60?

20. 78% of what number is 297?

21. 9 is what percent of 17?

22. What is 90% of 694?

23. Find 48.5% of 253.

24. Find $66\frac{2}{3}$% of $9.05.

Problem Solving

Estimate. Use the diagram on page 202.

25. If Harry weighs 87 pounds, how much of his weight is nitrogen?

26. If Winifred's carbon content is 18 pounds, what is her approximate weight?

27. If Lupe weighs 102 pounds, about how much of his weight is hydrogen?

28. **Use Data** Use the chart on page 194. Estimate what percent of Fahad's day was spent playing with friends.

ALGEBRA

Solving Percent Problems

Build Understanding

The recommended daily allowances (RDA) of some minerals and vitamins are shown in the table.

The allowances tell how much of certain vitamins and minerals you need each day to stay healthy.

One cup of milk contains 291 milligrams of calcium, 0.1 milligram of iron, 0.09 milligram of thiamin, and 0.4 milligram of riboflavin.

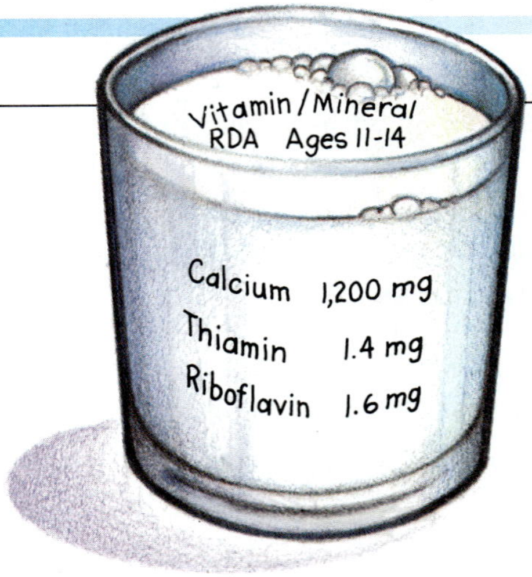

A. What percent of the RDA of calcium is in a cup of milk?

291 mg is what percent of 1,200 mg?

$291 = p \times 1{,}200$ — Write an equation.

$\dfrac{291}{1{,}200} = p \times \dfrac{1{,}200}{1{,}200}$ — Divide both sides of the equation by 1,200.

$0.2425 = p$

A cup of milk provides 24.25% of the RDA of calcium.

B. Does one cup of milk supply 25% of the RDA of riboflavin?

25% of 1.6 is what number?

$25\% \times 1.6 = x$ — Write an equation.

$0.25 \times 1.6 = x$ — Write the percent as a decimal.

$0.4 = x$

Yes, 25% of the RDA of riboflavin is 0.4 mg, which is in one cup of milk.

C. A tuna sandwich contains 14 grams of protein, or 30% of the RDA. How many grams of protein is the RDA?

14 is 30% of what number?

$14 = 30\% \times m$ — Write an equation.

$14 = 0.30 \times m$ — Write the percent as a decimal.

$\dfrac{14}{0.30} = \dfrac{0.30m}{0.30}$ — Divide both sides of the equation by 0.30.

$46.\overline{6} = m$

About 46.7 g is the RDA for protein.

D. There are two ways to use a calculator to solve the equation in Example A.

Calculator

Press: 291 [÷] 1200 [=]

Display: 0.2425

Then write the decimal as a percent.

0.2425 = 24.25%

Calculator

Press: 291 [÷] 1200 [%]

Display: 24.25

Talk About Math Explain the Press step in each calculator method shown in Example D. What does the percent key do?

Check Understanding

For another example, see Set H, pages 210–211.

Use the table and the information on page 204. Choose the correct equation for each problem. Then solve the problem.

1. Is 25% of the recommended daily allowance of calcium contained in one cup of milk?

a. $25\% = n \times 1{,}200$
b. $n = 25\% \times 1{,}200$

2. What percent of the recommended daily allowance of thiamin is provided by one cup of milk?

a. $k \times 1.4 = 0.09$
b. $k \times 0.09 = 1.4$

Practice

For More Practice, see Set H, pages 212–213.

Write and solve an equation for each problem.

3. 125 mg is what percent of 500 mg?

4. 4 gal is what percent of 64 gal?

5. 30% of 8.2 m is how much?

6. 72% of 35 oz is how much?

7. 15 in. is 60% of how much?

8. $4.25 is what percent of $34.00?

9. $7.50 is 15% of what amount?

10. 82% of 2.5 is what number?

11. 12 votes is what percent of 36 votes?

12. 36.1 g is 35% of how much?

13. 63% of $4,000 is how much?

14. 10 cm is what percent of 1 m?

Problem Solving

Solve each problem.

15. A diet calls for 2,000 calories per day. A 4-oz serving of baked ham contains 425 calories. What percent of the 2,000 calories is provided by the serving of ham?

16. A serving of corned beef contains about 1,975 mg of sodium. This amount is what percent of the average adult daily intake of sodium of 2,500 mg?

17. Mental Math A diet calls for 250 grams of carbohydrates per day. What percent of the carbohydrates is provided by a banana that contains 25 grams of carbohydrates?

18. Estimation A serving of shrimp contains about 238 mg of cholesterol. This is 78% of the amount per day allowed by a diet. About how many milligrams per day does the diet allow?

ALGEBRA

Write an Equation

PROBLEM SOLVING GUIDE

Understand
QUESTION
FACTS
KEY IDEA

Plan and Solve
STRATEGY
ANSWER

Look Back
SENSIBLE ANSWER
ALTERNATE APPROACH

Build Understanding

The 1988 Summer Olympics were held in Seoul, South Korea. Athletes from 161 nations competed for 237 gold medals. The Soviet Union won 23% of those medals. About how many gold medals were won by the Soviet Union?

Understand QUESTION About how many gold medals were won by the Soviet Union?

FACTS There were 237 gold medals awarded. The Soviet Union won 23% of them.

KEY IDEA The number of gold medals won by the Soviet Union can be calculated using the total number of gold medals awarded and the percent won by the Soviet Union. The number of nations that competed in the Olympics is extra information.

Plan and Solve STRATEGY *Write an equation* to find the number of gold medals won by the Soviet Union.

What number is 23% of 237?

$n = 23\% \times 237$ Write an equation.

$n = 0.23 \times 237$ Write the percent as a decimal.

$n = 54.51$

ANSWER Round 54.51 to the nearest whole number, 55. The Soviet Union won about 55 medals.

Look Back SENSIBLE ANSWER Estimate: 23% is close to 25%, and 237 is close to 200. 25% of 200 is 50, which is close to the number won by the Soviets.

■ **Write About Math** Show how you could solve this problem by using another method.

Check Understanding

Use the information on page 206. Write an equation. Then solve the problem.

1. France and Italy together won 5% of the gold medals. How many gold medals did they win?

2. Kenya won 5 gold medals. What percent of the total is this?

3. In the Winter Olympics, the Soviet Union earned a total of 29 medals. This was about 21% of all the Winter Olympic medals. How many Winter Olympic medals were there?

4. In the Winter Olympics, East Germany earned nine gold medals. This was about 43% of their Winter Olympics medals. How many Winter Olympics medals did they earn?

Practice

The table at the right shows medals won at the 1988 Summer Olympics. Use the table to solve Problems 5–7.

1988 Summer Olympics Medals

	Gold	Silver	Bronze
Soviet Union	55	31	46
E. Germany	37	35	30
United States	36	31	27
Others	109	140	134
Totals	**237**	**237**	**237**

5. What percent of the medals were silver?

6. Asian countries won about 11% of the medals. About how many medals did they win?

7. What percent of the medals did the Soviet Union win? East Germany? the United States?

8. European countries won 111 gold medals in the Summer Olympics. This was about 31% of all medals won by Europeans. About how many medals did the Europeans win that season?

9. In the Winter Olympics Europe won 33 gold medals, which was about 34% of all the Winter Olympics medals won by Europeans. How many Winter Olympics medals did the Europeans win?

Skills Review

Solve each proportion.

1. $\frac{3}{4} = \frac{n}{20}$
2. $\frac{15}{p} = \frac{3}{5}$
3. $\frac{8}{10} = \frac{x}{80}$
4. $\frac{5}{6} = \frac{30}{k}$
5. $\frac{n}{100} = \frac{6}{24}$
6. $\frac{120}{150} = \frac{n}{100}$
7. $\frac{45}{9} = \frac{n}{100}$
8. $\frac{n}{100} = \frac{17}{20}$

Estimate the diameter of each circle.

9. $C = 25.1$ in.
10. $C = 78.5$ cm

Write each as a percent.

11. $\frac{42}{80}$
12. $2\frac{7}{16}$
13. 0.025
14. 5.005

Solve each equation.

15. $r = 20\% \times 30$
16. $n \times 3.5 = 7$
17. $t \times 1.4 = 70\%$
18. $0.1\% \times 100 = p$

Use mental math to find each answer.

19. 14 is what percent of 70?
20. What number is 40% of 25?

Estimate each answer.

21. What is 52% of $39.98?
22. 9.8 is 20% of what number?

Write and solve an equation.

23. What percent of 300 cars is 120 cars?
24. 45 hats is 90% of what number?
25. 250% of 10 is what number?
26. What is 15% of 103?

Problem-Solving Review

Solve each problem.

27. Elise averages 2 hits out of every 5 times at bat. How many hits would you expect her to get in 18 times at bat?

28. A printer stand was originally priced at $45. The original price has been discounted 25%. What is the amount of the discount?

29. Lien needs 24 pounds of clay to make 5 sculptures. How much clay will she need for 45 sculptures?

30. A rectangular rug is in the shape of a golden rectangle (see page 192). If the rug is about 40 inches long, about how wide is it?

31. The science department has $2,400. If the department spends 22% of that amount on a microscope, how much money will be left?

32. Ernesto received a discount of $12 on shoes with a list price of $72. Find the percent of the discount.

33. **Data File** Use the data on pages 252–253. How many more people found their jobs through networking and personal contacts than found their jobs through advertisements?

34. **Make a Data File** Research the meaning of the baseball pitching statistic *earned run average* (E.R.A.). Find out how to compute this statistic. Then make a table listing the leading (lowest) earned run averages in both major leagues during each of the last 10 years. Be sure to include the names of the pitchers.

Cumulative Skills Review • Chapters 1–6

Tell whether the sequence is arithmetic, geometric, or neither. Then write the next 3 terms.

1. 4, 12, 36, 108 . . . **2.** 90, 84, 78, 72 . . . **3.** 100, 99, 97, 94 . . . **4.** 6, 12, 18, 24 . . .

Estimate each answer.

5. $98 + 45 + 103$ **6.** $624 \div 71$ **7.** $7{,}432 - 4{,}388$ **8.** 421×93

9. $45\frac{2}{3} + 15\frac{1}{2}$ **10.** $89\frac{5}{6} - 56\frac{3}{4}$ **11.** $12\frac{1}{16} + 8\frac{1}{12}$ **12.** $78\frac{9}{10} - 24\frac{1}{9}$

Multiply or divide.

13. 7.23×10 **14.** $0.0056 \times 10{,}000$ **15.** $1.3 \div 100$ **16.** $172.4 \div 1{,}000$

17. $54 \div -9$ **18.** $-9(-4)$ **19.** $-450 \div -50$ **20.** $-11(100)$

21. $-\frac{7}{8}(-\frac{8}{7})$ **22.** $8 \div -\frac{4}{5}$ **23.** $-\frac{1}{2} \times \frac{8}{11}$ **24.** $2\frac{2}{3} \div \frac{3}{8}$

Write a mathematical expression for each phrase.

25. 20 less than m **26.** the product of 8 and the sum of m and n

27. two-thirds the sum of f and g **28.** the quotient of r divided by t

Solve.

29. $t + 15 = 33$ **30.** $-11 = m - 4$ **31.** $y - 2.5 = 10$ **32.** $k + 1 = 4$

33. $\frac{3}{8} = \frac{n}{32}$ **34.** $\frac{v}{28} = \frac{3}{7}$ **35.** $\frac{14}{k} = \frac{42}{45}$ **36.** $\frac{7}{18} = \frac{21}{p}$

37. $\frac{c}{100} = \frac{23}{25}$ **38.** $\frac{5.5}{11} = \frac{n}{100}$ **39.** $\frac{16.8}{100} = \frac{4.2}{a}$ **40.** $\frac{n}{100} = \frac{3}{20}$

Graph each pair of equations on the same coordinate plane.

41. $y = \frac{1}{2}x$, $y = 2x$ **42.** $y = \frac{x}{2} + 1$, $y = x + 1$ **43.** $y = x + 3$, $y = 3x$ **44.** $y = x$, $y = -2x$

Write an equation for the table.

45.

x	0	1	2	3
y	4	5	6	7

Write each percent as a decimal.

46. 16% **47.** 0.2%

Write each solution set as an inequality.

48. $n - 3 > -10$ **49.** $-3a \leq -9$ **50.** $\frac{1}{4}m > -1$ **51.** $6 + a < 2.4$

Reteaching

Set A pages 184–187

Solve the proportion.

$\frac{9}{7} = \frac{45}{n}$

$9 \times n = 7 \times 45$ Find the cross-products.

$9n = 315$

$\frac{9n}{9} = \frac{315}{9}$

$n = 35$

Remember that a ratio is in simplest form when it is written as a fraction in lowest terms.

Solve each proportion.

1. $\frac{35}{42} = \frac{n}{12}$ **2.** $\frac{16}{25} = \frac{4}{x}$

3. $\frac{a}{36} = \frac{7}{12}$ **4.** $\frac{4.8}{d} = \frac{18}{21}$

Set B pages 188–189

25% of what number is 17?

$\frac{17}{x} = \frac{25}{100}$ Write a proportion.

$25x = 1{,}700$ Find the cross-products.

$\frac{25x}{25} = \frac{1{,}700}{25}$

$x = 68$

Remember that a percent is a ratio with 100 as the denominator.

Find each answer.

1. 6 is what percent of 75?

2. What is 60% of 17?

3. 40% of what number is 16?

4. 21.5% of what number is 8.6?

Set C pages 192–193

The ratio of the length of a golden rectangle to its width is about 1.6 to 1.

The ratio of the circumference of a circle to its diameter is about 3.14 to 1.

Remember that ratios can be written a to b, $a{:}b$, or $\frac{a}{b}$.

Find the length of a golden rectangle with the given width.

1. 8 in. **2.** 6.5 cm

Estimate the diameter of each circle.

3. $C = 47.1$ cm **4.** $C = 4$ in.

Set D pages 194–195

Write $\frac{7}{8}$ as a percent.

$$\begin{array}{r} 0.875 \\ 8\overline{)7.0} \\ \underline{6\,4} \\ 60 \\ \underline{56} \\ 40 \\ \underline{40} \\ 0 \end{array}$$

First, write $\frac{7}{8}$ as a decimal.

To write a decimal as a percent, move the decimal point 2 places to the right.

$0.875 = 87.5\%$

Remember that you can work backward to write a percent as a decimal.

Write each fraction as a percent.

1. $\frac{11}{20}$ **2.** $\frac{29}{40}$ **3.** $\frac{5}{6}$

Write each percent as a decimal.

4. 67.5% **5.** 19% **6.** 0.05%

Set E pages 198–199

Find 6% of 50.

You can write an equation to find what percent one number is of another number.

$6\% \times 50 = v$ Write 6% as a decimal.

$0.06 \times 50 = v$

$3 = v$

Remember to look for word clues that will help you write an equation.

Write an equation. Then solve the equation.

1. What number is 12% of 100?
2. Find 0.7% of 40.
3. 100 is what percent of 32?
4. 35% of what number is 4.2?
5. Find 60% of 25.

Set F pages 200–201

This table shows some common percents and their fractional equivalents.

Percent	100%	75%	50%	$33\frac{1}{3}$%	30%	25%	20%
Fraction	1	$\frac{3}{4}$	$\frac{1}{2}$	$\frac{1}{3}$	$\frac{3}{10}$	$\frac{1}{4}$	$\frac{1}{5}$

Remember that knowing the fractional equivalents of percents often makes mental computation easier.

Find each answer.

1. 12 is what percent of 16?
2. What percent of 40 is 32?
3. 75% of 20 is what number?
4. $33\frac{1}{3}$% of 15 is what number?

Set G pages 202–203

Use the table in Set F to help you estimate percents.

Remember to round to compatible numbers.

Estimate.

1. 53% of 19
2. 77% of 290
3. 12% of 92
4. 35% of 55

Set H pages 204–205

The average annual precipitation in Washington, D.C., is 39 inches. What percent of this amount is 3.5 inches?

What percent of 39 is 3.5?

$n \times 39 = 3.5$

$39n = 3.5$

$\frac{39n}{39} = \frac{3.5}{39}$

$n = 0.0897$

$0.0897 = 8.97\%$

3.5 inches is 8.97% of 39 inches.

Remember that writing a word statement first often helps you write an equation.

Write an equation and solve each problem.

1. Cheetahs can run up to 70 mph. A domestic cat can attain a speed of up to 20 mph. What percent of a cheetah's speed can a domestic cat attain?
2. One gallon of ColorFast paint covers about 450 square feet. This is about 82% of the area covered by a gallon of Marvelite paint. What area can be covered by one gallon of Marvelite?

More Practice

Set A pages 184–187

Write a ratio in simplest form.

1. 12 to 3 **2.** 850:1,000 **3.** \$9 out of \$63 **4.** 4 kids out of 20

Write a rate in simplest form.

5. 330 mi in 6 h **6.** \$110 for 4 tickets **7.** 270 km in 4.5 h

Solve each proportion.

8. $\frac{2}{3} = \frac{r}{24}$ **9.** $\frac{t}{10} = \frac{90}{120}$ **10.** $\frac{24}{72} = \frac{8}{c}$ **11.** $\frac{12}{g} = \frac{6}{17}$

Set B pages 188–189

Solve each proportion.

1. $\frac{n}{100} = \frac{9}{36}$ **2.** $\frac{n}{100} = \frac{322}{460}$ **3.** $\frac{4.5}{2.5} = \frac{n}{100}$ **4.** $\frac{72.5}{100} = \frac{2.9}{n}$

5. $\frac{62.5}{n} = \frac{25}{100}$ **6.** $\frac{3.5}{7} = \frac{n}{100}$ **7.** $\frac{n}{100} = \frac{9}{16}$ **8.** $\frac{n}{100} = \frac{4}{25}$

Write and solve a proportion.

9. $30\% = \frac{n}{10}$ **10.** $45\% = \frac{n}{60}$ **11.** $27\% = \frac{5.4}{n}$ **12.** $18\% = \frac{4.5}{n}$

13. $9\% = \frac{n}{4}$ **14.** $5\% = \frac{n}{160}$ **15.** $98\% = \frac{588}{n}$ **16.** $44\% = \frac{173.8}{n}$

Set C pages 192–193

Find the length of a golden rectangle with a width of

1. 4.5 inches. **2.** 15 millimeters. **3.** 3 ft **4.** 6.5 cm

Find the width of a golden rectangle with a length of

5. 19.2 feet. **6.** 33.6 meters. **7.** 5.6 in. **8.** 1 m

Estimate the diameter of each circle.

9. C = 109.9 cm **10.** C = 47.1 in. **11.** C = 235.5 cm **12.** C = 15.7 ft

13. C = 399 mm **14.** C = 7 ft **15.** C = 16 in. **16.** C = 25 cm

Set D pages 194–195

Write each fraction as a percent.

1. $\frac{29}{40}$ **2.** $2\frac{1}{3}$ **3.** $\frac{3}{8}$ **4.** $\frac{5}{16}$

Write each decimal as a percent.

5. 0.016 **6.** 2.01 **7.** 0.01 **8.** 0.833 **9.** 6

Write each percent as a decimal.

10. 42% **11.** 200% **12.** 0.016% **13.** $2\frac{1}{2}\%$ **14.** $\frac{4}{5}\%$

Set E pages 198–199

Solve each equation.

1. $25\% \times 50 = r$
2. $c \times 4.5 = 9$
3. $0.05\% \times 100 = m$
4. $d \times 35\% = 7$
5. $w \times 75 = 15\%$
6. $n = 125 \times 42\%$
7. $v \times 2.1 = 70\%$
8. $k \times 0.2 = 90\%$

Write an equation for each problem. Then solve the equation.

9. Find 3% of 20.
10. What number is 40% of 30?
11. 75% of 60 is what number?
12. 1 percent of what number is 8.1?
13. What percent of 12 is 15?
14. 24 is what percent of 160?

Set F pages 200–201

Use mental math to find each answer.

1. 20 is what percent of 40?
2. 40 is what percent of 20?
3. 20% of what number is 8?
4. What percent of 3 is 6?
5. 10% of what number is 4.5?
6. Find $4\frac{1}{2}\%$ of 60.
7. What number is 25% of 80?
8. Find 5% of 100.

Set G pages 202–203

Estimate each answer.

1. What is 47% of 90?
2. What is 73% of 12?
3. Find 27% of 60?
4. Find 15% of $29.95.
5. 10% of what number is 41.2?
6. 4.2 is 19% of what number?
7. 52% of 80 is what number?
8. Find 11% of 498

Set H pages 204–205

Write and solve an equation.

1. What percent of 625 students is 75 students?
2. What percent of 400 calories is 150 calories?
3. 195 grams is 60% of what quantity?
4. 95 men is 20% of what number?
5. 2,450 voters is what percent of 9,800 voters?
6. 73 days is what percent of a year?
7. 249 pages is what percent of 415 pages?
8. How many books is 35% of 120 books?
9. What percent is 12 out of 54?
10. 150% of 3 is what number?

Enrichment

Ratios in Music

Do you know how to "sing" these notes?

do-re-mi-fa-sol-la-ti-do

You may be more familiar with the letter names given to the notes represented by do, re, mi, and so forth: C, D, E, F, G, A, B, and C′. These notes form a **musical scale.** A musical scale is a sequence of notes.

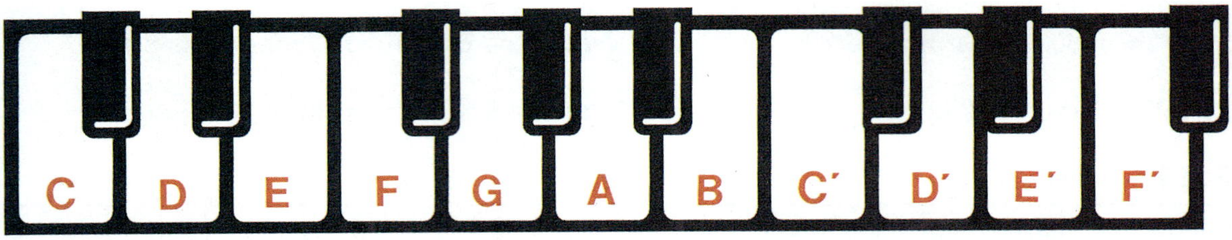

The table below shows the frequencies of the above notes. The ratio of the frequency of D to the frequency of C is $\frac{9}{8}$.

Find the remaining ratios.

Note	Letter name	Frequency (Hertz)	Frequency ratio
do	C	264	$\frac{D}{C} = \frac{297}{264} = \frac{9}{8}$
re	D	297	**1.** $\frac{E}{D}$
mi	E	330	**2.** $\frac{F}{E}$
fa	F	352	**3.** $\frac{G}{F}$
sol	G	396	**4.** $\frac{A}{G}$
la	A	440	**5.** $\frac{B}{A}$
ti	B	495	**6.** $\frac{C'}{B}$
do	C′	528	

The eight notes in the table create an **octave**. C′ is one octave higher than C. Notes that are exactly one octave apart have the same letter name. The same note in the next higher octave has a frequency that is twice the frequency of the note in the lower octave. For example, the frequency of D in the next octave is 594.

7. Find the frequencies of the other seven notes in the next higher octave.

8. Find the frequency ratios of successive notes in the next octave.

9. What is the frequency ratio of a note in one octave to the same note in the next higher octave?

10. There are eight octaves on a piano keyboard. What is the frequency ratio of a note in one octave, to the same note four octaves higher?

Chapter 6 Review/Test

Write the ratio in simplest form.

1. 8 to 10

2. 42:63

3. If Jean types 450 words in 10 minutes, what is her rate per minute?

Do the ratios form a proportion? Write *yes* or *no*.

4. $\frac{16}{34} \stackrel{?}{=} \frac{64}{136}$

5. $\frac{0.15}{4} \stackrel{?}{=} \frac{0.45}{20}$

Solve each proportion.

6. $\frac{m}{100} = \frac{8}{12.5}$

7. $\frac{15}{b} = \frac{25}{40}$

8. Write $37.5\% = \frac{c}{20}$ as a proportion. Then solve.

9. A golden rectangle's length to width ratio is about 1.6 to 1. If it has a width of 16 centimeters, find its length.

Write each number as a percent.

10. $\frac{5}{8}$

11. $\frac{27}{40}$

12. 0.045

13. 1.34

14. Write 250% as a decimal.

Solve each equation.

15. $30\% \times 80 = w$

16. $0.65\% \times 50 = a$

Find each answer.

17. 8% of what number is 4.2?

18. 2% of 95 is what number?

19. 30 is 20% of what number?

20. 4 is what percent of 5?

21. In a survey, 18% of the people said that they were very satisfied with a product. If there were 225 people in this category, how many customers took part in the survey?

Estimate each answer.

22. What is 48% of 60?

23. Find 30% of $48.95.

24. Which of these equations could you use to solve this problem?

Robin's starting pay was $42 per week. Then she received a 5% raise in pay. Then her pay was cut 5%. How much does she earn now?

a. $42(0.05) - 42(0.05) = p$
b. $[42 + 42(0.05)] - [42(0.05)] = p$
c. $[42 + 42(0.05)] - 0.05[42 + 42(0.05)] = p$

25. In the United States about $\frac{2}{5}$ of the population has Type A blood. A school has 375 students that have Type A blood. Write a proportion to find the total number of students enrolled in the school.

26. A store owner buys compact disks at 60% of the retail price. The retail price is $12.95. Write and solve an equation that shows how much it costs a store owner to buy a compact disk.

27. A $75 sweater is discounted 20%. Find the amount of the discount.

28. **Write About Math** Write a word problem for Problem 20.

Consumer Topics

7

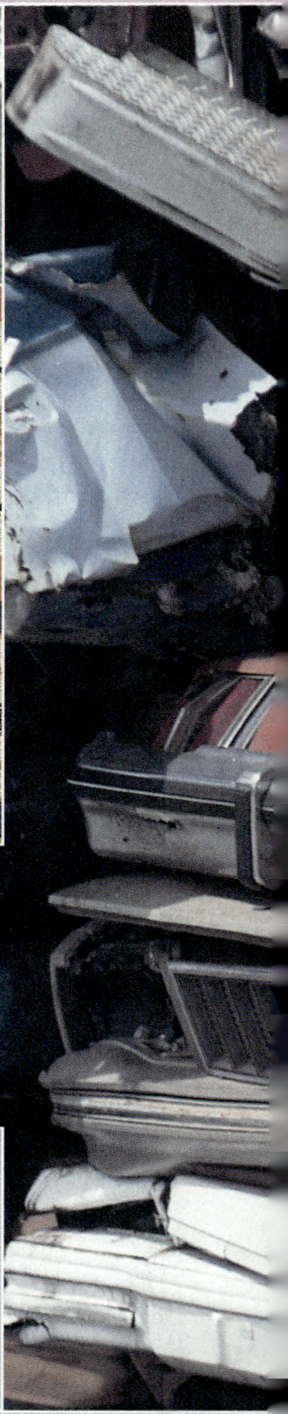

Did You Know: Recycling has been practiced around the world for many years. Sandals are made from old automobile tires, quilts from used clothing, famous sculptures from old bicycle parts, and musical instruments from old metal containers.

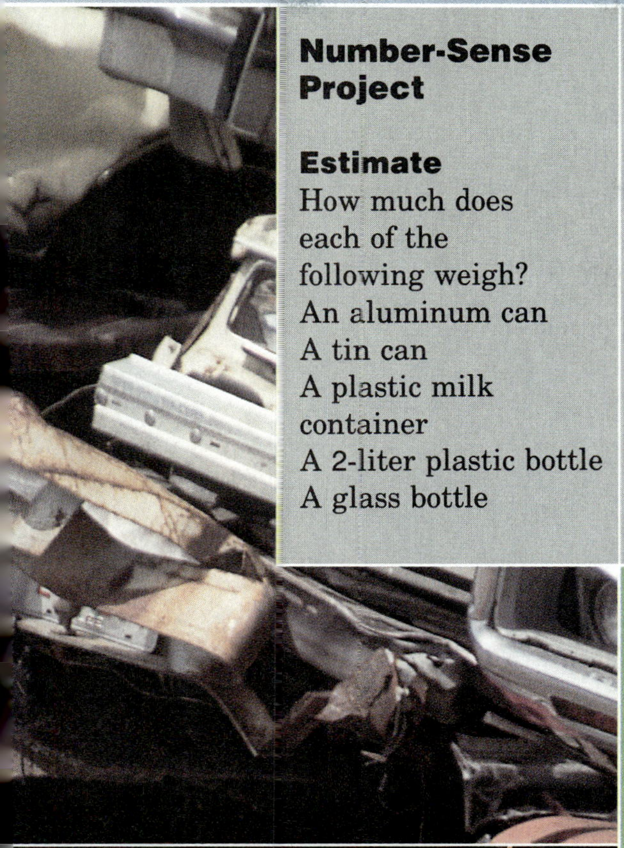

Number-Sense Project

Estimate
How much does each of the following weigh?
An aluminum can
A tin can
A plastic milk container
A 2-liter plastic bottle
A glass bottle

Gather Data
Household trash yields paper, glass, plastic, metal, and organic materials. How much does each weigh?

Analyze and Report
Find the average weekly weight of your family's recyclables. At this rate, how many pounds of material would your family recycle in a year?

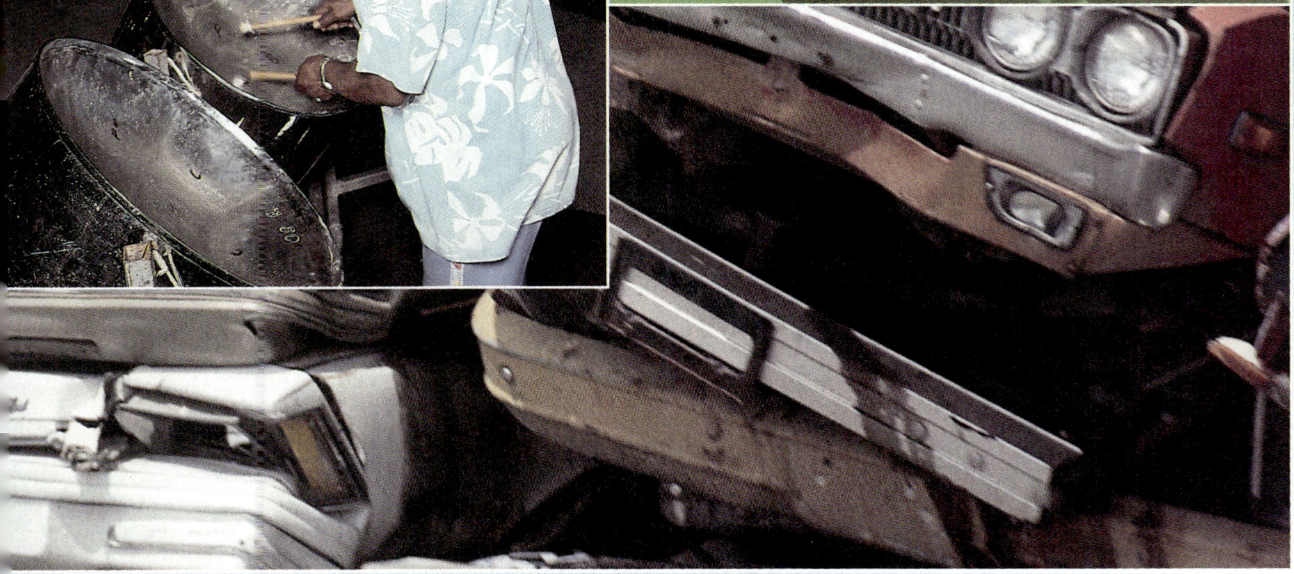

Income and Commissions

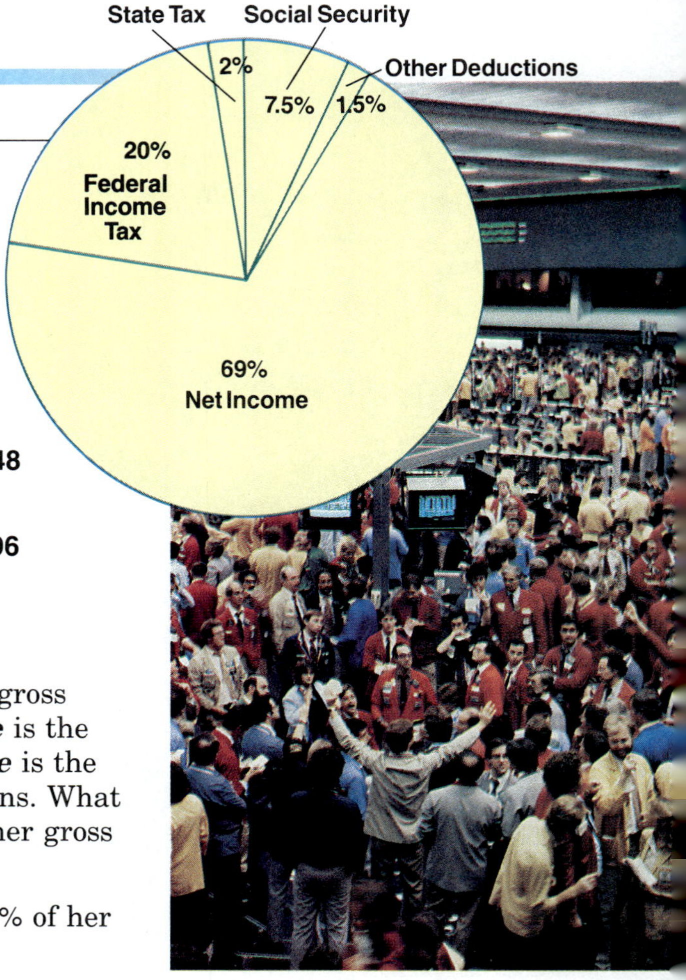

Build Understanding

A. Ms. Rosen is a stock broker. Each month she is paid a ***base salary*** of $1,667.67, plus a ***commission*** of 2% of the value of the stocks that she buys and sells for her clients. How much commission will she receive on a sale of 100 shares of a stock priced at $25.48 per share?

Value of the shares: **100 × $25.48 = $2,548**

Commission: **2% of 2,548**
0.02 × 2,548 = $50.96

She will receive a commission of $50.96.

B. Ms. Rosen uses a circle graph to show her gross income and her net income. ***Gross income*** is the total amount of money earned. ***Net income*** is the amount of money remaining after deductions. What was Ms. Rosen's net income last month if her gross income was $5,624?

The graph shows that her net income is 69% of her gross income. Find 69% of $5,624.

0.69 × 5,624 = 3,880.56

Her net income last month was $3,880.56.

Talk About Math Ms. Rosen was offered a lower base salary and a higher commission. What facts must she consider to make a decision?

Check Understanding

For another example, see Set A, pages 246–247.

Fill in the missing numbers and solve.

1. Ms. Rosen made $600 on a sale of $12,000 of bonds. What rate of commission did she receive?

▦ ÷ ▦ × ▦ = rate of commission

2. John Chung earns $200 a week plus 3% commission. With sales of $3,500 a week, what is his gross income?

▦ × ▦ + ▦ = gross income

Practice

For More Practice, see Set A, pages 248–249.

The table gives the earnings of several people. Find each person's gross income to the nearest cent.

Name	Total Sales	Rate of Commission	Weekly Salary	Gross Pay
Mary Horvath	$11,877	3%	$295	**3.**
Bill Bowen	$13,562	2%	$275	**4.**
Lorraine Hill	$14,415	1.5%	$305	**5.**
Grace Gagliardi	$11,333	2.5%	$187	**6.**

Use the information in Example B to answer Exercises 7–10.

7. How much was deducted from Ms. Rosen's gross income for state tax?

8. How much was deducted for other deductions?

9. How much was deducted for social security?

10. What were Ms. Rosen's total deductions?

Mixed Practice Complete the following.

11. 4% of $550 = ▒

12. ▒% of $1,200 = $72

13. 2.5% of ▒ = $20

14. ▒% of $400 = $26

15. 11% of $1,100 = ▒

16. 15% of ▒ = $582

17. ▒% of $4,500 = $630

18. 2.2% of ▒ = $1,430

19. 1% of $4,000,000 = ▒

20. 9% of ▒ = $7,200

21. ▒% of $2,345 = $2,345

22. 0.5% of $8,900 = ▒

Problem Solving

Solve each problem. **Remember** to check your work.

23. Jerry Cohen receives a salary of $255 a week plus 2% commission on all sales over $800. Last week he sold $1,500 worth of furniture. Find his gross pay.

24. In her best month so far this year, Ms. Rosen earned a commission of $1,379.48. This represented 2% of her total sales for that month. What were her total sales?

25. Ms. Rosen's gross income last year was $47,856.48. Find her net income to the nearest cent.

26. **Calculator** Last year Mr. Anderson earned $39,325.80. The amount withheld for state taxes was $1,966.29. What percent of his gross pay went to state taxes?

Budgets and Circle Graphs

Build Understanding

ACTIVITY

Graph That Budget
Materials: Protractor, compass, ruler
Groups: 2–4 students

An eighth-grade class has planned the budget for their science fair plant project. They made a list of their expenses and then calculated each one as a percent of the total.

Budget for Class Plant Project

Item	Cost($)	Percent
Plants	135	45
Potting Soil	24	
Containers	90	30
Plant Food		12
Other Expenses	15	5
TOTAL	$300	100%

a. Calculate what percent of the budget is for potting soil.

b. Make a circle graph in steps c and d using a protractor to draw each angle. Recall that there are 360° in a circle. The containers account for 30% of the budget, so they should account for 30% of the circle. Find the number of degrees in this sector of the circle graph. Find the number of degrees for the other items.

c. Draw a circle. Put the center of the protractor at the center of a circle, and mark 2 points on the circumference corresponding to the number of degrees. Using your ruler, draw a straight line from each point to the center of the circle.

d. Draw a circle graph for the class project budget. Give your graph a title and identify each sector by name and percent.

■ **Talk About Math** Why does a circle graph seem useful when looking at data?

Check Understanding

For another example, see Set B, pages 246–247.

Choose the correct answer.

1. What percent of the budget is for potting soil?
a. 12.5% **b.** 8% **c.** 0.08%

2. How much money did the class budget for plant food?
a. $12 **b.** $24 **c.** $36

3. How many degrees are there in the sector of the circle graph for plant food?
a. 43.2° **b.** 28.8° **c.** 18.0°

4. How many degrees are there in the sector for other expenses?
a. 8° **b.** 18° **c.** 108°

Practice

For More Practice, see Set B, pages 248–249.

Copy and complete the table below for another science project budget.

Item	Percent	Number of degrees
Food	30%	**5.**
Mice	20%	**6.**
Cages	**7.**	72
Mazes	**8.**	54
Other	15%	**9.**

10. Draw a circle graph for the data given in the table.

11. Why is it incorrect to mark 30° for food and 20° for mice?

12. Are cages more or less than one fourth of the project budget?

13. What fraction of the budget is for cages?

Find the number of degrees in a circle graph for the following parts of a project:

14. wire, 45% **15.** paper, 25% **16.** foil, 10% **17.** plywood, 8% **18.** paint, 12%

19. Make a circle graph for Exercises 14–18.

Problem Solving

Solve each problem.

Sam gets $6 a week in allowance, works part time, and wants to buy a dog, which will cost $100. His estimated budget is dog food, 35%; veterinary care, 20%; miscellaneous, 5%; savings, 40%.

20. Make a circle graph of Sam's budget.

21. Use the percent bar on the Math Sketcher to show Sam's budget.

22. If he makes an average of $36 a week, how long will it take him to save enough for the dog?

23. This year Sam estimates earnings of $1,800. How much will he budget for veterinary care? for dog food?

Skills Review

pages 56–57, 194–195

Copy and complete the table.

Fraction	$\frac{1}{2}$	**3.**	**5.**	**7.**	**9.**	$\frac{7}{8}$	**13.**
Decimal	**1.**	0.8	**6.**	1.45	**10.**	**11.**	**14.**
Percent	**2.**	**4.**	75%	**8.**	$66\frac{2}{3}\%$	**12.**	60%

ALGEBRA

Use a Formula

Build Understanding

Two years ago Eduardo deposited \$300 in a savings account. The first year the account earned ***simple interest*** (interest paid on the sum of money saved). The second year he received ***compound interest*** (interest paid on both the amount of money saved and the interest it earns). If Eduardo's account paid $5\frac{1}{2}\%$ interest per year and he made no deposits or withdrawals, how much interest did he earn if it was compounded annually for 2 years?

PROBLEM SOLVING GUIDE

Understand
QUESTION
FACTS
KEY IDEA

Plan and Solve
STRATEGY
ANSWER

Look Back
SENSIBLE ANSWER
ALTERNATE APPROACH

Understand QUESTION How much compound interest did Eduardo earn in 2 years?

KEY IDEA The amount of interest earned depends on the money in the account (the ***principal, p***), the percent of interest (the ***rate, r***), and how long the money is on deposit (the ***time, t***).

FACTS The principal is \$300. The rate is $5\frac{1}{2}\%$. The time is 2 years.

Plan and Solve STRATEGY *Use the simple interest formula* to find the interest Eduardo earned the first year.

$I = prt$

$I = 300 \times 0.055 \times 1$

$I = 16.5$

He earned \$16.50 the first year.

The second year he earned interest on both the principal and the first year's interest.

$(300 + 16.50) \times 0.055 = 17.41$

$16.50 + 17.41 = 33.91$ Add the interests earned each year.

ANSWER After 2 years Eduardo earned \$33.91 in interest.

Look Back SENSIBLE ANSWER The answer is sensible, since the simple interest for two years is \$33.

Talk About Math What number would you substitute for t if Eduardo's money were compounded every 6 months? Will he earn more or less than $16.50 the first year?

Check Understanding

Fill in the blanks.

1. If Eduardo had twice as much money in the bank, how much interest would he earn in a year?

   ▒ = ▒ × ▒ × ▒
   I p r t

2. Suppose the rate of interest doubled. How much interest would he earn in a year?

   ▒ = ▒ × ▒ × ▒
   I p r t

3. If Eduardo's bank compounded interest quarterly, how much interest would $300 earn in 6 months?

4. If Eduardo's bank compounded interest monthly, how much interest would $300 earn in 6 months?

Practice

For Exercises 5–8, find the amount of simple interest for each amount. Round each answer to the nearest cent. A calculator will help.

Principal	Annual rate of interest	Time	Interest
$50	5%	6 mo	**5.**
$200	5.75%	1 yr	**6.**
$350	6.5%	18 mo	**7.**
$3,210	6%	1 yr 9 mo	**8.**

TIPS FOR PROBLEM SOLVERS

Be flexible. If you get stuck, try another idea.

Calculator Use a calculator. Find the compound interest.

9. Find the interest on $600 at 8% compounded annually for 3 years.

10. Find the interest on $400 at 7% compounded semiannually (2 times per year) for 1 year.

11. SuperBank offers a rate of 5% compounded quarterly (4 times per year). Find your interest after one year if you start with $400.

12. About how long would it take to double $1,000 invested at 8% per year, compounded annually?

Comparison Shopping

Build Understanding

When Johanna goes shopping, she uses her calculator to find the best buy. She checks 3 bottles of a shampoo. Which is the best buy?

Johanna uses unit prices. *Unit pricing* is a method that shows both the total cost and the cost per unit of measure. She uses her calculator to find the cost of 1 oz of each size of shampoo. The size with the lowest unit price is the best buy.

Small size: $1.73 ÷ 4 = 0.4325 ≈ $0.43
Medium size: $2.73 ÷ 7 = 0.39 = $0.39
Large size: $3.57 ÷ 11 = 0.3245 ≈ $0.32

The large size for $3.57 is the best buy.

The best buys are often on the top or bottom shelves. The more expensive brands are frequently at eye level.

Talk About Math When comparison shopping for a product, why might you decide to buy the brand that is not the best buy?

Check Understanding

For another example, see Set C, pages 246–247.

Choose the correct way to find the unit price to the nearest tenth of a cent. Tell if you used mental math, paper and pencil, or a calculator.

1. 6.5 oz jar of skin cream for $4.99

a. 6.5 ÷ 4.99 **b.** 4.99 ÷ 6.5 **c.** 6.5 × 4.99

2. $0.79 for 4 oz bar of soap

a. 4 ÷ 0.79 **b.** 0.79 × 4 **c.** 0.79 ÷ 4

Find the unit price to the nearest tenth of a cent.

3. $6.79 for 3.5-oz bottle of sun screen

4. 4-oz can of first-aid spray for $4.89

Practice

For More Practice, see Set C, pages 248–249.

The table shows a number of items on Johanna's shopping list. For each brand, find the unit price to the nearest tenth of a cent.

Item	Name brand	Unit price	Generic brand	Unit price
Toothpaste	6.4-oz tube, \$2.19	**5.**	8.2-oz tube, \$2.65	**6.**
Vitamin C	100 tablets, \$1.99	**7.**	250 tablets, \$4.99	**8.**
Cotton balls	bag of 65, \$1.49	**9.**	bag of 130, \$2.09	**10.**
Bandages	can of 30, \$2.29	**11.**	can of 70, \$2.99	**12.**
Dental floss	300 yd, \$3.99	**13.**	100 yd, \$2.59	**14.**
Gauze pads	box of 25, \$4.79	**15.**	box of 10, \$2.29	**16.**

Choose the better buy. The symbol @ means "at".

17. 2 L of water @ \$1.49 or 3 L @ \$2.19

18. 200 tissues @ \$1.79 or 250 @ \$1.99

19. 22 oz of bread @ \$1.49 or 1 lb @ \$0.89

20. 1 gal of cider @ \$4.29 or 2 qt @ \$2.29

21. 5 kg of rice @ \$8.88 or 2 kg @ \$3.39

22. 15 ft of tape @ \$2.32 or 20 ft @ \$3.09

23. $\frac{1}{2}$ lb of lox @ \$5.59 or $\frac{1}{4}$ lb @ \$2.89

24. 1 lb of turkey @ \$3.49 or $\frac{1}{4}$ lb @ \$0.88

25. 2 lemons for \$0.98 or 12 for \$3.99

26. 3 notebooks for \$2.79 or 12 for \$9.89

Problem Solving

Solve each problem.

27. With a \$1 coupon which is the better buy: 8 oz of shampoo @ \$2.99, or 16 oz @ \$4.19?

28. Based on Exercises 5–16, what's generally true about generic and name brand prices?

29. With a 50¢ coupon for two 16-oz bottles of saline solution or one 30-oz bottle, which is the better buy: two 16-oz bottles @ \$1.89 each, or one 30-oz bottle @ \$3.49?

30. A 54-count package of diapers costs \$10.89 and has a \$1 mail-in rebate. A 40-count package costs \$8.29. If the 40 pack is purchased with a \$0.50 coupon, which is the better buy?

31. Which is a better value, \$2.49 for 8 oz of tea, or 5 oz for \$1.56?

32. **Critical Thinking** In Exercise 30 what other cost affects the 54-count package?

Multiple-Step Problems

PROBLEM SOLVING GUIDE

Understand
QUESTION
FACTS
KEY IDEA

Plan and Solve
STRATEGY
ANSWER

Look Back
SENSIBLE ANSWER
ALTERNATE APPROACH

Build Understanding

Every year the students at Lake Junior High raise money for a community project. This year they decided to buy a television set for the Senior Citizens' Center. The television set they want to buy is on sale at Bill's Bargainland for $33\frac{1}{3}\%$ off the listed price of $375. What is the sale price of the television?

Understand QUESTION What is the reduced price of the television?

FACTS The original price of $375 is reduced by $33\frac{1}{3}\%$.

Plan and Solve STRATEGY First find the amount of the discount. Then subtract the discount from the regular price to find the sale price.

Find $33\frac{1}{3}\%$ of $375. Since $33\frac{1}{3}\%$ is $\frac{1}{3}$, the amount of the discount is

$$\frac{1}{3} \times 375 = 125.$$

To find the sale price, subtract

$$375 - 125 = 250.$$

ANSWER The sale price of the television is $250, a savings of $125.

Look Back ALTERNATE APPROACH Another way to solve this problem is to work with the percents. If the discount is $33\frac{1}{3}\%$, then the sale price will be

$$100\% - 33\frac{1}{3}\% = 66\frac{2}{3}\%, \text{ or } \frac{2}{3}$$

of the regular price. To find the sale price, multiply

$$\frac{2}{3} \times 375 = 250.$$

The sale price of the television is $250.

Talk About Math Why might a store reduce the price of a television? When might be a good time to buy summer clothes?

Check Understanding

Choose the correct answer.

1. The students had to pay 6% sales tax when they bought the TV. How much sales tax did they pay on the TV?

a. \$5 **b.** \$15 **c.** \$25 **d.** \$50

2. How much sales tax would they have paid if they had bought the TV at the regular price?

a. \$12.50 **b.** \$22.50 **c.** \$25.50 **d.** \$52.50

Practice

Copy the table. Then fill in the missing values.

Item	Regular price	Rate of discount	Amount of discount	Sale price
Television cabinet	\$420.00	30%	**3.**	**4.**
Entertainment center	\$550.00	**5.**	\$275.00	**6.**
Wall unit	**7.**	$33\frac{1}{3}$%	\$90.00	**8.**
Television cart	\$175.00	**9.**	**10.**	\$140.00

Solve each problem.

11. The trees and shrubs that a class wants to buy cost \$340. Next week, the trees and shrubs will be discounted at 30%. If there is a sales tax of 5%, how much will the class have to pay for the trees and shrubs?

12. Number Sense Luisa tried to think of a shortcut for solving Exercise 11. She thought, "If there is a discount of 30% and then 5% tax is added, that should be the same as a discount of 30 − 5, or 25%." Is this correct? Explain.

Interpreting Utility Bills

Build Understanding

Utility bills show varying rates and charges and are based on the amount of electricity, gas, or water used. Many companies also add a monthly service charge. The electric company charges for the number of ***kilowatt hours*** used in one month. One kilowatt hour (1 kwh) is the amount of electricity needed to light a 100-watt light bulb for 10 hours. Here is an electric bill. Are the calculations correct?

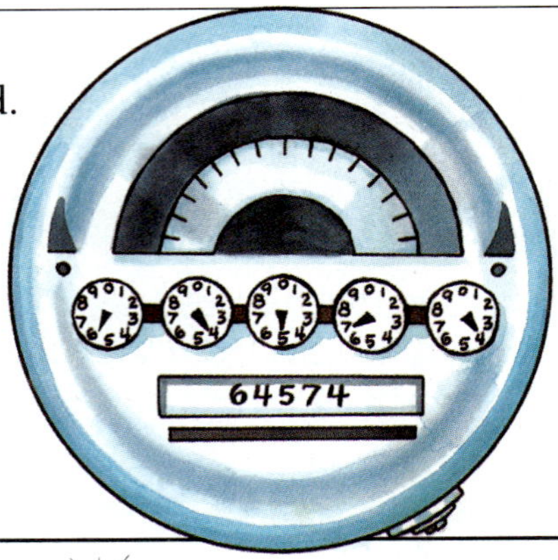

Subtract to calculate kwh used.

64574 − 64085 = 489

Multiply to calculate energy charge.

(400)(0.09208) = 36.832 ≈ 36.83
(89)(0.04627) = 4.11803 ≈ 4.12

Multiply to calculate tax.

(489)(0.00320) = 1.5648 ≈ 1.56

Add to find the total.

$11.24
36.83
4.12
+ 1.56
$53.75

The bill is correct.

Electric Company

Present meter reading	March 3	64574
Previous meter reading	January 31	64085
Total kilowatt-hours used		489
Customer charge		$11.24
Energy charge:	1st 400 kwh x $0.09208	$36.83
Remaining	89 kwh x $0.04627	$4.12
State tax	489 kwh x $0.00320	$1.56
Amount due		$53.75

If the total bill is paid before March 23, you may deduct $1.96 from the amount due

Talk About Math On an electric bill (or any similar bill) do you think the computations are usually correct? What figures would you check? Why?

Check Understanding

For another example, see Set D, pages 246–247.

Answer each question.

1. The customer used 489 kwh that month. What was the cost of the first 400 kwh? the remaining 89 kwh? the entire 489 kwh?

2. If the bill is paid on March 20, how much will it be? What percent discount does this represent?

Practice

For More Practice, see Set D, pages 248–249.

For Exercises 3–9, fill in the missing numbers in the bill below. Use a calculator. Round each result to the nearest cent.

Present meter reading	June 5	84175
Previous meter reading	April 30	83627
Total kilowatt-hours used		**3.** _____
Customer charge		$11.24
Energy charge: 1st 400 kwh × $0.0920		**4.** _____
Remaining **5.** _____ kwh × $0.04627		**6.** _____
State tax **7.** _____ kwh × $0.00320		**8.** _____
Amount due		**9.** _____

Mental Math For Exercises 10–13, estimate the annual cost of operating each appliance if a kilowatt-hour of electricity costs 7.704¢.

Appliance	Annual usage (kwh)	Annual Cost
Hair dryer	18	**10.**
Freezer	1195	**11.**
Air conditioner	1725	**12.**
Television	458	**13.**

Use the above bill to compute the electric cost for these meter readings. Round each result to the nearest $0.01.

14. Present: 54625
Previous: 53805

15. Present: 46020
Previous: 41999

16. Present: 00597
Previous: 98639

Problem Solving

The gas company charges per hundred cubic feet (CCF). Solve each problem.

17. How much is due on this bill?

Service Charge	$6.41
First 50 CCF	0.7714/CCF
Over 50 CCF	0.3788/CCF
Use in CCF	56

18. The gas company is changing its rates to $.8700/CCF for the first 50 CCF and $.8079/CCF for over 50 CCF. How much will this increase cost a family whose average use is 225 CCF per month?

Midchapter Checkup

Solve each problem.

1. Find Gerardo's gross income. Weekly salary: $225; total sales: $12,236; commission rate: 2.5%.

2. A $455 stereo is discounted by 29%. What is the total cost after a 6% tax is added?

3. Find the unit price for a 5-lb bag of flour selling for $1.05.

4. Gas rates are $.8100/CCF for the first 50, and $.7988/CCF for over 50 CCF. Find the fuel charge on 114 CCF.

5. One sector of a circle graph is 25%. How many degrees is this?

6. Find the interest on $345 at 7% compounded annually for 2 years.

Problem-Solving Workshop

Real-Life Decision Making

1. Which is the least expensive way to make chicken soup? Which is the most expensive?

2. Describe a situation in which it would be reasonable to buy each kind of soup shown.

MATH laugh

Before I take this job, please tell me, are the hours long?

No, only 60 minutes!

Explore with a Computer

Use the *Spreadsheet Workshop Project* for this activity.

When you buy an 18-ounce jar of peanut butter for $1.89, the unit cost is $0.105 per ounce. Suppose you buy a 48-ounce jar of the same brand of peanut butter for $3.75.

1. At the computer, change the price and number of ounces in the spreadsheet to represent the larger jar of peanut butter. What is the unit price for the 48-ounce jar? Which size is the better buy?

2. Compare the unit prices of a 32-ounce bottle of orange juice that costs $1.44 and a 24-ounce bottle that costs $0.99. Suppose you need to buy 96 ounces of orange juice. Which size would you buy and how many bottles do you need?

Price in dollars:	$ 1.89
Ounces in container	18

$$\frac{1.89\ \text{(dollars)}}{18\ \text{(ounces)}} = \frac{n\ \text{(dollars)}}{1\ \text{(ounce)}}$$

Number-Sense Project

Look back at pages 216–217.

1. If recycled aluminum cans bring $0.25 per pound, how many pounds would it take to net $100?

2. If each household contributes 8 pounds of aluminum cans, how many households would net $100?

3. If it takes each family 2 weeks to collect 8 pounds of aluminum cans, how much money could all these households earn in one year for recycled aluminum cans?

Using Credit Cards

Build Understanding

Patti's mother has a department store credit card. The unpaid balance on her account from last month is $87.50. This month she paid $20, her minimum payment, and charged $23.18 in new purchases. The ***annual interest rate*** for the card is 18.0%. What will her outstanding balance be at the end of the month?

First, find the balance after the payment of $20 was made.

$87.50 − $20.00 = $67.50

Second, find the monthly interest rate by dividing the annual interest by 12.

18.0% ÷ 12 = 1.5%

Third, find 1.5% of $67.50, the interest to be paid.

0.015 × 67.50 = 1.0125

The interest charge will be $1.01, to the nearest cent.

To find the new balance, add

67.50 + 1.01 + 23.18 = 91.69

The outstanding balance is $91.69.

Most credit card companies require at least a minimum payment on the ***outstanding (unpaid) balance*** of an account each month. They charge interest each month on the outstanding balance. The rate of interest varies, because each state's laws and credit card company's policies vary. It is wise to read the fine print before using a card.

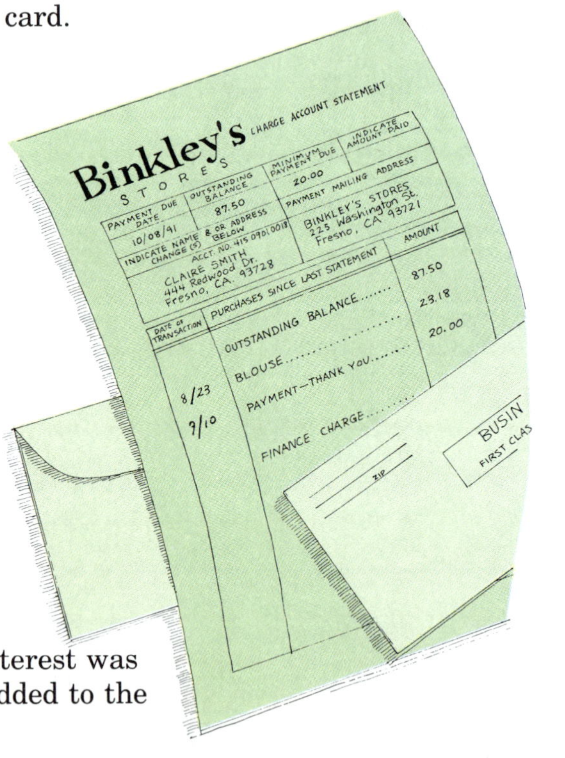

■ **Talk About Math** In the example, the interest was calculated before the new purchases were added to the account. Is this fair? Explain.

Check Understanding

For another example, see Set E, pages 246–247.

Tell whether the statement is true or false.

1. The rate of 1.7% interest per month as an annual rate of interest is written as 17%.

2. A credit card company usually offers the same interest rate in each state.

Practice

For More Practice, see Set E, pages 248–249.

Complete the table. Round the interest to the nearest $.01.
Use pencil and paper or a calculator for these exercises.

Unpaid balance	Payment	Balance after payment	Interest rate (per month)	Amount of interest	New purchases	New balance
$47.16	$0.00	**3.**	1.25%	**4.**	$0.00	**5.**
$79.62	$0.00	**6.**	1.25%	**7.**	$46.13	**8.**
$126.38	$20.00	**9.**	1.5%	**10.**	$0.00	**11.**
$148.18	$25.00	**12.**	1.5%	**13.**	$30.57	**14.**
$342.75	$70.00	**15.**	1.6%	**16.**	$16.62	**17.**

For each account find the balance after the payment was made, the amount of interest, and the new balance.

18. Unpaid balance $400, monthly interest 1.75%, new purchases $619.20

19. Unpaid balance $986.00, monthly interest 1%, no new purchases

Problem Solving

Solve each problem. **Remember** to line up the decimal points when adding or subtracting.

20. The unpaid balance on the Lis' C-Card account was $200. This month they charged $78 and paid $200. The monthly rate on the unpaid balance is 1.75%. What was the end-of-month balance?

21. Claire had an unpaid balance of $198.42 on her credit-card account. This month she paid $150, and charged $227.65 in clothing. The annual interest rate is 18%. What was her new end-of-month balance?

Choose a ________ Strategy

Phone Home The telephone company gives a discount of 35% off the regular rate on calls made between 6:00 P.M. and midnight, and a discount of 60% on calls made between midnight and 8:00 A.M. What is the cost of a 5-minute call made at 9:00 P.M. if the regular rate is $1.40 per minute?

22. How much will the call cost at the regular rate?

23. What is the amount of discount?

24. What is the cost with the discount?

PROBLEM SOLVING STRATEGIES

Choose an Operation
Solve a Simpler Problem
Use a Formula
Write an Equation
Make a Graph

ALGEBRA

Installment Buying

Build Understanding

A. Michele is buying her first car by borrowing the money from her parents. The car costs \$2,500. Michele repays her parents in 36 monthly installments of \$84 each. How much more will Michele pay for the car by paying for it in monthly installments?

Total cost over 36 months:
36 × \$84 = \$3,024

Subtract the car's price from the total cost.
\$3,024 − \$2,500 = \$524

Michele pays \$524 more.

B. About what rate of yearly interest is Michele paying on the installments?

You can use the simple interest formula, $I = prt$, to find the rate.

You know that I = \$524, p = \$2,500 and t = 36 months, or 3 years.

$$I = prt \rightarrow r = \frac{I}{pt}$$

$$r = \frac{(524)}{(2{,}500)(3)}$$

$$r \approx 0.069$$

Michele pays about 7% simple interest per year.

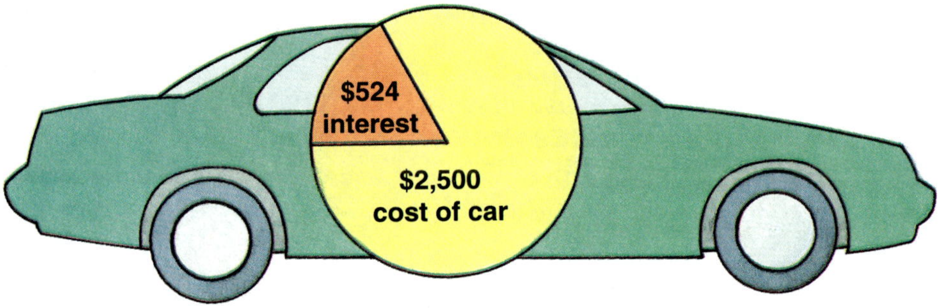

Talk About Math What are some of the advantages and disadvantages of buying expensive items in installments?

Check Understanding

For another example, see Set F, pages 246–247.

Fill in the missing numbers.

1. If Michele adds repairs, the car will cost \$700 more. How much more monthly interest will she pay?

$\frac{\$700}{36} \times$ ▒ = \$▒

2. How would the repairs in Exercise 1 affect Michele's monthly payment?

\$84 + $\frac{\$700}{36}$ + ▒ = \$▒

Practice

For More Practice, see Set F, pages 248–249.

Solve for the missing variable in the simple interest formula, $I = prt$.

3. p = \$7,825; r = 10%; t = 5 months; find I.

4. I = \$16.70; p = \$167; t = 2 years; find r.

5. I = \$2,550; p = \$15,000; $r = 8\frac{1}{2}\%$; find t.

6. I = \$2,937; r = 11%; t = 3 years; find p.

For each item, find the cost of financing and the rate of interest being charged.

Item	List price	Number of payments	Amount of each payment	Cost of financing	Annual interest rate
New car	\$ 13,980	60	\$ 333.46	**7.**	**8.**
Used car	\$ 5,478	60	\$ 132.50	**9.**	**10.**
Television set	\$ 649	36	\$ 25.60	**11.**	**12.**
Living room set	\$ 1,888	48	\$ 58.22	**13.**	**14.**
Canoe	\$ 479	18	\$ 30.00	**15.**	**16.**
Tractor	\$108,478	48	\$3,060.00	**17.**	**18.**
Carpeting	\$ 4,560	72	\$ 74.00	**19.**	**20.**
CD player	\$ 229	8	\$ 30.00	**21.**	**22.**
Computer	\$ 2,798	24	\$ 160.00	**23.**	**24.**

Problem Solving

Solve each problem.

25. **Calculator** The price of a camera is \$600. The payments are \$54 a month for 1 year. What is the simple interest rate?

26. On a \$455 freezer, Bob will make 24 monthly payments of \$21. Find the total interest paid.

27. Michele's parents bought a television on installment. The price plus tax was \$736.70. They paid 15% of the price as a down payment, and 25 monthly payments of \$41.16. How much did they pay for the set in all?

28. Michele's friend, Sarah, bought a car on installment. The list price was \$9,200. She made a down payment of \$1,400, and agreed to pay the balance in 36 monthly installments of \$278.42. How much interest will she pay on the remaining balance?

Multiple-Step Problems

PROBLEM SOLVING GUIDE

Understand
QUESTION
FACTS
KEY IDEA

Plan and Solve
STRATEGY
ANSWER

Look Back
SENSIBLE ANSWER
ALTERNATE APPROACH

Build Understanding

Suree is planning to visit her aunt in Thailand. Two years ago, the return airfare was $1,120 per person. Last year that price increased to $1,190. If the percent of increase remains the same, what will the airfare be this year, to the nearest dollar?

Understand QUESTION How much will the airfare increase this year?

FACTS Last year the airfare increased from $1,120 to $1,190.

KEY IDEA There are several steps.

Plan and Solve Find the amount of increase last year and express the increase as a percent.

$$\$1{,}190 - \$1{,}120 = \$70$$

$$\frac{70}{1{,}120} \times 100 = 6.25\%$$

To find the fare increase this year, find 6.25% of $1,190.

$$6.25\% \times 1{,}190 = 0.0625 \times 1{,}190$$
$$= 74.375 \approx \$74$$

To find the airfare this year, add $74 to last year's fare of $1,190.

$$\$1{,}190 + \$74 = \$1{,}264$$

ANSWER The airfare this year will probably be $1,264.

Look Back ALTERNATE APPROACH If the increase is 6.25%, the total fare is 106.25%.

$$(1{,}190)(106.25\%) = (1{,}190)(1.0625)$$
$$\approx \$1{,}264$$

Write About Math Does it make sense to talk about a price increase of more than 100%? a price decrease of more than 100%? Explain, using examples.

Check Understanding

Choose the best answer.

1. Last year, the airfare increased from $1,200 to $1,272. What was the percent increase?

a. 0.6% **b.** 6% **c.** 60%

2. If the fare increases at the same percent this year, what will the new fare be?

a. $1,348 **b.** $1,289 **c.** $1,276

Practice

Find the percent of the increase or decrease. I = increase; D = decrease.

3. 90 to 117 **4.** 56 to 84 **5.** 72 to 126 **6.** 59 to 118

7. 85 to 68 **8.** 120 to 90 **9.** 45 to 9 **10.** 250 to 100

11. 80 to 88 **12.** 45 to 60 **13.** 284 to 71 **14.** 128 to 80

Find the amount of increase or decrease and the new amount.

15. 88 with a 25% increase

16. 92 with a 50% increase

17. 185 with a 100% increase

18. 88 with a 25% decrease

19. 92 with a 50% decrease

20. 90 with a 40% decrease

21. 95 with a 120% increase

22. 27 with a $66\frac{2}{3}$% increase

23. Use Data Find this year's list price for the first four items given in the chart on page 235. The price increase is 7%.

Solve each problem. **Remember** to label the units in your answer.

24. In 1989, the Luna family paid $850 a month for rent. In 1990, their rent was 6% higher than it was in 1989. In 1991, their rent was 5% higher than it was in 1990. How much did they pay for rent in 1991? By what percent did their rent increase from 1989 to 1991?

25. The Ordonselli family is planning a camping trip. The trip will be about 3,000 miles long, and they want to estimate how much they will spend on gasoline. On their last two fill-ups, they used 42 gallons at a total cost of $43.64 and traveled 895 miles. At that rate, how much will gas for their trip cost?

Interpreting Data from a Graph

Build Understanding

A. Meteorologists use graphs to summarize and compute data. The ***broken-line graph*** at the right shows the temperature on the hour from 8 A.M. to noon. Such graphs are used to show trends over a period of time. When was the temperature highest? lowest?

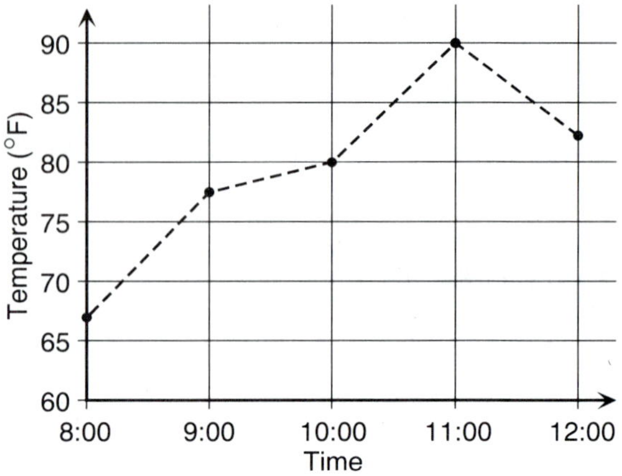

You can see from the graph that the temperature was highest at 11:00 A.M. and lowest at 8:00 A.M..

B. Graphs can be combined to make comparisons of several sets of data easier. The graph below compares the normal high and low temperatures for the first six months of the year.

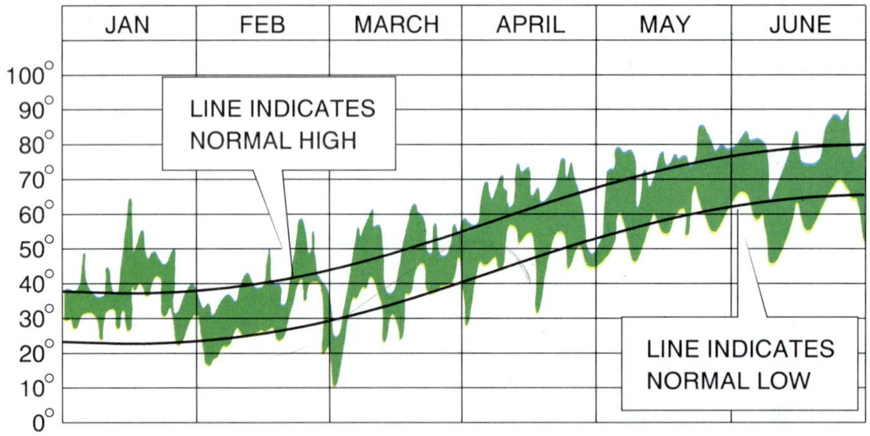

What is the normal range for June? What was the actual range for June? Was the actual range greater or less than the normal range?

From the graph, you can see that the normal low is about 62°. The normal high is about 80°, so the normal range is about 80° − 62°, or 18°.

The actual low was about 45° and the actual high was about 90°. So the actual range was about 45°, less than the normal range.

C. ***Circle graphs*** are used to compare parts of a whole. The graph shows the percent of days in June that were sunny, cloudy but not rainy, and rainy.

How many days were sunny?

60% × 30 = 0.6 × 30 = 18 days

How many days were rainy?

13% × 30 = 0.13 × 30 = 3.9 ≈ 4 days

Days of Sunshine, June

D. ***Bar graphs*** are used when data from one group or period are compared with data from another group or period. The bar graph below compares the amount of precipitation in Central City last year with the normal amount.

For which months was precipitation about normal? below normal?

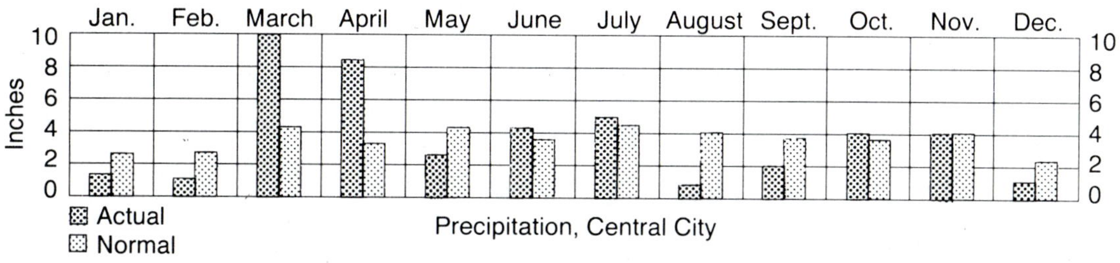

Precipitation, Central City

The Actual bar is about the same height as the Normal bar for November. The Actual bar is above the Normal bar for March, April, June, July, and October. The Actual bar is below the Normal bar for January, February, May, August, September, and December.

Talk About Math Can you tell from the broken line graph in Example A the time when the temperature was 75°? Explain.

Check Understanding

For another example, see Set G, pages 246–247.

Tell whether the statement is *true* or *false*. Use the graphs in Examples B and D.

1. The actual temperature range for the 6 months shown in the graph in Example B is 75°.

2. The total precipitation shown in the graph in Example D is less than normal for last year.

3. The coldest day shown in the graph in Example B was March 1.

Practice

For More Practice, see Set G, pages 248–249.

Use the graph in Example B for Exercises 4–6.

4. Describe in as much detail as you can what the weather was like in the last week of April and the first week of May.

5. Describe in as much detail as you can what the weather was like in the last week of March and the first week of April.

6. Describe the weather in January.

Use the graph in Example D for Exercises 7–8.

7. Which month had the most actual precipitation? About how much precipitation was it?

8. Which month is normally the driest? How much precipitation usually falls in that month?

Calculator Use the information in the graph at the right to answer Exercises 9–10. Round answers to the nearest whole day.

9. How many days were sunny?

10. How many days were cloudy with no precipitation?

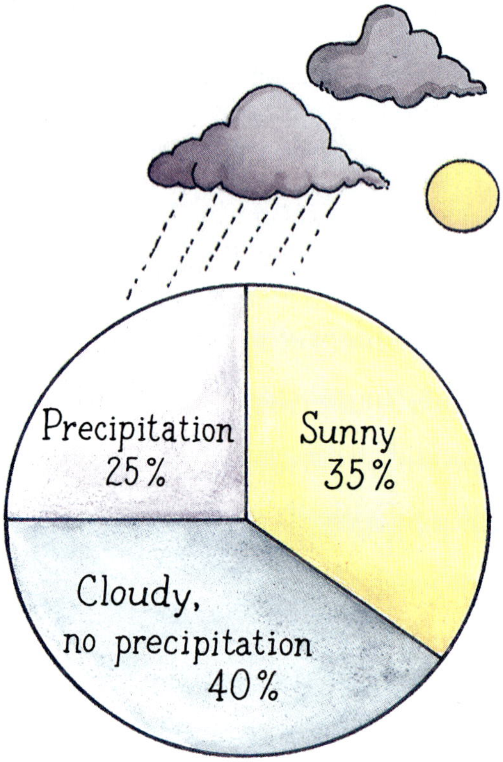

January Weather

Use the graphs in Examples A, B, C, and D to answer the following.

11. How much warmer was it at 11:00 A.M. than at 10:00 A.M.?

12. About how much colder was the coldest day in March than the warmest day in June?

13. Which month had the largest difference between high and low temperatures?

14. How many days were not sunny in the month of June?

15. Which month was wetter, April or August?

16. Which month had the smallest extreme in temperatures?

17. Between which hours was the smallest change in temperature?

18. In which month was the actual precipitation closest to normal?

19. Which month had the greatest difference between actual and normal precipitation?

Problem Solving

Explore ______ Math

Graphs can show trends. The Musichord Company made the graph below of its sales of records, cassettes, and compact discs (CDs).

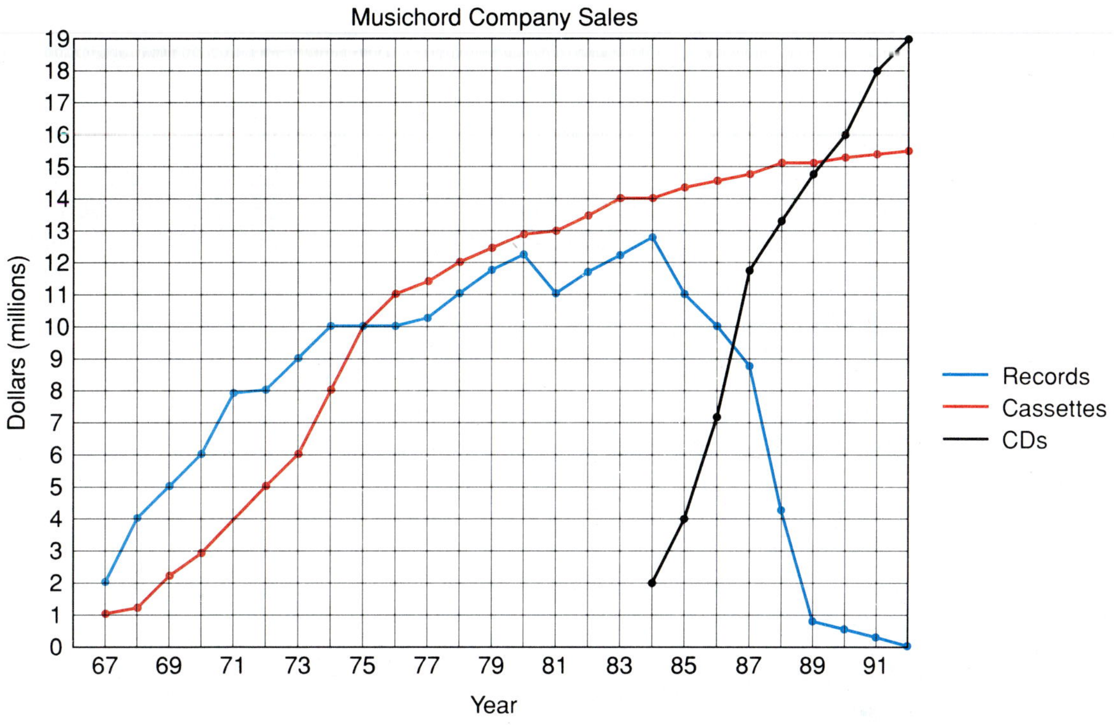

20. If you had been the company's marketing manager in 1970, what prediction about record sales might you have made?

21. What year had the highest combined sales for records and cassettes? Find the total.

22. In 1980, what recommendation would you have made about the production of records? Explain.

23. In 1985, what recommendation might you have made about production of cassettes?

24. Why do you suppose record sales dropped so quickly after 1984?

25. What prediction might you have made about cassette sales in 1970?

26. What year has the highest combined sale for records, CDs, and cassettes? What was the total?

27. Based on your findings in Problem 26, predict the total sales for 1993.

Deciding When an Estimate Is Enough

Build Understanding

If it takes 6 ounces of milk to make a 1-ounce cheese slice, about how many gallons of milk are needed to make 40 million slices? Estimate. You should estimate when an exact value is too tedious or impossible to compute, when an exact value is not necessary, or when an estimate is asked for.

PROBLEM SOLVING GUIDE

Understand
QUESTION
FACTS
KEY IDEA

Plan and Solve
STRATEGY
ANSWER

Look Back
SENSIBLE ANSWER
ALTERNATE APPROACH

Understand QUESTION How many gallons of milk are needed to make 40 million 1-ounce slices of cheese?

FACTS 6 oz milk = 1 oz cheese
1 gallon = 128 ounces of milk

KEY IDEA If you know how many cheese slices can be made from 1 gallon of milk, you can determine about how many gallons are needed for 40 million slices.

Plan and Solve STRATEGY How many slices of cheese can be made from 1 gallon of milk?

$$\frac{\textbf{128 ounces/gal}}{\textbf{6 ounces/slice}} \approx \textbf{21 slices/gal}$$

If there are 21 slices of cheese per gallon, then

$$\frac{\textbf{40 million slices}}{\textbf{21 slices/gal}} \approx \textbf{2 million gal}$$

ANSWER About 2 million gallons of milk are needed.

Look Back ALTERNATE APPROACH If 1 cheese slice needs 6 ounces of milk, then 40 million slices need (6 × 40) million ounces.

6 × 40 million = 240 million ounces

1 gallon = 128 ounces

240 million ÷ 128 = 1.875 million gallons

≈ 2 million gallons

In one year the U.S. produces enough American cheese to make 44,770,560,000 1-ounce slices, or about 180 slices for each American.

Talk About Math In the previous problem, is it better to estimate too high or too low? Why?

Check Understanding

Solve each problem.

1. Suppose 5 ounces of milk made one slice of cheese. About how many gallons of milk are needed to make 40 million 1-ounce slices of cheese?

2. Suppose 5,500 slices of cheese are sold each day. How many cows are needed to provide milk for cheese if each cow produces 5 gallons of milk a day? (Assume 5 oz of milk are in 1 slice of cheese.)

3. About how many 8-ounce glasses of milk do you drink in one day?

4. About how many gallons of milk do you drink in one year?

Practice

Solve. Use mental math, paper and pencil, or a calculator. Tell which method you used.

5. Estimate how many pounds of flour are needed to make buns for 40 million tuna melts. Estimate 10 buns per pound of flour.

6. At $5 an hour how long would you have to work to pay for 15 tuna melts? Each tuna melt costs $1.65.

Use the graphs to solve. Tell whether the answer is an estimate or exact.

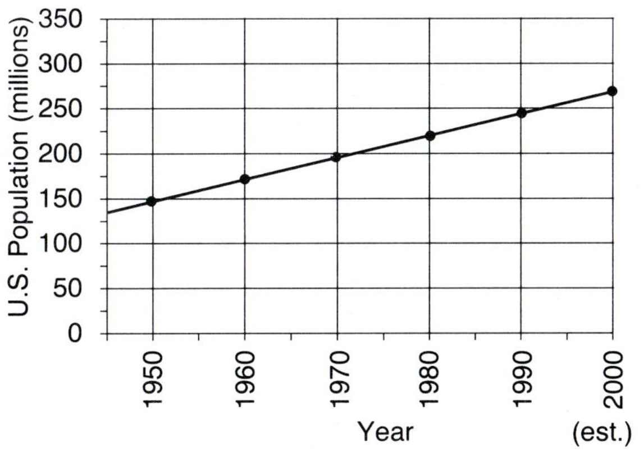

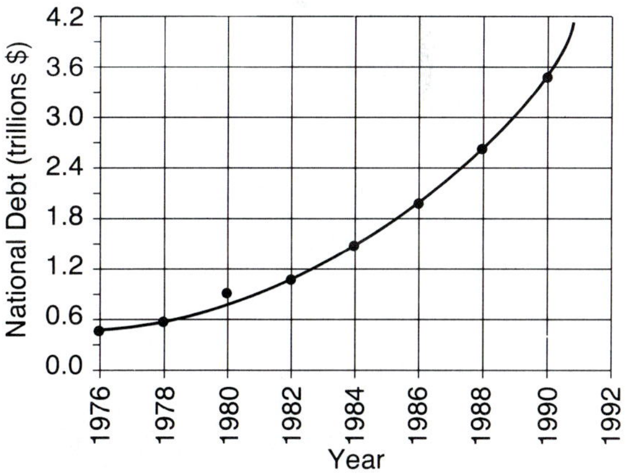

7. An almanac lists the 1980 U.S. population as 226,545,805. How does this figure compare to the graph?

8. Express the 1980 United States national debt in dollars per person.

9. If present trends continue, what will the U.S. population be in 2000?

10. Express the national debt for 1990 in dollars per person.

Skills Review

Use the data in the table. Find each person's gross pay to the nearest cent.

	Weekly Salary	Total Sales	Commission Rate
John	$400	$9,200	2%
Bev	$550	$7,422	1.5%
Les	$300	$5,600	3%

1. John **2.** Bev **3.** Les

The table shows the budget for the 8th grade play. Complete the table and make a circle graph.

Item	Percent	Degrees
Costumes	30%	**4.**
Set	40%	**5.**
Tickets	10%	**6.**
Programs	15%	**7.**
Other	5%	**8.**

Find the unit price to the nearest cent. Which is the best buy?

9. Mousse: 6 oz for $1.99 or 11 oz for $3.89

10. Baked beans: 16 oz for $0.69 or 28 oz for $0.97.

Use the graph to answer the questions.

11. During which month would you close for vacation?

12. Predict the February sales.

Problem-Solving Review

Solve each problem.

13. Denise receives $275 a week salary plus a commission of 5% on all appliance sales over $1,000. Last week she sold appliances worth $2,100. Find her gross salary.

14. Find the interest on $500 at 7.5% compounded annually for 2 years.

15. Roy bought $3,400 worth of carpeting on an installment plan. He made an $800 down payment and he agreed to pay the balance in 24 installments of $145. What rate of interest was Roy paying?

16. Running shoes sell for $40. Next week they go on sale at a discount of 20%. If sales tax is 8.25%, what will the total sales price be?

17. The airfare to Athens was $600 in 1988. It was 4% higher in 1989. In 1990 it was 5% higher than in 1989. What was the airfare to Athens in 1990? By what percent did it increase from 1988 to 1990?

18. **Data File** Use the data on pages 252–253. Suppose you and a friend order lunch. If the tax is 6% and you leave a 15% gratuity, what is the total for your lunch only?

19. **Make a Data File** Take a survey of local hardware stores to find the price per gallon of several different types of paint. Also, find out how many square feet each gallon of paint will cover. Determine the price per square foot for each. Display your findings in a table.

Cumulative Skills Review • Chapters 1–7

Write each decimal as a percent, and each percent as a decimal.

1. 0.008 **2.** 200% **3.** 9.5% **4.** 1.32

List the factors of each number.

5. 51 **6.** 75 **7.** 99 **8.** 107

Add or subtract.

9. $6\frac{3}{4} + 5\frac{1}{8}$ **10.** $12 - 5\frac{11}{12}$ **11.** $9\frac{5}{6} + 3\frac{2}{3}$ **12.** $60\frac{1}{2} - 29\frac{5}{8}$

13. $-9 + 6$ **14.** $45 - (-15)$ **15.** $-10 + (-5)$ **16.** $-22 - (-11)$

17. $\frac{6}{7} + (-\frac{1}{7})$ **18.** $-5 - (-2\frac{3}{4})$ **19.** $\frac{5}{9} + (-\frac{2}{3})$ **20.** $0 - (-1\frac{7}{11})$

Solve.

21. $\frac{4}{5}k = 16$ **22.** $7h = 84$ **23.** $\frac{1}{3}r + 6 = 1$ **24.** $8n - 7.5 = 32.5$

Find the interest on $2,000 at 7% compounded annually

25. for 1 year. **26.** for 18 months. **27.** for 2 years. **28.** for 3 years.

Use grid paper for Exercises 29–32.

29. Draw triangle *ABC*. $A(-1,1)$, $B(-4,5)$, $C(-4,0)$.

30. Translate triangle *ABC* so that (x, y) becomes $(-x, -y)$

31. Reflect triangle *ABC* over the x-axis.

32. Dilate triangle *ABC* using the rule (x, y) becomes $(2x, 2y)$.

Write an equation for each exercise. Then solve it.

33. Find 8% of 25. **34.** 18 is what percent of 45?

35. 2% of 30 is what number? **36.** 13 horses is 25% of what number?

Copy the electric bill and fill in the missing information.

Present meter reading	90138	
Previous meter reading	89472	
Total kilowatt-hours used	**37.** ______	
Energy charge	1st 351 kwh × 0.11439	**38.** ______
Over 351 kwh	**39.** ______ kwh × 0.13290	**40.** ______
Total		**41.** ______

Reteaching

Set A pages 218–219

This chart shows Trudy's weekly pay data for selling computers. Her weekly salary is $397.

Weekly salary	$397.00
Commission rate	6%
Sales amount	$5,249
Income taxes	$142.39
Social Security tax	$57.67

Remember that commission is rate times sales.

1. What is the amount of Trudy's commission?
2. What is Trudy's gross income?
3. What is Trudy's net income?
4. What percentage of gross income is income tax?
5. What percentage of gross income is Social Security tax?
6. What percentage of gross income is net income?

Set B pages 220–221

The circle graph shows Trudy's gross income as weekly salary and commission. The data are given in the chart in Set A. Her weekly salary as a percentage of gross income is 397 ÷ gross income.

Gross Income

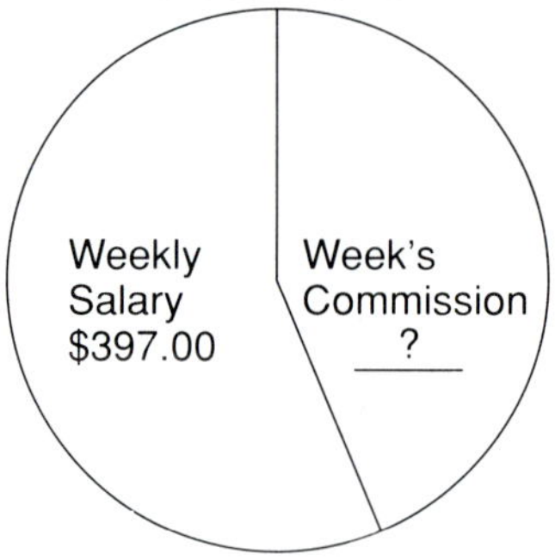

Remember that the percentage of the total is the specific amount divided by the total amount.

1. What percent of Trudy's gross income is her weekly salary?
2. What percent of her gross income is Trudy's commission amount?
3. Use estimation and the answers in Set A to draw a circle graph showing net income, income taxes, and Social Security tax as percents of gross income.

Set C pages 224–225

Kevin is shopping for pizza ingredients. The chart shows the results of his comparisons.

	Brand A	Brand B
Pizza cheese	$2.49 for 1 lb	$2.09 for 10 oz
Flour	$1.17 for 2 lb	$2.45 for 5 lb
Pizza spice	$2.53 for $2\frac{3}{4}$ oz	$1.30 for $1\frac{1}{2}$ oz

Remember that unit price is the cost per unit of measurement.

Find the unit price per ounce to the nearest tenth of a cent. (1 lb = 16 oz)

1. For each brand of pizza cheese
2. For each brand of flour
3. For each brand of pizza spice

Which brand is the best buy?

4. For pizza cheese
5. For flour
6. For pizza spice

Set D pages 228–229

The electric bill shows on-peak use (7 A.M. to 12 noon; 4 P.M. to 8 P.M.) and off-peak use.

Present reading	3519	
Previous reading	3017	
Customer charge, basic service		$5.25
On-peak use	141 @ .0963¢/kwh	?
Off-peak use	361 @ .0527¢/kwh	?
State tax (3¢/kwh for use over 450 kwh)		
Amount over 450 kwh ? ; charge @ 3¢/kwh		?
TOTAL		?

Remember that a kilowatt hour (kwh) is the amount of electricity used for a 100-watt appliance in 10 hours.

Find each answer.

1. Total kilowatt hours

2. Charge for on-peak use

3. Charge for off-peak use

4. Kilowatt hours over 450

5. State tax charges

6. Total cost of bill

Set E pages 232–233

Hanna received this credit card statement.

Previous Balance:	$75.56
Interest at 21%/year:	?
This month's charges:	
New Day Dept. Store	$29.96
Joe's Auto Repair	$42.08

Remember that the monthly interest rate is the annual rate divided by 12.

1. What is the monthly interest rate?

2. What is the interest on the previous balance?

3. If Hanna pays $20 this month, what will be the unpaid balance next month?

4. What will the interest charges be on next month's bill?

Set F pages 234–235

Francine buys a computer system on the terms shown below.

Price:	$5,385
Installments:	$184 per month
Number of payments:	48

Remember that simple interest is $I = prt$.

1. What is the total Francine will pay?

2. What is the total interest paid?

3. What is the interest rate per year?

Set G pages 238–241

The chart shows the mean monthly temperatures in Caribou, Maine. The temperature in March is about 25°F.

Monthly Temperatures: Caribou, Maine

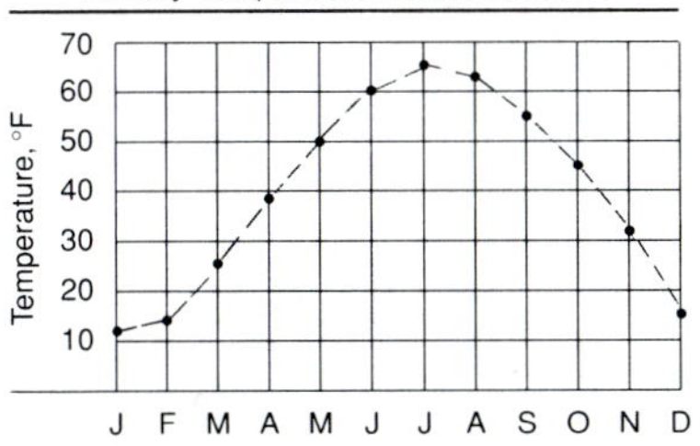

Remember to read all the scales and labels before you interpret a graph.

1. Which month is the temperature lowest?

2. Which month is the temperature highest?

3. How many months is the mean temperature below freezing (32°F)?

More Practice

Set A pages 218–219

The table gives earnings data for salespeople at Electronics Wholesale, Inc. Find each person's gross pay, to the nearest cent.

1. Pam's gross pay **2.** Mia's gross pay

3. Yan's gross pay **4.** Pat's gross pay

5. Which person has the largest gross pay? the smallest gross pay?

	Weekly Salary	Total Sales	Commission Rate
Pam	$250	$8,509	1.5%
Mia	$278	$7,682	2%
Yan	$311	$9,125	3%
Pat	$300	$8,916	2.5%

Set B pages 220–221

Yan's weekly expense budget is shown in the chart. Find the missing information.

Item	Rent	Food	Phone	Trans-portation	Clothing	Spending
Percent	32%	18%	**3.**	**4.**	22%	**6.**
No. of Degrees	**1.**	**2.**	10.8	39.6	**5.**	50.4

7. Construct a circle graph from the data in the table and from your answers for Exercises 1–6. Use a protractor to construct the angles.

Set C pages 224–225

Use the chart to find the unit price per ounce, to the nearest tenth of a cent, for each brand.

1. Mixed fruit **2.** Pears

3. Peaches **4.** Grapefruit

5. Pineapple

6. Which brand of pears is the best buy?

Canned Fruit	Store Brand	Name Brand
Peaches	16 oz, 98¢	15 oz, 95¢
Pears	14 oz, 83¢	16 oz, 99¢
Pineapple	8 oz, 55¢	10 oz, 69¢
Mixed fruit	16 oz, $1.03	8 oz, 59¢
Grapefruit	6 oz, 94¢	8 oz, $1.12

Set D pages 228–229

Copy the bills and fill in the missing information. Round your answers to the nearest cent.

Present 106348 Previous 105022 kwh used **1.** _______

Customer charge $7.89
Energy charge: $0.0861 × 500 kwh **2.** _______
Amount over 500 kwh **3.** _______
$0.0932 × kwh over 500 **4.** _______
Total **5.** _______

Previous 357811 Present 359656
On-peak use 758 Off-peak use 1087
Total use **6.** _______
Rates: 9.845¢ on-peak × 758 **7.** _______
4.976¢ off-peak × 1087 **8.** _______
Customer charge $9.85
Total **9.** _______

Set E pages 232–233

Copy and complete the table. Round interest to the nearest cent.

Unpaid balance	$52.32	$175.89	$519.22	$84.30	$257.08
Payment	$0	$65	$55	$10	$15
Balance after payment	**1.** ______	**2.** ______	**3.** ______	**4.** ______	**5.** ______
Interest rate (per month)	1%	1.25%	1.75%	1.1%	1.5%
Amount of interest	**6.** ______	**7.** ______	**8.** ______	**9.** ______	**10.** ______
New purchases	$78.06	$0	$45.19	$126.88	$59.99
New balance	**11.** ______	**12.** ______	**13.** ______	**14.** ______	**15.** ______

Set F pages 234–235

Round each answer to the nearest cent.

1. A stereo system is on sale for $1,095. It can be purchased on installment for 36 installments of $48.92. What is the total cost of the stereo system on the installment plan?

2. What is the cost of financing the stereo system in Exercise 1?

3. What is the annual interest rate for the stereo installment plan?

4. A VCR costs $689 list price. The installment plan requires payments of $33.88 per month for 24 months. What is the total cost of the VCR on the installment plan?

5. What is the cost of financing the VCR in Exercise 4?

6. What is the annual interest rate for the VCR installment plan?

Set G pages 238–241

The graph shows the mean monthly precipitation (in inches) for the month of June in several U.S. cities. Use the graph to answer the questions.

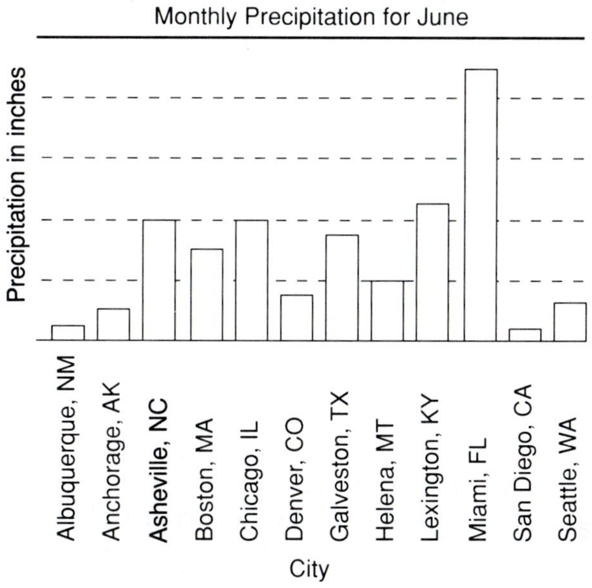

1. What city had the most precipitation in June?

2. What city had the least precipitation?

3. Which cities had about the same amount of precipitation?

4. How many cities had more precipitation than Boston, MA?

Enrichment

Compound Interest

Marsha deposited $1,000 in a savings account that paid 8% interest, compounded annually. At the end of one year she earned 8% of $1,000. At the end of the second year, however, she earned 8% of $1,080 (1,000 + 80).

Principal	$1,000.00
1st year interest (8% of $1,000)	80.00
Amount after 1 year	$1,080.00
2nd year interest (8% of $1,080)	86.40
Amount after 2 years	$1,166.40

Compound interest is paid on both the principal and the accumulated interest.

1. Find the interest that Marsha earned during the third year.

2. What was the total amount in her account after 3 years?

Compound interest can be determined on a calculator.

If $800 is invested at 6% compounded annually, how much will be in the account after 3 years?

To find the amount, press [+] [6] [%], three times. Each sequence will compound the interest by adding it onto the previous year's amount.

Press: 800 [+] [6] [%] [+] [6] [%] [+] [6] [%] **Display:** *952.8128*

1st year — 2nd year — 3rd year

To the nearest cent, the amount in the account will be $952.81.

Use a calculator or paper and pencil to find each total amount.

3. $500, 9%, 2 years

4. $1,200, 5%, 3 years

5. $2,000, 7%, 4 years

6. $3,600, 12%, 5 years

7. $8,250, 11%, 6 years

8. $4,400, 6.8%, 4 years

9. When interest is compounded **semiannually**, interest is added every 6 months at half the annual rate. If $1,600 is invested at 8.4% compounded semiannually, how much will be in the account after 3 years?

Chapter 7 Review/Test

1. Joan makes a base salary of $132 plus a commission of 5% on all her sales. What will be her total income on sales of $8,380?

2. The Jefferson family budget includes 35% for rent. In a circle graph showing their budget, how many degrees would be in the sector representing rent?

3. What is the *compound interest* on $400 at 6% compounded annually for 2 years?

a. $48.00 **b.** $49.44
c. $24.00 **d.** $13.00

4. Read the problem. Then decide which statement below is another way of asking the question.

Rose has $200 in a bank which pays 4.5% interest compounded annually. How much interest will Rose have in 4 years?

a. How much money will Rose have in 4 years?
b. How much money will Rose get every year?
c. How much will the bank pay Rose for leaving her money and its interest in the bank?
d. How much did the bank pay Rose in the fourth year?

5. What is the unit price for 5.5 ounces of cream for $1.32?

6. Alex's parents bought him a radio for graduation at 20% off the regular price of $128. How much did they pay for the radio?

7. What is the cost of 544 kwh of electricity if the cost of the first 500 kwh is $0.08 per kwh and the cost of remaining kwh is $0.06 per kwh?

8. Last month Mr. Jarad had an unpaid balance of $120 on his credit card. This month he paid $20. The annual rate is 18%. What will be his new unpaid balance?

9. Kathy bought a $630 television set and paid for it by making 24 payments of $30 each. How much was the cost of financing?

10. This year Max spent $145 on clothes. Last year he spent $125. What is the percent of increase in his spending?

11. Use the circle graph to find out about how many days of the year had some type of precipitation.

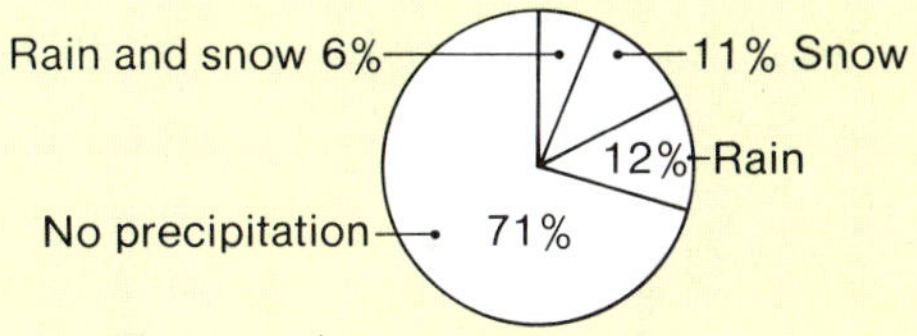

12. Solve the problem and tell whether the answer is an exact number or an estimate.

The ARB company advertises that it made over 5 million electric cords last year. If an average of 11 feet of wire is used for each cord, how many feet of wire did the company use last year?

13. **Write About Math** A newspaper reports that there are 1,200 deer in a forest preserve. Is 1,200 an estimate or an exact number? Why?

1. Menu

- Menu -

Lunch Sandwiches

Chicken Salad	3.75
Tuna Salad on light rye	3.45
Bacon, Lettuce, Tomato	3.75
Junior Club	4.95
Sloppy Joe with our own special sauce	4.45
BBQ Chicken	3.95
Charboiled Fish with lettuce, tomatoes, brown mustard	4.45

Lunch Salads

Mexican Fiesta	4.95
Salmon-Tomato on mixed greens	7.95
Chicken-Pineapple Bowl with poppyseed dressing	5.95

Drinks

Lowfat Milk	0.75
Orange, Grapefruit, or Cranberry Juice Small	0.75
Large	1.00
Apple Cider (in season)	1.25

1. Menu:
Most menu prices do not include tax or tips.

2. Chart:
The chicken dinner has more Calories, but it also provides more vitamins and minerals.

3. Line Graph:
The word *furlong* comes from "long furlow," produced by a farmer plowing his land.

4. Table:
Pin sizes show the measurements in sixteenths of an inch.

5. Circle Graph:
In a circle graph make sure the percents add up to 100.

2. Chart

Burning It Off

Time needed to burn the Calories in what you eat

	Bicycling	Swimming	Bowling
4 cups popcorn (150 Calories)	14 min	30 min	50 min
Peanut Butter sandwich (270 Calories)	25 min	54 min	80 min
2 pieces fried chicken, cole slaw and biscuit (920 Calories)	83 min	184 min	306 min

3. Line Graph

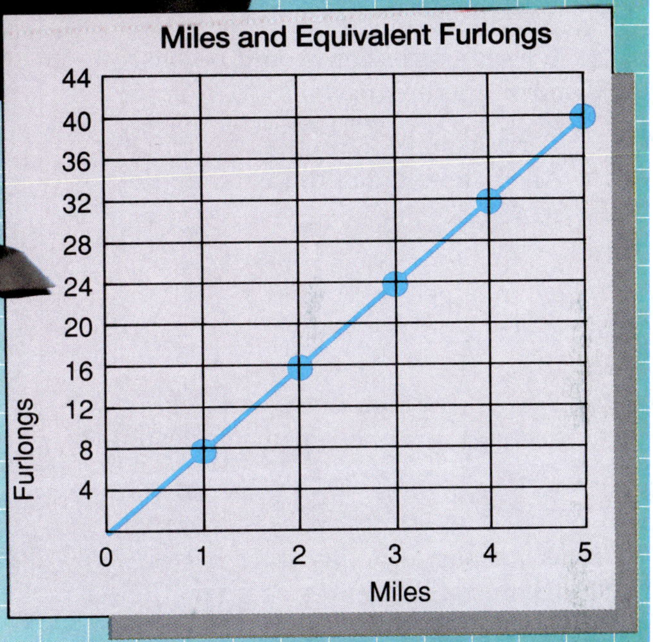

4. Table

Common Pin Sizes

Size	Length in.
6	$\frac{3}{8}$
8	$\frac{1}{2}$
14	$\frac{7}{8}$
16	1
17	$1\frac{1}{16}$
20	$1\frac{1}{4}$
24	$1\frac{1}{2}$
28	$1\frac{3}{4}$
32	2

5. Circle Graph

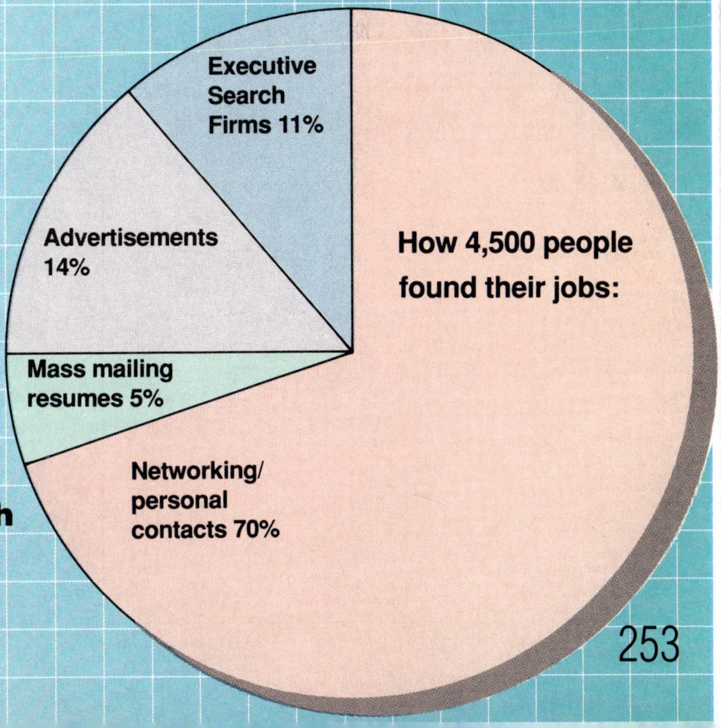

CUMULATIVE REVIEW/TEST

Cumulative Review/Test Chapters 1–7

Give the letter for the correct answer.

1. What is the prime factorization of 250?

a. $2^3 \times 5$ **b.** 2×5^2 **c.** 2×5^3

2. Choose the operation that should be performed first to evaluate this expression: $16 + 6 \div 3 - 1$.

a. $16 + 6$ **b.** $6 \div 3$ **c.** $3 - 1$

3. Which expression would be best to *estimate* the answer?

Terry bought 22 apples for $10.39. About how much did each apple cost?

a. $10 \div 20$
b. $10 \div 25$
c. $11 \div 20$

4. Which fraction, when written as a decimal, gives a repeating decimal?

a. $\frac{7}{50}$ **b.** $\frac{3}{8}$ **c.** $\frac{2}{9}$ **d.** $\frac{5}{16}$

5. What part of a day is 18 hours? Express the answer as a fraction, a decimal, and a percent.

a. $1\frac{1}{3}$, 1.33, 133%
b. $1\frac{1}{3}$, 1.33, 1.33%
c. $\frac{3}{4}$, 0.75, 0.75%
d. $\frac{3}{4}$, 0.75, 75%

6. Subtract.

$$5\frac{1}{4} - 2\frac{3}{8}$$

a. $3\frac{1}{8}$
b. $2\frac{7}{8}$
c. $2\frac{1}{8}$
d. not given

7. Multiply.

-32×0.4

a. -1.28
b. -12.8
c. 12.8
d. not given

8. Add.

$-\frac{1}{3} + -\frac{1}{6}$

a. $-\frac{2}{9}$
b. $\frac{2}{9}$
c. $\frac{1}{2}$
d. not given

9. Divide.

$-18.4 \div -23$

a. 0.8
b. -0.8
c. -0.08
d. not given

10. Evaluate the expression $2b(c - 2)$ when $b = -2$ and $c = 3$.

a. 4 **b.** -4 **c.** -14

11. Solve.

$3t - 9 = 27$

a. $t = 12$
b. $t = 6$
c. $t = -6$
d. not given

12. Solve.

$\frac{t}{21} = \frac{1}{7}$

a. $t = 147$
b. $t = 14$
c. $t = 3$
d. not given

13. Which equation could be used to solve this problem?

An eighth grade homeroom with 28 students sold 364 tickets to the Fall Festival. What was the average number of tickets sold per student?

a. $364n = 28$
b. $n = 364 - 28$
c. $n = 364 + 28$
d. $28n = 364$

14. Which is the solution set for $2x - 4 \le 8$?

a. $x \le 24$　　b. $x \le 6$
c. $x \le 2$　　d. $x \le 8$

15. In which quadrants of the coordinate plane are the x-coordinates positive?

a. II and III　　b. II and IV
c. I and III　　d. I and IV

16. Suppose the point (−5, 2) was translated 3 units to the right and then down 7 units. In which quadrant would the point then be located?

a. I　　b. II　　c. III　　d. IV

17. Choose the proportion that could be used to solve this problem.

Martin bought a coat for $12 off the usual price of $96. What percent of the original price was the coat marked down?

a. $\frac{12}{96} = \frac{x}{100}$
b. $\frac{84}{96} = \frac{x}{100}$
c. $\frac{12}{100} = \frac{x}{96}$

18. Choose the best estimate for 23% of 600.

a. 150　　b. 295
c. 250　　d. 623

19. 30% of which number is 600?

a. 180　　b. 18,000
c. 20　　d. 2,000

20. Which ratio could you use for the following problem?

Art received 50 votes for class president, but Anna received 52 votes. What part of the *total* votes did Art receive?

a. 52 to 50　　b. 52 to 102
c. 50 to 102　　d. 50 to 52

21. George makes a base salary of $1,500 plus a commission of 15% on all sales. What will be his total income on sales of $3,000?

a. $4,500　　b. $1,950
c. $2,175　　d. $3,225

22. How many degrees should you use in a circle graph to show that 60 out of 300 students ride the bus to school?

a. 60°　　b. 20°　　c. 360°　　d. 72°

23. What is the price for 1 pound of oranges if 4.4 pounds are on sale for $3.30?

a. $14.52　　b. $0.75
c. $1.33　　d. $7.70

24. Which is the appropriate *first step* in solving the following problem?

The principal said the gas bill for heating the school went up from $7,228 to $9,832 this year. What is the percent of the increase?

a. Find the amount of increase.
b. Find the percent of increase.
c. Subtract the percent of increase from the amount of increase.

Systems of Measurement

8

Did You Know: In 1990, the United States was the only major country that had not adopted the metric system. However, in 1990, many measurements in the United States were given in both metric and customary units.

Number-Sense Project

Estimate
If gasoline in your area were sold by the liter, how much do you think one liter would cost?

Gather Data
Find the cost per gallon for gasoline at three different stations. Also find the number of liters in a gallon.

Analyze and Report
Find the average cost per gallon of gasoline. At this price, what is the cost per liter? Give a rule for finding the approximate number of gallons equivalent to a given number of liters.

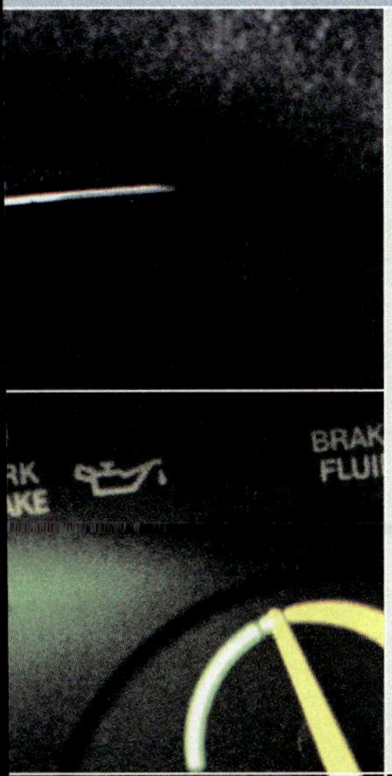

Customary Units of Measurement

Build Understanding

12 in.	=	1 foot (ft or ′)
3 ft	=	1 yard (yd)
36 in.	=	1 yd
5,280 ft	=	1 mile (mi)

Athletes and musicians develop their skills through practice. Estimation is another skill that you can develop through practice.

ACTIVITY

A. Measuring Up
Materials: Rulers, Math Sketcher
Groups: With a partner

a. Estimate the length of four objects in your classroom.

b. Measure each object, and fill in a chart like the one below.

Object	Estimated length	Actual length	Difference

B. In the customary system, the inch (in. or ″) is the smallest unit used to measure length. Area is expressed in square inches (sq in.), and volume is expressed in cubic inches (cu in.).

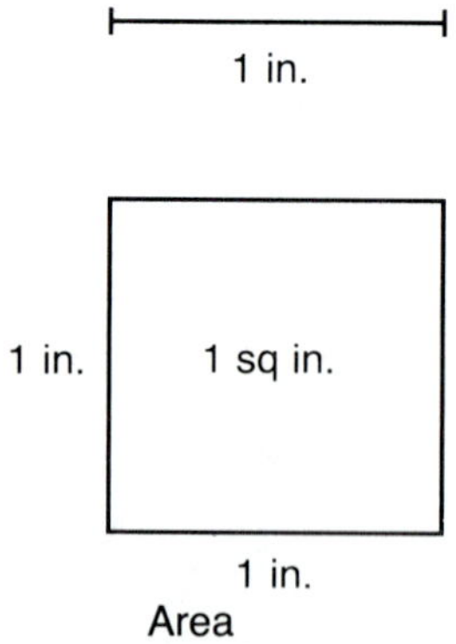

Area
$A = \ell \times w$

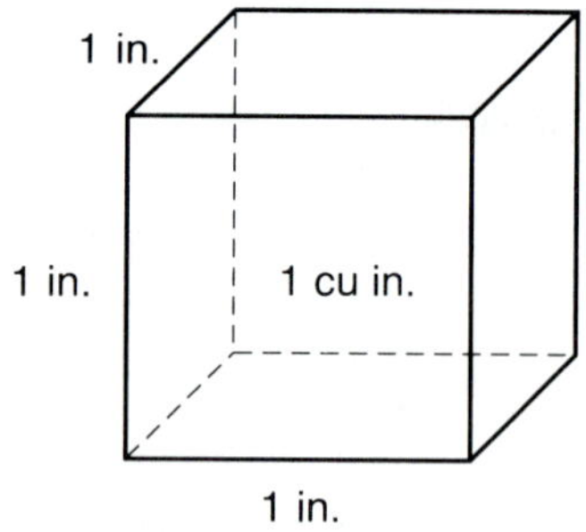

Volume
$V = \ell \times w \times h$

Kate has a dresser that is 4 ft long, 2 ft wide, and 3 ft high. How many square feet of glass does she need to buy to cover the top?

4 ft × 2 ft = 8 sq ft

C. Kate's mother has a table that is 4 feet long. How many inches long is it? How many yards long?

To change feet to inches—
Think: An inch is a smaller unit than a foot. Because you get more units when you change to a smaller unit, multiply.

4 ft = (4 × 12) in. = 48 in.

To change feet to yards—
Think: A yard is a larger unit than a foot. Because you get fewer units when you change to a larger unit, divide.

4 ft = (4 ÷ 3) yd = $\frac{4}{3}$ yd = $1\frac{1}{3}$ yd

D. Liquids are measured in units of ***capacity.***

9 qt = ▒ gal ▒ qt

Capacity	
8 fluid ounces (fl oz)	= 1 cup (c)
2 cups	= 1 pint (pt)
2 pints	= 1 quart (qt)
4 quarts	= 1 gallon (gal)

Divide 9 by 4, since 4 quarts equal 1 gallon.

9 ÷ 4 = 2 R1

9 qt = 2 gal 1 qt

E. Some substances are measured in units of ***weight.***

$2\frac{1}{2}$ lb = ▒ oz

Weight	
16 ounces (oz)	= 1 pound (lb)
2,000 pounds	= 1 ton

Multiply $2\frac{1}{2}$ by 16, since there are 16 ounces in 1 pound.

$2\frac{1}{2} \times 16 = \frac{5}{2} \times 16 = 40$

$2\frac{1}{2}$ lb = 40 oz

Talk About Math A pint of water weighs 16 ounces. Do all liquids weigh the same? What about motor oil? milk? corn syrup? mercury?

Check Understanding

For another example, see Set A, pages 286–287.

1. Estimation Without using a ruler, draw a segment that you think is about 1 in. long. Then measure it to check. Draw a segment that you think is 1 ft long and check.

Choose the best estimate of each measurement.

2. A man's height
a. 6″
b. 6′
c. 6 yd

3. Area of a book cover
a. 7 sq in.
b. 70 sq in.
c. 7 sq ft

4. Volume of a lunch box
a. $\frac{1}{5}$ cu ft
b. 2 cu ft
c. 10 cu in.

Find each missing number.

5. 3 gal = ▒ pt

6. 2 ft 1 in. = ▒ in.

7. 3 lb 7 oz = ▒ oz

8. Estimation Choose the best measurement for the weight of an empty gallon milk container (plastic).

a. 4 oz **b.** 4 lb **c.** 4 tons

Practice

For More Practice, see Set A, pages 288–289.

Number Sense Choose the best answer. Explain why your answers are reasonable.

9. Length of a pencil
- **a.** 6 in.
- **b.** 6 sq in.
- **c.** 6 cu in.

10. Floor area of den
- **a.** 1 sq ft
- **b.** 15 sq ft
- **c.** 150 sq ft

11. Volume of a room
- **a.** 45 cu yd
- **b.** 45 cu ft
- **c.** 45 sq ft

In Exercises 12–29 decide if the number of units in the answer will be greater than or less than the given number of units. Then find the missing number. Tell whether you use mental math, paper and pencil, or a calculator.

12. 2 ft = ▦ in.

13. 1 ft 1 in. = ▦ in.

14. 3 ft = ▦ in.

15. 65 in. = ▦ ft

16. 288 in. = ▦ ft

17. $\frac{1}{3}$ yd = ▦ ft

18. 10 c = ▦ pt

19. 20 oz = ▦ lb ▦ oz

20. 5 gal 5 qt = ▦ qt

21. 7 gal = ▦ qt

22. 33 pt = ▦ qt ▦ pt

23. 9 lb 1 oz = ▦ oz

24. 5 tons = ▦ lb

25. 54 oz = ▦ lb ▦ oz

26. 7 pt 5 c = ▦ c

27. 11 yd = ▦ ft ▦ in.

28. 17 pt = ▦ gal ▦ qt ▦ pt

29. $6\frac{1}{2}$ lb = ▦ oz

Estimation Choose the best measurement.

30. Capacity of a drinking glass
a. 8 qt **b.** 8 pt **c.** 8 fl oz

31. Weight of an artist's paintbrush
a. 1 oz **b.** 100 oz **c.** 1 lb

32. Length of a sofa
a. 50 ft **b.** 2 ft **c.** 6 ft

33. Capacity of a soup bowl
a. 8 oz **b.** 80 oz **c.** 2 oz

34. Area of a kitchen table
a. 2 sq ft **b.** 20 sq ft **c.** 200 sq ft

35. Volume of a suitcase
a. 6 cu ft **b.** 6 cu yd **c.** 12 cu ft

36. Height of one stair
a. 7 in. **b.** 17 in. **c.** 7 ft

37. Weight of a car
a. 1,800 lb **b.** 1,800 oz **c.** 80 lb

38. Height of a ladder
a. 2 cm **b.** 2 m **c.** 2 km

39. Weight of a baby
a. 8 lb **b.** 8 oz **c.** 0.8 oz

Copy the table. Insert the missing dimensions of each cube. Let n stand for any number.

Length	1 in.	2 in.	**40.**	**41.**	n in.
Base area	1 sq in.	**42.**	**43.**	16 sq in.	**44.**
Volume	1 cu in.	8 cu in.	27 cu in.	**45.**	**46.**

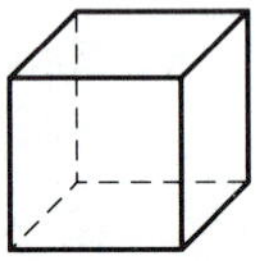

Problem Solving

Solve each problem.

47. Kate found pieces of carpeting that were 82 in., 5 ft 6 in., and 2 yd long. Which piece was the longest?

48. In order to register her car, Kate must find the weight in pounds. According to the manufacturer's manual, her car weighs 1.9 tons. How many pounds is this?

49. **Mental Math** A row of identical books on a shelf occupies 2,400 cubic inches. Each book measures 2 inches by 8 inches by 10 inches. How many books are on the shelf?

TIPS FOR PROBLEM SOLVERS

Compare problems to help you relate new problems to ones you've solved before.

50. Kate made an aquarium shaped like a cube with a volume of 8 cu ft. What is the length of each dimension in feet? in inches? Kate converted the volume to cubic inches and her result was 96 cu in. Is she correct? Why or why not?

51. Mrs. Choi is planning a party for Kate. She bought 3 containers of frozen yogurt each holding 1 gallon. How many quarts of frozen yogurt did she buy? If one quart contains 8 servings, how many servings did she buy?

52. Mrs. Choi used three 30-inch wide tables to form one long table. The tables were 4 feet, 64 inches, and 2 yards in length. How long was the new table?

53. In Problem 50, if 1 gallon equals approximately 231 cubic inches, about how many gallons can the aquarium hold?

54. In Problem 51, what part of a pint was each serving?

55. In Problem 52, what was the area of the new table?

Computing with Customary Measures

Build Understanding

A. Beth's pumpkin weighed 90 lb 3 oz in August. When harvested in September, it weighed 4 lb 14 oz more. What did the pumpkin weigh?

Find 90 lb 3 oz + 4 lb 14 oz.

90 lb 3 oz
+ 4 lb 14 oz
94 lb 17 oz = 94 lb + 1 lb 1 oz
= 95 lb 1 oz

One of the world's largest pumpkins—weighing in at 671 pounds and measuring almost 12 feet around—was grown in New Jersey in 1986.

B. Find 5 ft 1 in. − 4 ft 11 in.

You cannot subtract 11 in. from 1 in. Rename 5 ft 1 in. as 4 ft 13 in.

5 ft 1 in. =	**4 ft 13 in.**
− 4 ft 11 in.	**− 4 ft 11 in.**
	2 in.

C. Which is larger, 1 gal 1 pt or $6\frac{1}{2}$ qt?

1 gal = 4 qt = 8 pt

1 gal 1 pt = 9 pt

$6\frac{1}{2}$ qt = 13 pt

$6\frac{1}{2}$ qt is larger.

Talk About Math How is the subtraction problem in Example B like subtraction of mixed numbers and subtraction of whole numbers? How is it different?

Check Understanding

For another example, see Set B, pages 286–287.

Complete.

1. 45 lb 9 oz + 13 lb 12 oz = ▒ lb 21 oz = ▒ lb 5 oz

2. 14 gal 2 qt − 2 gal 3 qt = 11 gal ▒ qt

3. 23 ft − 12 ft 9 in. = 10 ft ▒ in.

Arrange the amounts in order from least to greatest.

4. 47 in. 3 ft 6 in. 2 yd

5. $\frac{1}{2}$ gal 100 oz 6 qt

Practice

For More Practice, see Set B, pages 288–289.

Add or subtract. **Remember** you may have to rename.

6. 4 ft 7 in. + 6 ft 3 in.

7. 37 lb 4 oz + 22 lb 11 oz

8. 7 lb 5 oz − 3 lb 8 oz

9. 9 gal 1 qt − 4 gal 3 qt

10. 6 yd 25 in. + 13 in.

11. 20 lb 12 oz + 14 oz

12. 19 lb − 8 lb 5 oz

13. 10 ft − 2 ft 9 in.

14. 4 yd 2 ft − 1 yd 9 in.

15. 6 gal 1 qt − 2 gal 1 pt

Arrange the amounts in order from least to greatest.

16. $1\frac{1}{2}$ ft   1 ft 4 in.   17 in.

17. $1\frac{1}{4}$ c   1 pt   11 fl oz

18. 2 ft 8 in.   29 in. $\frac{3}{4}$ yd

19. 8,000 pennies   40 quarters   80 dimes

20. 1.75 lb   20 oz $1\frac{1}{2}$ lb

21. 13 qt   3 gal   25 pt

Problem Solving

Solve each problem.

22. Maria gives her dog $3\frac{1}{3}$ tablespoons of medicine a day with a teaspoon. How many teaspoons does she give her dog each week? Hint: 3 teaspoons = 1 tablespoon.

23. Blood donors gave 3 gallons 3 quarts yesterday. Today donors gave 4 gallons 1 quart. How much more was collected today than yesterday?

Choose a ______ Strategy

Funny Money A penny weighs about 0.10 ounce, and a nickel weighs about 0.18 ounce. Which weighs more, $5 worth of pennies or $5 worth of nickels? How much more?

24. What is the weight of $5 worth of pennies?

25. What is the weight of $5 worth of nickels?

26. Which weighs more, $5 worth of pennies or $5 worth of nickels? How much more?

PROBLEM SOLVING **STRATEGIES**

- Choose an Operation
- Solve a Simpler Problem
- Use a Formula
- Write an Equation
- Make a Graph

Metric Units of Length, Area, and Volume

Build Understanding

Mr. Martinez is designing a large aquarium. The length and the width of the aquarium are given in meters. The floor area is measured in square meters, and the volume is measured in cubic meters. The charts below will help you work with metric units.

Metric Units of Length

To change to a smaller unit, multiply by 10, 100, and so on.

To change to a larger unit, multiply by 0.1, 0.01, and so on.

× 10 × 10 × 0.1 × 0.1

thousands	hundreds	tens	ones	tenths	hundredths	thousandths
*kilo*meter km	*hecto*meter hm	*deka*meter dam	meter m	*deci*meter dm	*centi*meter cm	*milli*meter mm

1 cm

1,000 mm = 1 m 100 cm = 1 m 1,000 m = 1 km

Metric Units of Area

To change to a smaller unit of area, multiply by 100, 10,000, and so on.

To change to a larger unit of area, multiply by 0.01, 0.0001, and so on.

× 100 × 100 × 0.01 × 0.01

square kilometer (km^2)	square hectometer (hm^2)	square dekameter (dam^2)	square meter (m^2)	square decimeter (dm^2)	square centimeter (cm^2)	square millimeter (mm^2)

1 cm

1 cm

$1\ cm^2$

$1\ cm^2 = 100\ mm^2$ $1\ m^2 = 100\ dm^2$ $1\ km^2 = 1{,}000{,}000\ m^2$

Metric Units of Volume

To change to a smaller unit of volume, multiply by 1,000, 1,000,000, and so on.

To change to a larger unit, multiply by 0.001, 0.000001, and so on.

× 1,000 × 1,000 × 0.001 × 0.001

cubic kilometer (km^3)	cubic hectometer (hm^3)	cubic dekameter (dam^3)	cubic meter (m^3)	cubic decimeter (dm^3)	cubic centimeter (cm^3)	cubic millimeter (mm^3)

1 cm

1 cm

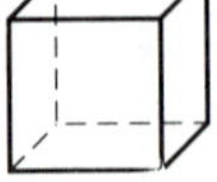

1 cm

$1\ cm^3$

$1\ cm^3 = 1{,}000\ mm^3$ $1\ m^3 = 1{,}000\ dm^3$ $1\ dam^3 = 1{,}000\ m^3$

Talk About Math A centimeter equals 10 mm. Therefore, a square centimeter equals $(10\ mm)^2$ or $100\ mm^2$. Does this line of reasoning work for volumes?

Check Understanding

For another example, see Set C, pages 286–287.

Choose the best measurement.

1. Thickness of a dime
a. 1 mm **b.** 10 mm **c.** 100 mm

2. Area of the city of Toledo
a. 70 cm^2 **b.** 70 m^2 **c.** 70 km^2

Find the missing number.

3. 5 m = ▒ cm

4. 2,100 cm^2 = ▒ m^2

Practice

For More Practice, see Set C, pages 288–289.

Find the missing number. Then explain why your answers are reasonable.

5. 924 cm = ▒ m

6. 3 m = ▒ mm

7. 0.32 cm = ▒ mm

8. 4 dm^2 = ▒ cm^2

9. 3,000 cm^2 = ▒ km^2

10. 892 m^2 = ▒ mm^2

11. 7 m^3 = ▒ mm^3

12. 5 cm^3 = ▒ m^3

13. 60,000 m^3 = ▒ km^3

14. 8,500 km^2 = ▒ m^2

15. 200 m^2 = ▒ cm^2

16. 4,876 m^2 = ▒ cm^2

17. 0.01358 m^2 = ▒ cm^2

18. 18 mm^2 = ▒ cm^2

19. 1 m^3 = ▒ mm^3

Mixed Practice Complete.

20. 27 sq ft = ▒ sq yd

21. 8 qt = ▒ gal

22. 103 mm = ▒ m

23. 1 cu yd = ▒ cu ft

24. 123 oz = ▒ lb ▒ oz

25. 95 m^2 = ▒ cm^2

26. 386 mL = ▒ L

27. 286 yd = ▒ ft

28. 441 m^2 = ▒ cm^2

29. 55 gal = ▒ qt

30. 36,288 sq in. = ▒ sq ft

31. 53 pt = ▒ gal ▒ qt ▒ pt

Problem Solving

Solve each problem.

32. Mr. Martinez's aquarium is 97 dm long and 73 dm wide. What are the dimensions in meters?

33. The area of one solar heating unit is 50,000 cm^2. Express the area in square meters.

34. Mr. Martinez's pocket phone directory is 69 mm wide and 124 mm long. What will be the area in square centimeters?

35. **Critical Thinking** Would a flagpole 8 meters tall fit into your classroom? Explain.

Metric Units of Capacity and Mass

Build Understanding

Suppose you had a hamburger and a glass of juice for lunch. The glass would hold about 200 milliliters and the hamburger would probably have a mass of about 0.22 kilograms (kg).

The mass of the paper clip is about 1 gram, the mass of the book is about 1 kilogram, and the pitcher contains about 1 liter of juice.

→ × 10 → × 10 → → ← × 0.1 ← × 0.1 ←

kiloliter (kL)	hectoliter (hL)	dekaliter (daL)	liter (L)	deciliter (dL)	centiliter (cL)	milliliter (mL)
kilogram (kg)	hectogram (hg)	dekagram (dag)	gram (g)	decigram (dg)	centigram (cg)	milligram (mg)

A. ***Milliliters*** are units of liquid measure or capacity. A ***gram*** is a unit of mass.

The mass of 1 liter of water is 1 ***kilogram***. The mass of 1 ***milliliter*** of water is 1 ***gram***.

A grain of sand has a mass of about 1 ***milligram***.

B. Convert 200 mL to liters.

Use the chart.

200 mL = ▒ L

200 mL = (200 × 0.1 × 0.1 × 0.1) L

200 mL = 0.2 L

C. Convert 0.67 kg to grams.

0.67 kg = ▒ g

0.67 kg = (0.67 × 10 × 10 × 10) g

0.67 kg = 670 g

■ **Talk About Math** Although the metric system is used commonly in science, it is not used much in everyday life in the U.S. How do you explain this?

Check Understanding

For another example, see Set D, pages 286–287.

Number Sense Choose the better unit, liter or gram.

1. Capacity of a jar **2.** A penny

Find the missing number.

3. 4.8 kg = ▒ g

Practice

For More Practice, see Set D, pages 288–289.

Estimation Choose the best measurement.
Remember to look at the units.

4. Mass of a science book
a. 1.8 mg **b.** 1.8 g **c.** 1.8 kg

5. Mass of a scientist
a. 7 kg **b.** 70 kg **c.** 700 kg

6. Capacity of a spoon
a. 5 mL **b.** 5 L **c.** 1.8 kg

7. Capacity of a kitchen sink
a. 0.4 L **b.** 40 L **c.** 400 L

8. Mass of a bicycle
a. 10 kg **b.** 10 g **c.** 100 kg

9. Capacity of an eyedropper
a. 0.1 L **b.** 0.01 kL **c.** 1 mL

10. Mass of a shoe
a. 0.4 kg **b.** 4 kg **c.** 40 g

11. Capacity of a fruit juice can
a. 177 mL **b.** 17 L **c.** 17 mL

In Exercises 12–27, decide if the number of units in the answer will be greater or less than the given number of units. Then solve.

12. 768 mL = ▦ L **13.** 32 L = ▦ mL **14.** 65.3 L = ▦ mL **15.** 14 g = ▦ mg

16. 518 kg = ▦ g **17.** 309 mg = ▦ g **18.** 15.5 kg = ▦ g **19.** 13,892 mg = ▦ kg

20. 3 L = ▦ mL **21.** 8.7 g = ▦ kg **22.** 566 mL = ▦ L **23.** 3.225 kg = ▦ g

24. 0.45 L = ▦ mL **25.** 47.74 g = ▦ kg **26.** 1.564 mL = ▦ L **27.** 76 kg = ▦ g

Problem Solving

Solve each problem.

28. A can of condensed soup has a capacity of 325 mL. How many liters of soup is this?

29. **Use Data** The mass of a bowling ball is about 7 kg. How many pounds is this? Use the table on page 274.

Skills Review

pages 156–157, 224–225

ALGEBRA

Find the intersection points by graphing.

1. $y = 2x + 2$
$y = -x - 1$

2. $y = x - 4$
$y = 3x$

Which is the better buy?

3. 3 lb of grapes for $2.69 or
2 lb of grapes for $1.89

Find the unit cost of each product. Round to the nearest $0.01.

4. 32 oz of juice at $1.68

5. 64 oz of detergent at $2.24

Computing with Metric Measures

Build Understanding

A. The pool area at the Fairlawn Swim Club is 3 dekameters long and 15 meters wide. How much fencing will the club manager need to fence in the entire pool area if the fence runs around all sides of the pool?

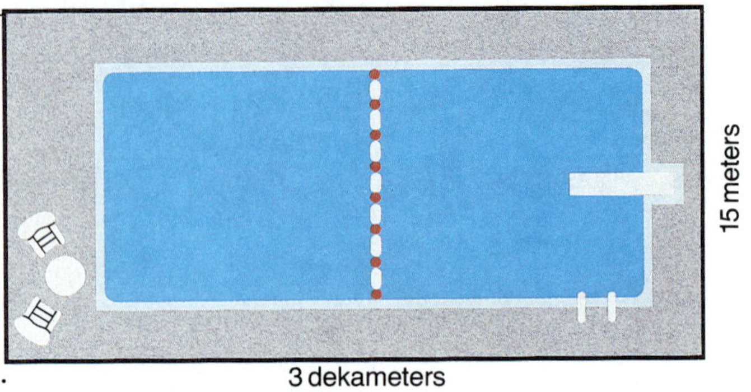

Find 3 dam + 15 m + 3 dam + 15 m.

Change to meters.

30 m + 15 m + 30 m + 15 m = 90 m

The manager needs 90 m of fencing.

B. The pool cover is 320 decimeters long and 18 meters wide. What is its area?

Find 320 dm × 18 m.

Make the units the same.

32 m × 18 m = 576 m^2

The area of the pool cover is 576 m^2.

C. The volume of the pool is 1,800 m^3. What is its average depth?

Volume = length × width × depth

1,800 m^3 = 30 m × 15 m × depth

depth $= \frac{1{,}800}{450} = 4$

The pool's average depth is 4 m.

Talk About Math Do you think it is generally easier to compute with metric units or customary units?

Check Understanding

For another example, see Set E, pages 286–287.

Find the missing number.

1. 6 m = ▒ dm **2.** 1,395 mL = ▒ L **3.** 250 cm = ▒ m

Compute.

4. 7 cm + 8 cm + 12 cm **5.** 1,546 mm − 845 mm

6. 312 mL + 146 cL = ▒ mL **7.** 12 × 475 g

8. 2.5 cm × 1.2 cm **9.** 0.455 kg ÷ 0.5

Explore With A Computer

Use the *Spreadsheet Workshop Project* for this activity.

When Javier and his family visited Germany, they wanted to compare metric measurements with customary units. Measurements they wanted to convert were for the height of a monument (10 meters), a bottle of juice (750 milliliters), the distance from their hotel to the city center (23 kilometers), gasoline (17 liters), and Javier's weight (58 kilograms).

1. At the computer, enter these measurements in the conversion chart.

2. Compare these measurements with other measurements, such as how much you weigh compared with Javier's weight.

Metric				Customary	
12	m	$\times$ 3.28 $\frac{ft}{m}$	=	39.36	ft
	L	$\times$ 33.8 $\frac{oz}{L}$	=		oz
	kg	$\times$ 2.2 $\frac{lbs}{kg}$	=		lbs
	km	$\times$ 0.6 $\frac{mi}{km}$	=		mi
	L	$\times$ 0.264 $\frac{gal}{L}$	=		gal

Number-Sense Project

Look back at pages 256–257.

For these problems, give approximate answers that do not require paper and pencil computation.

1. 50 km is about ■ miles.

2. 100 km is about ■ miles.

3. 10 km is about ■ miles.

4. Explain how you would change kilometers to miles mentally.

Give Sensible Answers

Build Understanding

Which of these estimates is the most sensible answer for the distance between Cleveland, Ohio, and Columbus, Ohio?

a. 760 m^2 **b.** 230 km **c.** 92 m

Understand QUESTION How far is it between Cleveland and Columbus?

KEY IDEA The answer must be sensible.

Plan and Solve STRATEGY 760 square meters is a measure of area. Both 230 kilometers and 92 meters are measures of length, but 92 meters is less than the distance of a 100-meter dash.

ANSWER The most sensible estimate for the distance between Cleveland and Columbus is 230 kilometers.

Look Back SENSIBLE ANSWER Consider the other choices: 760 m^2 is a measure of area, not length; 92 m is far too short to be the distance between two cities. Each kilometer is 1,000 meters.

Talk About Math In general, when would you use the kilometer, the meter, and the centimeter as the units of measure?

PROBLEM SOLVING GUIDE

Understand
QUESTION
FACTS
KEY IDEA

Plan and Solve
STRATEGY
ANSWER

Look Back
SENSIBLE ANSWER
ALTERNATE APPROACH

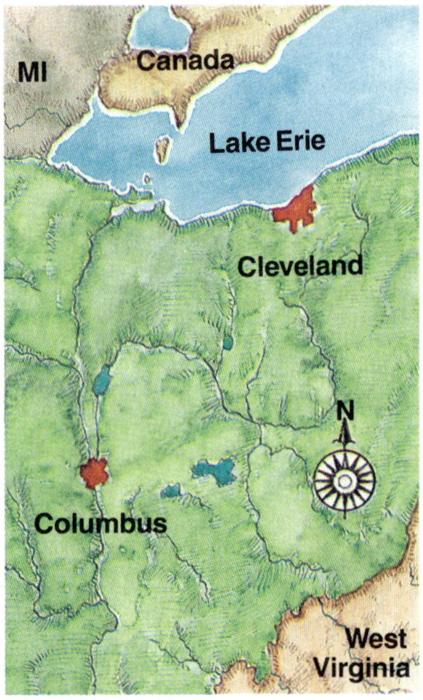

Check Understanding

Estimation Choose the most sensible estimate.

1. Length of a football field
   a. 1,100 cm **b.** 11 km **c.** 90 m

2. Capacity of a picnic cooler
   a. 20.2 L **b.** 2,400 cm **c.** 80 g

3. Weight of a car
   a. 500 T **b.** 1 T **c.** 20 lb

4. Area of an envelope
   a. 60 sq in. **b.** 2 sq mi **c.** 1 sq m

Practice

Number Sense From the list, choose the most sensible answer for each blank.

- 9,000 cm^2
- 5 m
- 650
- 0.56 L
- 15 mm
- 10 km^2
- 2,000 cm^3
- 7
- $65.25
- 0.3 kg
- 96 cm
- 24 h
- 1 m^2
- 1 L

Mike the Magician gave a performance before a crowd of ____5.____ people. During his act he used nine scarves, each ____6.____ long. Four of the scarves were sewn together to form a square with an approximate area of ____7.____.

For one trick, Mike used beakers filled with liquids of different colors. Each beaker contained ____8.____ of liquid. He poured the liquid from three beakers into a larger beaker having a capacity of ____9.____. The mixture of liquid changed to a different color every ten seconds.

Over a distance of ____10.____, Mike balanced ____11.____ spinning plates at once. The plates, each weighing about ____12.____, were perched on waist-high sticks that were no more than ____13.____ in diameter.

At the end of the show, Mike announced a second show the next night, only ____14.____ away.

Number Sense From the list, choose the most sensible answer for each blank.

- 1 qt
- #512
- 484 sq in.
- 7.5 cu ft
- 3 oz
- $52.50
- 1.5 cups
- 2 ft 3 in.
- $1\frac{1}{4}$ pt
- 344.12
- 25 lb
- $2\frac{1}{2}$ yd

Frannie was demonstrating woodworking and wood finishing techniques to a hobby class. She had constructed an end table ____15.____ high with a top surface area of ____16.____.

The table was enclosed and had two doors. The plans for the end table stated that the volume would be approximately ____17.____. The doors were made from one piece of wood ____18.____ long.

After describing the construction of the table, Frannie explained how she finished it with stain and sealer. She bought ____19.____ of stain, but used only ____20.____. ____21.____ of sealer were brushed on, and later the wood was rubbed down using about ____22.____ of fine steel wool.

When completed, Frannie estimated that the table weighed about ____23.____. She said she didn't know how much the table cost because she had used wood left over from other projects.

Number Sense in Measurement

Build Understanding

Otavalo, Ecuador, is one of Latin America's oldest and best-known market towns. Ponchos, wall hangings, shawls, woolen hats and gloves, pottery, and straw mats are just a few of the handmade products that can be purchased on market day.

Artisans in villages around Otavalo work during the week on fine weaving and embroidery, which they bring to town on Saturday to sell at the market.

A. Betty is shopping for a wall hanging to hang above her desk. It must be between 3 feet and 4 feet long. A vendor shows her one that is about one meter long. Is this length in the proper range?

Think: Since 1 yard (3 feet) is slightly shorter than 1 meter, the wall hanging is a little more than 3 feet long.

The length is in the proper range.

B. About how many kilograms is 120 pounds?

Think: 1 lb is about 0.5 kilograms.

So 120 pounds is about 60 kilograms.

C. About how many gallons are in 26 liters?

Think: 1 liter is a little more than 1 qt, so 26 liters is a little more than 26 qt.

Then 26 liters is a little more than $\frac{26}{4}$, or 6.5 gallons.

1 inch	≈	2.5 centimeters
1 yard	≈	0.9 meter
1 quart	≈	0.9 liter
1 mile	≈	1.6 kilometers
1 pound	≈	0.5 kilogram
2 pounds	≈	1 kilogram

Talk About Math In Example C, is 26 liters closer to 6 or 7 gallons?

Check Understanding

For another example, see Set F, pages 286–287.

Which is more?

1. 3 L or 3 qt

2. 5 mi or 10 km

3. 6 kg or 8 lb

4. 20 cm or 9 in.

5. 15 yd or 14 m

6. 55 km or 37 mi

7. About how many kilograms is 10 pounds?

Practice

For More Practice, see Set F, pages 288–289.

Estimate each measurement in the appropriate metric unit.

8. 12 in. **9.** 2 ft **10.** 1 in. **11.** 4 qt **12.** 10 lb

13. 12 ft **14.** 20 qt **15.** 2 yd **16.** 36 lb **17.** 5 mi

Estimate each measurement in the appropriate customary unit.

18. 5 cm **19.** 3 m **20.** 12 L **21.** 3 kg **22.** 100 L

23. 12 kg **24.** 16 km **25.** 10 m **26.** 18 km **27.** 22 cm

Arrange in order from least to greatest.

28. 150 ft, 50 m, 100 yd

29. 100 gal, 35 L, capacity of a teakettle

30. 4 kg, 8 lb, loaf of bread

31. 12 in., 20 cm, length of a teaspoon

Problem Solving

Solve each problem.

32. In Cotacachi, Ecuador, many people make and sell leather goods. Mark bought a 75-centimeter leather belt as a gift. His friends wear 30-inch, 34-inch, and 36-inch belts. Which of them would the belt fit?

33. While traveling in Mexico, Tom's dad stopped at a gas station and bought 32 L of gas. About how many gallons of gas did he buy?

The Asante and Ewe people of West Africa weave narrow strips to make a fabric called Kente cloth.

34. A Nigerian pottery bowl holds two liters of water. About how many quarts does it hold?

35. How many strips of 9-cm wide Kente cloth must a weaver sew together to make a fabric 1.62 meters wide?

36. A duty-free shop uses customary and metric units of measure. Which contains more, a 500-mL bottle or a bottle with 0.5 qt (16 oz)?

37. About 200 feet of 4-inch wide Kente cloth is needed to make a large man's garment. About how many square feet is this?

38. In the duty-free shop, a box of tea is labeled 10 oz; 284 grams. About how many grams are equivalent to 1 oz?

39. How many square centimeters are in a 3-foot-square shawl?

Use Data from a Table

PROBLEM SOLVING GUIDE

Understand
QUESTION
FACTS
KEY IDEA

Plan and Solve
STRATEGY
ANSWER

Look Back
SENSIBLE ANSWER
ALTERNATE APPROACH

Build Understanding

BOSTON TO NEW YORK TRAIN SCHEDULE

Train Number	95	17	16	73	75
Days of Operation	Daily	Ex. Su	Su only	Daily	Daily
Boston (Dp)	7 30A	8 25A	8 25A	10 15A	12 30P
Providence (Dp)	8 15A	9 08A	9 08A	11 01A	1 15P
New Haven (Ar)	10 08A	11 03A	11 06A	12 57P	3 05P
New Haven (Dp)	10 26A	11 21A	11 24A	1 15P	3 23P
New York (Ar)	12 04P	12 57P	1 00P	2 58P	5 05P

Mr. Kato is an engineer on train 95, which runs from Boston to New York daily. How long does this trip take?

Understand QUESTION How long is the trip on train 95 from Boston to New York?

FACTS The schedule shows that train 95 leaves Boston at 7:30 A.M. and arrives in New York at 12:04 P.M.

KEY IDEA Find the elapsed time between the departure and arrival.

Plan and Solve Subtract to find the elapsed time.

$$\begin{array}{r} 12{:}04 \\ -\ 7{:}30 \end{array} \rightarrow \begin{array}{r} 11{:}64 \\ -\ 7{:}30 \\ \hline 4{:}34 \end{array}$$

Think of 12 hours 4 minutes as 11 hours 64 minutes.

ANSWER The trip takes 4 hours 34 minutes.

Look Back SENSIBLE ANSWER Four and one half hours after 7:30 A.M. is 12:00 noon, so the answer is reasonable.

Talk About Math How can you calculate elapsed time mentally?

Check Understanding

Use the table on page 276.

1. How long does train 73 spend in New Haven?

2. Joe took train 17 from Boston to Providence and train 75 to New York. How long was he on the trains?

3. A train travels from Milan, Italy, to Rome in 238 minutes. How many hours and minutes is this?

4. The train ride from Sydney, Australia, to Perth takes 64 hours. How many days and hours is this?

Practice

Use the table on page 276.

5. Of the trains shown on the schedule, which one makes the trip from Boston to New York in the least amount of time?

6. Beatrig arrived at the station in New Haven 45 minutes before train 73 arrived. What time did she arrive at the station?

7. A train trip from Toronto to Winnipeg takes 18 hours. You leave Toronto at 1:00 P.M. Monday. What is the time in Toronto when you arrive in Winnipeg?

8. A train trip from Toronto to Vancouver takes 69 hours. You leave Toronto at 3:00 P.M. Tuesday. What is the time in Toronto when you get to Vancouver?

Calculator Use the table on page 601 to determine your age in

9. years. **10.** days. **11.** hours. **12.** minutes.

Choose a Strategy

Calendar Capers Two consecutive months in one year have a Friday the 13th. Answer the following questions about that year.

13. What month has the second Friday the 13th?

14. Make a table showing the 13th of each month until there is a third Friday the 13th. In which month does it occur?

15. Can you find another way to solve this problem? Explain your method.

PROBLEM SOLVING STRATEGIES

- Choose an Operation
- Solve a Simpler Problem
- Use a Formula
- Write an Equation
- Make a Graph

Precision and Greatest Possible Error

Build Understanding

A. In science class, Mia measured the height of a plant to the nearest quarter inch. Greta's measurement is to the nearest half inch; Jim's is to the nearest inch.

Since Mia used a smaller unit of measure, her measurement is more ***precise.*** The smaller the unit of measure, the greater the ***precision*** of the measurement.

Plant A	
Mia	$7\frac{1}{4}$ in.
Greta	$7\frac{1}{2}$ in.
Jim	7 in.

B. Jim's measurement tells you that the plant is between $6\frac{1}{2}$ inches and $7\frac{1}{2}$ inches tall. That is, the error of measurement, or ***greatest possible error (GPE),*** is $\frac{1}{2}$ inch. Measures are sometimes written like this:

$$7 \pm \frac{1}{2} \text{ (7 plus or minus } \tfrac{1}{2}\text{)}$$

Study the table below. What can you conclude about the GPE of a measurement?

Measurement	Unit of Measure	GPE
27 inches	inch	$\frac{1}{2}$ inch
3.8 meters	0.1 meter	0.05 meter
$12\frac{3}{16}$ inches	$\frac{1}{16}$ inch	$\frac{1}{32}$ inch

The GPE is always one half the unit of measure.

■ **Talk About Math** Greta and Jim measure the circumference of a tree. Greta's result is 0.9 meters and Jim's is 1.9 meters. What might explain the difference in measurements?

Check Understanding

For another example, see Set G, pages 286–287.

Measure each segment to the nearest centimeter and the nearest millimeter.

1. ______________________ **2.** ______________________________

3. Which of the following is precise to the nearest minute? Give its GPE.
a. 7 min 5 sec **b.** 61 min **c.** 0.1 min

Practice

For More Practice, see Set G, pages 288–289.

4. Which of the following is precise to the nearest $\frac{1}{2}$ inch?
a. $3\frac{1}{2}$ in. **b.** 9 feet **c.** 2 ft $1\frac{1}{2}$ inches

5. Which of the following is precise to the nearest meter?
a. 17 m **b.** 101 cm **c.** 15.5 m

Give the unit of measure and the GPE.

6. 5.1 cm **7.** 6.05 km **8.** 9 h 12 min **9.** 99 m

10. 2 L **11.** 99.3 oz **12.** 107 mL **13.** 5,900 mi

14. 9.234 kg **15.** 42.34 m **16.** 4 days 14 hours **17.** 279 mi

18. 5 lb 7 oz **19.** 0.8 km **20.** 2 min 45 sec **21.** 56 L

Which measurement is more precise?

22. 12.5 kg or 9 kg **23.** 8 mm or 37.1 mm **24.** 101 cm or 2 mm

25. $18\frac{1}{2}$ lb or 9 oz **26.** 3.9 kg or 12.80 kg **27.** 38 ft or 5 mi

28. 57.56 cm or 0.5 m **29.** 430 L or 43 mL **30.** 76 yd or 5.6 mi

31. 12 hr or 87 min **32.** 6.2 kg or 5,874 g **33.** 200 in. or 11 ft

Problem Solving

Solve each problem.

34. One Monday the science class found that one of their plants had grown $\frac{3}{4}$ inch over the weekend. What was the GPE of the measurement?

35. For an experiment, Caitlin needed 13.5 mL of a solvent. What is the unit of measure and the GPE?

Critical Thinking Solve each problem.

36. Numbers that are counted are exact. Numbers that are the results of measuring are approximate. Give an example of an exact number that is not counted.

37. A machinist is making a part that should be 1 inch long, $\pm\frac{1}{16}$ inch. Is a part $\frac{15}{16}$ inch long acceptable? Is a part $1\frac{3}{32}$ inches acceptable?

TIPS FOR PROBLEM SOLVERS

Share your thinking with others. Explaining your ideas helps you think better.

Relative Error and Accuracy

Build Understanding

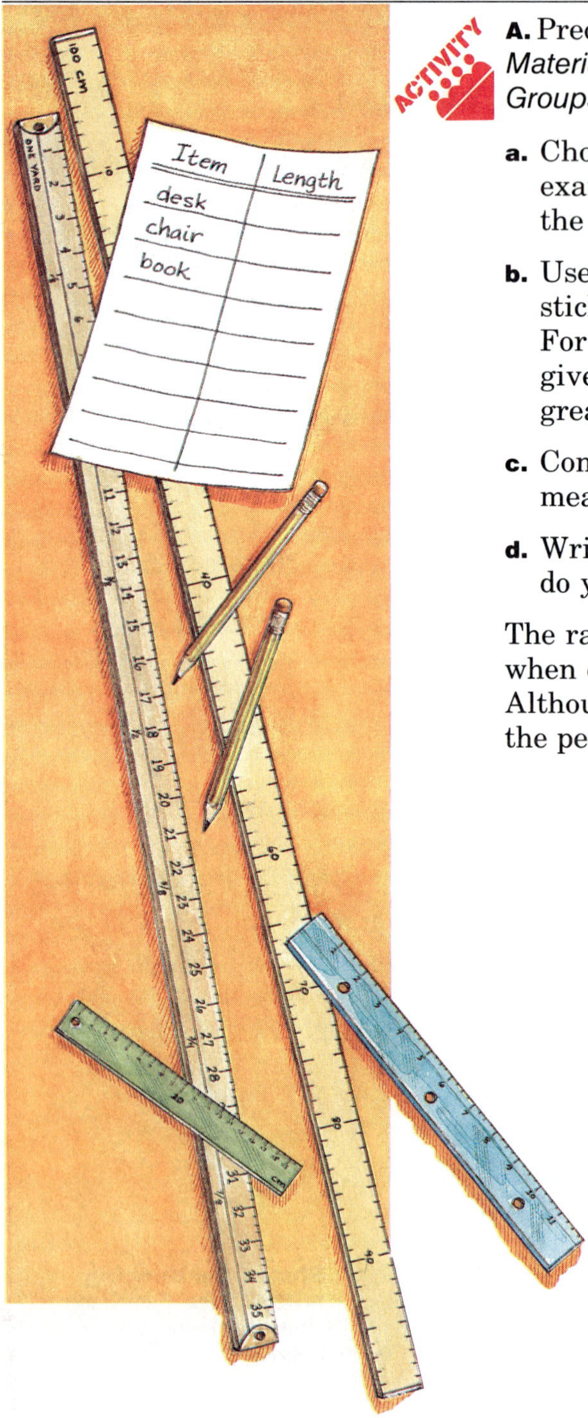

A. Precision Measuring
Materials: Yard sticks or meter sticks
Groups: 3–6 students

a. Choose two classroom items to measure. For example, measure the length of the room and the length of a desk.

b. Use the smallest division on your measuring stick. Record your findings in terms of that unit. For example, if the divisions are half inches, give your answer to the nearest half inch. The greatest possible error is one quarter inch.

c. Compute the ratio $\frac{\text{GPE}}{\text{measure}}$ for each measurement.

d. Write the resulting numbers as percents. What do you notice about the two percents?

The ratio you computed is the ***relative error*** or, when expressed as a percent, the ***percent error.*** Although both measurements were equally precise, the percent error was less for the greater length.

B. The *smaller the relative error,* the more **accurate** the measurement. Which is more accurate, a measurement of 5 centimeters or a measurement of 54 meters?

For 5 centimeters the GPE is 0.5 cm. For 54 meters, the GPE is 0.5 m.

$\frac{0.5}{5} = 0.1$, **or 10%** $\qquad \frac{0.5}{54} \approx 0.009$, **or 1%**

Thus, although 5 centimeters is more precise than 54 meters, 54 meters is more accurate.

Talk About Math Given two measurements, is the more accurate one necessarily more precise?

Check Understanding

For another example, see Set H, pages 286–287.

Copy and complete the chart. You may want to use a calculator to find the percent error.

Measurement	Unit	GPE	Percent Error
25 ft	1 ft	$\frac{1}{2}$ ft	$\frac{1}{2} \div 25 = 2\%$
48.3 km	0.1 km	**1.**	**2.**
0.05 L	0.01 L	**3.**	**4.**
15.2 mi	**5.**	**6.**	**7.**

Complete.

8. The GPE determines the ___?___ of a measurement.

9. The relative error determines the ___?___.

Practice

For More Practice, see Set H, pages 288–289.

Compute the percent error for each measurement. Then tell which measurement in each pair is more accurate.

10. $2\frac{1}{2}$ miles or 430 yards

11. 13.6 pounds or 13.60 pounds

12. 1.29 centimeters or 12.9 centimeters

Calculator For each measurement, give the GPE and the percent error to the nearest 0.1%. You may want to use a calculator.

13. 49.55 km

14. 5,459°C

15. 225 miles

16. 93.75 L

17. 0.05 m

18. 0.3 cm

19. $1\frac{3}{8}$ mi

20. 99.06 kg

21. 5.6 m

22. 28 ft

23. $12\frac{1}{4}$ in.

24. 165 lb

25. 4.2 cm

26. 603 mi

27. 10 h 15 min

28. 0.625 cL

Problem Solving

Solve each problem.

29. The diameter of Earth is often taken to be 8,000 miles to the nearest 1,000 miles. The diameter of a quarter is 1 inch to the nearest inch. Which measurement is more accurate?

30. Measure your height and the height of a friend to the nearest inch. Calculate the percent error of each measurement.

Significant Digits

Build Understanding

A. Paul measured his Go-Kart. It was 60 inches long. Can you tell whether he was measuring to the nearest 10 inches or to the nearest inch? Could he have been measuring to some smaller unit, such as one half inch?

Digits in a measurement are called ***significant*** when they tell us how many measured units there are—they show the ***accuracy*** of the measurement. You know that in 21.5 cm, the GPE is 0.05 cm, and 2, 1, and 5 are all significant digits.

When you know the basic unit of measure, you can identify the significant digits in the measurement. These rules will help you identify significant digits:

All nonzero digits are significant. Zero is also significant in these situations:

- When the zero is a placeholder between two nonzero digits (103)
- When the zero occurs at the end of a decimal fraction (6.20)
- When the final zero (or zeros) in a whole number are marked to show that they are significant ($3\underline{0}$)

B. For each quantity below, tell which digits are significant.

684 86.190 0.700 0.007 $\mathbf{3,2\underline{0}0}$

684: 3 significant digits: 6, 8, 4
86.190: 5 significant digits: 8, 6, 1, 9, 0
0.700: 3 significant digits: 7, 0, 0
0.007: 1 significant digit: 7
$3,2\underline{0}0$: 3 significant digits: 3, 2, 0

Talk About Math Explain the difference in accuracy between measures of 64.3 cm and 64.30 cm.

Check Understanding

For another example, see Set I, pages 286–287.

Complete each sentence.

1. The measurement 12.5 cm is more (*precise, accurate*) than 125 cm.

2. The number 32.01 has ___?___ significant digits.

3. The ___?___ error of a measurement is one half the unit.

4. Relative error is the ratio of ___?___ to the measurement.

Practice

For More Practice, see Set I, pages 288–289.

Copy and complete the table.

Measurement	Unit	Number of units	Number of significant digits	Significant digits	Greatest Possible Error (GPE)	Percent Error
360 miles	1 mile	360	**5.**	**6.**	**7.**	**8.**
360 miles	10 miles	36	**9.**	**10.**	**11.**	**12.**
4,500 miles	100 miles	**13.**	**14.**	**15.**	**16.**	**17.**
0.25 kg	0.01 kg	**18.**	**19.**	**20.**	**21.**	**22.**

Give the number of significant digits in each.

23. 48.3 L **24.** 0.03 kg **25.** 2,500°C **26.** 2,5$\underline{0}$0°C **27.** 2.54 in.

28. 20.04 g **29.** 139.06 **30.** 7.85×10^5 **31.** 0.009 **32.** 1.009

33. 35.8 ft **34.** 8.07 kg **35.** 7.008 **36.** 100 m **37.** 0.0101

38. 1.60 cm **39.** 4,$\underline{000,000}$ **40.** 5,004 mL **41.** 9.0 **42.** 7,564,000

43. 5.76 mi **44.** 219 yd **45.** 4×10^{-8} **46.** 19 g **47.** 1,728 in.^3

Problem Solving

Solve each problem.

48. Critical Thinking Which has the smaller relative error, a 1-meter measurement to the nearest centimeter, or a 1-yard measurement to the nearest $\frac{1}{16}$ inch?

49. Assume in Example A that Paul measured his Go-Kart to the nearest inch. What is the relative error?

50. If Paul had measured the Go-Kart in Example A to the nearest $\frac{1}{10}$ inch, how would he have written the measurement?

Explore Math

51. Each student should measure the same desk in your classroom to the same precision.

52. Make a graph. Plot the measurements on the horizontal axis and the number of people who made them on the vertical axis. What shape is your graph?

Skills Review

Find each missing number.

1. 4 ft 3 in. = ▦ in. **2.** 4 gal = ▦ qt

3. 7 lb 2 oz = ▦ oz **4.** $\frac{1}{3}$ yd = ▦ in.

5. 672 cm = ▦ m **6.** 4.6 L = ▦ mL

7. 900 dm^3 = ▦ m^3 **8.** 7 m = ▦ mm

Compute.

9. 20 lb − 14 lb 3 oz

10. 5 ft 10 in. + 3 ft 3 in.

11. 5 cm × 35 cm × 2 cm

12. 18 mm + 29 mm + 42 mm

Estimate each measurement in the appropriate metric measurement.

13. 20 in. **14.** 5 qt **15.** 3 mi

Estimate each measurement in the appropriate customary measurement.

16. 12 kg **17.** 40 cm **18.** 9 L

Give the unit of measure and the GPE (greatest possible error).

19. 2.5 L **20.** 470 mi. **21.** $2\frac{1}{2}$ in.

Compute the percent error for each measurement. Then tell which measurement in each pair is more accurate.

22. 7.2 km or 41 km

23. 5.8 cm or 6 cm

Name the number of significant digits in each measurement.

24. 0.02 g **25.** 72.1 m **26.** 200°C

27. 0.009 **28.** 2.34×10^3 **29.** 5.001

Problem-Solving Review

Solve each problem.

30. Dana has pieces of fabric that are 32 in. long, 2 ft 6 in. long, and 1 yard long. Which piece is the shortest?

31. Hannah said that a bowling ball weighs about 6 kg. Ricardo said it weighs about 0.6 kg. Who is right?

32. What is the mass of an aquarium if it holds 32.48 L of water?

33. Brad is hosting a party for 120 guests. He is using a 9-liter punch bowl. If 150-mL cups are used, how many times will the bowl need to be refilled if each person has one cup of punch?

34. Dolores finished a 5-kilometer race. About how many miles did she run?

35. Which is more precise, a measure of $4\underline{0}$ meters or a measure of 4 centimeters? Which is accurate to the nearest meter?

36. **Data File** Use the data on pages 426–427. Suppose you travel from Sacramento to Chicago. How long will your train ride take?

37. **Make a Data File** Choose a state. Use a road map to make a chart of the distances between 10 cities or towns within the state. List the distances in kilometers.

Cumulative Skills Review · Chapters 1–8

Use mental math to do each computation.

1. $478 - 98$ **2.** 12×21 **3.** $245 + 455$ **4.** 25×124

5. 9 is what percent of 90? **6.** 10% of what number is 9.8?

Multiply or divide.

7. $\frac{2}{3} \times \frac{3}{5}$ **8.** $\frac{3}{15} \div \frac{1}{5}$ **9.** $\frac{7}{8} \times 16$ **10.** $1\frac{7}{8} \div 2\frac{2}{3}$

11. $-\frac{15}{16} \times \frac{1}{2}$ **12.** $-10 \div 2\frac{3}{4}$ **13.** $-12 \times (-1.2)$ **14.** $0.9 \div (-0.6)$

Find the value of each expression when $t = -5$, $v = \frac{1}{2}$, and $a = 2$.

15. $t - a$ **16.** va **17.** $8v + a$ **18.** $(2v + a)t$

Graph each inequality on a coordinate grid.

19. $y \leq x - 1$ **20.** $y > 2x + 2$ **21.** $y < 2x - 4$ **22.** $y \geq -3x$

Estimate each answer.

23. What is 24% of 95? **24.** 5.3 is 21% of what number? **25.** Find 34% of 300.

Copy and complete the table. Round interest to the nearest cent.

Unpaid balance	\$75.00	\$345.90	\$880.80
Payment	\$40.00	\$100.00	\$ 80.00
Balance after payment	**26.**	**27.**	**28.**
Interest rate (per month)	1.6%	1.75%	1.3%
Amount of interest	**29.**	**30.**	**31.**
New purchases	\$94.85	\$149.20	\$313.02
New balance	**32.**	**33.**	**34.**

Choose the best answer.

35. Weight of a dog
a. 30 lb **b.** 30 in. **c.** 30 oz

36. Area of a dining room
a. 165 ft **b.** 165 cu ft **c.** 165 sq ft

37. Capacity of a fish tank
a. 50 kL **b.** 50 L **c.** 500 mL

38. Length of an automobile
a. 2.5 m **b.** 2.5 cm **c.** 250 mm

Which measurement is more precise?

39. 15 cm or 15 m **40.** 42 cm or 2.4 m **41.** 1.2 mi or 45 ft **42.** 12 in. or 1 ft

Reteaching

Set A pages 258–261

When estimating with measurements, use an appropriate unit. A door is about 3 *feet* wide, not 3 inches and not 3 yards.

Remember that inches, feet, and yards indicate linear measure. The term "square" suggests area measure. The term "cubic" suggests volume measure.

Choose the best answer. Explain why your answers are reasonable.

1. Width of a room
a. 10 in. **b.** 10 ft **c.** 10 sq ft

2. Area of the floor of a house
a. 1,000 ft **b.** 1,000 sq in. **c.** 1,000 sq ft

3. Volume of a toy chest
a. 6 cu ft **b.** 6 sq ft **c.** 6 cu in.

Set B pages 262–263

To subtract mixed units of measure, you may have to rename. Subtract 3 yd 15 in. from 8 yd 1 ft.

Write 1 ft as 12 in. Then write 8 yd 12 in. as 7 yd 48 in.

8 yd 1 ft → 8 yd 12 in. = 7 yd 48 in.
−3 yd 15 in. = −3 yd 15 in.
4 yd 33 in.

Remember equivalent measurements such as 12 in. = 1 ft, 3 ft = 1 yd, and 16 oz = 1 lb.

Add or subtract.

1. 10 ft 6 in. + 18 ft 7 in.

2. 9 lb 5 oz − 2 lb 9 oz

3. 18 gal 1 pt − 10 gal 1 qt

4. 8 ft 9 in. + 2 ft 7 in.

Set C pages 264–265

To change meters to kilometers you can divide by 1,000.

3,500 m = ▒ km

1 km = 1,000 m

$\frac{3{,}500}{1{,}000}$ **= 3.5 km**

Remember that to change to a smaller unit, multiply by 10, 100, or 1,000. To change to a larger unit, divide.

Find the missing number.

1. 52 m = ▒ mm **2.** 125 cm = ▒ m

3. 0.22 km = ▒ m **4.** 568 mm = ▒ m

5. 3.9 cm = ▒ mm **6.** 1,820 cm = ▒ m

7. 800 m = ▒ km **8.** 0.04 m = ▒ dm

Set D pages 266–267

The multiples of metric units (milli-, kilo-, and so on) can help you estimate.

A raisin has a mass of about 1 gram.
1,000 milligrams = 1 gram
1,000 grams = 1 kilogram

Remember, liters measure capacity.
1,000 milliliters = 1 liter
1,000 liters = 1 kiloliter

Find the missing number.

1. 46 g = ▒ kg **2.** 0.5 L = ▒ mL

3. 0.231 g = ▒ mg **4.** 25 mL = ▒ L

Set E pages 268–269

Five 170-mL glasses are filled with juice from a 1-L bottle. How much juice is left?

Multiply: 5 × 170 = 850; 850 mL are used.

Change 1 L to 1,000 mL.

Then subtract: 1,000 − 850 = 150

150 mL are left.

Remember to rename units when necessary. Compute.

1. 17 mm + 28 cm **2.** 6 L − 922 mL

3. 81 m × 5 km **4.** 7.2 kg ÷ 18 g

5. 386 mm − 29 cm **6.** 0.7 × 95 dam

Set F pages 274–275

What are the approximate dimensions of a 4-in. by 6-in. index card in centimeters?

Since 1 in. ≈ 2.5 cm, 2 in. ≈ 5 cm.

4 in. ≈ 10 cm 6 in. ≈ 15 cm

The index card is about 10 cm by 15 cm.

Remember that centimeters and inches measure length. Liters and quarts measure capacity.

Give an appropriate metric measurement.

1. 18 in. **2.** 10 ft **3.** 2 qt

Give an appropriate customary measurement.

4. 50 cm **5.** 10 kg **6.** 18 km

Set G pages 278–279

A bag of apples weighed 2.86 lb at the checkout counter. The unit of measure is 0.01 lb, and the GPE is 0.005 lb. The measure 2.86 is more precise than the measure 2.9.

Remember that GPE means the measure can be $\frac{1}{2}$ unit more or $\frac{1}{2}$ unit less.

Give the unit of measure and the GPE.

1. 4.3 ft **2.** 101 cm **3.** 25.83 g

Which measure is more precise?

4. 8 yd or 8.3 yd **5.** 0.4 L or 60 mL

Set H pages 280–281

A box of raisins is marked "15 oz—425 g." The GPE for 15 oz is 0.5 oz. The GPE for 425 g is 0.5 g. The percent errors are:

$\frac{0.5}{15} = 0.0\overline{3} = 3\frac{1}{3}\%$ $\frac{0.5}{425} = 0.001 = 0.1\%$

The gram is the more precise unit, and 425 g is the more accurate measure.

Remember that the more accurate measure has a smaller percent error.

Compare the percent error, and tell which measure is more accurate.

1. 11 in. or 111 in. **2.** 8 m or 80 cm

3. 570 mL or 0.57 L **4.** 32 oz or 2 lb

Set I pages 282–283

100 yards has 1 significant digit.
110 yards has 2 significant digits.
101 yards has 3 significant digits.
100.0 yards has 4 significant digits.
0.001 yard has 1 significant digit.

Remember that final zeros in a whole number are *not* significant unless marked.

Give the number of significant digits.

1. 11 **2.** 111 **3.** 0.11 **4.** 11,000

More Practice

Set A pages 258–261

Choose the best answer.

1. Height of a pear tree
   a. 20 in. **b.** 20 ft **c.** 200 yd
2. Weight of a pear
   a. 6 lb **b.** 6 pt **c.** 6 oz
3. Area of an orchard
   a. 2,500 sq ft **b.** 250 sq ft **c.** 2,500 cu ft

Find each missing number.

4. 39 in. = ▦ ft ▦ in.
5. 75 ft = ▦ yd
6. 2 ft 6 in. = ▦ in.
7. 20 c = ▦ qt
8. 42 oz = ▦ lb ▦ oz
9. 6,000 lb = ▦ tons

Set B pages 262–263

Add or subtract.

1. 5 ft 8 in. − 4 ft 10 in.
2. 12 lb 14 oz + 8 lb 6 oz
3. 2 qt 3 c + 3 qt 2 c
4. 24 yd 2 ft − 19 yd 18 in.

Set C pages 264–265

Find the missing number.

1. 12,000 mm = ▦ m
2. 4,000 mm^3 = ▦ cm^3
3. 250 m = ▦ km
4. 892 cm^2 = ▦ mm^2
5. 0.27 m = ▦ dm
6. 1,260 mm^2 = ▦ dam^2

Set D pages 266–267

Choose the best measurement.

1. Mass of a swim suit
   a. 15 kg **b.** 1.5 g **c.** 1,500 dg
2. Capacity of a swimming pool
   a. 150 kL **b.** 1.5 L **c.** 150 mL

Find the missing number.

3. 1,216 g = ▦ kg
4. 718 cg = ▦ g
5. 0.24 kg = ▦ mg
6. 5 daL ▦ dL
7. 4.3 L = ▦ mL
8. 39,000 mL = ▦ kL

Set E pages 268–269

Compute.

1. 341 mm + 297 mm + 509 mm = ▦ m
2. 8 kL − 1,615 L = ▦ L
3. 14 m × 8 m × 2 m
4. 4,540 g ÷ 16
5. 0.08 kL + 62 L + 4,200 mL = ▦ L
6. 720 mm^2 × 90 cm = ▦ cm^3
7. 9.72 g − 120 mg = ▦ g
8. 437 m^2 ÷ 19 m

Set F pages 274–275

Give an appropriate metric measurement.

1. 1 ft
2. 36 lb
3. 5 miles
4. 1 gal

Give an appropriate customary measurement.

5. 80 km
6. 10 L
7. 50 cm
8. 20 kg

Arrange in order from greatest to least.

9. 40 kg, 4 oz, 4 lb
10. 8 mi, 80 km, 800 m
11. 7 cm, 3 in., 30 mm
12. 7 ft, 2 yd, 2 m
13. 1 gal, 3 qt, 3 L
14. 350 m, 2 mi, 3 km

Set G pages 278–279

Give the unit of measure and the GPE.

1. $4\frac{1}{2}$ ft
2. 17 m
3. 9.3 g
4. 1.16 lb
5. 205 cm
6. 3 c
7. 94.6°
8. 2,800 mm

Which measurement is more precise?

9. 1.8 m or 38 cm
10. 4 mg or 28.2 mg
11. 9 in. or $\frac{3}{4}$ ft
12. 8 yd or 3.2 mi
13. $3\frac{1}{2}$ gal or 3 qt
14. 10 m or 12 cm

Set H pages 280–281

Compute the percent error for each measurement. Then tell which measurement in each pair is more accurate.

1. 3.6 cm or 36 mm
2. 2 kg or 259 g
3. 10 gal or 3 qt
4. $8\frac{1}{2}$ h or 20 min
5. 1.08 m or 90.5 cm
6. $3\frac{1}{2}$ lb or $3\frac{1}{2}$ oz

Find the GPE and the percent error to the nearest 0.01%. You may want to use your calculator.

7. $1\frac{1}{4}$ h
8. 18.5 m
9. 7 mg
10. 2.75 mm
11. 4,850 mi
12. 0.65 lb
13. 3.5 L
14. 92.1 kg

Set I pages 282–283

Name the number of significant digits in each measurement.

1. 256 mi
2. 42.1 g
3. 2.39 m
4. 8.125 in.
5. 50,$\underline{0}$00 lb
6. 0.003 L
7. 82 ft
8. 16.8 cm
9. 29.2 kg
10. 100 yd
11. 112.0 mm
12. 30 mL

Enrichment

Measurements and Computers

Today's typical computer takes about one billionth of a second, or one ***nanosecond,*** to perform a single operation.

1 nanosecond = 0.000000001 second = 10^{-9} second

Therefore, a billion (1,000,000,000) operations can be performed in one second. ENIAC, the world's first electronic digital computer, performed only 5,000 operations per second.

1. Today's typical computer is how many times as fast as ENIAC was?

2. How many operations could ENIAC perform in an hour?

3. How many operations can today's typical computer perform in an hour?

Today's supercomputers can perform a single operation in one trillionth of a second, or one ***picosecond.***

1 picosecond = 0.000000000001 second = 10^{-12} second

4. How many operations will a supercomputer perform in one second?

5. How many operations will a supercomputer perform in one nanosecond?

Computer memory is stored in units called ***bytes.*** The first personal computer disk could hold 140,000 bytes of memory. Currently, the most advanced disk, the CDROM, can store 56 megabytes. *Mega* means "one million" (10^6). Therefore, 56 megabytes means 56,000,000 bytes of memory or information.

6. If a disk held 26,000,000 bytes, how many megabytes would this be?

7. The CDROM's memory storage is how many times as great as the memory of the first personal computer disk?

8. *Giga* means "one billion" (10^9). If a disk could hold a gigabyte of memory, how many megabytes would it hold?

Chapter 8 Review/Test

Decide on the best estimate for each.

1. The length of a ten-speed bicycle

a. 5 yd **b.** 5 ft **c.** 500 cm

2. The weight of a horse

a. 900 lb **b.** 9 tons **c.** 9,000 lb

3. The capacity of a refrigerator

a. 10 ft
b. 10 cu ft
c. 1,000 cu in.

4. The area of a $20 bill

a. 10 cm^2
b. 100 mm^2
c. 100 cm^2

Solve.

5.
$$\begin{array}{r} 8 \text{ ft } 6 \text{ in.} \\ -4 \text{ ft } 9 \text{ in.} \\ \hline \end{array}$$

6.
$$\begin{array}{r} 85 \text{ lb } 4 \text{ oz.} \\ +14 \text{ lb } 12 \text{ oz.} \\ \hline \end{array}$$

7.
$$\begin{array}{r} 3 \text{ gal } 2 \text{ qt} \\ +2 \text{ gal } 3 \text{ qt} \\ \hline \end{array}$$

8.
$$\begin{array}{r} 4 \text{ yd } 1 \text{ ft} \\ -1 \text{ yd } 2 \text{ ft} \\ \hline \end{array}$$

Find the missing number.

9. 250 m = ▦ km **10.** 730 cm = ▦ m

11. 23 cm = ▦ mm

12. 15 mm = ▦ cm

13. 42,000 g = ▦ kg

14. 4.32 L = ▦mL

15. Arlene packs race cars into cartons for a toy factory. What is the volume of each carton if the dimensions are 40 centimeters, 30 centimeters, and 20 centimeters?

16. Carl was making baked apples for dessert. About how much cinnamon should he use for each apple?

a. $\frac{1}{4}$ kilogram **b.** $\frac{1}{2}$ cup
c. $\frac{1}{8}$ teaspoon **d.** $\frac{1}{4}$ pound

17. Jerry's car weighs about 3,000 pounds. About how many kilograms does the car weigh?

a. 4,000 kg **b.** 1,000 kg
c. 6,000 kg **d.** 1,500 kg

18. What pieces of information in the table must be used to solve the problem?

Schedule for Bus #105

Elm St.	7:30A	8:05A	9:21A
Rogers St.	7:51A	8:26A	9:42A
King Ave.	8:07A	8:42A	9:58A

Yvonne lives 10 minutes from the Elm Street bus stop. She leaves her home at 7:40 A.M. What time should she arrive by bus at King Avenue?

Give the unit of measure and the greatest possible error.

19. 4 yd **20.** 4.3 mL

21. The length of a room is 55 feet. Compute the percent of error for the measurement to the nearest 0.1%.

Give the number of significant digits in each measure.

22. 123 g **23.** 0.002 mg

24. **Write About Math** Why is it important to know about greatest possible error?

Geometry

9

Did You Know: A *lunar eclipse* occurs when the earth, moon, and sun all lie on the same line with the earth between the sun and the moon. Lunar eclipses usually occur about every 177 days, or every six *synodic months* (29.53 days). Not all eclipses are visible from all parts of the earth.

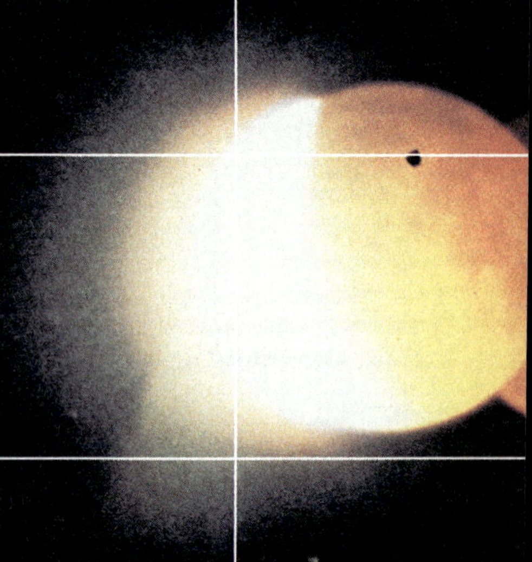

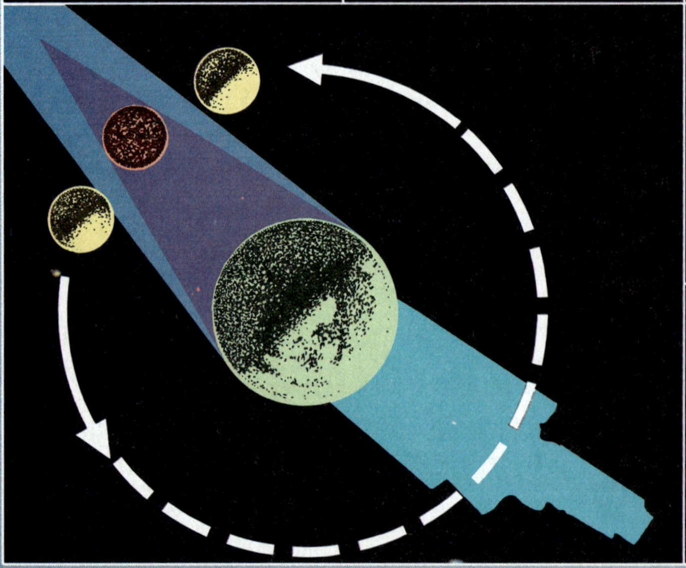

Number-Sense Project

Estimate

A lunar eclipse occurred on February 20, 1989. Estimate 177 days from February 20.

Gather Data

Find the dates of the lunar eclipses last year and this year. Tell where they could be seen.

Analyze and Report

Find the number of days between the two lunar eclipses last year and the two this year. Tell if any part of the eclipse can be seen in your area.

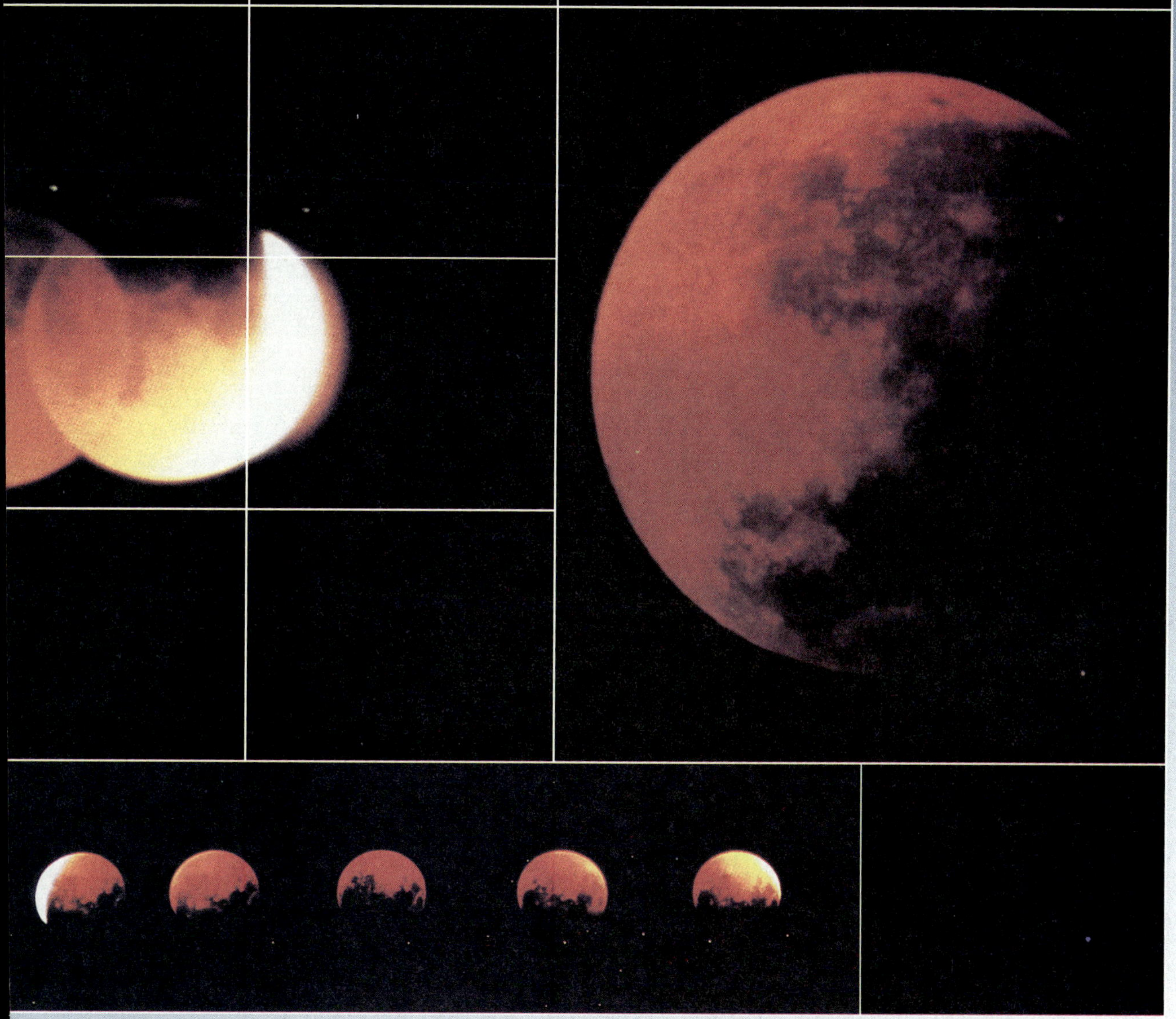

Relating Planes, Lines, and Points

Build Understanding

Look at a corner of a room. Each wall is part of a ***plane***. The flat surface of each wall has two dimensions: length and width. The place where two walls meet is a part of a ***line*** called a ***line segment***. Line segments have only one dimension: length.

The place where two walls and the floor meet is a ***point***. A point is a location. It has no dimension. ***Collinear points*** are points on the same line. ***Coplanar points*** are points in the same plane.

A point on a line divides a line into two ***half-lines***, or ***rays***. A line divides a plane into two ***half-planes***.

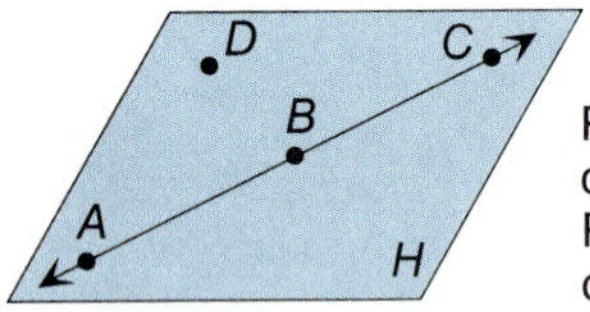

Points *A*, *B*, and *C* are collinear.
Points *A*, *B*, *C*, and *D* are coplanar.

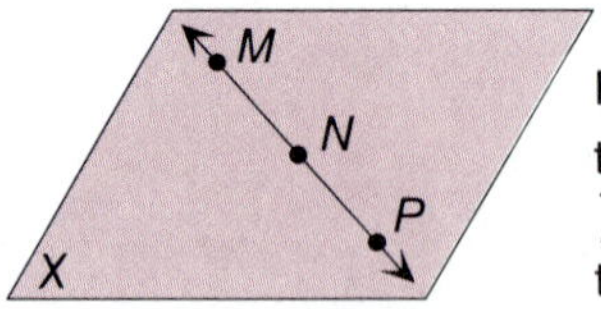

Point *N* divides the line into two rays, $\overrightarrow{NM}$ and $\overrightarrow{NP}$.
$\overleftrightarrow{MP}$ divides the plane *X* into two half-planes.

The room itself has three dimensions: length, width, and depth (or height). The entire room is part of ***space***.

Talk About Math What is the least number of planes needed to form a ray? a line segment? How can two lines not intersect and not be parallel? Use two pencils to illustrate your answer.

Check Understanding

For another example, see Set A, pages 334–335.

Match the items that name the same line, segment, or ray.

1. $\overline{PQ}$ **a.** $\overleftrightarrow{PR}$

2. $\overrightarrow{QS}$ **b.** $\overrightarrow{RP}$

3. $\overrightarrow{RQ}$ **c.** $\overline{QP}$

4. $\overleftrightarrow{QS}$ **d.** $\overrightarrow{QR}$

Practice

For More Practice, see Set A, pages 336–337.

Choose from the list at the right all the possible ways that the given items can intersect.

5. 2 lines in a plane

6. 2 planes

7. A line and a plane

8. 2 rays in a plane

9. 2 lines in space

10. A ray and a plane

a. 0 points
b. 1 point
c. 1 line

Problem Solving

Answer each question. Draw diagrams to illustrate your answers.

11. Are two points always collinear? 3 points?

12. Are 2 points always coplanar? 3 points? 4 points?

13. Are collinear points always coplanar?

The points *A*, *B*, *C*, and *D* in the illustration represent rides at an amusement park. The point *F* represents the location of the food stands. The segments represent paths between the rides and food stands.

14. List segments that describe at least two different routes you could take to go to all of the rides and the food stands.

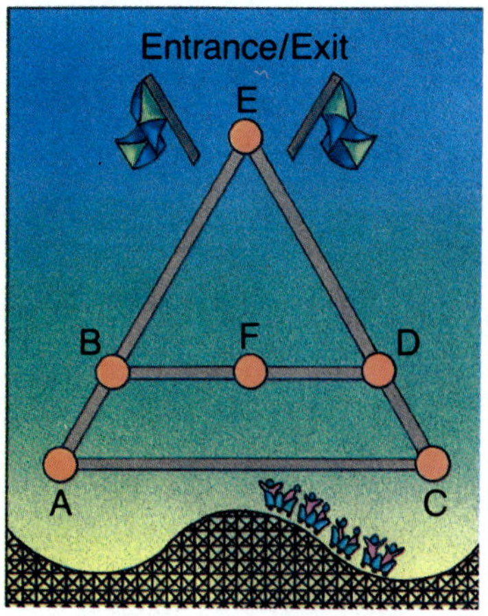

Visual Thinking Tell how a segment and also a ray can be created by putting the given figures together.

15. Plane, line, point

16. Line, point

17. 4 planes

Draw a Diagram

PROBLEM SOLVING GUIDE

Understand
QUESTION
FACTS
KEY IDEA

Plan and Solve
STRATEGY
ANSWER

Look Back
SENSIBLE ANSWER
ALTERNATE APPROACH

Build Understanding

Folk dancing is a popular pastime in many cultures. On May 1, in Old England, villagers would trim a tall pole with flowers and greens and ribbons for their annual maypole dance. The maypole is used in Swedish folk dancing as part of a Midsummer Day festival on June 24. If eight maypole dancers start the dance ten feet from the pole, locate and describe all the places they could be standing.

Understand QUESTION Where are the dancers in relation to the pole?

FACT Each of the eight dancers must be ten feet from the pole.

KEY IDEA A diagram will help to show all the possible locations for the dancers.

Plan and Solve STRATEGY *Draw a diagram* to test possible answers. Let 1 cm represent 1 ft. Draw 8 dots so that each dot is exactly 10 cm from the dot that represents the maypole. Using the same diagram, draw 8 new dots to show another formation that the dancers can take. Where will the dancers be located each time?

ANSWER The eight dancers will form a circle around the pole. This answer describes a ***locus,*** which is a point or set of points that satisfies a given condition. The locus is a circle.

Look Back SENSIBLE ANSWER Could the dancers be positioned inside or outside the circle?

Dancers of all ages celebrate the arrival of summer with the ancient dance around the maypole.

■ **Talk About Math** What is the locus if the dancers stand no more than ten feet from the pole? more than ten feet from the pole? Is the circle itself a part of either locus?

Check Understanding

Describe each locus. You may want to draw a diagram to help you.

1. In a plane, what is the locus of points located 2 inches from a line?

2. In a plane, what is the locus of points at least 1 inch from a point?

Practice

Solve each problem.

3. In the Danish folk dance Sonderburger Doppel Quadrille, dancers form two parallel lines. If the lines are 12 feet apart, locate points that are an equal distance from both lines.

4. Two lead dancers are positioned six feet apart. The remaining dancers must stand equidistant from each lead dancer. Where can the remaining dancers stand?

5. A troupe of 20 dancers forms a square, while holding hands. The dancers are 1 meter apart. What is the approximate area of the square?

6. The dancers stand in a row 15 feet long. The lead dancer must always be 3 feet from any of the other dancers. Where can the lead dancer stand?

7. A three-couple dance ensemble plans to purchase new costumes. The men's costume costs $249, and the women's costs $389. How much will they spend on costumes?

8. If each couple in a 20-dancer troupe practices together for 2 hours per week, and each individual practices for 3 hours per week, what is the total practice time for the entire troupe for one week?

9. Two lead dancers are positioned eight feet apart. Locate points that are ten feet from both lead dancers.

10. The guitar music for a Spanish dance is being transmitted by an omnidirectional microphone which picks up sounds in all directions within a certain range. If the range of an omnidirectional microphone is 15 feet and the microphone is suspended 16 feet above a stage, describe the locus where sound will be picked up.

Dancers from the La Mancha region of Spain celebrate their distinctive music.

Pairs of Angles

Build Understanding

The girders and beams of a building can meet to form different ***angles***. Architects use their knowledge of angles to help them design buildings.

Some angles have special names.

Acute angle
An angle that measures between 0° and 90°

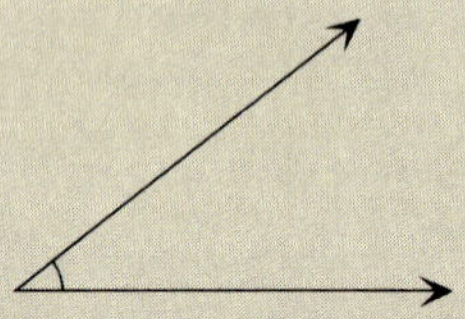

Right angle
An angle that measures 90°; formed by two perpendicular rays

Obtuse angle
An angle that measures between 90° and 180°

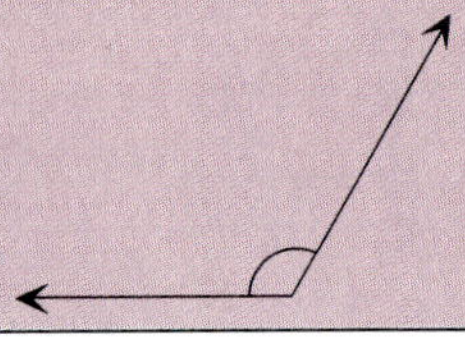

Straight angle
An angle that measures 180°

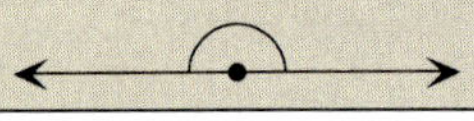

Architects also must have an understanding of how pairs of angles are related.

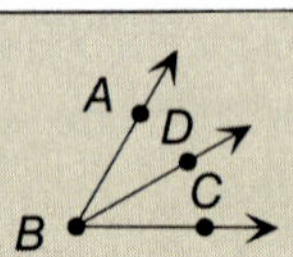

∠*ABD* is adjacent to ∠*DBC*. ∠*ABC* is not adjacent to ∠*ABD* or ∠*DBC*. Point B is a common vertex.

Adjacent angles
Angles that have a common vertex and a common side between them

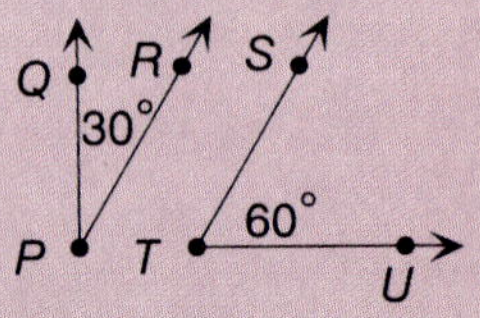

∠*QPR* and ∠*STU* are complementary.

Complementary angles
Two angles whose sum measures 90°

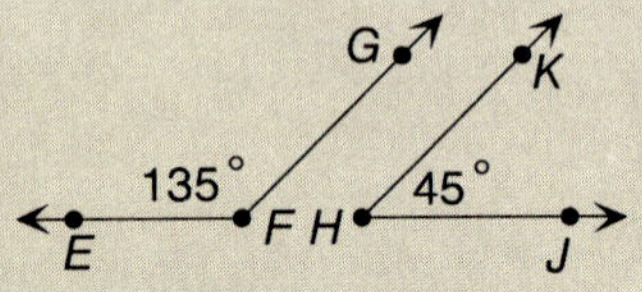

∠*EFG* and ∠*KHJ* are supplementary.

Supplementary angles
Two angles whose sum measures 180°

∠*WOX* and ∠*ZOY* are vertical angles;
∠*WOZ* and ∠*XOY* are vertical angles.

Vertical angles
Pairs of angles formed by two intersecting lines. The measures of vertical angles are equal.

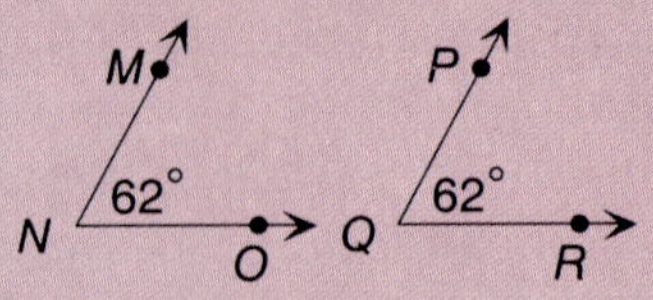

∠*MNO* and ∠*PQR* are congruent angles.
∠*MNO* ≅ ∠*PQR*

Congruent angles
Two angles that have the same measure

■ **Talk About Math** The sum of the angles of any triangle is 180 degrees. Can a triangle have more than one acute angle? more than one obtuse angle?

Check Understanding

For another example, see Set B, pages 334–335.

Name the different types of angles in the diagram.

1. Right angles **2.** Straight angles **3.** Acute angles **4.** Obtuse angles

5. Pairs of supplementary angles

6. Pairs of adjacent angles

7. Find the measure of $\angle WXY$.

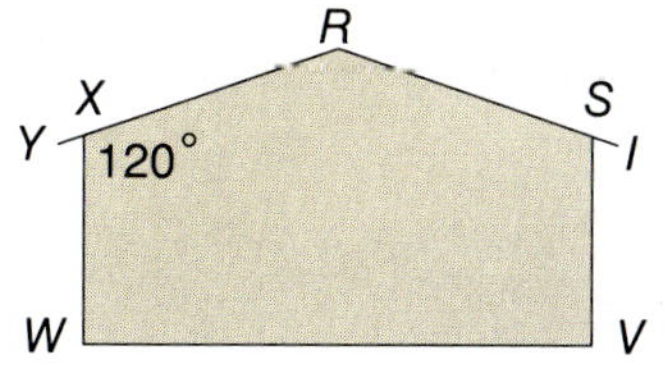

Practice

For More Practice, see Set B, pages 336–337.

Find the measure of each angle if $m\angle MKW = 50°$ and $\angle KRC$ is a right angle. **Remember** $m\angle MKW$ is read "the measure of angle MKW."

8. $\angle CKR$ **9.** $\angle WKC$ **10.** $\angle MKZ$ **11.** $\angle MCR$

12. $\angle KCQ$ **13.** $\angle ARK$ **14.** $\angle ARZ$ **15.** $\angle ZRC$

16. Which pairs of angles are congruent? complementary? supplementary?

17. Which pairs of angles are vertical angles?

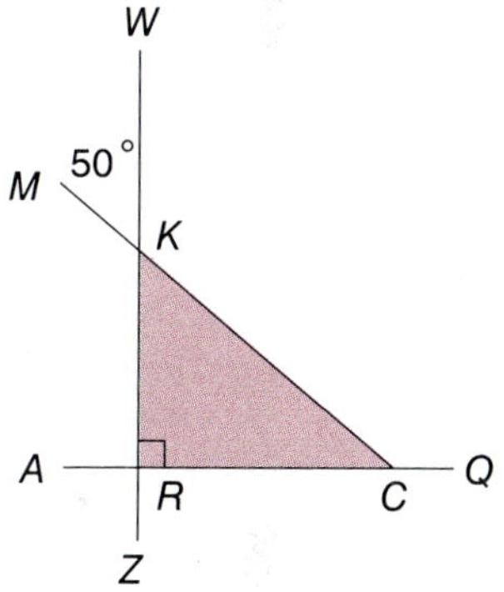

Problem Solving

Critical Thinking Use the diagram for Exercises 8–17 to solve Problems 18–20.

Suppose $m\angle MKW = 70°$. Tell how this would affect your answers to these exercises.

18. Exercise 15 **19.** Exercise 16 **20.** Exercise 17

21. What can you conclude about the two acute angles of a right triangle?

22. Find the measure of $\angle ABC$ on the outline of the roof shown at the right if $m\angle A = 60°$; $m\angle C = 100°$; and $m\angle CDB = 40°$.

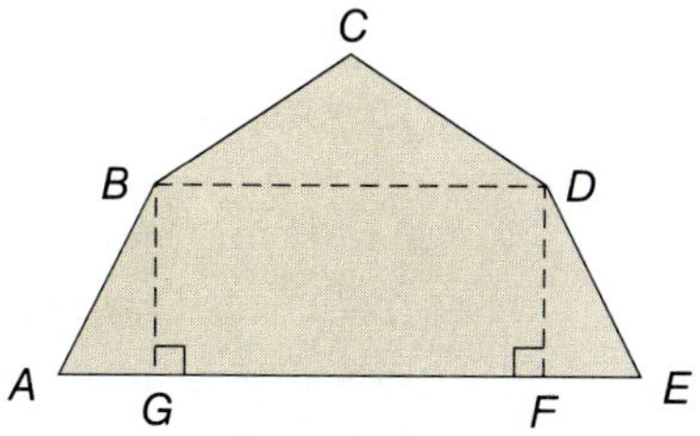

Parallel Lines and Angles

Build Understanding

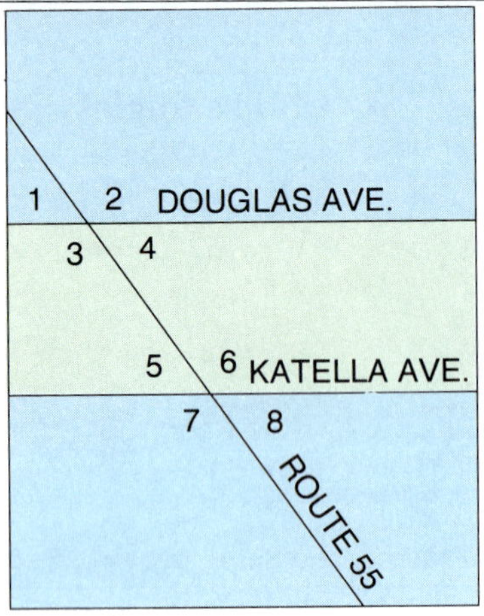

Civil engineers often use parallel lines when they design city streets.

On the map at the left, Douglas Avenue and Katella Avenue suggest parallel lines. Route 55, which intersects both streets, is a ***transversal***.

On the map, the green area between the two parallel lines is the ***interior region***. The blue areas are the ***exterior regions***.

The angles on the map are named by numbers.

Now look at some angle pairs with special names.

Alternate interior angles	Alternate exterior angles	Corresponding angles	
$\angle 3$ and $\angle 6$	$\angle 1$ and $\angle 8$	$\angle 1$ and $\angle 5$	$\angle 3$ and $\angle 7$
$\angle 4$ and $\angle 5$	$\angle 2$ and $\angle 7$	$\angle 2$ and $\angle 6$	$\angle 4$ and $\angle 8$

Alternate interior angles are congruent.

Alternate exterior angles are congruent.

Corresponding angles are congruent.

Talk About Math Suppose two nonparallel lines are cut by a transversal. How does this affect alternate interior angles? alternate exterior angles? corresponding angles?

Check Understanding

For another example, see Set C, pages 334–335.

Copy this diagram onto lined paper. Label the angles as shown.

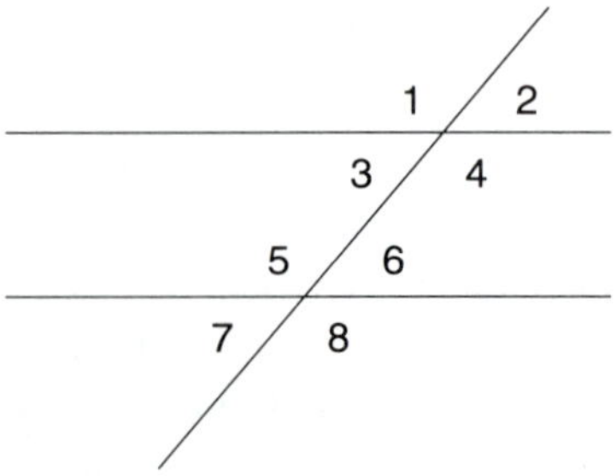

1. List all the angles with the same measure as $\angle 5$.
2. List all the angles with the same measure as $\angle 6$.
3. Use a protractor to measure each of the angles and to check your answers to Exercises 1 and 2.

Practice

For More Practice, see Set C, pages 336–337.

Draw a diagram to show whether each statement is true or false.

4. Horizontal lines are always parallel.

5. Interior angles on the same side of a transversal are always congruent.

6. In a plane, a line that is perpendicular to one of two parallel lines is perpendicular to the other.

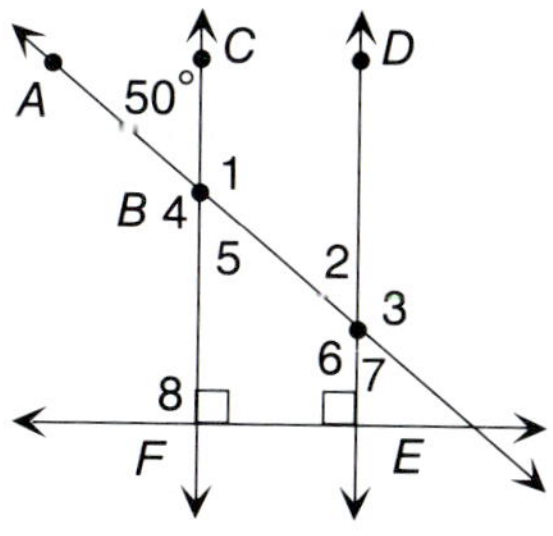

In the figure at the right, $\overleftrightarrow{CF}$ and $\overleftrightarrow{DE}$ are parallel, $m\angle ABC = 50°$, and $\angle DEF$ is a right angle. Find the measure of each angle without measuring.

7. $m\angle 1$ **8.** $m\angle 2$ **9.** $m\angle 3$ **10.** $m\angle 4$

11. $m\angle 5$ **12.** $m\angle 6$ **13.** $m\angle 7$ **14.** $m\angle 8$

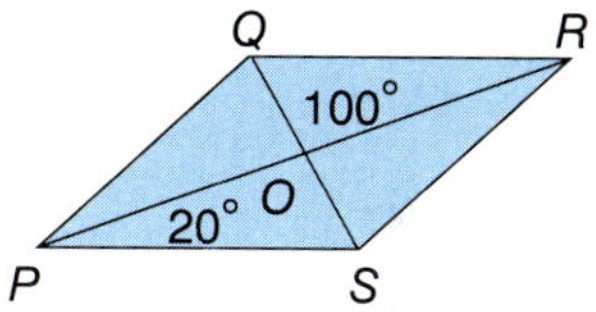

In the figure at the right, $\overline{PQ}$ is parallel to $\overline{SR}$, and $\overline{QR}$ is parallel to $\overline{PS}$; $m\angle RPS = 20°$; $m\angle QOR = 100°$. Find each measure.

15. $m\angle POS$ **16.** $m\angle PRQ$ **17.** $m\angle QOP$ **18.** $m\angle QSP$ **19.** $m\angle SQR$

Mixed Practice Use the figure for Exercises 7–14 to complete each statement.

20. $\angle 1$ and $\angle 3$ are __?__ angles.

21. $\overrightarrow{FE}$ is a(n) __?__ whose __?__ is F.

22. $\angle 3$ and $\angle 6$ are __?__ angles.

23. $\angle BFE$ is a(n) __?__ angle.

24. $\angle 1$ and $\angle 6$ are __?__ angles.

25. $\overline{BF}$ is a(n) __?__ whose endpoints are __?__ and __?__.

Problem Solving

On this map, First Avenue and Second Avenue are parallel. A city planner proposes to locate a small garden and park on the island formed by the intersections of the four streets shown. Find each measure.

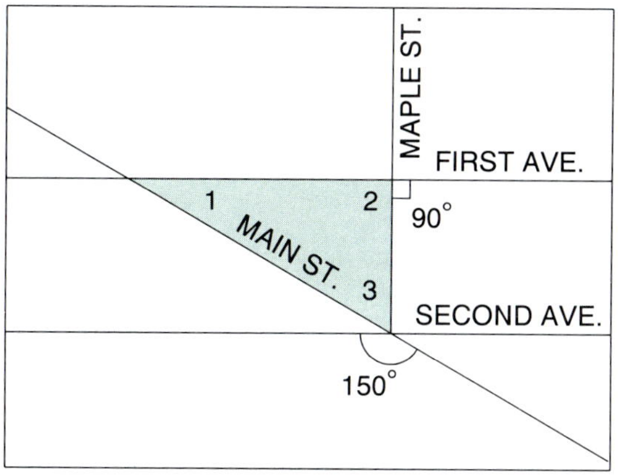

26. $m\angle 1$ **27.** $m\angle 2$ **28.** $m\angle 3$

29. The lengths of the sides of the garden are 2.1 cm, 2.8 cm, and 3.5 cm. If the map is enlarged so that the longest side is 14 cm, how long will each of the other sides be?

Angles in Polygons

Build Understanding

These shapes are ***polygons***. The sides of a polygon are line segments. The number of sides determines the name of the polygon.

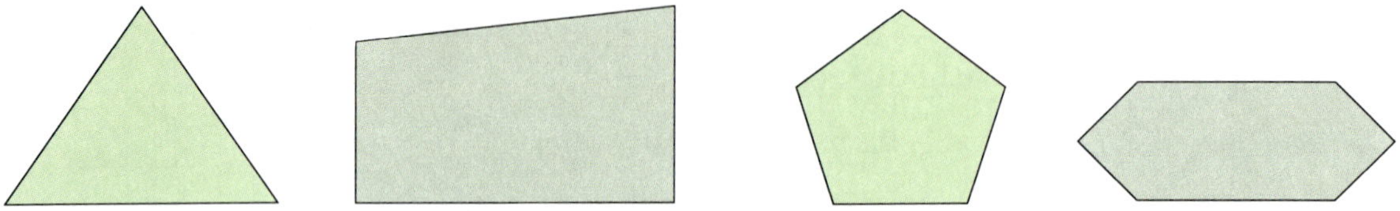

Triangle 3 sides | ***Quadrilateral*** 4 sides | ***Pentagon*** 5 sides | ***Hexagon*** 6 sides

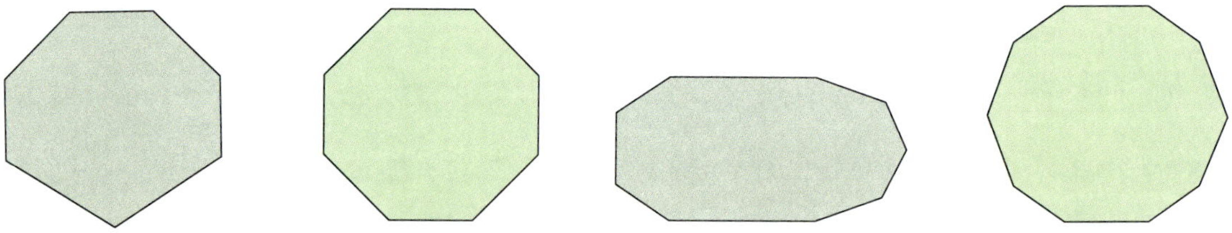

Heptagon 7 sides | ***Octagon*** 8 sides | ***Nonagon*** 9 sides | ***Decagon*** 10 sides

The sides and ***interior angles*** of a ***regular polygon*** are congruent. The pentagon and the octagon shown are regular polygons.

A. What is the sum of the measures of the angles in an octagon?

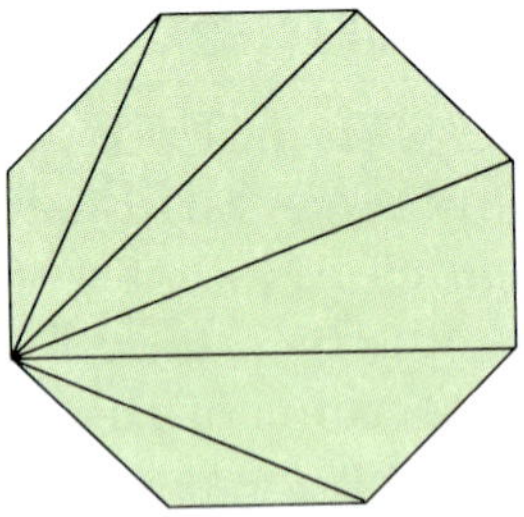

The ***diagonals*** drawn from one vertex of a polygon separate it into triangles. How many diagonals can be drawn from one vertex of an octagon? How many triangles are formed?

The five diagonals separate the octagon into six triangles. Since the sum of the measures of the angles of a triangle is 180°, the sum of the measures of the angles of an octagon is $6 \times 180°$, or 1,080°.

B. A regular polygon fits perfectly inside a circle. A ***central angle*** is formed by connecting the ***center*** of the circle with two adjacent vertices, or corners, of the polygon. Find the measure of each central angle of a regular hexagon.

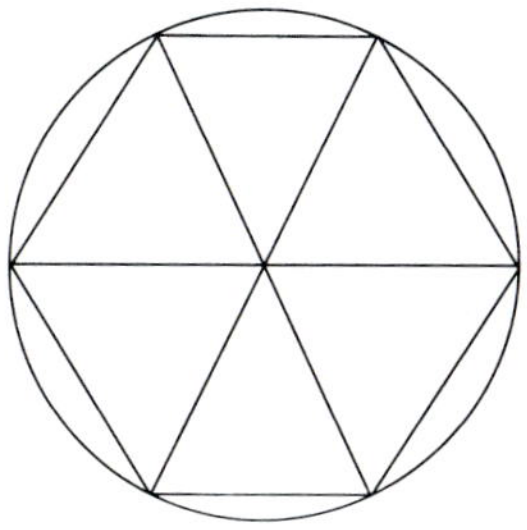

A regular hexagon has 6 equal central angles with a sum of 360°. Each central angle of a regular hexagon has a measure of 360° ÷ 6, or 60°.

C. Is it possible for a pentagon to have one right angle?

Draw a right angle with sides of any length. Then draw the 3 other sides.

D. Can a triangle be formed from line segments of 5 cm, 1 cm, and 2 cm?

Draw a segment 5 cm long. Mark off 1 cm and 2 cm segments from either end.

A triangle cannot be formed because 1 cm + 2 cm < 5 cm.

Talk About Math Suppose $\angle C$ of a hexagon measures 170°. What can you say about the hexagon?

Check Understanding

For another example, see Set D, pages 334–335.

For Exercises 1–8, draw each polygon listed in the table below. Then draw all the diagonals from one vertex of each polygon. Copy and complete the table.

Polygon	Number of sides	Number of angles	Number of triangles formed	Sum of measures of all angles
Triangle	3	3	1	180°
Quadrilateral	**1.**	**2.**	**3.**	**4.**
Pentagon	**5.**	**6.**	**7.**	**8.**

Use the table above to complete these statements.

9. The number of sides of a polygon ___?___ the number of angles.

10. The number of triangles formed by the diagonals from one vertex of a polygon is ___?___ less than the number of sides.

11. As the number of sides of a polygon increases by one, the sum of the measures of the angles increases by ___?___.

12. To find the sum of the measures of all the angles of a polygon, subtract ___?___ from the ___?___. Then multiply by ___?___.

Practice

For More Practice, see Set D, pages 336–337.

Complete the table.

Regular polygon	Number of sides	Number of central angles	Measure of each central angle
	3	3	120°
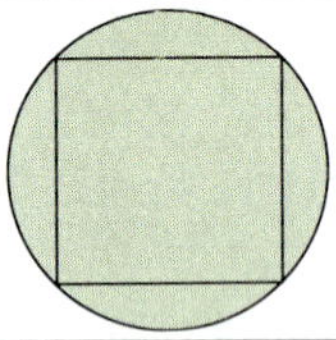	**13.**	**14.**	**15.**
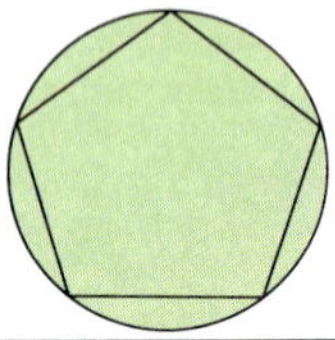	**16.**	**17.**	**18.**

Use the table above for Exercises 19–21.

19. The number of sides of a regular polygon ___?___ the number of central angles.

20. As the number of central angles of a regular polygon increases, the measure of each central angle ___?___.

21. To find the measure of each central angle of a regular polygon, divide ___?___ by ___?___.

Tell whether you would use mental math, paper and pencil, or a calculator. Determine the number of sides of the regular polygon with a central angle of the given measure.

22. 30° **23.** 10° **24.** 15° **25.** 18°

26. 45° **27.** 120° **28.** 72° **29.** 1°

Tell whether the following figures are possible. Explain.

30. A parallelogram with a right angle

31. A pentagon with four right angles

32. A regular decagon with a central angle of 60°

33. A regular hexagon with one right angle

34. A regular quadrilateral

35. A pentagon with one acute angle

Mixed Practice Tell whether each statement is *true* or *false*.

36. Two lines always intersect at a point.

37. Two planes can intersect in a line.

38. A line and a plane can intersect at a point.

39. The number of diagonals in a polygon never equals the number of its sides.

Problem Solving

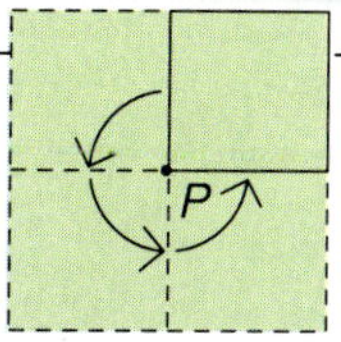

Polygons that completely cover a plane, with no gaps or overlapping, are said to ***tessellate.*** The square at the right tessellates because repeated tracings of the polygons at vertex P will completely cover the region.

40. The sum of the measures of all the angles about a point is 360°. The measure of one angle of a square is 90°. How can this information be used to determine if a square tessellates?

41. Name two regular polygons other than a square that tessellate.

42. A regular octagon does not tessellate the plane. What polygon can be combined with a regular octagon to tessellate the plane?

Explore ______ Math

What is the relationship between the measures of the angles of a triangle and the lengths of its sides?

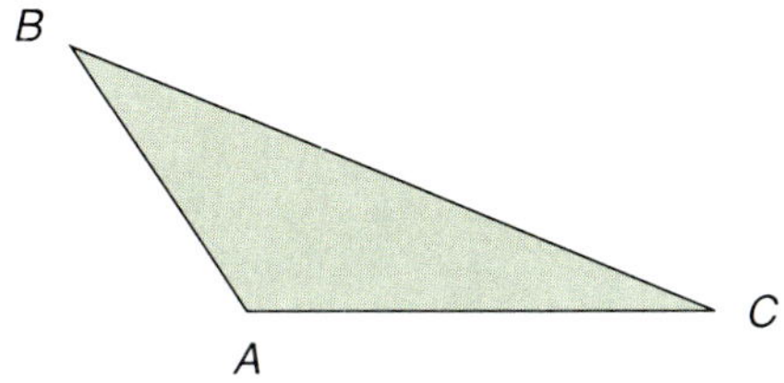

Side BC is **opposite** $\angle A$.

43. Draw an acute triangle. Measure each angle and each side. Make a table listing the angles and their opposite sides.

44. Repeat the procedure in Problem 43 for a right triangle and an obtuse triangle.

45. Make a conclusion from your tables. Where is the longest side of a triangle? the shortest side? Why is the hypotenuse the longest side of a right triangle?

46. Can a similar conclusion be made about other kinds of polygons?

Circles

Build Understanding

The Ancient Chinese, Babylonians, and Greeks all used properties of circles. They realized that the distance around the circle (the ***circumference***) is always equal to the product of the diameter, or twice the radius, and a certain number. That number is a little greater than 3. Today we call that number ***pi***. The symbol for pi is π. The most commonly used approximations for π are $\frac{22}{7}$, 3.14, and 3.1416.

A. Calculator Find the circumference of a circle with a radius of 1.52 m.

Circumference = $2 \times \pi \times$ radius

Press: 2 [×] 3.1416 [×] 1.52 [=]

Display: *9.550464*

The circumference is about 9.55 m.

B. A ***central angle*** of a circle is an angle whose vertex is the center of the circle.

A ***chord*** is a line segment whose endpoints are on the circle.

An ***inscribed angle*** is an angle whose vertex is on the circle and whose sides are chords of the circle.

The measure of an inscribed angle is $\frac{1}{2}$ the measure of the central angle that intercepts the same arc on the circle. If $m\angle 1 = 80°$, then $m\angle 2 = 40°$.

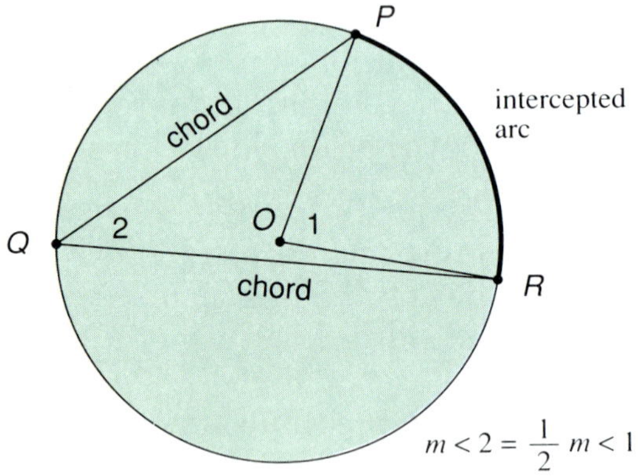

$\angle$O is a central angle.

$\angle$Q is an inscribed angle.

■ **Talk About Math** What kind of inscribed angle intercepts an arc that is a semicircle? an arc that is less than a semicircle? greater than a semicircle?

Check Understanding

For another example, see Set E, pages 334–335.

Use the diagram at the right for Exercises 1–7.
For Exercises 1–5, name these elements.

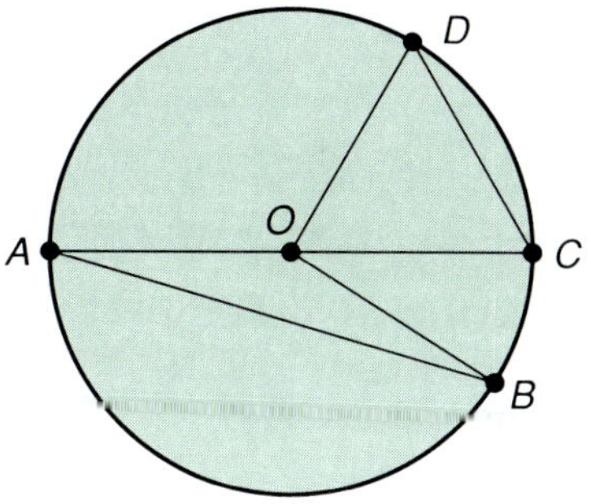

1. All diameters **2.** All radii **3.** All chords

4. All central angles **5.** All inscribed angles

Use a protractor to measure each angle. Then describe how the measures of each pair of angles are related.

6. $\angle ACD$ and $\angle AOD$ **7.** $\angle CAB$ and $\angle COB$

Practice

For More Practice, see Set E, pages 336–337.

Estimation For Exercises 8–11, estimate the circumference.

8. $r = 10$ in. **9.** $r = 2.1$ in. **10.** $d = 8$ in. **11.** $d = 3.9$ in.

For Exercises 12–15, use the given approximation for π to find the circumference. Tell whether you would use mental math, paper and pencil, or a calculator.

12. $r = 100$ cm, $\pi \approx 3.14$ **13.** $r = 14$ in., $\pi \approx \frac{22}{7}$ **14.** $r = 30.25$ ft, $\pi \approx 3.1416$ **15.** $d = 3$ m, $\pi \approx 3.14$

For Exercises 16–21, find the measure of each angle if $m\angle BOC = 140°$.

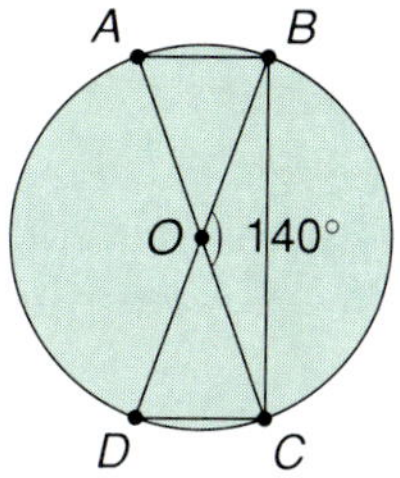

16. $\angle BAC$ **17.** $\angle BDC$ **18.** $\angle AOD$

19. $\angle AOB$ **20.** $\angle ABC$ **21.** $\angle BCD$

In the diagram for Exercises 1–5, find the measure of each angle given the following conditions.

22. $m\angle AOD = 110°$, $m\angle BOA = 160°$ **23.** $m\angle BOA = 150°$, $m\angle DOA = 130°$ **24.** $m\angle DOC = 66°$, $m\angle BOC = 25°$

25. Mental Math Without using a calculator, choose the best answer. The circumference of a circle with a radius of 8.2 cm is given by a calculator with which of the following displays?

a. 514.96 **b.** 11,429.6 **c.** 51.496 **d.** 25.748

26. Number Sense Choose the best answer. If the circumference of a circle is 60 cm, its radius is between which measurements?

a. 9 cm and 10 cm **b.** 10 cm and 11 cm **c.** 19 cm and 20 cm

Problem Solving

Many different approximations for π have been used over the centuries. Modern computers have calculated π to over a million decimal places.

Calculator Solve each problem.

27. Which of the above ancient values for π is closest to a modern approximation of 3.141597?

28. How many complete revolutions does a 15-inch diameter wheel make on a one-mile trip?

29. Does a 66-centimeter diameter wheel make more or less turns per kilometer than a 72-centimeter diameter wheel?

30. The fraction $\frac{355}{113}$ is a closer approximation of π than $\frac{22}{7}$. Calculate the difference between the two decimal numbers.

31. A circle has a radius of 25 cm. Using $\frac{22}{7}$ for π, calculate the circumference.

32. Calculate the circumference of the circle in Problem 31 using 3.1415927 for π.

33. What is the difference between the answers for Problems 31 and 32?

34. In Problems 31–32, what would be the difference in feet if the radius were 25 miles?

Explore ______ Math

Do you think the size of two circles determines the number of points of intersection?

35. Draw pairs of circles that intersect at 0 points, 1 point, and 2 points.

36. Show all intersection points for two circles of different sizes.

37. Show all possible intersection points for two congruent circles.

38. Were your results the same for Problems 36 and 37?

Midchapter Checkup

Tell whether each statement is true or false.

1. A line and a plane may intersect at one point.

2. Two parallel lines intersect at zero points.

3. Two planes can intersect at one point.

4. The locus of all points in a plane at the same distance from point *A* is a circle that has point *A* as its center.

Use the diagram to the right to name two of these types of angles.

5. Pairs of complementary angles

6. Pairs of supplementary angles

7. Acute angles

8. Obtuse angles

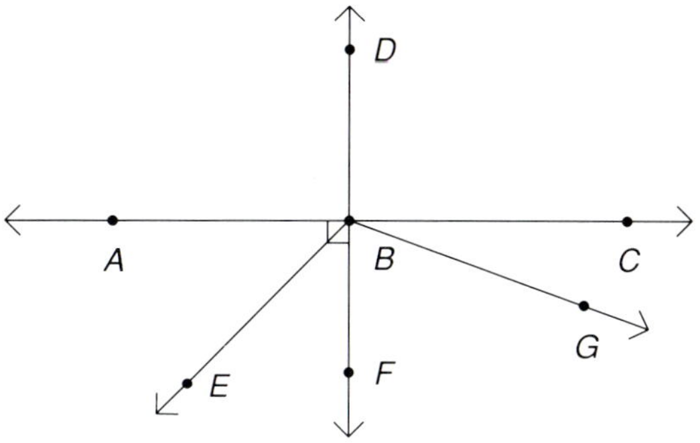

For Exercises 9 and 10, name the polygon and give the sum of the measures of its angles.

9.

10.

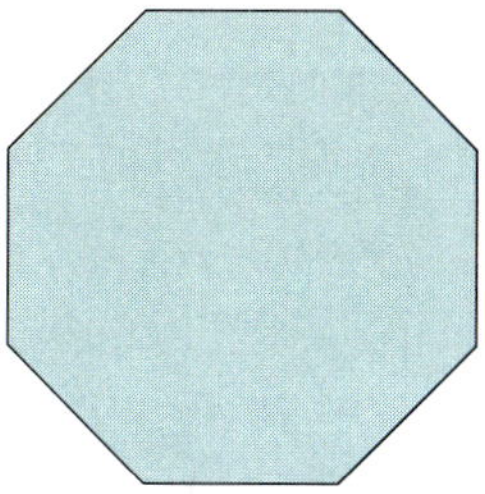

Lines *CD* and *EF* in the figure below are parallel.

11. Name two pairs of corresponding angles.

12. Name one pair of alternate exterior angles.

13. Name two pairs of alternate interior angles.

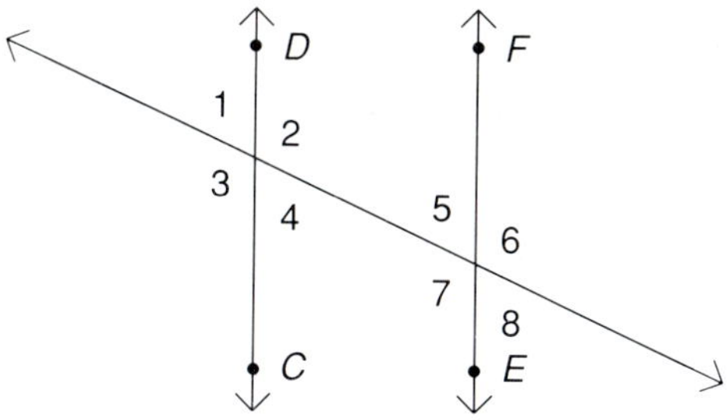

Explore as a Team

1. Tangrams can be used to form many geometric shapes.

a. Copy the square shown. Cut along the heavy lines.

b. Work as a team to form each polygon listed in the chart. Copy the chart and record the number of pieces used to make each polygon. Try to make each polygon using as many different number of pieces as possible.

c. Did your team find that some polygons could not be made with a certain number of pieces? Name them. Compare your team's results with those of another team. Are the results the same?

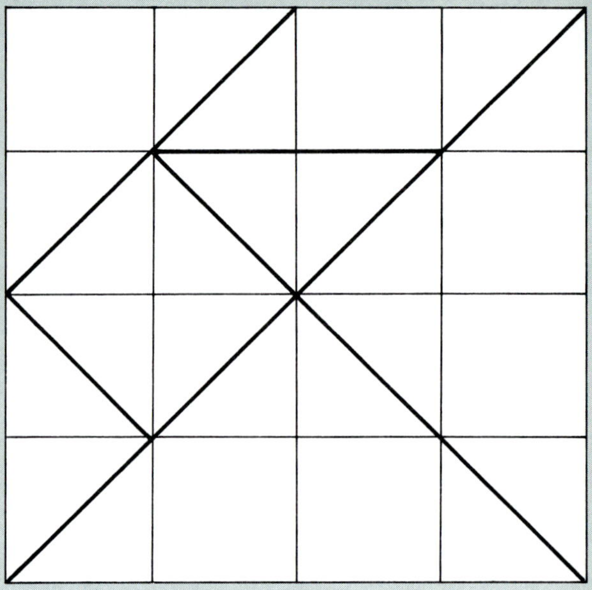

Shape	Number of pieces						
	1	2	3	4	5	6	7
square							
triangle							
rectangle							
parallelogram							
trapezoid							
pentagon							
hexagon							

Number Sense Project

Look back at pages 292–293.

1. During a solar eclipse, the sun cannot be seen from areas on the earth that lie in the moon's shadow. Here are some dates for solar eclipses. Find the number of days between each eclipse.

Date	Type	Days since last eclipse
10/3/86	Annular/total	177
3/29/87	Annular/total	■
3/17/88	Total	■

TIPS FOR WORKING TOGETHER

When you are unsure, ask someone in your group for help or say you don't understand.

Explore with a Computer

Use the *Geometry Workshop Project* for this activity.

Lydia wants to design a quilt using a pattern of polygons that originate from one central point. She drew her design using triangles, but decided it was too plain.

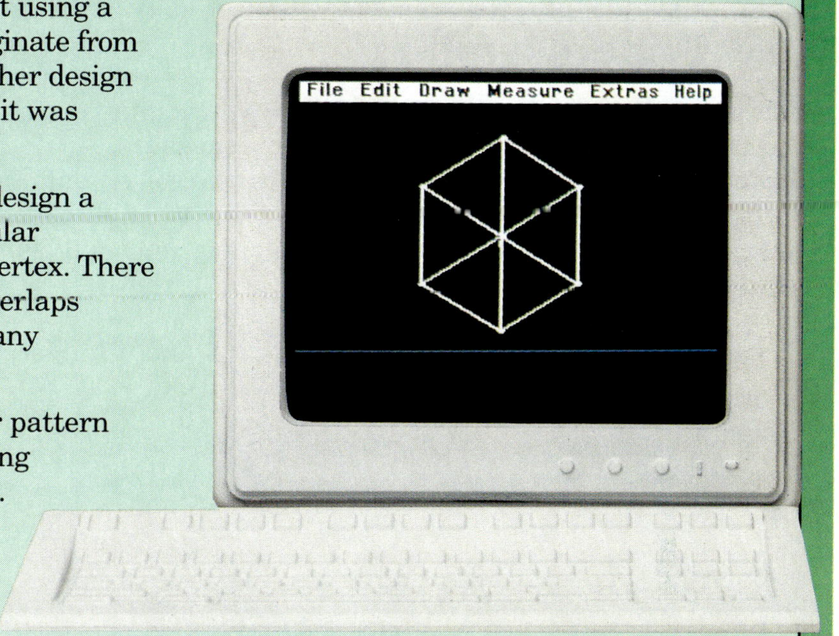

1. At the computer, design a pattern by placing regular hexagons around one vertex. There should be no gaps or overlaps between them. How many hexagons did you use?

2. Think of a similar pattern Lydia might create using other regular polygons. Try other polygons or combinations of polygons that can be placed around one vertex.

Visual Thinking Activity

For each exercise, compare the shape in column A to the shape in column B. Then look at the shape in column C. Decide which shape in columns 1–4 compares to the shape in column C in the same way.

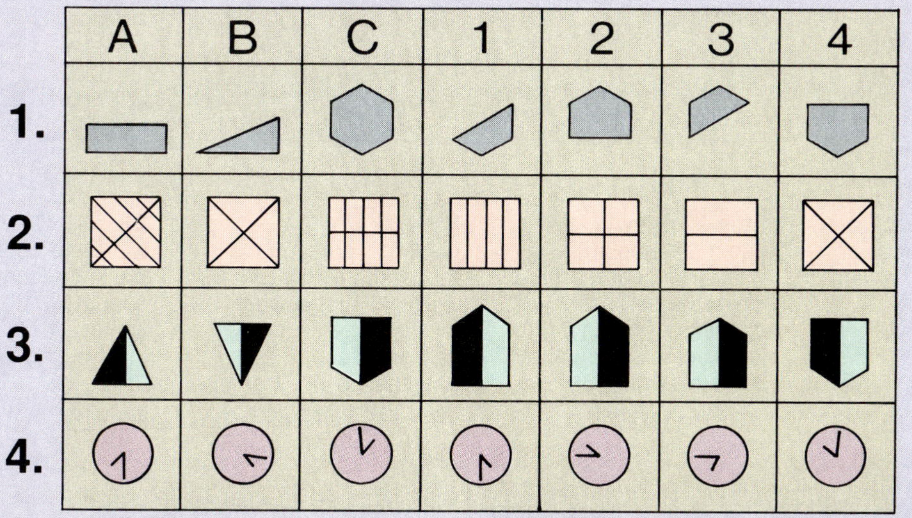

Basic Geometric Constructions

Build Understanding

You know that congruent segments have the same length and that congruent angles have the same measure. A ***bisector*** divides a segment or angle into two congruent parts. With just a compass and an unmarked straightedge, you can ***construct*** congruent segments, congruent angles, segment bisectors, and angle bisectors.

A. Construct a line that is perpendicular to $\overline{AB}$ and also bisects $\overline{AB}$.

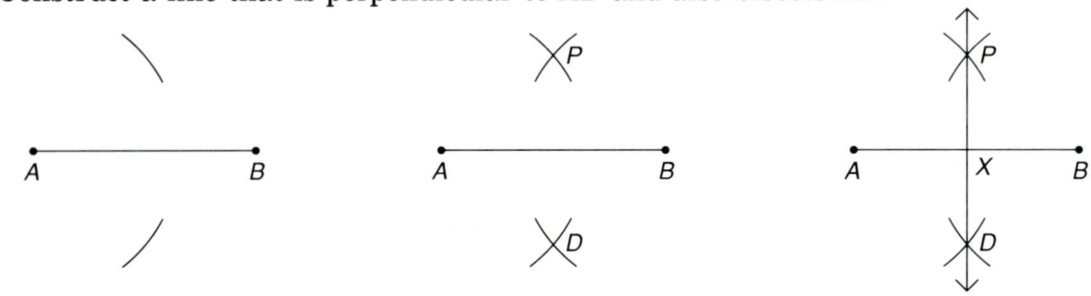

Step 1 With A as center, and using a compass with an opening greater than half $\overline{AB}$, draw an arc above and below $\overline{AB}$.

Step 2 Using the same compass opening and point B as center, draw arcs above and below $\overline{AB}$. Label the intersections of the arcs P and D.

Step 3 Draw $\overleftrightarrow{PD}$. Label the point of intersection X. $\overleftrightarrow{PD} \perp \overline{AB}$ and $\overleftrightarrow{PD}$ bisects $\overline{AB}$.

$\overleftrightarrow{PD}$ is the ***perpendicular bisector*** of $\overline{AB}$. $\overline{AX} \cong \overline{XB}$.

B. Construct an angle congruent to $\angle F$ and bisect it.

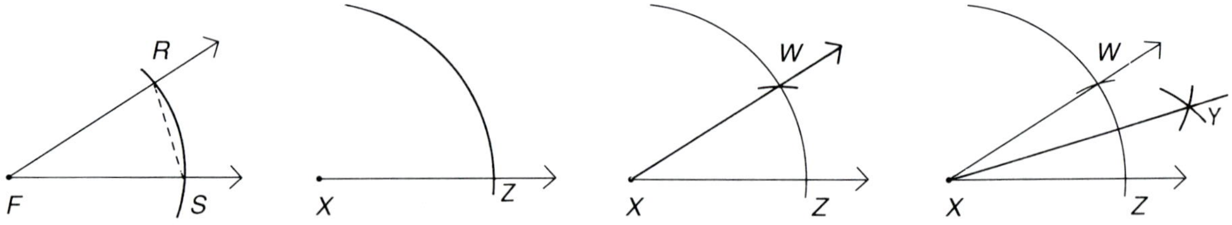

Step 1 With F as center, draw an arc that intersects both sides of $\angle F$.

Step 2 Draw a ray. Label its endpoint X. With X as center and the same compass opening, draw an arc to intersect the ray. Label the intersection Z.

Step 3 Set the compass opening to the length of $\overline{RS}$. With Z as center, draw an arc that intersects the first arc. Label the intersection W. Draw $\overrightarrow{XW}$. $\angle X \cong \angle F$.

Step 4 Draw an arc with Z as center. With the same compass opening and W as center, draw an intersecting arc. Label point Y. Draw $\overrightarrow{XY}$. $\overrightarrow{XY}$ bisects $\angle X$. $\angle WXY \cong \angle ZXY$.

■ **Talk About Math** Use the word *locus* to describe the construction of the perpendicular bisector of segment AB in Example A.

Check Understanding

For another example, see Set F, pages 334–335.

Construct the figure described.

1. Draw two points and label them K and Q. Construct the perpendicular bisector of $\overline{KQ}$.

2. Draw an obtuse angle with vertex V. Construct $\angle W$ so that it is congruent to $\angle V$.

3. Construct the angle bisector of $\angle W$ in Exercise 2.

4. Divide a segment MN into two congruent segments.

Practice

For More Practice, see Set F, pages 336–337.

For Exercises 5–10, copy or trace the figure and construct a congruent figure.

5. $\overline{GH}$ **6.** $\overline{JK}$ **7.** $\angle L$

8. $\angle M$ **9.** $\angle A$ **10.** $\overline{WZ}$

For Exercises 11–16, copy or trace the figure and construct the bisector.

11. $\overline{GH}$ **12.** $\overline{JK}$ **13.** $\angle L$

14. $\angle M$ **15.** $\angle A$ **16.** $\overline{WZ}$

17. Construct a right angle.

18. Construct a 45° angle.

19. Construct a 135° angle.

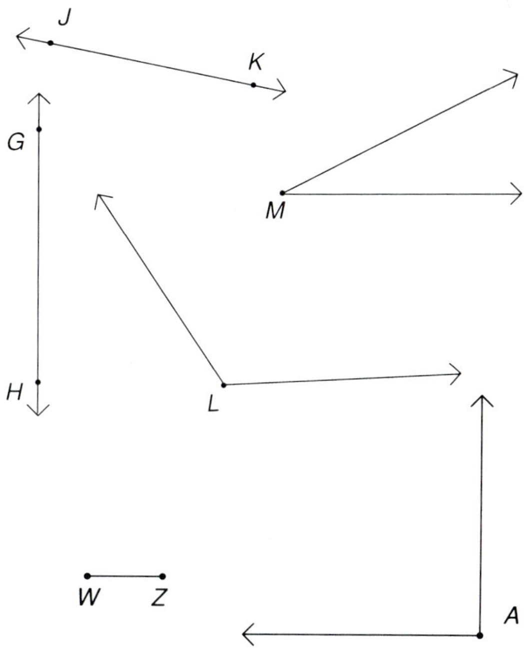

Problem Solving

Use only a compass and a straightedge to construct each figure.

20. Draw $\overline{QP}$. Construct a line through P that is perpendicular to $\overline{QP}$.

21. Draw $\overleftrightarrow{AB}$ and point C not on $\overleftrightarrow{AB}$. Construct a line through C that is parallel to $\overleftrightarrow{AB}$.

22. Construct a square.

23. Construct a parallelogram that is not a rectangle.

24. **Critical Thinking** Draw a circle. Construct a right inscribed angle. Explain why the angle must be a right angle.

25. **Critical Thinking** In the circle for Problem 24, also construct a central angle that is a right angle. Explain why it is a right angle.

Constructing Triangles

Build Understanding

ACTIVITY

Construction Site
Materials: Compass, straightedge, scissors

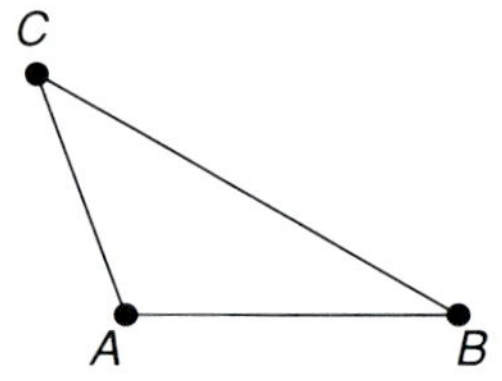

A. Trace or copy $\triangle ABC$.

a. On a line, construct $\overline{QR} \cong \overline{AB}$. At point Q, construct $\angle Q \cong \angle A$.

b. At point R, construct $\angle R \cong \angle B$. Label the intersection of the sides of $\angle Q$ and $\angle R$ point P.

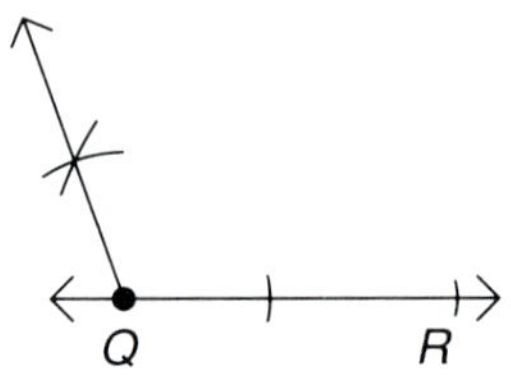

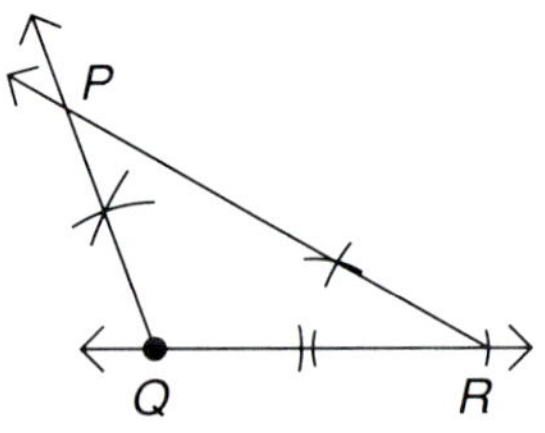

c. Cut out $\triangle QRP$ and slide it over $\triangle ABC$. Do all the sides and angles match? You used the ***angle-side-angle*** method ***(ASA)*** to construct $\triangle QRP \cong \triangle ABC$.

If two triangles are congruent, they have the same size and shape. The corresponding angles and sides are congruent. Pairs of congruent triangles may be in different positions.

B. Use the ***side-side-side (SSS)*** method to construct $\triangle GHK \cong \triangle ABC$. Construct $\triangle GHK$ with $\overline{AB} \cong \overline{GH}$, $\overline{AC} \cong \overline{GK}$, and $\overline{BC} \cong \overline{HK}$.

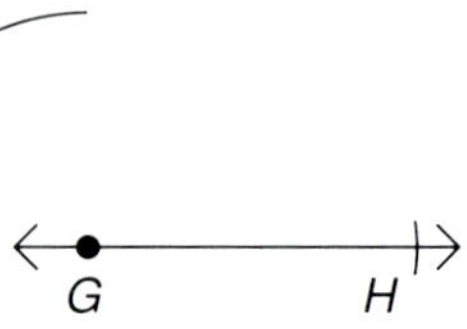

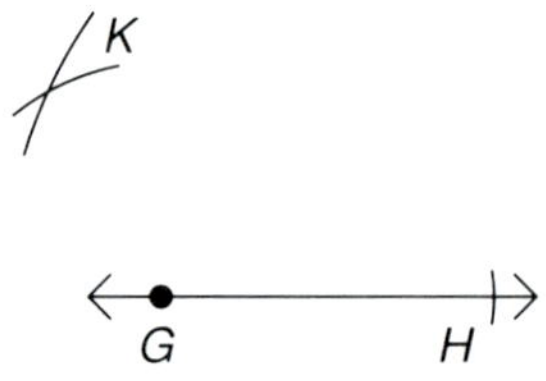

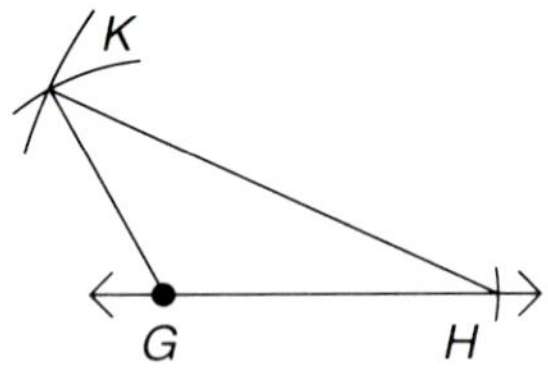

a. On a line, construct $\overline{GH} \cong \overline{AB}$. Open the compass to the length of $\overline{AC}$. With point G as center, draw an arc.

b. Open the compass to the length of $\overline{BC}$. With point H as center, draw an arc to intersect the first arc. Label point K.

c. Draw $\overline{GK}$ and $\overline{HK}$. $\triangle ABC \cong \triangle GHK$.

Two triangles are congruent if each of the three sides of one triangle is congruent to its corresponding side in the other triangle.

c. Construct $\triangle LNM \cong \triangle ABC$ using the ***side-angle-side (SAS)*** method. $\overline{LN} \cong \overline{AB}$, $\angle L \cong \angle A$, and $\overline{LM} \cong \overline{AC}$.

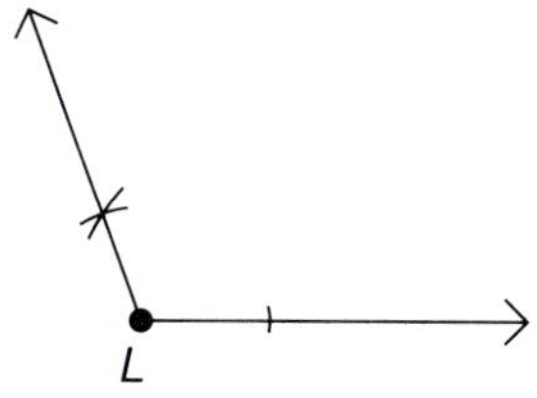

a. On a line, construct $\angle L \cong \angle A$. Extend the sides of $\angle L$.

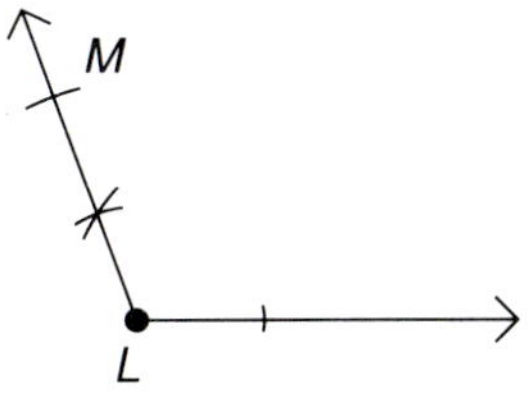

b. Construct $\overline{LM} \cong \overline{AC}$. Open the compass to the length of $\overline{AC}$. With point L as center, draw an arc intersecting a side of $\angle L$. Label point M.

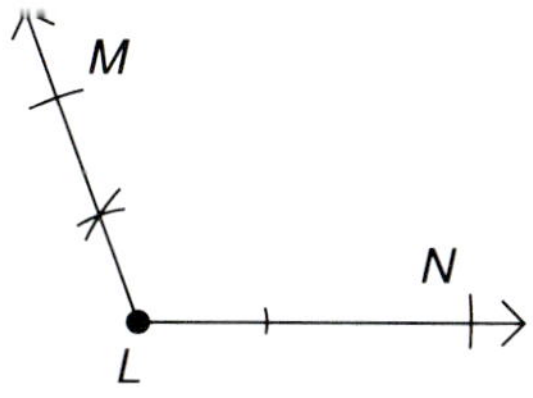

c. Construct $\overline{LN} \cong \overline{AB}$. Open the compass to the length of $\overline{AB}$. With point L as center, draw an arc intersecting the other side of $\angle L$. Label point N.

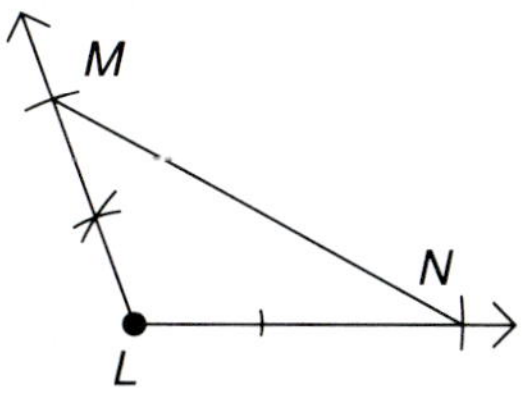

d. Draw $\overline{MN}$. $\triangle LNM \cong \triangle ABC$.

Two triangles are congruent if two sides and the included angle of one triangle are congruent to two sides and the included angle of the other triangle.

Write About Math Try to construct $\triangle JKL$ with $JK = 2$ cm, $KL = 3$ cm, and $JL = 6$ cm. Can it be done? Explain. How could you change the length of $\overline{KL}$ to construct $\triangle JKL$?

Check Understanding

For Exercises 1–4, trace the angles and segments shown below.

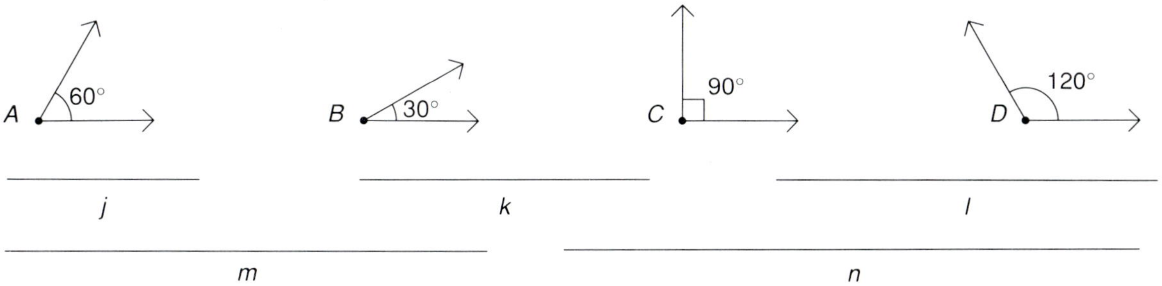

1. Use SSS to construct a triangle with sides k, l, and m.

2. Use ASA to construct a triangle with angle C, angle A, and side m.

3. Use SAS to construct a triangle with angle B, side n, and side k.

4. Can you construct a triangle with side j, side l, and side j? Explain.

Practice

Construct these triangles using the parts shown in Exercises 1–4. If the construction is impossible, explain why.

5. Use ASA to construct a triangle with angles C and D, and side k.

6. Use ASA to construct a triangle with angle B, angle C, and side m.

7. Use SSS to construct a triangle with three sides congruent to side k.

8. Equilateral triangle MXY with each side congruent to side m

9. $\triangle SNW$ with $\overline{SN} \perp \overline{NW}$, $\overline{SN} \cong$ side j, and $\overline{NW} \cong \frac{1}{2}$ side n

10. A triangle with sides j, k, and m

Trace $\triangle PQR$. Construct a congruent triangle using only the parts given.

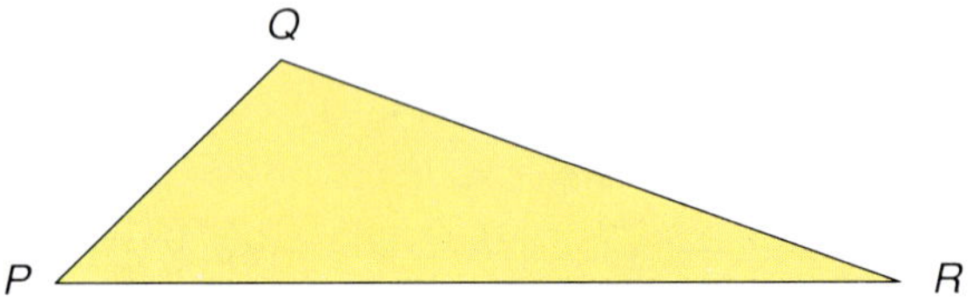

11. $\overline{PQ}, \overline{PR}, \overline{QR}$ **12.** $\angle P, \overline{PR}, \angle R$

Tell which method was used to construct $\triangle PQR \cong \triangle ABC$.

13.

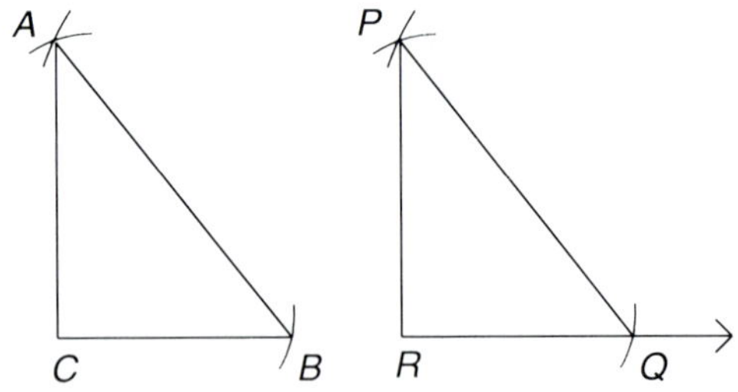

14.

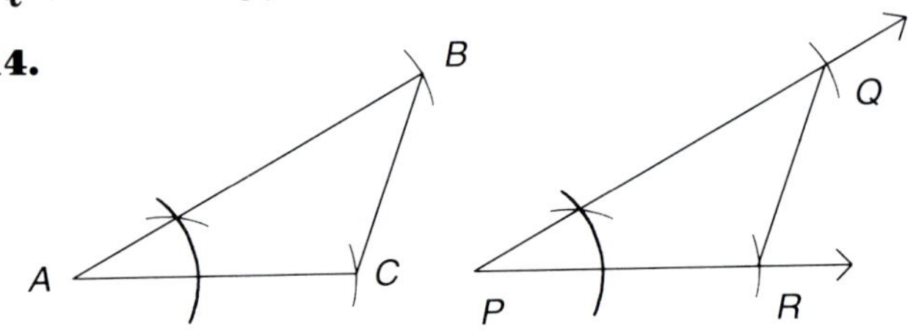

Name $\overline{AB}$ in each construction.

15.

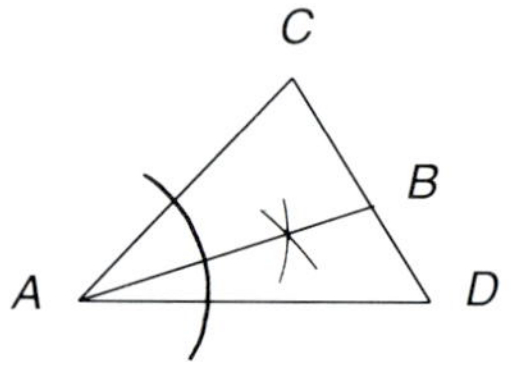

16.

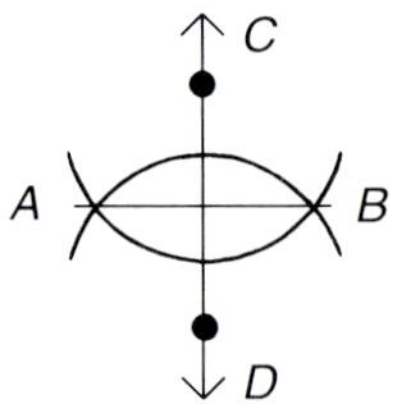

17.

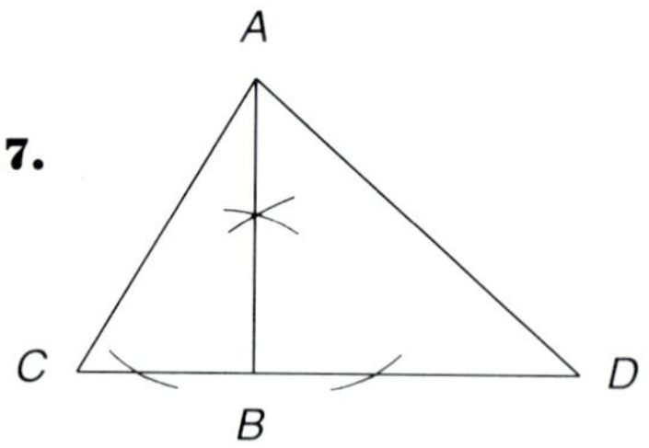

Critical Thinking Show each construction.

18. Draw any triangle ABC. Construct the perpendicular bisector of each side. What seems to be true about the perpendicular bisectors of the sides of a triangle?

19. Draw any triangle DEF. Bisect the angles. What seems to be true about the angle bisectors of a triangle?

20. Use your results from Exercise 18 to draw a circle that contains the vertices of triangle ABC.

21. Use the results from Exercise 19 to draw a circle that contains only one point from each side of $\triangle DEF$.

Problem Solving

Trace the points marked with a dot on the map. Use the map for Problem 22.

22. The Sail Race Committee for the Cold Harbor Yacht Club must map out three race courses. The courses must be of equal length and difficulty. To do this, they need to construct three congruent triangles using the map.

The first course they designed is from Great Ledge to White Rock to Dumpling Rock back to Great Ledge.

Use the SSS method to construct two other race courses using the markings on the map.

23. If the lengths of two sides of a triangular course are given, what other information do you need to determine the third side of the course?

TIPS FOR PROBLEM SOLVERS

Visualize the problem in your mind to help you understand it better.

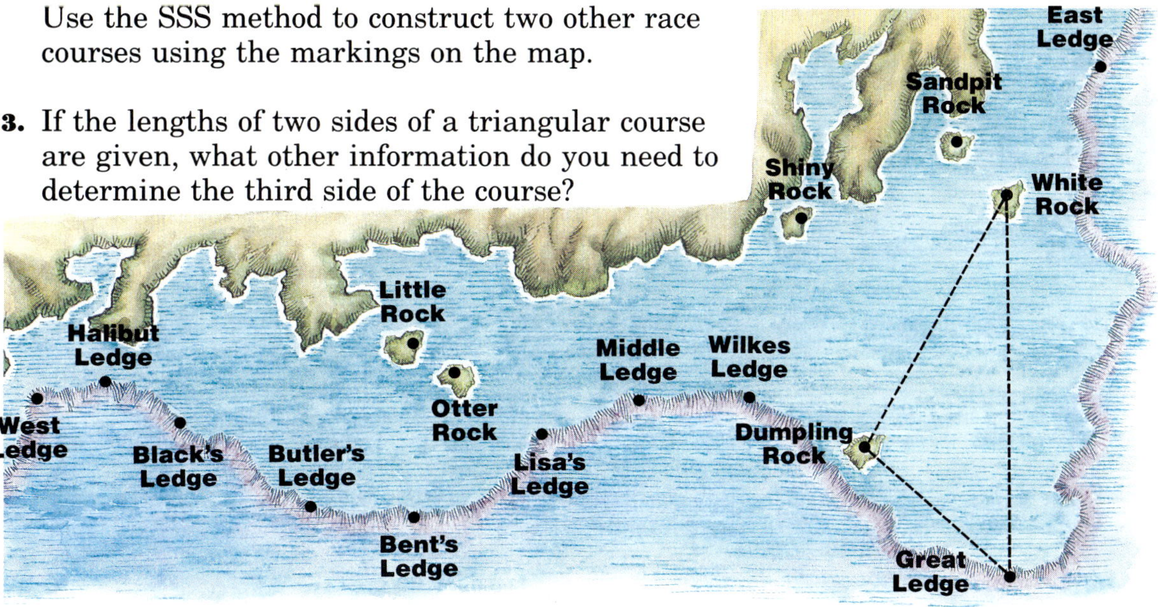

Skills Review pages 262–269

Add or subtract.

1. 14 gal − 2 gal 3 qt **2.** 26 oz + 6 lb 12 oz **3.** 7 yd 8 in. − 3 yd 5 in.

4. 6 gal 8 oz + 9 pt 7 oz **5.** 13 lb − 11 lb 3 oz **6.** 63 yd − 10 ft 8 in.

Tell whether you would use mental math, paper and pencil, or a calculator. Convert values to the same unit. Then perform the indicated operation.

7. 10 km + 100 m **8.** 150 mm − 0.6 cm **9.** 22.4 L + 175 mL

10. 2.2 kg − 1,630 g **11.** 788 mL + 4.5 L **12.** 7,630 g − 2.75 kg

Draw a Diagram

PROBLEM SOLVING GUIDE

Understand
QUESTION
FACTS
KEY IDEA

Plan and Solve
STRATEGY
ANSWER

Look Back
SENSIBLE ANSWER
ALTERNATE APPROACH

Build Understanding

Here is part of a script for a TV series.

Dan: (Gasping—these are the old prospector's last words) Sonny, listen. . . . Old Ray an' I found gold. Map's in cabin, . . . 'bout as far away from my place as from Ray's. . . . Less than 25 miles. . . . You'll be rich.

The distance from Nevermee, where Ray lives, to Minenot, where Dan lives, is $42\frac{1}{2}$ miles. Does Sonny have enough information to find the cabin?

Understand QUESTION How can Sonny find the cabin?

FACTS The cabin is equidistant from Nevermee and Minenot, and less than 25 miles from both. The towns are $42\frac{1}{2}$ miles apart.

KEY IDEA Narrow down the location by finding the locus of points that meet the conditions.

Plan and Solve STRATEGY *Draw a diagram.* The locus of points as far from Nevermee as from Minenot is the perpendicular bisector of $\overline{NM}$. Points less than 25 miles from each point are the points inside the intersection of circles N and M.

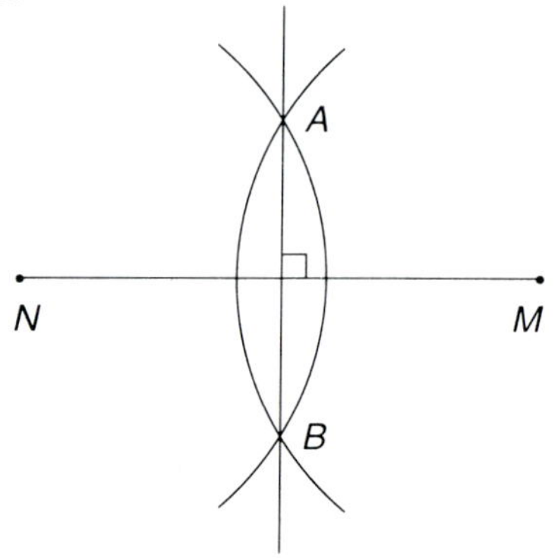

ANSWER Possible locations of the cabin are on $\overline{AB}$, excluding points A and B. Check all the cabins located on $\overline{AB}$.

Look Back SENSIBLE ANSWER Should other points be included or excluded? The locus of points on $\overline{AB}$ meets the conditions. The solution makes sense.

Talk About Math If the cabin was exactly 25 miles from each man's house, how would the solution change?

Check Understanding

1. Where could the cabin be if Dan also said it was 1 mile from the road that connects Nevermee and Minenot?

Practice

In another script for the series, a detective uses facts about the locations and ranges of police-band radio-transmitting stations to solve a case. There are stations at the courthouse, Dust Creek, Minenot, and Nevermee, and each transmitter has a 15-mile range.

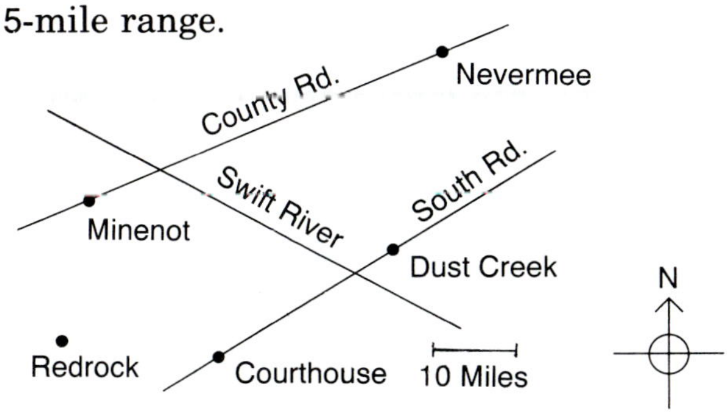

Trace the locations of the transmitters. Then answer each question.

2. Show the area covered by each radio transmitter. Which circles overlap? What do overlapping circles indicate?

3. Which circles do not overlap? What does this indicate?

4. **Estimation** About how many miles of County Road between Minenot and Nevermee are not within range of a police-band radio?

The prospector's map has instructions for finding the gold.

5. "Treasure is between Nevermee and Minenot on County Road as far from South Road as from Swift River." Trace the map given above. First construct the locus of points equidistant from South Road and Swift River. Then place an "X" to mark the location of the treasure.

6. "Treasure is buried equally distant from three largest trees found in that area just north of County Road." Draw a diagram to represent a possible arrangement for three trees and show how you could find the treasure.

Choose a ________ Strategy

Calling All Cars If a car radio can transmit 15 miles, for what percent of the distance between Minenot and Nevermee is this possible? Use the map above. Round to the nearest percent.

7. What is the distance between Minenot and Nevermee?

8. A radio can transmit 15 miles in all directions. What is the total transmission range for a vehicle on County Road?

9. The total transmission range is what percent of the distance between Minenot and Nevermee?

PROBLEM SOLVING STRATEGIES

- Choose an Operation
- Solve a Simpler Problem
- Use a Formula
- Write an Equation
- Make a Graph
- Draw a Diagram

Relating Geometric Solids to Real-World Objects

Build Understanding

How would you describe the shape of different buildings you have seen? Neuschwanstein Castle is an example of a building that contains many geometric shapes.

Neuschwanstein Castle took 18 years (1868–1886) to build.

A. A three-dimensional figure in which all the surfaces, or ***faces,*** are polygons is called a ***polyhedron.*** The plural of polyhedron is ***polyhedra. Prisms*** and ***pyramids*** are special kinds of polyhedra.

Prisms	Bases are parallel and congruent polygons; sides are parallelograms.
Pyramids	Base is a polygon; sides are triangles.

B. Prisms and pyramids are named by the shapes of their bases.

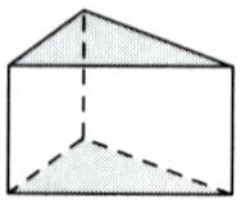

Triangular Prism

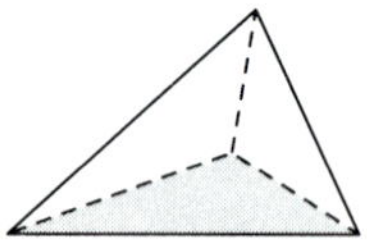

Triangular Pyramid

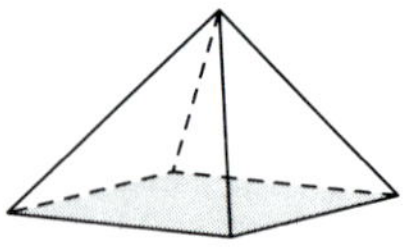

Square Pyramid

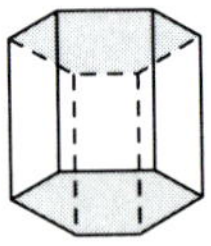

Hexagonal Prism

C. Two faces meet at an ***edge.*** The point at which three or more edges meet is called a ***vertex.***

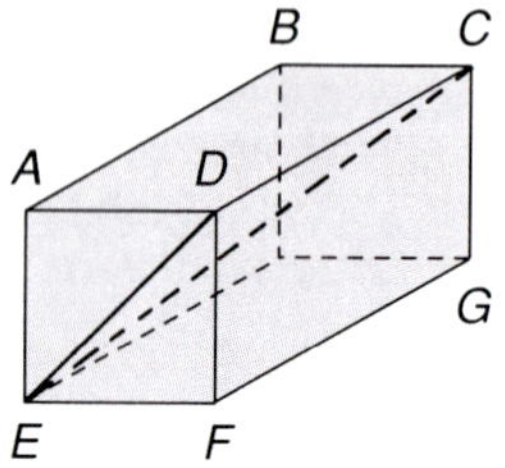

ABCD is a face.
$\overline{DF}$ is an edge.
C is a vertex.
$\overline{DE}$ is a diagonal of a face.
$\overline{CE}$ is a diagonal of the prism.

D. Is the shape of Epcot Center at Disney World a polyhedron?
No. Three-dimensional figures with curved surfaces are not polyhedra.

A perfect geodesic dome such as this one requires no internal supports.

Cylinder	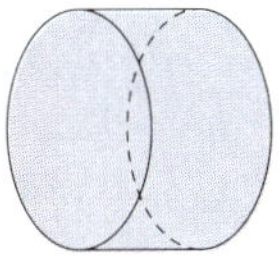 Two circular and congruent bases
Cone	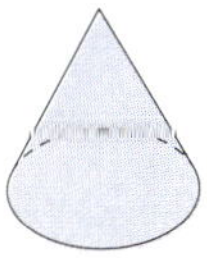 One circular base
Sphere	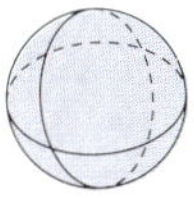 No base; every point on a sphere is the same distance from its center.

Cylinders, cones, and spheres are not polyhedra.

Talk About Math Suppose you had a cylinder made out of molding clay. What aspects of the cylinder would you change to reshape it into a polyhedron? What aspects of it would you keep?

Check Understanding

For another example, see Set G, pages 334–335.

Refer to the figures in Example B. Tell how many bases each figure has.

1. A pyramid

2. A prism

What is the name of each of these figures?

3. Prism with rectangular bases

4. Pyramid with a pentagonal base

5. Pyramid with an octagonal base

6. Prism with square bases

7. The shape of the base of a pyramid is a polygon. What are the shapes of the other faces?

8. The shape of the base of a prism is a polygon. What are the shapes of the other faces?

For each of Exercises 9–11, name a common three-dimensional object with the shape named.

9. A cone

10. A cylinder

11. A sphere

Practice

For More Practice, see Set G, pages 336–337.

This modern house in France uses a rectangular prism for its exterior shell.

The Gordon Wu Hall at Princeton University uses curved, as well as flat surfaces.

Sculptress Jackie Winsor combines the flat faces of prisms on the curve of a hemisphere.

12. What geometric solids from pages 320–321 can you find in the buildings pictured above?

13. What polyhedrons are on the surface of the hemisphere pictured above?

14. What two polyhedrons are joined to make the sculpture at the right?

15. Draw a building or sculpture that uses at least two geometric solids as parts.

Terry Haass makes lucite sculptures that join polyhedrons along a face or an edge.

Name each solid.

16.

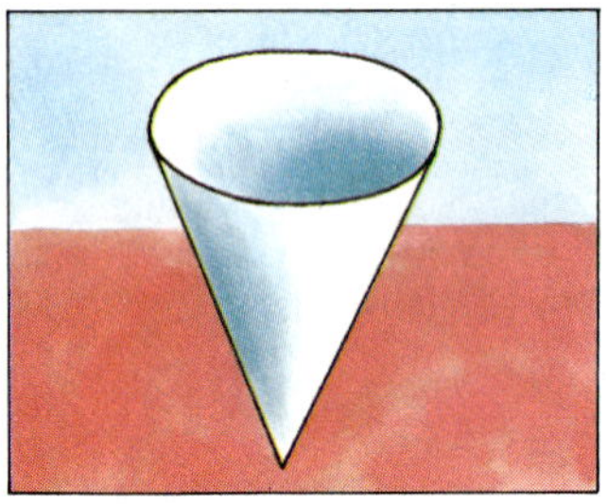

17.

18.

19.

20.

21.

22. If the base of a pyramid is octagonal, how many faces does the pyramid have?

23. If the bases of a prism are hexagonal, how many faces does the prism have?

Problem Solving

Solve each problem.

24. Refer to the photograph on page 320. What two geometric solids are used to create the shape of a tower on Neuschwanstein Castle?

25. Name two geometric solids needed to make the house shown in the photograph below.

Write one sentence to describe how the two solids in each pair are alike and one sentence to describe how they are different.

26. pyramid
prism

27. cone
cylinder

28. cylinder
prism

Reading ______ **Math**

Vocabulary Match each three-dimensional figure with its description.

Hexagonal prism
Cylinder
Triangular prism
Sphere
Triangular pyramid
Octagonal prism

1. The set of all points in space that are an equal distance from a given point

2. A polyhedron with two bases, each with six edges

3. A figure formed by two congruent circular regions joined by a curved surface

4. A polyhedron with a base having three edges and with triangular faces

5. A polyhedron with two bases, each with eight edges, and parallelogram faces

Make a Table

PROBLEM SOLVING GUIDE

Understand
QUESTION
FACTS
KEY IDEA

Plan and Solve
STRATEGY
ANSWER

Look Back
SENSIBLE ANSWER
ALTERNATE APPROACH

Build Understanding

How are the number of faces, edges, and vertices of a prism related? If the bases of a prism are 100-sided polygons, how many faces, edges, and vertices does the prism have?

An eighteenth-century mathematician named Leonard Euler discovered relationships among the number of faces, vertices, and edges of a polyhedron.

Understand QUESTION What is the relationship among the number of faces, vertices, and edges of a prism? How many faces, vertices, and edges does a prism with bases that are 100-sided polygons have?

KEY IDEA Every polyhedron has a countable number of faces, vertices, and edges.

Plan and Solve STRATEGY Count the number of faces, vertices, and edges of familiar prisms. Make a table to organize the data. Let n be the number of sides of the polygon that forms the base. Look for a pattern.

Kind of prism	n	Number of faces (F)	Number of vertices (V)	Number of edges (E)
Triangular	3	5	6	9
Rectangular	4	6	8	12
Pentagonal	5	7	10	15
Hexagonal	6	8	12	18

ANSWER It appears as though the number of faces is two more than n, the number of vertices is 2 times n, and the number of edges is 3 times n. So a prism with bases that are 100-sided polygons has 102 faces, 200 vertices, and 300 edges.

Look Back SENSIBLE ANSWER Since faces join at edges and intersect at vertices, there should be many more edges than vertices.

Talk About Math If a prism has bases with n sides, why does it have $n + 2$ faces, $2n$ vertices, and $3n$ edges?

Check Understanding

Use the triangular prism at the right to name these items.

1. Vertices **2.** Edges **3.** Faces

Extend the table on page 324 to include the following prisms.

4. Heptagonal **5.** Octagonal

6. Nonagonal **7.** Decagonal

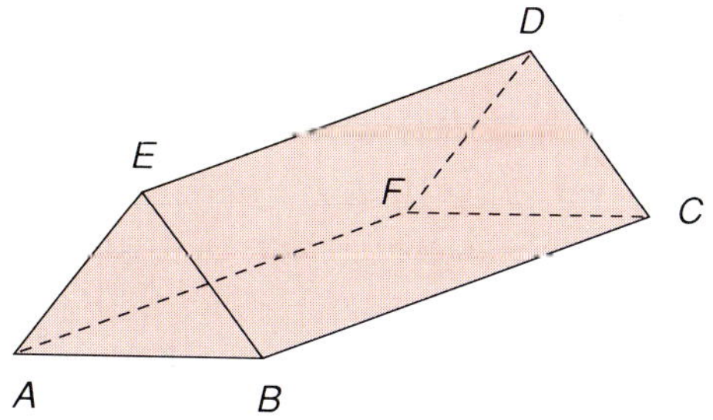

Practice

Complete the table for pyramids. Let n be the number of sides of the base.

Kind of pyramid	n	Number of faces (F)	Number of vertices (V)	Number of edges (E)
Triangular	3	4	**8.**	**9.**
Rectangular	4	**10.**	**11.**	**12.**
Pentagonal	**13.**	**14.**	**15.**	**16.**
Hexagonal	**17.**	**18.**	**19.**	**20.**

21. What pattern do you notice in the table for pyramids?

22. How many faces, vertices, and edges will a pyramid have if the base is a polygon with 100 sides?

Use the table on page 324 and the table you completed for Problems 8–20 to solve each problem.

23. To see the relationship between the data in both tables, make another column in which you show the sum $F + V$. How is $F + V$ related to E, the number of edges? Write a formula expressing the relationships among F, V, and E that is true for both kinds of polyhedra.

24. Suppose a polyhedron has F faces, V vertices, and E edges. Will a polyhedron with $2F$ faces have $2V$ vertices and $2E$ edges?

Patterns for Geometric Solids

Build Understanding

Customers at Marcy's Boutique can choose from among several shapes of boxes. The boxes are printed, but not cut, folded, or assembled.

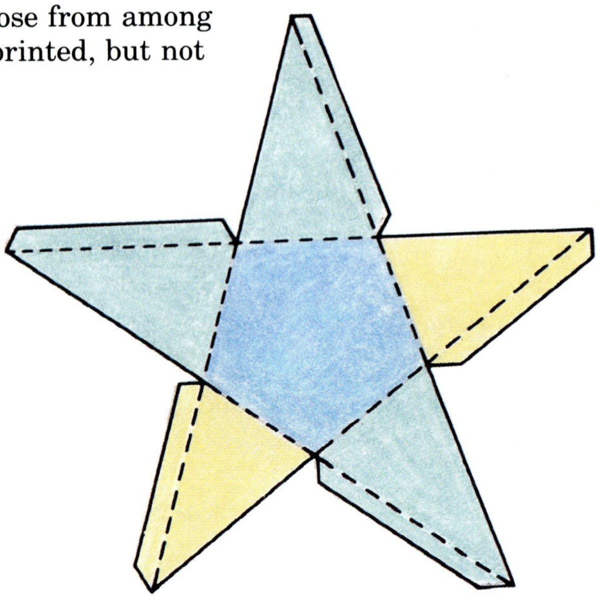

A. Boxing (No Gloves Necessary)
Materials: Scissors, glue, or tape

a. Trace the star.

b. Cut along the solid lines. Fold along the dotted lines. Fold the tabs inward and fasten the tabs.

c. What is the shape of the solid?

B. Prism Patterns for Pros
Materials: Rectangular prism
Groups: With a partner

How would you draw a pattern for a rectangular prism?

a. Trace the base of the prism.

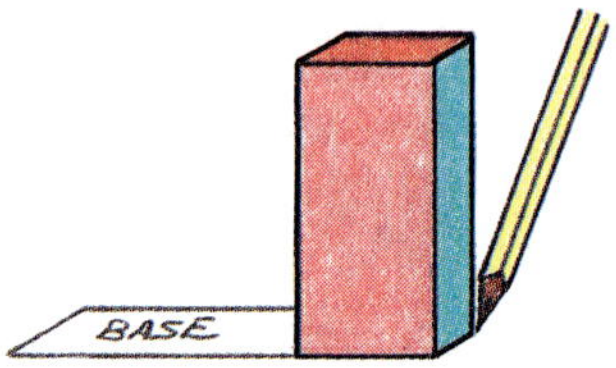

b. Lay the prism down along the adjoining edge. Trace that side.

c. Roll the prism off its base along each of its edges, making sure to trace the side it's lying on.

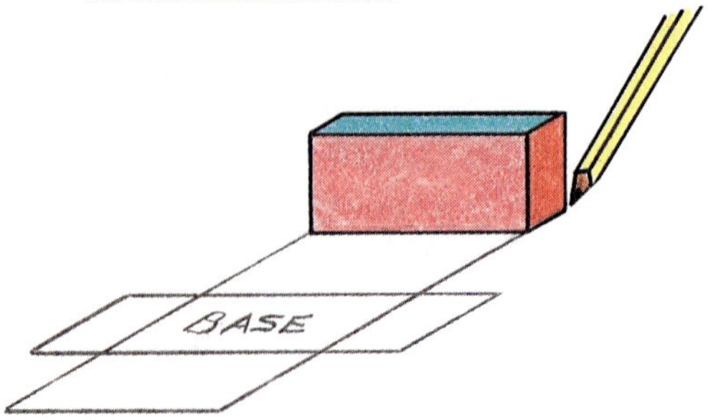

d. On the last side, tilt the prism onto its other base and trace it.

c. The shipment of boxes that arrived at the boutique this morning appears to be defective. What is wrong with the pattern on the right?

The pattern of a box needs six faces. Five faces are shown here. One more face is needed for a closed box.

Also, the ends of the boxes have an extra flap. The light blue rectangles should be removed.

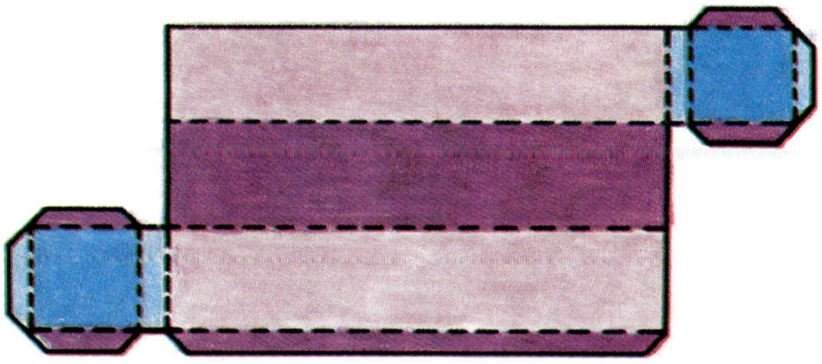

Talk About Math How can you tell the difference between a pattern for a prism and a pyramid?

Check Understanding

Use the pattern at the right for Exercises 1–5.

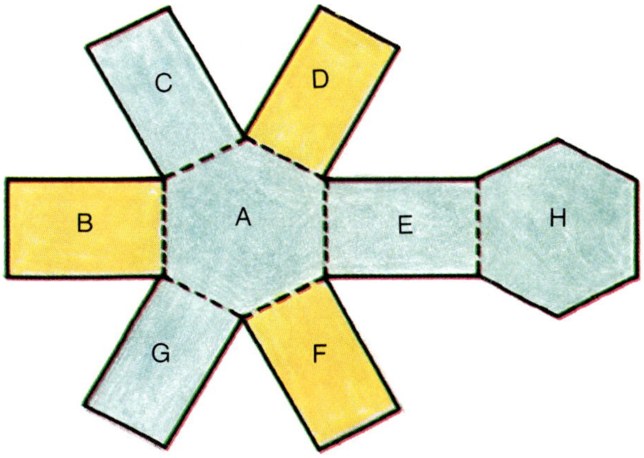

1. Name the solid that this pattern will form.
2. What are the bases of the figure?
3. Which face is opposite face *A*?
4. Which face is parallel to face *C*?
5. How many pairs of parallel faces are there?

Use the pattern at the right for Exercises 6–9.

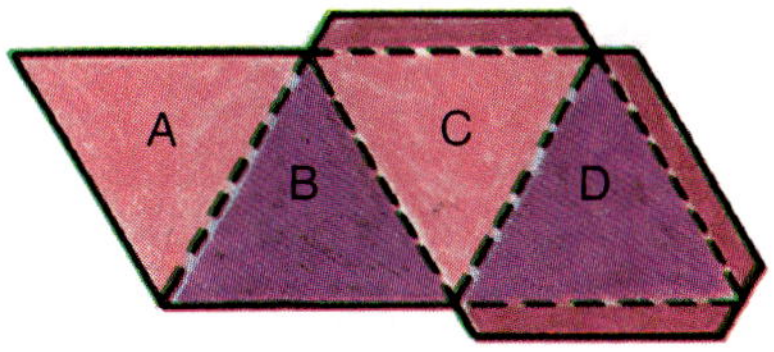

6. What solid will this pattern form?
7. Which face is opposite face *A*?
8. Can you tell which face is the base?
9. Sketch another pattern for this solid such that one face can be recognized as the base.

Practice

Match each solid on the left with a pattern on the right.

10.

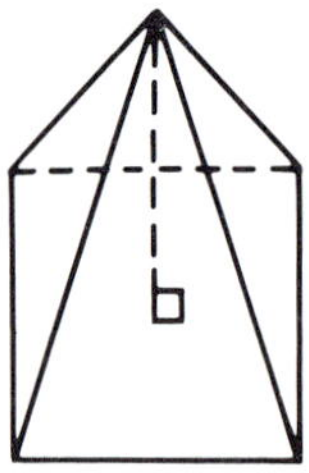

a.

11.

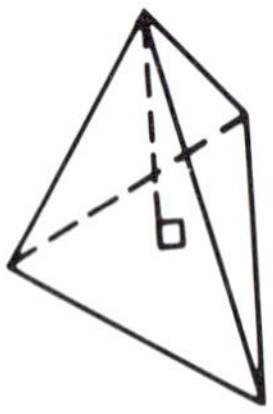

b.

12.

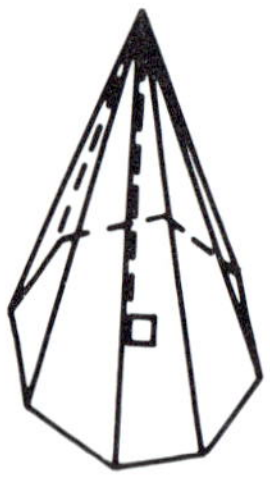

c.

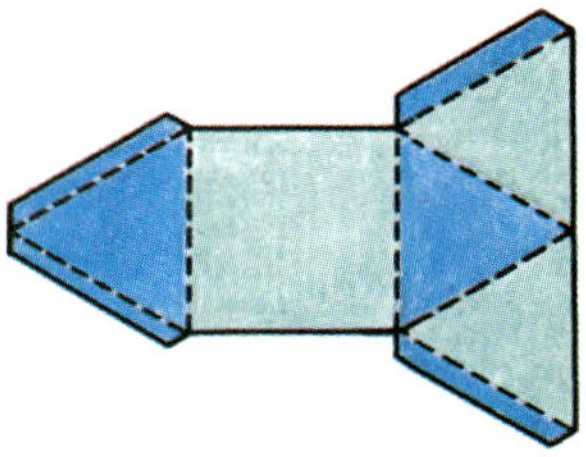

13.

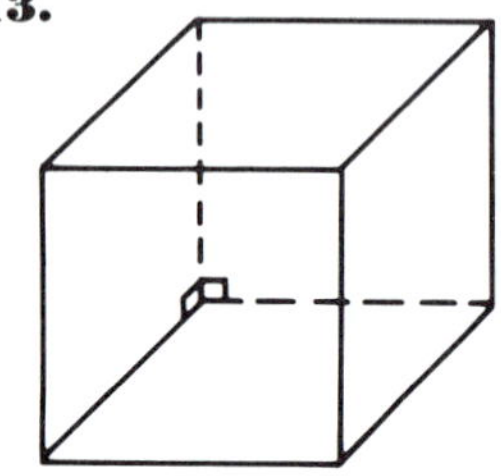

d.

14.

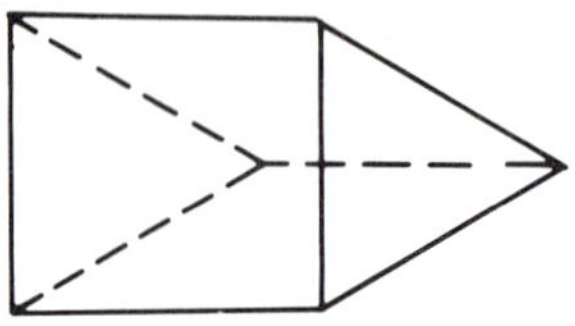

e.

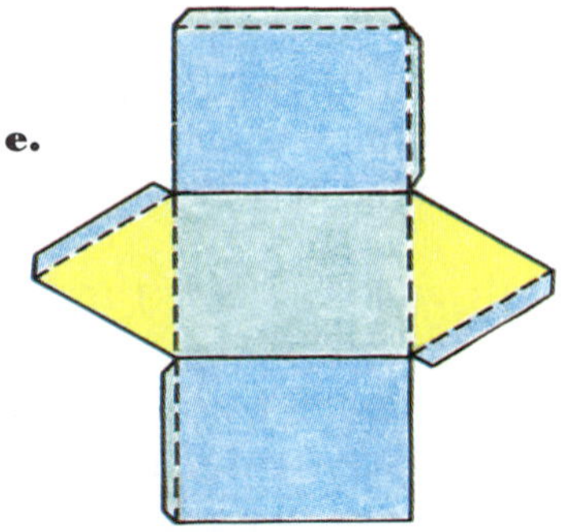

Describe the solids in Exercises 10–13 by completing the table.

	Exercise 10	Exercise 11	Exercise 12	Exercise 13
Name of solid	**15.**	**19.**	**23.**	**27.**
Shape of base	**16.**	**20.**	**24.**	**28.**
Number of faces	**17.**	**21.**	**25.**	**29.**
Number of edges	**18.**	**22.**	**26.**	**30.**

Name the solids that each pattern represents.

31.

32.

33.

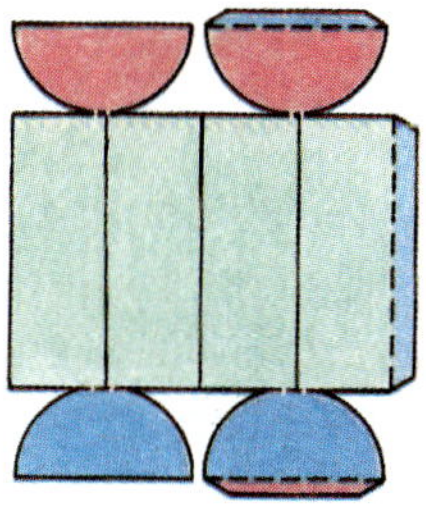

For Exercises 34–35, draw a pattern for each solid.

34.

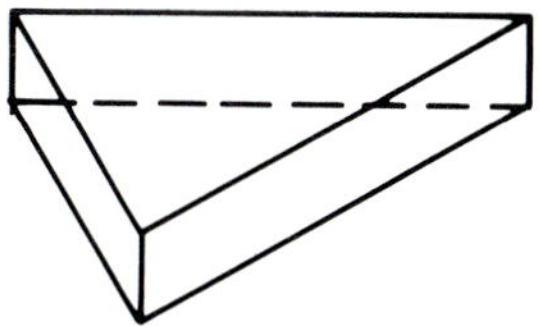

35.

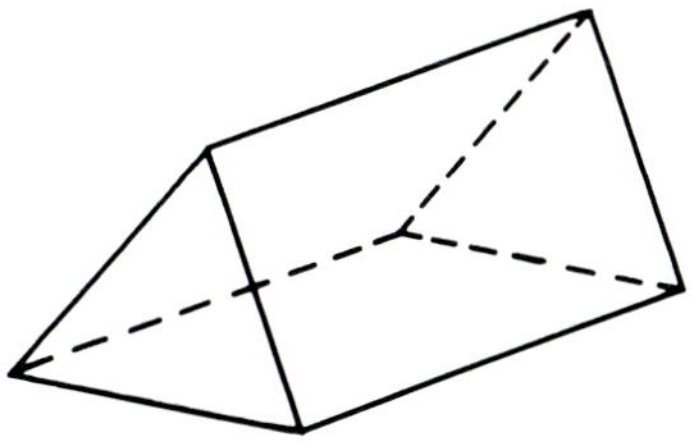

Problem Solving

Visual Thinking Solve each problem.

36. With some special purchases at Marcy's Boutique, these unusual containers are nested or placed inside one another. Which containers fit into one or more of the other containers? Which will be the outermost container?

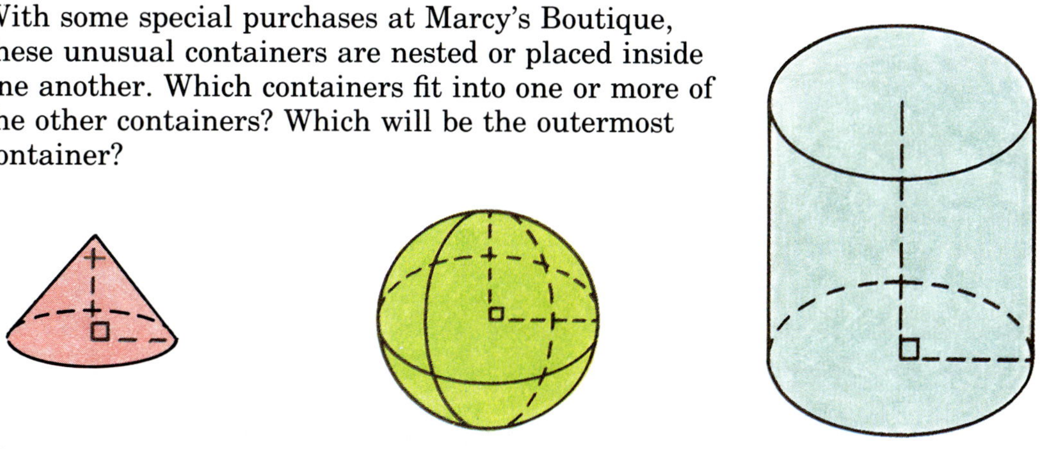

37. There is one pattern for a cube shown on page 328. Draw three other patterns for cubes. Be sure the patterns are different.

Drawing Three-Dimensional Figures

Build Understanding

"I never looked at it that way!" is a common response after seeing a mechanical drawing. A drafter makes drawings for architects, engineers, carpenters, and tool makers. A drafter must represent three-dimensional shapes in two-dimensional drawings.

When you look at a solid, you cannot see the whole object. A part of the object is always hidden from view. For this reason, a mechanical drawing will usually show several views of the same object. Often a view of an object will show only one surface.

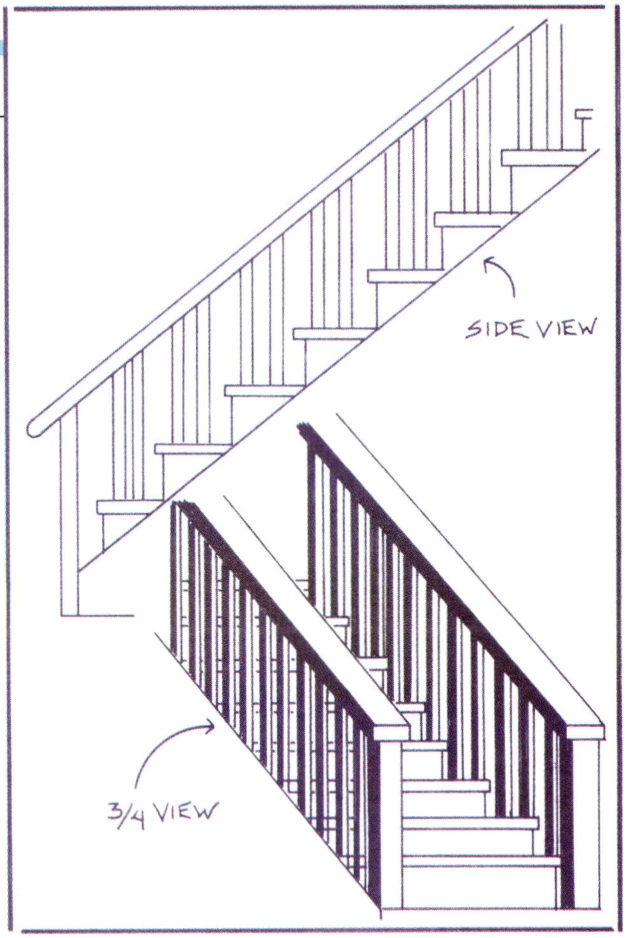

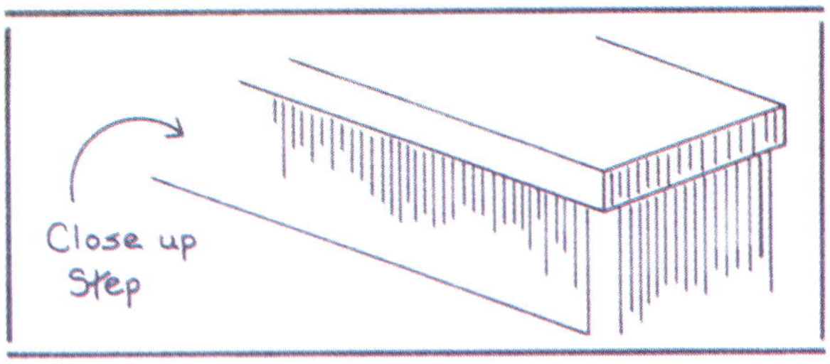

The two-dimensional drawings below show the same house from different views.

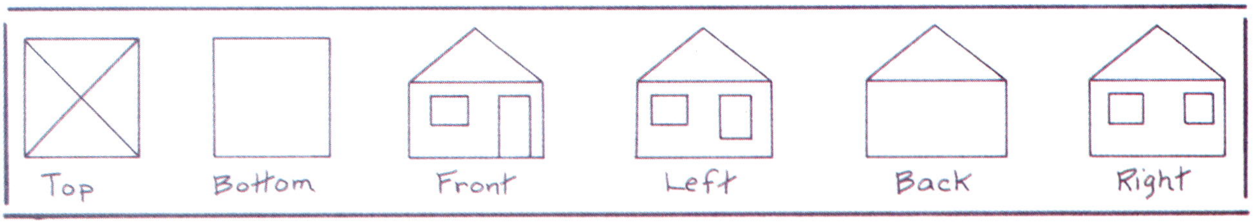

■ **Talk About Math** Why might a drafter omit a particular view of a proposed building?

Check Understanding

1. Which drawing shows a three-dimensional view of the above house?

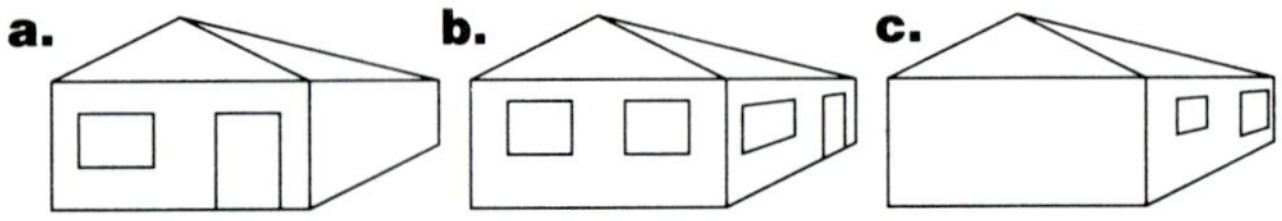

Practice

Name the geometric solid that is represented by the following top, bottom, and side views.

2.

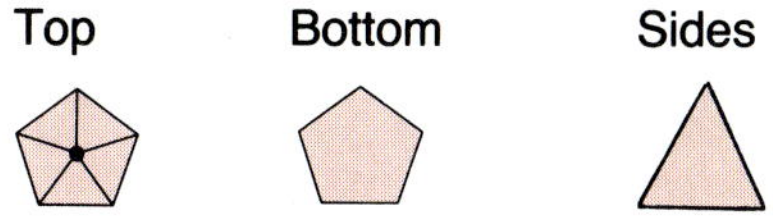

3.

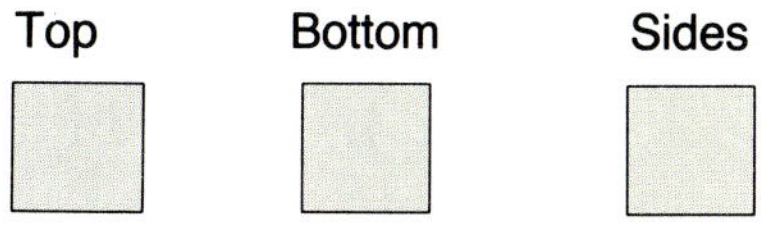

4.

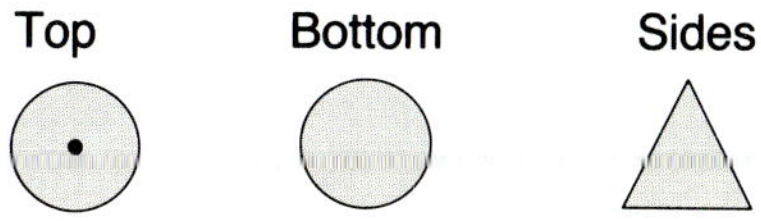

5.

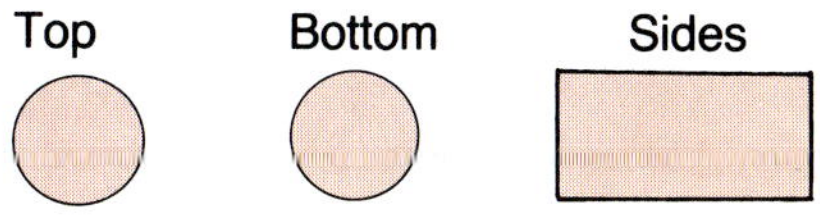

Draw the top, the bottom, and all side views necessary to give an accurate impression of the figure.

6.

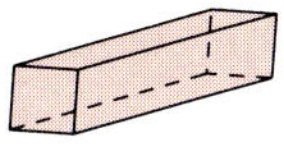

7.

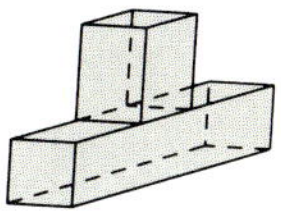

8.

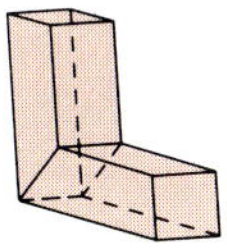

9.

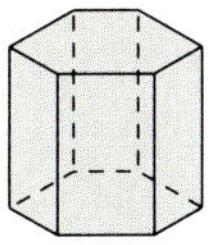

10.

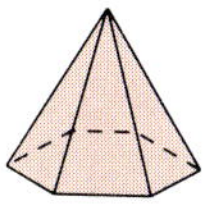

11.

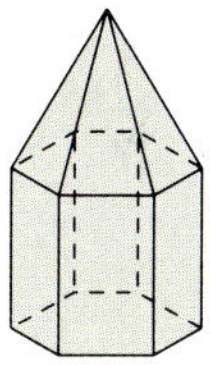

Problem Solving

Make a three-dimensional drawing of each building.

12.

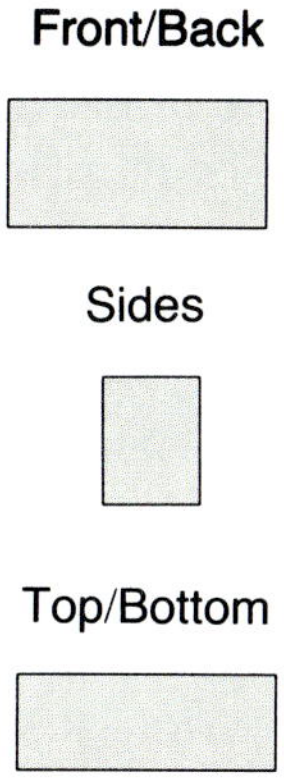

13.

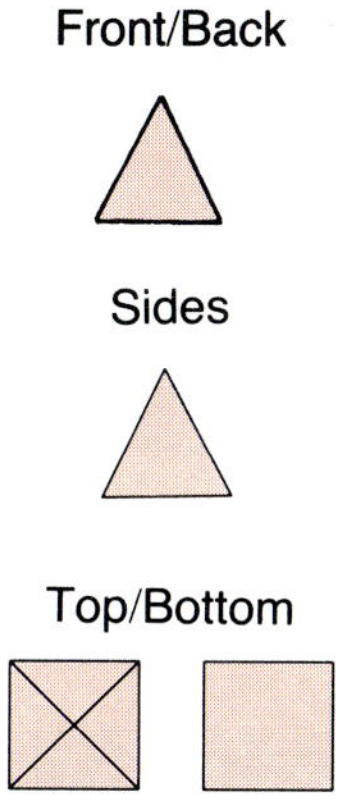

14.

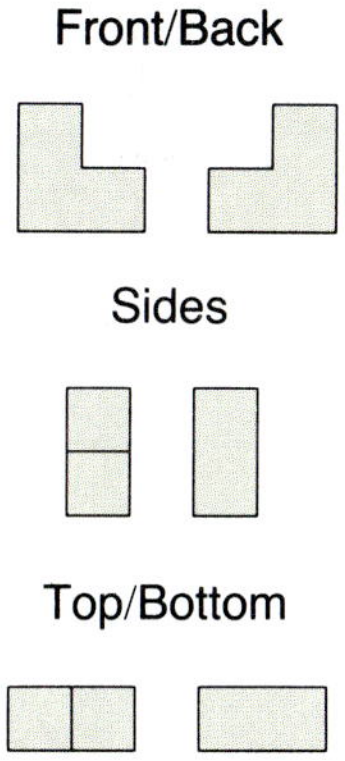

Critical Thinking One view of a three-dimensional figure is given. Make a three-dimensional drawing of the figure and then draw all the other views.

15.

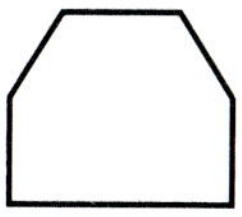

16.

17.

Skills Review

Select all possible ways the units named can intersect: 1 line, 1 point, or 0 points.

1. 2 planes **2.** A line and a plane

3. 2 lines in space **4.** 2 rays in a plane

Use the diagram for Exercises 5–12.

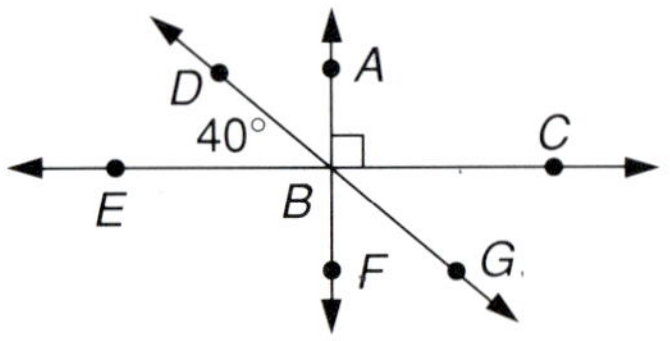

Find the measure of each angle.

5. $m\angle ABD$ **6.** $m\angle CBG$

7. $m\angle EBG$ **8.** $m\angle EBF$

Which pairs of angles are

9. vertical angles? **10.** congruent?

11. complementary? **12.** supplementary?

Find the measure of each angle.

13. $\angle ROQ$

14. $\angle RPQ$

15. $\angle PQO$

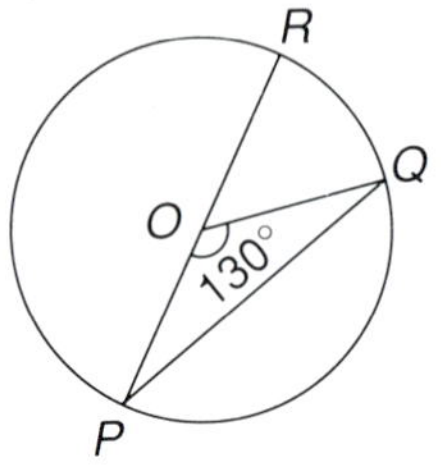

Use these angles and segments for Exercises 16 and 17.

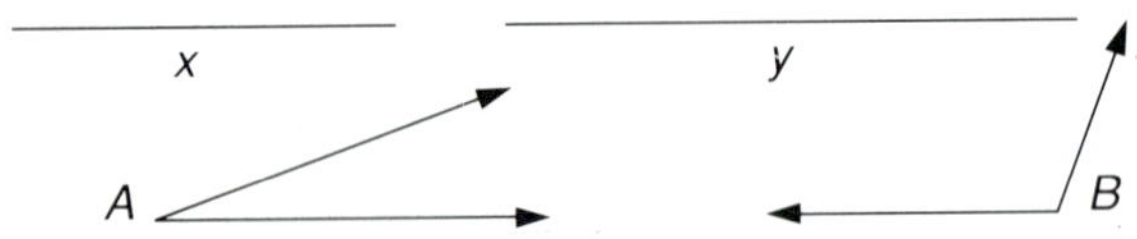

16. Use SAS to construct a triangle with side x, angle B, and side y.

17. Use ASA to construct a triangle with angle A, side y, and angle B.

Problem-Solving Review

Solve each problem.

18. A coach asks the gymnasts to form two parallel lines 15 ft apart. She tells one gymnast to move so that she is always an equal distance from both lines. Describe the locus of the moving gymnast.

19. What is the maximum number of obtuse angles in an obtuse triangle?

20. What is the sum of the measures of all angles in an octagon?

21. The circumference of a circle is 75 in. What is the approximate length of its radius?

22. Describe how to construct a 45° angle.

23. The sum of the measures of the interior angles of a polygon is 4,500 degrees. How many sides does the polygon have?

24. Give the number of faces, vertices, and edges in a hexagonal prism.

25. **Data File** Use the data on pages 426–427. Find the radius of the earth's outer core, the lower mantle, and the upper mantle. Use the scale 1 mm = 100 mi. Draw concentric circles to make a scale drawing of the inside of the earth if it were sliced through the equator.

26. **Make a Data File** Design a logo for an imaginary company to use on its products and advertising. Use geometric shapes to form the logo including different kinds of triangles, regular polygons, and circles. Use a compass and straightedge to make the logo.

Cumulative Skills Review • Chapters 1–9

Compute.

1. 2,312 + 4,192 + 533 **2.** (6 × 34) + (4 × 34) **3.** 26,897 − 14,442 **4.** 12 − −12

5. 0.00064 ÷ 8 **6.** 1.152 ÷ 45 **7.** 2284.08 ÷ 93 **8.** 9 × −23

9. 12 − (7 + 10) **10.** 15 ÷ 3 + 12 ÷ 4 **11.** 40 ÷ (2 × 4 − 3) **12.** −91 ÷ 7

Graph each equation.

13. $y = 4x - 4$ **14.** $y = \frac{x}{2} + 3$ **15.** $y = 5x$

Find the length of each golden rectangle. The width is given.

16. 8 inches **17.** 10.5 centimeters **18.** 18 millimeters

For each item, find the cost of financing and the rate of interest being charged.

Item	List Price	Number of Payments	Payment Amount	Total Interest	Annual Interest Rate
Car	$14,900.00	60	$346.43	**19.**	**20.**
Stereo	$ 1,499.00	24	$ 73.70	**21.**	**22.**

Compute.

23. 11 in. + 3 ft 7 in. **24.** 10 lb 4 oz − 2 lb 9 oz **25.** 5 gal − 3 gal 1 qt

26. 1 mi − 1 yd **27.** 8.94 g − 150 mg **28.** 15 cm × 11 cm × 5 cm

29. 0.9 kL + 3 L + 4,000 mL **30.** 1 km − 1 cm **31.** 5 yd − 4 yd 11 in.

Line *a* and line *b* are parallel. $\angle LMN = 55°$ and $\angle EFG$ is a right angle. Find the measure of each angle.

32. $m\angle 3$ **33.** $m\angle 12$

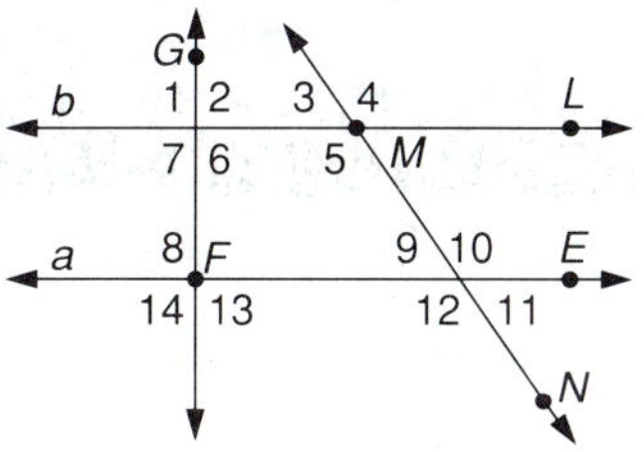

Complete each statement.

34. ∠3 and ∠9 are ____ angles **35.** ∠10 and ∠12 are ____ angles

36. ∠6 and ∠8 are ____ angles **37.** ∠1 and ∠2 are ____ angles

Use a compass and a straight edge.

38. Construct $\angle M \cong \angle N$ and bisect $\angle M$.

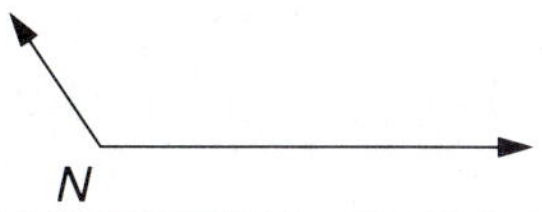

39. Construct $\overline{CD} \cong \overline{AB}$ and bisect $\overline{CD}$.

Reteaching

Set A pages 294–295

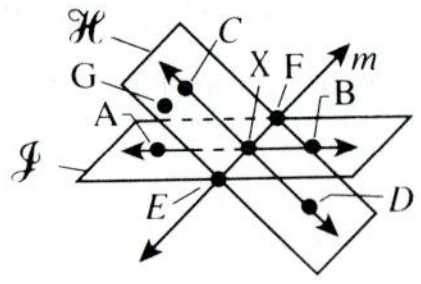

Planes $\mathcal{J}$ and $\mathcal{H}$ intersect in line *m*. $\overline{EF}$ is a line segment. Points *A*, *B*, and *X* are coplanar and collinear. Points *G*, *C*, *X*, and *A* are noncoplanar. Points *F*, *B*, and *X* are noncollinear. $\overleftrightarrow{AB}$ divides plane $\mathcal{J}$ into two half-planes.

Remember that planes have two dimensions.

Using the diagram at the right, name

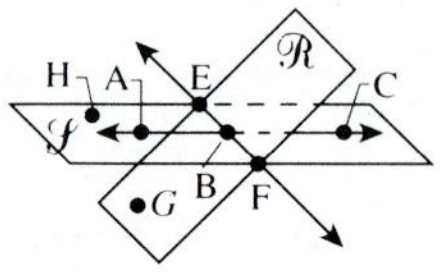

1. the intersection of planes $\mathcal{R}$ and $\mathcal{S}$.

2. the intersection of $\overleftrightarrow{AC}$ and $\overleftrightarrow{EF}$.

3. three noncollinear points.

4. four noncoplanar points.

Set B pages 298–299

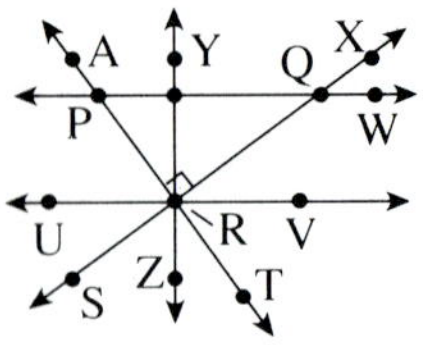

$m\angle XQW < 90$ (Acute)
$m\angle XQP > 90$ (Obtuse)
$m\angle PRX = 90$ (Right)
$m\angle VRT + m\angle TRU = 180$ (Supplementary)
$m\angle PRY + m\angle QRY = 90$ (Complementary)
$m\angle QRY = m\angle SRZ$ (Vertical)

Remember that congruent angles have the same measure.

In the diagram at the left, if $m\angle VRT = 75$, find

1. $m\angle TRU$. **2.** $m\angle URP$.

If $m\angle PQR = 60$, find

3. $m\angle QPR$. **4.** $m\angle XQP$.

5. $m\angle WQR$. **6.** $m\angle APW$.

Set C pages 300–301

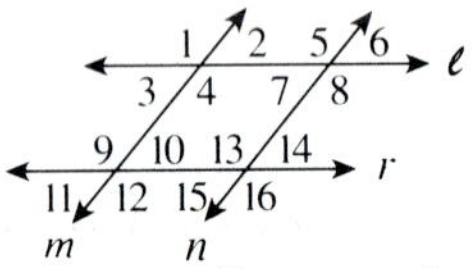

In the diagram above, $m \parallel n$ and $\ell \parallel r$.
$\angle 2$ and $\angle 7$ are alternate interior angles; $m\angle 2 = m\angle 7$.
$\angle 1$ and $\angle 8$ are alternate exterior angles; $m\angle 1 = m\angle 8$.
$\angle 4$ and $\angle 8$ are corresponding angles; $m\angle 4 = m\angle 8$.

Remember that alternate and corresponding angles are congruent when a transversal intersects two parallel lines.

In the diagram at the left, find each measure if $m\angle 12 = 110$.

1. $m\angle 11$ **2.** $m\angle 2$ **3.** $m\angle 16$

4. $m\angle 10$ **5.** $m\angle 13$ **6.** $m\angle 1$

Set D pages 302–305

Find the sum of the measures of the angles of a quadrilateral.

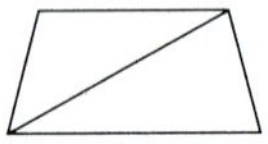

Two triangles are formed when you draw all the diagonals from one vertex of the polygon. The sum of the measures of the angles of a quadrilateral is $2 \times 180°$, or $360°$.

Remember that polygons are named by the number of sides they have.

Draw each polygon. Then draw all diagonals from one vertex of the polygon and give the sum of the measures of the angles.

1. Hexagon **2.** Pentagon **3.** Decagon

Set E pages 306–309

$\overline{DB}$ is a chord of circle A.
$\angle BAC$ is a central angle.
$\angle BDC$ is an inscribed angle.
$m\angle BDC = \frac{1}{2} m\angle BAC$

Remember that the circumference of a circle equals $2 \times \pi \times$ the radius.

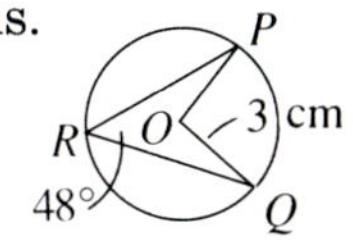

For the circle at the right,

1. find the circumference.

2. find $m\angle POQ$.

3. name a central angle.

4. name 2 chords.

Set F pages 312–313

Construct $\angle K \cong \angle D$ in Set E and bisect $\angle K$.

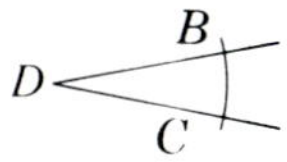

Step 1 With D as center, draw an arc that intersects both sides of $\angle D$.

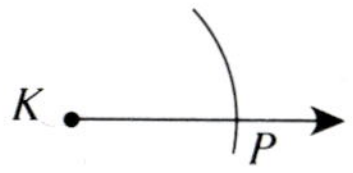

Step 2 Draw a ray. With K as center, draw an arc that intersects the ray at P.

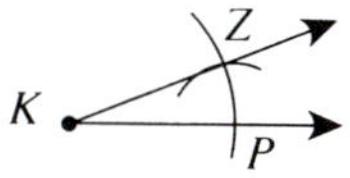

Step 3 Set the compass opening to the length of BC. With P as center, draw an arc that intersects the first arc at Z. Draw $\overrightarrow{KZ}$.

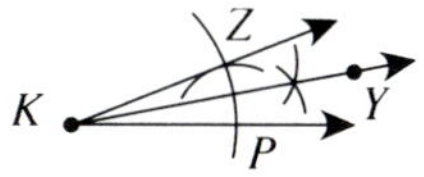

Step 4 With P as center, draw an arc. With the same compass opening and Z as center, intersect the first arc. Label the point Y and draw $\overrightarrow{KY}$.

Remember that you construct segments and angles to construct triangles.

Do each construction.

1. Construct $\overline{AB} \cong \overline{PW}$ in Set B.

2. Construct $\angle Y \cong \angle XRT$ in Set B.

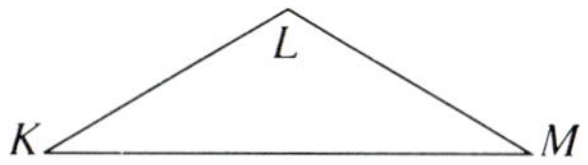

3. Construct $\angle A \cong \angle L$ above and bisect $\angle A$.

4. Construct $\overline{HJ} \cong \overline{KM}$ above and bisect $\overline{HJ}$.

5. Construct $\triangle SRO \cong \triangle KLM$ using $\overline{LM}$, $\overline{KL}$, and $\angle L$.

Set G pages 320–323

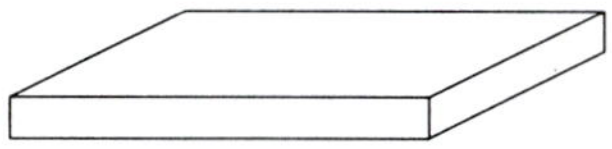

Each face is a polygon, so this solid is a polyhedron. The bases are parallel and congruent and the sides are parallelograms, so the solid is a prism.

This polyhedron is a pyramid; the base is a polygon and the sides are triangles.

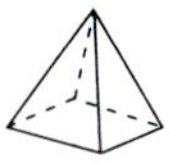

Cylinders, cones, and spheres are not polyhedra.

Remember that prisms and pyramids are named by the shape of their bases.

Give a real-world example for each geometric solid.

1. Triangular prism

2. Cone

3. Rectangular prism

4. Sphere

5. Square pyramid

6. Cylinder

More Practice

Set A pages 294–295

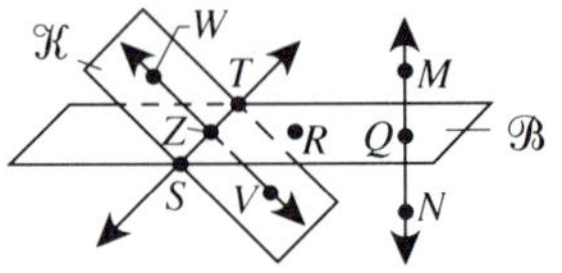

Using the diagram at the left, name

1. The intersection of planes $\mathcal{K}$ and $\mathcal{B}$.

2. The intersection of $\overleftrightarrow{MN}$ and plane $\mathcal{B}$.

3. Three collinear points.

4. Four noncoplanar points.

5. Two rays.

Set B pages 298–299

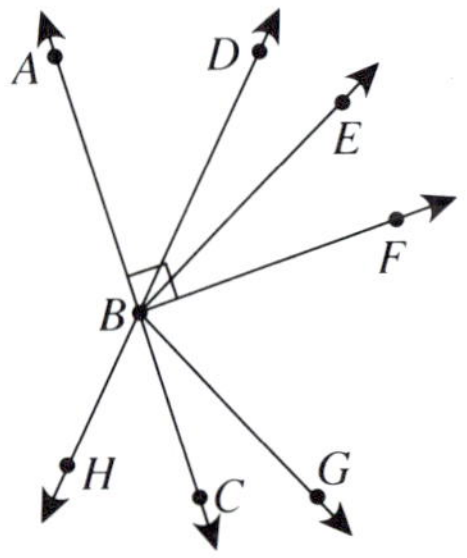

Use the diagram at the left to name

1. A pair of vertical angles.

2. A right angle.

3. Three obtuse angles.

4. Two pairs of adjacent angles.

Find each measure if $m\angle CBH = 52$.

5. $m\angle CBD$ **6.** $m\angle DBF$

7. $m\angle ABD$ **8.** $m\angle ABH$

Set C pages 300–301

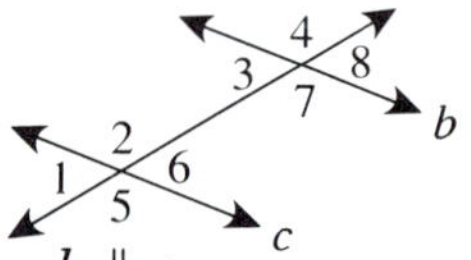

$b \parallel c$

Use the diagram at the left to find each measure if $m\angle 1 = 39$.

1. $m\angle 2$ **2.** $m\angle 3$ **3.** $m\angle 4$ **4.** $m\angle 5$

5. $m\angle 6$ **6.** $m\angle 7$ **7.** $m\angle 8$

Set D pages 302–305

The number of diagonals that can be drawn from one vertex of a polygon is shown. For each, tell how many sides the polygon has.

1. 0 **2.** 1 **3.** 4 **4.** 7

5. 8 **6.** 10 **7.** 12 **8.** 1000

The measure of each central angle of a regular polygon is shown. For each, tell how many sides the polygon has.

9. 20° **10.** 60° **11.** 120° **12.** 90°

13. 10° **14.** 15° **15.** 40° **16.** 8°

Set E pages 306–309

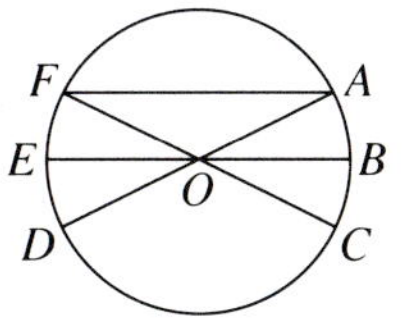

$m\angle FOA = 110$; $m\angle AOB = 30$

Use circle O at the left to name

1. a diameter.

2. all radii.

3. all chords.

4. two central angles.

Find each measure.

5. $m\angle EOD$

6. $m\angle AFC$

7. $m\angle DOC$

8. $m\angle FAD$

9. $m\angle BOC$

10. $m\angle DOF$

Find the circumference if the radius of a circle O is

11. 4.5 cm

12. 12 cm

13. 0.32 m

14. 10.5 km

Set F pages 312–313

Do each construction.

1. Construct $\angle Y \cong \angle F$ and bisect $\angle Y$.

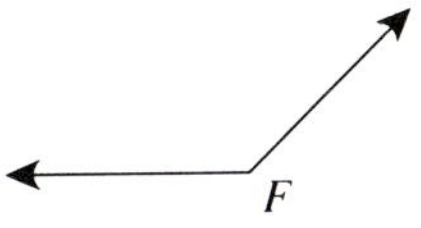

2. Construct $\overline{SW} \cong \overline{KM}$ and bisect $\overline{SW}$.

Use the angles and segments at the right for Problems 3–5.

3. Use SSS to construct a triangle with sides w, v, u.

4. Use SAS to construct a triangle with side w, side v, and $\angle T$.

5. Use ASA to construct a triangle with $\angle T$, $\angle Q$, and side v.

6. Use SAS to construct a triangle with $\angle Q$, side u, and side w.

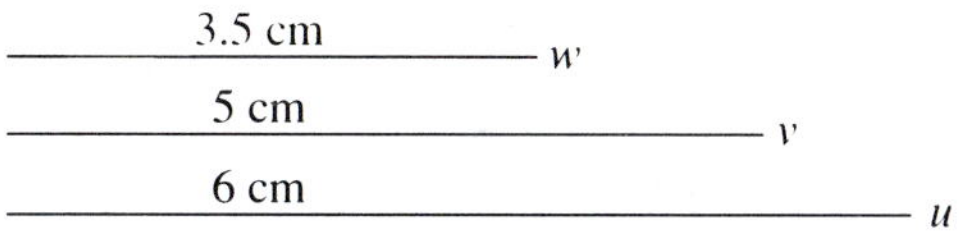

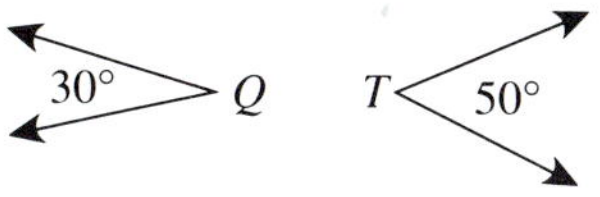

Set G pages 320–323

Name each solid.

1.

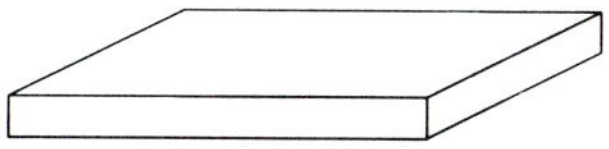

2.

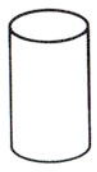

3.

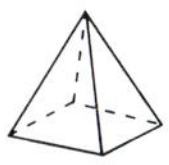

4.

5. Tell which of the solids above are polyhedra.

Enrichment

Three-Dimensional Locus

A locus in three dimensions is the set of all points *in space* that satisfy a given set of conditions.

Think about the locus of points in space equally distant from points A and B. The sketch helps show that the locus is a plane. It contains the midpoint of the segment that joins A and B, and it is perpendicular to this segment.

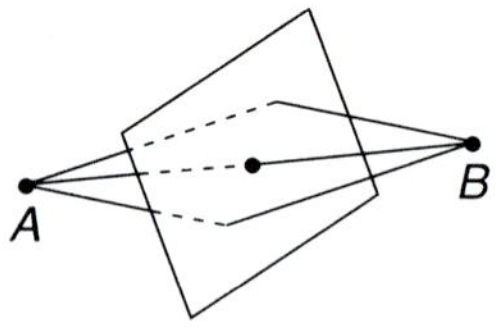

For each exercise, draw a picture and describe the three-dimensional locus.

1. All points that are 6 in. from a given point P
2. All points that are 12 in. from a plane
3. All points that are 1 m from segment XY
4. All points that are 1 m from line XY
5. All points equally distant from two parallel lines
6. All points equally distant from two parallel planes

Describe the two-dimensional locus that satisfies the conditions in

7. Exercise 1.
8. Exercise 3.
9. Exercise 4.

Examine each picture. Write a locus problem for which the part drawn in blue could be the answer.

10.

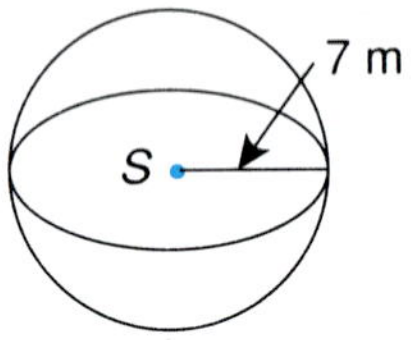

11.

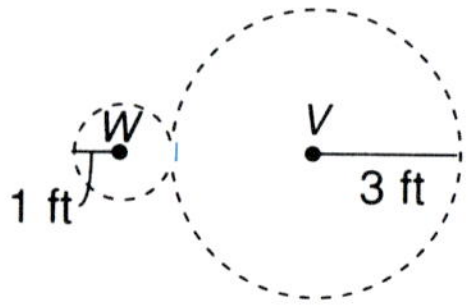

12.

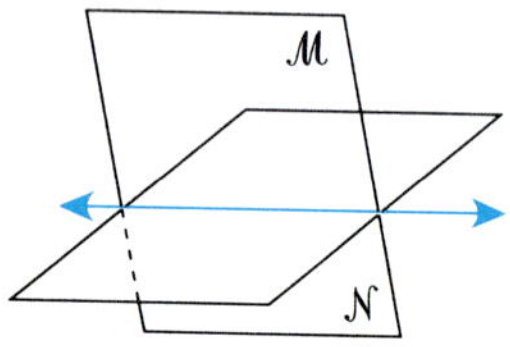

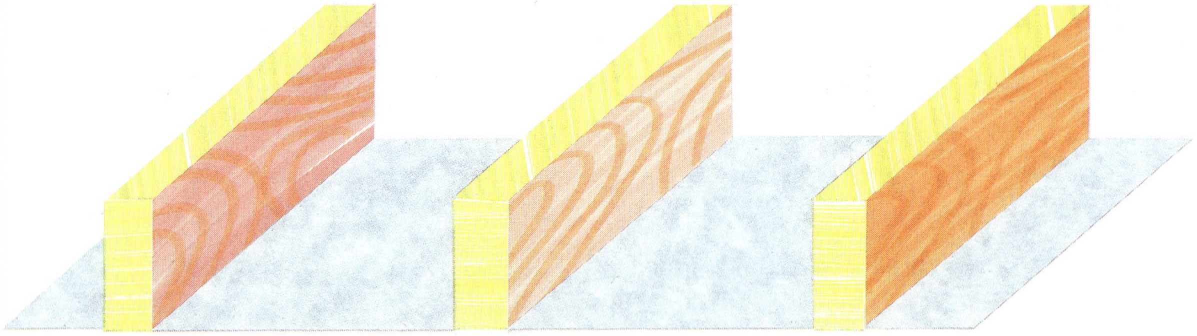

Chapter 9 Review/Test

1. Draw and describe the locus of all points in a plane that are $\frac{1}{2}$ inch from segment PQ.

2. Towns A and B are 10 mi apart. Draw and describe the locus of a beacon that is 5 mi from $\overline{AB}$ and is equally distant from A and B.

In the diagram below, $f \parallel g$.

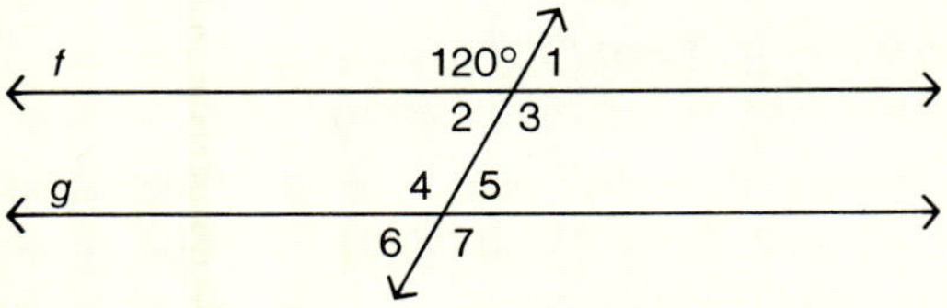

3. Name two pairs of vertical angles.

4. Name two pairs of supplementary angles.

5. Name all acute angles.

6. Find $m\angle 1$.

7. Find $m\angle 4$.

8. For the figure at the right, draw the top, bottom, and side views.

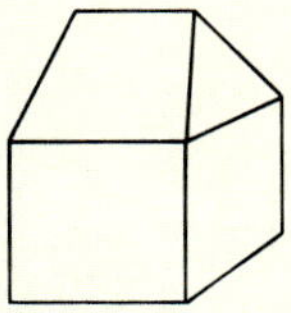

9. Tell which of these polygons tessellates in a plane: parallelogram, regular pentagon, regular hexagon.

Name each solid.

10.

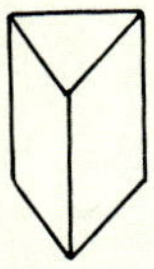

11.

12. Draw a pattern for the figure in Exercise 10.

Use the diagram for Problems 13–17.

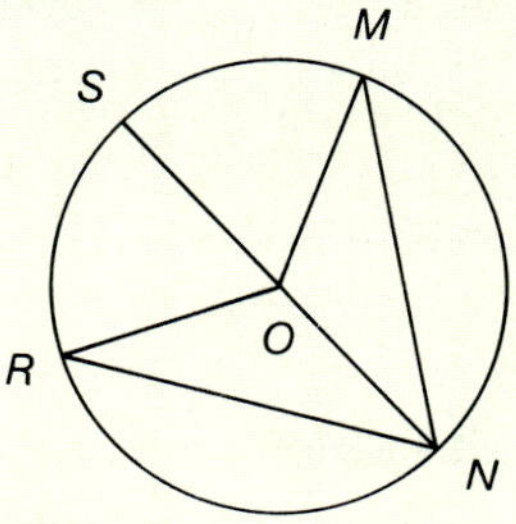

13. Name a chord.

14. Name a central angle.

15. Find the circumference of circle O above if the length of $\overline{OR}$ is 3.5 cm. Use $\pi = 3.14$.

16. Find $m\angle MOR$ in circle O if $m\angle MNR = 65°$.

17. In circle O above, $\overline{SN}$ bisects $\angle MNR$. If $m\angle MNR = 65°$, find $m\angle MNS$.

Do each construction.

18. Copy $\overline{XY}$ and construct the perpendicular bisector.

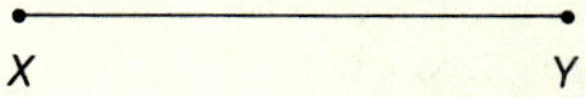

19. Use SSS to construct a triangle with sides a, b, and c.

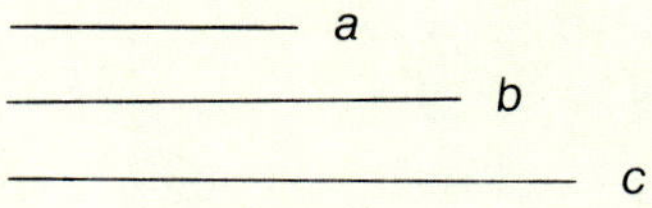

20. Make a table that lists the number of faces, edges, and vertices for the figures in Problems 8 and 10.

21. **Write About Math** Tell how you can use the definition of *prism* to determine whether your answer to Problem 12 is sensible.

Measurement in Geometry

10

Did You Know: Ayers Rock, the world's most famous monolith, is an isolated mass of rock rising 1,100 feet above the surrounding desert. The rock is 1.8 miles long, over 1,100 feet high, and almost 5.5 miles in circumference.

Number-Sense Project

Estimate
Estimate the perimeter (distance around) of your school building.

Gather Data
Devise a method to approximate the perimeter of your school. Then use it to find the perimeter.

Analyze and Report
Discuss the different methods used and compare the results. How far is it around your school?

ALGEBRA

Measurement and Circles

Build Understanding

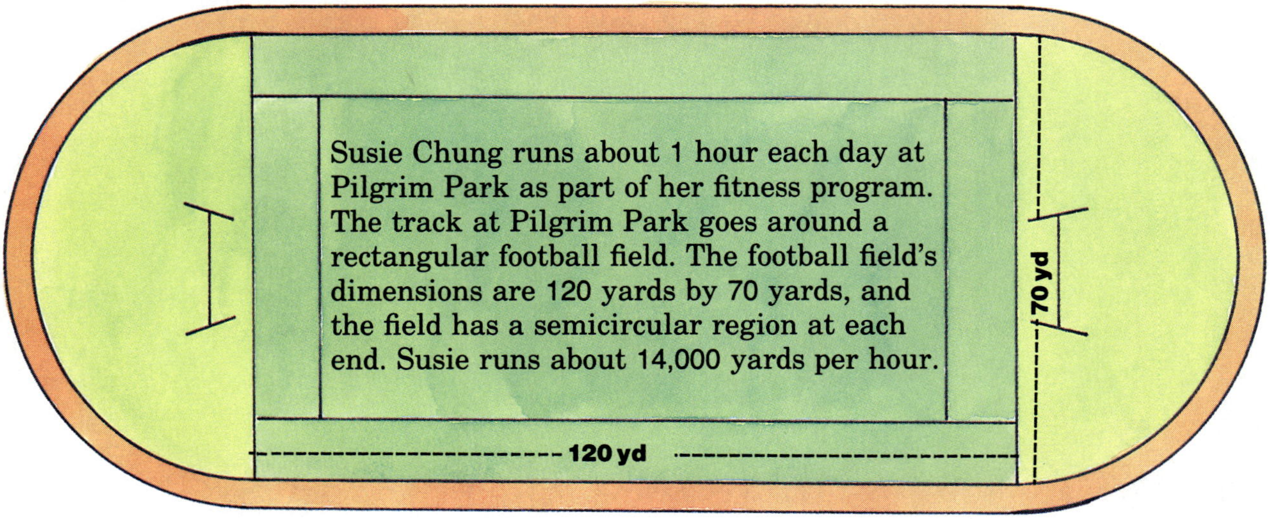

Susie Chung runs about 1 hour each day at Pilgrim Park as part of her fitness program. The track at Pilgrim Park goes around a rectangular football field. The football field's dimensions are 120 yards by 70 yards, and the field has a semicircular region at each end. Susie runs about 14,000 yards per hour.

A. About how many laps does Susie make around the track in 1 hour?

Find the perimeter of the inside edge of the track.

The perimeter of the track is the sum of the two straight lengths and the two semicircles. Together, the two semicircles are equivalent to 1 circle.

The circumference *(C)* of a circle is given by the formula:

$C = \pi d$ **where** $\pi \approx \frac{22}{7}$ **or** $\pi \approx 3.14$

$P = 2\ell + \pi d$

$P = (2)(120) + (\pi)(70)$

$P \approx 240 + \left(\frac{22}{7}\right)(70)$

$P \approx 460$

The perimeter of the track is 460 yards. Since Susie runs about 14,000 yards per hour, Susie makes about 14,000 ÷ 460, or about 30, laps around the track in 1 hour.

Think of the perimeter as the "top" and the "bottom" of the rectangular field plus the circumference of the circle formed by putting the two "ends" of the track together.

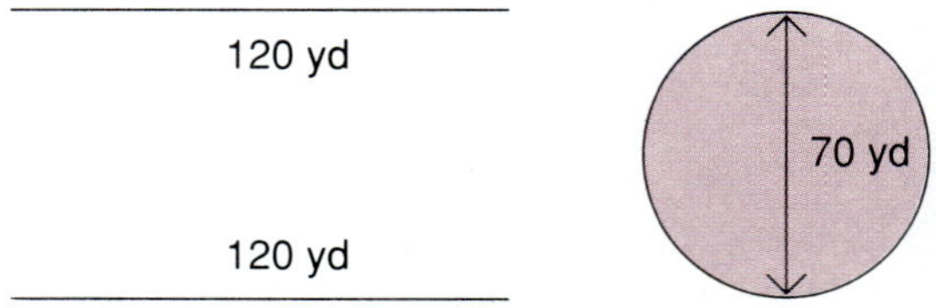

Recall that the diameter *(d)* equals 2 times the radius *(r)*. Another formula for circumference is $C = 2\pi r$.

B. Find the area inside the track.

The area inside the track is the sum of the area of the rectangle and the area of the circle formed by the two semicircles.

Use the formulas for the area of a rectangle and the area of a circle.

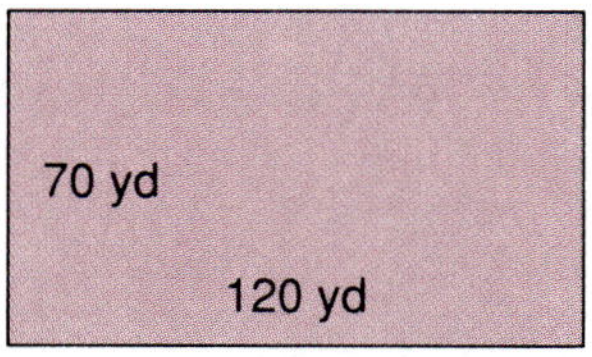

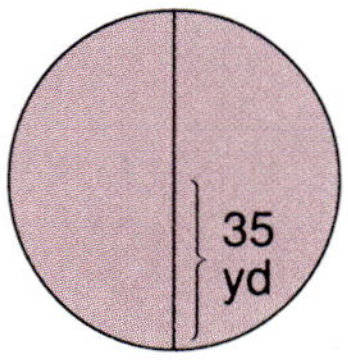

Area of rectangle	**Area of circle**
$A = \ell w$	$A = \pi r^2$
$A = (120)(70) = 8{,}400$	$A \approx (3.14)(35)^2 = 3{,}846.5$

The area inside the track is the sum of the two areas.

$A \approx 8{,}400 + 3{,}846.5 = 12{,}246.5$

The area is about 12,246.5 square yards.

Talk About Math When do you use $\frac{22}{7}$ instead of 3.14 for π?

Check Understanding

For another example, see Set A, pages 384–385.

For the given circle, find each indicated quantity.

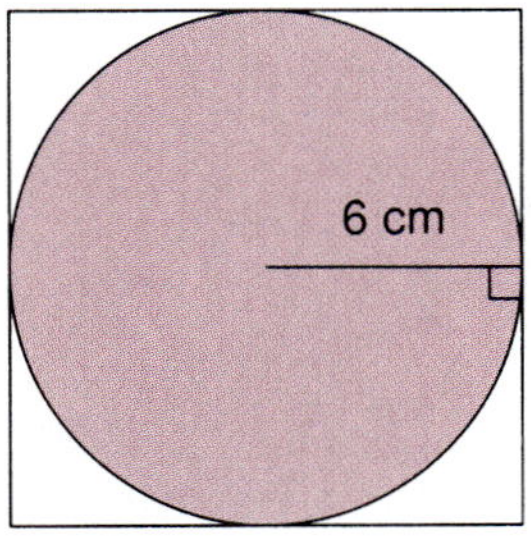

1. Diameter

2. Circumference

3. Area

4. Perimeter of square

5. Area of square

6. Area inside the square and outside the circle

Number Sense Decide whether each statement is always true, sometimes true, or never true. Give a reason for your answer.

7. If two circles have the same circumference, they are congruent.

8. If two circles have the same area, they are congruent.

9. If two rectangles have the same perimeter, they are congruent.

10. If two rectangles have the same area, they are congruent.

Practice

For More Practice, see Set A, pages 386–387.

Complete the following table, where r, d, C, and A represent the radius, diameter, circumference, and area of the circle. **Remember** to choose $\frac{22}{7}$ or 3.14 for π.

radius (r)	diameter (d)	circumference (C)	area (A)
4	**11.** ▦	**12.** ▦	**13.** ▦
14. ▦	6	**15.** ▦	**16.** ▦
8.4	**17.** ▦	**18.** ▦	**19.** ▦
20. ▦	14.08	**21.** ▦	**22.** ▦

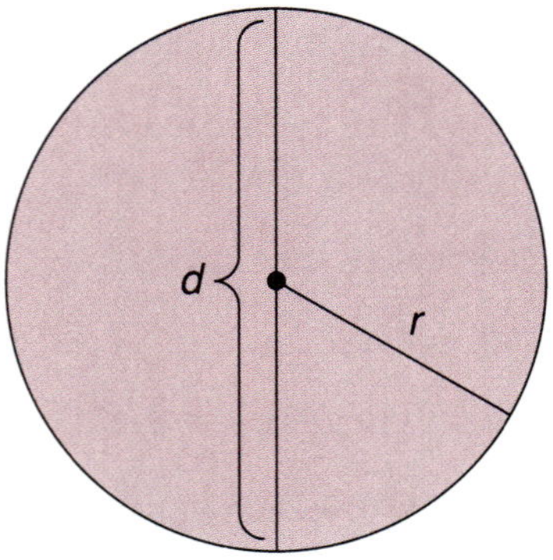

If the area of the square is 49 cm², what is the area of each circle?

23.

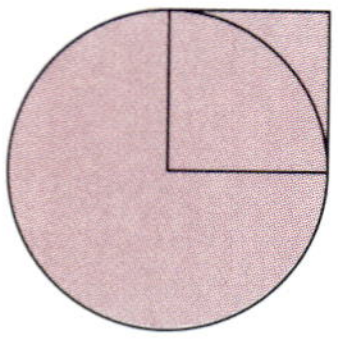

24.

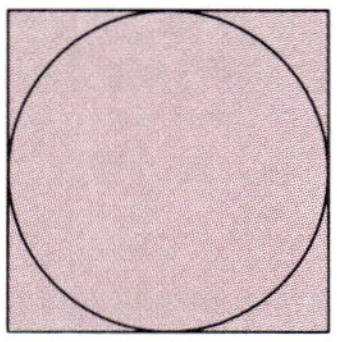

25.

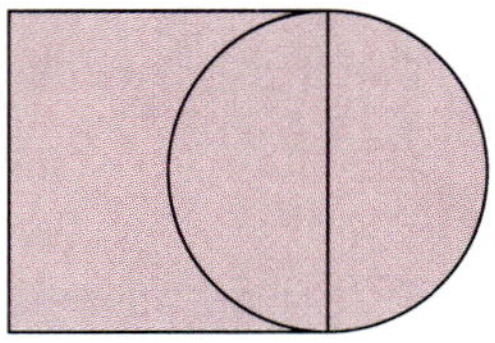

Find the area of the circle with the given dimension.

26. $r = 3.2$ ft

27. $d = 12.8$ in.

28. $C = 24\pi$ yd

29. $r = 1\frac{3}{4}$ ft

30. $d = 2\frac{5}{8}$ in.

31. $C = 314$ cm

32. $d = 140$ cm

33. $r = 0.03$ m

34. $C = 66$ yd

35. $r = 3\frac{1}{2}$ yd

36. $d = \frac{21}{32}$ in.

37. $C = 500\pi$ ft

38. The area of a circle is 154 square inches. Find r, the radius.

Problem Solving

Solve each problem.

39. How many complete revolutions does Kim Chung's 26-inch bicycle tire (diameter of the tire is 26 inches) make when he rides the bicycle for a distance of 1 mile?

40. Kim calculated that during the past three years the distance he rode is equivalent to riding once around a circular path with a radius of 6,940 km. How many kilometers did he ride?

TIPS FOR PROBLEM SOLVERS

Think about your own thinking. Pause to ask, "How is this going to help me solve the problem?"

41. **Calculator** The ancient Egyptians said that the area of a circle equals the area of a square whose side is $\frac{8}{9}$ the diameter of the circle. Use this formula to find the area of a circle with a radius of 9, of 27, of 100, and of 999.

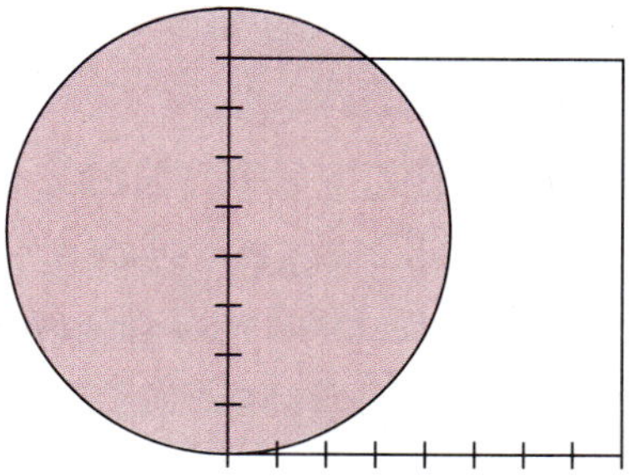

42. In Problem 40, what is Kim's average speed in kilometers per hour if he rode about 2,100 hours during the past three years?

43. Find the area and circumference of a circle with a diameter of 2. What happens to the area and circumference when the diameter is doubled? when the diameter is tripled?

44. If a circle has a radius of 3 in., by how much must you increase the radius to triple its circumference?

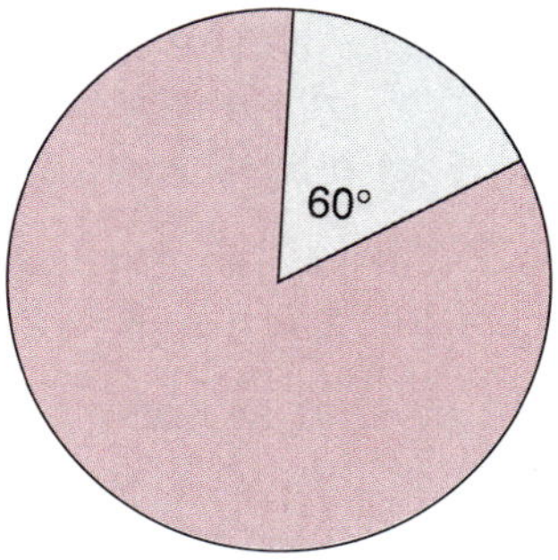

45. If the radius of the original circle is 5 in., by how much must you increase the radius to triple its circumference?

46. **Critical Thinking** By how much do you need to increase the radius of a circle to triple its circumference? Use the results of Problems 44 and 45.

47. If the area of the gray portion of the circle at the right is 12 cm^2, what is the area of the circle?

48. When Kim goes bike riding he leaves his dog tethered to a 10-foot rope which is tied to the corner of the 5-foot by 7-foot shed. Make a drawing of the region in which the dog can play and find its area to the nearest square foot.

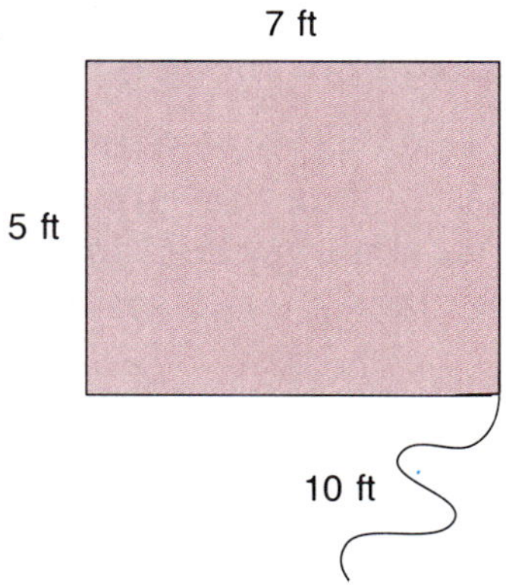

Skills Review pages 300–303

In the figure at the right, $\overline{AB} \parallel \overline{CD}$. What is the measure of each angle?

1. $\angle 1$ 2. $\angle 2$ 3. $\angle 3$ 4. $\angle 4$

5. $\angle 5$ 6. $\angle 6$ 7. $\angle 7$

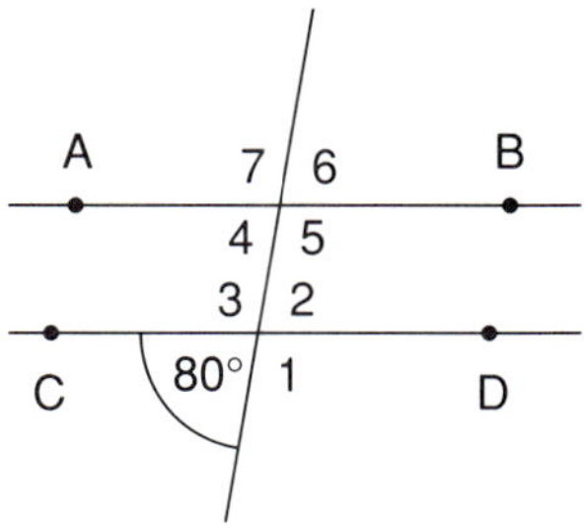

What is the measure of each angle of the polygon?

8. Regular hexagon 9. Rectangle 10. Equilateral triangle

ALGEBRA

Measurement of Parallelograms and Triangles

Build Understanding

A. If the lengths of two sides of a parallelogram are 8 units and 6 units, what values are possible for its area?

In Figure A, the parallelogram is a rectangle and its area is $8 \times 6 = 48$ sq units.

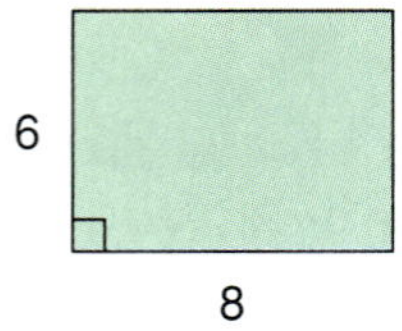

Figure A

In Figure B, the area is 8×5, since the parallelogram can be "rearranged" to form an 8 by 5 rectangle.

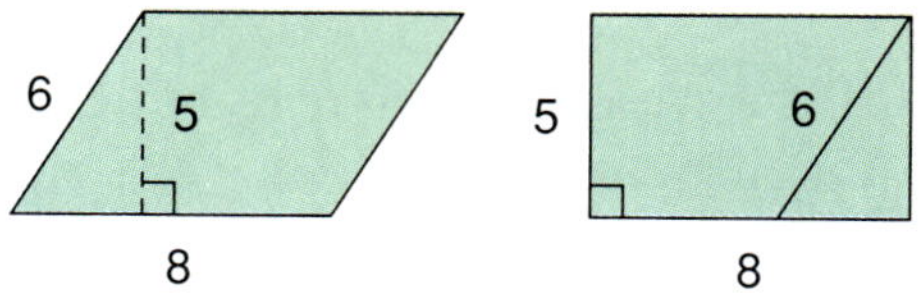

Figure B

In Figure C, the area of the parallelogram is $8 \times 2 = 16$ sq units.

Notice that as the angle between the sides of length 6 and 8 decreases, the area becomes smaller.

The area of a parallelogram equals the base times the height. ($A = bh$)

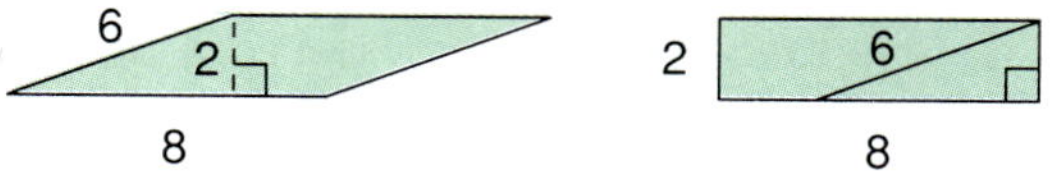

Figure C

Parallelograms with sides of 8 and 6 have areas that are positive numbers less than or equal to 48 sq units. The perimeter is always 28 units.

B. If the triangle at the right is rotated 180° about the midpoint M of a side, a parallelogram is formed. The area of the triangle is one-half the area of the parallelogram.

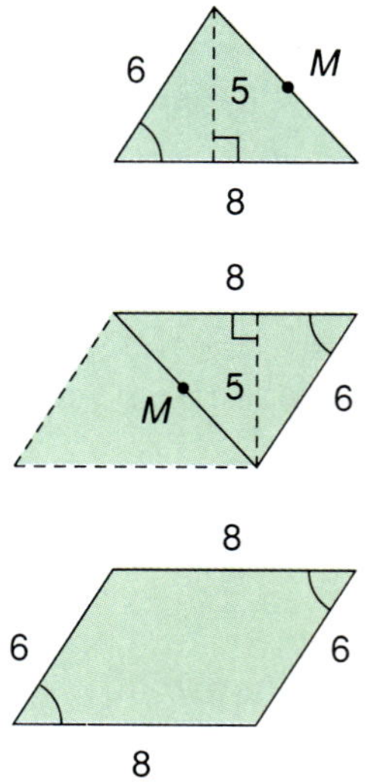

The area of any triangle equals one-half the area of the parallelogram, or one-half the base times the height.

$$A = \frac{1}{2}bh$$

$$A = \frac{1}{2}(8)(5) = 20$$

The area of this triangle is 20 sq units.

C. Mental Math The lengths of the sides of a triangle are 6 in., 8 in., and 6 in. What is the perimeter of a triangle with sides that are 2 times as long? 3 times as long? Use mental math to find the perimeters of the three triangles.

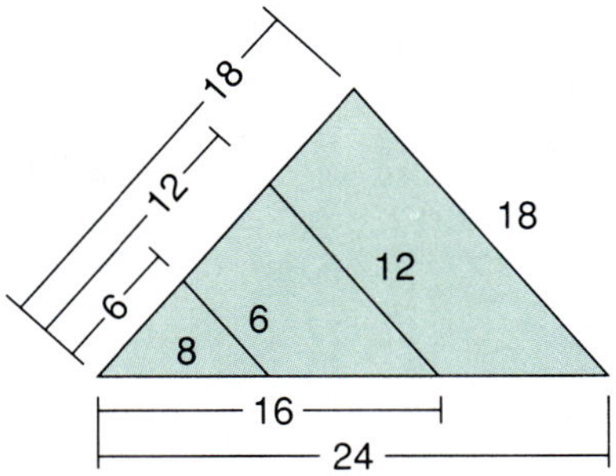

Think: P = sum of three lengths

Original triangle: $P = 6 + 6 + 8 = 20$ **in.**

Double the lengths: $P = 12 + 12 + 16 = 40$ **in.**

Triple the lengths: $P = 18 + 18 + 24 = 60$ **in.**

Notice that when the sides are doubled in length, the perimeter doubles. When the sides are tripled in length, the perimeter triples.

D. A rectangle has dimensions 6 in. by 8 in. What is the area of a rectangle with sides that are twice as long? 3 times as long? Find the areas of the three rectangles.

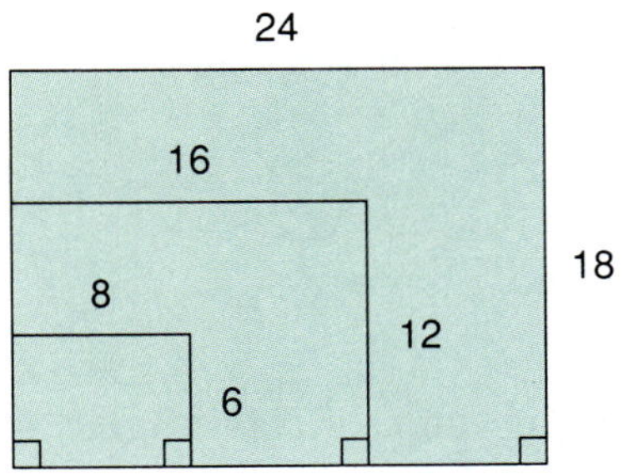

$A = \ell h$

Original rectangle: $A = (8)(6) = 48$ **sq in.**

Double the lengths: $A = (16)(12) = 192$ **sq in.**

Triple the lengths: $A = (24)(18) = 432$ **sq in.**

Notice that when the sides are doubled in length, the area is multiplied by 4, or 2^2. When the sides are tripled in length, the area is multiplied by 9, or 3^2.

■ **Talk About Math** What values are possible for the area and the perimeter of a triangle with two sides of lengths 7 units and 10 units?

Check Understanding

For another example, see Set B, pages 384–385.

Find the perimeter and area of each polygon.

1. Triangle

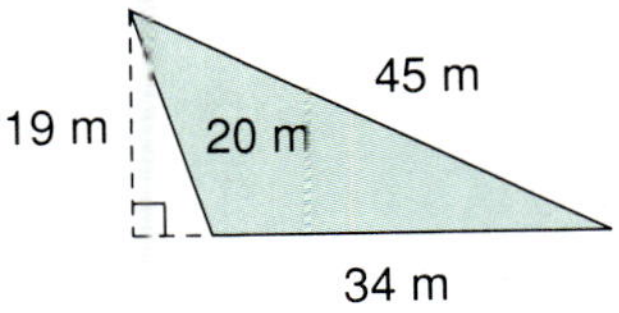

2. Parallelogram

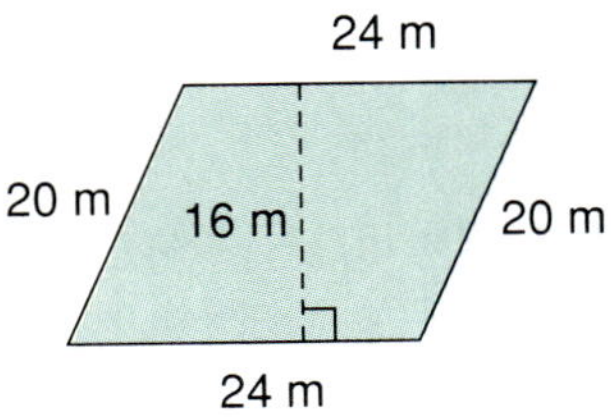

3. Rectangle

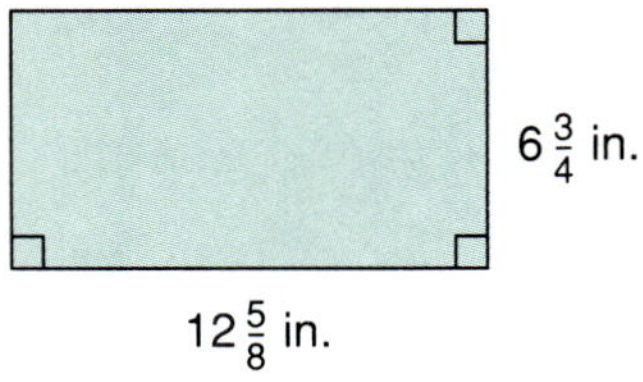

Practice

For More Practice, see Set B, pages 386–387.

Find the perimeter and the area of the polygon. Tell whether you use mental math, paper and pencil, or a calculator.

4.

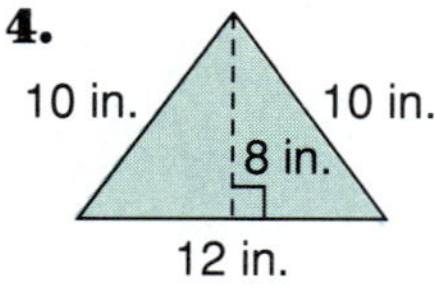

5.

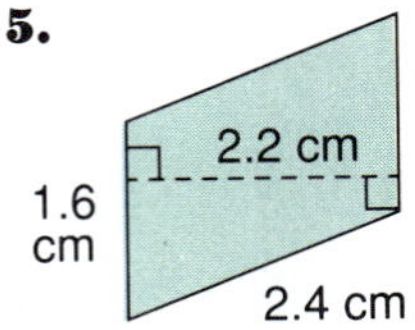

6.

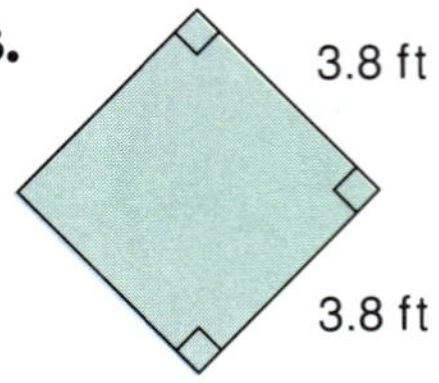

7.

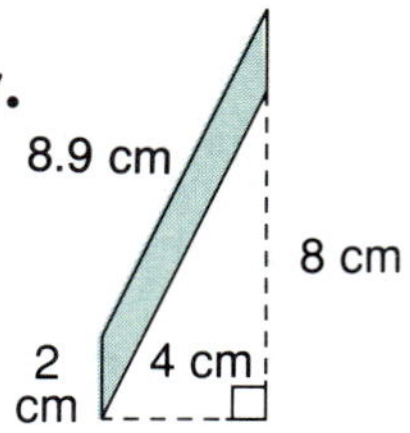

8.

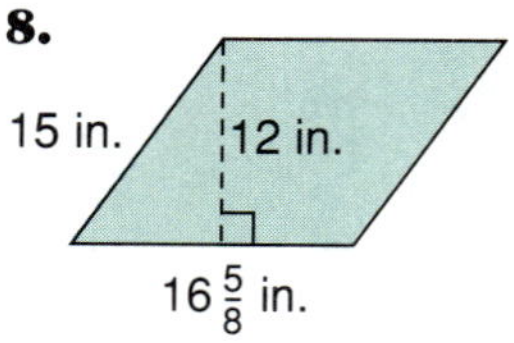

9.

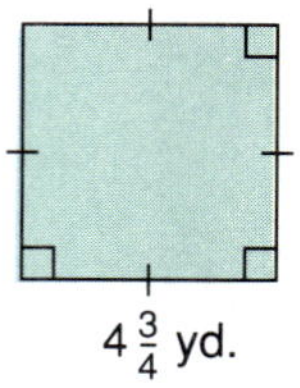

10.

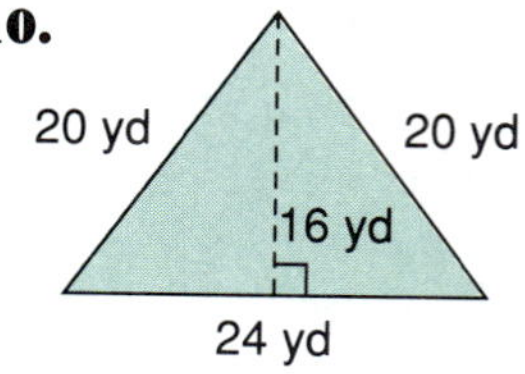

11.

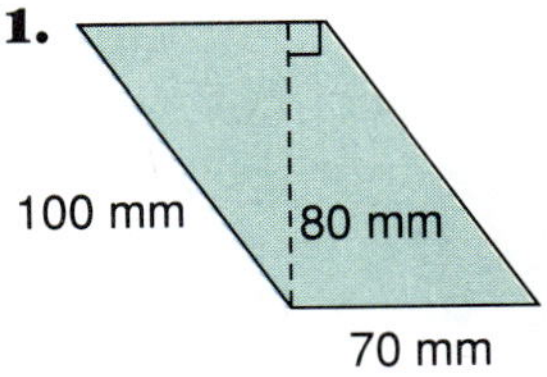

12.

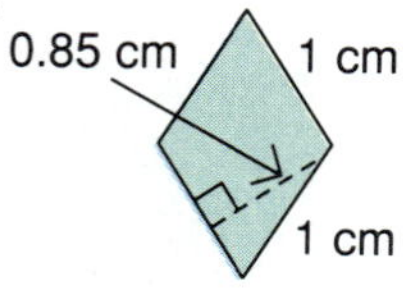

13.

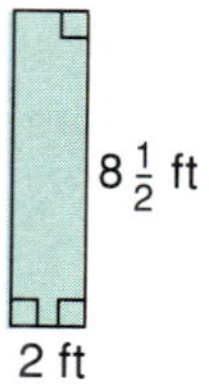

14.

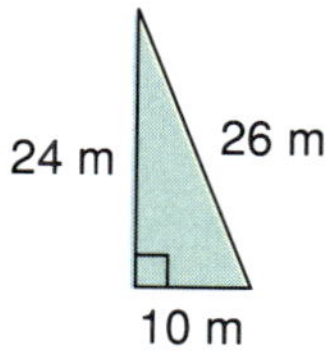

15.

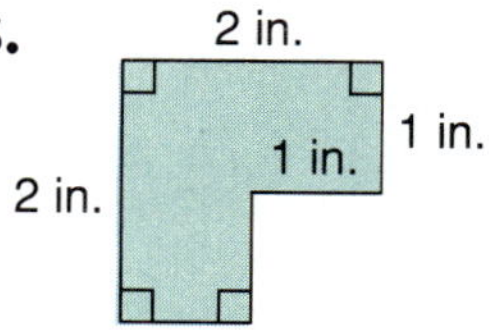

Each side of a triangle is multiplied by 4. By what number is

16. the perimeter multiplied?

17. the area multiplied?

Each side of a rectangle is halved. By what number is

18. the perimeter multiplied?

19. the area multiplied?

Answer each question.

20. **Mental Math** If the length of each side of a rectangle is tripled, by what factor is its perimeter multiplied?

21. **Visual Thinking** If the two parallelograms at the right are congruent, how are the areas of the shaded triangles related? Give a reason for your answer.

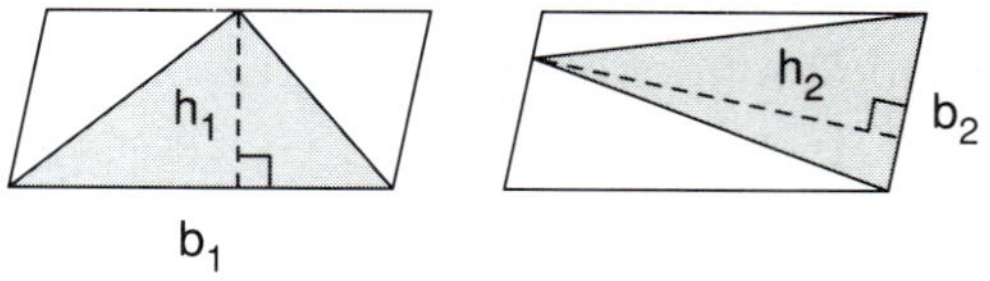

Find each answer.

22. The perimeter of a parallelogram is 36 cm. The bases are 12 cm. Find the lengths of the other two sides.

23. The area of a parallelogram is 36 cm. One base is 12 cm. Find the height to that base.

Problem Solving

Solve each problem.

24. A rectangular office is 18 feet by 24 feet. If carpeting costs $25 per square yard, how much will it cost to install wall-to-wall carpeting in this office? Hint: 9 sq ft = 1 sq yd

25. A circular Oriental rug with a radius of 5 feet is to be centered on a wooden square-shaped floor with sides of 12 feet. What is the area of the floor that is not covered by the rug?

26. A walk 2.5 meters wide surrounds a rectangular garden that is 40 m by 60 m. Find the area of the walk.

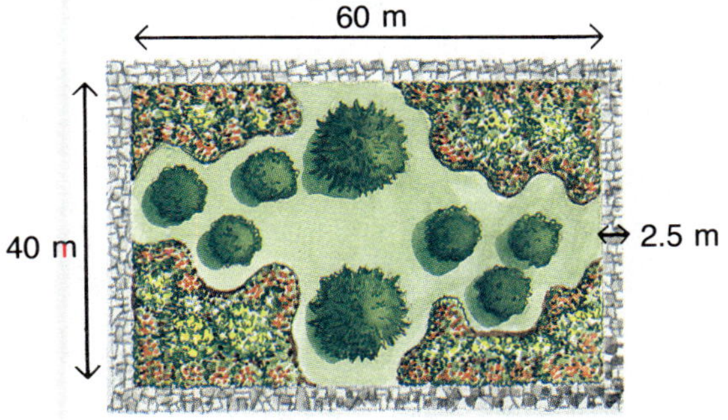

27. Find the area of the shaded region.

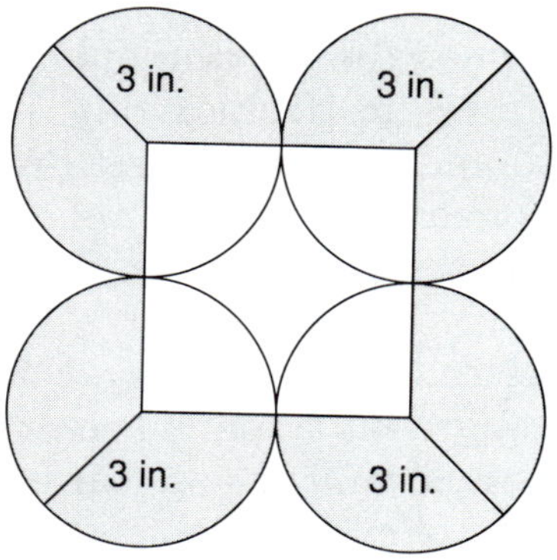

28. **Critical Thinking** Can you find the area and the perimeter of the L-shaped polygon with the information given? If you can, compute it. If you cannot, give reasonable values for the missing lengths needed, and then compute.

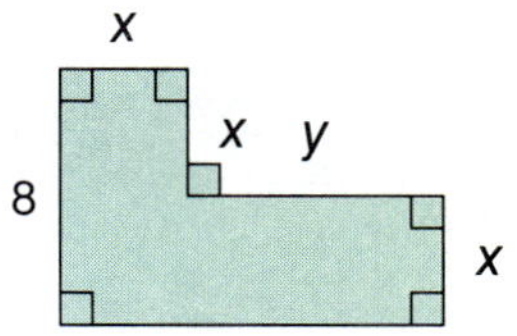

29. On a grid of 5 dots by 5 dots, draw as many triangles with an area of 2 square units as you can. Each vertex of the triangle should be a grid point. None of the triangles should be congruent.

The base and height of a parallelogram are each increased by 10%. By what percent is

30. the perimeter increased?

31. the area increased?

32. Draw a rectangle $ABCD$. Locate points E, F, and G so that the following conditions are satisfied.

a. Points C, D, E, F, and G are on the same side of line AB.

b. Triangle CDE is a right triangle; triangle CDF is acute; and triangle CDG is obtuse.

c. The areas of triangles CDE, CDF, and CDG are all equal.

33. Draw any triangle. Then draw three line segments that divide the original triangle into four triangles of equal area.

ALGEBRA

Measurement of Trapezoids and Irregular Figures

Build Understanding

Wood inlaying is an ancient craft that developed into a fine-art form. Early craftsmen in Africa and Asia used wood inlay on decorative boxes and religious ornaments. By the 15th century Botticelli had designed the wood-inlaid doors at Ducal Palace in Urbino, Italy. During the 17th and 18th centuries, French artisans had perfected the related technique of marquetry for furniture.

This portion of an inlaid wall design made during the 15th century uses perspective and realistic forms to achieve the idea of space.

A. Francisca, a woodworker, is using two congruent trapezoids as inlay pieces to form a parallelogram. Find the area of one trapezoid.

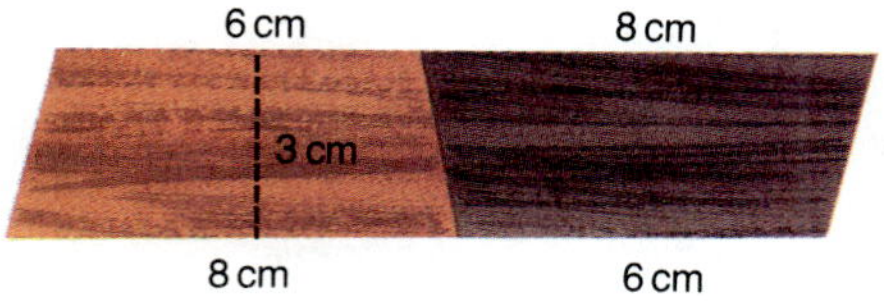

First find the area of the parallelogram. The parallelogram has a base of 8 + 6, or 14 cm, and a height of 3 cm.

$A = bh = (8 + 6)(3) = (14)(3) = 42$

Since the pieces are equal, the area of one piece is $\frac{1}{2}(42)$, or 21 cm^2.

The area of a trapezoid is one half times the sum of the lengths of the two parallel sides, b_1 and b_2, times the height, h.

$$\boldsymbol{A = \frac{1}{2}(b_1 + b_2)(h)}$$

B. Find the area of the figure.

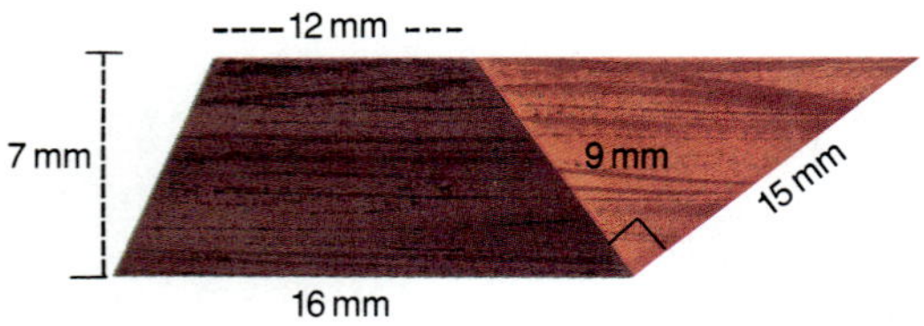

Find the area of each polygon and add the areas.

Trapezoid: $A = \frac{1}{2}(b_1 + b_2)(h) = \frac{1}{2}(16 + 12)(7) = 98$

Triangle: $A = \frac{1}{2}(b)(h) = \frac{1}{2}(9)(15) = 67\frac{1}{2}$

The area of the figure is $98 + 67\frac{1}{2}$, or $165\frac{1}{2}$ mm^2.

C. Use the formula to find the area of each trapezoid.

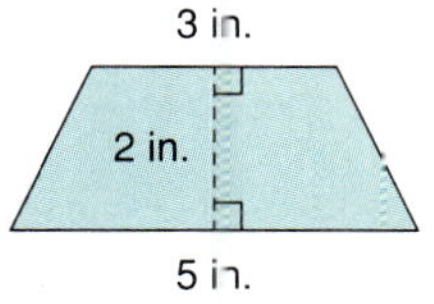

$A = \frac{1}{2}(b_1 + b_2)(h)$

$A = \frac{1}{2}(3 + 5)(2)$

$A = 8$

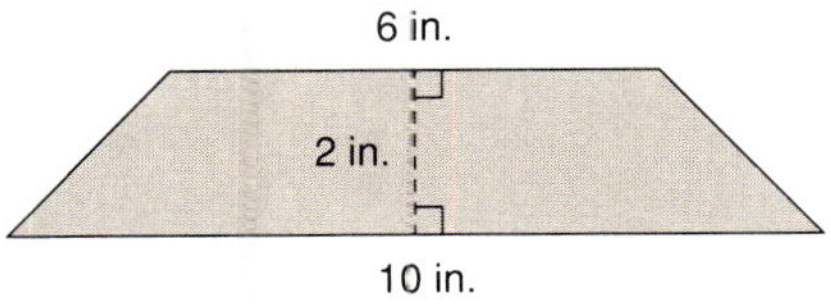

$A = \frac{1}{2}(b_1 + b_2)(h)$

$A = \frac{1}{2}(6 + 10)(2)$

$A = 16$

The areas are 8 square inches and 16 square inches. Notice that when the bases of a trapezoid are doubled and the height stays the same, the area doubles.

This parquet or wood-inlaid floor was installed in the Hall of Mirrors of the Palace of Versailles in France in 1678.

D. **Calculator** Write a calculator key sequence to find the area of the figure in Example B.

Press: 16 [+] 12 [=] [×] .5 [×] 7 [=] [M+] .5 [×] 9 [×] 15 [=] [+] [MRC] [=] **Display:** *165.5*

Talk About Math Can you find the perimeter of the trapezoid in Example A? If you can, find the answer. If you cannot, describe what additional information you need to find the perimeter.

Check Understanding

For another example, see Set C, pages 384–385.

Find the area of each polygon. Give your answer to the nearest tenth.

1.

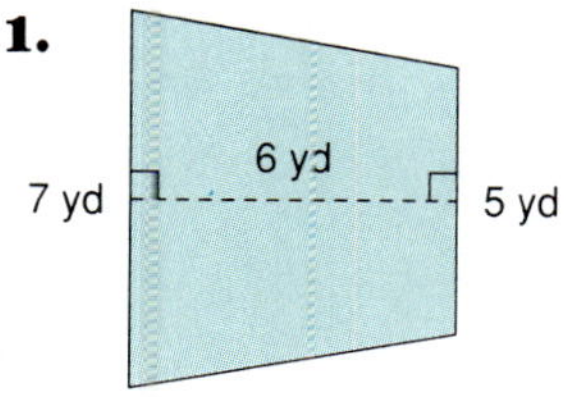

2.

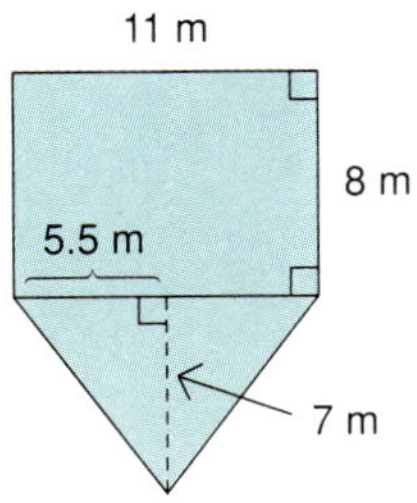

3.

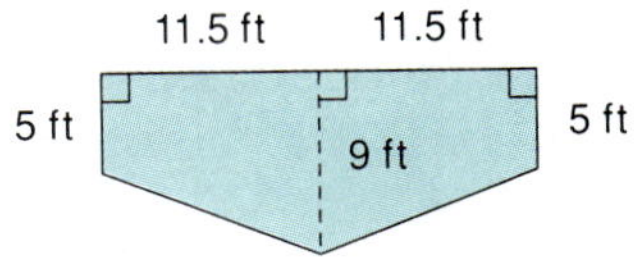

4. If the bases of a trapezoid are tripled in length, and the height stays the same, what happens to the area of the trapezoid?

Find the perimeter of each polygon.

5.

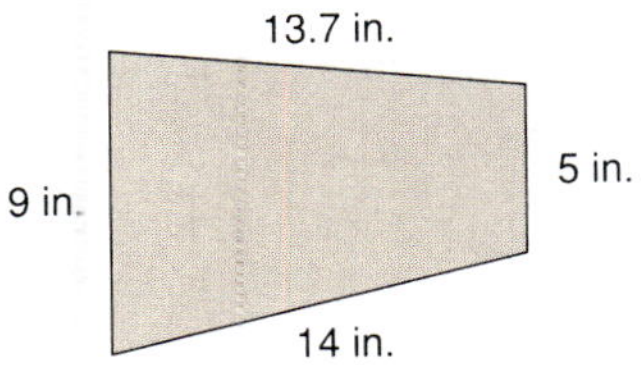

6.

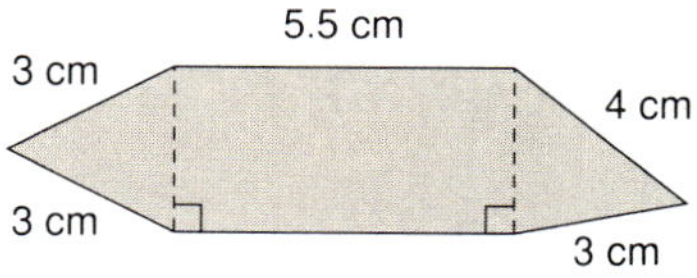

Practice

For More Practice, see Set C, pages 386–387.

Find the perimeter and the area to the nearest tenth. Tell whether you use mental math, paper and pencil, or a calculator.

7.

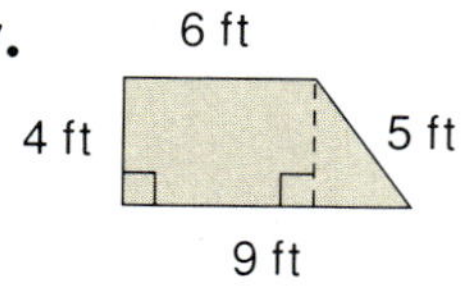

8.

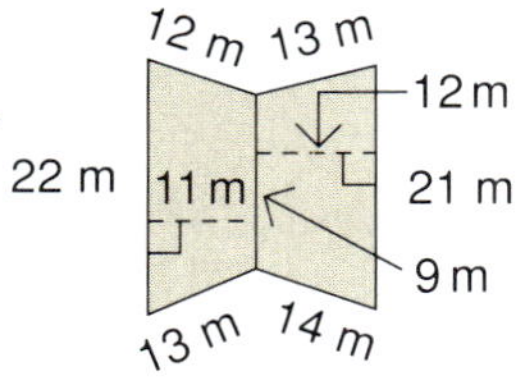

9.

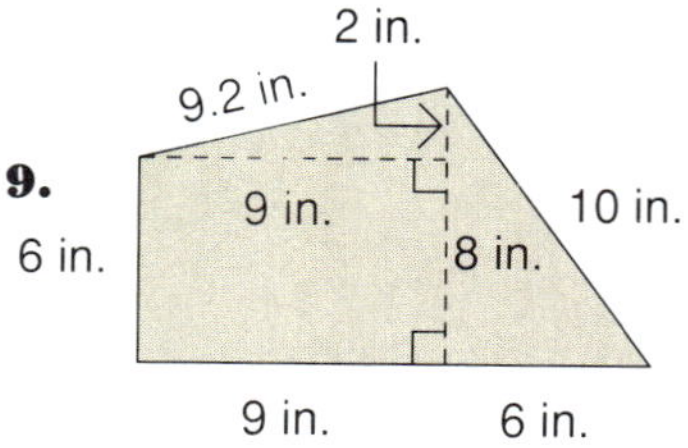

10.

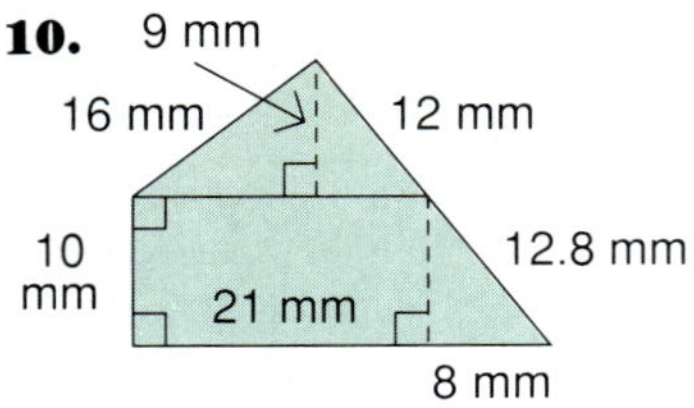

11.

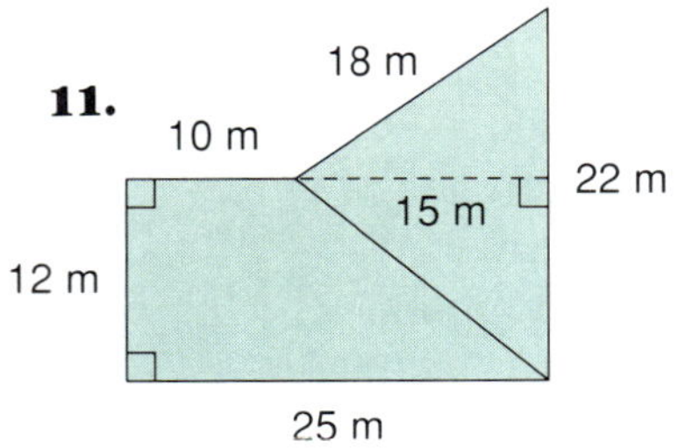

12.

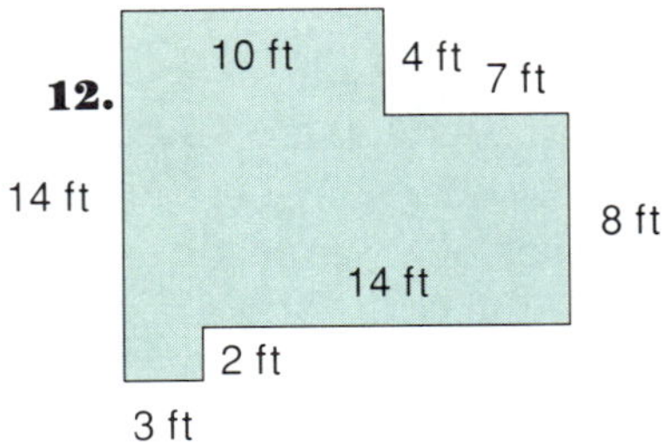

Mixed Practice Find each answer.

13. Critical Thinking A rectangle is divided into four rectangles, as shown in the figure. The areas of three of the rectangles are shown. If the dimensions are whole numbers, find the area of the fourth rectangle.

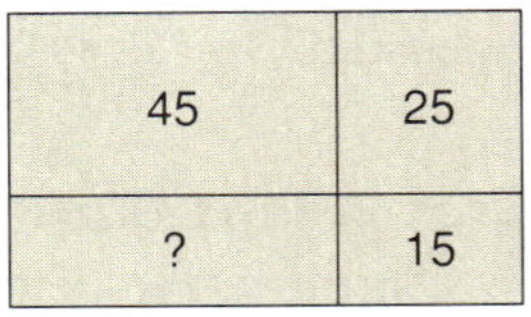

14. An 18 by 12 rectangular area is to be covered with small wood-veneer rectangles that each measure 3 by 2. If no two of the smaller rectangles overlap, how many of them are needed to cover the large one?

In the circular inlay to the right, each of the 16 triangles has two congruent sides and all the triangles are congruent.

15. What are the measures of the angles of the triangles?

Trace the figures. Then find a point X on $\overline{BC}$ so that $\overline{AX}$ divides the polygon into two regions of equal area.

16.

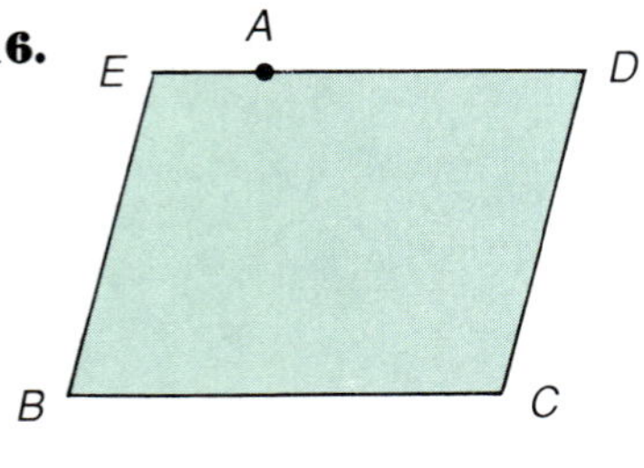

17.

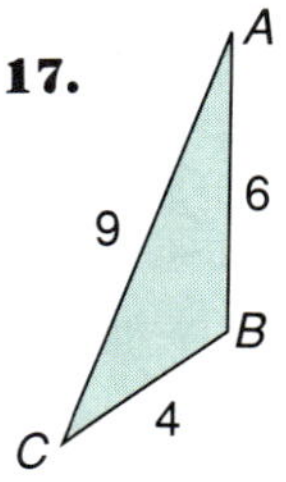

This circular-shaped inlay of triangles and trapezoids uses a variety of veneers.

Problem Solving

Solve each problem.

18. What happens to the area and the perimeter of a trapezoid if its height and bases are doubled?

19. Write a formula in terms of a, b, and c for the area and the perimeter of the polygon.

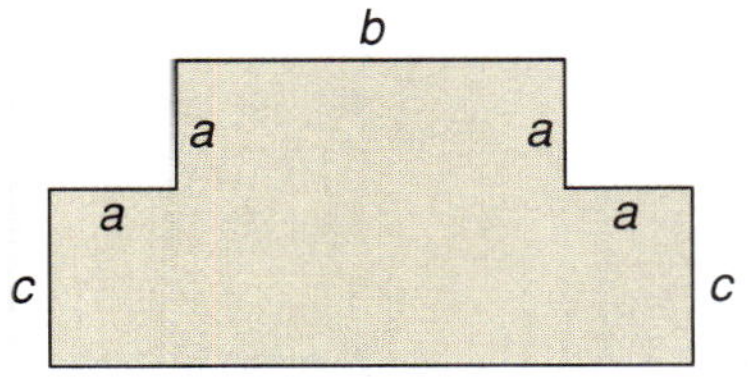

20. Write a formula in terms of a, b, and c for the area and the perimeter of the polygon.

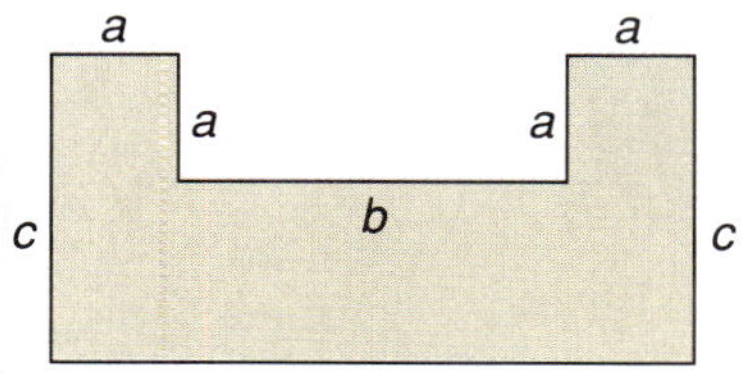

This is the back of an inlaid sandalwood *biwa* or lute that was made in Japan during the 8th century.

Explore ______ Math

Francisca designs inlaid strips as borders for table tops. Solve each problem.

21. For one design, Francisca combines right triangles and trapezoids to cover a rectangular area 5 in. by 84 in. Create a design using the shapes shown. How many of each shape are needed to cover the area?

The top of a table is made of two congruent cherry-wood trapezoids and four congruent triangular pieces, two of cherry and two of walnut.

22. What is the height of each trapezoid?

23. What is the area of each trapezoid?

24. What is the area of each triangular piece?

25. What is the total area of the table top?

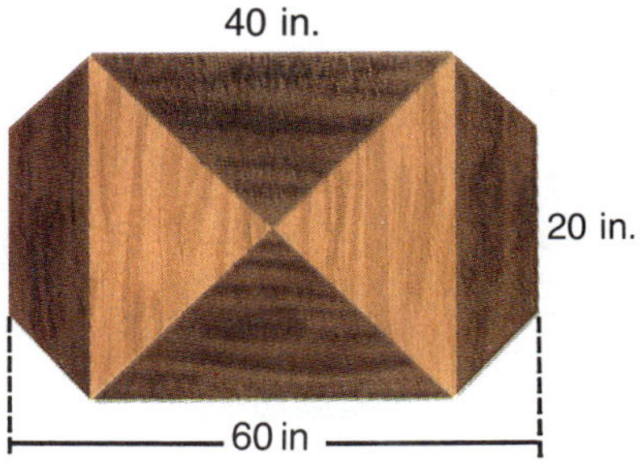

Use Data from a Diagram

PROBLEM SOLVING GUIDE

Understand
QUESTION
FACTS
KEY IDEA

Plan and Solve
STRATEGY
ANSWER

Look Back
SENSIBLE ANSWER
ALTERNATE APPROACH

Build Understanding

Oliver Doyle wants to estimate the area of Popp Island from the map. How can he do it?

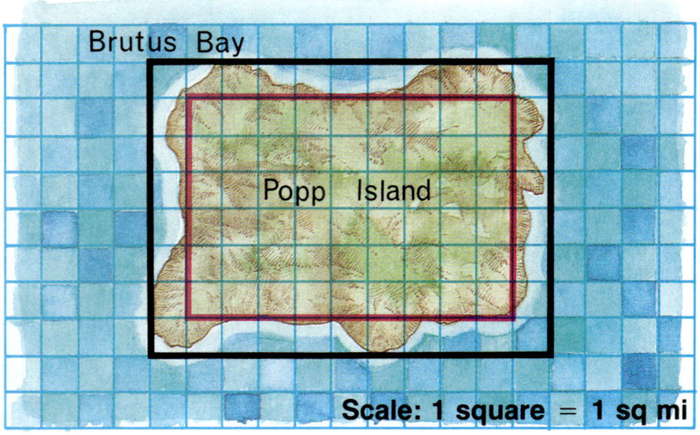

Understand QUESTION How can the area of Popp Island be estimated?

FACTS The shape of the island is irregular. You know how to find the area of a rectangle from the formula $A = \ell w$.

KEY IDEA Use the area of a simpler figure, such as a rectangle, to estimate the area of an irregular region.

Plan and Solve STRATEGY Trace the map of the island. Put your tracing over a grid so that one grid unit represents one square mile, as shown. Draw the largest possible rectangle inside the island. Then draw the smallest rectangle that encloses the island.

Area of inside rectangle = (6)(9) = 54 sq mi

Area of outside rectangle = (8)(11) = 88 sq mi

Finally, find the average of these two areas to estimate the area of the irregular shape.

Average $= \frac{54 + 88}{2} = 71$ **sq mi**

ANSWER The area of the island is approximately 71 square miles.

Look Back ALTERNATE APPROACH You could use the inside rectangle as a minimum estimate for the area. Then beginning at the lower left corner of the map, work your way around the map in a clockwise direction. Add (or subtract) $\frac{1}{2}$ or 1 square unit for each square on the border of the inside rectangle depending on where the island shape lies in that grid square.

Talk About Math
What other shape(s) could you use to get a closer estimate of the area of Popp Island?

Check Understanding

Describe the shape you could use to estimate each area. Tell whether you would draw the shape inside or outside, or average the areas both inside and outside.

1.

2.

3.

4.

5. The bottom of your foot

6. A leaf from a tree.

Practice

Trace the shapes in each problem on graph paper of 4 squares per inch. Let each square equal one square unit of the distance indicated. Estimate the area. **Remember** to label units in your answer.

7. Exercise 1

8. Exercise 2

9. Exercise 3

10. Exercise 4

11. What are the dimensions of a box just large enough to hold a million pennies in a single stack? Assume 16 pennies per inch.

12. How many pennies would there be in a stack as high as a skyscraper 1,454 feet high? Assume 16 pennies per inch.

ALGEBRA

Volume of Prisms and Cylinders

Build Understanding

A. The volume of a prism is the number of unit cubes that will fit inside the prism. You can find the volume of a prism by multiplying the number of cubic units in one layer by the number of layers. Find the volume of the figure at the right.

Each layer contains 16 unit cubes, and there are 4 layers. So the volume is $4 \times 16 = 64$ cubic units.

B. José has to find a box for packing 24 cans of juice. Each can has a diameter of 4 inches and a height of 7 inches. Find the volume of the 24 cans. Find the volume of the box.

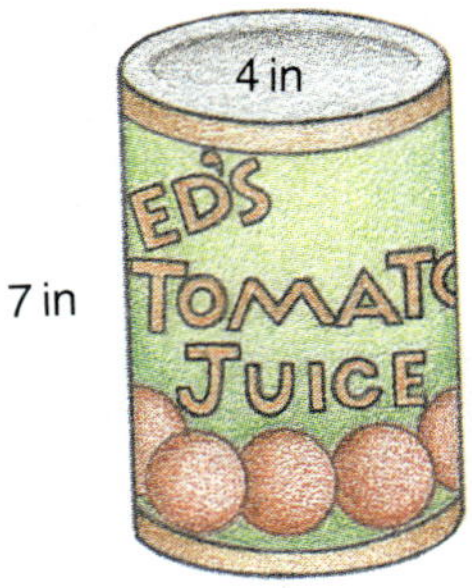

$V = Bh$
$B = \pi r^2$
$V = \pi r^2 h$

The volume of a prism or cylinder equals the area of the base times the height or $V = Bh$. Since the base of the can is a circle, the formula is $V = \pi r^2 h$.

Paper and Pencil

$V = \pi(2)^2(7)$

$\approx 3.14\,(4)(7) = 87.92$

Calculator

3.14 [×] 4 [×] 7 [=]

Display: *87.92*

The volume of each can is about 88 cu in. The volume of the 24 cans is about 24×88, or 2,112 cu in.

José could pack the cans in 6 rows of 4 each. The box would be 6×4 in. long, 4×4 in. wide, and 7 in. tall. The volume of the box is $24 \times 16 \times 7$, or 2,688 cu in.

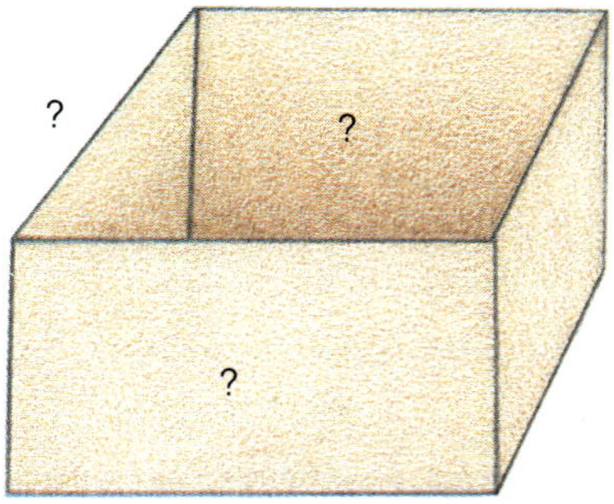

Talk About Math Find another box in which José could pack the 24 cans of juice. What is the volume of this box? How can José decide which shape is the best shape for the box?

Check Understanding

For another example, see Set D, pages 384–385.

Find the volume of each figure to the nearest hundredth. Let $\pi = 3.14$.

1. 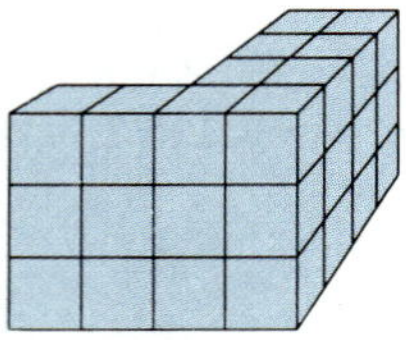

2. 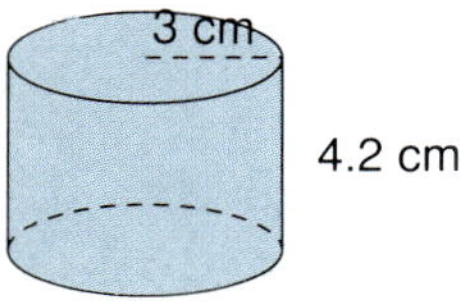

3. 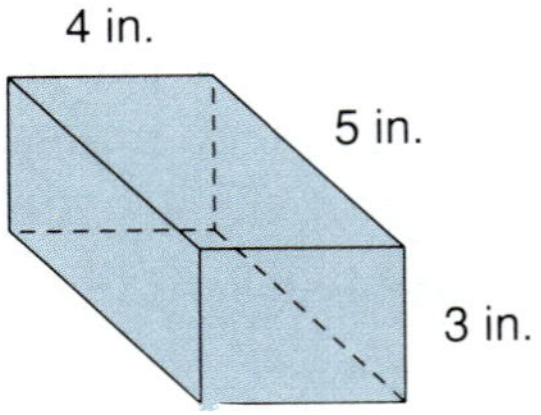

Practice

For More Practice, see Set D, pages 386–387.

Find the volume of each figure to the nearest hundredth. (Let $\pi = 3.14$.) **Remember** to label the units in your answer.

4. 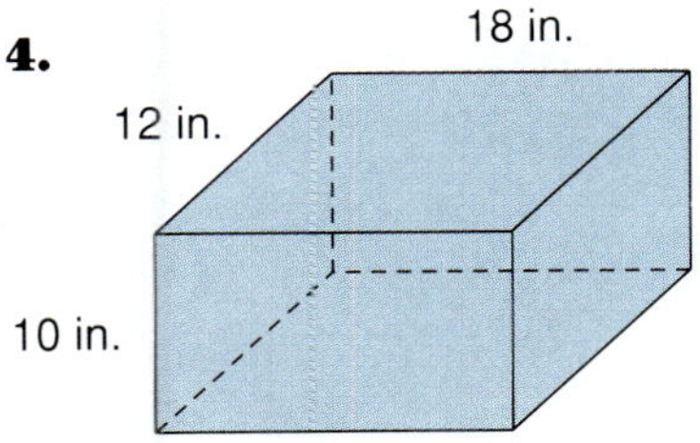

5. 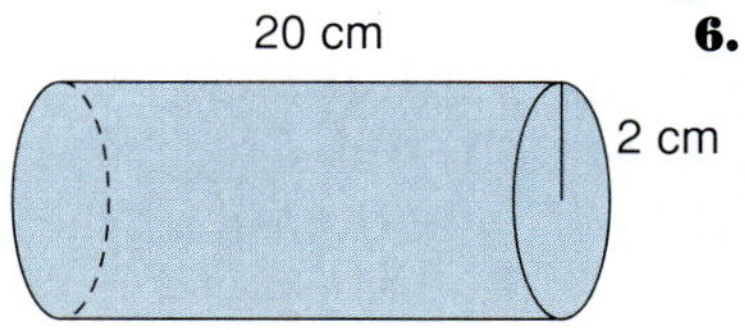

6. 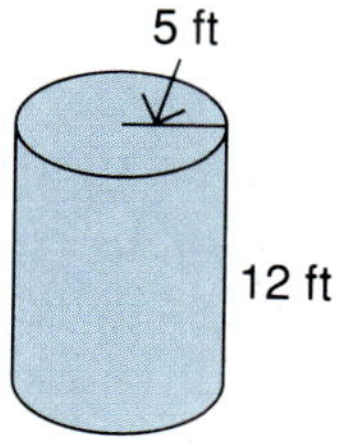

7. 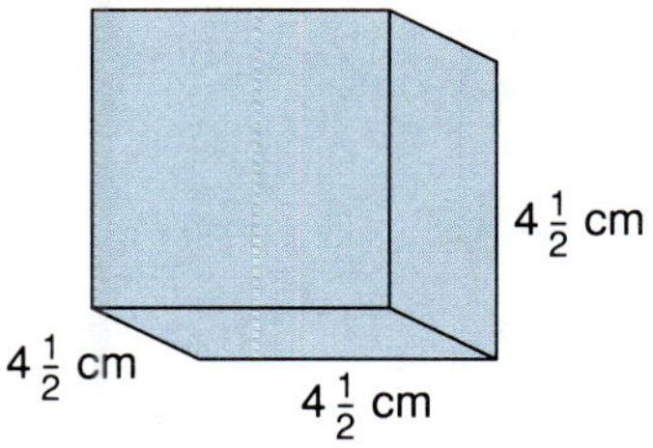

8. 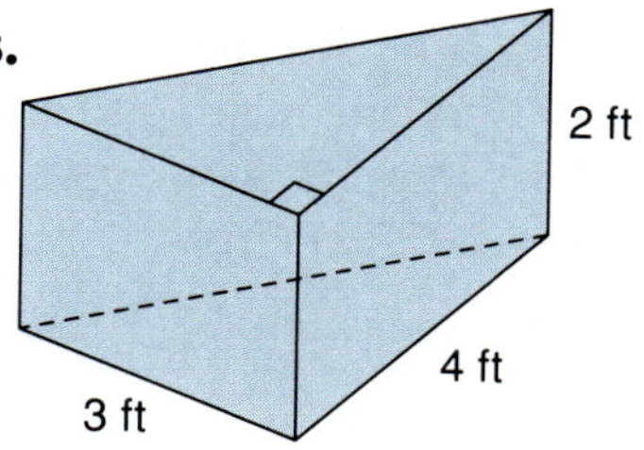

9. 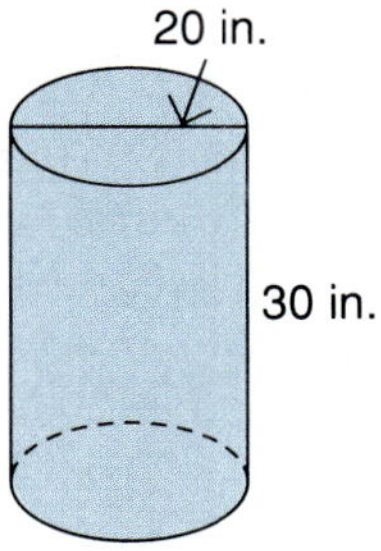

10. 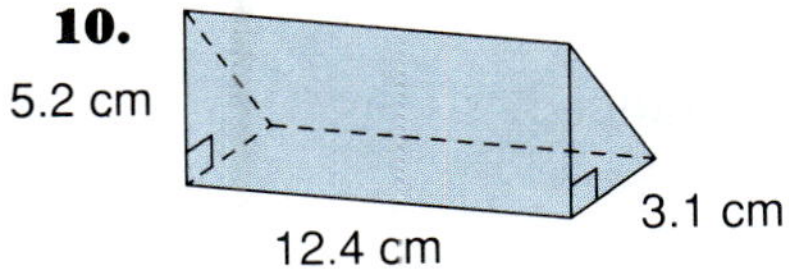

11. 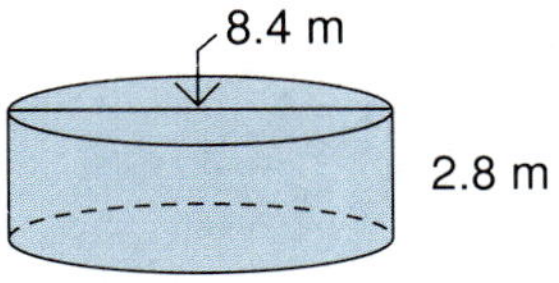

12. 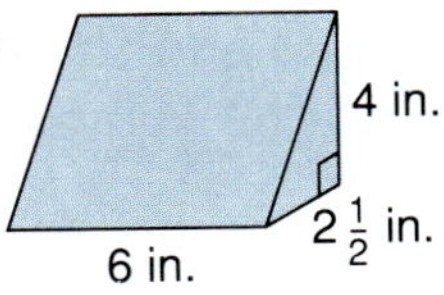

One ton of coal will fit in a rectangular bin 4 ft by 4 ft by 3 ft. Find the dimensions of a bin that will hold the given number of tons of coal. Use whole numbers for dimensions.

13. 2 tons **14.** 3 tons **15.** 4 tons **16.** 8 tons

17. **Visual Thinking** If you rotate this 12 by 18 rectangle about side AB or side AC, a cylinder will be formed. Which of these two cylinders do you think will have the greater volume?

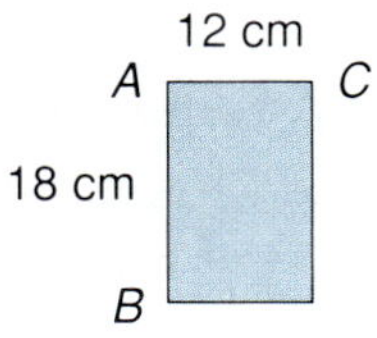

18. Find the volume of each cylinder in Exercise 17 to the nearest hundredth. (Let $\pi = 3.14$.)

Find the volume of each figure described.

19. A pentagonal prism with $B = 38\text{ cm}^2$ and $h = 4$ cm

20. A triangular prism with $B = 120\text{ cm}^2$ and $h = 8$ cm

21. A cylinder with $r = 7$ cm and $h = 6$ cm

22. A cylinder with $d = 2.1$ m and $h = 0.5$ m

Problem Solving

Solve each problem. **Remember** to draw a figure to help you solve the problem.

23. A 12-inch high concrete flower container is shaped like a cylinder. The outside diameter is 20 inches and the inside diameter is 18 inches. The bottom is one inch thick. What is the volume of concrete needed to make the container?

The interior dimensions of a small microwave oven are given in inches, but its "useful capacity," or interior volume, is given in cubic feet and expressed in decimal form. Find the volume of the microwave ovens with interior dimensions as given (in inches). Give the answer in cu ft. Hint: 1,728 cu in. = 1 cu ft.

24. $7\frac{1}{4} \times 12\frac{3}{4} \times 11$

25. $4\frac{3}{4} \times 16 \times 10\frac{1}{2}$

26. $6\frac{1}{4} \times 14\frac{1}{4} \times 10\frac{1}{2}$

27. An oil storage tank is shaped like a cylinder. The radius of the base is 15 feet and the height is 30 feet. Find the volume of the tank.

28. A 9-foot basement is being dug for a house that is 50 feet long by 28 feet wide. How many cubic feet of dirt must be removed?

29. A closet is $4\frac{1}{2}$ feet wide by 3 feet deep by 8 feet high. A packet of moth repellant will protect 2 cubic yards of space. How many packets are needed to fully protect the contents of the closet? Hint: 1 cu yd = 27 cu ft

30. A new concrete driveway is to be 8 feet wide, 30 feet long, and 6 inches deep ($\frac{1}{2}$ foot). Concrete is sold by the cubic yard. To the nearest cubic yard, how many cubic yards of concrete are needed for the driveway?

31. A metal box has outside dimensions of 20 cm by 30 cm by 15 cm, and inside dimensions of 18 cm by 28 cm by 13 cm. Find the volume of the metal used to make the box.

32. When this rock was put in the beaker below, the water level rose 2 cm. Find the volume of the rock if the radius of the beaker is 5 cm.

33. A cylindrical pipe 10 in. long is $\frac{1}{4}$ in. thick. The inside radius of the pipe is 3 in. Find the volume of the metal used to make the pipe.

34. A 21 by 28 cm piece of paper can be rolled two ways to form a cylinder. Which of these two cylinders do you think will have the larger volume? Find the volume of each cylinder.

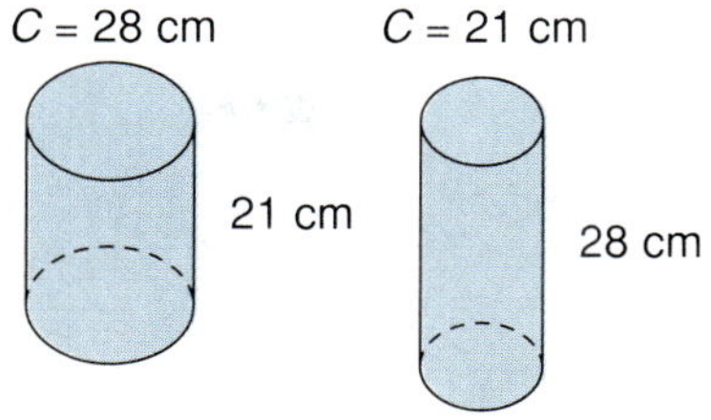

35. **Use Data** Which is greater, 1 cubic yard or 1 cubic meter? About how much greater? Use the table on page 274.

Critical Thinking Suppose each dimension of a box is changed as indicated below. In what way is the volume of the box changed? Try several examples for each case.

36. Doubled **37.** Tripled **38.** Quadrupled **39.** Halved

40. Write a general rule describing how the volume of a box is changed when its dimensions are multiplied by a number.

Choose a ________ Strategy

If you make 3 cuts in an orange, what is the maximum number of pieces you can make?

41. Suppose you make three parallel cuts through the orange. How many pieces will you get?

42. Consider other ways that you can make 3 cuts through an orange. How can you get the greatest number of pieces? How many pieces?

PROBLEM SOLVING STRATEGIES

- Choose an Operation
- Solve a Simpler Problem
- Use a Formula
- Write an Equation
- Make a Graph
- Draw a Diagram
- Make a Table

ALGEBRA

Volume of Pyramids and Cones

Build Understanding

ACTIVITY

A. Don't Spill the Beans
Materials: Pairs of containers in the shape of cylinders and cones (each pair having the same radius and height); bag of beans (lentils or split peas)
Groups: 3–6 students

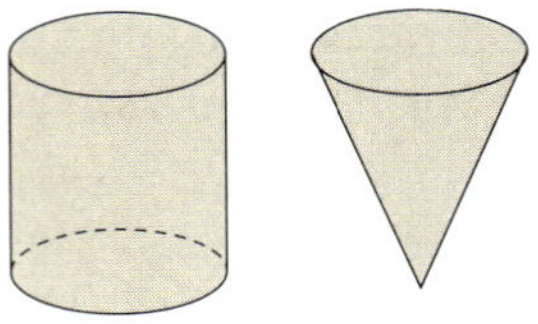

a. Place a cylinder and cone of the same radius and height on a table.

b. Fill the cone with beans and pour them into the cylinder. How many times can you do this before the cylinder overflows? Perform this experiment using different pairs of cones and cylinders with the same dimensions.

B. In the diagram at the right, the pyramid inside the cubical prism has its vertex at the center of the cube. The base of the pyramid is a face of the cube. Since the cube can be divided into 6 pyramids congruent to the one shown, the volume of each pyramid is one sixth the volume of the cube.

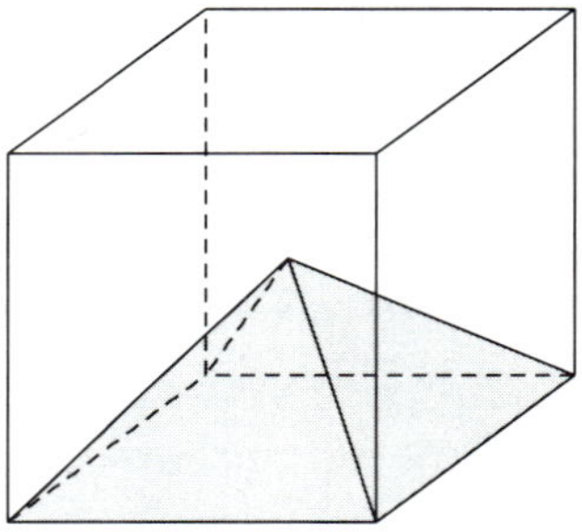

Let B represent the area of the base of the pyramid (and the base of the cube), and let h be the height of the pyramid. Then the height of the cube is $2h$. In terms of B and h, the volume of the cube is $2Bh$. So the volume of the pyramid must be $\frac{1}{6}(2Bh)$, or $\frac{1}{3}Bh$.

$V = \frac{1}{3}Bh$ The volume of any pyramid or cone is equal to one-third times the area of the base times the height.

Write About Math Both $V = \frac{1}{3}Bh$ and $V = \frac{1}{3}\pi r^2 h$ are formulas for the volume of a cone. Choose one that you prefer to use and write a paragraph explaining why.

Check Understanding

For another example, see Set E, pages 384–385.

Express the volume of each figure in terms of the indicated dimensions.

1.

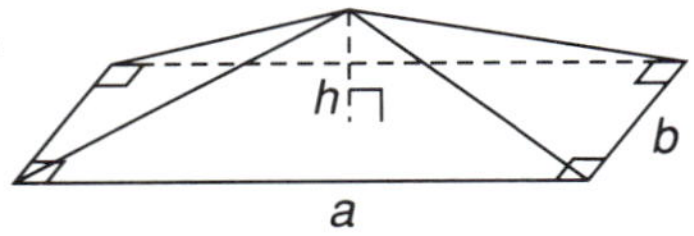

2.

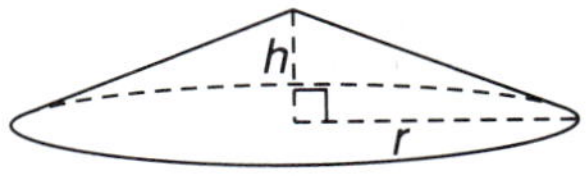

Practice

For More Practice, see Set E, pages 386–387.

Find the volume of each figure to the nearest hundredth. (Let $\pi = 3.14$.) Tell whether you use paper and pencil or a calculator.

3.

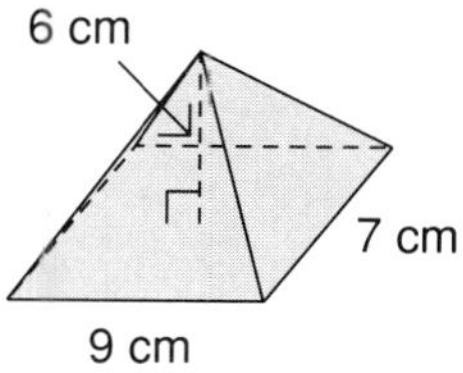

4.

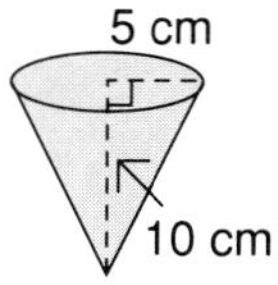

5.

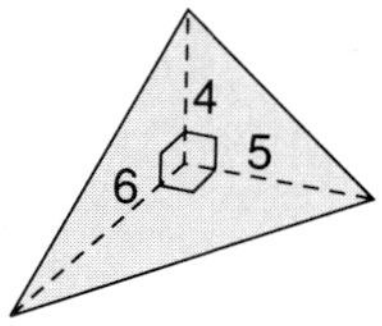

6.

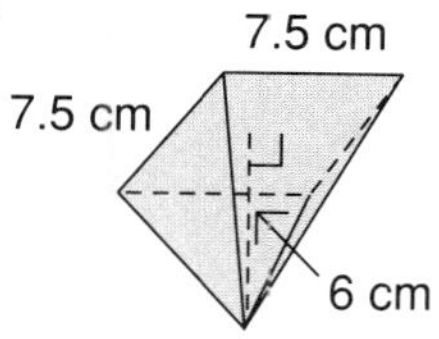

7.

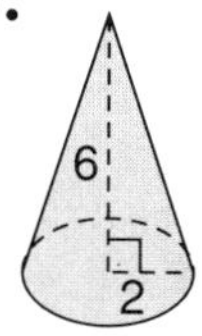

8.

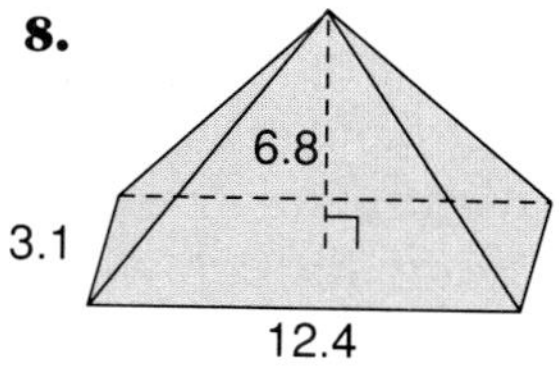

9.

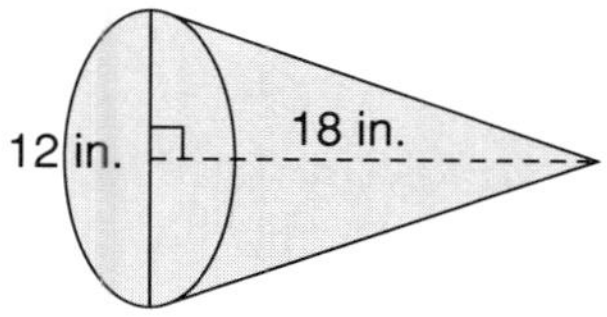

10.

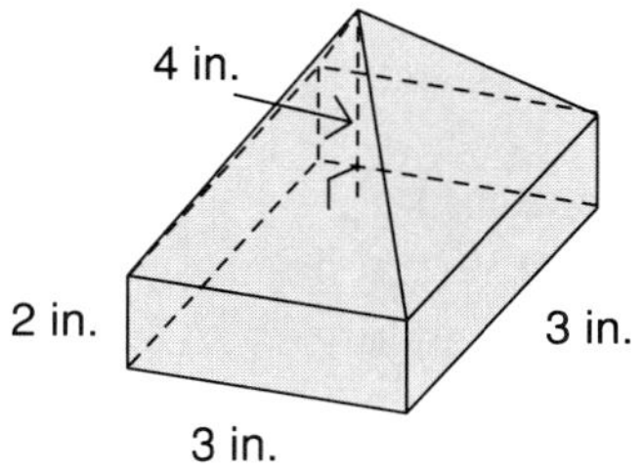

11.

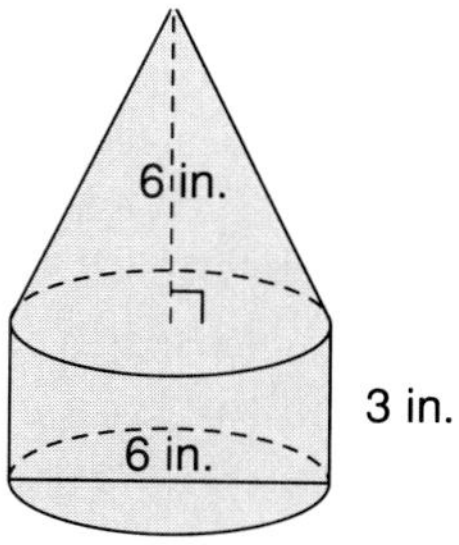

Answer each question.

12. If you double the radius and the height of a cone, by what factor do you increase the volume?

13. If you triple the radius and the height of a cone, by what factor do you increase the volume?

14. If you double the radius and triple the height of a cone, by what factor do you increase the volume?

15. If you double the height and triple the radius of a cone, by what factor do you increase the volume?

The cylinders at the right are congruent.

16. What is the volume of the two cones in Cylinder A?

17. What is the volume of the cone in Cylinder B?

18. Compare the volumes you found in Exercises 16 and 17. Explain the results.

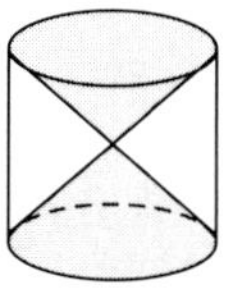

Cylinder A

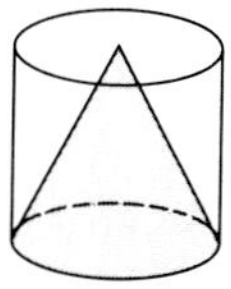

Cylinder B

Problem Solving

Solve each problem.

19. A crystal paperweight is shaped like a pyramid. Find the volume of the pyramid.

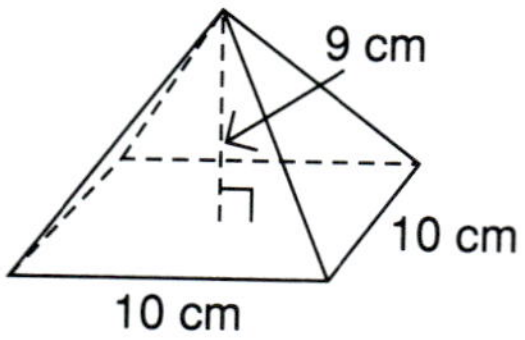

20. A glass vase shaped like a pyramid sits inside a cubical metal frame whose edge is 20 centimeters. What is the volume of the vase?

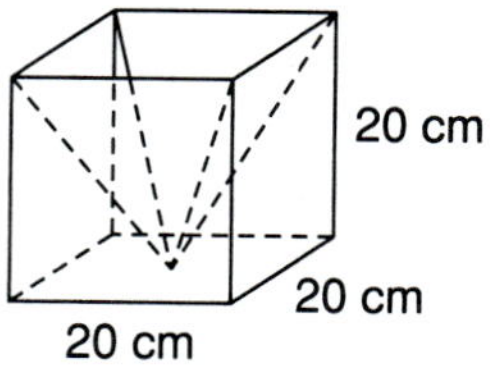

21. Grain is sometimes unloaded so that a cone is formed. Find the volume of the grain shown in the diagram below.

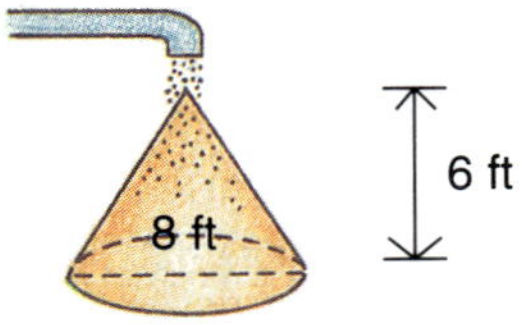

22. Find the volume of the coal hopper shown below.

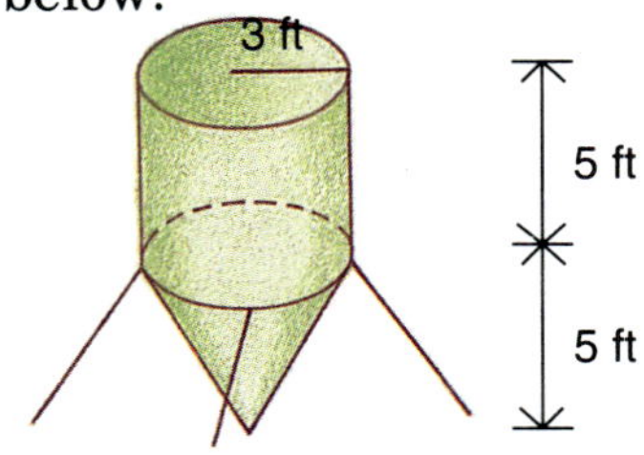

23. A pyramid fits tightly in a cube whose edge is 8 in., as shown. Find the volume of the region between the cube and the pyramid.

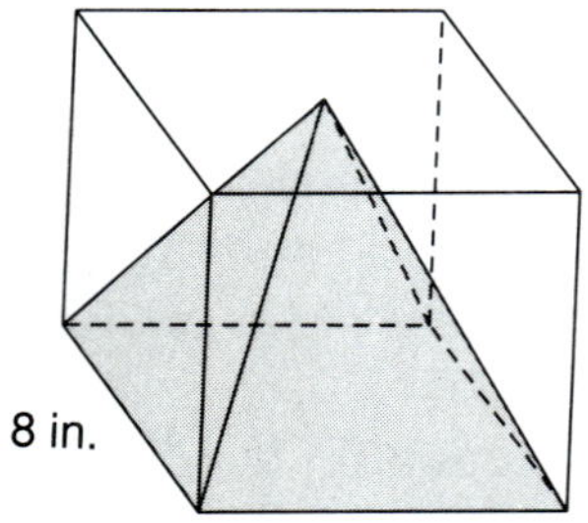

24. Find the ratio of the volume of the hourglass shape to the volume of the cylinder.

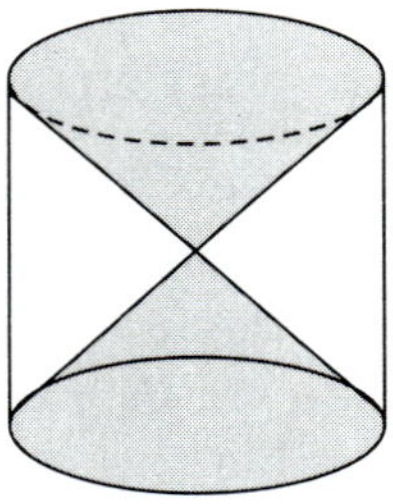

25. If you rotate this 3-4-5 right triangle about leg AB or leg AC, a cone will be formed. Which of these two cones do you think will have the greater volume? Find the volume of each cone.

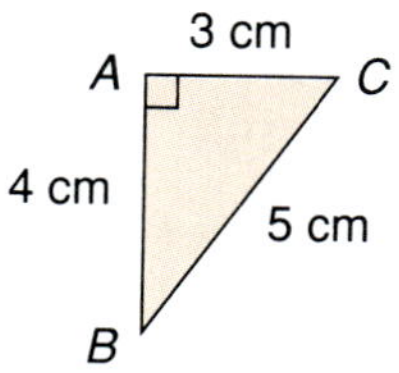

26. A cylinder and a cone have the same volume. If the base of the cone is congruent to the base of the cylinder, what is the ratio of the height of the cone to the height of the cylinder?

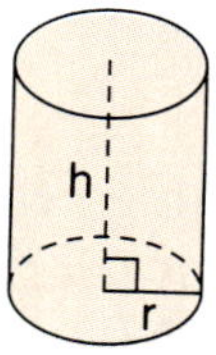

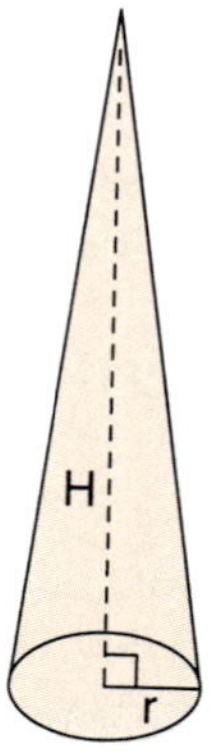

Midchapter ________ Checkup

A window consists of a rectangle and a semicircle, as shown. (Use $\pi = \frac{22}{7}$ or $\pi = 3.14$.)

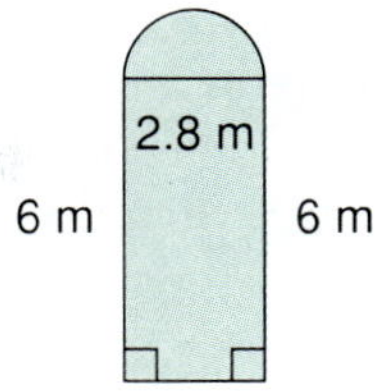

1. Find the perimeter of the window.

2. Find the area of the window.

Find the perimeter and area of each shape.

3.

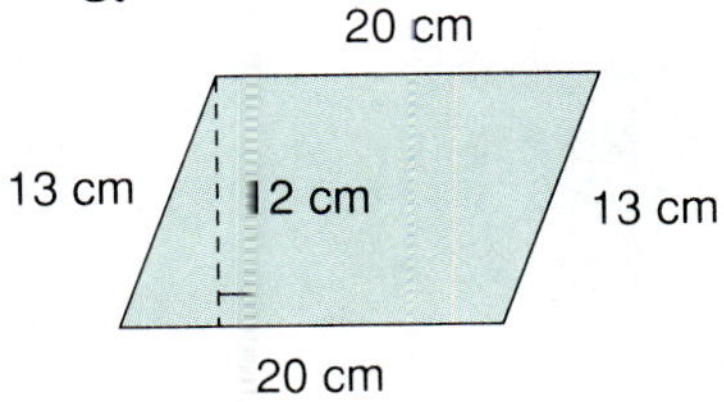

4.

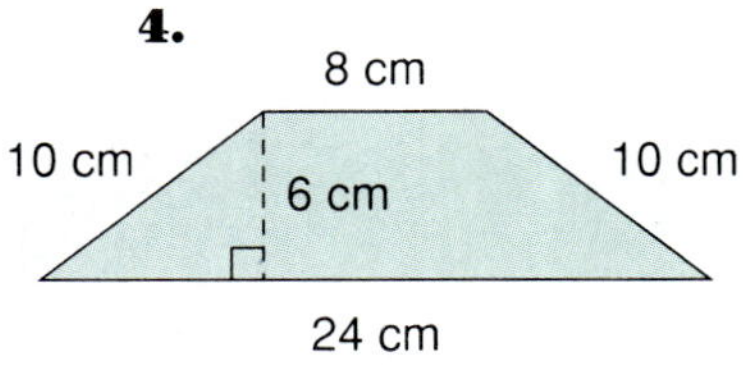

5.

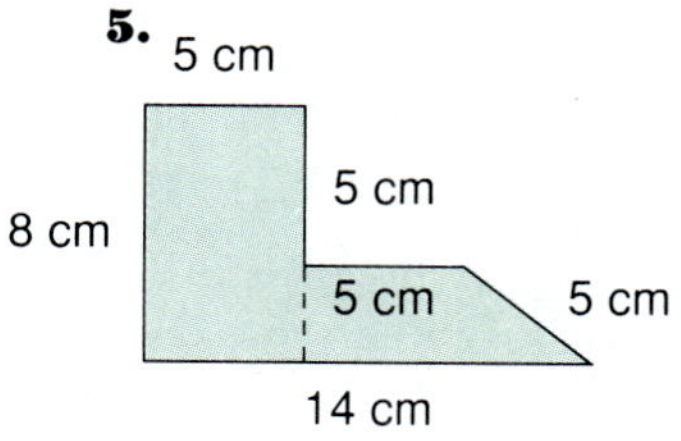

Find the volume of each solid. (Use $\pi = 3.14$.)

6.

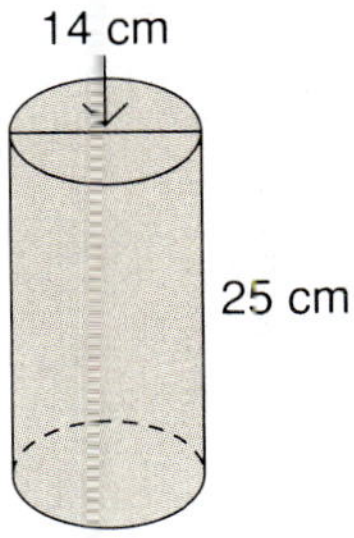

7.

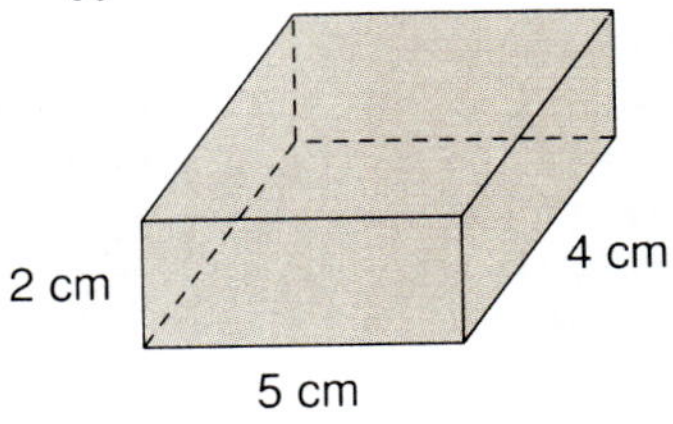

8.

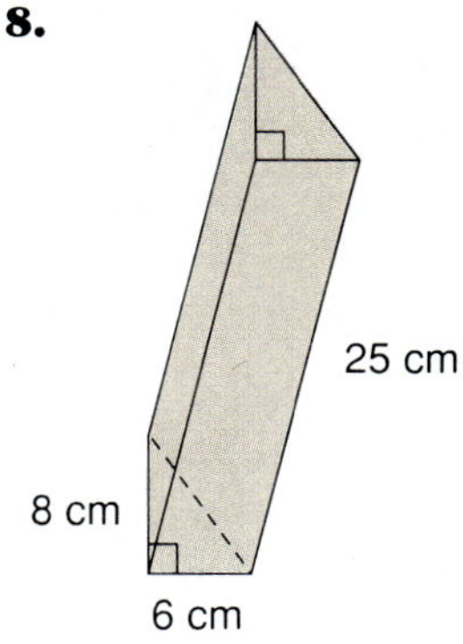

9.

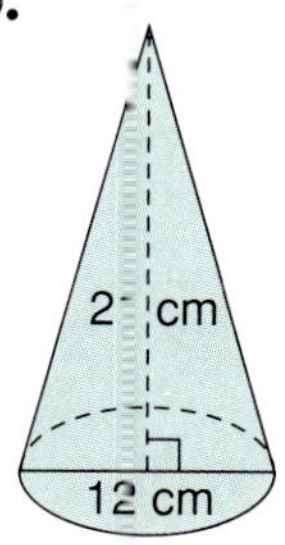

10.

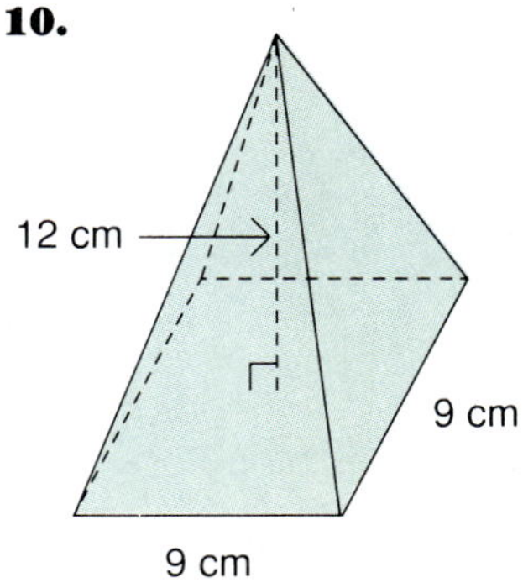

11.

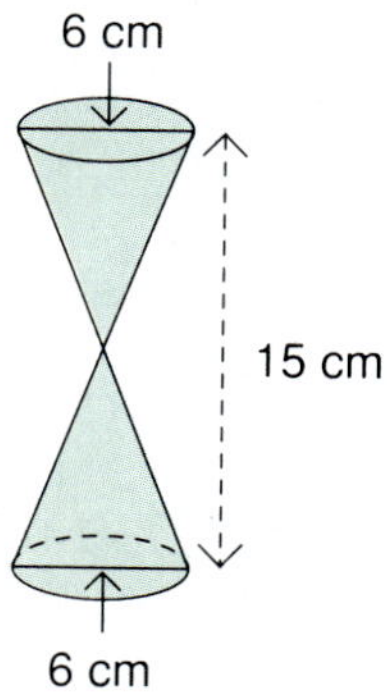

Real-Life Decision Making

Suppose you want to buy carpet for the living room area in your home. You measured the room and made the sketch shown at the right.

At most stores carpeting is sold by the yard in rolls that are 12 feet wide. Some stores also sell one-square-foot carpet tiles.

The carpeting you want to buy costs $22.50 a square yard. You have also found some carpet tiles that cost $1.95 a square foot.

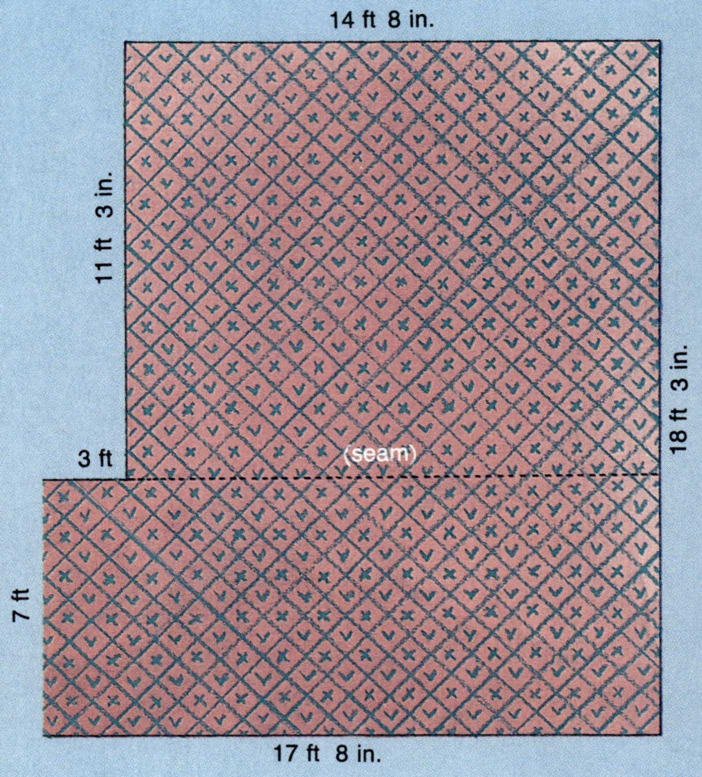

1. How much carpet do you need if you buy the carpet tiles? How much will it cost?

2. If the carpet is laid so that it has only one seam as shown in the drawing, how much carpeting do you need to buy if you buy it by the roll? How much will it cost?

3. What factors other than cost should you consider when deciding which carpet to buy?

4. Which carpet would you buy? Explain your decision.

MATH laugh

What are protractors?

People who vote yes for better tractors!

Explore with a Computer

Use the *Geometry Workshop Project* for this activity.

A modern architect is designing a building on an irregular lot of land. She wants to make the building the same shape as the lot. Think about how she might plan her building.

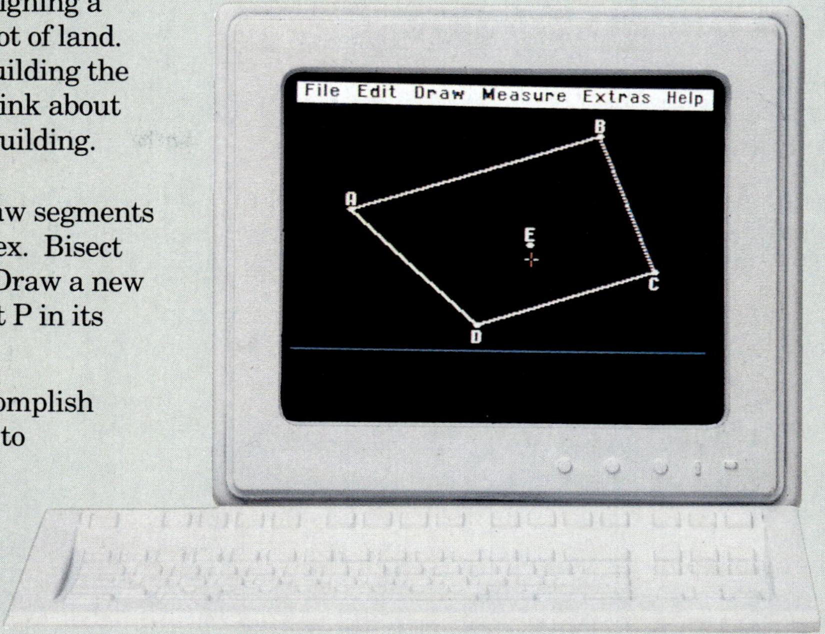

1. At the computer, draw segments from point E to each vertex. Bisect each of these segments. Draw a new quadrilateral with a point P in its interior.

2. Did this method accomplish what the architect wants to do? Draw a new quadrilateral with a point E in its interior. Repeat the steps in 1. Will this method work for any quadrilateral and any point E?

Number-Sense Project

Look back at pages 340–341.

Assume Ayers Rock is a perfect cylinder. Use the dimensions given to find each answer to the nearest tenth.

1. What is the radius?

2. What is the area of the base?

3. What is its volume? Remember to change the height to miles.

ALGEBRA

Use a Formula

Build Understanding

An Inuit igloo is in the shape of a hemisphere. Suppose the inside of the igloo is 12 ft in diameter. Find the volume of the inside living space.

In the last lesson you saw that volumes of different figures can be compared. The volume of a hemisphere is $\frac{2}{3}$ the volume of the smallest cylinder that contains it. The cylinder's height and the radius of its base both equal the radius of the hemisphere. The volume of the cylinder is:

$$V = \pi r^2 h$$
$$= \pi r^2(r) \quad \text{In this cylinder, } h = r.$$
$$= \pi r^3.$$

The hemisphere's volume is $V = \frac{2}{3}\pi r^3$.

Understand QUESTION What is the volume of the hemisphere?

FACTS The radius of the hemisphere is 6 ft. The formula for the volume of a hemisphere is $V = \frac{2}{3}\pi r^3$.

KEY IDEA You have enough information to use the volume formula.

Plan and Solve STRATEGY Use the formula for the volume of a hemisphere. Substitute the known facts (data) into the formula. Then evaluate the expression to find the volume.

$$V = \frac{2}{3}\pi r^3$$
$$V \approx \frac{2}{3}(3.14)(6)^3$$
$$= \frac{2}{3}(3.14)(216) = 452.16$$

ANSWER The volume of the living space is about 452.16 cu ft.

PROBLEM SOLVING GUIDE

Understand
QUESTION
FACTS
KEY IDEA

Plan and Solve
STRATEGY
ANSWER

Look Back
SENSIBLE ANSWER
ALTERNATE APPROACH

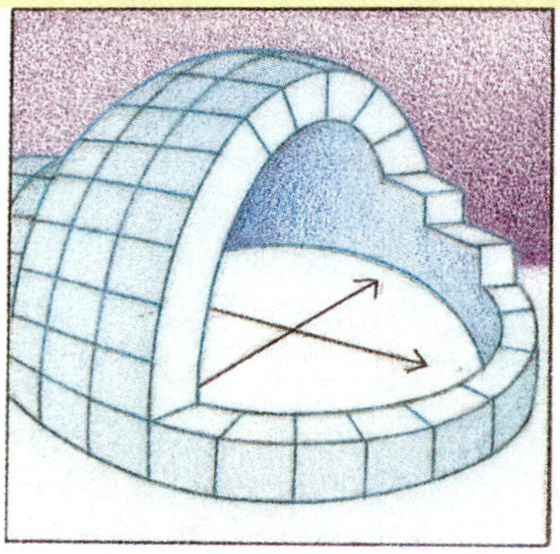

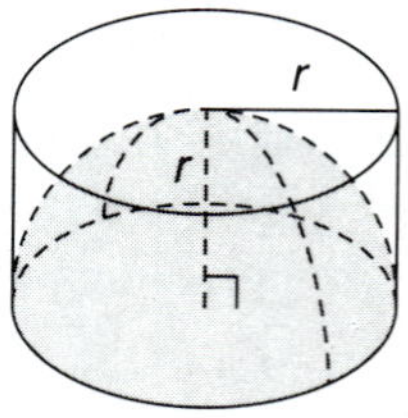

Look Back SENSIBLE ANSWER A cylinder with a base area of πr^2 and height r has a volume of πr^3, or about 3×6^3. The volume of the hemisphere is $\frac{2}{3}$ this volume. $\frac{2}{3} \times 3 \times 6^3 = 432$. The answer is sensible.

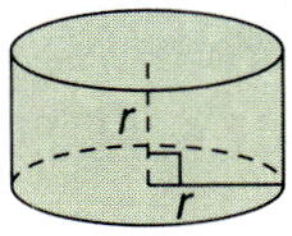

Talk About Math Assume each block of ice is 1.5 ft thick. Devise a strategy to find the volume of ice used to construct the igloo. Carry out your plan, and compute this volume.

Check Understanding

Write the formula.

1. A sphere has twice the volume of a hemisphere. Write a formula for the volume of a sphere.

Use the formula to find the volume of a sphere with the given radius or diameter.

2. $r = 3$ ft
3. $d = 18$ in.
4. $r = 3.5$ cm
5. $d = 14.8$ m

Practice

Use a formula to solve each problem.

6. **Calculator** Mimas, a satellite of Saturn, has a diameter of 390 km. Find its volume.

7. A sphere fits tightly in a cube with edges of 10 cm in length. Find the volume of the sphere.

8. A balloon with a diameter of 2.5 meters has 7 times the volume of a smaller balloon. Find the volume of the smaller balloon.

9. A tennis ball can holds three tennis balls. Find the ratio of the volume of the three balls to the volume of the can.

10. **Critical Thinking** Suppose the radius of a pink grapefruit is twice that of a white grapefruit, and the pink grapefruit costs seven times as much. Which one is the better buy?

11. Find the relationship, first discovered by Archimedes, among the volumes of a sphere, a cylinder, and a cone with equal radii and heights. (The height of the cone and cylinder is twice the radius.)

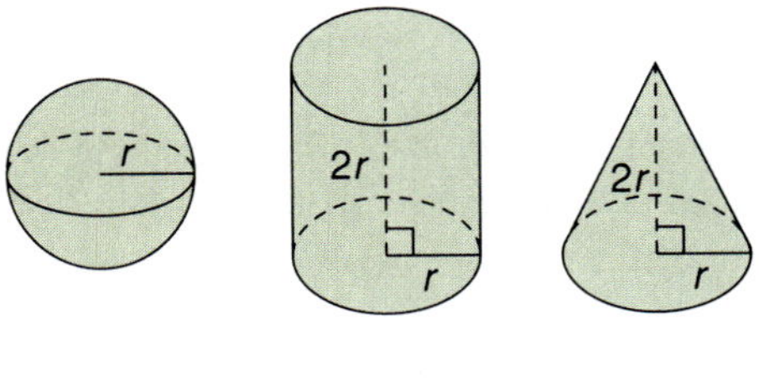

ALGEBRA

Surface Area of Prisms

Build Understanding

A. Prism Pastimes
Materials: 12 unit cubes
Groups: Small teams

a. These 12 cubes are arranged so that the surface area of the resulting figure is 36 square units.

b. Two other possible models are shown below. What other values are possible for the surface areas of figures constructed from these 12 cubes?

Area of a square	$A = s^2$
Area of a rectangle	$A = \ell w$
Area of a triangle	$A = \frac{1}{2} bh$

c. What figure made from the 12 cubes will have the largest possible surface area?

B. Each base of this prism is a regular hexagon with an area of 10.4 cm^2. Find the surface area.

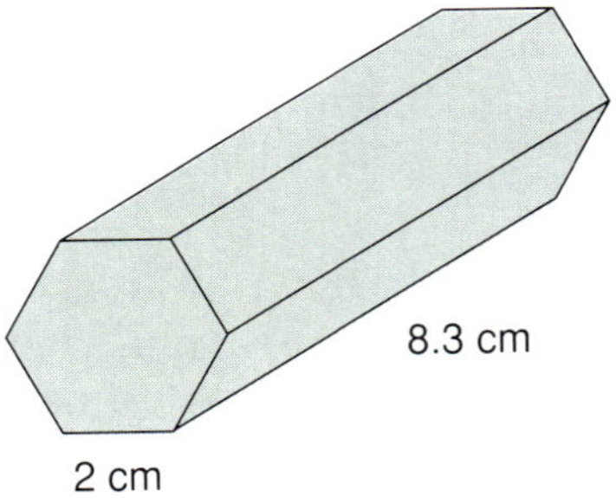

Each of the six rectangular faces has an area of 2×8.3, or 16.6 cm^2.

$$\text{Surface area} = \text{Area of two bases} + \text{Area of all the rectangular faces}$$
$$= 2(10.4) + 6(2 \times 8.3)$$
$$= 20.8 + 99.6$$
$$= 120.4$$

The surface area of the hexagonal prism is 120.4 cm^2.

■ **Talk About Math** How many of the figures that you made in Example A were prisms? What was the surface area of each one? Develop a formula for the surface area of a rectangular prism.

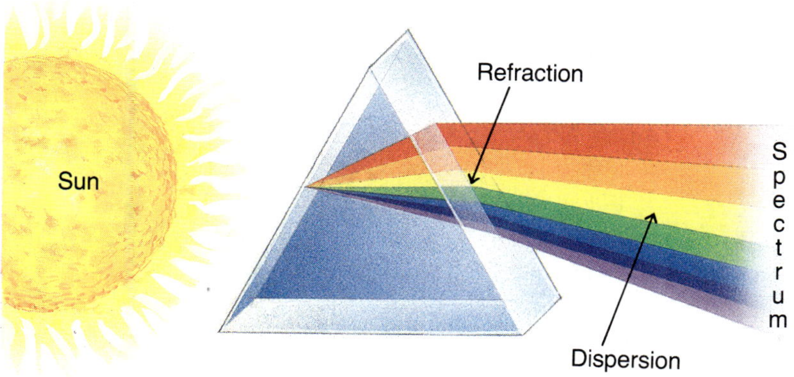

When sunlight passes through a glass prism, refraction occurs and disperses the light into a spectrum of seven different colors.

Check Understanding

For another example, see Set F, pages 384–385.

A pattern for a rectangular prism with dimensions ℓ, w, and h is shown.

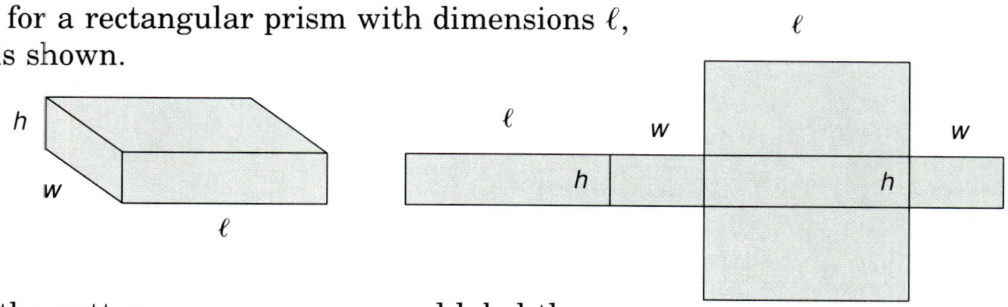

1. Copy the pattern on your paper, and label those sides not already labeled as ℓ, w, or h.

Use the formula $A = 2h\ell + 2hw + 2\ell w$ to compute the surface area for the rectangular prisms with the given measures.

2. $\ell = 5$ m, $w = 3$ m, $h = 2$ m

3. $\ell = 2.3$ in., $w = 1.8$ in., $h = 0.9$ in.

4. Draw a pattern for the prism at the right, and find its surface area.

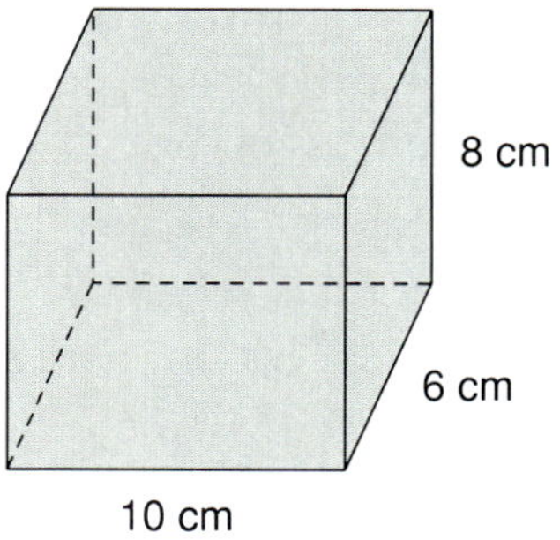

Use the triangular prism at the right for Exercises 5–8.

5. Find the area of each triangular base.

6. Find the area of the rectangular base on the bottom.

7. Find the area of each of the other two rectangular faces.

8. Find the surface area.

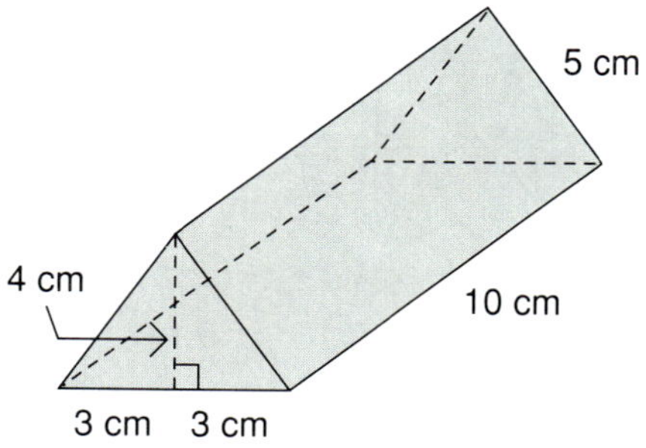

Practice

For More Practice, see Set F, pages 386–387.

The cube is made up of 27 unit cubes. Answer each question.

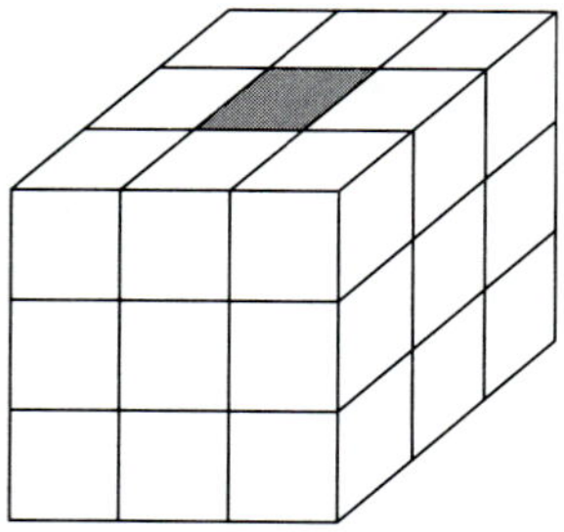

9. What is the surface area of the cube?

10. If the shaded cube and the ones below it are removed, what is the surface area of the remaining solid?

Which one of the cubes can you remove and have the surface area

11. remain unchanged? **12.** increase by 2? **13.** increase by 4?

Find each answer.

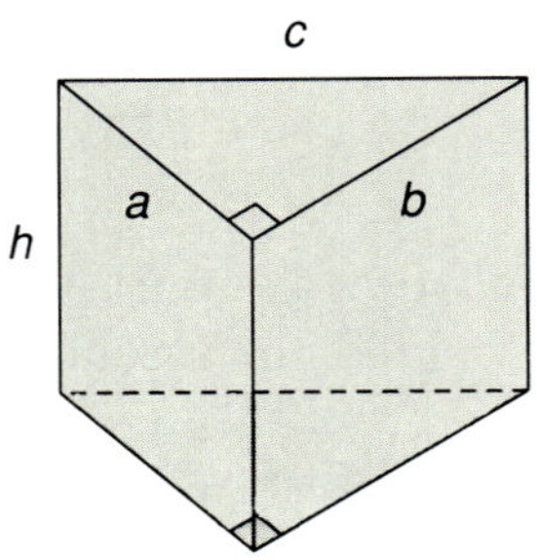

14. Draw a pattern for this triangular prism, and label the length of each segment *a*, *b*, *c*, or *h*.

15. Write a formula for the surface area of a right triangle prism with dimensions *a*, *b*, *c*, and *h*.

Use the formula from Problem 15 to help you find the surface area with the given measures. **Remember** to label units in your answers.

16. $a = 6$ ft, $b = 8$ ft, $c = 10$ ft, $h = 2$ ft

17. $a = 11.5$ mm, $b = 27.6$ mm, $c = 29.9$ mm, $h = 6.9$ mm

Mixed Practice Find the volume and surface area of each figure.

18.

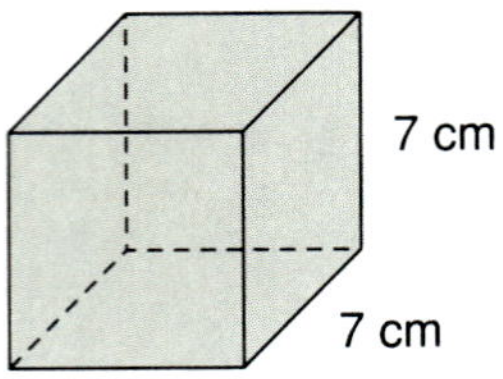

19.

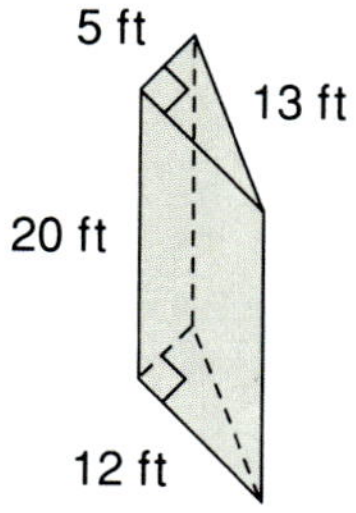

20.

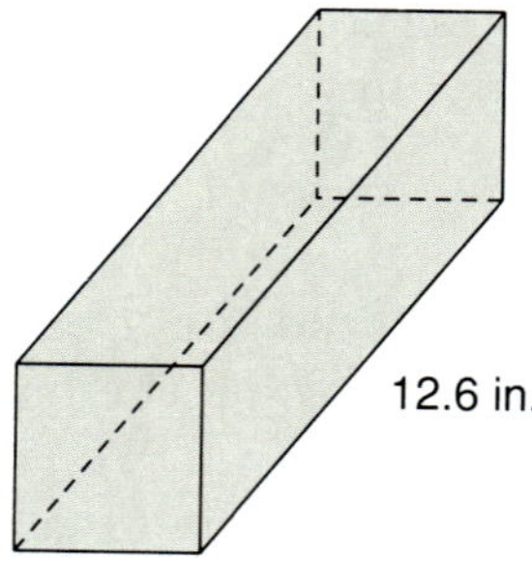

Problem Solving

Solve each problem.

21. What is the largest possible surface area of a solid constructed from n 1-in. cubes?

The surface area of a box is 144 cm^2. If each dimension of the box is changed as indicated, what is the surface area of the new box?

22. Doubled

23. Tripled

24. Halved

Estimation Estimate to solve Problems 25–27.

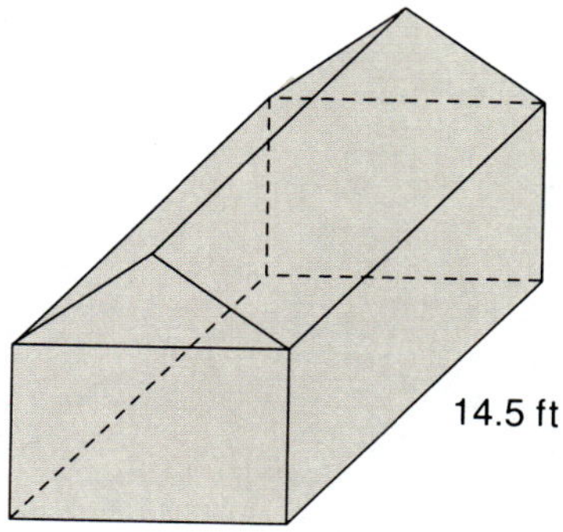

25. If one pint of paint covers 90 sq ft, estimate the amount of paint needed to paint the sides of the building shown at the right.

26. If one gallon of paint costs $12.99, and paint is sold by the gallon, estimate the cost of painting the building.

27. Estimate the number of pints of paint needed to paint each end of the building; each side of the building.

Reading **Math**

Diagrams and Pictures Dashed lines are often used in drawings to indicate hidden lines. Use the drawing at the right to answer the following.

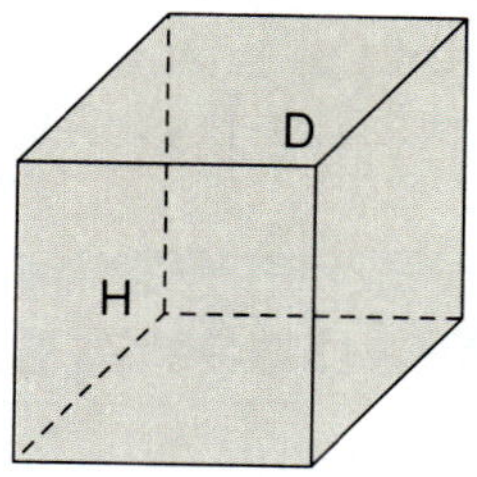

1. Name 3 edges that cannot be seen.

2. Name 3 faces that cannot be seen.

3. Name the face opposite face $ABCD$.

4. Name 2 faces that do not intersect.

Trace the diagram. Draw and name the following.

5. 2 diagonals of face $DCGF$

6. 4 diagonals of the cube

Surface Area of Pyramids

Build Understanding

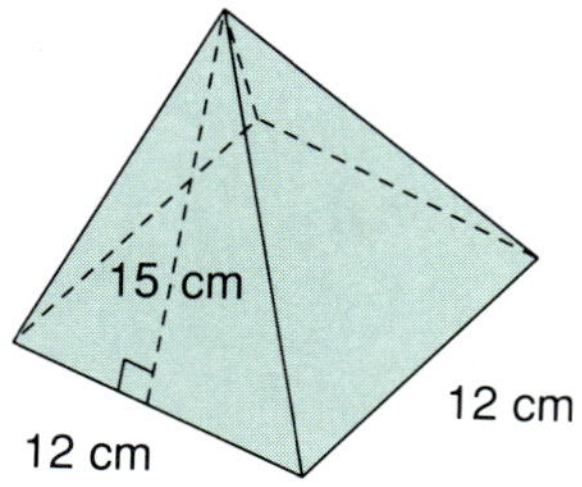

Charisse is making a model of an Egyptian pyramid. The pyramid has a 12-centimeter square base and the height of each triangular side is 15 centimeters. How much poster board does she need to make the model?

To find the amount of poster board needed, Charisse needs to find the surface area of the model. Imagine that the pyramid is opened up and flattened out, that is, a pattern is drawn for it.

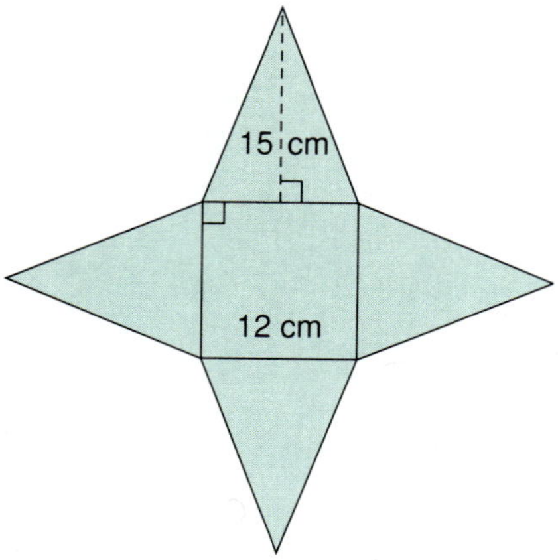

Area of a triangle: $A = \frac{1}{2}bh$

Area of a square: $A = s^2$

The sides of the pyramid, called its ***lateral faces,*** are triangles. The height of each triangular face, or the ***slant height*** of the pyramid, is 15 centimeters. The base is a square with sides of 12 centimeters.

$A = \frac{1}{2}bh = \frac{1}{2}(12)(15) = 90$ The area of each triangular face is 90 cm^2.

$A = s^2 = 12^2 = 144$ The area of the square base is 144 cm^2.

The ***surface area of a pyramid*** is the sum of the areas of all its faces.

$A = 4(90) + 144 = 504$

Charisse needs 504 cm^2 of poster board.

■ **Talk About Math** This is a ***regular pyramid*** since all of its lateral faces are congruent and its base is a regular polygon. Explain why $A = \frac{1}{2}ps + B$ represents the surface area of a regular pyramid where s is the slant height, p is the perimeter of the base, and B is the area of the base.

Check Understanding

For another example, see Set G, pages 384–385.

Answer each question about the pyramid.

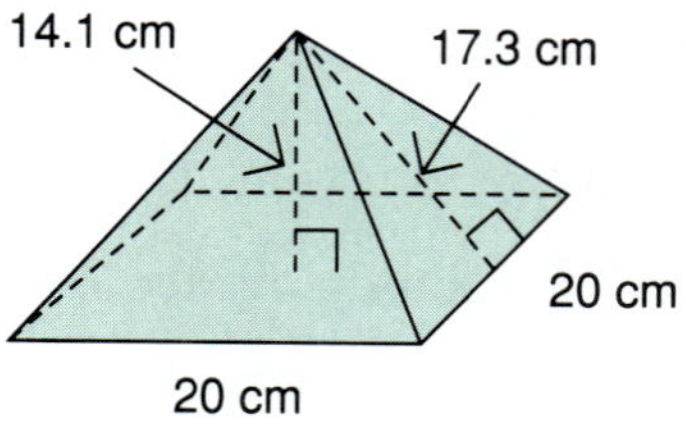

1. What is the area of one triangular face?

2. What is the area of the base?

3. What is the surface area of the pyramid?

Practice

For More Practice, see Set G, pages 386–387.

Find each answer.

4. Find the surface area of the model of a regular square pyramid with a base edge of 1.5 cm and a slant height of 9 cm.

5. Find the surface area of the rectangular pyramid in Figure 1.

6. Draw a pattern for the regular square pyramid in Figure 2. Label the lengths of the appropriate edges a or b.

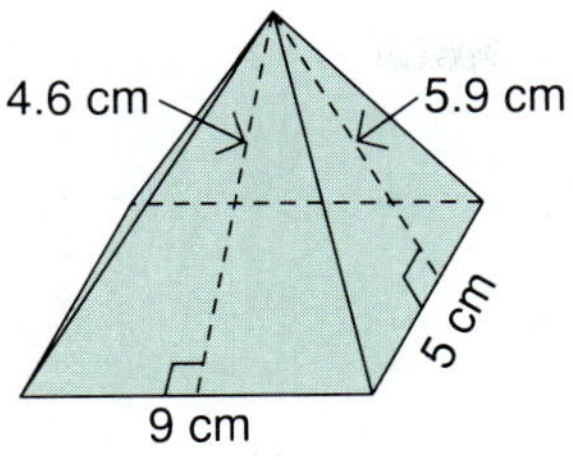

Figure 1

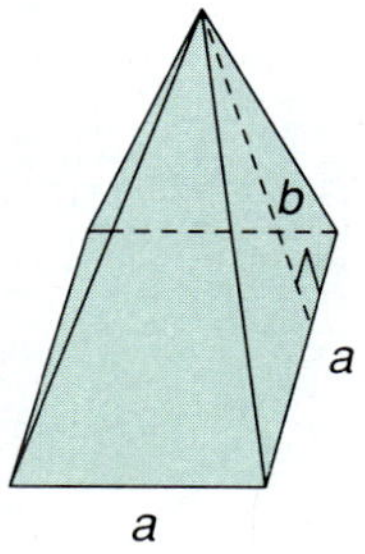

Figure 2

7. Express the surface area of Figure 2 in terms of a and b.

8. If you place two pyramids together base to base, an octahedron is formed. See Figure 3. Express the surface area of the octahedron in terms of a and b.

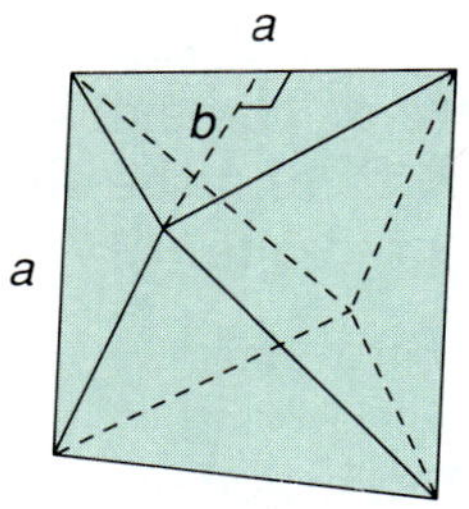

Figure 3

9. In Figure 2, find the surface area if a = 12 in. and b = 8 in.

10. In Figure 3, find the surface area if a = 30 mm and b = 20 mm.

Find the surface area of each pyramid. **Remember** to label the units in your answer.

11. Rectangular pyramid

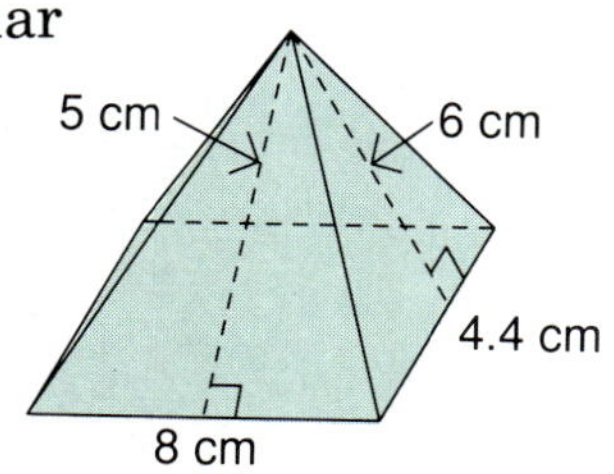

12. Regular square pyramid

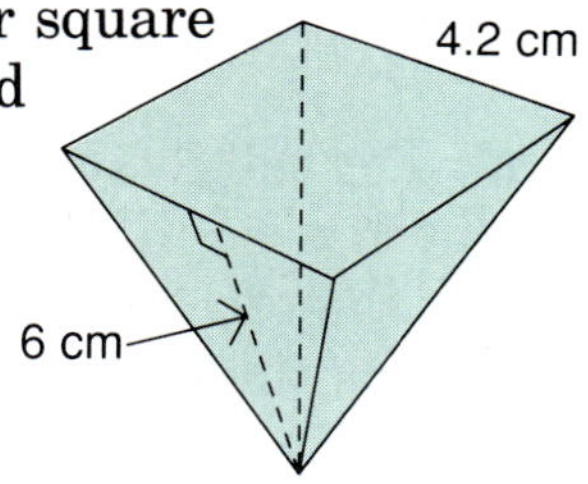

Mixed Practice Find the surface area and the volume of each pyramid. Tell whether you use paper and pencil or a calculator.

13. Square pyramid

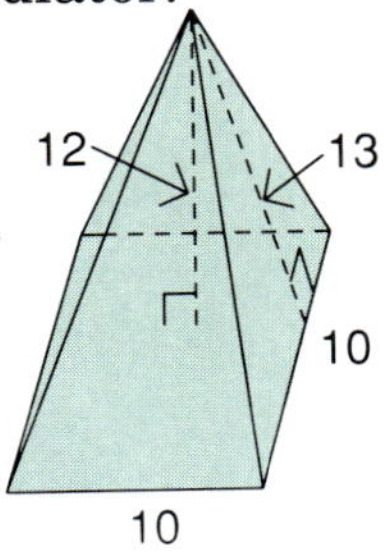

14. Rectangular pyramid

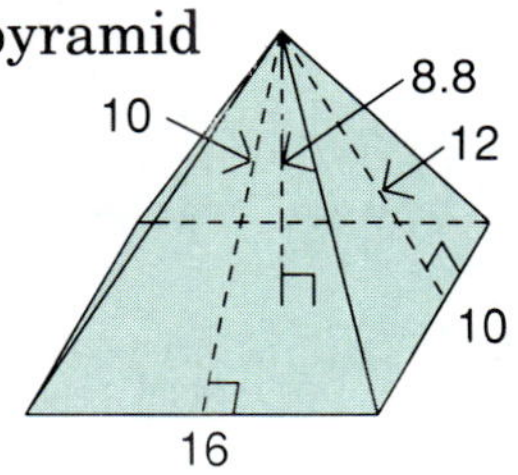

Problem Solving

Egyptian pyramids have four triangular sides that meet in a point at the top; New World "pyramids" are four-sided, flat-topped polyhedra.

The Great Pyramid in Egypt is a regular square pyramid. The sides of the base are 755 ft, the height is 481 ft, and the slant height is 611 ft. Find each indicated quantity for this pyramid.

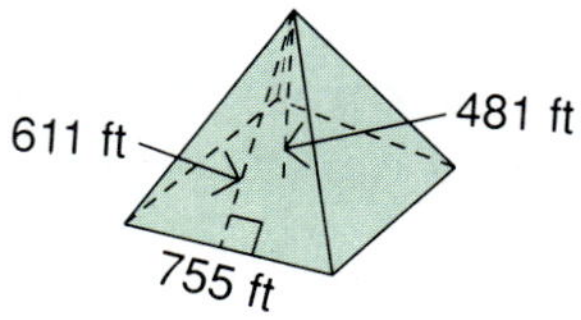

15. Volume

16. Surface area

17. **Estimation** Estimate the surface area of this cone by tightly fitting it inside a regular square pyramid.

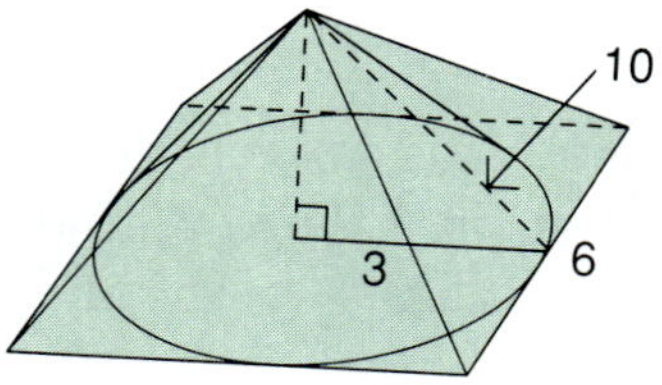

18. A courthouse steeple in the shape of a square pyramid has base sides of 12 feet, a height of 8 feet, and a slant height of 10 feet. How much copper sheeting is needed to cover the steeple roof?

Choose a _______ Strategy

Whoosh! For the Skateboard Derby the Wheelies built a hemispherical skateboard bowl 20 feet in diameter. They mounted it in a square frame. What is the total surface area of the frame?

19. Draw a diagram.

20. The formula for the surface area of a sphere is $4\pi r^2$. What is the surface area of the skateboard bowl?

21. What is the length of one side of the square frame?

22. What is the surface area of the frame?

PROBLEM SOLVING STRATEGIES

- Choose an Operation
- Solve a Simpler Problem
- Use a Formula
- Write an Equation
- Make a Graph
- Draw a Diagram
- Make a Table

The base of a pyramid may be any polygon. The pyramids shown below are regular pyramids because their bases are regular polygons and their lateral faces are congruent.

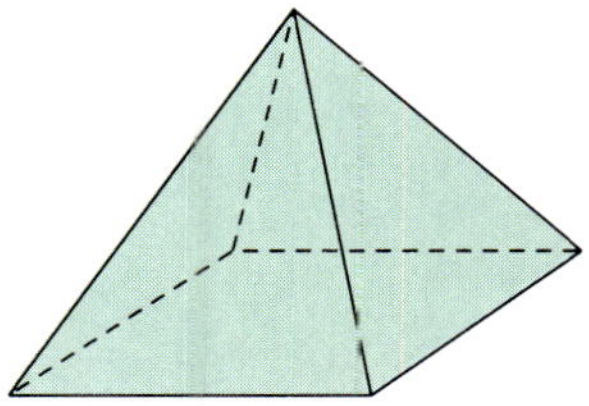

Square Pyramid

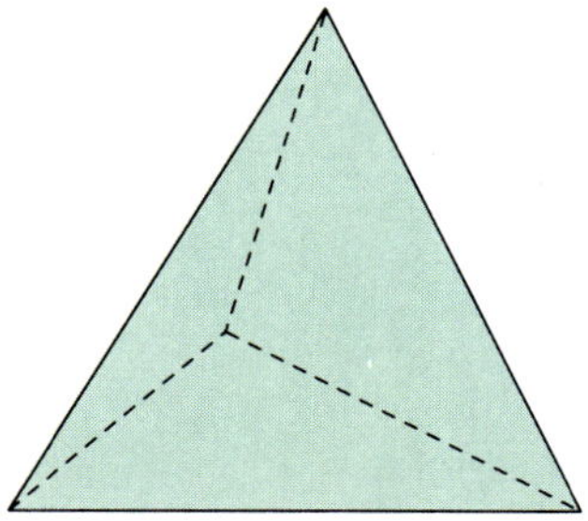

Triangular Pyramid

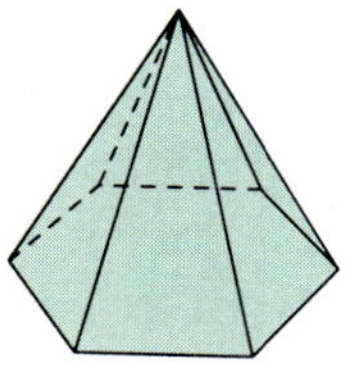

Hexagonal Pyramid

Trace each shape below on a separate sheet of paper. Using the shape as a base, construct a 3-dimensional model of each of the pyramids above. Use any convenient height for the triangular faces. You may want to add tabs for gluing, as shown on the pattern at the right.

23.

Square

24.

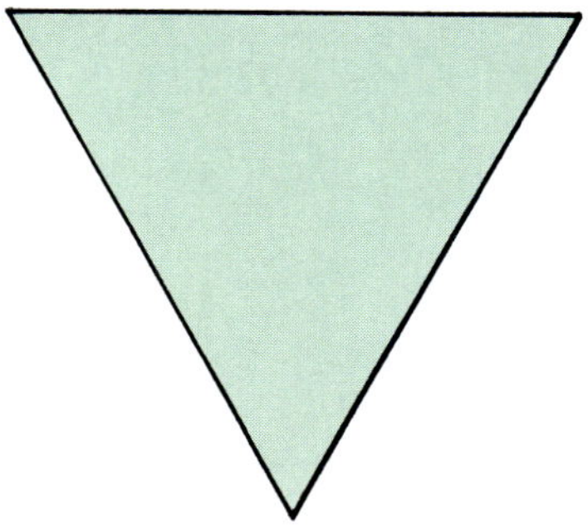

Equilateral Triangle

25.

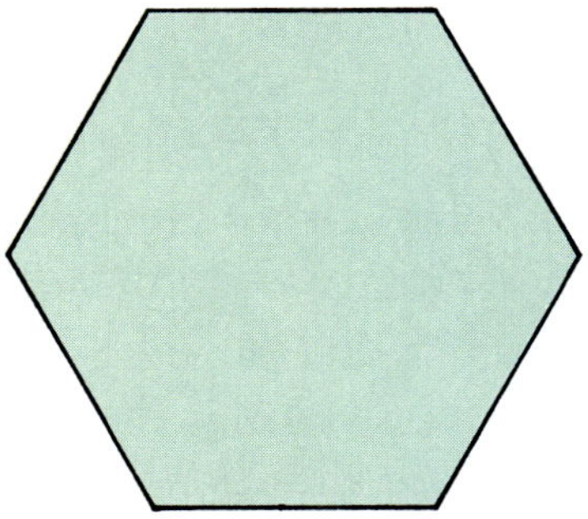

Regular Hexagon

26. Measure the dimensions of your models and calculate the surface area.

27. Calculate the volume of your pyramids.

28. How is the number of lateral faces of a pyramid related to the number of sides of the base?

29. How is the number of edges in a pyramid related to the number of sides of the base?

ALGEBRA

Surface Area of Cylinders

Build Understanding

Jody Gotkovsky is making a cylindrical scratching post for her Siamese cat, Coco. She wants to cover the post with carpet. How much carpet will she need to cover the entire post? If carpeting costs $7.95 per square yard, how much will Jody spend on carpeting? (1,296 sq in. = 1 sq yd)

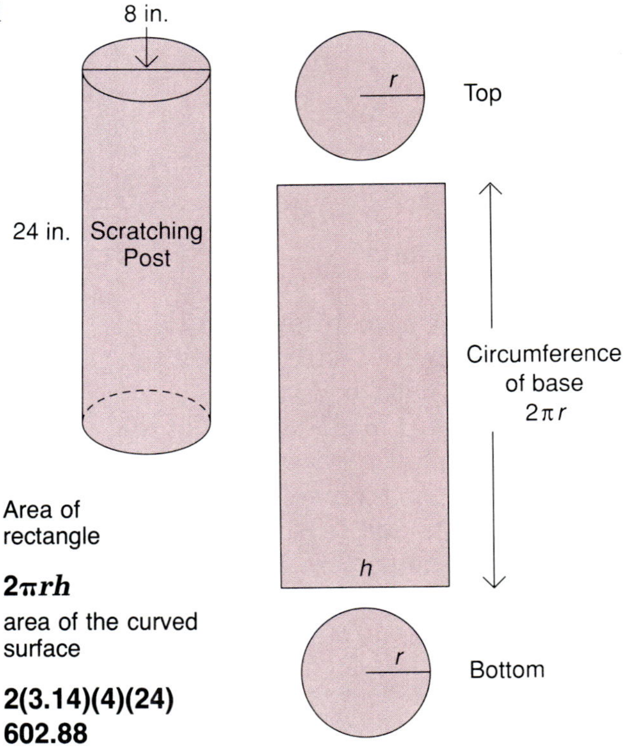

To find how much carpet Jody will need, you must find the surface area of the cylinder.

A pattern for this cylinder consists of two circles and a rectangle.

Surface area of a cylinder	=	Area of top	+	Area of bottom	+	Area of rectangle
A	=	πr^2	+	πr^2	+	$2\pi rh$
		area of the bases				area of the curved surface

$$\begin{aligned} A &= (3.14)(4^2) + (3.14)(4^2) + 2(3.14)(4)(24) \\ &= 50.24 + 50.24 + 602.88 \\ &= 703.36 \text{ sq in.} \end{aligned}$$

The total surface area of the cylindrical scratching post is 703.36 sq in.

Since 1,296 sq in. = 1 sq yd, you can divide the surface area of 703.36 sq in. by 1,296 sq in. to find the number of square yards of carpet Jody needs.

703.36 ÷ 1,296 = 0.54

Jody needs a little more than $\frac{1}{2}$ sq yd of carpet, not counting waste. She will spend at least $\left(\frac{1}{2}\right)$($7.95), or a little more than $4.00, on carpeting.

Talk About Math Explain why the formulas for the surface area of a cylinder and a prism can both be given by $A = ph + 2B$, where h is the height, p is the perimeter (circumference) of a base, and B is the area of a base.

Check Understanding

For another example, see Set H, pages 384–385.

Find the surface area of each cylinder.

1. r = 7 in. and h = 20 in.

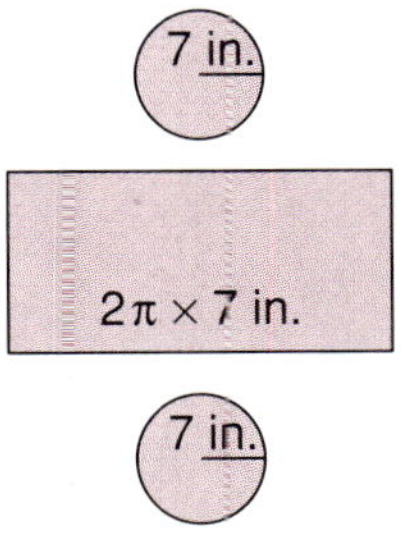

2.

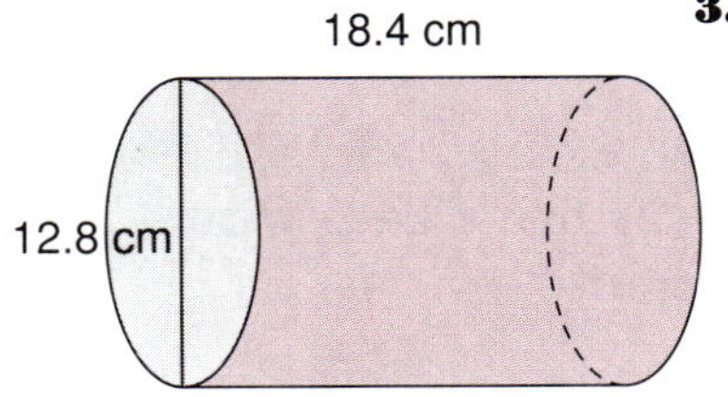

3.

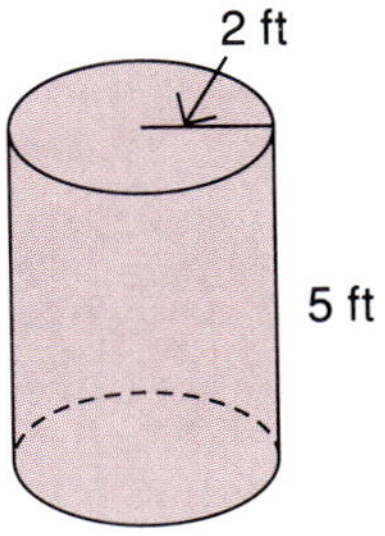

4. **Calculator** Write a calculator sequence for calculating the surface area of a cylinder.

If you rotate this 12 by 18 rectangle about either side AB or side AC, a cylinder will be formed.

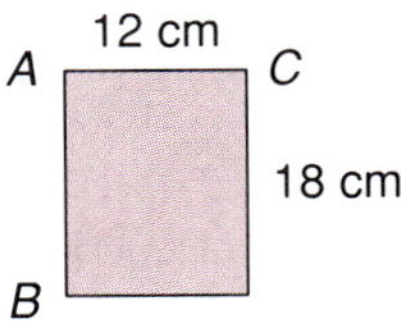

5. Which of these two cylinders do you think will have the greater surface area?

6. Find the ratio between the total surface areas of the cylinders.

Practice

For More Practice, see Set H, pages 386–387.

Find the surface area. Tell whether you use paper and pencil or a calculator. **Remember** to label units in your answers.

7.

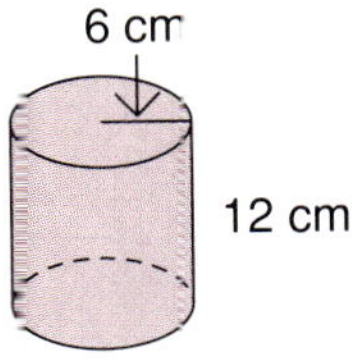

8.

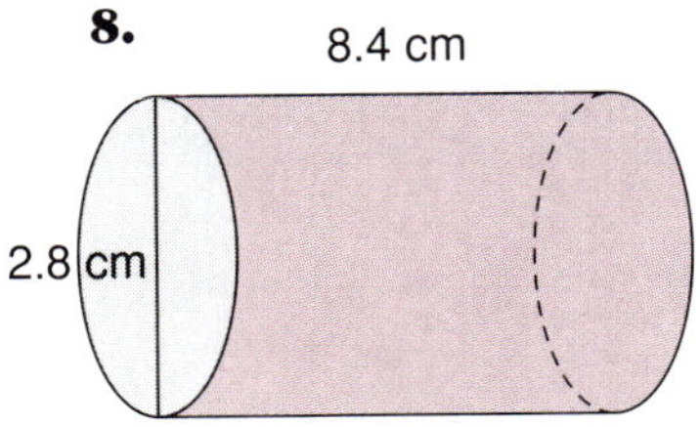

9.

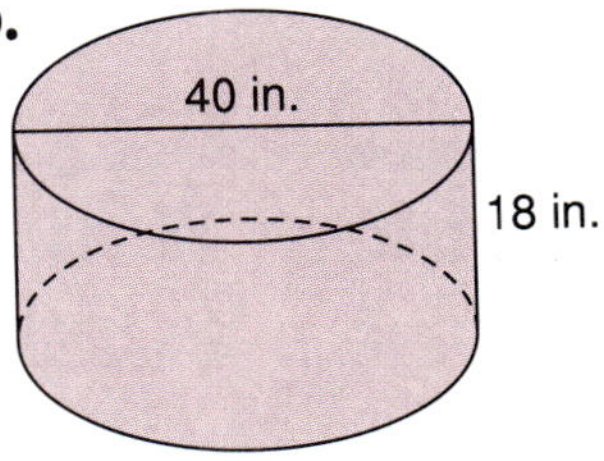

10. **Calculator** If the surface area of the cylinder at the right is 704 square feet, what is its height? Use $\pi = \frac{22}{7}$.

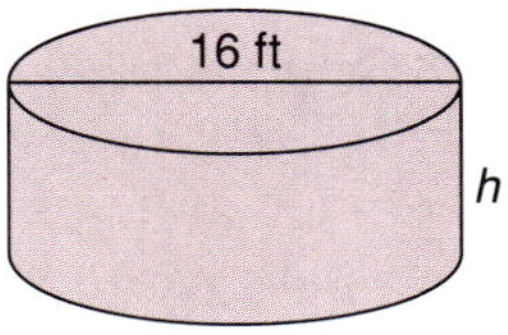

Mixed Practice Find the surface area and the volume of each cylinder.

11. 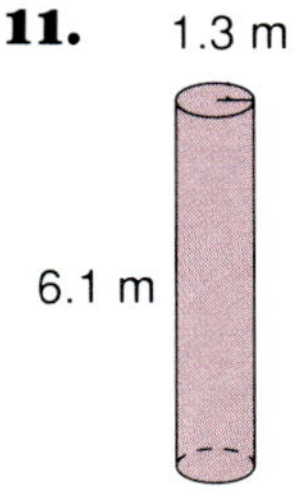

12. 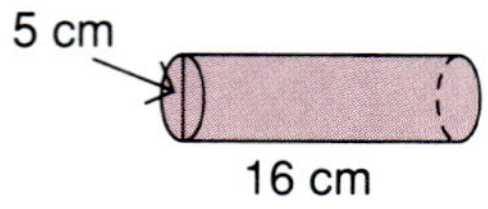

13. 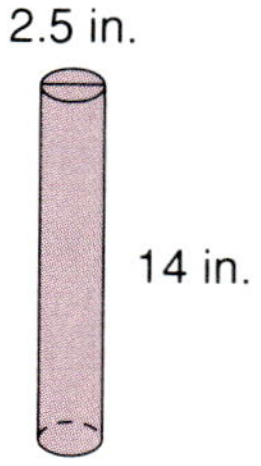

14. 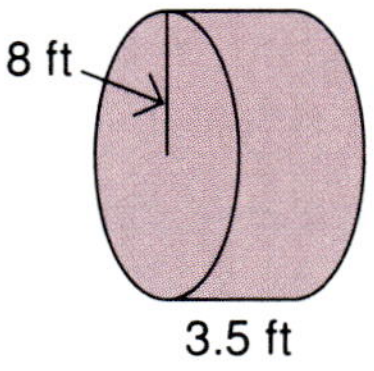

One cylinder has a base with a radius of 3 in. and a height of 5 in. A second cylinder has a base with a radius of 6 in. and a height of 10 in.

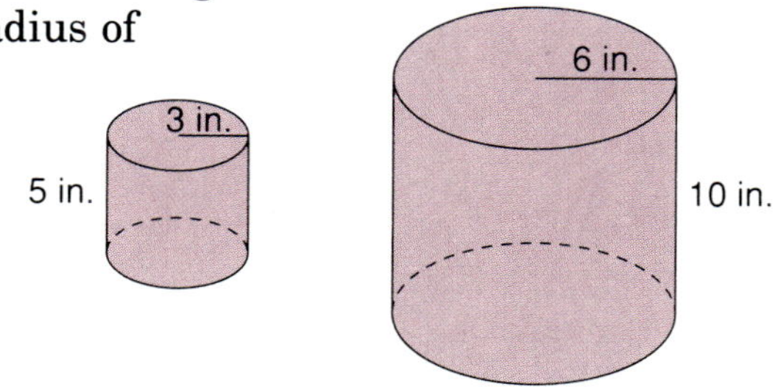

15. What is the ratio of their surface areas?

16. What is the ratio of their volumes?

A tennis ball can contains three tennis balls each with a radius of 3 cm. Find the following.

17. Ratio of the circumference of the top of the can to its height

18. Surface area of the can

19. Volume of the can

Problem Solving

Solve each problem.

20. A cylindrical cat toy is 7 inches in diameter and 10 inches high. If terry cloth costs $3.98 per square yard, how much will it cost to cover the toy?
(Hint: 1,296 sq in. = 1 sq yd.)

21. A lawn roller has a diameter of 21 in. and is 3 ft long. How much surface area is rolled with 10 full turns of the roller?

22. Calculate the amount of paint needed to paint the outside of six cylindrical storage drums, each with a diameter of 4.5 ft and a height of 8.75 ft. The tops and bottoms of the drums are also to be painted. One gallon of paint covers about 425 square feet.

23. A tin can has a base with a diameter of 3 inches and a height of 4.5 inches. About how many square inches of tin are needed to make the can?

24. Estimate the cost of the paint for Problem 22 if one gallon of paint costs $18.75.

25. **Use Data** Compare the surface areas of the two cylinders described in Exercise 17, page 357.

Suppose the radius and the height of a cylinder are changed, as indicated below. In what way is the surface area of the cylinder changed? Try several examples for each case.

26. Doubled **27.** Tripled **28.** Quadrupled **29.** Halved

30. **Critical Thinking** Examine the results of Problems 26–29. Write a general rule that describes how the surface area is changed when the radius and height of a cylinder are multiplied by a number, n.

Explore Math

Make a pattern for a three-dimensional model of a cylinder by following these steps. Use a compass and a metric ruler.

31. Construct a circle with a radius of 3 cm.

32. Find the circumference of the circle.

33. Construct a rectangle with two sides equal in length to the circumference of the circles, touching each circle at one point. (See drawing.)

34. Add tabs for gluing. Cut out the pattern and assemble the model.

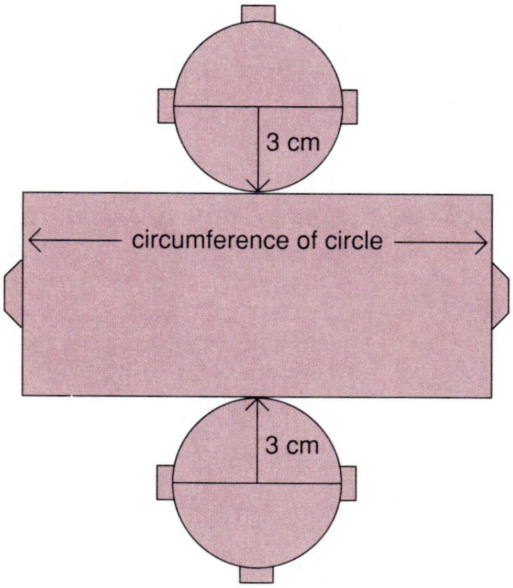

Try and Check

Build Understanding

The diagrams show how to construct an open box from an 18-inch square cardboard. What are the dimensions of the box of maximum volume that can be constructed in this way?

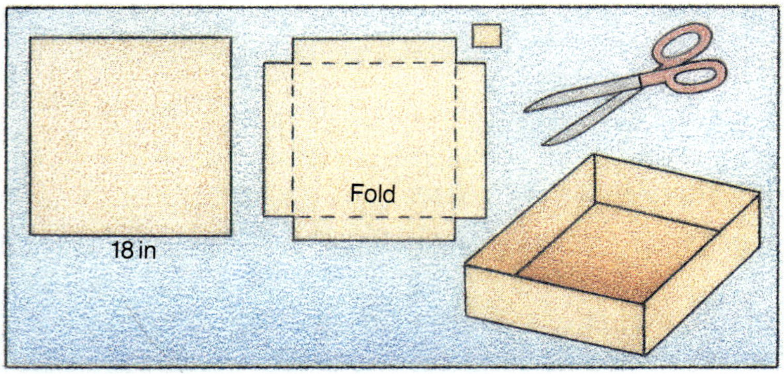

PROBLEM SOLVING GUIDE

Understand
QUESTION
FACTS
KEY IDEA

Plan and Solve
STRATEGY
ANSWER

Look Back
SENSIBLE ANSWER
ALTERNATE APPROACH

Understand QUESTION What are the dimensions of the box of maximum volume?

FACTS Four identical squares are cut from each corner of an 18-in. square.

KEY IDEA The size of the box depends on the size of the 4 squares.

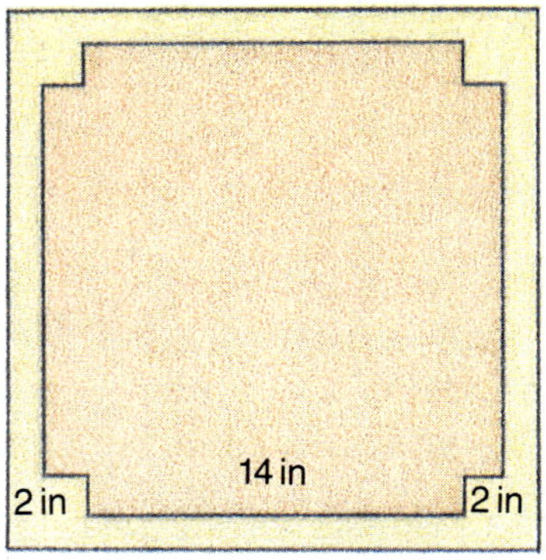

Plan and Solve STRATEGY Try various sizes for the cutout square and find the volume of the resulting prism. Organize your results in a table.

Side of cutout square	Height	Length	Width	Volume
1	1	16	16	256
2	2	14	14	392
3	3	12	12	432
4	4	10	10	400
5	5	8	8	320
6	6	6	6	216

If a 2-inch square is cut from each corner, then the height of the box is 2 in. The base of the box is a square, 14 in. by 14 in. The volume of the box is $V = h\ell w = 2 \times 14 \times 14$, or 392 cu in.

From the results in the table, the maximum volume is 432 cu in. for a box with dimensions 3 in. by 12 in. by 12 in.

ANSWER The dimensions of the box of the maximum volume are 12 in. by 12 in. by 3 in. Its volume is 432 cu in.

Look Back SENSIBLE ANSWER Could a larger volume be obtained by using decimal values for the side of the cut-out square? Try and check some decimal values near 3.

Talk About Math Suppose that you checked 2.5 inches and got a volume greater than 432 cubic inches. Could the answer be less than 2.5? equal to 2.5? greater than 2.5?

Check Understanding

Repeat the problem in the example for Exercises 1–4, but use the value given for the sides of the cardboard square. Give the dimensions for the greatest volume.

1. 12 inches **2.** 24 inches **3.** 30 centimeters **4.** 60 centimeters

Practice

Solve each problem.

5. The largest rectangular box that can be sent through the mail has, at most, a height plus the perimeter of the base equal to 108 inches. Find the dimensions for the greatest volume of a rectangular box with a square base that can be sent through the mail.

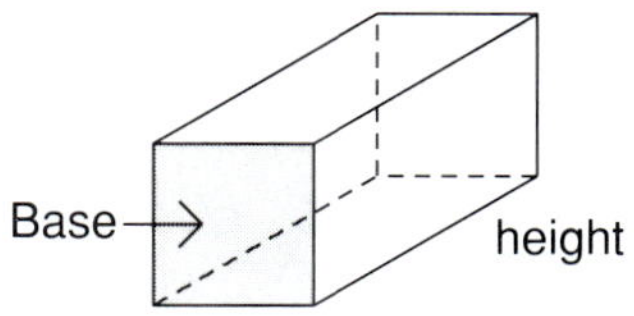

6. A basketball has a diameter of 9.5 inches. What is the surface area of the ball?

7. A grain silo is shaped like a cylinder. The diameter of the base is 12 feet and the height is 25 feet. What is the volume of the silo?

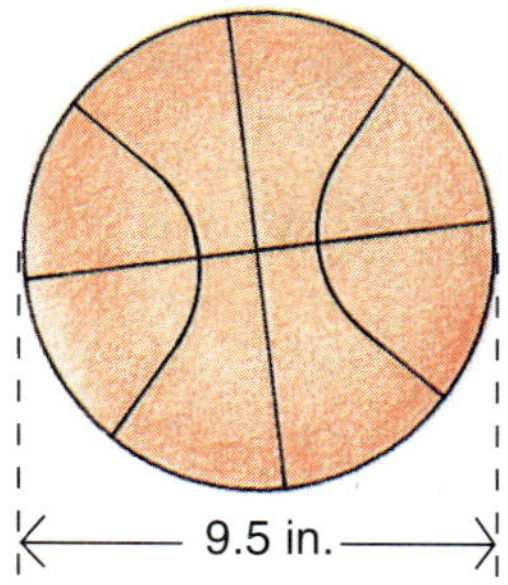

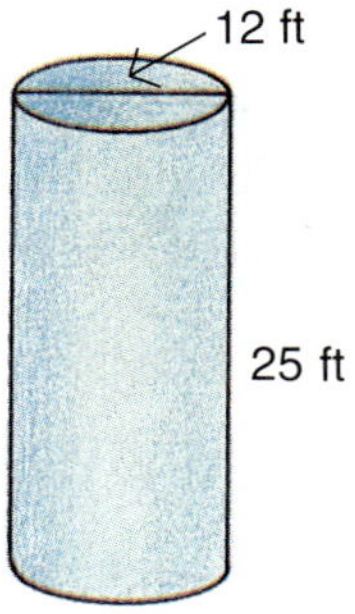

8. **Visual Thinking** Inez glued together 125 unit cubes to form a 5-by-5-by-5 cube. How many pairs of 1-by-1 faces did she glue together?

9. You are designing a box that will hold 100 one-inch cubes. The box has no top. What dimensions of the box will require the least amount of cardboard?

Skills Review

Find the circumference and the area for each circle. Use $\frac{22}{7}$ or 3.14 for π.

1. $r = 4.5$ cm

2. $d = 5$ in.

3. $d = 20$ ft

4. $r = 36$ m

Find the perimeter and the area of each figure.

5.

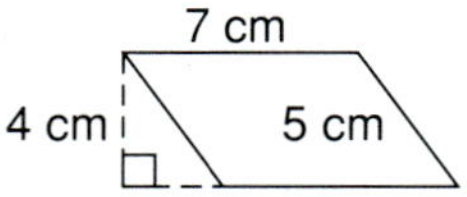

6.

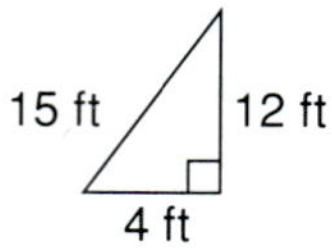

7.

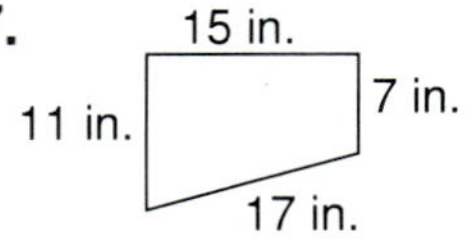

8.

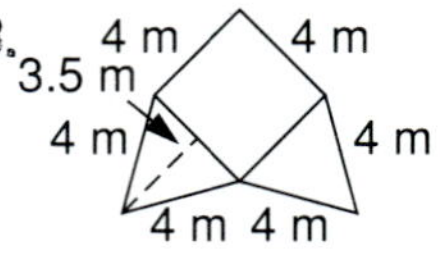

Find the volume of each figure. Use 3.14 for π.

9.

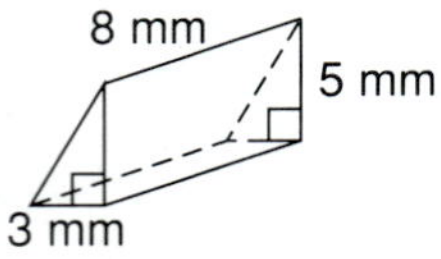

10.

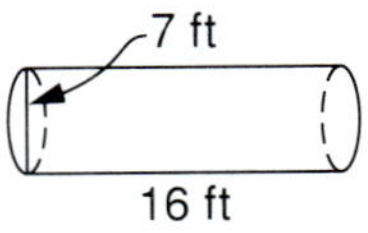

11.

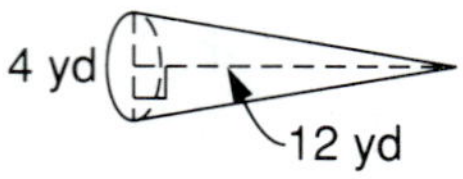

12.

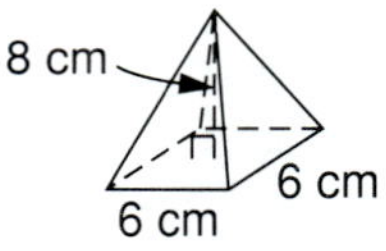

Find the surface area of each figure. Use 3.14 for π.

13.

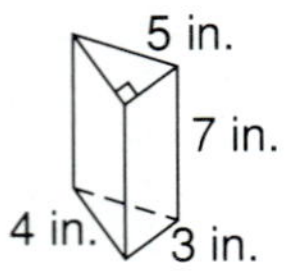

14.

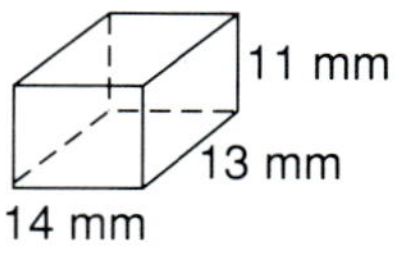

15.

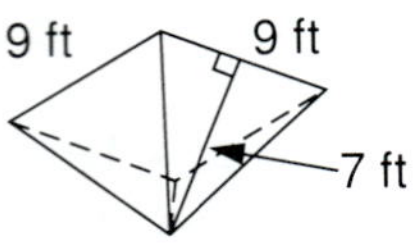

16.

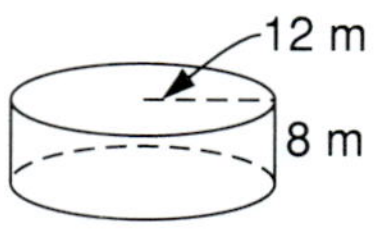

Problem-Solving Review

Solve each problem.

17. Jack's dog is tethered by rope to a post in the center of the backyard. If the rope is 30 feet long, what is the area in which the dog can roam?

18. A rectangular room is 15 feet by 27 feet. If carpeting costs $22 per square yard, how much will it cost to carpet the entire room?

19. A cylindrical pipe 20 inches long is $\frac{1}{2}$ inch thick. The inside diameter of the pipe is 4 inches. What is the volume of the metal used to make the pipe?

20. If you triple the radius and triple the height of a cone, by how many times do you increase the volume?

21. A greenhouse is in the shape of a hemisphere. The diameter of the floor is 18 feet. What is the volume of the living space?

22. A pet's toy is in the shape of a cylinder. The toy is 4 in. in diameter and 10 in. high. How much will it cost to cover the toy with cloth that costs $4.95 per square yard?

23. **Data File** Use the data on pages 426–427. What is the volume of the space under the stairs?

24. **Make a Data File** Do research to find the dimensions of one indoor sports court, such as a squash court, a volleyball court, or a basketball court. Draw a diagram, labeling all parts and dimensions.

Cumulative Skills Review • Chapters 1–10

Compare. Use <, >, or =.

1. $\frac{11}{16}$ ▦ $\frac{3}{4}$ **2.** $\frac{2}{3}$ ▦ $\frac{11}{15}$ **3.** $4\frac{2}{3}$ ▦ $4\frac{3}{5}$ **4.** −8.2 ▦ −2.8

Write a mathematical expression for each phrase.

5. $\frac{1}{2}$ the sum of 20 and n **6.** 5 times the square of v **7.** c plus 12 less than m

Write each number as a percent.

8. $\frac{19}{20}$ **9.** $6\frac{3}{5}$ **10.** 2.44 **11.** 0.03 **12.** 0.002

Find the unit price for each item. Which is the better buy?

13. 2 sweat shirts for \$39
3 sweat shirts for \$56

14. 4 pairs of socks for \$7
7 pairs of socks for \$13

15. 12 tennis balls for \$29
6 tennis balls for \$16

Find the greatest possible error (GPE) and the percent error to the nearest 0.01%.

16. $5\frac{1}{2}$ mi **17.** 0.75 lb **18.** 380 feet **19.** 17.8 mm

Use the pattern for Exercises 20–22.

20. What solid will this pattern form?

21. How many pairs of parallel faces are there?

22. Which face is opposite face F?

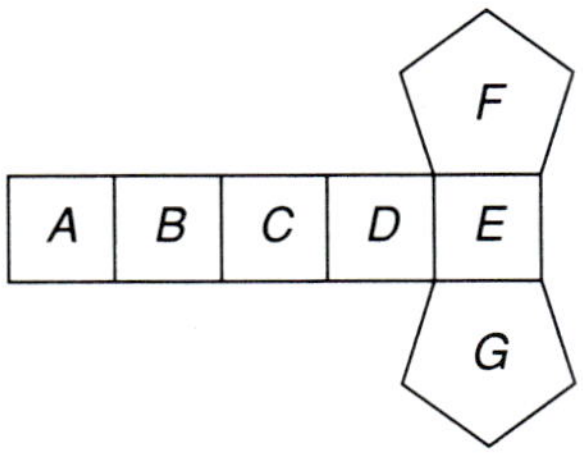

Find the perimeter and area of each figure.

23.
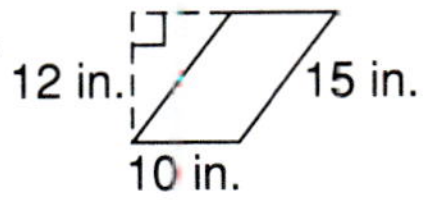

24.
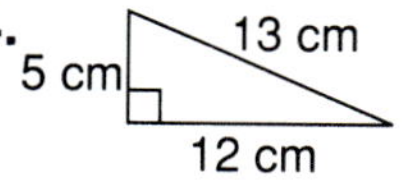

25.
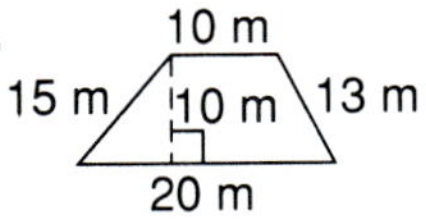

26.
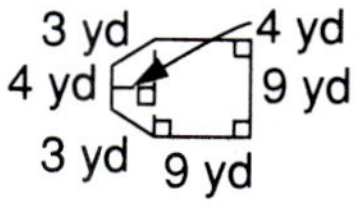

In the diagram at the right, $m \parallel n$ and $r \parallel s$. Find each measure if $m\angle 1 = 130°$.

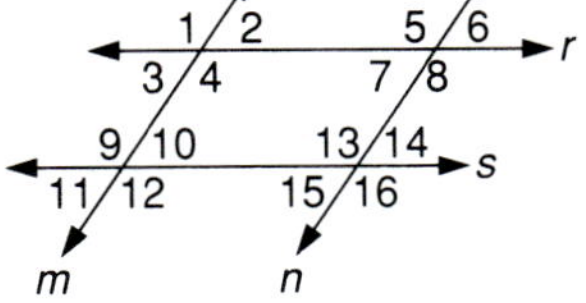

27. $m\angle 4$ **28.** $m\angle 10$

29. $m\angle 6$ **30.** $m\angle 16$

Find the surface area of each figure. Use 3.14 for π.

31.
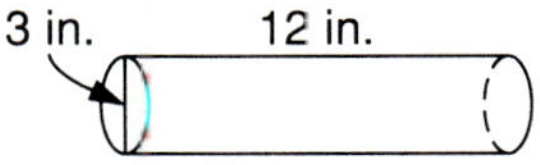

32.
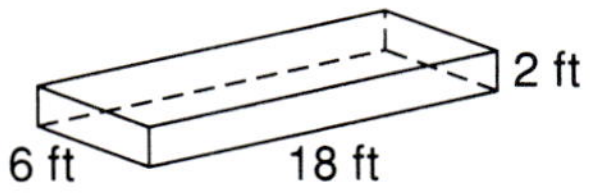

33.
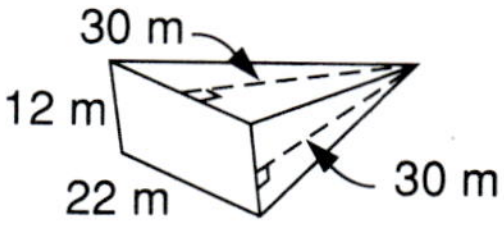

Reteaching

Set A pages 342–345

For this theater-in-the-round, find the circumference and area of the stage.

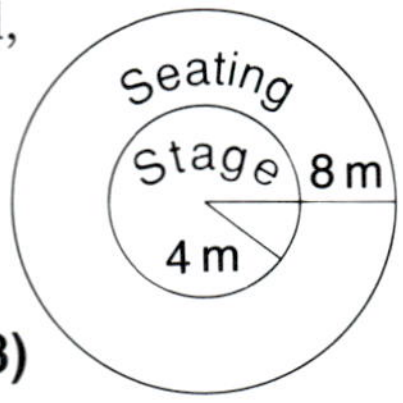

$A = \pi r^2$ $C = \pi d$

$A = (3.14)(4^2)$ $C = 3.14(8)$

$A = 50.24$ $C = 25.12$

Area: 50.24 m^2 Circumference: 25.12 m

Remember that the diameter of a circle is twice the radius.

1. What is the outside circumference of the seating portion?
2. What is the inside circumference of the seating portion?
3. What is the area of the seating portion?

Set B pages 346–349

Find the area and the perimeter of triangle *ABD*.

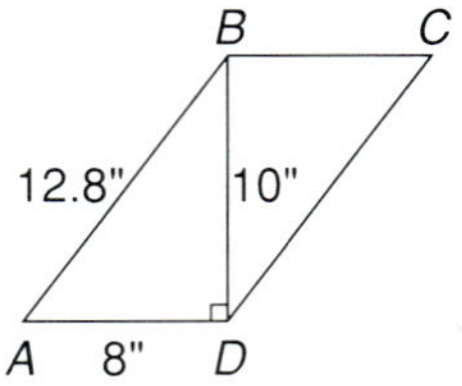

$A = \frac{1}{2}bh$

$A = \frac{1}{2}(8)(10)$ $P = AB + BD + DA$

$P = 12.8 + 10 + 8$

$A = 40$ $P = 30.8$

Area: 40 sq in. Perimeter: 30.8 in.

Remember that the area of a triangle is one half the area of a parallelogram with the same base and height.

1. Find the area of parallelogram *ABCD*.
2. Find the perimeter of the parallelogram.
3. Find the area of a parallelogram with a base of 15 in. and a height of 7 in.

Set C pages 350–353

Find the area of trapezoid $\overline{ABEF}$. The bases are $\overline{BE}$ and $\overline{AF}$.

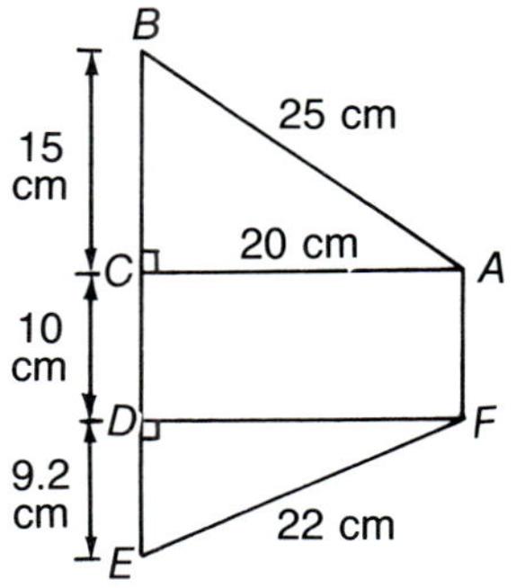

$A = \frac{1}{2}(b_1 + b_2)h$

$A = \frac{1}{2}(34.2 + 10)(20)$

$A = 442$ The area is 442 cm^2.

Remember that many irregular figures are made up of simpler figures.

Find each area.

1. Rectangle *ACDF*
2. Triangle *ABC*
3. Triangle *DEF*
4. Sum of the areas in Exercises 1–3.

Set D pages 356–359

The cylinder just fits inside the prism. Find the volume of each to the nearest tenth.

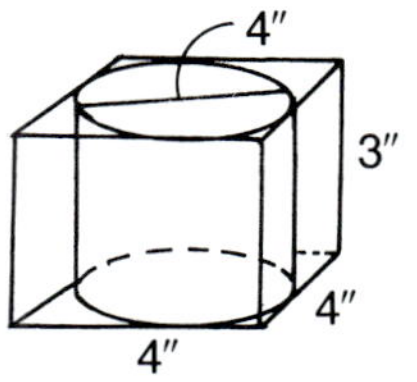

Cylinder:

$V = \pi r^2 h$

$V = (3.14)(2^2)(3)$

$V = 37.68 \approx 37.7$

Volume: 37.7 cu in.

Prism:

$V = \ell wh$

$V = (4)(4)(3)$

$V = 48$

Volume: 48 cu in.

Remember that in the formula $V = Bh$ for the volume of a cylinder or prism, *B* represents the area of the base.

1. Find the volume of a box that is 12 in. high, 8 inches long, and 8 inches wide.
2. Find the volume of a cylinder that just fits inside the box in Exercise 1.
3. What is the volume of the space inside the box surrounding the cylinder?

Set E pages 360–363

Find each volume.

Cone:

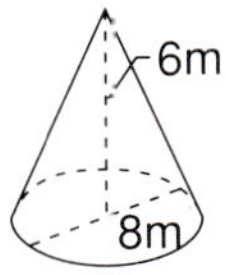

$V = \frac{1}{3} Bh$

$V = \frac{1}{3}(3.14)(4^2)(6)$

$V = 100.48 \approx 100.5$

Volume: 100.5 m³

Pyramid:

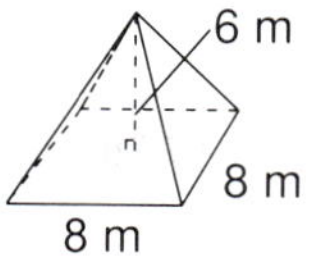

$V = \frac{1}{3} Bh$

$V = \frac{1}{3}(8^2)(6)$

$V = 128$

Volume: 128 m³

Remember that for a cylinder or prism, $V = Bh$, and for a cone or pyramid, $V = \frac{1}{3} Bh$.

1. What is the formula for the area of the base of a rectangular pyramid?

2. What is the formula for the volume of a rectangular pyramid?

3. Find the volume of a pyramid if the dimensions of the base are 8 cm by 10 cm and the height is 15 cm.

Set F pages 368–371

Find the area of the top face of the prism.

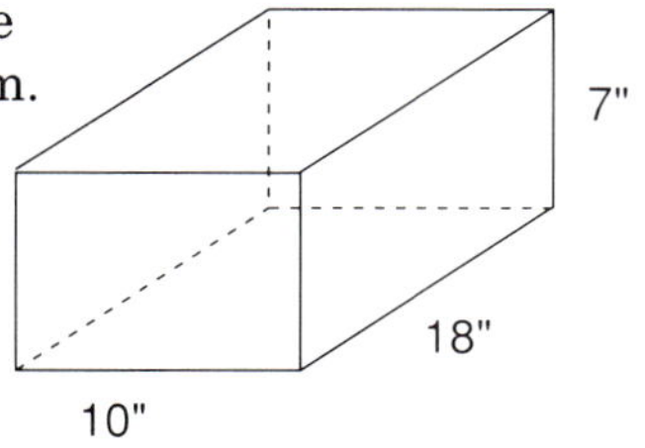

$A = \ell w$

$A = (18)(10)$

$A = 180$

The area of the top face is 180 sq in.

Remember that the surface area of a prism is the sum of the areas of the faces.

Use the rectangular prism shown.

1. How many rectangular faces are there?

2. How many square faces are there?

3. What is the surface area of the prism?

Set G pages 372–375

What is the height of the regular pyramid shown? What is the slant height of the pyramid?

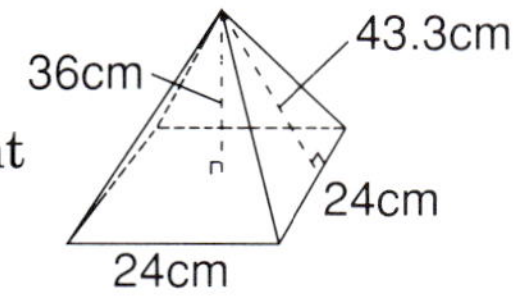

The height of the pyramid is 36 cm. The slant height is the height of each triangular face, or about 43.3 cm.

Remember that lateral faces are congruent in a regular pyramid.

1. What is the area of one triangular face of the pyramid shown?

2. What is the area of the base?

3. What is the surface area of the pyramid?

Set H pages 376–379

The base and top of a cylinder are congruent. Draw a pattern for the base and top of the cylinder shown.

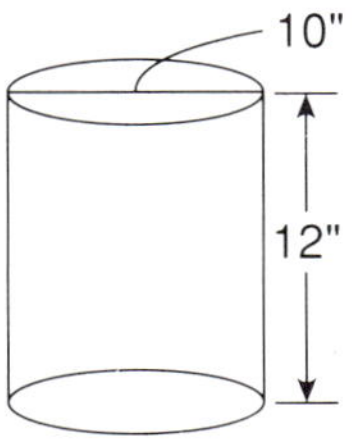

The pattern for the base and top is a circle with a radius of 5 in.

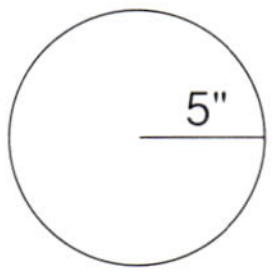

Remember that the lateral face of a cylinder is a rectangle of width $2\pi r$.

1. Find the area of the base and top of the cylinder shown.

2. Draw a pattern for the lateral face. Label the dimensions and find the area.

3. Find the surface area of the cylinder.

More Practice

Set A pages 342–345

Find the circumference and the area for each circle having the given dimension. Use $\frac{22}{7}$ or 3.14 for π.

1. $d = 14$ ft **2.** $d = 0.3$ dm **3.** $d = 136$ in. **4.** $r = 42$ m

5. $r = 1.5$ cm **6.** $d = 50$ dm **7.** $d = 12$ in. **8.** $r = 72$ m

9. $r = 1$ yd **10.** $r = 3.8$ m **11.** $r = 80$ mm **12.** $d = 31.8$ in.

13. $d = 25$ cm **14.** $r = 25$ cm **15.** $r = 4$ ft **16.** $d = 4$ ft

17. What is the diameter of a circle whose circumference is 66 mm?

18. What is the area of a circle whose circumference is 66 mm?

19. What is the diameter of a circle when circumference is 5 yd?

20. What is the area of a circle whose circumference is 5 yd?

21. What is the area of a circle whose circumference is 35 mm?

22. What is the area of a circle whose circumference is 25.12 cm?

Set B pages 346–349

Find the perimeter and the area of each figure.

1.
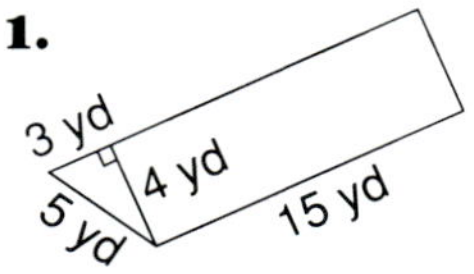

2.
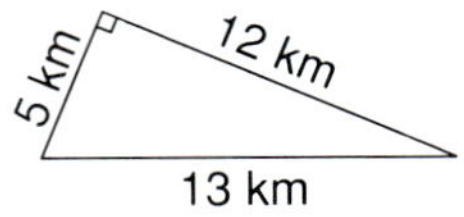

3.
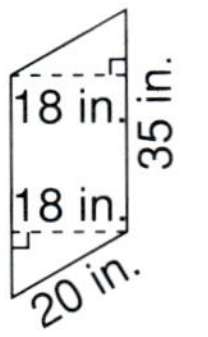

4.
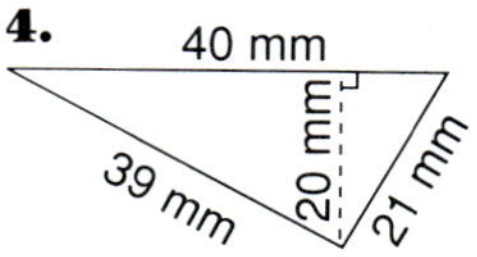

Set C pages 350–353

Find the perimeter and the area of each figure.

1.
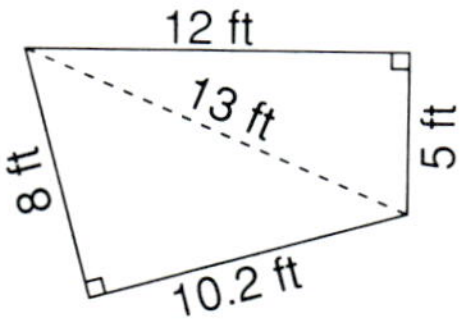

2.
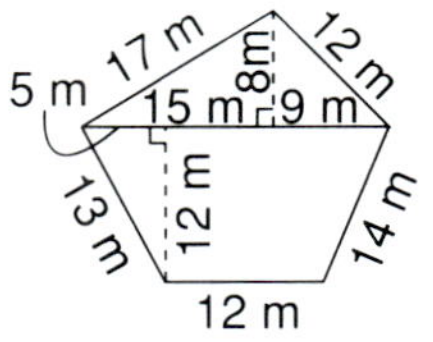

3.
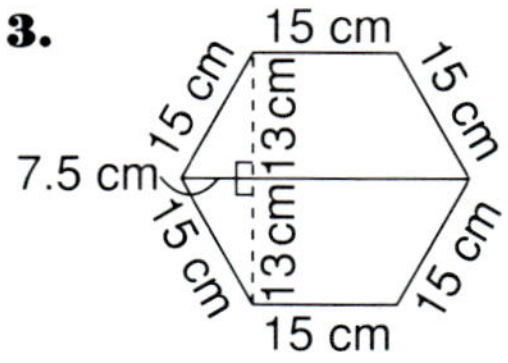

4.
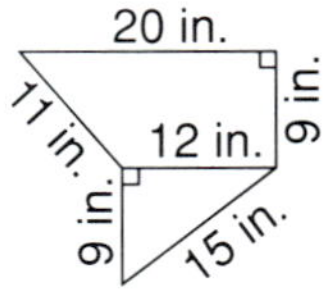

Set D pages 356–359

Find the volume of each prism or cylinder. Use 3.14 for π.

1.
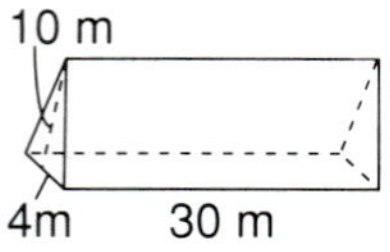

2.
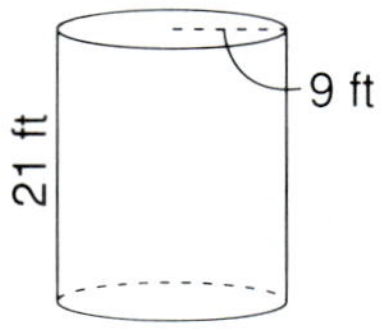

3.
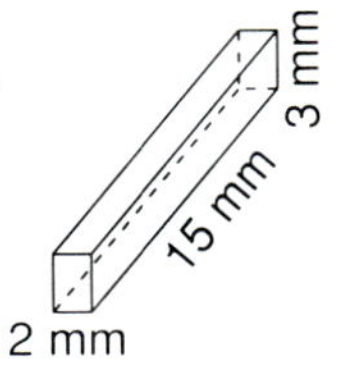

4.
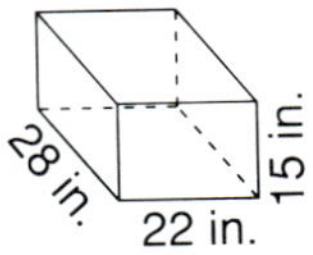

Set E pages 360–363

Find the volume of the pyramid or cone. Use 3.14 for π.

1. 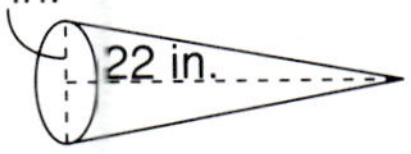

2. 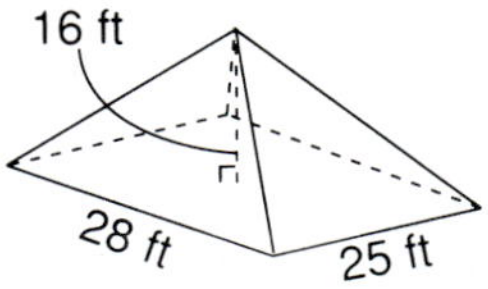

3. 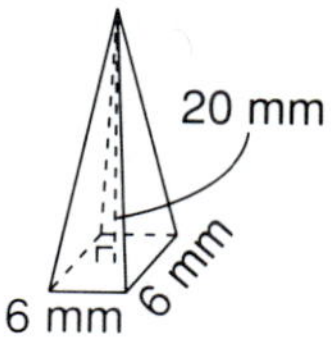

4. 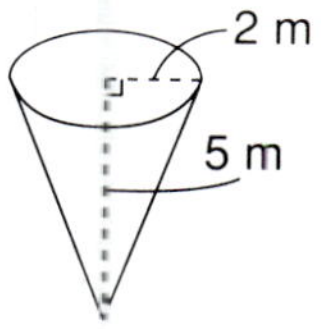

5. 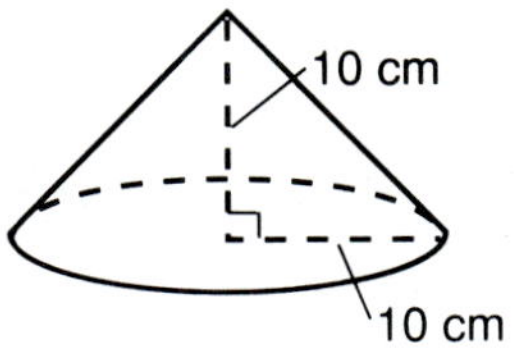

6. 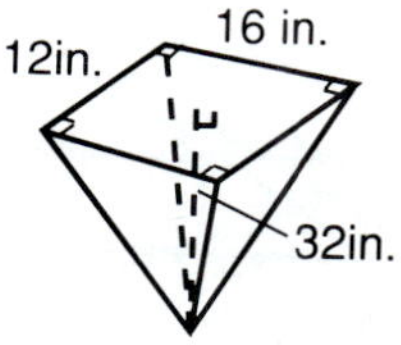

Set F pages 368–371

Find the surface area of each prism.

1. 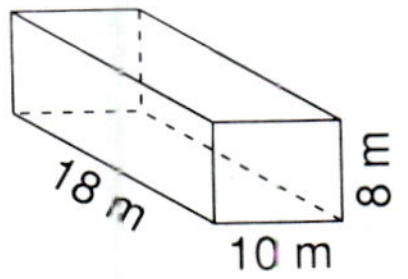

2. 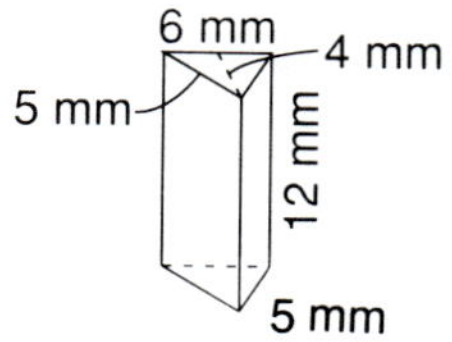

3. 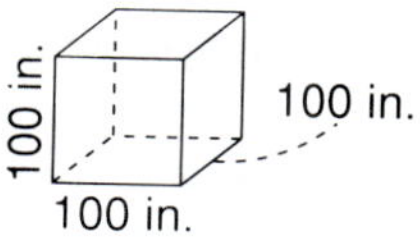

4. 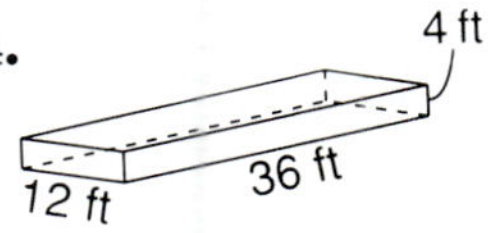

5. 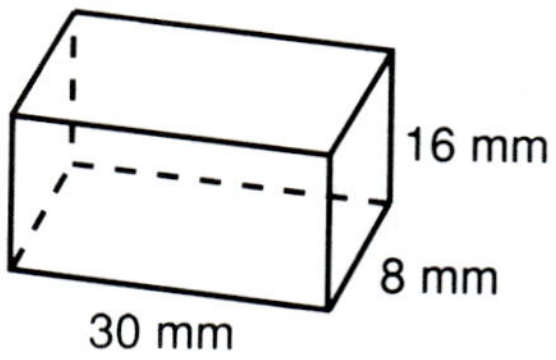

6. 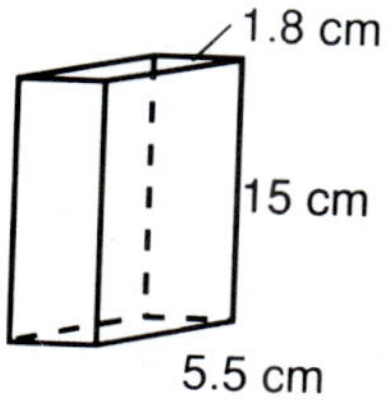

Set G pages 372–375

Find the surface area of each pyramid.

1. 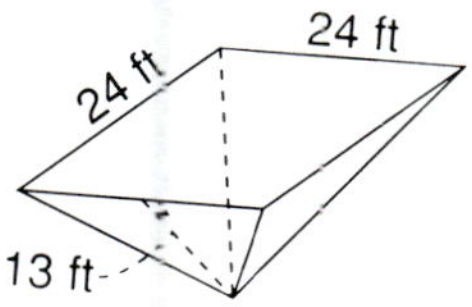

2. 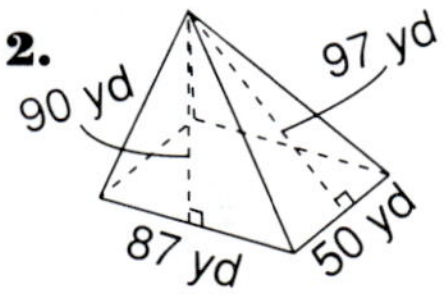

3. 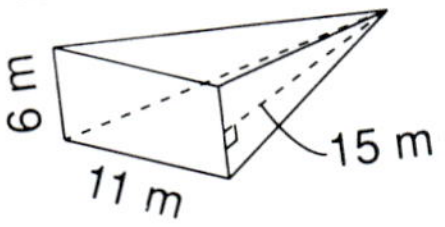

4. 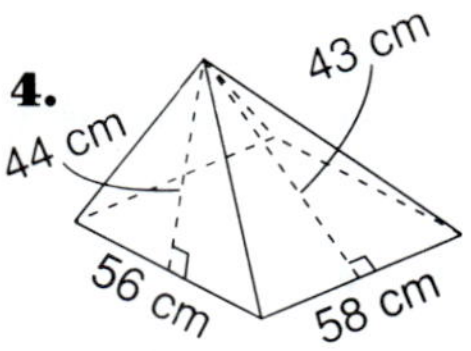

Set H pages 376–379

Find the surface area of each cylinder. Use 3.14 for π.

1. 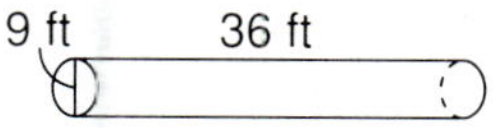

2. 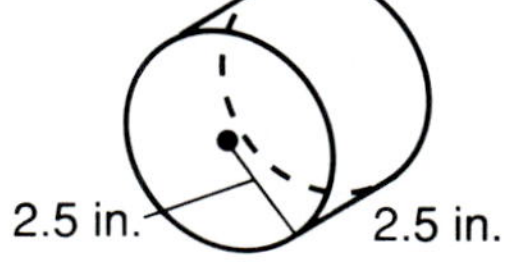

3. 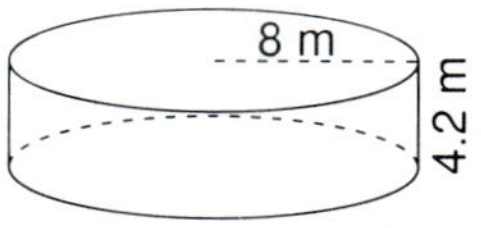

4. $r = 1.5$ cm
$h = 4.5$ cm

5. $d = 24$ in.
$h = 40$ in.

6. $r = 0.5$ m
$h = 3.5$ m

Independent Study ENRICHMENT

Enrichment

Cross Sections

For his mathematics project, Wyn will cut through 3-dimensional models to show the 2-dimensional cross sections that result.

For each exercise, make a sketch of the cross section if Wyn uses solid wooden models. Then sketch the cross section if he uses hollow plastic models.

1. Rectangular prism, vertical cut

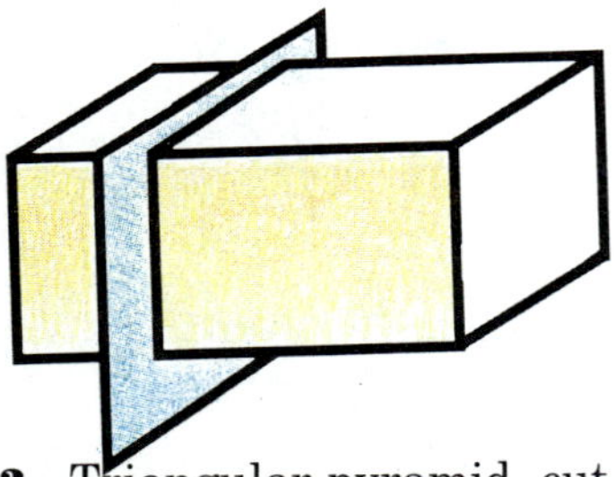

2. Rectangular prism, slanting cut

3. Triangular pyramid, cut parallel to base

4. Sphere

5. Cone, cut parallel to base

6. Cone, cut at angle to base

7. Cone, vertical cut

8. Cube, slanting cut

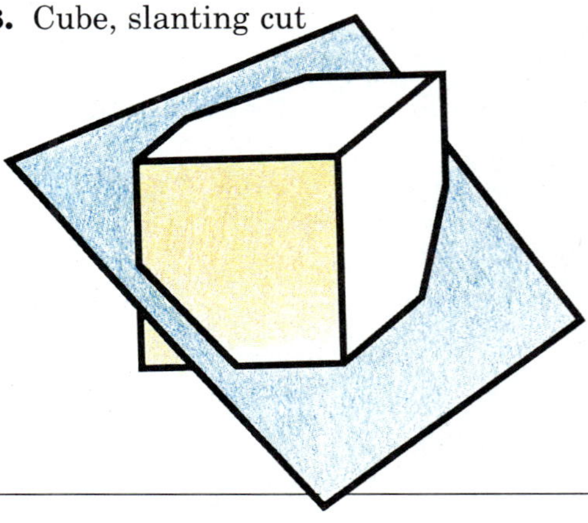

Chapter 10 Review/Test

Find the area of each polygon.

1.

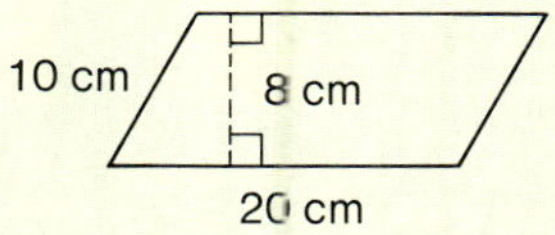

2.

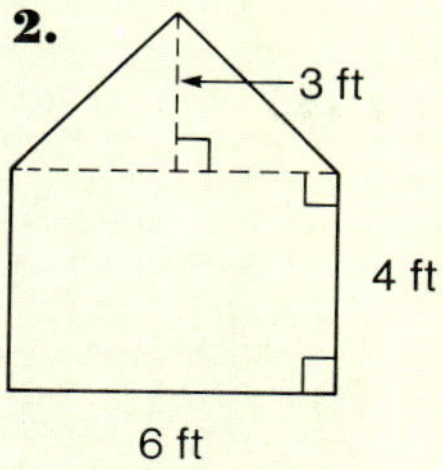

3. The circle has a radius of a units and an area of πa^2 square units. What is the area of a circle that has a radius that is twice as long as the radius of this circle?

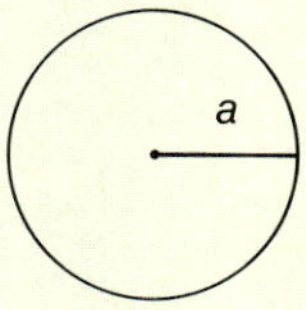

4. Robert needed to know the area of the palm of his hand for a science project. First he traced his palm on some paper. What shape could he use to estimate the area?

5. If the small box shown below is placed inside the big box, what is the volume of the space outside the small box but within the large box?

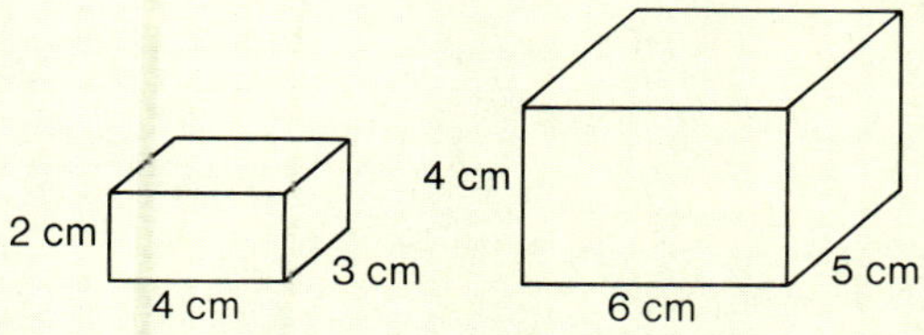

6. The volume of a cone is 42 cubic inches. What is the volume of a cylinder with a base congruent to that of the cone and equal to it in height?

Use the information below to answer Exercises 7 and 8.

Martha bought two rubber balls. One had a diameter of 2 inches and the other, a diameter of 4 inches.

7. Write the volume of each ball, using the formula $V = \frac{4}{3}\pi r^3$. Leave the symbol π in your answer; do *not* multiply by $\frac{22}{7}$ or 3.14.

8. What is the ratio of the volume of the smaller ball to the larger ball?

Find the volume and the surface area of each figure.

9. cube

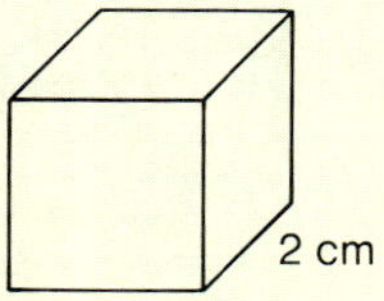

10. regular square pyramid

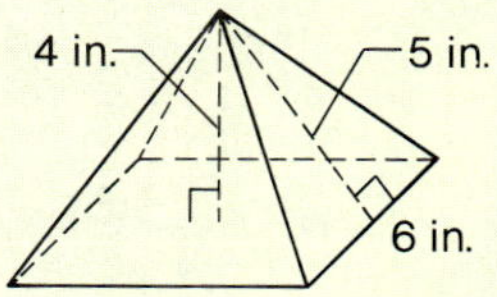

11. Debra is going to paint the curved surfaces of 10 cylindrical barrels that are 8 feet tall and have a diameter of 4 feet. (She will *not* paint the top or bottom.) The paint she is going to buy covers about 400 square feet per gallon. How many gallons of paint should she buy?

12. What are the dimensions of the largest rectangular box with a square base that can be made when the sum of the dimensions is 24 units? Hint: Try several dimensions until you get the largest volume. Use a chart to organize your work. Use only whole number values.

13. **Write About Math** What is similar about formulas for volumes of prisms, cylinders, and pyramids?

CHAPTER REVIEW/TEST

Rational and Irrational Numbers

11

Did You Know: Everything around us is made up of atoms. Atoms are extremely small—some are only one ten-millionth of a millimeter long.

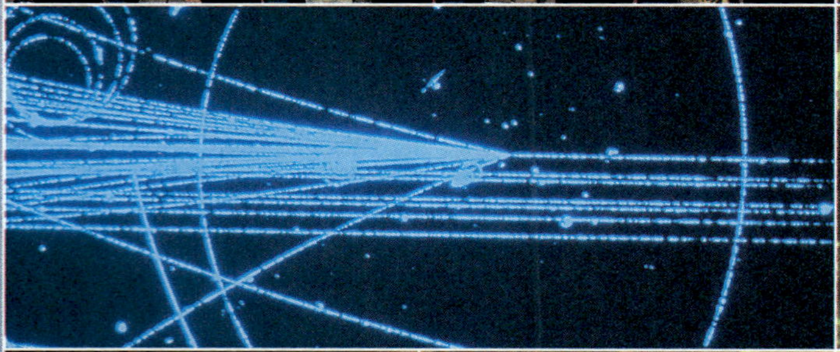

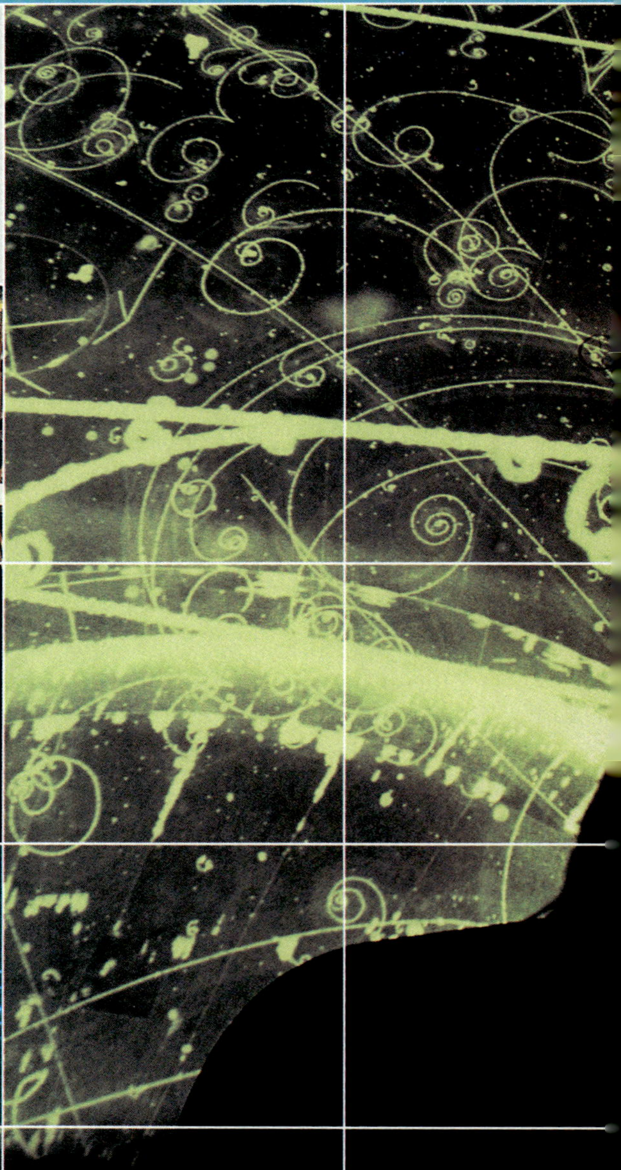

Number-Sense Project

Estimate
Do you think you could see an atom under an ordinary school microscope?

Gather Data
Find the names of various kinds of microscopes available to scientists and tell how many times each can magnify an object.

Analyze and Report
What kind of microscope would have to be used to magnify an atom so it could be seen by the human eye? How would the atom look?

A L G E B R A

Rational Number System

Build Understanding

A. In Chapter 3 you learned that numbers such as $\frac{5}{3}$ and $-\frac{1}{5}$ are called rational numbers. A ***rational number*** can be written in the form $\frac{a}{b}$, where a and b are integers and $b \neq 0$.

The set of rational numbers includes positive and negative integers, fractions, and decimals that terminate or repeat.

Examples of Rational Numbers

Integers: $5 = \frac{5}{1}$ and $-3 = \frac{-3}{1}$

Fractions and mixed numbers: $-4\frac{2}{3} = \frac{-14}{3}$ and $1\frac{1}{5} = \frac{6}{5}$

Decimals that terminate (end): $3.75 = 3\frac{3}{4} = \frac{15}{4}$

Decimals that repeat: $0.6666... = \frac{2}{3}$ and $0.\overline{45} = \frac{5}{11}$

B. This table shows properties that are true for rational numbers.

Property	Operation	Rule	Example
Commutative	+	$a + b = b + a$	$\frac{1}{2} + 3 = 3 + \frac{1}{2}$
Commutative	×	$a \times b = b \times a$	$-23 \times 4 = 4 \times (-23)$
Associative	+	$(a + b) + c = a + (b + c)$	$[39 + (-8)] + 4 = 39 + [(-8) + 4]$
Associative	×	$(a \times b) \times c = a \times (b \times c)$	$(8 \times 4) \times 25 = 8 \times (4 \times 25)$
Zero Property	+	$a + 0 = a$	$3.75 + 0 = 3.75$
Zero Property	×	$a \times 0 = 0$	$-3 \times 0 = 0$
One Property	×	$a \times 1 = a$	$\frac{22}{7} \times 1 = \frac{22}{7}$
Distributive	× and +	$a(b + c) = a \times b + a \times c$	$4\left(6 + \frac{3}{4}\right) = (4 \times 6) + \left(4 \times \frac{3}{4}\right)$ $-2(7 + 8) = [(-2) \times 7] + [(-2) \times 8]$

Talk About Math Explain how the examples given in the table show how you can use the properties to help you compute mentally.

Check Understanding

For another example, see Set A, pages 420–421.

Solve for s. Tell what property is illustrated.

1. $0 \times (-1.389) = s$

2. $(3 \times 20) + (3 \times 6) = s(20 + 6)$

3. $\frac{2}{3} \times \frac{1}{5} = \frac{1}{5} \times s$

4. $(12 \times 5) \times 4 = s \times (5 \times 4)$

Practice

For More Practice, see Set A, pages 422–423.

Answer each question. Write *yes* or *no*.

5. Does $5.3 - 6.7 = 6.7 - 5.3$?

6. Is $0.\overline{3}$ a rational number? Explain.

7. Does $(3 + 20) - 6 = 3 + (20 - 6)$?

8. Does $1.2\,(5 - 3) = (1.2 \times 5) - (1.2 \times 3)$?

Solve for n. Tell what property is illustrated.

9. $17.8 \times n = 0$

10. $\frac{4}{3} \times \frac{1}{2} = n \times \frac{4}{3}$

11. $n + 8.4 = 8.4 + 6.3$

12. $(0.2 \times 4) \times n = 0.2 \times (4 \times 2.5)$

13. $14 \times (n \times 5) = (14 \times 5) \times 5$

14. $1.2 \times 4 + 1.2 \times 6 = n(4 + 6)$

15. $\frac{1}{2} \times n = \frac{5}{8} \times \frac{1}{2}$

16. $n \times \left(\frac{3}{8} + \frac{1}{4}\right) = \left(\frac{2}{3} \times \frac{3}{8}\right) + \left(\frac{2}{3} \times \frac{1}{4}\right)$

17. $n \times 17.1 = 17.1$

18. $9.3 + (3.4 + 8.2) = (9.3 + 3.4) + n$

Mental Math Use mental math to compute. Tell what property you used.

19. 9.75×0

20. $23.4 + 0$

21. $28 + 92 + 8$

22. 3.873×1

23. $9 \times 3\frac{2}{9}$

24. $-0.8 \times 4 + 1.8 \times 4$

25. $\frac{-2}{5} + \left(\frac{2}{5} + \frac{2}{3}\right)$

26. $83 + 19 + 17$

27. $9 \times 0.6 + 9 \times 1.4$

28. $4.8 \times 3 + 4.8 \times -3$

29. $\left(2\frac{1}{2} \times \frac{1}{5}\right) \times 5$

30. $4 \times 6\frac{2}{5} \times \frac{1}{4}$

Problem Solving

Critical Thinking Write two examples to show each of the following.

31. Division is not commutative.

32. Division is not associative.

33. Multiplication distributes over subtraction.

34. Addition does not distribute over multiplication.

Give a rational number between

35. $\frac{-1}{2}$ and 0.

36. 0.44 and 0.48.

37. $\frac{1}{3}$ and $\frac{1}{2}$.

Tell whether each statement is *true* or *false*. Explain your answer.

38. Some negative rational numbers are integers.

39. All rational numbers can be written as terminating decimals.

ALGEBRA

Exponents and Powers of Ten

Build Understanding

Based on powers of 10, the metric system of measurement was designed to be easy to use.

This table shows how units of length in the metric system are related.

To change from one unit to the smaller unit shown to the right of it, multiply by 10.

To change from one unit to the larger unit shown to the left of it, multiply by 0.1.

× 10 × 10 × 0.1 × 0.1

thousands	hundreds	tens	ones	tenths	hundredths	thousandths
kilometer km	hectometer hm	dekameter dam	meter m	decimeter dm	centimeter cm	millimeter mm

A. How many millimeters are in 1 kilometer? Write the answer as a power of 10.

$\mathbf{1\ km = 10 \times 10 \times 10 \times 10 \times 10 \times 10 = 10^6\ mm}$

10^n means that 10 is a factor n times.
10^{-n} means $\frac{1}{10^n}$.

B. This table shows that when the exponent decreases by 1, the ***standard form*** of the number is divided by 10. When the exponent increases by 1, the standard form of the number is multiplied by 10.

Write the numbers 10^4 and 10^{-4} in standard form.

$$10^4 = 10 \times 10 \times 10 \times 10 = 10{,}000$$

$$10^{-4} = \frac{1}{10^4} = \frac{1}{10{,}000} = 0.0001$$

Powers of 10	
Exponential form	Standard form
10^3	1,000
10^2	100
10^1	10
10^0	1
10^{-1}	$\frac{1}{10} = 0.1$
10^{-2}	$\frac{1}{100} = 0.01$
10^{-3}	$\frac{1}{1{,}000} = 0.001$

C. Write the numbers 1,000,000 and 0.000001 in exponential form.

$$1{,}000{,}000 = 10 \times 10 \times 10 \times 10 \times 10 \times 10 = 10^6$$

$$0.000001 = \frac{1}{1{,}000{,}000} = \frac{1}{10^6} = 10^{-6}$$

■ **Talk About Math** How many zeros do 10^4 and 10^{-4} have in standard form? How many zeros are in 10^7 and 10^{-7}? What pattern do you see?

Check Understanding

For another example, see Set B, pages 420–421.

Tell how many zeros each number contains in standard form. Write the number in standard form.

1. 10^{-5} **2.** 10^{3} **3.** 10^{8} **4.** 10^{-7}

Give the exponent that would be used in the exponential form of each number. Then write the number in exponential form.

5. 0.01 **6.** 1,000 **7.** 0.000001 **8.** 100,000,000

Practice

For More Practice, see Set B, pages 422–423.

Write each number in standard form.

9. 10^{-5} **10.** 10^{-7} **11.** 10^{7} **12.** 10^{1} **13.** $\frac{1}{10^3}$ **14.** $\frac{1}{10^4}$

15. 10^{0} **16.** 10^{-1} **17.** $\frac{1}{10^6}$ **18.** 10^{-3} **19.** $\frac{1}{10^8}$ **20.** 10^{-9}

Write each number in exponential form.

21. 100 **22.** 10,000 **23.** 100,000 **24.** 10,000,000

25. 0.00001 **26.** 0.001 **27.** $\frac{1}{10{,}000}$ **28.** $\frac{1}{100{,}000}$

Compute. Write the answers in standard form.

29. $10^3 \times 10^4$ **30.** $10^3 \times 10^{-3}$ **31.** $10^2 \times 10^2$ **32.** $10^{-2} \times 10^2$

33. $10^{-4} \times 10^2$ **34.** $10^8 \times 10^{-4}$ **35.** $10^5 \times 10^{-1}$ **36.** $10^2 \times 10^{-3}$

Problem Solving

Solve each problem. Write your answer in exponential form.

37. How many centimeters are in 1 kilometer?

38. How many centimeters are in 10 kilometers?

39. ▒ millimeters = 1 meter

40. ▒ millimeters = 10 centimeters

41. ▒ kiloliters = 1 liter

42. ▒ centigrams = 1 kilogram

43. ▒ milligrams = 1 gram

44. ▒ milliliters = 1 kiloliter

45. Critical Thinking Evaluate 10^2 and $\frac{1}{10^{-2}}$. Then evaluate 10^4 and $\frac{1}{10^{-4}}$. Make a generalization.

ALGEBRA

Multiplying and Dividing Powers of 10

Build Understanding

DNA is the short name for deoxyribonucleic acid, a basic part of living cells. An appropriate microscopic unit of measure for DNA is the ***angstrom.*** There are about 10 billion, or 10^{10}, angstroms in a meter.

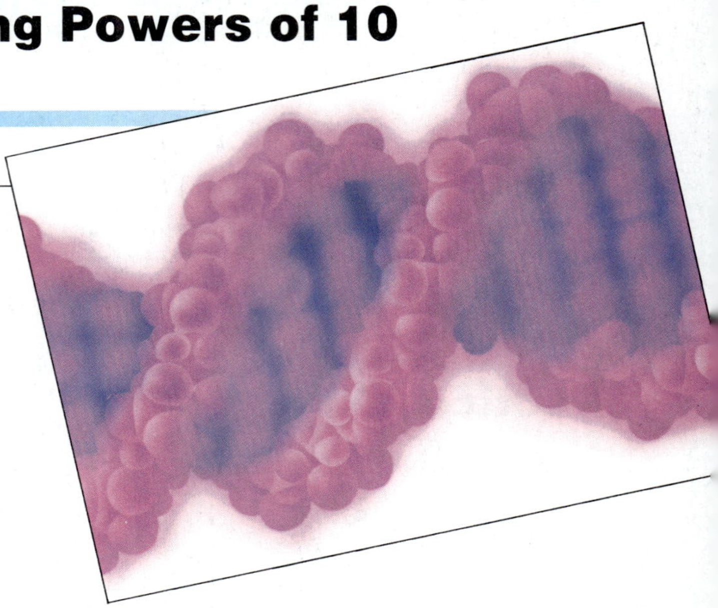

DNA is a large molecule, easily visible with modern microscopes. It is much too small to be measured in inches or even millimeters.

A. The length of the DNA strand in a cell is about 10^{-7} meters, or 1,000 angstrom units. The average human body contains about 10^{14} cells. If you laid all the cells in your body end to end, about how long would the string of DNA be?

Length of DNA in 1 cell → 10^{-7}; Number of cells → 10^{14}

$$10^{-7} \times 10^{14} = \frac{1}{10^7} \times \frac{10^{14}}{1} = \frac{10^{14}}{10^7}$$

$$\frac{10^{14}}{10^7} = \frac{100,000,000,000,000}{10,000,000}$$

$$\frac{100,000,000,000,000}{10,000,000} = 10,000,000 = 10^7$$

The string of DNA would be about 10,000,000 meters long.

You can also use the rules of exponents shown below to solve Example A.

$$10^a \times 10^b = 10^{(a+b)}$$

$$\frac{10^a}{10^b} = 10^{(a-b)}$$

$$10^{-7} \times 10^{14} = 10^{(-7+14)} = 10^7 = 10,000,000$$

The string of DNA would be about 10,000,000 meters long.

B. Find $10^3 \times 10^{15}$.

$$10^3 \times 10^{15} = 10^{(3+15)} = 10^{18}$$

C. Find $1,000,000 \times 10,000$.

$$1,000,000 \times 10,000 = 10^6 \times 10^4$$

$$10^6 \times 10^4 = 10^{(6+4)} = 10^{10}$$

D. Find $\frac{10^4}{10^7}$.

$$\frac{10^4}{10^7} = 10^{(4-7)} = 10^{-3}$$

E. Find $\frac{10,000,000}{1,000}$.

$$10,000,000 = 10^7 \quad 1,000 = 10^3$$

$$\frac{10^7}{10^3} = 10^{(7-3)} = 10^4$$

Talk About Math When is the product of two powers of 10 greater than 1? When is the quotient of two powers of 10 greater than 1?

Check Understanding

For another example, see Set C, pages 420–421.

Find the missing numbers.

1. $10^6 \times 10^3 = 10^{6+\square} = 10^{\square}$

2. $10^5 \times 10^{-2} = 10^{5+\square} = 10^{\square}$

3. $10^{-4} \times 10^{-2} = 10^{-4+\square} = 10^{\square}$

4. $\frac{10^{-7}}{10^3} = 10^{-7-\square} = 10^{\square}$

Practice

For More Practice, see Set C, pages 422–423.

Tell whether you would use mental math or pencil and paper. Then write the answer in exponential form.

5. $10^4 \times 10^3$

6. $10^{-11} \times 10^8$

7. $10^{-5} \times 10^{-14}$

8. $(10^4 \times 10^6) \times 10^{-3}$

9. $(10^7 \times 10^{-8}) \times 10^8$

10. $0.001 \times 1{,}000$

11. $100{,}000{,}000 \times 10{,}000$

12. $0.0001 \times 0.000000001$

13. $10{,}000{,}000 \times 100{,}000$

Divide. Write the answer in exponential form.

14. $\frac{10^5}{10^2}$

15. $\frac{10^6}{10^{-5}}$

16. $\frac{10^{-7}}{10^4}$

17. $\frac{10^{-4}}{10^{-5}}$

18. $\frac{10^5}{10^9}$

19. $\frac{100}{10{,}000}$

20. $\frac{0.001}{100}$

21. $\frac{0.0001}{0.000001}$

22. $\frac{100{,}000}{0.0001}$

23. $\frac{0.0001}{1{,}000}$

Problem Solving

Use the information on page 396 to solve.

24. $\square$ meters = 10^{12} angstrom units

25. $\square$ angstrom units = 1 mm

Number Sense Under what conditions of *a* and *b* is each of the following true?

26. $10^a \times 10^b < 1$

27. $10^a \times 10^b = 1$

28. $\frac{10^a}{10^b} > 1$

Explore Math

Use Data Use the table on page 394 to find the missing numbers.

29. 1 km = $\square$ m = $10^{\square}$ m

30. 1 m = $\square$ cm = $10^{\square}$ cm

31. 1 mm = $\square$ cm = $10^{\square}$ cm

32. Write a rule telling how to use powers of 10 to write equivalent measures in the metric system.

Scientific Notation for Large Numbers

Build Understanding

Using ***scientific notation***, social scientists can write large numbers in a more convenient form.

Populations of the World	
Continent	Population
Asia	3,031,000,000
Europe	684,000,000
Africa	615,000,000
North America	413,000,000
South America	282,200,000
Oceania	25,500,000
Antarctica	0

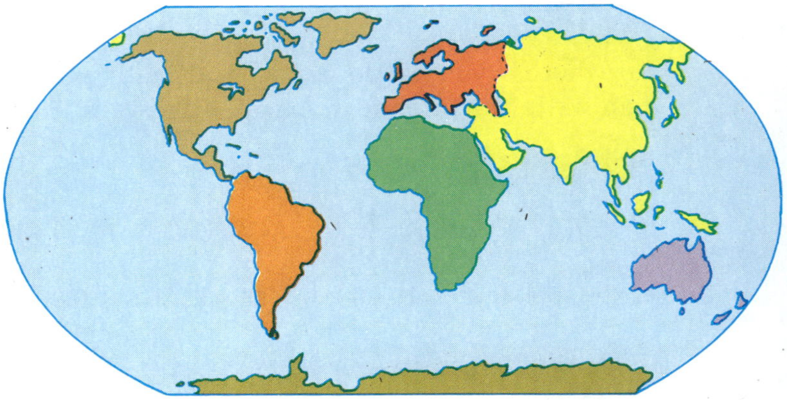

A. Show the population of Asia in scientific notation.

To express a number in scientific notation, write it as the product of

1. A number equal to or greater than 1 and less than 10.
2. A power of 10 in exponential form.

$3{,}031{,}000{,}000 = 3.031 \times 1{,}000{,}000{,}000$

$3.031 \times 1{,}\underbrace{000{,}000{,}000}_{\text{9 zeros}} = 3.031 \times 10^9$

B. Express Africa's population in scientific notation.

To change from standard to scientific notation, move the decimal point left until the number is at least 1 and less than 10. The number of places the decimal point moved is the exponent of the power of 10.

$615{,}000{,}000 = 6.15 \times 10^?$

$6\underbrace{15{,}000{,}000}_{\text{8 places}} = 6.15 \times 10^8$

C. Write 8.3×10^6 in standard form.

To change from scientific to standard form, move the decimal point right the number of places indicated by the exponent of the power of 10.

$8.3 \times 10^6 = 8\underbrace{300000}_{\text{6 places}} = 8{,}300{,}000$

■ **Talk About Math** Tell why 8.74×10^{100} is easier to read with exponents than it would be in standard form.

Check Understanding

For another example, see Set D, pages 420–421.

Tell whether each number is written in scientific notation. Answer *yes* or *no*.

1. 7.523×10^2 **2.** 10.1×10^3 **3.** 0.4×10^5 **4.** 5.26×10^8

Find the missing exponents.

5. $3{,}450 = 3.45 \times 10^{\square}$ **6.** $6{,}500{,}000 = 6.5 \times 10^{\square}$ **7.** 36 million $= 3.6 \times 10^{\square}$

Practice

For More Practice, see Set D, pages 422–423.

Write each number in standard form.

8. 3.2×10^4 **9.** 2.402×10^1 **10.** 1.25×10^4 **11.** 1.414×10^8

12. 6.8×10^5 **13.** 1.01×10^3 **14.** 4.3×10^7 **15.** 7.9×10^2

Write each number in scientific notation.

16. 175 **17.** 300,000 **18.** 54.15 **19.** 35,076.8

20. 67,100,000 **21.** 937.56 **22.** 6 **23.** 3,200,000

Write each number in standard form. Then write it in scientific notation.

24. 122×10^2 **25.** 0.63×10^3 **26.** 75.4×10^4 **27.** 0.00509×10^4

28. 0.785×10^5 **29.** 129×10^6 **30.** 0.00035×10^5 **31.** 6.007×10^4

Problem Solving

Use the population estimates in the table on page 398 as needed.

32. About how many more people are in Asia than in Africa?

33. The population of Asia is about how many times as great as the population of Oceania?

34. The population of Asia is predicted to be 4 billion in the year 2000. About how much of an increase is expected?

35. The population of Asia is about how many times as great as the population of North America?

36. Critical Thinking Suppose the population of each continent doubled. Express the population of each continent in scientific notation. Compare your results with your answers to Problems 32–35. Describe a method you can use to multiply a number written in scientific notation by 2.

Scientific Notation for Small Numbers

Build Understanding

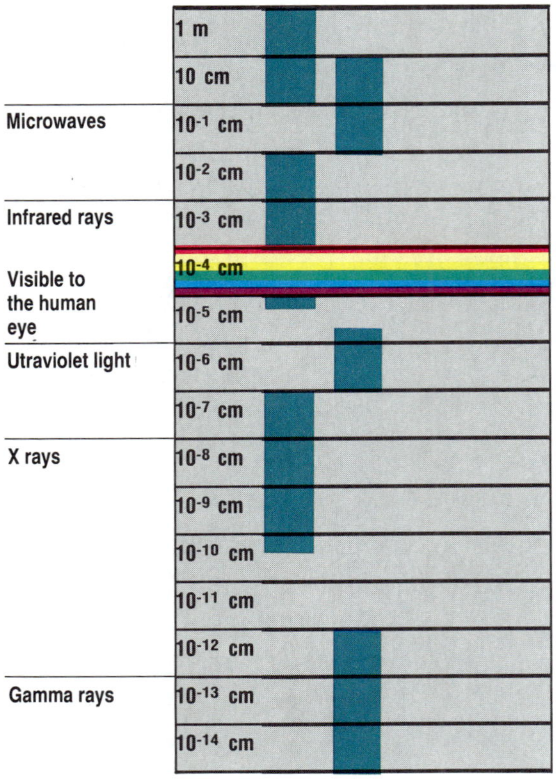

Light waves, the visible part of the electromagnetic spectrum, are near the beginning of the high energy, short wavelength portion of the spectrum.

Particles and waves too small to be seen can influence our environment. Scientific notation is used to describe these minute quantities.

A. Violet is the color of visible light with the shortest wavelength, about 0.00004 cm. Express 0.00004 in scientific notation.

$0.00004 = 4 \times 10^{-5}$ Imagine a decimal point after the nonzero digit 4. Moving the decimal point 5 places to the left is the same as multiplying by 0.00001 or 10^{-5}.

B. Light appears green when the wavelengths are between 4.912×10^{-5} cm and 5.75×10^{-5} cm. Write 5.06×10^{-5} cm in standard form.

$5.06 \times 10^{-5} = 0.0000506$

Multiplying by 10^{-5}, or 0.00001, moves the decimal point 5 places to the left.

Talk About Math Compare the procedures for writing large and small numbers in scientific notation. How are they the same? How are they different?

Check Understanding

For another example, see Set E, pages 420–421.

Find the missing number.

1. $1.02 \times 10^{-7} = \square$

2. $0.487 = \square \times 10^{-1}$

3. $0.00013 = 1.3 \times 10^{\square}$

Number Sense Which number is greater?

4. 7.5×10^{-4} or 4.92×10^{-4}

5. 1.62×10^{-3} or 1.62×10^{0}

6. 0.000099 or 6.3×10^{-2}

Practice

For More Practice, see Set E, pages 422–423.

Write each number in scientific notation.

7. 0.52 **8.** 0.003 **9.** 0.000502

10. 62.39 **11.** 0.00000000516 **12.** 278,000,000,000

13. 875,000,000 **14.** 576.5 **15.** 0.00000784

Write each number in standard form.

16. 2.3×10^{-2} **17.** 4.6×10^{-1} **18.** 5.01×10^{-5} **19.** 6.321×10^{-4}

20. 8.5×10^{-3} **21.** 7.004×10^{-6} **22.** 3.844×10^{-2} **23.** 1.005×10^{-5}

Mixed Practice Write each number in standard form.

24. 9.001×10^{6} **25.** 3.865×10^{-2} **26.** 3.865×10^{2} **27.** 5.83×10^{-8}

28. 3.72×10^{-4} **29.** 4.17×10^{8} **30.** 6.6×10^{9} **31.** 1.75×10^{-9}

Problem Solving

Solve each problem.

32. Gamma rays have wavelengths between 1.4×10^{-8} cm and 5×10^{-11} cm. Write these wavelengths in standard form.

33. Wavelengths between 0.00004 cm and 0.00007 cm are visible. Ultraviolet light has a wavelength of 2.9×10^{-5} cm. Show why ultraviolet light is not visible.

Midchapter Checkup

Write an equivalent expression. Tell which property of rational numbers you used.

1. $1.9 + 6.5 + 0$ **2.** 52.307×1 **3.** $9 \times 7 + 9 \times 3$ **4.** 7.5×0

Multiply or divide. Write the answer in standard form and in exponential form.

5. $10^{2} \times 10^{6}$ **6.** $10^{-3} \times 10^{5}$ **7.** $10^{-2} \div 10^{-5}$ **8.** $10 \div 10^{3}$

Write in standard form.

9. 2.37×10^{6} **10.** 1.07×10^{-2} **11.** $\frac{1}{10^4}$ **12.** 8.5×10^{-4}

Write in scientific notation.

13. 251,000 **14.** 0.0057 **15.** 364.27 **16.** 0.00000901

Math-at-Home Activity

Calculator Measure your own pulse and that of one or more family members for 10 seconds. Record your results.

1. How many times does each person's heart beat per

a. minute? **b.** hour?

c. day? **d.** year?

2. Whose pulse is the highest?

3. Whose pulse is the lowest?

4. Do you think your answers are exact? Why or why not?

Visual Thinking Activity

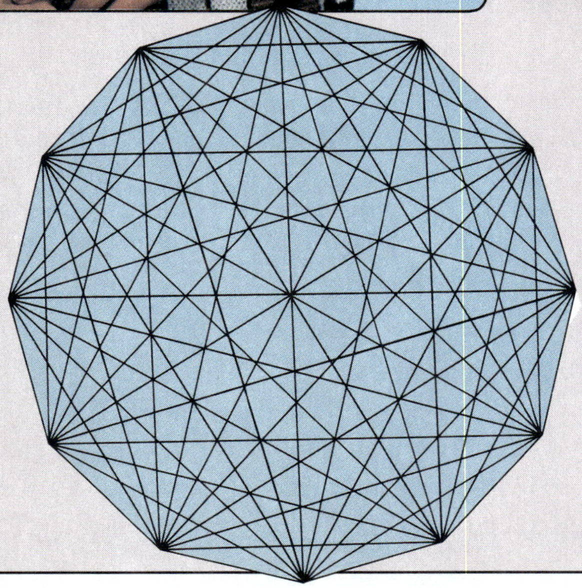

How many different line segments connect the 12 points on the circle?

Explore with a Computer

Use the *Spreadsheet Workshop Project* for this activity.

The square root of any number can be estimated as being between two numbers.

1. At the computer, complete the table by estimating the square root of each given number. Change your estimate to find each square root to the nearest tenth.

2. Which of the numbers in the table are perfect squares?

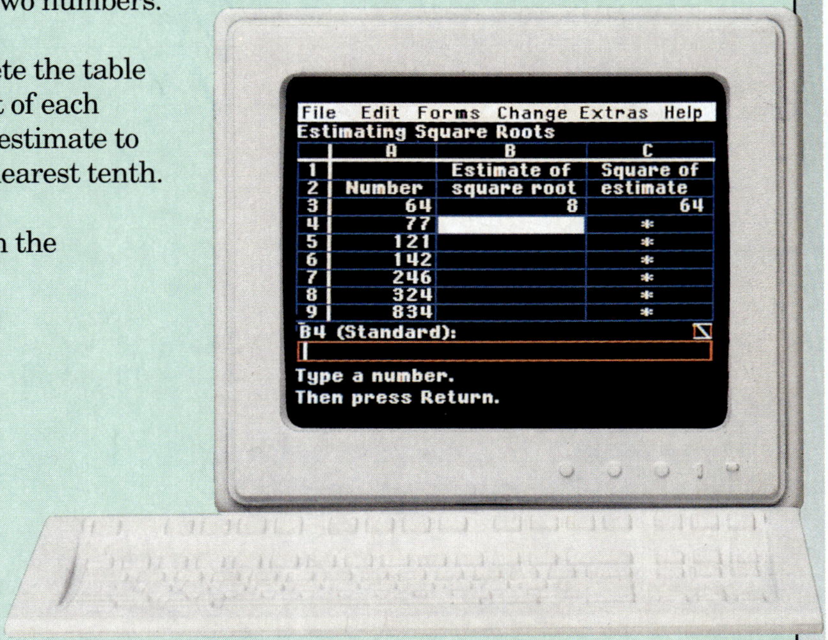

Number-Sense Project

Look back at pages 390–391.

The Euglena cell is about 3×10^{-2} mm long and is made up mostly of water molecules.

Use the diagram below and give the scientific notation for the measurement of each particle shown. The size of the Euglena cell is multiplied by $\frac{1}{100{,}000}$ to find the size of the water molecule and so on.

a. water molecule **b.** atom **c.** nucleus **d.** proton **e.** quark

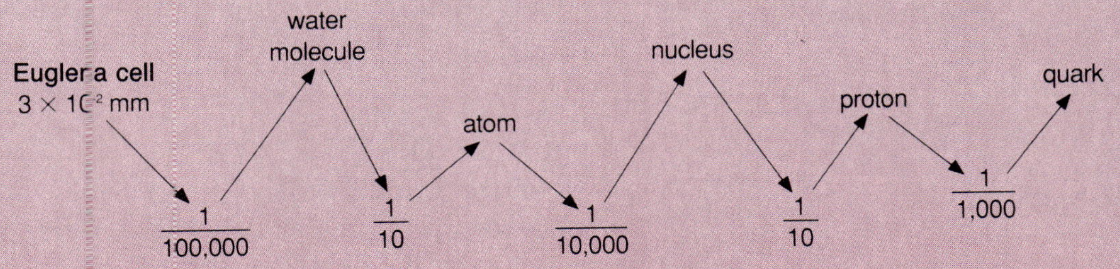

Computing in Scientific Notation

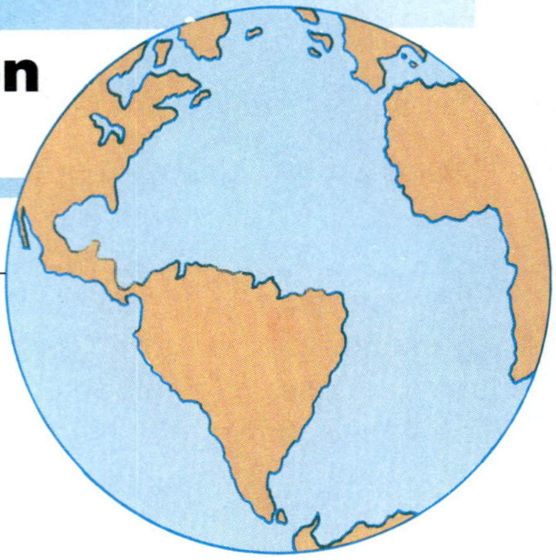

Build Understanding

A. Oceanic Detectives
Groups: 3–5 students

ACTIVITY

Use the clues shown to match the oceans of the world with their approximate areas in square miles.

Oceans of the World		*Areas of the Oceans*	
Arctic Ocean	**Indian Ocean**	**2.84×10^7 sq mi**	**5.44×10^6 sq mi**
Atlantic Ocean	**Pacific Ocean**	**3.18×10^7 sq mi**	**6.38×10^7 sq mi**

Clue 1
The Arctic Ocean is about 8.53×10^{-2} times as large as the Pacific Ocean.

Clue 2
If the Pacific Ocean were in the shape of a square, each side would be about 7.99×10^3 miles long.

Clue 3
The Atlantic Ocean covers about half the area the Pacific Ocean covers.

Clue 4
Side by side, the Atlantic Ocean and the Indian Ocean would cover 3.6×10^6 square miles less than the Pacific Ocean.

a. Name the oceans in order from largest to smallest.

b. Which ocean did you find first? Explain how you used each clue.

B. Use the properties of rational numbers and exponents to calculate in scientific notation. Find $(8.6 \times 10^6) + (3.2 \times 10^5)$.

Write both addends with the same power of 10:
$8.6 \times 10^6 = 8.6 \times 10^1 \times 10^5 = 86 \times 10^5$

$$(8.6 \times 10^6) + (3.2 \times 10^5)$$
$$= (86 \times 10^5) + (3.2 \times 10^5)$$
$$= (86 + 3.2) \times 10^5$$
$$= 89.2 \times 10^5$$
$$= 8.92 \times 10^1 \times 10^5$$
$$= 8.92 \times 10^6$$

C. Find $(5.3 \times 10^5) \times (2.0 \times 10^{-2})$. Use the associative property of multiplication. Write the answer in scientific notation.

$$(5.3 \times 10^5) \times (2.0 \times 10^{-2})$$
$$= (5.3 \times 2.0) \times (10^5 \times 10^{-2})$$
$$= 10.6 \times 10^{5-2}$$
$$= 10.6 \times 10^3$$
$$= 1.06 \times 10^1 \times 10^3$$
$$= 1.06 \times 10^4$$

Write About Math Describe a procedure for calculating with numbers in scientific notation. Include detailed examples to show each operation.

Check Understanding

For another example, see Set F, pages 420–421.

Find the missing numbers.

1. $(1.2 \times 10^6) - (6.5 \times 10^5)$

$= (1.2 \times \square \times 10^5) - (6.5 \times 10^5)$

$= (\square \times 10^5) - (6.5 \times 10^5)$

$= (\square - 6.5) \times 10^5$

$= \square \times 10^5$

2. $\dfrac{1.23 \times 10^7}{8.2 \times 10^3} = \dfrac{\square}{8.2} \times \dfrac{10^7}{10^{\square}}$

$= \square \times 10^{7-\square}$

$= (1.5 \times 10^{-1}) \times 10^{\square}$

$= \square \times 10^{\square}$

Practice

For More Practice, see Set F, pages 422–423.

Tell whether you would use mental math, paper and pencil, or a calculator. Then calculate and write answers in scientific notation.

3. $(4 \times 10^4) - (3 \times 10^4)$

4. $(8.4 \times 10^6) + (3.1 \times 10^6)$

5. $(6.7 \times 10^5) - (3.8 \times 10^5)$

6. $(5.2 \times 10^{-5}) + (3.9 \times 10^{-5})$

7. $(2.3 \times 10^6) \times (4 \times 10^5)$

8. $(3.3 \times 10^{-3}) \times (3 \times 10^2)$

9. $\dfrac{7.5 \times 10^4}{2.5 \times 10^1}$

10. $\dfrac{6.84 \times 10^{-4}}{2 \times 10^{-6}}$

11. $\dfrac{1.5 \times 10^4}{3 \times 10^{-2}}$

12. $(7.5 \times 10^5) + (7.2 \times 10^6)$

13. $(8.4 \times 10^6) \div (4 \times 10^3)$

14. $(3.8 \times 10^8) \times (1.4 \times 10^{-3})$

15. $(9.6 \times 10^5) - (7.2 \times 10^4)$

16. $(4.05 \times 10^{-3}) - (2 \times 10^{-3})$

17. $(5.7 \times 10^5) + (8.3 \times 10^5)$

18. $(5 \times 10^{-3}) - (2.25 \times 10^{-4})$

19. $\dfrac{(8.04 \times 10^{-3}) \times (1.2 \times 10^6)}{1.5 \times 10^{-4}}$

Problem Solving

Solve each problem. Use the information on page 404 as needed.

20. How much greater in area is the Atlantic Ocean than the Arctic Ocean?

21. The area of the Pacific Ocean is how many times as great as the 3.18×10^4 square miles covered by Lake Superior?

22. If the volume of the Pacific Ocean is about 1.63×10^8 cubic miles and the volume of the Arctic Ocean is about 4.03×10^6 cubic miles, the Arctic is about how many times as small as the Pacific?

23. If a teaspoon of water can cover about 4 square inches, or 9.96×10^{-10} square miles, it would take 3.26×10^{15} teaspoons of water to cover the Sahara Desert. About how large is the Sahara Desert?

Use Data from a Diagram

PROBLEM SOLVING GUIDE

Understand
QUESTION
FACTS
KEY IDEA

Plan and Solve
STRATEGY
ANSWER

Look Back
SENSIBLE ANSWER
ALTERNATE APPROACH

Build Understanding

Astronomers use scientific notation to express distances in our planetary system. If light travels at 1.86×10^5 miles per second, in how many minutes will light travel the maximum distance from the sun to Earth?

Understand

QUESTION How many minutes does it take light to travel the maximum distance from the sun to Earth?

FACTS Light travels 1.86×10^5 mi per sec. The maximum distance is given in the diagram.

KEY IDEA In the distance formula (*rate* × *time* = *distance*), you know the rate and the distance.

Plan and Solve

STRATEGY In the distance formula use the data from the diagram and the rate light travels.

ANSWER Since $rt = d$, use $t = \frac{d}{r}$.

$$t = \frac{9.45 \times 10^7}{1.86 \times 10^5}$$ Substitute the values given for d and r.

$$t = \frac{9.45}{1.86} \times \frac{10^7}{10^5}$$ Compute and round.

$$t \approx 5.08 \times 10^2$$

$$t \approx 508 \text{ seconds}$$

$$t \approx 8.47 \text{ minutes}$$

Sunlight takes about 8.5 minutes to reach Earth.

Look Back

ALTERNATE APPROACH You could use a calculator to do the computation.

Press: 9.45 [÷] 1.86 [×] 100 [÷] 60 [=]

Display: 8.4677418

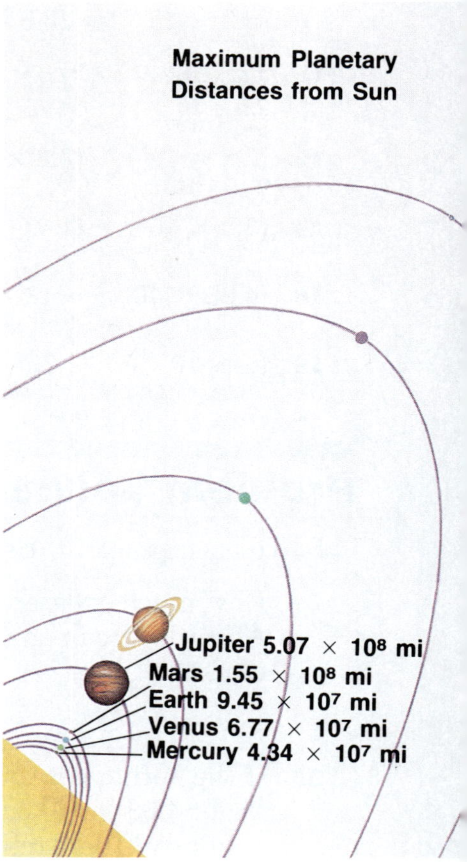

■ **Talk About Math** Recall what you learned about precision in Chapter 8. Why should you *not* give the answer as shown by the calculator?

Check Understanding

Number Sense Tell which numbers and operations you would use to solve. Use the diagram on page 406.

1. How much greater is the maximum distance from the sun to Mars than the maximum distance from the sun to Venus?

2. The maximum distance from the sun to Jupiter is how many times as great as the maximum distance from the sun to Earth?

3. If light travels at 1.86×10^5 mi per sec, how far will light travel in 1 minute? in 1 hour?

4. What is the maximum time light takes to travel from the sun to Jupiter?

5. How much greater is the maximum distance from the sun to Earth than the maximum distance from the sun to Mercury?

6. What is the maximum time light takes to travel from the sun to Mercury?

Practice

Solve. **Remember** to use the properties for rational numbers.

7. Problem 1 **8.** Problem 2 **9.** Problem 3

10. Problem 4 **11.** Problem 5 **12.** Problem 6

Choose a Strategy

Making a Solar System A scale model of the solar system uses 10 inches for the actual maximum distance from Earth to the sun. On the model, what will be the distance of each planet from the sun?

13. Complete the ratio of the scale distance to the actual distance from Earth to the sun. This is the scale ratio.

$$\frac{10}{x} \qquad \frac{\text{Scale distance in inches}}{\text{Actual distance in millions of miles}}$$

Use the scale ratio to find the scale distance from each planet to the sun.

14. Mercury **15.** Venus **16.** Mars **17.** Jupiter

PROBLEM SOLVING STRATEGIES

- Choose an Operation
- Solve a Simpler Problem
- Use a Formula
- Write an Equation
- Make a Graph
- Draw a Diagram
- Make a Table

Square Roots

The Great Pyramid was built about 2800 B.C. during the reign of Cheops, an Egyptian pharaoh.

Build Understanding

A. The base of the Great Pyramid of Cheops is a square with sides 756 feet long. The area of the base is $(756)^2$, or 571,536 square feet. The base of a scale model of the Great Pyramid has an area about one ten-thousandth of the actual base, or 57 square feet. What is the length of a side of the model's base?

The area of a square is given by the formula $A = s^2$. In the formula, if $A = 25$, then $s = 5$ because $25 = 5^2$. The ***square root*** of a number is one of its two equal factors. Integers such as 1, 4, 9, 16, and 25 are called ***perfect squares.*** The square roots of perfect squares are integers. For example, $\sqrt{81} = 9$ because $81 = 9 \times 9$.

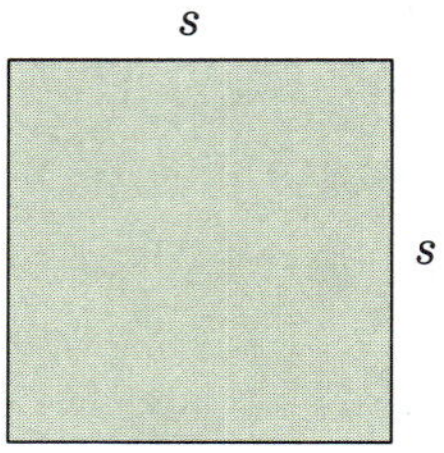

$A = s^2$
$\sqrt{A} = s$

On the model, $57 = s^2$. To find s, find the square root of 57, written $\sqrt{57}$. Although 57 is not a perfect square, you can estimate its square root.

Step 1: Estimate: Because 57 is between 49 and 64, $\sqrt{57}$ must be between $\sqrt{49}$ and $\sqrt{64}$, or between 7 and 8.

Average: $\frac{7 + 8}{2} = 7.5$ First approximation of $\sqrt{57}$

Step 2: **Divide:** $57 \div 7.5 = 7.6$

Average: $\frac{7.5 + 7.6}{2} \approx 7.6$ Second approximation

Step 3: **Divide:** $57 \div 7.6 = 7.5$

Average: $\frac{7.6 + 7.5}{2} \approx 7.6$ Third approximation

The second and third approximations equal 7.6 when rounded to the nearest tenth. Therefore, $\sqrt{57} \approx 7.6$.

The length of a side of the base is about 7.6 feet.

Calculator

Press: 57 [√]

Display: 7.5498344

B. Use this portion of a table to find $\sqrt{22}$ to the nearest thousandth. From line 2 of the table, $\sqrt{22} \approx 4.690$.

n	n^2	$\sqrt{n}$
21	441	4.583
22	484	4.690
23	529	4.796

Talk About Math How might you construct a list of perfect squares?

Check Understanding

For another example, see Set G, pages 420–421.

1. **Estimation** Using the divide-and-average method shown in Example A, estimate $\sqrt{85}$ to the nearest tenth.

2. $\sqrt{45}$ is between what two whole numbers?

3. Explain how you can use the table on page 602 to find $\sqrt{2{,}809}$.

Practice

For More Practice, see Set G, pages 422–423.

Find the square root. Round to the nearest hundredth when necessary.

4. $\sqrt{64}$
5. $\sqrt{400}$
6. $\sqrt{500}$
7. $\sqrt{8}$
8. $\sqrt{0.49}$
9. $\sqrt{9.6}$
10. $\sqrt{125}$
11. $\sqrt{800}$
12. $\sqrt{28}$
13. $\sqrt{39}$
14. $\sqrt{17.1}$
15. $\sqrt{198.25}$
16. $\sqrt{13{,}689}$
17. $\sqrt{0.01}$
18. $\sqrt{6.25}$

Estimation Estimate each square root to the nearest whole number.

19. $\sqrt{17}$
20. $\sqrt{85}$
21. $\sqrt{34}$
22. $\sqrt{105}$
23. $\sqrt{10}$
24. $\sqrt{66}$

Problem Solving

Calculator Solve each problem. Use $A = s^2$.

25. What is the length of a side of a square whose area is 1.44 sq in.?

26. Find the area of a square with a side that is $\sqrt{2.56}$ inches long.

27. The Mayans built pyramids with truncated tops in what is now known as Mexico. The Pyramid of the Sun at Teotihuacán, has a base of 213 meters. Find its area.

28. The square base of the Chepheren Pyramid in Egypt has an area of 501,264 square feet. What is the length of a side?

29. Ziggurats are stepped, pyramid-shaped towers. The average area of square-based ziggurats is 28,900 square feet. What is the average length of a side?

30. The largest ziggurat has a square base with an area of about 1[illegible]2,225 square feet. Find the length of a side to the nearest tenth of a yard.

Over 30 ziggurats are known to have been built in ancient Mesopotamia, the area now known as Iran and Iraq.

Irrational Numbers

Build Understanding

A. Every rational number can be written as a terminating decimal or as a repeating decimal. Decimals that do not terminate or repeat are called ***irrational numbers.***

Rational Numbers	Irrational Numbers
$\frac{-7}{2} = -3.5$	$\sqrt{2} = 1.4142135\ldots$
$\frac{1}{3} = 0.\overline{3}$	$\sqrt{3} = 1.7320508\ldots$
$1\frac{20}{99} = 1.\overline{20}$	$\pi = 3.1415926\ldots$

The square root of a perfect square is a positive or negative integer and therefore a rational number. $\sqrt{16}$ and $\sqrt{1{,}849}$ are rational numbers.

The square root of any positive integer that is not a perfect square is an irrational number. $\sqrt{17}$ and $\sqrt{90}$ are irrational numbers.

B. The rational numbers together with the irrational numbers make up the set of ***real numbers.*** Real numbers can be used to name all the points on the number line.

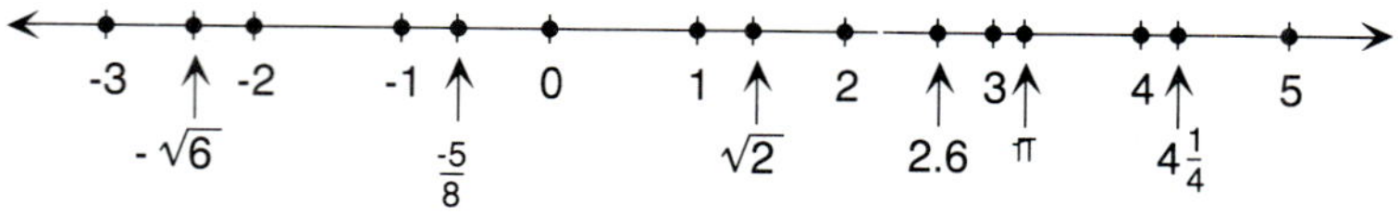

The properties of rational numbers are found on page 392. These properties are true for all real numbers.

C. Write $-4\frac{5}{6}$ as a repeating decimal.

$-4\frac{5}{6} = \frac{-29}{6}$

$$6\overline{)29.0000\ldots} = 4.8333\ldots$$

$-4\frac{5}{6} = -4.8\overline{3}$

D. Which number is greater, $\frac{22}{7}$ or π? Write the numbers as decimals.

$\frac{22}{7} = 3.1428571\ldots$

$\pi = 3.1415926\ldots$ Compare digits.

$\frac{22}{7}$ is greater than π.

■ **Write About Math** Refer to the list of properties on page 392. Write an example of each property using irrational numbers.

Check Understanding

For another example, see Set H, pages 420–421.

Tell whether each number is rational or irrational.

1. 4.7 **2.** $\frac{-5}{6}$ **3.** $\sqrt{23}$ **4.** $\sqrt{121}$ **5.** $3.\overline{14}$

Tell whether each statement is true or false.

6. Every rational number is a real number.

7. Every real number is a rational number.

8. Every integer is a rational number.

9. The number 0 is not a real number.

Practice

For More Practice, see Set H, pages 422–423.

Tell whether each number is rational or irrational.

10. $\frac{-3}{5}$ **11.** $\sqrt{16}$ **12.** $\sqrt{30}$ **13.** 0.4 **14.** $1\frac{3}{10}$

15. $\sqrt{64}$ **16.** $\sqrt{36}$ **17.** $\sqrt{50}$ **18.** $\sqrt{10}$ **19.** $\sqrt{400}$

Write each rational number as a repeating or a terminating decimal.

20. $\frac{1}{3}$ **21.** $\frac{-3}{11}$ **22.** $6\frac{1}{3}$ **23.** $-1\frac{7}{8}$ **24.** $\frac{20}{33}$

25. $\frac{15}{99}$ **26.** $\frac{5}{16}$ **27.** $\frac{-2}{3}$ **28.** $-2\frac{1}{9}$ **29.** $\frac{3}{80}$

Number Sense Tell which number is greater.

30. $3.\overline{82}$, $3.\overline{81}$ **31.** $\sqrt{90}$, $\sqrt{91}$ **32.** 3.14, $\frac{22}{7}$

33. 3.1416, π **34.** π, $\sqrt{12}$ **35.** π, $\frac{355}{113}$

Find a rational number between the pair of numbers in each exercise.

36. Exercise 30 **37.** Exercise 31 **38.** Exercise 32

39. Exercise 33 **40.** Exercise 34 **41.** Exercise 35

Problem Solving

Solve.

42. Consider the decimal 3.3030030003.... It neither terminates nor repeats, but it does follow a pattern. Write the next ten digits.

43. Write an irrational number between each of the pairs of numbers in Exercises 30–35.

ALGEBRA

Computing with Irrational Numbers

Build Understanding

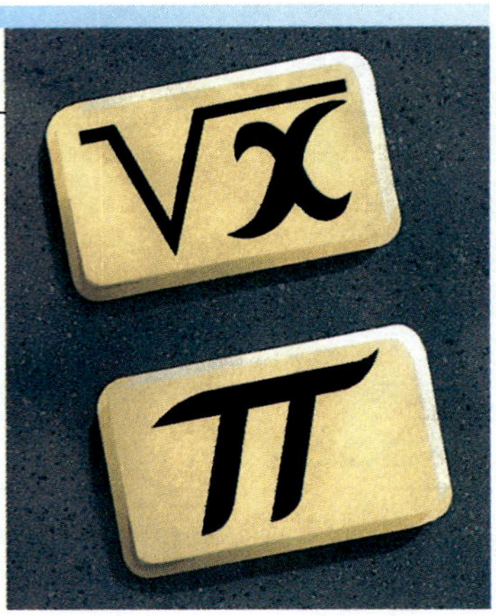

A. Root of the Problem
Materials: Calculator or square root table
Groups: With a partner

a. This key sequence shows how to compute $2\sqrt{5} \times \sqrt{7}$.

Press: 2 [×] 5 [√] [×] 7 [√] [=]

Display: *11.832159* ≈ *11.83*

b. Copy and complete the tables below. Use a calculator or the table of square roots on page 602 to give each answer. Round answers to the nearest hundredth.

$\sqrt{4} \times \sqrt{9} =$ ▦	$\sqrt{36} =$ ▦
$\sqrt{5} \times \sqrt{9} =$ ▦	$\sqrt{45} =$ ▦
$\sqrt{6} \times \sqrt{9} =$ ▦	$\sqrt{54} =$ ▦

$\sqrt{7} \times \sqrt{9} =$ ▦	$\sqrt{63} =$ ▦
$\sqrt{8} \times \sqrt{9} =$ ▦	$\sqrt{72} =$ ▦
$\sqrt{9} \times \sqrt{9} =$ ▦	$\sqrt{81} =$ ▦

$\sqrt{a} \times \sqrt{b} = \sqrt{▦}$

c. Copy and complete the tables below. Round answers to the nearest hundredth.

$3\sqrt{5} + \sqrt{5} =$ ▦	$4\sqrt{5} =$ ▦
$3\sqrt{5} + 2\sqrt{5} =$ ▦	$5\sqrt{5} =$ ▦
$3\sqrt{5} + 3\sqrt{5} =$ ▦	$6\sqrt{5} =$ ▦

$3\sqrt{5} + 4\sqrt{5} =$ ▦	$7\sqrt{5} =$ ▦
$3\sqrt{5} + 5\sqrt{5} =$ ▦	$8\sqrt{5} =$ ▦
$3\sqrt{5} + 6\sqrt{5} =$ ▦	$9\sqrt{5} =$ ▦

$a\sqrt{c} + b\sqrt{c} = (a + b)\sqrt{▦}$

d. What is true about $\frac{\sqrt{a}}{\sqrt{b}}$, when $b \neq 0$?

$\frac{\sqrt{a}}{\sqrt{b}} = \sqrt{\frac{▦}{▦}}$, **when $b \neq 0$**

B. Find $\sqrt{27}$.

$$\sqrt{27} = \sqrt{9 \times 3}$$
$$= \sqrt{9} \times \sqrt{3}$$
$$= 3\sqrt{3}$$
$$\approx 3 \times 1.732$$
$$\approx 5.196 \approx 5.20$$

C. Find $\sqrt{\frac{9}{16}}$.

$$\sqrt{\frac{9}{16}} = \frac{\sqrt{9}}{\sqrt{16}}$$
$$= \frac{3}{4}$$

Write About Math Give an example showing that the product of two irrational numbers does not have to be an irrational number.

Check Understanding

For another example, see Set I, pages 420–421.

Are the numbers equal? Answer *yes* or *no*.

1. $\sqrt{8} \times \sqrt{7} \stackrel{?}{=} \sqrt{56}$ **2.** $\dfrac{\sqrt{24}}{\sqrt{4}} \stackrel{?}{=} \sqrt{6}$ **3.** $\dfrac{\sqrt{20}}{2} \stackrel{?}{=} \sqrt{10}$

4. $2\sqrt{6} + 7\sqrt{6} \stackrel{?}{=} 9\sqrt{6}$ **5.** $3\sqrt{13} - 4\sqrt{13} \stackrel{?}{=} -1$ **6.** $\sqrt{3} \times \sqrt{2} \stackrel{?}{=} \sqrt{5}$

Complete each equation.

7. $\sqrt{40} = \sqrt{10} \times \sqrt{\square} = \square\sqrt{10}$ **8.** $3\sqrt{2} - 2\sqrt{2} = (3 - \square)\sqrt{2} = \square$

9. $\dfrac{\sqrt{20}}{\sqrt{5}} = \sqrt{\dfrac{20}{\square}} = \sqrt{\square} = \square$ **10.** $\dfrac{\sqrt{18}}{\sqrt{6}} + 3\dfrac{\sqrt{18}}{\sqrt{6}} = 4\sqrt{\dfrac{18}{\square}} = 4\sqrt{\square}$

Practice

For More Practice, see Set I, pages 422–423.

Compute. Round decimals to the hundredths place.

11. $\sqrt{8} \times \sqrt{2}$ **12.** $\sqrt{3} \times \sqrt{3}$ **13.** $\sqrt{50} \times \sqrt{2}$

14. $\sqrt{20} \div \sqrt{5}$ **15.** $\sqrt{18} \div \sqrt{2}$ **16.** $9\sqrt{4} - 3\sqrt{4}$

17. $\sqrt{2} \times \sqrt{4} \times \sqrt{2}$ **18.** $\sqrt{\dfrac{100}{49}}$ **19.** $7\sqrt{2} - 5\sqrt{2}$

20. $\sqrt{5} \times \sqrt{2}$ **21.** $\sqrt{16} \times \sqrt{9}$ **22.** $2\sqrt{3} + 2\sqrt{3} + 2\sqrt{3}$

23. $\sqrt{3} \times \sqrt{12}$ **24.** $5\sqrt{25} + 6\sqrt{25}$ **25.** $\sqrt{9} \times \sqrt{8}$

26. $\sqrt{\dfrac{25}{4}}$ **27.** $-\sqrt{\dfrac{100}{4}}$ **28.** $3\sqrt{6} + 6\sqrt{6}$

29. $\sqrt{2} \times \sqrt{8} \times \sqrt{4}$ **30.** $\sqrt{6} \times \sqrt{5} \times \sqrt{3}$ **31.** $2\sqrt{7} - 6\sqrt{7}$

32. $\sqrt{30} \div \sqrt{10}$ **33.** $\sqrt{17} \times \sqrt{17}$ **34.** $2\sqrt{13} + 3\sqrt{13} - \sqrt{13}$

35. $\sqrt{9} \times \sqrt{7}$ **36.** $\sqrt{\dfrac{81}{36}}$ **37.** $9\sqrt{2} - 4\sqrt{2}$

Estimation Estimate the value of each expression. Tell which point on the number line most closely approximates each number. Then compute each value to the nearest tenth to check your estimate.

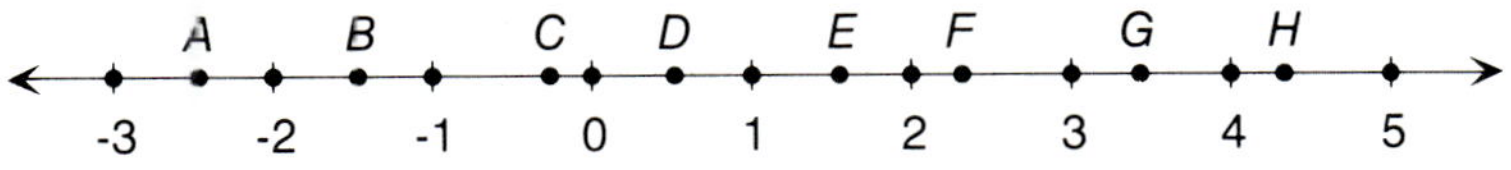

38. $3\sqrt{2}$ **39.** $-\sqrt{\dfrac{9}{4}}$ **40.** $\sqrt{12}$

41. $3\sqrt{8} - 4\sqrt{8}$ **42.** $\sqrt{\dfrac{24}{8}}$ **43.** $\frac{1}{2}(2\sqrt{3} - \sqrt{3})$

Problem Solving

Solve each problem.

44. The length of a rectangle is $\sqrt{8}$ in. and the width is $\sqrt{2}$ in. Find the area.

45. Find the perimeter of the rectangle in Problem 44.

46. The sides of a triangle have lengths $3\sqrt{5}$ cm, $4\sqrt{5}$ cm, and $2\sqrt{5}$ cm. Find the perimeter of the triangle.

47. The perimeter of a triangle is $18\sqrt{7}$ in. If two sides have lengths of $6\sqrt{7}$ in. and $5\sqrt{7}$ in., find the length of the third side.

48. Find the area of a circle with a radius of $4\sqrt{5}$ cm.

49. Find the area of a circle with a diameter of $10\sqrt{2}$ m.

50. An isosceles right triangle has an area of 8 cm^2. Find the lengths of the base and the height.

51. An isosceles right triangle has an area of 24 cm^2. Find the lengths of the base and the height to the nearest tenth of a centimeter.

52. **Calculator** A circle has an area of 50.27 cm^2. Find the radius of the circle to the nearest tenth of a centimeter.

53. The length of the base of a parallelogram is $18\sqrt{3}$ inches. The height is $9\sqrt{3}$ inches. Find the area of the parallelogram.

54. The height of a trapezoid is $3\sqrt{2}$ centimeters, and the lengths of the bases are $6\sqrt{2}$ and $8\sqrt{2}$ centimeters. Find the area of the trapezoid.

55. **Calculator** Eric has 200 square paving stones. Each stone is 1 foot long on a side. Eric wants to build a square patio having the largest possible area. How long will each side of the patio be? How many stones will be left?

56. **Calculator** A square picture has an area of 62 square inches. What is the length of each side of the picture?

TIPS FOR PROBLEM SOLVERS

Be confident so you can do your best.

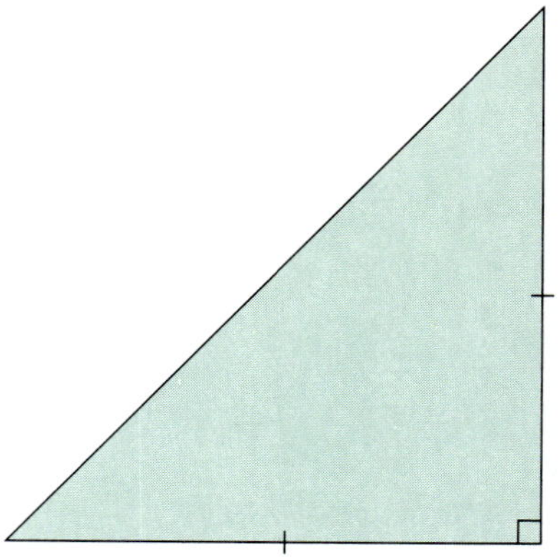

pages 342–379.

Find the perimeter and the area of each figure. **Remember** to include the unit of measure in your answer.

1.

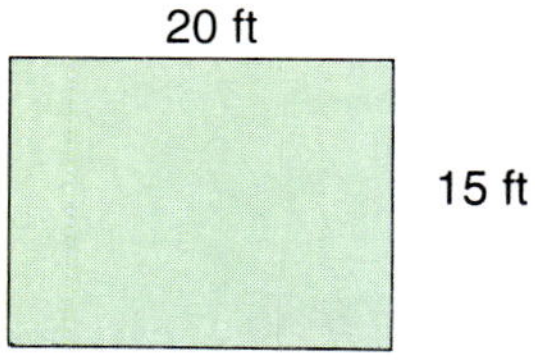

2.

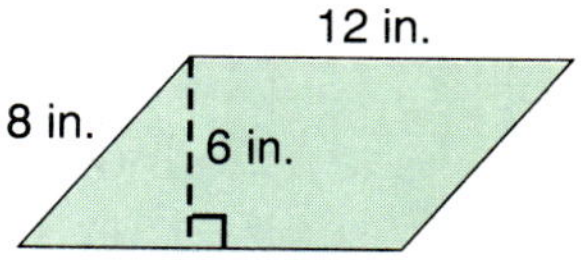

3.

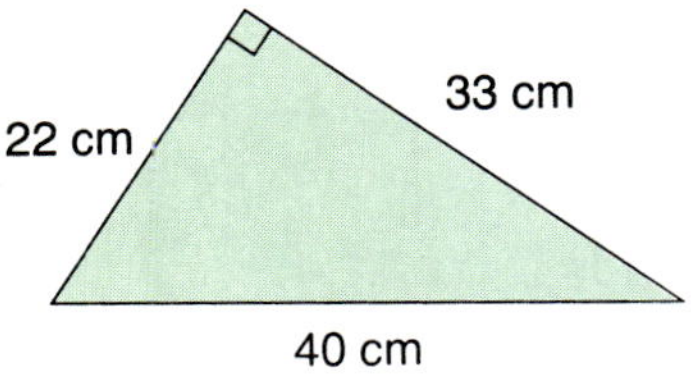

4.

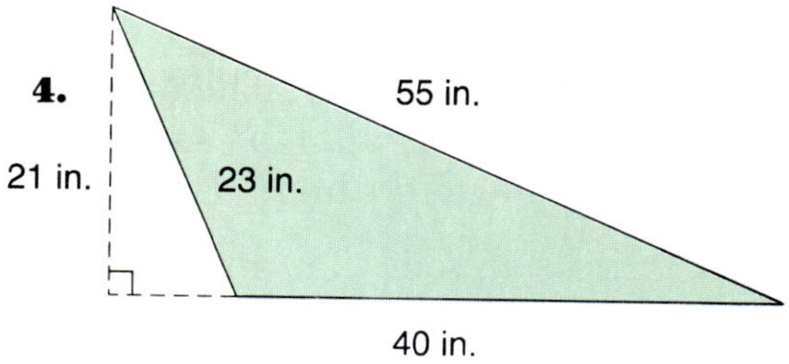

Find the circumference and the area of each circle. Use $\pi = 3.14$. Round answers to the nearest hundredth.

5.

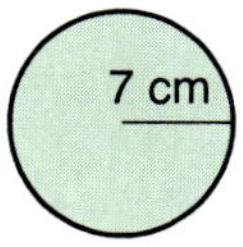

6.

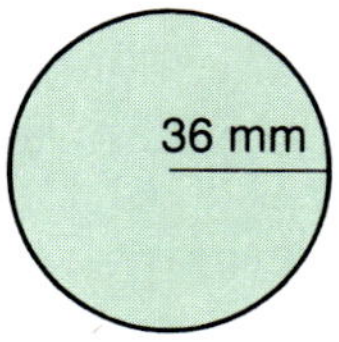

Find the surface area and the volume for Exercises 7–9. For Exercise 10, find only the volume. Use $\pi = \frac{22}{7}$. Round answers to the nearest tenth.

7.

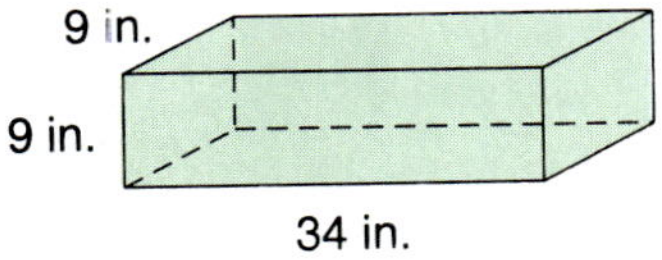

8.

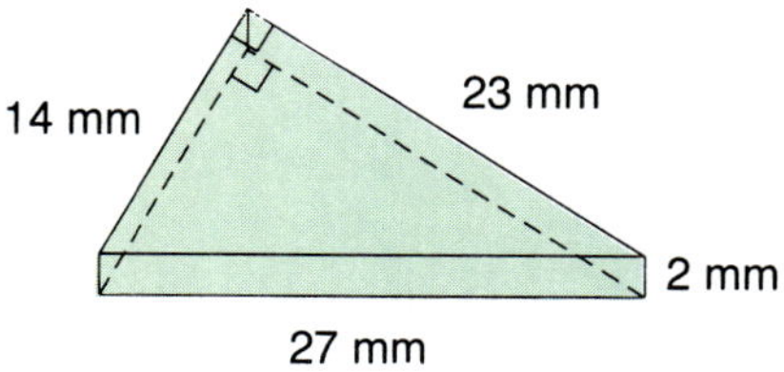

9.

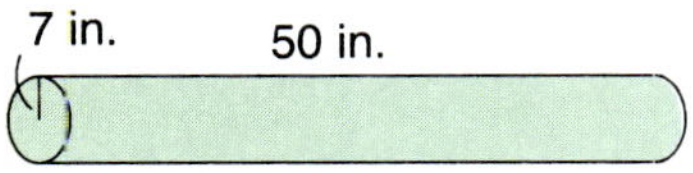

10.

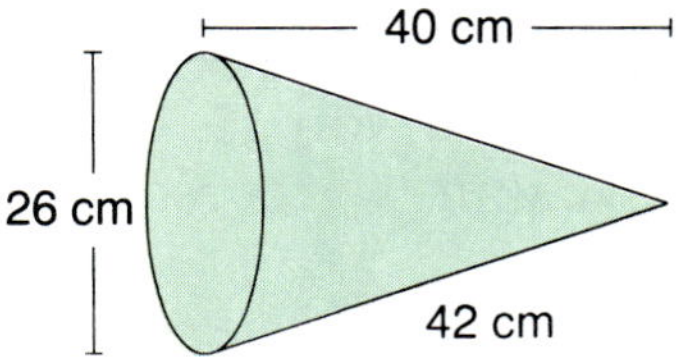

ALGEBRA

Use a Formula

PROBLEM SOLVING GUIDE

Understand
QUESTION
FACTS
KEY IDEA

Plan and Solve
STRATEGY
ANSWER

Look Back
SENSIBLE ANSWER
ALTERNATE APPROACH

Build Understanding

Did you know that the longer an object falls, the faster and farther it travels before hitting bottom? An object will fall 16 feet in 1 second. If the object continues falling for another second, it will travel another 48 feet. The distance an object falls varies with the square of the time it has been falling.

The distance d in feet that an object falls in t seconds is given by the formula $d = 16t^2$.

A redwood tree falls over Upper Yosemite Falls in a storm. How long will it be before the tree shatters on the granite rocks 1,450 feet below?

Understand QUESTION How long does it take an object to fall 1,450 feet?

Plan and Solve STRATEGY Use the distance formula.

$$d = 16t^2$$
$$1{,}450 = 16t^2$$
$$\frac{1{,}450}{16} = \frac{16t^2}{16}$$
$$90.625 = t^2$$
$$\sqrt{90.625} = t$$
$$9.5 \approx t$$

Use a calculator. Find $\sqrt{90.625}$ to the nearest tenth.

ANSWER The redwood takes about 9.5 seconds to fall from the top of Yosemite Falls.

Look Back SENSIBLE ANSWER In 10 seconds an object will fall 16×10^2, or 1,600, feet, so the answer is reasonable.

Talk About Math If an object takes 10 seconds to fall 1,600 feet, will it take 5 seconds to fall 800 feet? Check by using the formula. Discuss the result.

Check Understanding

Use one or more of the area formulas shown at the right to answer Exercises 1–4.

$A = \pi r^2$	The area of a circle is equal to π times the square of the radius of the circle.
$A = s^2$	The area of a square is equal to the square of any side of the square.
$SA = 6s^2$	The surface area of a cube is equal to 6 times the square of any edge of the cube.

1. What is the area of a square baseball diamond with bases 90 feet apart?

2. What is the surface area of a bouillon cube with edges 1 centimeter long?

3. What is the length of a wall in a square classroom with an area of 625 sq ft?

4. Explain why there is a 6 in the formula for the surface area of a cube.

Practice

Calculator Find answers to the nearest tenth. Use $d = 16t^2$.

5. The World Trade Center is 1,350 feet tall. How long will it take an object to fall from the roof to the ground?

6. A parachute opens 5 seconds after a skydiver leaves the plane. How far does she fall before the chute opens?

Use $d = 0.8t^2$, which describes the distance in meters an object falls on the moon in t seconds.

7. How long will it take a golf ball to fall to the moon from a lunar lander hovering 300 meters above the Sea of Tranquility?

8. A robot probe runs out of fuel and falls for 30 seconds before crashing into the moon's Mountains of Copernicus. How far did it fall?

9. If an object falls from a height of 20 meters on the moon, how long will it take the object to reach the surface of the moon?

10. Compare the distance an object falls in 5 seconds on earth with the distance the object falls in 5 seconds on the moon.

Reading ______ Math

Vocabulary Tell whether each statement is true or false.

1. All integers are whole numbers.

2. All whole numbers are integers.

3. All real numbers are irrational.

4. Rational numbers are never integers.

Skills Review

Solve for n. Tell what property is illustrated.

1. $n \times \left(\frac{1}{2} + 3\right) = \left(\frac{3}{4} \times \frac{1}{2}\right) + \left(\frac{3}{4} \times 3\right)$

2. $9.2 \times (6 \times n) = (9.2 \times 6) \times 1.3$

3. $\frac{15}{16} \times n = \frac{11}{12} \times \frac{15}{16}$

Write in standard form.

4. 10^{-4} 5. 10^{4} 6. $\frac{1}{10^5}$

7. 1.6×10^3 8. 2.343×10^6

9. 4.3×10^2 10. 6.07×10^{-2}

11. 1.112×10^{-4} 12. 5.5×10^{-6}

Multiply or divide. Write your answers in exponential form.

13. $10^3 \times 10^2$ 14. $10^{-6} \times 10^5$

15. $\frac{10^7}{10^4}$ 16. $\frac{10^{-8}}{10^3}$

Compute. Write your answers in scientific notation.

17. $(6 \times 10^4) - (4 \times 10^3)$

18. $\frac{(2.1 \times 10^{-3})}{(7 \times 10^2)}$

Estimate each square root to the nearest whole number.

19. $\sqrt{23}$ 20. $\sqrt{79}$ 21. $\sqrt{96}$

Tell whether each number is rational or irrational.

22. $\sqrt{17}$ 23. $-\frac{7}{8}$ 24. $\sqrt{121}$

Compute. Round decimals to the hundredths place.

25. $\sqrt{4} \times \sqrt{5}$ 26. $\sqrt{2} + \sqrt{2}$

27. $\sqrt{3} \times \sqrt{3}$ 28. $\sqrt{135} \div \sqrt{15}$

Problem-Solving Review

Solve each problem.

29. Write two examples to show that subtraction is not commutative.

30. Use exponential form to express the number of decimeters in two kilometers.

31. An estimated population of North America is 413,000,000. Write this number in scientific notation.

32. Light travels at a speed of 1.86×10^5 miles per second. The closest the planet Saturn comes to the sun is 8.384×10^8 miles. At that distance, how long does it take light from the sun to reach Saturn?

33. The area of a square is 3.24 sq in. What is the length of a side?

34. The length of a rectangle is $\sqrt{12}$ in. and the width is $\sqrt{3}$ in. Find the area.

35. An average human male breathes about 8.50×10^3 liters of air per day. Find the number of milliliters of air he would breathe per day. Write your answer in exponential form.

36. **Data File** Use the data on pages 426–427. The length of a giga unit is how many times the length of a micro unit?

37. **Make a Data File** Use an almanac or other source to find the mean distances of planets from the earth. List the distances in standard notation in one column of a table and in scientific notation in another column.

Cumulative Skills Review • Chapters 1–11

Write each fraction in lowest terms.

1. $\frac{26}{50}$ **2.** $\frac{150}{210}$ **3.** $\frac{39}{130}$ **4.** $\frac{77}{121}$

Divide. Round your answers to the nearest tenth.

5. $78.2 \div 6.1$ **6.** $8.7 \div 0.03$ **7.** $5{,}002 \div 45.5$ **8.** $26.7 \div 9.1$

Graph each inequality on a number line.

9. $m \leq 0$ **10.** $c \geq -2$ or $c = -3$ **11.** $r < 4$ **12.** $a < 1$ and $a > -3$

The Wesler family's vacation budget is shown below.
Copy and complete the chart. Then draw a circle graph.

Item	Auto/Gas	Lodging	Food	Amusement	Other
Percent	20%	35%	25%	15%	5%
Number of degrees	**13.**	**14.**	**15.**	**16.**	**17.**

Arrange in order from greatest to least.

18. 5 lb, 5 oz, 5 kg **19.** 3 ft, 3 m, 3 yd **20.** 5 in., 10 cm, 800 mm

Identify each figure.

21. 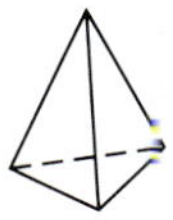

22. 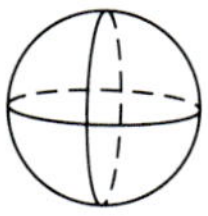

23. 

24. 

Find the volume of each figure. Use 3.14 for π.

25. 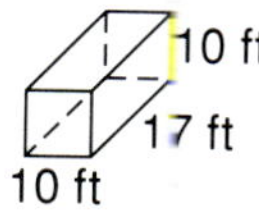

26. 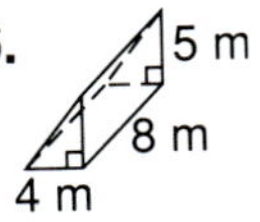

27. 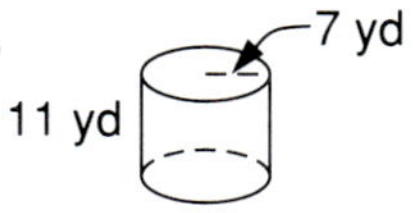

28. 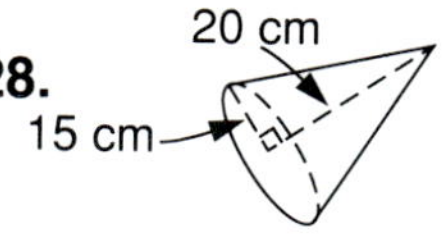

Find the area of each circle with the given dimension. Use 3.14 for π.

29. $d = 6$ in. **30.** $r = 1.5$ mm **31.** $d = 2$ yd **32.** $r = 30$ cm

Write each number in scientific notation.

33. 4,500,000 **34.** 17,900 **35.** 0.00805 **36.** 0.0000000332

Find each square root to the nearest hundredth.

37. $\sqrt{74}$ **38.** $\sqrt{529}$ **39.** $\sqrt{0.81}$ **40.** $\sqrt{300}$

Reteaching

Set A pages 392–393

Properties that are true for rational numbers are illustrated below.

Commutative: $5 + 3.1 = 3.1 + 5$; $6.7 \times 1.8 = 1.8 \times 6.7$

Associative: $\left(\frac{2}{3} + \frac{3}{5}\right) + \frac{1}{4} = \frac{2}{3} + \left(\frac{3}{5} + \frac{1}{4}\right)$; $(2.2 \times 3) \times 7.6 = 2.2 \times (3 \times 7.6)$

Distributive: $\frac{3}{8}\left(6 + \frac{4}{5}\right) = \left(\frac{3}{8} \times 6\right) + \left(\frac{3}{8} \times \frac{4}{5}\right)$

Properties of One and Zero: $4.1 \times 1 = 4.1$; $\frac{4}{9} + 0 = \frac{4}{9}$; $11 \times 0 = 0$

Remember that the commutative properties involve rearranging and the associative properties involve regrouping.

Solve for s. Tell what property is illustrated.

1. $s \times 1 = 19.8$ **2.** $\frac{2}{19} \times \frac{3}{7} = \frac{3}{7} \times s$

3. $(5 \times 6) + (5 \times 47.1) = s\,(6 + 47.1)$

4. $\left(\frac{1}{7} + \frac{2}{3}\right) + \frac{1}{6} = \frac{1}{7} + \left(s + \frac{1}{6}\right)$

Set B pages 394–395

Write 10^5 and 10^{-5} in standard form.

$10^5 = 100{,}000$ A positive exponent indicates the number of zeros in the number.

$10^{-5} = 0.00001$ When the exponent is negative, the number of zeros to the right of the decimal point is always 1 less than the absolute value of the exponent.

Remember that you can use the rules for positive and negative exponents to write numbers in standard form as powers of 10.

Write in standard form.

1. 10^1 **2.** 10^{-2} **3.** 10^7 **4.** 10^{-3}

Write in exponential form.

5. 0.01 **6.** 0.1 **7.** 100 **8.** 10,000

Set C pages 396–397

Compute $10^4 \times 10^7$.

$10^4 \times 10^7 = 10^{(4+7)}$ To multiply powers of 10, add the exponents.

$= 10^{11}$

Compute $\frac{10^9}{10^4}$.

$\frac{10^9}{10^4} = 10^{(9-4)}$ To divide powers of 10, subtract the exponents.

$= 10^5$

Remember that writing numbers that are in standard form as powers of 10 often makes computation easier.

Compute. Write answers in exponential form.

1. $10^{21} \times 10^6$ **2.** $\frac{10^{15}}{10^{12}}$ **3.** $10^4 \times 10^0$

4. $0.0001 \times 100{,}000$ **5.** $\frac{10^{-2}}{10^2}$

Set D pages 398–399

Write 3,972,000 in scientific notation.

$3.972 \times 10^?$ The number is between 1 and 10.

3972000.
3.972×10^6 You had to move the decimal point 6 places to the left.

Remember that to write a number that is in scientific notation in standard form, you move the decimal point the number of places indicated by the exponent.

Write each number in scientific notation.

1. 6,651 **2.** 24,000 **3.** 9,999,000

4. 226,000 **5.** 3,500,000

Write each number in standard form.

6. 7.678×10^4 **7.** 2.304×10^6

Set E pages 400–401

Write 0.0000179 in scientific notation.

$1.79 \times 10^{?}$ The number is between 1 and 10.

0.0000179 You had to move the decimal point 5 places to the right.

1.79×10^{-5}

Remember that any number between 0 and 1 written in scientific notation is the product of a number between 1 and 10 and a power of 10 with a negative exponent.

Write each number in scientific notation.

1. 0.007 **2.** 0.000014 **3.** 0.0003964

Write each number in standard form.

4. 6.27×10^{-3} **5.** 9.5×10^{-7}

Set F pages 404–405

Compute $(2.5 \times 10^3) + (3.2 \times 10^3)$.

$(2.5 \times 10^3) + (3.2 \times 10^3)$

$(2.5 + 3.2) \times 10^3$ Use the distributive property.

5.7×10^3

Remember, when you multiply numbers in scientific notation, you add the exponents.

Compute. Write answers in scientific notation.

1. $(9.5 \times 10^2) + (11.2 \times 10^2)$

2. $(4.2 \times 10^{-3}) \times (7.1 \times 10^7)$

3. $(5.1 \times 10^6) - (3.6 \times 10^5)$ **4.** $\frac{4.5 \times 10^6}{9 \times 10^{-2}}$

Set G pages 408–409

Estimate $\sqrt{30}$.

Estimate: 30 is between 25 and 36, so $\sqrt{30}$ must be between 5 and 6.

Average: $\frac{5+6}{2} = 5.5$

Divide: $30 \div 5.5 = 5.45$

Average: $\frac{5.5+5.45}{2} = 5.48$

Divide: $30 \div 5.48 = 5.47$

Average: $\frac{5.48+5.47}{2} = 5.48$ $\sqrt{30} \approx 5.48$

Remember that every number lies between a pair of perfect squares.

Use the divide-and-average method to estimate each square root. Round to the nearest hundredth.

1. $\sqrt{20}$ **2.** $\sqrt{34}$ **3.** $\sqrt{72}$ **4.** $\sqrt{44}$

Set H pages 410–411

Is $\sqrt{10}$ a rational number?

No, since 10 is not a perfect square, $\sqrt{10}$ is not a rational number.

Remember that the square root of a perfect square is a rational number.

Tell whether each number is rational or irrational.

1. $\sqrt{24}$ **2.** $\sqrt{25}$ **3.** $\sqrt{81}$

4. $\sqrt{169}$ **5.** $\sqrt{100}$ **6.** $\sqrt{150}$

Set I pages 412–415

Rules for computing with irrational numbers:

$$\sqrt{ab} = \sqrt{a} \times \sqrt{b}$$

$$\sqrt{\frac{a}{b}} = \frac{\sqrt{a}}{\sqrt{b}}$$

$$a\sqrt{c} + b\sqrt{c} = (a + b)\sqrt{c}$$

Remember to look for ways to use the rules at the left to make computing easier.

Compute. Round to the nearest hundredth.

1. $\sqrt{\frac{27}{4}}$ **2.** $3\sqrt{36} + 7\sqrt{36}$ **3.** $\sqrt{48} \times \sqrt{9}$

Independent Study MORE PRACTICE

More Practice

Set A pages 392–393

Solve for b. Tell what property is illustrated.

1. $23.0 \times 1 = b$

2. $6.4 \times (b \times 9) = (6.4 \times 10) \times 9$

3. $7.1 + 5.9 = 5.9 + b$

4. $12.1 \times 3 + 12.1 \times 9 = b(3 + 9)$

Compute.

5. $\frac{4}{5} + \left(\frac{3}{2} - \frac{4}{5}\right)$

6. $3.2 \times 3 - 3.2 \times 2$

7. $97 + 35 + 13$

8. $(32.9 + 12.2) - 32.9$

9. $18 + 11 + 32$

10. $(5 \times 0.4) \times 2$

11. $8.5 \times 7 + 8.5 \times 3$

12. $\frac{2}{11} \times \left(\frac{3}{11} \times \frac{11}{2}\right)$

13. $1.0049 \times 14 - 1.0049 \times 13$

Set B pages 394–395

Write in standard form.

1. 10^{-3} **2.** 10^{7} **3.** 10^{10} **4.** $\frac{1}{10^5}$ **5.** $\frac{1}{10^6}$ **6.** 10^{0}

Write in exponential form.

7. 0.0001 **8.** 10 **9.** 1,000,000 **10.** $\frac{1}{1,000}$ **11.** $\frac{1}{10}$

Compute. Write your answers in standard form.

12. $10^5 \times 10^3$ **13.** $10^4 \times 10^{-4}$ **14.** $10^3 \times 10^3$ **15.** $10^1 \times 10^{-1}$

Set C pages 396–397

Multiply. Write your answer in exponential form.

1. $10^8 \times 10^4$ **2.** $10^3 \times 10^{12}$ **3.** $10^{-10} \times 10^{11}$ **4.** $10^{16} \times 10^{16}$

5. $10,000 \times 100,000$ **6.** $1,000 \times 1,000$ **7.** 0.001×0.0001

Divide. Write your answer in exponential form.

8. $\frac{10^9}{10^2}$ **9.** $\frac{10^{-2}}{10^5}$ **10.** $\frac{10^9}{10^8}$ **11.** $\frac{10^{-7}}{10^{-3}}$ **12.** $\frac{0.0000001}{0.001}$ **13.** $\frac{1,000}{100,000}$

Set D pages 398–399

Write each number in standard form.

1. 9.573×10^4 **2.** 7.12×10^6 **3.** 3.76×10^3 **4.** 1.125×10^7

Write each number in scientific notation.

5. 500,000 **6.** 395.2 **7.** 1,254,000 **8.** 8,943

Write each number in standard form. Then write each number in scientific notation.

9. 379×10^4 **10.** 11.7×10^7 **11.** 0.17×10^6 **12.** $1,495 \times 10^3$

Set E pages 400–401

Write each number in scientific notation.

1. 0.017 **2.** 0.000925 **3.** 0.0023 **4.** 0.00000543

5. 0.0908 **6.** 0.000064 **7.** 0.53 **8.** 0.0006

Write each number in standard form.

9. 3.64×10^{-8} **10.** 8.37×10^{-4} **11.** 7.1×10^{-2} **12.** 1.019×10^{-5}

13. 4.205×10^{-2} **14.** 4.33×10^{-6} **15.** 7.0×10^{-1} **16.** 3.8×10^{-4}

Set F pages 404–405

Compute. Write your answer in scientific notation.

1. $(7 \times 10^3) - (3 \times 10^3)$ **2.** $(7.9 \times 10^2) \times (2.0 \times 10^3)$ **3.** $(4.2 \times 10^7) \div (6.0 \times 10^6)$

4. $\frac{2.4 \times 10^{-3}}{9.6 \times 10^{-5}}$ **5.** $\frac{3.6 \times 10^6}{1.2 \times 10^5}$ **6.** $\frac{7.2 \times 10^6}{2.4 \times 10^7}$

7. $(1.69 \times 10^{-6}) + (2.95 \times 10^{-6})$ **8.** $(9.3 \times 10^{-4}) + (2.2 \times 10^{-4})$

9. $(2.5 \times 10^5) - (2.15 \times 10^4)$ **10.** $8.9 \times 10^{-1} + 1.8 \times 10^{-2}$

11. $(4.24 \times 10^3) + (5.2 \times 10^3)$ **12.** $(5.39 \times 10^5) + (6.74 \times 10^5)$

Set G pages 408–409

Find each square root. Round to the nearest hundredth.

1. $\sqrt{700}$ **2.** $\sqrt{169}$ **3.** $\sqrt{0.64}$ **4.** $\sqrt{90}$

5. $\sqrt{243}$ **6.** $\sqrt{361}$ **7.** $\sqrt{48}$ **8.** $\sqrt{0.0001}$

9. $\sqrt{444}$ **10.** $\sqrt{0.09}$ **11.** $\sqrt{8}$ **12.** $\sqrt{0.0016}$

Set H pages 410–411

Tell whether each number is rational or irrational.

1. $\sqrt{39}$ **2.** $\frac{-6}{7}$ **3.** $\frac{4}{5}$ **4.** $\sqrt{225}$

5. $\sqrt{144}$ **6.** $2\frac{3}{8}$ **7.** $-4\frac{2}{9}$ **8.** $\frac{24}{37}$

9. $\sqrt{51}$ **10.** $\sqrt{113}$ **11.** $\sqrt{2500}$ **12.** $\sqrt{140}$

Set I pages 412–415

Compute. Round decimals to the hundredths place.

1. $-\sqrt{\frac{64}{25}}$ **2.** $3\sqrt{17} + 9\sqrt{17}$ **3.** $\sqrt{3} \times \sqrt{4} \times \sqrt{3}$ **4.** $-5\sqrt{11} + 11\sqrt{11}$

5. $\sqrt{\frac{75}{3}}$ **6.** $5\sqrt{23} + 9\sqrt{23}$ **7.** $\sqrt{16} \times \sqrt{4}$ **8.** $\sqrt{1} \times \sqrt{2} \times \sqrt{3}$

9. $3\sqrt{16} - 7\sqrt{16}$ **10.** $\sqrt{6} \times \sqrt{6}$ **11.** $8\sqrt{2} - 4\sqrt{2}$ **12.** $\sqrt{15} \times \sqrt{45} \times \sqrt{3}$

Enrichment

Examining Exponents

You know that when you multiply powers of 10, you add the exponents to find the product.

$$10^3 \times 10^2 = 10^{3+2} = 10^5$$

Check: $10^3 = 1{,}000$

$10^2 = 100$

$1{,}000 \times 100 = 100{,}000$

$100{,}000 = 10^5$

In various forms, exponents have been used by mathematicians since the fourteenth century. The system in use today was popularized in the seventeenth century by the French mathematician René Descartes.

In the example above, the ***base*** of the exponents is 10. You can add the exponents any time the bases of the numbers being multiplied are the same.

$$4^2 \times 4^3 = 4^{(2+3)} = 4^5$$

Check: $16 \times 64 = 1{,}024 = 4^5$

Find the following products. Write your answers in exponential form.

1. $3^4 \times 3^6$ **2.** $9^3 \times 9^4$ **3.** $13^2 \times 13^2$

4. $7^3 \times 7^9$ **5.** $2^6 \times 2^{-3}$ **6.** $6^5 \times 6^{-1}$

7. $5^{-7} \times 5^2 \times 5^2$ **8.** $9^4 \times 9^{11}$ **9.** $5^2 \times 5^{-4}$

10. $6^7 \times 5^5 \times 6^{-1}$ **11.** $2^3 \times 2^{-3}$ **12.** $3^9 \times 2^4 \times 2^{-3}$

13. $12.9^5 \times 12.9^{14}$ **14.** $16.08^7 \times 16.08^{-5}$ **15.** $42^{21} \times 42^3 \times 5^{19}$

If dividing, you can subtract exponents any time the bases of the numbers being divided are the same.

$$4^2 \div 4^3 = 4^{(2-3)} = 4^{-1} = \frac{1}{4}$$

Check: $16 \div 64 = \frac{1}{4}$

Find the following quotients. Write your answers in exponential form. Check your work.

16. $3^8 \div 3^3$ **17.** $7^4 \div 7^3$ **18.** $13^2 \div 13^2$

19. $9^4 \div 9^6$ **20.** $2^6 \div 2^8$ **21.** $5^4 \div 5^7$

22. $6^{-3} \div 6^3 \div 10^4$ **23.** $7^3 \div 7^{-2} \div 7^2$ **24.** $2^9 \div 2^8 \div 2^1$

25. $5^2 \div 5^2 \div 5^{-2}$ **26.** $5^2 \div 5^{-2} \div 5^2$ **27.** $5^{-2} \div 5^2 \div 5^2$

28. Write a general rule for multiplying with the same bases.

29. Write a general rule for dividing with the same bases.

30. Look at Exercises 25–27. How does the negative exponent affect the answer?

Chapter 11 Review/Test

Multiply or divide.

1. $10^{-17} \times 10^{6}$

2. $\frac{10^9}{10^2}$

3. $\frac{10^4}{10^{-6}}$

4. $\sqrt{12} \times \sqrt{3}$

5. What property is demonstrated by $3\left(\frac{1}{2} + \frac{2}{3}\right) = 3 \times \frac{1}{2} + 3 \times \frac{2}{3}$?

6. Find the number of millimeters in 1 kilometer.

Write each number in standard form.

7. 10^5

8. 6.83×10^{-3}

9. $\frac{1}{10^2}$

10. 10^9

11. 10^{-4}

12. 9.7×10^6

13. Find the area.

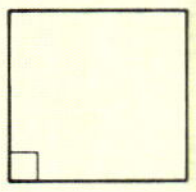

14. Find the perimeter.

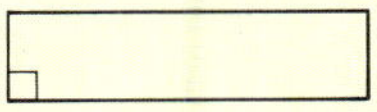

Compute.

15. $3\sqrt{19} - 4\sqrt{19}$

16. $\frac{9.6 \times 10^4}{8 \times 10^2}$

17. $(1.6 \times 10^{-7}) \times (3.8 \times 10^{-4})$

18. $(4.3 \times 10^5) - (4 \times 10^5)$

Write each number in scientific notation.

19. 0.0000000216

20. 727,000,000,000

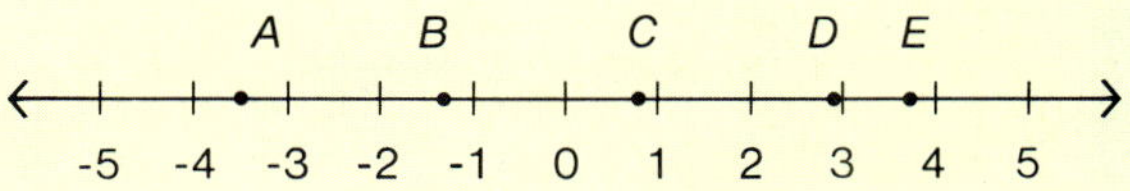

Tell which point on the number line above most closely approximates each number.

21. $\sqrt{8.7}$

22. $-\sqrt{\frac{16}{9}}$

23. $4\sqrt{3} - 6\sqrt{3}$

24. Use the divide-and-average method to estimate $\sqrt{77}$.

25. Select the most appropriate *first step* in solving the following problem.

The distance d in feet that an object falls in t seconds is given by the formula $d = 16t^2$. How long would it take an object dropped from the top of a 780-foot-tall building to hit the ground?

a. Find the square roots of both sides of the equation.
b. Substitute 780 for d.
c. Write 780 in scientific notation.

26. A proton has a mass of about 1.67×10^{-24} gram. An electron has a mass of about 9.1×10^{-28} gram. A proton is about how many times as heavy as an electron?

Solve for m.

27. $\left(\frac{5}{9} \times \frac{1}{4}\right) - \left(\frac{2}{3} \times \frac{1}{4}\right) = m\left(\frac{5}{9} - \frac{2}{3}\right)$

28. $(0.89 \times m) \times 4.02 = 0.89 \times (63 \times 4.02)$

29. **Write About Math** When a number is written in scientific notation, how can you easily tell if it is a large or small number?

Data File

Inside The Earth	
Thickness of sial[1]	0–18 miles
Thickness of sima[2]	8 miles
Thickness of upper mantle	430–18 miles
Thickness of lower mantle	1,370 miles
Thickness of outer core	1,400 miles
Radius of inner core	800 miles

[1]Light rocks of the crust that lie underneath the continents

[2]Dense rocks under the sial that form much of the ocean bed

1. Diagram and Table

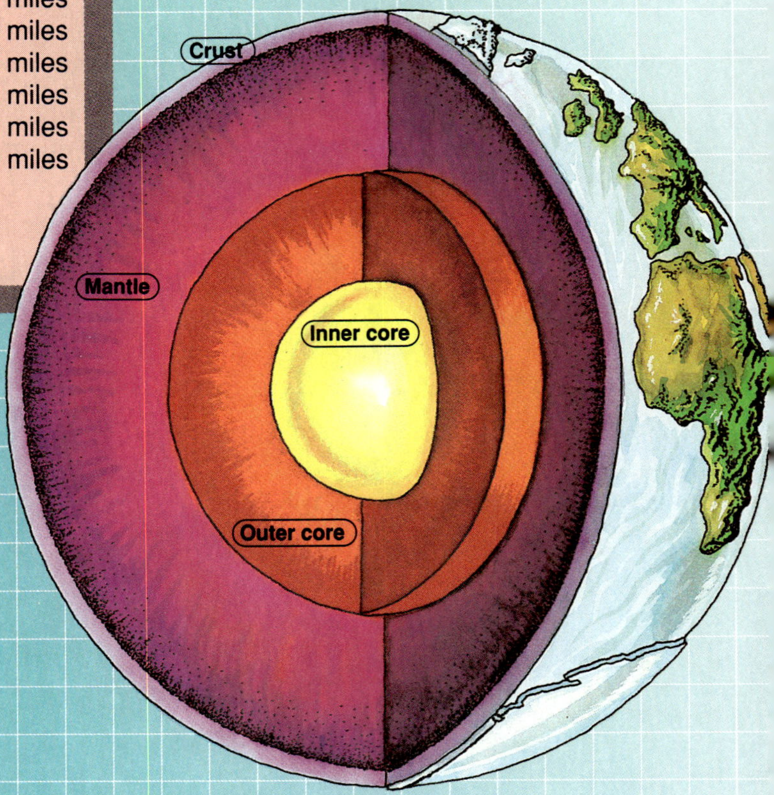

1. Diagram and Table:
Beneath a thin *crust* of rock is a hot, partly molten layer of rock called the *mantle*. The *outer core* forms a molten metal layer of iron and nickel. The *inner core* is solid metal under great pressure.

2. Pattern:
A set of stairs can be made from the pattern. To do this, copy the pattern. Cut on the solid lines. Fold one way on the red dashes and the opposite way on the black dashes.

3. Train Schedule:
One column shows the eastbound schedule; the other column shows westbound trains.

4. Table:
Many of the prefixes are used for metric measures.

5. Bar Graph:
The percents add up to more than 100. Some teenagers read more than one section.

2. Pattern

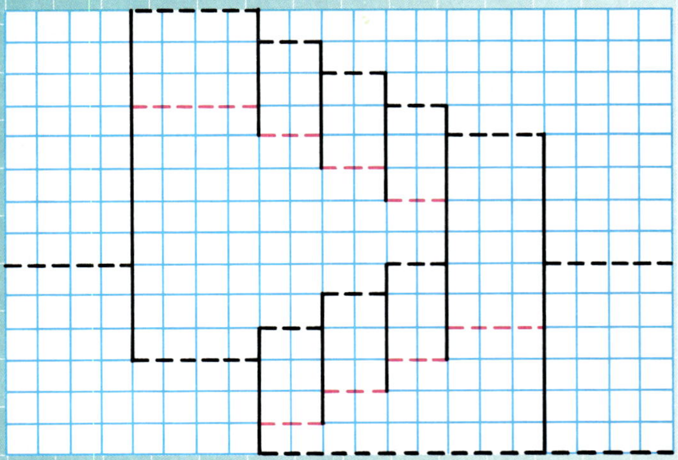

3. Train Schedule

San Francisco Transcontinental

California Zephyr 6

All trains daily

11:50a	Lv	Oakland (PST)	Ar	**4:05p**
12:03p	Lv	Richmond (PST)	Lv	**3:06p**
12:33p	Lv	Martinez (PST)	Lv	**2:37p**
12:53p	Lv	Suisun-Fairfield (PST)	Lv	**2:15p**
1:22p	Lv	Davis (PST)	Lv	**1:51p**
1:57p	Lv	Sacramento (PST)	Lv	**1:31p**
2:24p	Lv	Roseville (PST)	Lv	**12:41p**
3:09p	Lv	Colfax (PST)	Lv	11:35a
5:18p	Lv	Truckee (PST)	Lv	9:27a
6:11p	Ar	Reno (PST)	Lv	8:34a
6:40p	Ar	Sparks (PST)	Lv	8:28a
5:20a	Ar	Salt Lake City (MT)	Lv	**11:37p**
8:15p	Ar	Denver (MT)	Lv	8:55a
6:50a	Ar	Omaha (CT)	Lv	**11:25p**
4:25p	Ar	Chicago (CT)	Lv	**2:55p**

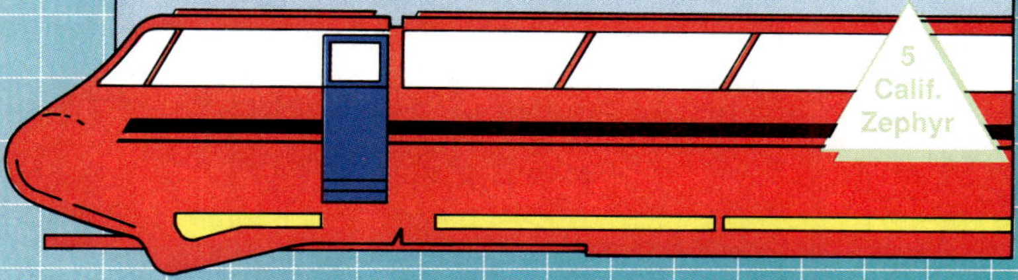

4. Table

Decimal Multiples

Factor	Name of prefix	Symbol
10	deca-	da
10^2	hecto-	h
10^3	kilo-	k
10^6	mega-	M
10^9	giga-	G
10^{12}	tera-	T
10^{-1}	deci-	d
10^{-2}	centi	c
10^{-3}	milli-	m
10^{-6}	micro-	μ
10^{-9}	nano-	n
10^{-12}	pico-	p
10^{-15}	femto-	f
10^{-16}	atto-	a

5. Bar Graph

Sunday newspaper reading by teens

Sections/pages read by 13- to 17-year-olds: (in percent surveyed)

Comics	75%
Sports	55%
Entertainment	50%
General News	45%
TV, radio listings	40%
Classified	30%
Editorial/opinion	25%
Business/Financial	20%

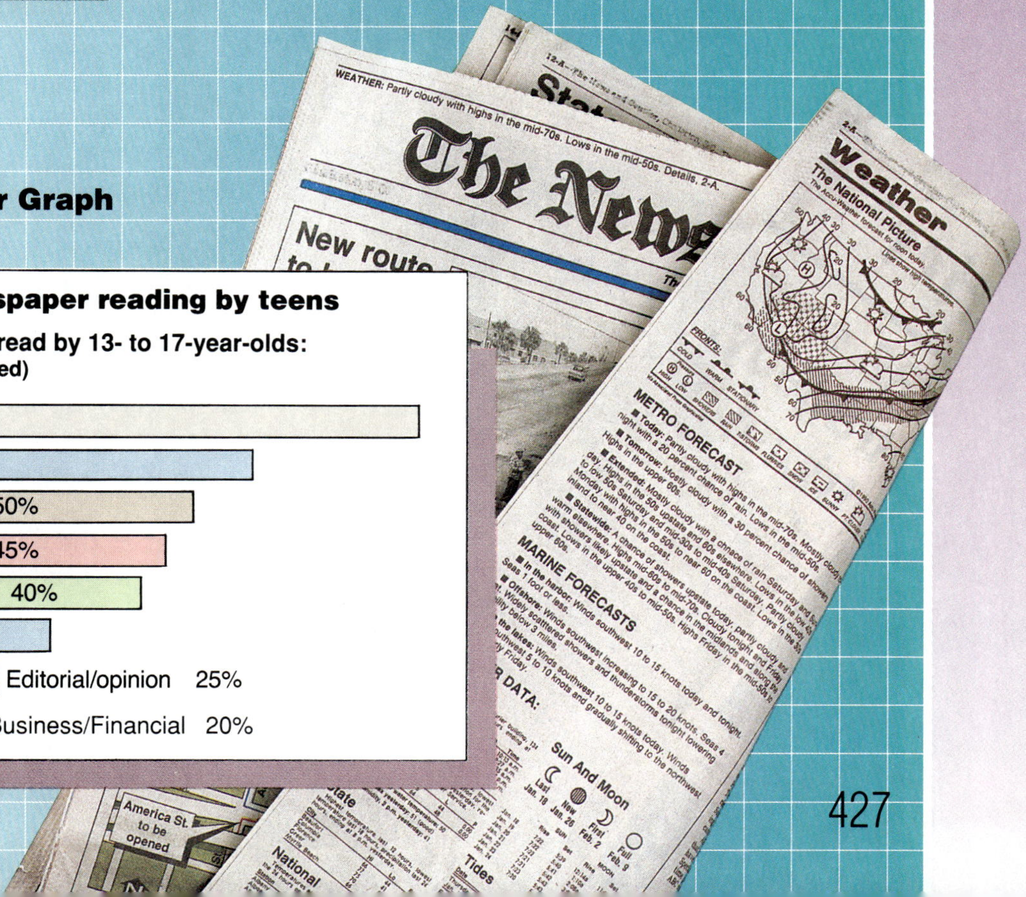

Cumulative Review/Test Chapters 1–11

Write the letter for the correct answer.

1. Mr. Kelsey has 3,982 beads for an art project he is doing with 43 students. Which of the following would be best for estimating how many beads each student can use?

a. $4{,}000 \div 50$ **b.** $3{,}000 \div 50$
c. $4{,}000 \div 40$ **d.** $3{,}000 \div 40$

2. Choose the best estimate for $3.32 \div 6.4$.

a. 50 **b.** 0.5
c. 0.05 **d.** 0.005

3. Subtract.
$-0.32 - 6.48$

a. 6.16
b. -6.16
c. -6.8
d. not given

4. Solve.
$6m = -42$

a. $m = -252$
b. $m = -7$
c. $m = 7$
d. not given

5. Which inequality is graphed?

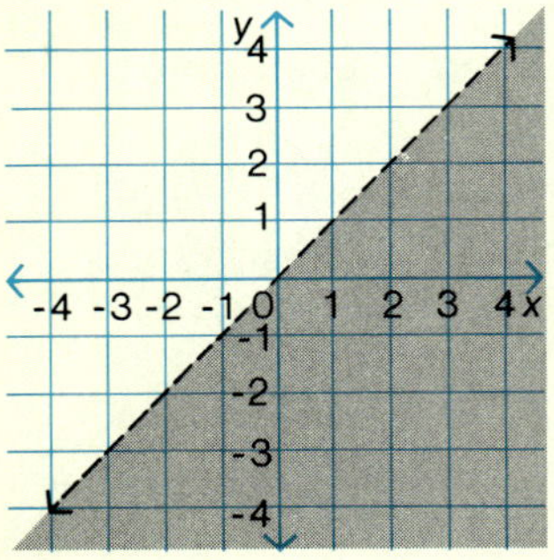

a. $y > -x$ **b.** $y > x$
c. $y < -x$ **d.** $y < x$

6. Which function table matches the equation $y = \frac{1}{4}x + 1$?

a.

x	y
4	17
5	21
6	25
7	29

b.

x	y
4	2
8	3
12	4
16	5

c.

x	y
4	0
8	1
12	2
16	3

7. Solve this proportion.
$\frac{26}{39} = \frac{x}{30}$

a. $x = 20$ **b.** $x = 33.8$
c. $x = 45$ **d.** $x = 90$

8. 12 is 25% of what number?

a. 3 **b.** 2.08 **c.** 4.8 **d.** 48

9. Mr. Jackson makes a base salary of \$250 plus a commission of 6% on all his sales. What will be his total income on sales of \$12,000?

a. \$12,250 **b.** \$1,500
c. \$720 **d.** \$970

10. Which statement best describes the meaning of the underlined phrase in this problem?

Ms. Morgan bought a car for \$7,350 with no down payment. What would the finance costs be if she made 48 payments of \$195 per month?

a. penalty for not having a down payment
b. cost of borrowing money to buy the car
c. cost of the down payment
d. cost with additional options

11. Angelo's science class was finding the mass of their schoolbooks. Which would be the best estimate of the mass of an eighth-grade math book?

a. 1 mg **b.** 10 g
c. 1 kg **d.** 10 kg

12. Solve this problem.

$$\begin{array}{r} 6\text{ lb} \\ -4\text{ lb }12\text{ oz} \\ \hline \end{array}$$

a. 1 lb 4 oz
b. 2 lb 12 oz
c. 2 lb
d. not given

13. A room is 5 yards long and 3 yards wide. What is the unit of measure and the greatest possible error?

a. yards; 1 yd
b. square yards; 1 sq yd
c. feet; 0.5 ft
d. yards; 0.5 yd

14. What is the circumference of the circle? Use 3.14 for π.

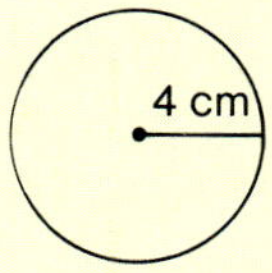

a. 12.56 cm
b. 12.56 cm^2
c. 25.12 cm
d. 25.12 cm^2

15. How many degrees are in an angle supplementary to a 75° angle?

a. 15° **b.** 105° **c.** 285° **d.** 75°

16. What is the area of a triangle with a height of 15 centimeters and a base of 10 centimeters?

a. 150 cm^3 **b.** 150 cm^2
c. 75 cm^2 **d.** 75 cm^3

17. What happens to the area of a triangle when the base is doubled but the height is not changed?

a. There is no change.
b. The area increases by one half.
c. The area doubles.

18. How many milligrams are in 1 kilogram?

a. 1,000,000 mg
b. 0 mg
c. 1,000 mg
d. 10,000,000 mg

19. Compute.

$\frac{10^6}{10^8}$

a. 10^{-2}
b. 10^2
c. $10^{0.75}$
d. not given

20. Write in standard form.

17.42×10^{-3}

a. 17,420
b. 1,742
c. 0.01742
d. 0.1742

21. What is $-\sqrt{\frac{49}{9}}$?

a. $2\frac{2}{3}$ **b.** $-2\frac{1}{3}$
c. $2\frac{1}{3}$ **d.** $-6\frac{1}{3}$

Indirect Measurement

12

Did You Know: This model of a heart in Philadelphia's Franklin Institute Science Museum is so large you can walk through it. A person would have to be 230 feet tall to have a heart this size.

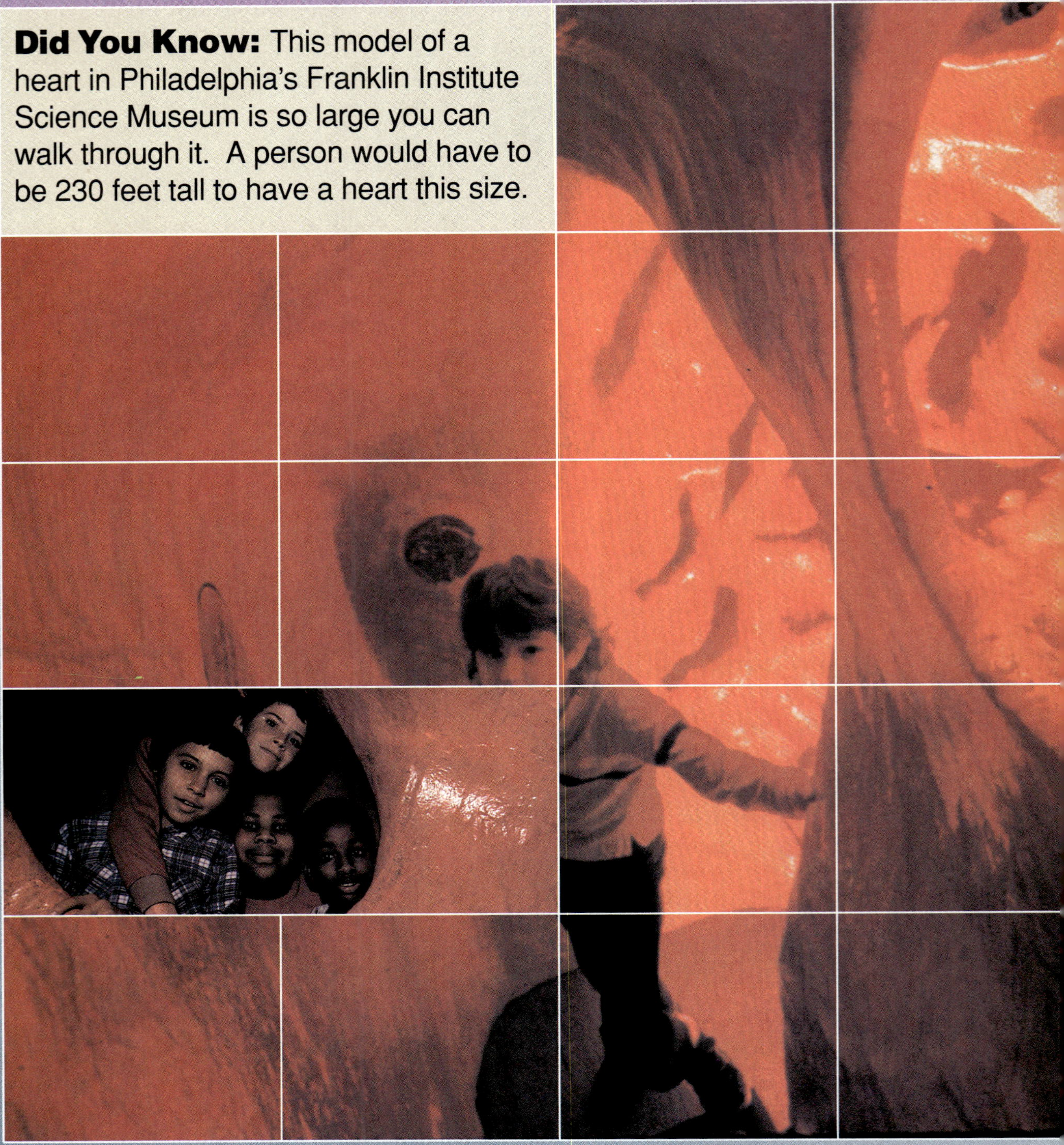

Number-Sense Project

Estimate

Estimate the weight of a person who is 230 feet tall.

Gather Data

Record the heights and weights of 5 people. Find the average height and weight. 230 feet is how many times this average height?

Analyze and Report

If each person's dimensions are multiplied by k, the volume and weight are multiplied by k^3. Why? What might a 230-foot person weigh?

ALGEBRA

Similar Figures

Build Understanding

Interior designers often use scale drawings to design the layout for rooms. A ***scale drawing*** uses figures that are similar to the original figures. ***Similar polygons*** are the same shape and have two important properties:

(1) Corresponding angles are congruent.

(2) Ratios of lengths of corresponding sides are equal.

A. Is $\triangle ABC \sim \triangle DEF$?

The symbol ~ means "is similar to."

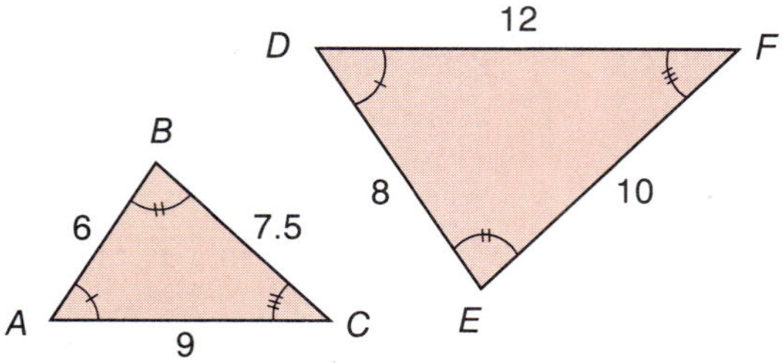

Corresponding angles are congruent.

Do the lengths of corresponding sides form equal ratios?

$\frac{6}{8} \stackrel{?}{=} \frac{9}{12}$ $\quad 6 \times 12 \stackrel{?}{=} 8 \times 9$

$\quad\quad\quad\quad 72 = 72$

$\frac{6}{8} \stackrel{?}{=} \frac{7.5}{10}$ $\quad 6 \times 10 \stackrel{?}{=} 8 \times 7.5$

$\quad\quad\quad\quad 60 = 60$

$\triangle ABC \sim \triangle DEF$ because corresponding angles are congruent and the lengths of corresponding sides form equal ratios.

B. Mental Math Trapezoid *PQRS* ~ trapezoid *WXYZ*. Find the measure of $\angle P$. How long is $\overline{XY}$?

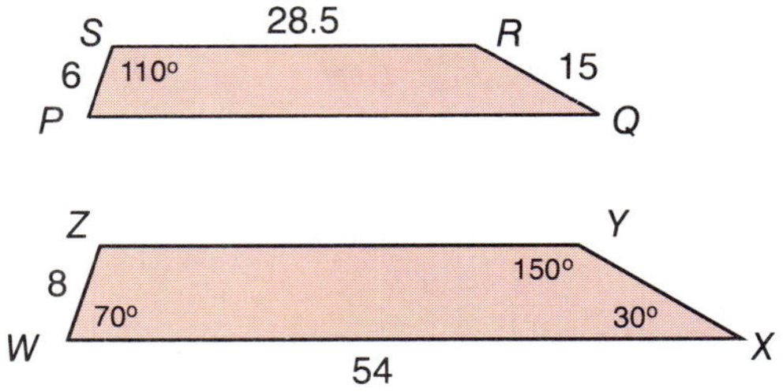

$m\angle P = 70°$ since $\angle P$ and $\angle W$ are corresponding angles.

$\frac{6}{8} = \frac{15}{x}$ $\quad 6x = 8 \times 15$

$\quad\quad\quad x = 20$

XY is 20 units.

■ **Talk About Math** Are all right triangles similar? Are all squares similar? Explain your answers.

Check Understanding

For another example, see Set A, pages 460–461.

Use the figures in Example B to complete each exercise.

1. QP = ▒ **2.** YZ = ▒ **3.** $m\angle R$ = ▒ **4.** $m\angle Z$ = ▒

Practice

For More Practice, see Set A, pages 462–463.

Find the missing measures of these similar polygons.

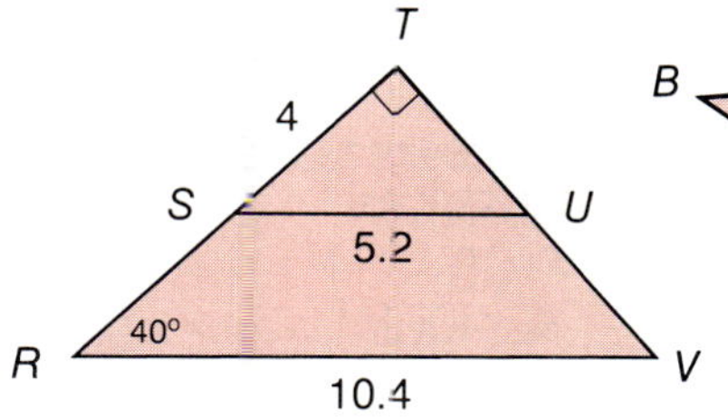

$\triangle RTV \sim \triangle STU$

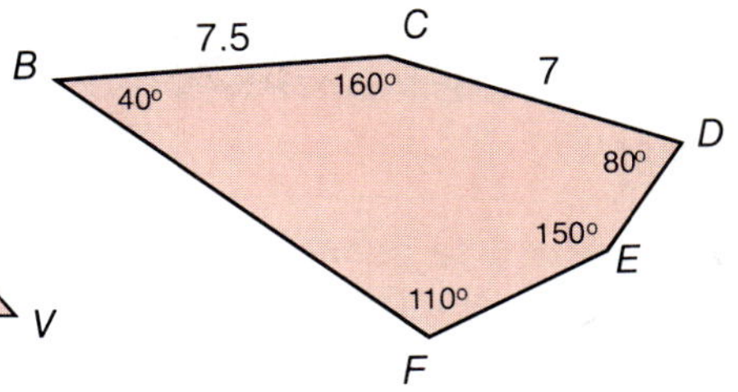

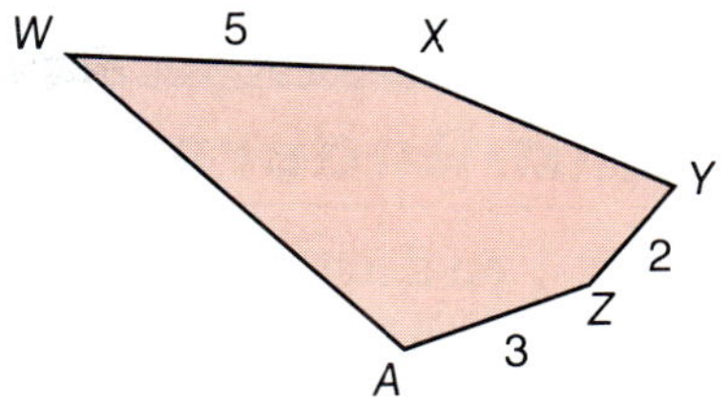

Polygon $BCDEF \sim$ Polygon $WXYZA$

5. $RT =$ ▒ **6.** $m\angle TSU =$ ▒ **7.** $m\angle TUS =$ ▒ **8.** $m\angle TVR =$ ▒

9. $m\angle W =$ ▒ **10.** $XY =$ ▒ **11.** $ED =$ ▒ **12.** $FE =$ ▒

13. $\angle SUV =$ ▒ **14.** $m\angle Y =$ ▒ **15.** $m\angle A =$ ▒ **16.** $RS =$ ▒

17. $m\angle X =$ ▒ **18.** $m\angle Z =$ ▒ **19.** $m\angle RSU =$ ▒ **20.** $m\angle RVU =$ ▒

21. If $BF = 9$, $WA =$ ▒. **22.** If $WA = 0.5$, $BF =$ ▒. **23.** If $BF = 1$, $WA =$ ▒.

Mental Math Use mental math to decide whether the polygons are similar.

24.

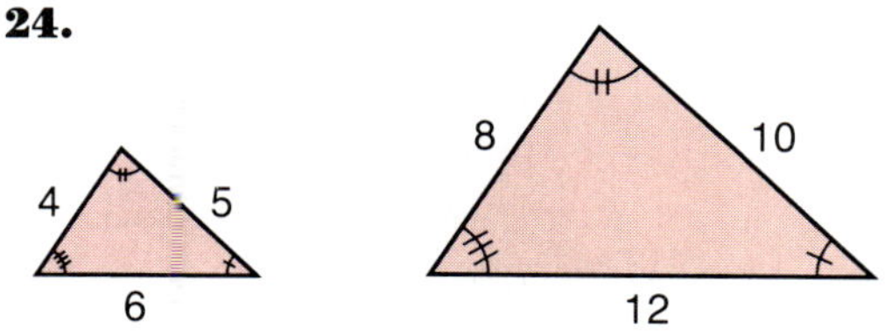

25.

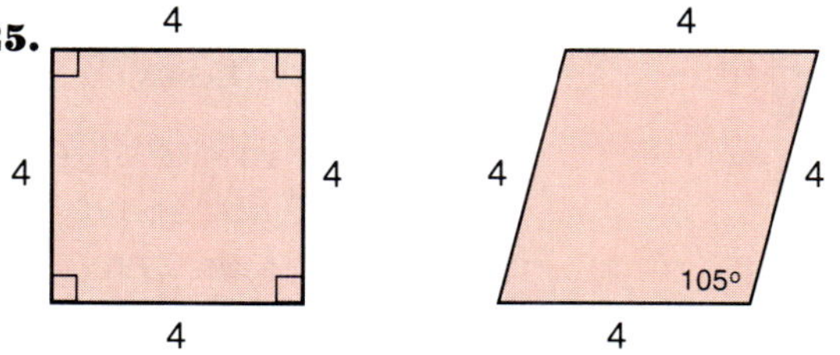

Problem Solving

Solve each problem. **Remember** that lengths of corresponding sides form equal ratios.

26. Use graph paper to draw a scale model of a rectangular room 15 ft by 12 ft. Let 1 unit represent 3 ft.

27. Make scale drawings for a 6-ft by 3-ft sofa, two 3-ft by 3-ft chairs, and a 4-ft by 2-ft TV. Add them to your scale model.

28. **Use Data** Use the information on page 192. Are all golden rectangles similar? Explain your answer.

29. On a blueprint, a rectangular closet is $\frac{7}{16}$ in. by $1\frac{1}{4}$ in. If the scale of the print is 1 inch to $6\frac{1}{2}$ ft, what are the dimensions of the closet?

ALGEBRA

Draw a Diagram

PROBLEM SOLVING GUIDE

Understand
QUESTION
FACTS
KEY IDEA

Plan and Solve
STRATEGY
ANSWER

Look Back
SENSIBLE ANSWER
ALTERNATE APPROACH

Build Understanding

Mr. Van's art class is going to paint the school mascot, a bear, on the gym wall. They will draw a diagram of the bear on graph paper and then transfer the bear's image, square by square, to a grid on the wall. The coach wants the bear's paw directly below his window. How high must the bear's image on the wall be?

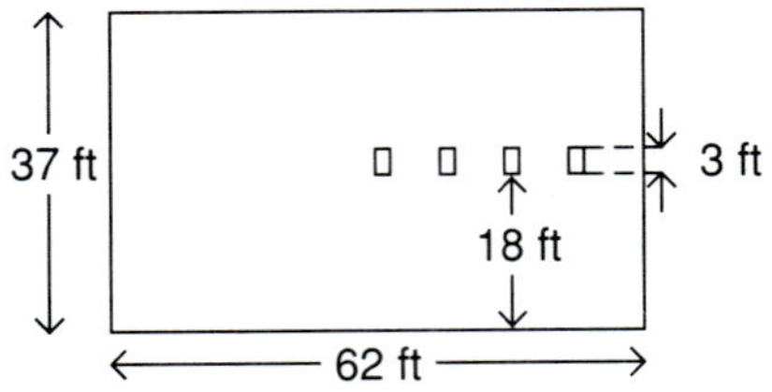

Understand QUESTION How high must the enlarged image of the bear be so that its paw will be below the coach's window?

FACTS In the diagram, the bear's paw is 2 in. above its feet and its head is 3 in. above its feet. The paw must be below the window, 18 ft above the floor.

The largest known bear was a Kodiak that died in captivity in 1955 weighing 1,670 lb.

Plan and Solve STRATEGY Write a proportion.

$$\frac{\text{ht of paw in diagram}}{\text{ht of head in diagram}} = \frac{\text{ht of paw on wall}}{\text{ht of head on wall}}$$

$$\frac{2}{3} = \frac{18}{n}$$

$$2n = 3 \times 18$$
$$2n = 54$$
$$n = 27$$

ANSWER The bear on the wall must be 27 feet high.

Look Back SENSIBLE ANSWER The height of the enlarged image of the bear, 27 ft, is less than 37 ft, the height of the gym wall.

■ **Talk About Math** Why could the proportion have been set up like this?

$$\frac{\text{height of paw in diagram}}{\text{height of paw on wall}} = \frac{\text{height of head in diagram}}{\text{height of head on wall}}$$

Check Understanding

1. What could be the maximum size of the bear's image without considering the location of the window?

2. Velma's method of transferring the bear's image was to calculate its size to be as big as the entire wall. What is wrong with this approach?

Practice

Solve each problem.

3. Mr. Van wants his students to reduce a figure on a 20-in. by 24-in. poster so that it fits in a $7\frac{1}{2}$-in. by $10\frac{1}{2}$-in. area. The figure is 21 in. tall and 11 in. wide. What will the reduced figure measure?

4. An 18-cm by 9-cm drawing of a raccoon on centimeter grid paper is to be enlarged to fit in a 90-cm by 45-cm space. What will you use for the dimensions of the new grid squares on the enlargement?

5. Draw a car that is 5 cm high and 12 cm long on centimeter grid paper. Reproduce the car in a 15-cm by 36-cm space.

6. A rectangular-shaped room has dimensions that are in a ratio of 4 to 3. What are some possible dimensions for the room?

7. Use one of your answers for Exercise 6 to make 2 scale drawings of the room, one using centimeter grid paper and the other using inch or half-inch grid paper.

8. Will a $1\frac{11}{16}$-inch by 3-inch drawing reduce to fit exactly in a 1-inch by 2-inch frame? Explain your answer.

The art class decides to make a parade of bears on the gymnasium wall. The bears will be as tall as the bottom of the windows, will be centered across the length of the wall, and will all be identical to the bear on page 434. There will be 2 feet of space between the bears.

9. How many bears will the students paint?

10. How much space will there be between the edge of the wall and the first bear? the last bear?

11. The drawing at the right is on a quarter-inch grid. Draw it in a 4-in. by 6-in. area.

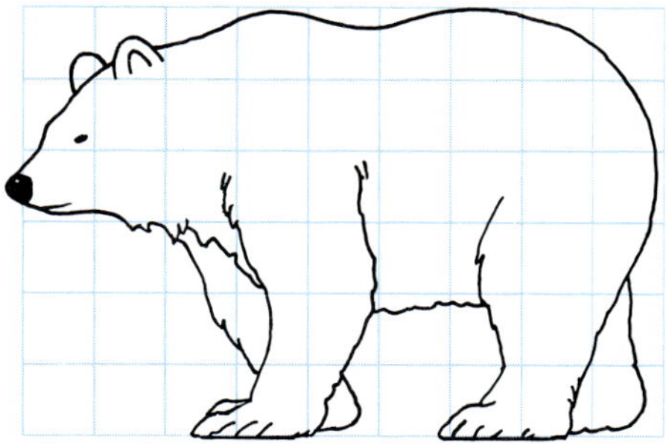

ALGEBRA

The Pythagorean Theorem

No drawing of Pythagoras exists, though this 18th-century engraving helps sustain his legend.

Build Understanding

In about 500 B.C., Pythagoras, a Greek mathematician, proved that a certain pattern exists in all right triangles. Pythagoras is credited for the theorem which bears his name, though Egyptian, Babylonian, and Chinese cultures were familiar with it as long ago as 2000 B.C.

A ***right triangle*** has one 90° angle. The side opposite the 90° angle is called the ***hypotenuse***. The remaining two sides are called ***legs***.

ACTIVITY

A. Squared Triangles
Materials: Grid paper, straightedge
Groups: With a partner

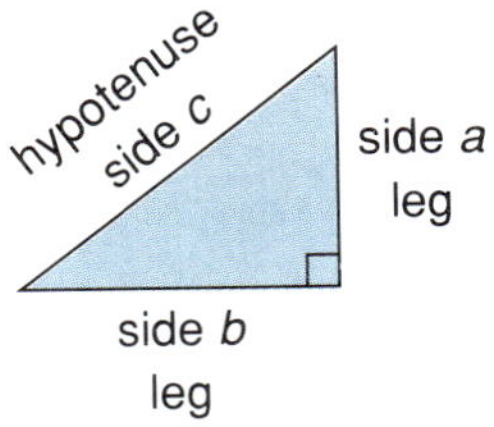

a. To find the relationship discovered by Pythagoras, copy the right triangle onto grid paper. Make squares on each side, as shown here.

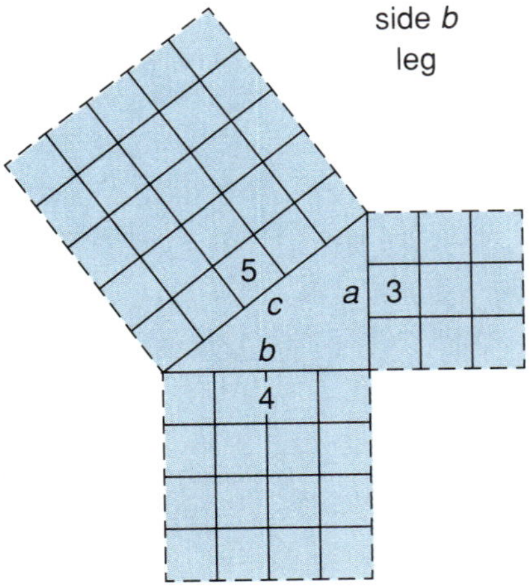

b. Count grid units to find the area of each square you constructed.

$a^2 =$ ▦ $b^2 =$ ▦ $c^2 =$ ▦

c. Repeat steps a and b for the two triangles shown below.

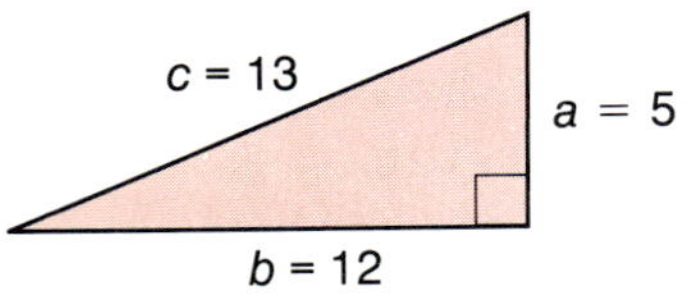

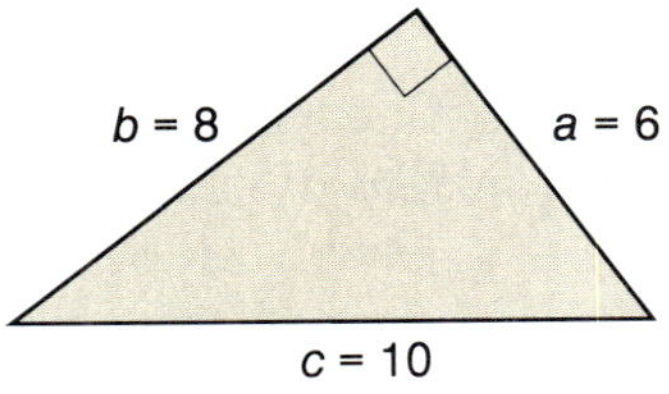

d. Organize your results from parts a through c in a table like the one shown.

Side *a*	Side *b*	Hypotenuse *c*	a^2	b^2	c^2

e. Use the results in the table to describe the relationship between the areas of the squares of the legs and the area of the square of the hypotenuse. Write an equation showing the relationship.

B. **Calculator** Test your theory from Example A on the triangles below by copying and completing the table.

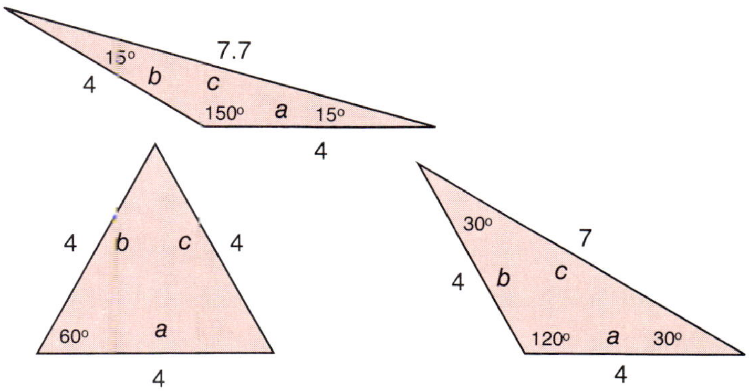

Measure of the largest angle	Side *a*	Side *b*	Side *c*	a^2	b^2	c^2
150°						
60°						
120°						

Does your theory work for all triangles?

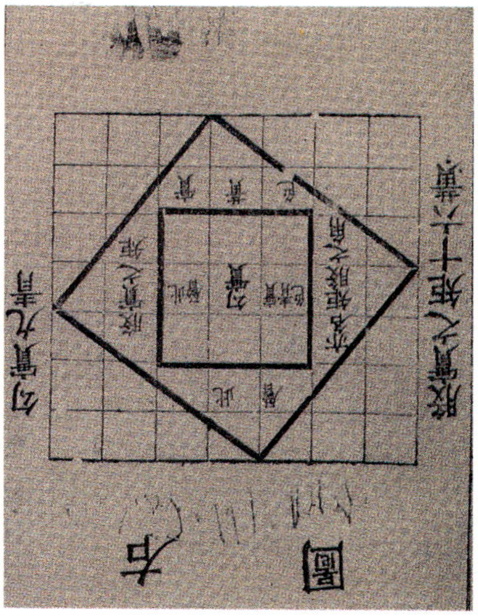

The Chou Pei, a mathematics text from China, may be 2,000 years old. This page shows that Chinese mathematicians knew that $c^2 = a^2 + b^2$ for all right triangles.

A ***theorem*** is a mathematical statement that can be proven by using already accepted ideas.

The ***Pythagorean Theorem*** states that the sum of the squares of the legs of a right triangle is equal to the square of the hypotenuse.

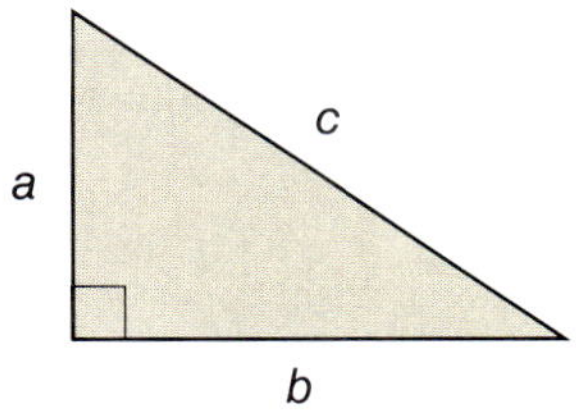

$a^2 + b^2 = c^2$

Write About Math From Example B, describe the relationship between the size of an angle and the square of the opposite side.

Check Understanding

For another example, see Set B, pages 460–461.

Use the Pythagorean Theorem to determine if these segments with the given lengths can be sides of a right triangle.

1. $a = 12$, $b = 16$, $c = 20$

2. $a = 2.5$, $b = 3.5$, $c = 4.5$

3. $a = 5$, $b = 7$, $c = 8$

4. $a = 10$, $b = 24$, $c = 26$

5. The square of the __?__ of a right triangle is equal to the sum of the squares of the __?__.

6. The longest side of a right triangle is called the __?__.

Practice

For More Practice, see Set B, pages 462–463.

Calculator Find each missing length to the nearest tenth using a calculator. **Remember** that the hypotenuse is opposite the 90° angle.

7.

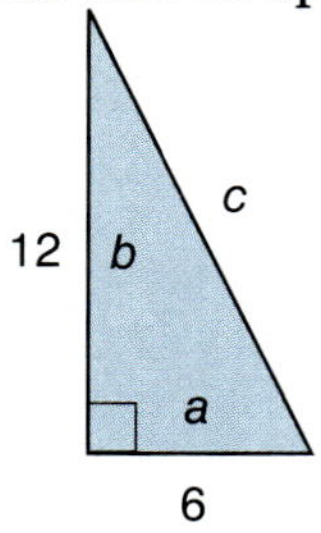

8.

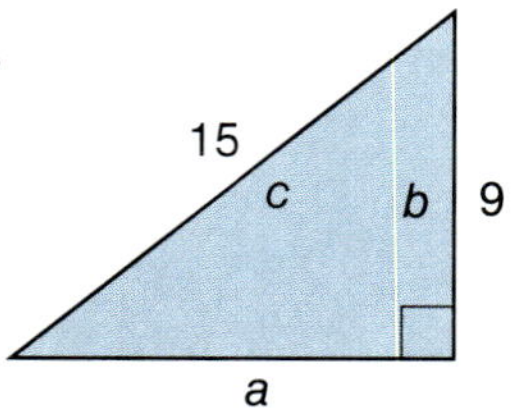

9.

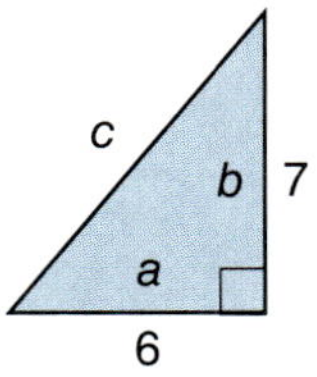

10.

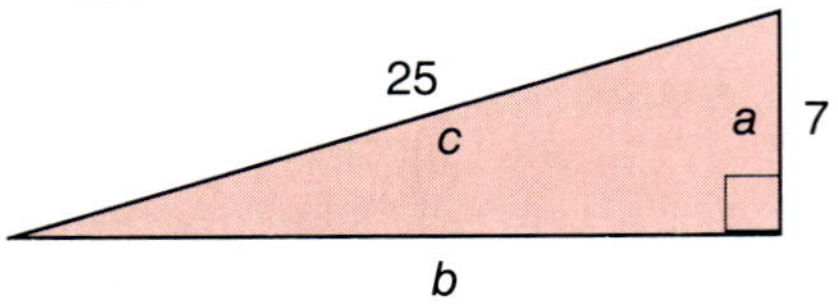

11.

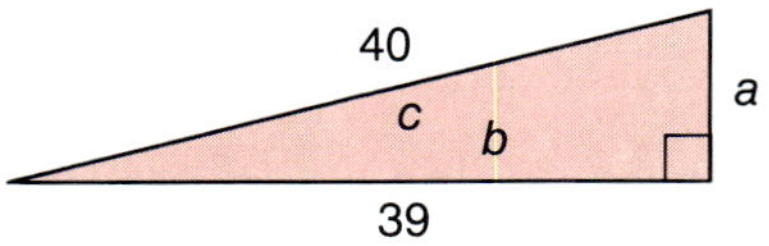

12.

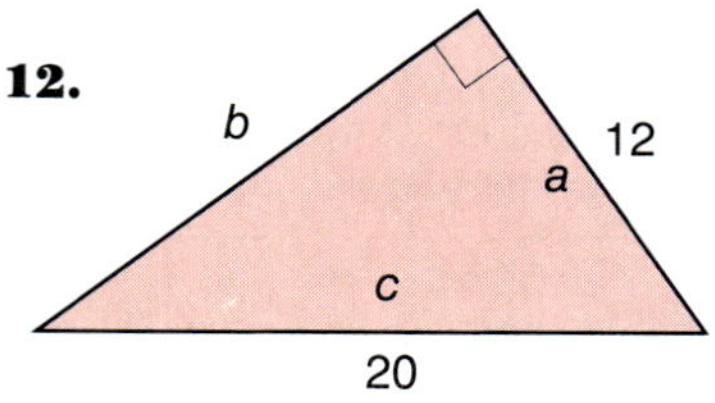

13. Which triangles in Exercises 7–12 have three sides with whole-number lengths?

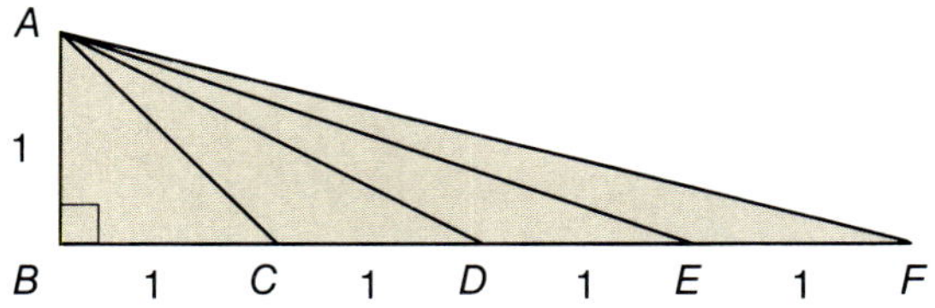

Express the length of each segment as a square root. Then approximate each square root as a decimal to the nearest thousandth.

14. *AC* **15.** *AD* **16.** *AE* **17.** *AF*

Mixed Practice Use the triangles shown below for Exercises 18–27.

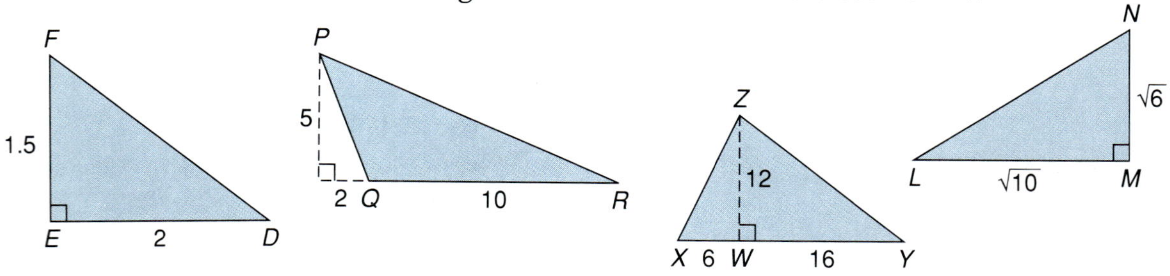

Find the area of each triangle.

18. $\triangle DEF$ **19.** $\triangle PQR$ **20.** $\triangle XYZ$ **21.** $\triangle XWZ$

Find the perimeter of each triangle.

22. $\triangle DEF$ **23.** $\triangle WYZ$ **24.** $\triangle WXZ$ **25.** $\triangle XYZ$

26. Find the area of $\triangle LMN$. **27.** Find the perimeter of $\triangle LMN$.

Problem Solving

Solve each problem.

28. Ancient Egyptian workers measured distances with ropes containing equally spaced knots. In order to make a right angle, they formed right triangles by counting the knots on the sides. Which of the rope triangles at the right will make a 90° angle at C?

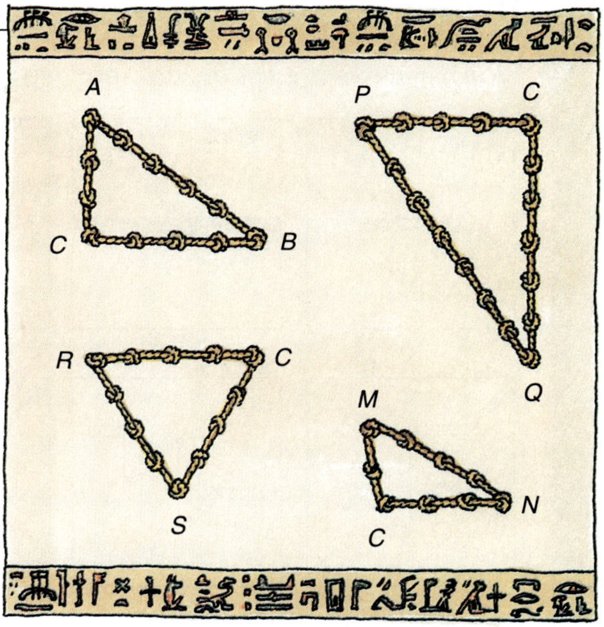

Ancient Egyptians used knotted ropes to construct right angles for land plots and buildings.

29. If an Egyptian right triangle has sides of 25 knots and 33 knots, how many knots must be in the longest side?

30. **Critical Thinking** How might the ancient Egyptians have used the knotted ropes to measure angles of 45°? 60°? 150°?

31. What is the length of a diagonal of a square with 6-centimeter sides?

32. The base of an isosceles triangle is 40 feet. Its base angles are 45°. Find the lengths of the other sides.

33. A flagpole is 20 ft high. One end of a guy wire is attached to the top of the pole. The other end of the wire is staked into the ground at the edge of a sidewalk 15 ft away from the pole. How long is the guy wire?

34. You want to reach the top edge of a 14-ft building with a 20-ft ladder. What is the maximum distance away from the base of the building that you can position the ladder?

Midchapter Checkup

The polygons are similar. Find the missing measures.

1. $FH = ▒$ **2.** $EG = ▒$

3. $m\angle A = ▒$ **4.** $m\angle E = ▒$

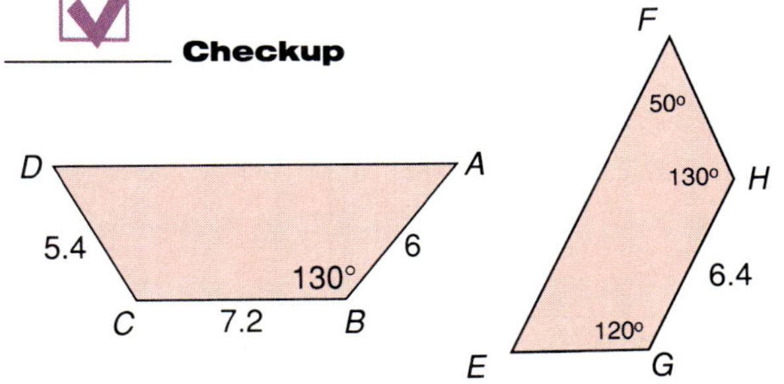

For Exercises 5–6, find each missing length by using the Pythagorean Theorem. Tell whether you used paper and pencil and the square root table on page 602 or a calculator.

5.

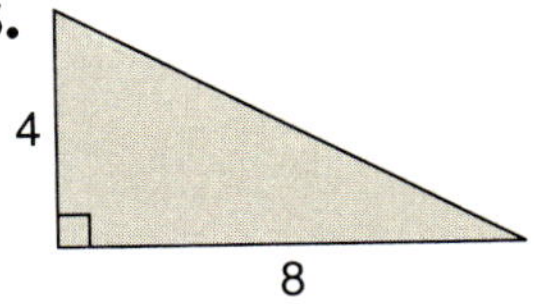

6.

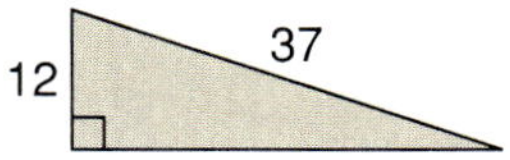

Problem-Solving Workshop

Visual Thinking Activity

Which squares are not divided into two congruent parts?

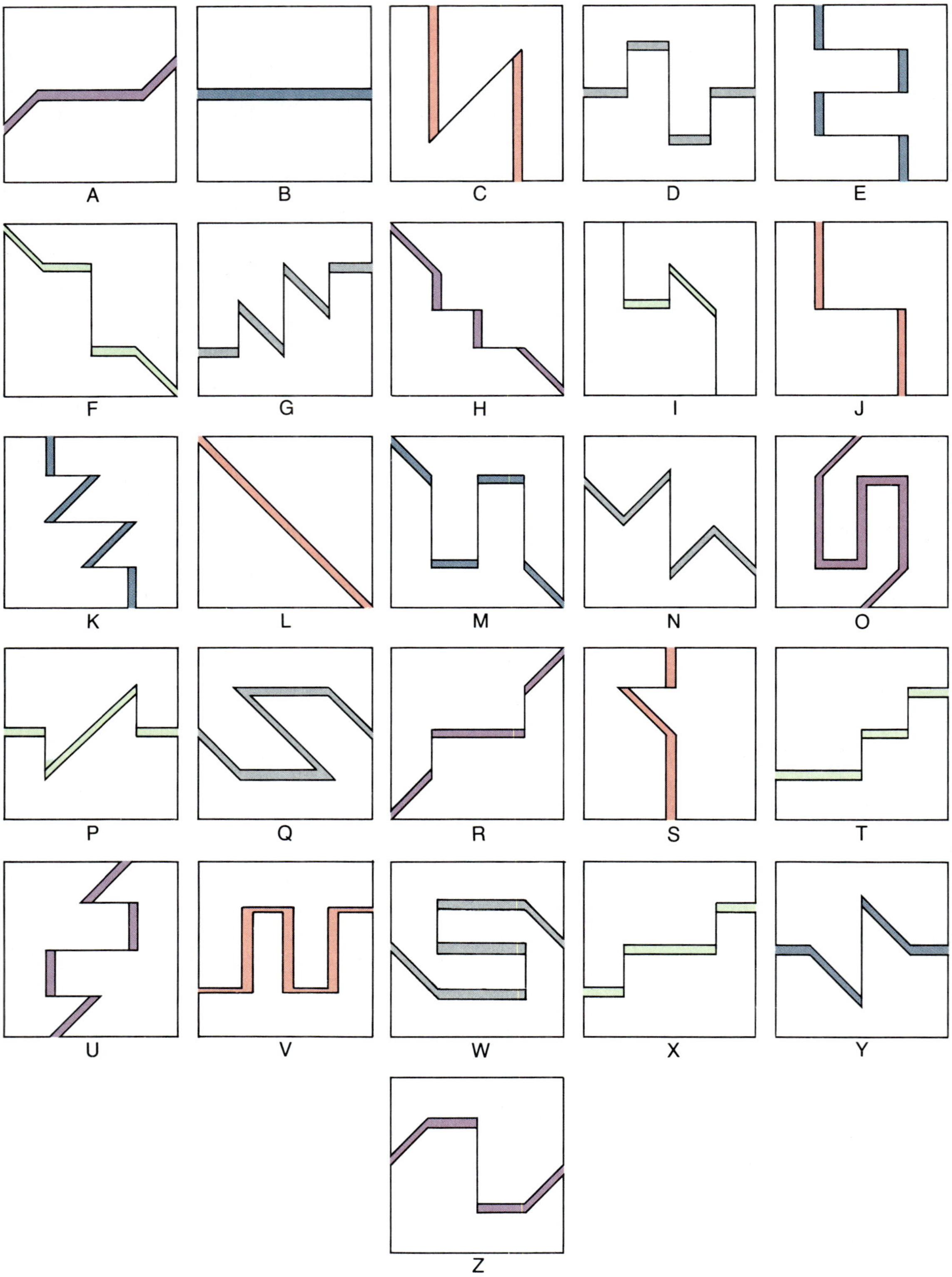

Explore with a Computer

Use the *Geometry Workshop Project* for this activity.

Suppose you have a game map. In the game, you can travel only on the grid lines or on the diagonals.

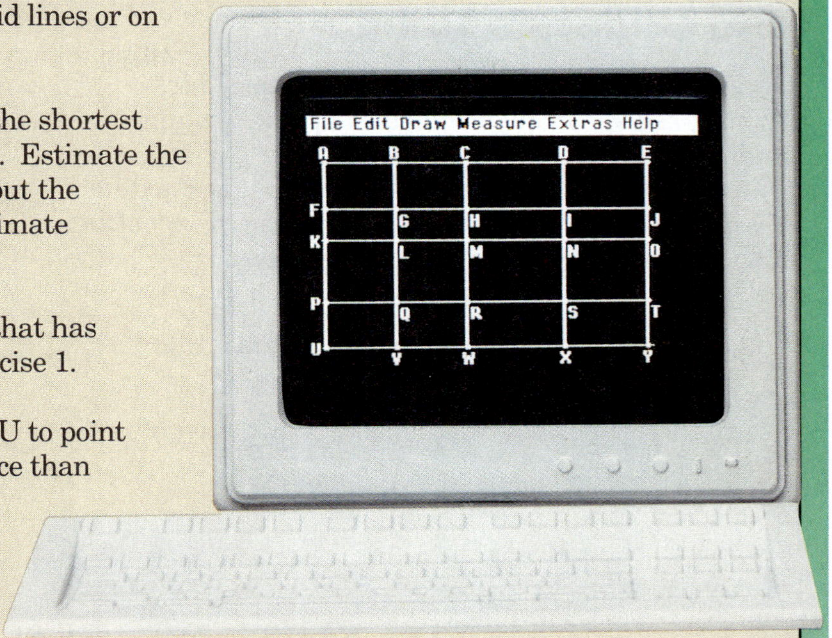

1. At the computer, draw the shortest route from point U to point J. Estimate the distance traveled. Think about the Pythagorean Theorem to estimate diagonal distances.

2. Draw a different route that has the same distance as in Exercise 1.

3. Can you get from point U to point D travelling a shorter distance than from point U to point J? Draw and measure the route to check your solution.

Number-Sense Project

Look back at pages 430–431.

Paul Bunyan of American folklore and the Brobdingnagians of *Gulliver's Travels* were giants. The Lilliputians of *Gulliver's Travels* were tiny people. Complete the chart so that the parts are proportioned to a 6-foot man.

Feature	6-foot human	Paul Bunyan	Brobdingnagian	Lilliputian
Height	6 ft	120 ft	72 ft	$\frac{1}{2}$ ft
Thumb	$2\frac{1}{2}$ in.	**1.**	**2.**	**3.**
Waistline	34 in.	**4.**	**5.**	**6.**
Foot	12 in.	**7.**	**8.**	**9.**

ALGEBRA

Using the Pythagorean Theorem

Build Understanding

Geraldo works for a building supply store. Mrs. Murray asked his advice about a canvas awning she wants to make for her picture window. The frame for the canvas begins at the edge of the roof and extends down to the top of the window 6 ft below. The bottom of the frame extends 4 ft beyond the window. What is the length of the awning?

You can draw a diagram to help you solve the problem. Label the known measurements.

Use the Pythagorean Theorem to find the hypotenuse of the triangle.

$$a^2 + b^2 = c^2$$

$$4^2 + 6^2 = c^2$$

$$16 + 36 = c^2$$

$$52 = c^2$$

$$\sqrt{52} = c$$

You can use a calculator or the square root table on page 602 to find $\sqrt{52}$.

$$7.2 \approx c$$

The awning is about 7.2 ft long.

Estimation You can estimate square roots by looking at differences and squares.

$7 \times 7 = 49$, so $\sqrt{52} > 7$.

$8 \times 8 = 64$, so $\sqrt{52} < 8$.

$52 - 49 = 3$ and $64 - 52 = 12$,

so $\sqrt{52}$ is closer to 7 than to 8.

Estimate: $\sqrt{52} \approx 7.2$

Talk About Math How do you know that the triangle in the example is a right triangle?

Check Understanding

For another example, see Set C, pages 460–461.

The diagonals of this parallelogram form right angles and bisect each other. Use the Pythagorean Theorem to find the measurements. The diagonal EG is 10 cm.

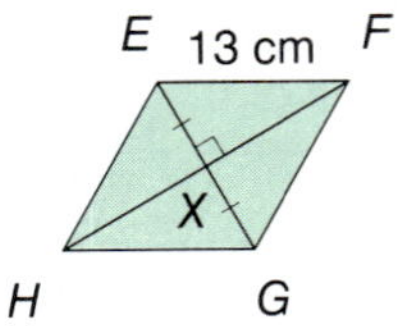

1. $EX =$ ▒ **2.** $FX =$ ▒ **3.** $EH =$ ▒

4. Find the base of a right triangle with a hypotenuse of 1.75 in. and an altitude of 0.875 in.

Practice

For More Practice, see Set C, pages 462–463.

Use the Pythagorean Theorem to find the missing measures to the nearest tenth. Tell whether you used mental math, a calculator, or the square root table on page 602.

5.

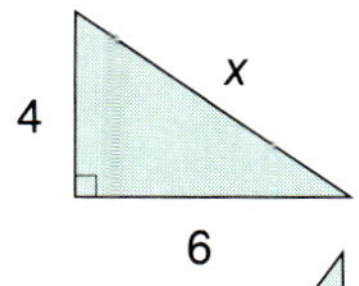

6.

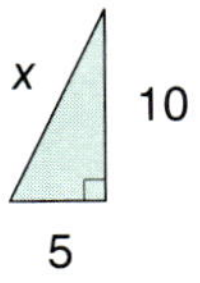

7.

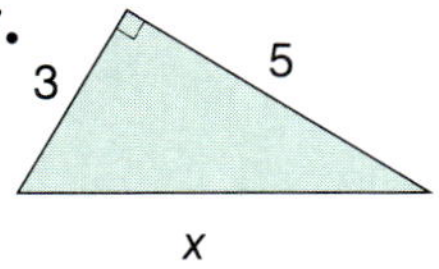

8.

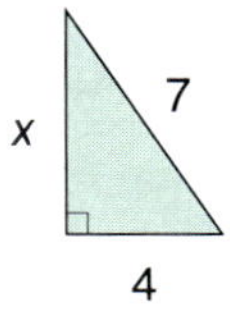

9.

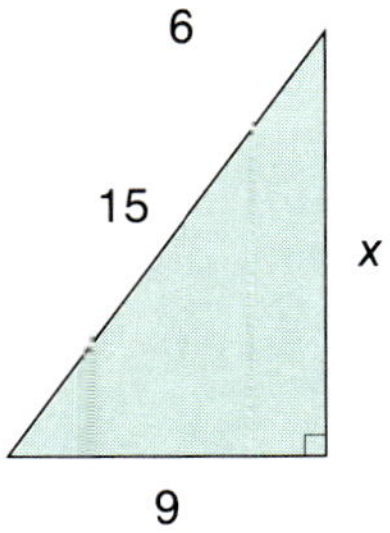

10.

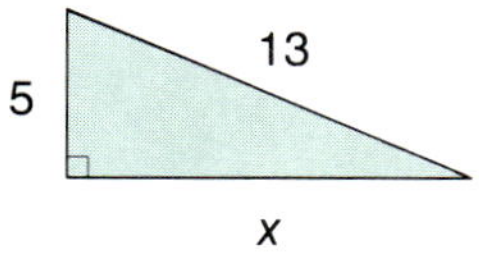

11.

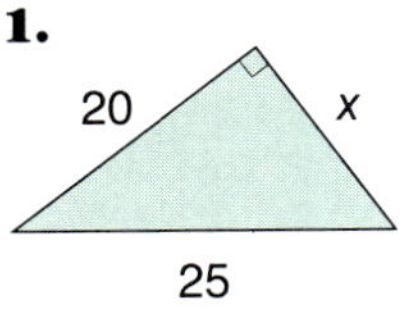

12.

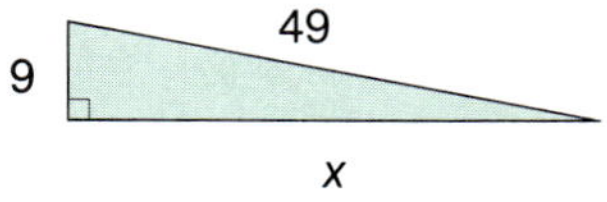

13.

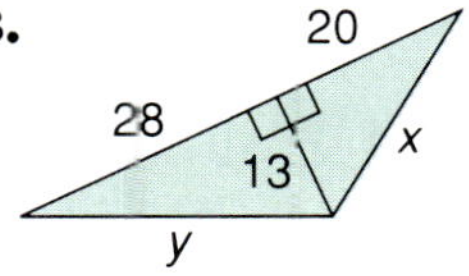

14.

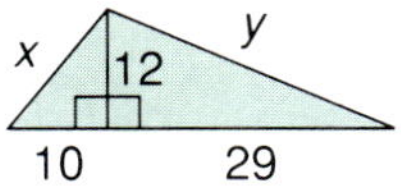

15.

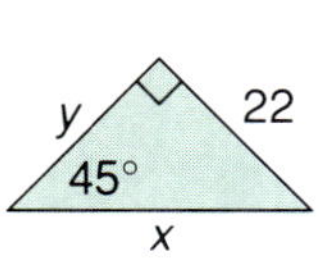

16.

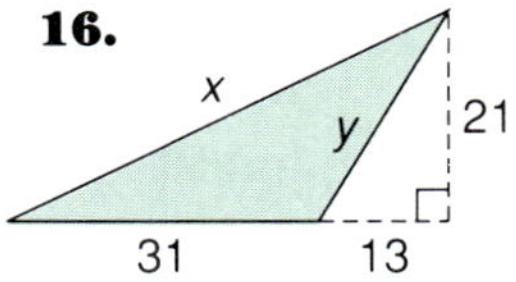

Problem Solving

Solve.

17. Ken is building a greenhouse. What is the length of the board for the frame he will need to buy at Geraldo's store?

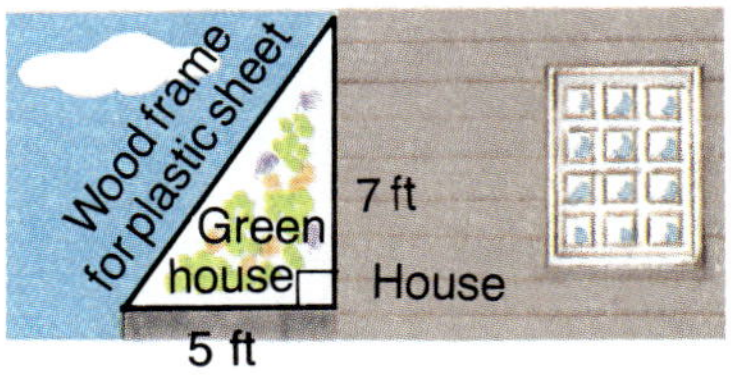

Choose a ________ Strategy

By Land or by Sea? What is the most economical way for Country Cable TV to lay a cable from Greenboro Junction to Trappsburg? Running the cable on land costs $10,000 per kilometer, and running it under water costs $18,000 per kilometer.

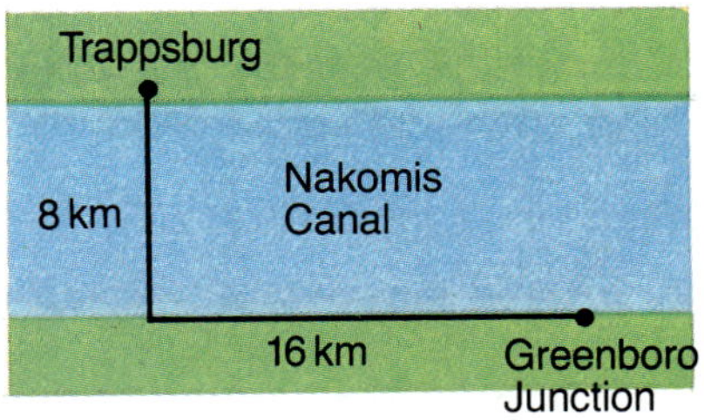

18. Find the shortest route for the cable to the nearest tenth of a kilometer. What is the cost?

19. Find the cost if 16 km of cable is laid on land to a point directly across from Trappsburg and then 8 km is laid under water.

20. Make a table of other routes and their costs. What is the cheapest way to lay a cable from Greensboro Junction to Trappsburg?

ALGEBRA

Pythagorean Triples

Build Understanding

A. Geo Trio
Materials: Geoboard, string, unit square
Groups: 3–5 students

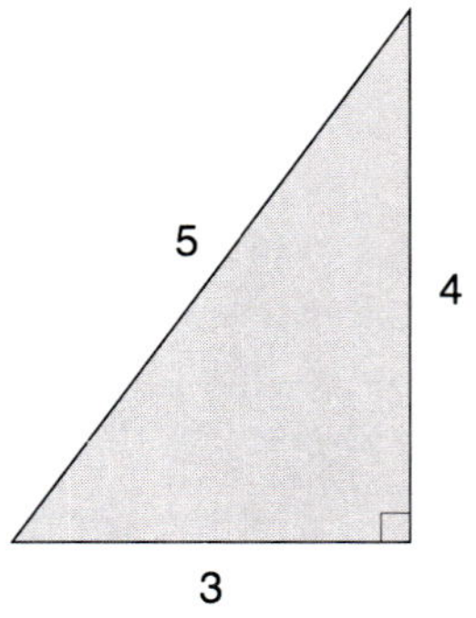

a. Using the geoboard and string, make a triangle with two sides that measure 3 units and 4 units.

b. Use the unit square to make the angle between the sides a right angle.

c. What is the measure of the hypotenuse?

d. Repeat steps a–c for legs of 6 and 8 units.

e. Repeat steps a–c for legs of 9 and 12 units.

f. Repeat steps a–c for legs of $1\frac{1}{2}$ and 2 units.

g. List your results in a table, with a the length of the shortest side, c the longest side, and b the third side. Find another right triangle triple.

a	b	c
3	4	5
6	8	
9	12	

h. Does 4, 5, 6 fit the pattern?

i. For each triple in the table, check to see if $a^2 + b^2 = c^2$.

B. Two right triangles have sides with the lengths shown. The triangles are similar, so the ratios of corresponding sides are equal.

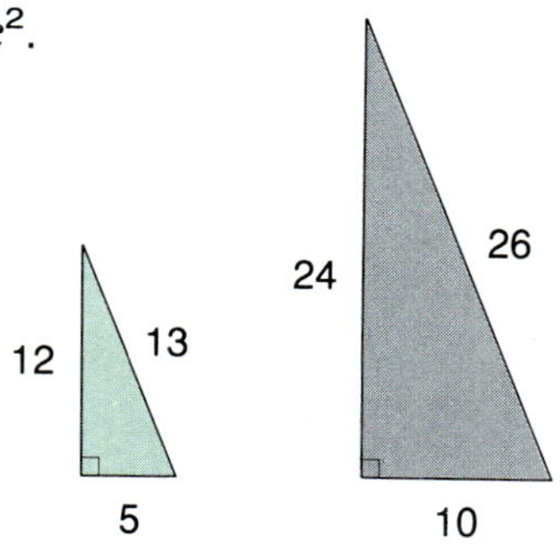

$$\frac{5}{10} = \frac{12}{24} = \frac{13}{26}$$

Pythagorean triples are three whole numbers (a, b, c) such that $a^2 + b^2 = c^2$.

From Examples A and B, two Pythagorean triples are 3, 4, 5 and 5, 12, 13.

■ **Talk About Math** Use the concept of similar triangles to explain why multiples of a Pythagorean triple are also Pythagorean triples.

Check Understanding

Which of these triples are Pythagorean triples?

1. 7, 24, 25 **2.** 5, 6, 7 **3.** 12, 16, 20 **4.** 10, 24, 27

Practice

Use the Pythagorean Theorem to verify whether these triples are Pythagorean triples. Answer *yes* or *no*.

5. 8, 15, 17 **6.** 1, $1\frac{2}{5}$, $2\frac{3}{5}$ **7.** 4, 7, 8 **8.** 11, 35, 37

9. 14, 48, 50 **10.** 20, 21, 29 **11.** 24, 45, 51 **12.** 16, 30, 34

13. 18, 20, 30 **14.** 27, 36, 45 **15.** 22, 27, 28 **16.** 300, 400, 500

17. 28, 29, 31 **18.** 24, 32, 40 **19.** 11, 60, 61 **20.** 66, 130, 112

Problem Solving

Solve each problem.

21. How far is it across the lake?

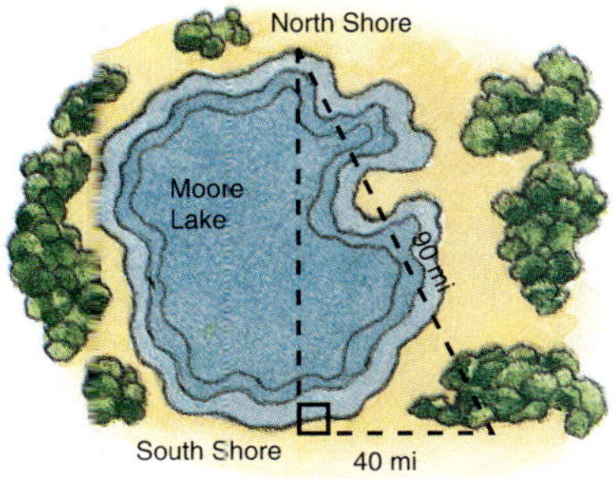

22. Elvira leaves the gas station at the intersection of State Street and Grove Road. How far must she go to reach the intersection of Route 92 and Grove?

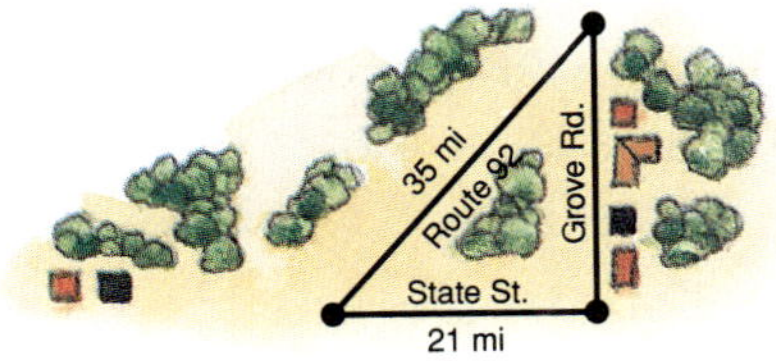

23. How tall is the tree pictured below?

24. Find the missing numbers in the triangle pictured below.

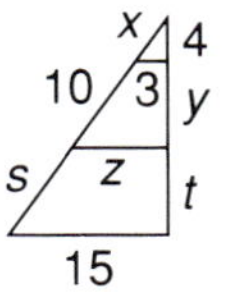

25. The diagonal of a rectangular hall mirror is 75 cm. What whole numbers can the lengths of the sides be?

26. A rectangular warehouse floor is 30 ft by 72 ft. What is the length of the diagonal of the floor?

Skills Review pages 32–33

Compute. Write answers in exponential notation.

1. $(1.2 \times 10^6) \times (3.0 \times 10^4)$ **2.** $(3.9 \times 10^8) \div (1.3 \times 10^3)$

3. $(9.8 \times 10^4) - (6.5 \times 10^4)$ **4.** $(2.9 \times 10^6) + (3.2 \times 10^6)$

ALGEBRA

30-60-90 Triples

Build Understanding

Lucia is working a physics problem about a car moving up an inclined plane. She must find the height of the plane.

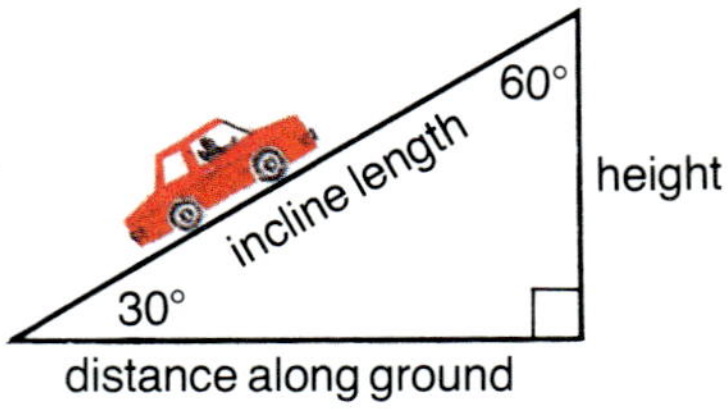

ACTIVITY

A. Halves Have It
Materials: Grid paper, Math Sketcher, scissors
Groups: Pairs of students

a. Draw an equilateral triangle on grid paper. Cut out the triangle.

b. Fold the triangle in half, as shown. Label the measure of each angle.

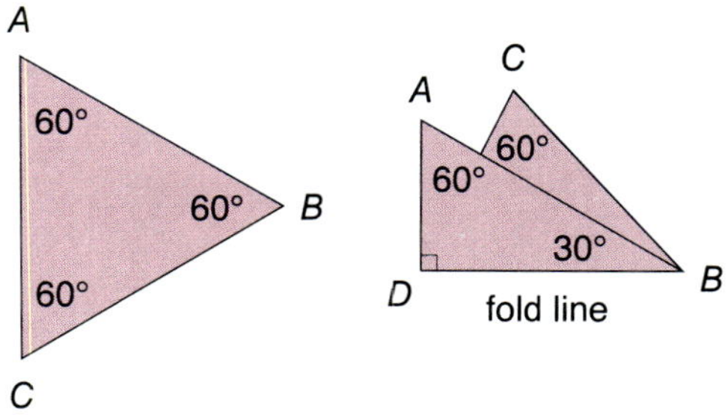

c. What is the relationship between AD and AB?

d. List the angle measurements of $\triangle ABD$ in increasing order.

e. Explain how Lucia can find the height of the inclined plane if she knows the length of the incline.

B. In a 30-60-90 triangle the shorter leg is one half as long as the hypotenuse. If the hypotenuse has length x, the other two sides have lengths of $\frac{1}{2}x$ and $\frac{\sqrt{3}}{2}x$.

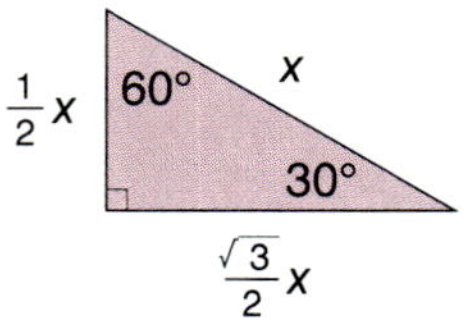

The hypotenuse of a 30-60-90 triangle is 4 ft long. How long are the other two sides?

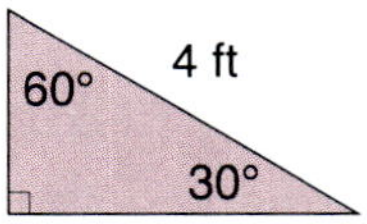

Hypotenuse	Short leg	Long leg
x	$\frac{1}{2}x$	$\frac{\sqrt{3}}{2}x$
4	$\frac{1}{2}(4) = 2$	$\frac{\sqrt{3}}{2}(4) = 2\sqrt{3} \approx 2(1.732)$, or about 3.5

The short leg is 2 ft long. The long leg is about 3.5 ft long.

■ **Talk About Math** What side of a 30-60-90 triangle is always opposite the 90° angle?

Check Understanding

For another example, see Set D, pages 460–461.

1. If the shorter leg of a 30-60-90 triangle is w, find the lengths of the other two sides.

2. What angle is always opposite the shorter leg in a 30-60-90 triangle?

Practice

For More Practice, see Set D, pages 462–463.

Calculator Find the measurements to the nearest tenth.

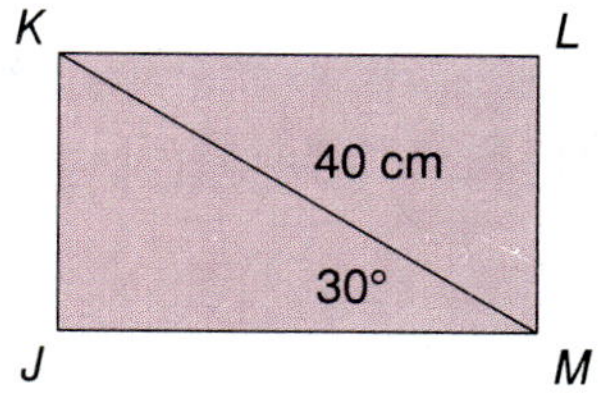

3. $m\angle JKM$ = ▦ **4.** $m\angle LMK$ = ▦ **5.** KJ = ▦

6. KL = ▦ **7.** Area of $JKLM$ = ▦

Find the missing side.

8.

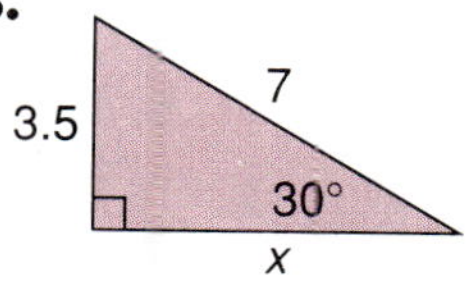

9.

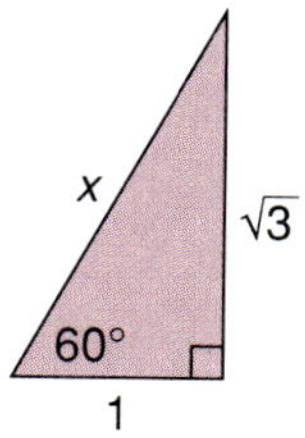

10.

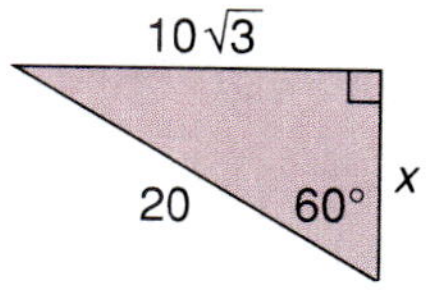

If $\triangle ABC \cong \triangle EFD$, and F is the midpoint of $\overline{BC}$, what is

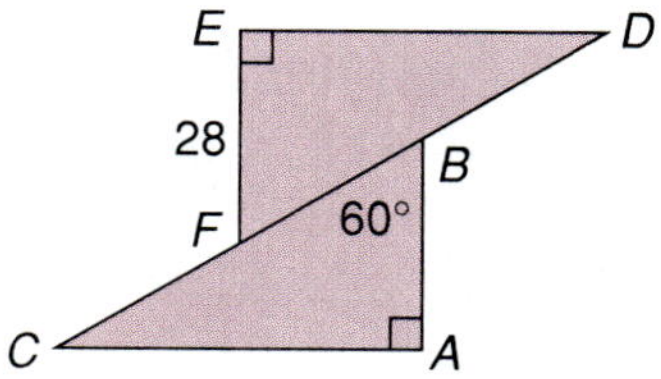

11. FD? **12.** ED? **13.** CA? **14.** CB?

15. $m\angle ACB$? **16.** $m\angle EFD$? **17.** $m\angle FDE$? **18.** CD?

Problem Solving

Solve each problem. Tell whether you used paper and pencil, mental math, or a calculator.

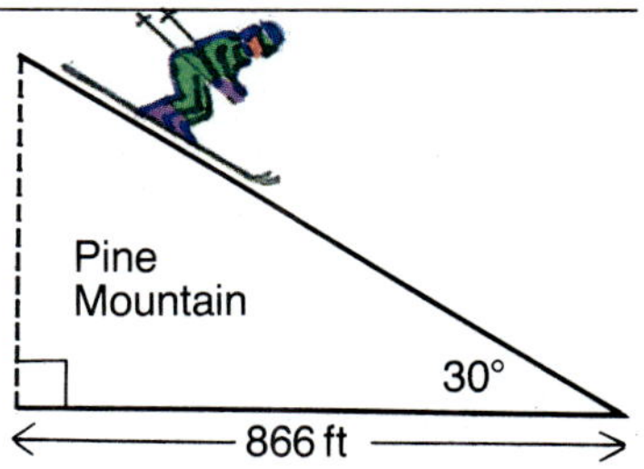

19. A downhill skier races down a mountainside. The mountainside is a 30-60-90 inclined plane, as shown. How far does the skier travel?

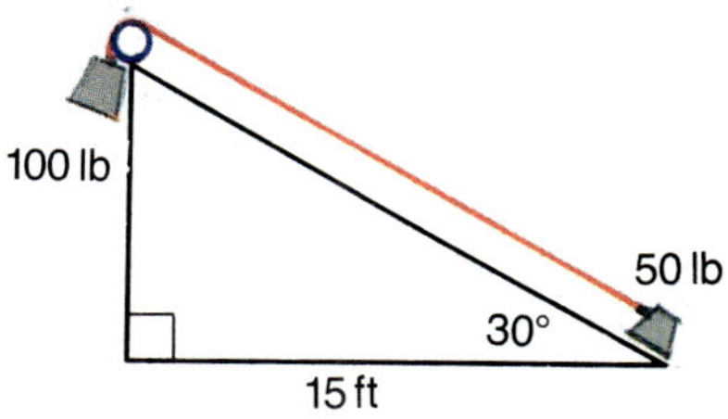

20. Critical Thinking Two weights are connected by a pulley, located at the top of the incline. The lighter weight rests on a 30-60-90 inclined plane. When the heavier weight falls vertically, it pulls the lighter weight up the incline. How far will the heavier weight fall?

Reading ____ Math

Following Examples Refer to Example B to answer the questions.

1. Why is the short leg 2 ft long?

2. Name the leg that is 2 ft long.

3. How do you know that the long leg is about equal to 2(1.732)?

4. Name the leg that is about 3.5 ft long.

ALGEBRA

45-45-90 Triples

Build Understanding

Each angle of a square is 90°. A diagonal of the square bisects two of the 90° angles and makes two triangles. The angles in each triangle are 45-45-90.

Pastry Dough Square

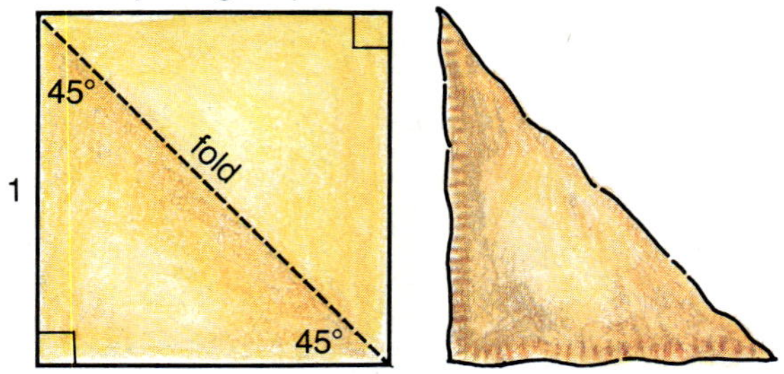

A. Giorgio is making pastry for meat and vegetable appetizers. For each appetizer he folds a square of pastry dough in half diagonally. How long is each appetizer if he uses 1-in. pastry squares?

The diagonal of each square is the length of the appetizer. You can use the Pythagorean Theorem to find the length of the diagonal.

$$a^2 + b^2 = c^2$$

$$1^2 + 1^2 = c^2$$

$$2 = c^2$$

$$\sqrt{2} = c$$

Because the pastry dough is square, $a = b$.

The length of each appetizer is $\sqrt{2}$ in.

B. One leg of an isosceles right triangle is a. How long are the other sides of the triangle?

In an ***isosceles triangle***, two sides are equal. So $AC = BC$ for the triangle shown. Side AB is the hypotenuse.

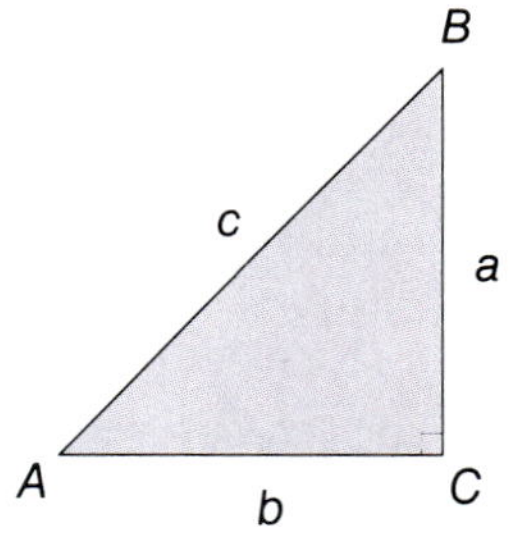

You can use the Pythagorean Theorem to find the length c in terms of the known length a.

$$a^2 + b^2 = c^2$$

$$a^2 + a^2 = c^2$$

$$2a^2 = c^2$$

$$a\sqrt{2} = c$$

In an isosceles right triangle, $a = b$.

The other leg of the isosceles right triangle is a. The hypotenuse is $a\sqrt{2}$.

In every isosceles right triangle:

—Both legs are the same length.
—The angles measure 45°, 45°, and 90°.
—The hypotenuse is $\sqrt{2}$ times the length of a leg.

■ **Write About Math** Write an expression for finding the area of a 45-45-90 triangle.

Check Understanding

For another example, see Set E, pages 460–461.

Use triangle *DEF* to complete each statement.

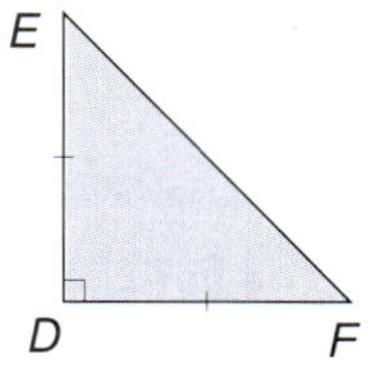

1. $m\angle D =$ ▦ **2.** $m\angle E =$ ▦ **3.** $m\angle F =$ ▦

Calculator Find each answer by using a calculator. Round your answers to the nearest tenth.

4. If $DE = 4$ cm, $DF =$ ▦ and $EF =$ ▦. **5.** If $DE = 10$ cm, $DF =$ ▦ and $EF =$ ▦.

6. If Giorgio makes small croissants from 6-in. squares, how long will each croissant be?

Practice

For More Practice, see Set E, pages 462–463.

Use the figure to find the indicated measurements. Leave the lengths in square root form.

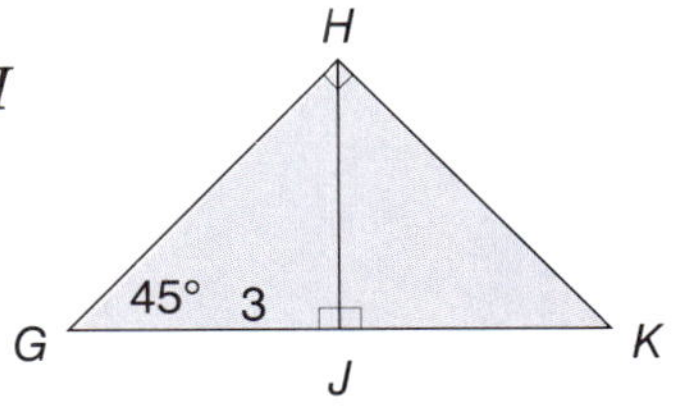

7. $m\angle GHK$ **8.** $m\angle JHK$ **9.** $m\angle HKJ$ **10.** *GH*

11. *HK* **12.** *GK* **13.** *HJ*

Mixed Practice Use the figures to find the indicated measurements to the nearest tenth. Use 45-45-90 triples, 30-60-90 triples, or Pythagorean triples.

14. *AC*

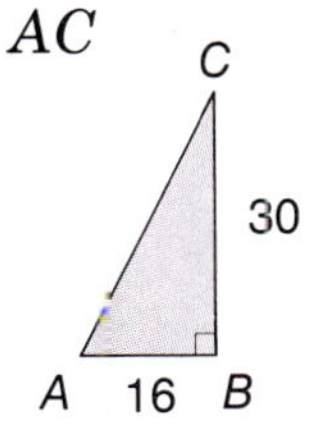

15. *XY* **16.** *YZ*

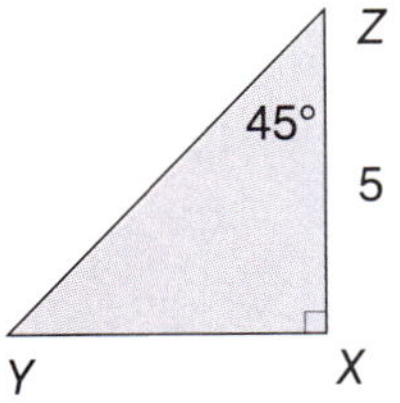

17. *RS* **18.** *SQ*

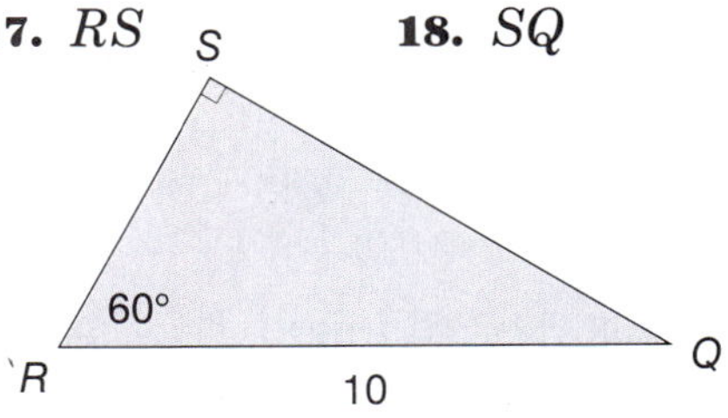

Problem Solving

Solve each problem. Round your answers to the nearest tenth.

19. Giorgio makes raspberry turnovers in two sizes, small and large. The small turnover is made by folding over a 3-in. square on the diagonal. The large turnover is made from a 5-in. square. How long is each turnover?

20. On Fridays, Giorgio sells individual pizza wedges made from squares cut in half on a diagonal. The small wedge is cut from a $3\frac{1}{2}$ in. square and sells for 99¢. The large wedge is cut from a $5\frac{1}{2}$ in. square and sells for \$1.89. Which wedge is the better buy?

ALGEBRA

Tangent Ratio

Build Understanding

For any right triangle, the following ratio can be written for each acute angle.

$$\frac{\text{length of opposite leg}}{\text{length of adjacent leg}}$$

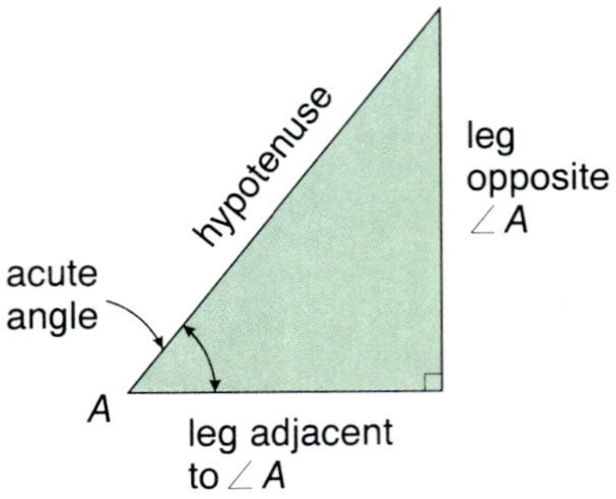

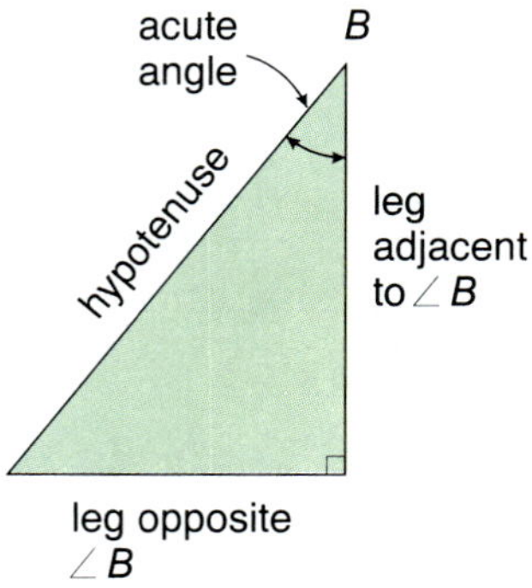

A. Jan Fong, a builder, is making plans for building a garage. She is considering 3 angles for the pitch of the roof: 30°, 45°, and 60°. The length of the incline will be 12 ft for all 3 angles. What happens to the ratio of the length of the opposite leg to the length of the adjacent leg as the angle of the incline increases?

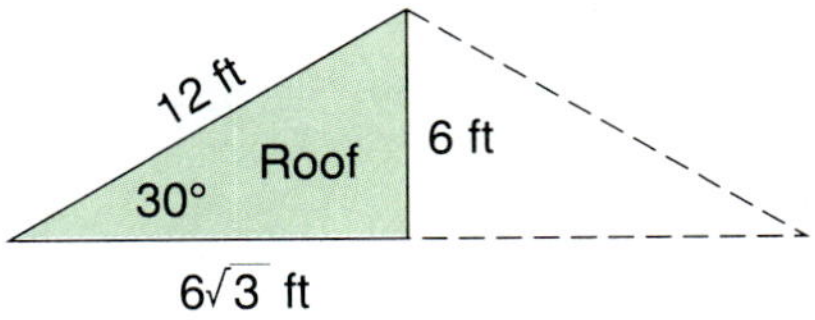

For the 30° angle, the ratio is:

$$\frac{\text{opposite leg}}{\text{adjacent leg}} = \frac{6}{6\sqrt{3}} = \frac{1}{\sqrt{3}} \approx 0.577$$

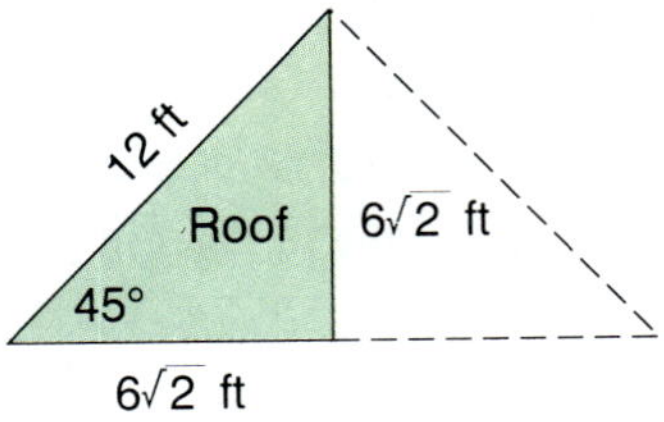

For the 45° angle, the ratio is:

$$\frac{\text{opposite leg}}{\text{adjacent leg}} = \frac{6\sqrt{2}}{6\sqrt{2}} = 1$$

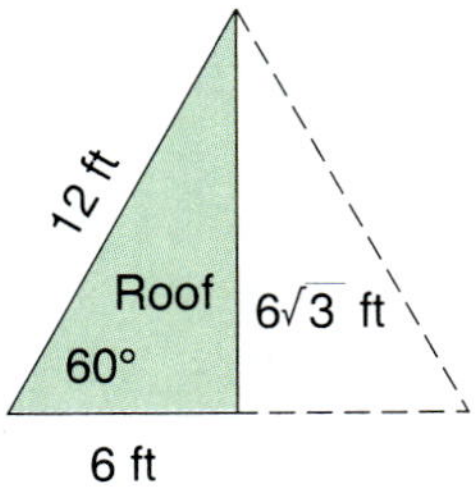

For the 60° angle, the ratio is:

$$\frac{\text{opposite leg}}{\text{adjacent leg}} = \frac{6\sqrt{3}}{6} = \sqrt{3} \approx 1.732$$

As the angle of the incline increases, the ratio of the length of the opposite leg to the length of the adjacent leg increases, from about 0.577, to 1, to about 1.732.

The ratio in Example A is called the ***tangent*** of the angle, which is shortened to ***tan***.

$$\tan A = \frac{\text{length of opposite leg}}{\text{length of adjacent leg}}$$

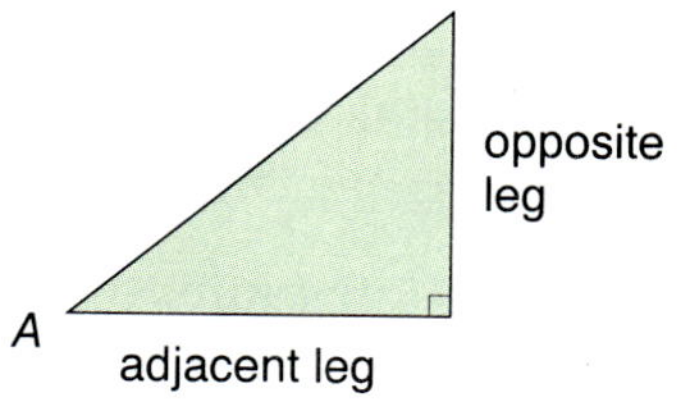

B. The table on page 603 gives tangent ratios. Use the table to find x to the nearest tenth.

$\mathbf{0.700 \approx \frac{x}{8}}$ $\tan 35 \approx 0.700$

$\mathbf{0.7 \times 8 \approx x}$ $\mathbf{5.6 \approx x}$

The length of x is about 5.6 cm.

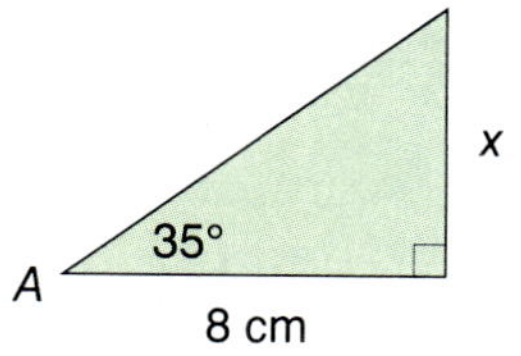

Talk About Math From Example A, describe what happens to the tangent of an angle as the angle increases in measure.

Check Understanding

For another example, see Set F, pages 460–461.

Match the description on the left with the correct term on the right.

1. The largest angle in a right triangle

2. The side of a right triangle that is opposite the largest angle

3. The leg of a right triangle that is opposite the smaller acute angle

4. The leg of a right triangle that is opposite the larger acute angle

a. shorter leg
b. 45° angle
c. hypotenuse
d. longer leg
e. 90° angle

Use the figure at the right to name the indicated part of the triangle.

5. hypotenuse

6. leg opposite $\angle K$

7. side opposite $\angle L$

8. leg adjacent to $\angle J$

9. leg opposite $\angle J$

10. leg adjacent to $\angle K$

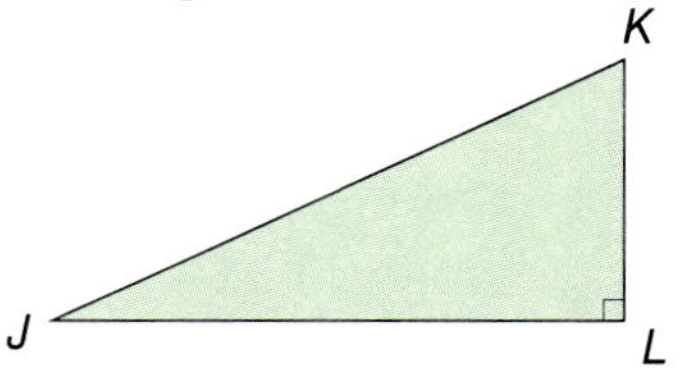

11. Find the length x to the nearest tenth.

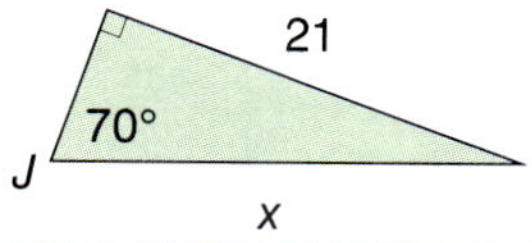

Practice

For More Practice, see Set F, pages 462–463.

Tell whether the statement is *always*, *sometimes*, or *never* true. Draw triangles to help you decide.

12. The leg opposite an acute angle in a right triangle is congruent to the leg adjacent to the acute angle.

13. The leg adjacent to an acute angle is shorter than the hypotenuse of the triangle.

14. The leg opposite an acute angle in a right triangle is shorter than the leg adjacent to that angle.

15. A right triangle has at least one obtuse angle.

16. A right triangle has at least one acute angle.

17. The hypotenuse is the longest side of a right triangle.

Use the table on page 603 to determine the size of each angle in the figures at the right.

18. $\angle A =$ ▦ **19.** $\angle C =$ ▦

20. $\angle E =$ ▦ **21.** $\angle H =$ ▦

22. $\angle D =$ ▦ **23.** $\angle M =$ ▦

24. $\angle G =$ ▦ **25.** $\angle K =$ ▦

26. $\angle V =$ ▦ **27.** $\angle T =$ ▦

28. $\angle N =$ ▦ **29.** $\angle J =$ ▦

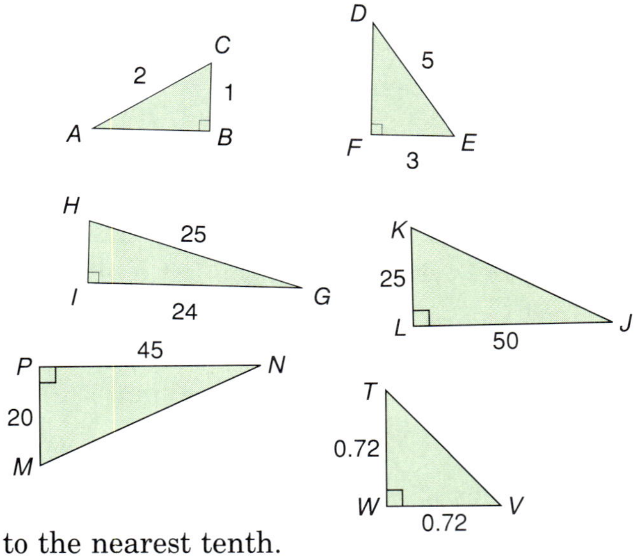

For each triangle, find the length of x to the nearest tenth. For Exercises 35 and 36, also find the length of y to the nearest tenth.

30.

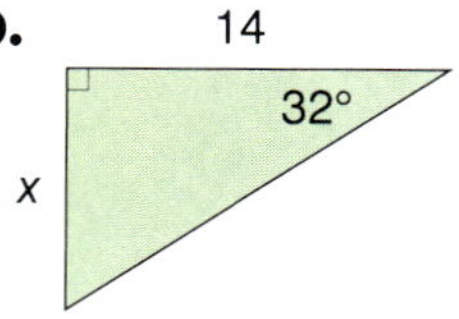

31.

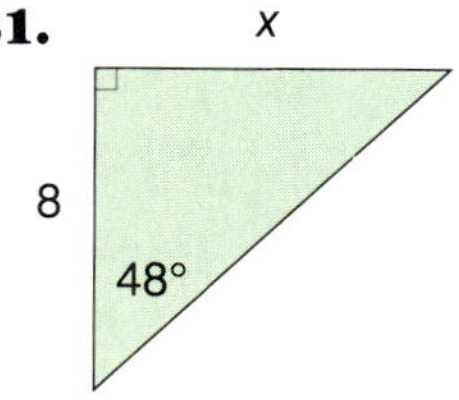

32.

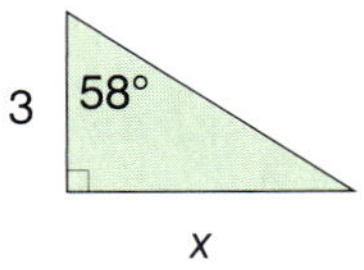

33.

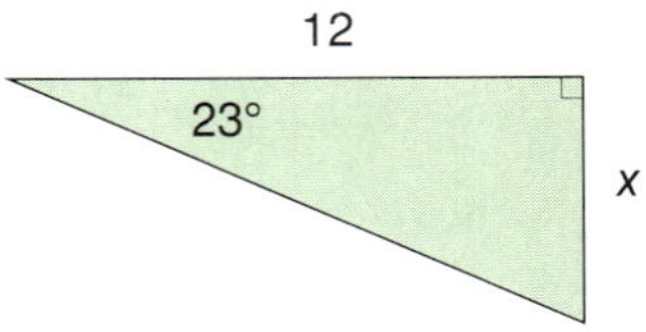

34.

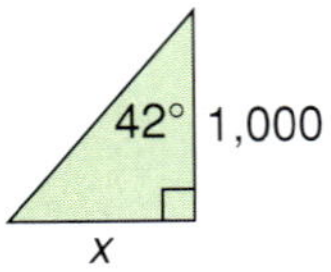

35.

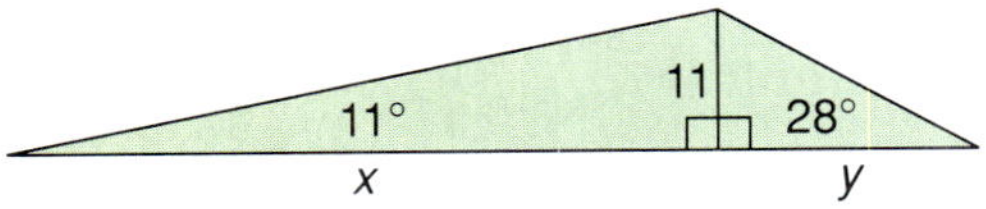

36.

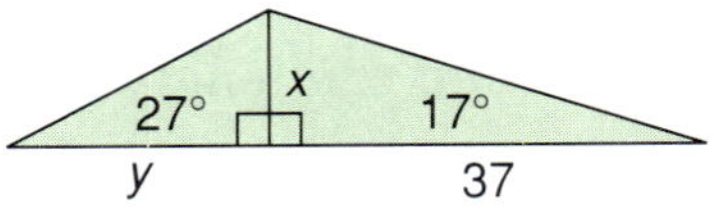

Problem Solving

Solve each problem. Round each answer to the nearest tenth.

37. Jan is constructing a greenhouse on the south side of the Kelsoes' home. The greenhouse extends 3 ft from the wall of the house. The distance along the wall from the top of the greenhouse to the point where the greenhouse roof meets the house is 3.5 ft. What is the size of the angle between the wall and the roof of the greenhouse?

38. Jan Fong is building a back porch for the Kelsoes. She wants the porch roof to rise 20° above the horizontal. The porch will be 10 ft front to back. How high will the porch roof be above the porch ceiling where the porch meets the house?

39. Critical Thinking A blueprint indicates a roof with a 24° angle above the ceiling. If the building is 30 ft wide, what is the distance from the ceiling to the peak of the roof?

TIPS FOR PROBLEM SOLVERS

Visualize the problem in your mind to help you understand it better.

Explore ______ Math

You can create your own Pythagorean triples. Any two positive whole numbers m and n, where $m > n$, can be selected. Copy and complete the following table to see how this method works.

m	n	$a = 2mn$	$b = m^2 - n^2$	$c = m^2 + n^2$
2	1	4	3	5
3	1	**40.**	**41.**	**42.**
3	2	**43.**	**44.**	**45.**
4	1	**46.**	**47.**	**48.**
4	2	**49.**	**50.**	**51.**
5	2	**52.**	**53.**	**54.**

55. How many Pythagorean triples do you think can be created by using this method?

56. Show why m and n cannot be the same number in this method for creating Pythagorean triples. Hint: (Look at the formulas for a, b, and c).

Use Alternate Strategies

Build Understanding

Faith wants to know the height of her office in Roth Towers. She can see a fountain from her window. With a transit, she finds that the angle of depression to the fountain is 53°. The distance from the building wall to the fountain is 90 ft. How high is her window?

PROBLEM SOLVING GUIDE

Understand
QUESTION
FACTS
KEY IDEA

Plan and Solve
STRATEGY
ANSWER

Look Back
SENSIBLE ANSWER
ALTERNATE APPROACH

Understand QUESTION How high is the window?

FACTS The ***angle of depression***—the angle between the window and the line of sight—is 53°. The fountain is 90 ft from the building.

KEY IDEA Determine the angle measures within the triangle, and then use the tangent formula to find the length of the leg opposite the angle.

Plan and Solve STRATEGY *Use logical reasoning.* Since $\overleftrightarrow{DB}$ is parallel to $\overleftrightarrow{AC}$, $\angle DBA \cong \angle BAC$. So, $m\angle BAC = 53°$.

You can *use the tangent formula* to find the length of the leg opposite the angle.

$$\tan 53° = \frac{n}{90} \quad \frac{\text{length of opposite leg}}{\text{length of adjacent leg}}$$

$$90 \times \tan 53° = n$$

$$90 \times 1.327 \approx n$$

$$119.4 \approx n$$

ANSWER The window is about 119.4 ft high.

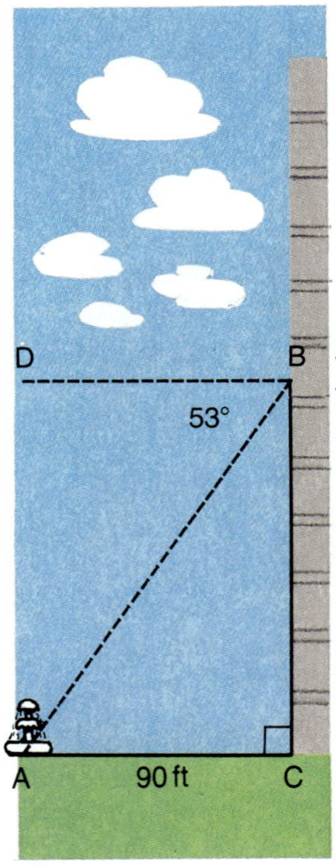

$$\frac{4}{3} = \frac{n}{90}$$

$$n = 120$$

Look Back ALTERNATE STRATEGY *Write an equation.* The angle opposite the longer leg of a 3-4-5 right triangle is about 53°. You can set up a proportion using this triple.

The answer of 119.4 ft is reasonable because it is close to 120 ft.

■ **Talk About Math** Can you use the Pythagorean theorem to solve this problem?

Check Understanding

Name two ways of finding each measurement.

1. $m\angle ACD$ **2.** $m\angle CAD$

3. AC **4.** $m\angle GJH$

5. $m\angle GJE$ **6.** $m\angle EGF$

7. EF **8.** GH

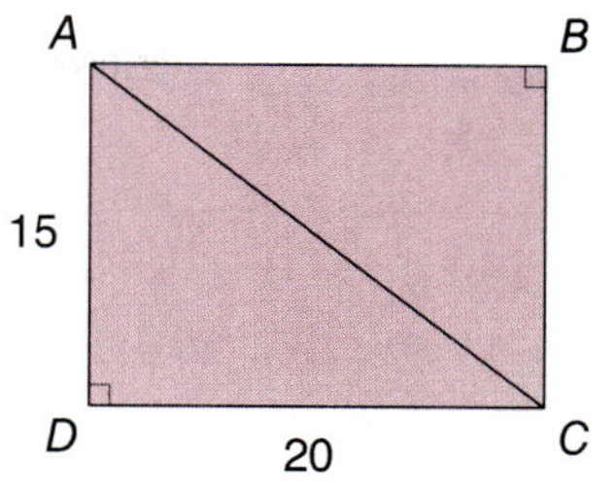

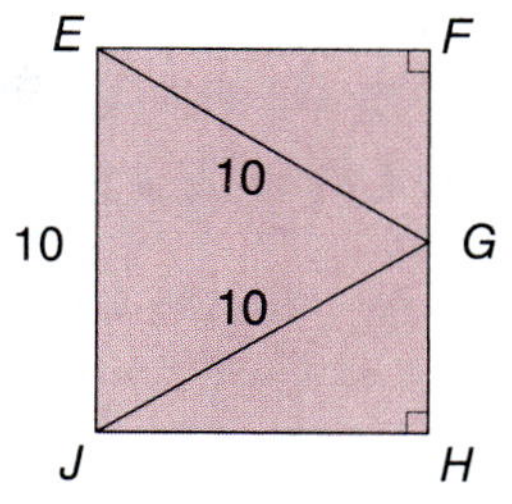

Practice

Solve each problem by using the Pythagorean Theorem, Pythagorean triples, or the tangent ratio. Tell which method you used.

9. The diagram pictures a bicycle race course. Find x.

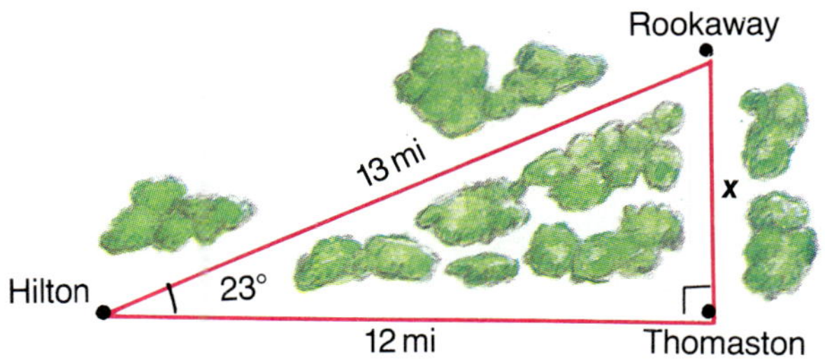

10. Find the sweep angle of the wing to the nearest whole degree.

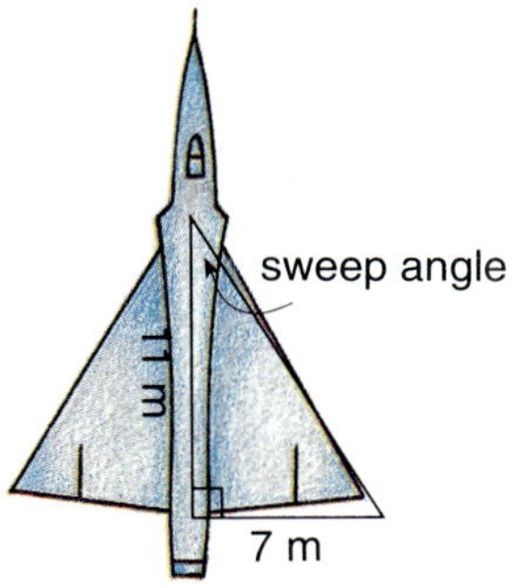

11. The shadow of a tree is 16 m long. The angle of the line of sight from the top of the shadow to the top of the tree is 55°. The distance along the line of sight is 28 m. A kite stuck in the top of the tree is attached to a string 20 m long. Can Josh reach the string without climbing the tree?

12. In the example, suppose Faith measured the distance along the line of sight with a laser measuring device instead of the transit. If the distance along the line of sight was 150 ft, how could Faith find the height of the window?

13. A work crew sets a guy wire 16 ft from a utility pole, and attaches it to the top of a 30 ft-tall pole. How long is the guy wire?

14. An airplane flying at an altitude of 1,000 ft is climbing at an angle of 5° above horizontal. The plane is flying toward a 13,000-ft mountain, 26 mi away. Will the aircraft clear the mountain at its present rate of climb? Explain your answer.

A L G E B R A

Sine and Cosine Ratios

Build Understanding

Two other ratios can help you identify the lengths of sides or the measures of angles in a right triangle. They are ***sine*** and ***cosine***, shortened to ***sin*** and ***cos***.

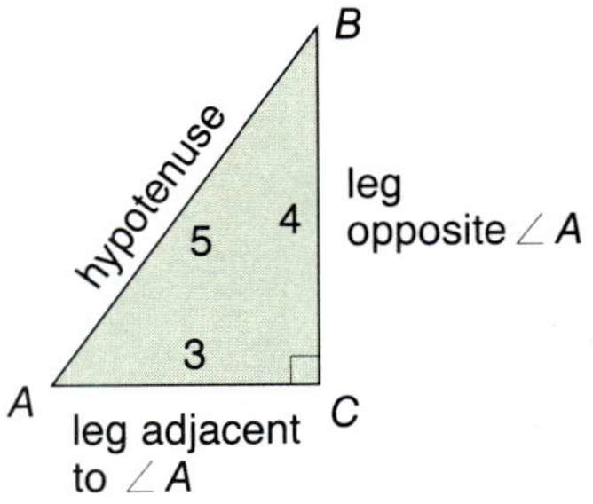

$$\sin A = \frac{\text{length of opposite leg}}{\text{length of hypotenuse}}$$

$$\cos A = \frac{\text{length of adjacent leg}}{\text{length of hypotenuse}}$$

A. Calculate the sine and the cosine for $\angle A$ above. Use the table on page 603 to find the measure of $\angle A$.

$\sin A = \frac{4}{5} = 0.8$

Look in the table. The sine of an angle of 53° is about 0.8. So the measure of angle A is about 53°.

$\cos A = \frac{3}{5} = 0.6$

The cosine of a 53° angle is about 0.6. This calculation verifies that the measure of $\angle A$ is about 53°.

B. Calculate the sine and the cosine of $\angle B$ above. Then compare the results with the sine and the cosine of $\angle A$ in Example A.

$\sin B = \frac{3}{5} = 0.6$

$\cos B = \frac{4}{5} = 0.8$

In Example A, $\sin A = 0.8$. So $\sin A = \cos B$.
Also, since $\cos A = 0.6$ and $\sin B = 0.6$, you know $\cos A = \sin B$.

Talk About Math Explain why $\sin A = \cos B$ and $\sin B = \cos A$ in Examples A and B.

Check Understanding

For another example, see Set G, pages 460–461.

Using the table on page 603, find the ratio or the angle.

1. sin 35° **2.** cos 80° **3.** $\cos A = 0.404$ **4.** $\sin B = 0.545$

5. Where in the table does $\sin A = \cos A$?

Practice

For More Practice, see Set G, pages 462–463.

Copy and complete the table by using $\triangle DEF$. Record the ratios and the angle measures. Tell whether you use paper and pencil or calculator.

	sin	cos	tan	angle measure
$\angle D$	**6.** ▦	**7.** ▦	**8.** ▦	**9.** ▦
$\angle E$	**10.** ▦	**11.** ▦	**12.** ▦	**13.** ▦

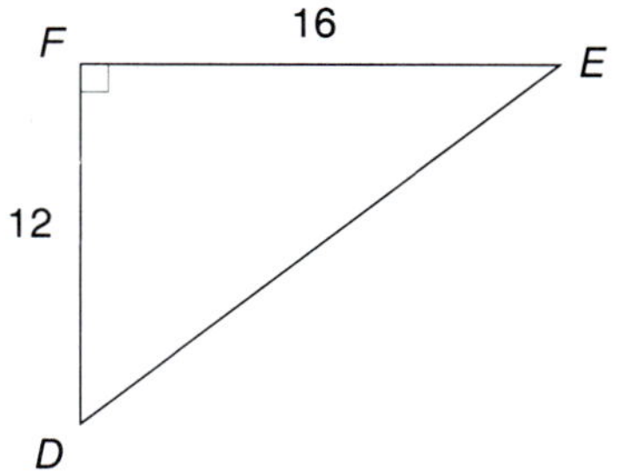

Find the side measures in $\triangle GHJ$. Then copy and complete the table. **Remember** that sin relates to "opposite leg" and cos relates to "adjacent leg."

14. GJ = ▦ **15.** HJ = ▦

	sin	cos	tan
$\angle H$	**16.** ▦	**17.** ▦	**18.** ▦
$\angle J$	**19.** ▦	**20.** ▦	**21.** ▦

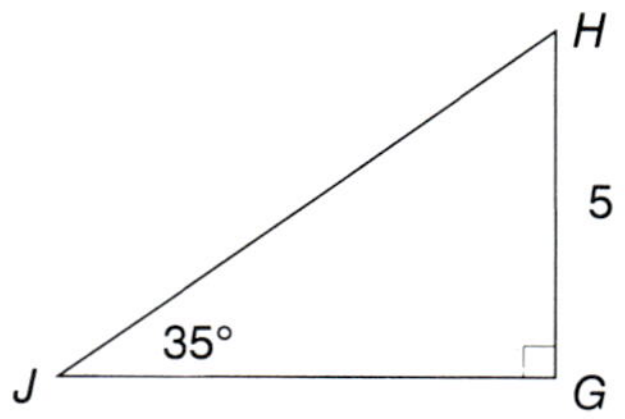

Mixed Practice Use sine, cosine, or tangent to find the measure of the angle, x, or the length of the side, n.

22.

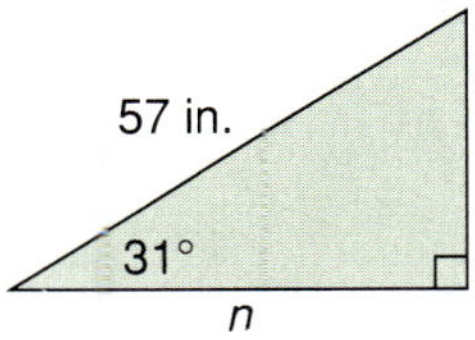

23.

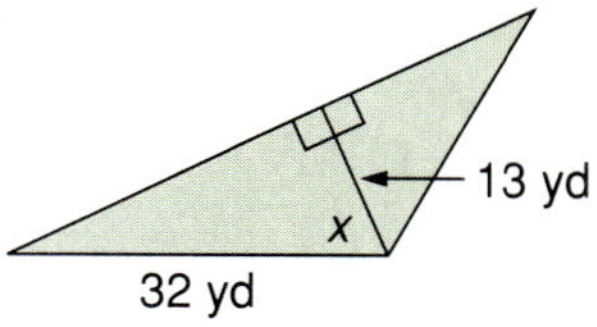

24.

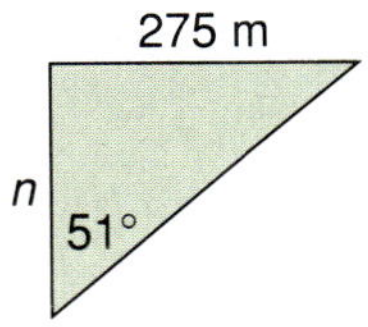

25.

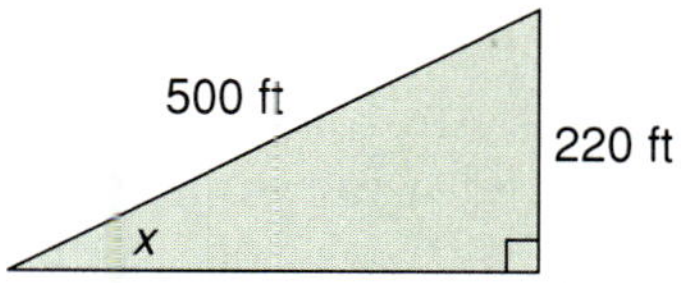

26.

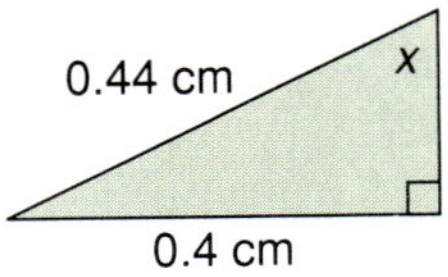

27.

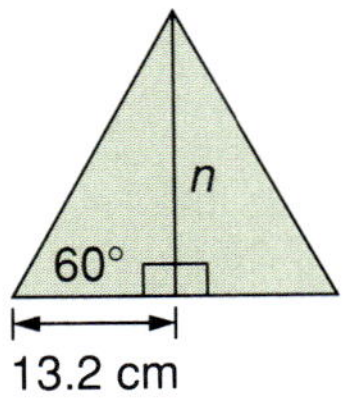

Problem Solving

Solve each problem.

28. The sign on the road leaving Heavenly Valley says: "5° hill ahead." The length of the hill is 6,200 ft. How far does the road rise above the valley floor?

29. The tailgate of a tractor-trailer rig is 1 m from the ground. The greatest incline for efficiently loading the truck is 10°. How long should the ramp be for a 10° incline? Write your answer to the nearest half meter.

Skills Review

The two polygons are similar. Find the missing measures.

1. $m\angle QRS$ **2.** QV

3. $m\angle QVU$ **4.** AB

5. $m\angle RST$ **6.** BC

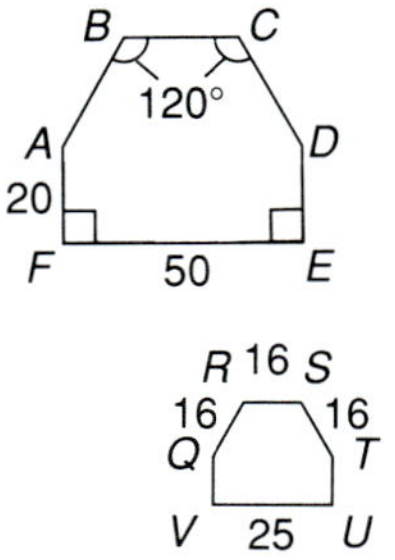

Find each missing length. Round answers to the nearest tenth.

7.

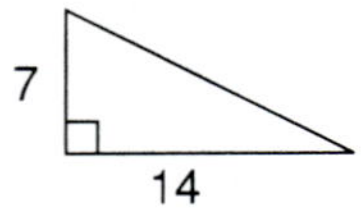

8.

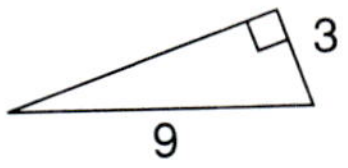

9.

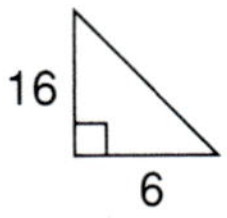

10.

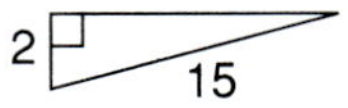

11.

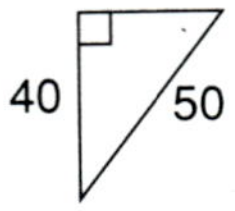

12.

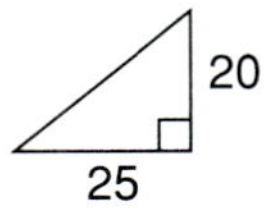

Use the Pythagorean Theorem to verify whether these triples are Pythagorean triples.

13. 4, 7.5, 8.5 **14.** 5, 7, 8

15. 40, 42, 58 **16.** $\frac{1}{2}, \frac{1}{3}, \frac{1}{4}$

Find each missing measurement. Round answers to the nearest tenth.

17. $m\angle DBC$ **18.** BD

19. $m\angle BAD$ **20.** AB

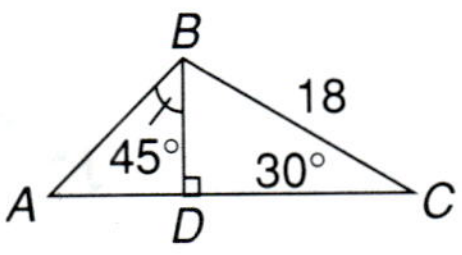

Find each answer by using the table on page 603 or a calculator.

21. tan B **22.** $m\angle B$

23. sin B **24.** BC

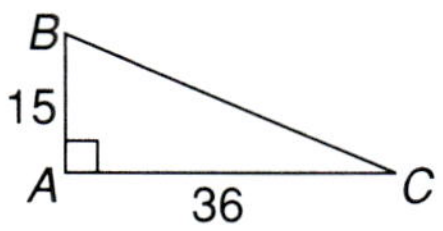

Problem-Solving Review

Solve each problem.

25. A rectangular room is 24 ft long and 16 ft wide. In a scale model of the room, 1 unit represents 4 ft. Find the length and width of the model.

26. Refer to the image of the bear on page 434. Suppose the base of the window was 12 ft high. How high must the enlarged image be so that the bear's paw will be below the window?

27. A storage bay is 5 ft off the ground. A ramp from the bay reaches a point on the floor 12 ft from the bay. How long is the ramp?

28. A rectangular dance studio is 48 ft long and 36 ft wide. What is the length of the diagonal of the floor?

29. Luigi makes a cheese turnover by folding a 7-in. square of dough along its diagonal. What is the length of the long side of the turnover?

30. An airplane takes off at an angle of 30° from the ground. How high above the ground is the plane when it has covered a horizontal distance of 400 ft? Use the table on page 603.

31. **Data File** Use the data on pages 572–573. What is the surface area of the 20-sided polyhedron formed by the pattern? Each edge is 2 cm.

32. **Make a Data File** Do research to find out the take-off and landing angles of various kinds of airplanes. Record your findings in a table. Use this information to determine horizontal and vertical distances during take-offs and landings.

Cumulative Skills Review • Chapters 1–12

Compare. Write <, >, or =.

1. −11 ▒ 7 **2.** −12 ▒ −14 **3.** 19 ▒ −19 **4.** 0 ▒ −6

Write a ratio in simplest form.

5. 15 to 40 **6.** \$36 out of \$60 **7.** 720:900 **8.** 24 cows out of 56

Name the number of significant digits in each measurement.

9. 300 lb **10.** 6.05 kg **11.** 0.008 L **12.** 90.06 m

The measure of each central angle of a regular polygon is given. Tell how many sides each polygon has.

13. 60° **14.** 72° **15.** 45° **16.** 30°

Find the surface area of each figure. Use 3.14 for π.

17.
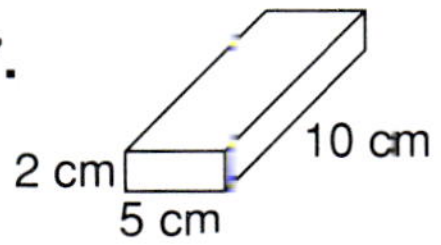

18.
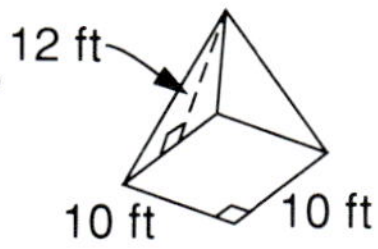

19.
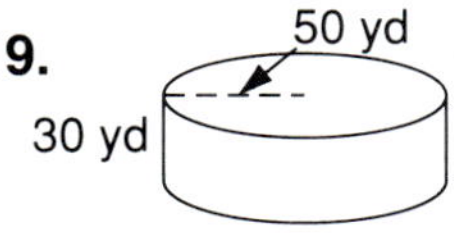

20.
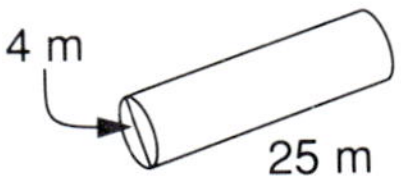

Compute.

21. $16 \div 2 + 4$ **22.** $14.75 \div 2.5$ **23.** $0.025 \times 8{,}000$ **24.** $20 - 3^2$

25. $8 \times 5\frac{3}{8}$ **26.** $15 \times -4 + -5 \times -4$ **27.** $-\frac{5}{6} + \left(6 + \frac{5}{6}\right)$

28. $\frac{5.6 \times 10^4}{2.8 \times 10^2}$ **29.** $(7.5 \times 10^5) - (4.5 \times 10^5)$ **30.** $(9.3 \times 10^{-3}) - (6 \times 10^{-4})$

31. $2\sqrt{36} + 3\sqrt{36}$ **32.** $\sqrt{7} \times \sqrt{7}$ **33.** $\sqrt{45} \div \sqrt{5}$

Find the missing measurements. Round your answers to the nearest tenth.

34. $m\angle CFD$ **35.** FD **36.** CD

37. $m\angle EAB$ **38.** EB **39.** AE

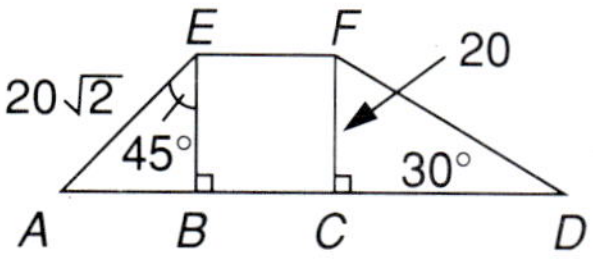

Copy and complete the table. Use $\triangle LMN$. Use the table on page 603 for Exercise 43.

	sin	cos	tan	angle measure
∠L	**40.**	**41.**	**42.**	**43.**

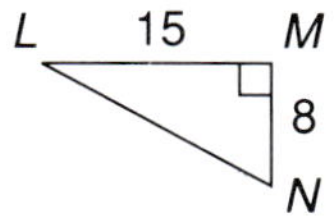

Reteaching

Set A pages 432–433

The two polygons are similar.

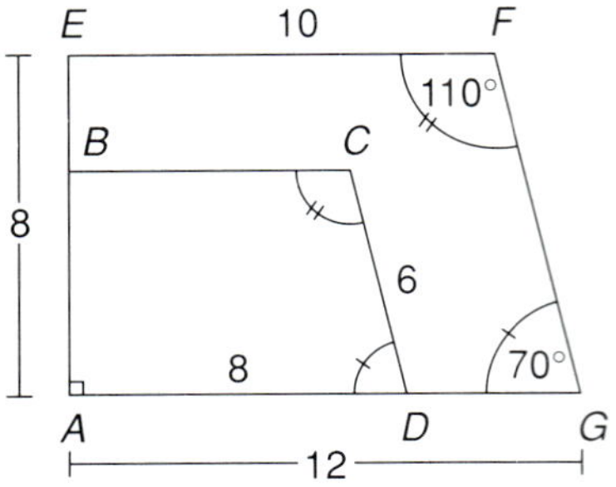

Since the polygons are similar, $\angle C \cong \angle F$. So $m\angle C = 110°$. By the same reasoning, $m\angle D = 70°$.

Remember that corresponding angles are congruent and lengths of corresponding sides have equal ratios in similar polygons.

Find the missing lengths.

1. Length of $\overline{AB}$ = ▦
2. Length of $\overline{FG}$ = ▦
3. Length of $\overline{BC}$ = ▦
4. Find $m\angle ABC$.
5. What angle in polygon $AEFG$ corresponds to $\angle C$?

Set B pages 436–439

The Pythagorean Theorem states that the sum of the squares of the lengths of the legs of a right triangle is equal to the square of the length of the hypotenuse.

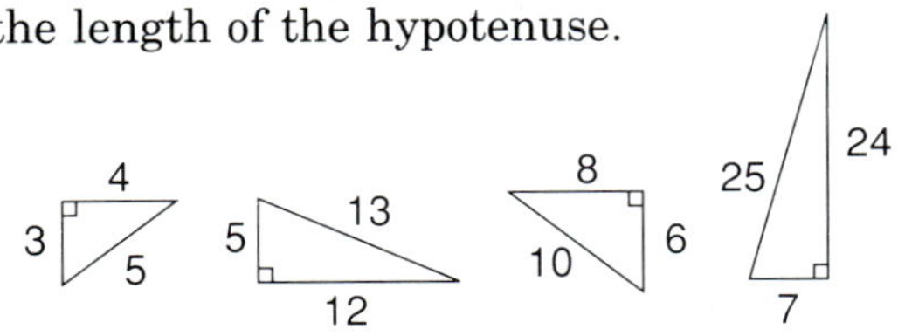

A *B* *C* *D*

In triangle *A*, the lengths of the legs are 3 and 4. The length of the hypotenuse is 5. So, according to the Pythagorean Theorem,

$$3^2 + 4^2 = 5^2$$

Check: $9 + 16 = 25$; the statement is correct.

Remember that the hypotenuse is opposite the right angle of a right triangle.

1. Find the lengths of the legs in triangle *B*.
2. Find the length of the hypotenuse in triangle *C*.

Write an equation for the Pythagorean Theorem for the indicated triangle. Does the equation check?

3. Triangle *B*
4. Triangle *D*
5. Use a calculator to find the length of the hypotenuse in a right triangle with sides $a = 4$ and $b = 5$. Round your answer to the nearest tenth.

Set C pages 442–443

The Pythagorean Theorem helps you find the length of any side of a right triangle. The hypotenuse in this right triangle has a length of 28.

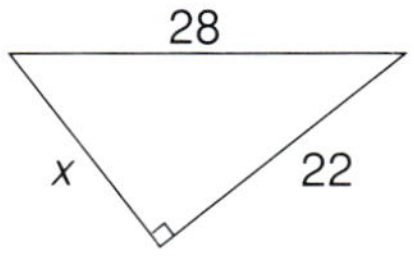

$$x^2 + (22)^2 = (28)^2$$
$$x^2 = (28)^2 - (22)^2$$
$$x^2 = 784 - 484$$
$$x^2 = 300$$
$$x = \sqrt{300} \approx 17.3$$

Remember that in $a^2 + b^2 = c^2$, c is the length of the hypotenuse.

Draw and label each triangle. Find the missing length. Round your answers to the nearest tenth.

1. $a = 19$, $b = 8$, $c =$ ▦
2. $a = 6.3$, $b =$ ▦, $c = 12.2$

Set D pages 446–447

A 30–60–90 triangle has sides whose lengths are expressed by the triple (x, $\sqrt{3}x$, $2x$), or approximately (x, $1.7x$, $2x$). Side b in this 30–60–90 triangle is

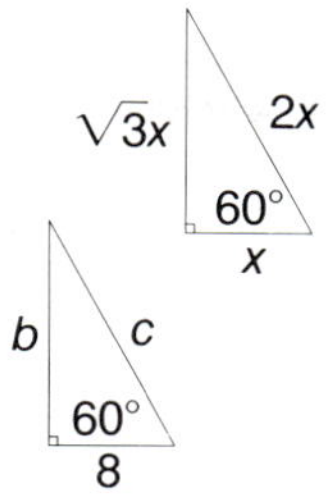

$(\sqrt{3})(8) \approx (1.7)(8) \approx 13.6$

Side b is opposite the 60° angle.

Remember that a 30–60–90 triangle is a right triangle whose acute angles measure 30° and 60°.

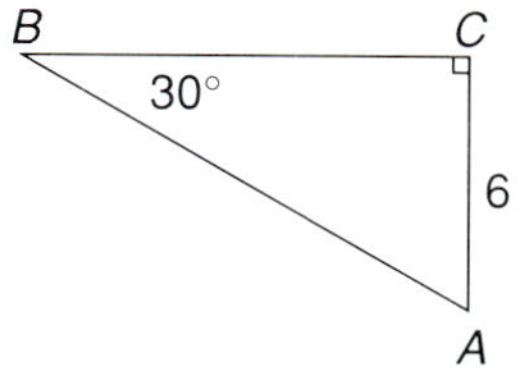

1. $m\angle A =$ ▦

2. $BC =$ ▦

3. $AB =$ ▦

Set E pages 448–449

A 45–45–90 triangle has sides whose lengths are expressed by the triple (x, x, $\sqrt{2}x$), or approximately (x, x, $1.4x$). Side c in this 45–45–90 triangle is

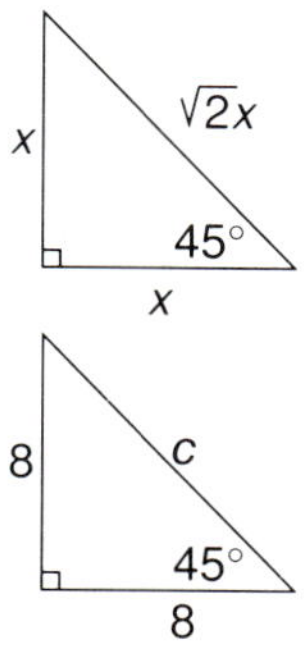

$(\sqrt{2})(8) \approx (1.4)(8) \approx 11.2$

Side c is opposite the 90° angle.

Remember that a 45–45–90 triangle is an isosceles triangle.

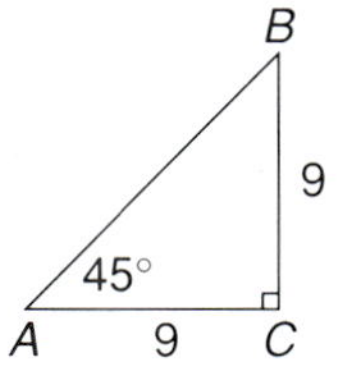

1. $m\angle B =$ ▦

2. $AB =$ ▦

Set F pages 450–453

In any right triangle, you can find the measures of the acute angles if you know the lengths of the legs. Use the tangent ratio and the table on page 603.

$$\tan A = \frac{\text{length of opposite leg}}{\text{length of adjacent leg}}$$

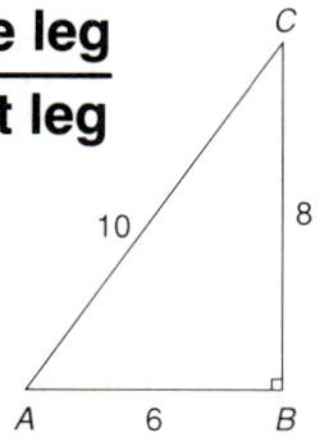

$\tan A = \frac{8}{6}$ $\tan A = 1.\overline{3}$

From the table, $m\angle A \approx 53°$.

Remember that the tangent ratio uses the measures of the legs of a right triangle.

1. What is the measure of the leg opposite angle C?

2. What is the measure of the leg adjacent to angle C?

3. Find tan C.

4. Find $m\angle C$. Use the table on page 603.

Set G pages 456–457

The sine ratio uses the side opposite an angle and the hypotenuse.

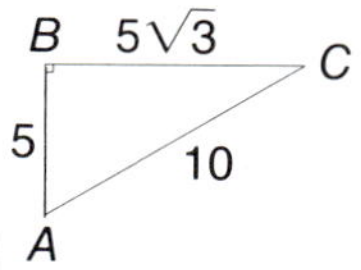

$$\sin A = \frac{\text{length of opposite leg}}{\text{length of hypotenuse}}$$

$\sin A = \frac{5\sqrt{3}}{10}$ $\sin A = \frac{\sqrt{3}}{2}$

The cosine ratio uses the side adjacent to an angle and the hypotenuse.

$$\cos A = \frac{\text{length of adjacent leg}}{\text{length of hypotenuse}}$$

Remember that both the sine ratio and the cosine ratio use the hypotenuse.

1. Find cos A.

2. Find sin C.

3. Find cos C.

4. Find $m\angle A$.

5. Find $m\angle C$.

6. Find tan A.

7. Find tan C.

8. Find $\frac{\sin A}{\cos A}$.

More Practice

Set A pages 432–433

Each pair of polygons is similar. Find the indicated measurements.

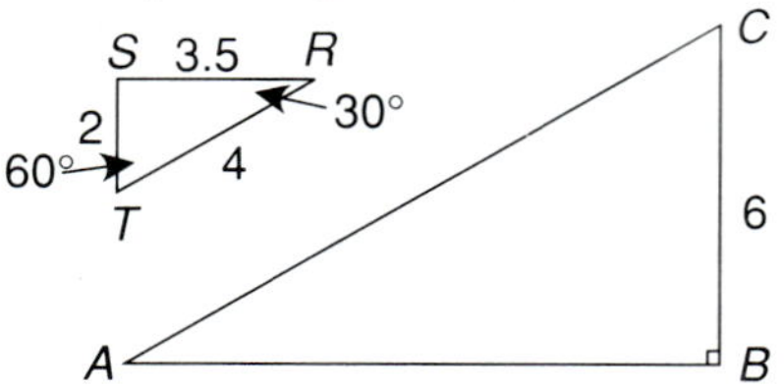

$\angle R \cong \angle A$
$\angle S \cong \angle B$
$\angle T \cong \angle C$

1. $m\angle A =$ ▒ **2.** $m\angle C =$ ▒

3. $AC =$ ▒ **4.** $AB =$ ▒

DEFG is a parallelogram.

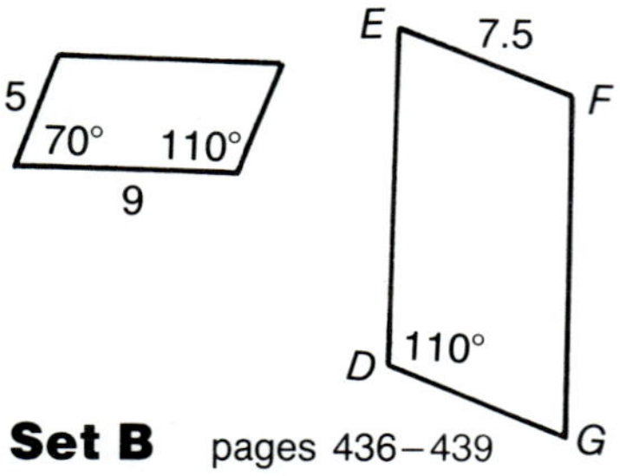

5. $m\angle E =$ ▒ **6.** $m\angle F =$ ▒

7. $m\angle G =$ ▒ **8.** $DE =$ ▒

Set B pages 436–439

Find the side lengths that are not given.
Round your answers to the nearest tenth.

1.

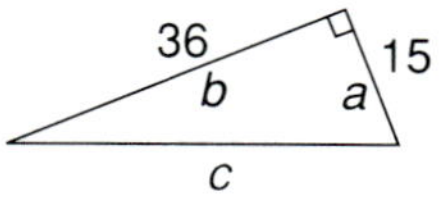

2.

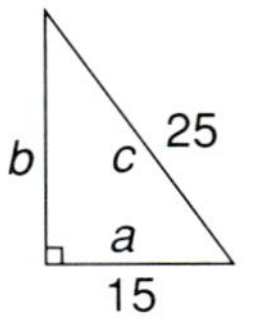

3.

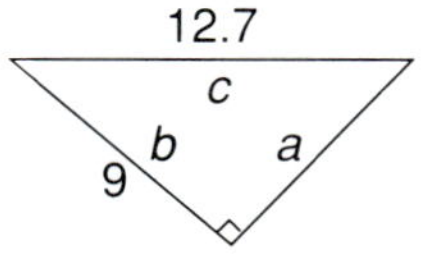

4.

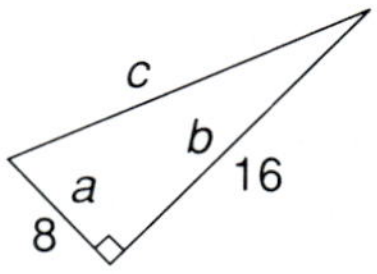

5.

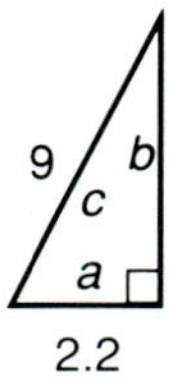

6.

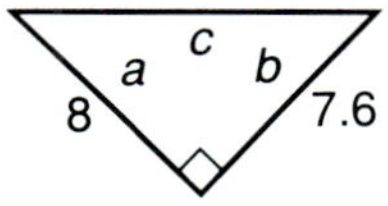

7.

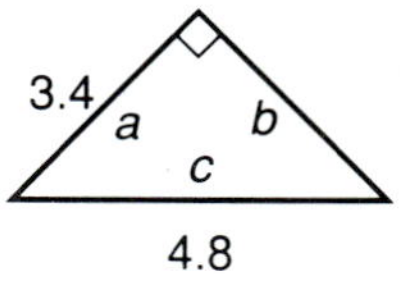

8.

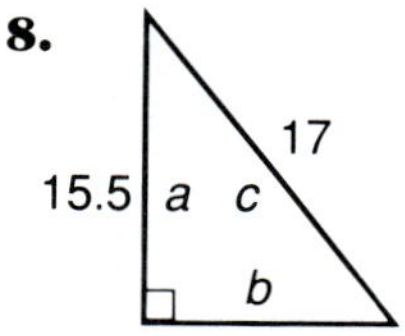

Set C pages 442–443

Use the Pythagorean Theorem to find the missing
measurements. Round your answers to the nearest tenth.

1.

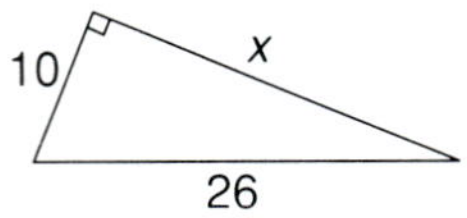

2.

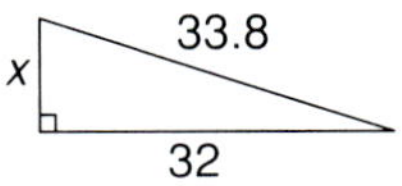

3.

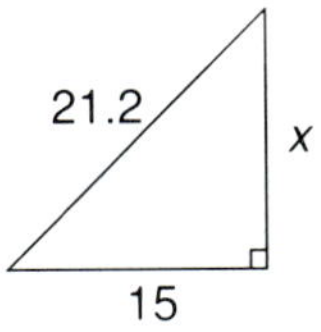

4.

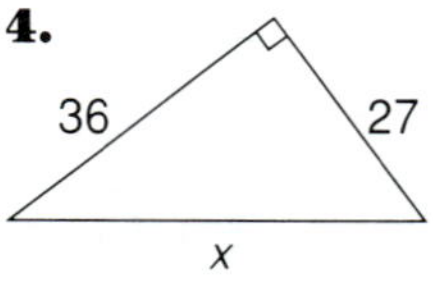

5.

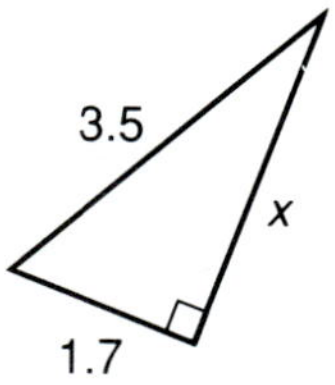

6.

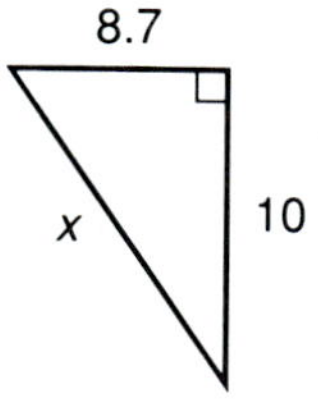

7.

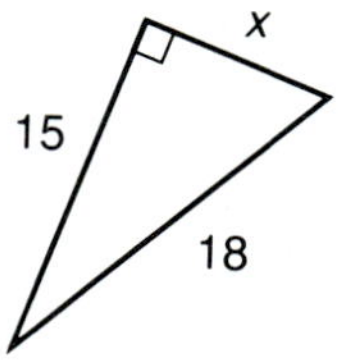

8.

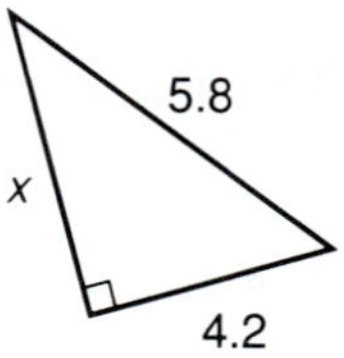

Set D pages 446–447

Find the missing measurements. Round your answers to the nearest tenth.

1. $m\angle BCA$ = ____ **2.** $m\angle ECF$ = ____

3. BC = ____ **4.** AC = ____

5. EC = ____ **6.** CF = ____

7. EF = ____ **8.** DF = ____
22.4

9. $m\angle D$ = ____ **10.** $m\angle ACE$ = ____

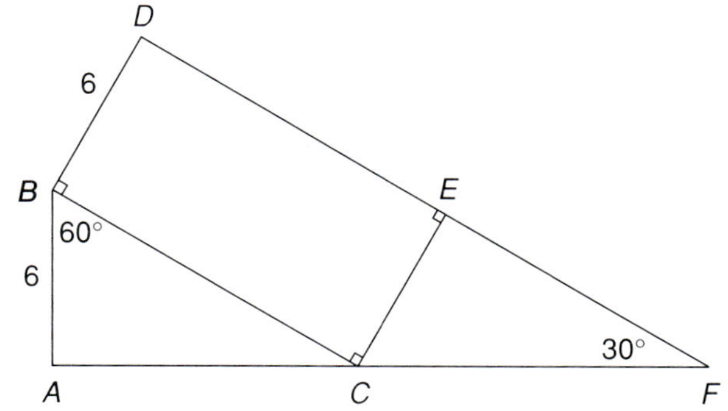

Set E pages 448–449

Use the figure to find the indicated measurements. Round your answers to the nearest tenth.

$AB = CD$
$AD = BC$

1. $m\angle ABD$ = ____ **2.** $m\angle BDC$ = ____

3. $m\angle CBD$ = ____ **4.** AB = ____

5. BD = ____ **6.** BC = ____

7. Area of $ABCD$ = ____ **8.** Area of ABD = ____

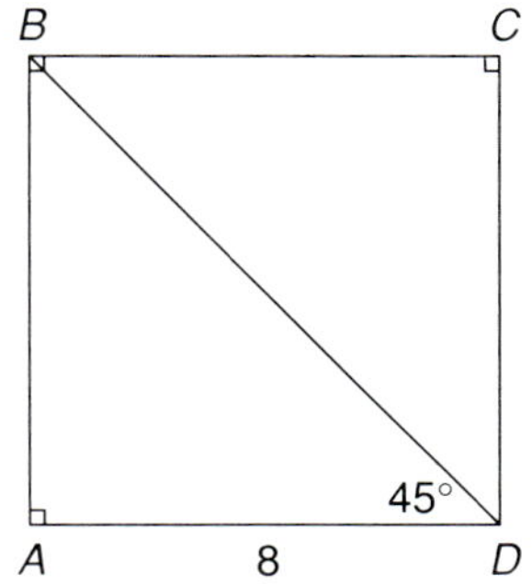

Set F pages 450–453

Write the tangent of the angle as a ratio. Then calculate the tangent. Finally, use the table on page 603 to determine the size of the angle.

1. tan A = $\frac{\_\_\_\_}{\_\_\_\_}$ **2.** tan A = ____ **3.** $m\angle A$ = ____

4. tan C = $\frac{\_\_\_\_}{\_\_\_\_}$ **5.** tan C = ____ **6.** $m\angle C$ = ____

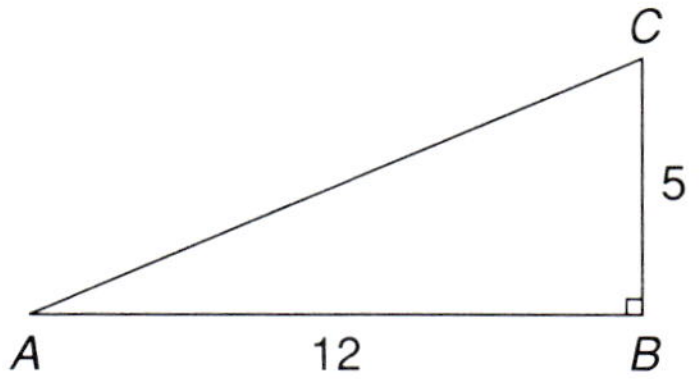

Set G pages 456–457

Find each answer by using a calculator or the table on page 603. Round your answers to the nearest thousandth.

1. BC = ____ **2.** sin B = ____

3. cos B = ____ **4.** tan B = ____

5. $m\angle B$ = ____ **6.** sin C = ____

7. cos C = ____ **8.** tan C = ____

9. $m\angle C$ = ____ **10.** Area ABC = ____

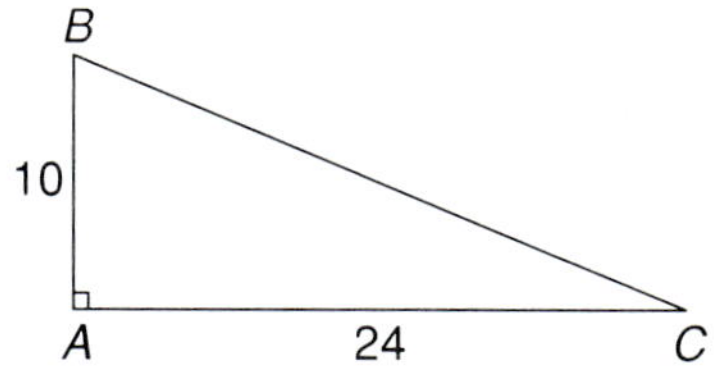

Enrichment

Waves

Ocean waves move in pulses with alternating high and low points. The distance between adjacent high points (or low points) is the **wavelength.** The distance that the wave travels in one second is its **velocity,** and the number of high or low points that pass a given point in one second is the **frequency** (sometimes called vibrations per second).

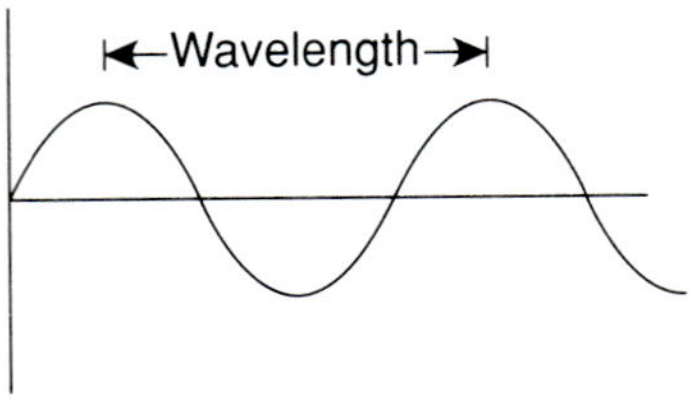

Wavelength, (w), velocity (v), and frequency (f) are related by the formula

$$w = \frac{v}{f} \quad \text{or} \quad v = fw \quad \text{or} \quad f = \frac{v}{w}$$

Jodie counted 6 ocean waves hitting the shore in one minute.

1. What was the frequency?

2. If the waves moved at a velocity of 5 feet per second, what was the wavelength?

3. Draw a graph, similar to the one pictured on the oscilloscope, of the waves Jodie observed. Use a scale on the horizontal axis that shows the measurement of the wavelength.

4. Why is it difficult to show frequency on the graph?

Sound waves are sometimes represented in the same way as ocean waves. At 0° C, sound travels at 331 m/sec in air.

A humpback whale underwater produced the sound graphed here.

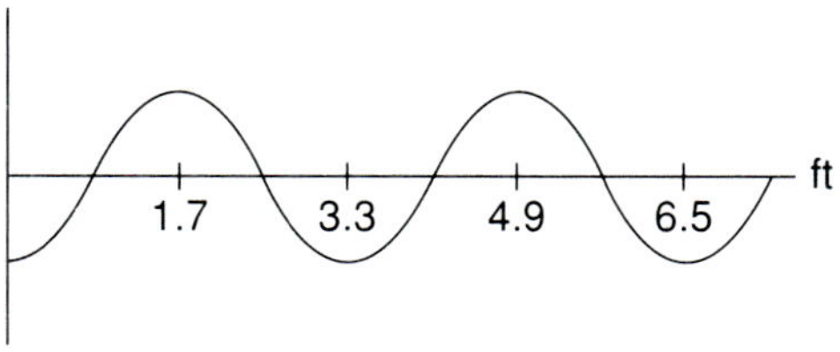

5. What was the wavelength of the sound?

6. In water, sound travels at a velocity of 4,760 ft/sec. What was the frequency of the sound produced by the whale?

Number-Sense Project

Estimate
Estimate the number of students in your school who like meat loaf, like mashed potatoes, try to eat Brussels sprouts, and drink milk often.

Gather Data
Survey ten people in the school not surveyed by other classmates. Ask if they like meat loaf, like mashed potatoes, will try Brussels sprouts, and drink milk often.

Analyze and Report
Give your findings as percents. Then pool data with other students' and compute the percents for each item. Compare the percents with the results on page 466.

ART CONNECTION

Organizing Data

Build Understanding

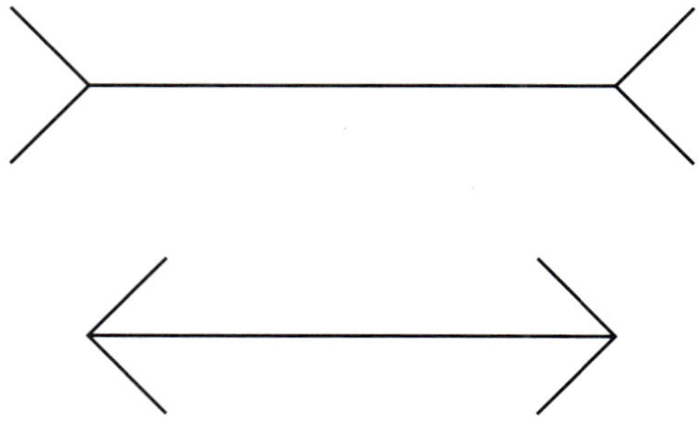

Look at these two lines. Without measuring, which one do you think is longer? Actually, the lines are the same length. The arrows on the ends of each line give the illusion that the top line is longer than the bottom line. Similarly, rearranging numbers in a set of data lets you see certain traits of the data more easily.

ACTIVITY

A. Your Number's Up!
Materials: Strips of paper

a. On a strip of paper, write a number from 1 through 8.

b. Place your strip with your classmates' strips in a pile at the front of the classroom.

c. As the number on each strip in the pile is read aloud, write the number on a sheet of paper.

d. You can make a ***frequency table*** to summarize the data. Copy the table and place a mark in the Tally column for each occurrence of a number in the data set. In the Frequency column, write the total number for each tally.

Number	Tally	Frequency
1		
2		
3		
4		
5		
6		
7		
8		

e. Another way to organize the data is to make a ***line plot.*** Divide a line into 8 equal segments and number each segment. In a single column above each number, mark an X for each occurrence of the number. When the line plot is complete, the height of each column of X's shows how frequently the number occurs.

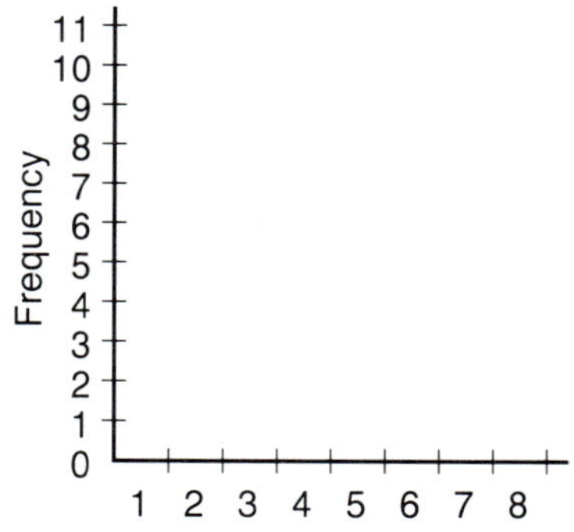

f. What do the frequency table and the line plot let you see more easily?

g. Try the activity again. Do you get the same results?

B. A set of data can be described by its ***measures of central tendency:*** the ***mean***, the ***median***, and the ***mode***.

When asked how much she spent for art supplies in each of the previous 6 months, Aisha wrote: \$23, \$17, \$25, \$48, \$32, \$29. Find the mean, the median, and the mode of the amounts she spent for art supplies.

The ***mean*** of a set of data is the average, or the sum of the items in the set divided by the number of items.

$$\frac{23 + 17 + 25 + 48 + 32 + 29}{6} = \frac{174}{6} = 29$$

The mean of the amounts Aisha spent is \$29.

When numbers are listed in increasing order, this arrangement is called an ***ordered list***. The ***median*** of an ordered list is the middle number. If there is an even number of items in the set, you divide the sum of the two middle numbers by 2 to find the median.

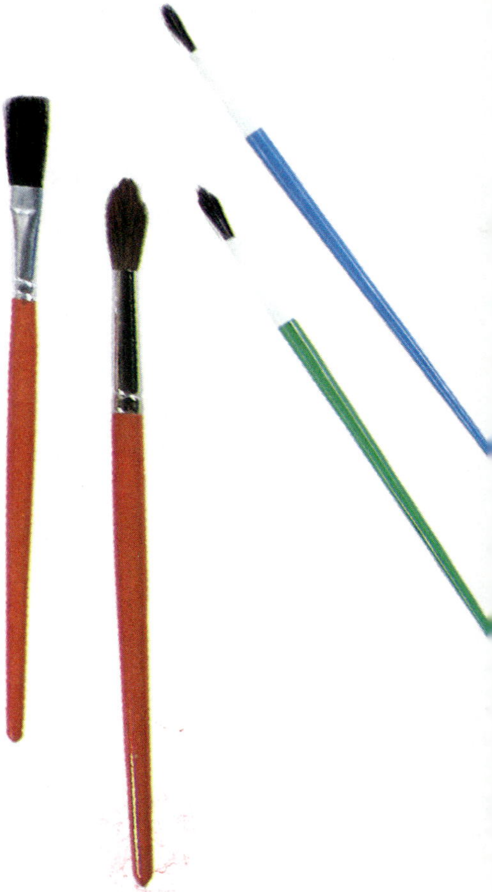

17 23 25 29 32 48

$$\frac{25 + 29}{2} = \frac{54}{2} = 27$$

The median of the amounts Aisha spent is \$27.

The ***mode*** of a set of data is the number that occurs most often. All the amounts Aisha spent for art supplies are different, so there is no mode.

In the set of data below, the mode is 67.

48 67 19 67 83 67 8

C. ***Quartiles*** divide a set of data into four equal groups. The ***upper quartile*** is the median of the numbers to the right of the median in an ordered list. The ***lower quartile*** is the median of the numbers to the left of the median in the ordered list.

Find the upper and lower quartiles for these numbers.

19, 8, 62, 5, 47, 18, 77, 7, 22, 13, 1, 54, 95, 6, 15

1, 5, 6, [7], 8, 13, 15, [18], 19, 22, 47, [54], 62, 77, 95 First you must put the numbers in increasing order.

Lower quartile (7) Median (18) Upper quartile (54)

Talk About Math Why might it be misleading to give someone the median when they ask you for the "average" number in a set of data?

Check Understanding

For another example, see Set A, pages 500–501.

Aisha made this line plot to find how frequently she uses the colors red, blue, green, and purple in her paintings. Which color does Aisha use

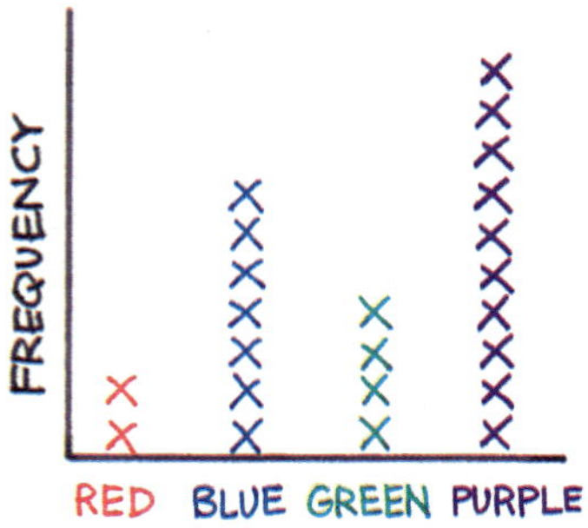

1. most often?

2. least often?

Complete.

3. The upper quartile of a data set is the ___?___ of the numbers to the right of the median.

4. Another name for the average of a set of data is the ___?___.

5. The ___?___ of a set of data occurs more often than any other number.

Practice

For More Practice, see Set A, pages 502–503.

Use the following list of the number of days it took Aisha to complete each of her last 20 paintings.

3, 3, 10, 7, 2, 5, 6, 5, 8, 3, 9, 7, 7, 5, 5, 3, 8, 8, 3, 4

6. Make a frequency table like the one in Example A.

7. Find the mean number of days it took Aisha to complete each painting.

8. Find the median of the data. **Remember** to list the data in order.

9. Find the mode of the data.

Find the mean, median, and mode for each set of data.

10. 18, 20, 16, 23, 18

11. 93, 92, 92, 83, 100, 98, 100

12. 9.5, 7.5, 3.5, 7, 6, 5.5

13. $2\frac{1}{2}$, $3\frac{3}{4}$, 6, $4\frac{1}{4}$, $2\frac{1}{2}$

Use the following data: **20, 16, 25, 25, 19, 19, 16, 23, 19, 18, 25, 17, 17, 25, 19, 20, 22, 19**

14. Make a frequency table.

15. Make a line plot.

16. Find the lower quartile.

17. Find the upper quartile.

Write a set of new data that consists of at least 10 numbers and that has

18. a mode of 12.

19. a mean of 50.

20. a median of −5.

21. a lower quartile of 3 and an upper quartile of 81.

22. a mean of 5, a median of 4, and a mode of 6.

Problem Solving

The ***range*** of a set of data is the difference between the highest and lowest values. The ***midrange*** of a set of data is the mean of the highest and lowest values.

The prices of 10 paintings for sale at an art gallery are listed below.

\$45, \$75, \$75, \$115, \$125, \$150, \$150, \$175, \$325, \$325

23. Find the range of the prices.

24. Find the midrange of the prices.

Critical Thinking Suppose the art gallery offered another \$325 painting for sale.

25. How would the addition of the \$325 painting change the mode?

26. How would the addition of \$325 change the other measures of central tendency?

27. Would the additional painting cause the range to change? the midrange? Explain.

Skills Review

pages 412–415

Solve each problem. Round answers to the nearest hundredth.

1. $\sqrt{19} \times \sqrt{2}$ **2.** $\sqrt{7} \times \sqrt{7}$ **3.** $2\sqrt{6} \times 2\sqrt{11}$ **4.** $\sqrt{16} \times \sqrt{15}$

5. $\frac{\sqrt{35}}{\sqrt{7}}$ **6.** $\sqrt{\frac{42}{7}}$ **7.** $\sqrt{\frac{4}{25}}$ **8.** $\frac{5\sqrt{72}}{\sqrt{8}}$

9. $9\sqrt{3} + 2\sqrt{3}$ **10.** $11\sqrt{31} - 7\sqrt{31}$ **11.** $\sqrt{14} - 12\sqrt{14}$ **12.** $4\sqrt{3} + 3\sqrt{4}$

13. $\sqrt{121} + \sqrt{169}$ **14.** $\frac{2\sqrt{51}}{\sqrt{17}}$ **15.** $\frac{12\sqrt{128} + 3\sqrt{128}}{3\sqrt{2}}$

Stem-and-Leaf Plots

Build Understanding

High and low temperatures for 15 U.S. cities for a January day are shown in the table.

City	High	Low
New York	42	32
Los Angeles	66	43
Chicago	26	8
Philadelphia	44	37
Detroit	31	19
San Diego	60	44
San Antonio	52	47
Phoenix	79	47
Baltimore	45	41
Indianapolis	38	29
San Jose, Cal.	64	45
Memphis	42	41
Jacksonville, Fla.	83	53
Milwaukee	21	7
Columbus, Ohio	38	30

A. A ***stem-and-leaf plot*** shows how often an outcome occurs and provides a "picture" of a set of data.

A stem-and-leaf plot of the high temperatures is shown below the table.

Stem	Leaves
2	1 6
3	1 8 8
4	2 2 4 5
5	2
6	0 4 6
7	9
8	3

The tens digit in a 2-digit number is the "stem." In a 1-digit number, the-stem is 0. The stems are written in a single column to the left of the vertical line, in increasing order from top to bottom.

The numbers in the bars to the right of the stems are the "leaves." The leaves are the ones digits, usually arranged in increasing order from left to right. On stem 3 the leaves 1, 8, and 8 represent temperatures of 31, 38, and 38. You can see that high temperatures in the forties were more common than any others on this particular day.

B. Make a ***back-to-back stem-and-leaf plot*** for the high and low temperatures for the 15 U.S. cities.

In a back-to-back stem-and-leaf plot, the stems are in the middle and the leaves are on the two sides.

Leaves for low temperatures	Stem	Leaves for high temperatures
8 7	0	
9	1	
9	2	1 6
7 2 0	3	1 8 8
7 7 5 4 3 1 1	4	2 2 4 5
3	5	2
	6	0 4 6
	7	9
	8	3

To plot 19, 7, and 8, the new stem-and-leaf plot includes stems of 1 and 0, because the stem for 19 is 1 and the stem for 7 and 8 is 0.

The leaves on the left side are arranged in increasing order from right to left.

■ **Write About Math** Make a frequency table for the high temperatures for the 15 U.S. cities. What information is easier to get from the frequency table than from the stem-and-leaf plot?

Check Understanding

For another example, see Set B, pages 500–501.

Use the stem-and-leaf plot in Example B to answer Exercises 1–4.

1. How many of the high temperatures were in the thirties?

2. How many cities had a low temperature of 47°?

3. What was the highest temperature? the lowest temperature?

4. Which temperatures are both high and low temperatures?

Practice

For More Practice, see Set B, pages 502–503.

For Exercises 5 and 6, use the data to make a stem-and-leaf plot. Hint: For Exercise 6, use 14 as the stem for 145.

5. 23, 56, 78, 54, 77, 31, 39, 67, 29, 62, 55, 50, 25, 44, 48, 34

6. 145, 156, 198, 143, 172, 165, 152, 145, 203

Mixed Practice Use these sets of data for Exercises 7–9.

1st set: 23, 65, 9, 0, 13, 45, 33, 42, 52, 14, 13, 65, 36, 43
2nd set: 43, 65, 87, 65, 26, 57, 52, 41, 61, 61, 47, 70, 60, 52

7. Make a back-to-back stem-and-leaf plot.

8. Find the median for each set of data.

9. Find the range and the midrange for each set of data.

Problem Solving

The following stem-and-leaf plots are for °F temperatures on a February day. One is for cities across the country; the other is for cities in the Midwest.

0	
1	
2	1 4 6 8
3	1 4 6 8 8 9
4	0 2
5	
6	
7	

First stem-and-leaf plot

0	4
1	0
2	1 6
3	3 4 8
4	0 5
5	4
6	3
7	6

Second stem-and-leaf plot

10. What is the lowest temperature in the first plot?

11. What is the lowest temperature in the second plot?

12. Which plot has the lowest temperature?

13. Which plot has the highest temperature?

14. Critical Thinking Which plot do you think is for the Midwest? Why?

Box Plots

Wildcats	Opponents
42	50
28	59
36	38
45	49
52	51
44	40
50	40
61	57
86	56
49	48
58	43
60	58
48	50

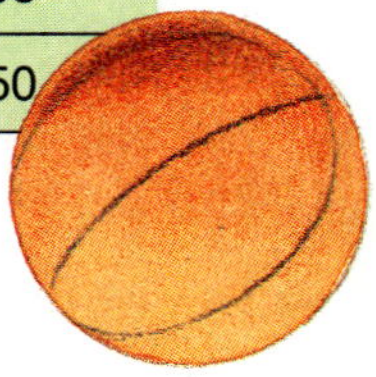

Build Understanding

This table gives a summary of the Wildcats girls' basketball team's scoring for the season.

A. Draw a box plot showing the Wildcats' scoring for the season. A ***box plot***, or ***box-and-whisker plot***, gives a visual summary of a set of data.

First, put the data in an ordered list. Determine the median, the lower quartile, and the upper quartile.

28 36 42 44 45 48 49 50 52 58 60 61 86

(42 + 44) ÷ 2 — Lower quartile = 43

49 — Median

(58 + 60) ÷ 2 — Upper quartile = 59

Draw a number line that includes the lowest and highest values. Above the line, draw a box whose ends line up with the lower and upper quartiles. Draw a segment through the box to show the median.

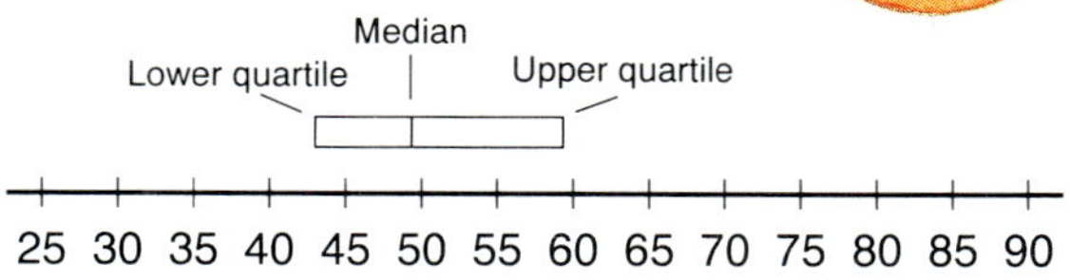

The value 86 is so far from the other values that it is called an ***outlier.*** Show it with an asterisk (*) above the number line. Then draw "whiskers" from the box to 28 and to 61 to show the extent of the remaining values.

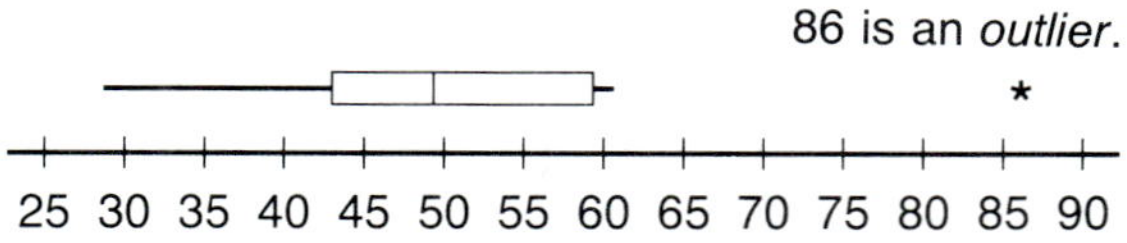

B. Box plots are especially useful for comparing data. This ***side-by-side box plot*** shows both the Wildcats' scoring and their opponents' scoring for the season. The Wildcats' scoring is shown by the plot on the bottom.

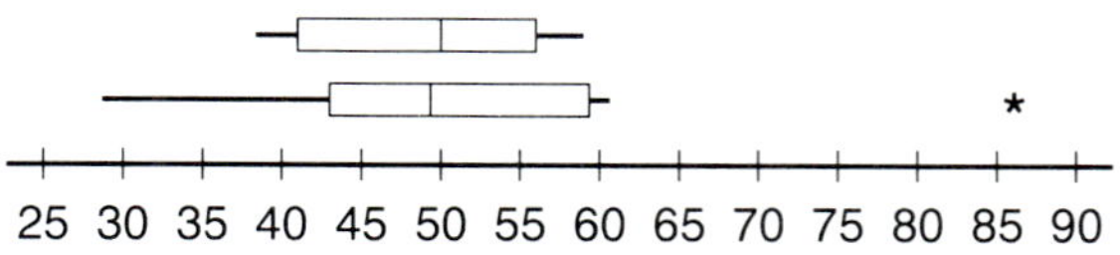

■ **Talk About Math** Which type of plot, a box plot or a stem-and-leaf plot, would be better to use with a large set of data? Why?

Check Understanding

For another example, see Set C, pages 500–501.

For Exercises 1–3, refer to this box plot showing Mariko's scoring for the Wildcats this season.

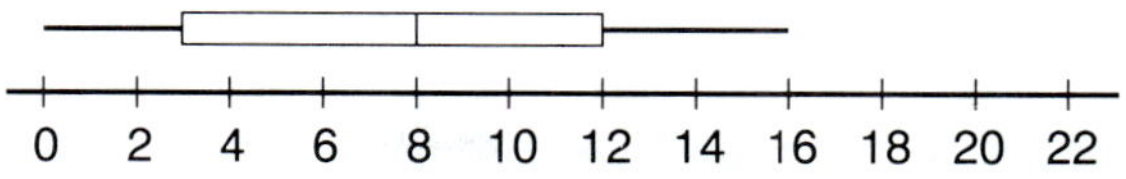

1. Find the most points Mariko scored in a game.

2. Find the fewest points Mariko scored all season in a game.

3. Find the median number of points Mariko scored.

Practice

For More Practice, see Set C, pages 502–503.

Make a box plot for each set of data. **Remember** to represent outliers with an asterisk (*).

4. 12, 13, 15, 17, 20, 21, 25, 29

5. 34, 56, 73, 65, 87, 88, 90, 91, 97

6. 19, 5, 9, 8, 9, 15, 12, 4, 7, 21

7. 89, 91, 97, 99, 80, 90, 93, 91, 85, 96, 99

8. 46, 61, 72, 77, 45, 56, 59, 97, 70, 69, 61, 60

9. 93, 40, 93, 50, 98, 69, 47, 90, 92, 47, 70, 50, 75, 86, 92, 50, 96

10. 126, 141, 132, 118, 127, 135, 178, 129, 137, 128, 123, 136, 140

Make a side-by-side box plot for these sets of data.

11. 1st set: 1, 3, 5, 7, 7, 9, 11
2nd set: 6, 8, 10, 12, 15, 19, 19

12. 1st set: 12.0, 12.4, 12.5, 12.5, 12.9, 13.0
2nd set: 8.9, 9.3, 10.1, 12.2, 13.6, 14.9

Problem Solving

Use the table on page 474 for Problem 13.

13. **Number Sense** The last 3 games in the table were post-season games. Describe how a box plot of only the 10 regular-season games would differ from the one showing all 13 games.

Here is the scoring per game by the Wildcats' center.

6, 12, 9, 8, 13, 10, 7, 17, 22, 12, 19, 20, 11

14. Make a box plot using the data.

15. In some box plots, the boxes cover the middle 80% of the data and the whiskers cover the top 10% and bottom 10%. Make this kind of plot for the data above.

16. Compare the two different plots. What happened to the whiskers? the box? the segment for the median?

Using Graphs to Display Data

Build Understanding

A. Eileen writes for a consumer magazine. She asked 1,254 adults what they would buy if they could buy anything. She used these data to make a ***bar graph*** and a ***circle graph***.

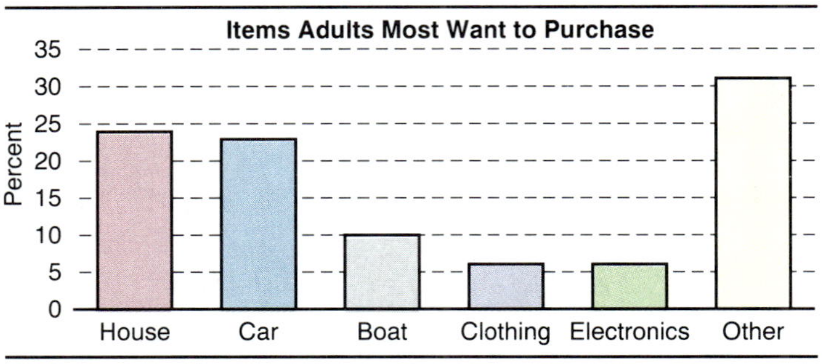

Items Adults Most Want to Purchase

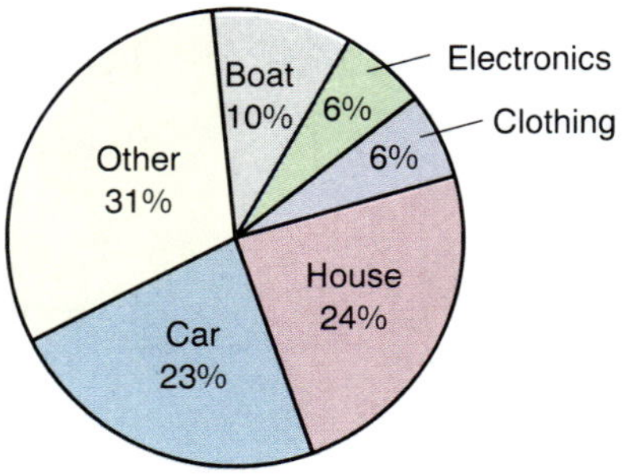

In general, bar graphs are used to show amounts in different categories, while circle graphs are used to show how one thing is divided.

B. Marta is making a graph to show how she budgets the \$160 she earns each month from her part-time job.

\$80 SAVINGS \$24 ENTERTAINMENT \$40 CLOTHES \$16 CONTRIBUTIONS

Since she is showing how she divides all her earnings, Marta chose to make a circle graph. To find the central angles, Marta finds what part of her money she budgets for each item. Then she multiplies by 360, the number of degrees in a circle.

Marta's Monthly Budget

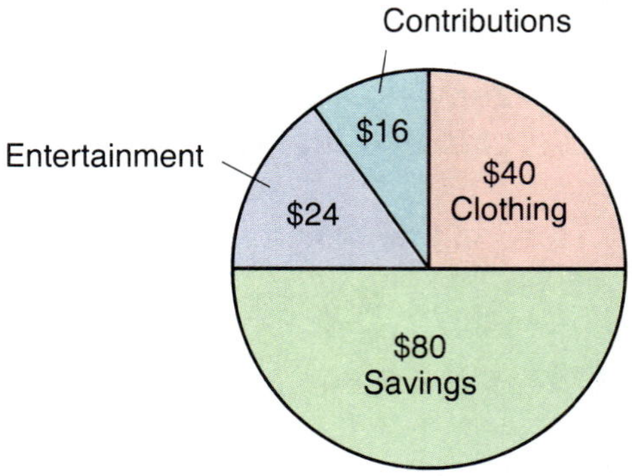

$\frac{80}{160} = 0.50 \qquad 0.50 \times 360° = 180°$

$\frac{24}{160} = 0.15 \qquad 0.15 \times 360° = 54°$

$\frac{40}{160} = 0.25 \qquad 0.25 \times 360° = 90°$

$\frac{16}{160} = 0.10 \qquad 0.10 \times 360° = 36°$

Marta then draws a circle and a radius. She uses the radius to draw the first angle. From the new radius, she draws the next angle.

■ **Talk About Math** In Example A, if Eileen wanted to display the number of people who wanted each item, would she use a bar graph or a circle graph? Why?

Check Understanding

For another example, see Set D, pages 500–501.

Tell whether you think Eileen should design a bar graph or a circle graph for each set of data. Then state the reason for your choice.

1. Favorite kind of music
2. Choice for U.S. President
3. Number of compact discs in five categories sold in the last year
4. High temperatures for the month of July in all the state capitals

Practice

For More Practice, see Set D, pages 502–503.

For each set of data, make a bar graph and a circle graph. Then state the advantage of each kind of graph.

5. Number of yards gained by the Panthers

Rushing	124 yards
Passing	56 yards
Penalties	20 yards

6. Monthly budget for the Ortega household

Housing	\$565
Food	\$175
Utilities	\$120
Insurance	\$ 80
Other costs	\$200

Is a bar graph or a circle graph more appropriate for each set of data? Draw the graph. In a circle graph, the sum of the percents must be 100%.

7. August movie rentals by category

Science Fiction	11%
Drama	28%
Action/Adventure	37%
Classics	5%
Comedy	19%

8. Results of customer satisfaction survey

Very satisfied	31
Satisfied	58
Dissatisfied	11
Very dissatisfied	2

9. Points scored per quarter

First quarter	17 points
Second quarter	19 points
Third quarter	20 points
Fourth quarter	21 points

10. Means of getting to school

Automobile	28%
Public transportation	15%
Walking	30%
School bus	27%

Problem Solving

Solve each problem.

11. **Critical Thinking** Suppose each amount in Marta's budget in Example B doubled. How would the circle graph change?
12. Eileen surveyed 100 more people. They all said they would buy cars. Using this new information, redraw the bar graph in Example A.

Bar Graphs and Histograms

Build Understanding

Most people in the urban areas of China travel by bicycle.

Over the past 40 years, many people around the world have moved from rural areas to cities. In 1950, only 34% of Brazil's population lived in cities. In 1988 that percent had grown to 71%. In China and India, there are still more people in rural areas than in cities, but even in these countries, the urban populations are growing rapidly.

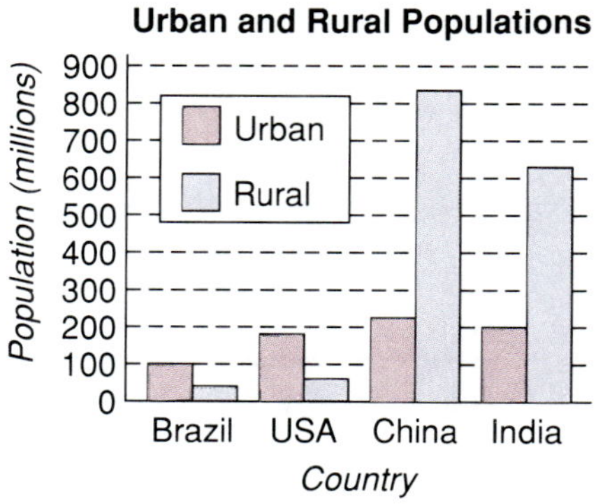

A. A bar graph can be used to compare data. This ***double bar graph*** compares the 1988 urban and rural populations of four countries.

B. A bar graph can also represent a set of data that contains negative values. Below is a bar graph for low temperatures during the first three weeks of December.

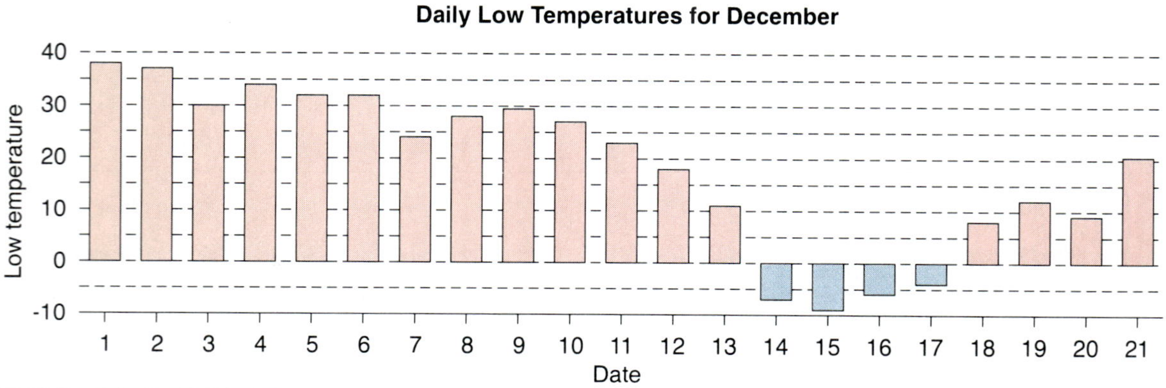

C. A ***histogram*** is a bar graph that shows frequencies within intervals. The width of each bar shows the width of the interval, and each bar shows intervals of the same width. In this histogram, the width of each interval is 10.

The height of the bars in a histogram shows how often outcomes within each interval occur. In the histogram at the right, the first bar shows that in 1989, 39 states each had 1 to 10 representatives in the House of Representatives.

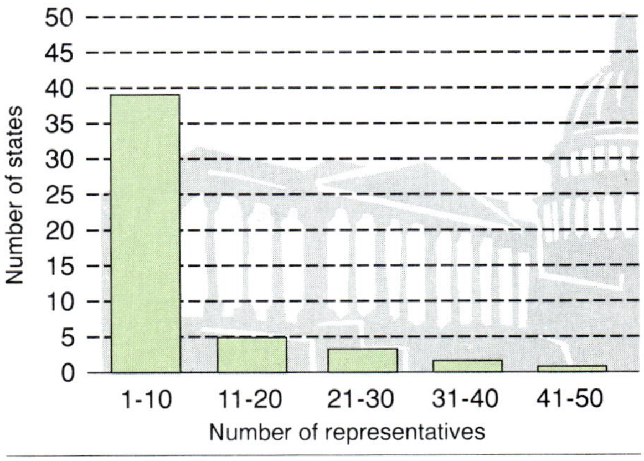

Talk About Math Look at the histogram above. Did any states have 0 representatives? Explain.

Check Understanding

Use the graphs on page 478 for Exercises 1–4.

1. In which country was the total 1988 population about 800 million?

2. In which country was the rural population the largest in 1988?

3. Use the graph in Example B to tell how many days had low temperatures below 0°F.

4. Describe a single bar graph you could make by combining certain data given in the double bar graph in Example A.

Practice

These are the average maximum and minimum temperatures in degrees Fahrenheit for the months of January, April, July, and October in Warsaw, Poland.
Maximum temperatures: 30°, 54°, 75°, 54°
Minimum temperatures: 21°, 38°, 56°, 41°

5. On a double bar graph, what two kinds of information would be graphed for each month?

6. Make a double bar graph of the data above.

7. In which month is the difference between the maximum and minimum temperatures the greatest? the least?

8. **Critical Thinking** With the information given, can you estimate Poland's average maximum and minimum temperatures in a year? Explain.

This is "old city" town square in Warsaw, Poland.

This graph compares the population growth rates of Europe to those of the world from 1950 to 1990. Supply the information asked for.

9. Population growth rate in Europe in 1970

10. Population growth rate in the world in 1990

11. In what year was the world's population growth rate 7 times greater than that of Europe's?

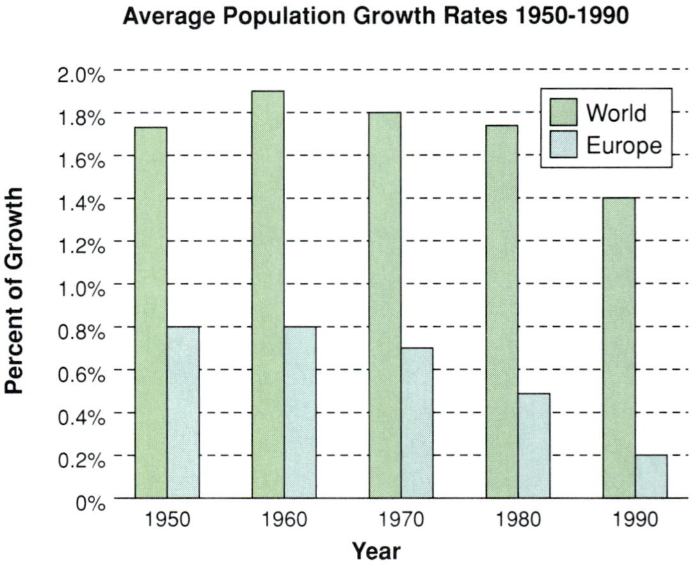

Look at the data in this histogram.

12. What is the most common range of precipitation?

13. How many cities average 2 inches or less precipitation?

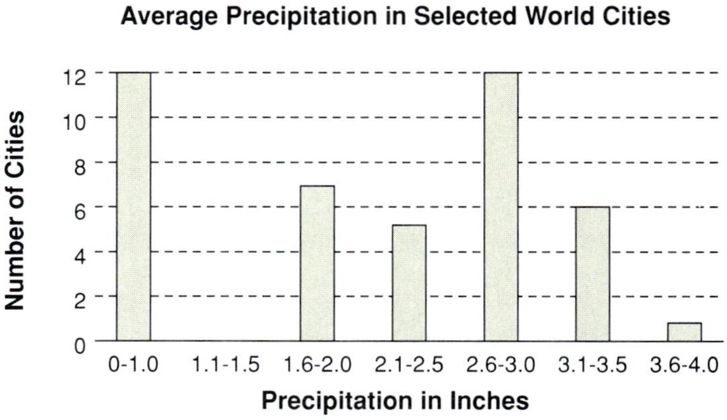

14. Use the information in the table below to make a bar graph.

Population Density (per square mile)	
Brazil	47
USA	69
China	306
India	686
Japan	850

15. **Critical Thinking** From the graph in Example A on page 478 you know that Brazil and the United States have high urban populations. Does a high urban population imply a high population density? Explain.

Japan has one of the highest population densities in the world. This street scene in Tokyo shows the Ginza, a popular shopping district. In Japan over 90% of the population lives in 20% of the land area.

Problem Solving

Make a graph.

16. **Use Data** Use the data on page 474 to make a histogram about the number of points the Wildcats scored. (Hint: Each bar should show a range of 5 points.)

17. The data at the right shows the populations, in millions, of Latin America and North America from 1950 to 1990. Graph the data by using a double bar graph.

Year	Latin America	North America
1950	166	166
1960	218	199
1970	286	226
1980	364	252
1990	450	277

Midchapter Checkup

Find the mean, median, and mode of each set of data.

1. 14, 8, 7, 14, 20, 9, 2

2. 48, 36, 45, 44, 38, 39, 49, 37, 42, 41

Use the frequency table for Exercises 3 and 4.

3. Make a line plot of the data.

4. What information is easier to see on the frequency table? on the line plot?

Height (inches)	Tally	Frequency
71–72	||	2
69–70	~~||||~~	5
67–68	~~||||~~ |	6
65–66	||||	4
63–64	~~||||~~	5
61–62	|||	3
59–60	|	1
57–58	||	2

Use this set of data for Exercises 5 and 6.

17, 21, 18, 43, 36, 36, 42, 27, 19, 26, 41, 33, 50

5. Draw a stem-and-leaf plot.

6. Make a histogram with each bar showing a range of 5.

Use this side-by-side box plot for Exercises 7–10. For each set of data, find the

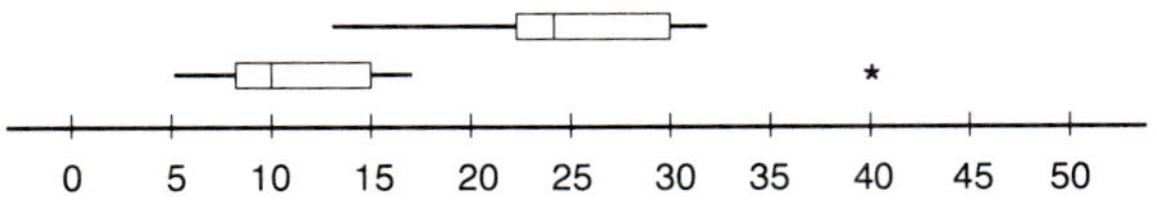

7. median. **8.** outlier. **9.** range. **10.** upper quartile.

Tell whether you would use a circle graph or a bar graph for each set of data.

11. Number of types of fish in a lake **12.** Hottest days in history

Critical Thinking Activity

Tom and Stephanie took a survey of the students at their school. On Tuesday, Tom surveyed half of the students. On Wednesday, Tom surveyed one-third of the remaining students. On Thursday, Tom and Stephanie each surveyed one-half of the remaining students. Stephanie did not survey anyone until Thursday.

What fraction of the students did Tom survey?

MATH laugh

What's the difference between an old nickel and a new penny?

ANSWER: Four cents!

Real-Life Decision Making

1. Suppose you would like to get a raise in your allowance.

a. Take a survey of at least 20 other students to find how much allowance they get per week. Record your results.

b. Find the mode, median, and mean of the data. Would you use the mean, median, or mode to try to convince your parents to increase your allowance? Explain your answer.

c. Present your survey results to your family by making a box plot, a stem-and-leaf plot, and a histogram.

d. Decide which graph would be the best way to display the data to your family.

Explore with a Computer

Use the *Graphing and Probability Workshop Project* for this activity.

Lee studied the price of one share of stock for two companies for a year. Help him decide which stock to buy.

1. At the computer, view the data in the table as a bar graph. View the data as a broken-line graph. View the data as a circle graph. Which type of graph is the best one to use with this information?

2. Study the graph that best shows the data. During the first 6 months, which company would have been a better investment? Which company's stock do you think he should buy?

	Cost per Share	
Month	**Company A**	**Company Z**
January	30	10
February	28	11
March	29	10
April	38	12
May	36	11
June	51	9
July	27	10
August	30	12
September	32	15
October	43	14
November	26	15
December	27	16

Number-Sense Project

Look back at pages 466–467.

Assume a population of 250 million and find the number of Americans who

1. like meat loaf.

2. like mashed potatoes.

3. try Brussels sprouts.

4. drink milk often.

Broken-Line Graphs

Build Understanding

A. Mrs. Gonzales, a physical education teacher, determined the number of push-ups boys and girls of various ages should be able to do in two minutes. She made ***broken-line graphs*** to show the trends of the data.

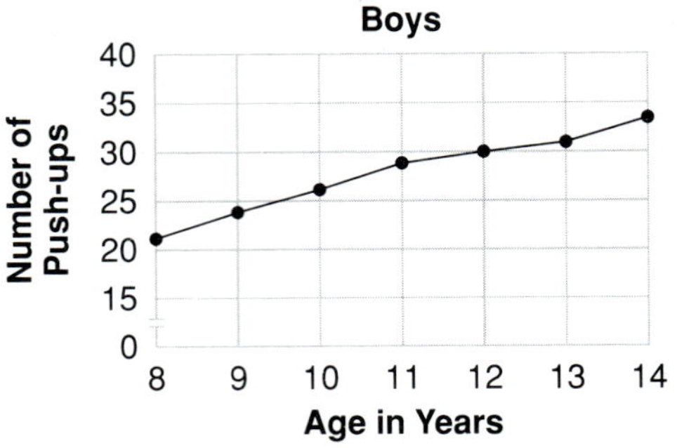

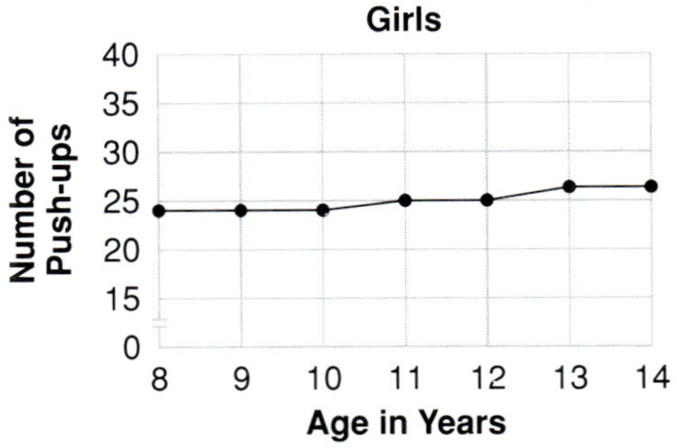

The horizontal scale shows the students' ages. Since her data began with 8-year-olds, the horizontal scale starts at 8. The number of push-ups is shown on the vertical scale with an interval of 5 so that the graph would be a reasonable size. Then Mrs. Gonzales plotted the points and drew segments to connect them.

B. To compare the boys' and girls' performances, Mrs. Gonzales plotted the two sets of data on the same axes. She made a ***double broken-line graph***.

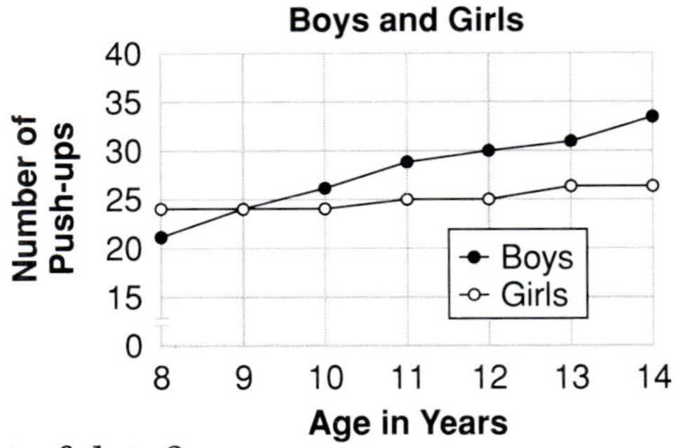

C. What type of graph would you make for each set of data?

School Enrollment	
School	Students
Finland	450
Clear View	398
Norwich	271
Brookpark	325

The data are in separate categories, in no particular order.

Make a bar graph.

Yearly Enrollment	
Year	Students
1989	1,444
1990	1,592
1991	1,832
1992	2,003

The data show changes over time.

Make a broken-line graph.

Current Enrollment in Finland School	
Grade	Students
6	180
7	150
8	120

The data show the whole divided into parts.

Make a circle graph.

Talk About Math In the graph in Example B, what does it mean if the slant is more vertical than horizontal? more horizontal than vertical?

Check Understanding

For another example, see Set E, pages 500–501.

Estimation Use the graphs in Examples A and B for Exercises 1–2.

1. At which age should girls be able to do more push-ups than boys?

2. Estimate the difference in the number of push-ups a 12-year-old boy and an 8-year-old boy can do.

Practice

For More Practice, see Set E, pages 502–503.

Refer to the graph for Exercises 3–6.

3. What do the letters mean on the horizontal axis?

4. Find the ranges of the precipitation for 1991 and 1993.

5. **Estimation** Estimate the total rainfall by April 30, 1991.

6. How much more rain fell in July of 1993 than in July of 1991?

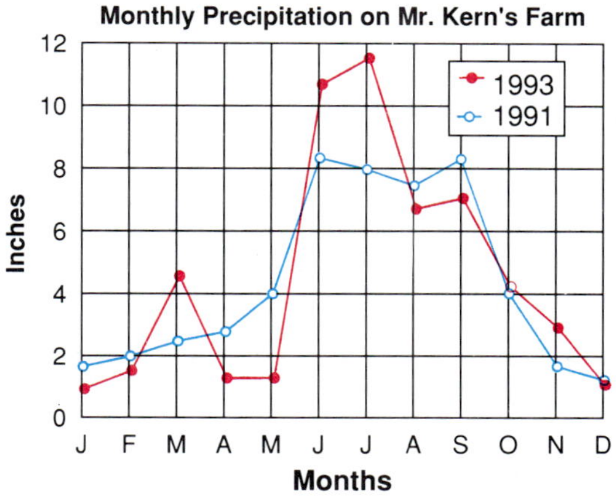

Refer to the graph for Exercises 7–10.

7. On which day were receipts the largest for Week 1? for Week 2?

8. On what day were the receipts the same?

9. Find the range of daily receipts for Week 1 and for Week 2.

10. Find the total receipts for Week 1 and for Week 2.

Problem Solving

Use the data at the right.

11. Using the same axes, make a double broken-line graph of the data in the table.

12. As age increases from 12 to 17, does time increase or decrease? How can you tell from the table? from the graph?

1-Mile Endurance Run

Age	Girls' Time	Boys' Time
12	10:18	8:52
13	10:04	8:12
14	10:01	7:54
15	10:00	7:50
16	9:54	7:42
17	9:51	7:24

Use Data from a Graph

PROBLEM SOLVING GUIDE

Understand
QUESTION
FACTS
KEY IDEA

Plan and Solve
STRATEGY
ANSWER

Look Back
SENSIBLE ANSWER
ALTERNATE APPROACH

Build Understanding

The graph shows Jason's average time for the 100-meter dash during a school year. The coach wants to know by what percent Jason's time decreased from September to June.

Jason's Average Time for 100-Meter Dash

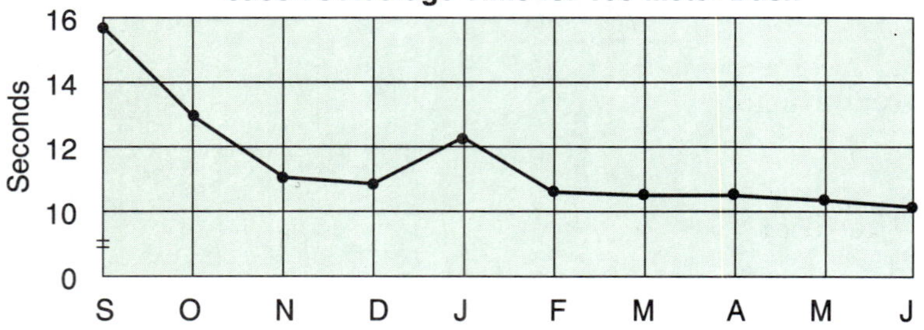

Understand QUESTION By what percent did Jason's time decrease from September to June?

FACTS Jason's time was about 15.8 seconds in September and about 10.2 seconds in June.

KEY IDEA The data can be used to create ratios comparing the time in September to the time in June. The ratios can be converted to percents.

Plan and Solve STRATEGY To find the percent decrease, find the difference between the two times and divide by the original time. Use this ratio and convert it to a percent. His time decreased by 5.6 seconds. ($15.8 - 10.2 = 5.6$)

$$\frac{5.6 \ (\text{Decrease})}{15.8 \ (\text{Original time})} = 0.35443 \approx 0.35$$

Round to the nearest hundredth.

$$0.35 = 35\%$$

Convert the decimal to a percent.

ANSWER Jason's time decreased by about 35%.

Look Back SENSIBLE ANSWER Jason's time in September was about 16 seconds, and 35% of 16 is a little more than 5.

Talk About Math If Jason's time decreased, how did his speed change?

Check Understanding

Use the graph on page 486 to solve each problem.

1. What was Jason's increase in time between December and January?

2. Find the percent increase in his time between December and January.

3. Find Jason's speed in meters per second during the month of June.

4. Write and solve an equation to find Jason's average time.

Practice

The graph shows Don's times at bat and hits for four years. Use the graph to answer each question.

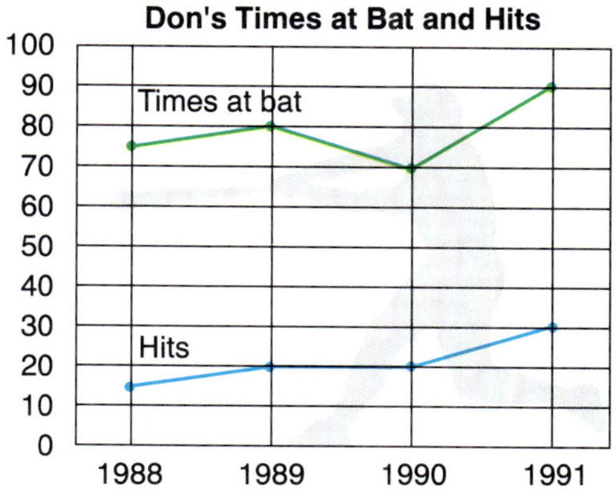

Write the ratio of hits to at-bats for each year as a decimal in hundredths.

5. 1988 **6.** 1989 **7.** 1990 **8.** 1991

9. **Estimation** What decimal will express Don's ratio for 1992?

Choose a ________ Strategy

Cancelled Stamps In 1968 it cost six cents to mail a letter. What was the average percent increase from 1968 to 1988?

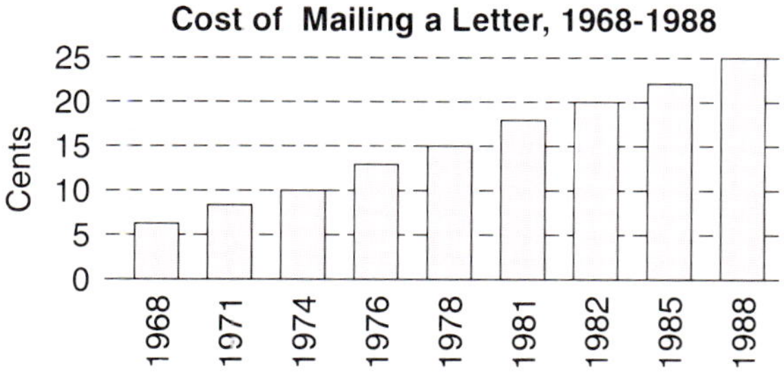

10. What was the percent of each increase?

11. What is the average of all the percents you found in Problem 10?

PROBLEM SOLVING
STRATEGIES

Choose an Operation
Solve a Simpler Problem
Use a Formula
Write an Equation
Make a Graph
Draw a Diagram
Make a Table
Try and Check

Scattergrams

Build Understanding

A. This ***scattergram*** shows the relationship between the population of a state and the number of U.S. congressional representatives it has.

The line on the scattergram is called the ***line of best fit***. A line of best fit is drawn as close to the points on the graph as possible. The points are very close to the line, so there is a high correlation between the population and the number of representatives. The upward slant of the line of best fit indicates a ***positive correlation*** between the variables.

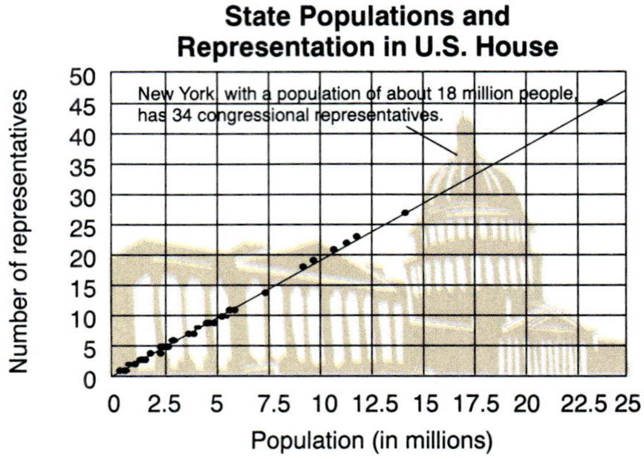

B. The scattergram at the right shows the relationship between the land area of a state and the population of the state.

The points are ***dispersed***, or scattered, so there is no line which fits the data very well. Therefore, there is ***little*** or ***no correlation*** between land area and population.

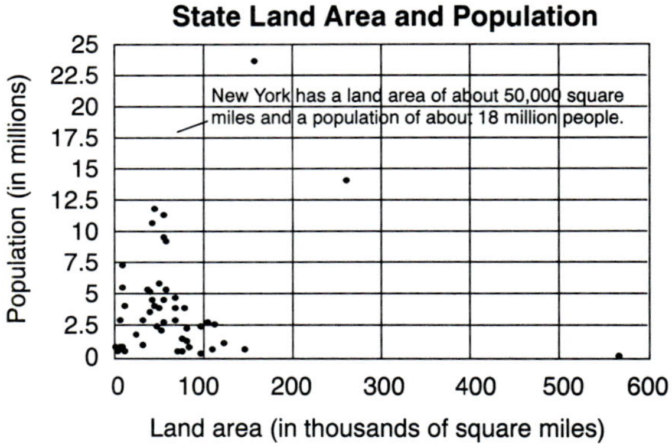

C. What relationship does the third graph show? There is a high correlation between the order in which a state entered the Union and the number of years of statehood. The downward slant of the line indicates a ***negative correlation*** between the variables.

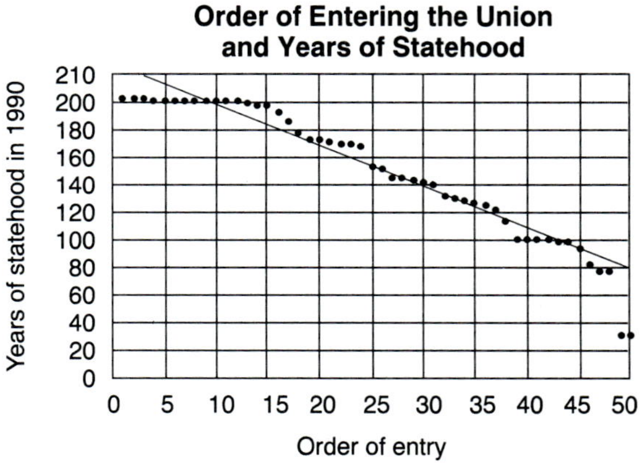

■ **Talk About Math** If the horizontal axis in Example A showed number of representatives and the vertical axis showed population, would there still be a positive correlation? Explain.

Check Understanding

For another example, see Set F, pages 500–501.

Tell whether each data set has a positive, negative, or no correlation. Explain.

1. The number of cars in Rhode Island and the number of crickets in Italy
2. The population of a state and its area
3. The area of a state and the density of its population
4. The population of a state and the number of post offices it has

Practice

For More Practice, see Set F, pages 502–503.

Use the scattergrams on page 488 to answer Exercises 5–11.

5. California has the greatest population. Where is the point for California?
6. How many congressional representatives does California have?
7. Is there a state without representatives? Explain.
8. Alaska has the greatest land area. Does it have the largest population? Explain.
9. If a dot is above the line of best fit in Example C, is the state older or younger than a state whose dot is below the line?
10. Locate the year of entry of the oldest state. How old will it be in the year 2000?
11. How many states will be over 50 years old in the year 2000?

Problem Solving

Use the chart at the right to solve each problem.

State	Order in which entered Union	West longitude
Delaware	1	75
S. Carolina	8	81
Alabama	22	87
Iowa	29	93
Oregon	33	121
Utah	45	112

12. Make a scattergram of the data. Draw a line of best fit.
13. What does the slant of the line indicate?
14. What correlation between the variables is shown?
15. If Hawaii were shown on the scattergram, where do you think the point would be? Explain.

Sample Statistics

Build Understanding

A. Elena Zachary owns the EZ Wheeling Bicycle Company. Before deciding to produce a new model called the EZ-6000 in large quantities, Elena needs to know what the ***population***, or every potential customer, thinks of it. Since she can't survey the entire population, she will survey a ***sample***, or some of the population.

To select 100 people for her survey, Elena can use a ***random sample:*** every potential customer has an equal chance of being selected. But, Elena knows that about 65% of her customers are from 9 to 18 years old. About 25% of her customers are between 18 and 32 years old. The rest of her customers are 32 years of age or older. So, Elena will select 65 people from 9 to 18 years old, 25 people between the ages of 18 and 32, and 10 people aged 32 or older. This sample is a ***stratified sample.*** She wants everyone in each age group to have an equal chance of being selected, so the sample will be a ***stratified random sample.***

B. Elena surveyed 30 shops that sell her bicycles to see if they were happy with the service they were receiving. The table below shows the results.

	Number	Percent
Satisfied	17	57%
Dissatisfied	11	37%
No response	2	7%
Total	30	101%

How could the total percent be 101?

Ratio		Percent		Rounded Percent
$\frac{17}{30}$	=	$56\frac{2}{3}\%$	=	57%
$\frac{11}{30}$	=	$36\frac{2}{3}\%$	=	37%
$\frac{2}{30}$	=	$6\frac{2}{3}\%$	=	7%
		100%		101%

Although $56\frac{2}{3} + 36\frac{2}{3} + 6\frac{2}{3} = 100$, the sum of the rounded percents is 101. The results have a ***round-off error*** of 1%.

Talk About Math Elena Zachary could have used her 14-year-old daughter or 100 of her daughter's classmates for the survey sample. Why didn't she?

Check Understanding

For another example, see Set G, pages 500–501.

Use the information in Examples A and B to complete each sentence.

1. The whole group you want information about is called the ___?___.

2. The part of the group you use to draw conclusions about the whole group is the ___?___.

3. When every person in the group has the same chance to be chosen, we are using a ___?___.

4. A random sample that has been taken from several specific groups of the population is called a ___?___.

Practice

For More Practice, see Set G, pages 502–503.

Describe the sample you would use to predict the sale of each of the following.

5. Basketballs **6.** Diapers **7.** Orange juice **8.** Sleds

9. Shampoo **10.** Compact discs **11.** Snow tires **12.** Dog food

Number Sense Explain whether you would survey a sample closest to 0%, 5%, or 100% of the population.

13. To test if regulators used for scuba diving work properly

14. To determine the favorite car of U.S. citizens

15. To see what TV programs are being watched in Helena, Montana, at 8 P.M. on Mondays

16. To see if people who fly an airline like the service

17. To test the appeal of a new perfume to be marketed nationwide

18. To determine the number of students who plan to go on a school trip

Of 35 customers, twenty preferred the EZ-6000, nine preferred the EZ-2000, and six preferred the EZ-5000.

19. Write ratios showing the customers' preferences.

20. Total the percents. What is the round-off error?

In a survey of 30 customers, 16 were satisfied with the product, 13 were dissatisfied, and 1 gave no response.

21. Find the percent for each.

22. Determine the round-off error.

In a survey of 500 people, 250 exercised less than 2 hours per week, 140 exercised 2 to 4 hours per week, and 110 exercised more than 4 hours per week.

23. Find the percent for each category.

24. Determine the round-off error.

Problem Solving

Elena gathered data about bicycle brakes. In Chicago, she surveyed 1,000 customers. In Phoenix and Seattle, Elena surveyed 100 customers each.

25. Why might Elena survey customers in 3 different areas?

26. How might weather and road conditions affect the results?

27. **Critical Thinking** Why is it necessary to survey 100% of the population in some cases, but only 5% or less in other cases?

Representing a Point of View

Build Understanding

A. The mayor of Sleepyville went on a four-week, all-expenses-paid tour of Europe in 1992 to promote tourism in Sleepyville.

The mayor used this graph to show the great improvement in tourism in 1993.

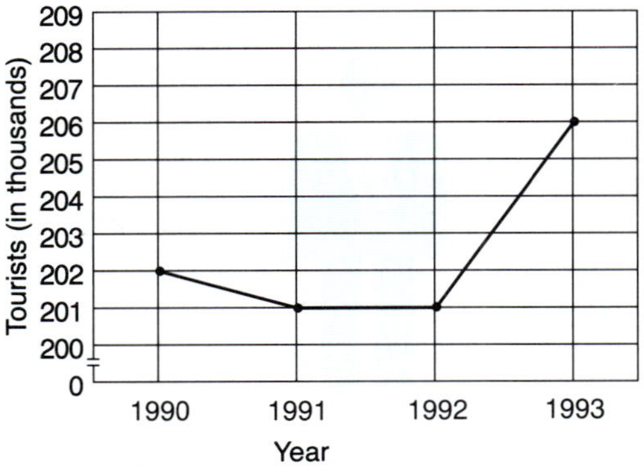

An opponent used this graph to show poor improvement in tourism in 1993.

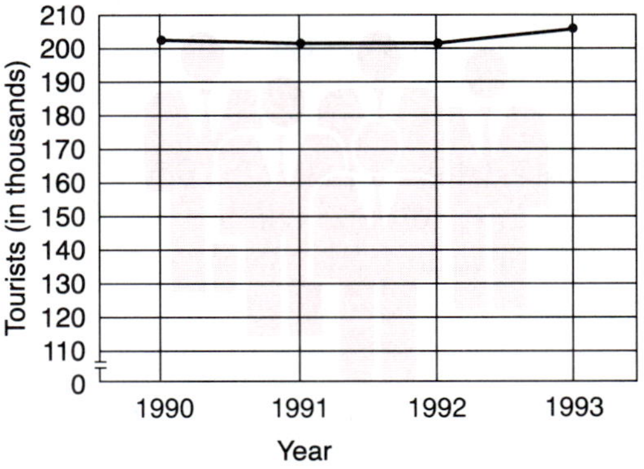

B. An ad for pain relievers used this graph to show that twice as many people prefer Painless over Paingo.

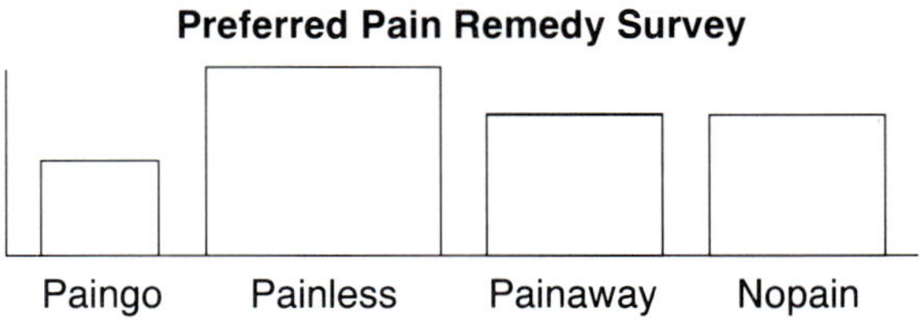

The bar for Painless is twice as tall and twice as wide as the bar for Paingo. The ratio of the areas of the bars is 4 to 1, not 2 to 1. This misleading impression could be corrected by making the bars of equal width.

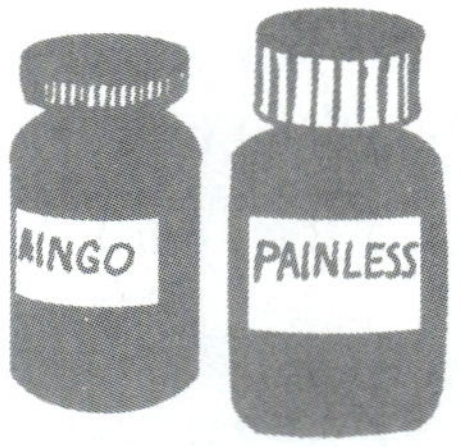

Talk About Math Explain which graph, the mayor's or the opponent's, gives the more accurate picture of the data.

Check Understanding

1. According to the mayor's graph, did tourism increase slowly or rapidly in Sleepyville from 1992 to 1993?

2. By about what percent did tourism actually increase in Sleepyville from 1992 to 1993?

3. In example B, the actual numbers of the survey were 10, 20, 15, and 15 people. Show these data in a bar graph.

Practice

Tell how each graph could be changed to represent a different point of view.

4.

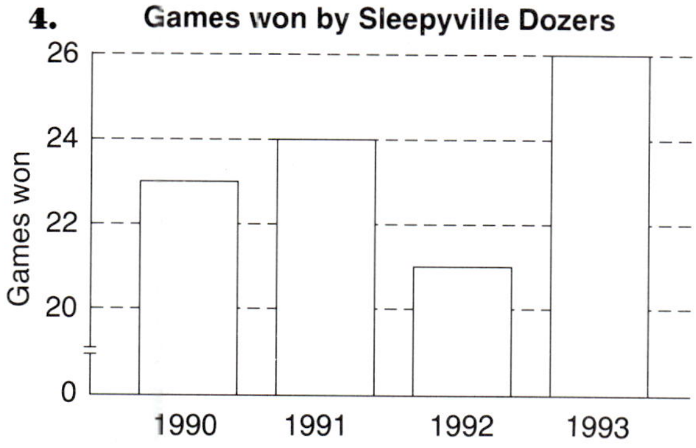

5.

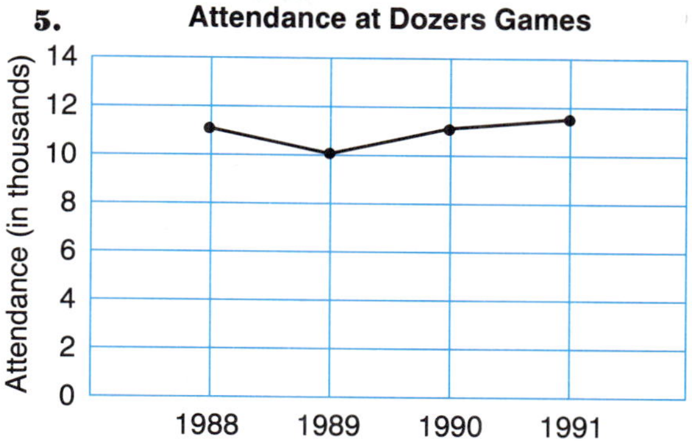

6.

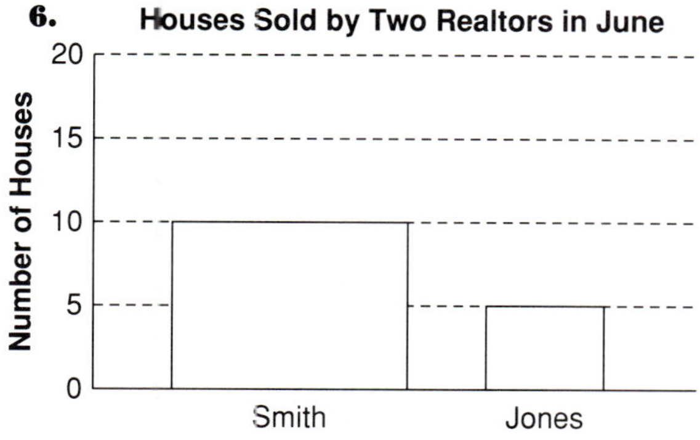

7.

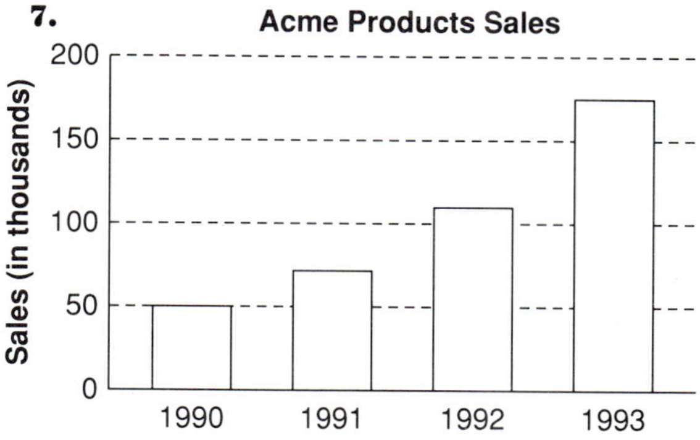

Problem Solving

Use the table to solve each problem.

Attendance at Sleepyville Water Park, 1990–1993

1990	135,000
1991	131,000
1992	118,000
1993	94,000

8. Make a broken-line graph showing that attendance at the Water Park stayed about the same between 1990 and 1993.

9. Make a broken-line graph showing that attendance at the Water Park dropped sharply between 1990 and 1993.

In 1992, 35,000 people attended Orchard View Water Park. In 1993, 47,000 people attended.

10. Make a bar graph that compares attendance at the two parks in 1992 and 1993.

11. Make a double broken-line graph that compares attendance at the two parks in 1992 and 1993.

12. Would Sleepyville officials prefer to use the bar graph or the broken-line graph?

Collecting Data

PROBLEM SOLVING GUIDE

Understand
QUESTION
FACTS
KEY IDEA

Plan and Solve
STRATEGY
ANSWER

Look Back
SENSIBLE ANSWER
ALTERNATE APPROACH

Build Understanding

ACTIVITY

A. Getting Around
Materials: Ruler
Groups: 3–6 students

a. Find out how each member of your group usually gets to school. Some possible means include walking, riding a bike, and riding in a car or bus.

b. Summarize your results in a frequency table.

c. Combine your results with the other groups'.

d. Use the combined data to make a bar graph.

B. The graph at the right shows the results of a survey of how 52 urban eighth graders get to school. Does the stratified sample accurately represent all U.S. students?

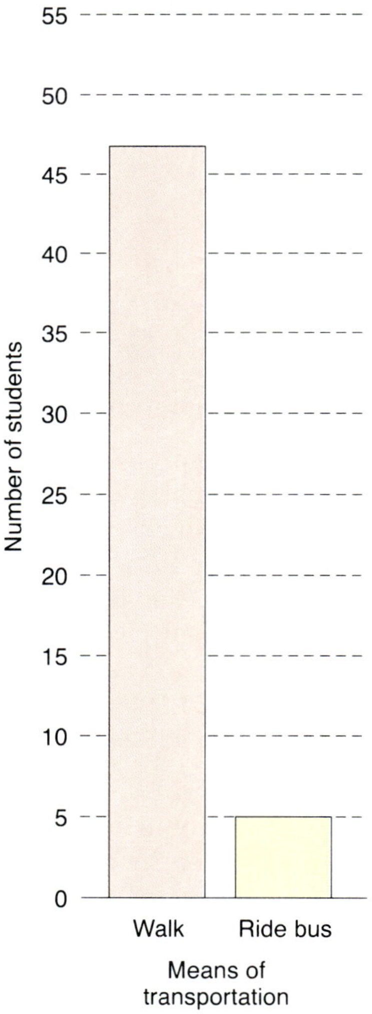

Understand QUESTION Does the group of students surveyed accurately represent all eighth graders in the United States?

FACTS All 52 surveyed were urban. All eighth graders use some means of transportation to get to school.

KEY IDEA Eighth graders in one area only were sampled.

Plan and Solve STRATEGY Compare your graph to the graph at the right. Consider whether other areas could be surveyed.

ANSWER Not all eighth graders are accurately represented. In some situations, walking is not practical—living in a rural area or attending a magnet school, for instance.

Look Back SENSIBLE ANSWER The students surveyed live in the city, where many of them can walk to school.

Talk About Math Describe the sample you would use if you wanted to determine the means of transportation used by all students in the United States.

Check Understanding

Use the graph in Example B for Exercises 1–4.

1. **Estimation** About how many students walk to school?

2. **Estimation** About how many students ride a bus?

3. How might the graph have been different if the sample had been taken at a rural school?

4. How might the graph have been different if half the students surveyed attended a rural school and half attended an urban school?

Practice

You want to determine the favorite sports of the students in your class.

5. Write the steps you would use to conduct the survey.

6. What type of graph would best show the results of your data?

7. List any weaknesses you see in the steps or sample you have described.

8. How would your sample change if you wanted to know the favorite sports of eighth-grade students in your city? in the United States?

Reading ——— Math

Vocabulary Match each term and its definition.

box plot
bar graph
stem-and-leaf plot
circle graph
outlier

1. A piece of data that is extreme or very different from the other data is a(n) ___?___.

2. A ___?___ uses digits of the data to provide a "picture" of how often something occurs.

3. A ___?___ shows the median, upper quartile, lower quartile, any outliers, and highs and lows of the data.

4. A ___?___ is used to show how something is divided and often uses percents.

ALGEBRA

Using Statistics to Make Estimates

Build Understanding

A team of naturalists wanted to estimate the number of deer in Wilderness Park. They captured, tagged, and released 200 deer. Later, they recaptured 100 deer to see how many of them had been tagged. They took 4 more samples, releasing the deer each time after counting the number that had been tagged.

						Total
Deer in the sample	100	50	50	50	100	350
Tagged deer	3	1	0	1	2	7

The naturalists found that 7 out of 350, or 1 out of every 50, deer were tagged. They used a proportion to estimate the total number of deer in Wilderness Park.

Tagged deer→ / Sampled deer→ $\frac{1}{50} = \frac{200}{n}$ ←Total tagged deer / ←Total deer in Wilderness Park

$$n = 200 \times 50$$

$$n = 10{,}000$$

There are about 10,000 deer in the park.

Talk About Math Why did the naturalists count the number of tagged deer in several samples rather than just one sample?

Check Understanding

For another example, see Set H, pages 500–501.

1. If the naturalists had gotten these results, what would their estimate of the number of deer in Wilderness Park have been?

Deer in the sample	100	50	50	50	100
Tagged deer	3	12	2	0	3

2. Suppose samples taken by naturalists at Wilderness Park show that 1 out of 40 deer is tagged. What would their estimate of the number of deer be?

Practice

For More Practice, see Set H, pages 502–503.

Naturalists tagged 300 goats on Goat Island. Predict the total number of goats on Goat Island if the samples show that the average number of tagged goats is as follows.

3. 3 out of 50 **4.** 7 out of 100 **5.** 1 out of 30 **6.** 7 out of 8

7. 5 out of 40 **8.** 9 out of 200 **9.** 16 out of 400 **10.** 11 out of 300

Naturalists tagged 500 fish in Loon Lake. Predict the total number of fish in Loon Lake if the samples show that the average number of tagged fish is as follows.

11. 6 out of 500 **12.** 14 out of 1,000 **13.** 18 out of 500 **14.** 19 out of 200

15. 9 out of 250 **16.** 13 out of 300 **17.** 50 out of 2,000 **18.** 23 out of 800

Problem Solving

Solve each problem. Naturalists estimate that about 1,000 ducks nest around Loon Lake. Two hundred of the ducks have been tagged.

19. How many tagged ducks should a naturalist expect to capture out of a total sample of 450?

20. How many tagged ducks should a naturalist expect to capture out of a sample of 100?

Explore Math

If the naturalists in the example on page 496 know that there is a 10% error in sampling, they can use this information to estimate a range. If the estimate is 10,000 deer, then a 10% error means that the actual number of deer could be as low as 9,000 (10,000 − 0.10(10,000) = 9,000) or as high as 11,000 (10,000 + 0.10(10,000) = 11,000).

21. What would the range of possible values be in Example A if the estimated number of deer was 800 and the error in sampling were 10%?

22. What would be the range of possible values for the estimate you made in Exercise 1 if there were a 5% sampling error?

23. Calculate the sampling error if the range of values determined in the example on page 496 were 9,300–10,700.

24. Is an estimate given as a range better than one given as a single number?

Skills Review

Use the data below for Exercises 1–4.
5, 7, 9, 6, 5, 7, 6, 8, 9, 9, 7, 6,
8, 9, 9, 5, 7, 5, 7, 9

1. Make a frequency table.
2. Make a line plot.
3. Find the mean, median and mode.
4. Find the upper and lower quartiles.

Use these data for Exercises 5–6: 22, 29, 40, 48, 37, 42, 33, 25, 41, 32, 45, 31, 39

5. Make a stem-and-leaf plot.
6. Make a box plot for the data.

Make a suitable graph for each table.

7.

Walnut content by weight	
Water	5%
Carbohydrate	16%
Fat	64%
Protein	15%

8.

Kite Sales by Month	
February	32
March	46
April	65
May	51

Describe the sample you would use to predict each of the following situations.

9. What percent of the U.S. population will be travelling over the summer?
10. What percent of teenagers will buy a certain cassette tape?

Predict how many of 6,000 radios will be faulty if the sample showed the ratio of faulty radios to total radios to be

11. 2 out of 75.
12. 1 out of 30.

Problem-Solving Review

Solve each problem.

13. The number of home runs Karen hit in her 10 years in the league are: 23, 17, 18, 29, 27, 21, 12, 17, 30 and 20. Give the range and midrange for this data.
14. Paul has kept a record of the number of sit-ups he has done each day for a week. Which kind of graph is best for displaying this data? Why?
15. In a survey of 30 workers, 14 were satisfied with their salaries, 11 were not, and 5 gave no response. Find the percent for each category and determine the round-off error.
16. In the last 5 years, the average salary of workers at ABC company was, in thousands of dollars, \$21, \$23, \$23.8, \$24.5, and \$25.6. Explain how to draw a line graph so that it appears that salaries rose dramatically.
17. Rangers estimate that of the 2,000 seals in Seal Lake, 400 are tagged. How many tagged seals would you expect to find in a sample of 400?
18. **Data File** Use the data on pages 572–573. Make a scattergram of the water temperatures in late August and early June. Describe any correlations.
19. **Make a Data File** Use an almanac or other source. Find the heights of the 10 buildings with the greatest number of stories in each of two American cities. List the data in a table and in a back-to-back stem-and-leaf plot.

Cumulative Skills Review • Chapters 1–13

Write the prime factorization of each number in exponential form.

1. 135 **2.** 1,225 **3.** 468 **4.** 1,615

List the numbers in order from greatest to least.

5. $5\frac{1}{2}, \frac{17}{6}, 4\frac{11}{12}, \frac{19}{4}$ **6.** $\frac{3}{4}, \frac{5}{9}, \frac{4}{7}, \frac{2}{3}$ **7.** $-\frac{5}{8}, \frac{1}{4}, -\frac{3}{5}, \frac{2}{7}$

Solve.

8. $y + 15 = 26$ **9.** $t - 30 = 18$ **10.** $\frac{4}{5}c = -16$ **11.** $12p = -60$

12. $2v - 8 = 20$ **13.** $h + 5 = 50$ **14.** $w - 3 < -2$ **15.** $f + 4 \geq 4$

Find the perimeter and area of each figure. Use 3.14 for π.

16.
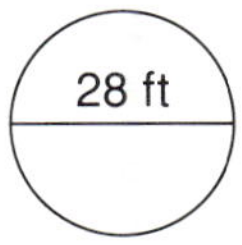

17.
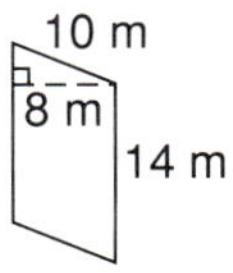

18.
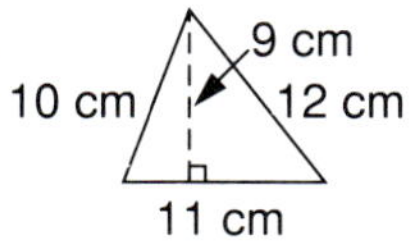

19.
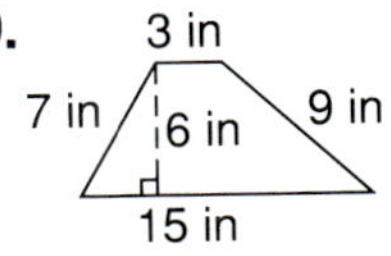

Write each number in standard form.

20. 10^6 **21.** 7.53×10^5 **22.** 10^{-5} **23.** 3.35×10^{-3}

Use the Pythagorean Theorem to verify whether these triples are Pythagorean Triples.

24. 10, 24, 26 **25.** 7, 8, 10 **26.** 12, 16, 20 **27.** 9, 9, 13

Use triangle *ABC* to find each measure.

28. $m\angle ABC$ **29.** AC **30.** AB

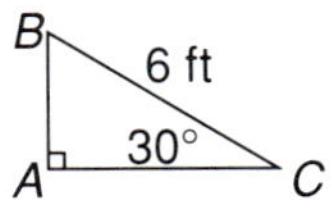

Use the data in the chart below for Exercises 31–36.

Study Time in Hours	5	3.5	2	1.5	4.5	3	3.5	4.5	2.5
Test Grade	94	87	74	75	90	80	85	99	88

31. Make a scattergram of the data.

32. Draw a line of best fit.

33. Is there a correlation between study time and test grade? If so, what is it?

34. What test grade would you expect for 5.5 hours of study time?

35. Find the median of the test grades.

36. Find the mean of the test grades.

Reteaching

Set A pages 468–471

Look at this set of data.

43 16 47 43 45 22 29

$$\text{Mean} = \frac{\text{Sum of numbers}}{\text{Number of numbers}} = \frac{245}{7} = 35$$

The median is the middle number in an ordered list: 43. The mode is the most frequently occurring number: 43.

Remember to divide the sum of the two middle numbers by 2 to find the median of a data set with an even number of items.

7 11 9 13 14 11

Using the set of data above, find the

1. mean. **2.** median. **3.** mode.

Set B pages 472–473

54 67 51 72 65 52 54 57 64 73 78

This stem-and-leaf plot represents the data above. The leaves 1, 2, 4, 4, and 7 on the stem 5 represent the numbers 51, 52, 54, 54, and 57. You can see that the numbers in the 50s occur most often.

Stem	Leaves
5	1 2 4 4 7
6	4 5 7
7	2 3 8

Remember that leaves represent digits in the ones place and that stems represent digits in the tens or hundreds place.

1. What are the highest and lowest numbers on the stem-and-leaf plot?

2. Make a stem-and-leaf plot for this set of data.

4 24 11 26 14 33 15 12 1

Set C pages 474–475

This box plot shows Jefferson's score for ten math quizzes.

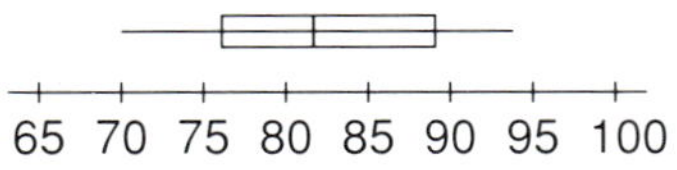

The scores range from 70 to 94. The median is 82. The upper quartile, 89, is the median to the right of the median 82. The lower quartile, 76, is the median to the left of the median 82.

Remember that an outlier, or a number that is very different from all the other numbers in a set of data, is not included in the whisker and is represented with an asterisk (*).

Draw a box plot for each set of data.

1. 19 28 21 24
2 17 30 31
23 29 24 27

2. 110 97 101 102
89 115 99 94
90 93 106 114

Set D pages 476–477

Tell whether a bar graph or a circle graph would best represent the data in this article.

Dr. Susan Vargas could not explain the sudden increase in donations. "Last year we collected 450 cans of food, and the two years before that, we collected 400 cans each year. This year's total of 725 cans was a nice surprise," Dr. Vargas said.

Because different amounts from different years are being compared, a bar graph would best represent the data.

Remember that in general, bar graphs are used for comparisons of amount in different categories and circle graphs are used to show how the parts of a whole are divided.

For each set of data, tell whether a bar graph or a circle graph would be more appropriate. Explain your answer.

1. Hottest days ever in New York City

2. Favorite type of food

Set E pages 484–485

This double broken-line graph shows enrollment at two junior high schools from 1986 to 1990.

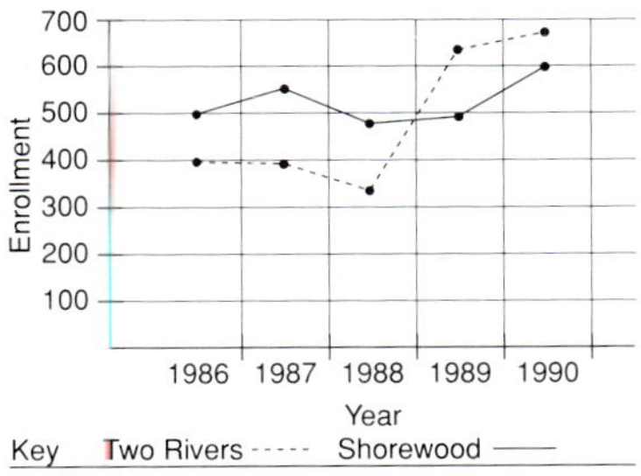

Remember that the lines on a broken-line graph simply connect the dots and do not represent any value.

1. In what year did both schools have a drop in enrollment?
2. Which school had an enrollment of 563 in 1987?
3. In what year were the enrollments the closest?

Set F pages 488–489

This scattergram shows the relationship between the record lowest temperatures in 14 of the 50 U.S. states and the elevation of the reporting station.

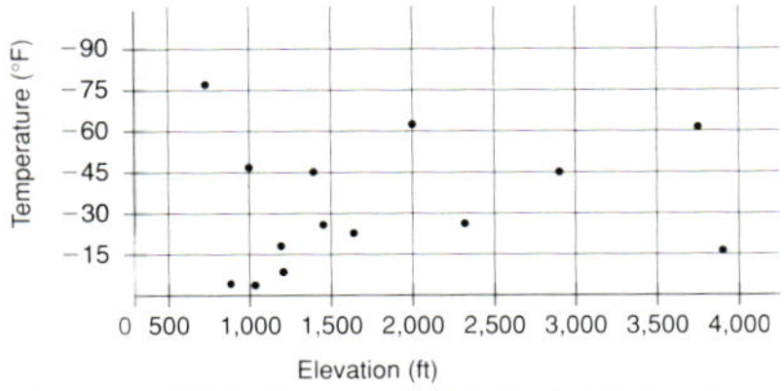

Remember, an upward slant of the line of best fit indicates a positive correlation.

1. What is the elevation of the location with the lowest temperature?
2. What is the record low temperature at the highest elevation?
3. Is there a positive, a negative, or no correlation between elevation and lowest temperature?

Set G pages 490–491

Population:
all cars shown
Sample:
cars in box
Random sample:
cars in circles
Stratified sample:
all white cars

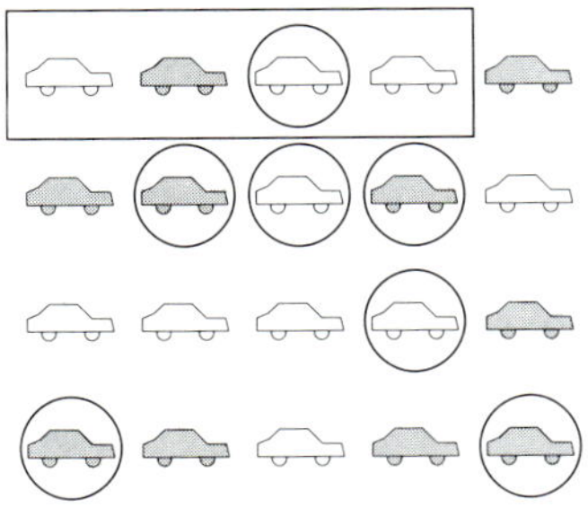

Remember that in statistics a population does not have to be a group of people, but can be a group of objects that you are interested in.

Tell what percent of the population at the left was surveyed for the

1. sample.
2. random sample.
3. Tell how a stratified sample and a random sample are similar. Tell how they are different.

Set H pages 496–497

Naturalists at a wildlife refuge tagged and released 250 deer. The results of five later samples of deer in the refuge are shown.

Sample	1	2	3	4	5	Total
Tagged deer	17	12	15	20	35	99
Deer in sample	50	50	50	50	50	250

Remember to write a proportion to solve this kind of problem.

1. Estimate the total number of deer in the refuge.
2. What would your estimate be if you used only the naturalists' first sample?

More Practice

Set A pages 468–471

Use the data below.
7, 8, 6, 9, 10,
7, 9, 8, 7, 6,
9, 9, 10, 7, 5,
10, 9, 8, 6, 5

1. Make a frequency table.

2. Make a line plot.

3. Find the mean.

4. Find the median.

5. Find the mode.

6. Find the upper quartile.

Set B pages 472–473

1. Make a stem-and-leaf plot for the data below.

21, 27, 39, 33, 34,
33, 23, 25, 39, 41,
38, 19, 45, 26, 31,
54, 39, 29, 33, 21

2. List the two sets of data used to make the following stem-and-leaf plot.

Leaves	Stem	Leaves
8 0 0	2	0 2 3 4
2	3	1 4 7 8 9
3 1	4	6

3. Make a stem-and-leaf plot for the data below.
6, 19, 17, 1, 19,
5, 4, 7, 13, 19,
8, 21, 7, 14, 7

4. List the two sets of data used to make the following stem-and-leaf plot.

Leaves	Stem	Leaves
6 4 4 2	8	1 2 9
4 3 0	9	8 9 9 9
7	10	2 3

Set C pages 474–475

1. Make a box plot from the data below.

19, 20, 35, 30, 32,
34, 16, 29, 37, 44,
32, 20, 40, 22, 29,
50, 36, 29, 28, 18

2. Make a side-by-side box plot for the sets of data below.

1st set:	61	62	65	2nd set:	22	48	53
	63	67	70		61	55	60
	59	61	66		49	62	57

3. Make a box plot from the data below.

99, 50, 74, 99, 85, 53,
56, 93, 73, 71, 83, 65,
91, 88, 88, 62, 90, 96

4. Make a side-by-side box plot for these data.

1st set:	30	36	29	2nd set:	34	50	49
	40	26	27		47	40	45
	41	45	36		44	35	47

Set D pages 476–477

Make the appropriate graph for each set of data.

1. Survey of taxicab drivers

Distance (mi)	No. of rides
0–5	91
6–10	76
11–15	19
16–20	8
20+	3

2. Earth's water

Body of water	Percent
Atlantic Ocean	23%
Pacific Ocean	46%
Indian Ocean	20%
Arctic Ocean	4%
Other	7%

3. Season ticket prices

Team	Price
Cougars	$60
Grizzlies	$65
Senators	$75
Panthers	$80
Cyclones	$100

Set E pages 484–485

The double broken-line graph below shows the number of riders for two rides at an amusement park.

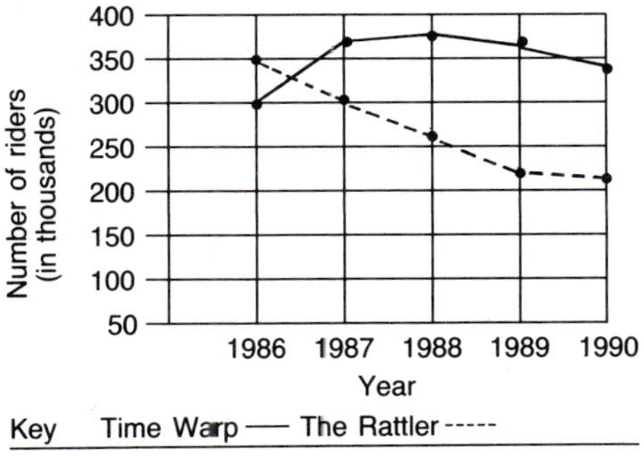

Use the double broken-line graph at the left for Exercises 1–4.

1. How many people rode The Rattler in 1986?

2. How many people rode Time Warp in 1989?

3. Between which two years did ridership on Time Warp increase the most?

4. In what year did more people ride The Rattler?

Set F pages 488–489

Use the scattergram at the right to answer the following questions.

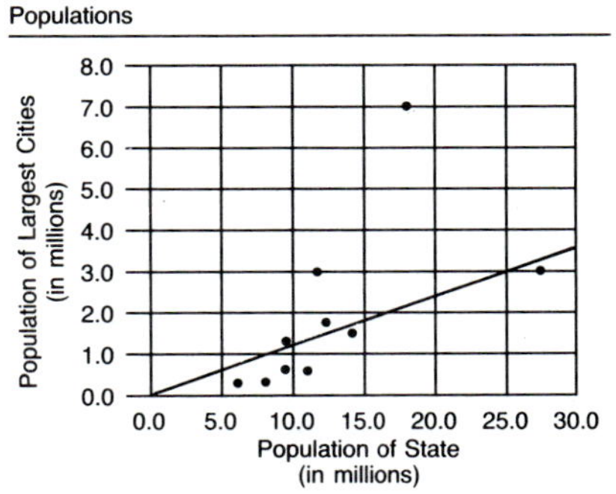

1. Is the city with the largest population located in the state with the largest population?

2. Is there a correlation between the population of a state and the population of that state's largest city? Is it negative or positive?

Set G pages 490–491

Describe the sample you would need to predict the sale of each of the following.

1. Mountain bikes
2. Toothpaste
3. Video games
4. Station wagons

Tell whether you would survey a sample closest to 0%, 5%, or 100% of the population. Explain your answers.

5. To determine whether parachutes open properly

6. To determine whether VCR buyers are satisfied with their purchase after a year

In a survey of 60 commuters, 36 drive to work alone, 17 take the train, 6 car pool, and 1 rides a bicycle.

7. Find the percent for each category.

8. Determine the round-off error.

Set H pages 496–497

Park rangers tagged 150 raccoons. Predict the total raccoon population in the park if samples show that the average number of tagged raccoons is

1. 4 out of 20.
2. 8 out of 100.
3. 1 out of 4.

Enrichment

Patterns in Histograms

Many businesses use patterns in histograms to determine if there are areas in need of improvement. Quality control experts examine **outliers** and **gaps** in histograms to find and correct problems in the business.

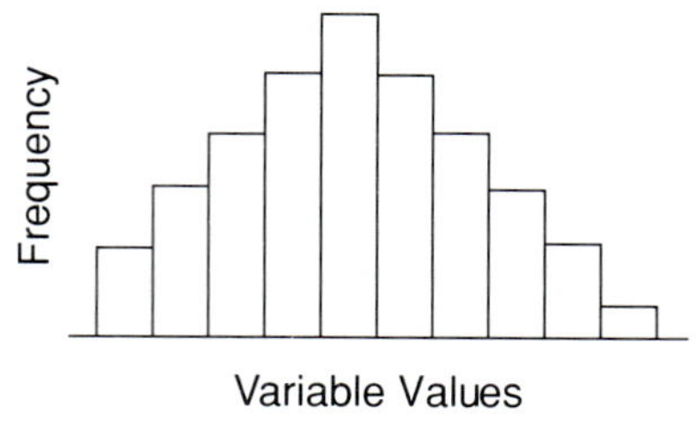

The histogram at the right shows a normal distribution pattern. The data decreases almost symmetrically on either side of the one most frequent outcome with no gaps or outliers.

This histogram shows a gap at 0.999 cm and the unexpected high outcome at 1.000 cm. The gap separates the 0.998 cm entry from the rest of the graph, making it look like an outlier.

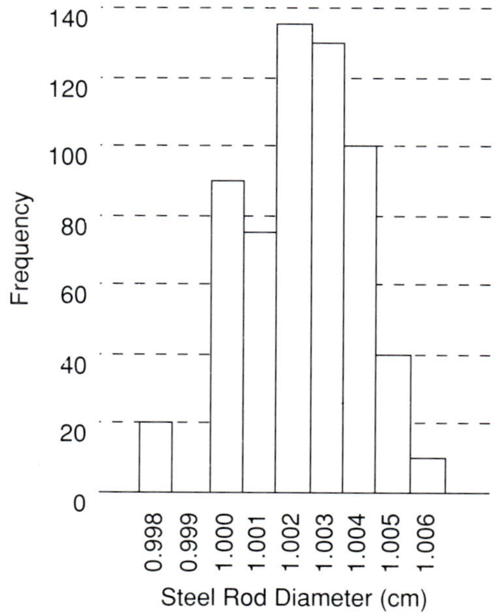

However, a quality control expert found that the gap was caused by incorrect grouping of the steel rods. Rods which should have been classified as 0.999 cm were grouped with the 1.000 cm rods. Knowing this, she could correct the problem.

Answer each question.

1. How are gaps and outliers different? How are they similar?

2. Which three entries did the quality control expert examine in the problem above?

Tell what parts of the histogram show a possible problem.

3.

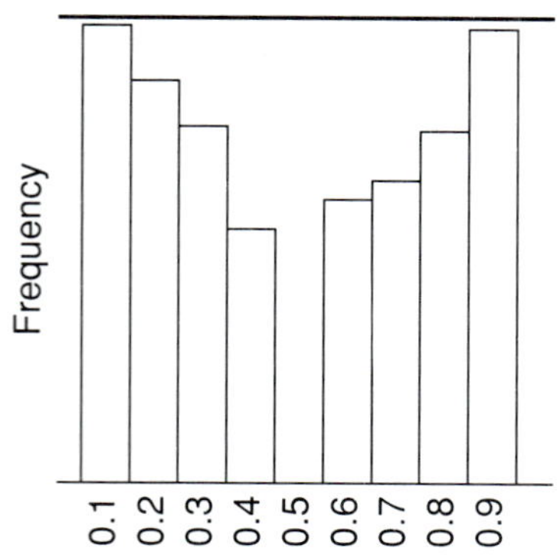

4.

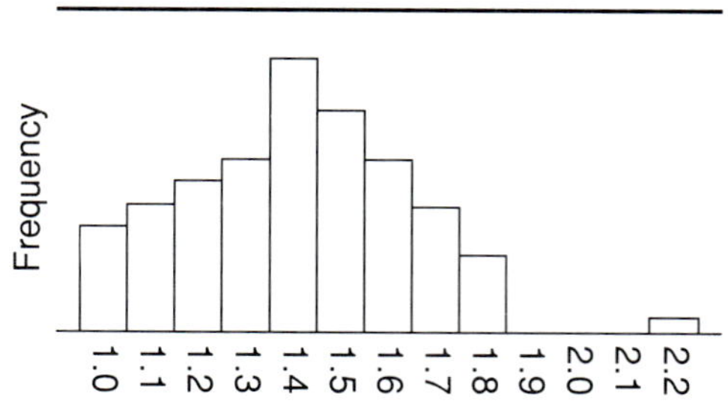

5. Name the gap in Problem 3.

6. Name the possible outlier in Problem 4.

Chapter 13 Review/Test

76 91 85 93 72 77 90 91 79

For the set of data above, find the

1. mean.

2. median.

3. mode.

4. range.

5. midrange.

6. upper quartile.

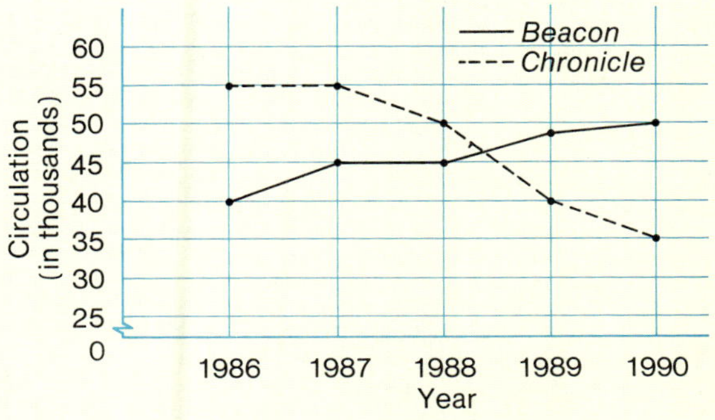

7. Between which two years did the circulation of the *Chronicle* decrease the most?

19 7 24 16 2 4 20 13 11 14 22 59

For the set of data above, make

8. a stem-and-leaf plot.

9. a box plot.

10. a histogram with a range of 10. Begin with 0–9.

11. Describe how you would reasonably collect data to find the percent of eighth-grade students in the United States who have ever attended a professional baseball game.

12. Out of 60 customers surveyed, 14 were disappointed with the service they had received. Find the measure of the central angle for this category on a circle graph.

City	1986 rank	Number of parks
Chicago	3	560
Cincinnati	39	96
Cleveland	22	41
Detroit	6	52
Indianapolis	13	134
Kansas City	29	174
Minneapolis	43	153
St. Louis	31	89

13. Use the data in the chart above to make a scattergram showing the relationship between a city's rank and the number of parks it has. Draw a line of best fit.

The data on the right show the number of takeoffs and landings per day at City Airport.

Year	Number
1987	36
1988	38
1989	44
1990	49

14. Tell which is the most appropriate *first step* in making a bar graph to show the above data.

a. Determine the range of the data.
b. Determine the mean of the data.
c. Determine the intervals of the horizontal axis.

15. Make the bar graph for Item 14.

16. A team of naturalists in a wilderness area tagged and released 20 hawks. The results of five later samples are shown below. Estimate the number of hawks in the wilderness area.

Sample	1	2	3	4	5	Total
Hawks in sample	10	15	20	10	10	65
Tagged hawks	4	9	13	6	7	39

17. Write About Math Tell how a stratified random sample and a random sample are different.

Probability

14

Did You Know: Because people pay more attention to the leading digits in a number, a price of $8.99 or $8,999 looks a lot lower to many people than a price of $9.00 or $9,000.

Number-Sense Project

Estimate
Out of 20 prices picked randomly, about how many would you expect to end in an 8 or a 9?

Gather Data
Pick a store, like a supermarket, or use a catalog. Randomly pick 20 items and record their prices.

Analyze and Report
About how many out of every 20 prices would you expect to end in an 8 or a 9? What did you and your classmates find in the prices you recorded? Do you feel prices tend to end in 8 or 9?

Probability Experiments

Build Understanding

A. Exploring Probability
Materials: Bag, ten 3″ × 5″ slips of paper: 4 marked *bear*, 3 marked *wolf*, 2 marked *raccoon*, 1 marked *lion*
Groups: 2 or more students

a. Put the slips of paper in a bag. Draw 1 slip from the bag without looking. Put a mark in the tally column for the animal name on your slip. Put the slip back in the bag.

Do this experiment 20 times. Add the tally marks for each name, and write that number in the frequency column.

Animal	Tally	Frequency
Bear		
Wolf		
Raccoon		
Lion		

b. In this experiment, a card was drawn 20 times, or the experiment had 20 trials. The result of drawing a certain desired card, such as *wolf*, is called a success. The experimental probability of drawing a certain card is given by this formula.

$$\textbf{Probability} = \frac{\textbf{Number of successes}}{\textbf{Number of trials}}$$

Using your data, find the experimental probability of drawing *wolf*. You can write "probability of drawing *wolf*" as *P*(*wolf*).

$$P(wolf) = \frac{\square}{20}$$

← The number in the frequency column for *wolf* from your table
← The number of trials

c. Use your table. Write the number of successes to complete each probability.

$P(bear) = \frac{\square}{20}$ $\quad P(raccoon) = \frac{\square}{20}$ $\quad P(lion) = \frac{\square}{20}$

B. The ***theoretical probability*** tells what *should* happen in an experiment and is given by this formula.

$$P = \frac{\text{number of favorable outcomes}}{\text{number of possible outcomes}}$$

In Example A, what is the theoretical probability of drawing *bear* or *lion*?

$$P(\textit{bear} \text{ or } \textit{lion}) = \frac{4+1}{10} = \frac{5}{10} = \frac{1}{2}$$

The theoretical probability of drawing *bear* or *lion* is $\frac{1}{2}$. You can expect the experimental probability of drawing either *bear* or *lion* to be about $\frac{1}{2}$. The more times you repeat the experiment, the closer your experimental probability will be to the theoretical probability.

Combine the results of the Activity for all the groups. Is the experimental probability of drawing *bear* or *lion* about $\frac{1}{2}$?

C. The probability of an outcome can be written as a number from 0 to 1. When an outcome is *certain* to happen, its probability is 1. When an outcome is *impossible*, its probability is 0.

In Example A, what is the theoretical probability of drawing either *bear, wolf, raccoon,* or *lion*? You are certain to pick either *bear, wolf, raccoon,* or *lion* because these are the only slips in the bag. Therefore, the probability is 1.

What is the theoretical probability of drawing *tiger*? Since there are no slips for *tiger*, the probability is 0.

Talk About Math In Example A, if the theoretical probability of drawing *wolf* is $\frac{3}{10}$, does this mean that you will draw *wolf* three times out of every ten draws? Explain.

Check Understanding

For another example, see Set A, pages 534–535.

Refer to Example A on page 508 for Exercises 1–10. Give the theoretical probability of each outcome.

1. $P(\textit{raccoon})$ **2.** $P(\textit{moose})$ **3.** $P(\textit{wolf} \text{ or } \textit{bear})$ **4.** $P(\textit{lion})$

Use the combined results from Example B to give the experimental probability of each outcome.

5. $P(\textit{raccoon})$ **6.** $P(\textit{moose})$ **7.** $P(\textit{wolf} \text{ or } \textit{bear})$ **8.** $P(\textit{lion})$

9. Draw two circle graphs: one that shows the theoretical probabilities and one that shows the experimental probabilities.

10. How would you explain a difference between the theoretical probability and the experimental probability?

Practice

For More Practice, see Set A, pages 536–537.

Give the theoretical probability for each outcome.

11. The sun will rise tomorrow.

12. It will either snow or not snow tomorrow.

Use the photo to give the theoretical probability for each outcome.

13. The item you randomly choose from the shelf is a mug.

14. You will randomly choose a blue mug from the shelf.

15. You will randomly choose a mug that is not blue from the shelf.

16. You will randomly choose a red mug from the shelf.

Mental Math Refer to the spinner. Find each theoretical probability.

17. $P(2)$

18. $P(3 \text{ or } 5)$

19. $P(\text{even number})$

20. $P(7)$

21. $P(\text{whole number})$

22. $P(\text{prime number})$

23. $P(\text{multiple of } 3)$

24. $P(\text{even or odd number})$

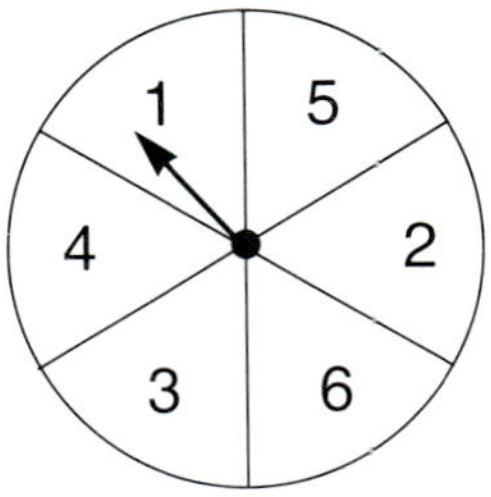

Estimation Choose a familiar song. For Exercises 25–29, estimate the probability of each outcome if you surveyed 30 people for their opinions: like very much, like, neutral, dislike, or strongly dislike.

25. $P(\text{like very much})$

26. $P(\text{like})$

27. $P(\text{neutral})$

28. $P(\text{dislike})$

29. $P(\text{strongly dislike})$

30. Draw a circle graph using your estimations from Exercises 25–29.

31. Are all of the outcomes equally likely? Explain.

Survey 30 people. Tally their opinions. For Exercises 32–36, find your experimental probability.

32. $P(\text{like very much})$

33. $P(\text{like})$

34. $P(\text{neutral})$

35. $P(\text{dislike})$

36. $P(\text{strongly dislike})$

Opinion	Tally
Like very much	
Like	
Neutral	
Dislike	
Strongly dislike	

Refer to your answers to Exercises 32–36 to solve each problem.

37. Draw a circle graph using the data from Exercises 32–36.

38. What is the probability that the next person you survey will like the song very much?

39. Are the estimated and experimental outcomes the same? Explain.

40. Were your estimated outcomes theoretical outcomes?

Problem Solving

Perform each experiment 10 times. Combine your results with your classmates. Then determine the experimental probability of each outcome. Draw a circle graph that shows each outcome's probability.

41. If you toss a paper cup in the air, it can land on its side, straight up, or upside down. Which is most likely? Make a guess, and then experiment to find out.

42. **Use Data** Refer to the coordinate points listed in Exercises 10–19 on page 154. What is the probability that a point randomly selected is in the fourth quadrant?

43. Write the letters A to Z on separate slips of paper of the same size, put the slips in a bag, and mix them up. What is the experimental probability that a letter chosen at random will be a vowel (*A, E, I, O,* or *U*)?

44. Write the numbers 1 through 25 on separate slips of paper of the same size, put them in a bag, and mix them up. What is the experimental probability that the number chosen at random will be a multiple of 5?

Choose a ________ Strategy

Overworked Vowels
In English, does one vowel appear more often than any of the others?

45. Decide whether you can use your answer to Problem 43 to determine whether one vowel occurs more frequently in English than others.

46. Randomly choose a page from a novel. Record the first 50 vowels which appear on the page.

47. Repeat the experiment five times. Use your results to determine the experimental probability of selecting each vowel from a randomly selected page.

PROBLEM SOLVING STRATEGIES

- Choose an Operation
- Solve a Simpler Problem
- Use a Formula
- Write an Equation
- Make a Graph
- Draw a Diagram
- Make a Table
- Try and Check

Use Data from a Table

PROBLEM SOLVING GUIDE

Understand
QUESTION
FACTS
KEY IDEA

Plan and Solve
STRATEGY
ANSWER

Look Back
SENSIBLE ANSWER
ALTERNATE APPROACH

Build Understanding

If you toss a number cube, each of the 6 numbers is equally likely to be on top when it lands. Since there are 3 even numbers, the theoretical probability that the top number is even is $\frac{3}{6}$, or $\frac{1}{2}$.

Suppose you toss a number cube 100 times. How many times out of 100 is the top number even? The theoretical probability of the top number being even is shown below.

Probability of even number		Number of tosses		Expected number of even results
$\frac{1}{2}$	×	100	=	50

Understand QUESTION Out of 100 tosses of the number cube, how many even numbers result?

FACT The result of tossing the number cube is either an odd or even number.

KEY IDEA A random number table like the one shown can be used to simulate tossing the number cube, since half of the digits from 0 through 9 are even.

Plan and Solve STRATEGY Let an even number on this random number table represent an even number landing on top of the number cube. Let an odd number on the table represent an odd number result.

5	6	7	8	6	5	8	9	9	0	2	2	3	5	4	9	3	4	2	2
2	4	7	9	4	5	4	4	7	9	1	7	4	2	0	5	8	6	5	8
4	3	1	3	7	8	9	0	8	3	9	8	6	2	8	6	4	6	7	3
5	8	8	5	5	4	2	1	8	3	1	5	9	7	5	3	9	0	7	2
3	3	1	7	8	5	3	3	0	4	1	2	5	3	6	5	4	8	3	4
7	2	0	6	3	2	1	2	3	8	5	4	0	8	4	1	2	5	3	8
4	2	8	5	6	5	2	1	5	7	8	5	1	3	4	5	5	1	8	3
8	4	1	8	6	8	1	5	6	0	6	3	1	3	0	7	7	4	4	3
1	3	5	5	2	1	5	2	5	1	9	3	5	1	8	3	4	5	7	4
6	7	2	0	7	7	9	7	3	0	7	5	3	3	4	5	1	5	4	2

ANSWER Of the first 100 digits on the random number table, 48 were even numbers and 52 were odd numbers. In this simulation, the top number of the number cube was even 48 out of 100 times.

Look Back SENSIBLE ANSWER The 48 even number and 52 odd number results in the simulation are close to the expected results of 50 even numbers and 50 odd numbers.

Talk About Math Why are the simulated results not the same as the theoretical results? If you used a random number table to simulate tossing the number cube 1,000 times, do you think the simulated results would be closer to the expected results?

Check Understanding

Suppose you flip a coin 20 times.

1. Predict how many times the coin will land heads up.
2. Is it possible for the coin to come up heads 20 times in a row?

Use the random number table on page 512 to simulate flipping a coin 20 times. Let even numbers equal heads and odd numbers equal tails. Record your results.

3. Are your simulated results the same as your predicted results?
4. Explain when and why random number tables are used.

Practice

Predict the results of each experiment. Then use the random number table on page 512 to simulate the experiment. Compare your predicted results with your experimental results.

5. Peggy put 10 counters numbered 0 through 9 in a box. Alex selects one counter at a time and then replaces it. How many times out of 25 will he select the number 7 counter?
6. If the probability of a boy wearing a plaid shirt is $\frac{1}{5}$, how many out of 200 boys are wearing plaid shirts? (Hint: Pick 2 numbers from 0 through 9 to represent plaid shirts.)
7. If the probability of rain on a spring day is $\frac{1}{2}$, how many times is it likely to rain in 90 days? (Hint: Pick 5 numbers from 0 through 9 to represent rainy days.)
8. **Number Sense** The probability that a randomly chosen person is a millionaire is about $\frac{1}{425}$. Out of a group of 300 people, how many are millionaires?

Solve each problem.

9. A stove is marked \$379, but it is on sale for 20% off. There is a sales tax of 8%. Find the total price.
10. A cylindrical barrel has a base with a radius of 16 inches and a height of 30 inches. Find the volume.

Fundamental Counting Principle

Build Understanding

Size	Color	Design
S M L	Red Yellow	Plain Fancy

BG Sporting Goods sells T-shirts with the store's logo printed on them. The T-shirts come in 3 sizes, 2 colors, and 2 designs. How many different T-shirts can they sell?

A. Use a ***tree diagram*** to count the T-shirts.

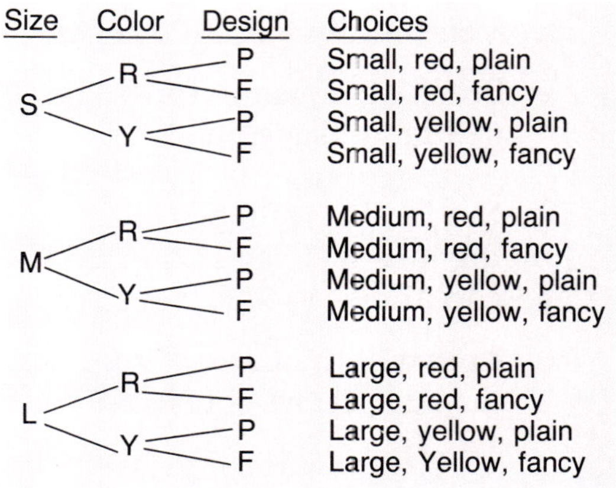

The top branch of the tree diagram shows one T-shirt: S, red, plain. Each branch ends under the Choices column, so count the number of items in that column to find all the choices.

There are 12 items in the Choices column, so there are 12 different kinds of T-shirts.

B. Use multiplication to find the number of choices.

This property is called the ***fundamental counting principle.***

If there are m choices for one category, n choices for another category, and z choices for a third category, there are $m \times n \times z$ different choices.

There are 3 sizes. For each size, there are 2 color choices. For each color choice, there are 2 design choices.

Number of choices for size		Number of choices for color		Number of choices for design		Total number of choices
3	×	**2**	×	**2**	=	**12**

There are 12 different T-shirts.

■ **Talk About Math** Flip a coin and toss a number cube. How could you use the fundamental counting principle to find all possible outcomes?

Check Understanding

For another example, see Set B, pages 534–535.

Suppose the tree diagram in Example A were rearranged so that Design came first.

1. Show the new tree diagram. How is your tree diagram different from the one in the example?

2. Can you still count the total number of choices? use the fundamental counting principle? Explain.

Practice

For More Practice, see Set B, pages 536–537.

Tell whether you would use mental math, a calculator, or paper and pencil. Then find the total number of choices.

3. A shoe factory makes running shoes in 24 sizes, 18 colors, and 12 widths.

4. A stationery store sells envelopes in 26 sizes, 48 colors, and 64 styles.

5. A department store sells pants in 12 sizes, 6 colors, and 5 lengths.

6. A paint store sells 6 kinds of paint in 436 different colors and 2 can sizes.

7. A furniture maker sells sofas in 3 sizes, 4 kinds of wood trim, and 10 fabrics.

8. In a class election, 4 people are running for president, 6 for vice-president, and 5 for treasurer.

9. A 3-letter code can be made from any letter in the alphabet. (Letters can be repeated.)

10. A combination lock uses 3 numbers from 1 through 36. (Numbers can be repeated.)

A car maker sells cars in eight 2-door or 4-door models, with either 4-cylinder or 6-cylinder engines, in 12 colors, in 4 styles, and with 3 upholstery options. How many choices are there for

11. engine, color, and upholstery?

12. doors, style, and color?

13. color, style, and upholstery?

14. doors, engine, color, and style?

15. How many different choices are there altogether?

Problem Solving

Use this table to solve each problem.

Sweatshirts		
Type	Size	Color
Crew neck, pullover Hood, pullover Hood, zipper	XS S M L XL XXL	White Red Navy Green Yellow

16. How many different sweatshirts are there from which to choose?

17. If one store carries all but the navy sweatshirts, how many different choices does it carry?

18. **Critical Thinking** An automobile dealer just received 432 vans from Zola Inc., which makes vans in 3 sizes (including minivans) and 9 colors (including red), with 8 different radios (including AM/FM). How many red Zola minivans with AM/FM radios does the dealer have? (Assume all the possible types were delivered in equal numbers.)

Permutations

Build Understanding

A ***permutation*** is an arrangement of the elements of a set in a particular order.

A. List the permutations of the letters A, B, and C.

ABC BCA ACB CAB BAC CBA

The letters A, B, and C can be arranged six different ways, so there are six permutations.

B. The director of a theater wants Huang, Ann, Sally, and John to stand in a row on stage at the end of the performance. How many different ways can the four performers be arranged?

The director can choose any of the 4 performers to be first. Then 3 choices remain for the second place, 2 for the third, and 1 for the fourth place.

Number of choices		Number of choices		Number of choices		Number of choices		Total number of choices
4	×	**3**	×	**2**	×	**1**	=	**24**

Altogether, there are 24 different ways in which the 4 performers can be arranged.

C. The product $4 \times 3 \times 2 \times 1$ is called ***4 factorial*** and is written **4!**. Notice that 4! describes the solution in Example B. Find 6! (6 factorial).

6! = 6 × 5 × 4 × 3 × 2 × 1 = 720

D. How many permutations are there for 5 students taken 3 at a time?

Choices for first student		Choices for second student		Choices for third student		Total number of choices
5	×	**4**	×	**3**	=	**60**

■ **Talk About Math** Describe a situation in which the permutation would be 6!.

Check Understanding

For another example, see Set C, pages 534–535.

Answer each question.

1. List the permutations for the numbers 5, 6, 7.

2. Find the value of 5!.

Practice

For More Practice, see Set C, page 536–537.

List the permutations. Then check your answer by calculating the number of permutations possible.

3. XYZ

4. 8 9 7 3

5. L O V E

6. Al, Bess, Chan

7. Maida, Miguel

8. 7 8 9

Tell whether you would use mental math, a calculator, or paper and pencil. Find the value of each of the following.

9. 3!

10. 8!

11. 10!

12. 2!

13. 7!

14. 5!

15. 6!

16. 9!

Calculate the number of permutations.

17. Six books on a shelf

18. Four people in a single-file line

19. P Q R S T

20. 1 2 3 4 5 6 7

Problem Solving

Solve each problem.

21. The 30 students on the Student Council have to elect a president, a vice-president, and a treasurer. In how many different ways can 3 students be selected to fill these offices?

22. **Calculator** Ms. Kim's class has 5 seats in the last row. She calculates that there are 14,250,600 different ways 5 students can be selected for the last row. How many students does she have?

Skills Review

pages 478–481, 484–485

Tell whether you would choose a bar graph, a double bar graph, a histogram, or a broken-line graph to represent these data sets. For each exercise, create your own set of data and draw the type of graph you select.

1. The price of milk in the cafeteria for each of the last 5 years

2. The number of times per week people of ages 10 to 20 exercise

3. Public high school and private high school enrollment from 1900 through 1990

4. Your math scores for this year

Independent Events

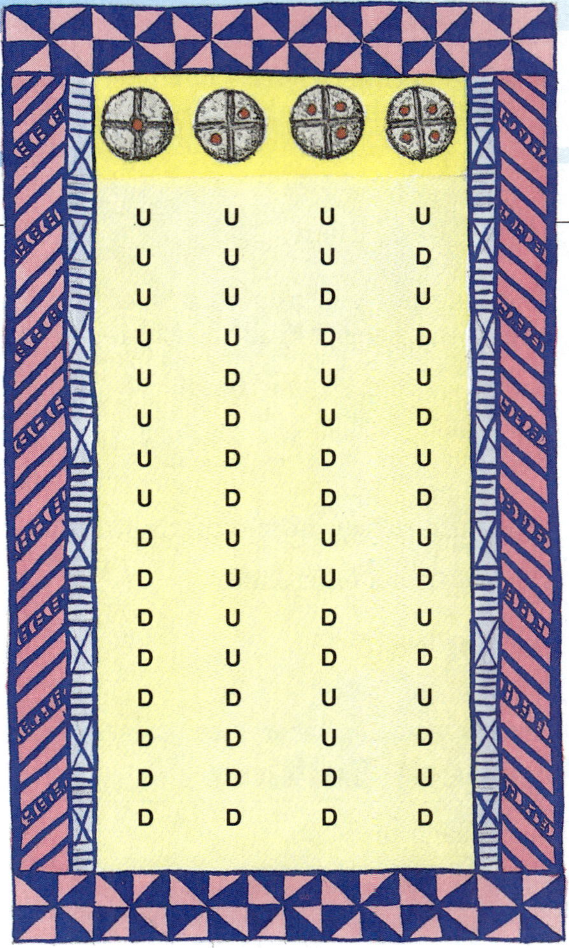

Build Understanding

The Polynesian settlers of Hawaii played a game call Lu-lu that used a set of 4 volcanic stone disks. Each disk had 1, 2, 3, or 4 markings on one side only. A player would toss the stones and get points for the number of marks on the stones landing faceup. The outcome of one stone did not affect the outcome of the others, so the tossing of the stones were ***independent events.***

A. Find $P(\text{U,U,U,U})$, or the probability that all four stones will land faceup, giving the player 10 points.

The list at the right shows all 16 possible outcomes. An outcome of (U,D,D,D) means that only the first stone lands faceup, giving the player 1 point. For 10 points, one outcome is favorable.

$$P(\text{U,U,U,U}) = \frac{1}{16}$$

B. You can use the fundamental counting principle to help you find $P(\text{U,U,U,U})$.

Since each toss has two possible outcomes, there are $2 \times 2 \times 2 \times 2$ possible outcomes for 4 stones.

$$P(\text{U,U,U,U}) = \frac{1}{2 \times 2 \times 2 \times 2} = \frac{1}{16}$$

C. You can also find the probability of two or more independent events by multiplying the probabilities of the individual favorable outcomes.

The probability that a stone will land face up is $\frac{1}{2}$.

$$P(\text{U,U,U,U}) = \frac{1}{2} \times \frac{1}{2} \times \frac{1}{2} \times \frac{1}{2} = \frac{1}{16}$$

Talk About Math Compare the three methods. When might you use the first method? When might that method be difficult?

Check Understanding

For another example, see Set D, pages 534–535.

A coin can land on heads (H) or tails (T). Suppose you toss a nickel, a dime, and a quarter. Find $P(\text{H,H,H})$ by

1. listing all the possibilities.

2. the fundamental counting principle.

3. the method given in Example C.

Practice

For More Practice, see Set D, pages 536–537.

In a version of Totolospi, a Hopi Indian game, players toss three sticks. The sticks have three different colors, but all of them are round on one side and flat on the other.

4. Make a list of the possible outcomes using R for "round" and F for "flat."

Use your list from Exercise 4 to find

5. P(R,F,F). **6.** P(R,F,R). **7.** P(F,F,F).

8. Use the method given in Example B or C to find P(F,F,R). Did you get the same answer?

This Totolospi game board is in the Southwest Museum in Los Angeles, California.

Problem Solving

In the game of Lu-lu, what is the probability of getting the following number of points in one turn? (Hint: For some cases, several different outcomes give the same point total.)

9. 1 point **10.** 2 points **11.** 3 points **12.** 0 points

13. Using the rules for Totolospi at the right, find the number of lines a player would advance in 5 turns with these outcomes: (R,F,F), (R,R,R), (F,R,F), (F,F,F), (R,R,R).

Totolospi Rules

- Advance 1 line on the gameboard for (F,F,F).
- Advance 2 lines for (R,R,R).
- Lose a turn for any combination of R and F.

Critical Thinking Solve each problem.

14. Suppose a bag contains green cubes and blue cubes. If the probability of drawing a green cube is $\frac{3}{4}$, what is the probability of drawing a blue cube?

15. In Problem 14, what is the least number of cubes that could be in the bag?

Midchapter Checkup

Use the spinner to find each theoretical probability.

1. P(2) **2.** P(even number) **3.** P(9)

4. Tim can choose from 4 restaurants and 3 activities afterwards. How many different choices does he have?

5. List the permutations for C A T.

6. A cube has 3 white faces, 2 blue faces, and 1 red face. Find P(red, white, blue) after 3 consecutive tosses.

Problem-Solving Workshop

Real-Life Decision Making

1. Suppose your school wants to order 50 pizzas for a PTA pizza party. How many different kinds of pizza combinations can you get if each pizza has two toppings and can be either thick or thin crust?

2. Survey friends and family members. Ask which type of crust and which toppings they prefer (if only two are allowed). Based on this information, make a list of the pizzas you would order. Justify your decision.

Math-at-Home Activity

Suppose you turn on the radio at a random time. Do you think there will be a commercial playing at that time?

1. Use a stop watch or a clock with a second hand. Select one radio station. Make a record of the total time spent on commercials during 30 minutes.

2. Determine the probability that there will be a commercial at any given time.

$$\text{Probability} = \frac{\text{time spent for commercials}}{\text{30 minutes}}$$

Number-Sense Project

Look back at pages 506–507.

A part of a supermarket receipt is shown below.

1. Make a frequency distribution of the last digits. Do you see a pattern?

2. Notice the items for which the prices do not end in an 8 or a 9. What do you notice about many of these products?

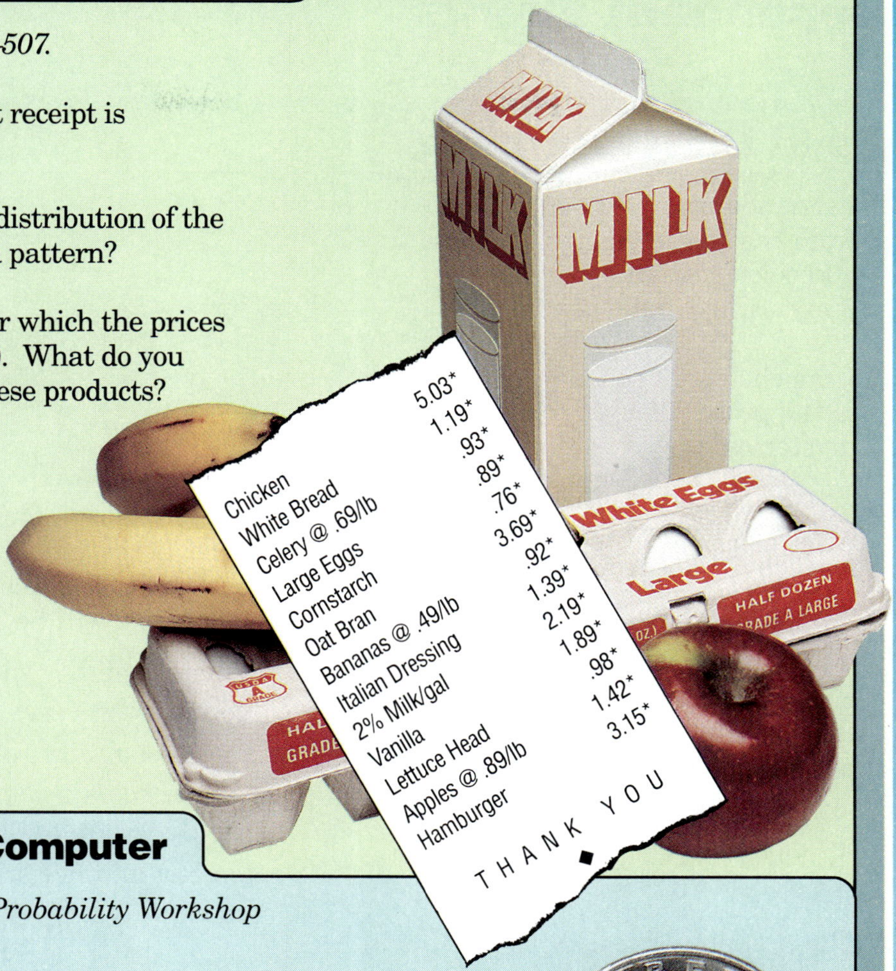

Explore with a Computer

Use the *Graphing and Probability Workshop Project* for this activity.

Jody and Larry are playing a coin tossing game. They toss four coins at a time. Jody gets a point if the result is 3 heads and 1 tail. Larry gets a point if the result is 4 tails.

1. Think about the possible combinations of heads and tails. What is the theoretical probability for each combination?

2. At the computer, toss four coins 100 times. Transform the data into fractions. What is the experimental probability for each combination?

3. Explain how the theoretical probability compares with the experimental probability. Predict who is likely to get the most points.

Dependent Events

Build Understanding

Fernando wants to borrow some books from the library. He will choose from 10 books: 5 science fiction, 3 mysteries, and 2 westerns.

A. If he chooses 2 books at random, what is the probability that both will be mysteries?

To find the probability that two or more events will occur one after the other, multiply their probabilities together.

The probability that the first book will be a mystery is $\frac{3}{10}$. If Fernando does pick a mystery book, then 9 books remain, 2 of which are mysteries. The probability that the second book is a mystery is $\frac{2}{9}$.

$$\frac{3}{10} \times \frac{2}{9} = \frac{6}{90} = \frac{1}{15}$$

The probability that both books will be mysteries is $\frac{1}{15}$. The outcome of the first book chosen influences the outcome of the second book chosen. The two choices are ***dependent events.***

B. If Fernando randomly chooses 3 books, what is the probability that the first book will be a western and the other two books will be science fiction?

The probability that the first book will be a western is $\frac{2}{10}$. Then 9 books remain. The probability that the second choice will be science fiction is $\frac{5}{9}$. Then eight books remain and the probability of getting another science fiction book is $\frac{4}{8}$.

$$\frac{2}{10} \times \frac{5}{9} \times \frac{4}{8} = \frac{40}{720} = \frac{1}{18}$$

The probability of choosing a western first, followed by 2 science fiction books, is $\frac{1}{18}$.

Talk About Math Why can't any probability be a number greater than 1?

Check Understanding

For another example, see Set E, pages 534–535.

A box of old books contains 6 mysteries, 4 westerns, and 2 children's books. Find and match probabilities, assuming that the books are selected randomly.

1. P(mystery, western)

2. P(western, mystery)

3. P(2 westerns, 1 mystery, 1 children's)

a. $\left(\frac{6}{12}\right)\left(\frac{4}{11}\right) = \frac{2}{11}$

b. $\left(\frac{4}{12}\right)\left(\frac{3}{11}\right)\left(\frac{6}{10}\right)\left(\frac{2}{9}\right) = \frac{2}{165}$

c. $\left(\frac{4}{12}\right)\left(\frac{6}{11}\right) = \frac{2}{11}$

d. $\left(\frac{4}{12}\right)\left(\frac{3}{12}\right)\left(\frac{6}{12}\right)\left(\frac{2}{12}\right) = \frac{1}{144}$

Practice

For More Practice, see Set E, pages 536–537.

Tell whether each pair of events is independent or dependent. Explain.

4. Drawing a name from a hat, replacing the name, and drawing another name

5. Drawing a name from a hat, then drawing another name without replacing the first name

You have 20 counters in a bag: 10 red, 6 white, and 4 blue. Once a counter is chosen, it is not replaced. Find each probability.

6. *P*(red, red) **7.** *P*(red, white) **8.** *P*(white, white)

9. *P*(white, red) **10.** *P*(red, red, blue) **11.** *P*(red, white, blue)

A set of 20 cards is labeled with ten 1's, four 2's, three 3's, two 4's, and one 5. Find the probability when the cards are selected one after another without being replaced.

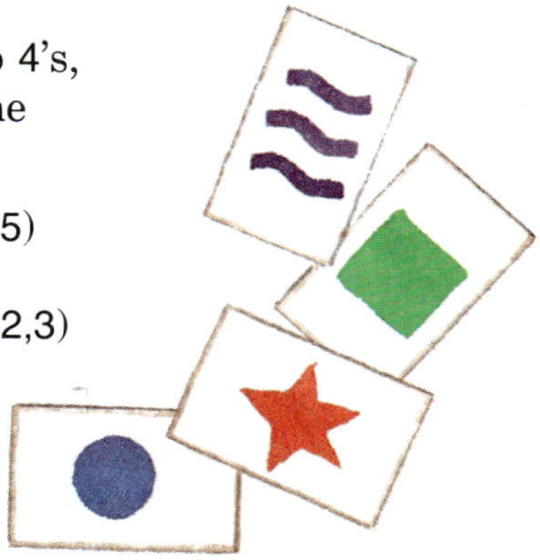

12. *P*(1,5) **13.** *P*(3,4) **14.** *P*(4,5)

15. *P*(2,3) **16.** *P*(3,4,5) **17.** *P*(1,2,3)

Mixed Practice A set of 22 cards has 8 circles, 6 squares, 5 stars, and 3 wavy lines. If no replacement is permitted, find each probability.

18. *P*(circle, circle) **19.** *P*(square, star) **20.** *P*(star, wavy line, square)

Find each probability if the card is replaced after each draw.

21. *P*(circle, circle) **22.** *P*(square, star) **23.** *P*(star, wavy line, square)

Tell if the following describe dependent or independent events.

24. Exercises 18–20

25. Exercises 21–23

Problem Solving

Olivia has collected 40 art books, 20 mysteries, and 10 classic novels.

26. If Olivia selects 3 books from her collection at random, find the probability that all 3 will be mysteries.

27. **Critical Thinking** Find the probability that 2 books Olivia selects at random will either both be art books or both be classic novels.

Solve each problem.

28. Ten students made the following quiz scores: 91, 87, 73, 80, 84, 80, 89, 92, 95, 86. Find the median score.

29. A rectangular field is 80 feet by 60 feet. Find the length of the diagonal distance across the field.

ALGEBRA

Find a Pattern

PROBLEM SOLVING GUIDE

Understand
QUESTION
FACTS
KEY IDEA

Plan and Solve
STRATEGY
ANSWER

Look Back
SENSIBLE ANSWER
ALTERNATE APPROACH

Build Understanding

A. Suppose you flip 4 coins: a penny, a nickel, a dime, and a quarter. In how many different ways can the coins result in 2 heads and 2 tails?

Understand QUESTION How many different arrangements are possible for 4 coins when 2 coins are heads and 2 coins are tails?

FACTS There are 4 coins. Since flipping the 4 coins are independent events the probability that each coin will come up heads (or tails) is $\frac{1}{2}$.

Plan and Solve STRATEGY *Draw a diagram* showing all the possibilities.

P N D Q	P N D Q	P N D Q	P N D Q	P N D Q
H H H H	T H H H	H H T T	H T T T	T T T T
	H T H H	T H H T	T H T T	
	H H T H	T T H H	T T H T	
	H H H T	H T H T	T T T H	
		T H T H		
		H T T H		
All heads, 0 tails **1** way	3 heads, 1 tail **4** ways	2 heads, 2 tails **6** ways	1 head, 3 tails **4** ways	0 heads, 4 tails **1** way

Do you see a familiar pattern?

The pattern is the same pattern found in row 4 of Pascal's triangle. You can use Pascal's triangle whenever the probability of each event in a group is $\frac{1}{2}$.

Pascal's Triangle	Row
1	0
1 1	1
1 2 1	2
1 3 3 1	3
1 4 6 4 1	4

Choose row 4 of the triangle for 4 coins. → **1 4 6 4 1**

↑

Number of tails → **0 1 2 3 4**

ANSWER There are 6 different ways 4 coins can come up 2 heads and 2 tails.

Look Back SENSIBLE ANSWER The diagram accounted for every possibility, so the answer is sensible.

B. How many different paths are there from C to T that spell the word COUNT? The blue line shows one path. You could trace all the other paths in the same way.

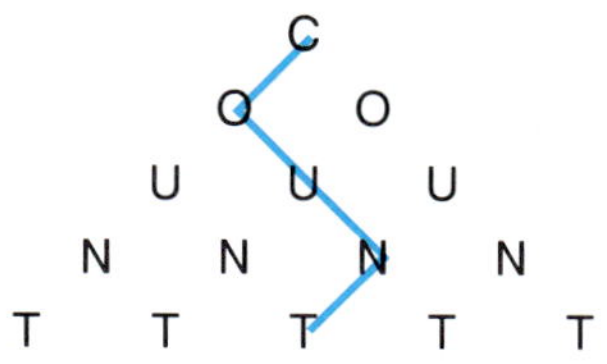

Use Pascal's triangle to find the number of different paths you can take to a certain point.

One shortcut is to substitute row 4 of Pascal's triangle for the fifth row of the diagram.

$$1 \quad 4 \quad 6 \quad 4 \quad 1$$

The number of different ways to get from C to any T is the sum of these numbers.

$$1 + 4 + 6 + 4 + 1 = 16$$

There are 16 different paths from C to T.

Talk About Math
Tell how finding the paths in Example B and tossing coins in Example A are similar.

Check Understanding

1. Explain why you can use Pascal's triangle to solve Example A.
2. In Example A, which row of Pascal's triangle would you use for 6 coins?
3. How could you determine the number of different paths from top to bottom in the word *probability* without drawing the diagram?

Practice

On a string of decorative lights, there is an equally likely probability that any light will be on or off. For 6 lights, how many different patterns are possible with 4 lights on and 2 lights off?

4. Which row of Pascal's triangle would you use to answer this question?
5. Write the numbers in the row you named in Exercise 4. Which number tells the number of different patterns for 4 on and 2 off?
6. What do the other numbers in the row you selected represent?
7. How many different possibilities are there for a string of 8 decorative lights having only 4 lights on?

Solve each problem.

8. A tabletop is shaped like a trapezoid with a height of 70 cm and bases of 80 cm and 100 cm. Find the area of the tabletop.
9. Miss Powell sold $8,000 worth of appliances last month. She receives a commission of 5% on all sales. Find her commission for last month.

ALGEBRA

Using Pascal's Triangle to Find Probability

Build Understanding

In a computer game, a treasure hunter must pass through 4 gates. Random numbers determine if each gate is open or closed. If the random number is even, the gate is open. If the number is odd, the gate is closed.

A. What is the probability that 4 gates will be found in this order: closed, open, open, closed?

You know that you multiply the probabilities of individual events when you want to find the probability that a series of events will occur. In this case, the events are independent and the probability of each event is $\frac{1}{2}$.

$$\left(\frac{1}{2}\right)\left(\frac{1}{2}\right)\left(\frac{1}{2}\right)\left(\frac{1}{2}\right) = \frac{1}{16}$$

The probability that the 4 gates will be closed, open, open, closed is $\frac{1}{16}$.

B. Find the probability that you will find 2 open gates and 2 closed gates in *any* order. Recall that

$$\textit{Probability} = \frac{\textit{Number of favorable outcomes}}{\textit{Total number of outcomes}}$$

Make a list of the possible ways 4 gates can be open or closed.

Key
○ open
● closed

○○○○	●○○○	●●○○	●●●○	●●●●
	○●○○	○●●○	●●○●	
	○○●○	○○●●	●○●●	
	○○○●	○●○●	○●●●	
		●○○●		
		●○●○		
4 open **1** way	3 open **4** ways	2 open **6** ways	1 open **4** ways	0 open **1** way

By listing, you can see that there are 6 ways to have 2 open gates and 2 closed gates, in any order. There are 16 possibilities altogether $(1 + 4 + 6 + 4 + 1 = 16)$. The probability of 2 open gates and 2 closed gates is 6 ways out of 16, which is $\frac{6}{16}$, or $\frac{3}{8}$.

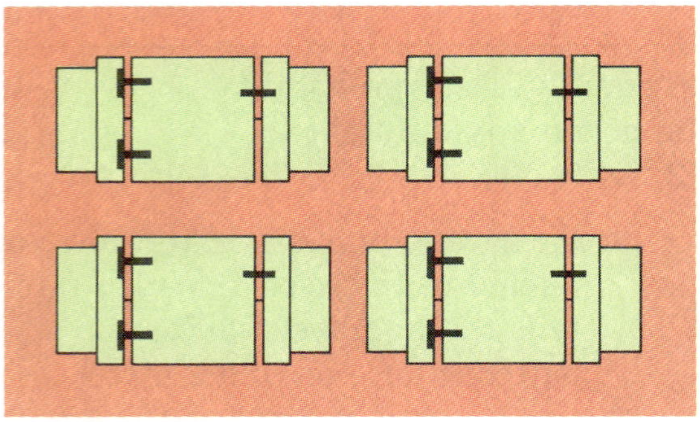

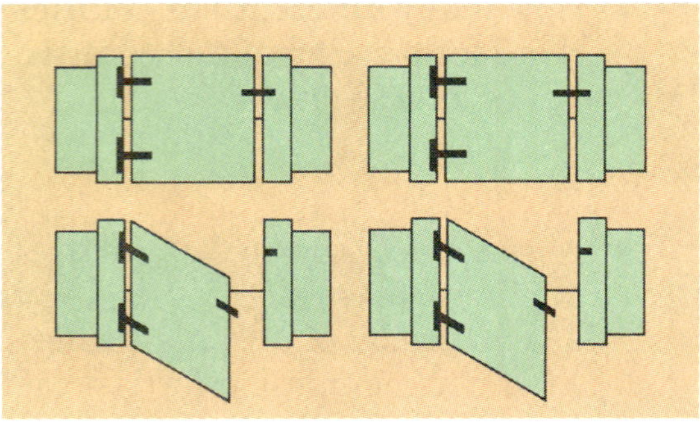

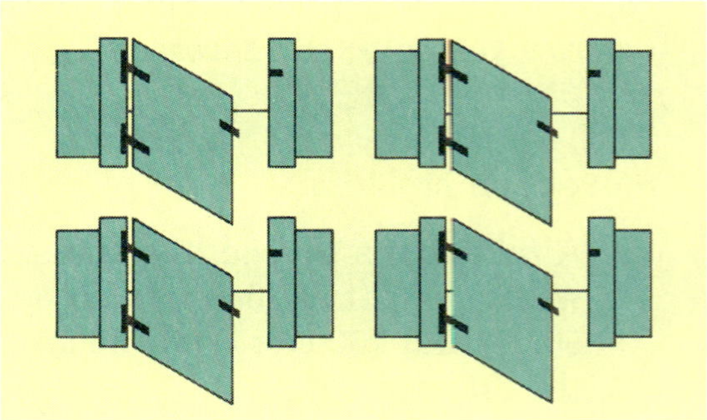

C. You can use Pascal's triangle to solve Example B since the probability for each gate being open or closed is $\frac{1}{2}$, and you are not looking for the gates to be open or closed in any particular order.

Row		Sum of all possible patterns
0	1	1
1	1 1	2
2	1 2 1	4
3	1 3 3 1	8
4	1 4 6 4 1	16
5	1 5 10 10 5 1	32
6	1 6 15 20 15 6 1	64

In Example B, since there are 4 gates, use Row 4 to represent the possible ways 4 gates can be open or closed.

1	**4**	**6**	**4**	**1**
4 open	3 open	2 open	1 open	0 open
1 way	4 ways	6 ways	4 ways	1 way

There are 6 ways that exactly 2 gates will be open. The sum of the numbers in Row 4 gives the number of possible outcomes, which is 16. The probability of 2 open gates and 2 closed gates in any order is $\frac{6}{16}$, or $\frac{3}{8}$.

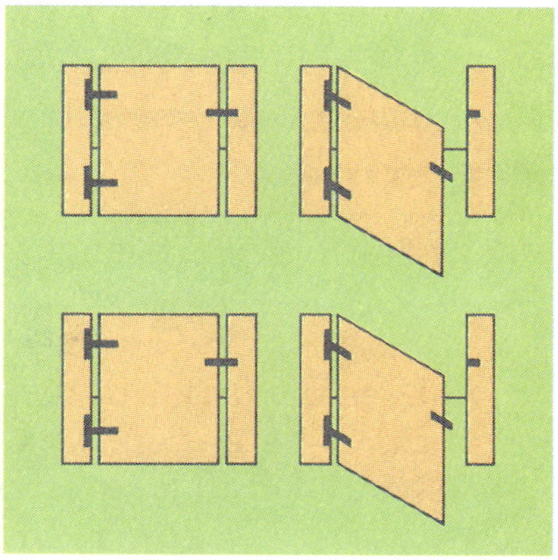

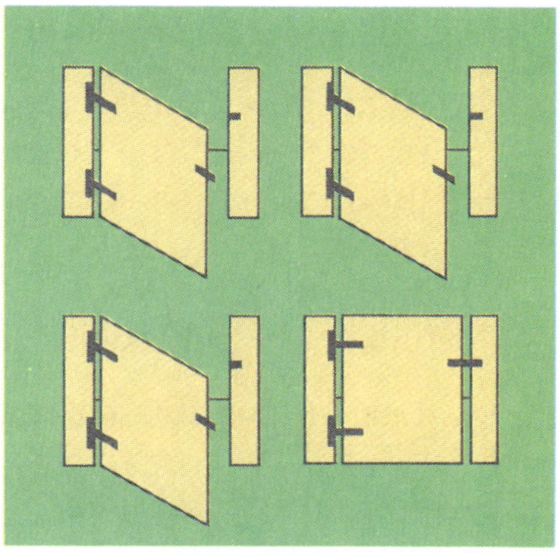

The first fully electronic computer was built in 1946 at the University of Pennsylvania by two engineers, J. Presper Eckert, Jr. and John W. Manchly.

D. What is the probability of finding gates that are either open, open, closed, open or open, closed, closed, open?

Look at the list in Example B. There is only one way in which either of these possibilities can occur. Since there are 16 total possibilities, the probability of either of these events is $\frac{1}{16} + \frac{1}{16}$, or $\frac{1}{8}$.

Talk About Math Why is the answer in Example A $\frac{1}{16}$, while the answer in Example B is $\frac{6}{16}$?

Check Understanding

For another example, see Set F, pages 534–535.

Find the probability of each of the following using 4 gates from the computer game.

1. 4 gates open

2. 4 gates closed

3. 3 gates closed, 1 open

4. Either 2 gates open or 3 gates open

5. 1 open, 3 closed in any order; or 2 open, 2 closed in any order

6. List all the possible outcomes if there were only 3 gates in the game.

Practice

For More Practice, see Set F, pages 536–537.

Row 5 of Pascal's triangle is shown below.

1 5 10 10 5 1

7. Does the first 1 in the pattern mean that 1 gate is open, or that there is 1 way for all 5 gates to be open?

8. Does the first 5 in the pattern mean that there are 5 ways for 4 gates to be open and 1 gate to be closed?

With 5 gates, there are 10 different ways 3 gates can be open and 2 closed, in any order.

9. What other information do you need to determine the probability of finding 3 gates open and 2 gates closed, in any order?

10. Find the probability for Exercise 9.

Each of the 3 light switches shown is equally likely to be on or off.

11. List all possible positions of the switches in the set.

Use Pascal's triangle or list possibilities to find each probability for 3 light switches.

12. All off

13. All on

14. 2 off, 1 on, in any order

15. On, on, off, in this order

16. 2 on, 1 off, in any order

A team is equally likely to win or lose each of 6 games. Use Pascal's triangle to find each probability.

17. Win half, lose half

18. Win 2, lose 4, in any order

19. Win 4, lose 2 in any order

20. Win 6

21. The probability that the team will win 1 out of their first 3 games and 2 out of their next 3 games

When you flip a coin 7 times in a row, heads or tails is equally likely on each toss. Use Pascal's triangle to find each probability.

22. All heads

23. All tails

24. 1 head and 6 tails

25. 4 heads and 3 tails

26. 5 heads and 2 tails

27. 2 heads and 5 tails

Problem Solving

Solve each problem.

28. A computer road race game has 4 intersections. At each intersection, the vehicle is equally likely to turn left or right. What is the probability that it will turn left twice and right twice in any order?

29. In a computer baseball game, the pitcher is equally likely to pitch a strike or a ball. What is the probability that the pitcher will pitch 5 strikes in a row?

30. In a safari computer game, you are equally likely to return with all your luggage as to return with none of it. You start with 6 pieces of luggage. What is the probability that you will return with 3 pieces?

In a computer track game, with 5 hurdles, you are equally likely to clear a hurdle as to knock the hurdle over.

31. What is the probability that you will clear 3 hurdles and knock 2 hurdles over, in any order?

32. What is the probability that your game will have the following result: clear, clear, miss, miss, clear?

33. What is the probability you will clear all 5 hurdles in a row?

34. What is the probability you will clear 4 hurdles and knock over 1 hurdle, in any order?

Reading ——— Math

Vocabulary Fill in the missing words.

1. The likelihood that an event will or will not occur is called the __?__.

2. If the probability of one event has an effect on the probability of another event, the events are __?__.

3. If the probability of one event has no effect on the probability of another event, the events are __?__.

4. The __?__ uses multiplication to find the number of choices.

Combinations

Build Understanding

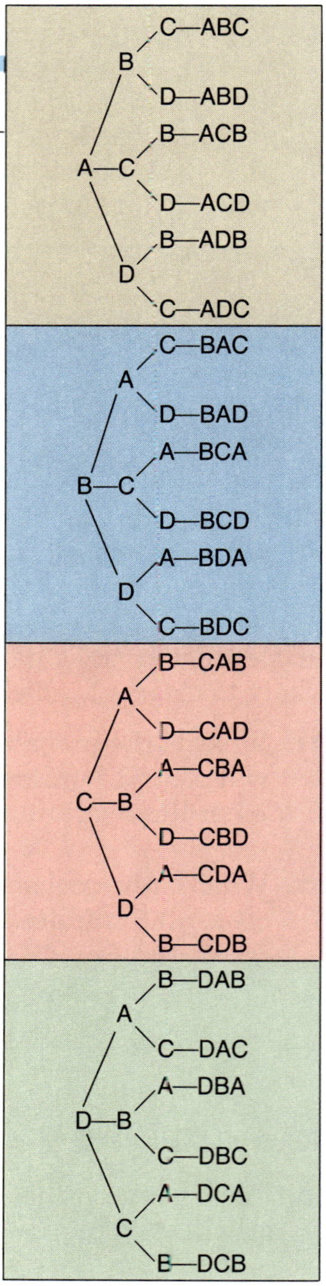

The 24 permutations, or ways to arrange the letters A, B, C, and D into groups of 3 are shown in the tree diagram at the right. A permutation is an arrangement of the elements of a set in a particular order.

Possibilities for 1st letter		Possibilities for 2nd letter		Possibilities for 3rd letter		Total possibilities
4	×	**3**	×	**2**	=	**24**

A. What do you notice about these 6 arrangements taken from the list?

ABC	BAC	ACB
CAB	BCA	CBA

Each arrangement is made up of the same 3 letters, A, B, and C. The only difference is the order in which the letters occur. A ***combination*** is a selection of elements from a set in which the order doesn't matter. Since the 6 permutations listed above are the same 3 letters in different orders, they represent only one combination: ABC.

B. How many 3-letter combinations can you make from the letters A, B, C, and D?

To find the number of combinations, eliminate any permutation that contains the same letters as another permutation. Begin with ABC. Cross out any other 3-letter arrangements that contain the letters A, B, and C. Do the same for ABD, ACD, and so on.

ABC	ABD	~~ACB~~	ACD	~~ADB~~	~~ADC~~
~~BAC~~	~~BAD~~	~~BCA~~	BCD	~~BDA~~	~~BDC~~
~~CAB~~	~~CAD~~	~~CBA~~	~~CBD~~	~~CDA~~	~~CDB~~
~~DAB~~	~~DAC~~	~~DBA~~	~~DBC~~	~~DCA~~	~~DCB~~

Once you have crossed out all the permutations that are rearrangements of the same 3 letters, you are left with the combinations. There are 4 three-letter combinations of A, B, C, and D.

Talk About Math

The examples show fewer combinations than permutations. Will this always be true? Why?

Check Understanding

For another example, see Set G, pages 534–535.

1. A selection in which order *does not* matter is called a ____?____.

2. A selection in which order *does* matter is called a ____?____.

3. The number of permutations is always ____?____ than the number of combinations.

4. The arrangements ABC, CAB, and ACB are three ____?____ and one ____?____.

Practice

For More Practice, see Set G, pages 536–537.

Use the words *NAP* and *PAN* for Exercises 5–8.

5. Are these words permutations of the letters A, N, and P? Explain.

6. Are these words combinations of the letters A, N, and P? Explain.

7. List all of the 3-letter permutations of the letters A, N, and P.

8. List all of the 3-letter combinations of the letters A, N, and P.

Problem Solving

Explore Math

Find the number of possible combinations of 18 items taken four at a time. You could make a list, but this would take a long time.

To find a more efficient method, *solve some simpler problems*.

9. Make a list to find the number of combinations for three letters, A, B, and C, taken two at a time.

10. Compute to find the number of permutations for three letters taken two at a time. (See page 516, Example D.)

11. Compute to find the number of permutations for two letters.

12. Divide the answer for Problem 10 by the answer for Problem 11.

13. Does your answer to Problem 12 match your answer to Problem 9?

14. Repeat the steps in Problems 9–13. Find the number of combinations for four letters taken two at a time.

15. Find the number of combinations for four letters taken three at a time.

16. Use this method to find the number of combinations for 18 letters taken four at a time.

Skills Review

Ted has 8 T-shirts: 2 blue, 3 white, 1 red and 2 black. Find each theoretical probability if he selects one at random.

1. P(blue) **2.** P(white)

3. P(blue or black) **4.** P(green)

Find the total number of choices.

5. A bicycle comes in 8 colors, 3 choices of handlebars, and 2 seat choices.

6. Balloons come in 5 sizes, 15 colors and 8 designs.

Calculate the number of permutations.

7. 6 horses **8.** 8 hats

A box contains 20 balls: 10 black, 6 white, and 4 blue. Find each probability.

9. P(blue, white) if the balls are replaced

10. P(blue, white) without replacement

11. P(blue, blue) if the balls are replaced

12. P(blue, blue) without replacement

Each of 5 light switches is equally likely to be on or off. Use Pascal's triangle to find each probability.

13. P(all on) **14.** P(1 on 4 off)

15. P(2 on, 3 off) **16.** P(at least 4 on)

Find the number of combinations and permutations for each.

17. 5 colors taken 2 at a time

18. 4 names taken 3 at a time

Problem-Solving Review

Solve each problem.

19. There are 2 red marbles, 3 yellow marbles, a green marble, and a blue marble in a bag. What is the theoretical probability of drawing a red or blue marble?

20. The probability of snow on a winter day in Frostbite is $\frac{1}{3}$. Predict how many times it will snow in 45 days.

21. Shirts come in 6 sizes, 7 colors, and 4 styles. Find the number of choices.

22. In how many ways can a captain, a co-captain, and an equipment manager be chosen from a team of 20 players?

23. In your sock drawer there are 5 red pairs of socks, 3 blue pairs, and 2 yellow pairs. Without looking, you reach into the drawer 3 times and pull out a pair of socks without replacing them. What is the probability that you will choose a red pair, then a blue pair, and then a yellow pair?

24. **Data File** Use the data on pages 572–573. In how many ways can 10 compact discs be loaded into the CD player? If you load CDs with 12, 12, 5, 10, 10, and 8 tracks in that order, what is the probability that track from disc 6 will play when the RANDOM button is pressed?

25. **Make a Data File** Use a reference source to write a 10-question multiple-choice test consisting of questions that force the test-taker to guess each answer. (For example: What is the Zip Code of Keswick, England?)

Cumulative Skills Review · Chapters 1–14

Write an equation to solve each problem. Then solve the equation.

1. 10% of what number is 9.4?

2. 40% of 80 is what number?

3. 54 is what percent of 60?

4. 64 is 25% of what number?

Compute.

5. $36 - 3 \times 3$

6. $20 \div 5 - 2$

7. $6.06 \div 1.01$

8. $-35 - (-17)$

Describe the sample you would need to predict the sale of each item.

9. Cereal

10. Cat food

11. Exercise bikes

12. Popcorn

13. Make a box plot using these data: 62, 65, 68, 75, 78, 80, 93, 85, 82.

Find the missing number.

14. 38 oz = ▒ lb ▒ oz

15. 3 ft 5 in. = ▒ in.

16. 27,000 mm = ▒ m

Write each solution set as an inequality.

17. $m - 7 \geq -5$

18. $-2x < -8$

19. $y - 3.4 \geq 0$

Tell whether each number is rational or irrational.

20. $-3\frac{2}{7}$

21. $\sqrt{130}$

22. $\sqrt{225}$

23. $\frac{29}{41}$

The two triangles are similar. Find the missing measurements.

24. $m\angle X$

25. $m\angle Z$

26. BC

27. XY

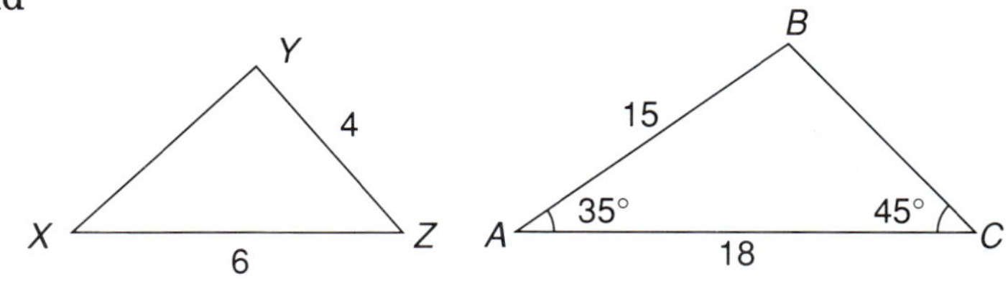

Make the appropriate graph for each set of data.

28.

Team	Bears	Lions	Sox	Jays
Games Won	9	12	5	7

29.

Week	1	2	3	4	5
Tickets Sold	28	45	70	94	115

Find the value of each of the following.

30. 5!

31. 3!

32. 10!

33. 7!

34. 2!

35. 4!

Use the letters P, L, A, N for Exercises 36–37.

36. How many 4 letter permutations are there?

37. How many 2 letter combinations are there?

Reteaching

Set A pages 508–511

The frequency table at the right shows the results of an experiment in which 25 colored slips of paper, five of each color, were drawn from a box, and replaced after each draw.

Color	Tally	Frequency
Red	𝍸 𝍸	10
Green	𝍸 ||||	9
Yellow	𝍸 𝍸 ||	12
Blue	𝍸 |	6
White	𝍸 𝍸 |||	13

Find the experimental and the theoretical probabilities of drawing a green slip.

Experimental: Favorable outcomes→ / Total outcomes→ $\frac{9}{50}$

Theoretical: Favorable outcomes→ / Possible outcomes→ $\frac{5}{25} = \frac{1}{5}$

Remember that the probability of any outcome is a number from 0 to 1.

Use the table at the left to find each experimental probability.

1. P(red) **2.** P(yellow)

3. P(blue) **4.** P(white)

5. P(red or blue) **6.** P(green or blue)

Find each theoretical probability.

7. P(red) **8.** P(yellow)

9. P(red or blue) **10.** P(yellow or white)

Set B pages 514–515

Fundamental Counting Principle
If there are *m* possibilities for one outcome, *n* possibilities for another outcome, and *z* possibilities for a third outcome, there are $m \times n \times z$ different possibilities.

Remember that you can use a tree diagram to check answers obtained with the Fundamental Counting Principle.

Find the total number of choices.

1. A dairy company makes custard-style and regular yogurt in 3 different sizes and 12 different flavors.

2. Ninth-graders choose from among 10 classes, 6 activities, and 8 sports.

Set C pages 516–517

A permutation is a unique arrangement of people or objects.

A	One permutation
AB ***BA***	Two permutations
ABC ***CBA*** ***BCA*** ***BAC*** ***CAB*** ***ACB***	Six permutations

You can find the number of permutations without listing them.

Number of choices for 1st letter		Number of choices for 2nd letter		Number of choices for 3rd letter		Total choices
3	×	**2**	×	**1**	=	**6**

Remember that you can write a product like 3 × 2 × 1 as a factorial: 3!.

List the permutations.

1. Miguel, Lisa, Mary **2.** 2 4 6 8

3. Calculate the number of permutations for A B C D E F G.

4. Find the value of 11!.

5. Tell why the number of choices decreases for each letter in the example at the left.

Set D pages 518–519

Use the spinner at the right to find each probability.

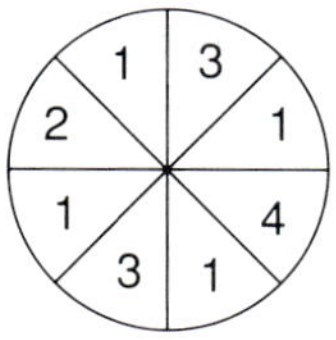

P(1) = $\frac{4}{8}$ ←Favorable outcomes ←Possible outcomes

P(3) = $\frac{2}{8}$ ←Favorable outcomes ←Possible outcomes

P(1, 3) = P(1) × P(3)

P(1, 3) = $\frac{4}{8} \times \frac{2}{8} = \frac{8}{64} = \frac{1}{8}$

Remember that two events are independent when the first event does not affect the second event.

Use the spinner at the left to find each probability.

1. P(1, 2) **2.** P(2, 3)

3. P(3, 3) **4.** P(2, 2)

5. P(1, 1) **6.** P(2 even numbers)

Set E pages 522–523

Find the probability of drawing a star and then a heart if two cards are drawn without replacement.

P(star) = $\frac{2}{5}$ ←Favorable outcomes ←Possible outcomes

P(heart) = $\frac{2}{4}$ ←Favorable outcomes ←Possible outcomes

P(star, heart) = P(star) × P(heart)

P(star, heart) = $\frac{2}{5} \times \frac{2}{4} = \frac{4}{20} = \frac{1}{5}$

Remember that two events are dependent when the outcome of the first event influences the outcome of the second event.

Use the cards at the left to find each probability.

1. P(heart, diamond)

2. P(2 hearts)

3. P(2 diamonds)

Set F pages 526–529

Use Pascal's Triangle to find the probability of getting 2 tails and 3 heads after five tosses of a coin.

Since there are 5 tosses, use row 5.

1	**5**	**10**	**10**	**5**	**1**
All heads	1 tail	2 tails	3 tails	4 tails	All tails
1 way	5 ways	10 ways	10 ways	5 ways	1 way

The sum of the patterns in row 5 is 32, so the probability of getting 2 tails and 3 heads is $\frac{10}{32}$, or $\frac{5}{16}$.

Remember that Pascal's Triangle can only be used with probability questions in which two equally likely outcomes are possible and the order of the outcomes is not important.

Find each probability for five tosses of a coin.

1. All heads **2.** All heads or all tails

3. 2 heads **4.** 1 head or 1 tail

Set G pages 530–531

Look at the six permutations of the letters A, B, and C in Set C.

A combination is a unique *selection* of people or objects. Each of the six permutations is made up of the same three letters A, B, and C, so the six permutations represent only one combination.

Remember that the number of combinations is always less than the number of permutations.

1. Find the number of two-letter combinations of A, B, and C.

2. Find the number of three-number combinations of 5, 8, 7, 2.

More Practice

Set A pages 508–511

Give the theoretical probability for each outcome.

1. You will ride a bike or not ride a bike tomorrow.

2. You will be selected at random from a group of 7 students to work a problem at the chalkboard.

The frequency table at the right shows the results of an opinion poll. Use the table to find each experimental probability.

3. P(Like) **4.** P(Neutral) **5.** P(Dislike)

Opinion	Tally	Frequency
Like	𝍸 𝍸 𝍸 ||	17
Neutral	𝍸 𝍸 ||||	14
Dislike	𝍸 ||||	9

Set B pages 514–515

Find the total number of choices a customer would have.

1. A delicatessen offers 3 choices of bread, 8 meats, and 4 cheeses for sandwiches.

2. Seven varieties of canned vegetables in three different sizes come packed in either a cream sauce or water.

3. A department store sells socks in 3 sizes, 6 colors, and 4 styles.

4. A paper company sells 15 kinds of paper in 42 colors and 2 sizes.

5. A cafeteria sells 4 different kinds of juice in 3 different sizes, with or without ice.

6. A store sells cabinets in 4 different types of wood, 10 different finishes, and 3 different styles.

7. A shoe store sells 111 different styles of shoes in 8 different colors and 12 sizes.

8. A department store sells T-shirts in 5 sizes, 8 colors and 4 styles.

Set C pages 516–517

List the permutations.

1. 7 9

2. R T C W

3. 2 4 6

4. ADN

5. 1 3 5 8

6. ILOS

Calculate the number of permutations.

7. A B C
D E F

8. 0 1 2 3 4
5 6 7 8 9

9. Four shrubs, three trees, in any order

10. Seven students

11. Five cars

12. Eleven hats

Find the value of each of the following.

13. 5!

14. 6!

15. 7!

16. 8!

17. 9!

18. 10!

Set D pages 518–519

A number chosen at random is either even (E) or odd (O).

1. Make a table showing all the possible ways you can pick three numbers in a row. One example is EOE.
2. Refer to the table you made for Exercise 1. What is the probability that the pattern will be EEO?
3. Show how you could have used another method to find the answer to Exercise 2.
4. What is the probability that the pattern will be EEE?
5. What is the probability that the pattern will be EEE or OOO?
6. What is the probability that the pattern will not be EEE?
7. What is the probability that the pattern will be EOE or OEO?
8. What is the probability that the pattern will have exactly 2 E's in it?

Set E pages 522–523

Exercises 1–8 refer to 25 lettered cards in a box: 13 A's, 4 B's, 4 C's, 3 D's, and 1 E. Find each probability when the cards are selected one after another without being replaced.

1. P(A, A)
2. P(A, E)
3. P(B, D)
4. P(C, C, A)
5. P(A, B)
6. P(B, C)
7. P(A, B, C)
8. P(C, D, E)

Set F pages 526–529

Each circle in a computer-generated design is equally likely to be black or white. Use Pascal's Triangle to find each probability for a row of four circles.

1. 2 white, 2 black in any order
2. All white
3. All black
4. 3 white, 1 black in any order

Suppose that boys and girls are equally likely to be born. Use Pascal's triangle to find each probability for a family with five children.

5. All girls
6. 3 boys, 2 girls in any order
7. At least 4 boys
8. Exactly 4 girls

Set G pages 530–531

List all the three-letter combinations of each group of letters.

1. N Q S
2. R D A Z
3. B T S V M

List all the three-letter permutations.

4. Exercise 1
5. Exercise 2

Enrichment

Random Walks and Fractals

The first square selected to begin a random walk may or may not ever reach the center square.

The photograph above shows a computer model of one type of **fractal.** This fractal is a random shape. Fractals occur frequently in nature—mountains, clouds, and coastlines, for example. Fractals cannot be described with the terms *point* and *line* that we use to describe geometric shapes.

A computer program that illustrates a fractal like the one above opens with a square, *A*, at the center of a circle. Another square, *B*, located on the circle is sent on a **random walk.** In a random walk, it is equally likely that each step will be taken up or down or left or right.

Square *B* continues its random walk until it either moves outside the circle or touches square *A*. Then square *B* is frozen, and another randomly selected square *C* begins its random walk on the circle, until it touches another square, and so on.

It can take hours for all the squares selected by a computer program to complete their random walks!

1. What is the probability that the first step of a random walk taken by the square at the right will cause it to disappear?

2. What is the probability that the random walk taken by the square at the right will consist of steps 1–5 exactly as shown?

3. Tell why you think a computer fractal illustration program takes so long to run. (Hint: Use your answers to Exercises 1 and 2 above.)

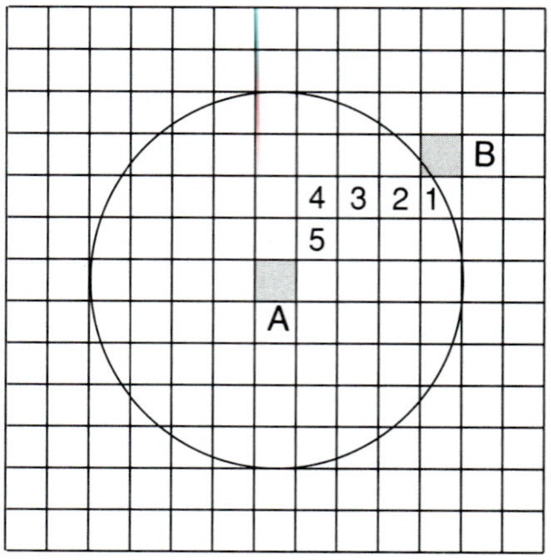

Chapter 14 Review/Test

4	5	6	0	8	5	1	4	5	5
9	7	8	8	0	3	5	6	6	3
2	8	3	2	4	8	3	3	4	2
5	2	4	5	3	7	4	8	1	6
0	9	3	3	4	8	7	0	1	0

A hospital wants to determine the probability of a boy or girl baby being born in the next 50 births.

1. Use the random table above to simulate the next 50 births. Use odd numbers to represent boys. Find the experimental probability that a boy was born.

2. What is the theoretical probability for the question in Item 1?

3. In how many different ways can 9 students sit in the first four seats on the school bus?

The table at the right shows the main courses and vegetables you can order at the cafeteria.

Main course	Vegetable
Fish	Peas
Beef	Carrots
Fowl	Broccoli
	Beans
	Lettuce

4. How many different ways could you order a main course and a vegetable?

5. If the cafeteria ran out of beans and carrots, how many ways could you order a main course and vegetable?

6. List the permutations and 3-letter combinations for TSU.

Find each value.

7. 5!

8. 7!

A single-serving package of mixed nuts contains 14 peanuts, 6 cashews, 5 filberts, and 3 brazil nuts. Find each probability for 2 nuts selected from the package at random, one after another.

9. P(2 peanuts)

10. P(1 cashew, 1 filbert)

11. Which is an appropriate method for solving the following problem?

In a computer game, your car is equally likely to clear a traffic cone or to hit the cone and knock it over. What is the probability that you will have this pattern: clear, hit, clear, hit, hit in any order?

a. Make a frequency table.
b. Use Pascal's Triangle.
c. Draw a probability tree diagram.

1
1 1
1 2 1
1 3 3 1
1 4 6 4 1

12. Use the diagram above to tell how many different ways four coins can come up 3 heads and 1 tail.

Use the spinner to find each probability.

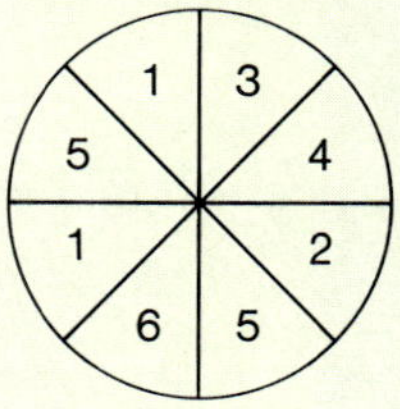

13. $P(1, 1)$

14. $P(4, 5)$

15. $P(\text{odd number})$

16. **Write About Math** Explain how the probability changes for Item 10 if the cashew is returned to the package before the filbert is drawn.

Mathematical Reasoning 15

Did You Know: Six common sailboats include the catboat, sloop, cutter, schooner, yawl, and ketch. You can classify them by considering such things as the number of masts and their positions, and the number of sails.

Number-Sense Project

Estimate
Look at the boat pictured below right. How many masts do you see? How many sails?

Gather Data
Determine some of the ways the six kinds of boats differ from one another.

Analyze and Report
Put your information in a chart. Use it to help you classify the boats in these pictures.

ALGEBRA

Sets and Subsets

Build Understanding

Soccer is the most popular sport in the world. Soccer as it is played today was developed in England in the 1800s. Today it is played by millions of people in more than 140 countries around the world.

The most famous soccer competition is the World Cup, an international competition that is held every four years. The following table shows the winners of all fourteen World Cup competitions.

The World Cup					
Year	Winner	Year	Winner	Year	Winner
1930	Uruguay	1958	Brazil	1978	Argentina
1934	Italy	1962	Brazil	1982	Italy
1938	Italy	1966	England	1986	Argentina
1950	Uruguay	1970	Brazil	1990	W. Germany
1954	W. Germany	1974	W. Germany		

Pelé, the famous Brazilian soccer player, scored 1,363 goals in his career, a record unapproached by anyone else.

A. Use both **roster notation** and **set builder notation** to name the countries that have won a World Cup. The roster notation lists each **element,** or member. The set builder notation describes the elements in words.

Roster notation:
{Uruguay, Italy, W. Germany, Brazil, England, Argentina}

Set builder notation:
$\{x \mid x \text{ is a country that has won the World Cup}\}$

This is read "The set of all x such that x is a country that has won the World Cup."

The largest soccer stadium in the world is Brazil's Maracana Stadium in Rio de Janeiro. It has a capacity of 200,000 people.

Another popular international sport is ice hockey. The modern rules for ice hockey originated in Canada, where it is the national sport.

A hockey puck often travels at a rate of over 100 miles per hour.

B. Suppose A and B are sets. Then $A \cap B$ is read, "the ***intersection*** of A and B" or "A ***intersection*** B." $A \cap B$ is the set of elements in both A and B.

Let A be the set of all hockey positions: goaltender (g), center (c), left wing (lw), right wing (rw), left defense (ld), and right defense (rd). Let B be the set of forwards—center, left wing, right wing—and the manager (m). Name the intersection of A and B in both roster notation and set builder notation.

Roster notation:	**Set builder notation:**
$A = \{g, c, lw, rw, ld, rd\}$	$A = \{x \mid x \text{ is one of the six hockey positions}\}$
$B = \{c, lw, rw, m\}$	$B = \{x \mid x \text{ is a forward position, and the manager}\}$
$A \cap B = \{c, lw, rw\}$	$A \cap B = \{x \mid x \text{ is an element of both Set } A \text{ and Set } B\}$

C. Suppose Q and R are sets. Then $Q \cup R$ is read, "the ***union*** of Q and R" or "Q ***union*** R." $Q \cup R$ is the set of all elements in Q and all elements in R.

Suppose Q is the set of the first five positive integers and R is the set of the first three positive even integers. Name $Q \cup R$ in both notations.

Roster notation:	**Set builder notation:**
$Q = \{1, 2, 3, 4, 5\}$	$Q = \{x \mid x \text{ is one of the first five positive integers}\}$
$R = \{2, 4, 6\}$	$R = \{x \mid x \text{ is one of the first three positive even integers}\}$
$Q \cup R = \{1, 2, 3, 4, 5, 6\}$	$Q \cup R = \{x \mid x \text{ is one of the first six positive integers}\}$

D. When every element in a set M is also an element in a set K, we say that M is a ***subset*** of K. For example, the set of all squares is a subset of the set of all rectangles. Also, every set is a subset of itself, and the ***empty set,*** $\varnothing$, a set which has no elements, is a subset of every set. The list of all subsets of $\{a,b\}$ is $\varnothing$, $\{a\}$, $\{b\}$, $\{a,b\}$.

Talk About Math How are each of the sets $\{a, a, b, c\}$, $\{b, a, c\}$, and $\{a, w, b\}$ related to the set $\{a, b, c\}$?

Check Understanding

For another example, see Set A, pages 566–567.

Consider these sets: $A = \{x \mid x \text{ is a positive integer less than } 10\}$ and $B = \{3, 6, 9, 12\}$.

1. Write A in roster notation.

2. Write B in set builder notation.

3. Write set $A \cap B$ and $A \cup B$ in roster notation.

4. Write all the subsets of set B.

Practice

For More Practice, see Set A, pages 568–569.

Write each set in roster notation.

5. $A = \{x \mid x$ is a prime number less than ten$\}$

6. $B = \{x \mid x$ is a positive odd number less than ten$\}$

7. $C = \{x \mid (x - 6)$ is a positive integer less than ten$\}$

8. $D = \{x \mid (x + 3)$ is a positive number less than 10$\}$

Determine all the sets from Exercises 5–8 to which each element belongs.

9. 2

10. 5

11. 9

12. 12

Next to sumo wrestling, the most popular sport in Japan is baseball.

Sets R and S represent the team sports in two schools.

R = {baseball, basketball, ice hockey, football, soccer}
S = {baseball, lacrosse, football, basketball}

13. Write $R \cap S$ in roster notation.

14. Write $R \cup S$ in roster notation.

Solve.

15. List all the subsets of {center, right wing, left wing}.

16. List all the subsets of $\{p, q, r, s\}$.

Use the sets A, B, C, and D in Exercises 5–8 to solve Exercises 17–30. **Remember** to include all members in the set.

17. Write set $A \cup C$ in roster notation.

18. Write set $A \cap C$ in roster notation.

19. Write set $B \cap C$ in roster notation.

20. Write set $B \cup C$ in roster notation.

21. Write set $B \cup D$ in roster notation.

22. Write set $B \cap D$ in roster notation.

23. Write set $A \cap B$ in roster notation.

24. Write set $A \cup B$ in roster notation.

25. Write set $C \cap D$ in roster notation.

26. Write set $C \cup D$ in roster notation.

27. Is it true that {6, 7, 8, 9} is a subset of $B \cap C$? Explain.

28. Is it true that {9, 11} is a subset of $A \cap C$? Explain.

29. Is it true that {3, 7} is a subset of $A \cap B$? Explain.

30. Is it true that {10, 11, 12} is a subset of $B \cup C$? Explain.

Problem Solving

Critical Thinking Find each answer. **Remember** to count the empty set as a subset of every set.

31. Find the total number of subsets possible for each given set. $\{p\}$; $\{p, q\}$; $\{p, q, r\}$; $\{p, q, r, s\}$

32. How many subsets are there for the set $\{p, q, r, s, t\}$? Hint: Find a pattern in your answer for Exercise 31.

33. Guess how many subsets there are for a set with 7 members. (Use the pattern from Exercise 32.)

Use your knowledge of sets and of probability to solve each problem.

34. If you pick a position at random from set A of Example B, what is the probability that it is the goaltender position?

35. If you pick a position at random from set A of Example B, what is the probability that it is a forward position?

36. If you choose a subset at random from Exercise 15, what is the probability that "center" is a member?

37. If you choose a subset at random from Exercise 16, what is the probability that it contains exactly two elements?

Explore ________ Math

The first team at the international hockey camp has six members. How many ways can a three-member committee be formed? To answer this question, first solve Problems 38–40.

38. For set $\{p\}$, how many 0-element (empty set) subsets are there? 1-element subsets?

39. For set $\{p, q\}$, how many 0-element subsets are there? 1-element subsets? 2-element subsets?

40. For set $\{p, q, r\}$, how many 0-element subsets are there? 1-element subsets? 2-element subsets? 3-element subsets?

Youth hockey programs worldwide help beginning players develop both team and individual skills.

Use Data Compare your answers to Problems 38–40 with Pascal's Triangle on page 12. Find and use a pattern to solve Problems 41 and 42.

41. For the hockey team with 6 members, how many ways could a 3-member committee be formed?

42. How many ways can a committee of four be formed from the members of the hockey team?

ALGEBRA

Venn Diagrams

Build Understanding

Venn diagrams use shapes to show how sets are related.

A. The school principal announced over the school's public address system: "All members of the football squad report to the auditorium at 2 P.M. All members of the orchestra report to the music room at 2 P.M." The six students who belong to both the football team and the orchestra are faced with a conflict. The relationship between the set of football players and the set of orchestra members is seen in the Venn diagram below.

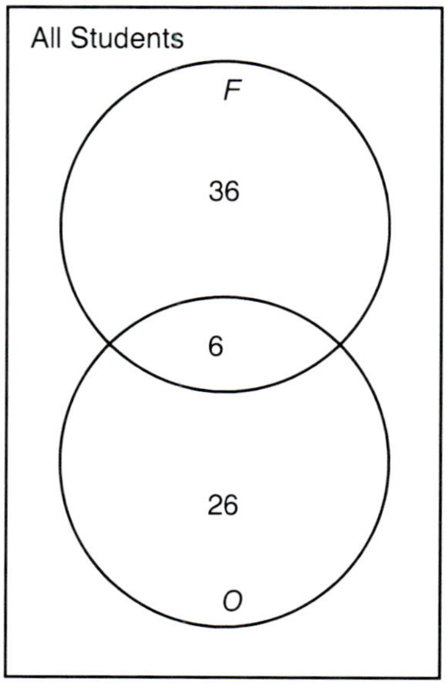

The rectangle represents all students in the school. Circle F shows students who are on the football squad (36 + 6). Circle O shows students who are in the orchestra (26 + 6). The portion where the circles overlap shows the students (6) who are in both groups. The Venn diagram shows the ***intersection*** of set F and set O, or

$F \cap O$ = {**6 students who are in the orchestra and on the football squad**}

B. What relationship does this Venn diagram show?

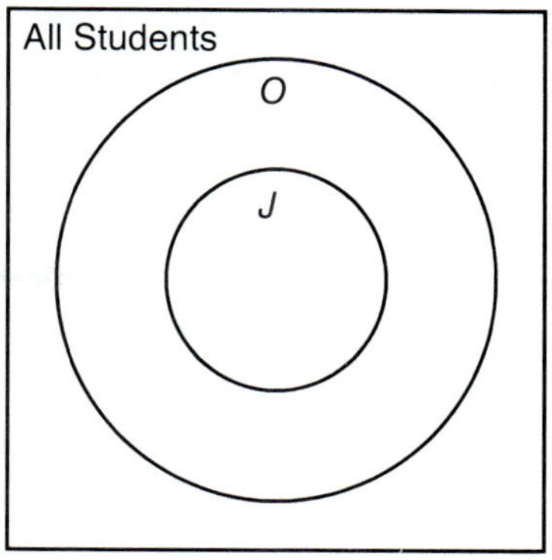

Rectangle	Set of all students
Circle *O*	Set of students in the orchestra
Circle *J*	Set of students in the jazz band

The Venn diagram shows that the set of students in the jazz band is a *subset* of the set of students in the orchestra. All members of the jazz band are also members of the orchestra.

C. This school year, no one in the jazz band is also in chorus. Draw a Venn diagram to show this relationship.

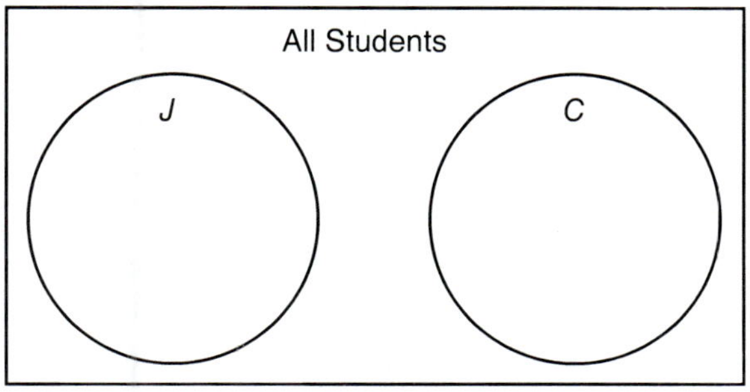

Rectangle	Set of all students
Circle *J*	Set of students in the jazz band
Circle *C*	Set of students in the chorus

The circles do not overlap, showing that no student is in both the jazz band and in the chorus. These two sets are called ***disjoint sets***. In set notation, these disjoint sets can be written as

$J \cap C = \varnothing$ — The intersection of disjoint sets is always the empty set ($\varnothing$).

Talk About Math Consider set *W* of all wooden objects in your classroom. Name some sets of objects in your classroom that are disjoint with set *W*. Name some sets of objects in your classroom that are subsets of *W*.

Check Understanding

For another example, see Set B, pages 566–567.

Find each answer.

1. Name two subsets of the set of food that would overlap in a Venn diagram.
2. Use a Venn diagram to show how the set of heavy metal music is related to the set of all music.
3. Use a Venn diagram to show how fiction is related to nonfiction in the set of literature.
4. Name three other sets of students that could be included in Example B.
5. In Example B, what does set $O \cup J$ represent?
6. In Examples A and C, what does $J \cup F$ represent?

Practice

For More Practice, see Set B, pages 568–569.

Find each answer. **Remember** to label your diagrams.

7. Draw a Venn diagram to show the set of all squares and the set of all rectangles as subsets of all parallelograms. Label each set.

8. Draw a Venn diagram to show the relationship between the set of all odd numbers and the set of all prime numbers as subsets of all positive numbers.

9. Use the set of whole numbers 1 through 12 to draw a Venn diagram showing the relationship between set T, all numbers divisible by 3, and set F, all numbers divisible by 4. How many elements does set $T \cap F$ have? How many elements does set $T \cup F$ have?

10. Draw a Venn diagram to show set W, all numbers that are divisible by 2, and set F, all numbers that are divisible by 4, as subsets of the whole numbers from 1 to 12. How many elements does set $W \cap F$ have? How many elements does set $W \cup F$ have?

11. **Number Sense** Draw a Venn diagram that shows the relationship between the odd numbers and the composite numbers in the set {5, 6, 7, 8, 9, 10, 11, 12, 13, 14, 15}.

12. Draw a Venn diagram to show the set S of scalene triangles, the set R of right triangles, and the set I of isosceles triangles as subsets of all triangles.

Mixed Practice Use your knowledge of sets and Venn diagrams to find each answer.

13. Use roster notation to show the intersection of all vowels in the words *violin* and *piano*.

14. Use a Venn diagram to show the intersection of all vowels in the words *violin* and *piano*.

15. Use roster notation to show the union of all consonants in the words *violin* and *piano*.

16. Use a Venn diagram to show the union of all consonants in the words *violin* and *piano*.

17. Use roster notation to list a subset of all words that can be made from the set of letters in the word *violin*.

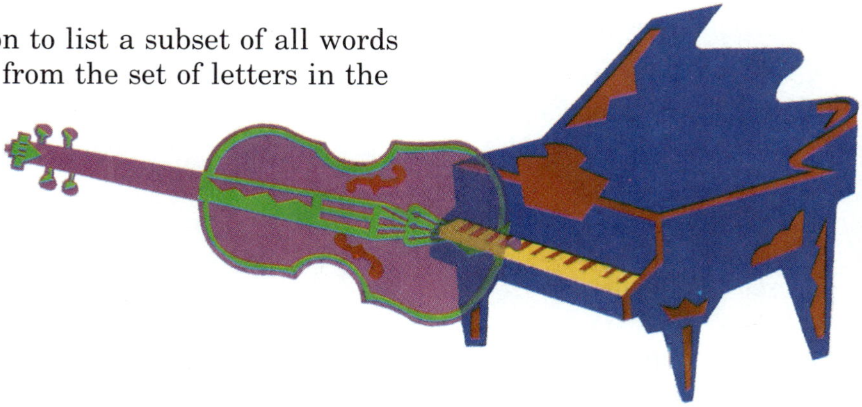

Problem Solving

Solve each problem.

18. Describe the information that the following Venn diagram shows.

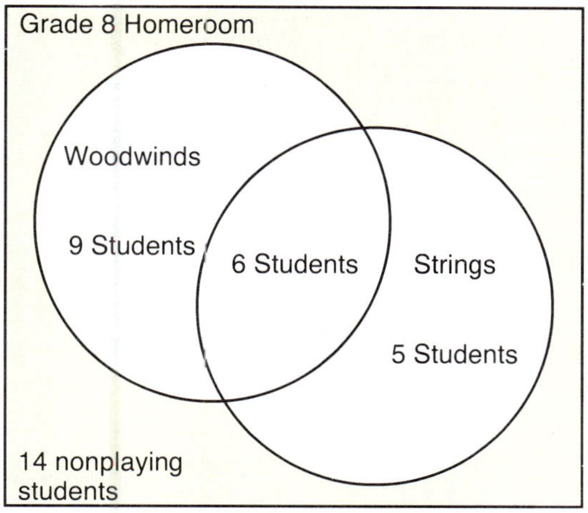

19. There are 34 students in the orchestra. Of these, 17 are also in the choir, 6 are in the choir and the glee club, and 10 are in neither. Use a Venn diagram to show how many orchestra students participate in exactly one other activity.

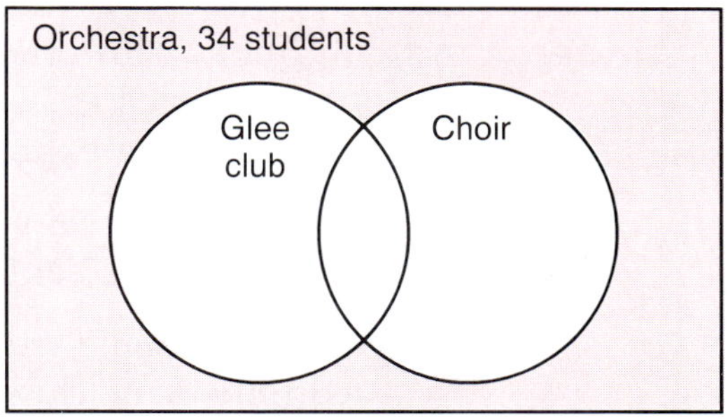

Skills Review pages 518–519, 522–523

A can holds 8 colored cubes: 2 red, 3 blue, 2 green, and 1 yellow. Suppose you draw one cube, replace it, and then draw another cube. Find each probability.

1. That both cubes you draw are red

2. That both cubes you draw are blue

3. That you draw a green cube and then a yellow cube

4. Are the events in Exercise 3 dependent or independent?

Now, suppose you draw one cube, keep it, and then draw another cube. Find each probability.

5. That both cubes you draw are red

6. That both cubes you draw are blue

7. That the first cube is green and the second is yellow

8. Are the events in Exercise 6 dependent or independent?

ALGEBRA

Draw a Diagram

PROBLEM SOLVING GUIDE

Understand
QUESTION
FACTS
KEY IDEA

Plan and Solve
STRATEGY
ANSWER

Look Back
SENSIBLE ANSWER
ALTERNATE APPROACH

Build Understanding

Of the 28 students in Mr. Aho's art class 15 entered in the modeling exhibit for the art show and 26 entered in the painting exhibit. How many students could have entered in both exhibits?

Understand

QUESTION How many students might have entered in both the painting and the modeling exhibits?

FACTS Out of 28 students, 15 entered models, and 26 entered paintings.

KEY IDEA Some students entered in both exhibits or neither exhibit.

Plan and Solve

STRATEGY *Draw a* Venn *diagram.* Circle M represents students in the modeling exhibit. Circle P represents students in the painting exhibit. The intersection of the circles represents students in both exhibits.

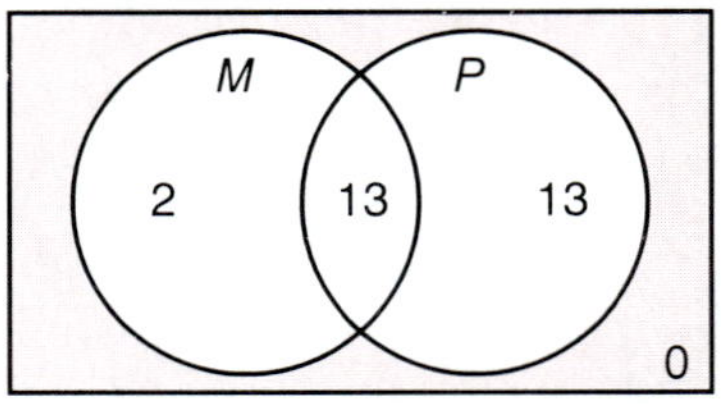

Case I: Two students entered only a model.

Since 26 of the 28 students entered paintings, two students did not. For those two students, consider three cases: **I:** both entered a model, **II:** only one entered a model, or **III:** neither entered a model. For Case **I,** write a 2 in circle M. A total of 15 students entered a model, so 13 students must have entered in both exhibits. Write 13 in the intersection. Then find $26 - 13$, or 13 to determine the number of students who entered only a painting. Put this number in circle P outside the intersection.

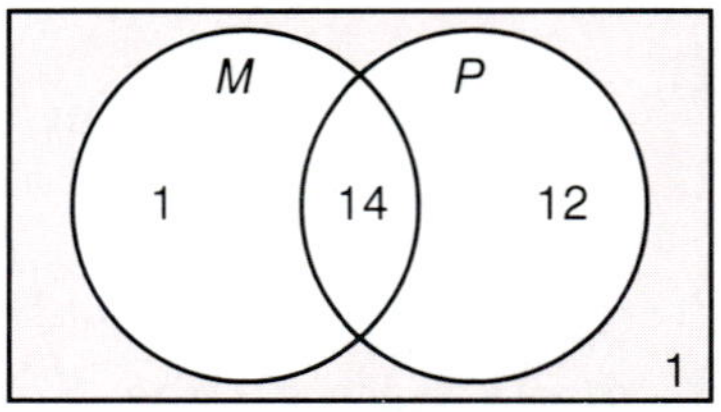

Case II: One student entered only a model.

Similarly, Venn diagrams can show Cases II and III.

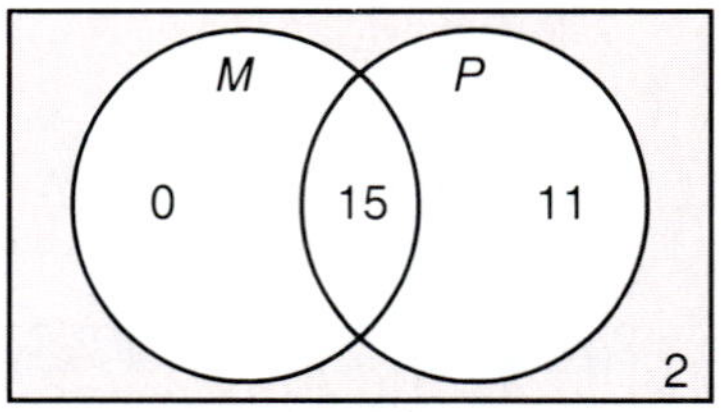

Case III: No students entered only a model.

ANSWER Students in both exhibits are represented in the intersection of the circles. Either 13, 14, or 15 students entered in both exhibits.

Look Back SENSIBLE ANSWER Check each diagram to see that the total number of students in the class is 28, that the number entering the modeling exhibit is 15, and that the number entering the painting exhibit is 26. The answers check.

Talk About Math What information would you need to know to give a single answer to the problem?

Check Understanding

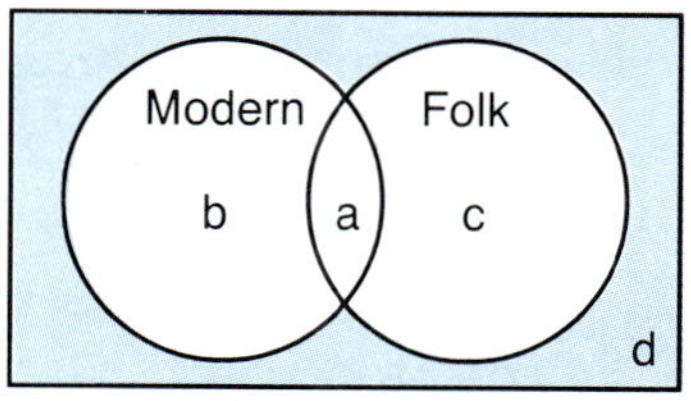

In a survey of 98 students, Mr. Aho found that 71 like modern art, 47 like folk art, and 32 like both. Copy the Venn diagram shown. Do Exercises 1–4 to find the number of students who like neither kind of art.

1. In section *a* write the number of students who like both kinds of art.

2. In section *b* write the number of students who like modern art but do not like folk art.

3. In section *c* write the number of students who like the folk art but do not like modern art.

4. How many students like neither kind of art? Enter this number in section *d*.

Practice

In a survey of 115 students, Mr. Aho found that 80 students like Andy Warhol's work, 65 like Georgia O'Keeffe's work, and 15 don't like either. Use a diagram to answer the questions.

5. How many students like the work of both artists?

6. How many like Warhol's work, but not O'Keeffe's?

7. How many like O'Keeffe's work, but not Warhol's?

8. How many like the work of only one of the two artists?

Copy and complete the Venn diagram to solve Problem 9.

9. Mr. Aho has 33 students in another art class. Twenty-nine students are oil painting (circle *O*), 14 are finger painting (circle *F*), 24 are painting in watercolors (circle *W*), and 10 of these students are using all three media. Every student who is painting in watercolors is also painting in oils, and only 3 students are using both oils and finger paints, but not watercolors. How many students are not doing any type of painting?

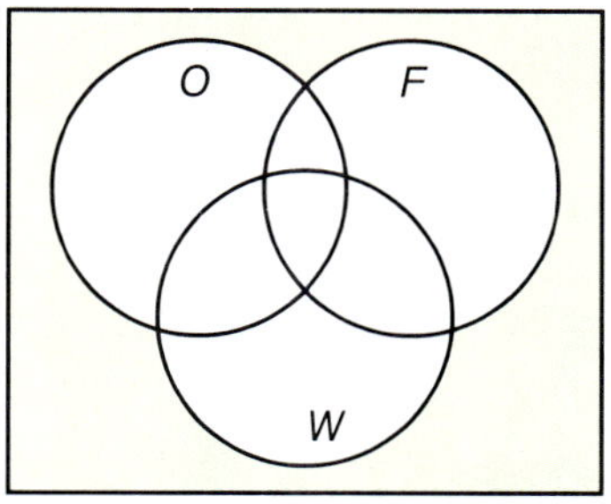

ALGEBRA

Compound Statements

Build Understanding

In mathematics, simple statements are often put together with the words *and* and *or*. The result is a ***compound statement.*** Compound statements, like simple statements, can be true or false.

A. An *and* statement is true when both parts of the statement are true. An *and* statement is false when one part or both parts of the statement are false.

and

P: 24 is composite **and** 24 is a multiple of 12.
Q: 19 is prime **and** 19 is even.

Statement P is true.
Statement Q is false.

B. An *or* statement is true when either one or both parts of it are true. An *or* statement is false when both parts of it are false.

or

R: 15 is a composite **or** 15 is a multiple of 6.
S: 9 is prime **or** 9 is even.

Statement R is true.
Statement S is false.

C. Another type of compound statement is the ***if-then*** statement. An *if-then* statement is true when both parts are false, or when the *if* part is false and the *then* part is true, or when both parts are true. An *if-then* statement is false only when the *if* part is true and the *then* part is false.

U: If 21 is even, then 21 is composite.
V: If 9 is even, then 9 is a multiple of 2.
W: If 15 is composite, then 15 is a multiple of 2.

Statement *U* is true because the *then* part is true, even though the *if* part is false.
Statement *V* is true because both parts are false.
Statement *W* is false because the *if* part is true and the *then* part is false.

The table at the right may help you determine when an *if-then* statement is true.

If part	*Then* part	*If-then*
True	True	True
True	False	False
False	True	True
False	False	True

if then

D. Every *if-then* statement has a corresponding statement that is its ***converse***. The converse of a statement is formed by reversing the two parts of the *if-then* statement. Statement Y below is the converse of statement X.

X: If a number is even, then 2 times that number is even.
Y: If 2 times a number is even, then the number is even.

Notice that statement X is true, but statement Y is false. For example, 2×3 is an even number, but 3 is an odd number. The converse of a true *if-then* statement is not necessarily true. Always check the converse of an *if-then* statement to determine if it is true.

Write About Math Write a true *if-then* statement whose converse is also true.

Check Understanding

For another example, see Set C, pages 566–567.

Tell whether the statement is true or false.

1. 9 is even and 7 is prime.

2. 5 is a whole number and 13 is odd.

3. $\frac{3}{4}$ is a proper fraction or $\frac{3}{4}$ is even.

4. $\frac{3}{4}$ is an integer or $\frac{3}{4}$ is odd.

Find a number that makes each statement true. Then find a number that makes each statement false.

5. ▒ is odd and ▒ is prime.

6. ▒ is composite or ▒ is a multiple of 5.

7. If ▒ is odd, then ▒ is prime.

8. If ▒ is prime, then ▒ is odd.

Practice

For More Practice, see Set C, pages 568–569.

Write the converse of each *if-then* statement. Then decide whether the converse is true or false.

9. If a polygon is a square, then it is a rectangle.

10. If n^2 is an even number, then n is an even number.

11. If a number is not prime, then it is composite.

12. If a triangle is equilateral, its sides are of equal length.

13. If a number is not composite, then it is prime.

14. If a number less than 10 is composite, then it is a square number.

Problem Solving

Solve each problem.

15. If you choose one of the numbers 1–10 at random, what is the probability that it is a composite number or a square number?

16. What is the probability that the number chosen in Exercise 15 is composite and square?

17. The Bukowski brothers made these statements. If Gordon told the truth, who else must have told the truth?

Gordon: "If the key is in the box, then it is in the kitchen."
Hank: "If the key is in the kitchen, then it is in the box."
Buddy: "If the key is not in the box, then it is not in the kitchen."
Patrick: "If the key is not in the kitchen, then it is not in the box."

18. The Santos sisters made these statements. If Vera told the truth, who else must have told the truth?

Lucy: "If the map is in the car, then it is not in the garage."
Sandy: "If the map is not in the car, then it is in the garage."
Vera: "If the map is in the garage, then it is in the car."
Clarice: "If the map is not in the car, then it is not in the garage."

TIPS FOR PROBLEM SOLVERS

Don't give up. Some problems take longer than others.

Reading ____ Math

Numbers and Symbols The Venn Diagram is divided into sections labeled 1–7. Each number can stand for any letter in its section. Find words for each group of numbers.

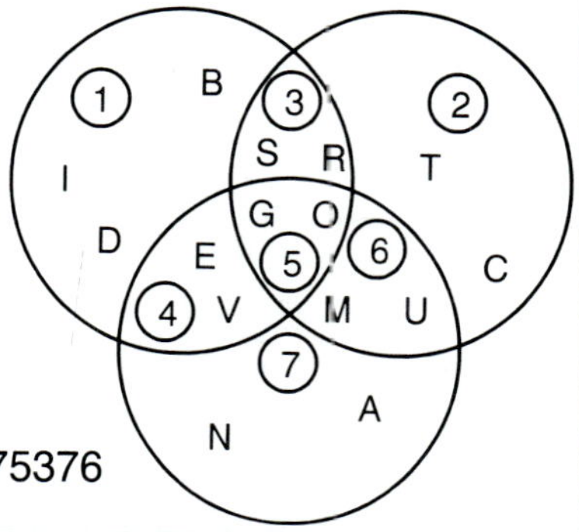

1. 342 **2.** 67157 **3.** 361342

4. 353243 **5.** 25744334 **6.** 4477 1175376

Midchapter Checkup

Solve the following problems using sets Q, R, S, and T.

$Q = \{1, 3, 5, 9\}$ $R = \{2, 4, 5, 8\}$ $S = \{1, 3, 6\}$ $T = \{5, 8, 9\}$

1. Write set $Q \cup R$ in roster notation.

2. List the subsets of $Q \cap S$.

3. Is the set $R \cup S$ equal to the set $\{x \mid x$ is the set of integers from 1 to 10$\}$?

4. List the subsets of $S \cap T$.

Use your knowledge of Venn diagrams to find each answer.

5. No one in the computer club is on the debate team, but some of the members of the computer club make up the entire chess club. Draw a Venn diagram to show this.

6. Draw a Venn diagram using the set of whole numbers 1 through 10 to show the relationship between set P, all prime numbers, and set I, all numbers that can be divided by 3. Which elements are not contained in $P \cup I$?

There are 47 superheroes in Heroland. Of these, 26 can fly, 15 have heat vision, and 10 only think they are superheroes and can do neither. Use a Venn diagram to answer the questions.

7. How many superheroes can both fly and have heat vision?

8. How many can fly, but don't have heat vision?

9. How many have heat vision but cannot fly?

10. How many have only one superpower?

Tell whether the statement is true or false.

11. 2 is odd or 10 is composite.

12. 17 is prime and 3 is a whole number.

13. If n is even, then $n + 1$ is odd.

14. 52 is a multiple of 4 or 23 is composite.

15. 8 is a square number and 8 is an integer.

16. If 2 is an odd number, then 12 is a composite number.

Write the converse of each if-then statement. Then decide whether the converse is true or false.

17. If a triangle is isoceles, then two of its sides are of equal length.

18. If n is negative, then n^2 is positive.

Explore as a Team

Suppose you have a 15-foot ladder. You want to determine where you can safely place the bottom of the ladder so that it doesn't slide or tip.

1. To simulate a ladder and a person climbing it, make five strips of cardboard that are each 6 inches long. Mark and label 5 dots as shown in the diagram.

Tape a nickel on each strip, each at a different position. The nickels will simulate people at different positions on the ladder. Tape the coins as shown.

2. Find a "wall" and a "floor" on which to lean your ladders. Place a centimeter ruler on the floor at right angles with the wall.

Take turns with your team members testing the ladders for the different positions of the nickels. For each position, find the closest distance (C) and the farthest distance (F) from the wall where the ladder won't fall. Determine the range where the ladder is safe ($F - C$).

3. Make a table of your results. What do you notice?

4. Explain how you could use your results to determine the safety range of a15-foot ladder.

TIPS FOR WORKING TOGETHER

Work as a group. If you understand, help another group member. Don't work ahead of the others.

Explore with a Computer

Use the *Spreadsheet Workshop Project* for this activity.

1. At the computer, use each of the numbers 1, 2, 3, 4, 5, 6, 7, 8, and 9 once to complete the magic square. The sum of each row, column, and diagonal must be the same.

2. Add a 5 to each of the numbers in your magic square. What happens to the sums?

3. Choose any number. Multiply each number in your magic square by that number. What happens to the sums?

4. What do you think will happen to the sums if you divide each number in your magic square by 12? by 15? by any number?

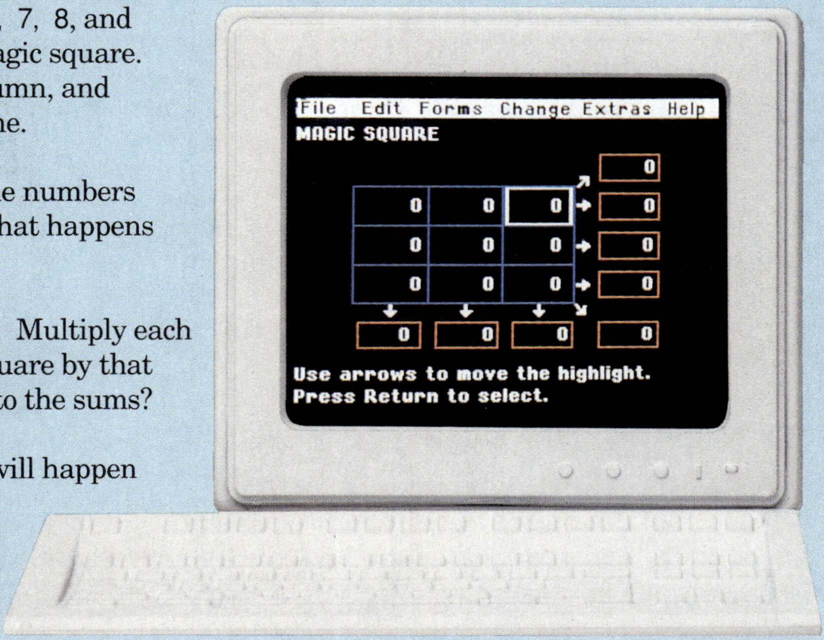

Number-Sense Project

Look back at pages 540–541.

Flow charts can also be used to classify numbers and polygons.

Use the chart below to classify each of the following numbers as prime or composite.

1. 28 **2.** 87 **3.** 61 **4.** 91

5. Make a flow chart to classify triangles according to sides.

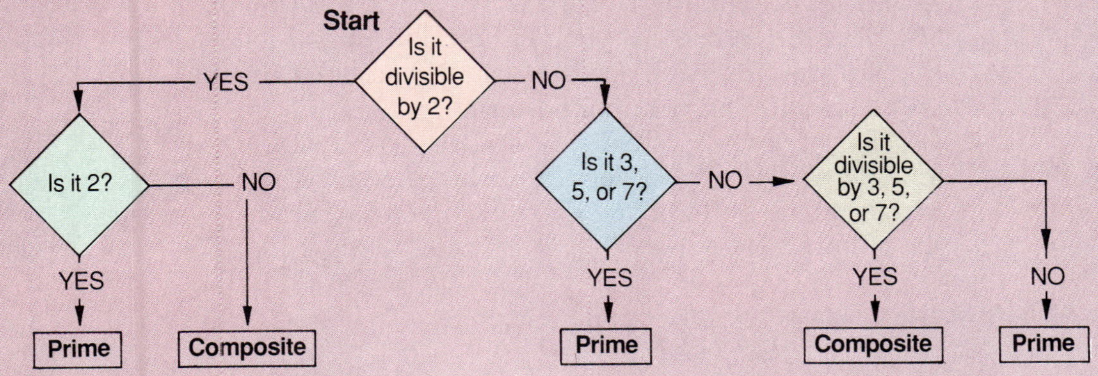

Work Backward

Build Understanding

ACTIVITY

The Dime-to-Dollar Auction
Materials: Markers to represent coins from 1¢ to 10¢
Groups: Teams of 3 or 4, each team playing the game

At a rummage-sale auction, the final bid of exactly $1 wins the item being sold. The opening bid and each following bid can range only from 1¢ to 10¢. What bidding strategy should you use to win? Play the game to see how it works.

PROBLEM SOLVING GUIDE

Understand
QUESTION
FACTS
KEY IDEA

Plan and Solve
STRATEGY
ANSWER

Look Back
SENSIBLE ANSWER
ALTERNATE APPROACH

Understand QUESTION How can you guarantee that you will make the final bid of $1?

FACTS Each bid can only be increased by 1¢, 2¢, and so on, up to 10¢. You win by being able to bid $1.

KEY IDEA Find a pattern in the bidding. Use this pattern to ensure that the final bid is $1.

Plan and Solve STRATEGY *Work backward* from the end of the bidding. If you bid 90¢ to 99¢, the next bidder will win. If you bid 89¢, the next bidder can bid only from 90¢ to 99¢, and you can win.

Next, look for a bid that will allow you to reach the 89¢ bid. If you bid 78¢, the next bid will be between 79¢ and 88¢, and you will then be able to bid 89¢ and then $1. Continue to work backward from 78¢. The next bid you want is 67¢, then 56¢, and so on. Note the pattern: You want bids 1¢ more than a multiple of 11¢.

ANSWER The winning pattern is 1¢, 12¢, 23¢, 34¢, 45¢, 56¢, 67¢, 78¢, 89¢, $1. If you bid first, bid 1¢ and follow the pattern after each opposing bid. If you bid second, try to bid into the winning pattern.

Look Back SENSIBLE ANSWER Work forward using the pattern. Increase bids by 1¢ to 10¢ to check if you can produce the winning bid.

■ **Talk About Math** How would the problem change if you could bid from 1¢ to 15¢?

Check Understanding

Manuel wants to share his marbles. He gives Yoko 3 more than $\frac{1}{2}$ of them. He then gives Benny 6 more than $\frac{1}{3}$ of what is left. He then gives Toshiko 12 more than $\frac{1}{4}$ of what is left. Manuel now has 24 marbles. How many did he start with?

1. Work backward. How many marbles did Manuel have before his gift to Toshiko? Hint: Guess and check.

2. Use your answer to Exercise 1 to find how many marbles Manuel had before his gift to Benny.

3. Use your answer to Exercise 2 to find how many marbles Manuel had before his gift to Yoko.

4. Check your answers by working forward from your answer to Exercise 3.

Practice

Solve each problem by working backward.

5. Suppose the auction is changed so that each bid is 1¢ to 20¢ higher. The goal is still \$1. What is the winning strategy?

6. If Manuel gave Yoko $\frac{1}{2}$ of his marbles plus 1 more marble, then gave Benny $\frac{1}{2}$ of what was left plus 1, then gave Toshiko $\frac{1}{2}$ of what was left plus 1, and then had 24 marbles left, how many marbles did he start with?

7. In the language club $\frac{2}{3}$ of the members take Spanish. Of the remaining members $\frac{1}{2}$ take French, $\frac{1}{3}$ take Japanese, and 4 people take German. How many members are in the club?

Choose a Strategy

Dog Days How old are these three dogs? The product of their ages (rounded to the nearest year) is 36. The sum of their ages equals Don's age. King and Rover are Rusty's puppies from the same litter.

8. Make a list of all sets of three whole numbers whose product is 36. Could one of the dogs be 7 years old?

9. Don knows his age, but couldn't find the ages of the dogs with the second clue. Why not?

10. How does the last clue help? How old are the dogs?

PROBLEM SOLVING STRATEGIES

- Choose an Operation
- Solve a Simpler Problem
- Use a Formula
- Write an Equation
- Make a Graph
- Draw a Diagram
- Make a Table
- Try and Check
- Find a Pattern
- Work Backward

Inductive and Deductive Reasoning

Build Understanding

Scientists and mathematicians use intuition and reasoning to help them understand the world we live in. Two types of reasoning used are called ***inductive*** and ***deductive.***

A. When you make several specific observations and then develop a general rule, you use ***inductive reasoning.*** A statement that is believed to be true but not yet proved is called a ***theory*** in science and a ***conjecture*** in mathematics.

Ms. Tchai's class substituted the numbers 1 through 11 into the expression $2n^2 + 1$. Each entry produced a multiple of 3 or a prime number. Using inductive reasoning, they conjectured that $2n^2 + 1$ would always produce a prime or a multiple of 3.

n	$2n^2 + 1$	
1	3	prime
2	9	3×3
3	19	prime
4	33	3×11
5	51	3×17
6	73	prime
7	99	3×33
8	129	3×43
9	163	prime
10	201	3×67
11	243	3×81
12	289	17×17

To see whether the conjecture was true, they extended the table to 12.

It fails at $n = 12$, since $2(12)^2 + 1 = 289$, which is neither a multiple of 3 nor prime.

A conjecture is often hard to prove. A conjecture can be disproved by finding one ***counterexample,*** which is an example that does not fit the pattern.

B. When you use a general rule to solve a problem, you use ***deductive reasoning.***

Eldon noticed that $n^2 + n + 2$ is even for every whole number value for n he tried. He used general rules to show that this will always hold true. He reasoned that the whole number n must be either even or odd.

(1) If n is even, then so is n^2. Then $n^2 + n$ is even and so is $n^2 + n + 2$.
(2) If n is odd, then so is n^2. Then $n^2 + n$ is even and so, $n^2 + n + 2$ is also even.

■ **Talk About Math** Suppose the expression in Example A did work for $n = 12$. What could the class conclude?

Check Understanding

For another example, see Set D, pages 566–567.

1. Why is solving the equation, $3x + 5 = 17$ an example of deductive reasoning?

2. Suppose you drew three different sets of two intersecting lines and measured all the angles. What might you conclude? Which type of reasoning did you use?

Practice

For More Practice, see Set D, pages 568–569.

Tell whether you would use inductive or deductive reasoning to decide if the statement is true or false.

3. If n is a whole number (but not 0), then $n^2 + 1$ is prime.

4. A number is ***abundant*** if the sum of its factors (excluding the number itself) is greater than the given number. Therefore, 20 is not abundant.

5. The sum of any two odd numbers is even. (Hint: An odd number equals an even number plus 1.)

6. The sum of any sequence of whole numbers starting with 1 is $(n)(n + 1) \div 2$.

Show that the indicated statement above is true or false. Use deductive or inductive reasoning.

7. Exercise 3
8. Exercise 4
9. Exercise 5
10. Exercise 6

Problem Solving

Calculator Test each conjecture. If you think the conjecture is true, show why. If you think it is false, find a counterexample to show that it is false. **Remember** that n is a whole number.

11. $2^n + 2n - 1$ is prime for $n \neq 0$.

12. $n^2 + 3$ is even or prime.

13. $n^2 + n + 11$ is always prime.

14. $2^n + n$ is prime if n is odd.

Solve. Tell whether you use deductive or inductive reasoning.

15. What is the next number in the sequence below?
1, 7, 3, 9, 5, . . .

16. Brothers and sisters I have none, but that man's father is my father's son. To whom am I referring?

17. What is the next letter in this sequence? **b, d, f, h, k, . . .**

18. What is the next number in this sequence? **1.5, 2.5, 4.0, 6.0, 8.5, . . .**

Use Logical Reasoning

Build Understanding

At a costume party Julio, Bert, Neil, and Larry asked Lin to guess which of them were dressed as an astronaut, a surgeon, a clown and a monster. He recognized Julio's voice as the monster's. Bert wasn't the surgeon and the astronaut was neither Larry nor Bert. Who was Larry?

Understand QUESTION What was Larry's costume?

FACTS Julio is the monster. Bert is not the surgeon. The astronaut is not Larry or Bert.

KEY IDEA Each boy is in a different costume.

Plan and Solve STRATEGY *Use logical reasoning.* Summarize the facts in a table. Place a √ in the table when you know who someone is. Put an X in the table when you know someone isn't in that costume.

	Astronaut	Surgeon	Clown	Monster
Julio	X	X	X	√
Bert	X	X		X
Neil				X
Larry	X			X

Since Julio is a monster, he can't be in any other costume and none of the other boys is a monster.

	Astronaut	Surgeon	Clown	Monster
Julio	X	X	X	√
Bert	X	X	√	X
Neil	√	X	X	X
Larry	X		X	X

The only possibility left for Bert is the clown. The only possibility left for the astronaut is Neil. Mark the possible √s and then all the possible Xs. This leaves Larry as the surgeon.

ANSWER Larry is the surgeon.

Look back SENSIBLE ANSWER Reread the problem to be sure that your answer does not contradict any of the given conditions.

PROBLEM SOLVING GUIDE

Understand
QUESTION
FACTS
KEY IDEA

Plan and Solve
STRATEGY
ANSWER

Look Back
SENSIBLE ANSWER
ALTERNATE APPROACH

■ **Write About Math** Make up a similar type of problem that deals with three people and their occupations. Check your problem so you are certain there is only one possible solution.

Check Understanding

Amy, Betsy, and Clarissa came to the party as a bride, a pilgrim and a pumpkin. Betsy is not the pumpkin. Either Amy or Betsy is the pilgrim. Answer each question.

1. Set up a table of rows and columns that considers all possibilities.
2. Fill in an X to show that Betsy is not the pumpkin.
3. Fill in an X to show that the pilgrim is either Amy or Betsy.
4. If Clarissa is the bride, who is Betsy?
5. If Betsy is the bride, who is Clarissa?

Practice

Holly tried to guess which of her friends was dressed as the rock star, gorilla, chicken, and rabbit. She knew that Dee was taller than the rock star or the gorilla. Elizabeth was either the gorilla or the rabbit, and either Jasmine or Stacy was the chicken. The rock star definitely wasn't Stacy.

6. Set up a table that shows the given information.
7. Use logical reasoning to decide who is wearing what costume.

"What would you see if you went to Texas?" To find out, solve this letter equation, $(\text{SEE})^2 = \text{TEXAS}$, where each letter represents a different digit from 0 through 9.

8. What are the possibilities for S if $(\text{SEE})^2$ is 5 digits?
9. What are the possibilities for S if it is the last digit of a square? (For example, no square ends in 7.)
10. From Problems 8 and 9, what is S?
11. What are the possible digits for E? (Hint: Try all possibilities by using a calculator.)
12. Give the value of each of the letters of $(\text{SEE})^2 = \text{TEXAS}$.
13. Use the values of the letters from the letter equation to decode this message: 0 13039!

Skills Review

Use sets A and B for Exercises 1–5.
$A = \{x|x \text{ is an even digit less than } 10\}$
$B = \{x|(x - 2) \text{ is a positive number less than } 9\}$.

1. Write set A in roster notation.

2. Write set B in roster notation.

3. Write set $A \cap B$ in roster notation.

4. Write set $A \cup B$ in roster notation.

5. Is {2, 4, 6} a subset of B?

Use sets M and N for Exercises 6–7.
$M = \{x|x \text{ is a positive number less than } 10\}$. $N = \{x|x \text{ is a composite number less than or equal to } 10\}$

6. Draw a Venn diagram for $M \cap N$.

7. How many elements does $M \cup N$ have?

Write the converse of each *if-then* statement. Then decide whether the converse is true or false.

8. If a triangle is equilateral, then it is isosceles.

9. If a number has only itself and 1 as factors, then it is prime.

10. If n is an even number, then $2n$ is an even number.

Tell whether you would use inductive or deductive reasoning to decide if the statement is true or false.

11. If line m is perpendicular to line n, then it is perpendicular to all lines parallel to line n in the same plane.

12. If n is a prime number other than 2, then $n + 1$ is an even number.

Problem-Solving Review

Solve each problem.

13. How many subsets are there for a set with 6 members?

14. What is the next number in the sequence below? Tell whether you used inductive or deductive reasoning. 0, 2, 5, 9, 14 . . .

15. Tell whether this statement is true or false: 8 is a prime number or $\frac{4}{5}$ is a proper fraction.

16. Ralph is giving away his baseball cards. He gave half of his cards to Annie. He gave $\frac{1}{4}$ of what was left plus 6 cards to George. Then he gave $\frac{1}{3}$ of the remaining cards plus 1 card to Ronnie. Ralph now has 15 cards left. How many did he have to begin with?

17. Ms. Lobe surveyed 85 of her music students. If 60 liked rock music, 35 liked classical music, and 10 didn't like either kind of music, how many liked both classical and rock music?

18. **Data File** Use the data on pages 572–573. Find the ratio of the shortest distance traveled by an animal to the longest distance traveled by an animal.

19. **Make a Data File** Choose two current popular television programs. Survey 60 7th- and 8th-grade students to find out which of the programs, if any, they like to watch. Record your results in a table. Show the number of students who liked one program, the other program, both programs, and neither program.

Cumulative Skills Review • Chapters 1–15

Plot the points on a coordinate grid and connect them in order.

1. (−5,0) **2.** (−3,5) **3.** (−1,0) **4.** (−5,3) **5.** (−1,3) **6.** (−5,0)

Draw the top, bottom, and all side views for each figure.

7. 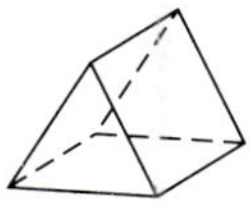

8. 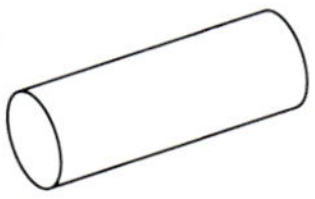

9. 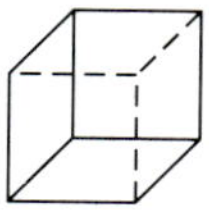

10. 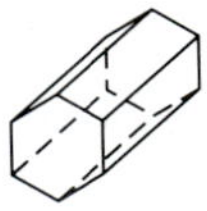

Find the volume of each figure. Use 3.14 for π.

11. 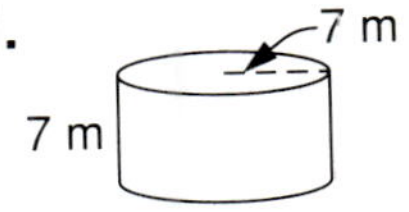

12. 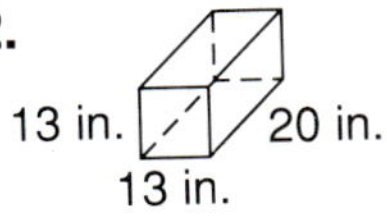

13. 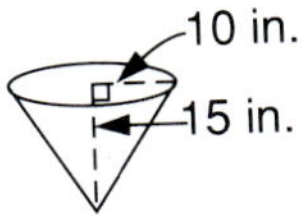

14. 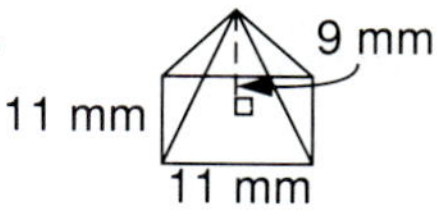

Are these Pythagorean triples? Write yes or no.

15. 16, 30, 34 **16.** 24, 28, 36 **17.** 18, 32, 50 **18.** $1\frac{1}{2}$, 2, $2\frac{1}{2}$

Use the data below for Exercises 19–21.

34, 41, 42, 37, 39, 44, 48, 30, 40

19. Make a box plot. **20.** Find the mean. **21.** Find the range.

Use the following information for Exercises 22–29.
A box contains 20 lettered cards: 10 Ms, 5 As, 3 Ts and 2 Hs.
Find each probablity when a card is drawn and then replaced.

22. P(M,M) **23.** P(M,A) **24.** P(M,A,T) **25.** P(M,A,T,H)

Find each probability when the cards are not replaced.

26. P(M,M) **27.** P(M,A) **28.** P(M,A,T) **29.** P(M,A,T,H)

Use the sets A, B, and C for Exercises 30–35.

$A = \{x|x$ is a positive odd number less than 15$\}$
$B = \{x|x$ is a composite number less than 15$\}$
$C = \{x|x$ is a whole number multiple of 5 less than 20$\}$

30. Write set A in roster notation.

31. Write set B in roster notation.

32. Write set C in roster notation.

33. Write set $B \cup C$ in roster notation.

34. Make a Venn Diagram to show $A \cap B$.

35. Make a Venn diagram to show $A \cap B \cap C$.

Reteaching

Set A pages 542–545

A set can be identified in set builder notation or in roster notation. In set builder notation, the set A of even numbers between 1 and 20 is written as

$A = \{x \mid x \text{ is an even number between 1 and 20}\}$

The { } symbols are called *braces*. The description of the set is put inside the braces.

Remember that set builder notation describes the set in words. Roster notation lists each element.

1. Write set A in roster notation.

2. Is 15 an element of set A?

3. Consider set $B = \{x \mid x \text{ is one of the first four positive odd numbers}\}$. Write set B in roster notation.

4. Consider set $C = \{0, 1, 2, 3, 4, 5\}$. Write set C in set builder notation.

5. Consider set $D = \{2, 4, 6, 8\}$. Write set D in set builder notation.

Set B pages 546–549

A Venn diagram can show relationships between sets.

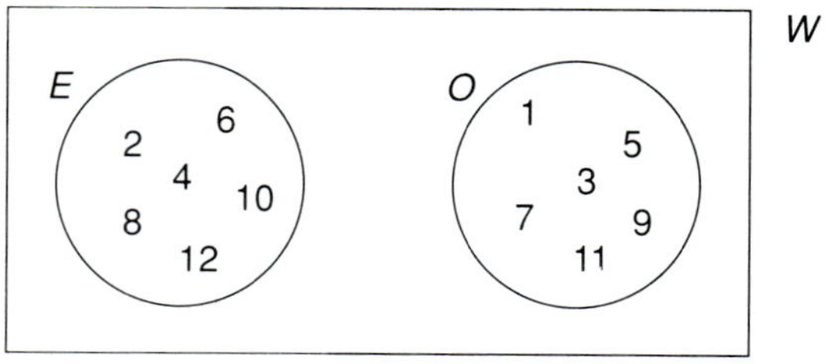

$W = \{x \mid x \text{ is a whole number between 0 and 13}\}$

The Venn diagram above shows that sets E and O are *disjoint*. That is, sets E and O have no elements in common.

The Venn diagram below shows that sets E and T have exactly two elements in common, 6 and 12.

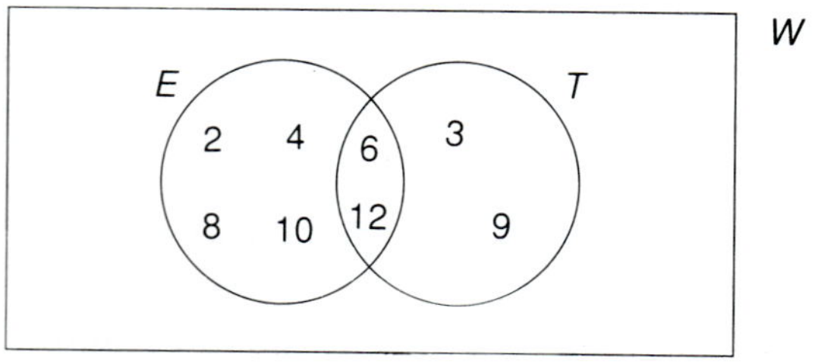

Remember that a Venn diagram uses a rectangle to show the large, universal set ("in the set of all numbers," for example). Circles show subsets of this universal set.

1. Write set E in set builder notation.

2. Write set W in roster notation.

3. Write set T in set builder notation.

4. Draw a Venn diagram to show $O \cap T$.

5. Find $E \cap O$.

Consider set $A = \{2, 3, 4, 7\}$.

6. Draw a Venn diagram to show the set A as a subset of set W.

7. Draw a Venn diagram to show the set $A \cap E$.

8. Draw a Venn diagram to show the set $A \cap O$.

9. Draw a Venn diagram to show the set $A \cap T$.

10. How many elements does set $A \cap E$ have?

11. How many elements does set $A \cap T$ have?

Set C pages 552–555

This table shows that an *and* compound statement is true only when both parts of it are true.

Part before *and*	Part after *and*	Complete *and* statement
True	True	True
True	False	False
False	True	False
False	False	False

Consider statement *P*:

P: 6 is even and 6 is a multiple of 4.

Statement P is false because the part after *and* is false.

The table below shows that an *or* compound statement is false only when both parts of it are false.

Part before *or*	Part after *or*	Complete *or* statement
True	True	True
True	False	True
False	True	True
False	False	False

See page 552 for the truth table for *If, then* statements.

Remember that there are two parts to consider for each *and* statement, each *or* statement, and each *if, then* statement.

Consider these statements.

p: 8 is even.
q: 8 is odd.
r: 7 is prime.
s: 11 is composite.
t: 16 is a perfect square.

Write T if the compound statement is true. Write F if the compound statement is false.

1. p and q **2.** p or q **3.** If p, then q

4. p and r **5.** p or r **6.** If p, then r

7. q and r **8.** q or r 9. If q, then r

10. r and q **11.** r or q **12.** If r, then q

13. t and p **14.** t or p **15.** If t, then p

16. s and t **17.** s or t **18.** If s, then t

19. q and s **20.** q or s **21.** If q, then s

22. t and r **23.** t or r **24.** If t, then r

25. s and p **26.** s or p **27.** If s, then p

Set D pages 560–561

Salvatore is finding the sum of even integers and makes this table.

n	Terms in sum	Sum
2	2 + 4	6
3	2 + 4 + 6	12
4	2 + 4 + 6 + 8	20
5	2 + 4 + 6 + 8 + 10	30

He notices a pattern and conjectures that the sum of the first n even integers is $n^2 + n$. Salvatore uses inductive reasoning.

Remember that a conjecture can be disproved by finding a counterexample.

1. Does Salvatore's conjecture work for $n = 6$?

2. Does Salvatore's conjecture work for $n = 10$?

3. Alice looked at the following list of numbers: 1 7 13 19. She conjectured that each number in the list is produced by the expression $2n^2 - 1$, where n is 1, 2, 3, and so on. Is she correct?

More Practice

Set A pages 542–545

Consider these sets:

$A = \{x \mid x \text{ is a units digit}\}$ $B = \{x \mid x = 2n + 1$, where n is a whole number less than 6$\}$

Solve.

1. Write set A in roster notation.
2. Write set B in roster notation.
3. Write set $A \cap B$ in roster notation.
4. Write set $A \cup B$ in roster notation.
5. Is $\{2, 4, 6, 8\}$ a subset of set A?
6. Is $\{2, 4, 6, 8\}$ a subset of set B?

Consider these sets:

$P = \{x \mid x \text{ is an integer between } -5 \text{ and } 5\}$ $Q = \{3, 6, 9\}$

Solve.

7. Write set P in roster notation.
8. Write set Q in set builder notation.
9. Write set $P \cap Q$ in roster notation.
10. Write set $P \cup Q$ in roster notation.
11. Write all the subsets of set $P \cap Q$.
12. Write all the subsets of set Q.

Set B pages 546–549

Solve. Identify and label your diagrams.

1. Draw a Venn diagram to show the relationship among the set of right triangles, the set of isosceles triangles, and the set of all triangles.
2. Draw a Venn diagram to show the relationship among the set of all equilateral triangles, the set of all isosceles triangles, and the set of all triangles.
3. Draw a Venn diagram to show the relationship among the set of prime digits, the set of all odd digits, and the set of whole numbers.
4. Draw a Venn diagram to show the relationship among the set of all even numbers, the set of all odd numbers, and the set of whole numbers.
5. Draw a Venn diagram to show the relationship among the set of positive integers, the set of negative integers, and the set of rational numbers.
6. Draw a Venn diagram to show the relationship among all units digits, curved units digits (such as 6), and non-curved units digits (such as 4).

Set C page 552–555

Consider these statements about the whole numbers between 10 and 40:

p: The first digit is odd.
q: The number is a multiple of 5.
r: The sum of the digits is 7.

Answer each question.

1. For what numbers is p or q true?
2. For what numbers is q and r true?
3. For what numbers is q or r true?
4. For what numbers is p and r true?
5. For what numbers is p and q true?
6. For what numbers is p or r true?

Write the converse of each if-then statement. Then decide whether the converse is true or false.

7. If the sum of the digits of a number is divisible by 3, then the given number is divisible by 3.
8. If the sum of two numbers is even, then the two numbers must be odd numbers.
9. If a number is divisible by 6, then it is an even number.

Set D pages 560–561

Tell whether you would use inductive or deductive reasoning to solve each problem. Then solve each problem. Use a calculator if you wish.

1. Test the conjecture that $n^2 + n + 17$ is always prime.
2. The area of a circle is πr^2. Therefore, the area of a circle with radius 3 is ▒. (Use $\pi = 3.14$.)
3. If the last digit of a number greater than 0 is 5 or 0, then the number is divisible by 5.
4. Since the volume of a cube is s^3, the volume of a cube with a side of length 3 m is ▒.
5. Since the volume of a sphere is $\frac{4}{3}\pi r^3$, the volume of a sphere with a radius of 6 in. is ▒.

Enrichment

Logic

Perkins, Smythe, Dinwiddie, Bloom, and Magoo are an airline pilot, a sea captain, a bus driver, a rodeo rider, and an engineer, though not necessarily in that order. In their spare time one reads mystery novels, one studies nuclear physics, one writes poetry, one composes symphonies, and one plays the ukulele.

Match each person with his profession and his pastime. Use logic boxes to help you unravel the following clues. If a clue allows you to eliminate a possible combination, write *No* in the correct box or boxes. Write *Yes* if a clue confirms a combination. A *Yes* entry means that all other boxes in that row and that column can be filled in with *No*.

- The pilot is either Smythe or Bloom.
- Dinwiddie knows nothing about music or poetry.
- Magoo once played Parcheesi with the sea captain, the rodeo rider, and the engineer.
- The first poem the bus driver wrote was "My Parents."
- Neither Bloom nor Perkins writes symphonies, and neither Perkins nor Dinwiddie reads novels.
- The rodeo rider plays his ukulele while busting broncos.
- The man who studies nuclear physics gets seasick.
- Smythe is the pilot's brother-in-law.

1.

	Pilot	Sea captain	Bus driver	Rodeo rider	Engineer
Perkins					
Smythe					
Dinwiddie					
Bloom					
Magoo					

2.

	Reads novels	Studies physics	Writes poetry	Composes symphonies	Plays ukelele
Perkins					
Smythe					
Dinwiddie					
Bloom					
Magoo					

Chapter 15 Review/Test

1. Using roster notation, write all the subsets of {x | x is a prime number between 10 and 18}.

2. Using roster notation, write the set that is the intersection of the set of all prime numbers and the set of all even numbers.

3. Using set builder notation, write the set that is the union of the first five odd numbers and the first five even numbers.

4. Use a Venn diagram to show how set B, boys in the math class, is related to set G, girls in the math class, within the set of all students.

5. Use a Venn diagram to show that, within the set of all students, some, but not all, of the students in set A, the math class, are also in set F, the football team.

6. Draw a Venn diagram that could be used to solve this problem.

   Of the 48 eligible students, 39 tried out for cheerleaders and 32 tried out for the pom-pon squad. How many students tried out for both if all but 1 of the eligible students tried out for at least one of the two events?

7. Which is the correct answer for the question in Item 6?
   a. 24 tried out for cheerleaders.
   b. 24 tried out for the pom-pon squad.
   c. 24 tried out for cheerleaders and the pom-pon squad.
   d. 24 students did not try out.

Tell whether each statement is true or false.

8. 24 is a multiple of 6 and 24 is a multiple of 5.

9. 100 is a multiple of 25 or 100 is a multiple of 28.

10. If 200 is a multiple of 20, then 200 is even.

11. The winning bid at the auction is exactly $50. The bids may be raised only by $1, $2, or $3. What should the first bid be in order to guarantee winning?

12. What kind of reasoning would you use when looking for a pattern in the first twenty prime numbers?

13. What kind of reasoning would you use when applying the formula for the area of a circle to solve some problems?

14. Stan has a red, a blue, and a green bag. Each bag contains one model: a sphere, a cube, or a pyramid. The cube is not in the green bag. The pyramid is not in the blue bag. If the sphere is in the green bag, what is in the blue bag? the red bag?

15. **Write About Math** The school newspaper said that a class of 28 students went on two field trips. Fifteen students went on the first trip only, 10 students went on the second trip only, and 8 students went on both trips. Is this possible? Explain.

Data File

1. Diagram

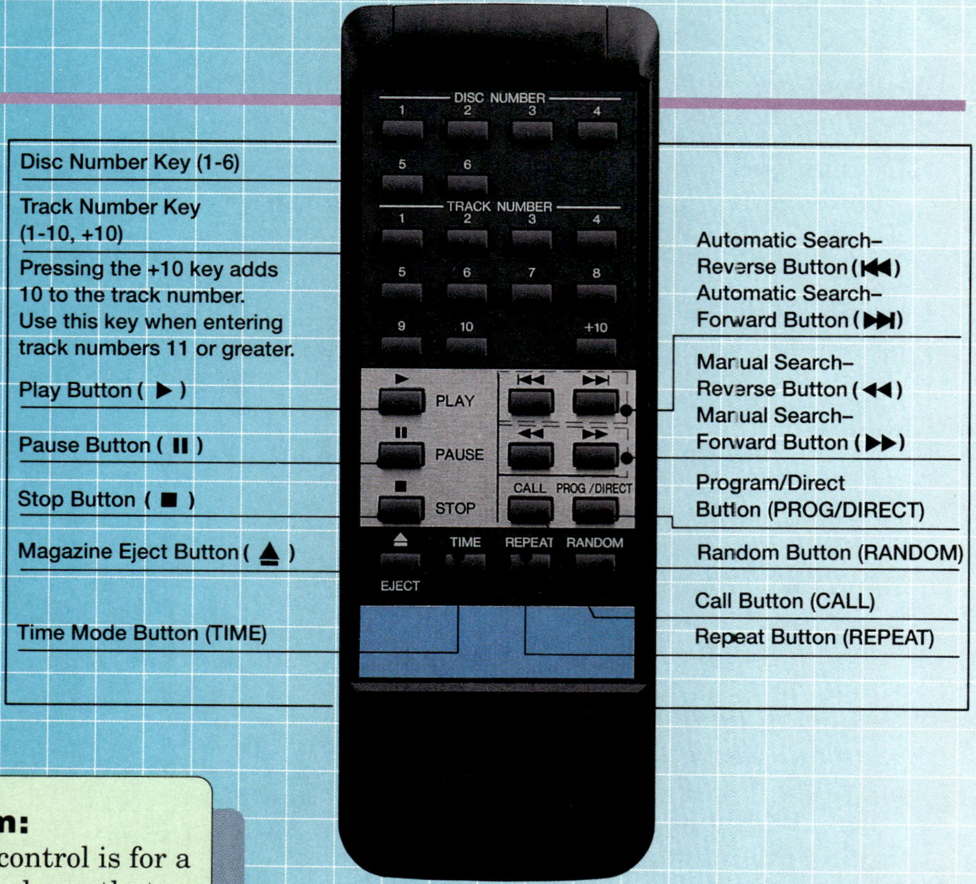

1. Diagram:
This remote control is for a compact disc player that holds six discs.

2. Circle Graph:
In 1987, Americans spent $75,000,000,000 on clothing.

3. Pattern:
A 20-sided polyhedron can be made from the pattern. To do so copy the pattern. Cut on solid lines and fold on dashes to make a 20-sided polyhedron.

4. Weather Statistics:
Swimmers usually prefer temperatures between 65° to 80°.

5. Almanac Entry:
There seems to be no correlation between the size of an animal and the distance it travels.

2. Circle Graph

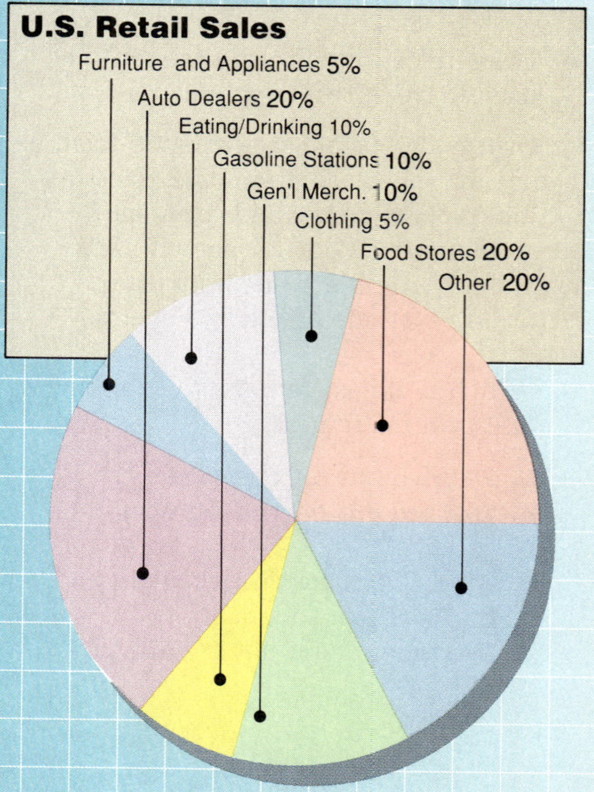

3. Pattern

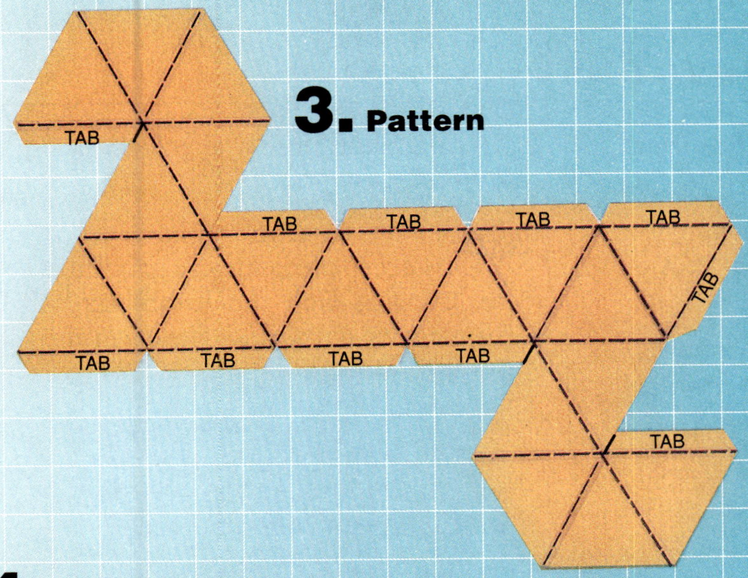

4. Weather Statistics

Average summer water temperatures at selected beaches (°F)

	Early June	Late August
Atlantic Coast		
Newport, R.I.	61	69
Atlantic City, NJ	62	83
Myrtle Beach, SC	77	82
Daytona Beach, FL	79	81
Pacific Coast		
Santa Cruz, CA	56	60
Morro Bay, CA	56	58
Ventura, CA	62	67
Oceanside, CA	63	69
Gulf Coast		
Key West, FL	86	87
St. Petersburg, FL	84	86
Galveston, TX	83	86
South Padre, TX	79	80

Animal	Distance	Territory
Monarch butterfly	2,000 miles round trip	Canada to California
Green turtle	2,800 miles round trip	South America to Ascension Island (Atlantic Ocean)
Caribou	800 miles	Northwest Territories to Islands in Arctic Circle
Elk	200 miles	Roam around Northern provinces of Canada

5. Almanac Entry

Cumulative Review/Test Chapters 1–15

Choose the letter for the correct answer.

1. The new highway is 4.2 miles long and cost 2.1 million dollars per mile to build. What was the total cost of the highway?

a. \$6.3 million **b.** \$2 million
c. \$8.82 million **d.** \$1.1 million

2. Add. $-0.25 + 0.75$

a. -0.5 **b.** 0.5
c. 1.0 **d.** not given

3. Solve. $\frac{x}{3} - 18 = -11$

a. $x = 54$ **b.** $x = -54$
c. $x = -21$ **d.** $x = 21$

4. Which equation is shown by the graph?

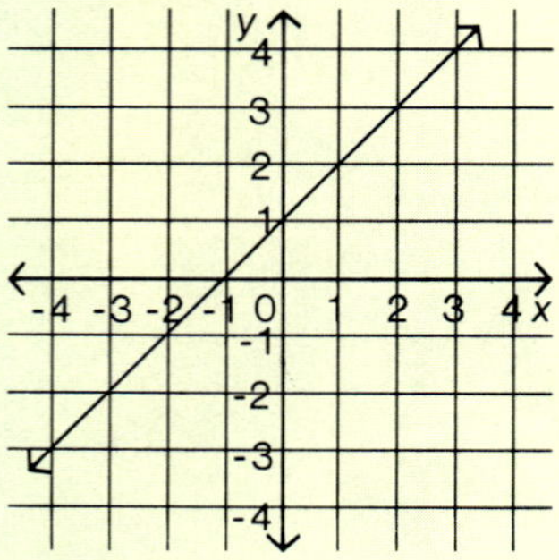

a. $y = x + 1$
b. $y = x - 1$
c. $y = 1 - x$
d. $y = -x - 1$

5. 140 is 35% of what number?

a. 400 **b.** 49
c. 189 **d.** not given

6. Jan's recipe calls for 2 kilograms of ground beef. About how many pounds should she buy?

a. 2 lb **b.** 0.75 lb
c. 4 lb **d.** 8 lb

7. Read the problem and select the correct answer.

Tomas put \$700 in the bank at 6% interest compounded annually for 3 years. How much interest will his money earn? Use the formula $I = prt$.

a. 133.71 percent for 3 years
b. 133.71 months
c. \$133.71
d. 133.71 compound percent

8. Line a is parallel to line b.

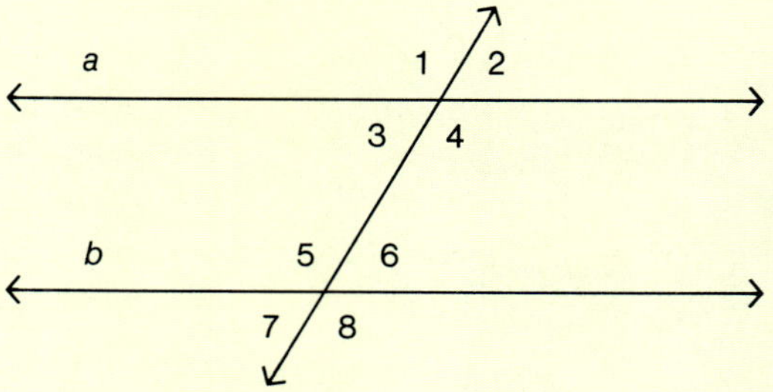

Which sets of angles are congruent?
a. $\angle 1$, $\angle 2$, $\angle 3$, and $\angle 4$
b. $\angle 1$, $\angle 3$, $\angle 5$, and $\angle 7$
c. $\angle 1$, $\angle 4$, $\angle 5$, and $\angle 8$
d. $\angle 1$, $\angle 4$, $\angle 6$, and $\angle 7$

9. The globe in the social studies room has a diameter of 10 inches. What is its volume? Use the formula $V = \frac{4}{3}\pi r^3$ and 3.14 for π.

a. 4,186.66 sq in.
b. 523.33 cu in.
c. 4,186.66 cu in.
d. 523.33 sq in.

10. Compute. $(4.5 \times 10^8) \div (3 \times 10^4)$

a. 1.5×10^4 **b.** 1.5×10^3
c. 1.5×10^2 **d.** not given

11.

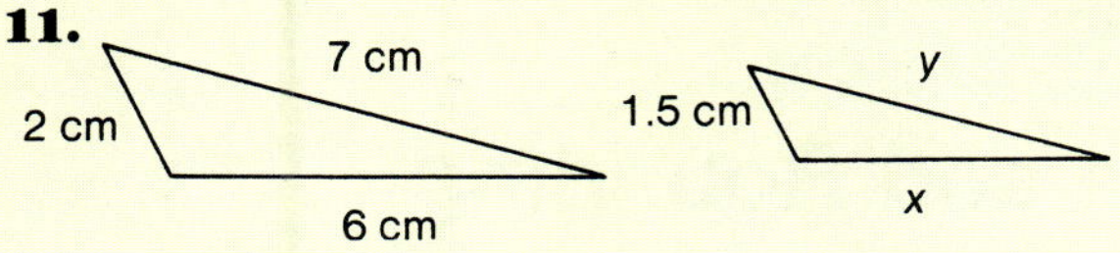

The two triangles are similar. What are the missing measurements, x and y?

a. x = 3 cm, y = 3.5 cm
b. x = 24 cm, y = 28 cm
c. x = 4.5 cm, y = 5.25 cm
d. x = 12 cm, y = 14 cm

12. Which of the following is a set of Pythagorean triples?

a. 12, 20, 30
b. 5, 12, 15
c. 12, 13, 16
d. 12, 16, 20

13. Which would you use to find the diagonal of a square?

a. 30–60–90 triple
b. 45–45–90 triple
c. Pythagorean triple

14. Find the mean, median, and mode of the following data.

4 8 12 4 8 12 4 8 12 4

a. mean = 7.6 median = 8
mode = 4
b. mean = 7.6 median = 8
mode = 36
c. mean = 8 median = 8
mode = 4
d. mean = 7.5 median = 8
mode = 36

15. How many degrees should be in the sector of a circle graph showing that 75 percent of the people surveyed prefer the color blue?

a. 75° **b.** 270° **c.** 27° **d.** 0.75°

16. How many different ways can 7 eighth graders stand in line to buy tickets to the school play?

a. 49 **b.** 40,320
c. 5,040 **d.** 42

17. A hat contains 2 red cards, 2 blue cards, 2 green cards, and 2 yellow cards. What is the probability of drawing a red card and then, without replacement, drawing a blue card?

a. $\frac{1}{8}$ **b.** $\frac{1}{4}$ **c.** $\frac{1}{16}$ **d.** $\frac{1}{14}$

18. What is the probability of getting all heads when flipping a coin 3 times?

a. $\frac{1}{8}$ **b.** $\frac{1}{4}$ **c.** $\frac{3}{4}$ **d.** $\frac{1}{2}$

19. Which of the following is the intersection of the set of all odd numbers and the set of all prime numbers less than 20?

a. {3, 5, 7, 11, 13, 17, 19}
b. {2, 3, 5, 7, 11, 13, 17, 19}
c. {1, 3, 5, 7, 11, 13, 17, 19}
d. {1, 2, 3, 5, 7, 11, 13, 17, 19}

20. How many numbers less than or equal to 10 are multiples of 2 *and* multiples of 3?

a. 2 numbers **b.** 1 number
c. 8 numbers **d.** 6 numbers

Whole Number Numeration and Rounding

Review

The total area of Bryce Canyon National Park in Utah is 35,835 acres.

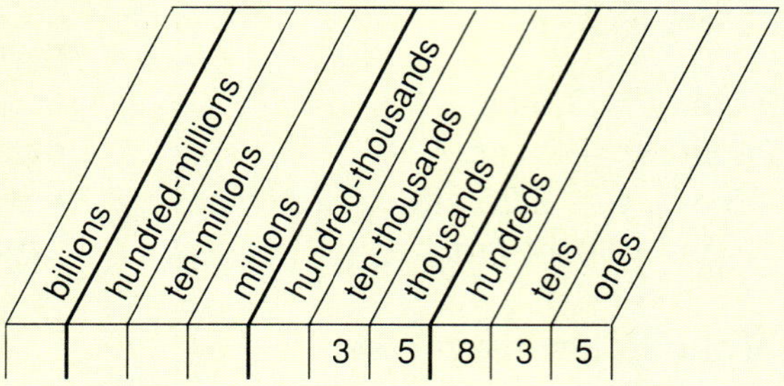

thirty-five thousand, eight hundred thirty-five

A. Write 35,835 in expanded form.

Standard form   Expanded form
35,835 = 30,000 + 5,000 + 800 + 30 + 5

B. Round 35,835 to the nearest ten-thousand, nearest thousand, and nearest hundred.

35,835 ↓ 40,000 The digit to the right of the ten-thousands place is 5, so round up.

35,835 ↓ 36,000 The digit to the right of the thousands place is greater than 5, so round up.

35,835 ↓ 35,800 Since the digit to the right of the hundreds place is less than 5, round down.

Practice

Write each number in words and in expanded form.

1. 5,974 **2.** 62,091 **3.** 79,020 **4.** 112,568 **5.** 30,147 **6.** 950,677

Round each number to the nearest million and to the nearest hundred-thousand.

7. 8,321,000 **8.** 13,597,222 **9.** 9,299,999 **10.** 681,837 **11.** 9,816,432

Round the area of each national park as directed.

National Park	Area in acres	Nearest ten-thousand	Nearest thousand	Nearest hundred
Rocky Mountain	263,809	**12.**	**13.**	**14.**
Mesa Verde	52,085	**15.**	**16.**	**17.**
Carlsbad Caverns	46,755	**18.**	**19.**	**20.**
Badlands	243,303	**21.**	**22.**	**23.**
Mammoth Cave	52,452	**24.**	**25.**	**26.**

Adding, Subtracting, and Multiplying Whole Numbers

Review

A. Find 63,492 + 19,868 + 3,871.

```
   12 21
  63,492
  19,868
+  3,871
--------
  87,231
```

Align the digits by place value. Add, beginning with the ones column. Rename as needed.

B. Find 108,963 − 89,597.

```
    9     15
  0 10 18  8 5 13
  1  0  8, 9 6  3
−    8  9, 5 9  7
-----------------
     1  9, 3 6  6
```

Align the digits by place value. Rename and subtract.

C. Find 506 × 3,493.

```
    3,493
  ×   506
---------
    20958   ←6 × 3,493
  1746500   ←500 × 3,493
---------
1,767,458
```

D. Find (30)(87)(63).
First multiply 30 × 87.
Then multiply 2,610 by 63.

```
   87        2,610
 × 30      ×    63
-----      -------
2,610         7830
            156600
           -------
           164,430
```

Practice

Add, subtract, or multiply. Watch the signs.

1. 837 + 519 **2.** 53,957 − 29,435 **3.** 1,965 + 715 **4.** 92 × 406

5. 8,514 + 3,168 **6.** 932 − 514 **7.** 961,978 − 504,321 **8.** 194 × 373

9. 550(76) **10.** 88(24,713) **11.** 583,802 + 966,410 **12.** 8,586 − 310

13. 3,310 − 1,121 **14.** 36,413 + 16,432 **15.** 86,713 − 16,555 **16.** 41 × 16 × 39

17. 707 × 530 **18.** 57,013 + 32,109 **19.** 98,000 − 17,632 **20.** 8,927 + 4,667

21. 899,418 − 777,765 **22.** 3,713 × 908 **23.** 416,725 + 504,321

24. 6,073 + 9,702 + 85 + 2,333 **25.** 28 × 97 × 84 **26.** 961,978 − 504,321

27. 30,015 + 13,344 + 19,278 **28.** (57)(32)(94) **29.** 372,956 − 247,013

30. 4,008 + 19 + 1,888 + 402 + 10,000 **31.** 18,907 + 1,690 + 3,492 + 700

32. 6,073 + 9,802 + 75 + 2,444 **33.** 30,015 + 13,344 + 9,278 + 89,230

Dividing Whole Numbers

Review

A. Find 1,760 ÷ 38.

4	Divide. THINK: 38 rounds to 40.
38)1,760	How many 4s in 17? 4
1 52	Multiply.
24	Subtract and compare.

46 R12	
38)1,760	
1 52↓	Bring down.
240	Divide.
228	Multiply.
12	Subtract and compare. The remainder is 12.

B. Find 22,321 ÷ 44.

5	Divide.
44)22,321	
22 0	Multiply.
3	Subtract and compare.

508	There are no 44s in 32, so write a zero in the quotient.
44)22,321	
22 0↓ ↓	Bring down.
321	Divide.
352	Multiply. 352 > 321, so 8 is too big.

507 R13	
44)22,321	Try 7.
22 0	
321	
308	Multiply.
13	Subtract and compare. The remainder is 13.

Practice

Divide.

1. 746 ÷ 7 **2.** 705 ÷ 8 **3.** 927 ÷ 4 **4.** 3,902 ÷ 5 **5.** 6,233 ÷ 6

6. 983 ÷ 27 **7.** 784 ÷ 92 **8.** 607 ÷ 44 **9.** 6,489 ÷ 86 **10.** 7,684 ÷ 67

11. 5,221 ÷ 18 **12.** 2,082 ÷ 85 **13.** 6,344 ÷ 21 **14.** 6,188 ÷ 38 **15.** 8,621 ÷ 91

16. 2,902 ÷ 87 **17.** 8,910 ÷ 76 **18.** 1,756 ÷ 31 **19.** 8,718 ÷ 42 **20.** 9,555 ÷ 40

21. 18,978 ÷ 38 **22.** 40,500 ÷ 55 **23.** 37,645 ÷ 51 **24.** 19,003 ÷ 14

25. 52,174 ÷ 84 **26.** 16,035 ÷ 28 **27.** 38,709 ÷ 60 **28.** 96,000 ÷ 51

29. 15,555 ÷ 36 **30.** 57,400 ÷ 66 **31.** 11,315 ÷ 25 **32.** 11,007 ÷ 72

33. 52,871 ÷ 82 **34.** 478,320 ÷ 41 **35.** 34,900 ÷ 57 **36.** 16,270 ÷ 23

37. 17,835 ÷ 605 **38.** 333,733 ÷ 786 **39.** 28,509 ÷ 361 **40.** 35,000 ÷ 190

Decimal Numeration

Review

A. Write 21.000306 in words.

millions	hundred-thousands	ten-thousands	thousands	hundreds	tens	ones	tenths	Hundredths	thousandths	ten-thousandths	Hundred-thousandths	millionths
					2	1	0	0	0	3	0	6

twenty-one and three hundred six millionths

B. List 6.3, 6.285, and 6.03 in order from least to greatest.

same   same

6.300   **6.285**   **6.030**

2 < 3, so 6.285 < 6.300   0 < 2, so 6.030 < 6.285

Write the numbers with the same number of decimal places. Then compare the digits from left to right.

6.03, 6.285, 6.3

Write the original numbers in order from least to greatest.

Practice

Write each number as a decimal.

1. Fifty-three hundredths **2.** Seventeen thousandths **3.** Four ten-thousandths

4. Two hundred fifty-one millionths **5.** Forty-one and forty-one millionths

Write each decimal in words.

6. 0.38 **7.** 2.85 **8.** 47.8 **9.** 41.008 **10.** 0.0034 **11.** 0.00003

For each number, write an equal decimal in hundredths.

12. 9.6 **13.** 4.340 **14.** 0.080 **15.** 7 **16.** 156 **17.** 4.000 **18.** 12

Write the numbers in order from least to greatest.

19. 0.247 0.24 0.2704 **20.** 0.3816 0.3628 0.36 **21.** 3.03 3.303 3.330

22. 5.63 5.66 5.6 **23.** 0.984 0.944 0.0984 **24.** 0.324 0.3024 0.342

Rounding Decimals

Review

A. Round 9.7524 to the nearest one, nearest tenth, and nearest hundredth.

Decimals are rounded in the same way as whole numbers.

Ones place → 9.7524 ← Greater than 5, so round up.
9.7524 → 10

Tenths place → 9.7524 ← Equal to 5, so round up.
9.7524 → 9.8

Hundredths place → 9.7524 ← Less than 5, so round down.
9.7524 → 9.75

Notice that you also drop all digits to the right of the place to which you are rounding.

B. Round 0.0475 so that only one digit is not zero.

First nonzero digit. → 0.0475 ← Greater than 5, so round up.
0.0475 → 0.05

Practice

Round each number to the place shown in parentheses.

1. 37.735 (hundredths) **2.** 15.623 (ones) **3.** 18.0154 (thousandths)

4. 0.22979 (thousandths) **5.** 0.801 (tenths) **6.** 11.0138 (hundredths)

7. 0.4338 (hundredths) **8.** 99.997 (ones) **9.** 0.0084297 (millionths)

Round each number so that only one digit is not zero.

10. 56.3998 **11.** 32.75 **12.** 0.0309 **13.** 0.9333 **14.** 3.7502 **15.** 0.08416

Round each number as directed.

Number	Nearest one	Nearest tenth	Nearest hundredth	Nearest thousandth
8.817	**16.**	**17.**	**18.**	
71.0090	**19.**	**20.**	**21.**	**22.**
0.9999	**23.**	**24.**	**25.**	**26.**
48.0556	**27.**	**28.**	**29.**	**30.**

Adding and Subtracting Decimals

Review

A. Find 3.4 + 0.63 + 1.457 + 6.78.

First estimate by rounding each number to the nearest whole number.
3 + 1 + 1 + 7 = 12

```
   2 1
   3.4      Line up the decimal
   0.63     points. Then add.
   1.457
+  6.78
 -------    Write the decimal point
  12.267    in the answer.
```

B. Find 18 − 9.756.

Estimate: 18 − 10 = 8

Write 18 as 18.000. Then line up the decimal points and subtract.

```
   17 9  9
  0 7 10 10 10
  1 8 . 0  0  0
 −  9 . 7  5  6
 ---------------
    8 . 2  4  4
```

C. Find 0.0345 − 0.0063.

```
        2 14
  0 . 0 3 4 5
 −0 . 0 0 6 3
 -------------
  0 . 0 2 8 2
```

To estimate, round both numbers to the same place.
0.035 − 0.006 = 0.029

Practice

Add or subtract.

1. 39.867 + 27.986 **2.** 32 − 14.306 **3.** 47 + 0.0569 **4.** 0.819 − 0.277

5. 0.247 − 0.0899 **6.** 10.6 + 8.44 **7.** 42.135 − 28.6 **8.** 13.2 − 0.572

9. 54 + 27.1314 **10.** 22 − 0.0003 **11.** 13.75 + 44 **12.** 9.475 − 6.131

13. 66.408 − 32.78 **14.** 2.8612 − 0.0087 **15.** 6.675 + 0.98003 **16.** 78 + 53.928

17. 0.112 + 96 + 3.48 + 9.7 **18.** 4.301 + 430 + 0.431 + 30.41 **19.** 156.8 − 9.986

Copy and complete this expense report.

Expenses	Monday	Tuesday	Wednesday	Thursday	Friday	Item Totals
Hotel	$39.95	$39.95	$44.85	$44.85	$0	**20.**
Meals	$35	$42.15	$28	$30.15	$16	**21.**
Daily Totals	**22.**	**23.**	**24.**	**25.**	**26.**	**27.**
				Cash Advance		−150.00
				Balance Due		**28.**

Multiplying Decimals

Review

A. Find 0.65 × 4.013.

To estimate, first round each number so that only one digit is not zero.
0.7 × 4 = 2.8

```
     4.013  ←3 decimal places
   × 0.65   ←2 decimal places
   ------
     20065
    240780
   -------
   2.60845  ←5 decimal places
```

B. Find 0.3 × 0.015.

Estimate: 0.3 × 0.02 = 0.06

Sometimes it is necessary to write extra zeros in the product.

```
    0.015  ←3 decimal places
  ×   0.3  ←1 decimal place
  -------
   0.0045  To show 4 decimal places,
           write 2 extra zeros.
```

Practice

Multiply.

1. 7.4 × 8.3 **2.** 44.1 × 7.02 **3.** 2.3 × 5.96 **4.** 50.09 × 28 **5.** 6.04 × 8.7

6. 17 × 0.3 **7.** 3.15 × 9.01 **8.** 0.057 × 8.8 **9.** 7.06 × 243 **10.** 0.72 × 0.04

11. 0.5 × 716 **12.** 8.73 × 0.08 **13.** 0.76 × 9.7 **14.** 8.4 × 0.012 **15.** 33 × 0.772

16. 7.6 × 0.19 **17.** 4.37 × 55.6 **18.** 93.7 × 1.2 **19.** 10.8 × 0.5 **20.** 6.7 × 8.92

21. $(0.12)^2$ **22.** $(8.7)^2$ **23.** $(0.023)^2$ **24.** $(0.37)^2$ **25.** $(28.4)^2$

26. 0.784(7.08) **27.** 0.11(18.95) **28.** 0.071(3.6) **29.** (0.875)(0.07)

30. (3.2)(5.4)(8.7) **31.** (0.9)(0.66)(0.8) **32.** 2(6.85)(3.4) **33.** 7(1.95)(0.02)

Copy and complete this produce bill.

Item	Quantity	Unit Price	Item Totals (to nearest cent)
Bananas	2.53 lb	$0.59 per lb	**34.**
Tomatoes	1.33 lb	$0.98 per lb	**35.**
Oranges	2.89 lb	$0.79 per lb	**36.**
Pears	2.49 lb	$0.98 per lb	**37.**
		Total	**38.**

Adding and Subtracting Fractions

Review

A. Find $\frac{3}{4} + \frac{5}{8}$.

$\frac{3}{4} = \frac{6}{8}$ Write the fractions with a common denominator.

$+\frac{5}{8} = \frac{5}{8}$ Add the numerators.

$\frac{11}{8} = 1\frac{3}{8}$ Rename the sum.

B. Find $\frac{2}{3} - \frac{1}{6}$.

$\frac{2}{3} = \frac{8}{12}$ Write the fractions with a common denominator.

$-\frac{1}{6} = \frac{2}{12}$ Subtract the numerators.

$\frac{6}{12} = \frac{1}{2}$ Write the difference in lowest terms.

Practice

Add or subtract.

1. $\frac{1}{8} + \frac{1}{3}$ **2.** $\frac{5}{8} - \frac{1}{2}$ **3.** $\frac{3}{4} + \frac{4}{5}$ **4.** $\frac{11}{12} - \frac{2}{3}$ **5.** $\frac{7}{8} - \frac{5}{6}$ **6.** $\frac{5}{6} + \frac{1}{4}$

7. $\frac{3}{8} - \frac{1}{3}$ **8.** $\frac{3}{5} - \frac{1}{2}$ **9.** $\frac{9}{16} + \frac{5}{8}$ **10.** $\frac{1}{12} + \frac{2}{3}$ **11.** $\frac{3}{4} - \frac{2}{5}$ **12.** $\frac{1}{3} - \frac{1}{4}$

13. $\frac{7}{8} + \frac{5}{12}$ **14.** $\frac{1}{2} - \frac{1}{3}$ **15.** $\frac{7}{8} + \frac{3}{16}$ **16.** $\frac{7}{8} + \frac{3}{5}$ **17.** $\frac{7}{12} - \frac{1}{2}$ **18.** $\frac{9}{10} + \frac{4}{5}$

19. $\frac{5}{16} + \frac{5}{8}$ **20.** $\frac{1}{4} + \frac{15}{16}$ **21.** $\frac{1}{8} - \frac{1}{12}$ **22.** $\frac{2}{3} + \frac{1}{2}$ **23.** $\frac{5}{6} - \frac{3}{8}$ **24.** $\frac{3}{4} + \frac{2}{3}$

25. $\frac{2}{3} - \frac{1}{4}$ **26.** $\frac{1}{2} + \frac{7}{10}$ **27.** $\frac{1}{8} + \frac{1}{10}$ **28.** $\frac{7}{12} - \frac{3}{8}$ **29.** $\frac{4}{5} + \frac{2}{3}$ **30.** $\frac{5}{8} + \frac{1}{6}$

31. $\frac{5}{6} + \frac{4}{5} + \frac{11}{15}$ **32.** $\frac{5}{8} - \frac{1}{10}$ **33.** $\frac{9}{10} + \frac{7}{8} + \frac{3}{5}$ **34.** $\frac{11}{25} - \frac{3}{10}$

35. $\frac{1}{8} + \frac{5}{16} + \frac{7}{32}$ **36.** $\frac{4}{9} - \frac{1}{6}$ **37.** $\frac{5}{9} + \frac{1}{3} + \frac{5}{6}$ **38.** $\frac{7}{8} - \frac{2}{3}$

Multiplying and Dividing Fractions

Review

To multiply fractions, multiply numerators and multiply denominators.

A. Find $\frac{1}{5} \times \frac{2}{3} \times \frac{1}{4}$.

$\frac{1}{5} \times \frac{2}{3} \times \frac{1}{4} = \frac{1 \times \overset{1}{\cancel{2}} \times 1}{5 \times 3 \times \underset{2}{\cancel{4}}}$

$= \frac{1}{30}$

Whenever possible, simplify your work by dividing a numerator and a denominator by a common factor.

B. Find $8 \times \frac{1}{8}$.

$8 \times \frac{1}{8}$

Two numbers whose product is 1 are reciprocals.

$\frac{\overset{1}{\cancel{8}}}{1} \times \frac{1}{\underset{1}{\cancel{8}}} = 1$

8 and $\frac{1}{8}$ are reciprocals of each other.

To divide by a fraction, multiply by its reciprocal.

C. Find $\frac{2}{3} \div \frac{1}{2}$.

$\frac{2}{3} \div \frac{1}{2} = \frac{2}{3} \times \frac{2}{1}$ The reciprocal of $\frac{1}{2}$ is $\frac{2}{1}$.

$= \frac{4}{3} = 1\frac{1}{3}$ Multiply. Write the answer as a mixed number.

D. Find $\frac{3}{4} \div \frac{1}{4}$.

$\frac{3}{4} \div \frac{1}{4} = \frac{3}{\underset{1}{\cancel{4}}} \times \frac{\overset{1}{\cancel{4}}}{1}$ The reciprocal of $\frac{1}{4}$ is $\frac{4}{1}$.

$= \frac{3}{1} = 3$ Multiply. Write the answer as a whole number.

Practice

Multiply.

1. $\frac{1}{2} \times \frac{1}{3}$ **2.** $\frac{1}{4} \times \frac{1}{2}$ **3.** $\frac{3}{4} \times \frac{1}{5}$ **4.** $\frac{1}{3} \times \frac{7}{8}$ **5.** $\frac{1}{2} \times \frac{5}{6}$ **6.** $\frac{1}{5} \times \frac{2}{3}$

7. $\frac{3}{4} \times 4$ **8.** $\frac{2}{3} \times 3$ **9.** $\frac{2}{5} \times \frac{1}{2} \times \frac{5}{6}$ **10.** $\frac{4}{5} \times \frac{1}{6} \times \frac{2}{3}$ **11.** $\frac{9}{10} \times \frac{2}{3}$ **12.** $\frac{5}{6} \times \frac{5}{6}$

Tell whether or not the pair of numbers are reciprocals.

13. $\frac{5}{6}$ and $\frac{6}{5}$ **14.** $\frac{1}{2}$ and 2 **15.** 6 and $\frac{6}{1}$ **16.** $\frac{1}{3}$ and $\frac{1}{2}$

Divide.

17. $\frac{5}{6} \div \frac{1}{3}$ **18.** $\frac{1}{2} \div \frac{3}{4}$ **19.** $\frac{2}{3} \div \frac{5}{6}$ **20.** $\frac{3}{16} \div \frac{5}{12}$ **21.** $\frac{1}{2} \div \frac{7}{16}$ **22.** $\frac{7}{8} \div \frac{1}{6}$

23. $5 \div \frac{3}{5}$ **24.** $\frac{4}{5} \div \frac{2}{3}$ **25.** $\frac{5}{8} \div 5$ **26.** $\frac{9}{16} \div 3$ **27.** $6 \div \frac{1}{6}$ **28.** $8 \div \frac{3}{4}$

Overview of the Metric System

Review

A. The metric system of measurement has three basic units of measure.

The *meter* is the basic unit of length. A door is about 1 meter wide.

The *liter* is the basic unit of capacity. Four drinking classes hold about 1 liter.

The *gram* is the basic unit of mass. The mass of a small grape is about 1 gram.

B. For units bigger and smaller than the basic units, prefixes are used with *meter, liter,* and *gram*. This table shows the most common prefixes and how they are used.

Prefix	Meaning	Length	Capacity	Mass
kilo-	1,000	kilometer (km)	kiloliter (kL)	kilogram (kg)
hecto-	100	hectometer (hm)	hectoliter (hL)	hectogram (hg)
deka-	10	dekameter (dam)	dekaliter (daL)	dekagram (dag)
	1	meter (m)	liter (L)	gram (g)
deci-	0.1	decimeter (dm)	deciliter (dL)	decigram (dg)
centi-	0.01	centimeter (cm)	centiliter (cL)	centigram (cg)
milli-	0.001	millimeter (mm)	milliliter (mL)	milligram (mg)

Practice

Give or complete each unit of measure.

1. Mass of an apple seed
milli ____

2. Diameter of an apple
centi ____

3. Height of an apple tree
____

4. Mass of an apple
____

5. Capacity of a pail
____

6. Length of an apple stem
milli ____

7. Capacity of a glass
milli ____

8. Mass of a pumpkin
kilo ____

9. Capacity of a barrel
deka ____

Write the metric unit for each symbol.

10. mm **11.** kg **12.** cm **13.** mg **14.** mL **15.** dm **16.** km **17.** daL

Find each missing number.

18. 1 mL = ____ L **19.** 1 cm = ____ m **20.** 1 mg = ____ g **21.** 1 mm = ____ m

22. 1 km = ____ m **23.** 1 hL = ____ L **24.** 1 daL = ____ L **25.** 1 kg = ____ g

Classifying Triangles

Review

A. Triangles can be classified according to the lengths of their sides. In the diagrams, congruent sides are marked with a slash.

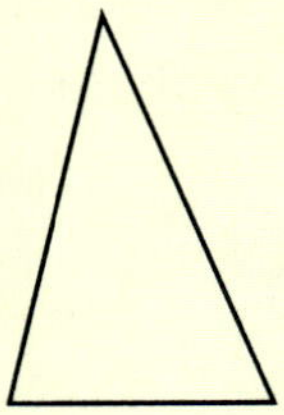

Scalene Triangle
No congruent sides

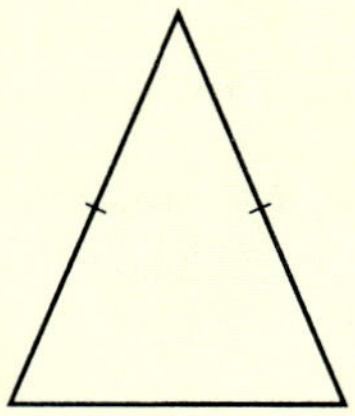

Isosceles Triangle
At least 2 congruent sides

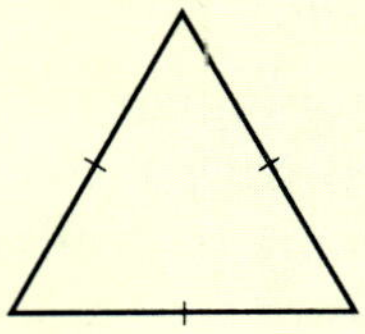

Equilateral Triangle
3 congruent sides

B. Triangles can also be classified according to the measures of their angles.

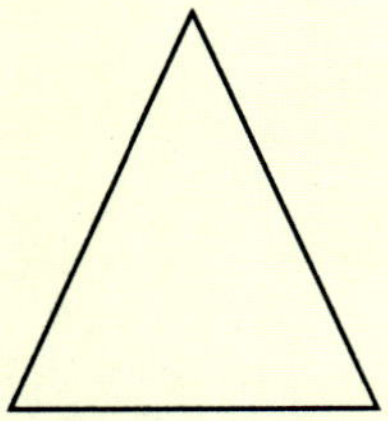

Acute Triangle
3 acute angles

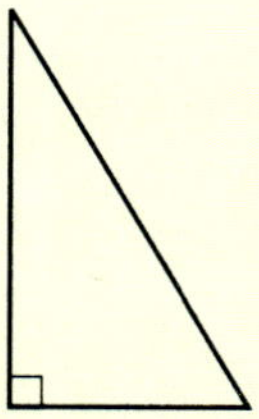

Right Triangle
1 right angle

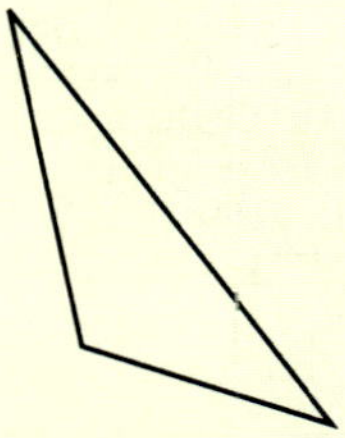

Obtuse Triangle
1 obtuse angle

When classifying triangles, it is helpful to know that the sum of the angle measures of any triangle is 180°.

C. In triangle ABC, $\angle A$ has a 95° measure. Can $\triangle ABC$ be a right triangle?

$180° - 95° = 85°$

Since the sum of the measures of angles B and C is only 85°, neither angle can be a right angle.

Since $\angle A$ is obtuse, $\triangle ABC$ fits the description of an obtuse triangle.

Practice

Classify each triangle as scalene, isosceles, or equilateral.
Congruent sides are marked with a slash.

1.

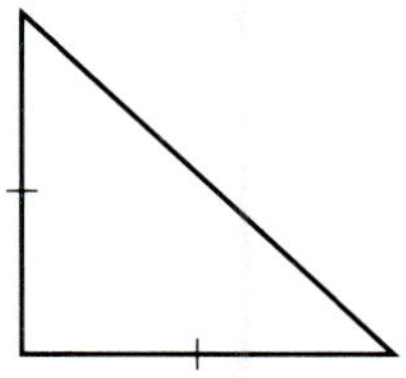

2.

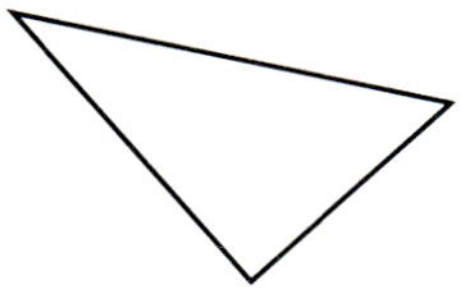

3.

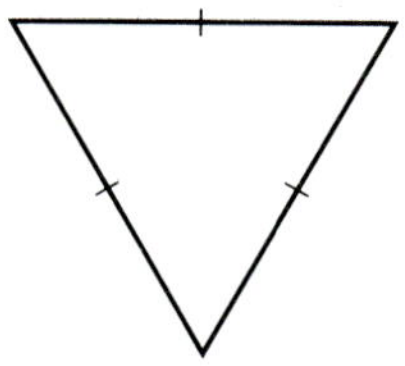

4.

5.

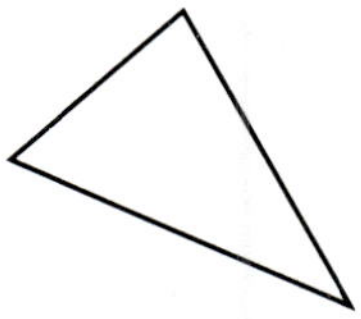

6.

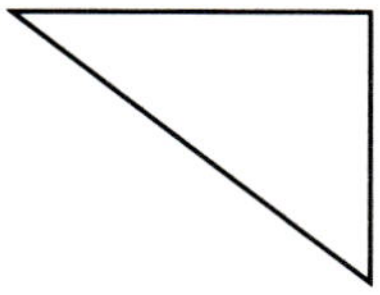

7.

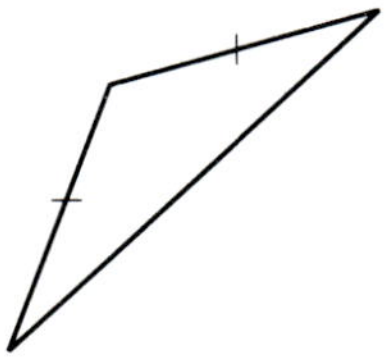

8.

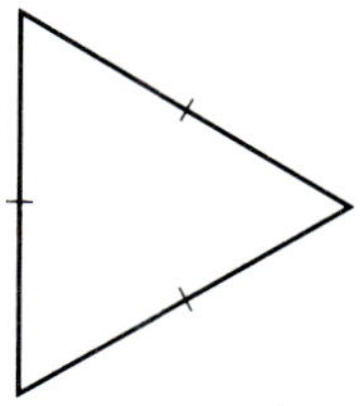

Classify each triangle as acute, right, or obtuse.

9.

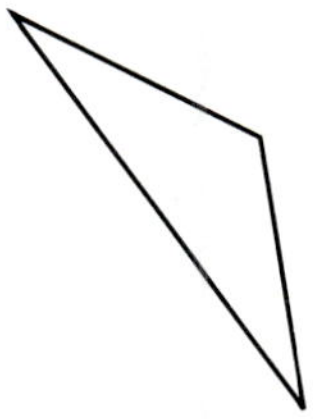

10.

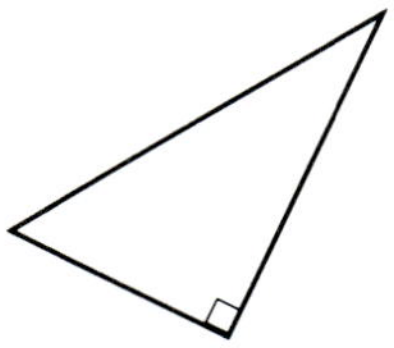

11.

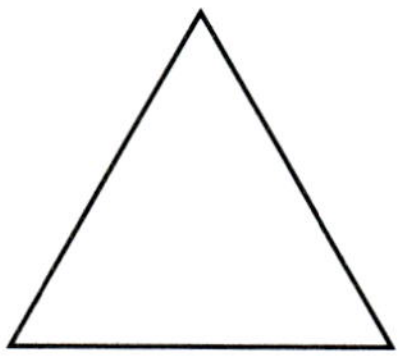

12.

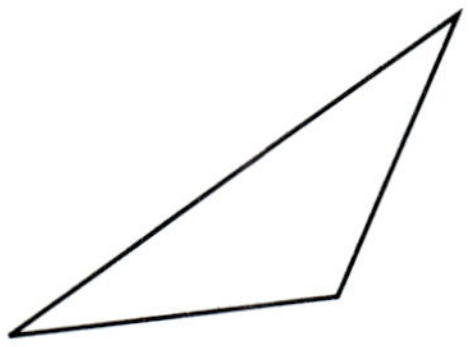

13.

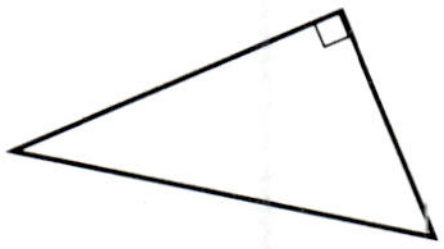

14.

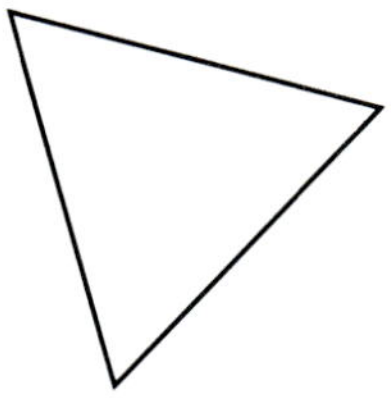

15.

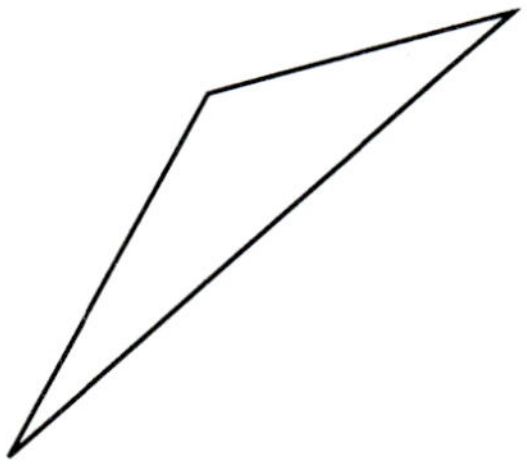

16.

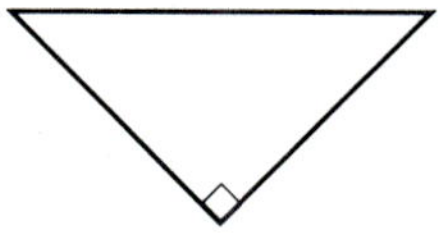

In Exercises 17–20, the measures of two angles of a triangle are given. Find the measure of the third angle.
Then classify the triangle as obtuse, acute, or right.

17. 75° and 35° **18.** 60° and 90° **19.** 45° and 45° **20.** 30° and 125°

Congruent Triangles

Review

Congruent triangles have the same size and shape. Their corresponding sides are the same length and their corresponding angles have the same measures.

A. Triangle ABC is congruent to triangle EDF. Name three pairs of corresponding sides and three pairs of corresponding angles.

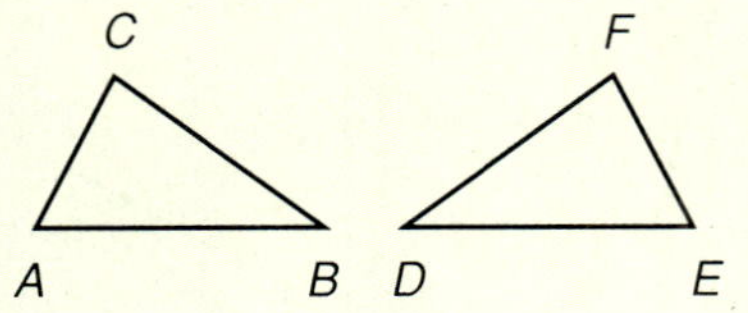

$\overline{AC} \cong \overline{EF}$ $\quad$ $\overline{AB} \cong \overline{ED}$ $\quad$ $\overline{BC} \cong \overline{DF}$

$\angle A \cong \angle E$ $\quad$ $\angle B \cong \angle D$ $\quad$ $\angle C \cong \angle F$

B. $\triangle JKM \cong \triangle NOM$

Corresponding sides and corresponding angles are marked with the same number of slashes.

Find the length of $\overline{MN}$ and the measures of $\angle K$, $\angle N$, and $\angle O$.

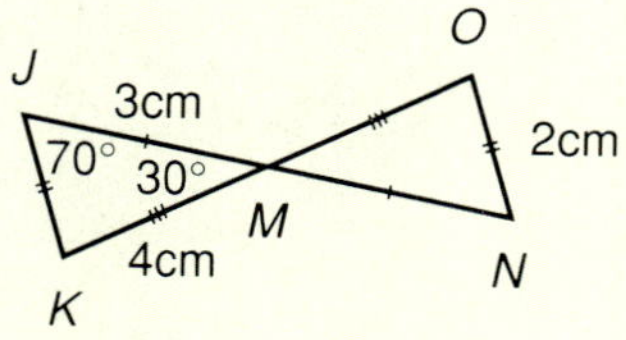

Since $\overline{MN}$ corresponds to $\overline{MJ}$, the length of $\overline{MN}$ is 3 centimeters.

Since $\angle N$ corresponds with $\angle J$, the measure of $\angle N$ is 70°.

$m\angle J + m\angle JMK = 70° + 30° = 100°$

$180° - 100° = 80°$

The measure of $\angle K$ is 80°.

$\angle K$ corresponds with $\angle O$, so the measure of $\angle O$ is 80°.

Practice

For each pair of congruent triangles, name three pairs of corresponding sides and three pairs of corresponding angles.

1. $\triangle ABC \cong \triangle DEF$

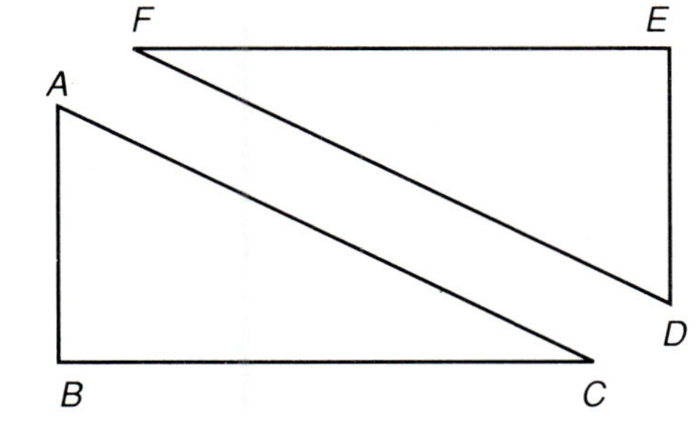

2. $\triangle OMN \cong \triangle IJK$

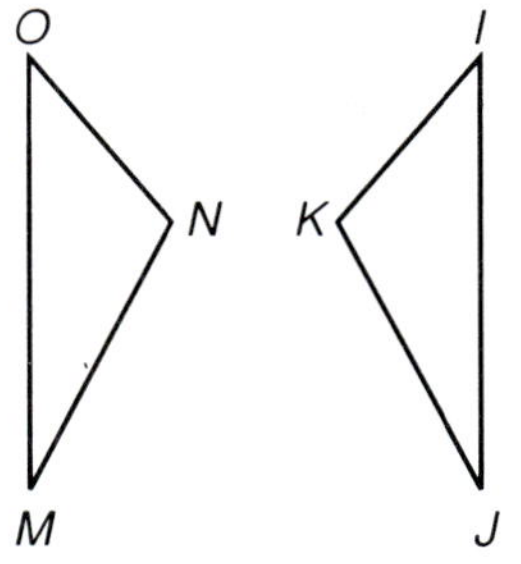

3. $\triangle XYZ \cong \triangle UVW$

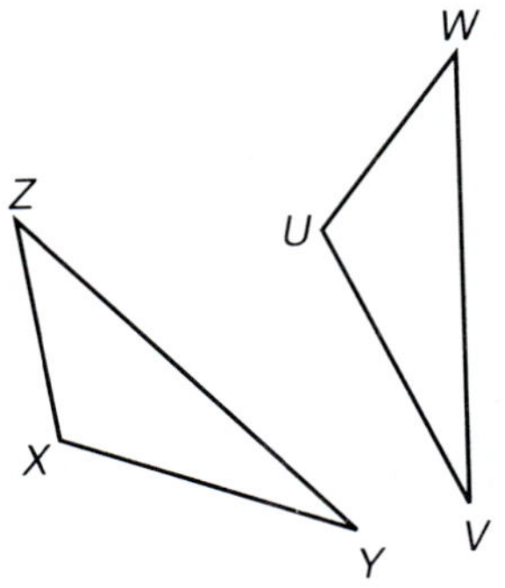

Use $\triangle GHI$ and $\triangle PQR$ for Exercises 4–9. $\triangle GHI \cong \triangle PRQ$.

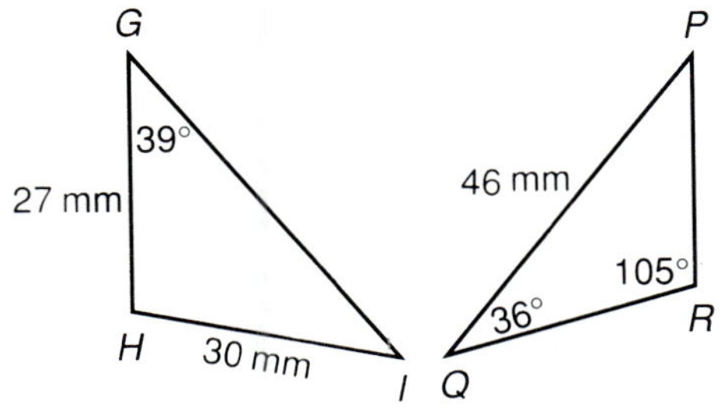

Find the length of each segment or the measure of each angle.

4. $\overline{QR}$ **5.** $\overline{IG}$ **6.** $\overline{PR}$ **7.** $\angle H$ **8.** $\angle I$ **9.** $\angle P$

In triangles RST and UVW, all three pairs of corresponding angles are congruent.

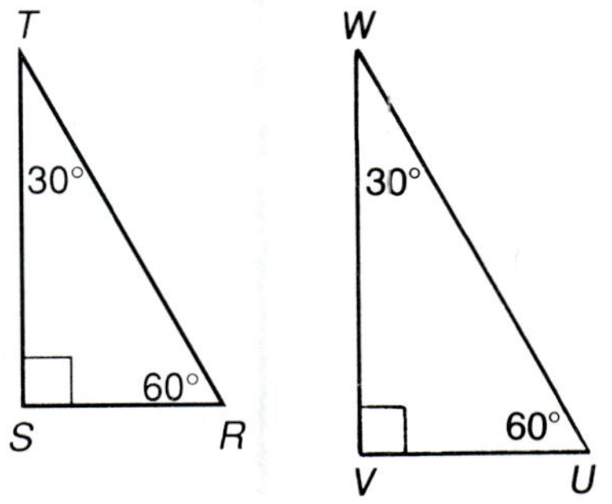

10. Is $\triangle RST \cong \triangle UVW$? Why or why not?

Independent Study Handbook

Contents

How to Use a Calculator

Calculators are used in everyday life at home and at work. They save time when solving problems with large numbers or problems with many numbers. *Remember*:

- **Do** estimate to check whether you pushed the correct buttons.
- **Don't** use a calculator when paper and pencil or mental math is faster.

Calculator displays

- **Number of digits** How many digits will your calculator display? If you press 99,999 × 99,999 to generate a number with more digits than the display can show, most calculators will show some kind of "error" message.
- **Unnecessary zeros** If you add 2.10 and 3.20, does your display show 5.3 or 5.30? Calculators usually drop unnecessary zeros.
- **Rounding** If you divide 2 by 3, do you see 0.6666666 or 0.6666667? Many calculators drop any digits after 8 digits, rather than round.

Calculator keys

Square Root
Finds the square root of the display.

Percent
Helps do percent problems.

Change Sign
Changes the display from positive to negative or negative to positive.

Memory Recall
Displays what is in memory. Push it twice to clear the memory.

Divide

Multiply

Subtract

Add

Equals

Decimal point

Memory Minus
Subtracts the display from what is in the memory.

Memory Plus
Adds the display to what is in the memory.

On-Off, Clear
Turns the calculator on. Press it once to clear the last number entered. Press it twice to clear everything.

Calculator key sequences

- **Order of operations** Press 2 [+] 3 [×] 4 [=]. If you get 20, your calculator does operations in the order they are pressed. If you get 14, your calculator does multiplication before addition.
- **Memory Keys** Press 28.4 [+] 16.2 [M+]. Then press 96 [−] [MRC]. Pressing the [M+] key completes an operation and adds the result to the memory. Pressing the [MRC] key displays the number in memory.

Problem-Solving Help File

Use these pages when you need help with problem solving.

Problem-Solving Guide

There is no recipe or magic formula for solving problems. But keeping a problem-solving guide in mind can help you become a better problem solver.

PROBLEM SOLVING GUIDE

Understand
QUESTION
FACTS
KEY IDEA

Plan and Solve
STRATEGY
ANSWER

Look Back
SENSIBLE ANSWER
ALTERNATE APPROACH

Understand

QUESTION

- What are you asked to find?
- Try to state the question in your own words.
- Is an exact answer needed?

FACTS

- What facts are given?
- Is there too much or too little information?
- Is data needed from a picture, table, or graph?
- Do you need to collect some data?

KEY IDEA

- How are the facts and the question related?
- Are there groups that are part of a whole?
- Are two groups being compared?
- Are there groups that are joining or separating?
- Are there groups of the same size?

Plan and Solve

STRATEGY

- What can you do to solve the problem?
- Can the problem be solved by computing?
- Estimate the answer.
- Choose a strategy. Try another, if needed.

ANSWER

- Give the answer in a sentence.
- Do you need to interpret a remainder?
- Is rounding needed?

Look Back

SENSIBLE ANSWER

- Did you check your work?
- Did you use all the needed data?
- Does your answer have the correct units?
- Is your answer close to the estimate?
- Is your answer reasonable for the situation?

ALTERNATE APPROACH

- Is there another way to get the same answer?
- Could you use the same strategy differently?
- Would another strategy be faster or simpler?

Problem-Solving Strategies

You might think of problem-solving strategies as problem-solving tools that you own and use when needed. One or more strategies might be used for a problem. And if one strategy doesn't work, try another one.

PROBLEM SOLVING STRATEGIES

Choose an Operation
Solve a Simpler Problem
Use a Formula
Write an Equation
Make a Graph
Draw a Diagram
Make a Table
Try and Check
Find a Pattern
Work Backward
Use Logical Reasoning

TIPS FOR PROBLEM SOLVERS

Don't give up. Some problems take longer than others.

Problem-Solving Behaviors and Attitudes

When you solve problems, do you give up quickly or lack confidence? Behaviors and attitudes can affect your work. So, remember these tips. They can help you become a better problem solver.

- **Don't give up.** Some problems take longer than others.
- **Be flexible.** If you get stuck, try another idea.
- **Be confident** so you can do your best.
- **Take risks.** Try your hunches. They often work.
- **Brainstorm to get started**—one idea will lead to another.
- **Visualize the problem** in your mind to help you understand it better.
- **Compare problems** to help you relate new problems to ones you've solved before.
- **Think about your thinking.** Pause to ask, "How is this going to help me solve the problem?"
- **Share your thinking with others.** Explaining your ideas helps you think better.
- **Organize your work** to help you think clearly.

Mental Math Strategies

Often the best calculator is your own mind. For simple calculations, mental math can be better than paper and pencil or a calculator. To sharpen your mental math skills, use the mental computation strategies shown on these pages.

Breaking Apart Numbers

Break apart one or more numbers to get numbers that are easier to use.

54 + 23
54 + 20 + 3
74 + 3
77

Break apart 23.
Use the associative property.

87 × 2
(80 + 7) × 2
(80 × 2) + (7 × 2)
160 + 14
174

Break apart 87.
Use the distributive property.

35 + 48
(30 + 5) + (40 + 8)
(30 + 40) + (5 + 8)
70 + 13
83

Break apart 35 and 48.
Regroup the numbers.

60% of 900
6 × 0.10 × 900
6 × 90
540

Break apart 60%.
Find 10% of 900.
Then multiply by 6.

Compatible Numbers

Compatible numbers are pairs of numbers that are easy to use. Look for numbers like 1, 10, 100 or 3, 30, 300 that are easy to use.

40 + 30
70

28.6 × 10
286

180 ÷ 60
3

When there are 3 or more numbers, look for pairs of numbers that are compatible.

−3 + 48 + −7
−3 + −7 + 48
−10 + 48
38

$\mathbf{\frac{1}{3} \times 7 \times 12}$
$\frac{1}{3} \times 12 \times 7$
4 × 7
28

Using Equivalent Forms

Divide to find "fraction of."

$\frac{1}{3} \times$ **180**

180 ÷ 3

60

Change decimals or percents to fractions to get a number that is easier to use.

25% of 32

$\frac{1}{4}$ of 32

32 ÷ 4

8

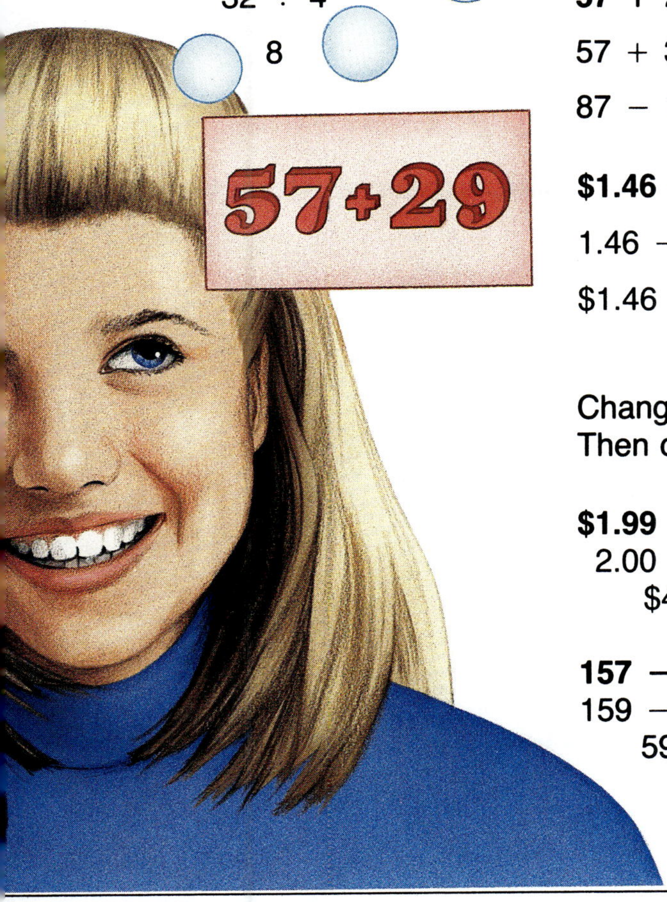

Compensation

Change one number to make it easy to use. Then change the answer to compensate.

57 + 29

57 + 30 = 87 Add 1 to 29 to get 30.

87 − 1 = 86 Subtract 1 from the answer.

\$1.46 − \$0.97

1.46 − 1.00 = 0.46 Add 3¢ to 97¢.

\$1.46 − \$0.97 = \$0.49 Add 3¢ to the answer.

Change one number to make it easy to use. Then change the other number to compensate.

\$1.99 + \$2.12

2.00 + 2.11

\$4.11

Add 1¢ to \$1.99 and subtract 1¢ from \$2.12.

157 − 98

159 − 100

59

Add 2 to 98 and to 157.

Estimation Strategies

In everyday life, an exact answer is often unnecessary. For example, you can estimate while shopping to see if you have enough money.

When you do need an exact answer, estimation helps you find possible errors. Estimation is especially important for checking whether you pushed a wrong button on a calculator.

To help you make good estimates, use the estimation strategies shown on these pages.

Front-End Digits

Use just the first digit in each number to help you make an estimate.

$$\begin{array}{r} \mathbf{173} \\ \mathbf{421} \\ \underline{+\mathbf{348}} \end{array} \qquad \begin{array}{r} 100 \\ 400 \\ \underline{+300} \\ 800 \end{array}$$

Since 73 + 21 + 48 is more than 100, you can adjust the estimate by adding 100 to get 900.

Rounding

Round to one nonzero digit.

$$\begin{array}{r} \mathbf{425} \\ \underline{\times \mathbf{28}} \end{array} \qquad \begin{array}{r} 400 \\ \underline{\times \quad 30} \\ 12{,}000 \end{array}$$

Round to the same place.

$$\begin{array}{r} \mathbf{28.45} \\ \underline{-\ \mathbf{3.79}} \end{array} \qquad \begin{array}{r} 28 \\ \underline{-\ \ 4} \\ 24 \end{array}$$

$$\mathbf{13\tfrac{1}{4}} + \mathbf{8\tfrac{7}{8}}$$
$$13 + 9$$
$$22$$

Round to the nearest half.

$$\mathbf{\tfrac{3}{8}} + \mathbf{2\tfrac{5}{8}} + \mathbf{\tfrac{1}{4}}$$
$$\tfrac{1}{2} + 2\tfrac{1}{2} + \tfrac{1}{2}$$
$$3\tfrac{1}{2}$$

Round both numbers up and both numbers down to get a range.

57 × 84 $\qquad 60 \times 90 = 5{,}400$
$\qquad\qquad\quad 50 \times 80 = 4{,}000$

57 × 84 is between 4,000 and 5,400.

Substituting Compatible Numbers

Use numbers that are close to the original numbers.

$\mathbf{23\overline{)476}}$

$24\overline{)480}$ or $23\overline{)460}$ or $25\overline{)500}$

$23\overline{)476}$ is about 20.

24 × 78 × 4

25 × 78 × 4

100 × 78

24 × 78 × 4 is about 7,800.

$\mathbf{\frac{1}{3} \times 187}$

$\frac{1}{3} \times 180$

$\frac{1}{3} \times 187$ is about 60.

26% of 32

25% of 32

$\frac{1}{4} \times 32$

26% of 32 is about 8.

Clustering

Look for groups of numbers that are close to the same number.

\$6.27 **\$6.58** **\$5.89** **+ \$6.13**	Each number is about \$6.00, so the sum is 4 × 6 or 24.

$\mathbf{4\frac{7}{8} + 5\frac{1}{5} + 4\frac{2}{3}}$

Each number is about 5, so the sum is about 3 × 5 or 15.

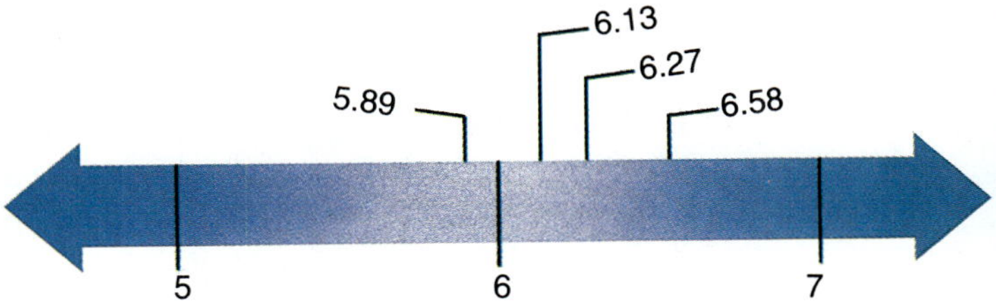

Comparing to a Reference Point

Compare the numbers to numbers you can work with easily.

346 **+ 438**	Both numbers are less than 500, so the sum is less than 1,000.
$\mathbf{\frac{5}{8} + \frac{3}{5}}$	Both numbers are greater than $\frac{1}{2}$, so the sum is greater than 1.

Math Study Skills

Try these math study skills to help you do your best.

Before a Lesson

- **Preview the lesson.** Look over the lesson to see what it's about.
- **Set a purpose.** Are you about to learn a new topic or revisit a familiar one?
- **Recall what you know.** What have you learned about this topic previously?

Build Understanding

Reading the lesson

- **Read slowly.** Don't try to read a math book as fast as a story book.
- **Learn vocabulary and symbols.** Note new math terms and symbols. Use the glossary and index. Watch for words like "product" that have other meanings outside of math.
- **Read diagrams, tables, graphs.** Use a ruler to help you read rows and columns.
- **Do the examples.** Work the examples yourself as you go through them.

Doing Activities

- **Use materials.** Keep the materials organized. Use them to explore new ideas.
- **Work with others.** When you work with others, use the tips for working together given on page 600.

Check Understanding

Trying on your own

- **Note what you don't understand.** When you try some exercises, be aware of what you don't understand.
- **Reread the lesson.** When you don't understand, reread the "Build Understanding" section.

Preventing errors

- **Find another example.** When you need another example, turn to the "Reteaching" set at the back of the chapter.
- **Try again.** Keep trying until you feel you understand.

Practice and Problem Solving

Reading the exercises

- **Read directions.** Read carefully.
- **Read word problems.** Read slowly and reread, if needed.

Doing written work

- **Show your work.** Record what you did. Make your solution easy to follow and the answer easy to find.
- **Check your work.** Review what you write.
- **Find more practice.** Use the "More Practice" at the back of the chapter when needed.

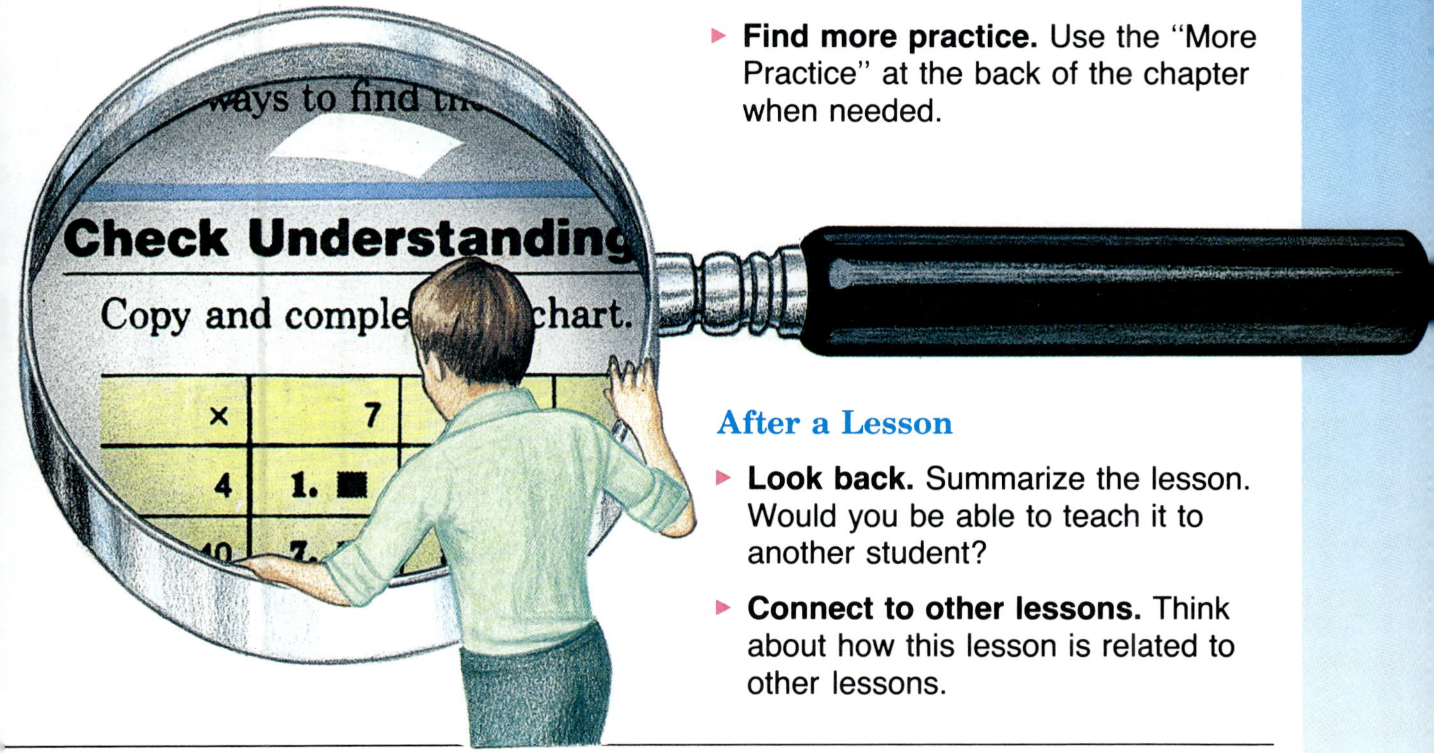

After a Lesson

- **Look back.** Summarize the lesson. Would you be able to teach it to another student?
- **Connect to other lessons.** Think about how this lesson is related to other lessons.

Working in Groups

When you do math working with others, you'll learn more math, you'll learn how to work as a team, and you'll enjoy math more.

TIPS FOR WORKING TOGETHER

You can disagree without being disagreeable.

Roles for Group Members

When you work in a group, it can be helpful for each person to have a role. Some roles are:

- **Reporter**—This person summarizes the group's thinking.
- **Encourager**—This person encourages group members to take part and to work together well.
- **Recorder**—This person records the group's work.
- **Checker**—This person asks group members to explain their thinking or may ask others if they agree.
- **Materials Manager**—This person gets any materials that are needed and returns them at the end of class.

Tips for Working Together

Here are some tips for working well with others in a group.

- Involve your whole group. Help everyone to participate.
- Help keep your group on task.
- To make sure your group understands the task or solution, have each group member say it in his or her own words, summarize the steps, or give an example.
- Work as a group. If you understand, help another group member. Don't work ahead of the others.
- Be a good tutor. Make up similar problems or easier ones to help someone understand.
- When you are unsure, ask someone in your group for help or say you don't understand.
- Tell someone when he or she does or says something that helps you.
- Don't decide by voting. Try to understand which might be the best solution and why.
- Remember, you can disagree without being disagreeable.

Tables

Metric System

Length	10 millimeters (mm)	=	1 centimeter (cm)
	10 centimeters 100 millimeters	=	1 decimeter (dm)
	10 decimeters 100 centimeters	=	1 meter (m)
	1,000 meters	=	1 kilometer (km)
Area	100 square millimeters (mm^2)	=	1 square centimeter (cm^2)
	10,000 square centimeters	=	1 square meter (m^2)
	100 square meters	=	1 are (a)
	10,000 square meters	=	1 hectare (ha)
Volume	1,000 cubic millimeters (mm^3)	=	1 cubic centimeter (cm^3)
	1,000 cubic centimeters	=	1 cubic decimeter (dm^3)
	1,000,000 cubic centimeters	=	1 cubic meter (m^3)
Mass (weight)	1,000 milligrams (mg)	=	1 gram (g)
	1,000 grams	=	1 kilogram (kg)
	1,000 kilograms	=	1 metric ton (t)
Capacity	1,000 milliliters (mL)	=	1 liter (L)

Time

60 seconds	=	1 minute
60 minutes	=	1 hour
24 hours	=	1 day
7 days	=	1 week
365 days 52 weeks 12 months	=	1 year
366 days	=	1 leap year

Geometric Formulas

Area	
rectangle	$A = \ell w$
parallelogram	$A = bh$
triangle	$A = \frac{1}{2}bh$
circle	$A = \pi r^2$
Surface Area	
cylinder	$A = 2\pi r^2 + 2\pi rh$
Circumference	
circle	$C = \pi d$ or $C = 2\pi r$
Perimeter	
rectangle	$P = 2\ell + 2w$
Volume	
rectangular prism	$V = \ell wh$
prism	$V = Bh$
cylinder	$V = \pi r^2 h$

Customary System

Length	12 inches (in.)	=	1 foot (ft)
	3 feet 36 inches	=	1 yard (yd)
	1,760 yards 5,280 feet	=	1 mile (mi)
	6,076 feet	=	1 nautical mile
Area	144 square inches (sq in.)	=	1 square foot (sq ft)
	9 square feet	=	1 square yard (sq yd)
	4,840 square yards	=	1 acre (A)
Volume	1,728 cubic inches (cu in.)	=	1 cubic foot (cu ft)
	27 cubic feet	=	1 cubic yard (cu yd)
Weight	16 ounces (oz)	=	1 pound (lb)
	2,000 pounds	=	1 ton (T)
Capacity	8 fluid ounces (fl oz)	=	1 cup (c)
	2 cups	=	1 pint (pt)
	2 pints	=	1 quart (qt)
	4 quarts	=	1 gallon (gal)

Tables

Squares and Square Roots

n	n^2	$\sqrt{n}$	n	n^2	$\sqrt{n}$	n	n^2	$\sqrt{n}$	n	n^2	$\sqrt{n}$
1	1	1.000	**51**	2,601	7.141	**101**	10,201	10.050	**151**	22,801	12.288
2	4	1.414	**52**	2,704	7.211	**102**	10,404	10.100	**152**	23,104	12.329
3	9	1.732	**53**	2,809	7.280	**103**	10,609	10.149	**153**	23,409	12.369
4	16	2.000	**54**	2,916	7.348	**104**	10,816	10.198	**154**	23,716	12.410
5	25	2.236	**55**	3,025	7.416	**105**	11,025	10.247	**155**	24,025	12.450
6	36	2.449	**56**	3,136	7.483	**106**	11,236	10.296	**156**	24,336	12.490
7	49	2.646	**57**	3,249	7.550	**107**	11,449	10.344	**157**	24,649	12.530
8	64	2.828	**58**	3,364	7.616	**108**	11,664	10.392	**158**	24,964	12.570
9	81	3.000	**59**	3,481	7.681	**109**	11,881	10.440	**159**	25,281	12.610
10	100	3.162	**60**	3,600	7.746	**110**	12,100	10.488	**160**	25,600	12.649
11	121	3.317	**61**	3,721	7.810	**111**	12,321	10.536	**161**	25,921	12.689
12	144	3.464	**62**	3,844	7.874	**112**	12,544	10.583	**162**	26,244	12.728
13	169	3.606	**63**	3,969	7.937	**113**	12,769	10.630	**163**	26,569	12.767
14	196	3.742	**64**	4,096	8.000	**114**	12,996	10.677	**164**	26,896	12.806
15	225	3.873	**65**	4,225	8.062	**115**	13,225	10.724	**165**	27,225	12.845
16	256	4.000	**66**	4,356	8.124	**116**	13,456	10.770	**166**	27,556	12.884
17	289	4.123	**67**	4,489	8.185	**117**	13,689	10.817	**167**	27,889	12.923
18	324	4.243	**68**	4,624	8.246	**118**	13,924	10.863	**168**	28,224	12.961
19	361	4.359	**69**	4,761	8.307	**119**	14,161	10.909	**169**	28,561	13.000
20	400	4.472	**70**	4,900	8.367	**120**	14,400	10.954	**170**	28,900	13.038
21	441	4.583	**71**	5,041	8.426	**121**	14,641	11.000	**171**	29,241	13.077
22	484	4.690	**72**	5,184	8.485	**122**	14,884	11.045	**172**	29,584	13.115
23	529	4.796	**73**	5,329	8.544	**123**	15,129	11.091	**173**	29,929	13.153
24	576	4.899	**74**	5,476	8.602	**124**	15,376	11.136	**174**	30,276	13.191
25	625	5.000	**75**	5,625	8.660	**125**	15,625	11.180	**175**	30,625	13.229
26	676	5.099	**76**	5,776	8.718	**126**	15,876	11.225	**176**	30,976	13.266
27	729	5.196	**77**	5,929	8.775	**127**	16,129	11.269	**177**	31,329	13.304
28	784	5.292	**78**	6,084	8.832	**128**	16,384	11.314	**178**	31,684	13.342
29	841	5.385	**79**	6,241	8.888	**129**	16,641	11.358	**179**	32,041	13.379
30	900	5.477	**80**	6,400	8.944	**130**	16,900	11.402	**180**	32,400	13.416
31	961	5.568	**81**	6,561	9.000	**131**	17,161	11.446	**181**	32,761	13.454
32	1,024	5.657	**82**	6,724	9.055	**132**	17,424	11.489	**182**	33,124	13.491
33	1,089	5.745	**83**	6,889	9.110	**133**	17,689	11.533	**183**	33,489	13.528
34	1,156	5.831	**84**	7,056	9.165	**134**	17,956	11.576	**184**	33,856	13.565
35	1,225	5.916	**85**	7,225	9.220	**135**	18,225	11.619	**185**	34,225	13.601
36	1,296	6.000	**86**	7,396	9.274	**136**	18,496	11.662	**186**	34,596	13.638
37	1,369	6.083	**87**	7,569	9.327	**137**	18,769	11.705	**187**	34,969	13.675
38	1,444	6.164	**88**	7,744	9.381	**138**	19,044	11.747	**188**	35,344	13.711
39	1,521	6.245	**89**	7,921	9.434	**139**	19,321	11.790	**189**	35,721	13.748
40	1,600	6.325	**90**	8,100	9.487	**140**	19,600	11.832	**190**	36,100	13.784
41	1,681	6.403	**91**	8,281	9.539	**141**	19,881	11.874	**191**	36,481	13.820
42	1,764	6.481	**92**	8,464	9.592	**142**	20,164	11.916	**192**	36,864	13.856
43	1,849	6.557	**93**	8,649	9.644	**143**	20,449	11.958	**193**	37,249	13.892
44	1,936	6.633	**94**	8,836	9.695	**144**	20,736	12.000	**194**	37,636	13.928
45	2,025	6.708	**95**	9,025	9.747	**145**	21,025	12.042	**195**	38,025	13.964
46	2,116	6.782	**96**	9,216	9.798	**146**	21,316	12.083	**196**	38,416	14.000
47	2,209	6.856	**97**	9,409	9.849	**147**	21,609	12.124	**197**	38,809	14.036
48	2,304	6.928	**98**	9,604	9.899	**148**	21,904	12.166	**198**	39,204	14.071
49	2,401	7.000	**99**	9,801	9.950	**149**	22,201	12.207	**199**	39,601	14.107
50	2,500	7.071	**100**	10,000	10.000	**150**	21,500	12.247	**200**	40,000	14.142

Trigonometric Ratios

Measure of angle	tan	sin	cos	Measure of angle	tan	sin	cos
1°	0.017	0.017	1.000	**46°**	1.036	0.719	0.695
2°	0.035	0.035	0.999	**47°**	1.072	0.731	0.682
3°	0.052	0.052	0.999	**48°**	1.111	0.743	0.669
4°	0.070	0.070	0.998	**49°**	1.150	0.755	0.656
5°	0.087	0.087	0.996	**50°**	1.192	0.766	0.643
6°	0.105	0.105	0.995	**51°**	1.235	0.777	0.629
7°	0.123	0.122	0.993	**52°**	1.280	0.788	0.616
8°	0.141	0.139	0.990	**53°**	1.327	0.799	0.602
9°	0.158	0.156	0.988	**54°**	1.376	0.809	0.588
10°	0.176	0.174	0.985	**55°**	1.428	0.819	0.574
11°	0.194	0.191	0.982	**56°**	1.483	0.829	0.559
12°	0.213	0.208	0.978	**57°**	1.540	0.839	0.545
13°	0.231	0.225	0.974	**58°**	1.600	0.848	0.530
14°	0.249	0.242	0.970	**59°**	1.664	0.857	0.515
15°	0.268	0.259	0.966	**60°**	1.732	0.866	0.500
16°	0.287	0.276	0.961	**61°**	1.804	0.875	0.485
17°	0.306	0.292	0.956	**62°**	1.881	0.883	0.469
18°	0.325	0.309	0.951	**63°**	1.963	0.891	0.454
19°	0.344	0.326	0.946	**64°**	2.050	0.899	0.438
20°	0.364	0.342	0.940	**65°**	2.145	0.906	0.423
21°	0.384	0.358	0.934	**66°**	2.246	0.914	0.407
22°	0.404	0.375	0.927	**67°**	2.356	0.921	0.391
23°	0.424	0.391	0.921	**68°**	2.475	0.927	0.375
24°	0.445	0.407	0.914	**69°**	2.605	0.934	0.358
25°	0.466	0.423	0.906	**70°**	2.748	0.940	0.342
26°	0.488	0.438	0.899	**71°**	2.904	0.946	0.326
27°	0.510	0.454	0.891	**72°**	3.078	0.951	0.309
28°	0.532	0.469	0.883	**73°**	3.271	0.956	0.292
29°	0.554	0.485	0.875	**74°**	3.487	0.961	0.276
30°	0.577	0.500	0.866	**75°**	3.732	0.966	0.259
31°	0.601	0.515	0.857	**76°**	4.011	0.970	0.242
32°	0.625	0.530	0.848	**77°**	4.332	0.974	0.225
33°	0.649	0.545	0.839	**78°**	4.705	0.978	0.208
34°	0.675	0.559	0.829	**79°**	5.145	0.982	0.191
35°	0.700	0.574	0.819	**80°**	5.671	0.985	0.174
36°	0.727	0.588	0.809	**81°**	6.314	0.988	0.156
37°	0.754	0.602	0.799	**82°**	7.115	0.990	0.139
38°	0.781	0.616	0.788	**83°**	8.144	0.993	0.122
39°	0.810	0.629	0.777	**84°**	9.514	0.995	0.105
40°	0.839	0.643	0.766	**85°**	11.430	0.996	0.087
41°	0.869	0.656	0.755	**86°**	14.301	0.998	0.070
42°	0.900	0.669	0.743	**87°**	19.081	0.999	0.052
43°	0.933	0.682	0.731	**88°**	28.636	0.999	0.035
44°	0.966	0.695	0.719	**89°**	57.290	1.000	0.017
45°	1.000	0.707	0.707				

Tangent

$$\frac{\text{length of opposite side}}{\text{length of adjacent side}}$$

Sine

$$\frac{\text{length of opposite side}}{\text{length of hypotenuse}}$$

Cosine

$$\frac{\text{length of adjacent side}}{\text{length of hypotenuse}}$$

Glossary

A

Absolute value The number of units a number is from 0 on a number line.

Acute angle An angle with a measure less than 90°.

Adjacent angles Angles that have a common vertex and a common side between them.

Alternate interior (exterior) angles Angles that are between (outside) two parallel lines intersected by a transversal and on opposite sides of the transversal

Angle (∠) A figure formed by two rays with the same endpoint.

Area A number given in *square units* that indicates the size of the inside of a plane figure.

Associative property The way in which addends (or factors) are grouped does not affect the sum (or product).
$(a + b) + c = a + (b + c)$
$(a \times b) \times c = a \times (b \times c)$

Average A number obtained by dividing the sum of two or more addends by the number of addends.

B

Base (1) (of an exponent) A number raised to a power. In 4^3, 4 is the base. (2) (geometry) A name used for a side of a polygon or surface of a space figure.

Bisect To divide into two congruent parts.

Broken-line graph A drawing that shows how quantities change over time.

C

Central angle An angle with its vertex at the center of a circle.

Chord A segment with both endpoints on a circle.

Circle A plane figure with all points the same distance from a given point called the *center*.

Circle graph A drawing that compares the parts of a quantity with the whole quantity.

Circumference The distance around a circle.

Closure property If a and b are rational numbers, then $a + b$ and $a \times b$ are unique rational numbers.

Combination A selection of objects without regard to order.

Common denominator A common multiple of two or more denominators. A common denominator for $\frac{1}{6}$ and $\frac{3}{8}$ is 48.

Common multiple A number that is a multiple of two or more numbers.

Commutative property The order in which numbers are added (or multiplied) does not affect the sum (or product).
$a + b = b + a$
$a \times b = b \times a$

Complementary angles Two angles whose measures add up to 90°.

Composite number A whole number, greater than 0, that has more than two factors.

Cone A solid figure formed by connecting a circle to a point not in the plane of the circle.

Congruent figures Two figures with the same size and shape.

Construction The drawing of a figure using only a compass and a straightedge.

Coordinate plane The plane formed by two intersecting perpendicular number lines.

Coordinates An ordered pair of numbers used to locate a point in a coordinate plane.

Corresponding parts Matching parts of similar figures.

Cosine For a given acute angle in a right triangle, the ratio:
$$\frac{\text{Length of side adjacent to } \angle X}{\text{Length of hypotenuse}}$$

Cross-products The cross-products of the ratios $\frac{3}{4}$ and $\frac{9}{12}$ are 3×12 and 4×9.

Cube A prism with all square faces.

Customary system of measurement A system for measuring length in *inches, feet, yards, miles;* capacity in *cups, pints, quarts, gallons;* weight in *ounces, pounds, tons;* temperature in *degrees Fahrenheit.*

Cylinder A solid figure with two circular bases that are parallel and congruent.

D

Data A collection of gathered information that has not been organized.

Decimal A number used to name a whole quantity and/or a fractional part.

Degree (of an angle) A unit for measuring angles.

Dependent events Events for which one outcome affects another outcome.

Diagonal A segment with two nonadjacent vertices of a polygon as its endpoints.

Diameter In a circle, a segment that passes through the center and that has both endpoints on the circle.

Dilation A transformation that changes a figure's size but not its shape.

Distributive property When a factor is a sum, multiplying each addend before adding does not change the product.

Divisible One number is divisible by another if the remainder is zero after dividing.

Divisor A number that is divided into another number, the *dividend.*

Edge Segment where two faces of a polyhedron meet.

Endpoint The point at the end of a segment or ray.

Equation A mathematical sentence that states the equality of expressions.

Equilateral triangle Triangle with three congruent sides.

Estimate A number that is close to another number. A name used for a calculation not requiring an exact answer.

Experimental probability Ratio of the number of successes to the number of trials.

Exponent A number that tells how many times the base is to be used as a factor. 4^3 means $4 \times 4 \times 4$, and is read 4 to the third *power.*

Expression A mathematical phrase that uses numbers, variables, and operation symbols to represent a value.

Face Flat surface that is part of a polyhedron.

Factor (1) A number to be multiplied. (2) A number that divides evenly into a given second number is a factor of that number.

Favorable outcome A result in a probability experiment that meets a specific condition.

Formula An equation that states a general fact or rule by using variables.

Fraction A number that names a part of a whole or of a set.

Frequency table A table that shows the number of times a particular item occurs in a set of data.

Fundamental Counting Principle If there are m possible outcomes for one event, n possible outcomes for a second event, and p possible outcomes for a third event, then the total number of possible outcomes is $m \times n \times p$.

Graph A drawing used to show information in an organized way.

Greatest common factor (GCF) (1) The greatest number that is a factor of two or more numbers. (2) The greatest number that divides two or more numbers with no remainder.

Greatest possible error (GPE) One half of the unit being used to find a measure.

Half-planes A line divides a plane into three distinct sets of points: the line itself and two half-planes.

Height The segment from a vertex perpendicular to the line containing the opposite side.

Hypotenuse In a right triangle, the side opposite the right angle.

Improper fraction A fraction whose numerator is greater than or equal to its denominator.

Independent events Events for which one outcome does not affect another outcome.

Inequality A mathematical sentence with one of the following symbols: $<, >, \leq, \geq$.

Inscribed angle An angle whose vertex is on the circle and whose sides are chords of the circle.

Integers The whole numbers and their opposites. Some integers are $+3$, -3, 0, $+16$, -16.

Intersecting lines Lines that meet at a point.

Irrational number A number that cannot be written as a fraction. A nonrepeating decimal.

Isosceles triangle Triangle with two congruent sides.

Least common multiple (LCM) The smallest number that is a common multiple of two or more given numbers.

Legs of a right triangle The two sides forming the right angle.

Line A set of points continuing without end in opposite directions.

Linear equation An equation with solutions which lie on a straight line when graphed.

Line plot A graph that uses Xs to show information and compare quantities.

Line segment Two points and the straight path between them.

Mean *See* average.

Median The middle number in a group of numbers when the numbers are listed in order.

Metric system A system of measures with basic units of: meter for length, liter for capacity, gram for mass, and degrees Celsius for temperature.

Midpoint A point that divides a segment into two congruent segments.

Mixed number A number that has a whole number part and a fraction part.

Mode Number that occurs most often in a set of data.

Multiple A multiple of a number is the product of that number and a whole number.

Obtuse angle An angle with a measure greater than 90° and less than 180°.

Octagon An eight-sided polygon.

Opposites Two numbers whose sum is 0.

Origin On a coordinate grid, the point, (0, 0), where the two axes intersect.

Outcome A possible result in a probability experiment.

Parallel lines Lines in a plane that never meet.

Parallelogram A quadrilateral with opposite sides parallel and congruent.

Pattern A general form by which things can be arranged in an organized way.

Percent (%) A ratio that compares a number to 100. 45% means 45 hundredths.

Perfect squares A number whose square root is an integer.

Perimeter The sum of the lengths of the sides of a polygon.

Permutation An ordered selection of items from a given group.

Perpendicular lines Lines that intersect to form right angles.

Pi (π) The number obtained by dividing the circumference of any circle by its diameter. A common approximation for π is 3.14.

Plane A flat surface that extends without end in all directions.

Point An exact location in space.

Polygon A closed plane figure made by line segments.

Polyhedron A solid figure made up of flat surfaces called *faces*. Each face is a polygon.

Precision A property of measurement based on the size of the unit of measure. The smaller the unit, the more precise the measurement.

Prime factorization A number written as the product of prime numbers. $30 = 2 \times 3 \times 5$

Prime number A whole number, greater than 1, that has exactly two factors: itself and 1.

Prism A polyhedron with two parallel, congruent faces, called *bases*. All other faces are parallelograms.

Probability A number from 0 to 1 that tells how likely it is that a given event will occur. The closer to 1, the *more likely* the event is to occur. The closer to 0, the *less likely* it is to occur.

Property of one The product of one and a number is that number.

Property of zero The sum of 0 and a number is that number. The product of 0 and a number is 0.

Proportion A statement that two ratios are equal. $\frac{2}{5} = \frac{12}{30}$

Pyramid The solid figure formed by connecting points of a polygon to a point not in the plane of the polygon. The polygon and its interior is the *base*.

Pythagorean Theorem In a right triangle, the sum of the squares of the legs equals the square of the hypotenuse. $a^2 + b^2 = c^2$

Quadrant One of the four parts into which a plane is divided by two perpendicular lines.

Quadrilateral A four-sided polygon.

Quotient The answer after dividing one number by another.

Radius (1) In a circle, a segment that connects the center of the circle with a point on the circle. (2) In a circle, the distance from the center to a point on the circle.

Range The difference between the greatest and the least numbers in a set of data.

Rate A ratio that compares one quantity to a different kind of quantity.

Ratio A pair of numbers that expresses a rate or a comparison.

Rational number Any number that can be written as a fraction. A terminating or repeating decimal.

Ray A set of points that has one endpoint and that extends without end in one direction.

Real numbers The set of numbers consisting of all rational and all irrational numbers.

Reciprocals Two numbers whose product is 1. $\frac{3}{4}$ and $\frac{4}{3}$ are reciprocals because $\frac{3}{4} \times \frac{4}{3} = 1$.

Rectangle A parallelogram with four right angles.

Regular polygon A polygon with all sides congruent and all angles congruent.

Relative error The ratio of the greatest possible error to the measurement.

Repeating decimal A decimal in which one or more digits repeats, such as 0.518181818...

Repetend The repeating digit or digits in a repeating decimal.

Rhombus A parallelogram with four congruent sides.

Right angle An angle with a measure of 90°.

Right triangle Triangle with one right angle.

Sample Part of a group upon which an experiment or survey is conducted.

Sample space A list of possible outcomes.

Scale drawing A drawing made so that distances in the drawing are proportional to actual distances.

Scalene triangle Triangle with no congruent sides.

Scientific notation A way to write a number as the product of a power of 10 and a number greater than or equal to 1 and less than 10.

Sequence A set of numbers in a certain order, usually formed by a pattern.
arithmetic: 0,2,4,6,8,...
geometric: 1,2,4,8,16,...
Fibonacci: 1,1,2,3,5,8,...

Significant digits The digits needed to express the number of units in a measure.

Similar figures Figures with the same shape but not necessarily the same size.

Simplest form A fraction for which the greatest common factor of both the numerator and denominator is 1.

Sine For a given acute angle in a right triangle, the ratio:
$\frac{\text{Length of side opposite } \angle X}{\text{Length of hypotenuse}}$

Skew lines Lines that are in two different planes.

Slant height In a cone, the distance from the vertex to a point on the circumference of the base. In a regular pyramid, the height of the triangular faces.

Solution A value of a variable that makes an equation true.

Sphere A solid figure with all points the same distance from a given point called the *center*.

Square (1) (geometry) a rectangle with four congruent sides. (2) (numeration) To multiply a number by itself.

Square root A number a is the square root of a number b if $a \times a = b$. 3 is the square root of 9.

Standard form The notation for writing numbers using the digits 0–9 and each place represents a power of ten.

Standard order of operations Rules for finding the value of an expression.

Statistics Numerical facts that are collected, organized, and analyzed.

Stem-and-leaf plot A way to display numerical data in which tens digits (stems) appear in a vertical line and ones digits (leaves) appear in horizontal lines.

Straight angle An angle whose measure is 180°.

Supplementary angles Two angles whose measures add up to 180°.

Surface area The sum of the areas of all the surfaces of a solid figure.

Symmetric figure A plane figure that can be folded into two congruent parts. The fold is the *line of symmetry*.

Tangent For a given acute angle in a right triangle, the ratio:
$\frac{\text{Length of side opposite } \angle X}{\text{Length of side adjacent to } \angle X}$

Term (1) The numbers in a sequence. (2) In the ratio $a{:}b$, a is the first term and b is the second term.

Terminating decimal A decimal with an exact number of nonzero digits, such as 0.375.

Theorem A mathematical statement that can be proven by using accepted ideas.

Theoretical probability Ratio of the favorable outcomes to the possible outcomes for an event.

Transformation A flip (reflection), slide (translation), or turn (rotation) that changes the location of a figure on a plane without changing its size or shape.

Transversal A line that intersects two or more lines in the same plane.

Trapezoid A quadrilateral with one pair of parallel sides.

Tree diagram An organized way to list all possible outcomes of an experiment.

Variable A letter or symbol used to represent a number.

Venn diagram A diagram using geometric figures to show how sets are related.

Vertex (1) The common endpoint of two rays that form an angle. (2) The point of intersection of two sides of a polygon. (3) The point of intersection of the edges of a polyhedron.

Vertical angles Angles formed by two intersecting lines and sharing only a vertex.

Volume A number given in cubic units that indicates the size of the inside of a space figure.

Whole number One of the numbers 0, 1, 2, 3, and so on.

X-axis The horizontal number line in the coordinate plane.

Y-axis The vertical number line in the coordinate plane.

Answers for Selected odd-Numbered Exercises

Chapter 1

Pages 4-5
1. Find the question to be answered. **3.** In the Strategy step **5.** Answers may vary. Samples: 558, 684, 909 **7.** 990; 981 **9.** Methods may vary. A sample is given. List the numbers for each hundred and add; 54 numbers **11.** 190 digits **13.** 20 **15.** 934,151,617,181,920 **17.** 501,111,111,111,920

Pages 6-9
1. 3, 4, 5, 6, 7, 8, 9, 10; arithmetic **3.** 68 triangles **5.** Neither; 24, 35, 48 **7.** 45, 60, 75 **9.** Arithmetic; 13, 15, 17 **11.** Geometric; 512, 2,048, 8,192 **13.** Neither; 25, 36, 49 **15.** Arithmetic; 20, 25, 30 **17.** Neither; 21, 34, 55 **19.** Neither; $\frac{1}{6}, \frac{1}{7}, \frac{1}{8}$ **Exercises 21-37,** method choices may vary. **21.** 5, 9; M **23.** 19, 51, 83; P **25.** 16, 22, 28; M **27.** 5, 25, 45; M **29.** 1, 25, 49; P **31.** 18, 36; P **33.** 3,300, 3,000; M **35.** 16, 4, 1; P **37.** 1, 296, 216, 1; P **39.** 35 squares **41.** 21, 28, 36, 45, 55 **43.** 8, 14, 20, 26, 32, 38 **45.** 100th **47.** Yes **49.** Yes **Skills Review 1.** 691 **3.** 954 **5.** 155 **7.** 144 **9.** 13 **11.** 1,330 **13.** 300 **15.** 1,268 **17.** 9,108 **19.** 5,895 **21.** 61,470 **23.** 9,101 **25.** 20,482 **27.** 548 **29.** 50

Pages 10-11
1. 1, 1, 2, 3, 5, 8, 13, 21, 34, 55, 89, 144, 233, 377, 610 **3.** 18th, 21st, 24th **5.** Positions that are multiples of 4 (4th, 8th, . . .) **7.** Every 7th position **9.** Every 12th position **11.** 521 **Exercises 13-23,** method choices may vary. **13.** 6, 11, 17, 28; M **15.** 12, 19, 31; M **17.** 5, 15, 40; P **19.** 19, 47, 75, 122; P **21.** 2, 5, 12, 19; P **23.** 11, 19, 30, 79; P **25.** Yes; the Fibonacci sequence, 1, 1, 2, 3, 5, 8, 13, . . ., multiplied by 5 is 5, 5, 10, 15, 25, 40, 65, . . ., and 5 + 5 = 10, 5 + 10 = 15, 10 + 15 = 25, and so on. **27.** 610 bees **29.** The product of two middle numbers is either one more or one less than the product of the first and last.

Pages 12-13
1. 1, 2, 3, 4, 5, 6, 7, 8, 9, 10, 11 **3.** 121; Row 2 **5.** 14,641; Row 4 **7.** 1, 2, 4, 8, 16, 32, 64, 128, 256, 512, 1,024 **9.** Rows 2, 4, 8; row 16(2^n) **11.** 1, 3, 7, 15, 31, 63, 127, 255, 511, 1,023 ($2^n - 1$) **13.** $2^0, 2^1, 2^2, 2^3, 2^4, 2^5, 2^6, 2^7, 2^8, 2^9, 2^{10}$ **15.** 1, 10, 45 **17.** 1, 3, 6, 10, 15, 21, 28, 36 **19.** 1, 5, 15, 35, 70, 126, 210, 330 **21.** Each sequence gives the next diagonal.

Pages 14-15
1. 89 arrangements; 610 arrangements **3.** 1,000,000 **5.** 500,500 **7.** 7 games **9.** 31 games

Pages 18-19
Exercises 1-3, answers will vary. Sample answers are given. **1.** 218 x 4.95, 200 x 5 = 1,000; Rounding to one nonzero digit **3.** 2,467 ÷ 49, 2,500 ÷ 50 = 50; compatible numbers **5.** 20 + 3 + 60 = 8; rounding **7.** 500 – 400 = 100; rounding **9.** $7\overline{)3{,}500}$ = 500; compatible numbers **11.** 40 x 400 = 16,000; rounding **13.** 30 x 100 x 60 = 180,000; rounding **15.** 500 x 40 = 20,000; rounding **17.** 5 x 40 = 200; rounding **19.** 2,000 – 700 = 1,300; rounding **21.** 10,000 ÷ 500 = 20; compatible numbers **23.** 325,000 – 200,000 = 125,000; rounding **25.** 20 x 200 x 200 = 800,000; rounding **27.** 50 x 4 = 200; clustering **29.** 400 + 300 = 700; 642 **31.** 100 + 300 = 400; 475 **33.** About 400 + 100 or 500 miles **35.** About 15 x 4 or $60.00 **37.** About 20 x 2 x 40 or 1,600 miles **39.** Wrong operation **41.** First digit of quotient misplaced

Pages 20-21
1. 20 **3.** 142 **5.** 2 **7.** 49 **9.** 31 **11.** 11 **13.** 92 **15.** 64 **17.** 21 **19.** 50 **21.** 51 **23.** 0 **25.** 0 **27.** 2 **29.** 2 **31.** 4 **33.** 22 **35.** 22 **37.** 4 **39.** (4 + 3) x 2 = 14 **41.** 6 x 9 ÷ (4 + 4) = 6 **43.** 8 x (10 + 2 + 3) = 64 **45.** $\frac{7 \times 1{,}250 + 5 \times 1{,}035}{12}$ = $1,160.42 **47.** (1 + 2) x (3 x 4) **49.** A fraction

Pages 22-23
1. 37 seconds; round down **3.** $18\frac{3}{4}$ seconds **5.** 1 hour 9 minutes 27 seconds **Choose a Strategy 7.** 49 bars **9.** 48 boys **11.** 24 boys

Pages 24-25
1.

n	10 x n	5 x n
2	20	10
4	40	20
5	50	25
10	100	50
12	120	60
24	240	120
124	1,240	620

3. Multiply n by 10. Divide by 2. Add both results. **5.** 468 **7.** Associative; 57 **9.** Associative; 120 **11.** Commutative; 99 **13.** 486 **15.** 424 **17.** 182 **19.** 24 **21.** 122 **23.** 0 **25.** 22,113 **27.** 7,425 **29.** 1, 2, 96,000 **31.** 13,700 **33.** Multiply n by 100, then divide by 4. **Exercises 35-37,** answers may vary.

Pages 26-27
Exercises 1-13, method choices may vary. **1.** 3,413; P **3.** .273; P **5.** $290,000; M **7.** 1,516,764; C **9.** 1,392; P **11.** 55,000; M **13.** 271,490,700; C **Exercises 15-23,** estimates may vary. **15.** 120,000; 121,130 **17.** 1,200,000; 1,468,175 **19.** 400,000; 408,018 **21.** 40,000;

36,739 **23.** 29,000; 30,000 **Exercises 25-27,** method choices may vary. **25.** \$34,700.40; C **27.** \$59,673.00; M

Pages 28-31

1. Even **3.** The number formed by the last two digits is divisible by 4. **5.** The number is even and divisible by both 2 and 3. **7.** 1, 3, 5, 7 **9.** 90: 1, 2, 3, 5, 6, 9, 10, 15, 18, 30, 45, 90; composite **11.** 92: 1, 2, 4, 23, 46, 92; composite **13.** 95: 1, 5 19, 95; composite **15.** 1, 7, 49; composite **17.** 1, 3, 5, 7, 15, 21, 35, 105; composite **19.** 1, 19, 361; composite **21.** 1, 2, 4, 5, 8, 10, 20, 40; composite **23.** 1, 3, 17, 51; composite **25.** 1, 2, 4, 7, 8, 14, 16, 28, 56, 112; composite **27.** 6, 12, 18, 24, 30, 36, 42, 48, 54, 60; No, there are infinitely many. **29.** False; 6 = 2 x 3 but 6 is not divisible by 9. **31.** False; 2 is even and prime. **33.** Rows 3 and 5; the odd numbered rows **35.** 2002; 2014; 2026 **37.** 3, 4, 6 **39.** Answers will vary. A sample is given for numbers 2, 3, 4, and 5. a. Their product is 120. b. Their sum is even. c. Three of the numbers are prime. **41.** 5 days **43.** S1: 1-12; S2: 2, 4, 6, 8, 10, 12; S3: 3, 6, 9, 12; S4: 4, 8, 12; S5: 5, 10; S6: 6, 12; S7: 7; S8: 8; S9: 9; S10: 10; S11: 11; S12: 12; They are multiples of the student number. Multiples of 20. **45.** L1, L2, L3, L4, L5 **47.** 1, 4, 9; 1, 4, 9, 16, 25; 1, 4, 9, 16, 25, 36, 49, 64, 81, 100

Pages 32-33

1. Yes (2 x 2 x 3 x 5) **3.** $2^2 \times 5 \times 11$ **5.** Yes, 35^2 = 1,225 **7.** $3^2 \times 5^2$ **9.** 3×11^2 **11.** $2^2 \times 3^5$ **13.** $2^2 \times 10^3$ **15.** 5 x 11 x 13 x 17 **17.** $3^3 \times 5^3 \times 7^2$ **19.** 7^5; M **21.** 7^8; M **23.** 7^{114}; M **25.** Prime factorization: $3^2 \times 5$; factors: 1, 3, 5, 3^2 or 9, 3 x 5 or 15, $3^2 \times 5$ or 45 **27.** 3 **29.** 4 **31.** 5 **33.** $\frac{n+1}{2}$ ways; $\frac{n+2}{2}$ ways **35.** $(3^1)(3^0) = 3^{1+0} = 3^1$; $(3^1)(3^0) = 3^1$ **37.** $4^4 + 4^4 = 4^4(1 + 1) = 4^4(2) = 2^8(2) = 2^9$; $4^4 + 4^4 = 2^9$

Pages 34-35

1. 3 **3.** 1 **5.** $\frac{3}{4}$ **7.** $\frac{4}{5}$ **9.** 6 **11.** 1 **13.** 15 **15.** 25 **17.** 1 **19.** 5 **21.** $\frac{1}{3}$ **23.** $\frac{2}{9}$ **25.** $\frac{3}{5}$ **27.** $\frac{3}{10}$ **29.** $\frac{39}{77}$ **31.** $\frac{1}{7}$ **33.** $\frac{5}{8}$ **35.** $\frac{2}{7}$ **Exercises 37-43,** answers may vary. Sample answers are given. **37.** Monday **39.** Thermometers **41.** Yes; 9 and 27 have a GCF of 9. **43.** 1

Pages 36-37

1. 56 **3.** 36 **5.** 45 **7.** 200 **9.** 490 **11.** $\frac{11}{15}$ **13.** $\frac{11}{18}$ **15.** $\frac{7}{12}$ **17.** $\frac{7}{32}$ **19.** $\frac{5}{11}, \frac{1}{2}, \frac{5}{8}$ **21.** $\frac{1}{9}, \frac{1}{5}, \frac{1}{3}$ **23.** $\frac{9}{14}, \frac{5}{7}, \frac{3}{4}$ **25.** $\frac{8}{15}, \frac{7}{12}, \frac{3}{5}$ **27.** 12; 2 **29.** 105; 1 **31.** 22; 1 **33.** 400; 1 **35.** June 12, June 24 **37.** Eagles won 18; Hawks won 16. **39.** *abc*

Chapter 2

Pages 48-49

1. 0.125 **3.** 50.3 **5.** 0.047 **7.** 400 ÷ 50 = 8; no **9.** 8 ÷ 16 = 0.5; yes **11.** 20 ÷ 50 = 0.4; yes **13.** 320 ÷ 80 = 4; yes **15.** 350 ÷ 35 = 10; no **17.** \$8.90 **19.** \$2.86 **Exercises 21-33,** methods may vary. **21.** 63.2; C **23.** 7.1525424; C **25.** 0.00425; C **27.** 7.1253; P **29.** 0.0405; P **31.** 0.06; P **33.** 1.95; P **35.** \$9.18 **37.** Vocalist tapes cost less.

Pages 50-51

1. 37,000 **3.** 1,000 **5.** Count the number of zeros in the power of 10. Move the decimal point the same number of places. **7.** M; 45 **9.** M; 1.05 **11.** M; 0.00037 **15.** 0.0002 **17.** 0.0034 **19.** 680 **21.** 68,000 **23.** 2,040 **25.** 0.068 **27.** 0.034 **29.** 564 **31.** 7 **33.** 2,350 **35.** To multiply a number by 500, first multiply it by 1,000 and then divide by 2. **37.** To multiply a number by 0.5 divide it by 2. **39.** 200 m **41.** \$8,880 **Skills Review 1.** 30 **3.** $2^2 \times 5^2$ **5.** 2×5^3

Pages 52-53

1. 10^1 **3.** 10^2 **Exercises 5-7,** estimates may vary. **5.** 550 ÷ 50 = 11 **7.** 400 ÷ 40 = 10 **9.** 4.68 **11.** 39.50 **13.** 32.75 **15.** 120.4 **17.** 0.85 **Exercises 19-33,** method choices may vary. **19.** 3.85; P **21.** 42.6; C **23.** 5.86; P **25.** 423; P **27.** 806; P **29.** 5.93; C **31.** 23.529412; C **33.** 1.6; P **35.** \$8.25 per hour **37.** \$11.55 per hour **39.** The first \$76.40; \$3,820

Pages 54-55

1. Division **3.** 26.23 points; subtraction **5.** 1,268.93 points; addition **7.** 47.5 sec; multiply **9.** Answers may vary. Sample: Using Exercise 5, students might ask what Wehling's average score was. [(413.34 + 423.39 + 432.20) ÷ 3 = 422.98] **11.** A: 210 m; B: 200 m; C: 190 m; D: 215 m; E: 195 m

Pages 56-57

1. 0.18 **3.** $0.3\overline{18}$ **5.** $\frac{33}{50}$ **Exercises 7-13,** method choices may vary. **7.** P; 0.25 **9.** P; 0.36 **11.** P; $0.4\overline{6}$ **13.** C; $0.\overline{36}$ **15.** $\frac{7}{10}$ **17.** $\frac{1}{4}$ **19.** $\frac{8}{9}$ **21.** $\frac{75}{100}$; 0.75 **23.** $\frac{35}{100}$; 0.35 **25.** $\frac{108}{1,000}$; 0.108 **27.** $\frac{48}{1,000}$; 0.048 **29.** < **31.** < **33.** When the denominator of a fraction is a factor of 10, 100, 1,000, and so on, multiply both the numerator and the denominator by the missing factor of 10, 100, 1,000, and so on. Then the numerator gives the digits in the decimal and the denominator tells where to place the decimal point.

Pages 60-61

1. $\frac{43}{3}$ **3.** $3\frac{3}{4}$ **Exercises 5-15,** method choices may vary. **5.** $5\frac{20}{3}$; M **7.** $\frac{61}{8}$; M **9.** $4\frac{5}{13}$; P **11.** $15\frac{3}{4}$; P **13.** 1; M **15.** 42; P **17.** > **19.** < **21.** = **23.** >

Pages 60-61 (continued)

25. $2\frac{3}{10}, 2\frac{3}{5}, 3\frac{5}{6}$ **27.** $1\frac{1}{6}, 1\frac{7}{12}, 1\frac{2}{3}, 1\frac{5}{6}$ **29.** 8.5625 **31.** 7.53 **33.** $6.\overline{714285}$ **35.** 7.07, $7\frac{7}{20}$, 7.7, $7\frac{7}{7}$ **37.** Buckeye, dog face, io, mourning cloak

Pages 62-65

1. $\frac{5}{10}, \frac{8}{16}$ **3.** $\frac{5}{6}, \frac{9}{10}, \frac{3}{4}$ **5.** Less than 1 **7.** Greater than 1 **9.** Greater than 1 **11.** Between 8 and 10 **13.** Between 13 and 15 **15.** $21 - 7 = 14$ **17.** $1 + 4 - 1 = 4$ **19.** $1 + 5 + 8 = 14$ **21.** $15 - 2 + 2 = 15$ **23.** 0 **25.** $\frac{1}{2}$ **27.** 1 **29.** 1 **31.** >1 **33.** >1 **35.** <1 **37.** $>\frac{9}{10}$ **39.** $>\frac{3}{5}$ **41.** $\frac{1}{8}, \frac{2}{8}, \frac{3}{8}$ **43.** $\frac{4}{8}$ **45.** 14; rounding **47.** 29; round to the nearest whole number **49.** 9; rounding **51.** 17; rounding **53.** 28; rounding **55.** 38; rounding **57.** 93; rounding **Exercises 59-65,** answers may vary according to estimation method. **59.** Greater than **61.** Less than **63.** Less than **65.** Cannot tell **67.** 1 **69.** 3 **71.** $a = b$ **73.** $2a = b$ **75.** $a > b$ **77.** 15 mi **79.** $12\frac{1}{2}$ mi

Pages 66-69

1. 24 **3.** 9 **5.** $15\frac{5}{18}$ **7.** $17\frac{2}{15}$ **9.** $8\frac{5}{12}$ **11.** $11\frac{11}{12}$ **13.** $1\frac{5}{12}$ **15.** $9\frac{5}{24}$ **17.** $\frac{21}{40}$ **19.** $18\frac{3}{14}$ **21.** $14\frac{2}{3}$ **23.** $7\frac{17}{20}$ **25.** $3\frac{10}{21}$ **27.** $68\frac{7}{10}$ **29.** $38\frac{7}{24}$ **31.** 70 **33.** $35\frac{7}{8}$ **35.** 1 **37.** 7 **39.** $\frac{7}{10}$ **41.** 1, $1\frac{11}{12}$ **43.** Bear Creek to Lookout Pass **45.** $\frac{13}{30}$ mi **47.** $2\frac{1}{5}$ **49.** $4\frac{8}{15}$ **51.** $1\frac{2}{5}$ **53.** $3\frac{11}{15}$ **55.** $1\frac{5}{6}$ **57.** $4\frac{7}{30}$ **59.** $3\frac{11}{15}$ **61.** $\frac{7}{10}$ mi **Explore Math** **63.** $\frac{53}{63}$ **65.** Yes **67.** Yes, if the whole numbers are kept separate or if the mixed numbers are rewritten as improper fractions.

Pages 70-71

1. $\frac{1}{10}$ **3.** $\frac{1}{4}$ **5.** $\frac{1}{8}$ **7.** $\frac{3}{17}$ **9.** 3 **11.** 1 **13.** $\frac{5}{9}$ **15.** $\frac{1}{4}$ **17.** $\frac{3}{16}$ **19.** $\frac{4}{5}$ **21.** $4\frac{1}{2}$ **23.** $\frac{3}{10}$ **25.** 1 **27.** $\frac{9}{16}$ **29.** $\frac{1}{2}$ **31.** $2\frac{4}{5}$ **33.** $\frac{13}{24}$ **35.** $\frac{4}{15}$ **37.** $\frac{3}{5}$ **39.** $1\frac{2}{75}$ **41.** 8 lots **43.** Write the division in fraction form. Multiply both terms by the reciprocal of the divisor to obtain an equivalent fraction with a denominator of 1.

Pages 72-73

1. Cost and population **3.** Dollars per person **5.** Methods choices may vary. P; 19 cities **7.** Too little information **9.** Too little information **11.** Methods choices may vary. M; 0.1 mile **13.** Methods choices may vary. C; 10,615,451 cu ft

Chapter 3

Pages 84-85

1. A setback of 12 yards **3.** –50 **5.** –2 **7.** –9 **9.** 6 **11.** 3 **13.** –5 **15.** 63 **17.** 23,501 **19.** 7 **21.** 66 **23.** –13 **25.** –8 **27.** x **29.** < **31.** > **33.** < **35.** < **37.** > **39.** > **41.** > **43.** < **45.** Yes, 1; no; yes, –1 **47.** Answers may vary.

Pages 86-87

1. $-8 + 7$ **3.** Negative **5.** –3 **7.** M; 14 **9.** M; 0 **11.** M; 16 **13.** M; 9 **15.** M; 12 **17.** P; –46 **19.** P or C; 0 **21.** 7 **23.** 3 **25.** 6 **27.** –8 **29.** 4 **31.** 0 **33.** 280°C **35.** –6, –2

Pages 88-89

1. Positive **3.** Positive **5.** Negative **7.** P; 126 **9.** M; 32 **11.** M or P; –8 **13.** M or P; –6 **15.** M or P; –13 **17.** M or P; 42 **19.** M or P; –6 **21.** M; –63 **23.** P; –78 **25.** P; –168 **27.** 50 **29.** 48 **31.** 0 **33.** –30 **35.** 5 **37.** –85 **39.** 96 **Explore Math** **41.** –27 **43.** -243 **44.** Positive; negative

Pages 90-91

1. –63°F **3.** –30°F **5.** 41°F **7.** About 40 mi/h **9.** Answers may vary. Sample: 29°F

Pages 94-95

1. Answers may vary. Sample: 60.25 in., $\frac{241}{4}$ in. **3.** 4; –4.25 **5.** $\frac{-7}{1}$ **7.** $\frac{-13}{5}$ **9.** $\frac{23}{10}$ **11.** –5.1 **13.** $1\frac{4}{5}$ **15.** < **17.** = **19.** $-\frac{1}{2}, 0, \frac{3}{4}$ **21.** $-1, \frac{3}{2}, 2\frac{4}{5}$ **23.** –14.5°F or $-14\frac{1}{2}$°F **25.** $2\frac{1}{2}, -1\frac{3}{4}, 3$

Pages 96-97

1. 5.97 **3.** $\frac{1}{8}$ **5.** 0 **7.** $-4\frac{3}{4}$ **9.** $\frac{5}{4} = 1\frac{1}{4}$ **11.** $\frac{1}{8}$ **13.** $-\frac{16}{21}$ **15.** $-\frac{1}{6}$ **17.** –3.82 **19.** –37.1 **21.** –1.12 **23.** 2 **25.** –13.55 **27.** An increase of 0.1°F **29.** Negative **Skills Review** **1.** 1.16 **3.** 1.87 **5.** 0.35

Pages 98-99

1. 7.5 lb **3.** 25.5 lb **5.** Negative **7.** Positive **9.** $\frac{1}{3}$ **11.** $\frac{-3}{16}$ **13.** $\frac{-49}{18} = -2\frac{13}{18}$ **15.** $\frac{6}{7}$ **17.** 2 **19.** –9 **21.** $\frac{5}{8}$ **23.** $-1\frac{7}{9}$ **25.** –6 **27.** 32 **29.** –80 **31.** 8.4 **33.** –340 **35.** –0.64 **37.** –4 **39.** $\frac{1}{2}$ **41.** 6.9 **43.** 0 **45.** 14 **47.** 1 **49.** 16 weeks **51.** Mrs. Chandler; $\frac{2}{3}$ weeks sooner

Pages 100-101

1. Less than 400°F **3.** $F = \frac{9}{5}C + 32$; $F = \frac{9}{5}(20) + 32$; $F = 68°$ **5.** $C = \frac{5}{9}(F - 32)$; $C = \frac{5}{9}(-5 - 32)$; $C = -20\frac{5°}{9}$ **7.** $C = \frac{5}{9}(F - 32)$; $C = \frac{5}{9}(77 - 32)$; $C = 25°$ **9.** 374°F

Choose a Strategy **11.** 1.9 min **13.** Wanda; by 0.2 min

Chapter 4

Pages 116-117

1. 10 **3.** 11 **5.** $1\frac{7}{12}$ **7.** 48 **9.** 6 **11.** 121 **13.** 1.2 **15.** 30 **17.** –10 **19.** 3 **21.** $4\frac{2}{3}$ **23.** $\frac{1}{100}$ **25.** 3 x (2 + 4) = 18 **27.** (7 - 4) - (2 - 1) = 2 **29.** (–7 + 8) x (5 – 3) = 2 **31.** $(3 + 4)^2 = 49$ **33.** 2 + 3 x (5 - 1) = 24 **35.** a **37.** Answers may vary. Example: Jennifer bought 5 pencils at $0.05 each and 3 packs of notebook paper at $0.98 each. Write an expression to tell how much she spent. (5 x 0.05) + (3 x 0.98) = $3.19

Pages 118-119

1. $7t$ means 7 times t: $4 + 7t = 4 + (7)(2) = 18$ **3.** Compute inside parentheses first: $(t + 3)^2 = (2 + 3)^2 = 25$ **5.** 28 **7.** $-4\frac{1}{2}$ **9.** $-2\frac{4}{5}$ **11.** –1 **13.** $52\frac{1}{2}$ **15.** –4.6 **17.** $-2\frac{1}{8}$ **19.** –12 **21.** –22 **23.** –45 **25.** $11\frac{1}{2}$ inches **Explore Math** **27.** True for all x **29.** True for all x

Pages 120-121

1. a **3.** $7x$ **5.** $x + 7$ or $7 + x$ **7.** $\frac{2}{3}p + q$ **9.** $\frac{22}{7}r^2$ **11.** $(mn)^2$ **13.** c **15.** Open **17.** True **19.** False **21.** Open **23.** $3 **25.** Noon: the wind makes it seem colder, or 18°F.

Pages 122-123

1. Add –5 to both sides; $k = 7$ **3.** Add –3.5 to both sides; $c = 16.5$ **5.** $n = 5$ **7.** $w = 4.2$ **9.** $w = 1.8$ **11.** $z = -60$ **13.** $p = 13$ **15.** $t = 104$ **17.** $d = -10$ **19.** $a = 34$ **21.** $k = -11$ **23.** $g = 3$ **25.** $n + 7 = 18$; $n = 11$ **27.** $b + 9 = 25$; $b = 16$ **29.** $-m - 1 = 1$; $m = -2$ **31.** $C + \frac{3}{10} = 5$; $C = 4\frac{7}{10}$ **33.** $n + 150 = 762$; $n = 612$ students **35.** Group together $n + 8 = 12$, $8 + n = 12$, $12 = n + 8$. By the commutative property and the definition of subtraction, $n + 8 = 8 + n$ and $n - 8 = n + (-8) = -8 + n$ Group together $n - 8 = 12$, $-8 + n = 12$, $12 = n + (-8)$ If two quantities are equal, the quantities can be on either side of the equal sign. So, if $n + 8 = 2$, then $12 = n + 8$

Pages 126-127

1. Multiply by $\frac{1}{5}$. **3.** Add –3. **5.** Multiply by $\frac{4}{9}$. **7.** $n = 2$ **9.** $x = 1\frac{1}{5}$ **11.** $t = 3\frac{1}{3}$ **13.** $m = 73.6$ **15.** $y = 8$ **17.** $q = -85$ **19.** $s = 1.5$ **21.** $f = -10$ **23.** $x = 11$ **25.** $y = 4$ **27.** $t = 0$ **29.** $c = -9.8$ **31.** $x = 6$ **33.** $x = 48$ **35.** 125 lb **37.** Answers will vary. About 138 lb

Pages 128-129

1. Variable (c) **3.** $\frac{2}{3}c = 192$ **5.** $4.5h = 90$; $h = 20$ (hours) **7.** $12w = 84$; $w = 7$ (weeks) **Choose a Strategy** **9.** 330 m/sec

Pages 130-131

1. Add 3; multiply by $\frac{1}{6}$. **3.** Add $\frac{2}{3}$; multiply by $\frac{3}{2}$. **5.** $n = 7$ **7.** $x = 7$ **9.** $c = 20$ **11.** $h = 9$ **13.** $k = 64$ **15.** $d = 42$ **17.** $z = -1$ **19.** $d = \frac{1}{4}$

21.

x	–3	–2	–1	0	1	2	3
y	–2	$-1\frac{1}{3}$	$-\frac{2}{3}$	0	$\frac{2}{3}$	$1\frac{1}{3}$	2

23.

x	–3	–2	–1	0	1	2	3
y	–1.5	–1	–0.5	0	0.5	1	1.5

25. $(2,3)m + 15 = 73$; $m = 87$ **27.** $5n + 7 = 62$; $n = 11$ **29.** Multiply each part of the equation to get $x - 8 = 4$. Then add 8 to get $x = 12$. **Skills Review** **1.** 2, 3, 5 **3.** 2, 3 **5.** 2 x 2 x 5 x 5

Pages 132-133

1. Money earned in 32 h **3.** $50 + (12)(35) = r$; $r =$ $470 **5.** $(325 - 40) + 57 = c$; $c =$ $5 **7.** $4x + 83 = 355$; $x = 68$ h **Choose a Strategy** **9.** 72 years old

Chapter 5

Pages 144-147

5. 7.5, 15 **7.** –2, 0, 2, $3\frac{1}{2}$ **23.** $x > -3$ and $x < 4$ **25.** $x \geq -6$ **27.** Answers may vary. A sample is given. $x < 2$ or $x > -2$ **29.** 29,000 ft **31.** -300 ft **33.** $x = -0.25$ **35.** $x > 1.9$ and $x \leq 3.8$ **37.** 4.4 mi **39.** 12.3 mi

Pages 148-149

1. –6; yes **3.** $x > 2$ **5.** $x \leq 2$ **7.** $y \leq -4$ **9.** $p < -10$ **11.** $k \geq 9.6$ **13.** $m \geq -4$ **15.** $x > -5$ **17.** $x > -3$ **19.** b **21.** g **23.** g **25.** b **27.** c **29.** f **31.** a **33.** Each inequality sign is reversed; each inequality remains the same. **35.** $t - 5 > 3.5$ **37.** $x + 1.2 > 3.8$

Pages 150-151

1. Route 55 and Ashland **3.** Stony Island **5.** 800W, 1600S **7.** 400E, 1200S **Exercises 9-13,** Answers may vary. **9.** 1 mi E, 6 mi S **11.** $\frac{1}{4}$ mi W, $4\frac{3}{8}$ mi S **13.** $\frac{3}{8}$ mi E, $\frac{1}{2}$ mi S **15.** Stadium **17.** Lincoln Park Zoo

Pages 152-155

1. Quadrant IV **3.** Quadrant I **5.** (1.5, 2.25), (–1.5, 2.25) **21.** x-axis **23.** y-axis **25.** IV **27.** x-axis **41.** The lines intersect at the origin and the greater the coefficient of x, the steeper the line rises from left to right. **43.** The first two lines are perpendicular and intersect on the y-axis at –3. The third and fourth lines are perpendicular and intersect at the origin. **45.** Negative **47.** $y = 0$ **53.** a, b, d, f, g, h **55.** b, c, f **57.** f, h **59.** d **Skills Review** **1.** $m = 8$ **3.** $n = 29$ **5.** $y = -9$ **7.** $x = 4.75$ **9.** $t = 13$ **11.** $n = 21\frac{1}{3}$ **13.** $b = 5$ **15.** $a = 8$ **17.** $b = -1$

Pages 156-157
1. Intersect at (0, 2) **15.** They are different. **17.** The constant term equals the y- coordinate of the point where the graph crosses the y-axis. **19.** Intersect **21.** Parallel **23.** –2, –4 **25.** Answers may vary. Sample is given. . 4.8, 1.2 **27.** $x + y = -4$ is parallel to $x + y = 4$ and $x - y = -1$ is parallel to $x - y = 1$.

Pages 158-159
1. Star Video will be cheaper. **3.** \$5, \$10, \$50 **7.** First 9 weeks; 11 weeks and beyond

Pages 162-163
1. $y = 2x$ **3.** $y = -x$ **5.** $y = x + 2$ **7.** $y = x$ **9.** $y = -2x$ **11.** Answers may vary. $y = x$ **13.** $y = -0.1x$ **15.** 35°C

Pages 164-165
1. No **Explore Math 29.** Solutions of both inequalities. **31.** All the single-shaded and double-shaded regions that were marked for $y > x$ and $y < 3 - x$

Pages 166-167
1. (6, -2) **3.** (3, 2) **5.** (-2, 3) **7.** $(x, y) \rightarrow (x + 8, y + 2)$ **17.** $(x, y) \rightarrow (x + 2, y + 3)$ **19.** $(x, y) \rightarrow (x + 2, y + 7)$ **21.** Purple

Pages 168-171
Exercises 1-3, Answers may vary. **7.** $D'(0, 0)$, $E'(4, -3)$, $F'(0, -3)$ **9.** 180° in either direction **13.** Translation or reflection **15.** $P'(-2, -4)$, Q'(2, 0), R'(–2, 4) **17.** 360° **19.** Yes; a vertical line from the top of the mask through the center down to the chin **Explore Math 21.** Circle, point, cone

Pages 172-173
1. (x, y) becomes $(3x, 3y)$. **3.** $A'(-12, 6)$ $B'(-12, 12)$ $C'(6, 12)$ $D'(6, 6)$ **5.** $A''(-2, 1)$, $B''(-2, 2)$, $C''(1, 2)$, $D''(1, 1)$ **7.** $A'''(-48, 24)$ $B'''(-48, 48)$ $C'''(24, 48)$ $D'''(24, 24)$ **9.** ΔW **11.** ΔZ **13.** 12 in. **15.** 20 in.

Chapter 6

Pages 184-187
1. $\frac{17}{3}$ **3.** $\frac{1}{4}$ **5.** $\frac{3}{1}$ **7.** True **9.** $\frac{5}{2}$ **11.** $\frac{9}{11}$ **13.** $\frac{3}{4}$ **15.** $\frac{1{,}000{,}000}{1}$ **Exercises 17-25,** method choices may vary. **17.** 15; M **19.** 14; C **21.** 60; P **23.** 312; C **25.** 168; P **27.** $\frac{120}{20} = \frac{6}{1}$; \$6 per ticket **29.** $\frac{385}{7} = \frac{55}{1}$; 55 mi/h **31.** $\frac{75}{3} = \frac{25}{1}$; 25 mi/gal **33.** Yes **35.** No **37.** 9 in. to 36 in.; $\frac{1}{4}$ **39.** 20 mg to 10,000 mg; $\frac{1}{500}$ **41.** 2 ft to 15 ft; $\frac{2}{15}$ **43.** 500 cm to 25 cm; $\frac{20}{1}$ **45.** 36 times **47.** 24 mi/h **49.** 24 points **51.** $\frac{15}{105} = \frac{1}{r}$; $r =$ 7 min **Exercises 53-55,** Answers may vary. **57.** Yes **59.** No **Skills Review 1.** $k = 90$ **3.** $f = 113$ **5.** $t = 4$ **7.** $x = 6$ **9.** $y = 56$

Pages 188-189
1. b **3.** 16 **5.** 83.3 **7.** 50 **9.** 66.7 **11.** 287.7 **13.** 9 **15.** 19 **17.** 400 **19.** $\frac{50}{100} = \frac{n}{12}$; $n = 24$ **21.** $\frac{87.5}{100} = \frac{8.4}{n}$; $n = 9.6$ **23.** $\frac{24.5}{100} = \frac{n}{30}$; $n = 7.35$ **25.** $\frac{n}{100} = \frac{12}{150}$; $n = 8$ **27.** $\frac{13.4}{100} = \frac{n}{950}$; $n = 127.3$ **29.** $\frac{2.5}{100} = \frac{n}{125}$; $n = 3.125$ **31.** $\frac{11}{100} = \frac{n}{111}$; $n = 12.21$ **33.** $\frac{7.5}{100} = \frac{n}{6{,}000}$; $n = 450$ **35.** $\frac{134}{100} = \frac{n}{55}$; $n = 73.7$ **37.** $\frac{x}{100} = \frac{3.99}{19.95}$; $x = 20\%$ **39.** $\frac{55}{100} = \frac{330}{x}$; $x = 600$ people **41.** Explanation may vary.

Pages 190-191
1. Yes; The comparison of dozen to cups is maintained in both ratios. **3.** No; the comparison of larger to smaller amounts in the left-hand ratio is reversed on the right. **5.** $\frac{3}{16} = \frac{x}{48}$; $x = 9$ teaspoons **7.** $\frac{6}{2} = \frac{x}{15}$; $x = 45$ cups **Choose a Strategy 9.** $\frac{3}{5}$

Pages 192-193
1. No **3.** Yes **5.** Yes **7.** 9.6 in. **9.** 12 in. **11.** 12.8 ft **13.** 68.8 cm **15.** 9 cm **17.** 16 m **19.** 3.75 ft **21.** 47.5 m **23.** About 120 cm **25.** About 40 mm **27.** About 6 to 1 **29.** $14\frac{2}{3}$ yd shorter **Explore Math 31.** 1 to 1.6, 1 to 1.625, 1 to 1.615, 1 to 1.619, 1 to 1.618; ≈ 1 to 1.6

Pages 194-195
1. $\frac{8}{24} = \frac{1}{3}$; 33.3% **3.** $\frac{3}{24} = \frac{1}{8}$; 12.5% **5.** $\frac{2}{25}$ **7.** $55\frac{5}{9}\%$ **9.** 75% **11.** 150% **13.** 28% **15.** 100% **17.** $123\frac{1}{3}\%$ **19.** 3 **21.** 0.085 **23.** 6.5% **25.** 0.37 **27.** 0.0075 **29.** 5.5 **31.** 90% **33.** 250% **35.** 1.2 **37.** 0.0013 **39.** 37.5% **41.** A fraction is less than 100% when the numerator is less than the denominator, equal to 100% when the numerator equals the denominator, and greater than 100% when the numerator is greater than the denominator

Pages 198-199
1. $\frac{7.5}{100} = \frac{x}{180}$; $x = 13.5$ **3.** M; 10 **5.** M or P; 0.5 **7.** $0.04 \times 20 = b$; $b = 0.8$ **9.** $30 = p \times 90$; $p = 33.3\%$ **11.** $0.66 \times 333 = t$; $t = 219.78$ **13.** $48 = 0.96 \times m$; $m = 50$ **15.** $8 = f \times 3{,}200$; $f = 0.0025$; 0.25% **17.** $\frac{n}{100} = \frac{80}{40}$; $80 = n \times 40$; 200% **19.** $\frac{25}{100} = \frac{6.4}{n}$; $0.25 \times n = 6.4$; $n = 25.6$ **21.** $\frac{n}{100} = \frac{25}{125}$; $25 = n \times 125$; 20% **23.** \$537.50 **25.** \$860 **27.** $860 - (0.35 \times 860) = b$; $b = \$559$

Pages 200-201
1. b **3.** a **5.** e **7.** b **9.** 15 **11.** 30 **13.** $66\frac{2}{3}\%$ **15.** 50% **17.** M; 50% **19.** P; 50 **21.** P; 48% **23.** M; $33\frac{1}{3}\%$ **25.** \$2,400 **27.** 25%

Pages 202-203
1. b **3.** a **5.** About 11 **7.** About 8 **9.** About 120 **11.** About 200 **13.** About 55 **15.** About 20 **17.** About 25% **19.** About 20% **21.** About 50% **23.** About 125 **25.** About 2.7 lb **27.** About 10 lb

Pages 204-205
1. b; $n = 300$; no **3.** $125 = n \times 500$; $n = 0.25$; 25% **5.** $0.30 \times 8.2 = n$; $n = 2.46m$ **7.** $15 = 0.60 \times n$; $n =$ 25 in. **9.** $7.50 = 0.15 \times n$; $n = \$50.00$ **11.** $12 = n \times 36$; $n = 0.33\frac{1}{3}$; $33\frac{1}{3}$ % **13.** $0.63 \times 4{,}000 = n$; $n = \$2{,}520$ **15.** 21.25% **17.** 10%

Pages 206-207
1. 12 medals **3.** 138 medals **5.** $33\frac{1}{3}$% **7.** 18.6%; 14.3%; 13.2% **9.** 97 medals

Chapter 7

Pages 218-219
1. 600; 12,000; 100; 5% **3.** $651.31 **5.** $521.23 **7.** $112.48 **9.** $421.80 **11.** $22 **13.** $800 **15.** $121 **17.** 14 **19.** $40,000 **21.** 100 **23.** $269.00 **25.** $33,020.97

Pages 220-221
1. a **3.** a **5.** 108 **7.** 20% **9.** 54 **11.** He confused percent with degrees. **13.** $\frac{1}{5}$ **15.** 90° **17.** 28.8° **23.** $360; $630 **Skills Review** **1.** 0.5 **3.** $\frac{4}{5}$ **5.** $\frac{3}{4}$ **7.** $1\frac{9}{20}$ **9.** $\frac{2}{3}$ **11.** 0.895 **13.** $\frac{3}{5}$

Pages 222-223
1. 33; 600; 0.055; 1 **3.** $8.31 **5.** $1.25 **7.** $34.13 **9.** $155.83 **11.** $20.38

Pages 224-225
1. b; $0.768; C **3.** $1.94 **5.** $0.342 **7.** $0.020 **9.** $0.023 **11.** $0.076 **13.** $0.013 **15.** $0.192 **17.** 3L @ $2.19 **19.** 1 lb @ $0.89 **21.** 2 kg @ $3.39 **23.** $\frac{1}{2}$ lb @ $5.59 **25.** 12 lemons for $3.99 **27.** 16 oz @ $4.19 **29.** The 30-oz bottle **31.** $2.49 for 8 oz

Pages 226-227
1. b **3.** $126.00 **5.** 50% **7.** $270.00 **9.** 20% **11.** $249.90

Pages 228-229
1. $36.83; $4.12; $40.95 **3.** 548 **5.** 148 **7.** 548 **9.** $56.64 **11.** $80.00 **13.** $40.00 **15.** $228.45 **17.** $47.25 **Midchapter Checkup** **1.** $530.90 **3.** $0.21/lb **5.** –90°

Pages 232-233
1. False **3.** $47.16 **5.** $47.75 **7.** $1.00 **9.** $106.38 **11.** $107.98 **13.** $1.85 **15.** $272.75 **17.** $293.73 **19.** $986.00; $9.86; $995.86 **21.** $276.80 **23.** $2.45

Pages 234-235
1. 0.07; 1.36 **3.** $326.04 **5.** 2 years **7.** $6,027.60 **9.** $2,472 **11.** 272.60 **13.** $906.56 **15.** $61 **17.** $38,402 **19.** $768 **21.** 11 **23.** $1,042 **25.** 8% **27.** $1,139.51

Pages 236-237
1. b **3.** 30%; I **5.** 75%; I **7.** 20%; D **9.** 80%; D **11.** 10%; I **13.** 75%; D **15.** 22; 110 **17.** 185; 370 **19.** 46; 46 **21.** 114; 209 **23.** $14,958.60; $5,861.46; $694.43; $2,020.16 **25.** $146.27

Pages 238-241
1. False **3.** True **5.** Low temperatures were near normal except for a cold night around April 1. High temperatures started below normal and ended above normal. **7.** March; over 10 inches **9.** 11 days **11.** 10° warmer **13.** March **15.** April **17.** Between 9:00 and 10:00 **19.** March **Explore Math** **21.** 1984; about $27 million **23.** To continue production, keeping careful watch on the sales of CDs **25.** They probably would continue to increase. **27.** If you assume the same ratios of increase that occurred from 1987 to 1988, sales would be about $15.5 million, $15 million, and $1 million, or about $31.5 million in all.

Pages 242-243
1. About 1.6 million gallons **3.** Answers may vary. **5.** 4 million lb; M **7.** 225 million; estimate **9.** 250 million; estimate

Chapter 8

Pages 258-261
1. Answers may vary. **3.** b **5.** 24 **7.** 55 **9.** a **11.** a **13.** >; 13; M **15.** <;$5\frac{5}{12}$ **17.** >; 1; M **19.** <;1, 4; P **21.** >; 28; M **23.** >; 145; C **25.** <; 3, 6; P **27.** >; 33; 0; M **29.** >; 104; C **31.** a **33.** a **35.** a **37.** a **39.** a **41.** 4 in. **43.** 9 sq in. **45.** 64 cu in. **47.** The 82-in. piece **49.** 15 books **51.** 12 qt; 96 servings **53.** 59.8 gal **55.** 5,520 sq in.

Pages 262-263
1. 58; 59 **3.** 3 **5.** $\frac{1}{2}$ gal; 100 oz; 6 qt **7.** 59 lb 15 oz **9.** 4 gal 2 qt **11.** 21 lb 10 oz **13.** 7 ft 3 in. **15.** 4 gal 1 pt **17.** $1\frac{1}{4}$ c; 11 fl oz; 1 pt **19.** 80 dimes; 40 quarters; 8,000 pennies **23.** 2 quarts **Choose a Strategy** **25.** 18 oz

Pages 264-265
1. a **3.** c **5.** 9.24 **7.** 3.2 **9.** 0.0000003 **11.** 7,000,000,000 **13.** 0.00006 **15.** 2,000,000 **17.** 135.8 **19.** 1,000,000,000 **21.** 2 **23.** 27 **25.** 950,000 **27.** 858 **29.** 220 **31.** 6; 2; 1 **33.** $5m^2$ **35.** Perhaps across the floor, but not upright. A room is usually about 3 m high.

Pages 266-267
1. Liter **3.** Gram **5.** b **7.** b **9.** c **11.** a **13.** >; 32,000 **15.** >; 14,000 **17.** <; 0.309 **19.** <; 0.013892 **21.** <; 0.0087 **23.** >; 3,225 **25.** <; 0.04774 **27.** >; 76,000 **29.** About 14 lb **Skills Review 1.** (–1,0) **3.** 3 lb for $2.69 **5.** $0.04 per oz

Pages 268-269
1. 60 **3.** 2.5 **5.** 701 mm **7.** 5,700 g **9.** 0.91 kg **11.** 16.3 mm **13.** 80 **15.** 19 **17.** 46,080 cm^3 **19.** 104 km **21.** 118,440,000 cm^3 **23.** 198,912 mm^3 = 198.912 cm^3 **25.** 34.5825 m^2 **27.** 27.2 km^2 **29.** 0.6 **31.** 4 bowls

Pages 272-273
1. c **3.** b **5.** 650 **7.** 9,000 cm^2 **9.** 2,000 cm^3 **11.** 7 **13.** 15 mm **15.** 2 ft 3 in. **17.** 7.5 cu ft **19.** 1 qt **21.** 1.5 cups **23.** 25 lb

Pages 274-275
1. 3 L **3.** 6 kg **5.** 14 m **7.** 5 **9.** 60 cm **11.** 3.6 L **13.** 4 m **15.** 2 m **17.** 8 km **19.** 10 ft or $3\frac{1}{3}$ yd **21.** 6 lb **23.** 24 lb **25.** 10 yd or 30 ft **27.** 9 in. **29.** Tea kettle; 35 L; 100 gal **31.** Teaspoon; 20 cm; 12 in. **33.** 8 gal **35.** 18 strips **37.** 67 sq ft **39.** 8,100 cm^2

Pages 276-277
1. 18 minutes **3.** 3 hours 58 minutes **5.** Train 17 **7.** 7:00 A.M. Tuesday **Exercises 9-11,** answers may vary. **9.** 12 years; 13 years; 14 years **11.** 105,192 hours; 113,952 hours; 122,736 hours **Choose a Strategy 13.** March **15.** Answers may vary. One solution is to add the number of days from March until you reach a number that is divisible by 7.

Pages 278-279
1. 5 cm; 54 mm **3.** b **5.** a **7.** 0.01 km; 0.005 km **9.** 1 m; 0.5 m **11.** 0.1 oz; 0.05 oz **13.** 100 mi; 50 mi **15.** 0.01 m; 0.005 m **17.** 1 mi; 0.5 mi **19.** 0.1 km; 0.05 km **21.** 1 L; 0.5 L **23.** 37.1 mm **25.** 9 oz **27.** 38 ft **29.** 43 mL **31.** 87 min **33.** 200 in. **35.** 0.1 mL; 0.05 mL **37.** Yes; no

Pages 280-281
1. 0.05 km **3.** 0.005 L **5.** 0.1 mi **7.** 0.05 ÷ 15.2 = 0.3% **9.** Accuracy **11.** 0.4%; 0.04%; 13.60 lb **13.** 0.005 km; 0.0% **15.** 0.5 mi; 0.2% **17.** 0.005 m; 10.0% **19.** $\frac{1}{16}$ mi; 4.5% **21.** 0.05 m; 0.9% **23.** $\frac{1}{8}$ in.; 1.0% **25.** 0.05 cm; 1.2% **27.** 0.5 min; 0.1% **29.** The measurement of Earth

Pages 282-283
1. Precise **3.** Greatest possible **5.** 3 **7.** $\frac{1}{2}$ mi **9.** 2 **11.** 5 mi **13.** 45 **15.** 4, 5 **17.** 1.1% **19.** 2 **21.** 0.005 kg **23.** 3 **25.** 2 **27.** 3 **29.** 5 **31.** 1 **33.** 3 **35.** 4 **37.** 3 **39.** 7 **41.** 2 **43.** 3 **45.** 1 **47.** 3 **49.** 0.8% **Explore Math 51.** Let students agree on which unit of measurement to use.

Chapter 9

Pages 294-295
1. c **3.** b **5.** a; b **7.** a; b; c **9.** a; b **11.** Yes; no **13.** Yes **Exercises 15-17,** answers may vary. **15.** Segment: Have a plane intersect the line for one end of the segment, and use point *R* on the line for the other endpoint. Ray: Let the plane intersect the line at point *R*. **17.** Segment: Intersect two planes to form a line; then have the other two planes intersect the line for the two endpoints. Ray: Intersect three planes in a line and intersect the line with the remaining plane.

Pages 296-297
1. Two lines parallel to the given line and 2 in. on either side of it. **3.** A line between the two given lines, 6 ft from each of them. **5.** 25m^2 **7.** $1,914 **9.** Points *C* and *D*, intersection of the circles with radius 10 ft and centers *A* and *B* (the two lead dancers)

Pages 298-299
1. $\angle XWV$; $\angle SVW$ **3.** $\angle ISV$; $\angle YXW$ **5.** $\angle WXY$, $\angle WXR$; $\angle VSR$, $\angle VSI$, $\angle XWV$, $\angle SVW$ **7.** 60° **9.** 130° **11.** 40° **13.** 90° **15.** 90° **17.** $\angle MKW$ and $\angle RKC$, $\angle WKC$ and $\angle MKR$, $\angle KRC$ and $\angle ARZ$, $\angle ARK$ and $\angle ZRC$ **19.** Same answer as Exercise 16 **21.** The acute angles of a right triangle are complementary.

Pages 300-301
1. $\angle 1$, $\angle 4$, $\angle 8$ **3.** Answers may vary. 130°, 50° **5.** False. $\angle 1$ is not congruent to $\angle 2$. **7.** 130° **9.** 130° **11.** 50° **13.** 50° **15.** 100° **17.** 80° **19.** 60° **21.** Ray; endpoint **23.** Right **25.** Line segment *B*; *F* **27.** 90° **29.** 8.4 cm; 11.2 cm

Pages 302-305
1. 4 **3.** 2 **5.** 5 **7.** 3 **9.** is the same as **11.** 180° **13.** 4 **15.** 90° **17.** 5 **19.** equals **21.** 360; the number of sides **Exercises 22-25,** method choices may vary. **23.** M; 36 **25.** P or C; 20 **27.** P; 3 **29.** P; 360 **31.** No. The fifth angle would have to be a straight angle. (4 x 90 = 360, 540 – 360 = 180) **33.** No. Each angle must be 120°. **35.** Yes. The other four angles would be right or obtuse. **37.** True **39.** True **41.** Equilateral triangle, hexagon **Explore Math 43.** Answers will vary. **45.** The largest side of a triangle is always opposite the largest angle. The shortest side is always opposite the smallest angle. The hypotenuse is always the longest side of a right triangle because it is opposite the largest angle.

Pages 306-309
1. $\overline{AC}$ **3.** $\overline{AB}$, $\overline{DC}$, $\overline{AC}$ **5.** $\angle BAC$ **7.** 20°; 40°, $m\angle COB = 2m\angle CAB$ **9.** 12 in. **11.** 12 in. **13.** 88 in.; P **15.** 9.42; P **17.** 70° **19.** 40° **21.** 90°

23. $m\angle OAB = m\angle OBA = 15°$; $m\angle BOC = 30°$; $m\angle COD = 50°$; $m\angle ODC = m\angle DCO = 65°$ **25.** C **27.** Greek **29.** More turns **31.** 157.14285 **33.** 0.06322 cm

Pages 314-317
5. Impossible; $m\angle C + m\angle D > 180°$ **13.** SSS **15.** $\overline{AB}$ is the angle bisector of $\angle A$. **17.** $\overline{AB}$ is a height of ΔACD **23.** The size of the angle between the sides. **Skills Review** **1.** 11 gal 1 qt **3.** 4 yd 3 in. **5.** 1 lb 13 oz **7.** M; 10,100 m **9.** P; 22,575 mL **11.** C; 5,288 mL

Pages 318-319
1. There would be only two possible locations for the cabin. It would be on AB and 1 mile either side of $\overline{MN}$. **Choose a Strategy** **7.** 42.5 miles **9.** 71%

Pages 320-323
1. 1 base **3.** Rectangular prism **5.** Octagonal pyramid **7.** Triangles **9.** Pencil point **11.** Basketball **13.** Rectangular prism **15.** Answers may vary. **17.** Octagonal prism **19.** Rectangular prism **21.** Square pyramid **23.** 8 faces **25.** Answers will vary. **27.** Both a cylinder and a cone have bases that are circles. The cylinder has two congruent bases whereas the cone has only one base.

Pages 324-325
1. *A, B, C, D, E, F,* **3.** *AEB, FDC, EBCD, EAFD, ABCF* **5.** *n*: 8; *F*: 10; *V*: 16; *E*: 24 **7.** *n*: 10; *F*: 12; *V*: 20; *E*: 30 **9.** 6 **11.** 5 **13.** 5 **15.** 6 **17.** 6 **19.** 7 **21.** $E = n + 1$; $V = n + 1$; $E = 2n$

23.

Prisms	Pyramids
$F + V$	$F + V$
11	8
14	10
17	12
20	14

$F + V = E + 2$

Pages 326-329
1. Hexagonal prism **3.** *H* **5.** 4 pairs **7.** No face is opposite face *A*. **11.** b **13.** a **15.** Square pyramid **17.** 5 **19.** Triangular pyramid **21.** 4 **23.** Octagonal prism **25.** 9 **27.** Cube **29.** 6 **31.** Cylinder **33.** Cylinder

Pages 330-331
1. c **3.** Cube **5.** Cylinder

Chapter 10

Pages 342-345
1. 12 cm **3.** 113.04 cm^2 or $113\frac{1}{7}$ cm^2 **5.** 144 cm^2 **7.** Always; the radius length must be the same so they must be the same size. **9.** Sometimes; a counterexample is 13 x 7 and 8 x 12. **11.** 8 **13.** 50.24 **15.** 18.84 **17.** 16.8 **19.** 221.56 **21.** 44.21 **23.** 153.86 cm^2 or 154 cm^2 **25.** 38.47 cm^2 or $38\frac{1}{2}$ cm^2 **27.** 128.61 sq in. **29.** $9\frac{5}{8}$ sq ft **31.** 7,850 cm^2 **33.** 0.0028 m^2 **35.** $38\frac{1}{2}$ yd **37.** 196,250 sq ft **39.** About 776 revolutions

Pages 346-349
1. 99 m **3.** 323 m^2 **5.** 3 **7.** First shaded area = $\frac{1}{2}b_1h_1$ and second shaded area = $\frac{1}{2}b_2h_2$. But congruent parallelograms have the same area, so $b_1h_1 = b_2h_2$. Therefore, the shaded areas are equal. **9.** 3.52 cm^2; C **11.** 8 cm^2; M **13.** $\frac{1}{4}$ **15.** 3 cm **17.** 525 m^2 **19.** 4^2, or 16 **23.** 21 percent

Pages 350-353
1. 36 sq yd **3.** 161 sq ft **5.** 41.7 in. **7.** $P = 24$ ft; $A = 30$ sq ft; M **9.** $P = 40.2$ in.; $A = 102$ sq in.; P **11.** $P = 87$ m; $A = 375$ m^2; P **13.** The area doubles. **15.** 36 **17.** $CX = EA$ **19.** $A = bc + ba + 2ac$; $P = 6a + 2c + 2b$ **Explore Math** **21.** Answers will vary.

Pages 354-355
Exercise 1-5, answers may vary. **1.** Circle; outside **3.** Triangle; outside **5.** Rectangle; outside **7.** 9 sq mi **9.** 7.5 km^2 **11.** $\frac{3}{4}$ in. x $\frac{3}{4}$ in. x 62,500 in.

Pages 356-359
1. 30 cubic units **3.** 60 cu in. **5.** 251.20 cm^3 **7.** $91\frac{1}{8}$ cm^3 **9.** 9,420 cu in. **11.** 155.09 cm^3 **13.** 8 x 4 x 3 **15.** 8 x 6 x 4 **19.** 152 cm^3 **21.** 923.16 cm^3 **23.** 309π cu in. or 970.26 cu in. **25.** 0.46 cu ft **27.** 21,195 cu ft **29.** 2 packets **31.** 2,448 cm^3 **33.** About 49 cu in. **35.** 1 m^3 is greater about 0.271 m^3. **37.** 3^3, or 27 times **39.** 0.5^3, or $\frac{1}{8}$ times **Choose a Strategy** **31.** 4 pieces

Pages 360-363
1. $V = \frac{1}{3}abh$ **Exercises 3-11,** method choices may vary. **3.** 126.0 cm^3; P **5.** 20.0 cu units; P **7.** 25.12 cu units; C **9.** 678.24 cu in.; C **11.** 141.3 cu in.; C **13.** By 27 **15.** By 18 **17.** $\frac{1}{3}\pi r^2h$ **19.** 300 cm^3 **21.** 100.48 cu ft **23.** $341\frac{1}{3}$ cu in. **25.** Answers may vary. Around $\overline{AB}$: 37.68 cm^3; Around $\overline{AC}$: 50.24 cm^3

Pages 366-367
1. $V = \frac{3}{4}\pi r^3$ **3.** 3,052.08 cu in. **5.** 1,696.54 m^3 **7.** $166\frac{2}{3}\pi$ cm^3, or $523\frac{1}{3}$ cm^3 **9.** 2:3 **11.** The ratios of the volumes, sphere to cylinder to cone, are $\frac{4}{3}$ to 2 to $\frac{2}{3}$.

Pages 368-371
3. 15.66 sq in. **5.** 12 cm^2 **7.** 50 cm^2 **9.** 54 sq units **11.** Any corner **13.** The center cube on any face **15.** $A = ah + bh + ch + ab$ **17.** 793.50 mm^2 **19.** V = 600 cu ft; A = 660 sq ft **21.** $4n + 2$ sq in. **23.** 1,296 cm^2 **25.** 5 pints **27.** A little less than a pint; a little more than a pint

Pages 372-375
1. 173 cm^2 **3.** 1,092 cm^2 **5.** 115.9 cm^2 **7.** $A = 2ab + a^2$ **9.** 336 sq in. **11.** 101.6 cm^2 **13.** Methods choices may vary. A = 360 sq units; V = 400 cu units; C **15.** $91{,}394{,}008\frac{1}{3}$ **17.** About 156 sq units **Choose a Strategy** **21.** 20 ft **Explore Math** **27.** Answers may vary. **29.** They are equal.

Pages 376-379
1. 1,186.92 sq in. **3.** 87.92 sq ft **5.** Answers may vary. The one rotated about side AC has 50% more surface area. **Exercises 7-9,** method choices may vary. **7.** 678.24 cm^2; C **9.** 4,772.8 sq in.; C **11.** A = 60.41 m^2; V = 32.37 m^3 **13.** A = 119.71 sq in. V = 68.69 cu in. **15.** 1 : 4 **17.** $\pi : 3$ **19.** 508.68 cm^3 **21.** 164.85 sq ft **23.** 56.52 sq in. **25.** The cylinder with the 18-in. radius has 50% more surface area. **27.** 9 times greater **29.** Quartered

Pages 380-381
1. 2 in. x 8 in. x 8 in. **3.** 5 in. x 20 in. x 20 in. **5.** 18 in. by 18 in. by 36 in. **7.** 2,826 cu ft **9.** 4 in. by 5 in. by 5 in.

Chapter 11

Pages 392-393
1. 0; zero prop. of mult. **3.** $\frac{2}{3}$; comm. prop. of mult. **5.** No **7.** Yes **9.** 0; zero prop. of mult. **11.** 6.3; comm. prop. of add. **13.** 5; assoc. prop. of mult. **15.** $\frac{5}{8}$ comm. prop. of mult. **17.** 1; one property of mult. **19.** 0; zero prop. of mult. **21.** 128; assoc. prop. of add. **23.** 29; dist. prop. **25.** $\frac{2}{3}$; assoc. prop. of add. **27.** 18; dist. prop. **29.** $2\frac{1}{2}$; assoc. prop. of mult.; one property **Exercises 31-39,** Answers may vary. **31.** $4 \div 2 = 2$; $2 \div 4 = \frac{1}{2}$; $6 \div 3 = 2$; $3 \div 6 = \frac{1}{2}$ **33.** $2(5 - 3) = 2\,(2) = 4$ $7(9 - 4) = 7(5) = 35$ **35.** $-\frac{1}{4}$ **37.** $\frac{3}{8}$ **39.** 0.66... .

Pages 394-395
1. 4; 0.00001 **3.** 8; 100,000,000 **5.** –2; 10^{-2} **7.** –6; 10^{-6} **9.** 0.00001 **11.** 10,000,000 **13.** 0.001 **15.** 1 **17.** 0.000001 **19.** 0.00000001 **21.** 10^2 **23.** 10^5 **25.** 10^{-5} **27.** 10^{-4} **29.** 10,000,000 **31.** 10,000 **33.** 0.01 **35.** 10,000 **37.** 10^5 **39.** 10^3 **41.** 10^{-3} **43.** 10^3 **45.** $10^2 = 100$ and $\frac{1}{10^{-2}} = \frac{1}{\frac{1}{100}} = 100$; $10^4 = 10{,}000$ and $\frac{1}{10^{-4}} = \frac{1}{\frac{1}{10{,}000}} = 10{,}000$; In general, $\frac{1}{10^{-n}} = 10^n$.

Pages 396-397
1. 3; 9 **3.** –2; – 6 **5.** 10^7; M **7.** 10^{-19}; M **9.** 10^7; P **11.** 10^{12}; P **13.** 10^{12}; P **15.** 10^{11} **17.** 10^1 **19.** 10^{-2} **21.** 10^2 **23.** 10^{-7} **25.** 10^7 **27.** $a = -b$ or $b = -a$ **Explore Math** **29.** 1,000; 3 **31.** 0.1; -1

Pages 398-399
1. Yes **3.** No **5.** 3 **7.** 7 **9.** 24.02 **11.** 141,400,000 **13.** 1,010 **15.** 790 **17.** 3×10^5 **19.** 3.50768×10^4 **21.** 9.3756×10^2 **23.** 3.2×10^6 **25.** 630; 6.3×10^2 **27.** 50.9; 5.09×10^1 **29.** 129,000,000; 1.29×10^8 **31.** 60,070; 6.007×10^4 **33.** About 120 times as great **35.** About 7 times as great

Pages 400-401
1. 0.000000102 **3.** -4 **5.** 1.62×10^0 **7.** 5.2×10^{-1} **9.** 5.02×10^{-4} **11.** 5.16×10^{-9} **13.** 8.75×10^8 **15.** 7.84×10^6 **17.** 0.46 **19.** 0.0006321 **21.** 0.000007004 **23.** 0.00001005 **25.** 0.03865 **27.** 0.0000000583 **29.** 417,000,000 **31.** 0.00000000175 **33.** 0.000029 cm is shorter than 0.00004 cm

Pages 404-405
1. 10^1; 12; 12; 5.5; **Exercises 3-19,** method choices may vary. **3.** M; 1×10^4 **5.** P; 2.9×10^5 **7.** P; 9.2×10^{11} **9.** P; 3×10^3 **11.** P; 5×10^5 **13.** P; 2.1×10^3 **15.** P; 8.88×10^5 **17.** P; 1.4×10^6 **19.** C; 6.432×10^7 **21.** About 2×10^3 times as great **23.** About 3.25×10^6 sq mi

Pages 406-407
1. Subtraction; 6.77×10^7, 1.55×10^8 **3.** Multiplication ; 1.86×10^5; 60; Multiplication; 1.86×10^5, 3600 **5.** Division; 9.45×10^7, 4.34×10^7 **7.** 8.73×10^7 mi **9.** 1.116×10^7 mi; 6.696×10^8 mi **11.** About 2.17 times as great **Choose a Strategy** **13.** 94.5 **15.** 7.16 in. **17.** 53.65 in.

Pages 408-409
1. 9.2 **3.** Find 2,809 in the n^2 column and look at the corresponding number in the n column. If $n^2 = 2{,}809$, and $n = 53$, then $\sqrt{2{,}809}$ is 53. **5.** 20 **7.** 2.83 **9.** 3.10 **11.** 28.28 **13.** 6.24 **15.** 14.08 **17.** 0.1 **19.** 4 **21.** 6 **23.** 3 **25.** 1.2 in. **27.** 45,369 m^2 **29.** 170 ft

Pages 410-411
1. Rational **3.** Irrational **5.** Rational **7.** False **9.** False **11.** Rational **13.** Rational **15.** Rational **17.** Irrational **19.** Rational **21.** $-0.\overline{27}$ **23.** –1.875 **25.** $0.\overline{15}$ **27.** $-0.\overline{6}$ **29.** 0.0375 **31.** $\sqrt{91}$

33. 3.1416 **35.** $\frac{355}{113}$ **Exercises 37-43,** answers may vary. **37.** 9.5 **39.** 3.141595 **41.** 3.1415928 **43.** $\sqrt{14.58}$; $\sqrt{90.5}$; π; $\sqrt{9.86965}$; $\sqrt{11.5}$; $\sqrt{9.86905}$

Pages 412-415
1. Yes **3.** No **5.** No **7.** 4; 2 **9.** 5; 4; 2 **11.** 4 **13.** 10 **15.** 3 **17.** 4 **19.** 2.83 **21.** 12 **23.** 6 **25.** 8.49 **27.** –5 **29.** 8 **31.** –10.58 **33.** 17. **35.** 7.94 **37.** 7.07 **39.** B; –1.5 **41.** A; –2.8 **43.** D; 0.9 **45.** About 8.49 in. **47.** $7\sqrt{7}$ in., or about 18.52 in. **49.** 50π m^2, or about 157.1 m^2 **51.** 6.9 cm; 6.9 cm **53.** 486 sq in. **55.** 14 ft; 4 stones **Skills Review** **1.** 70 ft; 300 sq ft **3.** 95 cm; 363 cm^2 **5.** 43.96 cm; 153.86 cm^2 **7.** 1,386 sq in.; 2,754 cu in. **9.** 2,508 sq in.; 7,700 cu in.

Pages 416-417
1. 8,100 sq ft **3.** 25 ft **5.** 9.2 sec **7.** 19.4 sec **9.** 5 sec

Chapter 12

Pages 432-433
1. 40.5 **3.** 150° **5.** 8 **7.** 50° **9.** 40° **11.** 3 **13.** 130° **15.** 110° **17.** 160° **19.** 140° **21.** 6 **23.** $0.\overline{6}$ **25.** No **29.** $34\frac{1}{8}$ in. by $97\frac{1}{2}$ in. = 2 ft $10\frac{1}{8}$ in. by 8 ft $1\frac{1}{2}$ in.

Pages 434-435
1. 37 ft x $24\frac{2}{3}$ ft **3.** $5\frac{1}{2}$ in. wide by $10\frac{1}{2}$ in. tall **9.** 4

Pages 436-439
1. Yes **3.** No **5.** Hypotenuse; legs **7.** 13.4 **9.** 9.2 **11.** 8.9 **13.** Exercises 8, 10, 12 **15.** $\sqrt{5}$; 2.236 **17.** $\sqrt{17}$; 4.123 **19.** 25 **21.** 36 **23.** 48 **25.** 42 + $6\sqrt{5}$ **27.** 4 + $\sqrt{6}$ + $\sqrt{10}$ **29.** 41 knots **31.** $6\sqrt{2}$, or 8.5 cm **33.** 25 feet

Pages 442-443
1. 5 cm **3.** 13 cm **Exercises 5-15,** method choices may vary. **5.** 72; C **7.** 5.8; T **9.** 12; M **11.** 15; C **13.** x = 23.9; y = 30.9 **15.** x = 31.1; y = 22 **17.** 8 ft 7 in. or 8.6 ft **Choose a Strategy** **19.** $304,000

Pages 444-445
1. Yes **3.** Yes **5.** Yes **7.** No **9.** Yes **11.** Yes **13.** No **15.** No **17.** No **19.** Yes **21.** 80.6 mi **23.** 60 ft **25.** 45 cm and 60 cm or 21cm and 72 cm **Skills Review** **1.** 3.6×10^{10} **3.** 3.3×10^4

Pages 446-447
1. $2w$, $\sqrt{3}\,w$ **3.** 60° **5.** 20 cm **7.** 692 cm^2 **9.** 2 **11.** 56 **13.** 48.5 **15.** 30° **17.** 30° **19.** Method choices may vary. A sample is given. 1,000 ft; P

Pages 448-449
1. 90° **3.** 45° **5.** 10 cm; 14.1 cm **7.** 90° **9.** 45° **11.** $3\sqrt{2}$ **13.** 3 **15.** 5 **17.** 5 **19.** 4.2 in., 7.1 in.

Pages 450-453
1. e **3.** a **5.** $\overline{JK}$ **7.** $\overline{JK}$ **9.** $\overline{KL}$ **11.** 22.3 **13.** Always **15.** Never **17.** Always **19.** 60° **21.** 74° **23.** 66° **25.** 64° **27.** 45° **29.** 27° **31.** 8.9 **33.** 5.1 **35.** x = 56.7; y = 20.7 **37.** About 41° **39.** 6.7 ft **Explore Math** **41.** 8 **43.** 12 **45.** 13 **47.** 15 **49.** 16 **51.** 20 **53.** 21 **55.** Infinitely many

Pages 454-455
1. Find tan ($\angle ACD$); 3-4-5 triple has smallest angle of 37° **3.** Pythagorean theorem; 3-4-5 triple **5.** Equilateral triangle; subtract the measure of angle *GJH* from 90. **7.** Pythagorean triple; 30-60-90 triangle **Exercises 9-13,** methods may vary. **9.** 5 miles; Pythagorean triples **11.** No; the height of the tree is $\sqrt{28^2 - 16^2}$, or nearly 23 meters. **13.** 34 ft; Pythagorean Theorem

Pages 456-457
1. 0.574 **3.** A = 66° **5.** At 45° **7.** 0.6 **9.** 53° **11.** 0.8 **13.** 37° **15.** 8.7 **17.** 0.57 **19.** 0.57 **21.** 0.70 **23.** 66° **25.** 26° **27.** 22.9 cm **29.** 6 m

Chapter 13

Pages 468-471
1. Purple **3.** Median **5.** Mode **7.** 5.55 days **9.** 3 **11.** 94; 93; 92 and 100 **13.** 3.8; $3\frac{3}{4}$; $2\frac{1}{2}$ **17.** 23 **Exercises 19-21,** answers will vary. A sample is given. **19.** 20, 30, 30, 40, 50, 60, 60, 60, 70, 80 **21.** 0, 1, 3, 5, 8, 10, 57, 72, 81, 92, 178 **23.** $280 **25.** The modes originally were $75, $150, and $325. Now the mode would be just $325. **27.** Neither the range nor midrange would change since the greatest and least values are not changing. **Skills Review** **1.** 6.16 **3.** 32.50 **5.** 2.24 **7.** 0.40 **9.** 19.05 **11.** –41.16 **13.** 24.00 **15.** 40.00

Pages 472-473
1. 3 temperatures **3.** 83°; 7°

5.

Stem	Leaves
2	3, 5, 9
3	1, 4, 9
4	4, 8
5	0, 4, 5, 6
6	2, 7
7	7, 8

7.

Leaves for 1st set	Stem	Leaves for 2nd set
9, 0	0	
4, 3, 3	1	
3	2	6
6, 3	3	
5, 3, 2	4	1, 3, 7
2	5	2, 2, 7
5, 5	6	0, 1, 1, 5, 5
	7	0
	8	7

Pages 472-473 (continued)
9. 1st set: 65 and 32.5; 2nd set: 61 and 56.5
11. 4° **13.** Second plot

Pages 474-475
1. 16 **3.** 8 **13.** The box plot would have the same high, low and outlier, but the median would be 47, the lower quartile would be 42 and the upper quartile would be 52.

Pages 476-477
1. Circle graph; circle would represent music with each section showing percentage of people favoring that particular type of music. **3.** Bar graph; bars can represent five categories of compact discs and height shows number sold. **11.** It would not change.

Pages 478-481
1. India **3.** 4 days **5.** Maximum and minimum temperatures **7.** April, January and July **9.** About 0.7% **11.** 1990 **13.** 19 **15.** No; since the population density is found by dividing the total population by the total land area of the country, a country with a large land area would have a population density much less than a country with a small land area.

5.

Stem	Leaves
1	7,8,9
2	1,6,7
3	3,6,6
4	1,2,3
5	0

7. 10; 24 **9.** 35; 20 **11.** Circle graph or bar graph

Pages 484-485
1. At 8 years **3.** The names of the months **5.** About 9 inches **7.** Saturday; Saturday **9.** $350; $500

Pages 486-487
1. About 1 sec **3.** About 8.3 m/sec **5.** 0.20 **7.** 0.29 **9.** Approximately 0.37 **Choose a Strategy** **11.** 19.8%

Pages 488-489
1. No correlation; since there is no relation between number of cars in Rhode Island and number of crickets in Italy. **3.** Negative; the larger the area the less dense is its population **5.** At the top right **7.** No; each state has population; therefore each state has representation. **9.** Older **11.** 48 states **13.** The slant of the line indicates that in general the later the state entered, the further west its longitude. **15.** Hawaii should be the entry farthest to the right, since it was the last state to enter the Union.

Pages 490-491
1. Population **3.** Random sample **5.** Children and adults interested in basketball **7.** Grocery shoppers **9.** General population **11.** Drivers in snowy climates **Exercises 13-17,** explanations may vary. **13.** 100% for safety reasons **15.** 5%; although population is small and therefore sample would be small, population is not extremely diversified. **17.** 5%; sample should be taken in stores in different parts of the country **19.** $\frac{20}{35}$; $\frac{9}{35}$; $\frac{6}{35}$
21. 53%; 43%; 3% **23.** 50%; 28%; 22%
25. Road conditions, climate hills might affect outcome of survey. **27.** Answers may vary; 5% may be sufficient for testing some new products, but 100% is necessary when accuracy is essential.

Pages 492-493
1. It increased rapidly **5.** Answers will vary. Show a gap in vertical scale and more divisions for attendance between 10,000 and 12,000. Vertical interval width could be 500 rather than 2,000. **7.** To show a larger increase in sales, show a gap in the vertical scale and number the vertical scale in tens.

Pages 494-495
1. 47 **3.** More students would ride the bus.
5. a. Decide size of sample to be surveyed.
b. Decide on question: What is your favorite sport?
c. Ask question and tally results. **7.** Questions may be too general and allow too many categories of answers.

Pages 496-497
1. 3,500 deer **3.** 5,000 **5.** 9,000 **7.** 2,400
9. 7,500 **11.** 41,667 **13.** 13,889 **15.** 13,889
17. 20,000 **19.** 90 **Explore Math** **21.** 720 to 880 **23.** 7%

Chapter 14

Pages 508-511
1. $\frac{2}{10}$ or $\frac{1}{5}$ **3.** $\frac{7}{10}$ **5.** Answers will vary. **7.** Answers may vary. **11.** 1 **13.** 1 **15.** $\frac{4}{5}$ **17.** $\frac{1}{6}$ **19.** $\frac{1}{2}$ **21.** 1
23. $\frac{1}{3}$ **Exercises 25.-37.** Answers may vary.
39. No. How a person feels about a song cannot be predicted with certainty. **Exercises 41-43.** Answers may vary. **Choose a Strategy** **Exercises 45-47.** Answers may vary.

Pages 512-513
1. 10 times **3.** Answers may vary. **5.** About 2 or 3 times **7.** About 45 days **9.** $327.46

Pages 514-515
Exercises 3-9, method choices may vary.
3. 5,184 choices; C **5.** 360 choices; P or C
7. 120 choices; M **9.** 17,576 choices; P or C
11. 72 choices **13.** 144 choices **15.** 576 choices
17. 72 sweatshirts

Pages 516-517
1. 657, 675, 756, 765 **3.** XYZ, YXZ, YZX, ZXY, XZY, ZYX; 6 permutations **5.** LOVE, LOEV, LVEO, LVOE, LEOV, LEVO, OVLE, OLVE, OVEL, OEVL, OLEV, OELV, VLOE, VLEO, VOEL, VOLE, VELO, VEOL, EVLO, EVOL, ELVO, ELOV, EOVL, EOLV; 24 permutations **7.** Maida, Miguel, Miguel, Maida; 2

permutations **Exercises 9-15,** method choices may vary. **9.** 6; M **11.** 3,628,800; C **13.** 5,040; C **15.** 720; C **17.** 720 permutations **19.** 120 permutations **21.** 24,360 ways or $30 \times 29 \times 28$ **Skills Review Exercises 1-3,** graphs will vary. **1.** Bar graph or broken-line graph **3.** Double bar graph or double broken-line graph

Pages 518-519
1. H, H, H; H, H, T; H, T, H; H, T, T; T, H, H; T, H, T; T, T, H; T, T, T; $P(\text{H, H, H, }) = \frac{1}{8}$ **3.** $P(\text{H, H, H}) = \frac{1}{2} \times \frac{1}{2} \times \frac{1}{2} = \frac{1}{8}$ **5.** $\frac{1}{8}$ **7.** $\frac{1}{8}$ **9.** $\frac{1}{16}$ **11.** $\frac{1}{8}$ **13.** 5 lines **15.** 4

Pages 522-523
1. a **3.** b **5.** Dependent; the name chosen first is not replaced, so there are fewer choices remaining. **7.** $\frac{3}{19}$ **9.** $\frac{3}{19}$ **11.** $\frac{2}{57}$ **13.** $\frac{3}{190}$ **15.** $\frac{3}{95}$ **17.** $\frac{1}{57}$ **19.** $\frac{5}{77}$ **21.** $\frac{16}{121}$ **23.** $\frac{45}{5,324}$ **25.** Independent **27.** $\frac{55}{161}$ **29.** 100 ft

Pages 524-525
1. Because the probability of each event is $\frac{1}{2}$ **3.** Add the terms in row 10 of Pascal's triangle. **5.** 1, 6, 15, 20, 15, 6, 1; 15 **7.** Use 1 8 28 56 70 56 28 8 1; 70 different possibilities **9.** $400

Pages 526-529
1. $\frac{1}{16}$ **3.** $\frac{1}{4}$ **5.** $\frac{5}{8}$ **7.** 1 way for all gates to be open **9.** Total number of possible patterns for 5 gates **11.** Off off off, off off on, off on off, off on on, on off off, on off on, on on off, on on on **13.** $\frac{1}{8}$ **15.** $\frac{1}{8}$ **17.** $\frac{5}{16}$ **19.** $\frac{15}{64}$ **21.** $\frac{9}{64}$ **23.** $\frac{1}{128}$ **25.** $\frac{35}{128}$ **27.** $\frac{21}{128}$ **29.** $\frac{1}{32}$ **31.** $\frac{5}{16}$ **33.** $\frac{1}{32}$

Pages 530-531
1. Combination **3.** Greater **5.** Yes, because the letters for NAP and PAN are in a particular order for each word. **7.** ANP, APN, NAP, NPA, PAN, PNA **Explore Math 1.** 3 combinations **3.** 2 **5.** Yes **7.** 4; 24; 6; 4; yes

Chapter 15

Pages 543-545
1. $A = \{1, 2, 3, 4, 5, 6, 7, 8, 9\}$ **3.** $A \cap B = \{3, 6, 9\}$; $A \cup B = \{1, 2, 3, 4, 5, 6, 7, 8, 9, 12\}$ **5.** $A = \{2, 3, 5, 7\}$ **7.** $C = \{7, 8, 9, 10, 11, 12, 13, 14, 15\}$ **9.** *A, D* **11.** *B, C* **13.** $R \cap S$ = {baseball, basketball, football} **15.** ∅; {center}; {right wing}; {center, right wing}; {center, left wing}; {right wing, left wing}; {center, left wing, right wing} **17.** {2, 3, 5, 7, 8, 9, 10, 11, 12, 13, 14, 15} **19.** {7, 9} **15.** {2, 3, 5, 7, 8, 9, 10, 11, 12, 13, 14, 15} **17.** {7, 9} **21.** {–2, –1, 0, 1, 2, 3, 4, 5, 6, 7, 9} **23.** {3, 5, 7} **25.** { } or ∅ **27.** No; 6 and 8 are not in $B \cap C$. **29.** Yes; 3 and 7 are contained in both *A* and *B*. **31.** {*p*}; {*p, q*}; {*p, q, r*}; {*p, q, r, s*} 2 subsets; 4 subsets; 8 subsets; 16 subsets **33.** $2^7 = 128$ subsets **35.** $\frac{1}{2}$ **37.** $\frac{3}{8}$ **Explore Math 39.** 1; 2; 1 **41.** 20 ways

Pages 546-549
1. Answers may vary. Sample is given. Fruit and desserts. **5.** The set of all students in orchestra, including students in jazz band. **13.** {i, o} **15.**{ℓ, n, p, v} **17.** {I , in, on, no, oil, viol, lion, loin, nil, violin} **Skills Review 1.** $\frac{1}{16}$ **3.** $\frac{1}{32}$ **5.** $\frac{2}{28}$ or $\frac{1}{14}$ **7.** $\frac{1}{28}$

Pages 550-551
5. 45 students **7.** 20 students **9.** 3 students

Pages 552-555
1. False **3.** True **5.** 3; 9 **7.** 3; 15 **9.** If a polygon is a rectangle, then it is a square; false **11.** If a number is composite, then it is not prime; true **13.** If a number is not composite, then it is prime; true **15.** $\frac{3}{5}$ **17.** Patrick

Pages 558-559
1. 48 (He gave Toshiko 24 marbles.) **3.** 168 (He gave Yoko 87 marbles.) **5.** 16¢, 37¢, 58¢, 79¢ **7.** 72 students **Choose a Strategy 9.** Because the numbers within (1, 6, 6) and (2, 2, 9) each add up to the same number 13.

Pages 560-561
1. Because logical principles (the properties of real numbers) are used to justify each step in solving the equation (a specific problem). **3.** Inductive **5.** Deductive **7.** False; $3^2 + 1 = 10$, 10 is not prime. **9.** We know that the sum of two even numbers is even. Suppose *k* and *n* are any two even numbers .Then $k + 1$ is odd and $n + 1$ is odd. If we add them, we get $k + n + 2$. $(k + n)$ is even and $(k + n) + 2$ is even. So, it is true that the sum of any two odd numbers is even. **11.** False. $2^6 + 2(6) - 1 = 75$, which is not prime. **13.** False. $10^2 + 10 + 11 = 121$, which is not prime. **15.** 11; inductive **17.** The letter I, the next letter that has an ascender inductive

Pages 562-563
1.-3.

	bride	pilgrim	pumpkin
Amy			
Betsy			X
Clarissa		X	

5. The pumpkin **7.** Dee is the rabbit, Elizabeth is the gorilla, Jasmine is the rock star, and Stacy is the chicken. **9.** 1, 4, 5, 6, 9 **11.** 3 **13.** A STATE!

INDEX

Index

INDEX

INDEX

ACKNOWLEDGMENTS

Design

Cover and Special Features: SHELDON COTLER + ASSOCIATES Lipman Hearne, Rosa + Wesley Design Associates, Jack Weiss Associates

Photographs

Cover: The Image Bank; Fred Schenk xi (tl): Tony Freeman, PhotoEdit xi (bl): Bob Daemmrich, The Image Works xi (tr): Bill Gallery, Stock Boston xi (br): Tony Freeman, PhotoEdit xii (b): Bob Burch, Bruce Coleman Inc. xv (bl): Dan McCoy, Rainbow xvi (t): Stephen Frisch, Stock Boston xvi (b): Charles Gupton. Stock Boston xvii (tr): Brent Jones xvii (bl): John Elk III, Stock Boston xix (tr): Reprinted with permission from: Peitgen, H.O./Richter, P. H.: *The Beauty of Fractals,* 1986. © 1986 Springer-Verlager Berlin-Heidelberg xx (tr): Brent Jones ScottForesman photographs by: Richard Chesnut 58, 59, 82–83, 110, 125, 230, 231, 253, 333, 466–467, 520, 521, 572; Arie deZanger 58, 209, 270, 402, 482, 483, 520; Fred Schenk 46–47, 92, 93, 142–143, 161, 216–217, 426, 427, 466–467; unless otherwise acknowledged, all photos are the property of ScottForesman. From *Art in Africa* by Tibor Bodrogi © Corvina, 1968: 169 Art Resource: Alinori 350; Museum of Anthropology, Mexico City 29 David Biedrzychi: 132 Courtesy Trustees of The British Library: 437; The British Museum: 30 Cameramann Int'l: Milt and Joan Mann 216–217 (steel drums, scrap cars, sandals), 480 Woodfin Camp & Associates, Inc.: Marc & Evelyne Bernheim 540–541; Robert Frerck 340–341; Kenneth Garrett 479; Stephanie 2–3; Mike Yamshita 114–115 Doug Chappell: 128, 198 Willard Clay: 416 Click/Chicago/Tony Stone: Wat Arun 236; Alan Smith 321; Tony Stone 320 Bruce Coleman: Eric Freedman 101; Jonathan Wright 100 Comstock: Jack J. Clark 142–143 Sterling Dimmitt: 188 Paula Cooper Gallery: Efraim Lev-er 322 "Brick Dome" sculpture by Jackie Winsor, 1971 DOT Photos: Dan Nerney 540–541 Duomo: David Madison 216–217 FPG: Jason Hailey 506–507; Fred Stein 506–507 Focus on Sports: 542, 543; Kobayakawa 544 The Franklin Institute: 430–431 Grant Heilman: A. C. Smith 496 The Image Bank: Hank Delespinasse 2–3; Grant V. Faint 182–183; Pat LaCroix 182–183; Mieke Maas 182–183; Joanna McCarthy 315; Marc Solomon 2–3; David Vance 182–183 Catherine Koehler: 171, 274 Doug Mindell: 48, 118, 120 Mt. Washington Observatory, Gorham, New Hampshire: Rusty Cook 92 Musée de Paris: "Bull's Head" by Pablo Picasso: 217 Odyssey Productions: Robert Frerck 190, 191, 192, 275 L'Oeil Magazine Oct. 1991: 322 (French house); Nov. 1991: 322 (Terry Haass lucite sculpture) Photo Researchers, Inc.: Richard Ellis 16; Dr. Fred Espenak/ Science Photo Library 292–293; John Giannicchi/Science Source 310; Ronald Royer/Science Photo Library 292–293 Princeton University: 322 Rainbow: Dan McCoy 390–391 Courtesy Reynolds Metal Company: 231 Rue Enterprises: Leonard Lee Rue 111 496 Satellite Data Services Division/ NCDC: 114–115 *Scripta Mathematica:* 424 Shoso-in Repository, Nara: 353 Frank Siteman: 20, 56, 171, 172 Southwest Museum: 519 Reprinted with permission from Peitgen, H. O./Richter, P. H.: *The Beauty of Fractals,* 1986. © 1986 Springer-Verlager Berlin-Heidelberg: 538 Stock Boston: Philip Jon Bailey 256–257; Jon Coletti 256–257; Owen Franken 256–257; R. Fried 351, 542; L. Migdale 296, 478 The Stock Market: David Ball 82–83, 340–341, 355; David Davidson 539; Brownie Harris 182–183; J. Paul Kennedy 271; Charles Krebs 2–3; Joan Menschenfreund 540–541; Roy Morsch 256–257; Barry O'Rourke 540–541; R. B. Sanchez 216–217 Ben Simmons 2–3; Stu Schwartzberg 253 Supreme Court Historical Society: 15 Sygma: Jay Mather/Sacramento Bee 46–47 Taurus Photos: Marilyn M. Pfaltz 323; Frank Siteman 408; Jim Walston 374 University of Pennsylvania: 290 From *Wood Inlay, Art and Craft,* an Art Horizons Book, Van Nostrand Reinhold Company, Division of Litton Educ. Publ., Inc. © 1973 Photo: Alfred Russo 352 Joe Viesti: 297 Noah Webster Foundation: 34

Illustrations

Elizabeth Allen, Diane Bennett, Eliott Bergman, Tom Briggs, Ken Call, Dan Collins, Susan Dodge, Cameron Eagle, Andrea Eberbach, Janice Fried, Bill Gerhold, Brad Hamann, Lipman Hearne, Monica Incisia, Dave Joly, Mike Jones, Robert Jones, Steven Klecker, Robert Korta, Jack Lefkowitz, Roger Layonmark, Brenda Losey, Judith Love, Chuck Ludeke, Jeff Mangiat, Susan Mills, Leonard Morgan, Mike Muir, Eileen Mueller Neill, Sharon O'Neil, Brenda Pepper, Ellen Rixford, Joe Rogers, Jada Rowland, Bruce Sanders, Elaine Sears, Judy Seckler, Dan Siculan, Suzanne Snider, Barton Stabler, Maria Strosier, Carol Stutz, Peggy Tagel, Heather Taylor, John Trotta, Paul Vaccarella, Kathleen Volp, John Walter Jr.

Data

p. 110, Deak International p. 111, American Demographics p. 253, National Center for Career Strategies p. 466, *100% American* by Daniel Weiss. Copyright © 1988 by Daniel Weiss. Reprinted with permission of Poseidon Press, a division of Simon & Schuster, Inc. p. 427, San Francisco Transcontinental Train Schedule courtesy of California Department of Transportation

SCOTTFORESMAN STAFF

ScottForesman gratefully acknowledges the contributions of the following individuals.

Editorial

Karen Usiskin, Janice Ziebka, Therese Smith, Clare Froemel, Nancy Baty, Diane Renner, Janet Heller, Mary Schaefer, John Selisky

Design

Barbara Schneider, Virginia Pierce, George Roth, David Dumo, Tom Gorman

Production

Mary Lou Beals, Joy Kelly, Barbara Albright, Kathy Oberfranc, Lois Nelson, Fran Simon, Sally Buehne

Marketing

Cathie Dillender, Nan Simpson, Muffet Fox

Business

Elizabeth A. Dietz, Elizabeth R. Semro

Picture Research/Photo Studio

Nina Page, Rosemary Hunter, John Moore, Phoebe Novak

Photo Lab/Keyline

Marilyn Sullivan, Mark Spears, Madeline Oton-Tarpey, Gwen Plogman